A Study of History was first planned by the author in 1921; volumes i–iii were published in 1934, volumes iv–v and the work reached completio publication in 1954 of volumes volume containing relevant maps gazetteer will supplement the *Stu*

In the course of the thirty-th separating the conception and the ⸾ompιction of an undertaking on a scale comparable with Gibbon's, Dr. Toynbee's outlook has inevitably undergone changes which have vitally affected the trend of his great work. The most significant of these changes, concerning his estimate of the role of Religion in History, has led him beyond the limits of his original purpose, though without disrupting the basic plan.

The final four volumes contain Parts VI–XIII of the book.

Parts VI–VIII deal with phenomena apt to accompany a disintegrating civilization: a universal state, a universal church, and an heroic age of the barbarians beyond the civilization's pale.

Parts IX–X consider the collisions in living civilizations between contemporaries and 'renaissances' of 'dead' civilizations.

Part XI questions how far mankind is free to make its own history and how far it is governed by either 'the Law of God' or 'laws of Nature'; and, arising from that, Part XII views the prospects of Western Civilization, which has involved the whole world-population in its own fortunes.

Part XIII inquires into the reasons why we are moved to study History.

While the first five Parts of Dr. Toynbee's *Study* dealt with phases in the internal histories of civilizations (genesis, growth, breakdown, and disintegration), the topics

continued on back flap

A STUDY OF
HISTORY

A STUDY OF
HISTORY

BY

ARNOLD J. TOYNBEE

*Director of Studies in the Royal Institute
of International Affairs
Research Professor of International History
in the University of London
(both on the Sir Daniel Stevenson Foundation)*

But at my back I always hear
Time's wingèd chariot hurrying near.
ANDREW MARVELL

ποιεῖν τι δεῖ ἇς γόνυ χλωρόν.
THEOCRITUS: Κυνίσκας Ἔρως, l. 70

γηράσκω δ' αἰεὶ πολλὰ διδασκόμενος.
SOLON

My times are in Thy hand.
Ps. xxxi. 15, in the A.V.

But Thou art the same, and Thy
years shall have no end.
Ps. cii. 27, in the A.V.

VOLUME IX

*Issued under the auspices of the
Royal Institute of International Affairs*

OXFORD UNIVERSITY PRESS
LONDON NEW YORK TORONTO
1954

Oxford University Press, Amen House, London E.C.4

GLASGOW NEW YORK TORONTO MELBOURNE WELLINGTON
BOMBAY CALCUTTA MADRAS KARACHI CAPE TOWN IBADAN

Geoffrey Cumberlege, Publisher to the University

PRINTED IN GREAT BRITAIN

CONTENTS

XI. LAW AND FREEDOM IN HISTORY

X

CONTACTS BETWEEN CIVILIZATIONS IN TIME
(*Renaissances*)

A. 'THE RENAISSANCE'

THE metaphorical application of the French word *renaissance* to denote the 'rebirth' of an extinct culture was a Modern Western usage; and, for Western minds whose vocabulary had come to include this term, the first association of the word 'renaissance', in this latter-day technical meaning of it, was in the singular, not in the plural, and as a proper name, not as the label of a species.[1]

Modern Western historians were apt thus to speak of 'the Renaissance' under the spell of the same egocentric illusion[2] that had prompted *Homo Terricola* in all societies and all ages to speak of 'the Earth', the 'Moon', 'the Sun'. Such *façons de parler* were, of course, as unscientific as they were insidious, and as insidious as they were subjective. They were expressions of an unsophisticated observer's uncritical assumption that his own ego is the centre of the Universe and that a panorama seen from his personal angle of vision is a true picture of the Universe as it really is. In this same egocentric frame of mind an inhabitant of another of 'the Planets' would use *Terricola*'s familiar term 'the Earth' to mean the planet whose surface happened to be *his* habitat. If, for example, he happened to be a Martian, 'the Earth' would mean for him the planet Mars and not the planet Terra. On the other hand, *Terricola*'s term 'the Moon' would not have any counterpart in other planetary vocabularies, since a diverse parochial experience would have accustomed inhabitants of Jupiter to speak of 'the Moons' in the plural and inhabitants of Saturn to speak, instead, of 'the Ring', while inhabitants of other planets, if unequipped with telescopes, would deny that such phenomena as either 'moons' or 'rings' were to be seen among the heavenly bodies. It is true that, when they spoke of 'the Sun', inhabitants of any of 'the Planets' would be referring to one and the same star; but, when a 'twentieth-century' *terricola* was reminded, by the spectacle of 'the Milky Way', that suns were as common as dirt, and when he went on to reflect that any of these innumerable suns might have numerous planets revolving round it, he was forced to realize that his habitual phrase 'the Planets' was as provincial an expression as 'the Moon', and 'the Sun' as crass a provincialism as 'the Earth'. Nor did 'the Milky Way' itself fare any better; for *Homo Terricola*'s latter-day astronomers had informed him that this smoke-ring composed of stars, including his native planet's sun, was, itself, simply one of a number of nebulae in diverse stages of

[1] In Larousse, P.: *Grand Dictionnaire Universel du xixe Siècle*, vol. xiii, p. 936, the earliest French author cited as having used the word 'renaissance' in this technical sense is E.-J. Delécluze (*vivebat* A.D. 1781–1863). In the *New English Dictionary* the earliest passage cited dates from as late as A.D. 1845.   [2] See I. i. 158–65.

condensation. These astronomical illustrations of the egocentric illusion's distorting effect upon the appearance of Reality were illuminating commentaries on the customary Modern Western usage of the word *renaissance*.

In ordinary Modern Western parlance the singular expression 'the Renaissance' was used to denote something that had happened in one local province of one civilization in one age of its history on two planes of its activity. The particular civilization in question was Western Christendom, the particular province was Northern and Central Italy,[1] the particular age was the Late Medieval period of Western history (*circa* A.D. 1275–1475), the particular activities were the literary and visual arts. The occurrence that was identified by being labelled with this name invented for it *ad hoc* was the evocation—at this time and place, and within these two spheres of cultural action—of the 'ghost' of a 'dead' civilization; and the *revenant* thus called up from Sheol by this feat of cultural necromancy was the shade of an Hellenic culture to which the Western culture was affiliated.[2]

If our reminder of the distorting effect of the egocentric illusion on our mental picture of the stellar universe has put us on the alert against the danger of error to which this besetting illusion exposes human minds in all their mental operations, we may feel it worth while to re-

[1] i.e. the aboriginally Western Christian parts of the Italian Peninsula, as distinct from a *ci-devant* Byzantine South (see I. i. 32 and 38).

[2] This evocation of two facets of the Hellenic culture in a Late Medieval Italy was the occurrence to which the label inscribed 'the Renaissance' properly attached; but in popular parlance the usage of the term was sometimes incorrectly narrowed and sometimes incorrectly widened. It was sometimes confined to denoting the enrichment of an Italian renaissance of Hellenism in Latin dress, at a date by which this was already a going concern, through the fifteenth-century Italian humanists' acquisition from Constantinople of original works of Hellenic literature in the medium of the Classical Greek language (see IX. viii. 102). In reality, this Greek contribution to a Late Medieval Italian renaissance of Hellenism was the by-product of a contact in the Space-dimension between a Late Medieval Italy and a contemporary Orthodox Christendom which happened to be a 'carrier' of those Greek elements of an extinct Hellenic culture that the Italians acquired from this Byzantine source in the fifteenth century. On the other hand the meaning of the term 'the Renaissance' was sometimes extended to include the radiation of a Late Medieval Italian sub-culture into the Transmarine and Transalpine provinces of Western Christendom at the transition from the Medieval to the Modern Age of Western history.

In thus transmitting its own special culture to 'the Barbarians', a Late Medieval Italy did, of course, transmit the achievements of her evocation of Hellenism among her other current cultural commodities. But the diffusion of the Italian culture at this date was, in itself, not a renaissance but an encounter between two diverse contemporary Western sub-cultures within the bosom of a Western body social that was their common social setting. (The measure of the gulf by which these two Late Medieval Western sub-cultures had come to be divided by the time when their encounter began was given in a striking visual form by the contrast in style, and still greater contrast in êthos, between the native English sculpture and the imported Florentine master Pietro Torrigiani's work in the English King Henry VII's chapel in Westminster Abbey). This Italianization of the non-Italian provinces of the Western World of the day was a consequence of the Italians' success in forging ahead of the rest of Western Christendom in the course of the two preceding centuries; Italy had already won this lead in a cultural race between the divers provinces of a Medieval Western Christendom before the Italian renaissance of Hellenism had started; and, in virtue of this lead, the eventual diffusion of a Late Medieval Italian culture beyond the Alps and across the Western Mediterranean would assuredly have taken place even if there had been no Italian renaissance of Hellenism at all, or if there had been one that had never gone beyond a mere revival of the second-hand Latin version of the Hellenic literature, without any fifteenth-century Italian recourse to Hellenism's Greek fountain-head (see IV. iv. 275, nn. 1 and 2, and 363, n. 1, and IX. viii. 102, n. 2).

CONTENTS

ANNEXES

TABLES

consider the customary Western conception of 'the Renaissance' in a critical spirit; and, as soon as we enter upon this re-examination, we shall find that the popular usage of the term in the singular, to describe a Late Medieval Italian literary and artistic movement, was at variance with the historical facts in at least three respects. In the first place it did not cover the whole field even of the Late Medieval Italian renaissance of Hellenism, since it left out of the picture a political facet that, in the twentieth century, was still dominating the social landscape of a Late Modern Western World in which the literary and artistic traces of 'the Renaissance' had been gradually fading out.[1] In the second place the use of the word *renaissance* as a proper name for the evocation of Hellenism in a Late Medieval Italy ignored the fact that there had been other renaissances of Hellenism, in other provinces of Western Christendom, at other times in Western history (later, as well as earlier, than the Late Middle Ages), and that these other Western renaissances of Hellen-

[1] A child of a Late Modern Western Civilization who had had the good fortune to have been born just in time to have received a Late Medieval Italian (*alias* Early Modern Western) Hellenic education in the Greek and Latin languages and literatures was sadly aware, by the year A.D. 1952 (if he had had the further good or bad fortune to have survived two world wars), that he and his class-mates might be all but the last Western initiates into an Hellenic *Weltanschauung* which had been a veritable 'Illumination of the Soul' (to use Acton's words, quoted above in I. i. 47) for all those children of the West who had been given the opportunity of participating in this inspiring intellectual experience. In the Western educational arena by the year A.D. 1952 the humanist's curriculum introduced through a Late Medieval Italian renaissance of Hellenism had been put out of the running and all but pushed off the track by a physicist's curriculum representing an aboriginal Western *Weltanschauung* which, after having been put out of countenance for a season by the dazzling splendour of the Hellenic *revenant*, had been progressively reasserting itself ever since a native Western genius for an empirical and experimental exploration and exploitation of the Physical Universe had achieved a counter-renaissance in winning 'the Battle of the Books' at the turn of the seventeenth and eighteenth centuries (see IV. iv. 363, n. 2, and pp. 62–73, below).

In appraising, *circa* A.D. 1952, the policy pursued by a Late Modern Western World in discriminating, and selecting for retention or discard, the divers elements of the Hellenic culture that had been recaptured for the Modern West by the Italian Humanists, the last survivors of this now all but exterminated intellectual tribe might feel inclined to pray and beseech their exterminators to say after them, in language taken from the Anglican Book of Common Prayer: 'We have left undone those things which we ought to have done, and we have done those things which we ought not to have done.' In the very generation in which the literary and artistic facets of an Italian renaissance of Hellenism were being finally discarded by a post-Modern Western Man, this Caliban was not only clinging to the political facet but was pushing this resuscitated political ideology of Hellenism to extremes that had never been approached by the Hellenes themselves in their own self-immolation on the altar of an idolized Leviathan.

This selective policy that was thus being pursued by twentieth-century Western Man was, of course, as logical as it was perverse. His determination to retain the political facet, while discarding the literary and artistic facets, of Hellenism was governed by the same impulse that was moving him at the same time to give rein to his own native bent for Physical Science. Like this native Western physical technique, an alien Hellenic political ideology ministered to an insatiable lust for power which was the inevitable ruling passion in hearts that had relapsed from Christianity into a pagan worship of a Collective Humanity. This point had been noted by a Late Modern Western student of Hellenism in a passage already quoted in a different context:

'Europe's infatuation for the Greeks and Romans dates from the sixteenth century, when she began her great political and military reorganisation. She admired them in all things . . . because they taught her how to organise armies, how to wage wars, and how to build up great states' (Ferrero, G.: *Peace and War* (London 1933, Macmillan), p. 194, quoted in VII. vii. 542).

It looked as if a self-deconsecrated Modern Western Society had taken the political ideals of the Italian renaissance more seriously than its aesthetic ideals just because these political ideals presented a more defiant challenge to a Christian êthos against which a latter-day Western Man had rebelled.

ism had extended to other facets of the Hellenic culture besides the
literary, artistic, and political. In the third place the customary usage
ignored the still more portentous fact that there had been other renaissances of Hellenism in the histories of at least one other Hellenistic
Civilization besides Western Christendom, and other renaissances of
other 'dead' cultures besides Hellenism in the histories of other civilizations of the third generation besides the two Hellenistic Christian
societies.

As soon as we have thus brought all the relevant phenomena into
view, we become aware that, in using the word *renaissance* as a proper
name, we have been allowing ourselves to fall into the error of seeing a
unique occurrence in an event which in reality was no more than one
particular instance of a recurrent historical phenomenon. The evocation
of a dead culture by the living representatives of a civilization that is still
a going concern proves to be a species of historical event for which the
proper label is, not 'the Renaissance', but 'renaissances'; and, in an
earlier context, we have already identified the genus to which this species
belongs. The raising of a ghost by a necromancer produces an encounter
between the medium and his oracle; and such encounters between the
living and the dead are one species of a generic phenomenon which presents itself in a different specific form in encounters in which both
parties are alive at the time when they collide with one another. The
species of encounter in which the contact takes place between contemporaries has been the subject of the immediately preceding part of
this Study; and, in finding our way into that field of inquiry, we have
already taken note of a specific difference between contacts—of the
species there examined—in which the characteristic and distinctive
aspect of the encounter is a collision in the Space-dimension between
contemporaries living side by side in different geographical habitats,
and contacts in which the pertinent difference of location between the
colliding parties is a distance measured in the Time-dimension of the
chronologist and not in the Space-dimension of the geographer[1].

In the same context we have also already observed that, among encounters of the species labelled 'contacts in Time', we can identify at
least three distinct varieties. There are encounters in the life, of the kind
that we have labelled 'Apparentation-and-Affiliation,[2] between parties
belonging to different, but consecutive, generations whose lives have
partly overlapped in the Time-dimension. There are other encounters
(and these are our present subject) in which the parties are the same,
but in which the encounter takes place at a date when the party representing an older generation is no longer alive, and is therefore only able
to participate as a ghost evoked by a living necromancer—in contrast to
its original encounter, in the life, with an 'affiliated' civilization whose
still living representatives are now awakening the dead in order to establish a fresh contact of a different kind.[3] There are other encounters,
again, in which one of the parts is likewise played by a ghost, but this by
a ghost of the necromancer's own past self, and not by the ghost of one

[1] See IX. viii. 97.   [2] See I. i. 44 and IX. viii. 97–98.
[3] See IX. viii. 97–98 and 101.

of his parents.[1] In this place there is no need to redefine these distinctions between an archaistic endeavour to revert to an earlier stage of the archaist's own history and the two varieties of encounter between civilizations of different generations that are distinguished from one another by the difference between the elder party's status when it participates as a living 'apparented' civilization and its status when it participates as a ghost evoked in a renaissance. There is no need, either, to reduplicate our previous examination of the phenomena of Archaism and of Apparentation-and-Affiliation; and accordingly, in the present Part of this Study, we can confine our attention to renaissances, with which we have not had occasion to deal so far, except incidentally.

Before proceeding to make an empirical survey of renaissances as a first step towards an analysis of their specific characteristics, we have only to take note of one point of difference *ex hypothesi* between renaissances and those diverse contacts in the Time-dimension that are represented by the other two varieties of the species.

In the relation of Apparentation-and-Affiliation between two living societies of different generations, as well as in a society's archaistic reversion to some phase of its own past experience, the two parties must be, *ex hypothesi*, in diverse and dissimilar stages of their life-history. In a case of Apparentation-and-Affiliation, for example,[2] the elder of the two parties must, not only have broken down, but have gone so far along the road of disintegration as to have split into the two factions that we have called a proletariat and a dominant minority, before the embryo of a younger civilization can be conceived in the womb of the elder civilization's proletariat; and, in consequence, the two parties to one of these encounters in the Time-dimension in which both parties are alive at the time are bound to find themselves, during the period of this encounter between them in the life, in extremely dissimilar phases of experience, at however early a stage of its growth the 'apparented' society may have broken down, and at however early a stage of its own subsequent growth the 'affiliated' society may suffer (if it does suffer) the antecedent society's fate. In a case of Archaism the *a priori* necessity of a corresponding difference between the respective psychological situations of the necromancer and the ghost of his own past self is still more obvious; for the very fact that the necromancer is recalling a past phase of his own life carries the implication that this resuscitated past and the living present represent different stages in the formation of a single cumulatively growing experience. On the other hand, when the ghost that the necromancer evokes is the ghost, not of his own, but of a different civilization, which, though 'apparented' to his own, is now no longer in the land of the living, it is equally open to him, at will, to evoke either a phase of this dead antecedent civilization's experience that is dissimilar from the necromancer's own present or a phase that is more or less on a psychological par with it.[3] This wider freedom of choice, and the use that the necromancer is apt to make of it, will prove to be important themes in the study of renaissances upon which we are now embarking.

[1] See IX. viii. 101. The way of life that we have labelled 'Archaism' has been examined in V. vi. 49–97.   [2] See IX. viii. 97.   [3] See IX. viii. 98–100, and pp.128–37 below.

B. A SURVEY OF RENAISSANCES

(I) A PLAN OF OPERATIONS

IF we have now succeeded in establishing our thesis that a Late Medieval Italian renaissance of Hellenism which had been known as 'the Renaissance' in Modern Western parlance was, after all, not a unique phenomenon but was one representative of one species within a genus labelled 'encounters', the next step that suggests itself is to take advantage of this widening of our horizon for the prosecution of our inquiry along our customary empirical lines. Let us first see how many instances we can collect of renaissances within the meaning of the term as we have now defined it, and then let us go on to use the results of this survey as the basis for an analytical study of this species of encounter by means of the comparative method of investigation.

In setting out to plan a survey of renaissances, we shall find at once that our foregoing critique of 'the Renaissance' has already placed in our hands some clues to the discovery of a procedure. We have noticed that this Italian resuscitation of Hellenism was neither comprehensive nor indiscriminate; it was a recapture of certain particular facets of the re-suscitated culture's life. A literary and an artistic facet were two aspects of this renaissance that were in the foreground of a latter-day Western observer's retrospective picture of the phenomenon, and we have also noticed a political facet that had perhaps always been paramount in fact, and that was undoubtedly the one aspect of the Italian renaissance of Hellenism which, in A.D. 1952, was showing an increasing, instead of a diminishing, potency for fascinating Western souls.[1] These three facets of this particular *revenante* culture in this particular evocation corre-spond to three of the elemental and sub-elemental rays into which we have found the integral radiation of a radioactive culture being diffracted in the process of diffusion in the dimension, not of Time, but of Space;[2] and, with this clue in our hands, we may push our search for instances of renaissances into the rest of those divers fields of human activity which have figured as separately distinguishable strips in our culture-spec-trum. On these lines we shall make successive searches for symptoms of renaissances in the fields of Politics, Law, Science and Philosophy, Language and Literature, the Visual Arts, and Religion.[3] Moreover, these inquiries will not be confined to renaissances of various aspects of Hellenism in the Western Christian Hellenistic World at different stages in this civilization's history. We shall also put into the witness box, one after another, all the other civilizations of the third generation that have come within our cognizance[4]—and these are all that come into question in our present inquiry, since these alone had been *en rapport* with their

[1] See p. 3, n. 1, above. [2] See IX. viii. 498–500.
[3] It will be noticed that Economics are absent from this list, in contrast to the impor-tance of the part that they have proved to play in encounters in the Space-dimension between contemporaries.
[4] A list of tertiary civilizations will be found in the table of primitive societies, civiliza-tions, and higher religions in serial order, in VII. vii. Table IV facing p. 772.

predecessors on the comparatively intimate terms required for making the feat of evocation a possibility.

While the resuscitation of a dead culture in the heart and mind of a living society may result in the necromancer's recollecting aspects of the resuscitated culture that he has forgotten, or even in his discovering aspects of which he has never before been aware, he could never have performed the initial act of materializing the nucleus of the wraith which he has thus afterwards gradually brought into focus if, before ever he set out to raise this ghost, he had not possessed some hold over the dead society. This indispensable preliminary hold consists, as we have seen,[1] in the possession of a stock of practices and ideas derived from the dead civilization's cultural heritage; and this key is not in the hands of any civilization of a younger generation that is not affiliated to the dead society in virtue of being the issue of a chrysalis church that has been constructed by the dead society's internal proletariat. This link of Apparentation-and-Affiliation, as we have called it, duly subsists between tertiary civilizations and their secondary predecessors; but we have found no more than abortive rudiments of it in the relation between secondary civilizations and the primary predecessors of these;[2] and, *ex hypothesi*, there can have been no relation of this kind between those primary civilizations themselves and the primitive societies out of which they must have arisen by some process of mutation.[3] On this showing, we may take it that we shall have covered the ground of our present inquiry when we have taken an inventory of the tertiary civilizations' performances in their resuscitations of facets of the lives of their secondary predecessors in the divers fields of activity that we have been able to distinguish for our present purpose.

(II) OPERATIONS ACCORDING TO PLAN

(a) RENAISSANCES OF POLITICAL IDEAS, IDEALS, AND INSTITUTIONS

We have already noticed that the Late Medieval Italian renaissance of Hellenism exerted a more enduring influence on Western life on the political plane than on either the literary or the artistic.[4] We may now go on to observe that the political manifestations of this renaissance not only outlived the aesthetic manifestations but had forestalled them. A renaissance which did not declare itself on the aesthetic plane earlier than the generations of Dante (*vivebat* A.D. 1265–1321) and Petrarch (*vivebat* A.D. 1304–74) had begun to take effect on the political plane as early as the eleventh century, when the government of the cities of Lombardy had passed out of the control of their bishops into the hands of communes administered by boards of magistrates who were appointed by, and responsible to, the citizens. The resuscitated Hellenic political ideal which made this impact on eleventh-century Western Christian urban communities in Northern Italy[5] proceeded, after the radiation

---

[1] In IX. viii. 98.
[2] See VII. vii. 421–2.
[3] See II. i. 302–30.
[4] See p. 3, n. 1, above.
[5] See III. iii. 344, n. 2; IV. iv. 352, n. 2; and pp. 645–8, below.

of a Late Medieval Italian sub-culture into the Transalpine and Trans-marine provinces of Western Christendom, to make a corresponding impact on the peoples of the feudal monarchies which this walking ghost of Hellenism encountered there.

In both its earlier and narrower and its later and wider field the influence of this Hellenic *revenant* on Western politics was the same. The superficial effect was to propagate a cult of constitutional self-government which was eventually to confer upon itself the flattering Attic title of 'Democracy'[1] after demonstrating its potency by precipitating successively an English, an American, and a French Revolution. By the year A.D. 1871 this 'Democracy' seemed to have won a conclusive victory over a post-Alexandrine Hellenic Absolute Monarchy which had been evoked by Late Medieval Italian and Early Modern Transalpine and Transmarine Western despots as an instrument for transposing a resuscitated Hellenic style of polity from a city-state to a nation-state scale.[2] But a lip-service to a Humanitarianism professedly dedicated to the welfare of individual human beings glozed over a demonic idolization of a tribal Collective Humanity whose juggernaut car was to ride roughshod over the rights of children, women, and men[3] when these rights were divested of their religious sanction. In a Christian society this sanction had been the sacrosanctity of each single soul in the eyes of a God who had revealed Himself to be the Father and Redeemer of every creature. In a post-Christian twentieth-century Western World a blasphemously idolatrous revival of the worship of an Athênê Poliûchus masquerading as the Goddess France and of an Athânâ Chalcioecus masquerading as the Goddess Prussia[4] was threatening to bring down upon the heads of *ci-devant* Christian Western idolators the nemesis that had once overtaken those pre-Christian Hellenic idolators whose abomination of desolation these Hellenizing Western neo-pagans had re-erected in order to fill a desolatingly vacant place on their own swept and garnished altars.

This ghost of an idolatrous Hellenic worship of a Collective Humanity embodied in a parochial state was thus evoked in Medieval Italy some three or four hundred years earlier than the ghosts of an Hellenic literature and visual art that, in their authentic original epiphanies in the fifth and fourth centuries B.C., had been raised to their highest level of achievement by Attic worshippers of a parochial Athênê Poliûchus. This Italian renaissance of Hellenic political parochialism was not, however, either the only or the earliest political renaissance of Hellenism in Western history. In the course of Hellenic history itself, a religion of state-worship that had begun to be known by its fruits[5] had temporarily salvaged its credit in the eyes of partially disillusioned worshippers by passing over from a pristine parochial to a latter-day oecumenical form; Athênê Poliûchus, Athânâ Chalcioecus, Tychê Antiocheôn, Fortuna Praenestina, and the other deified combatants in a mêlée of conflicting

---

[1] See IV. iv. 140.   [2] See III. iii. 350–61.
[3] This deplorable effect of the impact of Democracy upon Parochial Sovereignty has been noticed in IV. iv. 161–7.
[4] See I. i. 443–4 and IV. iv. 317–20 and 405–8.
[5] Matt. vii. 20 and xii. 33; Luke vi. 44.

parochial idols had eventually been called to order by being subordinated to the oecumenical supremacy of a Dea Roma and a Divus Augustus; and a post-Diocletianic absolute version of this consolidated worship of the concentrated power of a politically unified Mankind was formally re-vived in Western Christendom, a quarter of a millennium before the revival of city-state-worship in Lombardy, when Charlemagne was crowned as a Roman Emperor by Pope Leo III in Saint Peter's on Christmas Day A.D. 800.[1]

The memory of this Carolingian evocation of a 'holy' Roman ghost of an extinct Hellenic universal state cannot come into our minds without reminding us simultaneously that, since then, the same ghost had been re-evoked again and again in the Western World in the course of the eleven and a half centuries that had elapsed between the date of the coronation of Charlemagne at Rome and the time of the writing of these lines.

The all but fatal collapse of the nascent Western Christian Civiliza-tion itself, which had been the price of Charlemagne's failure to re-suscitate the Roman Empire in the West effectively, did not deter a Saxon Otto I[2] from repeating his Austrasian predecessor's attempt; and the subsequent failure of Otto's attempt in its turn did not deter a Swabian Frederick I from attempting, for his part, to undo the political effects of the humiliation of a Franconian Henry IV at Hildebrand's hands by employing against a triumphant Hildebrandine Church the refurbished spiritual weapon of a recently disinterred Justinianean Law.[3] Thereafter, when Frederick Barbarossa's experience had demonstrated that the necromancer's wand provided by his Bolognese legists was a broken reed, his grandson Frederick *Stupor Mundi* set himself to reverse, at the eleventh hour, the cumulative disaster of Charlemagne's, Henry IV's, and Frederick I's successive discomfitures[4]—though the weapon in which Frederick II trusted to conjure a victory out of his forlorn hope was one which had missed fire, more than two hundred years back, in the hands of his Saxon predecessor Otto III.[5]

This imaginative tenth-century forerunner of a thirteenth-century *Stupor Mundi* had sought to condense an insubstantial wraith of a de-funct *Imperium Romanum* into at least a similitude of flesh and blood by transferring the seat of a rehabilitated Western Christian 'Holy Roman Empire' from Western Christendom's Saxon marches over against the North European barbarians[6] to her Roman march over against Orthodox Christendom. At the turn of the tenth and eleventh centuries of the Christian Era the Ducatus Romanus was a patch of common ground on which the domains of the two Christendoms overlapped;[7] and, in install-ing himself in the *ci-devant* Imperial City, Otto III had hoped to fortify the sickly counterfeit of the Roman Imperial Power that had been

---

[1] Charlemagne's attempt to revive the Roman Empire in Western Christendom has been discussed in this Study in I. i. 343; III. iii. 276; IV. iv. 378–9; V. v. 477, n. 1; and VI. vii. 19.
[2] See II. ii. 167–8.   [3] See IV. iv. 557, and p. 31, below.
[4] See IV. iv. 560–7; VII. vii. 537–8; and IX. viii. 394–5.
[5] See IV. iv. 617, n. 2.   [6] See II. ii. 167–9.
[7] See IV. iv. 335–7, 521–2, and 599–600.

palmed off on Western Christendom by reinforcing it with tougher metal imported from a Byzantine mint. The success of Leo III Syrus's revival of the Roman Empire in Orthodox Christendom had been as conspicuous as the failure of Charlemagne's subsequent attempt to perform a corresponding feat of political necromancy in the West.[1] Could not a clumsy Western necromancer's abortive essay be salvaged by the Herodian expedient of turning to Western Christendom's account the achievements of an Orthodox Christian necromancer's virtuosity?

This complicated experiment of trying to raise the ghost of a dead civilization by employing a living civilization as a medium, which Otto III had failed to carry to success in the cultural crucible of a late-tenth-century City of Rome, was repeated by Frederick II under more promising conditions in a thirteenth-century Kingdom of Sicily which was the East Roman Empire's Transadriatic successor-state. The outcome of this more ambitious adventure in the black art of political alchemy was, as we have seen,[2] a war to the death between a pseudo-Byzantine 'Holy Roman Empire' and a Hildebrandine Papal Roman Church which brought the victorious ecclesiastical combatant to the ground in the same ruin as his vanquished secular adversary and thereby compromised the future of a promising Western Christian attempt to explore a previously untried approach towards the goal of the baffling enterprise of Civilization. Yet the ghost of an obsolete Hellenic institution that had been so inauspiciously raised at the close of the eighth century of the Christian Era by an Austrasian king and a Roman patriarch was still able to induce fresh Western victims to feed it with their life-blood within full view of their infatuated predecessors' unburied corpses.

By the time of the extirpation of Frederick II Hohenstaufen's brood, the cumulus of historic disasters, that had gradually come to be associated with academic pretensions to the imperial prerogative in the West, had gathered round a tragic imperial crown into a lowering nimbus which might have been expected to serve as an effective deterrent against any further repetition of Charlemagne's folly. Yet this scarecrow *Caesarea Maiestas* was eagerly appropriated by the architects of a Danubian Hapsburg Monarchy for the sake of the prestige that it could still lend to their strictly practical enterprise of providing an Early Modern Western World with a local carapace to protect it against Ottoman aggression in the Danube Basin;[3] and, after the decay of the Ottoman Power had rendered a Hapsburg Empire's service to the Western Civilization superfluous,[4] 'the Holy Roman Empire of the German Nation'—which had been preserved by the arts of Hapsburg statesmanship to weigh as an incubus on submissive German backs with a gravity that grew heavier century by century—was sedulously transferred to no-less-willing French backs by the policy of a Napoleon whose motives in thus posing as a traditionalist were the hard-headed calculations of *raison d'état*.

The immediate effect of the Corsican adventurer's usurpation of the imperial style and title in A.D. 1804 was to vulgarize a term of Western

[1] See I. i. 343; III. iii. 276; IV. iv. 378–9; V. v. 477, n. 1; and VI. vii. 19.
[2] In IV. iv. 560–7.   [3] See II. ii. 177–9.   [4] See II. ii. 179–90.

political art whose dignity had been the only one of its pristine virtues that had not by then long since departed from it. The reigning Danubian Hapsburg monarch Francis II's self-metamorphosis from a 'Roman Emperor' into an 'Hereditary Emperor of Austria' on the 10th August, 1804, was caricatured, on the 12th October, 1822, in the proclamation of Don Pedro I as Emperor of Brazil.[1] Yet this *reductio ad absurdum* of the value of a political coinage which a Napoleon I had debased did not deter a Napoleon III from assuming, on the 2nd December, 1852, a title that was to lure him into liquidating a Second French Empire in a more conclusive disaster than the First French Empire's débâcle. Nor did the conclusiveness of the French nation's failure in the nineteenth century to re-establish the reality of a Roman Empire on ex-Roman ground in Europe deter French imperialists from seeking a more propitious field on ex-Roman ground in North-West Africa for an experiment in political necromacy that never ceased to exact sacrifices without ever forfeiting its powers of fascination.[2]

Meanwhile a German nation that was taking its revenge on the Second French Empire for the sins of the First had not waited for the capitulation of a beleaguered Paris to reassume—as it did at Versailles on the 31st December, 1870—the incubus of which it had been relieved, 64 years back, by the fortuitous combined good offices of a Corsican usurper and a Hapsburg defeatist;[3] and even the demonic twentieth-century Austrian improviser of a momentary Third German Reich, in whose wild eyes a Prussian essay in a Second German Reich and an Austrian epilogue to a First German Reich were both alike anathema, eventually came under the spell of the Roman Empire's still unlaid ghost so far as to fly in the face of his own crazy ideology by perching his vulture's-nest on a crag overhanging an enchanted Barbarossa's holy cave at Berchtesgaden[4] and by accepting the regalia of Charlemagne, stolen from a Hapsburg treasure-house, as a tribute from the *Statthalter* of the lethal lunatic's own *gleichgeschaltet* Austrian homeland.[5]

During the 134 years that had elapsed between the date of Hitler's indulgence in this freak of historical fancy and the date of Napoleon I's assumption of a usurped imperial diadem, the now fast-fading phantom of a Roman oecumenical autocrat's *khvarenah*,[6] which by that time had been haunting a Western political waste-land for more than a thousand years, had been shining with too faint a flicker of light to be capable any longer of working more serious mischief than the will-o'-the-wisp's

---

[1] See VI. vii. 22, n. 1.

[2] The quest for a consolation prize in Africa to compensate for disappointments in Europe was a motive of nineteenth-century and twentieth-century French imperialism in the Maghrib that has been noticed in Toynbee, A. J., and Boulter, V. M.: *Survey of International Affairs, 1937*, vol. i (London 1938, Milford), pp. 489–90. See also the present Study, IX. viii. 258.

[3] Francis II Hapsburg had renounced the title of Holy Roman Emperor on the 6th August, 1806.

[4] See Bryce, James: *The Holy Roman Empire*, chap. xi, *ad finem*, quoted in III. iii. 463.

[5] The regalia of the Holy Roman Empire were presented to Hitler by Seyss-Inquart on the 6th September, 1938, at the National Socialist Party's annual rally at Nuremberg. Hitler placed these treasures in the hands of the civic authorities of Nuremberg, who had been the custodians of them before A.D. 1809.

[6] See IX. viii. 548, n. 1.

prank of enticing fools to follow a treacherous gleam to their deaths. But this ideal of oecumenical unity which, on Western soil, had hitherto invariably proved abortive was only one aspect of the ghost of a senile Hellenic universal state that had been raised in St. Peter's by Pope Leo and King Charles on Christmas Day, A.D. 800. The absolutism of the Diocletianic Roman Empire's demands upon its subjects had been as characteristic a feature of this Late Hellenic political institution as its claim to world-wide dominion; and the intensive, as well as the extensive, potency of the original had been reproduced in the wraith that had been raised to haunt a Western Christendom.

'The Carolingian Empire . . . was conceived as the society of the whole Christian people under the control of a theocratic monarchy, and [it] attempted to regulate every detail of life and thought, down to the method of ecclesiastical chant and the rules of the Monastic Order, by legislative decrees and governmental inspection. . . . The fusion of temporal and spiritual powers was far more complete in the Carolingian State than it had been in the Christian barbarian kingdoms, or even in the Byzantine Empire.'[1]

Charlemagne and his successors had condemned this resuscitated Constantinian absolutism to miscarry by attempting to bring, not only every plane of human activity, but also every geographical province of Western Christendom, under the sway of this 'unitary Church State';[2] but an auspicious difference in the circumstances in which the Carolingian *tour de force* was reattempted by Frederick II Hohenstaufen made it possible for Frederick's political oecumenicalism to fail as lamentably as Charlemagne's without involving his absolutism in the disaster which had overtaken both elements in the Carolingian enterprise.

When Charlemagne had ventured on his attempt to reinaugurate a Constantinian absolutism throughout his wide-spread and still fast-expanding dominions, he had had to start building up again, from the foundations, a sophisticated social structure that had long since been rased to the ground in all the former provinces of the Roman Empire that lay within his frontiers, and this perhaps the most thoroughly of all in his own ancestral patrimony, Austrasia. By contrast, the Emperor Frederick II inherited, in the Kingdom of Sicily, a base of operations in which absolutism was already a going concern, thanks to the effective local revival there of a Late Roman dispensation by the efficient hands of his father's Norman victims' Byzantine and Muslim predecessors.[3] And, although the difference in degree of political efficiency between a thirteenth-century Sicily and an eighth-century Austrasia proved not to be great enough—vast though it was—to compensate for Frederick II's handicap in entering the lists so late in the day, the consequent failure of his attempt to unite Central and Northern Italy with Southern Italy and Sicily under a centralized oecumenical autocratic rule did not prevent him from making, as King of Sicily, the mark on Western history that he found himself impotent to make as Holy Roman Emperor. In other

---

[1] Dawson, Christopher: *Religion and the Rise of Western Culture* (London 1950, Sheed & Ward), pp. 15 and 89. The quotations from this book have been made with the permission of the author, the Society of Authors, and the publishers.
[2] Dawson, op. cit., p. 89.　　　　　　　　　　　　[3] See IX. viii. 394–5.

contexts[1] we have already observed that the effective local revival of a
Late Roman absolutism in the Kingdom of Sicily, which did not avail in
Frederick II's lifetime to serve the King-Emperor as an instrument for
making the same resuscitated absolutism likewise effective on an oecumenical scale, did stimulate a host of Late Medieval and Early Modern
Western parochial diadochi and epigoni of the *Stupor Mundi* to honour
his memory by taking his autocracy as their ensample on the less ambitious Siculo-Neapolitan geographical scale on which it had achieved so
brilliant a success.

The earliest of these successful experiments in establishing counterparts of a Byzantine Kingdom of Sicily in other provinces of Western
Christendom were the work of despots who, in the course of the quarter
of a millennium following Frederick's death in A.D. 1250, swept up the
seventy or eighty self-governing city-states of Central and Northern
Italy into not more than ten miniature empires that were, all of them,
faithful reproductions of their Sicilian prototype in proving to be so
many local graves of Medieval Italian civic liberties.[2] This local Sicilian
culture of an antediluvian weed which had thus been bedded out in Late
Medieval North Italian nursery gardens[3] was one of the principal Italian
exports to the Transmarine and Transalpine parts of Western Christendom in the diffusion of the Late Medieval Italian sub-civilization at the
turn of the fifteenth and sixteenth centuries; and in this wider field the
propagators of an inauspiciously resuscitated Late Hellenic autocracy
did not have to reperform their North Italian instructors' arduous task
of fencing in new political enclosures for the cultivation of the exotic
plant of absolutism. Beyond the Alps and the Tyrrhene Sea the North
Italian cuttings of a Late Hellenic poison-ivy that had been successfully
recultivated in Sicily found ready-made garden-beds in the existing
feudal kingdoms and principalities; and in another context[4] we have
seen how, under the impact of this imported autocracy, the medieval
parliamentary liberties of the non-Italian parts of Western Christendom
came within an ace of suffering the fate that had already overtaken the
medieval civic liberties of Italy.

In the ex-feudal Kingdom of England alone the challenge presented
to an indigenous medieval parliamentarism by the infiltration of an
exotic Italianate autocracy was successfully met by a marriage between
parliamentary liberties and autocratic efficiency which bore fruit in the
creation of a Late Modern Western form of parliamentary constitutional
government. This was, however, merely a local exception to the general

---

[1] In VII. vii. 537–8 and IX. viii. 363 and 394–5.
[2] See III. iii. 354–6 and IV. iv. 353, n. 2. In Southern Italy these civic liberties had
been extinguished some two hundred years earlier by Norman pupils of Byzantine
avatars of Roman Justinians and Diocletians. The civic liberties of the once self-governing city-states of Northern and Central Italy were extinguished—with the two notable
exceptions of Venice and Genoa—as effectively when, like Milan and Florence, they
became capitals of miniature empires as when, like Pavia and Siena, they became provincial towns; and, though the yoke of political subjection might weigh less heavily on
the necks of *ci-devant* city-states which, like Padua and Verona, had lost their independence to a tyrant city and not to a tyrant dictator, dynasty, or Papal Crown, the cities
that became subject to Venice did lose their independence no less decisively than their
sisters that became subject to the Papal Monarchy, the Medici, and the Visconti.
[3] See I. i. 19.   [4] In III. iii. 358–63.

course of political development in Western Christendom in its Early
Modern Age. In the Western World of that age, outside England, the
stalking spectre of a reanimated Diocletianic Roman absolutism won a
sweeping victory; and, though all victories are wasting assets, it took two
hundred years for the tyranny of a Philip II (*regnabat* A.D. 1555–98) to
refine itself into the 'enlightened' absolutism of a Joseph (*imperabat*
A.D. 1765–90), and three centuries for 'the divine right' of kings, who had
converted their limited hereditary feudal rights into an unlimited adventitious Justinianean prerogative, to water itself down into the prosaic
'legitimacy' pleaded by the shell-shocked beneficiaries of a brief post-
Napoleonic Restoration.

> The kings crept out—the peoples sat at home,
> And finding the long-invocated peace
> (A pall embroidered with worn images
> Of rights divine) too scant to cover doom
> Such as they suffered, cursed the corn that grew
> Rankly, to bitter bread, on Waterloo.[1]

Yet, even after the judgement passed by 'the Ideas of 1789' on a Modern
Western ghost of a Late Hellenic absolutism had been executed in the
French Revolution's mid-nineteenth-century aftermath (*metabatur*
A.D. 1848–71), a vestige of autocracy still survived in the Western World
in the Hapsburg government of Austria-Hungary and the Hohenzollern
government of Prussia-Germany; and, even when these now patently
anachronistic vestigial autocracies were tardily overthrown as a consequence of their defeat in the War of A.D. 1914–18, the sequel was to
disappoint President Wilson's sanguine endeavour to 'make the World
safe for Democracy';[2] for, when the ghost of a resuscitated Justinian,
that had still been haunting the politically backward eastern marches of
a now almost ubiquitous Western Civilization, had thus at last been laid,
the victorious 'Anglo-Saxon' institution of responsible parliamentary
representative government did not succeed to the exorcised Hapsburg
and Hohenzollern Caesars' vacant heritage. In this hour of supreme
opportunity an English-grown parliamentarism proved to be a tender
plant, which might bear admirable fruits on its native soil in England
and her daughter commonwealths founded by English settlers overseas,
but which was apt to wilt under the ordeal of transplantation to non-
Anglo-Saxon Western ground.

The anti-parliamentarian denouement in Central Europe in the inter-
war years A.D. 1919–39 gave 'Anglo-Saxon' votaries of Parliamentarism
a shocking surprise; yet the replacement of an overthrown Justinianean
'legitimacy' by a dynamically militarist-minded Agathoclean tyranny,
which was the sign of these unhappy inter-war times, had been foreshadowed, long since, in Napoleon I's exploitation of 'the Ideas of 1789'
and in Napoleon III's occupation of the vacuum left by the fall of Louis
Philippe's constitutional monarchy; and on the morrow of a Second

---

[1] Browning, E. B.: *Crowned and Buried*, Stanza xii.
[2] 'The World must be made safe for Democracy'—President Wilson in his Address
to the Congress of the United States on the 2nd April, 1917, calling for a declaration of
war against Germany.

World War it was no longer possible for Western Liberals to blind their eyes to the truth that, after all, the ghost of a resuscitated Hellenic absolutism had not been laid in Western Christendom effectually. It had no sooner been banned in one epiphany than it had reasserted itself in another; and this second visitation of an unquiet spirit was more disturbing than the first, since the demonic powers latent in Human Nature, which, in the economy of an absolute monarchy, were let loose in one lost soul alone, were 'activated' *viritim* in the eruption of a 'totalitarian' democracy that was a veritable dictatorship of Leviathan.

This Frankenstein's monster was the latest product of a *karma* from which Western Man had never succeeded in releasing himself since he had wantonly incurred it, on Christmas Day A.D. 800, by raising the ghost of an antecedent society's universal state. We may now go on to remind ourselves that this particular exhibition of the necromancer's craft on the political plane was no monopoly of the Western practitioners of the Black Art.

A ghost of a Roman Empire that had served as the Hellenic Society's universal state was raised by an Orthodox as well as by a Western Christian Hellenistic Society; and we have seen[1] that in Orthodox Christendom this necromantic *tour de force* was performed with such virtuosity that the incubus of the East Roman Empire proved heavy enough to break the Orthodox Christian Society's back in the reign of the Emperor Basil the Bulgar-killer (*imperabat* A.D. 969–1025), little more than 250 years after the local evocation of the ghost of Roman imperialism by Leo Syrus (*imperabat* A.D. 717–41). We have likewise seen[2] that neither the disastrous aftermath of the Great Romano-Bulgarian War of A.D. 977–1019 nor the submergence of a surviving remnant of Orthodox Christendom in Western Anatolia, which was the promptly exacted price of the re-erection of a simulacrum of the East Roman Empire at Constantinople in A.D. 1261, nor even the capture of the vampire Imperial City in A.D. 1453 by the 'Osmanlis, made a sufficient impression on the Greeks to break the spell of their infatuation with the ghost of an Hellenic universal state which had been exacting from them these ghastly sacrifices. They required the crowning catastrophe of A.D. 1922, in which the submerged Orthodox Christian diasporà in Anatolia was exterminated, to rid them of 'the Great Idea' of crushing themselves to death for the third time in Orthodox Christian history by once again saddling themselves with a resuscitated Roman Empire.

We have also watched the ghosts of other universal states playing the malignant role played by the Hellenic universal state's ghost in the histories of the two Christian Hellenistic civilizations. The ghost of a Syriac universal state that had eventually been embodied in the 'Abbasid Caliphate was raised at Cairo[3] after the fall of Baghdad in A.D. 1258, and was translated to Constantinople, after the fall of Cairo in A.D. 1517, to ride there malignly on the shoulders of 'Osmanlis who had inadvertently acquired this political incubus among the spoils of their victory

[1] In I. i. 64, n. 3, 65, 66, and 70; IV. iv. 320; VI. vii. 19; and IX. viii. 103.
[2] In VI. vii. 29–31.
[3] See I. i. 67, n. 2, 70, 360, and 396; II. ii. 75–76; and VI. vii. 21.

over the Mamlūks.[1] The ghost of a Sinic universal state that had been embodied in the Ts'in and Han Empire[2] returned to haunt an affiliated Far Eastern Society in the shape of the Sui and T'ang Empire;[3] and, when the main body of the Far Eastern Society propagated an offshoot on to Japanese soil, this Sinic political incubus was exported to Yamato in A.D. 645 as an indispensable piece in the conventional suite of contemporary Chinese cultural furniture, to play a weird role in its doubly exotic new environment overseas.[4]

In the analogous propagation of an offshoot of Orthodox Christendom on to Russian soil at the turn of the tenth and eleventh centuries of the Christian Era, the converted Varangian war-lords' Scandinavian mother wit or heaven-sent good fortune preserved them from committing the political solecism of dressing themselves up in a re-conditioned Roman Imperial *skaramangion* which had been transmuted on eighth-century Greek shoulders from a silken robe into a leaden cope, and on tenth-century Bulgar shoulders from a leaden cope into a corrosive shirt of Nessus. Yet the Russian offshoot of Orthodox Christendom proved, after all, unable in the long run to escape its fate of having to take delivery of an Hellenic political incubus which had become the characteristic peculiar institution of the Orthodox Christian way of life since the evocation of this ghost by Leo Syrus's necromantic genius. The Muscovite epigoni of Rurik, who provided a broken-down Russian Orthodox Christendom with its universal state,[5] won for themselves the dubious privilege of catering for this now necessary social service by equipping themselves with the redoubtable apparatus of an autocracy that consecrated its home-grown institutions by dedicating them to a Byzantine ideal. The formidable mission of casting herself for the role of a Third Rome was the price at which Moscow purchased from malicious gods her licence to monopolize the grim business of empire-building on Russian ground.[6]

Our survey up to this point has made it evident that, in the histories of civilizations of the third generation, a renaissance of the universal state of an antecedent civilization has been a not uncommon event. Indeed, among all the civilizations of this third generation that were not abortive, the Hindu Civilization is perhaps the only one in whose history we do not find this particular institution re-emerging from the psychic storeroom of the affiliated society's memory of the apparented society's life and works; for, in the history of the Iranic Muslim Civilization, we can perhaps detect in Timur Lenk's warped empire-building activities a belated and abortive attempt at a revival of the antecedent Syriac Society's universal state if we follow up the clue offered to us by the resemblances between Timur's career and Charlemagne's.[7] If Timur's demonic temperament had not carried him to fatally farther lengths

---

[1] See VI. vii. 21–27.
[2] Points of likeness and difference between the renaissances of the Sinic and Hellenic universal states are examined on pp. 649–81, below.
[3] See II. ii. 376; III. iii. 449; and VI. vii. 19.
[4] See II. ii. 158–9 and VI. vii. 40–41.
[5] See IV. iv. 88; V. v. 312; V. vi. 191 and 309.
[6] See VI. vii. 31–40 and IX. viii. 676–8.
[7] See IV. iv. 488–504.

than Charlemagne's limit in committing the marchman's besetting sin of turning his arms against the interior of the world which it is his historical mission to defend, it is conceivable that the Transoxanian empire-builder might have emulated the achievement of his Austrasian counterpart, who raised a ghost of the Roman Empire in Western Christendom, by raising a ghost of the 'Abbasid Caliphate on Iranic Muslim ground—though we may also surmise that, even if Timur had achieved the utmost success within his power in this enterprise, the contrast between a Timurid caricature of the Baghdādī 'Abbasid Caliphate at Samarqand and a contemporary 'Abbasid reproduction of the Baghdādī 'Abbasid Caliphate at Cairo would have been even greater than the historic contrast between Charlemagne's caricature and Leo Syrus's reproduction of the Roman Empire.

In every instance of either an effectual or an abortive evocation of an antecedent civilization's universal state that we have examined up to this point, the society whose life this *revenant* has haunted has been linked through a chrysalis-church[1] with the society out of whose ashes the spectre has been conjured up. Is a chrysalis-church an indispensable officiant in the rite whereby this feat of evocation is accomplished? Or are there cases in which the ghost of an antecedent civilization's universal state has been evoked by a civilization which has been linked with its predecessor, not through a chrysalis-church constructed by the predecessor's internal proletariat, but through the predecessor's external proletariat or its dominant minority?[2] The answers to these questions likewise may prove to be indicated by the Carolingian clue which has just enabled us to detect an abortive evocation of a ghost of the 'Abbasid Caliphate on Iranic Muslim ground by Timur Lenk; for, in the early histories of at least three secondary civilizations derived from primary predecessors through these predecessors' external proletariats, we find polities that bear a closer apparent family likeness to Charlemagne's empire than Timur's empire displays. The polities in question are the Chóu Empire in Sinic history,[3] the Khatti Empire in Hittite history, and the Toltec Empire in Mexic history.[4]

All these three empires resemble the Carolingian Empire in being products of barbarian interlopers who had established themselves within the former frontiers of the universal state of an antecedent civilization. All three empires also resemble the Carolingian Empire in the further point of having their political centre of gravity in regions which, in the geography of the antecedent civilization and its universal state, had

[1] This conception of the role of churches in the histories of civilizations has been examined in VII. vii. 392–419.
[2] Our classification of societies in which these distinctions are drawn is set out in the table IV in vol. vii, facing p. 772.
[3] In the tables in vol. i, pp. 131–3 and 186, the Sinic Society has been wrongly classified as a primary civilization, in contradiction to the Sinic Society's own tradition that the Chóu culture was a secondary one which had been preceded by that of the Shang (*alias* Yin). Since the publication of the first three volumes of this Study in A.D. 1934, the Sinic Society's tradition about its own antecedents had been confirmed by the progress of archaeological discovery (see VI. vii. 213, n. 1).
[4] For the Toltec Empire, see Gann, Th.: *Mexico from the Earliest Times to the Conquest* (London 1936, Lovat Dickson), pp. 34–50; Vaillant, G. C.: *The Aztecs of Mexico* (London 1950, Penguin), pp. 65–82.

been, not central, but peripheral. The geographical situation of Charlemagne's Austrasia in what had been the Rhenish march of the Roman
Empire has manifest parallels in the geographical situations of these
other three empires' nuclei. The Chóu Dynasty's original patrimony lay
in the Wei Basin, which had been the western marchland of the Shang
culture and which was to continue to play the same role in the successive
histories of the Sinic and the Far Eastern Civilization.[1] The Khatti
Empire's metropolitan territory lay in the former western marchland of
a Sumeric universal state on the eastern fringe of the Anatolian Plateau.
The Toltec Empire's capital city, Tula, lay in the former north-western
hinterland of 'the First Empire' of the Mayas on the south-eastern fringe
of the Mexican Plateau.

The four empires that we are comparing bear a further and more intimate resemblance to one another in being, all alike, feudal in their
organization. All four were loose and unstable associations of divers
peoples constituting so many separate principalities or kingdoms that
were held together precariously under the never quite unchallenged
overlordship of one of their number.[2] This ramshackle constitution was
a birth-mark that was also a death-warrant; and the slow agony of the
Holy Roman Empire's decline and fall, in the course of the 1,005 years
and seven and a half months intervening between Charlemagne's coronation at Rome on Christmas Day A.D. 800 and Francis II's abdication
at Vienna on the 6th August, 1806, has a striking parallel in Sinic history
in the eight or nine hundred years[3] long *dégringolade* of a Chóu Empire
which received its Napoleonic *coup de grâce* in 249 B.C. at the brutal
hands of the revolutionary militarist principality of Ts'in. The ninth-
century collapse of the Carolingians, the eleventh-century humiliation
of the Carolingians' Franconian successors by Pope Gregory VII, and
the thirteenth-century overthrow of the Hohenstaufen by Pope Innocent
IV, are milestones on a leisurely yet unswerving road to ruin that have
their counterparts in the history of the Chóu in the successive catastrophes of 841 and 771–0 B.C.[4]

The four-hundred-years-long history of the Khatti Empire was
chequered by a corresponding series of collapses and recoveries ending
in the final cataclysm in the first decade of the twelfth century B.C.
Though the progress of Modern Western archaeological discovery in
South-West Asia during the second quarter of the twentieth century of
the Christian Era had brought to light evidence indicating that a supposed blank interval of 150 or 200 years between the fall of the First
Empire of Khatti and the rise of the Second Empire[5] was the figment of

---

[1] See VI. vii. 212, n. 4.

[2] For the structure of the Toltec Empire, see Gann, op. cit., pp. 35–36 and 44. The
similarity in point of structure between the Chóu Empire and the Carolingian Empire
leaps to the eye when the map on p. 13 in A. Herrmann's *Historical and Commercial
Atlas of China* (Cambridge, Mass. 1935, Harvard University Press) is placed side by
side with Maps No. 29 and No. 30 in K. von Spruner's and Th. Menke's *Hand-Atlas
für die Geschichte des Mittelalters und der Neueren Zeit* (Gotha 1880, Perthes).

[3] Our estimate of the Chóu Empire's duration will differ according to whether we
follow the Sinic official tradition in accepting 1122 B.C. as the date of the Chóu Dynasty's
overthrow of the Shang, or whether we adopt the shorter chronology which dates this
revolution *circa* 1050 B.C. (see VI. vii. 212, n. 4).

[4] See ibid.   [5] See I. i. 111.

an erroneous chronology,[1] this excision of an imaginary dark age did not invalidate the evidence indicating a break in the continuity of Hittite political history between the reign of a Telepinu who was the last emperor of the first line and the reign of a Tutkhaliya who was the first emperor of the second line—even though the time-interval between these two reigns had to be estimated, on a revised chronological reckoning, in terms of months or years instead of generations or centuries. Nor did the New Empire, once established, run its 250 years' course from the later decades of the fifteenth century to the first decade of the twelfth century without at least one muffled jolt; for the account, in the imperial archives at Boghazqal'eh, of the solution of an admittedly acute political crisis in the first decade of the fourteenth century through the association of Suppiluliuma on the imperial throne side by side with his 'father' Tutkhaliya the Weakling reads suspiciously like a notification, in the bland language of official historiography, of a change of dynasty[2] that would be a counterpart in Hittite history of the replacement of the Merovingians by the Carolingians in the discreetly managed Frankish dynastic revolution of A.D. 751.

These manifold and remarkable points of likeness between the Khatti, Toltec, and Chóu Empires and the Carolingian Empire lead a student of history to wonder whether they may not be due, at least in part, to some common element in the four empires' respective origins. The Chóu Empire actually represented itself as being what the Carolingian Empire likewise avowedly was; for the Chóu Empire professed to be a revival of an antecedent Shang Empire at the hands of the barbarian invaders by whom the Shang had been overthrown. This Sinic claim was duly vindicated by the progress of archaeological discovery after it had been contested at the tribunal of an arrogantly hypercritical school of latter-day Western historians; and these notoriously captious critics had never denied that the rise of the Khatti Empire had been preceded by the fall of an Empire of Sumer and Akkad which we have identified as being the Sumeric Civilization's universal state, or that an 'Old Empire' of the Mayas, which we have identified as being the Mayan universal state, had come and gone before the rise of the Empire of the Toltecs. On this showing, was it too rash a conjecture to surmise that the Toltec and Khatti Empires were not merely sequels to the Mayan and Sumero-Akkadian Empires in the bare chronological sense, but were also deliberate attempts—such as the Chóu and Carolingian Empires were known to have been—to bring these dead predecessors back to life by a feat of necromancy?

Our survey of renaissances of political ideas, ideals, and institutions would be incomplete if we were to confine it to the foregoing consideration of diverse types of polity. This would leave still unexplained, for example, the striking contrast between the incompetence that is a common characteristic of the Chóu Empire, the Khatti Empire, and the

[1] See the Note on Chronology in vol. x, on pp. 171–212.
[2] See Cavaignac, E.: *Le Problème Hittite* (Paris 1936, Leroux), p. 29, and Götze, A.: *Hethiter, Churriter, und Assyrer* (Oslo 1936, Aschenhoug; London 1936, Williams & Norgate), p. 56.

Carolingian Empire and the efficiency that is a no less patent common characteristic of the T'ang Empire and the East Roman Empire. The reason why we find our array of ghosts of universal states thus sorting itself out into two conspicuously diverse types does not become apparent until we go on to observe that the political necromancers who conjured up the T'ang Empire and the East Roman Empire were not content simply to revive the styles, titles, and pretensions of the defunct universal states that they were seeking to bring back to life. In both cases they went on to give substance to these resuscitated forms by recreating the classically educated lay professional civil service which had been the life and soul of the Han Empire and the Roman Empire when these universal states had been present on Earth in the flesh.

These evocations of a ghost of the Roman imperial civil service in the East Roman Empire in and after A.D. 864[1] and a ghost of the Han imperial civil service in the T'ang Empire in and after the reign of T'ai Tsung (*imperabat* A.D. 627–49)[2] have already been noticed in other contexts, and in this place we have merely to observe that this renaissance of a vital human instrument of imperial administration accounts satisfactorily for the solidity which so impressively distinguishes the T'ang and the East Roman body politic[3] from the general ruck of walking ghosts of universal states.[4] We may go on to observe that the Carolingian Empire attempted, without success, to fortify itself by the less laborious expedient of investing itself with a religious sanction, symbolized in the revival of a rite which was familiar to Early Western Christian minds, more than thirteen centuries after this rite had been put out of action as a consequence of the successive falls of the Kingdoms of Israel and Judah, because the memory of it had been preserved in historical records that had come to rank among the Holy Scriptures of the Christian Church before the Church had become a chrysalis for the incubation of a nascent Western Christendom out of the mortal coils of a dead Hellenic World.

The religious sanction given to the formal revival of the Roman Empire in the West on Christmas Day, A.D. 800, when a Frankish king was created Roman Emperor in virtue of being crowned by the Pope, had no precedent in the unconstitutional history of the authentic Roman Empire, in which the Caesar-making proxy of an impotent Roman Senate and People had been, not the Clergy, but the Army.[5] The

---

[1] See IV. iv. 345, with nn. 2, 3, and 4.

[2] See VI. vii. 357, n. 4, 365, n. 4, 369, and 370–2.

[3] In previous examinations of the genesis of the East Roman Empire we have already noticed the incentive that moved its architects first to raise a defunct Roman Empire from the dead and then to clothe this phantom in flesh and blood by recreating the Roman imperial civil service. These successive feats of necromancy were Orthodox Christendom's responses to the challenge of being bombarded at point-blank range by the explosive militancy of the Primitive Muslim Arabs (see II. ii. 369 and 384–5, and IV. iv. 323).

[4] The historical problem raised by the still more massive solidity of 'the Old Kingdom' of Egypt is discussed on pp. 682–92, below.

[5] The religious sanction that was not only explicit but was also all-important in the consecration of Charlemagne and his successors as Holy Roman Emperors in the West had been foreshadowed, however, in the political ideology of a Later Roman Empire when the abuse of the Caesar-making power by the soldiers during a century of anarchy (*saeviebat* A.D. 193–284) had revealed the full measure of the soldiers' contempt for a

ceremony performed on the 25th December, 800, at Rome had, how-ever, a pertinent precedent in a ceremony performed at Soissons in or about November, 751,[1] when the Austrasian major-domo Pepin had been created King of the Franks in virtue of being crowned and anointed by Pope Zacharias' representative Saint Boniface, and this consecration of Pepin, which had been recelebrated by Pope Stephen II in person at Saint Denis on the 28th July,[2] 754, was a Western Christian rite—already customary by that time in Visigothia—which was the revival of an Israelite institution commemorated in the Books of Samuel and Kings.

'There can be no question that its ultimate origin is to be found in the Old Testament, where it embodies the theocratic principle and the depen-dence of the secular power on the spiritual power of the prophet, as we see in the case of Samuel anointing David in place of Saul,[3] and in the even more dramatic story of Eliseus's [Elisha's] mission to anoint Jehu as king to destroy the house of Ahab.[4] In both of these cases the prophet as the representative of God intervenes to change the course of History by transferring the kingship to a new line, and we can hardly doubt that these precedents were in the minds of the Pope and Saint Boniface and the advisers of King Pepin when the new rite was introduced.'[5]

This Western Christian renaissance of an Israelite institution did not avail to give the Carolingian Empire the durability of its more solidly constructed East Roman counterpart and rival, but the unavailingly resuscitated Syriac rite was nevertheless to play an historic part in the Western World's political life.

'Henceforward it was to be a characteristic feature of Western kingship, so that the chrism or oil of consecration was held to confer a new sacred character on the person of the ruler. . . . The evolution of the English coronation rite takes us back with hardly any serious gaps to its Carolin-gian origins.'[6]

(b) RENAISSANCES OF SYSTEMS OF LAW

In proceeding with our survey of renaissances in divers fields of activity, we may now pass on from the province of political ideas, ideals, and institutions to the province of Law, in which the realities of ordinary life are reflected more faithfully than they are in Politics.

living god who was their own creature. This fearful experience had given birth to the idea that a divine ruler whose divinity could be liquidated by killing its human incarna-tion was more vulnerable than a ruler who did not profess to be more than a mortal himself, but who did claim to be the chosen instrument and protégé of a god whom the soldiers could neither assassinate nor intimidate, because this divine patron of a human ruler who was His vicegerent on Earth was Himself invisible and intangible. 'Aurelian . . . used to say that the soldiers deceived themselves in supposing that the destinies of the Emperors lay in their hands. For he used to aver that it was God who had bestowed the purple and . . . had decided the period of his reign' (*Auctor Anonymus post Dionem*, quoted in V. v. 649, n. 4).
[1] See Hodgkin, Th.: *Italy and her Invaders*, vol. vii (Oxford 1899, Clarendon Press), p. 134, n. 2.
[2] Doubt is cast upon this date by Hodgkin, ibid., pp. 230–1; but it rests on the authority of an abbot of Saint Denis—the scene of the ceremony—who died only sixty years after the event.
[3] 1 Sam. xvi. 1–13.   [4] 2 Kings ix. 1–10.
[5] Dawson, Christopher: *Religion and the Rise of Western Culture* (London 1950, Sheed & Ward), pp. 85–86.   [6] Dawson, op. cit., pp. 85 and 92.

We have seen that, after a post-Hellenic interregnum had declared itself on the political plane in the break-up of a unitary Roman Empire into a mosaic of indigenous and barbarian successor-states, the emergence of two new Hellenistic Christian civilizations found its political expression in attempts to raise the Roman Empire from the dead.[1] On the legal plane, as we have also noticed already in other contexts, a Roman Law, which, in the course of ten centuries ending in Justinian's generation, had been slowly and laboriously elaborated to meet the complicated requirements of a sophisticated oecumenical Hellenic Society,[2] was swiftly left stranded[3]—and this in the comparatively robust Centre and East, as well as in the sickly West, of a collapsing Hellenic World—by the rapid obsolescence of the whole way of life to which the Roman Law had come to be so nicely geared. Thereafter, the symptoms of decay and death were followed in due course by manifestations of fresh life on the legal, as on the political, plane; but, in a nascent Orthodox Christendom and a nascent Western Christendom alike, the impulse to provide a live law for a living society did not find its first vent in any move to reanimate a Roman Law that, in the eighth century of the Christian Era, was sitting perched, far above contemporary heads, on a pinnacle of the mighty mausoleum of an extinct Hellenic culture, like Noah's Ark when the subsidence of the Flood had left that now superfluous house-boat high and dry on the inaccessible summit of Mount Ararat. In the legal sphere the first move in both these new worlds was, not to raise a ghost, but to perform an act of creation. Each of these two Christian societies demonstrated the sincerity of its belief in a Christian dispensation by attempting to create a Christian Law for a would-be Christian people. In both Christendoms, however, this new departure in a would-be Christian direction was followed by a renaissance, first of the Israelitish law that was latent in Christianity's Scriptural heritage from Jewry, and then of a Justinianean Law which floated clear again when the level at which it had been stranded was reached by these resurgent civilizations' rising waters.

In Orthodox Christendom the Christian new departure was announced, in the joint reign of the two Syrian founders of the East Roman Empire, Leo III and his son Constantine V, in the promulgation, in March, A.D. 740,[4] of 'a Christian law book' which was 'a deliberate attempt to change the legal system of the Empire by an application of Christian principles'.[5] This revolutionary work was published under the conservative title of 'A Selection (ἐκλογή), in Abridgment, of the Institutes, Digest, Code, and Novels of the Great Justinian'; but its two imperial promulgators showed their hand and gave notice of their aspirations by adding in the same breath that the work was 'also a Rectification in the Direction of Greater Humanity (καὶ ἐπιδιόρθωσις εἰς τὸ φιλανθρωπότερον)'; and, in the first paragraph of the preface, the

---

[1] See pp. 9–15, above.   [2] See VI. vii. 265–8.
[3] See III. iii. 266, n. 1, and VI. vii. 279–80.
[4] For the date, see P. Collinet in *The Cambridge Medieval History*, vol. iv (Cambridge 1923, University Press), p. 708.
[5] Bury, J. B., in his edition of Edward Gibbon: *The History of the Decline and Fall of the Roman Empire*, Editio Minor, vol. v (London 1901, Methuen), Appendix 11, p. 526.

source of law was declared to be (not legislation enacted by the Roman People but) revelation vouchsafed by God, and the sanction of law to be (not human enforcement but) divine retribution.

'Our God who is the lord and maker of all things, the creator of Man who has endowed Man with the privilege of free will, has (in the language of prophecy) given Man, to help him, a law in which God has made known to Man everything that Man ought to do and to shun. The conduct prescribed by the law is to be adopted because it is a passport to salvation (ὡς σωτηρίας ὄντα πρόξενα); the conduct prohibited by the law is to be eschewed because it brings punishment on the transgressor. No one who keeps these commandments or who—save the mark—disregards them will fail to receive the appropriate recompense for his deeds of whatever character. For it is God who has proclaimed both the positive and the negative commandments in advance [of the human legislator]; and the power of God's words—a power that knows no variation and that rewards every man's works according to their deserts—shall (in gospel language) not pass away.'

This passage and its sequel drew the following pertinent comment from a Modern Western historian who was equally conversant with an East Roman and an Hellenic mental environment:

'What especially strikes one who is accustomed to the language of Gaius or Tribonian is the ecclesiastical note which characterises both the preface and other parts of the *Ecloga*. The point of view of the old Roman jurists had been almost completely lost, and the spirit of Roman Law had been transformed in the religious atmosphere of Christendom. Men tried now to base jurisdiction on Revelation, and to justify laws by verses of Scripture.'[1]

A Modern Western student of the *Ecloga*, if asked how far, in his opinion, its authors were justified in their claim to have humanized the Justinianean Law, would perhaps place his finger first on the mitigation, here at last, of the barbaric native Roman institution of the *Patria Potestas*,[2] after this enormity had successfully resisted all the expurgatory efforts of cultivated jurisconsults, steeped in the humane atmosphere of the Hellenic schools of philosophy, who had laboured, over a span of four centuries or more ending in the Severan Age,[3] to render an archaic Roman Law worthy of a post-Alexandrine Hellenic Civilization that had been constrained to receive this antiquated legal dispensation as

---

[1] Bury, J. B.: *A History of the Later Roman Empire from Arcadius to Irene (395 A.D. to 800 A.D.)*, 1st ed. (London 1889, Macmillan, 2 vols.), vol. ii, p. 414.

[2] 'The *Patria Potestas* still holds an important place in the Justinianean Law, although the rights which it gave the father over the children were small indeed compared with the absolute control which had been enjoyed in ancient times. The tendency was to diminish these rights and to modify the stern conception of *Patria Potestas* by substituting the conception of a natural guardianship: a change corresponding to the change (promoted by Christianity) in the conception of the family, as held together by the duties of affection rather than by legal obligations. The two most important points in the later transformation of the *Patria Potestas* were (1) its conversion into a parental *potestas*, the mother being recognized as having the same rights and duties as the father (thus her consent, as well as the father's, is necessary for the contraction of a marriage), and (2) the increased facilities for emancipation when the child came to years of discretion; emancipation seems to have been effected by the act of setting up a separate establishment. These principles were established by the Iconoclasts' (Bury, J. B., Appendix 11 to his minor edition of Gibbon's History, vol. v, p. 528).

[3] See VI. vii. 262–3 and 265–8.

a consequence of Rome's conquest of the Hellenic World. If asked, next, which was the chapter in which the influence of Christianity on the *Ecloga* was most conspicuous, the Modern Western student would assuredly have singled out the chapter on Marriage; for in this field the fundamental principles of the Roman Law, which, 'as accepted and interpreted by Justinian, laid down that no bond between human beings was indissoluble, and that separation of husband and wife was a private act, requiring no judicial permission',[1] were overridden in the *Ecloga* by provisions embodying the irreconcilably different Christian view[2] that marriage was a partnership for life and that to remarry after being divorced was to commit adultery.[3] These would not, however, have been the answers that the same two questions would have been likely to receive from Orthodox Christians, either jurists or laymen, in any

---

[1] Bury, Appendix, p. 527.

[2] The 'lofty conception of family life' (Collinet, op. cit., p. 709), which the authors of the *Ecloga* had imbibed from Christianity, had, of course, been derived by the Christian Church from a Jewry that had been its matrix. The very passage in the Gospels (Matt. xix. 3–9; Mark x. 2–9) criticizing the facility with which a husband could divorce his wife according to the provisions of the Deuteronomic Code (Deut. xxiv. 1) was an echo of domestic controversies within the bosom of a Jewry which had morally outgrown the Deuteronomic dispensation by the beginning of the Christian Era. This high standard in the sphere of family relations had been one of the most striking features by which the social life of the Jews in the diasporà had been distinguished, to its credit, from the contemporary life of a post-Alexandrine Hellenic Society in which the Jews had come to be dispersed abroad, and from which the vast majority of the converts to Christianity had subsequently been drawn. The fifth and seventh chapters of Saint Paul's First Epistle to the Corinthians bear witness to the difficulty of inducing Hellene Gentile Christians to rise, in this sphere, to contemporary Jewish standards. These standards were learnt from Judaism by Christianity at first hand, in the generation of the first Hellenic Gentile converts; and later generations of Gentile Christians, who might have been loath in any case to recognize that a Christian virtue had a Jewish origin, were the more easily able to forget their ethical debt to Jewry in the sphere of family relations because, in the canon of Scripture which the Church had taken over from Jewry as Christianity's 'Old Testament', the principles and practice of a post-Exilic Judaism in this province of life figured far less prominently than the luxuriant polygamy that had been the rule among the Israelites' Afrasian Nomad ancestors in their heroic age in the days of the dissolution of 'the New Empire' of Egypt and the foundering of the Minoan World.

It was left for the Latter-day Saints of the Mormon Church and other nineteenth-century sects of Protestant Christian origin in the New World to carry their Bibliolatry to the point of making a law unto themselves out of the polygamy of the Hebrew Patriarchs as portrayed in the Book of Genesis. These un-ironic-minded 'Bible Christians' do not seem to have taken cognisance of the significant historical fact that the particular Biblical way of family life to which they were piously harking back had by this date been eschewed by the Jews for twenty-four Post-Exilic centuries, at the shortest reckoning.

The tale of centuries would be twenty-five if it could be accepted as an established finding of Modern Western scholarship that a passage in 2 Kings (xxii. 3–xxiii. 25) is to be interpreted as implying that the Book of Deuteronomy was promulgated, under show of being rediscovered, in a Pre-Exilic Kingdom of Judah in the eighteenth year of the reign of King Josiah, i.e. in the year 621 B.C. (see Smith, J. M. P.: *The Origin and History of Hebrew Law* (Chicago 1931, University of Chicago Press), pp. 39–40); for a comparison of the stipulation in the Book of Deuteronomy, xvii. 17—'Neither shall he [the King] multiply wives to himself, that his heart turn not away; neither shall he greatly multiply to himself silver and gold'—with the account, in 1 Kings xi. 1–8, of the luxuriant idolatry into which King Solomon had been led astray by his luxuriant polygamy, indicates that, between Solomon's day and Josiah's, a Solomonian polygamy, which had been as costly to the Israelite tax-payer as its religious sequel had been abominable in the sight of the strict worshipper of Yahweh, had produced in Judah a disapproval of polygamy in high places which was bound after, if not before, the fall of the monarchy to broaden into a disapproval of polygamy in itself.

[3] 'The influence of the ecclesiastical view of Marriage as a *consortium vitae* can be seen too in the treatment of the property of the married partners' (Bury, ibid.; cp. Collinet, in op. cit., p. 709).

generation from the age of the authors of the *Ecloga* themselves down to the time of writing. Orthodox Christians, if thus interrogated, would have been apt to answer that the most humane and, on this evidence, the most Christian, chapter of the *Ecloga* was Chapter Seventeen, which lays down the penalties for crimes.

'The tendency of the *Ecloga* was to avoid capital punishment as far as possible. . . . Its distinguishing feature is the use of mutilation as a mode of punishment[1]—a penalty unknown in Roman Law. . . . Since mutilation was generally ordained in cases where the penalty had formerly been death, the law-givers could certainly claim that their code was more lenient. . . . [But] we may question whether this tendency was due so much to the growth of feelings of humanity as to ecclesiastical motives, namely the active maintenance of the asylum privileges of Christian sanctuaries, and the doctrine of repentance.'[2]

Whatever the origins of this tendency to substitute mutilation for capital punishment may have been,[3] it was certainly a radical new departure which had a profound and an enduring effect on the Orthodox Christian êthos; but, when a new departure in the domain of Law was inspired by a Christian theology which placed the Old Testament on a par with the New Testament at the infinite altitude of absolute authoritativeness which was the self-evident prerogative of all Scriptures that were accepted as being the divinely revealed Word of God, it was almost inevitable that the birth of a new Christian law should be followed by a renaissance of the latent law of an Israel to which the Christian Church had insisted on affiliating itself by the compromising act of including the Books of the Law and the Prophets among Christianity's spiritual *impedimenta*.

When we count up the references or allusions to the Bible in the pre-

[1] The table of penalties in *Ecloga*, chap. 17, is summarized in Bury, Appendix, p. 529.—A.J.T.

[2] Bury, Appendix, p. 529, following Zachariä von Lingenthal, K. E.: *Geschichte des Griechisch-Römischen Rechts* (Berlin 1892, Weidmann), pp. 330–3. When the writer of this Study was making the present footnote on the 10th March, 1950, he had at one elbow Bury's own copy of this work of Zachariä von Lingenthal's, marked with the notes in pencil, from Bury's hand, which the English historian had eventually used in writing his own appendix on Graeco-Roman Law, while at his other elbow he had the copy of the volume of Bury's edition of Gibbon, containing this appendix, which had been given to the writer by his Mother forty-five years back. The impression which this appendix had made on his mind at his first reading of it in A.D. 1905 had lost none of its vividness during the time that had passed between his receipt of this impression and his utilization of it.

[3] One source of this new type of punishment seems to have been existing customary practice. 'The Roman magistrates seem to have made occasional use of such discretion as was allowed to them in the determination of punishments in order to inflict punishments' consisting of some form of mutilation (Zachariä von Lingenthal, op. cit., p. 331; cp. Collinet, op. cit., pp. 709–10). Zachariä von Lingenthal (op. cit., p. 332) throws out the conjecture that the authors of the *Ecloga* may have been influenced by an exhortation —thrice repeated in the Gospels (Matt. v. 29–30; Matt. xviii. 8–9; Mark x. 43–47)—to cut off or pluck out a hand, foot, eye, or other offending member rather than condemn oneself to be cast into hell fire unmutilated. This remains no more than a guess, since none of these texts is actually cited in the *Ecloga*; but, if Orthodox Christian legislators did indeed take literally a piece of Primitive Christian poetry in which the problems of the Soul are approached in terms of physical symbolism, this unfortunate misinterpretation would be analogous, in its solemn innocence of irony, to the fortunate misinterpretation of Ovid's cynical prescriptions for the conduct of sordid amours which was one source of the Medieval Western troubadours' ideal of Romantic Love (see Lewis, C. S.: *The Allegory of Love: A Study in Medieval Tradition* (Oxford 1936, Clarendon Press)).

face to the *Ecloga*, we find that the Old Testament is cited half as many times again as the New Testament.[1] It is true that all the six citations from the Old Testament are taken from 'the Prophets' (in the comprehensive traditional Jewish usage of that label) and not from 'the Law'; and the Prophet Amos seems to have been especially venerated by Leo Syrus, to judge by the fact that this emperor not only cited one text from the Book of Amos in the preface to the *Ecloga* but also reproduced another[2] in mosaic over the chancel arch of the church of Saint Eirênê at Constantinople when he rebuilt it after a fire.[3] Yet, in this Orthodox Christian evocation of the Old Testament in the field of Law, it was inevitable that, in the long run, 'the Law', and not 'the Prophets', should prevail; and, sure enough, an *Ecloga Legis Mosaïcae* eventually made its appearance in the corpus of an *Ecloga ad Procheirum Mutata* derived from an *Ecloga Privata* which was itself an emanation from the original *Ecloga* promulgated by the Emperors Leo and Constantine in A.D. 740.[4]

If there is truth in the proverb that 'coming events cast their shadows before them', we should not be surprised to find in the original *Ecloga* some unacknowledged influence of a Mosaic Law that, in the gradual development of East Roman legislation, was to take perhaps as many as four centuries to rise naked to the surface; and, if we apply this clue to our search for the original inspiration of the *Ecloga*'s revolutionary partiality for punishments in the form of mutilations, commended as 'humanitarian' substitutes for the death penalty, we may come to the conclusion that the eighth-century legislator is more likely to have been inspired by a correctly literal interpretation of the *Lex Talionis*[5] as enunciated in 'the Covenant Code'[6] of the *Corpus Mosaïcum* than by an

---

[1] The passages cited from the New Testament are 1 Pet. i. 17; 1 Pet. v. 2; Luke xvi. 17; John vii. 24. Those cited from the Old Testament are Isa. viii. 20; Ps. lviii. 1–2 [in the Septuagint's version: Ps. lvii. 2–3]; Eccl. vii. 4 and 6; 1 Kings iii. 16–28; Isa. v. 23–24; Amos ii. 6.   [2] Amos ix. 6.

[3] See Freshfield, E. H.: *Roman Law in the Late Roman Empire* (Cambridge 1932, Bowes & Bowes), p. 46.   [4] See Collinet, op. cit., p. 717.

[5] The possibility that, in this point, the *Ecloga* may owe an unacknowledged debt to the *Corpus Mosaïcum* comes to look almost like a positive probability when we observe that the contrast between the *Ecloga* and the *Corpus Iustinianeum* in the matter of their respective philosophies of punishment had been anticipated by a corresponding contrast between Israel's 'Covenant Code' and the Sumeric Code of Hammurabi. 'The Code of Hammurabi is much the more severe of the two and uses the penalty of capital punishment to a much greater extent' (Smith, J. M. P.: *The Origin and History of Hebrew Law* (Chicago 1931, University of Chicago Press), p. 20, quoted already in Bk. VII. vii. 293, n. 1). On the other hand 'the rectification in the direction of greater humanity' which 'the Covenant Code', like the *Ecloga*, introduced in its departures from the provisions of the latest code of an antecedent civilization largely consisted, in the earlier case as well as in the later, in the replacement of the death penalty by various forms of mutilation: 'Eye for eye, tooth for tooth, hand for hand, foot for foot, burning for burning, wound for wound, stripe for stripe' (Exod. xxi. 24–25). We may also observe that the Code of Hammurabi and the *Corpus Iustinianeum* agreed with one another on a further point of common difference from the Mosaic Law and the *Ecloga* alike. 'The second decalogue of "the Covenant Code" (Exod. xxi. 12–27) deals with personal injuries. The Code of Hammurabi deals with the same class of offences (§§ 195–214). The greater number of the laws in Hammurabi's Code is due in part to the fact that the fine or penalty is graded according to the social and economic rank of the one injured' (Smith, op. cit., pp. 21–22). Correspondingly, 'it is worth while to observe in the *Ecloga* a democratic feature which marks a real advance, in the interests of justice, on the Justinianean code. The *Ecloga* metes out the same penalties to poor and rich, whereas the older law had constantly ordained different punishments for the same offence, according to the rank and fortune of the offender' (Bury, Appendix, p. 530).

[6] Exod. xxi. 23–25.

incorrectly literal interpretation of a piece of poetic symbolism in the New Testament.[1]

In contrast to the gradualness and unselfconsciousness of this renaissance of the Mosaic Law out of an Orthodox Christian Law's Israelite Scriptural heritage, the renaissance of the Roman Law out of Orthodox Christendom's own Hellenic antecedents[2] was both selfconscious and abrupt. In the preface to 'the Handbook' (ὁ πρόχειρος νόμος) promulgated between the years A.D. 870 and A.D. 879 by the founder of the Macedonian Dynasty of East Roman Emperors, Basil I, in conjunction with his sons and colleagues Constantine and Leo (VI), the new legislators gave notice[3] that the *Ecloga* was hereby abrogated, not indeed entirely, 'but to the requisite extent' (ἀλλ᾿ ὅσον ὤφειλεν), while, in the preface to a subsequent draft for a second edition (ἐπαναγωγή) of 'the Handbook' which was published between the years A.D. 879 and A.D. 886 in the names of the Emperors Basil I, Leo VI, and Alexander, notice was given that 'Our Imperial Majesty . . . has totally (πάντη) rejected and scrapped the imbecilities promulgated by the Isaurians[4] in defiance of the . . . Divine Dogma and to the undoing of the salutary laws'.

The *odium theologicum* which the Macedonian Emperors here advertise as their motive for setting themselves the task of superseding their Syrian predecessors' legislation either partially or completely might perhaps not have been a sufficiently powerful motive in itself to nerve them for the formidable positive enterprise of resuscitating the Justinianean Law if they had not already found their hands being forced by the mounting pressure of practical needs arising from an increasing complication and sophistication of life in the body social of a then rapidly advancing Orthodox Christian Civilization. The relatively simple 'Selection' that had satisfied the legal requirements of the nascent Orthodox Christendom of the eighth century of the Christian Era was inadequate to meet the additional demands made on the Law by the cumulative effect of a subsequent 130 years and more of social progress; and we may conjecture that, even if the Syrian Dynasty had not identified itself with Iconoclasm, or, alternatively, if the Iconoclastic Movement which the Syrian Emperors did promote had never been reversed by an Iconodule reaction, a ninth-century East Roman Imperial Government would still have found in a resuscitation of the Justinianean Law the most obvious method open to them for providing a more advanced Orthodox Christian Society with the more subtle legal apparatus which had now become one of its crying needs. In any case—whatever may have been the respective parts played by practical necessity and religious animus in stimulating the Macedonian legislators to engage in necromancy—their two preliminary experiments in the Black Art, of which 'the Handbook' and 'the Second Edition' were the trophies, were followed up promptly by the promulgation, *circa* A.D. 888–90,[5] of 'the Imperial Decisions' (τὰ βασιλικά) in no less than sixty books, and tardily[6]

---

[1] See p. 25, n. 3, above.   [2] See IX. viii. 103.
[3] *Procheirum,* Preface, § 2.
[4] i.e., by the Emperors of the Syrian Dynasty.—A.J.T.
[5] For the date, see Collinet, op. cit., p. 713.
[6] Constantine IX (X) Monomákhos's Law School had the same ironic fate as the

by the foundation of an Imperial School of Law at Constantinople in
A.D. 1045.[1]

The ninth-century Vasilican ghost of a sixth-century *Corpus Iustinianeum* resembles its original in presenting an imposing first appearance
which it is incapable of sustaining under closer examination. The only
touch of originality in the codificatory work of the Emperor Leo VI is
his substitution, in the *Vasiliká*, of a single unitary system of classification for Justinian's dispersion among four works (Code, Digest, Institutes, and Novels) of materials concerning the same subjects.[2] But

'within the titles, the laws (or chapters) are not the personal work of
Leo; their text was in no way revised by the commissioners for the
Basilics. They were all drawn from earlier works, chiefly from the Code
and the Digest, a very few from the Institutes, many from the Novels of
Justinian and his successors, a few also from the *Procheiron*. The laws are
all given in Greek; when they are derived from the three Latin works of
Justinian, they have been extracted, not from the originals, but from
Greek commentaries of the sixth and seventh centuries.'[3]

To quarrel with a renaissance for being unoriginal is a criticism that
might perhaps be discounted as captious; but the ineffectiveness that is
another characteristic of the Macedonian Dynasty's attempt to reinstate
the Roman Law is a more serious weakness; for a ghost, after all, is only
distinguishable from a nonentity in so far as he succeeds in making an
impression on the living men and women whom he haunts. The ninth-
century renaissance of Roman Law in Orthodox Christendom showed
itself conspicuously impotent to supersede in reality the Iconoclast
Emperors' new Christian Law which it was abrogating verbally, and
even impotent to exorcise the rival ghost of a Mosaic Law which was
re-emerging out of the Christian Law's Pentateuchal crypt.

It is significant that the Iconodule legislator Basil I's 'Handbook'
(πρόχειρος νόμος) 'in its second part also reproduced the provisions of
the *Ecloga*, in spite of the abuse of its authors in the prologue,'[4] and that
in Basil's 'Second Edition' (ἐπαναγωγή), which professed to have
abolished the *Ecloga*, no longer just partially, but entirely, the *Ecloga*
was actually followed even more closely than it had been in 'the Handbook'.[5] The strength of the *Ecloga*, in its encounter with a resuscitated
Roman Law, lay in the fact that the *Ecloga* was a faithful reflection of
the Orthodox Christian êthos—partly because it had successfully caught

Emperor Justinian's codification. The work had no sooner been accomplished than it
was left high and dry by a catastrophe that swept away a complicated and sophisticated
social life which was both the *raison d'être* and the *sine qua non* of a refined legal apparatus.
The foundation of the East Roman Imperial Law School in A.D. 1045 was followed
within twenty-six years by the simultaneous military disasters at Bari and Manzikert
(Melazkerd) in A.D. 1071 which heralded the débâcle, not only of the East Roman Empire,
but of the Orthodox Christian Civilization (see IV. iv. 354, n. 2), just as the completion
of Justinian's codificatory work in A.D. 534 had been followed within sixty-eight years
by the débâcle heralded by the assassination of the Emperor Maurice in A.D. 602 (see
VI. vii. 270).
  [1] See Collinet, op. cit., pp. 719–20, and the present Study, IV. iv. 345.
  [2] See Collinet, ibid., p. 713.
  [3] Collinet, ibid., p. 713.   [4] Collinet, ibid., p. 712.
  [5] See Zachariä von Lingenthal, C. E.: *Collectio Librorum Juris Graeco-Romani In-
editorum: Ecloga Leonis et Constantini; Epanagogê Basilii, Leonis et Alexandri* (Leipzig
1852, Barth), p. 62, n. 16.

the Byzantine spirit and partly also, no doubt, because it had done so much to make that spirit what it had come to be—whereas the Hellenic spirit expressed in the Late Roman Law was an alien presence in an Orthodox Christian environment. In the Law of Marriage, for example, 'Basil returned to the Justinianean system, but the doctrine of the *Ecloga* seems to have so firmly established itself in custom that Leo VI found it necessary to make a compromise and introduced a new system which was a mixture of the Iconoclastic and the Justinianean doctrines.'[1] Basil had a similar experience when he sought to undo his Syrian predecessors' beneficent work of humanizing the barbaric Roman institution of the *Patria Potestas*.[2] In this sphere, likewise, 'Basil revived the Justinianean legislation; here, however, as in many other cases, the letter of Basil's law books was not fully adopted in practice, and was modified by a novel of Leo VI which restored partly the law of the *Ecloga*'.[3] As for the criminal law, 'here the system established by the *Ecloga* is retained in most cases, and sometimes developed further',[4] against the grain of a Macedonian legislation which was consciously striving to depose the Iconoclast legislators and to reinstate Justinian.

'The system of punishments provided in the *Ecloga* continued on the whole to set the standard for later ages. The relevant passages of the *Ecloga* are for the most part incorporated into the *Procheiron*, into the *Epanagogê*, and even into the *Vasiliká*, some of them *verbatim*, some in rather different language or in a slightly modified form—though it is at the same time also true that the *Ecloga's* system of punishments is not retained or applied in its purity. The penal chapters of the [Justinianean] Digest and Code have on the whole also found their way into the *Vasiliká*, with the result that the *Vasiliká*—particularly in contexts in which they are concerned with crimes or misdemeanours not expressly dealt with in the *Ecloga*—prescribe the old [Roman] punishments which frequently contradict the spirit of the new system.'[5]

The vigour with which this would-be Christian spirit continued to assert itself against the would-be Roman spirit of an imperious Justinian's impotent ghost is betrayed in a sentence in the preface to the *Epanagogê* leading up to the passage, quoted above,[6] in which the Macedonian legislators denounce their Syrian predecessors and all their legal works.

'The experience by which Our Majesty has been aroused and stimulated to bestir itself to retrieve and proclaim the good world-saving law with the utmost zeal and utmost care is what we can only describe as our initiation in the secret chambers of the heart by the divine intervention of the Trinity in Unity (ἐκ τῆς φυσικῆς μοναρχίας καὶ τριαδικῆς δεσποτείας . . . θείως πως καὶ ἀπορρήτως μυηθεῖσα).'

Thus, though the Macedonian Emperors were bent on reinstating a Roman Law that had been disestablished—wrongfully, in their belief— by the preceding Syrian Emperors' innovations, it never occurred to

---

[1] Bury, Appendix, p. 527.   [2] See p. 23, n. 2, above.
[3] Bury, Appendix, p. 528.   [4] Bury, ibid.
[5] Zachariä von Lingenthal, K. E.: *Geschichte des Griechisch-Römischen Rechts* (Berlin 1892, Weidmann), pp. 333–4.   [6] On p. 27.

these Iconodules, any more than it would have occurred to their Iconoclast bugbears, to look for the sanction of Law in autonomous acts of
human volition. As a matter of historical fact, the Roman Law, whose
champions the Macedonian Emperors professed to be, had been the
man-made product of a well-documented series of legislative acts performed first by the Roman People in their lawfully constituted assemblies and latterly by Emperors to whom the People had formally dele-
gated their legislative power. Yet, in defiance of all recorded Roman
legal history, the Macedonians showed themselves true Orthodox Christians in displaying a veritably 'Isaurian' inability to imagine that any
law could be validated by any other sanction than the ordinance of a
God who had 'given Man a good law to salvage and blend and preserve' a Human Nature in which the polar and antithetical elements of
spirit and matter had been combined and compounded by the Creator.[1]
In other words, 'the salutary law' which the Macedonians were vindicating against the Iconoclasts was founded, in the Macedonians' belief
likewise, on 'the divine dogma', and their quarrel with these Syrian predecessors of theirs was a family quarrel in which the opposing theses that
were championed with so much zeal and bitterness by their respective
advocates were two closely related variants of one identical Orthodox
Christian creed.

The plot of a legal drama in which a Christian new departure was
dogged by the successively raised ghosts of Moses and Justinian can be
seen likewise working itself out on a Western stage on which Leo
Syrus's role was played by Charlemagne.

'The Carolingian legislation . . . marks the emergence of the new social
consciousness of Western Christendom. Hitherto the legislation of the
Western kingdoms had been of the nature of a Christian appendix to the
old barbarian tribal codes. Now, for the first time, a complete break was
made with the Past, and Christendom enacted its own laws, which covered
the whole field of social activity in Church and State and referred all
things to the single standard of the Christian êthos. This was inspired
neither by Germanic nor [by] Roman precedent.'[2]

In Western, as in Orthodox, Christendom, however, the ghost of
Moses trod hard on the Apostles' and Evangelists' heels.

'The Carolingian Emperors gave the law to the whole Christian people
in the spirit of the kings and judges of the Old Testament, declaring the
Law of God to the people of God. In the letter which Cathaulf addressed
to Charles at the beginning of his reign, the writer speaks of the king as
the earthly representative of God, and he counsels Charles to use the
Book of Divine Law as his manual of government, according to the precept of Deuteronomy xvii. 18–20, which commands the King to make a
copy of the Law from the books of the priests, to keep it always with him,
and to read it constantly, so that he may learn to fear the Lord and keep

---

[1] Ὁ τῶν ἀγαθῶν πάντων πρύτανις καὶ ταμιοῦχος εὖ βουληθείς, μετὰ τὴν τῶν νοητῶν
καὶ αἰσθητῶν ποίησιν, μικτῶν [MSS. μικτόν] τε κοινὸν σύνδεσμον [MSS. σύνδεστον] καὶ
τύπον κοινὸν τῶν ἀντικειμένων καὶ ἀντιθέτων φύσεων παράγει τὸν ἄνθρωπον, νόμον αὐτῷ
ἀγαθὸν δοὺς ὡς ἀναρρυσίν τινα καὶ κρᾶσιν καὶ διαμονὴν τῆς τοιαύτης διαθέσεως.—Epana-
gôgê, Preface, as emended by Zachariä von Lingenthal.
[2] Dawson, Christopher: Religion and the Rise of Western Culture (London 1950,
Sheed & Ward), p. 90.

His laws, lest his heart be lifted up in pride above his brethren and he turn aside to the right hand or to the left.'[1]

Yet, in Western, as in Orthodox, Christendom, a resurgent Moses was overtaken by a resurgent Justinian.

In the course of the eleventh century of the Christian Era the Imperial Law School established by official action at Constantinople in A.D. 1045[2] found its counterpart in Western Christendom at Bologna in the spontaneous emergence there of an autonomous university dedicated to the study of the Justinianean *Corpus Iuris*;[3] and the effect of this Western renaissance of the Roman Law was not confined to the abortive attempt —which was the Bolognese necromancers' first essay in the practical application of their art—to use the Constantinopolitan Roman Imperial Prerogative, in the form in which it had emerged from Justinian's hands, as a legal weapon to reinforce the armaments of Hohenstaufen Emperors in their twelfth-century renewal of the Holy Roman Empire's eleventh-century struggle with the Papacy.[4] Though in Western Christendom— in contrast to the course of Orthodox Christian history—a resuscitated Roman Law thus failed to serve the political purpose of under-pinning a resuscitated Roman Empire, it did potently serve the different political purpose of fostering the revival, on Western ground, of an earlier Hellenic political institution: the sovereign independent parochial state.[5]

In Western Christendom's sinister evocation of this formidable ghost of political parochialism from a defunct antecedent civilization's dead past, the graduates of the University of Bologna played parts comparable to those played in the evocation of ghosts of dead universal states by the

---

[1] Ibid., pp. 90–91. [2] See p. 28, above.

[3] Bury conjectures (Appendix, p. 526) that the foundation of the Constantinopolitan Law School in A.D. 1045 'may have possibly had some influence on the institution of the school at Bologna half a century later'. This is perhaps unlikely, considering the mutual hostility of Western and Orthodox Christendom towards one another in that age. It is true that the Romagna, of which Bologna was the principal city, had been, as was attested by its name, the last fragment of Italy to pass out of the political jurisdiction of a Roman Imperial Government at Constantinople. Yet in A.D. 1045 little less than three centuries had elapsed since the Constantinopolitan Government's definitive loss of the Exarchate in A.D. 751 (see VII. vii. 539, n. 3); and there is no ground for supposing that in the eleventh century the Romagna had not long since lost a familiarity with the Orthodox Christian World which Venice and Amalfi then still retained thanks to the importance of the part played in their economies by their trade with the Levant. This negative conclusion does not, of course, imply that the location of the earliest and greatest Western school of Justinianean Law at Bologna was nothing more than a geographical accident. It was assuredly not an accident that the study of the Justinianean Law in the West should have radiated from the principal city of an Italian province in which this law had been in force, *de facto* as well as *de jure*, for little less than two centuries running from the systematic reincorporation of Italy into the Constantinopolitan Roman body politic, after the final liquidation of an Ostrogoth resistance movement in A.D. 553, down to the final loss of the Ravennese Exarchate by the East Roman Emperor Constantine V in A.D. 751 (if we may assume that the *Ecloga* had not had time to supplant the *Corpus Iustinianeum* in the Exarchate during the eleven years that had elapsed since its promulgation in A.D. 740). Those two centuries of practical familiarity with the *Corpus Iustinianeum* must have enabled this version of the Roman Law to strike far deeper roots in 'the' Romagna than in an adjacent Po Basin which had been converted from a Romania into a Lombardia at intervals ranging from a period of no more than fifteen to a period of no more than fifty years (A.D. 568–603) after the date of the integral reincorporation of Italy into the Constantinopolitan Roman Empire in A.D. 553.

[4] See IV. iv. 557; VII. vii. 539; and p. 9, above.

[5] The Western renaissance of this Hellenic political institution has been noticed on pp. 7–8, above.

graduates of the East Roman academy founded by the Caesar Bardas at Constantinople *circa* A.D. 864[1] and the corresponding Far Eastern academy that the T'ang Emperor T'ai Tsung brought into existence at Si Ngan when in A.D. 622 he reinstituted the Han imperial régime's system of competitive examinations in the Confucian Classics as the method of selecting new recruits for the Imperial Civil Service.[2] The civil lawyers educated by Bologna and her daughter universities became the administrators, not of an abortive 'Holy Roman Empire', but of parochial sovereign states on Western ground, and the efficiency of their professional services was one of the secrets of this other resuscitated Hellenic political institution's progressive victory over all the alternative forms of political organization that were latent in Western Christendom's original social structure.

This victory was not won exclusively by the labours of the doctors of civil law whom Bologna began to breed in the generation of the pioneer Western civil lawyer, Irnerius (*florebat circa* A.D. 1090–1130). While the Bolognese civilians were providing the cities of North and Central Italy with administrators whose competence enabled the nascent communes to cut loose from their post-Carolingian prince-bishops' apron-strings and launch out upon a career of civic self-government,[3] the canonists, who were able to supplement the Bolognese school of civil law with a sister faculty of ecclesiastical law after the publication of Gratian's encyclopaedic *Decretum circa* A.D. 1140–50, made an indirect and unintentional contribution to the development of the Western Parochial Secular State in the course of their purposive organization of a Western Oecumenical Church under the sovereignty of the Papacy; and this unforeseen and unintended appropriation of the fruits of the Medieval Western canon lawyers' labours for the benefit of the Modern Western parochial sovereign states, that were eventually built out of the ruins of a fallen Medieval Western Papal Commonwealth,[4] is one of the ironies of history; for in A.D. 1268, on the morrow of the cold-blooded execution of the last of the Emperor Frederick II Hohenstaufen's heirs, it looked as if the perpetuation of this thirteenth-century triumph of a Western Papal commonwealth designed and built by Bolognese canonists had been assured by the now manifestly irretrievable overthrow of a Western oecumenical empire which the twelfth-century Bolognese civilians had vainly aspired to fortify by lending Justinianean flesh and blood to a Carolingian wraith.

On the Papal side in a struggle between the Papal Church and the Hohenstaufen Dynasty which had lasted for a hundred years, not only the rank-and-file, but the leaders themselves, had been recruited from the Bolognese school of Canon Law and had owed their victories to the weapons which their education had placed in their hands and trained them to use. Bologna was the *alma mater studiorum* and *mater saeva*

---

[1] See IV. iv. 345 and p. 20, above.
[2] See VI. vii. 357, n. 4, 365, n. 4, 369, and 370–2; and p. 20, above.
[3] The role of the Bolognese Faculty of Civil Law in providing civil servants for the nascent Italian city-states is brought out by Dawson in op. cit., pp. 224 and 227.
[4] This plundering of a Late Medieval Oecumenical Western Church's administrative armoury by the Papacy's parochial secular *diadochi* has been noticed in IV. iv. 577–8.

cupidinum[1] of Pope Alexander III (*fungebatur* A.D. 1159–81), Pope Lucius III (*fungebatur* A.D. 1181–5), Pope Innocent III (*fungebatur* A.D. 1198–1216), and Pope Innocent IV (*fungebatur* A.D. 1243–54), while Pope Honorius III (*fungebatur* A.D. 1216–27), Pope Urban IV (*fungebatur* A.D. 1261–4), and Pope Clement V (*fungebatur* A.D. 1265–8) were also likewise canonists.[2] Thus no less than half the number of the incumbents of Saint Peter's chair during the crucial years A.D. 1159–1268 had arrived at the apex of the Western ecclesiastical hierarchy by climbing a recently erected juristic ladder.[3] In the now decisively concluded struggle between the Papacy and the Holy Roman Empire the canonists had been both the principal agents of the Church's victory and the principal beneficiaries from the spoils; and in the third quarter of the thirteenth century it looked as if the civil lawyers whose loss gave the measure of the canonists' gain had obtained the poorest of consolation prizes for their failure to become the omnipotent civil servants of a Western avatar of a secular Roman imperial body politic. When they had been disappointed of the realization of this grandiosely ambitious dream of oecumenical jurisdiction, what did it signify that they had been finding obscure employment as the modest notaries and secretaries of fledgling parochial Italian city-states?

Even after a Pope Boniface VIII (*fungebatur* A.D. 1294–1303), who was both a trained canonist and trained civilian,[4] had brought to the ground in its turn the Papal *Respublica Christiana* that his canonist predecessors had reared so high upon the Holy Roman Empire's ruins, the oecumenical administrative machine which the canonists had been building up for the Papal Church was the one wing of the Innocentian edifice that not only survived intact but continued to grow. The financial organization to which an Innocent IV had given an impetus, in order to provide a militant Roman See with the sinews of war, was carried to its acme during a fourteenth-century 'Babylonish Captivity' (*durabat* A.D. 1309–77) which gave the Papacy's fiscal officers the advantage of operating from a headquarters situated near the geographical centre of communications of the Western Christendom of the day.[5]

After the return of the Papal Curia to Rome in A.D. 1377, yet another century had to pass before the 'Modern Western' type of parochial polity, which had come into being in the Late Medieval Italian city-states, thanks to the creative work of the civil lawyers who were these cities' public employees, made its fortune by imposing its exotic pattern of administrative practice and political theory on the feudal monarchies in the Transalpine and Transmarine provinces of the Western World; and this moment of transition from the 'Medieval' to the 'Modern' chapter of the history of the Western World at large, outside the narrow limits of a politically precocious Northern and Central Italy, at last revealed, for the first time, the ironic destiny of a Western Christian

---

[1] Horace: *Carmina*, Book I, Ode xix, l. 1. [2] See IV. iv. 530–1.
[3] Dawson points out, in op. cit., p. 227, that Alexander III was actually a pupil of Gratian and a commentator on his works, and that Innocent III, in his day, was a pupil of the Bolognese canonist Uguccio of Pisa. [4] See IV. iv. 532.
[5] The convenience of the location of Avignon from the Papal administrators' standpoint has been noticed in IV. iv. 520, n. 2, and 571, n. 1.

Canon Law which had been worked out at Bologna on the model of a pagan Roman Civil Law in order to give a Papal Church the victory over an abortive Western resuscitation of the Roman Empire. In the modern chapter of Western history the Canon Law continued to play a major part in Western life only in so far as its practical applications in the spheres of administration and finance were pressed into the service of the parochial secular states which boisterously held the stage in this noisy 'modern' act of a Western tragi-comedy.[1]

This Modern role of the Canon Law was, however, as unobtrusive as it was influential, and the legal triumph that attracted all the éclat was the 'reception' of the Justinianean Roman Law in one parochial state after another of a now rapidly and widely expanding Western body social. In the Western Civilization's European homelands a conquering Roman Law overleapt an intractable England to seize upon Scotland;[2] but the winning of this outpost in a European *Ultima Thule* was merely the prelude to a Transoceanic expansion. In the New World of the Americas, the Spanish Crown was as much indebted to the faithful services of its civil lawyers for its hard-won sixteenth-century victory over the truculent Castilian *conquistadores* as the Roman See had been to the services of its canonists for its thirteenth-century victory over the Hohenstaufen. In the New World of South Africa, Dutch colonists, planted there after the 'reception' of the Roman Law in their mother country, gave Justinian a fresh footing on a Continent from whose northern extremity he had been evicted a thousand years earlier by the artificers of an Islamic Law which had entered Egypt and the Maghrib in the train of seventh-century Arab Muslim conquerors.

The Islamic Law, like the Roman Law, had its renaissances in the

---

[1] If, at first sight, it might seem surprising that it should have been feasible thus to turn an oecumenical Canon Law to account for the benefit of parochial secular states that were the Civil Law's nurslings, an explanation of this apparent enigma is to be found in an illuminating passage of Christopher Dawson's *Religion and the Rise of Western Culture* (London 1950, Sheed & Ward), pp. 224–5 and 227:

'While the University of Paris throughout the Middle Ages was essentially a clerical institution, Bologna was largely a lay university where the lawyers and officials who played such a large part in the government of the Italian cities received their education.

'No doubt the development of the study of the Canon Law which was associated with the work of Gratian about 1140 made Bologna an equally important centre of training for the administrators and lawyers of the Mediaeval Church. But it was as a school of Roman Law that Bologna first became famous in the days of Irnerius (*circa* A.D. 1090–1130), and it was the civilians, not the canonists, who set the standard and determined the course of studies. . . .

'The fact that [the] work [of actually supplying the Mediaeval Church with its organisation] was done by men trained in the same school and the same traditions as the civilians who during the same period were organising and rationalising the Mediaeval State was of the first importance for the history of Western institutions; and it was in the life of the Italian cities that this process of interaction was most complete. The rulers and officials of the City-State and the administrators of the Church were drawn from the same classes, [were] educated in the same universities, and shared the same intellectual background, so that there was a continual process of mutual criticism which stimulated the growth of an educated public opinion, such as did not yet exist in Northern Europe.'

[2] 'It is clear that the Common Law of Scotland is in considerable measure derived from the Civil Law; to a less extent, but in important particulars, from the Canon Law. Though there was probably no period at which the Civil Law was accounted part of the law of Scotland, yet that law, as explained and in some respects amended by the Dutch and French commentators of the sixteenth and seventeenth centuries, is the basis of the Scots law of contract and of property, apart from feudal conveyancing' (Gloag, W. M., and Henderson, R. C.: *Introduction to the Law of Scotland*, 3rd ed. (Edinburgh 1939, Green), p. 8).

histories of civilizations of a new generation that eventually arose out of the ruins of the universal state in which the resuscitated law had formerly been current; but this broad general resemblance between the respective posthumous fortunes of the Justinianean *Corpus Iuris* and the Islamic *Sharī'ah* is diversified by differences of detail due to differences between the Roman Empire and the Arab Caliphate in the several points of their antecedents, their origins, their structures, and their relations to the higher religions that propagated themselves within these universal states' frontiers.

The difference between the Roman Empire and the Arab Caliphate that had the greatest effect in giving different turns to the posthumous histories of the Roman Civil Law and the *Sharī'ah* was that the Arab conquerors who built the Caliphate and gave this oecumenical empire an oecumenical law were likewise the missionaries of Islam, so that, in the Caliphate, Religion, Law, and Government were all in the same hands from the outset, in sharp contrast to the history of the relations between these three activities in the Roman Empire, where an oecumenical government and an oecumenical law, created by pagan hands, had set hard in their pagan mould before the Roman imperial régime found itself constrained to come to terms with an exotic Christian Church against which this pagan Hellenic universal state had been fighting a losing battle for a quarter of a millennium ending in the generation of Constantine.

The common purpose of providing the legal currency for a universal state was, it is true, reflected in certain similarities in the respective processes of evolution through which these two oecumenical systems of law arrived at their final forms. The *Sharī'ah* in the Age of the Caliphate, like the Roman Law in the Imperial Age, owed its development largely to jurists recruited, not from the ruling people itself, but from these empire-builders' subjects; and in both episodes of legal history the imperial jurists who had thus made their way up from below drew freely upon their indigenous social heritage in carrying out their arduous task of transfiguring the archaic and fragmentary traditional law of conquerors, who had been marchmen in the Roman case and transfrontier barbarians in the Arab case, by smoothing away its rugged edges and filling in its lacunæ until they had succeeded in making out of this unpromisingly incongruous material a legal system more or less capable of serving the complicated and sophisticated needs of the society on which the empire-builders had imposed their own law by right of conquest.[1] Owing, however, to the difference in the respective historical relations of Christianity and Islam to the founders of the oecumenical states that were their original political frameworks, the outcome of two otherwise more or less similar episodes of legal history was in the one case a still essentially pagan *Corpus Iuris Romani Iustinianeum* and in the other case a *Sharī'ah* in which the ingenuity of non-Arab jurists had not only eked out a most inadequate Arab customary law by surreptitiously introducing elements of Oriental Roman Law and other legal systems previously current

---

[1] The evolution of the Roman Law has been sketched in VI. vii. 262–3 and 265–8; the evolution of the *Sharī'ah* has been sketched ibid., 288–91.

among the populations that the Arabs had subjugated, but had presented the whole of this amalgam in the form of logical deductions and
inductions from the Qur'ān and the Traditions of the Prophet Muhammad.

It will be seen that, in thus resetting fragments of old secular law in
a new religious mould, the Islamic jurists of the Umayyad and 'Abbasid
ages who were the authors of the *Sharī'ah* were doing something
reminiscent, not so much of the interpretative and codificatory work of
the Roman jurists of the Imperial Age, as of the creative work of the
Orthodox Christian authors of the *Ecloga* and the Western Christian
authors of Charlemagne's would-be Christian legislation; and, in the
light of this analogy, it might perhaps have been expected *a priori* that
there would have been no occasion for a renaissance of the *Sharī'ah*
because there would have been no necessity for this already developed
and established Islamic Law to pass out of currency as a result of the
downfall of the Caliphate—considering that Islam itself survived the
dissolution of the Caliphate as robustly as Christianity had survived
the downfall of the Roman Empire.

If the Eurasian Nomad barbarians who overran the derelict provinces
of a dissolving Caliphate in the course of the two centuries ending in the
Mongols' sack of Baghdad in A.D. 1258 had all been as barbarous as the
Eurasian Nomad and North European sedentary barbarians who overran the Roman Empire's derelict western provinces in the fifth and sixth
centuries of the Christian Era, they might indeed all have taken the
option, which the eleventh-century Saljūq Turkish barbarian invaders
of the Caliphate did take, of 'receiving' the *Sharī'ah* as an automatic
consequence of their conversion to the faith of a rapidly growing Muslim majority of the ex-subjects of the universal state whose former territories these barbarians were now overrunning. As it happened, however,
the Mongols, who broke upon the shores of Dār-al-Islām in the last
and most violent wave of the Eurasian Nomad invasion of the Caliphate's derelict domain, and the Türkmen ancestors of the 'Osmanlis,
who fled westwards, before the Mongols' menacing advance, from
Central Asia into North-Western Anatolia, both resembled the Arab
founders of the Caliphate in being barbarians who were gifted with
exceptional capacities; and their ability displayed itself in the originality
of their creative work in the field of law as well as in the field of politics.

In previous contexts[1] we have already noticed that Chingis Khan
and his successors were so confident of the virtue and value of their
own traditional barbarian customary law that they made the audacious
attempt to impose it on their subjects by force, in place of the *Sharī'ah*
and the other legal systems under which the conquered peoples had been
living at the time when they had been overtaken by the Mongol conquest; and in an earlier Part of this Study[2] we have also taken a glance
at 'the peculiar institution' which the 'Osmanlis fashioned for themselves—as their instrument for conquering and holding an oecumenical
empire—out of elements of the Eurasian Nomad culture which were
just as independent of the *Sharī'ah* as was Chingis Khan's Mongol

---

[1] In VI. vii. 74 and 256–7; and IX. viii. 354–5.   [2] In III. iii. 22–50.

Yāsāq itself. The Mongol and the Ottoman attitude towards the *Sharīʿah* were, of course, very different; for, while the Mongol conquerors of the Old World remained—in some cases for as long as a hundred years after the conquest—either militant shamanists or militant Nestorian Christians who were bent upon suppressing the *Sharīʿah* and superseding it, the Ottoman 'Ghāzis of Rūm',[1] so far from being persecutors of Islam, were zealous propagators of it. Yet, though the peculiar and characteristic Ottoman institution of the Pādishāh's Slave-Household was built up, not as a substitute for the Islamic dispensation, but as an instrument for the enlargement of the domain of Dār-al-Islām by slaves of a Muslim potentate who were Muslims themselves, besides being peculiarly trained *qullar*, it was nevertheless also true that 'the Ottoman Ruling Institution', as it has been called by one of the most discerning of the Modern Western students of it,[2] was based on non-Islamic foundations, was set up alongside of 'the Muslim Institution' as an independent organization, and was the predominant organ in the Ottoman body social during the creative age of Ottoman history in the fourteenth and fifteenth centuries of the Christian Era.[3]

Both the independence and the predominance of the Pādishāh's Slave-Household were asserted by its members when they prevailed upon Sultan Bāyezīd II (*imperabat* A.D. 1481–1512) to grant their corporation the privilege of judicial autonomy.

'The members of the Ruling Institution had not always had their own system of justice; they had long been under the jurisdiction of the ordinary Muslim courts. This had led to an essential difficulty: the ordinary courts were part of another institution and were recruited in a wholly different way; their judges had risen through a rival system of education, and were men of letters rather than men of war; the favoured *qullar* of the Sultan had therefore come to feel averse to obeying them. Accordingly, Bāyezīd II had ordered that the members of his family should be judged by their own officers. This was a radical change; for it brought into prominence the distinction between the two institutions, and had the further effect of setting off the *qullar* from all the rest of the population of the Empire and of constituting them almost a separate nationality.'[4]

After the relative power of 'the Ruling Institution' of the Ottoman body politic had thus risen to its apogee at the turn of the fifteenth and sixteenth centuries of the Christian Era, the balance promptly began to swing over to 'the Muslim Institution's' side as a consequence of the

---

[1] The Timurid Mughal Emperor Bābur's habitual use of this periphrasis for describing the ʿOsmanlis has been noticed in I. i. 349, n. 1.

[2] See Lybyer, A. H.: *The Government of the Ottoman Empire in the Time of Suleiman the Magnificent* (Cambridge, Mass. 1913, Harvard University Press), p. 36.

[3] See ibid., pp. 233–5.

[4] Ibid., p. 116. As has been noticed in this Study in IX. viii. 186, n. 2, above, the practical effect of this exemption of the *qullar* from the jurisdiction of the Islamic judicial authorities was to confer on them the corporate status of a *millet* which, in the Ottoman Empire, was enjoyed likewise by another corporation of privileged Muslims, the Seyyids (see Lybyer, op. cit., pp. 206–7 and 216). The privilege of judicial autonomy which was thus obtained by the slave companions of the Ottoman Pādishāhs was also possessed by the free companions of the Macedonian Kings in the post-Alexandrine as well as in the pre-Alexandrine Age of Hellenic history—at any rate in any case in which one of the Companions was being tried on a capital charge (see Granier, F.: *Die Makedonische Heeresversammlung* (Munich 1931, Beck), pp. 51–52.

extension of direct or indirect Ottoman rule over five-sixths of the
Arabic Muslim World, including the dominions of the Mamlūks in
Syria, Egypt, and Arabia, in the course of the fifty-eight years running
from A.D. 1516, when Syria was occupied by Sultan Selīm I and Algiers
by the 'Osmanli corsair Khayr-ad-Dīn Barbarossa, and A.D. 1574,
which was the date of the 'Osmanlis' definitive eviction of the Spaniards
from Tunis.[1] In the Arab countries ruled by Mamlūks who had inherited from their extinct Ayyubid masters a tradition of serving as
defenders of the Islamic faith, and who had completed the expulsion
of the Crusaders from Syria in order to turn this liberated province of
Dār-al-Islām into a glacis covering the approaches to Islam's Egyptian
citadel in the quarter from which Egypt was under the threat of Mongol
attacks,[2] these *ci-devant* slaves who had entered into their former
masters' heritage had sought to legitimize their usurpation of power by
ruling in the name of a Cairene ghost of a Baghdādī 'Abbasid Caliphate;[3]
and, though these Mamlūks had, like the 'Osmanlis, developed 'a
peculiar institution' of their own which, in their case, likewise, had been
the secret of their success,[4] the reign of the Islamic *Sharī'ah* had
been maintained unbroken and unimpaired in the Mamlūks' dominions
by the Mamlūks' policy of wielding their power in a puppet 'Abbasid
Caliph's name and by their prowess in preserving Syria and Egypt from
being swept by a tornado of Mongol conquest that had devastated all
the eastern provinces of Dār-al-Islām from Farghānah as far westward
as the eastern bank of the Middle Euphrates.[5] The conquest of the
Mamlūk Empire by the Ottoman Sultan Selīm I in A.D. 1516–17 thus
produced a sudden and drastic change in the demographic constitution
of the Ottoman body politic by bringing under the Pādishāh's rule a
mass of new Arabic-speaking Muslim subjects who knew no other dispensation than the *Sharī'ah*;[6] and this demographic change was quickly
reflected in the field of law.

Already, nearly half a century before Selīm I (*imperabat* A.D. 1512–20)
burst through the Taurus and descended upon the Arabic World in
A.D. 1516, his predecessor Mehmed II the Conqueror (*imperabat* A.D.
1451–81) had found that the requirements of his Muslim subjects in
an Ottoman Empire which in his reign was still confined to originally
Orthodox Christian ground called for a new codification of the *Sharī'ah*
as expounded by a Hanafī school of Islamic jurists, whose presentation
of the Islamic Law was the one that had been officially 'received' in the
Ottoman dominions; and Mehmed II had accordingly put in hand a
new Ottoman redaction of the *Sharī'ah* according to Abu Hanīfah.[7]
'This work, finished in A.D. 1470, was not sufficient in the days of
Suleymān (*imperabat* A.D. 1520–66). At the time of its preparation the
Ottoman Empire had been still wholly within territory that had re-

---

[1] See I. i. 69–70, 348, and 396, n. 5; II. ii. 444–5; IX. viii. 105, n. 1; and IX. viii. 220–1.
[2] See I. i. 350; IV. iv. 447; and V. v. 248.
[3] See VI. vii. 20.   [4] See III. iii. 30–31.
[5] On the 2nd September, 1929, the writer of this Study swam the Euphrates from its
Mamlūk shore below the bluff crowned by the castle of Qal'at-an-Najm to the Mongol
shore opposite.   [6] See Lybyer, op. cit., pp. 152–3 and 233–4.
[7] See Lybyer, op. cit., p. 152, following d'Ohsson, I. M.: *Tableau Général de l'Empire
Ottoman* (Paris 1788–1824, Didot, 7 vols.), vol. i, p. 21.

mained Christian during all the early brilliant period of Islam';[1] and Sultan Mehmed's choice of a Christian renegade, Khosrev Pasha,[2] as his codifier of the *Sharī'ah* for the use of an Iranic Muslim community *in partibus Christianorum* was a characteristic stroke of the Ottoman political genius in its pre-Selimian Age, however inappropriate the choice might look from a conservative Hanafite Sunnī Muslim standpoint. Since Mehmed II's day, however, the 'Osmanlis

'had conquered three seats of the later Caliphate—Damascus, Baghdad, and Cairo—and had come to hold the protectorate of the Holy Cities, where Muhammad and the early Caliphs had ruled. A new code of law, therefore, better adapted to the more widely Muslim character which the Empire had assumed, was [now] demanded. Suleymān charged Shaykh Ibrahīm Halabī with the task of preparing such a code; and the result, prepared before A.D. 1549, was the *Multeqā el-Ebhār* ('the Confluence of the Seas'), which remained the foundation of Ottoman Law until the reforms of the nineteenth century.'[3]

It was no accident that the work of replacing a redaction of the *Sharī'ah* which had been made for Sultan Mehmed II by a Christian renegade should have been entrusted by Sultan Suleymān I to a Muslim-born doctor of the Islamic Law whose home was Aleppo—an Arabic-speaking Muslim city which was the nearest of all the seats of theological learning in an Arabic Muslim World to the new domain in Anatolia which had been won by Turkish Eurasian Nomad converts to Islam for an Iranic Muslim World at the expense of Orthodox Christendom.

This progressive renaissance of the Islamic Law in an expanding Ottoman Empire was achieved, as has just been observed, on the initiative of converted descendants of the local Eurasian Nomad barbarian interlopers when these 'Osmanlis eventually extended their rule over the Arabic-speaking portion of the former dominions of the 'Abbasid Caliphate. In the Transoxanian marches of a defunct 'Abbasid Caliphate and a nascent Iranic Muslim World the local Eurasian barbarian interlopers became converts to Islam in their turn in the fourteenth century of the Christian Era;[4] but this tardy conversion of the Mongols of the Chaghatāy Horde was not sufficiently thorough or wholehearted to reconcile their sedentary Iranic Muslim subjects to an oppressive Nomad domination; and accordingly in Transoxania, in contrast to the course of events in the Ottoman World, the local renaissance of the *Sharī'ah* was achieved in the teeth of the converted descendants of the barbarian conquerors, and not through their agency. In a previous context[5] we have noticed that Timur Lenk rose to power by becoming the military leader of an anti-Nomad cultural reaction on

---

[1] Lybyer, loc. cit.

[2] See Hammer-Purgstall, J. von: *Des Osmanischen Reichs Staatsverfassung und Staatsverwaltung* (Vienna 1815, Camesinasche Buchhandlung, 2 vols.), vol. i, p. 9.

[3] Lybyer, op. cit., pp. 152–3 (cp. p. 318), following d'Ohsson, op. cit., vol. i, pp. 22–24, and Hammer-Purgstall, J. von: *Des Osmanischen Reichs Staatsverfassung und Staatsverwaltung* (Vienna 1815, Camesinasche Buchhandlung, 2 vols.), vol. i, p. 10. 'The *Multeqā* is the basis of d'Ohsson's excellent work, which consists [in vols. i–vi—A.J.T.] of a translation of the code with its comments, to which he has added [in vol. vii—A.J.T.] observations of great value based on historical studies and on his own investigations during many years' residence in Turkey' (Lybyer, op. cit., p. 153, n. 1).

[4] See II. ii. 145.   [5] In II. ii. 147–8.

the part of the Transoxanian townspeople and 'ulamā which began as an insurrection against a Chaghatāy ascendancy and was followed up by Timur's military genius with a counter-offensive in which Cain took his long overdue revenge on a provocative Abel. In this place we have only to notice that Timur followed up his overt assumption of sovereign power at Balkh on the 8th April, 1369, by re-validating the *Sharī'ah* in all fields that came within the *Sharī'ah's* cognizance; and, though he seems to have refrained from following up this positive act by the negative one of expressly abrogating the Mongol *Yāsāq*, its abrogation was accomplished in effect by the reinstatement of an Islamic Law in whose sight *nihil humanum* was *alienum*.[1]

(c) RENAISSANCES OF PHILOSOPHIES

In other contexts[2] we have watched the Confucian litterati surviving the dissolution of a Sinic universal state embodied in the Han Empire and eventually regaining their monopoly of an imperial civil service after a ghost of the Han Empire had been raised by the Sui Dynasty and kept on foot by the Sui's successors the T'ang; and in the same contexts we have also observed that, in achieving this remarkable recovery of lost ground on the plane of public administration, the Confucians were winning a political victory over Taoist and Mahayanian Buddhist contemporaries and rivals. The reestablishment by T'ang T'ai Tsung, in A.D. 622, of an official examination in the Confucian Classics as the method of selecting new recruits for the imperial civil service signified that, in this political field, the Taoists and Buddhists had let slip an opportunity for supplanting the Confucians which had seemed to be within the grasp of these upstart competitors for public office during a post-Sinic interregnum, when the prestige of the Confucians had been damaged by the collapse of the universal state with which they were identified, while, in a defunct Han Empire's former northern provinces, which had been the cradle of the Sinic culture, Taoists and Buddhists were enjoying the political patronage of barbarian rulers of local successor-states who found the Mahāyāna more attractive than Confucianism and who would have been glad in any case to recruit their civil servants from any non-Confucian community that might be qualified for office by possessing the necessary standard of education, rather than place themselves in the hands of Confucians whose loyalty they sagely doubted.

The contrast between this political failure of the Mahāyāna in Northern China in a post-Sinic Age and the success with which the Christian Church seized and harvested its corresponding opportunities in Western Europe in a post-Hellenic Age brings out the fact that—at any rate by comparison with Christianity—the Mahāyāna was a politically incompetent religion. The patronage of the parochial princes in Northern China during the best part of three centuries, running from

[1] Terence: *Hautontimorumenus*, l. 77 (Act I, scene i, line 25). See Cahun, L.: *Introduction à l'Histoire de l'Asie: Turcs et Mongols des Origines à 1405* (Paris 1896, Colin), pp. 469–72, and Bouvat, L.: *L'Empire Mongol, Deuxième Phase* (Paris 1927, Boccard), pp. 66–69.   [2] See VI. vii. 355–8, and pp. 649–81, below.

the break-up of the United Tsin Empire to its reconstitution by the Sui, was of no more avail than the more potent patronage of the Kushan Emperor Kanishka had been at the turn of the first and second centuries of the Christian Era. Even this royal aid failed to give the followers of the Mahāyāna a firm seat in a political saddle. As soon, however, as the encounter on Far Eastern ground between the Mahāyāna and Confucianism was transferred from an alien political plane to a spiritual plane on which both were breathing their native air, the fortunes of their almost bloodless war were dramatically reversed.

The Confucians exposed themselves to the risk of experiencing this *peripeteia* when they followed up the political triumph of securing the reinstatement of the Confucian Classics, as the shibboleth for admission into the civil service of an avatar of the Sinic universal state, by attempting to reanimate the thought latent in their literary canon. This process of re-eliciting a philosophy out of a cut-and-dried official examination-subject was started, after the T'ang régime's partial recovery from its first convulsion half way through the eighth century of the Christian Era, by the Neoconfucian thinkers Han Yü (*vivebat* A.D. 768–824) and Li Ao (*mortuus circa* A.D. 844);[1] and, after this Neoconfucianism had branched in the eleventh century into two schools that were first differentiated by the brothers Ch'eng Yi (*vivebat* A.D. 1033–1108) and Ch'eng Hao (*vivebat* A.D. 1032–85), the younger brother's 'School of Principles' was carried to its culmination by Chu Hsi (*vivebat* A.D. 1130–1200), while the elder brother's 'School of Mind' culminated in the thought of Wang Shou-jen[2] (*vivebat* A.D. 1473–1529).[3] This Far Eastern Neoconfucianism began and ended[4] with declarations of dissent from both Taoism and the Mahāyāna. Yet

'we can say that the Neoconfucianists more consistently adhere to the fundamental ideas of Taoism and Buddhism than do the Taoists and Buddhists themselves. They are more Taoistic than the Taoists, and more Buddhistic than the Buddhists.'[5]

The channel through which a would-be revival of Confucianism imbibed the spirit of the Mahāyāna was the Ch'an[6] School of Mahayanian Buddhism, which had struck root on Far Eastern ground in the Early T'ang Age.[7]

'There are three lines of thought that can be traced as the main sources of Neoconfucianism. The first, of course, is Confucianism itself. The second is Buddhism, together with Taoism, via the medium of Ch'anism; for, of all the schools of Buddhism, Ch'anism was the most influential at the time of the formation of Neoconfucianism. To the Neoconfucianists, Ch'anism and Buddhism are synonymous terms, and . . . in one sense Neoconfucianism may be said to be the logical development of Ch'anism. Finally, the third is the Taoist Religion, of which the cosmological views

---

[1] See Fung Yu-lan: *A Short History of Chinese Philosophy* (New York 1948, Macmillan), p. 267.
[2] Commonly known as 'the Master of Yang-ming' (Fung Yu-lan, op. cit., p. 308) or as Wang Yang-ming.   [3] See Fung Yu-lan, op. cit., p. 281.
[4] See ibid., pp. 267–8 and 316–18.   [5] Ibid., p. 318.
[6] A Chinese rendering of the Sanskrit word 'Dhyāna' which, in turn, was rendered as 'Zen' in Japanese (see V. v. 96–103).
[7] See Fung Yu-lan, op. cit., pp. 255–65.

of the Yin-Yang School[1] formed an important element. The cosmology of the Neoconfucianists is chiefly connected with this line of thought.'[2]

The particular potency of the Ch'an School of Mahayanian philosophy in informing and inspiring a post-Buddhaic Confucian school of Far Eastern thought was due, not merely to the external accident that Ch'anism happened to be in fashion in the Far East at the time when the Neoconfucian Movement was initiated, but also to the fact that an Indic Dhyāna which had struck root on Far Eastern ground had gone a long way, in this new cultural environment, towards adapting its ethics to a Confucian moral climate.

'The most important development in Chinese Buddhism was its attempt to depreciate the Otherworldliness of original Buddhism. This attempt came close to success when the Ch'an masters stated that "in carrying water and chopping firewood, therein lies the wonderful Tao". But . . . they did not push this idea to its logical conclusion by saying that, in serving one's family and the state, therein also lies the wonderful Tao. The reason, of course, is that, once they had said this, their teaching would have ceased to be Buddhism.'[3]

Yet, while developing this affinity with Confucianism on the ethical plane and thereby qualifying itself to exert an unacknowledged influence on the thought of professedly anti-Buddhist Neoconfucian philosophers, the Ch'an School of the Mahāyāna *in partibus Confucianorum* remained faithful, on the metaphysical plane, to its Mahayanian origins; and, after insinuating itself into Neoconfucianism through an ethical door, it gave this ghost of Confucianism a metaphysical substance which had been lacking in Confucianism in its original authentic form.[4] 'The Neoconfucianists developed a point of view from which all the moral activities valued by the Confucianists acquire a further value that is "supermoral" ';[5] and, without this infusion of Mahayanian metaphysics through a Ch'an Mahayanian channel, Neoconfucianism might have remained a stranger in its own Far Eastern house; for the impact of the Mahāyāna on a moribund Sinic Society, at a time when the inhabitants of this dissolving world were undergoing the harrowing experience of living through a social interregnum, had produced in their souls a profound and enduring change of spiritual outlook which recalls to the mind of a Western student of History the similar change produced in his own forebears' souls by the impact of Christianity on a moribund Hellenic Society.

'After the revival of Taoism and the introduction of Buddhism, people had become more interested in metaphysical problems and in . . . "super-

---

[1] See the present Study, II. i. 201–3. The Neoconfucians translated the notion of Yin and Yang into intellectual terms (Forke, A.: *The World-Conception of the Chinese* (London 1925, Probsthain), p. 200).—A.J.T.

[2] Fung Yu-lan, op. cit., p. 268. [3] Ibid., p. 271. Cp. pp. 264–5.

[4] Chu Hsi's debt to Mahayanian Buddhist metaphysics is pointed out by Hackmann, H.: *Chinesische Philosophie* (Munich 1927, Reinhardt), pp. 346–7, in a passage cited in this Study in II. i. 202, n. 2. For Chu Hsi's Buddhist solution of the logico-metaphysical problem of the relation between the intellectual unity of an idea (in the Platonic sense of the term) and the multiplicity of its manifestations in the World of Sense, see Fung Yu-lan, op. cit., p. 298.

[5] Fung Yu-lan, op. cit., p. 280.

moral values", or, as they were then phrased, the problems of the nature and destiny [of Man].'[1]

The influence on Neoconfucianism of these aspects of the Mahāyāna made itself felt not only in the adoption of the peculiarly Ch'anist theory and practice of 'sudden enlightenment',[2] but also—at least according to the doctrine of the Neoconfucian 'School of Mind'—in an identification, *more Indico*, of the mind of each individual human being with a Cosmic Intelligence.[3]

It is true that Neoconfucianism did make some motion to break away from its Mahāyanian moorings in the metaphysical sphere, in which the Mahāyāna on Sinic soil had remained true to its original Indic genius, in contrast to its concessions to the Sinic genius in the sphere of Ethics. For example, in prescribing a method of spiritual cultivation, the Neoconfucians departed from Ch'anism by substituting an active 'attentiveness' for a passive 'quiescence' as the requisite state of mind for a neophyte.[4] Yet attempts, such as this, to recapture the authentic spirit of a Confucianism which these Far Eastern intellectual necromancers had set out to resuscitate were feeble and fitful by comparison with the force and copiousness with which a fountain of Mahayanian Buddhist thought continued to well up through a Neoconfucian conduit-pipe that had been designed to perform the quite different intellectual service of tapping the buried springs of a genuine pre-Buddhist Confucian philosophy; and this captivation of the Neoconfucian philosophical renaissance itself by the spirit of the Mahāyāna made nonsense of the reinstated Confucian imperial civil servants' efforts to reduce the strength of an exotic Mahayanian universal church's hold on the spiritual allegiance of a now politically reunited and socially advancing Far Eastern World.

Even before the reunification of the whole former domain of the Han Empire by Sui Wên-ti in A.D. 589 and the reinauguration of the public examinations in the Confucian Classics by T'ang T'ai Tsung in A.D. 622, the Confucians had seized an opportunity offered to them in the North by their own captivation of the *ci-devant* barbarian To Pa 'Wei' dynasty. In A.D. 446 they had induced the reigning emperor of this house to issue an anti-Buddhist edict;[5] and they had no sooner acquired a hold upon the government of a resuscitated oecumenical

[1] Ibid., p. 266.
[2] For the role of 'sudden enlightenment' in Ch'anism, see ibid., pp. 261-2; for its adoption by the Neoconfucian 'School of Principles', see ibid., p. 306. 'Sudden enlightenment' was likewise adopted by 'the School of Mind' (ibid., pp. 307, 308-9, and 312). Other Ch'anist elements in Neoconfucianism are noticed ibid., pp. 272 and 290.
[3] See ibid., pp. 309, 312, and 315. In this Neoconfucian identification of individual human selves with a Cosmic Self we may perhaps discern one of the key-ideas of Early Indic thought which had reasserted itself in the Mahāyāna after having been rejected by the historical Buddha Siddhārtha Gautama as being the arch-impediment to an acceptance of his own key-doctrine that an individual's self was a mere continuum of intrinsically separate and ephemeral psychological states inauspiciously held together by the sinister force of *Karma* in a complex that could be dissolved and dissipated by going through a prescribed course of spiritual *askêsis* which the Buddha himself had worked out in order to put it within the power of his suffering fellow sentient beings to purge the cumulus of this tormenting *Karma* away.
[4] See Fung Yu-lan, op. cit., p. 286.
[5] See Fitzgerald, C. P.: *China, A Short Cultural History* (London 1935, Cresset Press), pp. 275-6, quoted on p. 678, n. 4, below.

empire than they began to abuse this power for the purpose of repressing their hated Buddhist rivals. From A.D. 626 onwards, Buddhist monasteries in the T'ang Imperial Crown's dominions were placed under a Confucian official control that grew progressively more severe;[1] and a series of anti-Buddhist memorials addressed to the T'ang Imperial Throne by Confucian high officials—by Fu Yi in A.D. 624,[2] by Yao Ch'ung in A.D. 713,[3] and by Han Yü in A.D. 819[4]—at length produced their cumulative effect in a systematic official persecution, started in A.D. 845,[5] which, though mild and indeed almost humane compared to many of the persecutions of which a Christian Church was either a victim or a perpetrator, was an exceptionally violent and bloody incident in the less unhappy history of the relations between Church and State in the Far Eastern World.

As it turned out, this Confucian attempt to repress, and if possible eradicate, the Mahāyāna in the Far East was abortive; and, mid-way through the twentieth century of the Christian Era, the Mahāyāna was still a living spiritual force in China as well as in Indo-China, Korea, and Japan. Even, however, if the Mahāyāna, as an institution, had been successfully extirpated in China eleven hundred years before that date, a discreditable political success that would then have been achieved by Confucian civil servants would have been stultified in advance by a then already consummated surrender to the Mahāyāna on the metaphysical plane which did credit to the intellectual integrity of a Neoconfucian School of Far Eastern philosophers. The pioneers of this Buddhistic Neoconfucianism had already set their course on these Mahayanian lines before the Great Persecution of A.D. 845 was launched; and, when a Neoconfucian philosophy that had been duly approved by a Confucian imperial régime had thus taken the Ch'an version of the Mahāyāna to heart, an authentic renaissance of unadulterated Confucianism would still have been as far off as ever if, before the final downfall of the T'ang Dynasty, the Confucian civil servants had succeeded in their efforts to suppress the external manifestations of an exotic higher religion which had now found an inviolable sanctuary and an ideal base of spiritual operations in Neoconfucian bosoms that were both unsuspect and unsuspecting.

When a Zealot-minded Ming Dynasty (*imperabant* A.D. 1368–1644) conferred on Chu Hsi the posthumous canonization that Han Wuti (*imperabat* 140–87 B.C.) had conferred on Confucius, and added the works of this prince of the Neoconfucian 'School of Principles' to the 'set books' prescribed for the official examinations, to serve thenceforth as the sole authorized commentary on the Confucian Classics,[6] these

---

[1] See Hackmann, H.: *Chinesische Philosophie* (Munich 1927, Reinhardt), pp. 272–3.
[2] See Hackmann, op. cit., p. 272; Franke, O.: *Geschichte des Chinesischen Reiches*, vol. ii (Berlin and Leipzig 1936, de Gruyter), pp. 390 and 570; Goodrich, L. C.: *A Short History of the Chinese People* (London 1948, Allen & Unwin), pp. 122–3.
[3] See Franke, op. cit., p. 572; Hackmann, op. cit., p. 272 (who gives the date as A.D. 714).
[4] See Franke, op. cit., pp. 490 and 572; Hackmann, op. cit., p. 273.
[5] See Franke, op. cit., pp. 497–9; Goodrich, op. cit., pp. 125–7; Hackmann, op. cit., p. 273 (who gives the date as A.D. 844).
[6] See Hackmann, op. cit., p. 357.

Zealots were unconsciously and unintentionally defeating their own purposes by enthroning a thinly disguised Ch'an Buddhism in an authentic Confucianism's never reoccupied place; and, when Wang Shou-jen committed what had now become the political offence of attacking Chu Hsi's version of a Buddhistic Neoconfucian philosophy on behalf of the rival 'School of Mind',[1] one incidental effect of his polemics was to plunge the bows of his own craft deeper than ever into Mahayanian Buddhist waters.

It will be seen that the Neoconfucian philosophers' *odium philosophicum* towards an Indic Mahāyāna was as ironically self-frustrating an essay in the perverse exercise of kicking against the pricks[2] as the Macedonian legislators' *odium theologicum* towards the would-be Christian legislation of an antecedent Syrian Dynasty;[3] and there is a common moral to be drawn from this common failure of two similar attempts, in different provinces of life, to substitute ghosts raised from Sheol for living ideas or institutions. It is all very well for a necromancer to evoke a wraith; but he courts failure if he goes on to try to merge his own identity in the spectral form that he has succeeded in conjuring up; for a phantom is nothing if not transparent; and a creature of flesh and blood that seeks to take cover behind a *revenant* from the world of shades will remain conspicuously visible through the tenuous wisps of this ghastly fancy dress. The shape of the Mahāyāna shows through the shimmer of Neoconfucianism as plainly as the solid substance of the Syrian Emperors' would-be Christian legislation can be discerned beneath the patches of a Justinianean veneer with which its nakedness was partially covered by the Syrians' Macedonian successors.

When we pass from the renaissance of a Sinic Confucian philosophy in Far Eastern history to the renaissance of an Hellenic Aristotelian philosophy in Western Christian history,[4] we find the plot of the play taking a piquantly different turn on this other stage. Whereas Neoconfucianism succumbed to a Mahāyāna that, in the official view of a Confucian imperial régime, was a trespasser squatting on demesne land to which it could not show any legal title, Neo-Aristotelianism imposed itself on the theology of a Christian Church in whose official view Aristotle—even when the paragon of Medieval Western theologians had fallen into the habit of referring to him as 'the Philosopher' *sans phrase*—nevertheless still remained a son of perdition who was to be kept under mistrustful surveillance on the precarious footing of an enemy alien provisionally permitted to reside within the terrestrial bridgehead of the *Civitas Dei*. In fact, the Hellenic philosopher's ghost captivated a Christian Church that had readmitted this pagan *revenant* on sufferance

---

[1] See ibid., p. 360, and Fung Yu-lan, op. cit., pp. 308–10.
[2] Acts ix. 5 and xxvi. 14.   [3] See pp. 27–30, above.
[4] An illuminating account of this Aristotelian intellectual renaissance in Medieval Western Christendom will be found in the following works of the Modern Western scholar C. H. Haskins: *Studies in the History of Mediaeval Science*, 2nd ed. (Cambridge, Mass. 1927, Harvard University Press); *The Renaissance of the Twelfth Century* (Cambridge, Mass. 1927, Harvard University Press); *Studies in Mediaeval Culture* (Oxford 1929, University Press). A psychological question concerning the Andalusian and Sicilian Muslim and the Byzantine Greek Orthodox Christian channels through which a knowledge of Aristotle's philosophical works was acquired by a Medieval Western Christendom is discussed in the present Study on pp. 130–35, below.

into a Western Earthly Paradise after the Church had gained possession of the title deeds, while, conversely, the Sinic philosopher's ghost was captivated by a Mahāyāna on which it had served notice to quit on the strength of title deeds which the Confucians had never let out of their hands. It will be seen that these two otherwise antithetical versions of a ghost-story have one common feature. In either variant of the tale, a party which can claim to have the law on its side is worsted by an opponent who has to rely solely on his merits because, at law, he has no case.

In these at first sight adverse circumstances, a ghostly Neo-Aristotelianism in Western Christendom displayed the same astonishing intellectual potency as a living Mahāyāna in the Far Eastern World.

'It was not [from the Roman tradition] that [Western] Europe derived the critical intelligence and the restless spirit of scientific inquiry which have made [the] Western Civilisation the heir and successor of the Greeks. It is usual to date the coming of this new element from the [Italian] Renaissance and the revival of Greek studies in the fifteenth century, but the real turning-point must be placed three centuries earlier. . . . Already at Paris in the days of Abelard (*vivebat* A.D. 1079–1142) and John of Salisbury (*vivebat circa* A.D. 1115–1180) the passion for dialectic and the spirit of philosophical speculation had begun to transform the intellectual atmosphere of [Western] Christendom; and from that time forward the higher studies were dominated by the technique of logical discussion— the *quaestio* and the public disputation which so largely determined the *form* of Mediaeval [Western] Philosophy even in its greatest representatives. "Nothing", says Robert of Sorbonne, "is known perfectly which has not been masticated by the teeth of disputation;" and the tendency to submit every question, from the most obvious to the most abstruse, to this process of mastication not only encouraged readiness of wit and exactness of thought but, above all, developed that spirit of criticism and methodic doubt to which Western culture and Modern Science have owed so much.'[1]

A ghost of Aristotle that set this abiding impress on the spirit, as well as on the form, of Western thought also produced a passing effect on its substance; and, though the impress here was less durable, it nevertheless went deep enough to require a long and arduous campaign of mental strife as the price of its eventual effacement.

'In [the] whole picture of the Universe [as seen by Medieval Western eyes] there is more of Aristotle than of Christianity. It was the authority of Aristotle and his successors which was responsible even for those features of this teaching which might seem to us to carry something of an ecclesiastical flavour—the hierarchy of heavens, the revolving spheres, the intelligences which moved the planets, the grading of the elements in the order of their nobility and the view that the celestial bodies were composed of an incorruptible fifth essence. Indeed, we may say [that] it was Aristotle rather than Ptolemy who had to be overthrown in the sixteenth century, and it was Aristotle who provided the great obstruction to the Copernican theory.'[2]

[1] Dawson, Christopher: *Religion and the Rise of Western Culture* (London 1950, Sheed & Ward), pp. 229–30.
[2] Butterfield, H.: *The Origins of Modern Science, 1300–1800* (London 1949, Bell), pp. 21–22.

By the seventeenth century of the Christian Era, when the native intellectual genius of the West reasserted itself, in its own characteristically empirical and utilitarian vein,[1] by setting out on a hazardous intellectual pioneering expedition in a carriage-and-pair in which the two steeds yoked in double harness were a technological-minded Natural Science and a scientific-minded Technology, the theology of the Western Christian Church had become so closely entwined with the Aristotelian espalier on which it had been industriously trained by the cumulative labours of twelve generations of Schoolmen that a post-Christian Occidental secular faith's historic martyr, Giordano Bruno, forfeited his life in A.D. 1600 for an intellectual offence which was a flagrant crime of *lèse majesté* against the sovereignty of Aristotle without being explicitly incompatible with Christian theological doctrine.[2] And, when the Medieval Western Frankenstein's monster whose offended dignity had exacted this sixteenth-century burnt-offering was at last brought to bay by Bruno's scientific successors and avengers,[3] Aristotle died as hard in Padua as Jezebel in Jezreel.[4]

'To the Humanists of the [Italian] Renaissance, Padua was an object of particular derision because it was the hotbed of Aristotelianism; and it was one of the paradoxes of the Scientific Revolution that so important a part was played in it by a university in which Aristotle was so much the tradition and for centuries had been so greatly adored.'[5]

Before the seventeenth-century Transalpine Western scientists and philosophers had attacked the Schoolmen for their subservience to 'Aristotle their dictator',[6] the fifteenth-century Italian Humanists had despised them for their bad Latin; but a ghost of Aristotle which had been raised by the serious-minded heralds of an Early Medieval Western Renaissance of Hellenic philosophy could not be driven out of a Western intellectual arena by such finnikin weapons as the darts, culled from a Ciceronian quiver, that were shot at 'the Philosopher's' heroic wraith by frivolous heralds of a Late Medieval Western Renaissance of the 'classical' Latin and Greek languages and literatures. When, in the course of the seventeenth century, Aristotle's ghost was laid at last in a Western World which this formidable *revenant* had been haunting by that time for not much less than six hundred years, the indignantly recalcitrant spectre did not beat its sullen retreat into the Cimmerian Darkness, from which it had been released for so long a term

---

[1] See III. iii. 385–6.
[2] The indiscretion through which Bruno brought on himself a fate that did not overtake Copernicus is explained in Butterfield, op. cit., p. 50.
[3] The positive assertion of the existence of a plurality of worlds, which had cost Bruno his life in A.D. 1600, was repeated with impunity in A.D. 1686 by Fontenelle in an *œuvre de vulgarisation*, his *Conversations on the Plurality of Worlds*, which immediately became a 'best seller' (see Bury, J. B.: *The Idea of Progress* (London 1924, Macmillan), pp. 113–15). Yet in the eighth book of *Paradise Lost* Milton did 'not venture to affirm the Copernican system' (Bury, ibid., p. 114), any more than Copernicus himself had ventured to affirm the infinity of the Physical Universe (see Butterfield, op. cit., p. 50), though the date of publication of Milton's poem was only nineteen years earlier than that of Fontenelle's dialogue.
[4] 2 Kings ix. 30–37.   [5] Butterfield, op. cit., p. 42.
[6] Bacon, Francis: *Of the Proficience and Advancement of Learning, Divine and Human*, Book I, chap. iii, § 3.

of probation, without enjoying the satisfaction of seeing the crestfallen shades of an ornamental Cicero and an academic Isocrates simultaneously rebanished at the expiry of a very much briefer ticket of leave.

(d) RENAISSANCES OF LANGUAGES AND LITERATURES

A Revenante *Literature's Psychological Appeal*

When our progressive survey of renaissances carries us into the field of languages and literatures, it confronts us here with an apparent paradox. In this field we meet on the one hand with grotesquely blatant revelations of a vein of pedantry or frivolity, or both, which has caught our eye here and there in our foregoing review of renaissances in the fields of Law and Politics, and which may well be latent in all renaissances as a perhaps inevitable effect of their intrinsic artificiality. On the other hand, this is the field in which the *tours de force* of the cultural necromancer's art win the most enthusiastic acclamation and esteem and are able to count on the most devoted and most uncritical support in setting at defiance the exorcist's salutary summons to an unduly long lingering ghost to return to the nether regions from which it has been conjured up.

The solution of this puzzle is to be found in a feature of the literary and visual 'Fine Arts' that distinguishes them from the social activities of life as well as from Mathematics, Natural Science, and Technology. In the field of the 'Fine Arts' the artist's gift and the critic's taste are independent—to a degree unknown in either of those two other provinces of human culture—of the temporary local circumstances of the historical time and place; and the aesthetic faculties enjoy this unparalleled measure of freedom because they have their roots in the subconscious depths of the Psyche, in whose sight 'a thousand years are but as yesterday when it is past, and as a watch in the night'.[1] The pace of psychic evolution is indeed immeasurably slower in this psychic abyss than on the conscious and volitional surface of the Soul. On the Time-scale of the Subconscious the span of five or six thousand years, counting back from the time of writing, which had seen human societies of the species known as civilizations come and go in a series that had by then already arrived at the third generation, was no more than 'the twinkling of an eye'[2] in which the hidden light of the 'collective subconscious' human spirit had known 'no variableness, neither shadow of turning'.[3]

The products of this 'Collective Subconscious' which had been welling up from the depths to the surface of the Psyche in creative works of Literary and Visual Art were thus, in one aspect, virtually eternal, universal, impersonal, and inevitable[4] by reason of the characteristics of the

---

[1] Ps. xc. 4. Cp. 2 Pet. iii. 8.
[2] 1 Cor. xv. 52.   [3] Jas. i. 17.
[4] The word 'virtually' in this sentence perhaps needs underlining, since the appearance of eternity, universality, impersonality, and inevitability which the subconscious abyss of the Human Psyche presented, at its 'collective' depth, to conscious individual human intelligences was, of course, no more than an illusory trick of Relativity. If a human intelligence became capable of viewing 'the Collective Subconscious' with the eyes, not of an individual human being, but of God, it would, no doubt, then become aware that, by comparison with the veritable Absolute, the human 'Collective Sub-

subconscious source from which they sprang, while in another aspect they were also actually ephemeral, parochial, personal, and arbitrary owing to their having to make their epiphanies on the surface of Life at some particular moment in the history of some particular body social, through the action of some individual man or woman who happened to have a genius for giving expression to a *Zeitgeist* in the medium of 'the Primordial Images'.[1]

In an earlier context[2] we have noticed that such expressions of something temporary and local in terms of something lasting and ubiquitous are apt to be so distinctive that the aesthetic test proves to be the surest as well as the subtlest method of ascertaining the limits of a society's extension in the dimensions of Time and Space. Yet this aesthetic monogram which is an almost infallible token for establishing the identity of a social milieu is nevertheless not an intrinsic feature of the body social on whose lineaments it displays itself; it is an arbitrary imprint in the sense that a style of art is not constrained to the same extent as is a system of government or law to reflect the practical exigencies of a particular time and place, while on the other hand it is free from the intellectual servitude which compels a system of Mathematics or Natural Science or Technology to conform to an already acquired and accepted body of knowledge or 'know-how' in order to qualify for finding its

conscious' was a creature of the same parochial and ephemeral kind as the individual human intelligence itself.

The Collective Subconscious's illusory appearance of absoluteness in the individual's intellectual sight was an optical illusion of the same order as the illusory appearance of immobility which a growing plant presents to the physical vision of a human observer. When the growth of a plant has been photographed in a cine-camera with a time-exposure of several weeks' or months' duration, and when a motion that is imperceptible to human eyes in real life has been rendered visible to them on the film by the device of reeling off the tale of weeks and months in so many seconds, it becomes manifest, even to an observer whose powers of vision are limited by the obtuseness of so crude an organ as the human eye, that a plant is in truth no less limber and lithe a living creature than an animal. When the tempo is artificially speeded up on the screen to this degree, the human spectator can watch the roots of a growing plant twisting and turning, like wriggling worms or writhing snakes, as they feel their way round stones and other obstacles in their feverishly eager search for nutriment, while the spectacle of the frantic competitive upward growth of the flowers and grasses under a hedgerow in springtime, and the successive sudden wilting of each competitor when it reaches the limits of its staying power in this struggle for access to a light and an air that are necessities of life, will remind the onlooker of the tragic competition for survival between the human prisoners in the Black Hole of Calcutta. Thus, on the Time-scale of the twinkling of even a human eye, when this Time-scale has been artificially substituted for a normal pace that is of an incommensurably slower order of velocity, the normally apparent distinction between the seeming immobility of a plant and mobility of an animal can be perceived to be illusory; and on this physical analogy we may infer that, in the psychic universe, the corresponding distinction, normally apparent in the mental vision of a human intelligence, between the flux of human life on its conscious and volitional surface and its seeming invariability in its subconscious depths is an illusion which does not cloud the clear sight of an Almighty God.

In the writer's world in his generation, in which 'the Collective Subconscious' was a recent, and therefore an imposing, discovery of a post-Modern Western Science, it was important to be constantly mindful of the truth that the godlike appearance of this deep level of the abyss of the Psyche was no less illusory than the spurious divinity of individual human mannikins of the stature of a Cheops or a Chephren or an Alexander or a Caesar; for, considering the strength and persistence of men's impulse to worship their own latest creations or discoveries, it was to be apprehended that a Twentieth-Century Western Man might mistake a human 'Collective Subconscious' for God (see VII. vii. 514).

[1] For this concept of 'Primordial Images', see the works of C. G. Jung, *passim*.
[2] In III. iii. 378–80.

place in the cumulatively growing structure of the Human Spirit's 'collective intelligence'.[1] The Fine Arts thus contrive to make the best of both the worlds between which they serve as mediators. Like the voice of the Pythia delivering oracles to Hellas from the Omphalos, they overawe the Conscious Mind and Will by intoning with all the authority of Absolute Necessity, and at the same time delight them by babbling with all the licence of Perfect Freedom. The logically incompatible categories of Necessity and Freedom are, in fact, miraculously reconciled in these oracular artistic intimations of the Primordial Images.

This ambivalent Freedom-in-Necessity or Necessity-in-Freedom, which is the peculiar quality of the Fine Arts and is the secret of the influence that a literature or a visual art is able to exercise over the life of the society in which this art has originally lived and moved and had its being,[2] makes its magic power felt with a heightened potency in the life of an affiliated society in which the ghost of an antecedent society's art has been conjured up. An aesthetic style that has been arbitrary in one sense even in its original social milieu becomes doubly arbitrary when it is imposed on an alien body social which has already created for itself a native style of its own; yet the exponents of this native aesthetic style which is the haunted society's blazon find the ground give way under their feet when they try to stand up to the spectral trespasser upon their patrimony; for the familiar native style, no less than the uncanny *revenant*, is an arbitrary coinage of the Primordial Images into the aesthetic currency of a particular time and place. A native style of art cannot plead, like a native system of government or law, that it is the only practicable solution of local contemporary social problems; and it cannot plead either, like a current system of Mathematics or Natural Science or Technology, that it is the only rational integration of the sum of knowledge within its field that has been accumulated up to date. When the native art of a haunted society is waging its defensive war against a stalking ghost of the art of an antecedent civilization, it finds itself destitute of Law's or Science's natural defences in the realm of Here and Now, and it is therefore easily driven out of such forward positions into a last ditch in the realm of *Semper et Ubique* where the phantom aggressor is able to contend with the assaulted living art on equal terms.

The issue on which the battle will be decided in this last ditch will be the question which of the two contending arts presents the identical substance of unvarying Primordial Images in an alternative form that better satisfies the abiding and ubiquitous spiritual needs of the souls of men and women, without regard to the local temporary social milieu in which their lot has been cast in their mortal life as individuals; and, on this issue, a live art has no advantage over a ghost; for the accident of the live art's happening to be alive at the moment when the combat is taking place is irrelevant to the determination of the respective merits of the combatants if these merits are being weighed in balances that render their account in terms of eternal and universal values, without being

---

[1] The respective relations of the Fine Arts and the Mathematical and Natural Sciences to the social milieu are examined further on pp. 697–704, below.
[2] Acts xvii. 28.

subject to the distorting gravitational pulls of Date or Locality. Under these conditions the odds are even. The ghostly invader has just as good a chance as the living defender of an open city to be awarded the crown of victory by the suffrages of the living generation of the society in whose life the combat is taking place. In the emotional depths of their spiritual experience, in which they are citizens of a Commonwealth of the Subconscious which has likewise been the spiritual home of every other human being who has ever lived—whatever may have been the particular time and place of his conscious volitional life on the surface of human existence—the voters in the forum have no closer affinity and no more compelling obligation to the literature or visual art that they happen to have created for themselves out of the Primordial Images than they have to the arts which their predecessors, in their day, have created out of the same abiding and ubiquitous psychic *hylê*. On the plane of the Subconscious it is incontestably true that *nihil humanum* is *alienum* from any human soul.[1]

•The considerations which we have just set out will perhaps suffice to explain why it is that *revenantes* literatures and visual arts present such markedly ambivalent appearances and arouse such bitterly violent and stubborn controversies; and we may now pass on from this preface to a review of the facts to which it applies.

The Resuscitation of a Classical Literature in an Anthology, Thesaurus, or Encyclopaedia

A survey of renaissances of languages and literatures that require resuscitation because they are 'dead', and demand it on the score of being 'classical',[2] is in one respect easier to undertake than our foregoing surveys of those living languages that have served as *lingue franche*[3] or as the official languages of universal states[4] or the liturgical languages of churches,[5] and than our accompanying surveys of living literatures which have used those living languages as their media. A living language has a life of its own; for it is not only *ex hypothesi* 'a going concern' before the birth of any literature that may eventually employ this living language as its medium; it may also continue thereafter to go its own way in the vocal and audible realm of the tongue and the ear on lines independent of its literary career in the scriven and legible realm of the penman's hand and the reader's eye into which it has now been translated. This original relation between a literature that uses a language and the language that is used by this literature is inverted when the ghosts of the same literature and same language are raised from the dead; for the ghost of a language can haunt the living world only as a parasite on the ghost of a literature which will originally have been an excrescence on the language in the days when the two have both been alive; and therefore, in surveying the renaissances of languages and literatures, we need not, and indeed cannot, deal with the *revenantes* languages apart from the *revenantes*

---

1 Terence: *Hautontimorumenus*, Act I, scene 1, line 25.
2 An attempt to define the distinctive characteristics of a 'classical' language and literature is made on pp. 705–17, below.   3 See V. vi. 62–83.
4 See VI. vii. 239–53.   5 See VI. vii. 253–5.

literatures which provide these 'dead' languages with their librettos for catching the eye of the audience of deaf mutes that confronts them when they reappear on the stage of History. Down to the time of writing, the hard labour of recapturing a 'dead' language had seldom been undertaken except for the sake of regaining access to monuments of literature in which this language had been enshrined;[1] and the usual course of a literary renaissance had been a series of steps towards a goal which was not the interpreter's *tour de force* of speaking a dead language as it had originally been spoken, but the scribe's *tour de force* of writing it as it had originally been written.

The first step in this arduous and unpromising enterprise was to retrieve the dead literature's remains; the second step was to remaster their meaning; the third step was to reproduce them in counterfeits which might be mistaken for maliciously adroit parodies if they were not patently inspired by a superstitious reverence for the originals which convicts them of being solemnly clumsy tributes of admiration.[2] In our survey of renaissances in this field, it will be convenient to follow *gradatim* in the footsteps of the literary necromancers whose procedure is the present object of our curiosity; but, as we investigate the three stages of this procedure in their historical order, it will become evident that they overlap with one another in the Time-dimension, and also that they are distinguished from one another by differences that are not mere corollaries of their chronological sequence.

For instance, when we come to look at the attempts to reproduce a 'classical' literature, we shall find that these imitative works of art, uninspired and uninspiring though they may be, do genuinely have at least one thing in common with their originals. Like these, they are the personal creations of individual human beings, not the mechanically assembled products of collective man-power. On the other hand we shall find team-work counting for more, and individual enterprise for less, in the execution of the preliminary and preparatory tasks of scholarship.

It is true that, here too, we shall meet with culture-heroes who have performed prodigies single-handed. The type is well exemplified in Photius (*vivebat circa* A.D. 820–91), the pioneer Orthodox Christian explorer of an Hellenic literature which, for a nascent Orthodox Christian Society, had been a *terra incognita* during a social interregnum that, on the cultural plane, had held the field continuously for two centuries down to Photius's own generation. The failure of the historical record to name anyone who was Photius's teacher is as eloquent as is its catalogue of his goodly company of pupils.[3] His *Library* (*Vivliothíki*) or *Host of Books* (*Myrióvivlon*) became a mine of information for later Orthodox

---

[1] It is true that in the Modern Western World there had been several attempts—which, down to the time of writing, had met with diverse degrees of success—to re-animate a 'dead' language viva voce as well as in the visual medium of script. Some of these experiments have been noticed in this Study already in V. vi. 62–71.

[2] In the realm of the Fine Arts the faculty of mimêsis is, of course, a two-edged sword which can be made to serve either as the sincerest form of flattery or as the deadliest form of exposure. The choice between these opposite uses is determined, not by any variation in the nature of the weapon, but by a difference in the temper of its wielder.

[3] This point is made by Krumbacher, K.: *Geschichte der Byzantinischen Literatur*, 2nd ed. (Munich 1897, Beck), p. 515.

Christian students of the Hellenic literature, and thereafter for Western students of it in their turn; the actual number of works noticed in this literary digest is 280; and, according to Photius's own account, these were merely the books that happened to have been read, studied, discussed, and appraised in his literary circle during the temporary absence of his brother, to whom the *Library* is dedicated as a *compte rendu* of the transactions in which the absentee had been unable to participate personally. Even if we were to suspect that this dedication was a literary *jeu d'esprit*, and that the contents of the Library represented a larger part of Photius's life-long literary output than the small fraction that they purport to be,[1] the extent of Photius's acquaintance with the Hellenic literature would still remain portentous by comparison with the ignorance of this pioneer scholar's own immediate predecessors.

An independent private scholar of the stature of a Photius is not, however, the characteristic figure in the landscape of a dawning literary renaissance. The pioneer enterprise of reoccupying a long since derelict literary empire is a piece of titan's work that may require the mobilization of a living political empire's organized collective resources; the typical monument of a literary renaissance in its first or second phase is an anthology, thesaurus, corpus, lexicon, or encyclopaedia compiled by a team of scholars at the instance of a prince; and the princely patron of such works of co-operative scholarship as these has, more often than not, been the ruler of a resuscitated universal state that has, itself, been the product of a renaissance on the political plane. Of the five outstandingly eminent representatives of the type who had appeared on the stage of History down to the time of writing—namely, Asshurbanipal, Constantine Porphyrogenitus, Yung Lo, K'ang Hsi, and Ch'ien Lung—the last four had all been emperors of *imperia rediviva*.

In the execution of the preliminary task of collecting, editing, annotating, and publishing the surviving works of a 'dead' classical literature, the Far Eastern emperors of a resuscitated Sinic universal state had not only far outdistanced all their competitors up to date but had raised paper monuments whose pyramid-like mass could not easily have been equalled even by the output of a post-Modern Western World with its unprecedented capacity for material production.

It is true that the size of Asshurbanipal's two clay libraries of Sumerian and Akkadian classical literature was an unknown and unknowable quantity for the latter-day Western archaeologists who had learnt of the assemblage and dispersal of these two great Assyrian collections by recovering some of the tablets in the course of their excavations on the site of Nineveh; for, within perhaps not more than sixteen years of the royal scholar-criminal's death, the contents of both his libraries had been 'scattered broadcast over the ruins'[2] of a hateful city that had been stormed, sacked, and devastated in 612 B.C. by the infuriated victims of the last and most atrocious bout of Assyrian militarism.[3] Asshurbanipal's collection may have been larger than the Confucian Canon of the Sinic

---

[1] See Krumbacher, op. cit., p. 519.
[2] Thompson, R. Campbell, in *The Cambridge Ancient History*, vol. iii (Cambridge 1925, University Press), p. 206.　　　　[3] See IV. iv. 468-70 and 483-4.

Classics which was, not facilely impressed on soft clay, but laboriously engraved on hard stone, at Si Ngan, the imperial capital of the T'ang Dynasty,[1] between A.D. 836 and A.D. 841,[2] and was printed between A.D. 932 and A.D. 953—during the bout of political anarchy between the extinction of the T'ang and the establishment of the Sung—in an edition which, including the commentary as well as the text, filled 130 volumes.[3] Yet we may guess with some confidence that the number of the cuneiform characters contained in Asshurbanipal's collection during the brief period of its existence as a going concern was small by comparison with the number of the Sinic characters contained in the comprehensive collection of works of a Sinic and Sinistic literature which Yung Lo, the third emperor of the Ming Dynasty,[4] assembled in A.D. 1403–7; for the revised version of Yung Lo's *Ta Tien* ran to no fewer than 22,877 books filling 11,095 volumes, without reckoning in the table of contents.[5]

This gigantic *Corpus Sinicum*, which had required the services of 2,180 or more scholars for the task of selection and transcription,[6] was beyond the printing capacity[7] even of a Far Eastern World whose enthusiasm for its Sinic cultural heritage had been reinforced by a Zealot hatred of alien Mongol conquerors[8] whom the Ming had recently succeeded in expelling from Intramural China; and, according to one account, a set of the *Ta Tien* in manuscript that had become, if it had not always been, unique was eventually destroyed by fire during the fighting in Peking in A.D. 1900 when the Legation Quarter was besieged by 'the Boxers' and relieved by an international expeditionary force.[9]

---

[1] See VI. vii. 213.

[2] See Goodrich, L. C.: *A Short History of the Chinese People* (London 1948, Allen & Unwin), p. 132.

[3] See Goodrich, op. cit., p. 141. This task was executed by the Hanlin Academy of Letters, which had been founded by the T'ang Emperor Hsüan Tsung on the eve of the troubles of A.D. 755–65, and which survived into the nineteenth century (ibid., p. 132).

[4] Some of Yung Lo's achievements in other fields have been noticed already in II. ii. 122 and in VI. vii. 264, n. 6.

[5] See Goodrich, L. C.: *A Short History of the Chinese People* (London 1948, Allen & Unwin), p. 201. The table of contents, running to sixty books, accounts for the discrepancy between the figure of 22,877 books given in *Der Grosse Brockhaus* (Leipzig 1929, Brockhaus, 20 vols.), vol. iv, p. 54, s.v. 'Chinesische Literatur', and the figure of 22,937 given in *The Encyclopaedia Britannica*, 1929, vol. v, p. 573, s.v. 'Chinese Literature'. These figures are derived from the Manchu Emperor Ch'ien Lung's notice of the *Ta Tien* in his catalogue of his own collection. An English translation of this notice by W. F. Mayers will be found in *The China Review*, vol. vi (1877–8), pp. 215–17.

[6] See Goodrich, ibid. The number is stated to have been 2,169 in the notice of the *Ta Tien* in Ch'ien Lung's catalogue of his own collection, cited in the preceding footnote.

[7] Though the work could not be printed as a whole, a number of its component parts were printed separately (see Goodrich, ibid.).   [8] See V. v. 348–52.

[9] This is the account given in Wilhelm, R.: *Geschichte der Chinesischen Kultur* (Munich 1928, Bruckmann), pp. 14 and 41. According to Goodrich, op. cit., loc. cit., and to *The Encyclopaedia Britannica*, 1929, loc. cit., there had once been three manuscript sets of the complete work. Out of these three sets, only 368 volumes were known to be in existence in A.D. 1940, according to Goodrich, ibid. According to the notice, cited already, in Ch'ien Lung's catalogue of his own collection, one duplicate manuscript set of the *Ta Tien* was made in the years A.D. 1407–9 for the printer's use before the project of printing the *Ta Tien* was abandoned; the whole collection was moved from Nanking to Peking when the imperial capital was transferred thither by Yung Lo in A.D. 1421 (see II. ii. 122); two more manuscript sets were made at Peking in A.D. 1562–7; the two original sets were then sent back to Nanking; but, out of the four, one Peking copy alone survived the disturbances that accompanied the fall of the Ming Dynasty. At the time when the notice in Ch'ien Lung's catalogue was drawn up (i.e. at some date between A.D. 1772 and A.D. 1782), only 2,422 books were missing in this surviving set, out of the original total of 22,937 (including the table of contents). At the date when Mayers was

When the Manchu Emperors K'ang Hsi (*imperabat* A.D. 1662–1722) and
Ch'ien Lung (*imperabat* A.D. 1736–96) emulated their Ming predecessor
Yung Lo's achievement, they endowed their own collection of the Sinic
classical literature with better expectations of life. K'ang Hsi's *K'in
Ting Ku Chin T'u Shu Chi Ch'êng* ('Compendium of Literature and
Illustrations, Ancient and Modern, drawn up under Imperial Authority')[1]
was more fortunate than Yung Lo's *Ta Tien* in duly finding its way into
print, thanks to the comparative modesty of its compass of 10,000 books
in 5,000 volumes (not including a table of contents running to 40 books
in 20 volumes) and to the adoption of a suggestion, made by the Jesuit
mission in Peking, that a fount of movable metal type should be cast
for it as a cheaper alternative method of printing than the cutting of
wooden blocks. K'ang Hsi's collection was eventually printed—in a
hundred sets according to one account, and in thirty according to another—in A.D. 1726 under the auspices of his successor Yung Chang
(*imperabat* A.D. 1723–35).[2]

The printing *in extenso* of Ch'ien Lung's *Ssu-k'u Ch'üan Shu*[3] was out
of the question, for this was a collection, not of extracts, like Yung Lo's
and K'ang Hsi's, but of complete works[4] of all genres, which were collected by the imperial officials throughout the Empire in pursuance of a
decree issued by Ch'ien Lung in A.D. 1772, and were collated with the
materials already assembled in Yung Lo's and K'ang Hsi's collections
by an editorial commission appointed in A.D. 1773.[5] The commission
eventually incorporated in the collection, according to one account,
3,511 works in 78,731 books, or, according to another account, 3,460
works in 75,854 books.[6] The commission also produced an analytical

writing (A.D. 1877–8), this copy was still extant in the Hanlin College at Peking, in a
building erected there for the housing of imperial collections of literature (see Mayers,
ibid., p. 217).

[1] See Mayers, ibid., pp. 218–23.

[2] 'The editors of the famous encyclopaedia *Ku Chin T'u Shu Chi Ch'êng*, whom his
father had pardoned for political offences, were put in danger of their lives in order that
he might enjoy the cheap satisfaction of having the work brought out under editors of
his own choosing, though it was probably already complete' (Goodrich, L. C.: *The
Literary Inquisition of Ch'ien-lung* (Baltimore 1935, Waverley Press), p. 21).

[3] See Mayers, ibid., pp. 291–9. Goodrich, op. cit., pp. 31 and 36, cites an unprinted
essay, on deposit in the library of Columbia University, by Wen-yu Yen, entitled
'*Ssu-k'u Ch'üan Shu*, "The Four Treasuries Library" and its Influence upon Chinese
Culture' (dated June 1932).

[4] See Goodrich, op. cit., p. 30; Mayers, op. cit., p. 293.

[5] 'The same officials who were appointed to invite book-collectors to lend or sell rare
texts to the Emperor were likewise required to search out and demand volumes and
manuscripts thought inimical to dynastic interests; and . . . for nearly ten years the same
officials in Peking who made the selections of books to be copied into *The Four Treasuries*
also made note of censorable items and reported them to the Throne.

'Ch'ien Lung . . . for all the munificence of his gifts to literature . . . stands accused
before the bar of public opinion for his open interference with the independence of the
scholars of his day, for his deliberate falsification of history, for his malice towards a
score of authors (several deceased long before) and their descendants, and for his
repeated burning of hundreds of books, wood blocks of many of them included . . .
a destruction of literary matter which one modern Chinese writer [Wang Kuang-wei in
the *Bulletin de l'Institut de l'Université Nationale* (Peking) for the 3rd February, 1926,
17] has no hesitation in classing as second only to the holocaust under Ts'in Shih Hwang'
—Goodrich, L. C.: *The Literary Inquisition of Ch'ien-lung* (Baltimore 1935, Waverley
Press), pp. 31 and 36.

[6] See Mayers, ibid., pp. 297–8 and 295. Mayers considers the larger of these two
alternative sets of figures to be the more authoritative. The material taken from the
Yung Lo Ta Tien consisted of 85 complete works and 284 fragmentary works (Mayers,
ibid., p. 298), running to 4,946 books (Mayers, ibid., p. 217).

catalogue, running to 200 books, giving a calendar of works submitted but rejected, as well as one of works included. This catalogue, an abridgement of it, and 147 of the collected works themselves,[1] were eventually printed. The preservation of the collection as a whole was provided for by the multiplication and dispersion of manuscript sets. In addition to the original fair copy, three others were made for official use, and these four were deposited in buildings, specially erected to house them, in the precincts of the Imperial Palace at Peking, at Yüan-ming Yüan, at Jehol, and at Mukden.[2] Three further complete manuscript sets were deposited in existing libraries at Yangchow, Chinkiang, and Hangchow. The rough copy was presented to the Hanlin Academy. Two manuscript sets of an anthology containing about a third of the complete collection were also lodged in the Imperial Palace at Peking and at Yüan-ming Yüan respectively.

These huge collections of the remains of the Sinic classical literature that were assembled by rulers of a Far Eastern oecumenical empire dwarf the corresponding works of the East Roman Emperor Constantine Porphyrogenitus (*imperabat* A.D. 912–59). Constantine organized the extraction of excerpts, classified under divers heads,[3] with the object of thereby making accessible to an intellectually awakening Orthodox Christian Society the cream of an Hellenic classical literature which—even in the shreds and tatters to which its remains had been reduced already by the storm and stress of a post-Hellenic interregnum—was still, in the tenth century of the Christian Era, quite 'immeasurable' and 'unmanageable' in its bulk[4] when this was pitted against the narrowly limited receptive powers of an individual human intellect. These Byzantine works of collective scholarship that were produced on Constantine Porphyrogenitus's initiative and under his auspices shrink into insignificance under the shadow of the mighty works of a Yung Lo and a Ch'ien Lung; and, if the East Roman scholar-emperor could challenge comparison with his giant Far Eastern counterparts on any ground at all, he would have a better prospect of holding his own as an author of original works[5]

---

[1] See Goodrich, op. cit., p. 148. Mayers, loc. cit., p. 296, gives the number as 'some 130 in all'.　　　　　　　　　　　　　　　　　　　[2] See VI. vii. 199, n. 4.

[3] i.e. *Diplomatic Missions, Virtues and Vices, Sententious Sayings* (περὶ γνωμῶν), *and Conspiracies against Sovereign Princes*, to mention only the heads under which Constantine Porphyrogenitus is known for a certainty to have made collections of extracts from the Hellenic Classics (see Krumbacher, op. cit., pp. 258–61). Constantine also arranged for the production of new editions of two late Hellenic works of the same character as his own collections: namely, the sixth-century compiler Cassianus Bassus's *Information about Agriculture* (Γεωπονικά) and the fourth-century compiler Oreibasius's *Concise Survey of Medical Theories* (Ἐπιτομὴ τῶν Ἰατρικῶν Θεωρημάτων) (see Krumbacher, op. cit., pp. 261–4).

[4] Ἐπ' ἄπειρόν τε καὶ ἀμήχανον ἡ τῆς ἱστορίας εὐρύνετο συμπλοκή.—Constantine Porphyrogenitus: περὶ Ἀρετῆς καὶ Κακίας, Introduction, quoted by Krumbacher, op. cit., pp. 258–9.

[5] Constantine Porphyrogenitus wrote *An Historical Narration of the Life and Acts of the Emperor Basil of Glorious Memory* [i.e. the author's grandfather Basil I (*imperabat* A.D. 867–86), the founder of the Macedonian Dynasty]; *The Administration of the Empire*; *The Army Corps Districts* (θέματα) *appertaining to the Empire of the Romans and the Origins and Etymologies of their Names, bringing out the distinction between the Names that have been Newly Coined and those that have been Resuscitated from the Ancient Nomenclature*; and *An Exposition and Outline of the Imperial Rules and Regulations* (Ἡ τῆς Βασιλείου Τάξεως Ἔκθεσίς τε καὶ Ὑποτύπωσις), labelled *De Caerimoniis Aulae Byzantinae* by Modern Western scholars.

In the foregoing list, the order in which Constantine's original works have been

than as a 'captain of literary industry' directing and organizing the labours of 'intellectual workers'.[1]

The Byzantine scholar-Heraclês who could have looked Ch'ien Lung in the face without being abashed was not the Emperor Constantine Porphyrogenitus but his commoner-namesake and approximate contemporary Constantine Kephalás, who, without having at his command the resources of an imperial secretariat and an imperial exchequer, succeeded in accomplishing the formidable task of collecting and arranging under subject-headings a vast anthology of the Hellenic poetry written in elegiac verse that had been produced in the course of the twelve or thirteen hundred years ending in the sixth century of the Christian Era. Nor was Kephalás the only private Byzantine scholar who distinguished himself as a collector of Hellenic poems of this genre. At the turn of the thirteenth and fourteenth centuries he found a worthy successor in Maximos Planoúdhis, whose anthology proclaims its independence of Kephalàs' work in its arrangement as well as in its contents.[2]

When we pass from the preliminary work of collecting and editing a classical literature to the subsequent task of interpreting its meaning, we find Far Eastern scholarship here again putting all competitors into the shade. At least three notable encyclopaedias of Sinic knowledge were compiled during the T'ang régime[3] and four during the Sung.[4] Three of these became classics under the collective title *San T'ung* ('The Three Encyclopaedias').[5] In the Ming Age, six such works dating from the T'ang and Sung Age were used by Yü Ngan-k'i for the compilation of a thesaurus of literary extracts;[6] and his work, in its turn, was capped by the Manchu Emperor K'ang Hsi's dictionary of universal reference, *Yuan Kien Lei Hai*, published in A.D. 1710.[7] The Sung Age had seen the compilation of two notable lexicons, one of which dealt with no less than 53,525 characters.[8] The *Tzŭ-Hui*, published in A.D. 1615 at a time when the Ming Dynasty was declining towards its fall, dealt with not more

mentioned is a descending order of originality. The *De Caerimoniis* owes its great historical value to the fact that it is little more than a new edition of an old handbook in which the date and authorship of a number of the earlier component parts are still recognizable. The *De Thematibus* likewise draws largely, and in many passages *verbatim*, on previously existing works; but in this case, unfortunately, the sources on which Constantine has chosen to draw are descriptions of the administrative organization of the Late Roman Empire as it was before the great administrative interregnum in the seventh century of the Christian Era, with the result that this disappointing work of Constantine's tells us much less than its title promises about the origin and development of the actual administrative organization, based on army-corps districts, which was the new and distinctive system current in the East Roman Empire (see Krumbacher, op. cit., pp. 253–4). We have noticed in another context (in IV. iv. 342) that the East Roman Empire had been generated by the union of the two army-corps districts of the Anatolici and the Armeniaci with one another and with the imperial city of Constantinople in the eighth century of the Christian Era.

[1] The comparable 'industrialization' of historical scholarship in a post-Modern Western World has been noticed in I. i. 3–8.

[2] Though Planoúdhis left out of his collection many epigrams that Kephalàs had included in his, he also included a number that Kephalàs had left out; and he arranged his own selection on a new plan, under a larger number of heads which he divided into sub-heads (see Krumbacher, op. cit., pp. 727–8).

[3] See Goodrich, op. cit., pp. 135–6.   [4] See ibid., pp. 152–3.

[5] See Mayers, W. F.: 'Bibliography of the Chinese Imperial Collections of Literature', in *The China Review*, vol. vi (1877–8), pp. 214–15.

[6] See Mayers, ibid., p. 287.   [7] See Mayers, ibid., pp. 287–8.

[8] See Goodrich, op. cit., p. 166.

than 33,179 characters but was remarkable for the achievement of arranging these under not more than 214 radicals, in contrast to the 540 that was the lowest figure to which the number had been reduced in any previous analysis.[1] K'ang Hsi (*imperabat* A.D. 1662–1722) organized the production of a lexicon dealing with more than 40,000 characters[2] (the *K'ang Hsi Tsi-Tien*, published in A.D. 1716) and two concordances (the *P'ei-Wen Yün-Fu*, published in A.D. 1711 in 444 books, with a supplement of 112 books published in A.D. 1716, and the *P'ien-Tsi-Lei-Pien*, published in A.D. 1726 in 240 books) that were designed for the same use as the Modern Western Humanist's *Gradus ad Parnassum*.[3] There are corresponding works to the credit of private Byzantine scholars— Photius's lexicon,[4] Souïdhas' encyclopaedia,[5] and a number of etymological dictionaries of unknown authorship[6]—but, if these Byzantine scholars could have had any inkling of the scale on which K'ang Hsi was to do for the Sinic classics what they were trying to do for the Hellenic classics in the lexicographer's line, there would have been no more spirit in them than there was in the Queen of Sheba when she had seen all Solomon's wisdom.[7]

When we pass from lexicography to criticism and exegesis, Orthodox Christendom can produce one outstanding figure in the person of the twelfth-century scholar-bishop Eustathius, whose commentary on the Homeric poems had proved of lasting value to succeeding Byzantine and Western students down to the time of writing. Eustathius's intellect was no less eminent than his moral character.[8] But how could one single champion be expected to prove a match for the legion of Western scholars who invaded the field of Hellenic studies in the fifteenth century of the Christian Era, or for the two waves of Far Eastern scholars who made progressive conquests in the field of Sinic studies in the age of the Sung and the age of the Manchu Dynasty?[9]

Critical scholarship in China under the Manchu domination was the child of abortive political endeavours that, in failing, moved the scholar-administrators who had made them to transfer their energies to an intellectual field in which they could count on finding themselves still masters of the situation. In the early decades of the seventeenth century of the Christian Era, when the Ming imperial régime in China was in its death agonies, the Confucian civil servants made two successive attempts —which were as honourable and as unsuccessful as the similar attempts that these latter-day imperial administrators' predecessors had made in the last days of the Posterior Han[10]—to save the régime from collapse

---

[1] See Goodrich, op. cit., p. 205.

[2] According to *Der Grosse Brockhaus*, 1929, vol. iv, p. 55, the number was 40,545; according to *The Encyclopaedia Britannica*, 1929, vol. v, p. 573, this lexicon ran to 49,000 characters arranged under 214 radicals (like Mei Ying-tso's *Tzŭ-Hui*).

[3] *Der Grosse Brockhaus*, 1929, vol. iv, p. 55. Details will be found in Mayers, loc. cit., pp. 288–91.

[4] See Krumbacher, op. cit., pp. 519–21.   [5] See ibid., pp. 562–70.

[6] See ibid., pp. 573–6.   [7] 1 Kings x. 5 and 4.

[8] In A.D. 1185 even the obscene Western Christian conquerors of Salonica, the Orthodox Christian city that was Eustathius's archiepiscopal see, were unable to resist the spell of this 'schismatic' prelate's saintliness; and, as far as his unfortunate flock did receive any mercy, they owed it to his intrepid intercession on their behalf (see IX. viii. 375, n.3).

[9] See *Der Grosse Brockhaus*, 1929, vol. iv, p. 55.   [10] See VI. vii. 371, n. 3.

by rescuing it from the hands of the palace eunuchs.[1] Thereafter, when the incurable corruption and incompetence of an effete indigenous dynasty brought extinction upon them and subjugation upon their subjects at the hands of Manchu barbarians, the Confucian litterati once again played an honourable part in the political arena—first by taking their share in an eventually unsuccessful Zealot resistance movement in the South, and then by engaging in an eventually successful manœuvre to captivate a resuscitated Sinic universal state's Manchu barbarian conquerors by making their own administrative services indispensable to the Empire's new masters.[2] In this 'cold war' between litterati and barbarians the intellectual attractiveness of the Confucian literary culture was as potent a weapon in the hands of the mandarins as the political utility of the Confucian administrative tradition; and, in this light, the outburst of critical scholarship in China in the seventeenth century may be regarded as a by-product, on the intellectual plane, of a movement of withdrawal-and-return that was to end on the political plane on which it had begun.[3]

The critical scholarship of the Manchu Age was not an entirely new departure, since the Neoconfucian philosophers of the Sung Age[4] had already cast doubt on the authenticity of some of the works that had come to be included in the canon of the Classics.[5] But, if the seventeenth-century and eighteenth-century Confucian scholars were indebted to the twelfth-century and thirteenth-century Neoconfucian philosophers for their critical approach to the Classics, they found their chief stimulus in exercising these awakened critical faculties at the Neoconfucians' expense. After having exposed the Buddhist and Taoist provenance of the Neoconfucians' cosmology, ethics, and psychology, they went on to condemn their scholarship itself as being unscientifically subjective;[6] and they justified their censoriousness by the exactness and exhaustiveness of their own work on the Sinic classical literature not only in the fields of phonetics, semantics, and textual criticism but in the less pedestrian enterprise of higher criticism as well.[7]

The Counterfeiting of a Resuscitated Classical Literature

When we pass from these preliminary and preparatory tasks of scholarship to the scholar's conceit of producing counterfeits of a classical literature that he is striving to raise from the dead, we must leave it to statisticians to determine whether the number of essays in the Sinic classical style that were produced by candidates for the imperial civil service examinations in China in the course of the 1,283 years that

[1] See Hu Hsih: 'The Chinese Renaissance', in *The China Year Book*, 1924–5 (London N.D., Simpkin Marshall), p. 633.
[2] See Hu Hsih. ibid. p. 634.
[3] On this showing, it would appear that the seventeenth-century Chinese scholars who performed such prodigies in the exegesis of the Sinic classical literature were following in the footsteps of Confucius himself and were thereby also taking the same course as the Pleiad of historians—a Thucydides, Xenophon, Josephus, Ollivier, Machiavelli, Polybius, Clarendon, and Ibn Khaldūn—whose auspiciously broken careers we have examined in an earlier context (see III. iii. 248–377).
[4] See pp. 41–43, above.
[5] See Hu Hsih, ibid., p. 634.
[6] See Hu Hsih, ibid., p. 635.
[7] See Hu Hsih, ibid., pp. 635–6.

elapsed between their reinstitution by T'ang T'ai Tsung in A.D. 622[1] and their abolition in A.D. 1905 in the last days of the Manchu régime was greater or less than the number of exercises in the writing of classical Latin and Greek prose and verse that had been produced by scholars and schoolboys in the Western World between the fifteenth century of the Christian Era and the time of writing. But, whatever might prove to be the answer to this statistical conundrum, it could be predicted that, in a competition in the use of resuscitated classical languages for literary purposes, mere volume of production would not avail to wrest into Chinese or Western hands the palm held by a band of Byzantine historians who found their medium of literary expression in the renaissance of an Attic Greek κοινή.

'The authors who brought historiography back to life after the fatal interregnum, extending from the middle of the seventh to the middle of the ninth century of the Christian Era, promptly addressed themselves to the ancient models; and the Age of the Comneni and the Palaeologi brings with it the spectacle of a marked increase in this subservience to [Hellenic] Antiquity. It would be a legitimate generalisation to say that the only substantial difference that distinguishes the [Byzantine] historians of the eleventh to the fifteenth century from the [Late Hellenic] historians of the sixth and seventh centuries is to be found in their respective ways of using a common external medium of exposition. As used by the historians of the Byzantine School, this literary instrument is much more artificial and much more obviously something that has been learnt by rote like a schoolboy's lesson. Procopius, Agathias, Menander Protector, Evagrius, and Theophylactus Simocatta may indulge in all kinds of mannerism and apishness, yet they have none of them quite lost their foothold in the living [Greek] speech of the cultivated society of their time, whereas an Anna Comnena studies her Ancient Greek as a foreign language, and this predicament of Anna's is the common embarrassment of all Byzantine historians from the twelfth century onwards. By their time the living [Modern Greek] language had departed so far from Ancient Greek in its morphology, its vocabulary and its syntax that the traditional language of belles lettres had come to be no longer even intelligible except at the price of a thorough preparatory grounding in it. This is the sole really generic formal difference that distinguishes the Byzantine historians in the strict sense of the term from the Late Hellenic historians.'[2]

This linguistic and literary make-believe was carried to its preposterous *reductio ad absurdum* by two of the four last cultivators of the genre: a fifteenth-century Athenian Nicholas Khalkokondhýlis who transposed his Christian name into an Hellenic-looking 'Laónikos', and a fifteenth-century Imbrian Kritópoulos who, by a more adroit change of just two letters of the Alphabet,[3] coined a likewise Hellenic-looking 'Kritóvoulos' out of a surname that advertised the bearer's Cretan origin. Not content

---

[1] 'After A.D. 681, the final examination for the highest degree, conducted 262 times during the [period of the] T'ang régime, included: (1) five essays on current events, (2) essays on the Confucian classics and history, (3) an original poem and a composition in rhythmic prose, and (4) special tests covering such topics as Mathematics and Law' (Goodrich, L. C.: *A Short History of the Chinese People* (London 1948, Allen & Unwin), p. 131, n. 18, following A. W. Hummel in *Report of the Librarian of Congress, 1938,* p. 222).   [2] Krumbacher, op. cit., pp. 226-7.

[3] Κρητόπουλος could be transformed into Κριτόβουλος by substituting an ι for an η and a β for a π.

—as an Anna Comnena and a Nikítas Khoniátis had been—with trying to write an Attic κοινή that might be mistaken by a charitable reader for the language of a Diodorus or a Procopius, the latter-day Athenian aspired to be a second Herodotus, and the latter-day Imbrian to be a second Thucydides; and each of these would-be mimics of the most elusive of all Hellenic originals rashly proclaimed his pretensions in an exordium aping his august ensample's famous opening words—only to fall into solecisms of syntax, vocabulary, and morphology for which a classically educated Modern Western schoolboy would have blushed if he had been convicted of having made such gross mistakes in such countless numbers. Yet the classically educated reader of these Byzantine historians' works whose teeth are set on edge by the stridency of the discord between their pretensions and their performance on the linguistic and literary plane would be guilty of the very frivolity by which these unsuccessful mimics offend him if he were to allow a wanton injury to his aesthetic sensibilities to blind him to the serious merits of the intellectual substance that is masked by an excruciatingly affected linguistic and literary form. A Malvolio-like Kritópoulos or Khalkokondhýlis can challenge comparison with an unpretentious Dhoúkas or Phrantzìs when he offers himself for appraisal, not as an author of a work written in Attic or Ionic Greek in the classical Hellenic style, but as a writer of the history of his own time. A Phrantzìs and a Khalkokondhýlis in the service of the Palaiológhi, a Dhoúkas in the service of the Gattilusi, and a Kritópoulos in the service of the 'Osmanli all succeeded, from their divers angles of vision, in appreciating and conveying the historic importance of the rise of an Ottoman Power that, in their day, was imposing an alien universal state upon their own Orthodox Christian Society; and a comparable historical insight had been shown by a number of their predecessors.

The first of the series, Léon Dhiakónos, whose work covers the history of seventeen years (A.D. 959–75) ending shortly before the outbreak of the Great Romano-Bulgarian War (gerebatur A.D. 977–1019), fully deserved a tribute that had been paid to him by Bury;[1] and, within the span of nearly five hundred years that separates Leo's generation from Kritópoulos's, Leo had a number of notable successors, among whom we may pick out, for mention here,[2] the Emperor Alexius Comnenus's

---

[1] 'With the history of Leo Diaconus (Leo Asiaticus) we enter upon a new period of historiography. After an interval of more than three hundred years, he seems to reopen the series which closed with Theophylactus Simocatta. His history . . . is . . . a contemporary work in a good sense, depending on personal knowledge and information derived from living people, not on previous writers' (Bury, J. B., in his edition of Edward Gibbon's *The History of the Decline and Fall of the Roman Empire*, Editio Minor, vol. v (London 1901, Methuen), p. 504).

[2] In refusing an honourable mention to Léon Dhiakónos's immediate successor Michael Psellos, the writer of this Study was conscious of his temerity in challenging the verdict of a scholar who was far better versed than he was in Medieval Greek literature. In Miss J. M. Hussey's judgement, Psellos's work was so excellent that the highest praise which she could bestow on Leo's was to rate this only one degree lower than the Psellan level. 'Leo's story of the tenth century is almost as delightful as Psellus's of the eleventh, although quite different in style and outlook' (*Church and Learning in the Byzantine Empire, 867–1185* (London 1937, Milford), p. 27). It is different indeed; and, though, by the date at which this note was being written, eighteen years had passed since the writer had had his own experience of reading Leo's history and Psellos's continuation of it one after the other, the passage of time had not taken the edge off the sharpness of

learned daughter Anna (*vivebat* A.D. 1083–*post* 1148), who continued and completed a history of the restoration of the East Roman Empire in her father's generation which had been begun by her husband the Caesar Nikiphóros Vryénnios (*vivebat circa* A.D. 1062–*post* 1137); a Ioánnis Kínnamos who wrote the history of the Comnenan régime during its 'Indian Summer' (A.D. 1118–76); a Nikítas Khoniátis who lived to see and describe the catastrophe of A.D. 1204; and a fourteenth-century Ioánnis Kandakouzinòs whose plausible *apologia pro vitâ suâ* could not cover the tracks of the truth that, in usurping the East Roman imperial crown and thereby precipitating a civil war (*saeviebat* A.D. 1341–54), he had opened the way for the 'Osmanlis to leap the Dardanelles and entrench themselves in Rumelia.

The Discomfiture of an Hellenic Ghost by a Western Vernacular Literature

If we now extend our synoptic view of the Far Eastern, Orthodox Christian, and Western renaissances of a classical language and literature to embrace the whole course of each of these three movements from beginning to end, we shall notice that the Far Eastern and the Orthodox Christian renaissance resemble one another and differ alike from the Western renaissance in two respects. In the first place, each of the two non-Western movements succeeded, when once it had got under way, in going forward, not indeed without occasional pauses, but at least without any serious set-backs, whereas the Western literary renaissance that got under way in Italy in the fourteenth and fifteenth centuries had had an eighth-century precursor of Northumbrian origin which had been abortive.[1] In the second place the counter-movement by which each of the two non-Western literary renaissances was eventually overcome was not any domestic reaction against it in favour of the native genius of the civilization which had put itself under a self-imposed ban by conjuring up this ghost of an antecedent society's culture. In the Far Eastern World and Orthodox Christendom, the haunted society never even attempted to exorcize the domineering *revenant*, and was not relieved of its oppressive presence until one masterful alien intruder was expelled by another in the shape of a contemporary Western Civilization which captivated Orthodox Christendom in the course of the seventeenth century, and China at the turn of the nineteenth and twentieth centuries,

the disappointment that he had suffered then in finding Psellos belying his high reputation by showing himself quite destitute of Leo's flair for what is historically interesting and important.

It is true enough that 'scholarship in the eleventh century is often unconsciously considered in terms of Michael Psellus' and that he is 'the most prominent figure of the revival of learning [in Greek Orthodox Christendom] in the eleventh century' (Hussey, op. cit., p. 43); but the conspicuousness of the position which Psellos undoubtedly succeeded in securing for himself in the Hall of Fame certifies nothing beyond his ability to impress Posterity. He achieved this by his facility as a writer; but this very facility convicts him of superficiality in the sight of a reader who measures the felicity of his pen against the jejuneness of his intellect. On this test the present writer inclines towards Krumbacher's harsh judgement on Psellos (Krumbacher, op. cit., p. 435, cited in Hussey, op. cit., pp. 43–44) rather than towards Miss Hussey's more indulgent appreciation of him; and he remains of the opinion that, without prejudice to the question whether Psellos's loss of his academic chair was or was not deserved (see Hussey, op. cit., pp. 65–71), the professor of Hellenic philosophy cannot hold a candle to his predecessor the deacon as a writer of the history of his own times.

[1] This difference has been noticed in IV. iv. 363, with n. 1.

of the Christian Era.[1] By contrast, the Modern Western renaissance of an Hellenic literature represented by the surviving remains of the Greek and Latin Classics was exorcized by the native genius of the Western Civilization, without the help of any alien cultural ally, in a *Kulturkampf* between the respective champions of 'the Ancients' and 'the Moderns' which resulted, before the close of the seventeenth century of the Christian Era, in a decisive victory for an anti-Hellenic 'Counter-Renaissance'.[2]

The abortive first attempt at a literary renaissance of Hellenism in Western Christendom was coeval with the birth of the Western Christian Civilization itself. The insular prophet of the movement in Northumbria[3] was the Venerable Bede of Jarrow (*vivebat* A.D. 673–735); its continental apostle in Carolingia was Alcuin of York (*vivebat* A.D. 735–804);[4] and, before it was prematurely extinguished by a blast of barbarism from Scandinavia, its exponents had not only begun to revive the Hellenic literary culture in its Latin dress, but had even acquired a smattering of the original Greek.[5] Alcuin had dared to dream that, in partnership with Charlemagne, he would be able to conjure up a ghost of Athens on the soil of Frankland;[6] but this Carolingian vision was as fleeting as it was splendid; it had no sooner made this first momentary epiphany than it vanished again without giving its dupes the time to test it; and, when, after a seven-hundred-years-long night-watch,[7] it was recaptured at last, at the turn of the fourteenth and fifteenth centuries of the Christian Era, by an exultant band of sanguine-minded Italian Humanists,[8] their longer hold upon it merely served to demonstrate that its fabric was baseless, and that, in persistently clutching at this elusive wraith of Hellenism, *Homo Occidentalis* was courting the poignant frustration that Aeneas brought upon himself when he thrice endeavoured to embrace the shade of Creüsa.[9]

[1] See IX. viii. 182–4 and 324–30.
[2] This Modern Western cultural civil war has been noticed in IV. iv. 363, with n. 2.
[3] An appreciation of this Northumbrian renaissance and a notice of its propagation in the Carolingian Empire will be found in Dawson, Ch.: *Religion and the Rise of Western Culture* (London 1950, Sheed & Ward), pp. 63–66 and 69–72.
[4] See Duckett, E. S.: *Alcuin, Friend of Charlemagne* (London 1952, Macmillan).
[5] The Carolingian Hellenists, such as they were, may have been the Irish Hellenists' teachers. At any rate, the Irish scholars who are known to have had some acquaintance with Greek seem all to have been ninth-century Irish residents in Continental Western Europe (see II. ii. 327, n. 1).
[6] Alcuin: *Correspondence*, Letter No. 170, addressed to Charlemagne (see Dawson, op. cit., p. 71).
[7] In a thirteenth-century University of Paris that was given over to the study of the Aristotelian philosophy, the arts and *belles lettres* were despised; and, in a thirteenth-century University of Oxford, Robert Grosseteste and his disciple Roger Bacon studied Ancient Greek (see pp. 133–5, below), not with a view to gaining any wide acquaintance with the Hellenic literature, but solely with an eye to a more accurate understanding of the works of Aristotle and the Scriptures of the Christian Church. This was a revulsion from the aftermath of a Carolingian literary renaissance which had left Western scholars destitute of any source of knowledge beyond the Latin *belles lettres* that had been preserved in the West to serve as textbooks for grammar and rhetoric; but a shift of interest from literature to metaphysics that was so marked in a twelfth-century and thirteenth-century Transalpine Western Christendom had no counterpart in a contemporary Italy, where, as we have seen (on pp. 31–34, above), the academically ablest minds turned in this age to the study, not of the Aristotelian philosophy, but of the Civil and the Canon Law (see Taylor, H. O.: *The Mediaeval Mind* (London 1911, Macmillan, 2 vols.), vol. ii, pp. 118–21). [8] See IV. iv. 275, n. 1, and 363, n. 1.
[9] Virgil: *Aeneid*, Book II, ll. 792–5.

The illusory semblance of solidity which this phantom displayed at its long-delayed second appearance was so well simulated in its first flush that the pioneers of Humanism might be forgiven, in their day, for flattering themselves that they had been privileged to make Alcuin's noble dream come true; but this sanguine fifteenth-century Italian belief could only have been justified by the event if the Humanists had been right in their underlying assumption that the genii of the western Civilization and Hellenism were two persons of one substance; and this was, indeed, the crucial article of faith in the creed of these Modern Western Hellenists.

In making this assumption the Humanists were simply applying to their own essay in the art of necromancy one of the necessary tenets of the necromancer's ideology. The motive for raising a ghost is to produce some change in the outlook and conduct of the living people whom the ghost is intended to haunt. If the haunted party were to show no sign of being affected by the apparition of the *revenant*, the evocation of this spectre would have been so much labour lost; the measure of the necromancer's success is the degree to which the ghost's intrusion effectually deflects the haunted party from his previous course; but, while the necromancer is thus bound to do his utmost to produce a deflection which will be notable enough to show that he has not exerted himself in vain, he also cannot afford to lay himself open to the charge that he is leading his patient astray from a course which is this wayfarer's high road; for to admit this would be tantamount to confessing that the necromancer's familiar spirit is a misleading will-o'-the-wisp and that the human object of his magical operations is, not his patient, but his victim.

For this reason, every successful necromancer has to justify what he has done by contending that, at the moment when he took it upon himself to raise a ghost from the Past, the living individual or society for whose benefit he professes to have been acting was wandering in the wilderness off the beaten track, and that therefore the magician, when he deflected the wayfarer from his course, was doing him the beneficent service of guiding him back out of a side-track into the highroad. This was the view of their work which the authors of a Modern Western literary renaissance of Hellenism endeavoured to impose on their contemporaries; and the power of the impression that this Late Medieval Italian cultural doctrine was able to make upon the Western tradition is indicated by the confidence with which this fifteenth-century dogma is reasserted in a work, published no less than a quarter of a millennium after the decisive defeat of 'the Ancients' in their seventeenth-century battle with 'the Moderns', by a latter-day Western historian-philosopher who was a contemporary of the writer of this Study.

'Western Civilisation has formed itself by . . . reconstructing within its own mind the mind of the Hellenic World and developing the wealth of that mind in new directions. Thus Western Civilisation is not related to Hellenic in any merely external way. The relation is an internal one. Western Civilisation expresses, and indeed achieves, its individuality, not by distinguishing itself from Hellenic Civilisation, but by identifying itself therewith.'[1]

[1] Collingwood, R. G.: *The Idea of History* (Oxford 1946, Clarendon Press), p. 163.

In *The Knights* of Aristophanes, Demosthenes has the happy thought[1] of routing Cleon by enlisting against him a sausage-monger who out-Cleons Cleon and so vanquishes him; and, if we take this cue from an Athenian playwright, our first retort to Collingwood's *ipse dixit*[2] will be to pit against it one of Spengler's which makes a precisely contrary assertion in terms that are even more magisterial.

'The Renaissance was . . . a rebellion against the spirit of [a] Faustian music, cast in the form of the fugue and breathing the spirit of the woods, which was at that moment on the point of asserting its dictatorship over the whole orchestra of the Western Civilisation's divers forms of self-expression (*über die gesamte Formensprache der abendländischen Kultur*). It [? i.e. the Renaissance] was a logically consistent consequence of the mature Gothic style in which this [Faustian spirit's] will to power had emerged undisguised. It [? i.e. the Renaissance] never attempted to deny either that its genesis was this or that its nature was (as in fact it was) that of a mere counter-movement; and the character of such a counter-movement was bound to be determined from first to last by the contours of the original movement whose negative effect upon the hesitant soul had declared itself in this reaction.

'It is consistent with the origin and nature of the Renaissance that this movement should lack (as it does lack) all genuine depth—and this in the double sense of a shallowness in its ideas and a shallowness in their manifestations. In point of ideas, one need only remind himself of the passionateness of the *abandon* with which the Gothic spirit (*Weltgefühl*) discharged itself over the whole landscape of the Western Culture in order to appreciate the character of the movement that was started, about the year 1420, by a little group of chosen spirits: scholars, artists and humanists. In the outburst of the Gothic spirit, it was a question of "to be or not to be" for a new type of spiritual life (*eines neuen Seelentums*); in the Renaissance it was just a question of taste. The Gothic spirit seizes in its grip the whole of Life, and penetrates into its most secret recesses. It created a new kind of human being and a new kind of world. . . . The Renaissance took possession of a few of the arts, and that was the whole story. It produced no change at all in Western Europe's intellectual outlook or emotional attitude to life. It made itself felt in matters of costume and mannerism without penetrating to the roots of existence. Between Dante and Michael Angelo—both of whom already overstep the Renaissance's chronological limits—this movement cannot muster any representative who can claim to rank as a genius. And, as for the manifestations in which the ideas of the Renaissance expressed themselves, these never gained any hold on the people—no, not even in Florence. In the depths of the people's soul—and this alone makes it possible for us to understand the epiphany of Savonarola and the power, of a wholly different order of potency, that he was able to exert over men's feelings—in the depths of the people's soul the Gothic undercurrent flows serenely along its musical course to its Baroque fulfilment. . . .[3]

[1] See ll. 141–9.

[2] In the passage quoted above, Collingwood adopts and asserts, without entering into any argument of the case, a disputable, and in fact long since successfully disputed, view of the role of the Italian Renaissance in Western history. The context shows that he has been moved to take up this dogmatic position by a belief that, in the Renaissance of Hellenism, the Western World was doing 'exactly' [*sic*] what is done by 'the historian who studies a civilisation other than his own'. Collingwood's view of the historian's relation to the objects that he studies is examined on pp. 718–37, below.

[3] Spengler, O.: *Der Untergang des Abendlandes*, vol. i (Munich 1920, Beck), pp. 320–1; cp. pp. 591–2.

'The Renaissance is a movement which is both anti-Gothic and antagonistic to the spirit of [Modern Western] instrumental music, and in this role it has an exact counterpart in Hellenic history (*in der Antike*) in a Dionysiac spirit (*Weltgefühl*) which is anti-Doric and at loggerheads with the plastic Apollinean spirit. . . . The great insurrection occurred in Hellas *circa* 700–600 B.C. and in Italy *circa* A.D. 1400–1500. In both cases we are witnessing a war in the soul; a rift in the foundations of the civilisation (*Kultur*) which has found its outward visible expression (*seinen physiognomischen Ausdruck*) in an entire epoch of [the society's] history, and especially in that epoch's universe of artistic forms; a revolt of the soul against its destiny (*Schicksal*), of which it has now taken the measure in its full compass. The recalcitrant forces in the society's bosom—Faust's second soul, which would fain dissever itself from his other soul—are attempting to do violence to the civilisation's intrinsic spirit; something that is an ineluctable necessity is to be repudiated, rescinded, evaded; the inwardness of the movement is a shrinking from the completion of the society's history in the pre-ordained terms of the Ionic style and of the Baroque style [respectively].

'In Hellenic history this revulsion attaches itself to an orgiastic worship of Dionysus which finds its medium in music and its goal in conjuring away Reality and dissipating corporeal objects (*den Körper vergeudenden*); in Western history it attaches itself to the literary tradition of "Antiquity" and to its cult of the plastic arts, and these two [elements of Hellenic culture] are brought to the rescue in the hope that, through powers of suggestion inherent in antagonistic forms of expression, these alien influences may provide the repressed feeling with a rallying point, may invest it with a pathos of its own, and may thereby obstruct the current which flows in Hellenic history from Homer and the geometric style [of painting] to Pheidias, and flows in Western history from the Gothic cathedrals through Rembrandt to Beethoven.'[1]

In these characteristic passages Spengler stigmatizes as an unsuccessful revolt against a manifest destiny the self-same movement that Collingwood commends as the successful fulfilment of a manifest destiny in words that are perhaps no less characteristic of their author's êthos. The same dogmatism asserts itself through the piquantly diverse English and German styles of two fine minds whose common foible has brought them into this head-on collision; and, if we were condemned to choose blindfold between one of these two unsupported asseverations and the other, we might find ourselves hard put to it to break the deadlock. As it happens, Collingwood contradicts his own pronouncement, quoted above, in another passage of the same work of his in which he pronounces that the philosophy of the Italian renaissance of Hellenism was as Christian at heart, under an Hellenic mask, as we have found[2] the Far Eastern Neoconfucian philosophy of the Sung Age to have been Buddhist at heart under a mask of Confucianism.

'In spite of the new interest in Graeco-Roman thought, the Renaissance conception of Man was profoundly different from the Graeco-Roman; and, when a writer like Machiavelli, in the early sixteenth century, expressed his ideas about History in the shape of a commentary on the first ten books of Livy, he was not reinstating Livy's own view of History.

[1] Spengler, O.: *Der Untergang des Abendlandes*, vol. i (Munich 1920, Beck), p. 321.
[2] On pp. 41-43, above.

Man, for the Renaissance historian, was not Man as depicted by Ancient Philosophy, controlling his actions and creating his destiny by the work of his intellect, but Man as depicted by Christian thought, a creature of passion and impulse. History thus became the history of human passions, regarded as necessary manifestations of Human Nature.'[1]

Collingwood's two pronouncements manifestly cancel one another out; yet, since both alike are unsupported assertions, the question which they raise is left still calling for a reasoned answer. Fortunately there are other voices to be heard in this debate; and, if, after listening to them, we find ourselves coming to the conclusion that happens to coincide with Spengler's thesis, this will not be because we have taken the hierophant's oracular dicta on faith; it will be because we have been convinced by the reasoning of soberly empirical-minded historians who have not disdained to argue their case by appealing to the relevant facts.

After having heard Spengler and Collingwood, let us listen to the following critique of the Modern Western literary renaissance of Hellenism from Bury's pen:

'In discarding mediaeval naïveté and superstition, in assuming a freer attitude towards theological authority, and in developing a new conception of the value of individual personality, men looked to the guidance of Greek and Roman thinkers and called up the spirit of the Ancient World to exorcise the ghosts of the Dark Ages. Their minds were thus directed backwards to a past civilisation which, in the ardour of new discovery and in the reaction against Mediaevalism, they enthroned as ideal; and a new authority was set up—the authority of ancient writers. In general speculation the men of the Renaissance followed the tendencies and adopted many of the prejudices of Greek philosophy. Although some great discoveries, with far-reaching, revolutionary consequences, were made in this period, most active minds were engaged in rediscovering, elaborating, criticising and imitating what was old. It was not till the closing years of the Renaissance that speculation began to seek and feel its way towards new points of departure.'[2]

While Bury thus gives reason for Spengler's characterization of 'the Renaissance' as a revolt against the medieval manifestations of the Western Civilization's native genius, Butterfield enlarges Spengler's *aperçu* of a seventeenth-century counter-revolution against the tyranny of a rebel Renaissance. The eruption of a Baroque visual art and music, which occupies the whole of Spengler's field of vision, is overshadowed in Butterfield's panorama by the eruption of a Late Modern Western Science as this presents itself in the Time-perspective of an observer looking back at it from the chronological vantage-point of a date near the middle of the twentieth century.

'We of the year 1949 . . . are in a position to see [the] implications . . . of the Scientific Revolution . . . much more clearly than the men who flourished fifty or even twenty years before us. . . . The very strength of our conviction that ours was a Graeco-Roman civilisation—the very way in which we allowed the art-historians and the philologists to make us

[1] Collingwood, R. G.: *The Idea of History* (Oxford 1946, Clarendon Press), p. 57.
[2] Bury, J. B.: *The Idea of Progress* (London 1924, Macmillan), p. 30. Cp. Butterfield, H.: *The Origins of Modern Science, 1300–1800* (London 1949, Bell), p. 162.

think that this thing which we call "the Modern World" was the product of the Renaissance—the inelasticity of our historical concepts, in fact—helped to conceal the radical nature of the changes that had taken place.'[1]

If, in the light of Butterfield's and Bury's reasoning, we give judgement in favour of the Spenglerian thesis in the issue between Spengler and Collingwood, our verdict will be that, before the close of the seventeenth century, the Western World did exorcize a ghost of Hellenism which it had conjured up some two or three hundred years earlier, but that, before the ghost was laid, this *revenant's* hold upon a living society's imagination had become so strong that another two or three hundred years had to pass before the epigoni of the victors in a seventeenth-century *Kulturkampf* could become fully alive to the truth that Queen Anne was dead.[2]

The issue between a ghost of Hellenism and the native genius of the Western Civilization had actually been decided before Queen Anne's accession to the throne; for a counter-attack that had been opened cautiously by Bodin (*vivebat* A.D. 1530–96),[3] and been carried on more boldly by Bacon (*vivebat* A.D. 1561–1626)[4] and Descartes (*vivebat* A.D. 1596–1650),[5] was pressed home to a decisive victory for the living Western culture's cause, and an irretrievable defeat for the Hellenic ghost's, by Fontenelle (*vivebat* A.D. 1657–1757)[6] in France and William Wotton (*vivebat* A.D. 1666–1727)[7] in England. The two telling shots to which

---

[1] Butterfield, op. cit., p. 173.

[2] The writer of this Study would be guilty of odious ingratitude to Hellenism itself, as well as to the Late Medieval Italian Humanists who raised its ghost to haunt a Modern Western World, if at this point he forbore to acknowledge and confess how thankful he was that one of 'those surprising overlaps and time-lags which so often disguise the direction things are taking' (to quote Butterfield, ibid.) had inhibited the arbiters of educational fashions in his own country from laying sacrilegious hands on the humane study of Greek and Latin letters for more than two centuries after this once sacrosanct curriculum had been implicitly condemned, as a logical consequence of the defeat that had overtaken 'the Ancients' in their seventeenth-century contest with 'the Moderns'. Whatever might be the verdict, from other points of view, on the 'classical' education instituted by the fifteenth-century Western Humanists, this was unquestionably the best education conceivable for a Westerner who wanted to be an historian; for a study of *Litterae Humaniores* was the one school of education open to a Westerner in the Modern Age in which he could learn to look at the society into which he happened to have been born with the alien eyes of an outsider whose spiritual home was Hellas, not Hesperia; and, for an historian, no training could be more valuable than this, since the first accomplishment that is required of an historian is an ability to jump clear of his own fortuitous Here and Now.

In having been born just in time to share in this boon, the writer might count himself fortunate indeed, considering that, by the date of his birth, the leaven of Fontenelle's *Digression* had already been working in Western minds for no less than 201 years. Though pedagogues are notorious for being arch-conservatives, even they do eventually respond to influences that have been in the ascendant for a very long time in the rest of the body social, and in England the bastions of a traditional Late Medieval Italian system of education in the Greek and Latin Classics at last duly began to crumble under the fire of Fontenelle's seventeenth-century batteries only a few years after the present writer's fifteen-years-long education in Latin and twelve-years-long education in Greek had been safely completed in A.D. 1911. In later life he thanked his stars for having permitted him to be so *felix opportunitate natûs*.

[3] See Bury, J. B.: *The Idea of Progress* (London 1924, Macmillan), p. 43. In the precise form of a comparison of merits, the controversy opened in Italy in A.D. 1620, and in France in A.D. 1635 (see ibid., pp. 80–1).

[4] See ibid., pp. 53–56.

[5] See ibid., pp. 67–69. 'He was proud of having forgotten the Greek which he had learnt as a boy. The inspiration of his work was the idea of breaking sharply with the Past, and constructing a system which borrows nothing from the dead.'

[6] See ibid., pp. 98–126.

[7] See ibid., pp. 119–23.

'the Ancients' had finally succumbed had been Fontenelle's *Une Digres-sion sur les Anciens et les Modernes* (*editum* A.D. 1688)[1] and William Wotton's *Reflections upon Ancient and Modern Learning* (*editum* A.D. 1694). Sir William Temple had played into Fontenelle's hands when he had attempted to answer the *Digression* in 'An Essay upon the Ancient and Modern Learning' which he had published in A.D. 1690 in the second volume of his *Miscellanea*; for he had not only provoked Wotton's able rejoinder but had brought his own cause into derision by rashly declaring his belief in the authenticity of the spurious *Epistles of Phalaris* and thereby drawing an annihilating broadside from a classical scholar of the calibre of Richard Bentley. Temple had not succeeded in rehabilitating himself in 'Some Thoughts upon Reviewing the Essay of Ancient and Modern Learning';[2] but his discomfiture had evoked the one immortal work indited in the course of this seventeenth-century controversy; for it had moved the hard-pressed scholar-statesman's brilliant protégé Jonathan Swift to come to his patron's support by writing in A.D. 1697 *The Battle of the Books* (*editum* A.D. 1704).

In this cultural civil war, whose outcome carried the Western Civiliza-tion out of an Early Modern into a Late Modern chapter of its history, one of the signs of the times was the publication at Rotterdam, in A.D. 1695–7, of Pierre Bayle's *Dictionnaire Historique et Critique*; for Bayle, the *déraciné* Southern French Protestant who had found his congenial second home at the meeting-point of an expanding Western World's oceanic and inland waterways at Rotterdam, was one of the prophets of a Rationalism which was a revulsion from the Wars of Religion,[3] and one of the founding fathers of a 'Republic of Letters' which was a secular substitute for a lost Medieval Western *Respublica Christiana*,[4] while Bayle's dictionary was the parent of Diderot's and d'Alembert's *Ency-clopédie* (*editum* A.D. 1751–65)[5] and thus the grandparent of all subse-quent Western works of co-operative intellectual engineering[6] whose promoters acknowledged their debt to the mother of Modern Western encyclopaedias by converting its title into a generic name for a line of literary production.

Dictionaries and encyclopaedias were not, of course, trophies of Late Modern Western Man's versatile inventive genius. They had been invented in a disintegrating Hellenic World in its post-Diocletianic Age

---

[1] 'La Lecture des Anciens a dissipé l'ignorance et la barbarie des siècles précédens, je le crois bien. Elle nous rendit tout d'un coup des idées du Vrai et du Beau que nous aurions été longtemps à ratraper, mais que nous eussions ratrapées à la fin sans le secours des Grecs et des Latins si nous les avions bien cherchées. Et où les eussions-nous prises ? Où les avoient prises les Anciens. Les Anciens mêmes, avant que de les prendre, tâton-nèrent bien longtemps. . . . Si l'on nous avoit mis en leur place, nous aurions inventé; s'ils étoient en la nôtre, ils ajouteroient à ce qu'ils trouveroient inventé; il n'y a pas là grand mystère' (Fontenelle, B. le Bovier de (*vivebat* A.D. 1657–1757): *Poësies Pastorales, avec un Traité sur la Nature de l'Eglogue et une Digression sur les Anciens et les Modernes*, 4th ed. (Amsterdam 1716, Etienne Roger), pp. 147 and 138).

[2] This essay is to be found in *The Works of Sir William Temple* (London 1720, Churchill and others), vol. i, pp. 290–304.

[3] See IV. iv 142–3, 150, 184, 227–8, and 643–5; V. v. 669–71; and V. vi. 317.

[4] An illuminating appreciation of Bayle's personality, outlook, and work will be found in Hazard, P.: *La Crise de la Conscience Européenne, 1680–1713* (Paris 1935, Boivin), pp. 101–18.

[5] In eighteen volumes of text and four volumes of plates.

[6] See I. i. 4.

and in a disintegrating Sinic World in the Age of the Posterior Han as strong-boxes for preserving an accumulated cultural wealth that was under threat of being lost through oblivion, and they had been revived, as we have seen,[1] in Orthodox Christendom and in the Far East as a first step towards recovering command of the buried treasures of an antecedent culture with a view to eventually bringing them back into circulation out of these golden treasuries. In sheer physical bulk, the monuments of a Far Eastern encyclopaedism dwarfed the most imposing structures of the kind that the technological resources of the Modern West had been able to produce down to the time of writing, as royally as the Pyramids at Gīzah dwarfed the 'sky-scrapers' on Manhattan Island. The novelty of the Late Modern Western encyclopaedias lay, not in their structure or in their scale, but in their purpose and in their spirit; for, in stealing this weapon from the armoury of a post-Diocletianic Hellenism, the Western champions of 'the Moderns' against 'the Ancients' in a seventeenth-century Western *Kulturkampf* were employing it neither for the preservation nor for the resuscitation of a 'dead' culture but for the assertion of a living culture's pretensions to be worth more than its predecessor's ghost.

The successive encyclopaedias that were published and republished, on an ever larger scale and at ever shorter intervals, in a Late Modern Western World from A.D. 1695 onwards, were so many manifestos giving notice of the Westerners' claim to have outstripped the wisdom of the Hellenes, and so many *comptes rendus* of the progress achieved by Western mental pioneers in virgin fields of knowledge, thought, and understanding. In the intellectual field of Mathematics, Natural Science, and Technology, which was the realm of an Impersonal Collective Consciousness, these self-confident Late Modern Westerners might prove in retrospect to have been justified in their belief that they had made original and momentous contributions to the cumulative wealth of Mankind. In aesthetic, moral, and religious fields in which a Collective Intellect's privilege of earning compound interest was denied to the seekers after spiritual treasure, and in which every society, and indeed every individual human being, was therefore forced to begin afresh Man's perennial search for the Pearl of Great Price,[2] Time alone would show whether an Occidental Faust was any more acceptable candidate for God's grace than an Hellenic Prometheus. Meanwhile, one thing was certain; and this was that before the close of the seventeenth century of the Christian Era a living and lively Western World had given a dead Hellenism's imperious ghost an unequivocally clear notice to quit.

Can we put our finger on any distinctive feature in the linguistic and literary renaissance of an antecedent civilization in the history of the Western World that might account for the Westerners' success in eventually shaking off this cultural incubus by their own unaided efforts, when this feat proved to be beyond the strength of both the Greek Orthodox Christians and the Chinese? We shall find at any rate one clue in the contrast, which we have noticed already,[3] between the spasmodic course

---

[1] On pp. 57–58, above.   [2] Matt. xiii. 45–46.
[3] On pp. 62–63, above.

of the linguistic and literary renaissance of Hellenism in the West and the uninterrupted progress of the corresponding renaissances in Greek Orthodox Christendom and in China; for the interruptions of the importunate activity of a ghost of the Hellenic culture in the West were so many opportunities for an original literature in the living vernacular languages of the Western peoples to spring up too high to be overshadowed, and strike root too deeply to be overthrown, when a temporarily banished spectre returned to try once again to captivate the Western World after a spell of quiescence following the failure of its first attempt. The new native Western poetry in the vulgar tongue had discarded an Hellenic mode of versification based on the quantitative value of syllables in favour of a mode, based on the accentuation of words, which was the natural mode for poetry in the living Romance[1] and Teutonic languages of the Western Christian peoples; and this native Western accentual verse had been enriched by the adoption of a contemporary Arabic poetry's device of rhyme, which was alien to the literary tradition of the Hellenic World and Western Christendom alike.[2] Yet, revolutionary as this Western new departure was, its triumph was portended in the success of the rhymed accentual Provençal poetry of the troubadours, and was assured when Dante made his historic decision to indite his *Divina Commedia*, not in Latin hexameters, but in rhymed accentual poetry in which he correctly took the troubadours' cue by using as his linguistic medium, not the troubadours' Provençal, but a Tuscan that was his own mother tongue.

It is true that the moral courage and aesthetic imagination here displayed by Dante had their counterparts, in the history of another civilization, in Ikhnaton's decision to discard, in favour of a living New Egyptian language, the long since dead Classical Egyptian which, down to Ikhnaton's day, had continued to be the obligatory medium of literary expression in the Egyptiac World because once, some 1,500 years before Ikhnaton's generation, this had been the living language of that world in the Age of 'the Old Kingdom'. It is also significant that, of all the sweeping reforms that Ikhnaton tried to impose upon the Egyptiac Society of his day, this linguistic reform alone survived his death.[3] Yet

---

[1] The natural bent of the Romance languages towards accentual, as opposed to quantitative, verse was part of their heritage from Latin. The 'Saturnian' verse of the oldest surviving specimens of Latin literature had been based on accent, not on quantity; and, although part of the price of the Romans' 'reception' of the Hellenic culture had been the banishment of this pristine native mode of Latin verse from the 'high-brow' Hellenizing Latin poetry of the Classical Age, the constriction of so strongly accented a language as Latin in the strait-waistcoat of a quantitative verse, reflecting the alien genius of Ancient Greek, could never—even in a Virgil's masterly hands—be anything but a *tour de force*. The unnaturalness of this imposition of an Ancient Greek prosody upon a Latin linguistic medium received its conclusive exposure when, some four centuries after the 'Saturnian' mode of versification had been driven off the field, an accentual prosody reasserted itself in a Christian Latin popular poetry produced by poets who were more keenly concerned to express themselves in a way that would be congenial to their public than they were to uphold any exotic literary canon.

[2] While a Medieval Western vernacular poetry adopted from a contemporary Arabic poetry the device of rhyme, which could be applied to accentual verse as readily as to quantitative, it is noteworthy that the Medieval Western vernacular poets were not inveigled by their admiration for their Arabic models into doing violence to the genius of their own mother tongues by going on to borrow from the Arabic a quantitative basis of versification which was common to the Arabic school and the Hellenic.

[3] See V. v. 496, and cp. IV. iv. 413.

these points in common between Ikhnaton's act and Dante's bring out all the more sharply the contrast between the respective relations in which these two men of genius stood to their social milieux.

Ikhnaton was spiritually at war with the êthos of the Past-ridden society into which he had been born; and, in this milieu, the weight of the incubus was so crushingly heavy that a would-be saviour of society could not afford to compromise. If he was to win any relief from pressure for his contemporaries and for Posterity, he could only hope to succeed by rejecting the Past *in toto*. By contrast, Dante was not faced with this desperate choice between two extreme alternatives. Living, as he had the good fortune to live, in an age of Western history in which the pressure of a resurgent Hellenism happened to be down in the trough between the sundered crests of a Carolingian wave that had already receded and a Medicean wave that was still beyond a fourteenth-century Florentine poet's temporal horizon, Dante was able to achieve his life-work as an exponent of the *Zeitgeist* instead of being forced, as Ikhnaton found himself forced, to resort to the hazardous *ultima ratio* of declaring war on it. Dante was able to express the spirit of his world and age by combining the cultivation of a vernacular poetry with a cult for a resuscitated Hellenic cultural past. He contrived—and this without strain, because without selfconsciousness—to be the exponent of a renaissance and of a new life simultaneously. And his ability to achieve this magically creative harmony was at least partly due to the auspicious fact that, in the Italy of his age, at the turn of the thirteenth and fourteenth centuries of the Christian Era, the influence of a resuscitated Hellenic culture was not overwhelmingly potent.

The impotence of this ghost to stifle the growth of a new and original culture that was springing up under its shadow is revealed in the success with which the living creature turned the tables on the *revenant* from a dead world; for in this case the spectre was dexterously captivated by its intended victim. When we examine the poetry composed in Latin in Western Christendom from the turn of the eleventh and twelfth centuries onward, we hear the accents of Jacob's voice while we are feeling the hands of Esau.[1] This medieval Latin poetry, as it was written from the twelfth century to the fifteenth, may be described not inaptly as vernacular poetry masquerading in a Latin dress. Though the words are Latin, the rhythm, rhyme, sentiment, and *je-ne-sais-quoi* of this ostensibly Latin poetry have all been breathed into it by the creative spirit of a contemporary Western literature in the vulgar tongue[2]—as Man became a living soul when the breath of life was breathed by the Lord God into a receptacle that he had formed of the dust of the ground.[3] And, when fifteenth-century Italian Humanists, in their injudiciously pedantic enthusiasm for a genuinely Hellenic article, proved clever enough to

[1] Gen. xxvii. 22.
[2] On this point see H. O. Taylor: *The Mediaeval Mind* (London 1911, Macmillan, 2 vols.), vol. ii, p. 154. In this connexion it is significant that the quarter of Western Christendom in which the finest works of Medieval Latin poetry were produced was a region lying to the north of the Loire, in what had been the north-western fringes of an Hellenic World of the Imperial Age, and not any of the Romance-speaking countries adjoining a Mediterranean Sea that had once been the Roman Empire's *mare nostrum* (see ibid., p. 122).
[3] Gen. ii. 7.

write classical Latin quantitative verse that might occasionally pass for the work of a Lucan or even an Ovid, they merely succeeded in killing a vernacular poetry in Latin fancy dress without ever coming within sight of their ulterior objective of installing a resuscitated literature in the classical Latin and Greek idiom and vein in the place of a long since securely established vernacular poetry in the unaffected medium of the vulgar tongue. The Humanists' revival of the art of writing quantitative Latin and Greek verse in a correct Hellenic style was followed, not by an eclipse of a native Western literature that was flying its own proper colours unabashed, but by a fresh outburst of it in a blaze which effectively took the shine out of the Humanists' frigid academic exercises.

The Discomfiture of an Orthodox Christian Greek Vernacular Literature by an Hellenic Ghost

The spontaneously generated native literature in the vulgar tongue which came to this fine flower in a Western World had its counterparts in a Greek Orthodox Christendom and in the Chinese main body of a Far Eastern Society; but here the seed fell among the thorns of the resuscitated language and literature of an antecedent civilization,[1] 'and the thorns sprang up with it, and choked it'.[2]

The Modern Greek language resembled Latin and Latin's Romance offspring, and differed, like them, from Ancient Greek, in being accentual and not quantitative, and it duly found for itself a congenial form of accentual versification—the so-called 'Metropolitan[3] Metre'—which was as alien in its technique from the Ancient Greek quantitative verse of a Homer or a Theognis as the contemporary accentual verse of Western Christendom was from the Latin quantitative verse of Homer's imitator Virgil or Theognis' imitator Ovid. As we have seen in another context,[4] this Modern Greek accentual verse provided the literary vehicle for a tenth-century epic poem celebrating the exploits of the Greek borderers in an East Anatolian no-man's-land beyond the Antitauran frontier of the 'Abbasid Caliphate; and this Byzantine Greek Epic of Basil Digénis (Dhiyénis) Akritas was thus, on both the literary and the social plane,[5] a true counterpart of the *Chanson de Roland*. Yet, whereas an eleventh-century *Chanson de Roland* was able to become the parent of a vernacular literature, in all the living languages of the Western World,[6] which was still bearing fruit nine hundred years later, the tenth-century Byzantine Greek Epic was cheated out of its manifest destiny through being sterilized by the triumph of a Greek Orthodox Christian renaissance of the Ancient Greek language and literature;[7] and, though the living Modern Greek language and its native accentual style of versification were emboldened, thereafter, to reassert themselves by the example of a Medieval Western vernacular literature which made its influence felt

---

[1] The successive vicissitudes in the history of an Orthodox Christian Greek literature, from its emergence during a post-Hellenic cultural interregnum down to the twentieth century, can be studied in the life in Trypánis, C. A.: *Medieval and Modern Greek Poetry, An Anthology* (Oxford 1951, Clarendon Press).
[2] Luke viii. 7. Cp. Matt. xiii. 7.
[3] i.e. Constantinopolitan (*Graecè:* στίχοι πολιτικοί).   [4] In V. v. 252–9.
[5] See ibid., pp. 260–1.   [6] See ibid., pp. 252–3.
[7] This has been noticed by anticipation in VII. vii. 409, n. 9.

in Greek Orthodox Christendom as a consequence of the ascendancy which the Franks progressively established over the Greeks from the close of the eleventh century onwards,[1] the price of this Frankish cultural assistance in revolting against an Hellenic cultural tyranny was the heavy one of being constrained to submit to a mere change of masters instead of recovering a lost cultural liberty. In Crete, where the Medieval Greek vernacular literature went farther, because the Medieval Frankish ascendancy here lasted longer, than in any other province of Greek Orthodox Christendom except the Ionian Islands, it flourished in virtue of resigning itself to becoming a version, in the Modern Greek language, of the contemporary literature of the West, while the Italianate Greek Orthodox Christian Ionian Islanders came to find it easier to make contributions to a Western literature in its native Italian medium than to transpose their literary compositions into their own Modern Greek mother tongue.[2]

It might perhaps have been expected that, after the Greek Orthodox Christians' feelings towards the West had changed, as they did change in the seventeenth century,[3] from contempt and hostility to admiration and receptivity, and after this revulsion had culminated, as it did culminate in the nineteenth century, in a resolve, on the Greek people's part, to become naturalized members of the Western Society of the day without any lingering Byzantine xenophobe reservations, one of the first fruits of this process of cultural conversion would have been the liberation of the Modern Greek language from the dead hand of a Hellenism that had been resuscitated in Greek Orthodox Christendom before the beginning of this Christian civilization's long and momentous encounter with a sister Christian society. Unhappily for the Greeks, the Western Society with which they threw in their lot in the nineteenth century was by then already infected with the spiritual malady of Nationalism, which had been engendered in the Western World by the impact of a Classical Hellenic ideal of political parochialism[4] on the Western World's parochially variegated linguistic map. It was not surprising that the nineteenth-century Greek proselytes to the altar of a Modern Western culture should succumb to this Modern Western Nationalism and should develop the linguistic symptoms that were characteristic of this cultural disease; but it was unfortunate that, in adopting a Western-minded linguistic Nationalism, the Modern Greeks should have elected to combine this, as they did, with a Byzantine-minded linguistic Archaism.

Instead of learning, as they might have learnt, from the troubadours and Dante the invaluable lesson that the poetry of the West had come to flower so finely just because the poets of the West had not been ashamed of their living mother tongues, the nineteenth-century Greek Orthodox Christian converts to a contemporary Western culture were obsessed by a haunting consciousness that the Modern Greek language was lineally descended from the Ancient Greek and that their ancestral Orthodox Christian Civilization was affiliated to the Hellenic; and these irrelevant historical facts imposed upon them so imperiously that, in their lin-

---

[1] See IX. viii. 392–4.
[2] See IX. viii. 679–80.
[3] See IX. viii. 165–8.
[4] See pp. 7–8, above.

guistic policy, they dared not live up to the ideals of the Western cultural faith to which they had formally declared their allegiance. They could not summon up the moral courage to take their own language as they found it and to rely on their own literary genius to fashion this language into a worthy instrument for conveying whatever they might prove to have it in them to express. They chose the untoward alternative course of taking refuge in the cultivation of a linguistic Archaism; and, though they refrained from carrying this folly to the lengths to which it had been carried by Byzantines who on paper had discarded their living Modern Greek mother tongue altogether in favour of an artificially resuscitated Attic,[1] the nineteenth-century Westernizing Greeks did the next worst thing when, like callous manufacturers of *foie gras*, they set themselves to denature their mother tongue by grouting into it as gross an infusion of the Attic Greek vocabulary, inflexion, and syntax as they could compel a tortured living language to swallow.[2]

Thus, on the linguistic and literary plane, the Greeks' 'reception' of a Modern Western culture, whose distinctive gift was to use living vernaculars as its literary vehicles, had the paradoxical result of fettering a living Greek language instead of liberating it.

The Sinic Classical Incubus on a Chinese Vernacular Literature

In the Chinese heart of a Far Eastern World, as in Greek Orthodox Christendom, a popular literature in the living vulgar tongue had succeeded in springing up, under the shadow of an antecedent culture's classical language and literature, before an expanding Western Civilization had appeared on the scene. A living 'mandarin' *lingua franca*[3] had become a vehicle not only for folk-songs[4] but also for drama since the thirteenth century of the Christian Era,[5] and for novels in the sixteenth, seventeenth, and eighteenth centuries.[6] In China, again, the same

---

[1] See pp. 73–74, above.
[2] This Modern Greek linguistic and literary Archaism and the *Kulturkampf* to which it gave rise have been noticed in V. vi. 68–70. Though the anti-archaistic movement in favour of the living language was abortive, it managed to keep the field in just sufficient strength to condemn a politically reunited Modern Greek people to live in a state of chronic cultural schism between the respective adherents of the καθαρεύουσα and the δημοτική. Either school of Modern Greek linguistic doctrine could cite on its own behalf the authority of a Modern Western Civilization whose example was law for Modern Greeks of both schools alike. The δημοτική answered to a Modern Western dogma, begotten by a sixteenth-century Protestant Reformation, that a national language ought to be 'understanded of the people'; the καθαρεύουσα answered to another Modern Western dogma, begotten by a nineteenth-century Romantic Movement, that a national language ought to have roots in the national past. In the native social milieu of the Western Society in which this pair of dogmas had originated, they did not conflict; for the local Western vernaculars—Italian, French, English, Dutch, German, and the rest —answered to both dogmas alike, in opposition to a Latin that had been the linguistic vehicle of a Western chrysalis-church. When, however, the same two dogmas were applied in the alien social milieu of a Modern Greek Orthodox Christian community which had 'received' the Modern Western culture by an act of conversion, the two dogmas here proved irreconcilable owing to the success previously achieved by a Byzantine renaissance of a dead Attic Greek in blighting the literary cultivation of the living Modern Greek language in an earlier chapter of Modern Greek cultural history.
[3] See V. v. 512–14.
[4] See Hu Shih: *The Chinese Renaissance: The Haskell Lectures, 1933* (Chicago 1934, University Press), p. 60. The quotations from this book have been made with the permission of the author and the publishers.
[5] See Hu Shih, op. cit., pp. 45 and 53.   [6] See ibid., p. 51.

negative, unintentional, and unconscious, yet none the less valuable, literary service had been performed by Mongol invaders as had been performed in Greek Orthodox Christendom by the Frankish conquerors of an East Roman Empire. Here, as there, an irruption of militant barbarians had been a cultural and social as well as a political and military catastrophe; here, as there, it had hit a small highly cultivated official class more severely than it had hit the uncultivated merchants, artisans, and peasantry;[1] here, as there, the shock dealt to this classically educated officialdom had broken 'the cake of custom'[2] which this governing class had imposed on the lower strata of society; and, since, in a resuscitated Sinic and a resuscitated Hellenic universal state alike, the linguistic and literary custom hitherto upheld by the now crestfallen pandits had been the cult of a dead classical language and literature at the expense of a living vulgar tongue and the popular literature conveyed in it, the cultural effect, in China as in Greek Orthodox Christendom, was to liberate this popular literature from the incubus of a classical ideal and thereby give it a chance to invigorate itself by gaining access to the air and to the light.

While the Chinese popular literature had the same history as its Modern Greek counterpart in these respects, it gave proof of a greater vitality by emulating the Medieval Western vernacular literature's feat of 'haunting the haunter'. As Hu Shih tells the story of how his own eyes were opened:

'I found that the history of Chinese literature consisted of two parallel movements: there was the classical literature of the scholars, the men of letters, the poets of the imperial courts, and of the *élite*; but there was in every age an undercurrent of literary development among the common people which produced the folk songs of love and heroism, the songs of the dancer, the epic stories of the street reciter, the drama of the village theatre and, most important of all, the novels. I found that every new form, every innovation in literature, had come never from the imitative classical writers of the upper classes, but always from the unlettered class of the country-side, the village inn and the market-place. I found that it was always these new forms and patterns of the common people that, from time to time, furnished the new blood and fresh vigour to the literature of the litterati, and rescued it from the perpetual danger of fossilisation. All the great periods of Chinese Literature were those when the master minds of the age were attracted by these new literary forms of the people and produced their best works, not only in the new patterns, but in close imitation of the fresh and simple language of the people. And such great epochs died away only when those new forms from the people had again

---

[1] After the sack of Constantinople by the Crusaders in A.D. 1204, some of the previously well-to-do Greek refugees from the sacked city were ill-treated by the Greek rural population in the hinterland, who forcibly relieved them of the money that they had been able to bring away with them, and gloated over the spectacle of grandees reduced to an equality with themselves on a common level of destitution. The poorer Greek inhabitants of Constantinople, who did not take flight, enriched themselves by buying from the Latin conquerors, at derisory prices, valuable articles of property that the Latins had plundered from the Greek purchasers' wealthy fellow-citizens (see the indignant comments on these proceedings in Nikítas Khoniátis' *Khroniki Dhiiyisis*, Epilogue on the Aftermath of the Catastrophe, chap. 5, on pp. 784–5 of I. Bekker's edition (Bonn 1835, Weber)).

[2] Bagehot, W.: *Physics and Politics*, 10th ed. (London 1894, Kegan Paul), pp. 27 and 35, quoted in II. i. 192.

become fixed and fossilised through long periods of slavish imitation by the uncreative litterati. . . .

'It was the anonymous folk songs of Antiquity that formed the bulk of the great *Book of Poetry* and created the first epoch of Chinese Literature. It was again the anonymous folk songs of the people that gave the form and the inspiration in the developments of the new poetry in the Three Kingdoms and later in the T'ang Dynasty. It was the songs of the dancing and singing girls that began the new era of *ts'ĭ* or songs in the Sung Dynasty. It was the people that first produced the plays which led to the great dramas of the Mongol period and the Mings. It was the street reciters of epic stories that gave rise to the great novels, some of which have been "best sellers" for three or four centuries.'[1]

Yet, in striking contrast to the attitude of a Dante, a Petrarch, or a Boccacio, the Chinese literary artists who owed so much to artless master-pieces in the vulgar tongue, and who turned their borrowed talent to such good account,[2] were as anxious to hide their light under a bushel[3] as if they had to fear the pains and penalties of failing to conform to some rigidly imposed cultural 'black-out'. 'They were so ashamed of what they had done that many of the earlier novelists published their works anonymously or under strange *noms de plume*';[4] and we may infer that no self-respecting Chinese litteratus would have dreamt of asking for trouble by putting his name to a work on the lines of Dante's *De Vulgari Eloquentiâ*, in which this sublime Western vulgarian indited, in the sacrosanct classical language, an appreciation of contemporary Western poetry in the living Provençal and Tuscan vernaculars, and garnished his shocking dissertation with quotations *verbatim* from this unmentionable literary garbage, to illustrate points of vulgar style that ought to have been beneath the notice of a properly instructed clerk. All the same, the breach of literary etiquette which a Dante dared to commit openly was perpetrated by Dante's Chinese counterparts in secret; for 'all these great novels have been most widely read by almost everybody who can read at all', and 'even the litterati who pretended to condemn them as vulgar and cheap know them well through reading them stealthily in their boyhood days'.[5]

'Why did it take so long for this living language of such wide currency and with such a rich output in literature to receive due recognition as the most fitting instrumentality for education and for literary composition? . . . The explanation is simple. The authority of the language of the Classics was truly too great to be easily overcome in the days of the [resuscitated Sinic oecumenical] empire. This authority became almost invincible when it was enforced by the power of a long united empire and reinforced by the universal system of state examinations, under which the only channel of civil advancement for any man was through the mastery of the classical language and literature. The rise of the national languages in Modern Europe was greatly facilitated by the absence of a united empire and of a universal system of classical examination. Yet the two great churches in Rome and in East Europe—the shadowy counterparts of the Roman Empire[6]—with their rigid requirements for advancement in clerical life,

---

[1] Hu Shih, op. cit., pp. 52–53.   [2] Matt. xxv. 14–30; Luke xix. 12–27.
[3] Matt. v. 15; Mark iv. 21; Luke viii. 16 and xi. 33.
[4] Hu Shih, op. cit., p. 61.   [5] Ibid., p. 60.
[6] See Hobbes' description of the Papacy, quoted in VII. vii. 696.—A.J.T.

have been able to maintain the use of two dead classical languages throughout these many centuries. It is therefore no mere accident that the revolution in Chinese Literature came ten years after the abolition of the literary
examinations in A.D. 1905, and several years after the political revolution
of A.D. 1911–1912.'[1]

It is likewise no accident that the impact of an alien Western culture,
which was the *primum mobile* at work in the overthrow of a resuscitated
Sinic imperial régime in China, should also have given the initial impulse
to the literary revolution which here followed so close upon the political
revolution's heels.

'Contact with strange civilisations brings new standards of value with
which the native culture is re-examined and re-evaluated, and conscious
reformation and regeneration are the natural outcome of such transvalua-
tion of values. . . . The novels which were read by the millions of Chinese,
but which were always despised by the Chinese litterati, have in recent
decades been elevated to the position of respectable literature, chiefly
through the influence of the European literature.'[2]

This tardy cultural enfranchisement of a notable living genre of
literary composition was an incident in the revolutionary exaltation[3] of
the whole of this formerly humiliated body of living literature, together
with the living 'mandarin' *lingua franca* that was its linguistic vehicle,
into the seat of the once mighty mummy of a dead Sinic language in
which the Confucian Classics were embalmed. In a feat of cultural
iconoclasm which was as salutary as it was sacrilegious, the bull who led
the way into the china shop was the eminent scholar, man of letters, and
philosopher who has been so largely quoted in the last few pages of the
present chapter; and anyone who is curious to know the details of this
fascinating episode of cultural history[4] should read Hu Shih's own
authoritative account[5] of the events of which he himself was *magna pars*.[6]
To whet the curiosity of readers of this Study, it will suffice to quote the
opening sentence of Hu Shih's personal narrative, in which he records
that 'the solution of this problem came from the dormitories in the
American universities'.[7]

The Entente between the Vernacular Languages of the Hindu World and a Perennial Sanskrit

The severity of this *Kulturkampf* that had to be fought out in China in
order to liberate a popular literature in the living 'mandarin' language
from the incubus of the Sinic classics presents a piquant contrast to the
auspiciously fruitful relations in the history of a contemporary Hindu
World between a classical Sanskrit language and literature and a pleiad
of popular literatures in living vernacular languages.

---

[1] Hu Shih, op. cit., pp. 60–61.   [2] Ibid., p. 47.   [3] Luke i. 52.
[4] This latter-day Chinese revolt against the incubus of a classical Sinic language and
literature is itself 'the Chinese Renaissance' according to Hu Shih's terminology,
whereas, according to the usage followed in this Study, it would figure as 'the Chinese
Anti-Renaissance' in reaction against a previous resuscitation of the language and literature of an antecedent civilization which would rank as 'the Chinese Renaissance' according to our usage of the term.   [5] In op. cit., pp. 50–57.
[6] Virgil: *Aeneid*, Book II, l. 6.   [7] Hu Shih, op. cit., p. 50.

This happier Hindu experience is the more remarkable, considering that, *a priori*, the Sanskrit language and literature might have been expected to weigh even more heavily than the Sinic upon the neck of an affiliated society. The Sanskrit's Cronos-like feat of devouring its own children, the prākrits, in a post-Açokan Age of Indic history[1] had endowed the cannibal tongue with such an irrepressible vitality that in the history of a Hindu Civilization, affiliated to the Indic, there was never any question of a renaissance of Sanskrit, because the successfully reinstated archaic Indic language and literature had never tasted death[2] during an intervening social interregnum which had seen the end of so many other elements of a dissolving Indic Civilization's cultural heritage. In a subsequently born Hindu World this ever-green Sanskrit language and literature enjoyed two signal advantages, neither of which was possessed by the Sinic classics in the Far Eastern World in which these had been resuscitated.

In the first place, Sanskrit was a sacred language, and the literature enshrined in it therefore holy writ, in the eyes of all pious Hindus, whereas in China the classics conveyed in the Sinic characters were merely the canonical expositions of the philosophy of an esoterically cultivated corporation of civil servants. This Confucian guild's influence on the masses was not comparable, either in range of diffusion or in degree of intensity, with the influence of the Brahman caste that was the custodian of a Hindu Society's Sanskrit heritage from an Indic past; and the Brahmans had turned their social prestige to account by achieving two feats which, if they had not been achieved both at once, might have been imagined to be incompatible. On the one hand the Brahmans had incorporated into their canon of holy scripture the profane works of Sanskrit literature, including the epics, by dint of copiously interpolating incongruous theological matter;[3] and on the other hand they had managed to save a drastically 'doctored' heroic poetry from losing its popular appeal. An interpolated *Mahābhārata* and *Rāmāyana* were never relegated to the shelves of Brahmanic theological libraries; throughout the course of Hindu history they never ceased to 'flit alive from mouth to mouth'.[4]

An early twentieth-century Confucian litteratus would have been dumbfounded if on an oecumenical grand tour he had found, at the annual *paniyiris* on the Aegean island of Tínos, crowds of Modern Greek Orthodox Christian pilgrims listening spellbound to a recital of the *Odyssey* interpolated with passages of Neoplatonic theology in a passable imitation of the Homeric diction, or if, at some gathering of a similar kind in Algarve or in Hainault, he had come across Portuguese or Walloon peasants drinking in, with equal eagerness, a recital of the *Aeneid* interpolated with an exposition of Saint Augustine's arguments against Pelagianism in Latin verse which Augustine, if not Virgil himself, might have allowed to pass muster. Even in a latter-day Chinese setting, not to speak of a latter-day Greek Orthodox Christian or

---

[1] See V. vi. 75–78. [2] Matt. xvi. 28; Mark ix. 1; Luke ix. 27.
[3] See V. v. 597 and 605–6.
[4] 'Volito vivo' per ora virum'.—Quintus Ennius's anticipatory epitaph for himself.

Romance Western secular setting, such imaginary scenes are, of course, wildly fantastic. The epic stories of the street reciter and the drama of the village theatre (with its auditorium open, *more Hellenico*, to the sky), with which our cultivated Chinese scholar-traveller would have been contemptuously familiar at home, would have been products, not of the pre-Confucian Age of an antecedent Sinic Civilization, but of the Confucian licentiate's own living Far Eastern Society's still recent Time of Troubles. The oldest of them would not yet have been seven hundred years old by the year A.D. 1900.[1] If, however, our traveller from Tientsin had visited, *en route* for the West, the festival annually celebrated in Rāma's honour at Benares, he would have had to confess that his own Sinic classics had been put out of countenance by Indic classics that had never ceased to be cherished by the people as well as by the pandits; for at Benares at this season of the year he would have witnessed[2] in the every-day life of a living Hindu Society an exact counterpart of those imaginary scenes that look so fantastic when set against even a Far Eastern, not to speak of a Near Eastern or a Western, back-cloth.

Where the classical language and literature of a dead antecedent civilization had thus managed to retain their hold on the imagination and affection of an affiliated society as living treasure-houses of both theological authority and popular entertainment, what chance might the living vernacular languages of the Hindu World be expected to find of securing employment for themselves as alternative vehicles for literature? When Sanskrit was so securely and completely in possession of this field, could any living language aspire to play even a modest and subordinate literary role? Had not Sanskrit already driven its own children, the prākrits, out of the literary field before the close of the history of an antecedent Indic Civilization? And, if this world-conquering classical language's diadochi had suffered this fate at Sanskrit's hands, did not this precedent spell in advance the doom of the epigoni?

Any alien observer who had ventured to make such prognostications on the basis of Indic experience would, however, have found them falsified by the event; for the effect of the vitality of Sanskrit on the fortunes of the Hindu World's vernaculars was not a withering blight but was, on the contrary, a potent stimulus.[3] In the Archaic Age of Hindu history,

---

[1] See Hu Shih: *The Chinese Renaissance* (Chicago 1934, University Press), pp. 53 and 61, cited on pp. 77 and 78, above.

[2] See MacDonell, A. A.: *A History of Sanskrit Literature* (London 1900, Heinemann), p. 317.

[3] In seeking to account for the difference in the respective literary fortunes of the prākrits—which, save for the survival of Pāli as the medium of the Hinayanian Buddhist scriptures, were driven off the field of literary usage by their Sanskrit parent's counteroffensive—and of the latter-day parochial vernacular languages of a Hindu World which were fertilized by their encounter with the Sanskrit language and literature, instead of being blighted by it, we have to allow for one pertinent consideration of a linguistic, not a literary, order. The prākrits' chances of victory in their competition with their Sanskrit parent were no doubt compromised by the linguistic fact that the degree of their differentiation from a common Sanskrit stock was slight enough to allow anyone who was literate in any prākrit to take to reading and writing Sanskrit, instead, with little difficulty. In departing from the pattern of Sanskrit, the prākrits had not gone so far as to break with the habit of expressing relations by the inflexion of the verbs and nouns that were the vehicles of meaning, instead of hitting upon the use of separate auxiliary words. The prākrits, like their Sanskrit parent, were inflective languages of the primitive Indo-European type. On the other hand the vernaculars of the next generation, derived

between the first emergence of a Hindu Civilization out of a post-Indic interregnum towards the end of the eighth century of the Christian Era and the Muslim conquest of the Ganges-Jumna Basin towards the end of the twelfth century,[1] we find the heroic poetry at the courts of parochial Rājpūt princes, descended from Hun and Gurjara Eurasian Nomad barbarian invaders, being composed, not in the classical Sanskrit of the *Mahābhārata*, but in a vernacular Hindī which was the living language caught by the interloping alien conquerors from their Hindu subjects.[2] If now—racing the drum round which our film of Hindu history unwinds—we pass on, in a flash, to the first phase of a universal state in which the Hindu Society temporarily arrested its disintegration after having gone through the experiences of a breakdown and a Time of Troubles, we shall find the Hindu genius embodied, in this generation, not in the alien Timurid Turkish Muslim empire-builder Akbar (*vivebat* A.D. 1542–1605), but in his contemporary and subject—probably unknown to Akbar himself—the Hindī poet Tulsī Dās (*vivebat circa* A.D. 1530–1623).[3]

A priori an alien observer might have expected that a Hindu man of genius, whose mission in life was to do in the Hindī language what was done in Latin by an Augustan Hellenic Virgil and in Tuscan by an Early Modern Western Ariosto, would have chosen for his own literary epic in Hindī any subject rather than the theme of a *Rāmāyana* whose Sanskrit *çlokas* were still 'flitting alive from mouth to mouth' in the latter-day poet's own time. Tulsī Dās, however, had a truer intuition of both the inclinations and the capacities of a catholic-hearted Hindu soul. He correctly divined that his people's devotion to a Sanskrit *Rāmāyana* would open, and not close, their hearts to the appeal of a Hindī *Rāmcharit Mānas*; and a Late Modern Western student of the Sanskrit literature has seen the culminating triumph of the *Rāmāyana* in this Sanskrit epic's ability, more than a thousand years after it had set hard in its own definitive form, to inspire the composition of a Hindī epic 'which, with its ideal standard of virtue and purity, is a kind of bible to a hundred millions of the people of Northern India'.[4]

from the prakrits, did sharply differentiate themselves from their parents by taking the revolutionary step that was taken by the Romance languages when they broke out of Latin, and by English when it broke out of Anglian (see III. iii. 176–9). In crossing this great linguistic 'divide', these Indo-Aryan languages of the third generation had cut themselves off from their prākrit parents and their Sanskrit grandparent alike, and had thereby ensured their hold, more effectively than the prākrits had ever ensured theirs, against the risk of an attempt on the part of Sanskrit to capture for itself exclusively the entire literary allegiance of the peoples speaking these derivative languages as their mother tongues. *A fortiori* it was difficult for Sanskrit to deprive of their literary birthright the Dravidian languages of Southern India which, like the Ugro-Finnish languages in Hungary, Finland, and the domain of the Soviet Union, were non-Indo-European. The Hindu devotional poetry in the Dravidian languages was even less in danger than a Hindī *Rāmcharit Mānas* was of ever being supplanted by a classical Sanskrit equivalent.

[1] See I. i. 85, with n. 2, and II. ii. 130–1.
[2] See Rawlinson, H. G.: *India, A Short Cultural History* (London 1948, Cresset Press), pp. 214–15.
[3] See Rawlinson, op. cit., pp. 373–5, and the present Study, V. v. 518, with n. 3.
[4] Macdonell, op. cit., p. 317. Compare the appreciation in Sir Charles Eliot: *Hinduism and Buddhism* (London 1921, Arnold, 3 vols.), vol. ii, pp. 245–7. His Râmâyana [i.e. the *Râmchârit Mânas*], which is an original composition and not a translation of Vâlmîki's work, is one of the great religious poems of the World and not unworthy to be set beside *Paradise Lost*' (p. 246).

Tulsī Dās' happy experience of an immortal Sanskrit epic's genially fructifying effect on the literary use of a living vernacular language would assuredly have given him no inkling of the hardness of the battle that a Hu Shih would have to fight in order to liberate a living 'mandarin' *lingua franca* from the tyranny of the Sinic classics.

(e) RENAISSANCES OF VISUAL ARTS

The renaissance of one or other of the visual arts of a dead civilization in the history of an affiliated civilization of the next generation is a not uncommon phenomenon. Among the more familiar instances of it we may mention the renaissance of 'the Old Kingdom's' style of sculpture and painting, after a two-thousand-years-long lapse, in a latter-day Egyptiac World of the Saïte Age in the seventh and sixth centuries B.C.;[1] the renaissance of a Sumeric style of carving in bas-relief—of which the finest specimen retrieved by Modern Western archaeologists was the stele of the Akkadian war-lord Naramsin (*dominabatur circa* 2422–2367 or 2358–2303 B.C.)—in a Babylonic World of the ninth, eighth, and seventh centuries B.C. in which this resuscitated Sumeric art was practised with the greatest virtuosity in Assyria; and the renaissance, in miniature, of an Hellenic style of carving in bas-relief, of which the most exquisite exemplars were Attic masterpieces of the fifth and fourth centuries B.C., on Byzantine diptychs—carved, not in stone but in ivory, in the tenth, eleventh, and twelfth centuries of the Christian Era[2]—in which the folds of the drapery of the Theotókos are nostalgically Hellenic in the beautiful severity of their lines. These three visual renaissances, however, were all left far behind, both in the range of the ground covered and in the ruthlessness of the eviction of the previous occupants, by a renaissance of Hellenic visual arts in Western Christendom which made its first epiphany in a Late Medieval Italy and spread thence to the rest of the Western World during a Modern Age of Western history. This evocation of ghosts of Hellenic visual arts was practised in the three fields of Architecture, Sculpture, and Painting; and, in every one of these three fields, the *revenant* style of art made so clean a sweep of the style that it found in possession of the corresponding sector of a Western artistic arena that, by the time when the aggressive ghost had spent his formidable force, Western Man had become so thoroughly used to living his aesthetic life under this alien ascendancy that he did not know what to do with a liberty that was not recovered for him by his own exertions, but was reimposed upon him by the senile decay of a pertinaciously tyrannical intruder. When the evaporation of an Hellenic spectre presented Western souls with an aesthetic vacuum, they found themselves at first unable, for the life of them, to say what was the proper visual expression for the West's long-suppressed native artistic genius.

The same strange tale of a house swept and garnished[3] by the drastic hands of ghostly visitants has to be told of each of the three provinces of

---

[1] See V. vi. 61–62. The peculiar relation of a post-Hyksos epilogue to an Egyptiac history which had reached its natural term after the dissolution of 'the Middle Empire' makes it hard to know whether to label the artistic revival of the Saïte Age a renaissance or a manifestation of Archaism.

[2] See IX. viii. 103.

[3] Matt. xii. 44; Luke xi. 25.

Western visual art that have been mentioned; but the most extraordinary episode of the three was the triumph of an Hellenic *revenant* over the native genius of the West in the province of Sculpture in the Round; for, in this field of artistic endeavour, the thirteenth-century Northern French exponents of an original Western style had produced masterpieces that could look in the face those of the Hellenic, Egyptiac, and Mahayanian Buddhist schools at their zeniths, whereas in the field of Painting, by the time when a *revenant* Hellenic style invaded it, Western artists had not yet shaken off the tutelage of the more precocious art of a sister Orthodox Christian Society, while in the field of Architecture the Romanesque style—which, as its latter-day label indicates, was a nascent Western World's variation on an architectural theme inherited from the latest age of an antecedent Hellenic Civilization—had already been overwhelmed by an intrusive 'Gothic' style which, contrary to the implication of its misnomer, had originated, not among the barbarians in a no-man's-land beyond the European *limes* of the Roman Empire, but in a Syriac World which, *in articulo mortis*, had made a cultural conquest of the savage Western Christian military conquerors who had seized upon fragments of a dissolving 'Abbasid and a dissolving Andalusian Umayyad Caliphate.

For a twentieth-century Londoner's enlightenment the combatants in a mortal struggle between a doubly defeated native Western visual art and its alien Syriac and Hellenic assailants were still standing, turned to stone in the postures of the last act in their encounter, in the architecture and sculpture of the chapel (*aedificatum* A.D. 1503–19) that had been built on to Westminster Abbey under the auspices of King Henry VII of England (*regnabat* A.D. 1485–1509). In the vaulting of the roof the 'Gothic' style had achieved a *tour de force* which, though manifestly its *ne plus ultra*, was a *chef-d'œuvre* capable of still holding at bay the waxing Hellenic invader who was now treading so importunately on a waning Syriac invader's heels. In the host of erect stone figures *in excelsis*, which declared in dumb-show *morituri te salutamus* as they gazed down at an Italian Hellenomime's trinity of recumbent bronze figures on the tombs below,[1] a Transalpine school of native Western Christian sculpture was singing a silent swan-song between frozen lips. The centre of the stage was held by the Hellenizing masterpieces of a Torrigiani (*vivebat* A.D. 1472–1522) who—contemptuously ignoring the uncouth milieu in which he had deigned to execute his own competently polished work for the sake of the lucrative profits to be earned from a royal patron *in partibus Barbarorum*—was looking round him complacently in the confident expectation that, *in saecula saeculorum*, these fruits of a Florentine master's voluntary exile would be the cynosure of every Transalpine sight-seer's eyes.[2]

[1] The contrast between these respective products of a surviving Transalpine native Western school and a contemporary Hellenizing Italian school of sculpture in Henry VII's Chapel came out dramatically when, after the War of A.D. 1939–45, the pensive English-carved figures usually marooned at Westminster up aloft were placed on exhibition at the Victoria and Albert Museum at South Kensington on a level with the spectator's eye and face to face with Torrigiani's accomplished gilt angels.

[2] 'This man had a splendid person and a most arrogant spirit, with the air of a great soldier more than of a sculptor, especially in . . . his vehement gestures and his resonant

A 'Gothic' architecture which thus continued to hold its own until the first quarter of the sixteenth century of the Christian Era in London—and the first half of the seventeenth century in Oxford—had by then long since been driven off the field in Northern and Central Italy; for here it had never succeeded, so decisively as in Transalpine Europe, in supplanting a Romanesque style which, in the realm of Architecture, was the native expression of the Western spirit. Italy was the bridgehead in which an alien presence, conjured up from a dead Hellenic World, first entrenched itself on Western soil; and the successive stages in the triumphal progress of a Hellenizing style of architecture, which was eventually to replace the Romanesque and the 'Gothic' alike in all quarters of the Western World, could be followed in the history, running from A.D. 1296 to A.D. 1461, of the building of the Cathedral of Santa Maria del Fiore at Florence. The Florentines' decision, taken in A.D. 1294, to 'scrap' their medieval cathedral dedicated to Saint Reparata in order to erect a modern building on the site may be taken as a symbolic act signifying a resuscitated Hellenism's declaration of aggressive war upon a Medieval Western *status quo ante*. The climax of an architectural drama which did not become tedious through being spun out over a span of 167 years was the victory of Filippo Brunelleschi (*vivebat* A.D. 1377–1446) in a public competition, opened in A.D. 1418, for designs for the construction of a cupola to crown the fane of a goddess who, to tell the truth, was not Mary the mother of Christ but was Venus the mother of Cupid.[1]

Brunelleschi's cupola made so deep an impression on the imagination of a duly astonished Western World that the homely Italian word duomo, signifying 'the house [of God]', thereafter acquired, in Western parlance, the secondary meaning of an architectural structure which Western builders had lacked the skill to execute before Brunelleschi elicited the secret from the testament of a dead Hellenic Society that had mastered this difficult art in its own extreme old age.[2] Yet Brunelleschi's cautiously high-pitched 'dome', which created this sensation in the West after it had been translated from an idea into a reality by the labours of fourteen years (A.D. 1420–34), would have looked clumsy to the eye of the contemporary Ottoman architect of a Green Mosque at Brusa[3] which was built for Sultan Mehmed I (*imperabat* A.D. 1413–21);[4] and, four hun-

voice—together, with a habit he had of knitting his brows, enough to frighten any man of courage. He kept talking every day about his gallant feats among those beasts of Englishmen' (Benvenuto Cellini: *Autobiography*, English translation by J. A. Symonds (London 1949, Phaidon Press), Book I, chap xii, p. 18).

[1] The prominence of the role which the Florentines assigned to their own city in the 'reception' of a *revenant* Hellenism in Italy and in the Western World at large was symbolized in the picture, painted by Sandro Botticelli (*vivebat* A.D. 1444–1510), of Florence hospitably running forward to cast a magnificent cloak over the shoulders of a naked Venus, newly risen from the foam and serenely riding on a fabulously gigantic sea-shell, who was being blown inshore by obstreperous puffs from the Winds.

[2] See IV. iv. 21 and 54–55.

[3] If the Ottoman architect Hajjī Ayvas, son of Ahī Bāyezīd, whose name appears in the inscription in the porch above the main entrance to the Green Mosque, had been given an opportunity of inspecting Brunelleschi's work, his verdict would probably have been that this was not even a genuine cupola.

[4] The inscription in the porch of the Green Mosque bears a date A.H. corresponding approximately to A.D. 1419 (see *Bursa*, published by la Direction Générale de la Presse, Ankara, 1949). The inscription over the Sultan's upper chamber, within, records that

dred years after the Feringī Brunelleschi's day, when his successors had
run through all the resources of a resuscitated Hellenic technique, and
had gone on to apply them to the revolutionizing of domestic as well
as public architecture, the ultimate effect of their technical ingenuity
was to make an aesthetic desert, since they had quenched both a native
Romanesque and an exotic 'Gothic' vein long before they had emptied
an Hellenic Amalthea's imported cornucopia.

The sterility with which the Western genius had been afflicted by a
renaissance of Hellenism in the domain of Architecture was proclaimed
in the West's surprising failure to reap any architectural harvest from
the birth-pangs of the Industrial Revolution. In Great Britain at the
turn of the eighteenth and nineteenth centuries, and in the Western
World as a whole before the nineteenth century reached its close, a
mutation in industrial technique that had begotten the iron girder had
suddenly thrust into the Western architect's hands an incomparably
versatile new building-material; and this gift of the grimy gods might
have been expected to inspire the favoured Western human recipient to
break even the toughest cake of inherited architectural custom in an
eager exploration of the potentialities of a hitherto untried instrument.
As it happened, no great effort was required of a Western architect of
that generation to break a Hellenizing architectural tradition that was
then already crumbling between his fingers; yet the architect who had
been presented by a blacksmith with the iron girder, and by Providence
with a clean slate, could think of no better ways of filling an opportune
vacuum than to cap an Hellenic Renaissance with 'a Gothic Revival' and
to recoil from the 'Gothic' ironmongery of Ruskin's Science Museum
at Oxford and the Woolworth Building in New York into a 'Colonial'
brickwork[1] reproducing the Hellenizing Western style of architecture as
this had been practised during an eighteenth-century North American
'Indian Summer'.

The first Westerner to think of frankly turning the iron girder to
account as a building material without bashfully drawing a 'Gothic' veil
over his Volcanic vulgarity was not a professional architect but an
imaginative amateur; and, though he was a citizen of the United States,
the site on which he erected his historic structure overlooked the shores
of the Bosphorus, not the banks of the Hudson. The nucleus of Robert
College—Hamlin Hall, dominating Mehmed the Conqueror's Castle of
Europe—was built by Cyrus Hamlin in A.D. 1869–71;[2] yet it was only
within the life-time of the writer of this Study, who was born in A.D.
1889 and was writing these lines in A.D. 1950, that the seed sown by

the work was completed in A.D. 1423 (see *Konstantinopel und das Westliche Kleinasien*
(Leipzig 1905, Baedeker), p. 144).   [1] See V. vi. 60.
   [2] 'The building is 113 feet by 103. . . . The stone is the same as that of the fortress
built in A.D. 1452–3. . . . It is fire-proof, the floors being of iron beams with brick arches'
(Hamlin, Cyrus: *Among the Turks* (London 1878, Sampson Low), p. 297).
   'While the work of construction was going on, Dr. Hamlin . . . might be in the water
at the bottom of the well mending the force pump, or at the top of the building standing
on an iron girder with forty feet of empty space below him. . . . He . . . was never daunted
by any new and unthought-of problem which presented itself in the building. . . . The
public opening was postponed to the 4th July [, 1871], just two years from the laying of
the corner stone' (Washburn, D.: *Fifty Years in Constantinople* (Boston and New York
1909, Houghton Mifflin), pp. 28–29 and 47).

Hamlin in Constantinople bore fruit in a Western World that was Brunel's as well as Hamlin's homeland.

This sterilization of the West's artistic genius, which was the nemesis of a Hellenizing renaissance in the realm of Architecture, was no less conspicuous in the realms of Painting and Sculpture. Over a span of more than half a millennium running from the generation of Dante's contemporary Giotto (*decessit* A.D. 1337), a Modern Western school of Painting, which had unquestioningly accepted the naturalistic ideals of an Hellenic visual art in its post-archaic phase, had worked out, one after another, divers methods of conveying the visual impressions made by light and shade until this long-sustained effort to produce the effects of photography through prodigies of artistic technique had been stultified, on the eve of its consummation, by the invention of photography itself. After the ground had thus inconsiderately been cut away from under their feet by the shears of Modern Western Science, Modern Western painters made a 'Pre-Raphaelite' Movement,[1] in the direction of their long since repudiated Byzantine provenance, before they thought of exploring a new world of Psychology which Science had given them to conquer in compensation for the old world of Physical Nature which she had stolen from the painter in order to hand it over to the photographer. After the invention of photography the best part of a century had to pass before the rise of an apocalyptic school of Western painters who made a genuinely new departure by frankly using paint—veritably *more Byzantino*—to convey the spiritual experiences of Psyche instead of the visual impressions of Argus;[2] but the increasing sureness of foot with which the Western painters were advancing along this new road by the close of the first half of the twentieth century seemed to augur that the Western sculptors, in their turn, would eventually set their faces in the same direction after discovering, by trial and error, that the broken road to Athens, which they had been following ever since a Niccolò Pisano had swerved into it in the thirteenth century, could not, after all, be regained by a detour through either Byzantium or Benin.

Thus, at the time of writing, it looked as if, in all three visual arts, the sterilization of a native Western genius by an exotic Hellenizing renaissance might eventually be overcome; but the slowness and the difficulty of the cure showed how serious the damage had been.

(*f*) RENAISSANCES OF RELIGIOUS IDEALS AND INSTITUTIONS

In the Realm of Religion the classical example of a renaissance was Judaism's perennial trick of springing up, like an accusatory jack-in-the-box, out of Christianity's Ark of a New Covenant.

The relation of Christianity to Judaism was as damningly clear to Jewish eyes as it was embarrassingly ambiguous for Christian consciences. In Jewish eyes the Christian Church was a renegade Jewish sect which, on the evidence of its own unauthorized appendix to the

---

[1] See V. vi. 60.

[2] In IV. iv. 52, this positive aim of a revolutionary twentieth-century school of Western painting has not been given due recognition.

Canon of Scripture, had sinned against the teaching of the obscure, misguided, and unfortunate, but undeniably idealistic, Galilean Pharisee whose name these traitors to Pharisaism had impudently taken in vain. As Jewish witnesses saw it, Christianity's allegedly miraculous captivation of an Hellenic *oikoumenê* was not the Lord's doing and was not marvellous;[1] for this was assuredly no repetition of what Yahweh had done for Israel in the days of Moses and Joshua, when He had led His Chosen People through the Wilderness and given them the Promised Land. The posthumous triumph of a Jewish rabbi who had been saluted by his followers, *more Hellenico*, as the son of a god by a human mother, was a pagan exploit of the same order as the historic conquests of an Alexander and a Caesar or the legendary conquests of a Bacchus and a Hêraklês. Judaism herself could have anticipated Christianity's conquest of the Hellenic World before Christianity had ever been heard of, if Judaism had stooped to conquer by descending to Christianity's level; but 'what shall it profit a man if he shall gain the whole World and lose his own soul?'[2] A Christianity which had never repudiated the authority of the Jewish Scriptures, and which had the audacity to declare itself to be the fulfilment of the Law, had made a facile conquest of a whole Hellenizing World—with the outstanding exception of a faithful remnant of Jewry—by betraying Judaism's two cardinal principles, Monotheism and Aniconism, which were Yahweh's supreme revelations. If Jewry had been willing thus to betray the Lord's trust by compromising with an Hellenic Polytheism and an Hellenic Idolatry, Jewry, too, could have cajoled the Hellenes into a nominal acceptance of Judaism at the price of Judaism's capitulating to Hellenism on the two crucial points of substance. And now, in face of a still impenitent Hellenic paganism, whose unchanged Ethiop skin[3] remained indecently visible through a transparent Christian dress, the watchword for Jewry was to persevere in bearing her witness to the Lord's everlasting revelations and commandments. In the words of a renegade disciple of Gamaliel's:

'Take unto you the whole armour of God, that ye may be able to withstand in the evil day, and, having done all, to stand. Stand therefore, having your loins girt about with truth.'[4]

This 'patient deep disdain'[5] with which a sensationally triumphant Christianity continued to be regarded by an unimpressed and unshaken Jewry was an annoyance which a victorious Church could perhaps have afforded to discount as the expression of a discomfited competitor's inevitable pique, if Christianity herself had not combined a sincere theoretical loyalty to a Jewish legacy of Monotheism and Aniconism with those politic practical concessions to an Hellenic Polytheism and Idolatry for which she was being arraigned by her Jewish critics. A Christian Church's reconsecration of the Jewish Scriptures as the Old Testament of a Christian Faith was the weak spot in Christianity's armour through which the shafts of Jewish criticism went home to Christianity's heart. 'Thou shalt have no other gods before Me' and 'Thou shalt not make

---

[1] Ps. cxviii. 23.   [2] Mark viii. 36. Cp. Matt. xvi. 26; Luke ix. 25.
[3] Jer. xiii. 23.   [4] Eph. vi. 13–14.
[5] Matthew Arnold: *Obermann Once More*, Stanza 28, l. 2.

unto thee any graven image, or any likeness of anything that is in Heaven above or that is in the Earth beneath or that is in the water under the Earth, thou shalt not bow down thyself to them nor serve them',[1] were commandments which the Christian believed, just as unquestioningly as the Jew, to be words of God which Man was required to obey without any reservations.

The Ten Commandments were of the essence of an Old Testament which the New Testament was perpetually invoking as its authority and hallowing as the Scripture that Christ had come to fulfil. The Old Testament was consequently one of the foundation stones on which the edifice of Christianity rested; but so, too, was the doctrine of the Trinity, so again was the cult of the Saints, and so likewise was the visual representation of the Saints and of all three Persons of the Trinity in three-dimensional as well as two-dimensional works of visual art. None of these foundation stones could be pulled out from under the building without danger of bringing it down. Yet how could Christian apologists answer the Jewish taunt that the Church's Hellenic practice was irreconcilable with her Judaic theory? Some reply was required that would convince Christian minds that there was no substance in Jewish arguments; for the tellingness of the Jewish exposure of the hypocrisy of the Christian Church lay in the responsive conviction of sin which this Jewish indictment evoked in Christian souls. Judaism was thus able to take its revenge on Christianity by forcing the Church to fight on two fronts simultaneously; and the foreign war against an obstinately unconverted Jewry was less formidable for the Christian ecclesiastical authorities than the domestic struggle, waged within the *penetralia* of each individual Christian soul, between an Hellenically easy-going Christian paganism and a Judaically tender Christian conscience.

The duality of the conflict is reflected in Christian polemical literature in the distinction between the genre of apologias for Christianity against Jewish attacks upon it and the genre of controversies within the bosom of the Church between Christian iconodules and Christian iconoclasts, though the arguments bandied about in both genres, and taken over, on either side, by successive generations of controversial writers from the works of their predecessors, are, of course, identical to a large extent.[2]

---

[1] Exod. xx. 3–5. Cp. Lev. xxvi. 1; Deut. v. 7–9 and vi. 14.

[2] Stock arguments in the armoury of Christian iconodule apologetics were: (i) that God's veto, communicated to Moses on the Tables of the Law, forbidding the visual representation of human beings and animals, must have been at least tacitly rescinded by Solomon's time, since Solomon is recorded in the Bible (see 1 Kings vi. 23–29, 32, 35, and vii. 25, 29, 36, 44) to have included graven images among the paraphernalia that he introduced into his temple, but is not recorded to have got into trouble with the Lord for having done this, though he is frankly recorded to have got into trouble in the same quarter for other doings of his (see 1 Kings xi. 9–40); (ii) that Christian iconodules differed decisively from the pagan idolators in the capital point that, unlike them, they did not make the images into objects of worship in themselves, but merely paid them reverence out of regard for the living beings of which they were lifeless representations, and reserved their worship for God alone in His invisible spiritual essence.

Iconodule arguments used at the turn of the sixth and seventh centuries in a tract against the Jews published by the Cypriot Archbishop Leontius of Neapolis in Greek also appear in the Armenian text of a tract against Christian iconoclasts that is attributed to Leontius's contemporary Vrt'anes K'ert'ogh (*florebat circa* A.D. 600). A French translation of Vrt'anes' tract is given by S. Der Nersessian, in 'Une Apologie des Images du viie Siècle', in *Byzantion*, vol. xvii, 1944–5 (Baltimore, Md. 1945, Byzantine Institute and

After the nominal conversion, *en masse*, of an Hellenic Gentile World in the course of the fourth century of the Christian Era, the domestic controversy within the bosom of a now Pan-Hellenic Church tended to overshadow the polemics between Christians and Jews; but the theological warfare on this older front seems to have flared up again in the sixth and seventh centuries in consequence of a puritanical house-cleaning in Jewry which, in the Palestinian Jewish community, had been taken in hand towards the close of the fifth century. This domestic campaign, within Jewry's bosom, against a Christian-like laxity that had latterly been tolerating the visual representation of animals, and even of human beings, in the mural decorations of synagogues,[1] had its repercussions on a Jewish-Christian battle-front in a resumption of offensive-defensive Christian polemical operations against the Jewish denunciation of Christian idolatry. When we turn to the parallel controversy between Christian iconophiles and Christian iconophobes, we shall be struck by its persistence and its ubiquity. From the morrow, and indeed from the eve, of the Christian Church's victory over a pagan Diocletianic imperial régime, we find this 'irrepressible conflict between opposing and enduring forces'[2] bursting out in almost every province of Christendom in almost every succeeding century of the Christian Era.

In a still unfissured Catholic Church a ferment of Iconophobia can be seen spreading in and after the fourth century. The exhibition of pictures in churches was forbidden by the thirty-sixth canon[3] of the Council of Elvira (*sedebat circa* A.D. 300/11).[4] Eusebius of Caesarea (*vivebat circa* A.D. 264–340) refused to oblige Constantine the Great's sister, Constantia, by granting a request of hers to him to send her a holy image. Epiphanius, Bishop of Constantia (alias Salamis) and Metropolitan of Cyprus (*vivebat circa* A.D. 315–402; *thronum conscendit* A.D. 367), tore up a curtain with a picture embroidered on it which he found hanging in a church.[5] In a Syriac Orient an attack against image-worship

---

Mediaeval Academy of America), pp. 58–69. A confrontation of parallel passages in Vrt'anes' and Leontius's tracts will be found ibid., p. 76. See also N. H. Baynes: 'The Icons before Iconoclasm', in *The Harvard Theological Review*, vol. xliv, No. 2 (Cambridge, Mass. 1951, Harvard University Press), pp. 93–106. It was Professor Baynes who first called the present writer's attention to Miss Der Nersessian's paper. See now also Alexander, P. J.: 'Hypatius of Ephesus, A Note on Image Worship in the Sixth Century', in *H.T.R.*, vol. xlv, No. 3 (1952), pp. 177–84.

[1] See Der Nersessian, S.: 'Une Apologie des Images du viie Siècle' in *Byzantion*, vol. xvii, 1944–5 (Baltimore, Md. 1945, Byzantine Institute and Mediaeval Academy of America), p. 79, citing, in n. 92, Frey, J. B., 'La Question des Images chez les Juifs', in *Biblia*, vol. xv, 1934, p. 298. The date of this domestic campaign in Jewry against intrusive idolatrous practices is historically significant. Coming, as it did, in the fifth century of the Christian Era, on the heels of the successive Nestorian and Monophysite reactions, inside the Christian Church, against the Hellenic element in Christianity, this puritanical Jewish drive against an infection of Hellenism in Jewry's bosom can be seen to have had its origin in the wave of Hellenophobia that began, in that century, to rise from the depths of a submerged Syriac Society, and that continued thereafter to swell up until it eventually broke upon the Hellenic World in an Islamic cataclysm.

[2] William H. Seward at Rochester, N.Y., on the 25th October, 1858.

[3] 'Placuit picturas in ecclesiâ esse non debere, ne quod colitur et adoratur in parietibus depingatur.'

[4] *Circa* A.D. 300 according to Zeiller, J., in Lebreton, J., and Zeiller, J.: *Histoire de l'Église*, vol. ii (Paris 1938, Bloud et Gay), p. 399; *circa* A.D. 311 according to Vogt, J.: *Constantin der Grosse und sein Jahrhundert* (Munich 1949, Münchner Verlag), p. 169.

[5] In this connexion it is perhaps significant that Epiphanius was a Palestinian of Jewish origin.

was launched, *circa* A.D. 488, by Xenaïas the Monophysite bishop of Mabbūg (*Graecè* Bambycê-Hierapolis); and in the sixth century there were iconoclast riots at Edessa and at Antioch. In the same century in the Greek heart of a Christian *oikoumenê* the strength of iconoclastic feeling is indicated by the recorded fact that Julian, bishop of Adramyttium, prohibited the exhibition, in churches of his diocese, of any visual representations in the round and of any two-dimensional representations in the media of stone and wood, and permitted sculpture-work on the doors only.[1] In the same century in the Latin West the strength of iconoclastic feeling is indicated by the recorded facts that a sixth-century bishop of Narbonne found it politic to drape a picture of Christ on the Cross, and that Pope Gregory the Great's contemporary, Bishop Serenus of Marseilles, broke or removed all images found by him in churches in his diocese.[2] *Circa* A.D. 670, in the citadel of Melchite orthodoxy at Constantinople, the Western Christian pilgrim Arculf was told a story of a man (vilified by him, or by his recorder Adamnan, as *ille Iudeus incredulus*) tearing down an image of the Theotókos from the wall of a house on which it was hanging, when he had learnt who it was that the image represented, and carrying it—apparently without making any concealment of what he was doing and also without exciting any protest—to a neighbouring public latrine, where,

'ob Christi ex Mariâ nati dehonorationem, imaginem matris eius per foramen super humanum stercus inferius iacens proiecit et ipse supersedens, per idem foramen alvum purgans, proprii stercus ventris super thoracidem beate Marie paulo ante ibi depositam dimittens, stolidissime agens profudit.'[3]

In Cyprus, where the iconophobe persuasion in the Christian Church's controversy found a champion in the fourth century in an Epiphanius of Constantia, and where the iconodule cause was championed at the turn of the sixth and seventh centuries by a Leontius of Neapolis in a polemical tract addressed to the Jews,[4] the question seems to have been a burning one; and we may hazard the guess that the perennial interest in it, and sharp division of opinion over it, in Cypriot Christian circles may have been a legacy from the former presence of an influential Jewish community on an island which the Roman imperial authorities had subsequently placed out of bounds for Jews, in retaliation for the Jewish insurrection there in A.D. 115–17.[5] There was not, however, any com-

[1] See Alexander, op. cit., p. 179. A tract addressed to Bishop Julian by his ecclesiastical superior Hypatius, Metropolitan of Ephesus, putting the case for visual representations in churches, will be found in *Orientalia Christiana Analecta*, vol. cxvii (Rome 1938, Pontificale Institutum Orientalium Studiorum), pp. 127–9. A translation, with notes and commentary, is given by Alexander, in loc. cit.

[2] Gregory's correspondence with Serenus about these proceedings is printed by J. P. Migne in his *Patrologia Latina*, vol. lxxvii, cols. 1027–8 and 1128–30.

[3] *Arculfi Relatio de Locis Sanctis ab Adamnano Scripta*, Book III, chap. 5 (in Tobler, T., and Molinier, A.: *Itinera Hierosolymitana et Descriptiones Terrae Sanctae Bellis Sacris Anteriora et Latinâ Linguâ Exarata* (Geneva 1879, Fick, 2 vols.), vol. i, pp. 199–201). All the cases of Iconophobia, except for Julian's case, that have been cited in this paragraph have been collected by S. Der Nersessian in op. cit., pp. 69–70, and the references to the original sources will be found there.

[4] See p. 88, n. 2, above. The surviving fragments of this tract are printed by J. P. Migne in his *Patrologia Graeca*, vol. xciii, cols. 1597–1609. Extracts—apparently from a different version—are quoted by Saint John of Damascus (see Baynes, op. cit., p. 97, n. 10). A résumé of Leontius's arguments is given by Baynes, ibid., pp. 97–103.   [5] See V. v. 68.

parably potent local Jewish stimulus, either present or past, to account for the sixth-century and seventh-century skirmishes between Christian iconophiles and Christian iconophobes in Armenia and Transcaucasia which have left their mark on the surviving local historical records; and these traces of the controversy in this outlying province of a Christian *oikoumenê* at this date suggest that an iconophobe reaction against a prevailing Iconophilia must by then have become endemic throughout an oecumenical Christian body ecclesiastic.

In the days of the Catholicos Nerses II of Albania[1] (*fungebatur* A.D. 548–57), local iconoclasts, whom this pontiff had expelled from his patriarchate, sought an asylum, beyond the limits of their persecutor's ecclesiastical jurisdiction, in Armenia.[2] Their advent presumably accounts for the anti-iconoclast measures that were taken at an Armenian church council held at Dvin, the capital of Persarmenia,[3] in A.D. 554.[4] These measures, however, proved ineffective; for, after the cession of Persarmenia to the Roman Empire in A.D. 591 and the election, in the same year, of a pro-Calchedonian Melchite Catholicos of Armenia, John, at Karin (alias Theodosiopolis, alias Erzerum), the capital of the section of Armenia that had always been in Roman hands since the partition in the reign of the Emperor Theodosius I, three iconoclast monks fled eastwards from Dvin, where they had hitherto been taking their stand under the nose of the anti-Calchedonian Monophysite Catholicos of Armenia, Moses. After seeking asylum first at Sot'k' in Siunik, and then at Artsakh, just on the Armenian side of the Armenian-Albanian frontier, the fugitives were eventually arrested in Ut'i by the Baron of Gardman and were sent back by him in chains to the Armenian ecclesiastical authorities.[5]

Nevertheless, Iconophobia was still rife in Albania nearly a hundred years later, in the eighth and ninth decades of the seventh century;[6] and who knows whether this unextinguished ember in Transcaucasia may not have been the source of the spark which flared up at Constantinople in A.D. 726 in a blaze of Greek fire? In A.D 686 a Roman expeditionary force commanded by the Emperor Justinian II's general Leontius had not

---

[1] This Transcaucasian Albania was approximately conterminous with the Shirwān of the Islamic geographers and with the Republic of Azerbaijan in the political geography of the U.S.S.R.

[2] Der Nersessian, op. cit. pp. 70–71, on the authority of the Armenian Catholicos John of Odsun (*fungebatur* A.D. 717–28), who mentions this episode in a tract of his against the Paulicians.

[3] The Kingdom of Armenia had been partitioned, by agreement, between the Sasanian and the Roman Empire *circa* A.D. 387–90 (see IX. viii. 413, n. 1). The Roman Imperial Government had ceded the lion's share of these spoils to the Sasanidae in the hope of thereby purchasing a relaxation of pressure on their Asiatic frontier which would allow them to concentrate their military efforts on the defence of their hard pressed frontier in Europe.   [4] See Der Nersessian, op. cit., p. 71.

[5] This episode is recorded in a letter, written in A.D. 682 or 683 (see Der Nersessian, ibid., p. 72) by Vardapat John Mayragometsi, the text of which has been preserved by Moses Kaghankavatsis in his *History of the Albanians*. A French translation of the Armenian text of this letter is given by Der Nersessian, ibid., pp. 71–72. The three iconoclast monks' names, according to John Mayragometsi, were Thaddaeus, 'Hesu', and Gregory. Thaddaeus is also mentioned as a prominent iconoclast in the tract attributed to Vrt'anes K'ert'ogh (see p. 88, n. 2, above); and Vrt'anes' 'Isaiah' is perhaps identical with John's 'Hesu', though, in John's text, 'Hesu' probably stands for 'Joshua' (see Der Nersessian, ibid., pp. 71 and 73).

[6] John Mayragometsi, op. cit., translated by Der Nersessian, ibid., p. 71.

only recovered from the Primitive Muslim Arab invaders whatever part of Roman Armenia these may have occupied by that date, but had pushed on eastwards as far in that quarter as Roman arms had ever previously been carried even by Marcus Antonius or by Heraclius; and Albania, as well as Armenia, is named among the countries thus momentarily brought under Roman rule.[1] The local Romano-Arab hostilities that had been restarted by this Roman counter-offensive had continued until A.D. 693, when Armenia and Transcaucasia had been reconquered by the Arabs and been incorporated into the Umayyad Empire definitively.[2] We may guess that on this Armenian-Caucasian front, as on the Syrian front, the retreating Roman troops had been accompanied by civilian refugees, and that some of the Albanian and Armenian refugees may have been iconophobes who carried their doctrine with them westwards into the Armeniac and Anatolic army corps districts of the East Roman Empire. Moreover, Caucasia, as we have noticed in other contexts,[3] was the scene of the romantic exploits in which, *circa* A.D. 710-13,[4] Leo Syrus won his spurs and paved his way to the East Roman imperial throne; and, according to the story, when Leo re-entered East Roman territory in order to become the Empire's saviour, he arrived, not alone, but at the head of a marooned East Roman force, extricated by him from the Western Caucasus, which was partly composed of Armenian troops.

In any case the evidence, cited above, attesting the vitality of the iconoclast cause in the Gallic and Caucasian extremities of Christendom, as well as in its Greek heart, during a period of some four hundred years precedent to the date at which an all-powerful East Roman Emperor made this cause his own, would explain how it was that, in Orthodox Christendom in A.D. 726, the ghost of a Judaic Iconophobia was able to assert itself so brusquely. In A.D. 726 this *revenant* did not have to be called up in a trice from the depths of Sheol; for by that date it had been hovering already for centuries round the flanks of a renegade Jewish Christian pilgrim's consciousness, on the wait for any opportunity to fasten upon his conscience.

In Orthodox Christendom the renaissance of a Judaic Iconophobia had a history not unlike that of the literary renaissance of Hellenism in the West. It broke out in two distinct eruptions (*aestuabant* A.D. 726-87 *et* A.D. 815-43),[5] separated chronologically by an interval of quiescence;

---

[1] The names in the list given by Theophanes in his *Chronographia*, *sub Anno Mundi* 6178 (= A.D. 685-6), are Armenia, Iberia, Albania, 'Voukania', 'Media'. Since Iberia (= Eastern Georgia) and Albania (= Northern Azerbaijan) could not have been reached by a Roman army overland except via Persarmenia, the term 'Armenia' in this passage must be interpreted as including the whole country and not as being limited to the Roman territory of Erzerum. Theophanes' 'Media' may then be identified with Southern Azerbaijan, and his 'Voukania' with Varkāna (*Graecè* Hyrcania), i.e. the eastern section of the strip of territory between the Elburz Mountains and the Caspian Sea in which the Zoroastrians up to that time had kept the Arabs at bay (see II. ii. 446-7).

[2] See Bury, J. B.: *A History of the Later Roman Empire* (London 1889, Macmillan, 2 vols.), vol. ii, p. 322, n. 4, following St. Martin.

[3] In I. i. 64, n. 3, and III. iii. 274-6.

[4] For the date, see Bury, op. cit., vol. ii, p. 376, n. 1.

[5] The East Roman Emperor Leo V (*imperabat* A.D. 813-20), who re-inaugurated Leo Syrus's policy, was an Armenian, and his provenance may account for his proclivities, in the light of the evidence, noticed above, indicating that Iconophobia had been rife in Armenia already in the sixth and seventh centuries of the Christian Era.

and the augury of eventual failure that might be discerned in the intervening set-back was fulfilled when the illogical but statesmanlike compromise on which an iconoclast administration and an iconodule opposition in the East Roman Empire came to terms in A.D. 843[1] proved to have won for the Orthodox Church no mere ephemeral truce but a lasting peace in a theatre of ecclesiastical warfare in which the polemics had been flaring up, off and on, by that time for no less than five centuries.

This apparently permanent settlement of the controversy over images in Orthodox Christendom was not, however, the last that was to be heard of this vexed question in Christendom at large. The temporary re-establishment of the cult of images in Orthodox Christendom by the decisions of a council held at Nicaea in A.D. 787 evoked expressions of dissent and disapproval in Charlemagne's dominions;[2] and, though this protest in Frankland against Iconodulia was quashed at Rome by Pope Hadrian I (*fungebatur* A.D. 772–95), when he rejected Charlemagne's suggestion that he should co-operate with him in a joint condemnation of the Second Nicene Council's acts,[3] the eruption in Transalpine Western Europe which these anticipatory rumblings portended did burst out at long last. A slow-growing Western Christendom had to wait, it is true, some eight hundred years longer for its Martin Luther than a precocious Orthodox Christendom had had to wait for its Leo Syrus; but, when the renaissance of a Jewish Iconophobia did break out in Western Christendom at length, the sixteenth-century explosion in

---

[1] See IV. iv. 364.

[2] In the *Libri Karolini* composed in Charlemagne's name by his ecclesiastical advisers in A.D. 790, the Fathers of the Second Nicene Council were taken to task on the ground that they had taken it upon themselves to declare the cult of images to be obligatory under pain of anathema, whereas, according to the iconodule Greek theologians' Frankish critics, the correct view was that the exhibition of pictures in churches was neither obligatory nor unlawful. Thereafter, at the council of Frankish bishops held at Frankfurt in A.D. 794, the acts of the Second Nicene Council were formally condemned on the false assumption (due apparently to a mistranslation) that the Fathers had awarded the same honours to the images as to the Holy Trinity (see Hodgkin, Th.: *Italy and her Invaders*, vol. viii, Book IX: *The Frankish Empire* (Oxford 1899, Clarendon Press), pp. 17–18).

This unfriendly reaction in Frankland to the Second Nicene Council's decisions was, no doubt, to some extent the reflection of a cultural antipathy between Western and Orthodox Christendom and a political rivalry between the Carolingian and the East Roman Power. In the intercourse between the two churches it was a cardinal principle of policy on either side that the other party must never be admitted to be in the right; and the position taken up by Frankish theologians in the *Libri Karolini* was nicely calculated to put Greek iconodules and Greek iconoclasts equally in the wrong. It is suggested by Hodgkin, ibid., that Charlemagne's hostility to the full-blooded Christian Iconodulia of the Nicene Fathers may also have been partly inspired by his own personal experience in wrestling with the pagan idolatry of Saxon barbarians whom he was finding it difficult to subdue and convert. Though there seems to be no positive evidence to corroborate this conjecture, it is supported by an analogy between Charlemagne's experience and Muhammad's; for Muhammad's uncompromising Iconophobia was undoubtedly a reaction to the stubbornness of the Quraysh in clinging to their pagan worship of the idols in the Ka'bah. Yet, when all due allowance has been made for local and temporary considerations of a religious order, as well as for non-religious considerations of a cultural and political order, which may have played some part in inclining the Frankish Church to react unfavourably to the Second Nicene Council's Iconophilism, a recollection of the instances, noticed on pp. 89–90, above, of iconophobe feeling in Gaul as early as the sixth century of the Christian Era may lead us to look for the main cause of the manifestations of Iconophobia in Frankland in A.D. 790 and 794 beyond the horizon of current affairs, in an original and abiding Judaic element in Christianity. We must not leave out of our reckoning here the gadfly ghost of a Judaic Aniconism.

[3] See Hodgkin, ibid., pp. 18–19.

Germany was no less violent than the eighth-century explosion had been in Anatolia, while, as far as could be seen at the time of writing, rather more than four hundred years later, its effects showed signs of being much more persistent. This long delayed discharge of pent-up iconophobe feelings in a Western quarter of Christendom in which there had been evidence of such feelings since as early a date as the beginning of the fourth century, when they had found expression at the Council of Elvira, suggests that Christian consciences were haunted by the presence of a Judaic Iconophobia *semper et ubique*.

In a Protestant Reformation in Western Christendom an Aniconism that was one of the two fundamental tenets of Judaism was not the only Judaic ghost that succeeded in reasserting itself. A Judaic Sabbatarianism simultaneously captivated the sixteenth-century secessionists from the Roman Catholic Church; and the renaissance of this other element of Judaism in a Protestant Western Christianity is less easy to explain, since the extreme meticulousness to which a post-Exilic Jewry in diasporà had carried its observance of a Sabbath Day's rest prescribed in the Mosaic Law was a peculiar people's response to a peculiar challenge. Ritualism had been a Jewish diasporà's effective elixir for preserving its corporate existence as a community under conditions of adversity under which most other similarly placed communities had dissolved;[1] but, in a Modern Western Protestant Christian World, the triumph of a Judaizing Sabbatarianism was not confined to those Protestant communities which, like the Calvinist minorities in France and in Hungary, found themselves scattered abroad, *more Iudaico*, among a Roman Catholic Gentile majority; the same Sabbatarianism captivated those Protestant communities in the Northern Netherlands, England, Scotland, the Scandinavian countries, and a number of autonomous Swiss cantons and German principalities and city-states in which the Protestants were masters in their own house.

It has been suggested that, in some, at least, of these cases, the 'reception' of a Judaic Sabbatarianism was an unconscious act of self protection against a demonic obsession with gainful economic activities which was so intense that it might soon have worn its votaries out if they had not providently reserved for themselves a salutary minimum of leisure by placing this under the sanction of a no less demonic superstition. But this psychological explanation of a Protestant Western Christian Sabbatarianism would appear to be ruled out by the historical fact that these Modern Western Protestant Christian communities had already become slaves of the Sabbath long before their enslavement to a power-driven mechanized industry capable of keeping its human slaves' noses to the grindstone for all the 168 hours in the week. What, then, are we to make of this paradoxical spectacle?

The Protestants' paramount objective was to return to the pristine practice of a Primitive Church; yet here we see them obliterating a difference of practice between Primitive Christianity and Judaism which the Primitive Church had introduced expressly to serve as a distinguishing mark. The Primitive Church had advertised its secession from Jewry by

[1] See IX. viii. 274.

transferring its weekly holy day from the Sabbath to the first day of the week; and the Protestants were now doing their best to cancel the intended effect of this Primitive Christian new departure by applying to 'the Lord's Day' both the Judaic name of the Sabbath and the Judaic tabu associated with it. Could these 'Bible Christians' be unaware of the logion 'the Sabbath was made for Man, and not Man for the Sabbath'?[1] Could they have read, without marking, the numerous passages in the Gospels,[2] illustrating this thesis, in which Jesus was reported to have gone out of his way to break the Sabbatarian tabu, and to have taken the offensive against the Pharisees by exposing the heartlessness of their legalistic observance of it? Could it have escaped the Protestants' notice that Paul, whom they delighted to honour above all the other Apostles, had made himself notorious by repudiating and denouncing the Mosaic Law, root and branch? The answer to all these questions is that, in appealing from the authority of the Papacy to the authority of the Bible, the Protestants had reanimated, not only the New Testament, but the Old Testament as well, and that, in a contest between these two resuscitated spirits for the dominion over Protestant souls, the spirit of Judaism had prevailed. The consequent renaissance of a Judaic Sabbatarianism was an impressive piece of testimony to the abiding potency of a ghost of Judaism by whose presence a Gentile Christianity had been haunted and harassed ever since its birth.

These renaissances of Judaic elements in Christianity, impressive though they may be, are not, of course, the only examples of the phenomenon in the field of Religion; and this chapter would be incomplete if we did not remind ourselves of other revivals of religious ideals and institutions in the histories of Christianity and of other higher religions. A Christianity which had eventually committed itself to a 'Conceptionist' Christology lived to be haunted by a repressed 'Adoptionism' when a Paulician fossil of a submerged Adoptionist Church struck sparks of Bogomilism by its impact on Slavonic-speaking Orthodox Christians in South-Eastern Europe, and sparks of Catharism by its subsequent impact on Romance-speaking Western Catholic Christians in Lombardy and Languedoc.[3] And a Western Christian Church that had barely succeeded in exorcizing Catharism by the simultaneous practice of a Dominican violence and a Franciscan gentleness lived on to be haunted by a ghost of Augustinian predestinarianism which Jansen raised within the newly fortified precincts of a Tridentine Catholicism after Calvin had raised it in the camp of a rebellious Protestantism.[4] In the history of Islam an Iranic Muslim Society that had emerged out of a post-'Abbasid social interregnum was rent asunder, in the spring of its growth, by the Safawīs' sudden evocation of a ghost of Imāmī Shiʿism at the turn of the fifteenth and sixteenth centuries of the Christian Era;[5] and thereafter an Arabic Muslim Society which had been forcibly incorporated into an Ottoman World, as a consequence of a 'war of religion' between the ʿOsmanlīs and

---

[1] Mark ii. 27.
[2] e.g., Matt. xii. 1–13; Mark ii. 23–28 and iii. 1–6; Luke xiii. 11–17; John v. 1–18 and vii. 23.   [3] See IV. iv. 364–9 and 624–34.
[4] See V. v. 426–7 and 615–18, and pp. 304–5, below.
[5] See I. i. 366–400.

the Safawīs, raised ghosts of a Primitive Muslim puritanism in the successive explosions of Wahhābī, Sanūsī, Mahdist, and Idrīsī Zealots.[1]

(III) THE ROLE OF PILGRIMAGES IN RENAISSANCES

In our survey of renaissances down to this point, we have been reconnoitring, one by one, the principal channels of social life and taking note of the instances, in each line of activity, of the phenomenon that we are studying in this Part. The necromancer's feat of evoking ghosts from the dead pasts of extinct civilizations has been found to have different effects in these divers departments of a living social milieu; but there is one feature, of a geographical order, that is common to all the cases that we have reviewed so far. Whatever differences these divers kinds of renaissance may display in other respects, they all uniformly manifest themselves in changes in the life of a living society that take place within the limits of the society's native geographical habitat. If our survey is to be complete, we must now go on to notice a geographical effect, beyond those limits, that may also be produced by a renaissance of any kind. The evocation of a ghost of some element, whatever it may be, in an antecedent culture may move the haunted society to break its own geographical bounds by trespassing on ground that lies outside these but within the former habitat of the dead predecessor with which the living trespasser is seeking to enter into communion.

Such attempts to translate renaissances from the Time-dimension into the Space-dimension had played an important part in the history of the contacts between civilizations because, as we have seen in an earlier context, the breach of temporal continuity between an antecedent society and its successor or successors in the next generation had often been accompanied by a breach of spatial continuity between the earlier and the later society's respective territorial domains. Though there had been affiliated societies whose habitats had been virtually co-extensive with those of their predecessors, there seemed to have been a greater number of cases—perhaps nine, as against six—in which the geographical coincidence had been only partial, or in which there had been no geographical coincidence at all.[2] In cases of these two latter kinds, a cultural renaissance is apt to produce a geographical tension; for a living society that is haunted by a ghost is prone to treat as holy ground[3] the scene of the *revenant*'s acts and experiences in its original epiphany as a creature of flesh and blood; and holy ground exerts a potent attraction, because it seems to offer a tangible medium of communication between a pious living votary and the elusively spectral object of his devotion. If the votary can continue to set foot in the holy land, he will be able to stand in the footprints of the saints and perhaps to see, touch, and adore their bones, their tombs, and other abiding material relics of their transitory life on Earth. Thus, in all cases where there has been a total or partial geographical displacement of an affiliated civilization's habitat from the

---

[1] See V. v. 295 and 329; V. vi. 227; IX. viii. 250 and 602.
[2] See the table in I. i. 132.　　　　　　　　　　　　[3] Exod. iii. 5.

locus of its predecessor's habitat, one of the ways in which a renaissance is apt to seek expression and satisfaction is through the institution of Pilgrimage.

This institution is not, of course, a by-product of renaissances; it is much older and far more widespread. Pilgrimages must have begun to be made by Mankind wherever and whenever one local shrine came to surpass its neighbours in prestige to a degree that moved the regular local votaries of the neighbouring shrines to reinsure their claim on the good graces of the *numina* by paying occasional or periodical visits to the pre-eminent shrine as well. This practice is not peculiar to any single species of society. We find it rife in the primitive societies as well as in the civilizations, and the greatest dimensions ever attained by any pilgrimages down to the time of writing had been in the lives of universal churches embodying 'higher religions'. Whether we measure these dimensions in quantitative terms of the numbers of the pilgrims, the linear mileage of their travels, and the square mileage of their catchment area, or whether we reckon in qualitative terms of the spiritual effect on the corporate life of a church and on the individual lives of its adherents, we shall arrive at the conclusion that the pilgrimages instituted by Buddhism, Christianity, Hinduism, and Islam, and by the divers sects into which each of these oecumenical religious societies had broken up, were to be reckoned among the most important human institutions of any kind that had been in operation within the two millennia ending *circa* A.D. 1950. In a Judaic religious *oikoumenê* a Jerusalem which had been hallowed by Jews, Christians, and Muslims alike had outstripped the exclusively Christian holy cities Bethlehem and Nazareth, as well as the exclusively Muslim Mecca and Medina. But who shall say whether the *mana* of the Haram-ash-Sharīf and the Church of the Holy Sepulchre and the Wailing Wall was greater in the aggregate than the *mana* of a Bodh Gayā which, in an Indic religious *oikoumenê*, was the supreme goal of every Buddhist pilgrim's aspirations?

The inauguration of pilgrimages on an oecumenical scale which accompanied the propagation of the higher religions to the ends of the Earth was inevitably followed by a reaction in favour of pilgrimages of a narrower range. Any pilgrims would be tempted to travel less far afield, into less strange and hostile social milieux, if they could be assured that, in choosing an easier option, they would be earning an undiminished amount of spiritual merit; and their ecclesiastical pastors and masters might be inclined to give them such assurances under the influence of mixed motives, including a circumspect reluctance to lay on their sheep's shoulders a burden too grievous to be borne,[1] as well as a politic desire to keep their flock within geographical bounds within which they would not be exposed to any rival religious influences. For these reasons, every secession of a sect from a universal church, and every emergence of a secular civilization from an ecclesiastical chrysalis, was apt to be followed by the establishment of new goals of pilgrimage, nearer home, as at least partial substitutes for the Haramayn, Jerusalem, or Bodh Gayā.

[1] Matt. xxiii. 4.

A classic example of the narrowing of a pilgrimage-horizon was to be found in the history of the holy places of the Shīʿah. Within less than a hundred years of the date of the Hijrah, Mecca and Medina, the two oecumenical Islamic holy cities in the Hijāz, had been partially supplanted, as goals of pilgrimage for Shīʿī Muslims, by two sectarian holy cities in ʿIrāq—Najaf and Karbalā—that had been sanctified by the martyrdoms of an ʿAlī and a Husayn; and these ʿIrāqī cynosures of the Shīʿah had afterwards been supplemented by the tombs of an Imāmī Shīʿah's seventh and ninth imāms, Mūsā al-Kāzim and Muhammad al-Jawād, at Kāzimayn. When, in the sixteenth century of the Christian Era, the career of the Safawī Imāmī Shīʿite empire-builder Shāh Ismāʿīl resulted in ʿIrāq's losing to Iran the position, enjoyed by ʿIrāq for more than eight hundred years down to that date, of being the principal stronghold of this 'Twelve-Imām' variety of Shīʿism,[1] and when, thereafter, ʿIrāq itself fell under the dominion of the Safawīs' Sunnī archenemies the ʿOsmanlis,[2] it became the policy of a Safawī imperial régime to discourage its Shīʿī subjects from making pilgrimages even to the historic holy places of the Shīʿah in an Arab ʿIrāq that was now in hostile Ottoman Turkish Sunnī hands, and to divert their hungry eyes with the lure of competitive cynosures inside the Safawī Empire's political frontiers. Persian pilgrims heading for Karbalā and Mecca were provided with alternative goals en route at Qumm and Qāshān in a Persian ʿIrāq where they could slake their spiritual thirst at a lower cost in money, fatigue, and danger without having to descend from their temperate native plateau to the sultry lowlands at its western foot, or to make the arduous transit of the Arabian desert between the Shīʿī Muslim holy cities on the Lower Euphrates and the oecumenical Muslim holy cities in the neighbourhood of the Red Sea. Better still, these Persian Shīʿī pilgrims could be induced not merely to stop short of the Qiblah, but to turn their backs on it, by being directed towards the Mashhad of the Imām Rizā in Khurāsān, in the north-eastern corner of the Safawī dominions.[3]

This Shīʿite Muslim story has Far Eastern Buddhist and Western and Orthodox Christian parallels.

After the propagation of the Mahāyāna into the domain of a disintegrating Sinic Civilization, the converts to this oecumenical higher religion in a nascent Far Eastern World were inspired with a zeal to visit the scenes of the Buddha's life and work in Northern India; and surviving records of journeys made by Chinese pilgrims to the holy land of Buddhism in the course of a span of years beginning in A.D. 259 and ending circa A.D. 1050[4] showed that the practice had been at its height in the fifth, sixth, and seventh centuries of the Christian Era. This floruit is surprising at first sight, considering that the more frequented pilgrims' way was not the sea-route from the south-east coast of China to the Bay of Bengal but the land-route via the Tarim Basin and the Oxus-Jaxartes

[1] See I. i. 366–400, together with the note by Professor H. A. R. Gibb, ibid., pp. 400–2.
[2] See I. i. 389–90.   [3] See I. i. 392.
[4] See Goodrich, L. C.: A Short History of the Chinese People (London 1948, Allen & Unwin), pp. 64 and 156.

Basin and the passes into the Indus Basin over the Hindu Kush; for the period during which the overland pilgrimage from China to India was enjoying its *floruit* approximately coincided with a period, running from *circa* A.D. 375 to *circa* A.D. 675, when the Eurasian Nomads were in a state of effervescence,[1] and when the perils braved by pilgrims on the overland route were consequently at a maximum.

Why should this route have been frequented by Chinese pilgrims during these particularly hazardous centuries, and deserted in the course of the next three hundred years, though these were times in which the Nomads were relatively quiescent? No doubt, one element in the answer is that the incentive of the merit to be earned by making the pilgrimage counted for more in Chinese Buddhist minds than the deterrent of the dangers that had to be faced. On this reckoning, the greater the peril, the greater the virtue of braving it; and accordingly the pilgrimage from China to India flourished, in spite, or perhaps rather because, of its hazardousness, so long as a distant holy land in Bihār was the only pilgrimage-resort where the Chinese pilgrim could hope to earn the merit that was the object of his quest. From the same angle of vision, we can also see that the stream of Chinese pilgrims to Bodh Gayā would be likely to dwindle, and finally to run dry, when a Mahāyāna that had long since taken root on Chinese soil begat there, in the fullness of time, a number of local Far Eastern Buddhist holy places—Wu-T'ai Shan in Shansi, Omei in Szechwan, and the like—whose gradually accumulated *mana*[2] eventually came to rival in the Chinese Buddhist community's estimation the *mana* of a Bodh Gayā in a once Buddhist Hindustan where in the meantime Buddhism had been progressively giving place to Hinduism.

In the same fashion, both an Orthodox and a Western Christendom eventually begat substitutes, within their own respective ecclesiastical bounds, for an oecumenical Christianity's original holy places in a Palestine that had fallen under Muslim rule in the seventh century of the Christian Era. In the tenth century, Orthodox Christendom provided itself with an equivalent of the Chinese Buddhists' Wu-t'ai Shan in 'The Holy Mountain' Athos, lapped by the waters of the Aegean, where in later times Russian pilgrims *en route* for Palestine could be induced to break their journey and to part with a portion of their offerings. A Russian pilgrim who wished to earn his merit still nearer home, without having to cross the sea, could content himself with visiting the shrine of a local theotókos in a north-eastern outpost of the Islamic World at Qāzān which had been won for Muscovy and Orthodoxy by the Tsar Ivan IV in A.D. 1552. A Greek pilgrim who did not wish to venture beyond the landlocked waters of an Archipelago which he had hallowed for himself as 'the Sacred Sea' could earn his merit no less conveniently by making his pilgrimage to the island of Tínos. In Western Christendom, *pari passu*, the Papacy encouraged a pilgrim *en route* for Jerusalem from the Transalpine ecclesiastical dominions of the Holy See

[1] See III. iii. 414.
[2] Wu-t'ai Shan, for instance, had already acquired such sanctity by the time of the great persecution of Buddhism in China in A.D. 845 that it was rehabilitated thereafter as early as A.D. 857 (Goodrich, op. cit., p. 127).

to break his journey, and lighten his purse, at Rome;[1] but Rome, in her
turn, had to part with some of the custom thus captured by her from
Jerusalem to younger holy places more conveniently placed than Rome
herself. A pilgrim heading towards Rome from Lombardy might earn
his merit and spend his money nearer home at Loreto; and a devout
native of England might make his pilgrimage to Canterbury or Wal-
singham without having to leave the shores of his insular *alter orbis*.[2] It
was left for France to emulate in a nineteenth-century Western Christendom the feat achieved by Khurāsān in a sixteenth-century Shi'ite
fraction of Dār-al-Islām. At Mashhad, Khurāsān had given birth to a
shrine that would draw Shī'ī Muslim pilgrims in the opposite direction
from Qarbalā and Mecca. At Lourdes and at Lisieux, France similarly
gave birth to shrines that could draw Roman Catholic Christian pilgrims
in the opposite direction from Rome and Jerusalem.

The foregoing examples illustrate the tendency of a pilgrimage-horizon to contract from the oecumenical range set for it by the world-wide
expansion of a universal church to the parochial limits of sects, civilizations, and states. This tendency towards a narrowing of the horizon on the
religious plane had, however, sometimes been checked or reversed by a
counter-tendency on the military, political, and economic planes. This
counter-movement would be set in motion by an impulse to recapture
by main force a lost hold upon some site that was still holy ground in the
now militant pilgrims' eyes in virtue of its having been the birthplace of
their society's chrysalis-church; and such impulses were the offspring
of renaissances, since they were responses to the appeal of a ghost who
had risen from the dead to exercise his powers of fascination upon the
living.

A classic example of a renaissance thus expressing itself geographically
in a militant movement of expansion is the explosion of a Medieval
Western Christendom in the Mediterranean in the Crusades.[3] In effect
the Crusades were assaults made by Medieval Western Christian agres-
sors on the contemporary domains of their living Muslim and Orthodox
Christian neighbours; but the conscious motive of these Western Christian invasions of Dār-al-Islām and Orthodox Christendom was a yearning
to incorporate in the Western Christian body social the birthplace of
another society that was not a rival civilization but was the Western
Civilization's own mother church. The Crusaders were seeking to gain
possession of a Palestine that was prized by them not so much on account
of its present strategic and economic value as for the sake of those historical associations with the origins and antecedents of Christianity that had
long since made Bethlehem, Nazareth, and Jerusalem the goals of pacific
Christian pilgrims. 'It was the pilgrimage to Jerusalem, and not the
Levant trade of Pisa and Genoa, that inspired the Crusading Movement'.[4]

---

[1] Rome had become a goal of Western Christian pilgrims before the end of the fourth
century. See Bardy, G.: 'Pèlerinages à Rome vers la Fin du ive Siècle', in *Analecta
Bollandiana*, vol. i, pp. 224–35.
[2] See I. i. 17–18.   [3] See I. i. 38 and IX. viii. 346–63.
[4] Dawson, Christopher: *Religion and the Rise of Western Culture* (London 1950,
Sheed & Ward), p. 203.

In taking up arms under the impulse of this homesickness for their pristine holy land, the Crusaders not only made for Christendom's oldest and most sacred pilgrimage-resort as their ultimate objective; they also set themselves intermediate goals to draw their flagging feet forward along the intervening stages of their long war-path by throwing out, *en route*, new pilgrimage-resorts in advanced posts just beyond an expanding Western Christendom's previous borders. Norman pilgrimages to the shrine of Saint Michael the Archangel on Monte Gargano, in the Apulian dominions of the East Roman Empire, were reconnaissances that became preludes to a Norman conquest of the bridgeheads of Orthodox Christendom and Dār-al-Islām in Southern Italy and Sicily,[1] and French pilgrimages to the shrine of Saint James the Apostle at Compostela, in a Galician no-man's-land between a Western Christian fastness in Asturia[2] and the former domain of a dissolving Andalusian Umayyad Caliphate, provided successive new drafts of military manpower for the progressive conquest of the Iberian Peninsula by the joint efforts of Cispyrenean and Transpyrenean Frankish aggressors.[3]

The perilous exposure of the shrine at Compostela on the fringe of a Medieval Western Christendom's *dār-al-ḥarb* had the same effect in spurring the Crusaders into making superhuman exertions as the desperate deed of a Scottish knight who, on an Andalusian battlefield where he had broken his pilgrimage in order to fight under a Castilian banner, turned the fortunes of a day which had been going against the Franks by flinging into the midst of the all-but-victorious Muslims a silver casket containing Robert the Bruce's heart, and rushing forward after it to conquer or die for the sake of rescuing a treasure, entrusted to his safekeeping, which he had thus deliberately thrown into jeopardy as a last resort for calling out his own supreme reserves of vigour and valour.[4] This incident was an omen; for the mission which the Bruce on his death-bed had charged his companion in arms, James Douglas, to fulfil had been to carry his heart to Jerusalem in order to bury it there in the Church of the Holy Sepulchre; the attainment of this Palestinian objective was sacrificed for the sake of a Frankish victory on Andalusian ground which was won by Douglas at the cost of the martial pilgrim's own life; and this personal story repeated itself on an oecumenical scale. While the last of the Crusaders' bridgeheads on the coast of Syria was lost within less than two hundred years of the Frankish invaders' first descent upon Palestine, their conquests in the Iberian Peninsula, Southern Italy, and Sicily under the auspices of the far-flung shrines at Compostela and Gargano were the two abiding gains of territory that were made by Western Christendom in the Crusades at Dār-al-Islām's and Orthodox Christendom's expense.

Elsewhere, and above all in Palestine, the Crusades were the failure that is the usual nemesis of attempts to reach religious goals by military short-cuts; but the Western Christians' yearning for the holy land of Christendom, which had found its earliest expression in these misguided

---

[1] See IV. iv. 401–2.   [2] See II. ii. 446.   [3] See V. v. 259–60.
[4] The tale is told by the writer's mother, Edith Toynbee, in *True Stories from Scottish History* (London 1896, Griffith Farran Browne), pp. 90–91.

Frankish military enterprises, was too deeply ingrained in Western Christian hearts to be expunged by the mortification of a military fiasco. More than five and a half centuries after the Mamlūks had evicted the last of the Crusaders from Acre, a dispute between Western Christian and Orthodox Christian ecclesiastical authorities over their respective rights in Christendom's Palestinian holy places provided the diplomacy of a *ci-devant* Christian World with an occasion for making the Crimean War. The same abiding Western Christian interest in the Christian Holy Land also found sincere and innocent expressions in the same century in the inauguration of The Palestine Exploration Fund by British 'Bible Christians' in A.D. 1864 and the establishment of a Protestant bishopric at Jerusalem under the joint auspices of the English and Prussian Crowns in A.D. 1841.[1] In the twentieth century the fascination of the Christian Holy Land was still strong enough to lure Victorian British 'Bible Christians' ' grandchildren into implicating themselves in a shirt of Nessus when they succumbed to the temptation to undertake a mandate for the administration of Palestine on terms that were bound to disappoint either the Arab natives of the country or the Zionist immigrants of the great expectations which these ambiguous terms could not fail to create in the minds of both parties.[2]

Perhaps the most impressive of all latter-day testimonies to the tenacity of the Christian Holy Land's hold on Western Christian imaginations and affections were the North American Protestant mission-stations which, in the course of the nineteenth century, were established at key-points in the Ottoman countries and in Persia. The founders and propagators of these American Protestant missions in South-East Europe and South-West Asia were descendants of pioneers who had plucked up their roots in the Old World and shaken its dust from off their feet[3] in order to clear the ground for the creation of a New World on the other side of the Atlantic. These transoceanic emigrants from England who had put their hand to the plough that was to call a New England into existence were duly inhibited, by a warning text,[4] from looking back over their shoulder towards their English mother land; but, in boldly choosing and steadfastly following this arduous course, the Pilgrim Fathers had been inspired by the Biblical myth of a Chosen People enduring the ordeal of the wilderness for the sake of making their way into a Promised Land;[5] and, in thus identifying the *Mayflower's* historic

---

[1] 'There is an Anglican bishop resident in Jerusalem. Previous to A.D. 1887 he was appointed by the Queen of England and the King of Prussia alternately. Three bishops held office under this arrangement (A.D. 1841–1881)' (British Admiralty, Naval Staff, Intelligence Division, Geographical Section: *A Handbook of Syria (including Palestine)* (London, N.D., H.M. Stationery Office), p. 209).

'As to the project of a Jerusalem bishopric, I never heard of any good or harm it has ever done, except what it has done for me' (Newman, J. H.: *Apologia pro Vitâ Suâ* (London 1890, Longmans Green), p. 146).

For Newman, the crucial points were that this concerted action of the English and Prussian crowns convicted the Established Church of England of being in communion with the united Lutheran-Calvinist Protestant Church of Prussia, and that in an Act of the Parliament at Westminster, in execution of the project, the Church of England was labelled 'Protestant' expressly (see ibid., pp. 141–6).

[2] See IX. viii. 303–6.
[3] Matt. x. 14; Mark vi. 11; Luke ix. 5; Acts xiii. 51. Cp. Acts xviii. 6 and Neh. v. 13.
[4] Luke ix. 62.   [5] See I. i. 211–12.

Gentile Christian human freight with a legendary Mosaic Israel, they were fortifying one of their emotional links with the Old World in the act of nerving themselves to sever another; for, though any lingering home-sickness for England that might have persisted in their hearts would have been condemned by their consciences and repressed by their wills as a hankering after the fleshpots of Egypt[1] which would indeed have proved them unfit for the Kingdom of God, there was no counter-text in the Bible to harden their hearts against the appeal of texts[2] summoning them to succour scattered and shepherdless Christian sheep in 'Bible Lands' where the labourers were few. The nineteenth-century descendants of seventeenth-century Pilgrim Fathers who dedicated their lives, from father to daughter and from mother to son, to the service of American missionary institutions at Bayrūt, Smyrna, Constantinople, Merzifūn, and a dozen other stations in the Near and Middle East were pilgrims still, as their fathers had been before them;[3] and, when they thus turned right-about-face, to make the return-voyage eastward-ho across the Atlantic from the Fair Havens[4] of an American New Canaan[5] to Levantine scalas at which Saint Paul had once embarked and disembarked, instead of pressing on westward to a Salt Lake or a Klondyke, they were showing their loyalty to their ancestral faith by responding to a call of 'Bible Lands' which was stronger than their dread of re-entangling themselves in an Old-World city of destruction.

The call of a holy land *in partibus alienis*, which thus continued to re-echo in Western Christian ears down a corridor of Time stretching from 'the Dark Ages' to the twentieth century of the Christian Era, likewise availed, in the ninth century of the Islamic Era, to move the Iranic Muslim 'Ghāzis of Rūm'[6] to trespass on Arabic Muslim ground by annexing an Egyptian Mamlūk Empire which included among its dominions the Islamic Holy Land in the Hijāz. The last Egyptian Mamlūk Sultan Tūmān Bey's Ottoman conqueror, Sultan Selīm I, who did not deign to relieve the Mamlūks' puppet Cairene 'Abbasid Caliph of a Caliphial title which Selīm I's forebears had already usurped,[7] was proud to number among the fruits of his portentous victory the privilege of becoming the guardian of the Holy Places of Islam;[8] and, some three hundred years later, his successor Sultan Selīm III (*imperabat* A.D. 1789–1807) was confronted with the choice between vindicating his claim to this still-treasured ancestral office by effective action or else suffering a politically disastrous loss of face in orthodox Sunnī Muslim eyes when, in A.D. 1803, the Sunnī Muslim World was cut to the heart by the shocking news that the impiously militant Wahhābī sectaries had made a descent upon the Hijāz. The Pādishāh at Constantinople was constrained to discharge his bounden duty vicariously by instructing his virtually self-appointed viceroy in Egypt, Mehmed 'Alī,[9] to act on his

[1] See II. ii. 24–25.
[2] Matt. ix. 36–38; Mark vi. 34; Luke x. 2; John iv. 34–35.
[3] Ps. xxxix. 12.   [4] Acts xxvii. 8.   [5] See I. i. 212, n. 1.
[6] The 'Osmanlis are thus designated by their Timurid Turkish kinsman Zahīr-ad-Dīn Muhammad Bābur in his *Memoirs* (see I. i. 349, n. 1).
[7] See VI. vii. 21–22.
[8] See Arnold, Sir T. W.: *The Caliphate* (Oxford 1924, Clarendon Press), pp. 148–53.
[9] For a notice of Mehmed 'Alī's career, see IX. viii. 239–49.

nominal lord and master's behalf; and, though the ensuing conquest of the Wahhābīs' homeland and fastness in the Najd by Egyptian Ottoman arms proved ephemeral,[1] Mehmed 'Alī's execution of the Sublime Porte's commands did have the effect of making the Hijāz safe again for Sunnī Muslim pilgrims by liberating the Islamic Holy Land in A.D. 1812 from a Wahhābī domination that was not re-established thereafter until A.D. 1924–5.

The intermission of the annual pilgrimage to the Holy Cities of the Hijāz under threat of Wahhābī attack had been singled out by the eminent Egyptian Muslim historian Jabartī as being, in his estimation, the most important event of a year A.H. 1213 (A.D. 1798–9) which had also witnessed the descent on Egypt of a French expeditionary force;[2] and neither the eventual reconquest of the Hijāz by a resurgent Wahhābī Power in A.D. 1924–5 nor the simultaneous triumph of a secularizing movement *alla Franca* in the Ottoman Empire's republican Turkish successor-state availed to dry up a pilgrimage-stream whose convergent waters were fed from a catchment area extending as far west as the Senegal and as far east as Indonesia.

The military measures twice taken by an Ottoman Sunnī Muslim Power in order to bring the Hijāz under its aegis, and thereby ensure due access to Mecca and Medina for Sunnī Muslim pilgrims from all parts of a Sunnī Muslim World, had their counterparts in the repeated attempts of the Safawīs and their successor Nādir Shāh to reverse the military decisions of the years A.D. 1534 and 1546[3] by reconquering from their 'Osmanli adversaries an Arab 'Irāq which contained the oldest and most venerable holy cities of the Shī'ah; and in the present context we may also remind ourselves that the 'Osmanlis' descent from the Anatolian Plateau upon the lowlands to the south of the Taurus in A.D. 1516–17 had been anticipated by the East Romans in and after A.D. 926[4] in a repeatedly renewed offensive culminating in A.D. 999 in a raid which had brought East Roman armies as far south as Tarabulus—more than half the length of the road from the Cilician Gates to Jerusalem—a hundred years before any Western Christian Crusader set foot on Syrian ground.

This expansion of the East Roman Empire southward into Syria in the tenth century of the Christian Era, like the expansion of the Ottoman Empire in the same direction in the sixteenth century, was, no doubt, partly the almost automatic consequence of a local change in a balance of military and political power. The decline of the Mamlūk polity, which gave the opening for the 'Osmanlis' sixteenth-century swoop upon Syria and Egypt, had its counterpart in the tenth century in an enfeeblement of Islam through the break-up of the 'Abbasid Caliphate. Is there any evidence that the East Roman aggressors, too, were partly moved, as the 'Osmanli aggressors appear to have been, by an aspiration to bring under their aegis the holy places of their religion? A longing to wrest the Holy Land of Christendom out of non-Christian hands had once inspired the

---

[1] See V. vi. 233, with n. 5, and IX. viii. 250.
[2] See IV. iv. 462, n. 2.   [3] See I. i. 390.
[4] See IV. iv. 399–400 and V. v. 242, 246, 253–4, and 256.

Roman Emperor Heraclius and his subjects to persevere, in the face of an apparently irretrievable defeat, in waging the last and worst of the Romano-Persian wars (*gerebatur* A.D. 603–28) until they had liberated Christendom's holy city Jerusalem from a Zoroastrian domination and had recovered a Holy Rood which had been removed by sacrilegious Persian hands in A.D. 614. The same ardent feeling for the same Christian Holy Land was to be the loadstone of Western Christian Crusaders' efforts a hundred years after the time of Basil II's two Syrian campaigns. When the Eastern Orthodox Christian warrior-emperors Nikiphóros Phokàs (*imperabat* A.D. 963–9), John Tzimisces (*imperabat* A.D. 969–76), and Basil II (*imperabat* A.D. 969–1025) successively invaded Syria, were they moved in part by the same nostalgia for the cradle of Christianity?

If the master-motive of Basil's raid in the direction of Palestine in A.D. 999 had indeed been a crusader's zeal, it would be difficult—even after making full allowance for Basil's double preoccupation with the Great Romano-Bulgarian war on a distant European front and with the repeated rebellions of feudal magnates in the Anatolian heart of his dominions[1]—to understand how in A.D. 1001 Basil could have brought himself to conclude a ten-years' truce with the 'Fātimid' Power under which the Syrian arena was partitioned between the two empires along a line running, far out of range of Jerusalem, from a point on the shore of the Mediterranean, just to the north of Tartūs (Antaradus), to a point on the bank of the River Orontes just to the south of Shayzar (Caesarea).[2] It would be even more difficult to understand why in A.D. 1009 Basil did not break the truce, even at the cost of interrupting his war-to-the-death with Bulgaria, as he had interrupted it once before in A.D. 995, in order to transfer his striking force to a Syrian theatre of operations. In A.D. 995 Basil had made a forced march across Anatolia for the sake of saving Aleppo from falling into the hands of the 'Fātimid' Power; in A.D. 1009 what was at stake in Syria was not the fortress of Aleppo but the Church of the Holy Sepulchre at Jerusalem. In A.D. 1009 this Christian holy place was pillaged and rased by order of the 'Fātimid' Caliph Hākim (*imperabat* A.D. 996–1020).[3] Yet Basil made no military move either to prevent the outrage or to avenge it.

There are, nevertheless, some indications that Basil II, as well as his successors Constantine VIII (IX) (*imperabat solus* A.D. 1025–8) and Constantine IX (X) Monomákhos (*imperabat* A.D. 1042–54), was partly moved by a genuine concern for the Palestinian holy places. In A.D. 987–8, seven years before his first Syrian campaign, Basil himself had sent a mission to Cairo charged with funds for the upkeep of the Church of the Holy Sepulchre at Jerusalem.[4] In A.D. 1027 Constantine VIII negotiated with the 'Fātimid' Government a treaty empowering him to undertake the restoration of the church, which Hākim had destroyed in the meantime. This treaty was renewed in A.D. 1036; and the actual work of

[1] See IV. iv. 390–3 and 396–7.
[2] See Runciman, S.: *A History of the Crusades*, vol. i (Cambridge 1951, University Press), p. 33.
[3] See V. v. 683–5.
[4] See Runciman, op. cit., p. 34, n. 1.

rebuilding was carried out by Constantine Monomákhos some ten years after that.[1]

'To supervise the work, imperial officials voyaged freely to Jerusalem, where, to the disgust of Muslim citizens and travellers, the Christians seemed to be in complete control. So many Byzantines were to be seen in its streets that the rumour arose amongst the Muslims that the Emperor himself had made the journey.'[2]

These facts suggest that the East Romans were not indifferent to the appeal of the Christian Holy Land; yet the full strength of its hold on Orthodox Christian affections and imaginations was only to be demonstrated some three hundred years and more after the last vestiges of the East Roman Empire had been obliterated by an Ottoman conqueror, when a 'Holy Russia' that had not been converted till A.D. 989,[3] six years before the date of the first of the East Roman Emperor Basil II's two raids into Palestine, tardily vindicated her pretension to be 'the Third Rome'[4] by constituting herself the champion of the Orthodox Church throughout the Ottoman Empire,[5] and, above all, in the Palestinian holy places.

In taking up this cause on the morrow of the decisive Russian victory in the Great Russo-Turkish War of A.D. 1768–74, a secular-minded Westernizing Petrine Imperial Russian Government was, no doubt, exploiting its subjects' religious feelings for the furtherance of political ambitions of its own which, in the Crimean War, were eventually to lead the Russian Empire into military and political disaster; but the sincerity of the Russian peasantry's devotion to the Holy Land was attested by the volume of an annual pilgrimage-stream that used to roll through the Bosphorus and Dardanelles till it broke on the coast of Palestine after sweeping over the promontory of Athos. The aspiration to make the pilgrimage to their holy places came to play as dominant a part in the Russians' life as in the Muslims'; and in the World War of A.D. 1914–18 an Imperial Russian Government at its last gasp obstinately vetoed all Western suggestions for establishing a Jewish National Home in Palestine on the ground that this would create an intolerable eye-sore for Russian pilgrims to Orthodox Christendom's Holy Land. In A.D. 1917 the Tsardom had to fall on the 12th March before the Balfour Declaration could be published on the 2nd November.

If we now pass on to inquire whether there are examples of renaissances expressing themselves in geographical terms in cases in which two civilizations of different generations have been related to one another in some other way than through the link of a chrysalis-church, we may glance first at instances in which the successor-society has been a civilization of the second generation, and the predecessor-society a civilization of the first generation which has not bequeathed any universal church to the affiliated civilization, and we may then proceed to examine instances in which a civilization of the third generation that has been related to an antecedent civilization of the second generation through a chrysalis-church has also come into direct contact with its predecessor

[1] See Runciman, op. cit., p. 36.   [2] Ibid., pp. 36–37.   [3] See II. ii. 352.
[4] See VI. vii. 31–40 and 577–9.   [5] See IX. viii. 127, n. 2.

outside the field in which the chrysalis-church has served as an inter-
mediary.

The south-eastward movement of expansion out of an Anatolian
homeland into 'the Fertile Crescent' between the Taurus and the North
Arabian Desert, which we have seen a Sunnī Iranic Muslim Ottoman
Empire making in the sixteenth century of the Christian Era, and an
Orthodox Christian East Roman Empire in the tenth century, had been
anticipated in the fourteenth and thirteenth centuries B.C. by a Khatti
Empire that had established its hegemony over an Anatolian Hittite
World; but there is nothing to suggest that this Hittite Power's aggressive expansion south-east of the Taurus in this age, or even its earlier
raid on Babylon, was consciously inspired by any pious yearning to gain
possession of an antecedent Sumeric Civilization's birthplace in the
Land of Shinar. We have still less warrant for imagining that the Toltec
military adventurers from a Mexic World who established themselves,
first as mercenaries and then as masters, in the domain of a sister society
in Yucatan[1] had been drawn in this direction by any yearning to set eyes
on the Guatemalan homeland of an antecedent Mayan Civilization to
which the Yucatec and the Mexic Society were both affiliated.

Orthodox Christian and Western Christian military adventurers conquered and reconquered the Continental European Greek homeland of an
Hellenic Civilization which was the parent of both these mutually anti-
pathetic Christian Hellenistic societies, and here the evidence would seem
to give us grounds for pronouncing, with some confidence, that these
efforts to seize and hold Greece, energetic and persistent though they
were, were not inspired by any conscious feeling of piety towards a
treasured past such as moved the Western Crusaders to seize and hold
Palestine.

When the Byzantines conquered Greece from pagan Slav barbarian
squatters there in the reign of the East Roman Emperor Basil I (*imperabat* A.D. 867–86), and again when they afterwards recaptured it from
schismatic Western Christian usurpers, foot by foot, in the course of
168 years running from A.D. 1262 to A.D. 1430, the value of Greece in
Byzantine eyes, which induced the Byzantines to make these strenuous
military efforts for the sake of gaining possession of it, did not, as far as
we can judge, reside in the historic role that Greece had once played as
the birthplace of Hellenism. The motive that moved Basil I to conquer
Greece seems to have been, not cultural piety, but a strategico-political
calculation. He appears to have been seeking to forestall the danger that,
if he did not occupy Greece himself, it might fall into the hands of a
rival Bulgarian Power, which, during Basil's reign, was rapidly appropriating the lion's share of the hitherto independent Slavinias in the
interior of the Balkan Peninsula;[2] and, when the Palaiológhi persisted in
squandering the rapidly dwindling resources of a precariously restored
East Roman Empire on the luxury of reconquering the Morea from the
Latins, instead of concentrating their military efforts on the defence of
their last bridgeheads in Anatolia against Turkish assailants whose
knife was then already at Byzantium's throat, they would appear to have

[1] See I. i. 123–4 and IX. viii. 315.   [2] See IV. iv. 343.

been moved by a short-sighted eagerness to turn to immediate account the military weakness of Frankish trespassers on East Roman ground who had become even more decrepit than the Byzantine lawful owners. In reconquering the Morea from the Latins, the Palaiológhi were improvidently securing the twofold immediate satisfaction of taking their revenge for grievous wrongs suffered in the past at the hands of hated schismatic Christian aggressors and at the same time momentarily conpensating themselves for irreparable losses of strategically invaluable territory in Anatolia with ephemeral gains of strategically valueless territory in Rumelia. The Palaiológhi chose to act on this short view without reflecting that, in expelling the Franks from the Morea, they were working, not for themselves, but for their future Ottoman successors. Yet, unstatesmanlike though their preoccupation with the Morea may look in retrospect to an historian's eye, there is no evidence that the warping of their political judgement was the effect of any sentimental attachment to a country that had once been the cradle of Hellenism.

In the vocabulary of a Greek Orthodox Christendom the word 'Hellene' had acquired the opprobriously pejorative connotation of the English Western Christian word 'heathen';[1] and, in the sixth, no less than in the first, century of a progressive renaissance of the Ancient Greek language and literature in Byzantium that had started in the generation of Photius (*vivebat circa* A.D. 820–91), this was still the first association that the word 'Hellene' would spontaneously suggest in the minds of Byzantine Hellenists, however pedantically they might have schooled themselves to conform to the literary affectation of using the term in its original laudatory sense, in imitation of its usage in the classical works of Hellenic literature which they had consciously taken as their models. Moreover, even the most affectedly self-conscious Byzantine votary of an Hellenic literary culture would never have answered 'Hellas' if he had been asked to name his cultural holy land; for, though the East Roman garrisons in Central Greece which had kept their heads above the flood-waters of a Slav Völkerwanderung had been christened 'the Helladhikí', neither a mouldering Athens nor a desolate Delphi and Olympia were the sites which, in the vision of a Photius or a Souídhas, were hallowed by the visibly abiding presence of the Hellenic genius.

The temenos which every Byzantine votary of Hellenism would have named as his cultural holy of holies was not an Athens that had been 'the education of Hellas'[2] at the Hellenic Civilization's apogee; it was a Constantinople that had become Hellenism's city of refuge in the last chapter of Hellenic history. This transference of a cultural halo from the city of Cecrops to the city of Constantine was registered in the language of every-day life in Constantinople's arrogation to herself of Athens' former privilege of being designated 'the City'[3] (ἡ πόλις) *par excellence*;

[1] See the passage in chap. 50 of Constantine Porphyrogenitus's *De Imperio Administrando* that has been quoted in II. ii. 259, n. 1.
[2] Thucydides, Book II, chap. 41.
[3] The common noun that thus became Constantinople's distinctive appellation eventually provided 'the City' with a new proper name. The Ottoman Turkish 'Istanbul' reproduces a Megarian Doric Greek εἰς τὰν πόλιν (pronounced 'stambólin'), signifying 'to the city' in the sense of 'to Constantinople'. This would be the context in which the term would first come to the ears of non-Greek-speaking strangers who had asked the

and a patriotic Byzantine 'metropolitan' (πολίτης) in the age of the Macedonian and Comnenian dynasties could, and would, have pointed out, to any Helladic provincial who had ventured to challenge 'the City's' claim to her title, that Constantinople's heritage from Athens was 'an enduring substance'[1] and not an empty name. From the days of Constantine the Great onwards the later Roman Emperors who had reigned at Constantinople had collected there the surviving masterpieces of Hellenic visual art; and these original monuments of the Hellenic culture, together with the Constantinopolitan collections of manuscripts reproducing the surviving masterpieces of Hellenic literature, were visible proofs that Constantinople's assumption of Athens' proud title had been no unwarrantable usurpation.

It was, indeed, true that from the year A.D. 529, in which Justinian had closed the University of Athens,[2] to the year A.D. 1203, in which Constantinople was captured for the first time by the Frankish perpetrators of 'the Fourth Crusade', an imperial city which, down to the latter of those two dates, had never seen an alien conqueror within her walls, had justified her claim to be called 'the City' by being the unique sanctuary of Hellenism, of which the like was not to be found in Hellas or anywhere else. This hitherto inviolate treasury stored with choice works of Hellenic literature and visual art was under Western Christian military occupation from A.D. 1204 to A.D. 1261; and there could be no more conclusive proof of the Crusaders' indifference to a Hellenistic Western Christian Civilization's cultural birthright than their almost complete failure to turn to any cultural account their fifty-seven-years-long tenancy of Hellenism's Constantinopolitan store-house. When these thirteenth-century Western French and Venetian barbarians broke into 'the City', they found it adorned with masterpieces of the classical Hellenic sculptors; and any fifteenth-century Italian pope or despot would have gone and sold all that he had[3] if he had ever been offered the chance of buying a single one of these treasures; yet these Humanists' thirteenth-century forebears, who held the whole priceless collection in their grasp, could think of no better way of turning Hellenic bronzes to account than to break them up and melt the base metal down for coinage into petty cash.

A record of some of the masterpieces that fell victims to these atavistic Frankish acts of Vandalism was made, for the information of Posterity, by a contemporary Greek historian.[4] It is astonishing that French men-at-arms should have had no eye for the beauty of these Hellenic statues in a century in which figures of comparable aesthetic merit in their own style were being carved by French sculptors. It is perhaps still more astonishing that, among the Western Christian clerics who accompanied the Frankish expeditionary force and who wielded, for good or evil,

way and had been given the answer in a phrase surviving from the locally prevalent dialect of Ancient Greek.
[1] Heb. x. 34.
[2] See IV. iv. 272–3; V. vi. 115 and 223–4.
[3] Matt. xiii. 46.
[4] Nikítas Khoniátis' memorandum on Hellenic works of art destroyed by the Frankish conquerors of Constantinople is printed on pages 854–68 of I. Bekker's edition of Nikítas' *Khroniki Dhiíyisis* (Bonn 1835, Weber).

a considerable moral influence over their combatant comrades,[1] not one,
so far as we know, should ever have thought of employing himself at
Constantinople in learning Ancient Greek in order to read in the original
language those philosophical works of Aristotle's that were being studied
so minutely and discussed so eagerly by these military chaplains' fellow
clerks in the universities of Western Christendom during both the century preceding and the century following the establishment of a Latin
imperial régime at Constantinople in A.D. 1204.

. This barbarous indifference to dazzling cultural opportunities was
not, of course, displayed by all contemporary Western Christian clerks.
Medieval Western students of the philosophy of Aristotle did not neglect
the chance offered to them in a Frank-ridden thirteenth-century Romania
of verifying and revising from the original Greek text the Latin translations of Aristotle's works that they had already been making from Arabic
translations in a Frank-ridden Sicily and Andalusia that had been overrun
by the Crusaders more than a hundred years earlier. It is significant,
however, that the translators who laboured with such devotion at Toledo
and at Corinth were not native local 'fresh-water Franks' of the lineage
of the *conquistadores*, but were 'salt-water Franks' born and bred in
Lombardy, Germany, Britain, Brabant, and other provinces of the
Crusaders' Western Christian homeland, whose enthusiasm for the
study of Aristotelianism had been passionate enough to nerve them, for
the sake of it, to make a long and perilous journey over the passes of the
Pyrenees or across the waters of the Mediterranean. These Medieval
Western culture-heroes will demand our attention in a later chapter.[2]
In the present context we have merely to observe that the indifference
to the opportunities for tapping the living waters of Hellenism at the
fountain-head which was displayed by the thirteenth-century Western
conquerors of Constantinople is cogent evidence that the predatory
Frankish adventurers who sallied out from a conquered imperial capital
to overrun outlying provinces of Romania in a Cis-isthmian European
Hellas and a Peloponnesus were not drawn in that direction by the spell
of classic ground, but were moved solely by the Medieval Western man-
at-arms' insatiable hunger to acquire for himself a feudal lordship over
some patch of rent-producing agricultural land where there was a
peasantry that he could use as serfs.[3]

If, on this showing, we find no evidence that a yearning to set eyes on
the homeland of an antecedent Hellenic culture was one of the motives
in the minds of the French and Venetian conquerors of Constantinople,
Central Greece, and the Morea in the thirteenth century of the Christian
Era, we shall not find any grounds for imagining that a cult of Hellenism

---

[1] See, *passim*, Villehardouin, Geoffroi de: *Conquête de Constantinople*, ed. by Wailly,
N. de (3rd ed., Paris 1882, Firmin-Didot), and Clari, Robert de: *La Conquête de Constantinople*, ed. by Lauer, P. (Paris 1924, Champion).
[2] On pp. 133–5, below.
[3] The only product of an occupied Greece that a Medieval Frankish 'ascendancy'
there can claim credit for having popularized in the Western European homeland of
those Levantine *conquistadores* was—not the Greek text of Aristotle's works which was
translated at Corinth by a scholar from Brabant, William of Moerbeke (see pp. 133–5,
below), but a 'Malmesey' wine exported from the Laconian port of Monemvasía
(Frenchified as 'Malvoisie').

played a greater part in moving the Venetians to reconquer the Morea in
the ninth decade of the seventeenth century. This seventeenth-century
Frankish reoccupation was, however, followed by secular pilgrimages of
a new-fangled kind of which the thirteenth century had seen no trace;
and the trickle of Late Modern Western connoisseurs of Hellenic art
and students of Hellenic literature on pilgrimage to the homeland of
Hellenism round the shores of the Aegean Sea did not cease to flow
when the short interlude of Venetian rule in the Morea was abruptly
terminated by an Ottoman reconquest in A.D 1715.

This difference between the respective cultural sequels to two Frankish
conquests of the Morea that were separated from one another by a
Time-span of nearly five hundred years was due, of course, to the intervening captivation of the Modern Western World as a whole by a
renaissance of Hellenism in the literary and aesthetic spheres which had
been initiated in Italy in the fourteenth and fifteenth centuries; for a
modern tendency towards the secularization of a Western way of life
which had previously been lived within a Christian religious chrysalis
had its effect upon the originally religious institution of Pilgrimage. Since
an early stage in the growth of this institution, pilgrimage-resorts had
tended to become museums of the visual arts; for, in wholly or mainly
illiterate societies, it was a commonplace that pictures and sculptures
were the books of an unlettered majority. In another context[1] we have
quoted a passage in the *Ion* of Euripides in which a party of Athenian
women pilgrims to Delphi are brought on to the stage as sightseers
perambulating the precincts of the temple of Apollo. The interest that
these visitors find in looking at the works of art with which the temenos
is adorned lies in identifying these portrayals of mythical characters and
scenes that are part of the familiar furniture of the spectators' own imaginations. This delight in the visual satisfactions that a pilgrimage-resort
can provide was inherited from naïve and illiterate religious pilgrims to
the holy places of Paganism and Higher Religion by sophisticated and
erudite secular pilgrims to relics of the works of Hellenic art, and sites
and scenes of events celebrated in surviving records of Hellenic history,
when a fifteenth-century Italian renaissance of Hellenism had invested
these visible and tangible 'antiquities' with an aura of pseudo-religious
sanctity in the sight of a cultivated ruling minority in a Modern Western
World.

This secularized Modern Western version of an ancient religious institution took the form of a 'grand tour' that, for the polite society of the
Transalpine and Transmarine countries of a Modern Western World,
found its earliest goal in a Roma Profana from whose long-obscured
virgin countenance a pious Humanism had been gingerly stripping away
Roma Sacra's meretricious enamel mask. A classic example of the genre
was Goethe's *Italienische Reise* (*peregrinabatar* A.D. 1786–8).

'In Italy Goethe directed his attention above all to the artistic treasures.
The works of art that captivated him were, however, almost exclusively
confined to the relics of Antiquity and those modern works which, like

1 In V. vi. 521–2.

Palladio's buildings, have brought Ancient forms back to life.[1] The concentration of his interest on this genre was carried by him to such extremes that at Venice he had no eye for Titian's pictures, and at Assisi none for the celebrated Franciscan Church with its picture-covered walls and ceiling.[2] The nearer Goethe approached to Rome, the more passionate and tempestuous became his yearning to set foot in the Capital of the World.[3] After his arrival there on the 20th October [, 1786], he lived through his Roman days in a state of high beatitude. Here he found himself renewing his youth. He felt himself regenerated and endowed with a new capacity for the enjoyment of Life, the enjoyment of History, Art and Antiquity.'[4]

[1] 'Palladio was penetrated (durchdrungen), through and through, by the essence of the Ancients, and was conscious of the pettiness and narrowness of his own age—in the spirit of a great man who is resolved not to resign himself but to re-mould the rest of Creation (das Uebrige) as far as possible in accordance with his own noble concepts.'— Goethe: Italienische Reise, ed. by Schuchardt, Chr. (Stuttgart 1862, Cotta, 2 vols.), vol. i, p. 117.

[2] 'The monstrous substructures of the churches—piled one on top of another, Babylonian fashion—in which Saint Francis rests, did not detain me. I gave them a wide berth to my left, with a feeling of aversion. . . . Then I asked a handsome youngster the way to the Maria della Minerva [the ci-devant pagan Hellenic temple in the heart of the city]. . . . The growth in spiritual stature that I owe to the contemplation of this work of art is something ineffable. It will bear everlasting fruit. . . . [As I made my way down again,] the dear Minerva gave me one more last glimpse of her benign and consoling countenance, and then I took a side glance to my left at the melancholy cathedral of Saint Francis' (ibid., pp. 159–61).

[3] 'My yearning (Begierde) to reach Rome was so great, and was increasing by such leaps and bounds from moment to moment, that it would brook no further delay; so I made no more than a three-hours' stop in Florence. . . . I hurried through the place post-haste—the cathedral, the baptistery and all that. Here, once again, an entirely new and unknown world confronts me—and it is a world on which I have no inclination to linger (verweilen). The lay-out of the Boboli Gardens is exquisite. At Florence my exit was as rapid as my entry' (ibid., pp. 168 and 156).

Students of Goethe's outlook and êthos will be reminded of a more famous passage in which the same verb verweilen is employed apropos of the same temptation to linger on the course of a journey—heading, in this case, not towards a physical Rome, but towards a spiritual goal of human endeavours. In agreeing the terms of his fateful wager with Mephistopheles, Faust makes the following commitment:

> Werd' ich zum Augenblicke sagen:
> 'Verweile doch! Du bist so schön!'
> Dann magst du mich in Fesseln schlagen,
> Dann will ich gern zugrunde gehen!
>   Goethe: Faust, ll. 1699–1702, quoted in II. i. 281.

[4] Karl Alt in Goethe's Werke: Auswahl (Berlin, N.D., Bong, 4 vols.), vol. i, pp. xxix–xxx. While the paramount objective of the Modern Western 'grand tour' was to venerate the relics, and set eyes upon the scenes, of an antecedent Hellenic culture whose legacy to an affiliated Western Civilization had at last come to be appreciated at its full value by latter-day Western Humanists, this was not, of course, the cultivated traveller's sole concern. The typical Modern French, Dutch, English, German, Scandinavian, or American visitor to Italy was, unlike Goethe, eager also to acquaint himself at first hand with the Italian monuments of an earlier phase of his own Western culture, and also to improve his own mastery of this culture in its contemporary phase by sampling other contemporary local varieties of it besides the one in which he himself had been educated owing to the accident of his having been born in the particular province of the Western World of which he happened to be a native.

The interest in the tourist's own civilization's past which was one of the attractions exercised by Italy on a Transalpine or Transmarine Modern Western secular pilgrim was a manifestation, not of the renaissance of an antecedent culture, but of a different vein of nostalgia which we have labelled 'Archaism' (see V. vi. 49–97). This Modern Western transposition of an archaistic yearning from the Time-dimension into the Space-dimension by giving vent to it by way of a secular pilgrimage had had its counterpart in Hellenic history in the grand tours that had been in the fashion for cultivated Romans from the second century B.C. until the onset of the paroxysm with which an elderly Hellenic Society was afflicted in the third century of the Christian Era. After the Hellenic World had recovered from this stroke—in so far as it ever did recover from it—the secular Hesperian pilgrim to Greece, in the wake of a Titus Flamininus, a Cicero, a Nero, a Hadrian, and an Aulus Gellius, gave way to the religious Hesperian pilgrim to Palestine

Yet, fruitful though this sojourn in Rome was to prove for all the future literary labours of a *Bürger-höfling* man of genius, Goethe's comfortable journey to Rome from Karlsbad in A.D. 1786 was prosaic compared with the veritable pilgrimage to a now profanely holy city that had been made in A.D. 1755 *in formâ pauperis* by Goethe's revered[1] plebeian forerunner Johann Joachim Winckelmann, the shoemaker's son.

Meanwhile, from the close of the seventeenth century onwards, a gradually increasing band of more adventurous Western spirits had been pushing their reconnaissances of profanely holy ground beyond a Rome that had been saluted as a πόλις Ἑλληνίς by Heracleides Ponticus[2] and been vituperated as a *Graeca urbs* by Juvenal[3] into a Greece that, for these classically instructed Western eyes, was Hellenism's authentic holy of holies. After a grand tour culminating at Rome had been celebrated in Goethe's *Italienische Reise*, one in which Greece was the first objective and Rome was an afterthought and anticlimax was celebrated in *Childe Harold's Pilgrimage* (*in Graeciâ peregrinabatur* A.D. 1809–11) in language that simulated the rapture of a Christian pilgrim's more spontaneous feelings at the sight of Bethlehem and Galilee.[4]

on a new course set by an Aetheria and a Jerome. In a Western World in the modern chapter of its history, a Gibbon and a Goethe and a Byron and a Leake reverted, under the auspices of a fifteenth-century Italian renaissance of Hellenism, from Aetheria's and Jerome's religious pilgrimage to Hadrian's and Gellius's cultural tour.

[1] See Goethe's appreciation of Winckelmann in *Dichtung und Wahrheit*, Book VIII (vol. iv, pp. 279–80, in Karl Alt's *Auswahl*).

[2] See V. v. 212.   [3] See V. v. 67.

[4] The writer of this Study had to confess that he himself had been a life-long addict to this sentiment for Hellenic ground. It had led him to make the traditional Modern Western Humanist's pilgrimage to 'classical lands' as soon as he had finished his studies at home, *in partibus Barbarorum*, at the Medieval Western Christian University of Oxford, and he had been confirmed in his devotion to this profanely sacred soil by the inexhaustible benefits that he had found himself deriving, ever after, from a ten-months' stay, first in Rome and then in Greece, in A.D. 1911–12. He could never forget his feelings on the 30th September, 1911, when, for the first time, he had made the journey from Genoa to Rome by the coastal railway. After returning, with indifference, the stare of a Leaning Tower of Pisa, which had peered in at him through his railway-carriage window looking just as it had always looked in the pictures of it, he was thrilled to find himself crossing the Arno into territory that had lain within the frontiers of the Roman Commonwealth since before the outbreak of the First Romano-Punic War. 'Henceforth', he found on the 20th May, 1950, that he had entered in his *ephemerides* for the 30th September, 1911, 'I know every stage of the way, and can always tell where we are by the look of the country. Cecina, with distant Volterra mountains to the left . . . O pulcherrima Maritima Tusciae—haec vera Italia, non Ligures neque Taurini.' At that moment he had the strange experience of setting eyes on his spiritual home for the first time in his life when he was in his twenty-third year; and the effect was heightened when, on the 20th November, 1911, he found his ship travelling up the Gulf of Corinth, threading its way through an isthmian canal, and breaking out into the Saronic Gulf of the Aegean Sea, to confront the pilgrim dramatically with the converging view of serried classic sites closing in round him at point-blank range: Salamis, Aegina, Methana, Megara, Cithaeron, Peiraeus, Lycabettus, Hymettus, Laurium. This was the spectacle that had overwhelmed Servius Sulpicius Rufus one day in the year 45 B.C. when he had run into it from the opposite direction (see his letter to Cicero (*Ad Familiares*, iv, 5) quoted in IV. iv. 315).

The present writer had also to confess that, in his neglect of a 'post-classical' Italy, he had gone to farther extremes than Goethe's worst extravagances. Goethe had at least set foot in Assisi, whereas the writer, down to the 13th August, 1952, had been content with a Pisgah sight of Assisi caught from Spello on the 30th October, 1911. Moreover, though he had three times been shunted into and out of Venice by train *en route* between Calais and Constantinople, he had not set foot in Venice till the third of these occasions—on the 30th April, 1923, between the hours of 5.0 and 6.0 A.M.—and had then failed to advance farther than the pair of Late Roman Emperors in porphyry who embrace one another on the threshold of St. Mark's. His third offence against his native Western

Where'er we tread, 'tis haunted, holy ground;
No earth of thine is lost in vulgar mould,
But one vast realm of wonder spreads around,
And all the Muse's tales seem truly told,
Till the sense aches with gazing to behold
The scenes our earliest dreams have dwelt upon;
Each hill and dale, each deepening glen and wold,
Defies the power which crushed thy temples gone:
Age shakes Athena's tower, but spares gray Marathon.

Yet to the remnants of the splendour past
Shall pilgrims, pensive but unwearied, throng;
Long shall the voyager, with th' Ionian blast,
Hail the bright clime of battle and of song;
Long shall thine annals and immortal tongue
Fill with thy fame the youth of many a shore;
Boast of the aged! Lesson of the young!
Which sages venerate and bards adore,
As Pallas and the Muse unveil their awful lore.[1]

If, as perhaps it might have pleased Gibbon to remark, the sincerity of a cult can be measured by its capacity for breeding illusions, we may gauge the strength of a Modern Western *Schwärmerei* for the classic landscape of Greece by the vitality of a nineteenth-century Western Philhellenism. When, in A.D. 1821, the Ottoman Porte's Greek Orthodox Christian *ra'īyeh* in the Morea revolted against the Pādishāh, Metternich's disapprobatory interpretation of the event as an inexcusable defiance of a legitimate sovereign's lawful authority[2] might perhaps have won the day in a reactionary-minded post-Napoleonic Western Society if the romantic lighting of a Byronic stage had not availed instantaneously to transfigure a 'now degenerate horde' into 'spitten images'[3] of 'hero sires' whom they had so recently still 'shamed'.[4] Thereafter, Byron lived to rectify one volte face by making another; and the final estimate of the character of the Modern Greek people which he was led to form by bitter experience on a grim second pilgrimage to their country was far harsher than an earlier verdict which had been the light-hearted by-product of a poet's brilliant child's play. Yet, if Byron was thus cured of his illusion about the living inhabitants of his Hellas by less than four months' intimate intercourse with them in A.D. 1824, he never lost his illusion about Hellas herself; and his devotion to this idealized ghost of a dead world, that, for good or ill, could not ever disappoint him by confronting him in the flesh, moved the Frankish poet to spend the remains of his fortune, and crown the sacrifice by laying down his life, on behalf of the unworthy living human fauna of a latter-day Western Hellenist's brazenly undiscredited profane Holy Land.

cultural past was that he had always so far deliberately refused to break any journey in Tuscany, for fear that the siren charms of a Medieval and Early Modern Italy might detain him from pressing on into Hellenic holy ground in a 'Roman Italy', a Greece, and a Turkey that had been the goal of his pilgrimages up to date.
[1] Byron: *Childe Harold's Pilgrimage*, Canto II, Stanzas lxxxviii and xci.
[2] See II. ii. 185–6.
[3] See Wright, J.: *The English Dialect Dictionary*, vol. v (London 1904, Frowde), pp. 670–1, s. vv. 'spit an image' and 'spitten image'.
[4] *Childe Harold's Pilgrimage*, Canto II (published in March 1812), Stanza lxxxiii.

C. THE DRAMA OF RENAISSANCES

(I) THE STAGE OF THE DRAMA OF RENAISSANCES

NOW that we have concluded our survey of renaissances, it is time to examine the stage on which the dramatis personae play their parts.

If an encounter of any kind is to take place, there must be some common ground on which the parties can meet. In all the encounters with which we are concerned in this Study, the parties are living souls or their wraiths, and the interaction between them is therefore always some form of action on the psychic plane, even when, as in warfare, this operates through the medium of physical collisions and combats. In 'encounters in the flesh', however, in which all the parties engaged are simultaneously alive at the time, the meeting-place in which they make their psychic contact with one another is the external physical world, whereas in renaissances the encounters are not only of a psychic order in themselves but are also experienced in a psychic meeting-place, not a physical one. A renaissance takes place in the *for intérieur* of a living actor, who provokes the encounter by waking in his own mind a memory, dormant there, of a party who is no longer alive. To recall to mind something that one has forgotten is equivalent, as has been pointed out by Socrates,[1] to learning something new; and a recollection thus precipitates an event.

The difference in the setting of the respective stages of renaissances and encounters in the flesh generates a corresponding difference in their respective ranges of action in the two dimensions of Space and Time. In the Space-dimension, 'encounters in the flesh' have the wider range; for they can occur between any parties that happen to be alive simultaneously on the face of the planet, even if these parties have been unknown to one another previously—as, for example, the indigenous societies of the New World and a Western Christian Society in the Old World were unknown to one another until they collided at and after the turn of the fifteenth and sixteenth centuries of the Christian Era as a result of the Western Christian maritime explorers' physical feat of making the transit of the Atlantic Ocean. In renaissances there is no such possibility of encounters on the geographical plane between parties previously quite unacquainted, since, in the psychic medium in which a renaissance takes place, the living party to the encounter can, as we have seen, resuscitate only those elements of the life of a dead party that happen to be already latent in the living party's memory. In the Time-dimension, on the other hand, 'encounters in the flesh' have a narrower range than renaissances; for in 'encounters in the flesh' the parties can only encounter one another at the moments in their respective lives at which they happen to meet in the Space-dimension, whereas in renaissances the living necromancer—likewise confined in the Time-dimension, though he is, to the moment of his own life at which he is

---

[1] See Plato: *Phaedo*, 72 E–76 C, and *Meno*, 81 A–86 C.

performing his act of magic—is at the same time able to call up, at will, out of the storehouse of his memory, elements of the dead party's life taken from all stages of this dead party's history that are on mental record there. Moreover, the evocator has it in his power to bring on to his inner mental stage simultaneously any number of events in the dead party's history that in real life were not simultaneous but were successive.

The difference in the setting of the stages of renaissances and 'encounters in the flesh' also sets different limits to the number of the characters that can take part in the play. In 'encounters in the flesh' the possible number is limited only by the capacity of the habitable surface of the planet for simultaneously providing coexisting human societies with the habitat and subsistence requisite for keeping them all alive, side by side, on minimum scales of *Lebensraum* and welfare. In renaissances the maximum possible number of dramatis personae is three, since *ex hypothesi* there can be no more than two dead civilizations whose ghosts the living necromancer will be able to conjure up out of the Sheol of his own subconscious psyche by animating some memory of them that has been lying entranced there. There cannot be an intact mental record where there is not an unbroken cultural tradition; and there can be only two dead antecedent civilizations with which a living society will have been able to maintain this necessary cultural contact across the gulf of an intervening social interregnum.

One of the two will be the civilization to which the living society is 'affiliated';[1] the other will be a contemporary of this antecedent civilization which has been implicated with it through an 'encounter in the flesh' at the time when those two now dead civilizations were simultaneously alive, and which, in the course of this encounter, has imparted to the 'apparented' civilization's internal proletariat the 'spark of life' or 'germ of creative power' inspiring a church, incubated in the bosom of this proletariat, which has eventually served the 'affiliated' society as a chrysalis.[2] In the history of the Western Civilization, for example, the renaissances that our foregoing survey has brought to light will be found to be revivals of some element of the life either of an antecedent Hellenic Civilization, to which the Western Civilization is 'affiliated', or else of an antecedent Syriac Civilization, contemporary with, and implicated with, the Hellenic, to which the Western Civilization is related through a germ of creative power derived from the Syriac Civilization by a Christian Church that has served the Western Civilization as its chrysalis.

Until not much more than a hundred and fifty years before A.D. 1952, renaissances and 'encounters in the flesh' were the only kinds of contact between one civilization and another of which there had been historical instances within the Time-span of some five or six thousand years during which societies of this species had been in existence up to date. But, within a period inaugurated by the French invasion of Egypt in A.D. 1798 (to give this new era a convenient, though conventional, initial date), a third kind of contact had been established through the enterprise of Late Modern and post-Modern Western archaeologists. These brilliant pioneers of historical exploration had succeeded in

---

[1] See I. i. 43–44.   [2] See I. i. 57.

making contact with civilizations that were neither living contemporaries of their own society, whom it could meet in the flesh, nor dead predecessors related to it by an unbroken tradition of the kind that linked the Western Society with a dead antecedent Hellenic Civilization to which it was 'affiliated' and also with a dead antecedent Syriac Civilization with which it was in liaison through the Christian Church.

The first of these 'lost' or 'forgotten' civilizations to be retrieved by Western ingenuity was the Egyptiac; and this was hardly an accident, since the Egyptiac was, for several reasons, less difficult than other castaways were to recapture. For one thing, the Egyptiac culture did not have to be literally disinterred, since it had left physical monuments that not only stood above ground but towered into the sky. The Pyramids at Gīzah did not have to wait for the arrival of a French expeditionary force in A.D. 1798 to loom large in the minds of living men. Ever since their erection in the third millennium B.C. they had made an overwhelming impression on the imaginations of non-Egyptiac sight-seers; and Western and Greek Orthodox Christian scholars who had never set eyes on them were familiar with the fact of their existence—and with the further fact that they were the abiding products of a now long since extinct Egyptiac Civilization—thanks to the accounts of the Egyptiac Society's culture and history in the records of an Hellenic Civilization which, throughout its own life-span, had been in contact in the Space-dimension with an Egyptiac Tithonus.[1] One of the incidental products of this Helleno-Egyptiac encounter had been the bilingual inscription in the Greek Alphabet and in two Egyptiac scripts on 'the Rosetta Stone' (incisus est 196 B.C.) which had given Modern Western scholars their key to the deciphering of both the Hieroglyphic and the Demotic Egyptiac characters; but the task of proceeding from the reading of scripts to the interpretation of a dead language conveyed in them might have been still more arduous than it actually was if in the nineteenth century of the Christian Era a language descended from the demotic Egyptian had not been still in daily use as the liturgical language of a Coptic Monophysite Christian Church.

Western scholars had more ado to recapture a Babylonic and an antecedent Sumeric Civilization whose still visible monuments were shapeless mounds of disintegrating sun-dried brick that could not compare with granite-built pyramids in impressiveness; yet here, too, living languages furnished valuable clues. The Achaemenian inscriptions in a simplified version of the cuneiform script, which provided the keys for this script's decipherment, conveyed a language of the Indo-European family from which a still living Modern Persian was descended;[2] the Akkadian language, conveyed in parallel columns of cuneiform script in the Achaemenian inscriptions, proved to be a member of the same Semitic family as the already familiar Arabic, Syriac, Aramaic, Hebrew, Amharic, and Ge'ez; an already acquired knowledge of Old Persian and Akkadian made it possible to decipher the Elamite language, which was the third of those employed in the Achaemenids' trilingual inscriptions,

---

[1] The doom of Tithonus has been observed in VI. vii. 47–52.
[2] See VI. vii. 247–8.

though Elamite had no affinity with any previously known language, living or dead; and bilingual texts in Asshurbanipal's library[1] enabled philologists who had already mastered a Semitic Akkadian language to interpret a Sumerian language which, like Elamite, had no known affinities, but which was of much greater historical importance than Elamite, since it proved to be the mother tongue of the creators of a Sumeric Civilization into whose heritage the speakers of Elamite and Akkadian had entered belatedly as proselytes.

Perhaps the most remarkable of all the triumphs of a Modern Western Archaeology was the disinterment of civilizations that had not only been long since dead and buried but had fallen into complete oblivion. The Minoan Civilization and the Indus Culture, both of which had been disinterred within the present writer's lifetime in the Old World, and the Mayan Civilization in the New World, were the most notable cases of dead civilizations that had suffered this total eclipse; and the recapture of the marvellously accurate but formidably complicated Mayan system of chronological reckoning and notation was perhaps the greatest feat of archaeological skill so far achieved.

The vividness of the life with which these dead, buried, and in some cases entirely forgotten civilizations were endowed in the consciousness of a latter-day Western Society that had succeeded in recapturing them was piquantly illustrated by the vitality of Ikhnaton's ghost, which, after a *vitai pausa*[2] of more than thirty-two centuries' duration, aroused the same controversially conflicting feelings of sympathy and antipathy in Western academic circles in the nineteenth century of the Christian Era that the Egyptiac records testified to his having aroused in the flesh in Egyptiac clerical circles when he was living, reigning, and innovating in the fourteenth century B.C.

In thus establishing a third kind of contact between one civilization and another, the Modern Western archaeologists had done contemporary Modern Western historians the invaluable service of raising the number of known civilizations to a figure at which it had become just feasible to make this species of human society a subject of comparative study.[3]

(II) THE OCCASION OF THE DRAMA OF RENAISSANCES

'Encounters in the flesh' may be precipitated by deliberate acts of will —inspired by aggressiveness, piety, curiosity, or other incentives—on the part of one or more of the parties. Curiosity, for example, was the motive of Herodotus's, Marco Polo's, and Ibn Baṭṭūtah's travels; piety the motive of Goethe's and Byron's, as well as Fa Hsien's and Arculf's, pilgrimages; aggressiveness the motive of Alexander's, Demetrius's, the Cid's, and Chingis' conquests. It is also possible, however, for these encounters between contemporaries in the Space-dimension to come about by accident. For example, contact between a Tari Furora Society and a

[1] See pp. 53–54, above.
[2] Lucretius: *De Rerum Naturâ*, Book III, ll. 860 and 930.
[3] See pp. 205–6, below.

Western Society that had previously had no knowledge of one another was established in A.D. 1935 when the natural fortifications of the Tari Furora's secluded fastness in Papua were penetrated by an enterprising Western explorer[1] who had not been attracted by any rumour of the existence of a mysterious people behind a barrier of knife-edged mountains, but had been impelled by a desire to fill in one of the few still remaining blanks in a Western map of the World plotted out by predecessors of Hides' who, by his day, had been at work continuously for some four and a half centuries.

The encounters negotiated by Modern Western archaeologists with dead civilizations, not related by any unbroken thread of tradition with either the Western or any other living civilization, might likewise be the outcomes of either accident or design. Schliemann, for example, made it the master-purpose of his career to identify and excavate the site of a Troy whose fame had been immortalized in the Homeric Epic,[2] whereas nothing but the play of Chance could have thrust into the hands of expert and imaginative investigators the clues that led to the discovery of the previously quite forgotten Minoan Civilization and Indus Culture. A renaissance, on the other hand, cannot ever come about in this accidental way; for the evocation of a ghost by a necromancer is, by definition, a deliberate act of will on the necromancer's part; and, in practising his grim and perilous art, the necromancer is always inspired by a conscious purpose.

If the wizard screws up his courage to the pitch required for subjecting himself to the self-imposed ordeal of awaking the dead, he embarks on this desperate enterprise as a last resort, under pressure of an urgent need to solve some current problem in his own life which he has failed to solve by drawing upon his native resources. The ghost of a universal state, for example, is usually evoked in the hope that its presence may quell the anarchy of a current Dark Age by the application of a remedy which, in the now dead antecedent civilization's history, did once effectively quell the anarchy of a Time of Troubles. The evocation of ghosts of the Roman Empire in the shapes of an East Roman Empire[3] and a Danubian Hapsburg Monarchy,[4] and the installation, at Cairo, of a simulacrum of an 'Abbasid Caliphate that had just been extinguished at Baghdad,[5] were mainly inspired by the need for a united military and political front against an alien aggressor. The installation in Japan,

---

[1] See V. v. 197, with n. 1. The assumption, made by the writer of this Study in this earlier passage, that the Tari Furora must have acquired some elements of their material culture from abroad before the Westerners' advent is corroborated in a letter written on the spot by Mr. C. R. Stonor on the 25th January, 1950, when he was engaged in carrying out a survey of the economy of the Tari Furora people for the Government of the Territory of Papua. 'They grew maize before we discovered them—a crop which, without doubt, they obtained by occasional trading with coastal tribes, who, in turn, obtained it from Europeans.' On the other hand, Mr. Stonor writes that, apart from the acquisition of this simple American crop from some alien source, he 'can find nothing in the indigenous system of agriculture to justify the views of the late Mr. Hides, or of any popular accounts of this region, wherein it is assumed that people so low in the cultural scale could not have evolved their system of cultivation' [for themselves, independently of any of the agricultural civilizations].   [2] See XIII. x. 12–16, 155, and 163.

[3] See II. ii. 367–9; IV. iv. 323; and VI. vii. 19–21.
[4] See II. ii. 177–88; V. v. 325–7; and VI. vii. 28.
[5] See I. i. 67, n. 2, 70, and 349–50; and VI. vii. 21.

in A.D. 645, of a copy of the Sinic Han imperial régime, that had just been reinstated in China, was designed to foster the planting out of the Far Eastern Civilization, *de toutes pièces*, on the virgin soil of the Japanese Isles;[1] and the corresponding purpose of taming German, Scandinavian, and Slav barbarians beyond the north-eastern frontier of Western Christendom was likewise one of the motives for the evocation of the Holy Roman Empire.[2] The ghost of a pre-Alexandrine Hellenic city-state was revived in a Medieval Italy, and the ghost of a post-Alexandrine Hellenic absolute monarchy in the Modern Western World at large, in the hope of thereby enabling a potentially progressive Western Society to achieve its own latent possibilities on the political plane beyond the limits of the modest capacity of the clumsy native Western institution of Feudalism. The ghost of a Roman Law was evoked first in Orthodox and then in Western Christendom in the hope of providing a native economy that was rapidly increasing in complexity with a correspondingly elaborate legal framework which could not be pieced together out of a juvenile Christian society's rudimentary native law derived from Christian and Judaic sources. Aristotle's ghost in the West, and Confucius's ghost in the Far East, were evoked in the hope of enabling a Western and a Far Eastern intellect to break out of the shell of a Christian and a Mahayanian Buddhist patristic theology. The ghost of a Sinic Literature was evoked in the Far East, and a ghost of an Hellenic Literature in a Greek Orthodox and a Western Christendom, in the hope of thereby irrigating an arid native vein of literary genius. The ghosts of an Hellenic Sculpture and an Hellenic Architecture were evoked in a Modern Western World which was painfully aware that the medieval school of native Western and borrowed Syriac visual art had no more arrows left in its quiver.

A renaissance is thus always deliberately produced for a consciously conceived purpose by a living agent who is awaking the dead from their sleep; and, if the living party to the relation did not thus deliberately take the initiative, an encounter of this kind could never occur; for a ghost cannot raise itself on its own initiative, to haunt the living uninvited; nor can the dead and the living meet one another by chance, as two or more living individuals or societies can, if they happen to be alive simultaneously on the face of the same planet.

(III) THE PLOT OF THE DRAMA OF
RENAISSANCES

The distinctive feature of a renaissance that determines its occasion is also the key to its plot; and our inquiry into the occasion has shown us what this distinctive feature is. In an encounter between a necromancer and a ghost the dramatis personae can never exchange their roles, because, in contrast to the dramatis personae in an encounter in the flesh between parties who are all alike alive at the time, the parties to a renaissance are not 'of like passions'[3] with one another.[4]

---

[1] See II. ii. 158–9.   [2] See II ii. 166–70.   [3] Acts xiv. 15.
[4] This difference between an encounter in the flesh between contemporaries and an encounter between a necromancer and a ghost is analogous to the difference between a

Of course, in an encounter of either, or indeed of any, kind, the initiative will have come from one side only; but, in an encounter between the living, the party which happens to have been the victim of the first assault, no less than the party by whom the first assault happens to have been delivered, has it in him to take the initiative if occasion offers. In an encounter of this kind the assaulted party's passivity and inferiority and the assailant's activity and superiority at the opening of the first act of the play are not due to intrinsic qualities in the parties' respective natures which, in virtue of being immutable, make the effects that follow from them irreversible. In 'encounters in the flesh' the assailant's ascendancy usually proves to be a wasting asset, while the assaulted party usually demonstrates his potentialities from the outset. As soon as the encounter begins, there is, as we have observed elsewhere,[1] a reciprocal exertion of influences and a concomitant tendency for the initiative to change hands through being captured from the original aggressor by the party that has been his victim at the moment when the curtain has risen on the first scene. This 'reversal of roles' (*Graecè* περιπέτεια) is, in fact, the distinctive feature of this genre of encounters; and *ex hypothesi* a corresponding exchange of parts cannot occur in encounters of the different genre in which one party only is a living individual or living generation of a society, while the other party is a wraith. We have already noticed that, in an encounter of this latter kind, the living party alone has the power to take the initiative; and we may now go on to observe that, when once, thanks to the necromancer's initiative, the ghost has been raised, the ghost alone has the power to exert an influence. The spectre's uncanny presence cannot fail to affect the haunted living soul, while the necromancer cannot retort by exercising any counter-influence on the ghost that he has raised; for the living can influence only the living, and it is impossible for the necromancer to catch alive the dead individual or society whose ghost he has called up, since, in order to catch him alive, he would have to have been his contemporary and to have encountered him in the flesh instead of in his own haunted psychic inner world. When the ghost gets on his nerves he has no means of retaliating. In an encounter of this uncanny genre the channel of influence is a 'one-way street' which admits no counter-flow of traffic; and the haunted necromancer will find cold comfort in reflecting that he has only himself to blame, and quoting *ad hominem*: 'Vous l'avez voulu!'[2]

An influence to which there can be no retort in kind is a challenge (indeed a formidable one); and the plot of the play which the evocation of a ghost sets in action can be summed up in the formula that the necromancer seeks to find aid for coping with one challenge at the price of exposing himself to another. He is responding to a challenge from a living contemporary by inviting a challenge from the ghost of a dead

sedentary society, in which every member is inherently capable of exchanging roles with every other, in spite of the institutional impediments of class or caste, and a Nomadic society consisting of three non-interchangeable components: the shepherds or herdsmen, the dogs, horses, and camels that are their non-human auxiliaries, and their flocks and herds (see III. iii. 7–22).

[1] In IX. viii. 464–80.
[2] Molière: *Georges Dandin*, Act I, scene ix.

predecessor. In every renaissance this is the structure of the plot; and the structure is necessarily rigid and invariable because the dramatis personae are incapable of exchanging their parts. Since there can be no *peripeteia* there can be no second act—and no 'concatenation',[1] either, between a series of one-act plays. In contrast to an encounter between contemporaries, which is apt to run into several acts and to link up with previous and subsequent dramas of its own genre, a renaissance is bound to be an insulated experience.

The only element of elasticity in the plot of a renaissance is the diversity of the possible denouements of a situation in which one of the parties is confronted with two challenges at once; for the doubling of the challenge raises the number of possible alternative responses to four.

One alternative, which the necromancer may bring to pass if he is sufficiently cool-headed and adroit, is for him to play off his two adversaries against one another. If he can first succeed in getting the better of the living adversary whom he is encountering in the flesh by mobilizing against him the ghost that he has evoked with that intent, he may then perhaps succeed in exorcizing the now superfluous *revenant* with the aid of the now subjugated living party. A classic example of this tricky feat of prestidigitation is the Western Civilization's success in exploiting an Italian renaissance of the Hellenic culture to retrieve a breakdown in its own native cultural growth, and then shaking off the incubus of a resuscitated Hellenism by reverting to its own distinctive Western vein.[2] On the other hand—and this is the second alternative—the ingenious necromancer may get the worst, and not the best, of both worlds, as a latter-day Persia found to her cost when she was constricted by the strait-waistcoat of an Imāmī Shī'ism which her Safawī conquerors had called up from Sheol to serve them as a spiritual weapon in a competition for political supremacy in an Iranic Muslim World in which the 'Osmanlīs, and not the Safawīs, eventually won the day.[3] As this example shows, the necromancer may both fail to solve the problem confronting him in his own social milieu which has tempted him into resorting to the necromancer's art, and may also fail to rid himself of a ghostly incubus which in this case he will have imposed on himself in vain. The third alternative is a failure to meet the challenge of a contemporary problem combined with a success in escaping the challenge of the vainly resuscitated ghost—as a nascent Western Christendom was compensated by the fiasco of the Carolingian evocation of a ghost of the Roman Empire for the failure of this abortive act of necromancy to quell the anarchy of a Dark Age.[4] The fourth alternative—which is the inverse of the third—is exemplified in the fatal success of a Leo Syrus and a Sui Yang Chien in solving the same problem of anarchy in a nascent Orthodox Christendom and in a nascent Far Eastern World at the price of saddling the salvaged society with an incubus that defied all subsequent efforts to throw it off and that progressively increased its pressure until

---

[1] The phenomenon of 'concatenations' of encounters between contemporaries has been examined in IX. viii. 454–63.
[2] See pp. 62–73, above.
[3] See I. i. 366–400.
[4] See p. 9, above.

it eventually broke the back of the society that had deliberately assumed this fatal burden.[1]

After taking this bird's-eye view of the plot of the drama of renaissances, it may be convenient to glance at the process of evocation before looking further into the nature of a challenge from the *revenant* which is the nemesis of recourse to the necromancer's art.

[1] See pp. 15 and 16, above.

D. THE PROCESS OF EVOCATION

(I) THE INVERSION OF AN ORIGINAL
HISTORICAL ORDER

AT first sight it might seem possible to call up the whole culture of a dead antecedent society *en bloc*, since *ex hypothesi* the whole of this dead society's history has already been played out to a finish, and, just because it is all now dead, and is extant only in the tradition of a living society, it might be expected to be also all now revocable simultaneously. Actually, as we have found in our survey of renaissances,[1] the elements of a dead antecedent culture are apt to be resuscitated piecemeal; and there are two reasons for this. One reason, as we have seen,[2] is that a ghost is never raised except for the immediate practical purpose of obtaining its assistance for the solution of some pressing problem in the necromancer's own life; and the element which, with this purpose in view, he selects for reanimation out of the comprehensive spectrum of a dead civilization's accumulated experience will be only what is relevant to the current problem that is exercising the necromancer himself at the time. If, however, the necromancer were nevertheless to overstep the limit of his immediate requirements by trying to resuscitate the dead culture in its entirety, a positive obstacle to an integral renaissance would then present itself. The simultaneous presence of elements of human action and experience that have never been in existence simultaneously 'in real life' is only possible in a psychic world in which these elements have been reduced to the tenuous consistency of disembodied memories. As soon as the Will takes delivery of these ghosts from the Intellect in order to translate them into real life again, they once again become amenable to a law of real life which debars incompatible institutions, ideas, and ideals from reigning simultaneously in one and the same social milieu.

The most crack-brained Medieval Western votary of Hellenism would never, for example, have dreamed of deliberately resuscitating, side by side, a bevy of sovereign independent parochial city-states *alla Greca* and an oecumenical Roman Empire which, in the history of the Hellenic Civilization, had been the tardily applied antidote to the fatal anarchy which the licence of parochial sovereignty had eventually let loose upon the Hellenic World. When, in the twelfth century of the Christian Era, these two resuscitated Hellenic institutions did come face to face with one another in a Western arena as a result of the unco-ordinated operations of rival schools of Medieval Western necromancers, their inherent incompatibility promptly brought them into violent collision; and it proved impossible to make a Medieval Northern and Central Italy safe for a plenary indulgence in the Greek vice of parochial sovereignty without reducing 'the Holy Roman Empire' to nonentity.

For these reasons the ghosts of elements which, in the life of a dead

---

[1] On pp. 6–114, above. [2] On pp. 118–20, above.

antecedent civilization, have come and gone in succession to one another, without ever having appeared on the stage simultaneously, are apt likewise to be resuscitated successively, and not simultaneously, in the history of an affiliated society. When this happens, the chronological order in which these ghosts are evoked is neither the original order nor a haphazard one bearing no relation to it; it is the original order in reverse.[1]

In the political field, for example, a Roman Empire which had been the last political institution to be thrown up in the course of Hellenic history was the first to be resuscitated in the history of a Hellenistic Western Christendom. 'The Holy Roman Empire' was inaugurated at Rome a week before the eighth century of the Christian Era ran out, and in Charlemagne's life-time its writ ran in all provinces of the Western World of the day except Britain and Asturia. On the other hand the sovereign city-state whose emergence in Hellenic history had been almost coeval with the birth of the Hellenic Civilization itself was not resuscitated in the Western World until after the beginning of the eleventh century, and even then its first effective reappearance was confined to a Northern and Central Italian province of the Western World.[2] Two or three hundred years had to pass, after that, to give an expanding Medieval Western cosmos of city-states time to establish secondary strongholds in Flanders and in Germany,[3] and some two hundred years more to give the resuscitated Hellenic ideal of parochial sovereignty time to translate itself from the city-state to the nation-state scale by captivating the feudal monarchies of Transalpine and Transmarine Western Europe;[4] and it was not till after the outbreak and exacerbation of the French Revolution in Paris, little less than a thousand years after the date of the coronation of Charlemagne at Rome on Christmas Day A.D. 800, that the Hellenomane nations of a Late Modern Western World finally capitulated to the Periclean Attic political ideals of absolute sovereignty for each parochial state, *vis-à-vis* the rest of the body social, and absolute democracy for the citizens of each parochial state in the management of their own parochial domestic affairs.[5]

In this instance the reason why the original chronological order was reversed in the evolution of a renaissance is perhaps not difficult to descry. The explanation is to be found in the utilitarian considerations which are the motive of every renaissance, as we have already noticed. In Charlemagne's generation throughout Western Christendom, a nascent civilization's most urgent political need was to extricate itself from the anarchy of a Dark Age; and the obvious institutional instrument for the purpose was a universal state which had been instituted originally by a disintegrating antecedent civilization as a means of

---

[1] This phenomenon has been touched upon already in IX. viii. 98–101.
[2] 'The State in the Classical and Modern sense of the word first re-emerged in the Italian city-state with its intensive political life, its strong civic consciousness, and its complex and artificial constitutional systems' (Dawson, Chr.: *Religion and the Rise of Western Culture* (London 1950, Sheed & Ward), p. 214).
[3] See III. iii. 299–300 and 344–7.
[4] See III. iii. 360–3.   [5] See pp. 7–15, above.

extricating itself from the anarchy of a Time of Troubles. So long as the Roman Empire had been an effective régime, a mortally wounded Hellenic body social had enjoyed a reprieve. When the Roman Empire had been stricken with its second and final paralytic stroke—which, in the western provinces, had incapacitated it at the turn of the fourth and fifth centuries of the Christian Era—the Hellenic Civilization had dissolved into the resurgent anarchy of a social interregnum with which a nascent Western Christendom was still battling in the eighth century. The Western Hellenistic Society of Charlemagne's day did not have far to seek in order to hit upon the happy thought that, if only it could now revive the Roman Empire in the form in which this had existed in the West from Augustus's reign to Theodosius the Great's (save for an interlude of recurrent anarchy between Alexander Severus's reign and Diocletian's), it might be able to recapture the blessed *pax oecumenica* which the Western Christian Society's Hellenic predecessor had enjoyed for the greater part of those four centuries.

On the other hand, Charlemagne's generation in Western Christendom, and *a fortiori* Charles the Fat's, would have found nothing attractive in the international anarchy of a pre-Alexandrine Hellenic cosmos of sovereign parochial city-states and a post-Alexandrine Hellenic cosmos of sovereign parochial 'enlightened monarchies' which were to prove so attractive in their turns to the Medieval Italians and to the Modern peoples of the Transalpine Western countries; for this international anarchy, which the Roman Empire had temporarily quelled, was the crying evil with which the Carolingians were contending. Parochial liberties bought at the price of oecumenical chaos could appeal only to communities whose energies had accumulated a head of steam strong enough to need a vent, but not yet strong enough to blow Society to pieces; and this new set of social circumstances—which differed from those of a Carolingian Western Christendom in almost every point except the significant point of being transitory—was the situation in which the pre-Augustan Hellenic ideal of parochial absolute sovereignty ran riot through the Western World in the course of some eight or nine centuries following its first revival on the city-state scale in an eleventh-century Italy.

Corresponding considerations explain the reversals of an original chronological order in the evolutions of renaissances in divers non-political fields of activity.

In the linguistic and literary field, for example, the collection of texts of works of the antecedent culture's literature, which we have found[1] to be the earliest symptom of a dawning cultural renaissance, is the latest cultural pursuit of an antecedent civilization in its death agonies. The manuscript-hunting fifteenth-century Italian Humanists were crossing pens with the manuscript-copying sixth-century monks in Cassiodorus's *vivarium* at Squillace, where the last of the great Roman imperial civil servants in the West had spent his old age in providently lading a monastic Noah's ark with samples of the Latin version of an Hellenic literature after he had retired from his thankless secular pro-

---

[1] On pp. 52–57, above.

fessional task of trying to make an Ostrogothic barbarian successor-state of the Roman Empire work.

The compilation of encyclopaedias and dictionaries, which is apt to follow after the collection of texts in the evolution of a renaissance,[1] comes before them in an antecedent society's cultural history; for, even when a disintegrating civilization has reached a stage of cultural decay at which it gives up the attempt at further creation in order to concentrate its dwindling energies on trying to preserve the cultural legacy of the Past, it makes, at first, an effort to bequeath the quintessence of this heritage to Posterity in a systematized form worthy of a rational mind, before eventually resigning itself to the *ultima ratio* of a mere mechanical reproduction of texts. Lexicographical activities thus occupy not the last, but the penultimate, chapter in the cultural history of a disintegrating civilization, whereas, in the evolution of a renaissance, they come, as we have observed, not first, but second, after the texts of the antecedent society's literature have been retrieved and explored. The fourth-century commentators Servius and Macrobius, the fourth-century grammarian Aelius Donatus, and the fifth-century encyclopaedist Martianus Capella, who were labouring for the preservation of the Latin version of the Hellenic literature in the western provinces of the Roman Empire on the eve of a fifth-century collapse, had to wait for their Modern Western avatars until the sixteenth century and after. In the Greek-speaking heart of the Roman Empire, where Hellenism survived for some two hundred years longer than in the western provinces, a sixth-century Hesychius of Miletus was the encyclopaedist who, in a Byzantine renaissance of Hellenism, found his avatar in a tenth-century Souïdhas;[2] and Hsü Shên's *Shuo Wên*, comprising 10,000 characters arranged under 540 radicals,[3] which was the model for all the dictionaries compiled in a Far Eastern renaissance of Sinic letters from the T'ang Age onwards, had been produced at some date during the first half of the second century of the Christian Era, before the collapse of a Posterior Han Dynasty which was the Sinic counterpart of the Hellenic Civilization's post-Diocletianic régime.

The inversion of an original chronological order persists as a cultural renaissance continues to unfold itself. The writing of original works in the antecedent culture's literary language, which, in the antecedent civilization's own history, is apt, as we have seen, to be on the wane by the time when lexicography comes to the fore, is apt, in the evolution of a renaissance, to hang fire until the reincarnate lexicographers have prepared the ground for it.[4] We have noticed this sequence in the history of a Byzantine renaissance of Hellenic letters,[5] and we have also noticed[6] that the Byzantine writers in the medium of Ancient Greek were content to imitate a Neo-Attic κοινή which had been the vehicle

---

[1] See pp. 57–58, above.
[2] See Sandys, J. E.: *A History of Classical Scholarship from the Sixth Century B.C. to the End of the Middle Ages* (Cambridge 1903, University Press), p. 371.
[3] See *Der Grosse Brockhaus* (Leipzig 1929, Brockhaus, 20 vols.), vol. iv, p. 55, and *The Encyclopaedia Britannica*, 1929, vol. v, p. 573.
[4] See pp. 59–62, above.   [5] See pp. 60–62, above.
[6] See pp. 60–61, above.

of the Hellenic literature of a post-Augustan Imperial Age before they had the temerity to produce caricatures of the language and style of a Thucydides and an Herodotus. In a parallel Western renaissance of Hellenism in a Latin dress, the sequence was likewise the inverse of the original order. Medieval Western Latinists were content to reproduce the Latin of a post-Diocletianic Age before they ventured to try their hand at imitating the works of an antecedent Silver Age of Latin literature, or those of a Golden Age by which the Silver Age itself had been preceded.[1]

This inversion of an original chronological order can also be observed in the evolution of renaissances in the field of visual art. For example, in the evolution of a Western renaissance of Hellenic architecture, an Andrea Palladio (*vivebat* A.D. 1518–80) made his appearance 141 years later than a Filippo Brunelleschi (*vivebat* A.D. 1377–1446). In other words, a series of Western architects who were turning their eyes towards Hellenic sources of inspiration, because they were no longer finding scope for their creative powers either in a native Western Romanesque style or in an imported 'Gothic', sought to reproduce the cupola of the Ayía Sophía[2] before they thought of reproducing the columns and pediment of the Parthenon, though the Parthenon was the *chef-d'œuvre* of the native style of Hellenic architecture at its zenith, whereas the Ayía Sophía was a *tour de force* of Ionian epigoni of Ictinus who, after discarding their already worked-out native style as impiously as Brunelleschi and Palladio were discarding theirs, had sought their own fresh inspiration abroad in an exotic Syriac style which was the native Hellenic style's antithesis.[3] In the long-drawn-out epilogue to the history of an Egyptiac Civilization which had been galvanized into an unnatural life-in-death after it had run through all the phases of disintegration to the very verge of dissolution,[4] the artistic as well as the political style of a 'Middle Empire' which had played the senile role of an Egyptiac universal state was promptly revived, after an abortive interregnum, under 'the New Empire' in the sixteenth and fifteenth centuries B.C.,[5] whereas the revival of the artistic style of 'the Old Kingdom', whose floruit had come and gone some seven or eight hundred years before 'the Middle Empire's', was not attempted until the advent of the Saïte Age in the seventh and sixth centuries B.C.

If, as the sequence of renaissances of Hellenic political institutions in Western history suggests, the order in which a living society evokes ghosts out of the past life of a dead predecessor is determined by the living society's estimate of the ability of divers ghosts to help it to meet its own successive pressing needs, how are we to account for the apparently well-attested fact that this utilitarian order of evocation turns out to be correlated with the order in which these elements of the life of the dead civilization had originally succeeded one another in the flesh? If the order of evocation is, as it appears to be, the inverse of the

[1] See Taylor, H. O.: *The Mediaeval Mind* (London 1911, Macmillan, 2 vols.), vol. ii, p. 152.
[2] See p. 84, above.   [3] See IV. iv. 54–55.
[4] See I. i. 133–9; II. ii. 112; V. v. 351–3; V. vi. 190; and VI. vii. 49–50.
[5] See further pp. 350–1, below.

historical order, how are we to explain a correlation which is apparently an historical reality and yet does not appear to serve any useful purpose in itself and is certainly not deliberately intended? The explanation is perhaps to be found in the consideration that the living party to the encounter is apt to be still in process of growth during the time when it is making its successive renaissances of divers elements drawn from a dead antecedent society's past life, whereas, *ex hypothesi*, the dead society whose experiences and achievements are thus being laid under contribution one after another will have passed through all the successive stages of a disintegration into which it will have fallen as a result of having had its growth cut short by a breakdown. If we may assume that, in the living society's memory, the traditions of the archaic stage of the dead antecedent society's growth will have left no abiding impression, then, of all the phases of the dead society's history that the living society does still recollect, the last phase of its disintegration, in which it will have entered into 'a second childhood', will be the phase which will display the closest affinity with the infantile first phase of the living society's growth, whereas the adult last phase of the dead society's growth, in which it was standing at its zenith on the eve of its breakdown, will be the last phase of its history to become intelligible to its living successor, though it will be the oldest phase of the dead civilization's history that is still within the living society's ken. The living society will not begin to become capable of understanding or appreciating this adult phase of its dead predecessor's history until, in the course of its own growth, it has passed out of childhood through adolescence into a corresponding state of spiritual maturity; and, whatever may be the potential fruitfulness of some other individual's or society's recorded experience, this experience cannot become of any practical use to us unless we have learnt to understand its significance and appreciate its value.

Even a talent that we have inherited as our birthright will remain barren so long as we ourselves remain incapable of turning it to account. Just as the potential agricultural wealth of North America was inaccessible to native hunting peoples who lacked the iron axes needed for cutting down the forests,[1] or as the potential agricultural wealth of the clay soils of Britain was inaccessible to husbandmen who had not yet mastered the technique of deep ploughing,[2] so the spiritual experience of social maturity is inaccessible to a society that is still spiritually juvenile. And, since a treasure, so long as it remains inaccessible, is for practical purposes non-existent, it is not, after all, surprising that a living civilization which is still in its own childhood should neglect the mature achievements of a dead predecessor's manhood, and should start its course of successive renaissances by exploiting the senile products of a subsequent 'second childhood' which even a child can already comprehend and, in consequence, already utilize. The growing civilization will have to be increased in wisdom and stature[3] to an altitude of approximate parity with its dead predecessor's altitude at its zenith before it can profitably bring out of its mental storehouse those choice

[1] See II. ii. 278-8.   [2] See VIII. viii. 38-39.   [3] Luke ii. 52.

treasures that the dead society ultimately created in a period of ripeness which, in the dead society's own history, came long before the period of its senile decay.

(II) THE ECLECTICISM OF
WAHLVERWANDTSCHAFTEN

If this explanation[1] hits the mark, our phenomenon of chronological inversion will have proved to be a variation on Goethe's theme of *Wahlverwandtschaften* ('elective affinities', 'congenialities'). In the language of the Gospels,

'Whosoever hath, to him shall be given, and he shall have more abundance; but whosoever hath not, from him shall be taken away even that he hath.'[2]

The hard truth proclaimed in this ruthlessly illuminating text is pointedly illustrated in the cultural history of Western Christendom.

For example, there was never a time—not even at the blackest nadir of a Western Dark Age—at which this Hellenistic Christian civilization did not 'have' the poetry of Virgil in the sense of possessing manuscripts of the text and retaining a sufficient knowledge of the Latin language to be able still to construe the literal meaning of the words. Yet there were at least eight centuries, running from the seventh to the fourteenth century of the Christian Era inclusive, during which Virgil's poetry was beyond the comprehension of even the most gifted, pious, and industrious Western Christian students of it, if we take, as our standard of what constitutes a genuine understanding, an ability to divine in Virgil's poetry the meaning that had been intended by the poet himself and that had been duly apprehended by kindred spirits in his own world, from a contemporary Horace down to a fourth-century Servius and Augustine. Even a Dante, in whose spirit the first glimmer of an Italian renaissance of Hellenism was already beginning to dawn, saw in Virgil a figure which the historical Virgil would have taken, not for his own unassumingly human self, but for some augustly mythical Orpheus or Musaeus; and, in the mental vision of less enlightened Medieval Western souls, the true lineaments of the classical poet were still further transmogrified into the quite unrecognizable shape of a wonder-working magician who had left his mark on a Neapolitan landscape where the historical poet had lived a quiet life of literary seclusion and where his mortal remains had eventually been laid to rest in a tomb on the road between Naples and Puteoli.[3]

Similarly, there was never a time at which the Western Civilization did not 'have' the philosophy of Aristotle in the sense of possessing the texts of the Hellenic philosopher's principal treatises on logic in competent translations by a Late Hellenic man of letters, Boëthius (*vivebat circa* A.D. 480–524), who combined a mastery of Aristotle's thought with a mastery of the Ancient Greek language in which this thought had

---

[1] Suggested already, by anticipation, in IX. viii. 99–100.
[2] Matt. xiii. 12. Cp. Matt. xxv. 29; Mark iv. 25; Luke viii. 18 and xix. 26.
[3] See Comparetti, D.: *Virgilio nel Medio Evo*, 2nd ed. (Florence 1896, Seeber), Parte Seconda: 'Virgilio nella Leggenda Popolare.'

originally been conveyed.[1] Yet there were six centuries, reckoning from the date of Boëthius's death, during which his translations of these works of Aristotle's were beyond the comprehension of the most acute Western Christian thinkers, notwithstanding Boëthius's foresight in leaving them keys in the shape of Latin commentaries of his own and a Latin translation of a commentary of Porphyry's.[2]

Moreover, there was once a time—between the date of the Crusaders' capture of Toledo in A.D. 1085 and the date of their loss of Constantinople in A.D. 1261—during which a Medieval Christendom 'had', in the sense of holding physically in its grasp, the whole philosophical, scientific, and literary legacy of Hellenism that was extant, in that age, in Dār-al-Islām in Arabic translations and at Constantinople in the Ancient Greek originals;[3] yet Western Christian scholars failed to make any use of their opportunity for winning a knowledge and understanding of Hellenic poetry in the original Greek during those fifty-seven years for which the Constantinopolitan store-house of Hellenism was under Western Christian rule, whereas their fifteenth-century Humanist successors in Italy, who were debarred from the Crusaders' potentially invaluable direct access to the springs of Helicon by the successive counter-strokes of a Greek Orthodox Christian *revanche* and a consequent Ottoman Muslim conquest of an ephemerally liberated Romania, succeeded nevertheless in acquiring a mastery of the Ancient Greek language and literature as a κτῆμ' ἐς αἰεί[4] for a Modern Western World, thanks to their zest, energy, and acumen in profiting to the utmost from the imperfect scholarship of a dozen Byzantine Greek refugees who had found asylum in Italy from the Ottoman conquerors of their homeland and had managed to bring away with them a handful of manuscripts of Ancient Greek texts.

Considering the effectiveness of the fifteenth-century Italian Humanists' exploitation of these slender opportunities that were all that came their way, how are we to explain their thirteenth-century Venetian and French predecessors' signal failure to harvest their own immense opportunities for gathering in all the fruits of an Hellenic literary culture in Greece itself?

In seeking an explanation of this apparent paradox, we have, no doubt, to take into account the bitterness of the two sister Christian Hellenistic civilizations' animosity towards one another from the close of the twelfth century of the Christian Era to the later decades of the seventeenth.[5] Their mutual estrangement went to farther lengths than their common quarrel with Islam, and either of these Christendoms found it easier to enter into fruitful pacific intercourse with its Muslim neighbours than with its schismatic Christian co-religionists. For this reason, a Palermo captured in A.D. 1072 and a Toledo captured in A.D. 1085 by the Western Christian Crusaders from the Muslims turned out in the sequel to be more favourable forums for cultural intercourse

---

[1] See Sandys, J. E.: *A History of Classical Scholarship* (Cambridge 1903, University Press), pp. 239 and 507.
[2] See ibid., pp. 239–40; Taylor, H. O.: *The Mediaeval Mind* (London 1911, Macmillan, 2 vols.), vol. i, p. 92.   [3] See p. 110, above.
[4] Thucydides, Book I, chap. 22.   [5] See IX. viii. 151–65 and 380–92.

between the conquerors and the conquered than a Constantinople that was captured by another band of the same Western Christian aggressors in A.D. 1204. It was thus psychologically easier for Medieval Western Christian scholars to take delivery of Hellenic cultural treasures of which the Muslims happened to be 'carriers' than it was for them to incur a corresponding cultural debt to other alien 'carriers' who were schismatic Byzantine Greek Orthodox Christians; and subjugated Byzantine Greeks, on their side, may have been less ready than subjugated Muslims were to share their Hellenic cultural riches with their new Frankish masters.

In another context[1] we have noticed that, when, under the successively unfurled banners of Nestorianism, Monophysitism, and Islam, a Syriac World that was progressively liberating itself from an Hellenic ascendancy had simultaneously opened its mind to receive the Hellenic culture, it had not taken delivery of this alien culture as a whole, but had confined its interest in Hellenism to the two intellectual provinces of Philosophy and Physical Science. An Hellenic philosophy and physical science, not an integral Hellenic culture, was thus the legacy of Hellenism that Medieval Western scholars found accessible to them, through the good offices of Muslim middlemen, in the cultural forum of an eleventh-century Palermo or Toledo, and it is notorious that, in the twelfth and thirteenth centuries, a Western scholarship that had previously failed to take advantage of the legacy of an Hellenic Boëthius did show the same zest, energy, and acumen in profiting by its opportunities of mastering Hellenic philosophy and science through an Arabic medium at Palermo and Toledo as it was to show thereafter, in the fifteenth century, in acquiring the literary culture of Hellenism, in its Ancient Greek original dress, from a handful of Byzantine Greek refugees.

The speed, enterprise, and determination with which Western scholarship turned to account the opportunities offered at Toledo are particularly impressive.[2] One of the earliest of the series of translators who laboured there, Dominic Gondisalvi, who set to work at the instigation of the Western Catholic Christian Archbishop of Toledo, Raymond (*fungebatur circa* A.D. 1130–50), translated into Latin a running translation—made for him orally, into Castilian out of Arabic, by a bilingual Andalusian Jew, Johanan ben David ('Avendeath') of Seville—of the Muslim *savants'* commentaries on Aristotle and original works in the philosophical and scientific fields.[3] The earliest maker, at Toledo, of Latin translations of the existing Arabic translations of Hellenic philosophical and scientific works was a Gerard of Cremona (*obiit* A.D. 1187); and this Lombard translator at Toledo was followed by a Michael Scot (who is believed to have learnt his Arabic at Palermo), by a German Hermann, and by an English Alfred (*florebat* A.D. 1215–70).[4]

---

[1] In IX. viii. 408.
[2] See Sandys, J. E.: *A History of Classical Scholarship from the Sixth Century B.C. to the End of the Middle Ages* (Cambridge 1903, University Press), pp. 539–47. See ibid., p. 507, n. 5, for Sandys' debt to A. Jourdain: *Recherches critiques sur l'âge et l'origine des traductions latines d'Aristote, et sur les commentaires grecs ou arabes employés par les docteurs scholastiques* (1st ed. 1817; 2nd ed. 1843).
[3] See Sandys, ibid., pp. 539–40.   [4] See ibid., pp. 540 and 543–7.

If this were the whole story, we might imagine that we had now fully explained the contrast between the imperviousness of Medieval Western Christian minds to the classical works of Hellenic literature which lay at their disposal in the original Greek at Constantinople and other points in Greek Orthodox Christendom, that were conquered by Western Christian arms in and after A.D. 1204, and the eagerness with which the same Medieval Western Christian minds seized upon and mastered the philosophical and scientific works of Aristotle which were accessible to them, in Arabic translations, at Palermo and Toledo. We might jump to the conclusion that this contrast was simply the corollary of a difference in degree of intimacy and cordiality between the respective relations in which the Medieval Western Christians stood to their Arab Muslim and to their Greek Orthodox Christian contemporaries. We might not suspect that a Medieval Western mind's selection of the works of Aristotle, and rejection of the works of Plato, the Attic dramatists, Pindar, and the authors of the Homeric Epic in the twelfth and thirteenth centuries of the Christian Era had anything to do with any differences in degree of psychological affinity between the respective relations in which a Medieval Western culture stood to divers successive phases of the Hellenic culture itself, as these were represented by the various works of an Hellenic intellect and imagination that have just been mentioned. There would, however, be two palpable flaws in any answer to our question which ignored the play of *Wahlverwandtschaften* in the contact in the Time-dimension between an affiliated Western Christian Hellenistic Civilization and its Hellenic predecessor, in order to offer an explanation solely in terms of the contacts in the Space-dimension between a Medieval Western Christendom and its Muslim and Greek Orthodox Christian contemporaries that were the dead Hellenic culture's two living 'carriers'.

Any answer that was confined within these limits would have failed to take account of two intractable historical facts. One of these facts is that in the fifteenth century, when Italian Humanists were eagerly acquiring from refugee Byzantine Greek 'carriers' their knowledge of the Ancient Greek language and literature, the religious and cultural animosity between Western and Orthodox Christians was even more violent than it had been in the thirteenth century,[1] when Medieval Western Christian scholars were showing themselves insensible to the attractions of Ancient Greek poetry. The other relevant fact is that in the thirteenth century the Western Christian enthusiasts for the study of Aristotle's philosophy, who were making such good use of the opportunities offered at Toledo for studying it through an Arabic medium, did not, as a matter of fact, neglect the simultaneous opportunities offered at Constantinople and elsewhere in the Frankish principalities on Greek Orthodox Christian soil for gaining access to texts of Aristotle's works in the Hellenic philosopher's own original Ancient Greek. Though the Frankish conquerors of Romania, including the clerks as well as the fighting-men, would appear to have been barbarously indifferent to the Hellenic cultural treasures of all kinds—philosophical as well as poetic and plastic—that they held in their insensitive hands,[2] the contemporary Frankish

---

[1] See IX. viii. 151–2.   [2] See p. 110, above.

Aristotelians in the Crusaders' West European homeland did make serious efforts to supplement their Palermitan and Toledan translations of Aristotle's works into Latin from Arabic with better translations into Latin from the original Greek which the Frankish conquest of Romania in and after A.D. 1204 made it possible thereafter to produce.[1]

'The Schoolmen, no longer satisfied with renderings from the Arabic versions of Aristotle, began to obtain translations taken directly from the Greek. Thus the *De Anima* was known to William of Auvergne (who became a bishop of Paris in A.D. 1228 and was still alive in A.D. 1248) in a translation from the Greek, before the Schools of Paris had received Michael Scot's translation either of the Arabic text or [of] the commentary by Averroës. The *Rhetoric*, the *Politics*, the first four books of the *Nicomachean Ethics*, the *Magna Moralia*, part at least of the *Metaphysics*, and the *Parva Naturalia*, were known from the first in Latin translations from the original.[2] . . . It may . . . be inferred[3] that a Latin translation of the Greek text of the *Ethics* was known under the name of [Robert] Grosseteste [*vivebat circa* A.D. 1175–1253], having probably been executed under his direction between A.D. 1240 and A.D. 1244 by one of the Greeks whom he had invited to England.[4]. . . Thomas Aquinas . . . in quoting Aristotle . . . uses translations from the Greek alone, and not from the Arabic.[5] It was at his own instance that "William of Brabant" is said to have produced in A.D. 1273 (doubtless with the help of others) a literal Latin translation of the Greek text of "all the works of Aristotle", which superseded the old renderings from the Arabic.[6] "William of Brabant", [who] is none other than William of Moerbeke or Meerbeke, . . . was probably one of the young Dominicans annually sent to Greece to learn the language. After his return (*circa* A.D. 1268) he was chaplain to Clement IV and Gregory X, and acted as Greek secretary at the Council of Lyons [A.D. 1274].[7] . . . Towards the close of his life he became [Latin Catholic] Archbishop of Corinth (A.D. 1277–1281) and continued the work of executing (and possibly superintending) translations from Greek into Latin.'[8]

---

[1] See Sandys, op. cit., pp. 547–64.   [2] Ibid., p. 548.

[3] From the two facts (i) that Hermann, the Toledan translator from the Arabic, 'who finished his translation of the Arabic commentary of Averroës on the *Ethics* in A.D. 1240, states, in the preface to his rendering of Al-Fārābī's comments on the *Rhetoric* in A.D. 1256, that his work on the *Ethics* had been rendered useless by Grosseteste's translations of the latter from the original Greek' (Sandys, op. cit., pp. 554–5, citing Hermann's: 'Reverendus pater, magister Robertus, Lincolniensis episcopus, ex primo fonte, unde emanaverat, Graeco videlicet, ipsum librum est completius interpretatus et, Graecorum commentis praecipuas annexens [*sic apud Sandysium*—A.J.T.] notulas, commentatus.'); and (ii) that Grosseteste's 'great admirer, Roger Bacon, . . . assures us that . . . [Grosseteste] could never translate from either Greek or Hebrew without assistance' (Sandys, op. cit., p. 553)).

[4] Ibid., p. 555.   [5] Jourdain, op. cit., p. 40.

[6] ' "[*Sub anno* A.D.] 1273: Wilhelmus de Brabantiâ, Ordinis Praedicatorum, transtulit omnes libros Aristotelis de Graeco in Latinum, verbum ex verbo, quâ translatione scholares adhuc hodiernâ die utuntur in scholis, ad instantiam domini Thomae de Aquino" (Slav. Chron. in Lindenbrog's *Scriptores Rerum Germ. Septent.*, 1706, p. 206; cp. Jourdain, p. 675).'

According to Taylor, H. O.: *The Mediaeval Mind* (London 1911, Macmillan, 2 vols.), vol. ii, p. 391, a series of Latin translations of Aristotle's works made from the Greek text, direct, was produced by collaborators of Saint Thomas Aquinas from A.D. 1263 onwards.—A.J.T.

[7] See the present Study, IV. iv. 532, 569, 616, and 622.—A.J.T.

[8] Sandys, op. cit., pp. 562–3. A list of works of Hippocrates and of Galen and of Simplicius, Ammonius, and Proclus, besides Aristotle himself, that were either certainly or probably translated by William of Moerbeke into Latin out of the original Greek, will be found ibid., p. 563.

This historical evidence makes it clear that the mutual antagonism of the two Christian Hellenistic societies did not, in fact, prevent thirteenth-century Western Christian scholars from acquiring from their Orthodox Christian contemporaries any elements in Orthodox Christendom's cultural heritage from Hellenism on which any thirteenth-century Western Christian hearts were set.

'In the course of about 130 years, i.e. in the interval between the early translations at Toledo in A.D. 1150 and the death of William of Moerbeke in A.D. 1281, the knowledge of Aristotle's philosophy had passed in [Western Christian] Europe from a phase of almost total darkness to one of nearly perfect light;'[1]

and, in this thorough, as well as rapid, Medieval Western Christian intellectual conquest of Aristotelianism which culminated in William of Moerbeke's labours at Corinth, the pacific *conquistadores* were not deterred by any psychological inhibitions from drawing upon a Byzantine Greek as well as an Andalusian Arab storehouse of Hellenic culture. How came it, then, that, when they were so eagerly pulling out the original Greek texts of Aristotle's works from thirteenth-century Byzantine shelves, they were content to leave untouched the works of Ancient Greek poetry, stacked there side by side with the *Corpus Aristotelicum*, which were to be pulled out in their turn some two hundred years later by fifteenth-century Italian Humanists with an eagerness as lively as the thirteenth-century Western Schoolmen's passion for the philosophy of Aristotle?

Considering that, in the interval, the already bad relations between the Franks and their living Greek contemporaries the Byzantines were steadily deteriorating, we can only account for the subsequent awakening of Western imaginations to an appreciation of the beauty of a dead Ancient Greek poetry on the supposition that, in the course of those intervening two centuries, some cultural *épanouissement* in Frankish souls in Northern and Central Italy had been attuning them to Ancient Greek melodies to which the thirteenth-century Frankish Aristotelo-maniacs had remained deaf when their ears had been opened to the clicking Morse Code of an Aristotelian logic that had been equally inaudible to them till then; and, as soon as we find ourselves having to allow for this unknown quantity, we can identify it, with some assurance, with a familiar historical event. In Italy between Dante Alighieri's day (*vivebat* A.D. 1265–1321) and Poggio Bracciolini's (*vivebat* A.D. 1380–1459), a growing school of Humanists had been successfully 'tuning in' to the melodies of a dead Hellenic poetry in the Latin rendering into which the original Greek cadences had been transposed by Virgil and the lesser denizens of a Latin Muse's transported Parnassus. We can watch this cultural process of recapturing an appreciation of Hellenic poetry in a Latin dress in the act of accomplishment in the fourteenth-century Italian soul of Petrarch (*vivebat* A.D. 1304–74). By the fifteenth century the process was complete; and this long and arduous apprenticeship in a Latin medium had elicited, in the souls of the fifteenth-century Italian

---

[1] Sandys, op. cit., p. 565.

Humanists who had served it, the aesthetic capacity to appreciate Hellenic poetry in the Greek original.

The door of a Medieval Western mental prison-house was thus by that time unlocked and ajar; and one touch from the fumbling hand of a dimly enlightened Byzantine Greek refugee therefore now sufficed to push this door wide open. The ease with which the fifteenth-century Italian Humanists in a Latin medium made themselves Humanists in the original Greek vindicates the truth of the aphorism 'Whosoever hath, to him shall be given, and he shall have more abundance'.[1] The Italians' successful cultivation of their native Latin legacy from Hellenism in the course of the Later Middle Ages of Western history had assimilated the mental atmosphere of the precocious fifteenth-century Italian province of an embryonic Modern Western World to the cultural climate which a by then long since dead Hellenic World had once enjoyed in the times in which the Greek and Latin masterpieces of an Hellenic literature had been created.

This episode of Medieval Western cultural history points to the explanation of a phenomenon which has come to our notice as a matter of historical fact. If, in the history of a living civilization, the divers phases of a dead antecedent culture are apt to be conjured up in a sequence which is the inverse of the order in which these same phases have originally appeared in the antecedent society's own life, the reason, as we can now discern, is because a ghost does not become amenable to a necromancer's incantations unless and until the would-be wizard has learnt the art of invoking the departed spirit in the dead soul's own familiar language. The necromancer will never be able to raise a ghost with which he is not already psychologically in sympathy; for, even if the shades in Sheol were willing to answer to the summons of a discordant living voice, it would be impossible for a necromancer to have addressed a summons to a shade with which he had not already acquired some psychic affinity. Without this bond of pre-established harmony to place him *en rapport*, the necromancer would be disablingly insensitive to the aura of the ghostly presence.

A truth which, in this Study, we have approached empirically, through a survey of historical embodiments of it, has been apprehended by Plato intuitively and been presented by him in a myth. Plato's account, in the *Critias*, of an imaginary civilization of the first generation flowering on the subsequently lost continent of Atlantis, out in the Ocean somewhere to the west of the Straits of Gibraltar, is prefaced by a passage purporting to explain why it is that no more than the most jejune tradition of this dead civilization's character and achievements has been preserved by its successors through an intervening series of social interregna caused by recurrent cataclysms.

'While the names of [the great men of this dead Atlantic Civilization] have been preserved, the memory of their achievements has been obliterated by the catastrophes that have overtaken their successors and by the immensity of the periods of the time that has since elapsed. We

---

[1] Matt. xiii. 12, quoted on p. 130, above.

have already observed[1] that the survivors of the periodic catastrophes have always been a remnant consisting only of illiterate highlanders whose knowledge of the past rulers of their world has been virtually confined to a bare list of names. These famous names have still had a strong enough hold on their affections to move them to bestow them on their own children, but they have had no knowledge of their predecessors' qualities and institutions beyond the faintest echoes of hearsay. The reason is that, from father to son for many generations running, they have suffered from a shortage of the sheer necessities of life, and that their attention—and consequently their intellectual activity—has been concentrated on these shortages to the neglect of Ancient History. Mythology and historical research are a pair of activities that only gains a footing in communities in process of civilization (πόλεις) *pari passu* with a margin of leisure. Their opportunity arrives when a community has reached a stage at which the necessities of life have been provided for; until that stage is reached, there is no opening for them; and this is the reason why only the names of the famous men of Antiquity have been preserved, without any accompanying memory of their achievements.'[2]

In other words, there can be no renaissance of a dead culture except in the bosom of an affiliated society that has raised itself to the cultural level at which its predecessor was standing at the time when it was accomplishing these achievements that have now become candidates for resuscitation; and (Plato reminds us), even if the affiliated society does eventually attain this degree of cultural maturity, the possibility of a renaissance is not thereby automatically guaranteed; for, in the meantime, the tradition of the antecedent culture in the affiliated society's heritage from its predecessor may have worn so thin that a tardily established cultural affinity may find itself neutralized by the lack of even the most etherial medium for establishing communications between the living society in the current phase of its history and the corresponding phase of the history of the dead civilization.

[1] In the *Timaeus*, 21E–23C, quoted in this Study in IV. iv. 24–25.
[2] Plato: *Critias*, 109D–110A.

E. THE CONSEQUENCES OF NECROMANCY

(I) THE TRANSFUSION OF PSYCHIC ENERGY

WHAT rites are required for establishing effective contact with a
ghost with whom a necromancer has business to transact?
According to a legend in the *Odyssey*, the technique of raising the
dead was found to be a dangerous game by the hero of the epic when,
some twenty-seven centuries before Columbus's day, he cast off from
the land of the living and made the untried westward transit of Ocean
Stream in quest, not of gold and spices in the workaday markets of a
terrestrial Cathay, but of oracles from a phantom seer's uncanny lips in
a mouldering House of Hades.[1] Though Odysseus showed his usual prudence by following, to the letter, the professional instructions of the
sorceress Circe,[2] even so he had considerable difficulty in extricating himself from his hazardous psychic adventure; and Odysseus' experience, as
narrated in the epic in the adventurer's *oratio recta*, is doubly disconcerting to the reader; for the hero of the *Odyssey* was granted a privilege
which we cannot hope to share if we venture in his wake in real life.

The crux of necromancy lies in the hard fact that a psychically depotentiated ghost cannot hold converse with the living unless its vitality
has been momentarily raised again to the level of consciousness;[3] the
sole means of administering this indispensable temporary reinvigora-
tion to the shades of the departed is to give them a restorative draught,
and for this purpose such insipid ingredients as honey, milk, wine, water,
and barley meal[4] are not enough; in order to bring a ghost back to an
effective state of animation, the vivifying brew has to be 'laced' with the
sinister infusion of some living creature's freshly shed blood. This is a
prescription *sine qua non* without which no business can be transacted;
'no blood-offering, no oracle';[5] and Odysseus duly provided the life-
taking life-giving draught; but the legendary Achaean hero was allowed
to reanimate the shades of Teiresias and the rest of the ghastly rout by a
vicarious sacrifice. The operative blood that Odysseus infused into the
innocent but ineffective bloodless offerings in his sacrificial trench
spurted from the sword-slashed throats of a young ram and a black ewe,[6]
whereas the blood that has to be contributed in real life is not an amenable substitute's but is the necromancer's own—with which he parts at a
risk, for himself, of succumbing to pernicious anaemia.

Thus, in real life, the necromancer can restore a ghost's vitality only at
the cost of lowering his own by the exact degree to which he raises his
phantom beneficiary's; and the venturesome necromancer's plight becomes more and more precarious as the difference in psychic potency
between the souls of the two parties to this ghoulish encounter is progressively reduced by the living party's deliberately performed self-

[1] *Odyssey*, Book XI, 'Necyïa', *passim*.
[2] For these, see *Odyssey*, Book X, ll. 504–40.
[3] See *Od.* XI, ll. 140–54.   [4] *Od.* X, ll. 518–20; *Od.* XI, ll. 26–28.
[5] The shade of Teiresias in *Od.* XI, ll. 147–9.
[6] *Od.* X, ll. 527–8; *Od.* XI, ll. 35–36.

devitalizing ritual act. At the beginning of the proceedings, when the spectre's potency registers zero, while the necromancer's registers a still undiminished plenitude of normal human blood-pressure, the difference is of a magnitude at which it constitutes a securely impassable gulf;[1] but, as the original difference approaches parity, this gulf dwindles to the narrowness of a strait across which the reanimated ghost can leap; and at that stage the necromancer has both attained the result for which he has been working and has incurred the peril which, in his profession, is inseparable from success. The reanimated ghost is now at the successful necromancer's disposal for him to command if he can; but, in consequence, the necromancer himself is now exposed to a risk of having the tables turned on him by the reanimated ghost.

The truth seems to be that a ghost which is impotent to take the initiative in engineering its own revival does not feel any moral obligation towards a necromancer whose motive in taking the necessary initiative and in making the indispensable blood-sacrifice has not, after all, been a disinterested one. The first use that the ghost will make of the vitality that the blood-transfusion is restoring to him will be to reassert a will of his own. In the language of a nascent post-Modern Western Science of Psychology,

'An autonomous complex pursues its way and goes through its paces, repeating its own special performance quite regardless of any human consideration. It is a kind of ghost haunting the corridors of the Mind, and, like a ghost, it enters the sphere of the Present from the still living Past. It is elusive and hard to challenge, like the ghost. Only analytical insight, with fair appraisal of its historical significance, can break through the intangible envelope and release the energy informing it.'[2]

In real life a necromancer seldom has the legendary Odysseus' luck of drawing as his 'opposite number' in the lottery a Teiresias who honours a gentleman's agreement by delivering his oracle in exchange for the draught of revivifying blood and then tactfully relieving the necromancer of his presence.[3] And, even when the shade with which the necromancer has business to transact does behave in this gentlemanly way, his unwanted fellow phantoms neutralize his tact by their importunity. When Odysseus was engaged in raising the ghost of Teiresias, the dark life-blood had no sooner spurted into the sacrificial trench than

'they came flocking up from Erebus, the souls of the lifeless dead: brides and their grooms; old men with a tale of sufferings to match their tale of years; and maidens in the springtide of their sorrow, which was as fresh as the bloom of their youth. There came warriors, too, slain in battle, with their armour bedabbled in gore. All these in their multitudes came crowding round the trench from every quarter, with an unearthly clamour; and I, at their onset, was gripped by a blanching fear.'[4]

[1] Luke xvi. 26.
[2] Baynes, H. G.: *Mythology of the Soul* (London 1940, Baillière, Tindall & Cox; 1949, Methuen), p. 862.
[3] *Od.* XI, ll. 150–1.
[4] *Od.* XI, ll. 36–43. Lines 38–43 were rejected as spurious by the Alexandrian critics Zenodotus and Aristophanes on the unconvincing ground of an alleged inconsistency with what follows them.

Odysseus, being Odysseus, did not lose his nerve, disconcerted though he was. As Circe had counselled him, he drew his sword and, squatting behind his trench with the weapon outstretched over it at arm's length, he 'fended off the feeble forms of the dead from approaching the blood' until he had done his business with Teiresias.[1] In thus inflexibly carrying out his instructions, this man of many sufferings and superhuman powers[2] performed a prodigy of strongmindedness; for, in the uneasy interval before the gentlemanly seer Teiresias presented himself, the first ghost to importune him was his unburied comrade Elpenor's,[3] while the second was his mother Anticleia's.[4] After Teiresias' ghost had duly appeared and delivered his oracle and withdrawn, Odysseus let down his guard over the blood-offering and gave access to other ghosts in a queue, with his own mother inevitably at the head of it;[5] but in the end he found it advisable to beat a hasty retreat for fear that the hazardous situation might get out of hand.

'After saying his say, Hêraklês went back to the House of Hades, while I stood my ground by the trench in case I might be approached by yet another of the hero warriors who had met their deaths aforetime. And, as like as not, I might have gone on seeing warriors of olden times according to my choice; but, before I could sate my curiosity, there came flocking upon me countless hordes of the dead with an unearthly din, and I, at their onset, was gripped by a blanching fear lest queenly Persephone might send upon me from Hades the Gorgon's head—fell monster's countenance.'[6]

Odysseus thereupon acted with a characteristic promptness which saved him from the fate that Pandora had brought upon Mankind when she had let loose all the scourges of human life by lifting the lid of her jar.[7] Odysseus made off in a trice, got his crew and himself back on board, and baffled his spectral assailants, as a living German army was to be baffled one day at Dunkirk, by putting the insulating breadth of Ocean Stream between the pursuers and the pursued.[8] This happy ending is not, however, a guaranteed outcome of the necromancer's adventure. A legendary Odysseus has his historical fellow adventurers who have not escaped so lightly.

(II) THE CHALLENGE FROM THE *REVENANT* AND A PAIR OF ALTERNATIVE POSSIBLE RESPONSES

(a) THE ANTAEAN REBOUND AND THE ATLANTEAN STANCE

When Odysseus had the temerity to trespass on the threshold of the Underworld, he duly won his sought-for oracle from the reanimated ghost of Teiresias, but, in winning it, also put himself in jeopardy of being made to pay for his impertinence by being confronted with the Gorgon's head. What was this *visio malefica* that Odysseus thus both

[1] *Od.* XI, ll. 48–50 and 82.   [2] Πολύτλας δῖος 'Οδυσσεύς.—*Odyssey, passim.*
[3] *Od.* XI, ll. 51–83.   [4] *Od.* XI, ll. 84–89.
[5] *Od.* XI, ll. 152–625.   [6] *Od.* XI, ll. 626–35.
[7] Hesiod: *Works and Days,* ll. 42–105, especially ll. 90–104.
[8] *Od.* XI, ll. 636–40.

courted and dreaded? It was the nemesis to which every necromancer exposes himself whenever he scores a success in playing his dangerous professional game. Thanks to his successful interrogation of Teiresias' obliging shade, Odysseus secured invaluable information in advance[1] about his own stormy future; it was invaluable because this uncanny foreknowledge just enabled the hero to master his fate by winning his way home to Ithaca and there recovering possession of his lost wife, property, house, and kingdom. Odysseus thus 'got away with' what he wanted in playing his game with the Infernal Powers; but other players, of hardly less note, have proved either less adroit or else perhaps merely more unfortunate.

Jacob, for example, in his nocturnal encounter at Peniel,[2] where he 'was left alone and there wrestled a man with him until the breaking of the day', won a blessing from this formidable jinn that was no less precious than a gracious Teiresias' oracle; but a legendary Canaanite Jacob brought tribulation on himself for lack of a legendary Hellenic Odysseus' saving sense of measure. Jacob did not know when he had had enough; and his insufferably obstinate terms to his foiled supernatural adversary— 'I will not let thee go except thou bless me'—cost him the dislocation of a major joint which left him lame for life. Jacob's retrospective boast— 'I have seen God face to face and my life is preserved'—though it may perhaps have been no exaggeration of the truth, was at the same time admittedly no cure for the boaster's permanent disablement. His fateful adversary had left an abiding mark on Jacob for evil as well as for good.

A legendary Canaanite Pygmalion, who fell in love with a statue that was the work of his own art, was extricated by the gods from the predicament into which this princely artificer had brought himself through an idolization of his own technique[3] by their gracious act of breathing the breath of life into the nostrils of an ivory ikòn which, thanks to this auspicious supernatural intervention, miraculously became a living soul.[4] As for a legendary post-Christian Western Frankenstein, who had no claim upon God's grace, this eponymous hero of a latter-day society came to an awful end which both a Pygmalion and a Jacob had escaped. Frankenstein's monster, like Jacob's jinn, did eventually take his departure; but in this Modern Western version of a Syriac myth the roles were reversed; for in this latter-day encounter it was the necromancer, and not the ghost, that took the initiative in breaking off the engagement, and the inhuman creature of a human creator's science made off with a curse instead of a blessing on his lips. 'I go, but remember: I shall be with you on your wedding night.'[5] While Jacob got off from his wrestling match with the Powers of Darkness none the worse for it beyond being lamed for life, Frankenstein's penalty was the loss of his birthright of creativity.

Is it possible to define more closely this terrifying challenge from the *revenant* which is the price of invoking the *revenant's* aid in seeking a response to some pressing challenge in the realm of current life? Such

[1] Detailed in *Od.* XI, ll. 92–137.   [2] Gen. xxxii. 24–32.
[3] See IV. iv. 423–65.   [4] Gen. ii. 7.
[5] Shelley, Mary: *Frankenstein, or the Modern Prometheus*, chap. 20.

a definition is perhaps implicit in the words in which Frankenstein was addressed by the monster whom he had conjured into life: 'You are my creator, but I am your master;—obey!'[1] It looks as if the relation between the necromancer and the ghost that he has raised can never be one of psychic parity. One or other of the two parties must be master, and one or other slave; and the shade of the departed has no sooner been reanimated by the sorcerer's *tour de force* than the live man and the *revenant* find themselves plunged—and this inevitably and immediately —into a contest which is deadly because a vital issue is at stake.

What is going to be the gruesome blood-transfusion's ultimate effect? Is the necromancer going to gain more by giving the reanimated ghost the strength to work for him, supposing that the ghost proves amenable, than he is going to lose by proportionately diminishing his own strength and thereby affording the ghost an opening for establishing an ascendancy over the living man who has recalled the dead to life, supposing that the ghost chooses thus to take advantage of his resuscitator's self-inflicted weakness? Is the rash communicant with the dread powers of an Underworld to return inspired by a muse or possessed by a devil? Is his encounter with the dead to be a stimulus or an obsession? Manifestly either of these alternatives is a possible outcome, since it is already manifest that the challenge from a *revenant* is a particular form of a general phenomenon, discernible in encounters of all kinds, that has come to our attention in more than one previous context. A personality's response to the psychic impact of another personality may be the kindling of a creative 'light caught from a leaping flame',[2] or it may be a submission to the deadening 'social drill' which we have labelled 'mimesis'.[3] A military uniform that may stiffen a soldier's plastic human nature into the superhuman inflexibility of a hero under fire may also stiffen it into the sub-human lifelessness of an automaton on the parade-ground; and the same pair of alternative possible outcomes presents itself when the challenger happens to be a *revenant* from the Underworld of a Dead Past as when he happens to be a living contemporary.

In the language of a nascent post-Modern Western science of Psychology,

'The atavistic attraction of a primordial image can become so overpowering at certain crises that only a disciplined devotion to reality, a devotion that cannot be uprooted or deflected, is able to withstand it. . . . The alternative possibility contained in the symbol can be apprehended by the term "psychological creation". . . . The ambivalence of the anima-figure now appears as an alternative to which Consciousness is able to respond in two ways. To . . . become identified with the archaic image would be one way. To express the Unconscious creatively, but to maintain psychological responsibility towards the expression, would be the other. Both ways are possible; the choice is fundamentally a question of attitude.'[4]

These two alternative possible attitudes have been given classical expressions in an Hellenic mythology.

---

[1] Shelley, Mary: *Frankenstein, or the Modern Prometheus*, chap. 20.
[2] Plato's Letters, No. 7, 341B–E, quoted in III. iii. 245.
[3] See III. iii. 245–8 and 374; IV. iv. 123–9, 131–2, and 234; V. v. 20; and V. vi. 255.
[4] Baynes, H. G.: *Mythology of the Soul* (London 1940, Baillière, Tindall & Cox; 1949, Methuen), pp. 701–2.

When Hêraklês was making his westward trek along the length of North Africa to find the Garden of the Hesperides and bring back thence the guardian nymphs' life-giving apples, he ran across two giants, Antaeus and Atlas. Before Hêraklês' advent, Antaeus had proved an invincible adversary for all comers who had ever been so rash as to join battle with him; for this sanguine giant was a son of Mother Earth; and, if ever, in any wrestling-match, his antagonist contrived to throw him, the momentary victor was merely defeating himself; for, in thus causing Antaeus to renew his contact with his mother, he was giving him the opportunity to replenish his vitality from its original source, and the giant refreshed invariably scored a decisive victory on the rebound from his momentary prostration. When Hêraklês accepted Antaeus's challenge and was baffled, in his turn, by this Earth-child's buoyant recoveries, he found a solution for the Antaean problem by strangling the wretch to death while holding him aloft off the ground. In sharp contrast to the series of triumphs that Antaeus had won before Hêraklês' advent, the experience with which Atlas had met had been the discouraging one of defeat. This giant Atlas was the child, not of the goddess Earth, but of the titan Iapetos;[1] he had taken part, together with the rest of Iapetos's brood, in the Titans' unsuccessful assault on the Olympian citadel of the usurper high god Zeus; and, when the battle was over, the malicious leader of a victorious war-band of interloping barbarian gods had exercised his ingenuity in devising retaliatory torments for his defeated adversaries. Whatever we may think of the dooms of Menoetius and Prometheus, we must admit that, in the sentence passed on Atlas, Zeus did 'make the punishment fit the crime'.[2]

'The baleful mind of Atlas plumbs the depths of all the seas, but the giant's own frame holds up the tall pillars that keep Earth and Heaven asunder.'[3]

'Atlas, compelled by an overmastering constraint, holds up wide Heaven, supporting it with his head and his unwearying hands in his station at the ends of the Earth, just on the hither side of the shrill Hesperides; for this was the doom that was dealt out to him by the wit of Zeus.'[4]

Atlas's crime had been an attempt to scale high Heaven; the punishment inflicted on him was to hold high Heaven up; and this was the stance in which the melancholy giant was eventually found by his visitor Hêraklês. In order to grasp the relation between an Atlantean stance and an Antaean rebound, we have to recognize that the Earth, off whose fostering breast a buoyant Antaeus was perpetually bouncing up like an india-rubber ball, and the Firmament whose dead weight was constantly pressing down upon the head and hands of an immobilized Atlas, are merely two different aspects of one and the same psychic continent as seen from opposite quarters of the spiritual compass. This depressing Firmament and refreshing Earth are, in psychic reality, identical. 'The choice' between falling into an Atlantean stance and making an Antaean rebound is in truth 'fundamentally a question of attitude'.

---

[1] Hesiod: *Theogony*, l. 509. This Hellenic Iapetos is the Japheth of the Book of Genesis. [2] Gilbert, W. S., in *The Mikado*.
[3] *Od.*, Book I, ll. 52–54. [4] Hesiod: *Theogony*, ll. 517–20.

The antithesis between the Antaean and the Atlantean attitude has
been traced out in a Platonic dialogue, staged in a post-Marxian Russian
social setting, which is no less illuminating if it is myth than if it happens to be history.[1]

'In the summer of A.D. 1920 the two philosophers, M. Gershenson and
V. Ivanov, were living in the Convalescent Home for Scientific and
Literary Workers in Moscow. Each of them was installed in a corner of
the common room. From one corner to the other they exchanged twelve
letters about problems of the Philosophy of History. . . .

'The standpoint represented by Gershenson was one of an anarchic
hostility to Culture.

' "All the spiritual achievements of Mankind, [he wrote] all the
wealth of intuitions, factual knowledge and moral standards that has been
garnered and fortified in the course of the centuries—all this has latterly
become burdensome to me. It weighs on me like some throttling yoke,
like some dress that is excessively heavy and excessively warm.[2] This
feeling has been distressing me for a long time past; but it used to descend
on me only occasionally, and even then never for long at a time, while
now it has become a chronic experience. As I see it, it would really be the
greatest possible blessing if one could plunge into Lethe and, in those
waters, flush out of one's soul, without leaving a trace, the recollection of
all religions and systems of philosophy, all factual knowledge, all arts and
all poetry, in order to step out on to the [farther] bank as naked as
Primaeval Man, and there—naked, unencumbered, and joyful—stretch
out one's bare arms, in freedom, till they touched Heaven. There would
be only one thought out of the Past that one would wish to retain in one's
consciousness, and that is: How burdensome, how oppressively hot, it was
in those [now discarded] clothes! How blissfully unencumbered one feels
without them!" '

We may pause at this point in our quotation to observe in parenthesis
that both the depression and the yearning which Gershenson has here

[1] The dialogue, as reproduced here, is a translation from the German text of Ernst
Robert Curtius's *Deutsche Geist in Gefahr* (Stuttgart and Berlin 1932, Deutsche Verlags-
Anstalt), pp. 116–19. Professor Curtius records that he had extracted it from the journal
Die Kreatur, Jahrgang I, Heft 2 (1926). The passages here translated have been quoted
with the permission of the author and the publishers.

[2] This inhibiting effect of the incubus of the Past has been noticed by Hume in his
essay *Of the Rise and Progress of the Arts and Sciences*. In Hume's opinion, however, the
impositions of a dead antecedent civilization are not so paralysing as those of some living
community in one's own world which has forged ahead of its neighbours and consequently made an impact on them comparable to that of an alien culture.

'Perhaps it may not be for the advantage of any nation to have the arts imported from
their neighbours in too great perfection. This extinguishes emulation and sinks the
ardour of the generous youth. So many models of Italian painting brought into England,
instead of exciting our artists, is the cause of their small progress in that noble art. The
same, perhaps, was the case of Rome when it received the arts from Greece. That multitude of polite productions in the French language, dispersed all over Germany and the
North, hinder these nations from cultivating their own language, and keep them still
dependent on their neighbours for those elegant entertainments.

'It is true, the Ancients had left us models, in every kind of writing, which are highly
worthy of admiration. But, besides that they were written in languages known only to
the learned—besides this, I say, the comparison is not so perfect or entire between
modern wits and those who lived in so remote an age. Had Waller been born in Rome
during the reign of Tiberius, his first productions had been despised when compared to
the finished odes of Horace. But in this island the superiority of the Roman poet
diminished nothing from the fame of the English. We esteemed ourselves sufficiently
happy that our climate and language could produce but a faint copy of so excellent an
original.'

depicted in the light of his own experience are sensations that Atlas is experiencing while he is performing his interminable fatigue-duty of holding up the Firmament.

The melancholy giant's state of depression can be taken for granted; his longing for release is attested by the alacrity with which he accepted Hêraklês' offer when the wayfaring demigod proposed to give Atlas a holiday by temporarily taking the giant's burden on his own shoulders, on the understanding that Atlas would employ his ticket of leave on the mission of collecting for his temporary liberator a basketful of life-giving apples from the neighbouring Garden of the Hesperides. Atlas duly performed this part of the bargain; but, when he came back, apples in hand, and, standing, for once, at ease, saw his intolerable load resting on other stalwart shoulders, he was seized by a sudden overwhelming temptation to play on his obliging visitor the mean trick of leaving him eternally *planté là* in a stance in which it was impossible for the living pillar to get out from under his incubus unless some voluntary substitute should first step in under to relieve him. According to the Hellenic myth, Hêraklês—stimulated to an unwonted intellectual activity by an emergency in which brawn could not serve instead of brain—hit upon a ruse for tricking the dishonest Titan into reassuming his pristine burden and thereby enabling his temporary *remplaçant* to slip out again after all.

We can now see, however, from a chance disclosure in Gershenson's account of the Atlantean state of mind, that Atlas would inevitably have retrapped himself, even if Hêraklês had not had his uncharacteristic 'brain-wave'. For Gershenson's one idea of how to use an imaginarily recaptured liberty is to reach up and touch the very Firmament from whose pressure he imagines himself released; and the Atlantean touch has a magic effect which is the opposite of the Antaean. When Antaeus touches a motherly Earth, he rebounds from her bosom; but, when Atlas touches a step-fatherly Heaven, he clamps the load down upon his head. Atlas' predicament looks rather like a hopeless case. At infinity, Atlas' interminable stance seems bound to lose him his life, either by freezing him into the state of petrifaction that is a living creature's penalty for having beheld the Gorgon's head,[1] or alternatively by goading him into Samson's suicidal act of pulling down the roof in order to die with the Philistines.[2] But we must not anticipate the sequel to the story in our post-Marxian Russian version of it.

'Ivanov's answer to Gershenson contains the following significant passages:

' "I will tell you what is the real origin of the mood to which you are so painfully subject at the moment. It is a reflection of a particular attitude towards Culture—an attitude in which Culture is experienced, not as a live treasure-house of gifts, but as a system of exquisitely subtle constraints. That is not surprising; for, after all, the goal that Human Culture has pursued has been precisely to make itself into a strait-waistcoat. As I see it, though, Culture is something very different: it is a guide of Erôs and a hierarchy of venerations."

---

[1] This is the common fate of 'arrested civilizations' (see III. iii. 1–111), 'fossils' (see I. i. 35 and 90–92), and 'Tithoni' (see VI. vii. 47–52).
[2] Judges xvi. 30.

'Gershenson, however, insists upon Primitivism like the true blue Rousseauite that he is:

' "I would give up [he writes] all the factual knowledge and all the ideas that I have gleaned from books, and would sacrifice, into the bargain, the whole of my own intellectual superstructure that I have succeeded in erecting on those academic foundations, in exchange for the joy of personally achieving, entirely out of my own experience, one single original act of knowledge. It might be as simple as you please, but it would have the freshness of a summer's morn."

'The discussion is then carried to a deeper level by Ivanov's passing beyond the limits of a merely cultural ideal and introducing the transcendence of the Absolute.

' "A man who has faith in God [he writes] will not consent at any price to see in his faith merely one of the constituents of Culture. On the other hand, a man who has become a slave of Culture will inevitably diagnose Faith as a cultural phenomenon, whatever may be the exact definition of Faith that he goes on to work out. He may define it as an inherited outlook and an historically determined psychic *habitus*, or define it in terms of Metaphysics and Poetry, or define it, again, as a socially formative force and an ethical standard: it all comes to the same thing. . . . The real point is this: our faith in an Absolute—in which we are already in touch with something that is not Culture—is the issue on which our destiny hangs. If we have this faith it gives us an inward freedom which is veritably Life itself; if we do not have it, our unbelief condemns us to an inward enslavement by a Culture that has long since become godless in principle through the effect that it has had of imprisoning Man in himself (as has been definitively expounded by Kant). Faith alone—and, by 'faith', I mean a complete renunciation of the Fall of Man, for which 'Culture' is another name[1]—will enable you to overcome that 'temptation' of yours which you have felt so deeply. But Original Sin cannot be eradicated by a superficial obliteration of its outward marks and manifestations. To un-learn our literacy and to 'expel the Muses' (to speak with Plato's words) would be merely a palliative; the letters of the Alphabet would reflect, all over again, the old unalterable spiritual constitution of the prisoner fettered to the rock in the Platonic Cave.[2] Rousseau's dream is the offspring of unbelief. On the other hand, living in God means living no longer entirely in the realm of Relativity which is the realm of Human Culture; it means rising above Culture into Freedom in one part of one's own being."

'The two friends did not succeed in arriving at an understanding with one another; but Ivanov's way of working out the idea implicit in Humanism is a clarification that is of such truly decisive significance for ourselves that I will take the liberty of quoting one last utterance of his.

' "Culture itself, in the true sense of the word, is, as I see it, no dead level, no plain bestrewn with ruins, no field sown with dead men's bones. Culture has in it, moreover, something veritably hallowed; for Culture is a recollection, not only of our forefathers' terrestrial form and outward appearance, but also of their spiritual achievements in dedicating Mankind to ideals. It is a live, everlasting recollection which, in souls that become participants in these dedications, is undying. These dedications have been bequeathed by our forefathers for the benefit of their remotest

---

[1] See the passages of works of Plato's that have been discussed in the present Study, IV. iv. 585–8.—A.J.T.
[2] Plato: *Respublica*, 514A–521C, quoted in this Study in III. iii. 249–52.—A.J.T.

descendants; and no jot of the once new letters shall pass away;[1] for the Spirit of Mankind on which they are stamped is one and indivisible. In this sense, Culture is not just something monumental; over and above that, it is a spiritual initiative; for the faculty of recollection, which is Culture's sovereign ruler, permits the true servants of Culture to become participants in our forefathers' 'initiations' and communicates to these faithful servants, in the act of renewing these initiations in their souls, the power to make new beginnings and new departures.

' "Recollection is a dynamic principle, in contrast to an oblivion that signifies lassitude, cessation of movement, decline, and regression to a condition of relative torpidity. We share Nietzsche's determination to keep a sharp watch on ourselves, to make sure that we do not harbour in our souls the poison of disintegration, infection, and 'decadence'. What is 'decadence'? It is a sense of an exquisitely subtle organic bond with the monumental tradition of a dead civilisation (*hohen Kultur*), combined with an oppressively proud consciousness of being, ourselves, the last epigoni in the series. In other words, a recollection that no longer has any life in it because it has lost its spirit of initiative, and therefore does not any longer give us any power of participating in the initiations of our forefathers or any impulse towards taking the initiative effectively, is tantamount to an awareness that 'the oracles are dumb'[2]—which is, as a matter of fact, the title given by a decadent Plutarch to one of his works (*De Defectu Oraculorum*)".'

In this last-quoted passage, Ivanov is diagnosing the nature of 'the Antaean rebound' in terms of Socrates' doctrine of ἀνάμνησις[3] and Jung's concept of Primordial Images. 'If the Soul is to achieve this recovery of self-possession (*diese Selbstbesinnung*), it has, as we can learn from Ivanov, to comply with one indispensable condition: it must go back into the very innermost depths;'[4] and then, when it has risen again from this pearl-fishing diver's descent into Hell, it has to resist an Atlantean temptation 'to become identified with the archaic image'[5] that it has retrieved from the Abyss, in order 'to express the Unconscious creatively'[6] in a masterful act of metabolization that is 'the alternative possibility'.[7] A living soul that does thus succeed in accomplishing an Antaean rebound from the renaissance of a dead antecedent culture acquires thereby 'the power to make new beginnings and new departures' because its creative way of handling what it has resuscitated generates the *élan* that is the gait of growth[8]—in contrast to the mechanicalness of the mimesis[9] that is the inadequate Atlantean response to an identical challenge from the same *revenant*.

If to 'have life and have it more abundantly',[10] in the spiritual and not merely in the physical sense of the word, is the true end of Man, the possibility, opened up by a renaissance, of making an Antaean rebound is an opportunity that is not too dearly bought at the price of incurring the inevitable risk of stiffening, instead, into an Atlantean stance. We can also now perhaps see why it was that, in Modern Western minds, the renaissance of a dead antecedent culture, which in reality is no more

[1] Matt. v. 18. Cp. Luke xvi. 17.—A.J.T.
[2] Milton, John: *Hymn on the Morning of Christ's Nativity*, Stanza 19.—A.J.T.
[3] See p. 115, above. [4] Curtius, op. cit., p. 119.
[5] Baynes, op. cit., quoted on p. 142, above. [6] Ibid. [7] Ibid.
[8] See III. iii. 112-27. [9] See IV. iv. 119-33. [10] John x. 10.

than a neutral event in the issue between Life and Death, should have so incongruously acquired a connotation that associated it with a spring-like outburst of fresh vitality. In the history of a fifteenth-century Italian renaissance of the Hellenic culture, which had been canonized as 'the Renaissance' *sans phrase* in a subsequent Modern Western tradition,[1] the repetitive rebirth of something that had been born before was followed, *resiliente Antaeo*, by the unprecedented new birth of something that was now being born for the first time. These two events were so far from being identical that the second of them had to fight for its life—in a strenuous 'Battle of the Books'[2]—in order to make good its debatable birthright. In the sequel to this fifteenth-century renaissance in the Western World there were unmistakably Atlantean tendencies warring against those that were manifestly Antaean; but, by dint of ignoring these Atlantean symptoms, having no eye for any except the Antaean, and identifying these with the foregoing renaissance[3] of Hellenism that had provided the occasion of this mighty Antaean rebound in Modern Western history, Western minds had contrived to invest 'the Renaissance', and therefore the generic term 'renaissance' as well, with an aura of vitality and creativity strangely out of keeping with a Cimmerian fog that is the genuine atmosphere of the Odyssean and all other 'necyïa'.

(*b*) A SURVEY OF ANTAEAN AND ATLANTEAN REACTIONS[4]

If we now take a survey of responses to the challenge presented by renaissances, we shall find the examples of Atlantean stances preponderating over those of Antaean rebounds in the ubiquity of their distribution among the divers provinces of social life, if not in the sheer weight of their numbers. Whereas the unequivocal examples of the Antaean rebound seem to be confined to the two fields of Religion and Literature, we find the Atlantean stance not only likewise strongly represented in both these fields, but also presenting itself in the fields of Politics, the Visual Arts, and Pilgrimages, in which no examples of the Antaean rebound are forthcoming. In surveying the Soul's reactions to renaissances, we shall also find, as we have already found in surveying its reactions to encounters between contemporaries, that there are instances—and these perhaps not the least interesting and important of those on our muster-roll—which cannot be classified exclusively under either of two antithetical heads, but have to be pronounced ambivalent. In the array of reactions to renaissances, cases of ambivalency present themselves in the fields of Religion, Politics, the Visual Arts, Philosophy, and Law; and in Philosophy and Law they seem to have the field to themselves.

The supreme example of an Antaean rebound is the sequel, in the soul

---

[1] See pp. 1-5, above.   [2] See pp. 68-69, above.

[3] In thus identifying a birth of something new with a new birth of something old, the Modern Western literary purveyors of the French word *renaissance* were doing what had been done with the Greek word *palingenesia* in a post-Alexandrine chapter of Hellenic history (see V. v. 27, n. 2, and V. vi. 172-3). They were taking liberties with the literal meaning—a new birth of something old—which had been the original usage of the word, in order to invest it with a new significance that was hardly legitimate.

[4] In order to avoid an unnecessary multiplication of footnotes, the writer has refrained, in this chapter, from giving references to the survey of renaissances in X. B (ii), above.

of Saint Francis of Assisi, to his evocation of the spirit of Christ. An *imitatio Christi* which would have been intolerably presumptuous if it had not been unselfconsciously humble was proved to have been no mechanical act of mimesis by the light of the leaping flame that seared the saint's body with the stigmata of its lightning-like passage as it kindled Christ's spirit in his soul. In the histories of the civilizations of the third generation it would be hard to descry any other soul that had won such grace from so hazardously high a spiritual venture; but, when we pass from this unique evocation of Christ's own spirit to evocations of the spirit of His Apostles, we find more than one example of the Antaean rebound from this still lofty yet not quite Everestian spiritual altitude. This creative reaction is exemplified in the souls of those other Western saints who set themselves to lead an apostolic life, both outside the fold of the Western Christian Church of the day, as heretics, and inside it, as friars of the Orders of Saint Francis and Saint Dominic, in the twelfth and thirteenth centuries of the Christian Era;[1] and it is exemplified again in the souls of a John Wesley and his companions and successors, who in the eighteenth and nineteenth centuries were moved with the same compassion[2] for shepherdless sheep scattered abroad in urban wildernesses.

An Antaean rebound was likewise the sequel to the evocation of a ghost of Jewish Aniconism in the Protestant fraction of a fissured Modern Western Christian Church; for this resuscitated tabu on the representation of the Godhead in visual form was a reminder of the greatness of the spiritual gulf across which the encounter between God and Man takes place; and, the keener the human soul's sense of the distance between these two spiritual poles, the higher the tension of the current that streams between them in a vaulting arc.

Iconoclasm, however, is not enough in itself to ensure an Antaean rebound—as is attested by its Atlantean outcome in the history of a sister Christian Church. Though the Iconoclastic Movement in Orthodox Christendom petered out, as we have seen, in a compromise in which the Iconodules had the best of the bargain, it did not fail to fulfil its first imperial patron Leo Syrus's purpose of disciplining the Orthodox Christian Church into becoming an obedient humble servant of an East Roman *imperium redivivum*.[3] Nor was this bitted and bridled Church afterwards any more happily inspired when it evoked the ghost of a Jewry in diasporà[4] in order to keep itself still in existence after its subjugation by an East Roman Imperial Government had resulted in the breakdown and disintegration of the Orthodox Christian Civilization and the imposition of peace on the main body of Orthodox Christendom by an alien universal state in the shape of the Ottoman Empire. In eventually consenting to serve in an Ottoman régime as a *millet*, as in previously consenting to serve in an East Roman régime as a department of state, the Orthodox Church was accepting the sentence passed on Atlas by Zeus in the Hellenic myth.

[1] See IV. iv. 369–71, 558–60, 562, and 652–6.
[2] Matt. ix. 36 and xiv. 14; Mark vi. 34.
[3] See IV. iv. 346–53 and 592–623.
[4] This diasporan organization of Jewry has been noticed in IX. viii. 272–313.

Moreover, a Western Protestantism that had reacted with an Antaean rebound to an evocation of a Jewish tabu on graven images, from which an Orthodox Christendom had recoiled into an Atlantean stance, did not escape Atlas' fate when it evoked another ghost of Judaism in the shape of Sabbatarianism; and a similar fate overtook a latter-day Islamic Society when it evoked, out of the past of Islam, a pristine puritanism in and after the eighteenth century of the Christian Era[1] and a pristine Shi'ism at the turn of the fifteenth and sixteenth centuries.[2] These successive revivals of two movements in the history of Primitive Islam, which had been at daggers drawn in their original epiphanies, both had the uniform effect of drawing down upon a latter-day Islamic Society's devoted head the incubus of a pair of spiritual maladies—militancy and formalism—which had always been Islam's besetting sins, and which had never failed to seize any opportunity of fastening upon her again whenever she had succeeded for a season in rising above them and momentarily shaking them off.

It is impossible to guess which type of reaction might have been precipitated by the evocation, first in Orthodox and then in Western Christendom, of the ghost of an 'Adoptionism' that appears to have preceded the 'Conceptionist' presentation of Christianity and to have survived in an Antitauran fastness in order to re-emerge from there, in the ninth century of the Christian Era, in the shape of Paulicianism. A ninth-century Paulician movement in Eastern Anatolia, and a Bogomilism and a Catharism whose subsequent invasions of Europe were a murdered Paulicianism's posthumous revenge, were each in turn repressed by physical force[3] at too early a stage for it to be possible for us to know them by their fruits.[4] There are other reactions to the evocation of a ghost from the Past in the field of Religion which compel us to classify them, not as unidentifiable, but as ambivalent, by displaying unmistakably Antaean and unmistakably Atlantean symptoms side by side.

In a modern chapter of Western history, for example, we have seen a renaissance of an Augustinian predestinarianism, which had persistently reasserted itself in the successive forms of a Protestant Calvinism, a Tridentine Roman Catholic Jansenism, and a post-Christian and anti-Christian Marxism, first generating Antaean outbursts of energy and enterprise and then freezing the Western body social into an Atlantean posture[5] in which this colossus's feet of clay were sundered by an unbridgeable gulf of 'unplumb'd, salt, estranging sea'[6] insulating race from race, whether these were the spiritual races of the Elect and the Damned,

---

[1] See IX. viii. 250 and 602.   [2] See I. i. 366–400.
[3] See IV. iv. 364–9 and 624–34. The 'manifest destiny' of Paulicianism had been to take the place, in Orthodox Christendom, of a 'Conceptionist' Christianity which, in both its Iconoclast and its Iconodule vein, had failed to save the Church from becoming the servant of a resuscitated Hellenic universal state. The 'manifest destiny' of Catharism had been to take the place, in Western Christendom, of a Catholic Christianity which had been failing to serve as a good shepherd for sheep astray in the strange social milieu that had been conjured up in Western Christendom by a resuscitation of the Hellenic political institution of the idolized city-state.
[4] Matt. vii. 16–20 and xii. 33; Luke vi. 43–44.
[5] See V. v. 426–7 and 615–18.
[6] Arnold, Matthew: Isolation, quoted in II. i. 326.

or the social races of the Proletariat and the Bourgeoisie, or the physical races of the Albinos and the Negroes.[1]

A Modern Western Protestant Christian bibliolatry had had a no less ambivalent effect. In evoking this ghost from the Sheol of Christianity's Judaic past, Protestantism had released hidden waters of life in a galaxy of new fountains that had irrigated not only the Protestant countries in which they had welled up, but the whole of the Modern Western World. The translation of the Bible into the vernacular languages of the Protestant Western peoples had conferred on all Western vernacular languages alike, in Catholic as well as Protestant eyes,[2] a prestige that had previously been the monopoly of a dead Latin and Greek; the literary cultivation of a people's mother-tongue had prepared the ground for universal education; the microscopic study of a sacred text had been an apprenticeship in a higher criticism which could be, and duly was, applied thereafter in all fields of scholarship. These reactions to a Judaic idolization of the Bible had been Antaean indeed; yet the Atlantean responses to the same challenge had been no less portentous. The political nemesis of hallowing the local vernaculars of a society which was a linguistic Babel had been the grim epiphany of a Gorgon's head in the guise of a Linguistic Nationalism.[3] The moral and intellectual nemesis of deifying holy scriptures was a Protestant servitude, from which a still priest-ridden Tridentine Catholicism had remained free, to 'the letter that killeth'.[4] The Protestant deification of the Bible in the sixteenth century of the Christian Era had had the same deadening effect on spiritual life as the Muslim deification of the Qur'ān in the ninth century, and as the Sikh Granth-worshippers' caricature of this Muslim lapse into the mortal sin of polytheism (*shirk*).[5]

When we pass from Religion to Language and Literature, we find both a fifteenth-century Italian revival of Classical Latin and Ancient Greek in a Western World, and the perennial survival of Sanskrit in a Hindu World, uniformly giving rise to an Antaean outburst of literary creativity in living vernacular languages. As a Sanskrit Rāmāyana inspired a Hindī *Rām-charit Mānas*, so the Ancient Greek and Latin classics in divers literary genres inspired corresponding works in Tuscan, Castilian, and Portuguese, in Northern French and Midland English, in High German and Low Dutch. So far from checking the progress of a Western polyglot vernacular literature which, since its birth in the eleventh century, had blossomed in French, Provençal, and Tuscan in turn, the fifteenth-century Italian renaissance of Latin and Greek gave an impetus to the vernacular literary movement that carried it from Italy and France into all the other linguistic provinces of an Early Modern Western World. The new mastery of Ciceronian Latin which was achieved by an Erasmus did not lure his fellow Westerners into abandoning the literary cultivation of their own mother tongues in order

---

[1] See II. i. 207–49.
[2] For example, the literary form of a High German language that had been created by Luther in his act of translating the Bible had been adopted by German-speaking Catholics as well as by German-speaking Protestants.
[3] See IV. iv. 185–90 and IX. viii. 536–8.
[4] 2 Cor. iii. 6.   [5] See I. i. 9, n. 3.

to revert to a reanimated dead language which had been shown, by the great Humanist's performance, to be a superb medium for conveying all the thoughts and feelings that Erasmus's contemporaries in the Western World might be moved to express in prose; it inspired them with the ambition to develop their divers living vernaculars into adequately massive vehicles for carrying a Ciceronian load, and, *a fortiori*, to refine them into adequately subtle instruments for catching, from a Horace or a Virgil, strains that could find a convincing echo only in some language that was still alive on the lips of a latter-day Western poet. An Erasmian Latin prose found its *métier*, and kept it for some two hundred years, as the *lingua franca* of an early Modern Western Republic of Letters; but, when, towards the end of the seventeenth century of the Christian Era, the Humanists' cult of Hellenism suffered its decisive defeat in the controversy between the respective champions of 'the Ancients' and 'the Moderns', even this limited function of serving as an oecumenical linguistic medium for Western philosophy, science, and scholarship was captured from Erasmus's Latin by Bossuet's French. The transition may be caught in the act in the table of contents of the collected works of Leibnitz (*vivebat* A.D. 1646–1716).

These incidents in a Modern Western reaction to a Late Medieval Italian renaissance of Latin and Greek were Antaean indeed; but they were also Antaean with a vengeance. A living French vernacular which, in the *grand siècle* of Modern French history, came to be elevated above its peers to an invidious eminence, in order to play a discarded Latin's oecumenical role, had neither the literary prestige nor the political neutrality that had made Latin so apt an instrument for this indispensable Western cultural purpose. The failure of French fully to fill the formidable linguistic vacuum produced by the abandonment of Latin was the first symptom, in this cultural encounter between the Modern West and a ghost of Hellenism, of the stiffening of an Antaean rebound into an Atlantean stance; and this tragic *peripeteia* declared itself unmistakably when, in a Late Modern chapter of Western history, the local vernacular languages of the Western World began to prostitute to the political service of a parochial nationalism the literary gifts that had accrued to them in double measure from the Humanists' cult of the Hellenic classics and from the Protestants' cult of the Bible.[1]

This Atlantean aspect of the sequel to a fifteenth-century renaissance of Hellenism in the Western World was, however, relatively incon-

---

[1] Down to A.D. 1952 it looked as if the Hindu World might succeed in avoiding a corresponding aberration. There seemed to be little sign of any tendency for a polyglot Hindu Society's sense of oecumenical solidarity to disrupt itself into parochial national movements animated by the perverse ideal of manufacturing so many political fatherlands out of the areas in which the divers living vernacular languages of the Hindu World happened respectively to be current. If it were indeed true that the Hindus had not reacted in this unfortunate Western way to the literary cultivation of local living vernaculars under the stimulus of a classical language and literature derived from an antecedent civilization, the Hindus' happier record in this respect was perhaps the consequence of external pressure rather than the fruit of innate virtue. Whereas the Modern Western World had been virtually free from external pressure from A.D. 1683, when the 'Osmanlis had met with their second, and decisive, reverse before the walls of Vienna, down to A.D. 1917, when the Bolsheviks had entered into the heritage of a Petrine Russian Empire, the Hindu World had been under Muslim pressure since the tenth century of the Christian Era, and under Western pressure since the eighteenth.

spicuous by comparison with the portentousness of the Atlantean reaction to a ninth-century renaissance of Hellenism in a Greek Orthodox
Christendom; for here, as we have seen, the recultivation of the Ancient
Greek classics stifled, instead of stimulating, the growth of a literature
in a living Modern Greek language. The few stunted shoots that had
succeeded in forcing their way up in competition with the choking
thorns[1] of a resurgent Hellenism would hardly have survived if the field
had not been drastically ploughed up again by aggressive Western
trespassers. A Modern Greek vernacular literature held its own—as far
as it did hold its own—against Byzantinism at the price of following a
Western lead; and, in the latest chapter of the history of this Graeco-
Occidental cultural intercourse, the archaizing Romanticism in which
the indigenous vernacular literatures of a Late Modern Western World
had proclaimed their self-enslavement to the service of a parochial
Nationalism was caricatured in a new-born Kingdom of Greece by the
perpetration of the καθαρεύουσα. A Modern Greek people that had just
liberated itself from an Ottoman political ascendancy promptly used its
newly won powers of self-determination to put its Modern Greek
mother tongue in Ancient Greek irons.

If this Atlantean reaction to a renaissance of Hellenism in Greek
Orthodox Christendom carried to extremes an Atlantean tendency that
is likewise discernible in the Western response to a challenge from the
same *revenant*, the whole-heartedly Antaean rebound of the living
vernacular languages of the Hindu World from their contact with a
maternal Sanskrit is offset by the hyper-Byzantine stance of the Chinese
main body of a Far Eastern World under the petrifying Gorgon stare
of the resuscitated Sinic classics. It will be seen that the field of Language
and Literature, like the field of Religion, was a debatable ground on
which an Antaean-minded Ivanov and an Atlantean-minded Gershenson
had fought inconclusive battles.

When we turn to Politics and the Visual Arts, we here find the
Atlantean reaction holding the field, save for one or two cases of ambivalence.

The classic political examples of the Atlantean stance are the avatars
of an antecedent civilization's universal state in the shapes of the Sui
and T'ang Empire in the Chinese main body of a Far Eastern World,
the East Roman Empire in a Greek Orthodox Christendom, and the
Cairene Caliphate in an Arabic Muslim World; and, if the Danubian
Hapsburg Monarchy, the Carolingian and Timurid empires, and the
caricature of a Chinese T'ang régime in the Far Eastern Civilization's
Japanese offshoot failed to play the same disastrously momentous part
in the histories of the Western Christian, Iranic Muslim, and Japanese
societies, this was merely because the Danubian Monarchy never succeeded in making itself more than nominally oecumenical,[2] while the

[1] Matt. xiii. 7; Luke viii. 7.
[2] See V. v. 325–7. The Danubian Hapsburg Monarchy had been called into existence
after the collapse of the Kingdom of Hungary in A.D. 1526 to serve as a carapace for
protecting the south-eastern land-frontier of the Western World against Ottoman aggression (see II. ii. 177–88); a union of the remnant of Hungary with the lands of the
Bohemian Crown and with the hereditary dominions of the House of Hapsburg proved

other three evocations all happened to prove expensively abortive.[1] In contrast to the social effect of a universal state in its original epiphany in the flesh, when it secures a postponement, though not a permanent remission, of the execution of a self-imposed sentence for a society that has already inflicted mortal wounds on itself, the social effect of the evocation of a dead and buried universal state's ghost is to force the growth of the evoking society to a hot-house pace at which it is condemning itself in advance to pay for a spell of artificially induced precocity by a premature breakdown in which Atlas involuntarily betrays and stultifies his mission by doing Samson's suicidally vindictive deed.

In the history of Western Christendom up to the date of writing mid-way through the twentieth century of the Christian Era, the same penalty had been paid already three times over for the sin of resuscitating the pre-Augustan Hellenic political institution of the deified parochial state; and in this parochial three-act play of Western political

to be a sufficient mobilization of Western strength to prevent the 'Osmanlis from making further continental conquests at Western expense; and the rest of the Western World therefore left it to the Danubian Hapsburg Monarchy to perform this public service for the Western common weal, without acknowledging its obligation to the Monarchy by submitting to the hegemony of a *Caesarea Maiestas* whose suzerainty, even within the limits of the Holy Roman Empire, had never been more than nominal, outside the frontiers of the hereditary dominions of the imperial house of the day, since 'the Great Interregnum' (*vacabat* A.D. 1254–73).

The role of unprofitable servants, who had done that which it was their duty to do, without having earned thereby any claim to recognition or reward (Luke xvii. 7–10), was naturally resented by the Hapsburgs of the Danubian line when it was imposed upon them by their Western beneficiaries, and they expressed this resentment by making their weight felt in the interior of the Western World whenever any slackening of the pressure from their Ottoman adversaries gave them an opportunity to neglect their task of serving as wardens of the West's anti-Ottoman marches. Such opportunities for occasional intervention in the domestic politics of the Western World were expended by the Danubian Hapsburg Power, with remarkable consistency, on Atlantean efforts to uphold lost causes. The ninety-years-long eclipse of the Ottoman Power from the death of Sultan Suleymān I in A.D. 1566 to the appointment of Mehmed Köprülü to be Grand Vezir in A.D. 1656—an eclipse that was only momentarily relieved by the meteoric career of Sultan Murād IV (*imperabat* A.D. 1623–40)—was spent by a Viennese *Caesarea Maiestas* in Counter-Reformational activities culminating in the Thirty Years' War (*gerebatur* A.D. 1618–48). The temporary exhaustion of the Ottoman Power after the Great War of A.D. 1682–99 was taken by the Danubian Hapsburg Power as an opportunity for joining forces with the Netherlands and Great Britain in order to repress King Louis XIV of France for the benefit of British interests. The relief from Ottoman pressure after the collapse of the Ottoman Power in the Russo-Turkish War of A.D. 1768–74 tempted the Danubian Hapsburg Monarchy into committing itself to the forlorn hope of repressing the hydra-headed 'Ideas of Seventeen Eighty-Nine', which had no sooner been crushed in their first avatar in the form of a Napoleonic imperialism than they reasserted themselves in the form of a nineteenth-century Romantic Nationalism which the Danubian Hapsburg Monarchy was so far from being able to repress that it was first encircled and finally disrupted by it.

It is true that these Atlantean reactions to the raising of a ghost of a Roman *Caesarea Maiestas* at Vienna were not entirely unaccompanied by Antaean symptoms. The most lively of these was the role which Vienna came to play as a melting-pot for transforming Orthodox Christians or ex-Orthodox Christian Uniates into Westerners. An eloquent memorial of this Antaean activity was the Vienna telephone directory (see VI. vii. 235 and IX. viii. 529–30); yet, when the history of the Danubian Hapsburg Monarchy from A.D. 1526 to A.D. 1918 is viewed as a whole in perspective, this Antaean twitch does not perceptibly relax the rigidity of the Monarchy's Atlantean stance.

[1] Charlemagne's abortive empire-building cost a nascent Western Society the recrudescence of a post-Hellenic social interregnum (see IV. iv. 490); Timūr's cost a nascent Iranic Muslim Society the loss of its opportunity to make itself the heir of the Eurasian Nomad World (see IV. iv. 496–500); the pseudo-T'ang régime that had been installed *de toutes pièces* in Yamato cost a nascent Japanese Society the harsh experience of subjection to the ascendancy of the unexotically crude marchmen who opened up the Kwanto (see II. ii. 158–9).

necromancy the tragedy had been more ironic than in the drama of resuscitated universal states, since, each time, the first effect had been an Antaean enhancement of vitality which had tempted self-betrayed Western victims of the Black Art to leap like rabbits into a noose which they themselves had set to wring their own necks. This had been the unvarying outcome of the successive resuscitations of a pre-Alexandrine Hellenic city-state in a Medieval Western Italy, Germany, and Flanders,[1] a post-Alexandrine Hellenic absolute monarchy in almost all provinces of an Early Modern Western World,[2] and an Hellenic Democracy in Late Modern Western states in which parliamentary constitutions of an indigenous Medieval Western pattern had either succeeded, as in England and her daughter communities, in surviving the impact of the two earlier waves of political Hellenization or else, as in other Western countries, had eventually reasserted themselves, under English inspiration, against the renaissance of a post-Alexandrine Hellenic absolutism.[3] The offspring of a resuscitated Hellenic Democracy's impact upon an indigenous Western Parliamentarism was a Nationalism from whose deadly toils a self-tormented Western World was struggling, for dear life, to extricate itself on the morrow of a Second World War.[4]

In the field of the Visual Arts a spectacular example of the Atlantean stance is presented by the sequel to the Modern Western World's reception of the Hellenic order of Architecture. The same Atlantean posture can be detected by a discerning eye in an Assyrian renaissance of a Sumeric style of bas-relief and in a Saïte renaissance of the minor arts of an Egyptiac 'Old Kingdom', while the tragi-comedy of an Atlantean snare set with an Antaean bait, which we have witnessed in the sequel to successive Western resuscitations of parochial Hellenic political institutions, is reproduced in the sequel to the abandonment of

[1] See III. iii. 299–310, 341–50, and 355–7; and V. v. 619–42.
[2] See III. iii. 357–9.
[3] See III. iii. 359–63. In the English-inspired revivals of a Medieval Western Parliamentarism in Late Modern Continental European Western countries, beginning with the reconvocation of the States General in France in A.D. 1789, there was a vein of academic artificiality which betrayed itself in France in the successive collapses of parliamentary government in A.D. 1799, A.D. 1852, and A.D. 1940; in Germany in the fiasco of 'the Revolution of the Intellectuals' in A.D. 1848, in the discomfiture of the Prussian Liberals by Bismarck in A.D. 1862–3, and in the collapse of the Weimar régime in A.D. 1933; and in Italy in the *de facto* liquidation, in A.D. 1922, of the Sardinian constitution of A.D. 1848. 'The Frankfort Parliament was a highly academic assembly—it contained 49 university professors and lecturers, and 57 schoolmasters, and at least three-fourths of its members had been to a university' (Namier, L. B.: *The Revolution of the Intellectuals* (London 1944, Cumberlege), p. 86, n. 1). In the retrospect of 160 years of disappointing experience, the artificial revival of an indigenous Western Parliamentarism in Continental Western Europe could be seen to be a sickly plant. In the same Time-perspective, however, it was also manifest that the resuscitation of Hellenic Democracy, in the sense of the rival self-deification of parochial human tribes, had been as effective as it had been disastrous. 'The *Volksgeist* of mass-movements replaced the *Zeitgeist* of the intellectuals, and came to be worshipped by the modern *clercs*' (Namier, op. cit., p. 73). 'Democracy', in this archaeologically correct parochial and idolatrous interpretation of a resuscitated pre-Augustan Hellenic ideal, was worshipped by the Napoleons, Mussolinis, Hitlers, and other Late Modern and post-Modern Continental European Western war-lords and dictators as fanatically as it was by any professorial member of the abortive German Parliament at Frankfort in A.D. 1848. What is more significant, it was also worshipped with a no less pagan bigotry, though usually with a greater show of discretion, by better seasoned and less incompetent parliamentarians in Great Britain and in the overseas Western countries of British origin.
[4] See IV. iv. 156–67.

an indigenous style of Western painting in favour of a resuscitated Hellenic Naturalism. The aesthetic petrifaction to which a Western school of painting had condemned itself in adopting a dead Hellenic style in place of its own indigenous Western aesthetic ideals is attested by the frustration of the genius of a Dhomínikos Theotokópoulos (*vivebat* A.D. 1541-1614), who tried to bring to the rescue of his Hellenizing Western contemporaries the aesthetic ideals of a Byzantine culture that had been tardily relieved of the incubus of the East Roman Empire. As we have noticed in another context,[1] the vista which a Byzantine Greek Theotokópoulos had opened up for Western painters was obstructed for no less than three centuries by the wraith of an Hellenic Greek Apelles, until the eventual exhaustion of an artificially administered Hellenic stimulus at last enabled latter-day Western eyes to see through the mirage by which Giotto had been bemused.

In the field of Philosophy the same ironic denouement was the sequel to the renaissances of a Sinic Confucianism in the Far Eastern World and an Hellenic Aristotelianism in Western Christendom. In the epilogues to both these tales the immediate effect was an Antaean outburst of intellectual energy, and the eventual effect a stiffening into the Atlantean stance of a dogmatic scholasticism.

The intellectual petrifaction which was the ultimate effect of an intellectual renaissance in the histories of both these societies is attested in either case by the frustration of a creative genius. In China in the Sung Age, Wang An-shih (*vivebat* A.D. 1021-86), who had foreseen that the Sung Empire would succumb to a barbarian onslaught unless it quickly put its house in order, and who had gone on to work out and translate into action the social reforms required in order to rally the people to the support of the Sung régime and the Far Eastern way of life, lived to see his work undone—with immediate catastrophic consequences—by Confucian litterati in whose eyes he had committed the unpardonable offence of breaking away from preconceived ideas in wrestling with unprecedented problems.[2] In Western Christendom in the thirteenth century of the Christian Era, Wang An-shih's frustration in the field of Public Administration had its counterpart in Roger Bacon's in the field of Physical Science. The vista which Bacon (*vivebat circa* A.D. 1214-94) opened up by looking at Nature as she was, with the unprejudiced eyes of an empirical observer, was obstructed for no less than four centuries by the straw-stuffed skin and bones of a dead Aristotle posted by the Schoolmen between the jambs of the door which Bacon had unlocked and opened. The obstruction was not removed by the fifteenth-century Italian Humanists' jeering exposure of the truth that this imposingly resuscitated Hellenic figure was a corpse; and Western Man had to wait for admission into a realm that was his own peculiar discovery till an obsolete Hellenic frame of mind was blown away at last by a mine laid and exploded by René Descartes (*vivebat* A.D. 1596–1650). While philosophers may question whether Descartes

---

[1] In IV. iv. 360-1.
[2] See Williamson, H. R.: *Wang An Shih* (London 1935-7, Probsthain, 2 vols.), and the present Study, V. vi. 306, with n. 6.

did, or could, divest his mind of all preconceived ideas and set it to work again, *ab initio*, on a genuinely clean slate, historians will not doubt that his naïve belief in the possibility of a new intellectual start, and his bold attempt to put this idea and ideal into practice, did effectually reopen the way for the resumption of a Baconian advance which an Aristotelian obstruction had arrested at the outset of the first day's march.

To the historian's eye, Descartes' supposedly clean slate reveals an unobliterated Christian inscription;[1] for, fortunately for the intellectual future of the two societies that had rashly evoked the ghosts of philosophies created by their predecessors, their uncritical enthusiasm had not availed to make a clean sweep of a living theology in order to enthrone a resuscitated philosophy in its place. In Western Christendom a Saint Thomas Aquinas had been at liberty to enfeoff Aristotle only in so far as he could contrive to do this without trespassing on the already established tenures of those Fathers and Councils of the Christian Church whose authority was recognized in the West; in China the Neoconfucians' nominally integral reinstatement of Confucianism had been achieved only by the sleight of hand with which they preserved, *en masse*, under a Confucian veneer, the tenets of a Mahayanian Buddhist theology which they professed to be rejecting *in toto*. Thus, when the renaissance of a dead philosophy had spent its force and taken its toll, this dubious intellectual adventure did not leave the society that had indulged in it altogether destitute of resources for making a fresh intellectual start; and, though in China this new departure was not taken without the help of a push from alien hands, a Western World which gave a twentieth-century China a salutary intellectual shock was able to perform this service for one of its contemporaries by that date because by then it had already succeeded in throwing off its own intellectual incubus by its own unaided intellectual prowess.

In the field of Law, Greek Orthodox Christendom in the Age of the Macedonian Dynasty partially insured itself against the risks of its evocation of the *Corpus Iustinianeum* in the *Vasilikà* by condescending to the same trick that was practised in the China of the Sung Age in the Neoconfucian renaissance of Confucianism. We have noticed already that the compilers of the *Vasilikà* tacitly retained the Christian essence of the legislation of an Iconoclast Syrian Dynasty whose works they were professedly execrating and rejecting. The truth was that, notwithstanding the retrospective anathema that the Iconoclasts had incurred, the Biblical elements out of which they had created their new system of law were sympathetic to the genius of an Orthodox Christian Society to which the pagan Hellenic spirit of a classical Roman Law had become morally repugnant; and the East Roman legislators of the Macedonian Age must have been aware at least intuitively, if not consciously, that the Orthodox Christian public for whom they were legislating would not be able to bear the dead weight of a genuinely integral Justinianean juristic renaissance. They therefore deftly lightened the incubus of the resuscitated Roman Law that they were imposing on the social life of Orthodox

---

[1] On this point see Butterfield, H.: *The Origins of Modern Science, 1300–1800* (London 1949, Bell), pp. 98–99.

Christendom by resorting to a device that had been employed by the Late Roman Emperor Justinian's own architect Anthemius of Tralles as his solution for the physical problem of imposing a cupola on the cathedral church of the Ayía Sophía without risking a collapse of the supporting pilasters. The light Rhodian bricks of which, according to the legend,[1] Anthemius's etherial cupola was ingeniously constructed, found their Byzantine juristic counterpart in *Vasilikà* whose ponderous-sounding Justinianean titles were affixed to contents covertly fabricated from the more etherial substance of the *Ecloga*.

In a Western Christendom where the resuscitation of the Justinianean Roman Law in Orthodox Christendom under the Macedonian Dynasty was emulated, some two hundred years after the time of the East Roman Emperor Basil I (*imperabat* A.D. 867–86), by academic enthusiasts, no corresponding precautions were taken to temper the rigour of an obsolete legal system to the exigencies of a social *terrain* with which it was still more out of keeping than it was with the life of a ninth-century Orthodox Christian World; and it is therefore not surprising to find the 'reception' of the Civil Law in the West having Atlantean sequels. We have seen[2] how the Hohenstaufen Dynasty's academic pretension to benefit by a post-Diocletianic Roman imperial prerogative, which, in the West, had never been exercised effectively since the death of the Emperor Theodosius I in A.D. 395, committed the Holy Roman Empire to a policy of self-assertion that was so ludicrously beyond its strength that it inevitably resulted in the collapse registered in 'the Great Interregnum' of A.D. 1254–73. This Atlantean doom which the Holy Roman Empire thus brought down upon its own head might have seemed at the time to be offset by an Antaean sequel to the contemporary reception of the Civil Law in the North and Central Italian city-states. Yet, though the first effect may have been stimulating both in a Late Medieval Western cosmos of city-states and in an Early Modern Western chaos of nation-states, it could be seen in retrospect that the ultimate effect had been Atlantean here likewise; for the reception of an oecumenical Roman Law within the cramping framework of a parochial state had manifestly aggravated the explosiveness of an idolization of parochial sovereignty which the Western World had resuscitated from the charnel house of a pre-imperial Age of Hellenic history.

If, in conclusion of our present survey of Antaean and Atlantean reactions, we now take a second glance at some of those pilgrimages in which renaissances of elements of dead cultures had been transposed from the Time-dimension into the Space-dimension, we shall observe

---

[1] According to Lethaby, W. R., and Swainson, H.: *The Church of Sancta Sophia, Constantinople* (London 1894, Macmillan), p. 156, 'there was no trace [in the dome] of the light bricks made in Rhodes which the Anonymous mentions, although in the pendentives a light substance, whitish, with impressions of plants in it, was used in irregular masses'.

An English translation of this *Anonymus Combefisii* (or *Bandurii* or *Lambecii*) will be found ibid., pp. 129–43, and the passage about the Rhodian bricks appears on pp. 136–7:

'The Emperor sent Troilus the cubicular, Theodosius the prefect, and Basileidês the quaestor to Rhodes to have bricks of Rhodian clay made, all equal in weight and length. ... And they sent bricks of measured sizes to the Emperor—twelve of them weigh [the weight of] one of ours; for the clay is light, spongy, fine, and white.'

[2] In II. ii. 170–1.

that the auspicious failure of the Crusades saved Western Christendom from the Atlantean fate that it was courting when it tried to slake its thirst for the fountain-head of Christianity by mistranslating a spiritual nostalgia into a military occupation. The Ayyubid and Mamlūk defenders of an embryonic Arabic Muslim Society who evicted the Crusaders from Palestine and their other conquests in Syria, and the Nicene Greek and Ottoman Turkish defenders of a disintegrating Orthodox Christendom who evicted these Western Christian intruders from Constantinople and Greece, compelled the Franks to divert from the Levant to the Baltic and the Atlantic most of the energies that Frankland had to spare for navigation, piracy, maritime trade, and overseas conquest; and this compulsory diversion of energies made the Franks' fortunes in spite of themselves and contrary to the intentions of their victorious Muslim and Orthodox Christian adversaries. In wresting out of Frankish hands the mastery of the Mediterranean, the Mamlūks and the 'Osmanlis pushed the Franks into mastering the Ocean, taking Dār-al-Islām in the rear,[1] winning two new worlds for Western Christendom in the Americas, and establishing a temporary Western ascendancy over the whole face of the planet.

The undesired and unintended benefit that the repulse of the Crusades thus thrust upon the Franks on the whole is demonstrated by a Venetian and a Genoese exception. The Late Medieval Italians' superiority in efficiency over their Transalpine and Transmarine Frankish contemporaries resulted, as we have noticed in another context,[2] in their gathering into their hands such fragments of the Crusaders' conquests *outre mer* as were not liberated by force of Greek and Turkish arms; and this exceptional success of the maritime Italian city-states in the hour of the Crusaders' general failure in the Levant was one cause of the Italians' own subsequent failure in the hour of the great *peripeteia* in which a Frankish discomfiture was converted into a Frankish triumph through the conquest of the Ocean by the maritime nation-states of Western Europe.

In these feats of West European maritime enterprise individual Venetian and Genoese seamen played parts of outstanding importance. When a progressive exploration of the West Coast of Africa, that had been initiated by the Portuguese Prince Henry the Navigator *circa* A.D. 1421,[3] had petered out in A.D. 1448,[4] the fresh impetus which saved this Portuguese enterprise from missing its manifest destiny was given to it in A.D. 1455–6 by the Venetian Alvise da Ca' da Mosto, who in two successive voyages[5] turned the flank of Dār-al-Islām by establishing contact, beyond its southern limits, with still pagan Negro African peoples; reached and explored the River Gambia; and perhaps discovered the Cape Verde Islands.[6] As for a Genoese Columbus who carried the Castilian flag across the Atlantic to the Caribbean threshold of the Mexic and Andean

---

[1] See IX. viii. 216–19.   [2] In III. iii. 347, n. 1.
[3] See Prestage, E.: *The Portuguese Pioneers* (London 1933, Black), p. 54.
[4] See Prestage, op. cit., pp. 92–93.   [5] See Prestage, op. cit., pp. 94–125.
[6] Alvise da Ca' da Mosto's, Diogo Gomez's, and Antonio da Noli's rival claims to have been the discoverer of the Cape Verde Islands are discussed by Prestage in op. cit., pp. 122, 140, and 143–4.

worlds, he was Fortune's favoured child among a goodly company of his Genoese fellow countrymen who had been lending their expert professional services to the Iberian Christian kingdoms since A.D. 1317.[1]

When individual Genoese and Venetian maritime adventurers were so keenly alive to Western Christendom's possible future on the Ocean, and were so effectively active in helping to translate this possibility into accomplished fact, how came it that the Genoese and Venetian commonwealths let slip, with such fatal consequences for themselves, their own opportunity of playing in this immense new field of Western maritime enterprise the leading part that was theirs for the taking, in virtue of their then still unchallenged supremacy over all other maritime Western Christian states in skill, experience, and wealth? Their geographical location within the basin of an inland sea is not, in itself, enough to account for their failure to compete in the new Oceanic race; for a Mediterranean Sea that was landlocked over against the Indian Ocean had an egress into the Atlantic, and at least a modest share in an Early Modern Western World's oceanic activities was afterwards taken by the Grand Duchy of Courland,[2] whose location within the basin of the Baltic was quite as serious a geographical handicap in the oceanic race as any to which Genoa and Venice were subject. The underlying explanation of the two Italian maritime commonwealths' failure to respond to the challenge of the Ocean was not a Mediterranean geographical location but was a Levantine commercial, political, and military commitment which was the modern legacy of their medieval success. At the critical moment at the turn of the fifteenth and sixteenth centuries, Venice and Genoa were still being held fast in an Atlantean stance by the baneful incubus of a Medieval Western Christian reversion to Western Christendom's Levantine past out of which these successful Italians had never been shaken by disasters such as had opportunely overtaken their French and Catalan fellow adventurers in that unpromising quarter.

This Atlantean doom was thus Genoa's and Venice's exceptional fate in the sequel to a failure of the Crusades in which the rest of Western Christendom had been saved, in its own despite, by a timely defeat. When however, a nascent Iranic Muslim Society was dragged at the heels of Timur Lenk's war-horse into turning its face away from lands of promise round the shores of the Great Eurasian Steppe towards the cradle of a dead antecedent Syriac Civilization,[3] the whole of the aberrant society paid the Atlantean penalty for its demonically wayward war-lord's commission of a sin that had once been the undoing of Lot's wife.[4] When Timur's conquests in the interior of the Iranic and Arabic Muslim worlds had proved to be as ephemeral as they had been devastating, the Iranic Muslim Society stood as stiff as any pillar of salt while the Mongol and Calmuck pagan Nomads were being converted to the Tibetan Tantric form of Mahayanian Buddhism instead of being converted to the Sunnī form of Islam, and while the political dominion over the shores of the Eurasian Steppe was being partitioned between Sinified Manchus and Orthodox Christian Muscovites. This *gran rifiuto*, through which

---

[1] See Prestage, op. cit., pp. 4–5.   [2] See IX. viii. 129.
[3] See IV. iv. 493–5.   [4] Gen. xix. 26.

Timur Lenk arbitrarily cheated of its manifest destiny an Iranic Muslim World that he had just liberated from a Chaghatāy Nomad ascendancy, is a classic example of an Atlantean sequel to a renaissance translated into the geographical terms of a physical return to an antecedent civilization's cradle.

(III) THE BLESSEDNESS OF IMMUNITY, MERCIFULNESS OF MORTALITY, AND UNTOWARDNESS OF PRECOCITY

An Attic tragedian in a celebrated chorus[1] has declared his conviction that

> Not to be born, by all acclaim,
> Were best; but, once that gate be passed,
> To hasten thither whence he came
> Is Man's next prize—and fast, Oh fast![2]

Whether we do or do not agree with Sophocles in his pessimistic verdict on the predicament of being born into This World, we can hardly have arrived at the present point in our study of renaissances without feeling sure that at any rate it is best not wantonly to provoke the re-birth of something that has already been born once and that is now obligingly dead, buried, and in abeyance, and that, if on any occasion we have had the temerity to raise the dead, the least awkward denouement to which we can look forward in this ill-advised escapade is to see the *revenant*'s disturbing presence laid again as hastily as Fate may allow; for our survey of the courses and consequences of renaissances in the histories of civilizations of the third generation has made it clear that the severity of the penalty that the necromancer will have to pay for having indulged a disembodied ghost's yearning to haunt the land of the living will be proportionate to the vehemence of the craving of the shade in Sheol to be reanimated by a draught of life-blood drawn from a living creature's veins.

The blessedness of immunity from renaissances was attested by the contrasts between the respective fortunes of the Visual Arts and Literature in the Chinese main body of a Far Eastern World, of Architecture and Literature in the main body of Orthodox Christendom, and of Music and Architecture in the West; for the Visual Arts in China, Architecture in Orthodox Christendom, and Music in the West had manifestly each been the master-art of its own culture; and in the history of each of them a renaissance of elements from the past life of an antecedent civilization was conspicuous by its absence. In China an Indo-Hellenic school of art that had been introduced into the Far Eastern World at a pre-natal stage by a Mahāyāna which had served as a chrysalis for the embryo of a Far Eastern Civilization was never disturbed by the re-emergence of a pre-Mahayanian Sinic art. In Orthodox Christendom a Syriac school of Architecture whose archetype was the church of the Ayía Sophía at Constantinople was never disturbed by a revival of the

---

[1] Sophocles: *Oedipus at Colonus*, ll. 1227–8.
[2] Gilbert Murray's translation (London 1948, Allen & Unwin), p. 93.

incompatible ideal embodied in the Parthenon at Athens. In the West a school of music that had discarded all but two of the numerous Hellenic 'modes', and, out of these two, had concentrated its efforts on one, was never disturbed by any resurgence of the Hellenic Babel that it had repressed. On the other hand a renaissance was, as we have seen, the dominating event in the histories of a Chinese Far Eastern and a Greek Orthodox Christian literature, as well as in the history of a Western architecture; and it was assuredly no accident that these activities that had been potently haunted by reanimated ghosts were all convicted of having been dismal failures by confrontation with the brilliant success of contemporary activities in which a living society's native genius had not been blighted by the malign influence of a *revenant*.

The mercifulness of mortality, when the dead have been ill-advisedly brought back to life, is illustrated in the history of a Western Civilization that repeatedly escaped the due penalties for its own perverse feats of necromancy thanks to the premature dissipation of the haunting spectre either by the necromancer's own ruthless hand or by the indulgence of Fate. The Western Civilization earned by its own efforts the relief from an incubus that it won for itself by sending back to limbo, in a seventeenth-century victory of 'the Moderns' over 'the Ancients', the ghost of the Hellenic classics that had been raised in a fifteenth-century Italian renaissance, and by shattering, in the thirteenth-century victory of a Hildebrandine *Respublica Christiana* over a Frederician Holy Roman Empire, the simulacrum of an Hellenic universal state that had been imposed on Western Christendom for the second time at the hands of Otto I. On the other hand the West owed to Fate rather than to any Western foresight or forcefulness the fortunate premature collapse of the Holy Roman Empire after its original installation by Charlemagne, and likewise the fortunate premature expiry of the Carolingian renaissance of an Hellenic literature in its Latin version. Fate was equally kind to Western Christendom in making a fiasco of the Crusades and thereby liberating Western energies from an atavistic adventure in the blind alley of the Mediterranean Basin in order to set them free for encircling the Globe by mastering the Ocean. How much the Western Civilization did gain by the timely reinternment of these inopportune *revenants* in the Sheol from which they had been evoked can be measured by the extent of the damage which the same civilization suffered from a resuscitated Hellenic art and architecture that inopportunely escaped the guillotine, and from a resuscitated Hellenic parochial state that seemed to have an inexhaustible reserve of hydra-heads.[1]

At the time of writing in the first century of a post-Modern Age of Western history, the Western Society's continuing failure to exorcize a demon that was as assiduous as it was insidious presented the most formidable of all the pending threats to the Western Civilization's future. Yet, even in this field of Politics, in which it had thus paid so heavy a penalty for having revived an Hellenic parochialism, the Western Society had at least been more fortunate than a sister Orthodox Christian Society in being saved by the successive collapses of the Carolingian and Otto-

[1] See VII. vii. 542–3.

nian resuscitations of an Hellenic universal state from the incubus which had been imposed on the Orthodox Christian Society at the dawn of its history by the disastrous efficacity of Leo Syrus's resuscitation of this oecumenical Hellenic political spectre. A similar comparison between the fortunes of two other sister societies likewise indicated that the Japanese offshoot of a Buddhistic Far Eastern Society had been more fortunate than the main body of the same society in China in being saved by the collapse of a pseudo-T'ang régime in Yamato from the doom which the disastrous efficacity of the T'ang régime itself had eventually brought upon China.

In this connexion we may also notice that even a quasi-immunity is rewarded by a modicum of beatitude. The partial successes of a Maha-yanian Buddhist theology in foiling the renaissance of a Confucian Sinic philosophy in the Far East, and of a Syrian Dynasty's Christian legisla-tion in foiling a Macedonian Dynasty's renaissance of a Justinianean Hellenic law in Orthodox Christendom, had, as we have seen, the auspi-cious effect of attenuating the untoward consequences of these two renaissances for the societies that had done their worst to evoke them.

The untowardness of precocity is likewise illustrated by synoptic views that have already come under our eyes.

For example, in the field of Language and Literature, where the negative or positive value of a renaissance of dead classics can be measured by the blight or stimulus of its influence on the creation of a literature in living vernacular languages, we can see that the effective renaissance of Hellenism in a Greek Orthodox Christendom as early as the ninth century of the Christian Era, less than two hundred years after the emergence of an infant Orthodox Christian Civilization out of a post-Hellenic interregnum, was far more noxious than the effective renaissance of the same Hellenism in the fifteenth century in a Western World which had enjoyed a six hundred years longer immunity from the haunting presence of this Hellenic ghost, thanks to a Carolingian re-naissance's fortunate failure. We can also see that, when a Modern Greek people conjured up a ghost of the Attic Greek language at the very moment of its entry as a proselyte into a Western Society's gates, the chimaera of a 'purist' Greek language (ἡ καθαρεύουσα), with which it saddled itself in the act, was a still more grievous incubus than an Anna Comnena's Attic κοινή or even than a Nicholas Khalkokondhýlis' pseudo-Herodotean Ionic.

In the field of Religion, where the negative or positive value of a re-naissance can be measured by its influence in hindering or helping the Soul in its perennial struggle with the sin of Idolatry, we can see that an effective renaissance of a Judaic Aniconism in a Greek Orthodox Christendom as early as the eighth century of the Christian Era par-tially cured an infant Orthodox Christian Church of image-worship at the cost of committing an Orthodox Christian Society to the likewise idolatrous worship of a ghost of an Hellenic universal state, whereas the renaissance of the same Judaic Aniconism in Western Christen-dom some eight hundred years later wholly cured a Protestant Western Church of image-worship—though this at the cost of helping to commit a Modern Western World to the idolatrous worship of a ghost of an Hellenic parochial state.

In the field of political ideas and institutions we can see that the fortunate successive Western fiascos of a Carolingian resuscitation of the Hellenic universal state which collapsed in the ninth century, and of an Ottonian resuscitation of it which collapsed in the thirteenth century, gave the Western Christian Civilization at any rate a longer lease of life than was enjoyed by an Orthodox Christendom which had succumbed to the suicidal sin of state-worship in the eighth century when it had deified the East Roman Empire. The similarly suicidal self-commitment of the Western World to a state-worship in which the idol was a parochial one and in which the idolatry was polytheistic had not captivated the Western World as a whole until the turn of the fifteenth and sixteenth centuries, when this brand of idolatry, with which the Italians had marked their foreheads[1] as early as the eleventh century of the Christian Era, was painstakingly reproduced by all the other peoples of a ci-devant Christian Western World.

If we now go on to ask ourselves why the most prudent counsels for any living soul that is playing with the Black Art should be—as History shows them to be—'That thou doest, do slowly [sic]'[2] and 'Better late, best never', we may find an answer to our question in the principle 'One man's meat is another man's poison' which our foregoing study of encounters between contemporaries[3] has brought to light; for this 'law' is also operative in encounters in which the parties are a necromancer and a ghost.

In an encounter of any kind, an invasion of the life of one of the dramatis personae by some element in the life of another of them which has been torn out of its original context and has been introduced in isolation into an alien social milieu can, indeed, hardly fail to be a highly disturbing event in the history of the invaded party. The effect of a twelfth-century Western renaissance of Aristotelianism in suspending the creative activity of Western Christian thought has been noticed by a distinguished Modern Western student of the Medieval Western Mind;[4] and the consequences of a renaissance may be still more baneful when its influence is stimulating than when it is repressive. Great, for example, as was the havoc wrought in Hellenic history by the Hellenes' sin of idolizing their parochial states, the havoc was still greater[5] when this particular form of Hellenic idolatry was resuscitated in a Western Christendom where the vein of Judaic fanaticism inherent in Christianity was lying in wait, ready to inspire an Hellenic parochial state-worship imported from the shadow-realm of Hades with a demonic intensity which it had never attained in even the deadliest of its pristine manifestations on its native heath in a heathen Hellenic World whose life it had brought to a premature bad end.

The extent, however, of the ravages which a renaissance will thus, in

---

[1] Rev. xiii. 16; xiv. 9; xix. 20; xx. 4.
[2] Cp. John xiii. 27.   [3] See IX. viii. 530–42.
[4] Taylor, H. O.: *The Mediaeval Mind* (London 1911, Macmillan, 2 vols.), vol. i, p. 17.
[5] See the passage on p. 194 of Guglielmo Ferrero's *Peace and War*, English translation, London 1933, Macmillan), that has been quoted in VII. vii. 542–3.

the nature of the event, be apt to make in the psychic constitution of the necromancer will manifestly be apt to vary in accordance with the degree of the patient's powers of resistance at the time when he wantonly infects himself with the bacillus; and in the history of a healthily growing civilization, so long as the growth has not been cut short by a breakdown, we may presume that every further decade, generation, and century of growth will enhance the robustness of the growing body social's constitution and accordingly will, to that degree, increase its capacity for carrying Atlas' load without collapsing under the weight of the incubus, even if the patient's vitality, in the hour of crisis, does not prove lively enough to enable him to avoid falling into an Atlantean stance by responding to the challenge with an Antaean rebound. The better the spiritual health of the victim of a renaissance at the time of his self-inflicted ordeal, the better his chance of metabolizing the uncanny treasure that he has wrested from the coffers of Hades, and, in metabolizing it, constraining it to serve his weal as an elixir instead of working his woe as a cancer. A subconscious awareness of these saving truths reveals itself in phenomena that have already come to our notice in the present Part of this Study. This is, in fact, the reason why divers elements in the culture of a dead antecedent civilization are apt to be resuscitated in a chronological order that is the inverse of their original sequence in the history of the civilization that has been their native milieu.[1] It is also the reason why a necromantically inclined society is apt to discriminate among the ghosts that are within range of its magician's wand by studiously ignoring shades whose psychic stature would dwarf the wizard's if he were so foolhardy as to reanimate them, while at the same time he may be eagerly courting other shades whose psychic stature is not thus unmanageably incommensurate with his own.[2]

(IV) THE STERILITY OF THE BLACK ART

Even, however, when a necromancer avoids or escapes the nemesis of being enslaved by a ghost that he has reanimated at his own expense by nurturing it with a transfusion of his own life-blood, the sterility to which even the least noxious achievements of the Black Art are condemned *ex officio originis* is exposed remorselessly when these are compared with the contemporary achievements of a necromantic society's native genius.

In the field of politics, for example, it is evident that, in the Medieval chapter of Western history, the master-institution was not an *Imperium Romanum Redivivum* but was a newly created Papal Roman *Respublica Christiana*,[3] and that in Arabic Muslim history it was, not the Cairene ghost of an ʿAbbasid Caliphate, but a novel self-recruiting Mamlūk corps, that endowed this society, in its infancy, with the strength to hold its own even against the world-conquering Mongols.[4] In the modern chapter of Western history, again, the indigenous Western institution of parliamentary representative government eclipsed the resuscitated Hellenic

---

[1] See pp. 124–30, above.
[2] See pp. 130–7, above.
[3] See IV. iv. 405.
[4] See IV. iv. 446–50.

institution of a demagogic Democracy that was apt—first in city-states in Italy after A.D. 1254 and then in a nation-state in France after A.D. 1789—to turn, as fast as milk turns in thundery weather, into the sour brew of a plebiscitary dictatorship. In the field of Law the genius of an Orthodox Christian Civilization revealed itself, not in a Macedonian Dynasty's revival of a dead Justinianean Hellenic law, but in an antecedent Syrian Dynasty's new creation of an East Roman law inspired by Christian principles. In the field of Philosophy, likewise, the genius of a Far Eastern Civilization revealed itself, not in the revival of a dead Confucianism, but in the foregoing new creation of indigenous Far Eastern philosophies inspired by Mahayanian Buddhist thought, while, in the intellectual history of a Medieval Western Christendom, the genius of Saint Thomas Aquinas revealed itself, in his *Summa Theologica*, not in the resuscitation of Aristotelian theses but in the construction of a system that was the Angelic Doctor's own.[1] In the field of Physical Science the Medieval Western Schoolmen's revival of the intellectually vicious Hellenic practice of arguing about the phenomena of Physical Nature *in vacuo*, as if Logic could do duty for verification, threatened to sterilize, and succeeded in retarding, the harvest that was to be garnered from the application of an experimental method of research in accordance with the Western Civilization's native bent.[2] In the field of Language and Literature the all but flawlessly Ciceronian Latinity of an Erasmus, who had taught himself to speak with the tongues of men and of angels, was become as sounding brass or a tinkling cymbal[3] in a Modern Western house of many mansions[4] that had been filled with a sound as of a rushing mighty wind[5] by a vernacular poetry in a chorus of divers living Western languages, while, in a contemporary Far Eastern World, a creative art of the Drama and the Novel, conveyed in a living 'mandarin' *lingua franca*, had likewise eventually taken the light out of a pedantic reproduction of the style and themes of the Sinic classics. In the field of the Visual Arts an Orthodox Christian Civilization's miniature reminiscences in ivory of an Hellenic style of bas-relief carving in marble turn deathly pale, exquisite though they are, in the presence of mosaics glowing and vibrating with a veritable life engendered by the fruitful marriage of an indigenous Byzantine creativity with an indigenous Byzantine technique.

The last word on the comparative merits of the realm of Hades and the land of the living was spoken to Odysseus by the shade of Achilles:

'I would rather be a wretched peasant on the land, labouring as a serf with a poor portionless man for my master, than be sovereign lord of all the legions of the shades of the dead and departed.'[6]

---

[1] This point is made by Taylor, H. O.: *The Mediaeval Mind* (London 1911, Macmillan, 2 vols.), vol. i, p. 18, and vol. ii, p. 437.

[2] See III. iii. 385-6. [3] 1 Cor. xiii. 1. [4] John xiv. 2.

[5] Acts ii. 2. [6] *Od.*, Book XI, ll. 489-91.

XI

LAW AND FREEDOM IN HISTORY

A. THE PROBLEM

(I) THE STATE OF THE QUESTION

WHEN the writer was planning the present Study in the summer of
A.D. 1927, he saw that he would have to grapple with the problem
of the respective roles of Law and Freedom in human history before
he could attempt to win a Pisgah sight of the prospects of the Western
Civilization. Yet in the winter of A.D. 1928–9, when, with that ulterior
objective in mind, he was drafting his notes for eventually writing the
present Part, he was conscious that the fateful question then still seemed
academic to most people in Western countries that had been either neutral
or on the winning side in the World War of A.D. 1914–18. In the June
of A.D. 1950, when, after a seven-years-long interruption extending over
the years 1939–46, he at last reached this point in the writing of the
book, he found himself working in a new atmosphere that was decidedly
more congenial to his theme.

By the year A.D. 1950 the survivors of a generation of Westerners that
had fought two fratricidal world wars in one lifetime had emerged from
the second of these unprecedentedly destructive conflicts of a traditional
military kind only to find itself engaged in a 'cold war' which was neither
less arduous nor less critical for being less barbarous than a twice-
played military overture in which the *encore* had surpassed the first performance; and these disillusioning and disquieting experiences had
brought about, in most living Western souls, a revolutionary change of
feeling and outlook. By this time, most Westerners had become aware
that their own civilization was in danger of coming to grief; and reflection had then reminded them that this was, after all, no novel prospect
in an historical arena in which most, if not all, other human societies of
the same species had come to grief already. The living generation in the
West was, in fact, beginning to look at the facts of History as these presented themselves to the naked eye, instead of continuing to peer at this
formidable spectacle through smoked glasses inherited from its grandparents; and, in the light of luminous facts which they were at last
allowing themselves to see, they were asking themselves questions that
would have shocked their grandparents if these could ever have dreamed
of formulating them.

The generation of *Homo Occidentalis* that had already been in its
dotage in A.D. 1914 had been the latest generation to hold, with an
unquestioning faith, a dogma which, by then, had been serving for a
quarter of a millennium as the gist of a Late Modern Western Man's
mechanically desiccated and peptonized religion. This fallaciously comfortable doctrine was that the Western Society could see ahead of it an
unbroken vista of progress towards an Earthly Paradise, and that its

triumphant advance along this open avenue was inevitable, since the only 'law' binding upon a *Homo Sapiens* who was free to shape his own future in every other respect was 'a law of progress' rendering a wishful thinker's desires inevitable.

In A.D. 1950 the grandchildren of these Victorian Last of the Mohicans were asking themselves questions that had been formulated for Western inquirers on the morrow of the First World War by Oswald Spengler, a pontifical-minded man of genius thinking and writing in the psychological milieu of a country which had then just suffered what, by the still moderate standards of the day, had been a shattering military defeat. Some thirty years after the publication of the first edition of *Der Untergang des Abendlandes* in A.D. 1919, a chorus of Western voices was echoing Spengler's prescient questionnaire. Are the great tribulations that we have suffered, and the greater tribulations that we forebode, the products of 'laws', beyond our control, that turn out to be no 'laws of progress'? If such unpleasant laws are, in truth, in operation, do these govern the whole of Human Life, or are there some provinces or planes of Life in which Man is his own master—free, within those limits, to find remedies, through his own action, for evils that are of his own making? If human affairs should prove to be thus under dual control, then what affairs are under our own control and what are governed by 'Law'? And, if we do find that Man's stable contains a loose-box, can we use this islet of freedom as a ὅπου στῶμεν from which—by virtue, wisdom, and work—we may perhaps succeed in enlarging the borders of the province under Man's control at the expense of the province under the dominion of 'Law'?

The German philosopher who led the way in putting these disturbing new questions into once complacently sluggish Western minds went on to give to all of them one comprehensive dogmatic answer of his own. The true law of Human Social Life, he laid down, was not a law of inevitable progress; it was a law of inevitable breakdown, disintegration, and dissolution—and this within a Time-span which was perhaps even more inflexibly uniform than the life-spans of living organisms. Happily, the adoption of Spengler's fateful questions did not commit his fellow Westerners to endorsing, in advance, the German hierophant's oracular response to his own shrewd inquiry; and, since in other contexts we have already exposed the fallacy of Spengler's confusion of societies with organisms[1] and the groundlessness of his belief in the omnipotence of the savage goddess Necessity,[2] we can regard the questions asked and answered by Spengler as being, *pace Spengleri*, still open.

(II) DEFINITIONS OF TERMS

In venturing, without prejudice, to seek a fresh answer of our own to the question whether human affairs are governed by laws, our first step must be to define what we mean by 'laws' and by 'human affairs'.

In the context of our present Study, 'human affairs' manifestly mean, not Medicine, but the Humanities; not the organic chemistry, biology,

---

[1] See III. iii. 219–23.   [2] See IV. iv. 7–39.

and physiology of the human body, but the affairs of human beings in that spiritual aspect of Humanity in which Man is a person with a consciousness and a will moving on the face of the waters[1] of a subconscious psychic abyss, and not in the physical aspect in which Man is a body whose chemical constituents can be analysed, weighed, measured, and priced at their current value in the market for material commodities. If, for our purposes in this Study, we define the term 'human affairs' in the spiritual sense, we can see that our field of human affairs articulates itself into four provinces occupied respectively by the Soul's diverse relations with God, with its own self, with a relatively small circle of other human beings with whom it is in direct personal communion, and with a relatively large circle of people with whom it is in indirect impersonal contact through the mechanism of institutions.[2] We shall be reconnoitring all four provinces in this Part of our Study.

In this same context, 'law' manifestly does not mean the man-made legislation which is, of course, the only authentic 'law' in the literal sense of the word, and which is also the only law with which we have a direct acquaintance in our immediate day-to-day human experience. The 'law' with which we are concerned in this Study resembles this familiar man-made institution in being a set of rules governing human affairs; but the differentia of this so-called 'law' is that it is not made by Man; and, in using the term with this transference of meaning, we are attributing the characteristics of a known human institution to the enigmatic working of a mysterious Universe. In resorting to this linguistic expedient of metaphor we are flagrantly guilty of Anthropomorphism; and, if we cannot—as indeed we cannot—reach our goal without taking this flight of the imagination, we must recognize that, in transporting a word from the social to the metaphysical sphere, we cannot help transporting the word's connotations together with the label to which these notions adhere. The inherent threat to the accuracy, as well as to the clarity, of our thought is as evident as it is unavoidable; and the most effective safeguard against it will be to remind ourselves, in advance, what these *a priori* connotations of the word 'law' are.

The most striking characteristic of man-made law is that it is intended to apply consistently in uniform circumstances in all human situations that are deemed to fall within the scope of whatever the particular law may be. By implication the law is intended to be imposed impartially, and to be enforced effectively, upon all and sundry who come within its ambit. Furthermore, the law is intended, not only to be consistently formulated and applied and to be impartially and effectively administered, but also to be, and to be recognized by all concerned as being, morally right. Since, however, Human Nature is lamentably imperfect in morals, intelligence, and practice alike, and since this all-pervasive imperfection is ubiquitously reflected in the unsatisfactoriness of Man's conduct of his human affairs, even the best law known to History is never quite just, never quite effectively or impartially administered, and never quite consistently applied or formulated.[3] A perfectly consistent

---

[1] Gen. i. 2.   [2] See I. i. 454–5 and III. iii. 223–30.
[3] There were on record notorious cases in which a community's will or power, or

formulation of the law is indeed inherently impossible, since the most acute and supple intellectual operations of the most consummate legal genius would be unequal to coping with the subtlety and complexity of the concrete human affairs with which a lawyer's abstractions have to deal.

This intractability of Life to Law accounts for the moral ambivalence which is an ineradicable trait of Law and an irrefutable testimony to the power of Original Sin. The impersonal objectivity that is the Law's acknowledged ideal had been mocked, in every actual law that had ever been enacted since the dawn of legislation, by the unmistakable reflection in it of some personal bias unjustly favouring one 'interest' by unjustly penalizing another. The perfect justice of a God who 'is no respecter of persons',[1] and 'who, without respect of persons, judgeth according to every man's work',[2] had never been exhibited by any human legislator. Even the least unscrupulous and most disinterested human legislation had always perceptibly reflected in some degree the play of current religious, economic, political, military, and other social forces. Yet, even if we could imagine the advent of an omnipotent human legislator who was at the same time perfect in every faculty of the Human Spirit, the disinterested impersonality that would be the glory of this imaginary paragon's legislation and dispensation of justice would be concurrently the scandal of his work, since a law that can never be sufficiently impersonal in the sense of ignoring the personal interests of the legislator, the judge, and the administrator can also never be sufficiently personal in the sense of allowing sufficiently for the personal circumstances of each and every human soul who is subject to this law and whose case is *sub judice*. The inherent, and consequently inescapable, dilemma of all human legislation and legal proceedings is that, in so far as the Law succeeds in being impersonal, it necessarily achieves this at the odious price of treating human souls—which are individual and unique—as if they were mass-produced, standardized non-human objects like coins or bricks or pounds of butter or sacks of coal, while, in so far as it succeeds in making allowances for personal circumstances, it necessarily achieves this at a risk of grievously departing from an impartiality that is of the essence of human justice.

This was the historical human social context from which the name and notion of 'law' had been transferred to a metaphysical context by a resort to the perilous yet unavoidable expedient of Anthropomorphism. At an earlier point in this Study[3] we have noticed that the social milieu in which this flight of the human imagination is apt to be made is the experience of a disintegrating society that has won a reprieve for itself by a political union within the framework of a universal state; and we have observed that, in these social circumstances, the idea of law is apt, in

both, to administer the law impartially and effectively had lagged far behind its will or power, or both, to formulate and apply the law consistently. One instance was the state of the municipal law of the Icelanders in the tenth century of the Christian Era; another was the state of the international law of the sovereign states of the Western Society in the twentieth century of the same era. The sequel in Iceland (see II. ii. 357, n. 2) suggests that an anarchy of this repulsively sophisticated type is apt to bring itself to a speedy end by inviting the intervention of some masterful alien hand.

[1] Acts x. 34.   [2] 1 Pet. i. 17.   [3] In V. vi. 15–17.

the act of being translated from the social to the metaphysical plane, to become polarized into two apparently antithetical concepts. For minds in whose mental vision the personality of the human legislator, judge, and administrator looms larger than the law of which he is at once the master and the servant, the metaphysical 'law' governing the Universe is the law of a unique and omnipotent God pictured in the image of a human Caesar.[1] For other minds, in whose vision Caesar's figure is eclipsed by a human law that is impersonally formulated, applied, administered, and enforced—such as 'the Law of the Medes and Persians which altereth not',[2] that was the oecumenical law of the Achaemenian Empire—the metaphysical 'law' governing the Universe is the law of a uniform and inexorable Nature. In this diffracted vision, metaphysical 'law' in the guise of 'a Law of God' and metaphysical 'law' in the guise of 'laws of Nature' present between them the double-faced countenance of a Janus, and in either face there are—as in the human law of every-day life —both consoling and horrifying features.

The horrifying feature in 'the laws of Nature' is their inexorability; for, although, in theory, these 'laws' may be scheduled as being *de jure* mere 'by-laws' or 'secondary causes' subject to the fiat of a 'First Cause' that will then be identified with God, in practice they will be taken as being *de facto* autonomous. 'The laws of Nature', in fact, fulfil the Medes' and Persians' ideal of laws that cannot ever be repealed or ever even be revised in the light of experience.[3] This inhuman quality of inexorability is horrifying indeed, yet its moral enormity carries with it an intellectual compensation; for laws in which there 'is no variableness, neither shadow of turning',[4] will on that very account be ascertainable, both exactly and definitively, by a human intelligence; and, while no more than isolated fragments of these 'laws of Nature' may be thus ascertainable at any particular time and place by any particular human mind, their intrinsic stability and permanence render them accessible to a process of progressive exploration by a Collective Human Intellect.[5] A knowledge of Nature thus appears to be within Man's mental grasp, and there is a sense in which this knowledge is power; for human beings who know Nature's unvarying laws and who can therefore predict with certainty which way she is going to jump will not only be able to dodge this inhuman monster's aimless blows; they will also be able to harness the energy generated, released, and expended in these undesigned operations, and so to turn this energy to account for serving human purposes (in so far, of course, as individual human wills can agree on what their common purposes shall be). And thus a Collective Human Intellect, which cannot divert the inexorable course of Nature by a hair's breadth, can nevertheless make a world of difference, for good or for evil, to the effect of the play of laws of Nature on human affairs by bringing into action technological devices that can effectively control, not the operation of these laws, but the incidence of their operation on Man's life.

[1] See V. vi. 33–36. [2] Dan. vi. 8 and 12.
[3] 'Biological progress exists as a fact of Nature external to Man' (Julian Huxley, in his 'Conclusion' to T. H. and J. Huxley: *Evolution and Ethics, 1893–1943* (London 1947, Pilot Press), p. 182).
[4] Jas. i. 17. [5] See pp. 697 and 701, below.

All the same, the limits within which even the most ingenious human technology can outmanœuvre a railbound Nature are narrowly circumscribed.

'Canst thou draw out Leviathan with an hook? Or his tongue with a cord which thou lettest down? Canst thou put an hook into his nose? Or bore his jaw through with a thorn? Will he make many supplications unto thee? Will he speak soft words unto thee? Will he make a covenant with thee? Wilt thou take him for a servant for ever? Wilt thou play with him as with a bird? Or wilt thou bind him for thy maidens? Shall the companions make a banquet of him? Shall they part him among the merchants?'[1]

The Stellar Universe, which was the first field in which any exact and systematic discovery of 'laws of Nature' was ever made by the Collective Intellect of Man in Process of Civilization, had not yet been made amenable to technological manipulation at the time of writing; and a Late Modern Western Man's world-conquering intelligence had liberated him from the astrologer's mistaken belief that human affairs were at the mercy of malignant influences emanating from the inexorable courses of the stars, only to convince him of a truth that convicted him of sin. The successive discoveries of a 'know-how' for navigating the air and splitting the atom in a society that had not yet rid itself of the institution of War had made it manifest to a technologically triumphant generation that the malignity of Leviathan 'is not in our stars but in ourselves'.[2]

A human soul that has been convicted of sin, and been convinced that it cannot achieve its own reformation without the help of God's grace, will opt, like David, to fall into the hand of the Lord and not into the hand of Man.[3] An inexorability in punishing, as well as in exposing, Man's sin, which is the Last Judgement of 'the laws of Nature', can be overcome only by accepting the jurisdiction of a 'Law of God'. The price of this transfer of spiritual allegiance is a forfeiture of that exact and definitive intellectual knowledge, with its attendant technological power, which is the material prize and the spiritual burden of human souls that are content to be Nature's masters at the cost of being her slaves. 'It is a fearful thing to fall into the hands of the living God';[4] for, if God is a spirit,[5] His dealings with human spirits will be unpredictable and inscrutable, as the acts of any personality always are for any other personality that has to meet its kind in an encounter. In appealing to the Law of God, a human soul has to abandon certainty in order to embrace Hope and Fear; for a law that is the expression of a will is animated by a spiritual freedom which is the very antithesis of the *saeva necessitas* of laws of Nature, and an arbitrary law may be inspired either by redemptive Love or by vindictive Hate, may be administered either by making a winning appeal or by exerting an overbearing compulsion, and may be designed to promote either good or evil. In casting itself upon the Law of God, a human soul is apt to find in this what it brings to it; for in the mirror of God's perfection it will see a reflection of itself, and hence Man's notions of the Law of God have run to irreconcilable extremes of

---

[1] Job. xli. 1–6.   [2] Shakspeare: *Julius Caesar*, Act I, scene ii.
[3] 2 Sam. xxiv. 14.   [4] Hebrews x. 31.   [5] John iv. 24.

diversity, in which a *visio beatifica* of God the Father wars with a *visio malefica* of God the Tyrant. This conflict of incompatible visions will exercise us throughout this Part. At the present stage we have merely to take note of the indisputable truth that both visions alike are consonant with the image of God as a personality pictured in the anthropomorphic guise beyond which the human imagination seems to be impotent to penetrate even in its farthest flights of intuition.

(III) THE ANTINOMIANISM OF LATE MODERN WESTERN HISTORIANS

(a) THE REPUDIATION OF THE BELIEF IN A 'LAW OF GOD' BY LATE MODERN WESTERN MINDS

The idea of a 'Law of God' had been wrought out by the travail of the souls[1] of Israelite and Iranian prophets in intuitive responses to the challenges of Babylonic and Syriac history, while the classical expositions of the concept of 'laws of Nature' had been blue-printed by philosophic observers of the disintegration of an Indic and an Hellenic World. Yet, though these might be the illustrations of the two possible schools of metaphysics that would occur most readily to a twentieth-century Western mind, we have already observed[2] that one or other of the two concepts had been embraced in some form by the children of almost all civilizations that had met with the experiences of breakdown and disintegration.

Moreover, both concepts can be entertained by the same mind at the same time without any prohibitive inconsistency; for, even if they were incompatible in the theoretical sense of being logically irreducible to unity,[3] this would not *ipso facto* make them incompatible in the practical sense of its being inconceivable that these two kinds of Law should be in force simultaneously side by side. We can, indeed, conceive of them as being co-regnant, not only without conflict, but in positive co-operation

---

[1] Isa. xliii. 11.   [2] In V. vi. 15-49.

[3] Actually, the gulf between the repetitive recurrent regularity of 'a law of Nature' and the purposively, and therefore non-repetitively, persistent regularity of the Law of God appears to be unbridgeable only so long as we forget that, in thinking of the phenomena in which 'a law of Nature' manifests itself, the thinking human mind itself is a party to the situation.

There is a sense in which the mind's faculty of memory—reinforced and amplified in its range by the social technique of making and preserving records—converts every repetitive cyclic movement into a unique one-way movement (i.e. a movement of the same character, in this respect, as the movement manifested in the Law of God). When the repetitions of the phenomena are not unrealistically abstracted from their subjective setting, it is manifest that Repetition No. x+1 differs from Repetition No. x not merely quantitatively but also qualitatively, because the apprehension of it carries with it a memory of x previous instances, whereas the apprehension of No. x carries with it a memory of x—1 instances only.

'Let us take the most stable of all internal states: the visual perception of an exterior object at rest. It is in vain that the object remains the same, and that I look at it from the same side, from the same angle, in the same light: the vision that I have of it differs, none the less, from the vision that I had of it just now—if only because it has aged by the quantum of one instant. My memory is there, and my memory injects something from this past into this present. My mental state, as it advances along the track of Time, is constantly swelling its bulk with the duration that it is amassing; it is making, so to speak, a snowball of itself' (Bergson, H.: *L'Évolution Créatrice*, 24th ed. (Paris 1921, Alcan), p. 2).

with one another, in virtue of the very diversity between the two notions of regularity which they respectively embody. 'The Law of God' reveals the regularity of a single constant aim pursued unwaveringly, in the face of all obstacles and in response to all challenges, by the intelligence and will of a personality. 'Laws of Nature' display the regularity of a recurrent movement—for instance, the motion of a wheel revolving any number of times round its axis. If we could imagine a wheel coming into existence without owing its creation to a wheelwright, and then revolving *ad infinitum* without ever serving any purpose, these 'repetitions' would indeed seem 'vain';[1] and this was the pessimistic conclusion drawn by Indic and Hellenic philosophers from a *Weltanschauung* in which, by a *tour de force* of intellectual abstraction, they had set 'the sorrowful wheel of existence' turning for ever *in vacuo*. In real life, of course, we find no wheels without wheelwrights, and no wheelwrights without drivers who commission these artificers to build wheels and fit them to carts in order that the wheels' repetitive revolutions may recur, not in vain, but for the practical and practicable purpose of conveying a cart towards the driver's intended goal. 'Laws of Nature' make sense when they are pictured as being the wheels that God has fitted to His own chariot;[2] and a truth that is true of the orbits of the stars in courses laid down for them by an act of God's power is no less manifestly true of recurrent spiritual responses to the challenges of God's love, such as a human soul's experience of sin, fall, penitence, and grace, or a human society's experience of breakdown, disintegration, and illumination by the spark of creativity that announces the epiphany of a higher religion.[3]

In fact, the apparent incompatibility between the two kinds of regularity is merely a mirage in the shadow-world of abstract logic; in real life they are not only compatible with one another but are inseparably complementary in a divinely inspired interplay in which, at divers levels of Reality, cyclic movements according to laws of Nature are successively transcended in experiences and endeavours that, in turn, are subject to cyclic movements at a higher level from which, in turn, still higher experiences and endeavours spring. The astronomical day-cycle and year-cycle are transcended in the cumulative experience and endeavour of a human being's life-time. A life-time is subject to the biological generation-cycle, and this in turn is transcended in the cumulative experience and endeavour of a human society in process of civilization. A civilization is subject to a menacing possibility (though not to an inexorably predetermined doom) of breaking down and disintegrating, and the breakdowns and disintegrations of civilizations in turn are transcended in the cumulative spiritual progress of Religion through learning by suffering. This cumulative progress of Religion—which is the spiritually highest kind of experience and endeavour within the range of Man on Earth—is a progress in the provision for Man, in his passage through This World, of means of illumination and grace for helping the pilgrim, while still engaged on his earthly pilgrimage, to attain a closer communion with God and to become less unlike Him.[4]

---

[1] Matt. vi. 7.
[3] See I. i. 57 and VII. vii. 551–5.
[2] See IV. iv. 34–38.
[4] See VII. vii. 563–4.

If our two concepts of the character of metaphysical 'law' can thus both be held simultaneously by the same mind, and if at any rate one or other of them has actually been held by the children of most of the civilizations known to History, it is not surprising to find that the Western Christian Civilization was originally no exception to this rule. A belief that the whole life of the Universe was governed by 'the Law of God' was the *qiblah* of a Judaic *Weltanschauung* that was the common heritage of the Orthodox Christian, the Western Christian, the Arabic Muslim, and the Iranic Muslim societies; and a theocentric philosophy of history derived from the intuitions or inspirations of the Prophets of Israel and Judah and the Iranian Prophet Zarathustra was bequeathed to Western Christendom in Saint Augustine's *De Civitate Dei* and to the Arab Muslim World in Ibn Khaldūn's *Prolegomena* to his *History of the Berbers*—two works of spiritual genius which unmistakably reflect one single common outlook and whose mutual affinity can only be accounted for by their indebtedness to a common source, since Ibn Khaldūn was as ignorant of his Christian predecessor and fellow Maghribī's theodicy as Augustine was of *Muqaddamāt* that did not see the light till more than nine hundred years after the Christian North African Father's death.

The Augustinian version of a Judaic view of history was taken for granted by Western Christian thinkers throughout the first millennium (*circa* A.D. 675–1675) of the Western Civilization's life and was reformulated—to incorporate the additions made to Western knowledge since the fifteenth century of the Christian Era by an Italian renaissance of Hellenism and an Iberian conquest of the Ocean—in a *Discours sur l'Histoire Universelle* published in A.D. 1681 by Jacques-Bénigne Bossuet (*vivebat* A.D. 1627–1704). The Eagle of Meaux's majestic variation on a traditional Judaic theme was, however, the last serious Western performance of this spiritual masterpiece; for, while Bossuet was in the act of writing his classic discourse, a spiritual revolution was taking place around him in his world. Within the brief span of the last few decades of the seventeenth century of the Christian Era, a Western World that was exorcizing a stalking ghost of Hellenism[1] was at the same time liquidating its own ancestral Judaic *Weltanschauung*.

This Late Modern Western act of apostasy has an explanation which is also an excuse. The Western exponents of the view that History was governed by a 'Law of God' had 'given great occasion to the enemies of the Lord to blaspheme'[2] by allowing themselves to fall into an anthropomorphic misconstruction and misrepresentation of the Prophets' and Evangelists' insight into the relation established between God and Man by God. The heart of the Judaic discovery—or revelation—had been an intuition of the truth that, in virtue of a love, forbearance, and self-abnegation (κένωσις)[3] that were the stigmata of God's divine creativity, God's service is Man's perfect freedom[4] and God's Law is a perfect law of liberty;[5] but this revelation had become blurred in human hearts and

---

[1] See pp. 62–73, above. [2] 2 Sam. xii. 14.
[3] Phil. ii. 7–8 (as translated in the Revised Version).
[4] The Second Collect, for Peace, in the order for Morning Prayer in the Book of Common Prayer according to the Use of the Church of England.
[5] Jas. i. 25 and ii. 12.

minds because the mystical experience of the relation between Man and God was not, and could not be, reproduced in the practical experience of any relation between Man and Man in an exclusively human social milieu. A coercive justice that vindicated an imperfect freedom by usurping a perfect freedom's place was the best that Man, following his own devices, had found himself able to make of the bad business of try-ing to hold together a society of sinners who showed themselves humanly ungodlike in standing upon their own rights and in envying their neigh-bours' prosperity even when it was inoffensive and legitimate; and the Prophets' God-given vision of God had only to falter and fade for the bleared eyes of the Prophets' children to misread 'the Law of God' by interpreting the word 'law' literally in terms of a familiar human law in which the Prophets had found their inadequate but indispensable human symbol for speaking of divine thoughts and ways that, being God's, were ineffable.[1]

This travesty of a Christian intuition of 'the Law of God' has been accurately described and erroneously identified with the reality in the following summary account of it by a post-Modern Western historian-philosopher.

'Any history written on Christian principles will be of necessity univer-sal, providential, apocalyptic, and periodized. . . . If challenged to explain how he knew that there was in History any objective plan at all, the mediaeval historian would have replied that he knew it by revelation; it was part of what Christ had revealed to Man concerning God. And this revelation not only gave the key to what God had done in the past; it showed us what God was going to do in the future. The Christian revela-tion thus gave us a view of the entire history of the World, from its creation in the past to its end in the future, as seen in the timeless and eternal vision of God. Thus mediaeval historiography looked forward to the end of History as something fore-ordained by God and through revelation foreknown to Man. It thus contained in itself an eschatology.'[2]

While we may challenge our historian-philosopher's claim to have expounded the theology of the Bible, we must concede that his picture is a trenchant *exposé* of the misconception entertained by Bossuet; for the guileless bishop of Meaux has furnished us with inculpatory evi-dence against himself.

'Ce long enchaînement des causes particulières qui font et défont les empires dépend des ordres secrets de la divine Providence. Dieu tient du plus haut des cieux les rênes de tous les royaumes; il a tous les cœurs en sa main: tantôt il retient les passions, tantôt il leur lâche la bride, et par là il remue tout le genre humain. . . . Dieu exerce par ce moyen ses redoutables jugements, selon les règles de sa justice toujours infaillible. C'est lui qui prépare les effets dans les causes les plus éloignées et qui frappe ces grands coups dont le contre-coup porte si loin.'[3]

In Bossuet's picture a Medieval Western Christian imaginary portrait

---

[1] Is. lv. 8.
[2] Collingwood, R. G.: *The Idea of History* (Oxford 1946, Clarendon Press), pp. 49 and 54.
[3] Bossuet, J.-B.: *Discours sur l'Histoire Universelle*, 3rd ed. (Paris 1700), Troisième Partie, chap. viii.

of God the Tyrant has been brought up to date by painting over the naïve original the more sophisticated lineaments of a Louis XIV; and our historian-philosopher has good ground for asserting that

'In Mediaeval thought the complete opposition between the objective purpose of God and the subjective purpose of Man, so conceived that God's purpose appears as the imposition of a certain objective plan upon History quite irrespective of Man's subjective purposes, leads inevitably to the idea that Man's purposes make no difference to the course of History, and that the only force which determines it is the Divine Nature.'[1]

This reading of a distorted Medieval Western Christian *Weltanschauung* is borne out by a scrutiny of Early Modern Western reproductions of it.

Bossuet, for example, delivers himself into his critics' hands when he seeks to justify his picture of God's plan by placing this under a magnifying glass.

'Vous voyez un ordre constant dans tous les desseins de Dieu, et une marque visible de sa puissance dans la durée perpétuelle de son peuple. . . .

'Plus vous vous accoutumerez à suivre les grandes choses et à les rappeler à leurs principes, plus vous serez en admiration de ces conseils de la Providence. Il importe que vous en preniez de bonne heure les idées, qui s'éclairciront tous les jours de plus en plus dans votre esprit, et que vous appreniez à rapporter les choses humaines aux ordres de cette sagesse éternelle dont elles dépendent. . . .

'Trois choses devaient . . . concourir ensemble : l'envoi du Fils de Dieu, la réprobation des Juifs, et la vocation des Gentils. . . . L'Église, victorieuse des siècles et des erreurs, ne pourra-t-elle pas vaincre dans nos esprits les pitoyables raisonnements qu'on lui oppose ; et les promesses divines, que nous voyons tous les jours s'y accomplir, ne pourront-elles nous élever au-dessus des sens ? Et qu'on ne nous dise pas que ces promesses demeurent encore en suspens, et que, comme elles s'étendent jusqu'à la fin du Monde, ce ne sera qu'à la fin du Monde que nous pourrons nous vanter d'en avoir vu l'accomplissement. Car, au contraire, ce qui s'est passé nous assure de l'avenir : tant d'anciennes prédictions si visiblement accomplies nous font voir qu'il n'y aura rien qui ne s'accomplisse, et que l'Église, contre qui l'enfer, selon la promesse du Fils de Dieu, ne peut jamais prévaloir, sera toujours subsistante jusqu'à la consommation des siècles, puisque Jésus-Christ, véritable en tout, n'a point donné d'autres bornes à sa durée. . . .

'Si on ne découvre pas ici un dessein toujours soutenu et toujours suivi ; si on n'y voit pas un même ordre des conseils de Dieu qui prépare dès l'origine du Monde ce qu'il achève à la fin des temps, et qui, sous divers états, mais avec une succession toujours constante, perpétue aux yeux de tout l'univers la sainte société où il veut être servi, on mérite de ne rien voir, et d'être livré à son propre endurcissement comme au plus juste et au plus rigoureux de tous les supplices.'[2]

The Eagle of Meaux is able to carry off this travesty of the authentic Christian revelation on the wings of a magnificent style; but, when

---

[1] Collingwood, R. G.: *The Idea of History* (Oxford 1946, Clarendon Press), p. 55. Cp. p. 48.

[2] Bossuet, J.-B.: *Discours sur l'Histoire Universelle*, 3rd ed. (Paris 1700), Seconde Partie, chap. xxx; Troisième Partie, chap. i; Seconde Partie, chaps xxix and xxx.

Bossuet's theme is handled by pedestrian representatives of the same Medieval school of Early Modern Western historical thought, the ridiculous bathos to which a sublime Biblical doctrine has been reduced becomes prosaically apparent.[1] Archbishop Ussher[2] (*vivebat* A.D. 1581–1656) makes the Medieval Western Christian *Weltanschauung* chronologically ludicrous when he mobilizes the heavy artillery of Early Modern Western scholarship to demonstrate that the date of the Creation was 4004 (*sic*, not 4000) B.C.,[3] Old Style, at 6 p.m. on the evening before the 23 October;[4] and Dr. Hartmann Schedel, the learned compiler of the Nuremberg Chronicle,[5] makes it visually ludicrous when, between a preview of the Last Things that are to bring History to its meticulously predetermined end and the colophon of a record of already accomplished events, that he has carried down to the moment at which the manuscript was sent to the printer, he inserts three blank folios in order to give an industrious owner of the tome the necessary space, if he is willing to write on both sides of each sheet, for completing the record between the year 1493 of the Christian Era and God's fore-appointed 'D-Day' for the sounding of the Last Trump.[6] When all due allowance has been made

---

[1] 'Du sublime au ridicule il n'y a qu'un pas' (Napoleon to de Pratt, after the Grand Army's retreat from Moscow in A.D. 1812).   [2] See VI. vii. 299.

[3] 'In hanc concessi sententiam: a vesperâ primum Mundi diem aperiente ad mediam noctem primum Christianae aerae diem inchoantem, annos fluxisse 4003, dies 70, et horas temporarias 6, verumque Christi Domini natalem, quadriennio toto (quod mortis Herodis tempus demonstrat) vulgaris aerae Christianae principio anteriorem extitisse. Juxta rationes enim nostras, et Salomonici Templi structura 3000 Mundi anno est absoluta; et 4000 Mundi anno, impletis diebus quibus Virgo Θεοτόκος erat paritura, Christus in perfectâ carne, cujus Templum fuerat typus, hominibus primum apparuit et manifestatus est. Unde ad annos aerae Christianae 4 additis, et ab annis ante eandem totidem detractis, pro communi et vulgatâ vera et germana obtinebitur Nativitatis Christi epocha' (Ussher, J.: *Annales Veteris Testamenti a Primâ Mundi Origine Deducti* (London 1650, Flesher), *Lectori*).

[4]

	Anno Periodi Juliani	Anno ante aeram Christianam
'In principio creavit Deus Coelum et Terram' [Genes. i, 2], quod temporis principium (juxta nostram Chronologiam) incidit in noctis illius initium quae xxiii diem Octobris praecessit, in anno Periodi Julianae 710. 'Primo igitur seculi die (Oct. 23, feriâ 1) cum supremo Coelo creavit Deus angelos,' etcetera.	710	4004

Ibid., p. 1.

[5] Schedel, Hartmann: *Liber Chronicarum* (Nuremberg, 12th July, 1493, Anton Koberger).

[6] After bringing his narrative of the *Sexta Etas Mundi* down to the moment (ka'as Junias Anno ab incarnatione salvatoris xp̃i Millesimo quadringentesimo nonagesimo tercio) of going to press, Dr. Schedel addresses the reader as follows in his last paragraph on the reverse side of his folio cclviii:
'Cartas aliquas sine scriptura pro sexta etate deinceps relinquere convenit. indicio posterio ψ. q̃ emẽdare addere. atq; gesta principum ƺ privatorum succedentium perscribere possunt. Non em̃ omnia possumus omnes. Et quando ꝙ bonus dormitat homerus. In terra em̃ aurum queritur. ƺ de fluviorum alveis splendens profertur gloria. pactolus qƺ ditior est ceno ꝙƺ fluento. Varii quoqƺ mirabiles qƺ motus in orbe in dies exoriuntur. Qui novos requirunt libros. quibus ordine referantur. Pauca tamen de ultima etate ut perfectum opus relinquatur in fine operis adjiciemus.'
The three immediately following folios, Nos. cclviiii, cclx, and cclxi, are duly blank on both sides except for the page number at the head of the recto side of each of them; and these blank folios are followed in turn by an illustrated account of the *Septima etas mũdi.* This occupies folios cclxii to cclxvi inclusive, and consists of four and a half pages of

for the margin of elasticity which the use of the pen instead of the press would confer on an owner-chronicler by permitting him to contract or expand his hand-writing to fit the chronological length of the lacuna, whatever this might turn out to be,[1] Dr. Schedel can hardly be acquitted, even so, of having come impiously near to playing Providence in venturing to cast up the number of pages that would be required for completing the record of 'the times before appointed'[2] on the same scale as the already past and printed portion of the story. What would an earthly autocrat have said to one of his subjects who had thus presumed to indulge in public speculation on the timing of a future act of state when the intended date had been expressly docketed 'top secret'? And had not Christ rebuffed the importunate curiosity of the Apostles with the chastening words 'It is not for you to know the times or the seasons, which the Father hath put in His own power'?[3]

In presenting a travesty of the Christian revelation in such quaintly ridiculous caricatures as these, the Medieval-minded Early Modern Western historians were inviting decimation by a cross-fire from a Late Modern scientific dogmatism on the one flank and from a Late Modern agnostic scepticism on the other; and they are defenceless against the strictures with which their 'abstract and one-sided theocentric view' has been castigated by a post-Modern Western historian-philosopher. The Medieval historians 'fell', according to this harsh but not unmerited verdict, 'into the error of thinking that they could forecast the future', and, 'in their anxiety to detect the general plan of History, and their belief that this plan was God's and not Man's, they tended to look for the essence of History outside History itself, by looking away from Man's actions in order to detect the plan of God.'

'Consequently the actual detail of human actions became for them

---

narrative *De Antichristo, De morte ac fine rerum*, and *De extremo iudicio ac fine mundi*; a commentary in Latin verse on a half-page woodcut of the Dance of Death; and two full-page woodcuts: one of the epiphany of Antichrist and the other of the Last Judgement.

The awe-inspiring effect of this *finale* is somewhat diminished by the addition of the supplement, occupying folios cclxvii to ccc inclusive, that is advertised in the last sentence of the last paragraph on folio cclviii, quoted above; but it is plain that the learned doctor could not restrain himself from providing this unseasonable receptacle for a windfall of information about Poland and for a map of Europe.

The writer of this Study had come across a copy of Dr. Schedel's *magnum opus* at Blellach House, Dinnet, Aberdeenshire, in July 1908, and the blank folio pages had made an indelible impression on his memory; but, being then still at an unmethodical age, he had neglected to take a note of what the book containing these blank pages had been. He identified the work as the Nuremberg Chronicle on the 23rd June, 1952, when he was allowed, by the courtesy of the keepers of the New York Public Library's rare books, to inspect the second of the copies in the Library's possession.

[1] 'Sometimes a copy comes to light in which an owner did accept the challenge. Usually written in sixteenth-century hands, they record all-but-forgotten wars which were bitterly important, no doubt, to the people who wrote them. The carelessness of later binders who could not read the text and saw no point to including blank leaves in a volume, or who had, perhaps, a desire for a few sheets of fine, old, handsome paper, has cost many a copy of the Chronicle its famed three blank leaves. But in perfect copies they still remain, their white, unblemished surfaces questioning a future which has already extended nearly half a millennium beyond the time when Hartmann Schedel arranged to put them there for the accommodation of his readers' (Shaffer, Ellen: *The Nuremberg Chronicle* (Los Angeles 1950, Plantin Press, for Dawson Book Shop, Los Angeles), pp. 31–32).

[2] Acts xvii. 26.   [3] Acts i. 7.

relatively unimportant, and they neglected that prime duty of the historian, a willingness to bestow infinite pains on discovering what actually happened. This is why mediaeval historiography is so weak in critical method. That weakness was not an accident. It did not depend on the limitation of the sources and materials at the disposal of scholars. It depended on a limitation, not of what they could do, but of what they wanted to do. They did not want an accurate and scientific study of the actual facts of History; what they wanted was an accurate and scientific study of the divine attributes, a theology . . . which should enable them to determine *a priori* what must have happened and what must be going to happen in the historical process.

'The consequence of this is that, when Mediaeval historiography is looked at from the point of view of a merely scholarly historian, the kind of historian who cares for nothing except accuracy in facts, it seems not only unsatisfactory but deliberately and repulsively wrong-headed; and the nineteenth-century [Western] historians, who did in general take a merely scholarly view of the nature of History, regarded it with extreme lack of sympathy.'[1]

This hostility towards a Medieval Western *Weltanschauung* was not peculiar to a generation of latter-day Western historians whose complacent agnosticism facilely reflected the pleasant tranquillity of the places in which the lines had happened to be fallen unto them;[2] at a higher temperature it also animated both their epigoni and their predecessors. A twentieth-century generation of Mankind, that was tasting the extremely unpleasant experience of being driven from pillar to post by the whips of human dictators bent on putting their subjects through four-years' and five-years' plans, would have revolted, as from a chastisement of scorpions,[3] against any seriously intended suggestion that a six-thousand-years' plan was being imposed on them by a dictatorial Deity. The grotesque precision with which the term of this alleged sentence of penal servitude on Mankind had been dated by the pedantry of an archbishop, who had constituted himself the self-appointed clerk of God's court, would have been the last straw on a twentieth-century camel's back if this human beast of burden had any longer taken Ussher's calculations seriously. A seventeenth-century Western Man who had had to pay for his fidelity to a Medieval *Weltanschauung* by inflicting on himself the agony of the Wars of Religion could not afford either to dismiss Bossuet's thesis, in the biting twentieth-century manner, as a bad joke or to ignore it, in the conceited nineteenth-century manner, as the negligibly irrelevant error of a securely transcended ignorance. The seventeenth-century Western intellectual rebel was defiantly up in arms, and the unacceptable words of his mouth[4] soared, instead of condescending, when he proclaimed his resolve

> To wage by force or guile eternal war,
> Irreconcileable to our grand foe,
> Who now triumphs, and in th' excess of joy
> Sole reigning holds the tyranny of Heaven.[5]

---

[1] Collingwood, R. G.: *The Idea of History* (Oxford 1946, Clarendon Press), pp. 55–56.
[2] Ps. xvi. 6.   [3] See 1 Kings xii. 1–16.
[4] Ps. xix. 14.   [5] Milton: *Paradise Lost*, Book I, ll. 121–4.

Like the Satan in whose indomitable perversity the spirit of Late Modern Western Man had been prefigured by Milton's foreboding genius, the heralds of a mundane *Aufklärung* opened their campaign by fastening upon hostages that their adversary had given to Fortune. A Bossuet who had consciously followed the lead of his Christian and Jewish masters, and had unconsciously kept in step with his Muslim contemporaries, in taking for his metaphysical pole star a 'Law of God' governing the whole Life of the Universe, had at the same time found a place in the divine economy of human affairs for 'laws of Nature' which, in Bossuet's belief, were enacted by God as by-laws and were administered by the same divine legislator and potentate to suit the exigencies of His own paramount plan. According to this view the normal cyclically recurrent regularity of these 'by-laws of Nature' could be, and duly was on occasion, interrupted by 'miraculous' acts of personal intervention not unlike those performed by the human driver of a wheeled vehicle when he puts on the brake in descending a hill or even temporarily unships the wheels from the body of the coach in order to negotiate its passage through a strait gate or over a precipitous portage.[1] The first of the new departures made by Bossuet's revolutionary-minded contemporaries was to deny that the wheels of the Universe were ever unshipped, or even braked, in this unceremoniously purposeful fashion. Without prejudice to the questions whether God existed and whether, if He were deemed to exist, He might or might not be deemed to have the same mastery over His Universe as a human coachman has over his coach, the intellectual heralds of a Late Modern Age of Western history declared with one voice that in fact there was no evidence of any deity exercising any such divine prerogative.

There was no essential difference in outlook between Late Modern Western 'deists', who took their cue from 'the Glorious Revolution' of A.D. 1688 in England and Scotland by allowing the deity still to reign on the understanding that he should no longer aspire to govern, and Late Modern Western atheists, who, taking their cue from subsequent political revolutions in North America and in France, professed to have dethroned and perhaps even decapitated a Capetian God as the necessary preface to a declaration of Nature's independence. In thus banishing God from the cosmic scene and, in the act, eliminating miracles, Late Modern Western deists and atheists joined forces to release 'the laws of Nature' from their ancient servitude to arbitrary divine checks and balances. Henceforward these 'laws of Nature' were to be free to be entirely inexorable and were consequently to be subject to becoming completely intelligible to the Collective Intellect of Man.

'Avec l'éclat du génie, Newton marque ce passage du transcendant au positif qu'un Pufendorf essayait d'opérer dans le droit, un Richard Simon

---

[1] 'Ce même Dieu qui a fait l'enchaînement de l'univers, et qui, tout-puissant par lui-même, a voulu, pour établir l'ordre, que les parties d'un si grand tout dépendissent les unes des autres, ce même Dieu a voulu aussi que le cours des choses humaines eût sa suite et ses proportions . . . et qu'à la réserve de certains coups extraordinaires où Dieu voulait que sa main parût toute seule, il n'est point arrivé de grand changement qui n'ait eu ses causes dans les siècles précédents.'—Bossuet, J.-B.: *Discours sur l'Histoire Universelle*, 3rd ed. (Paris 1700), Troisième Partie, chap. ii.

dans l'exégèse, un Locke dans la philosophie, un Shaftesbury dans la morale. Avec assurance, il écarte les craintes qu'on pouvait concevoir au sujet des excès d'une raison qui, pendant un temps, se concevait comme destructive. Il réalise l'union, si difficile qu'on pouvait la croire impossible, entre les exigences critiques et les faits d'expérience. L'homme repart à la conquête de l'univers.'[1]

(b) THE CONTEST BETWEEN SCIENCE AND ANTINOMIANISM FOR THE POSSESSION OF AN INTELLECTUALLY DERELICT REALM OF HUMAN AFFAIRS

The realm of Nature which a Late Modern Western Man thus claimed to call 'mine' embraced, in his acquisitive vision, the whole range of non-human phenomena, including the physical composition, structure, and working of the human body—which, in our own definitions of terms,[2] we have duly excluded from the domain of human affairs in adopting a usage in which the word 'human' has the connotation of meaning something spiritual. At this point, however, on his light-hearted aerial voyage, Late Modern Western Man dashed his foot against a stony paradox from which he could not be steered clear by the absent hands of evicted angels.[3] The human priests of Reason, who had divested God of His divine privilege of arbitrary intervention in order to assert the counter-omnipotence of their own rival goddess, had no sooner subjected the formerly recalcitrant province of Non-Human Nature to Reason's rule than they made a second revolutionary new departure by paradoxically proclaiming another province which had hitherto been submissive to Reason's sway to be, after all, outside the bounds of her jurisdiction.

Late Modern Western minds that had risen in rebellion against the alleged arbitrariness of God now found Man usurping a prerogative that the Deity was deemed to have forfeited; for, if this was Reason's hour, it was also the power of Darkness.[4] Even these ingeniously rational minds had not the wit to make the sovereignty of Nature effective in every nook and corner of a Universe throughout which they had now abrogated the sovereignty of God; and one of these newly created residual Alsatias which eighteenth-century Western philosophers ruefully found themselves compelled to abandon to the anarchy of Chaos and Ancient Night[5] was the field of human history in the conventionally restricted sense of the history of those human societies that had been in process of civilization for the past few thousand years. In the vision bequeathed by Amos, Hosea, and Isaiah to Augustine, Ibn Khaldūn, and Bossuet, this episode of history had raised no insuperable moral or intellectual stumbling-block, since a faith that had been 'the evidence of things not seen'[6] had not doubted that 'all things work together for good to them that love God, to them who are the called according to His purpose';[7] but the Late Modern Western philosophers had now swept off the altar of Destiny a living cloth[8] woven on a divine pattern; and, in

---

[1] Hazard, P.: *La Crise de la Conscience Européenne* (*1680–1715*) (Paris 1935, Boivin), p. 328.
[2] See pp. 168–9, above.   [3] Ps. xci. 11–12.   [4] Luke xxii. 53.
[5] Milton: *Paradise Lost*, Book II, l. 970.
[6] Heb. xi. 1.   [7] Rom. viii. 28.
[8] See Goethe: *Faust*, l. 509, quoted in II. i. 204 and in V. vi. 324.

hastily setting themselves to cover a shockingly denuded surface with their own blue-print of 'the laws of Nature', they were disconcerted to find that this paper substitute could not be stretched, however mercilessly they might rack the scientific imagination, to extend over the particular field of events that concerned Man more than any other in virtue of its being the field in which Man's own life was at stake.

'In the eighteenth century, scientific inquiry concerned itself with what was "natural", to the exclusion of what was judged to be "unnatural", "monstrous", "accidental" and "unusual". . . . The humanists of the eighteenth century . . . assumed that the scientific study of change must have for its aim the determination of the "natural" or normal course of development of social groups, abstraction being made from the "accidental" interferences or hindrances occasioned by historical "events". . . . If we adopt this point of view . . . historical events will be conceived [of] merely as interferences with the "natural order". . . . What this mode of approach entailed was that the investigator should ignore, or rather eliminate from consideration, the intrusive influences which had interfered with the operations of the "natural order" in the course of Time. The point of view was thus arrived at which regarded historical "events" as unimportant and irrelevant for the purposes of scientific inquiry in the investigation of "progress" and of "evolution".'[1]

The stand thus taken by eighteenth-century Western philosophers was a logical corollary of their metaphysical policy; for, when once they had placarded on the door of Nature's power-house the notice 'No admittance except on Nature's business', they had left themselves no excuse for putting up with interferences by Man in precincts where they had shut the door in the face of an interfering God. Logic constrained rational minds to give to 'historic events' the short shrift given by them to 'miracles'. Yet, logical though this eighteenth-century Western attitude might be, it was not on that account at all less quaint, and its nineteenth-century sequel was quainter; for the subsequent evolution of the film of a Late Modern Western *Weltanschauung* brought on to the screen the spectacle of nineteenth-century and twentieth-century Western historians still clinging, in the name of Science, to the eighteenth-century philosophers' tenet that History does not make sense.[2] The quaintness of this self-stultifying eighteenth-century-mindedness of latter-day Western historians[3] lay in their apparently weather-proof imperviousness to the influences of a number of radical nineteenth-century and twentieth-

---

[1] Teggart, F. J.: *Theory of History* (New Haven, Conn. 1925, Yale University Press), pp. 84–87.
[2] The statement of this tenet had been reduced from five words to three in an epigram —'History is bunk'—that had been maliciously attributed to Mr. Henry Ford the First.
[3] General statements, such as this and those that follow, about the tenets, views, and attitudes of Late Modern and post-Modern Western historians are, of course, merely descriptions of what, as the present writer saw it, was the *predominant* school of thought among them; and therefore these statements, even if they were found to be correct in the main, would never be more than approximately accurate in the sense of being all-embracing. In every generation in this age, it would be possible to point to distinguished individuals of whom these statements were not true. The purpose of the present part of this Study is to trace, analyse, and appraise the prevailing line of historical thought in a Late Modern and a post-Modern Western World, at the risk of perhaps doing some injustice to a perennially dissident minority.

century changes in the climate of thought in their own Western intellectual milieu.

The first of these changes was a revolutionary improvement in the intellectual status of the historians' own mental activity. In the eighteenth century the depreciation of History in theory for the metaphysical reasons expounded by the latter-day student of History whom we have just cited had been accompanied, as was to be expected, by a contempt for, and neglect of, the pursuit of History in practice; and the acclamation with which Gibbon's work of genius (*edebatur* A.D. 1776–88) was greeted by that great eighteenth-century historian's contemporaries was the exception that proved the eighteenth-century rule. Gibbon's contemporary fame and vogue were, however, also portents of an approaching avalanche into a new geological age; for, within twenty-five years of the publication of the last instalment of *The History of the Decline and Fall of The Roman Empire* in A.D. 1788, the valuation of History had begun to appreciate on the Western intellectual stock exchange, and thereafter the boom had been buoyed up progressively to ever higher levels until, at the time of writing mid-way through the twentieth century of the Christian Era, a school of post-Modern Western scientists, whose own prestige was then perhaps only just passing its zenith, had paid their tribute of sincere flattery to the still rising prestige of the history of human affairs by condescending to take observations of their non-human objects of study in an historical perspective.

The latter-day Western physical scientists who were thus courteously dipping their flag to latter-day Western historians of human affairs, as their ships glided past one another, were, however, at the same time slyly committing against their fellow mariners a series of acts of piracy on high seas that had been left lawless through having been released from the jurisdiction of God without having been brought within the three-mile limit of any human intellectual discipline's territorial waters.

Eighteenth-century metaphysical cartographers had partitioned the Universe on the one side into an orderly province of non-human affairs in which 'the laws of Nature' were believed to be in force, and which was therefore held to be accessible to progressive exploration by the cumulative enterprise of a Collective Human Intellect, and on the other side into a chaotic province of human history which was dogmatically declared to be intrinsically unchartable. This arbitrary division of the Apple of Life was as pretentious a gesture as the disreputable Early Modern Western Pope Alexander VI's pretension to divide the surface of one planet between the Borgia's Castilian fellow-countrymen and their Portuguese competitors; and the eighteenth-century metaphysical operation also suffered from two incurable flaws which had made Pope Alexander's cartographical bulls a dead letter. Like these, it was influenced by a human bias and, like these again, it failed to allow for the extent and configuration of still undiscovered seas and lands. The eighteenth-century Western partition of the Universe did not, in fact, account for all that therein is.[1] It did not cover the whole area of even the single province of human affairs. There were branches or aspects of

[1] Ps. cxlvi. 6.

human affairs that were left by this imperfect partition in a no-man's-land; and, in the course of a quarter of a millennium running from the date of Bossuet's death to the time of writing, stretches of this post-Bossuetan Western intellectual no-man's-land had been occupied, polder by polder, by predatory pioneers of a Late Modern Western Science and had been progressively annexed by these intellectual pirates to the domain of 'the laws of Nature'.

In embarking on these empire-building intellectual enterprises, these aggressive-minded Western civil engineers had found a base of operations long since prepared for them, and invitingly awaiting their installation, in one science of human affairs that had been inherited by these post-Christian scientists from Christian predecessors to whom this property had been bequeathed by Hellenic philosophers. In the seventeenth and eighteenth centuries, Western minds had continued, on the strength of an acquiescence in tradition which was as uncritical as it was unacknowledged, to believe that the conscious human mind was effectively governed by 'laws of thought'; Descartes himself had never dreamed of retreating from this venerably green polder on to the forbiddingly bleak metaphysical *terra firma* in its rear; and, since the Hellenes had remained unaware of their Indic contemporaries' discovery of the Subconscious, while the Franks did not begin to make their own independent discovery of this until they had been enlightened by shell-shock after their catastrophe in A.D. 1914, Science's Modern Western empire-builders in the domain of human affairs were able to benefit for more than two hundred years by a mental illusion which made the science of 'Logic' and 'the Theory of Knowledge' loom decidedly larger than Life.

From this antique base, between the opening of the nineteenth century of the Christian Era and the middle of the twentieth, Western *conquistadores* whose war-cry was the vindication of Nature's legitimate rights had already reclaimed and annexed at least four further polders from the Modern Western no-man's-land of human affairs without being challenged, or perhaps even observed, by contemporary Western historians. These newly staked-out sciences in the field of human affairs, which a Late Modern Western embodiment of the Collective Human Intellect had succeeded in adding to the orthodoxly ancient science of Logic, were Psychology, Anthropology, Political Economy, and Sociology.

In the field of Psychology—the youngest of these four new sciences of human affairs and, on a superficial view, also the least obviously open, among the four, to the charge of encroaching on the traditional domain of History—the post-Modern Western scientific mind was verifying by observation Pascal's intuition that 'the Heart has its reasons, of which the Reason has no knowledge'.[1] In the twentieth century of the Christian Era a post-Christian Western science of Psychology was beginning to explore the subconscious abyss of the Human Psyche and to discover 'laws of Nature', reigning there, which were not the laws of Logic but were laws of Poetry and Mythology.

---

[1] 'Le cœur a ses raisons, que la raison ne connaît point' (Pascal, B.: *Pensées*, No. 277, in the text as arranged by L. Brunschvicg). In Pascal's vocabulary, 'the Heart' includes 'intuition' as well as 'feeling'.

In the field of Anthropology, Western Science had begun, before the close of the eighteenth century,[1] to bring to light 'laws of Nature' governing the social, cultural, and spiritual life of surviving representatives of Primitive Man who were still lying torpid—after an arduous climb from a sub-human to a human level which it had taken their ancestors hundreds of thousands of years to accomplish—on a ledge from which Man in Process of Civilization had begun, within the last five to six thousand years, to make a number of attempts to climb the cliff-face above.[2]

The label 'Anthropology', that had been assigned to this science of human affairs in the Yin-state into which the primitive societies had latterly subsided, bore on its face the unintended yet psychologically none the less significant implication that Man could only vindicate his title to call himself human so long as he remained torpid, and that Man in Process of Civilization had divested himself of his humanity in the act of crying 'excelsior' and resuming Mankind's temporarily interrupted ascent. In reality, however, it was impracticable for the science of Anthropology to boycott the study of the civilizations, even if that had been its intention, since, long before the enterprise of Civilization had entered on its fifth or sixth millennium, the radiation of one or other of the historical civilizations that had come and gone by that time had penetrated, affected, and modified the social fabric and life of all primitive societies that had survived the impact of this formidable *parvenue* social force.[3]

As a consequence of these encounters with civilizations, to which the primitive societies had been exposed in the course of their latter-day sabbath rest, and through which an epilogue that was not of these primitives' own making or choosing had been added to the closed dynamic chapter of their history, it was impossible for latter-day Western anthropologists to lay hands on any pure specimens of the primitive species of human society that could be certified to be free from all social contamination by the radioactivity of some civilization or other; and the presence of this tincture of Civilization in all the primitive social fabric that was accessible to the anthropologists signified that, if the new science of Anthropology had really been successful—as, admittedly, it had been[4]— in discovering 'laws of Nature' governing the surviving semi-primitive or ex-primitive societies in the contaminated state in which these now presented themselves, a scientific method of ascertaining laws of human affairs that had thus justified itself empirically by proving to be valid in this field of ex-primitive culture would also be, to say the least, a promising line of scientific attack upon the study of societies of the species, known as civilizations, by which all the surviving primitive societies studied by the anthropologists had been contaminated in some degree. In a lull between two world wars, a pair of experienced students of surviving primitive societies had deliberately applied the technique of Anthropology to the study of contemporary life in a typical city in one

[1] The classical pioneer work in the literature of the science of Anthropology was Martin Dobritzhofer's (Dobrizhoffer's) *Historia de Abiponibus, Equestri Bellicosâque Paraquariae Natione* (Vienna 1784, de Kurzbek, 3 vols.).
[2] See II. i. 192–5.   [3] See II. i. 187.   [4] See I. i. 179.

section of the North American province of a Western World;[1] but these anthropologists' dashing reconnaissance into the domain of the civilizations had been anticipated by two other expeditions organized by latter-day Western intellectual *conquistadores* who had never deigned to concern themselves with the conquest of primitive Caribs and Comanches, but had concentrated from the start, with the vaulting ambition of a Cortés or a Pizarro, on the conquest of the Mexicos and Perus.

The first of these scientific attacks on the life of Man in Process of Civilization had been made by what, at the time of writing, it had become fashionable to describe as a 'functional' approach. The eruption of Industrialism out of a social crater in Great Britain in the latter decades of the eighteenth century of the Christian Era, and the wide-spread devastation inflicted by the cataclysmic lava-flow, had produced enormities of material power, social injustice, and spiritual suffering[2] that had caught a horrified Frankenstein's imagination and, in moving his feelings, had spurred his collective intellect to work on the problem of ascertaining what 'laws of Nature' these might be that had thus suddenly asserted their tyrannical rule over Late Modern Western affairs. It was true that, within the century and three-quarters that had elapsed, by the time of writing, since Adam Smith's publication of *The Wealth of Nations* in A.D. 1776, the new Western science of Political Economy had hardly begun to extend its horizon beyond the spatial limits of the Western World or the chronological limits of the industrial phase of the Western Civilization's history; and this was, of course, an almost derisorily small fragment of the total history, already running to five or six millennia, of a species of society of which the Western Civilization was merely one of more than twenty known specimens. The intellectual importance of this new Modern Western science of human affairs was not, however, to be measured by the narrowness of the range of the data that it had brought within its purview so far. In a Late Modern Western World the establishment of a science of Economics had been an intellectually revolutionary event because, on one plane of social[3] activity, within the limits of one society in one chapter of its history, Political Economy had translated into an accomplished reality the eighteenth-century Western philosophers' dream of bringing to light the laws governing 'the natural order'[4] in the affairs of Man in Process of Civilization.

Moreover, the 'classical' nineteenth-century Scottish and English political economists had not been content merely to report the discovery of 'laws of Nature' in their newly reclaimed polder; they had gone on to proclaim to an awe-struck British Israel that these commandments which they had adventurously brought down from the goddess Science's holy mount were 'iron laws' of an adamantine severity; and this timely psychological substitute for the terrors of Hell had been swallowed with

---

[1] See Lynd, Robert S. and Helen M.: *Middletown* (New York 1929, Harcourt Brace) and *Middletown in Transition* (New York 1937, Harcourt Brace).
[2] See IV. iv. 137–92.
[3] In the eighteenth-century term 'Political Economy', the word 'political' had been employed to convey the meaning expressed by the word 'social' in twentieth-century Western usage.
[4] See the passages quoted from Teggart's work on p. 183, above.

a ravenous credulity by an ex-Christian people that was suffering the discomfort of a spiritual vacuum as a consequence of the decay of its ancestral Christian religious beliefs. In the year 1952 of the Christian Era, few Western children were being kept awake at night by a fear of suddenly hearing the blast of the Last Trump, but many chronologically adult Western men and women were living in terror, night and day, of seeing 'the iron laws of Economics' inexorably ordain a catastrophic slump in which the wretched votaries of Free Enterprise would be carried off by the gleefully pouncing demons of Communism to suffer torments, predestined for the economically damned, against which there were no known means of insurance or moral rights of appeal.

After the invading Myrmidons of Science had thus triumphantly established an apparently impregnable strong-point, at the economic level, in the hitherto inviolately irrational domain of Civilization, it would have been surprising if they had not followed up this signal first success in a virgin field by breaking into a general advance at every level and all along the line. This ambitious attempt to assert the sovereignty of 'the laws of Nature' over the life of Man in Process of Civilization in all its aspects and all its dimensions had been initiated by the pioneers of a new human science that had been labelled 'Sociology', though the cause of intellectual clarity might have been served better if this department of the science of Man had been explicitly distinguished from the sociology of Primitive Man by being designated 'the Anthropology of Man in Process of Civilization'. The truth was that the two latter-day Western sciences which had come to be known by the conventional names 'Anthropology' and 'Sociology' were distinguishable from one another, not by any intrinsic difference between their respective methods and aims, but merely by a fortuitous difference between their respective objects of study. They were at one with one another in being endeavours to discover 'laws of Nature' governing Human Life.

This affinity between the sciences of Primitive Human Life and of Human Life in Process of Civilization had been tacitly but eloquently recognized in the practice of research and teaching, and this practical rapprochement between the two academic disciplines had gone so far by A.D. 1948 that in that year the opening sentences of a paper by a sociologist on 'the limitations of anthropological methods in Sociology'[1] could be conceived as follows:

'One of the more interesting of contemporary developments in the

---

[1] This discussion of 'the Limitations of Anthropological Methods in Sociology' by Robert Bierstedt, with a comment on Bierstedt's paper by Clyde Kluckhohn, will be found in *The American Journal of Sociology*, vol. liv, No. 1, July 1948 (Chicago 1948, University of Chicago Press), pp. 22–30. Bierstedt's thesis is summarized as follows in his own abstract of it:

'Profound differences between primitive and civilised societies restrict the efficacy of anthropological methods when applied to the latter. Among the more important of these differences are the following: (1) civilised societies are literate; (2) they have histories; (3) they are susceptible to comprehensive causal analysis in historical terms; (4) their cultural diversity and variety are incomparably great; (5) their relations with other societies are constant and pervasive in both Time and Space. Anthropological methods in general are designed to answer questions whose sociological significance is limited when the subject of inquiry is a civilised society.'

The present writer's comment on Bierstedt's thesis would be: (1) the antithesis

social sciences is the increasingly intimate relationship between Sociology and Anthropology. The influence of anthropological methods, concepts, and even theories has become so powerful in recent years that for many purposes and in many areas of investigation the two sciences have become indistinguishable. In a number of academic departments the personnel is the same; and, in the universities where separate departments are maintained, research and teaching in Social Anthropology and Sociology are characterised by ever closer cooperation.'

It might be added that, in all Western universities mid-way through the twentieth century of the Christian Era, officially established chairs of Logic, Psychology, Anthropology, Political Economy, and Sociology were to be seen 'parked' side by side with no less officially established chairs of History, without any apparent recognition of the academically awkward fact that, if the intellectual creeds of either the professors of History on the one side or the professors of the sciences of human affairs on the other side were to be taken at all seriously by the academic authorities, a decent regard for intellectual integrity would constrain them to rase from the parquet of their aula either one or the other of these two rows of professorial cathedrae. In other periods of Western history than an intellectually anarchic Late Modern and post-Modern Age, Western opinion would indeed have revolted against an intellectual inconsistency and a moral laxity of this cynical enormity; for the intellectual creeds respectively professed by the historians and by the mental and social scientists were irreconcilably contradictory; and, if either creed were ever to be canonized as a sacrosanct orthodoxy, the contrary creed would have to be anathematized in the same breath as a damnable heresy.

'literate' versus 'non-literate' is not a valid differentia between societies in process of civilization and primitive societies: we have at least one instance of a non-literate civilization, i.e. the Andean Society; (2) and (3) the 'historylessness' of primitive societies is not a valid differentia either, for they must have had a lively history once upon a time, though the record of this had been lost and though the surviving primitive societies had become static by the time when the civilizations made their first impacts on them (see the present Study, I. i. 179–80 and II. i. 192–5); (4) the cultural diversity and variety of the civilizations is not incomparably, but only comparatively, greater than that of the primitive societies; (5) the surviving primitive societies had *ex hypothesi* had relations with those civilizations that had made the records of the histories of their encounters with them, and these relations had actually been constant and pervasive in both Time and Space since an early date in the histories of the civilizations of the first generation.

In short, the likenesses between the two sciences of Sociology and Anthropology seemed to the present writer to cut deeper than the differences. On the other hand, in the present Study, in I. i. 148, 455, and 458–61, we have come across what looks like a pertinent point of difference that is not discussed in Bierstedt's paper, and that is the difference in the respective numbers of the specimens of the two species of human society that happened to be at the disposal of Western scientists in the twentieth century of the Christian Era. The sociologists had at their command perhaps no more than twenty-one specimens of their object of investigation, whereas the anthropologists had more than six hundred specimens of theirs. This numerical point of difference was not a difference between the respective methods and aims of the two sciences, and was not a difference, either, between the intrinsic natures of the two species of society that the two sciences were respectively investigating. It was a difference in the extent of the respective current facilities for studying the two species of society scientifically. In practice, this difference was assuredly an important one—even in a generation in which Archaeology had at last brought the civilizations just within the range of scientific investigation by raising the number of specimens to the still meagre figure of twenty-one.

In truth the two schools of latter-day Western scholars held quite incompatible views about the methods and aims that were necessary for intellectual salvation in the study of the affairs of Man in Process of Civilization during the last five or six thousand years; and, since in the twentieth-century phase of their long and hitherto inconclusive controversy the word 'scientific', like the word 'democratic', was a fig-leaf which no Western *savant* could discard without falling foul of a cultural watch committee, the ideological argument between Western scientists and Western historians had to be conducted, like the argument between Russian Communists and Western Old Believers, in the form of a dispute about the meaning to be attached to a word whose sacrosanctity neither party dared impugn. In the political forum the word 'democratic' meant in Russian parlance 'egalitarian' at the expense of liberty, while in Western parlance it meant 'libertarian' at the expense of equality. Neither usage ventured to discard completely either of the two explosive ideas—Equality and Liberty—which the word 'democratic' held together at high tension, but the difference in relative emphasis was a difference of degree that went so far as to be tantamount to a difference of kind for practical purposes. The no less blessed word 'scientific', which was the football in the intellectual arena, likewise held together two ideas—the idea of ascertaining the facts of Nature and the idea of inferring the laws of Nature from an unprejudiced, accurate, and exhaustive study of the facts—and here the difference of doctrine was uncompromisingly sharp.

In this twentieth-century Western intellectual disputation, the writer of this Study was aware that he himself was a combatant and not a neutral spectator; and therefore, in order to neutralize as far as possible the effect of any personal bias that might have influenced his own convictions on the subject, he preferred to refrain from attempting to expound in his own words the doctrinal point at issue, and to lay before his readers, instead, a pair of expositions—the one more favourable and the other less favourable to the thesis which was orthodox for contemporary Western historians—from the pens of two contemporary Western scholars, one of whom was an historian as well as a philosopher, while the other was an historian who had made a special study of the history of Western science.

The philosopher-champion of the historians' thesis sums up and gives judgement as follows:

'Every natural science, said the Positivists, began by ascertaining facts and then went on to discover their causal connexions. Accepting this assertion, Comte proposed that there should be a new science called Sociology, which was to begin by discovering the facts about Human Life (this being the work of the historians) and then go on to discover the causal connexions between these facts. The sociologist would thus be a kind of super-historian, raising History to the rank of a science by thinking scientifically about the same facts about which the historian thought only empirically. . . . The claims of Comtian Sociology were quietly set aside by the abler and more conscientious historians, who came to regard it as sufficient for them to discover and state the facts themselves: in the famous words of Ranke, *wie es eigentlich gewesen.*[1] History as the knowledge of individual facts was gradually detaching itself as an autonomous study from Science as the knowledge of general laws.'[2]

The contemporary historian-critic of the historians' thesis presents an identical picture in a different light:

'In historical science, and particularly in the upper regions of the study, a . . . policy of abstraction has become customary. Historians, limited by the kind of apparatus they use and the concrete evidence on which they must rely, restrict their realm to what we might almost call the mechanism of historical processes: the tangible factors involved in an episode, the displacements produced in human affairs by an observed event or a specific influence, even the kind of movements that can be recorded in statistics.'[3]

The difference, brought out in this pair of passages, between the twentieth-century Western historians' and the contemporary Western scientists' respective usages of the word 'scientific' is driven home by our historian-philosopher in the following hammer-strokes with which he batters the devoted heads of 'positivistic historians . . . who have conceived the true or highest task of History as the discovery of causal laws connecting certain constant types of historical phenomena':

'Perversions of History on these lines all share one characteristic in common, namely a distinction between two kinds of History: empirical history which merely discharges the humble office of ascertaining the facts, and philosophical or scientific history, which has the nobler task of discovering the laws connecting the facts. . . .'

At this point the philosopher-historian deals the unphilosophic historians a blow in the face with his left fist, and the scientists a blow in the face with his right:

'There is no such thing as empirical history, for the facts are not empirically present to the historian's mind: They are past events, to be apprehended not empirically but by a process of inference according to rational principles from data given or rather discovered in the light of these principles; and there is no such thing as the supposed further stage of philosophical or scientific history which discovers their causes or laws or in general explains them, because an historical fact, once genuinely ascertained, grasped by the historian's re-enactment of the agent's thought in his own mind, is already explained. For the historian there is no difference between discovering what happened and discovering why it happened.'[4]

It will be seen that this philosopher-historian's exposition of the twentieth-century Western historians' creed comes near to asserting that

---

[1] *Geschichten der Romanischen und Germanischen Völker*, preface to the 1st ed. (Leopold Ranke's *Werke*, vol. xxxiii–xxxiv, 2nd ed. (Leipzig 1874, Duncker and Humblot), p. vii).—A.J.T.

[2] Collingwood, R. G.: *The Idea of History* (Oxford 1946, Clarendon Press), pp. 128 and 130–1.

[3] Butterfield, Herbert: *Christianity and History* (London 1949, Bell), p. 19. The quotations from this book have been made with the permission of the author and the publishers.

[4] Collingwood, R. G.: *The Idea of History* (Oxford 1946, Clarendon Press), pp. 176–7. Cp. pp. 263–6.

the genius of History lies, not simply in 'not trying', but actually in 'trying not', to make sense of historical facts. Ignoring the consensus of sociologists, economists, psychologists, epistemologists, and logicians, whose scientific activities all alike presupposed the feasibility of studying scientifically the affairs of Man in Process of Civilization, as well as those of a *Homo Sapiens Pristinus* who was the anthropologists' target, most twentieth-century Western historians were in truth still maintaining that anyone who might venture to profess any such science of Man in Process of Civilization would be at best a heretic and at worst a charlatan.

For an interested spectator of this contest, it might be a delicate operation to declare which of the two parties was in the right, but it was not a difficult forecast to foretell which of the two, rightly or wrongly, would be approved as orthodox, and which condemned as heretical, if the case were ever to be brought before the bar of an oecumenical council of the Western Republic of Letters by some controversialist who had the courage of his convictions. It could be predicted with confidence that in that event the anathema would fall upon the historians, for it was manifest that the main line of Western thought was represented, not by them, but by the believers in the possibility of a scientific study of the affairs of Man in Process of Civilization in the sense of an attempt, in this province of Reality as in others, to discover 'laws of Nature' by inference from ascertained facts.

The fundamental faith of Western Man had always been a belief that the Universe was subject to Law and was not given over to Chaos, and a deist or atheist Late Modern Western Man's version of this Western faith was (as we have seen) that the Law of the Universe was a system of 'laws of Nature' which were accessible to progressive investigation, discovery, and formulation by a Collective Human Intellect. Grand discoveries of hitherto latent 'laws of Nature' had been the essential triumphs of a Late Modern Western Civilization's intellectual heroes: Galileo, Newton, Lavoisier, Buffon, Lamarck, Cuvier,[1] Darwin, Einstein —to cite eight of the more famous names. Who would presume to draw a line beyond which these intellectual *conquistadores* must not extend their operations, or, in other words, presume to confine the jurisdiction of 'the laws of Nature' within some conventional limit? A proclamation that one province of the Universe—and this the metropolitan province occupied by Man in Process of Civilization—had been reserved once for all, by some undesignated higher authority, as a sanctuary for Chaos which was to be for ever immune from the jurisdiction of all law, natural or divine, would be odious treason and horrible blasphemy in the judgement of all scientifically *bien pensants* twentieth-century minds; and, if

---

[1] Any reader of Herbert Butterfield's *The Origins of Modern Science, 1300–1800* (London 1949, Bell) will observe that, in the notices of the work of these first six heroes on pp. 61, 125, 186, 203, 207, and 208–9, there is a common feature which in every case is the hero's essential feat. In every case his life-work is the vindication of the reign of 'laws of Nature' in provinces of Reality in which the evidences of Nature's jurisdiction had hitherto been invisible to Mankind's mental vision. While some of these six men of scientific genius did also distinguish themselves by ascertaining or verifying facts, they were famous, not for this, but for 'the discovery of causal laws, connecting certain constant types of . . . phenomena', which, in the province of historical phenomena, was, as we have seen, an illegitimate activity in the eyes of twentieth-century Western historians.

ever the antinomian historians were to be 'put on the spot', an explicit public confession of their shocking atavistic eighteenth-century belief that the life of Man in Process of Civilization was 'a tale told by an idiot, signifying nothing',[1] would inevitably provoke a conviction on the charge of heresy and a sentence to whatever punishment might await a convicted heretic in a post-Modern Western World in which the Late Modern Western virtue of tolerance had fallen back several degrees below an eighteenth-century standard of 'politeness'.

It could be predicted with no less confidence that, if, in our imaginary oecumenical council, some trick of oratory or freak of fortune were to win a majority of the votes for the antinomian historians, the sociologists on whom the tables would then be turned would be no less rightly combustible heretics according to the verdict of an historian-inquisitor. Indeed, if the historians had not yet asked for trouble by taking the offensive against the social scientists and denouncing them on the very charge of heresy that was hanging over the historians' own heads, this tactful tolerance of theirs seemed to be the genial product of an infinite capacity, not for holding their own passions in check, but for ignoring their aggressive adversaries' existence. Mid-way through the twentieth century of the Christian Era, most Western historians seemed still to be contriving to turn as blind an eye to the social scientists' successive trespasses on the historians' pointedly placarded preserve as a Neville Chamberlain had turned in A.D. 1938 to the Third Reich's successive aggressions in the Western World's political arena. In an era of appeasement the historians were allowing the economists to rob the Antinomian World of an Austria, and the sociologists to rob it of a Czechoslovakia, from under the Antinomians' very eyes, without betraying, by even the flicker of an eyelid, any consciousness of these impudent depredations that were being committed at the historians' expense.

One day in the winter of A.D. 1949–50, when the writer of this Study, with the present chapter in mind, was meditating in his native city of London on this strange comedy that was being played within his sight on a contemporary human stage, his legs carried him to the brink of the Round Pond in Kensington Gardens to enjoy a spectacle of which he had never grown tired since the abnormally severe weather in the early months of the year A.D. 1894 had taught the sea-gulls bred in the provinces and abroad to spend their winters in the London parks as the uninvited but pampered guests of the human inhabitants of the metropolis. While he was listening, on this particular afternoon, to the familiar screaming of the excited gulls, as they wheeled and dived, like fighter planes, and jostled with one another to catch in the air the morsels of bread that their human benefactors were, as usual, tossing to them, his eye was caught by the comically 'know-nothing' air of the domesticated ducks, officially domiciled in the Royal Parks and Gardens, who were placidly riding on the water just below the scene of the gulls' frantic aerial manœuvres. 'Too proud to fight',[2] these lawful denizens of the

---

[1] Shakspeare: *Macbeth*, Act. V, scene v.
[2] 'There is such a thing as a man being too proud to fight' (President Woodrow Wilson at Philadelphia on the 10th May, 1915).

pond were saving their face by pretending not to notice how aggressively the boisterous trespassers were behaving. Even when one of the rare crusts that fell into the water without having been intercepted by a gull's beak in its short aerial trajectory was snatched from right under the beak of a lazily floating duck by one of the swooping screeching marauders, the insulted duck, as it bobbed up and down on the wavelets that the gull's swoop had rudely raised, betrayed no sign of awareness that any irregularity was being committed. When the writer heard his wife's voice asking him, in a tone of amused surprise, why he had suddenly burst out laughing, he realized that this comic encounter between ducks and gulls on the Round Pond in Kensington Gardens had moved him to mirth by presenting itself to his imagination as an animated allegory of a drolly similar encounter between historians and social scientists.

(c) THE UNCONSCIOUS CREDULITY OF PROFESSED AGNOSTICS

Did those historians who, duck-like, ignored the gull-like scientists' predatory descents on the historians' preserve live up, in real life, to their own antinomian interpretation of the sacred word 'scientific'? The answers to this question would appear to be that they did not translate their profession of faith into practice and that they failed because the ideal which they had set themselves was impracticable *a priori*; but, in finding the answers to one question, we shall have confronted ourselves with another; and that is the deeper question why a majority of this particular generation of historians in this particular social milieu should ever have taken their antinomian stand at all.

An ironic feature of the latter-day Western historians' failure to honour their own antinomian principles was their unawareness that they were refuting their professions by their practice.

'The men of a given generation are generally unaware of the degree to which they envisage their contemporary history within an assumed frame-work, ranging events into certain shapes or running them into certain moulds which are sometimes adopted almost as in a day-dream. They may be sublimely unconscious of the way their minds are constricted by their routine formulation of the story; and only when the World is different, and there emerges a new generation not locked from birth in the accepted framework, does the narrowness of that framework become apparent to everybody. . . . It is a mistake for writers of history and other teachers to imagine that if they are not Christian they are refraining from committing themselves, or working without any doctrine at all, discussing History without any presuppositions. Amongst historians, as in other fields, the blindest of all the blind are those who are unable to examine their own presuppositions, and blithely imagine therefore that they do not possess any.'[1]

This tragi-comic figure of the prisoner who pronounces himself free because he is unconscious of his chains has crossed our path once already. In an earlier context we have quoted a profession of unbelief

[1] Butterfield, Herbert: *Christianity and History* (London 1949, Bell), pp. 140 and 46.

which its distinguished author manifestly felt to be an effective declaration of intellectual independence:

'One intellectual excitement has . . . been denied me. Men wiser and more learned than I have discerned in History a plot, a rhythm, a pre-determined pattern. These harmonies are concealed from me. I can see only one emergency following upon another as wave follows upon wave; only one great fact with respect to which, since it is unique, there can be no generalisations; only one safe rule for the historian: that he should recognise in the development of human destinies the play of the contingent and the unforeseen.'[1]

This declaration had become a *locus classicus* within seventeen years of the date of its publication;[2] yet, before it was published, it had already been put out of court by its author's choice of his title for the book in which this prefatory passage was intended to strike the key-note. An historian who had thus publicly declared his allegiance to the dogma that 'Life is just one damned thing after another' might have been expected to give his work some such conformably non-committal title as 'A History of Some Emergencies in Some Human Affairs'; but, in calling it, as he did, 'A History of Europe', he was recanting in his title his own denial in his preface that he had 'discerned in History a plot, a rhythm, a pre-determined pattern'; for the portmanteau word[3] 'Europe' is a whole *Corpus Juris Naturae* in itself.

In writing into his title this one word 'Europe', the historian was compromising himself inextricably by subscribing implicitly to at least thirty-nine articles of a submerged Western *religio historici*.

Article One of this traditional Act of Faith is an endorsement of a glaring pattern of cultural geography in which the *Oikoumenê* is dismembered, by a Procrustean operation, into fragments labelled 'Europe' and the rest of 'the continents'.[4] Article Two is an act of homage to an egocentric illusion which was shared by the children of a Western Society with the children of all other societies known to History, and which had misled them all into the identical, and therefore in every case incongruous, assumption that each society's own culture was 'Civilization' with a capital 'C'.[5] Article Three is the detection of a plot in which the emergencies that follow 'upon one another as wave follows upon

---

[1] Fisher, H. A. L.: *A History of Europe* (London 1935, Eyre & Spottiswoode, 3 vols.), vol. i, p. vii, quoted in the present Study, V. v. 414.

[2] The brilliance with which, in this passage, the *Weltanschauung* of an antinomian school of Late Modern Western historians is propounded by a master of the art of History, and the force of the impression made on the minds of contemporaries by so challenging an exposition of a sharply controversial thesis by an eminent authority, were the considerations that moved the present writer at this point in his argument to illustrate his theme by citing an historian of an older generation for whom he felt an abiding professional respect and personal regard. Herbert Fisher's kindness to him as a young man had been one of the happy circumstances in his life, and one of the milestones in his education had been *Napoleonic Statesmanship in Germany*—a book that, in his judgement, was a masterpiece in the practice of the delicate art of distilling History out of public archives.

[3] 'You see, it's like a portmanteau—there are two meanings packed up into one word' (Humpty Dumpty in *Alice Through the Looking Glass*, by Lewis Carroll).

[4] A critique of this traditional pattern of cultural geography will be found in IX. viii. 708–29. For the purposes of the present argument, it makes no difference whether this pattern is, or is not, a reflection of historical realities.

[5] This egocentric illusion had been examined in I. i. 157–64.

wave' wash up the historian's own culture, country, and clan on to a pinnacle on which History finds its denouement and its consummation.[1] Article Four is a no longer avowed, yet none the less patently implied, ascription of this plot of Human Destiny to a divine playwright and stage-manager who, by a sovereign act of predetermination, has selected the historian's tribe to be God's own Chosen People. Article Five is the Christian doctrine that God's choice has been transferred from Israel to the Christian Church. Article Six is the Medieval Western Christian dogma that the truly orthodox Christian Church is not the canonically Orthodox Church but the Western (notwithstanding any play that a Photius may make with the *filioque*). Article Seven is the Late Modern Western postulate that the mantle of a Medieval Western Christendom has fallen upon the shoulders of an ex-Christian Modern Western Society by the divine oversight of a God who has now ceased to govern and perhaps even ceased to reign. Article Eight is the equation of this de-consecrated shadow of a defunct Western Christendom with the imaginary cultural continent already labelled 'Europe'. Article Nine is a parrot cry that was being refuted by fresh strokes of the anthropologist's pencil and the orientalist's pen and the archaeologist's spade as often as it was being repeated by the tongues of Western historians. Its burden was that 'Europe' was distinguished alike from an 'Unchanging East'[2] and from primitive 'peoples that have no history'[3] by being History's only possible subject; and it will be seen that this slogan was an assertion that the only possible history was the history of Europe because European affairs alone had a rhythm.

A citation of the remaining thirty articles of religion that still lie packed in an expanding Pandora's Box labelled 'Europe' might tax the reader's patience without being strictly necessary for clinching the present argument. On the strength of Articles I–IX, as these have been recited above, we may perhaps take it as having been already demonstrated that an historian's professed inability to discern in History any plot, rhythm, or predetermined pattern is no evidence that blind Samson has actually won his boasted freedom from the bondage of 'laws of Nature'. The presumption is, indeed, the opposite; for, when bonds are imperceptible to the wearer of them, they are likely to prove more difficult to shake off than when they betray their presence and reveal something of their shape and texture by clanking and galling.

It is, no doubt, also true that, even when a thinker is salutarily aware of an intellectual pattern in his mind, this awareness is not in itself any guarantee that he will be able to get rid even of the particular pattern that is obsessing him, not to speak of his finding himself able to dispense with intellectual pattern-making altogether. Yet, short of that, Man's consciousness is likely to prove itself Man's guardian angel in this pass as in others; for, in so far as he manages to bring one of these patterns within

---

[1] This misconception of the process of growth as being a movement in a straight line culminating in the historian's own time and place has been examined in I. i. 168–71.

[2] The catchword of 'the Unchanging East' has been dissected in this Study in I. i. 164–8.

[3] The grounds for rejecting this opprobious label as a misnomer have been examined in I. i. 179–80.

the focus of consciousness, he is winning for himself at least a chance of managing to discern whether this image in his mind is a reflection of Reality or a baseless hallucination; and, even if he finds that he cannot think at all except on the lines of some pattern or other, he will at any rate have an opportunity, in the light of consciousness, of sorting his intellectual stock, comparing one pattern with another, discarding the patterns that seem to him counterfeit, and retaining those that seem to him true copies of 'laws of Nature'. By contrast, when a thinker can boast that, whether wilfully or by act of God (in an insurance company's usage of that phrase), he is unconscious of any plot, rhythm, or pattern in his panorama of the Universe, he is telling us in effect that he is at the mercy of whatever pattern, rhythm, or plot may be in invisible occupation of his professedly empty, swept, and garnished[1] mental house. This occupying pattern may be so archaic, infantile, crude, and far-fetched that, if the occupied mind ever could or would look its masked master-ideology in the face, it would be horrified to see itself in bondage to an ape, child, Caliban, or Chimaera.[2] Yet, so long as this master is able to rule the blind soul by an invisible *acte de présence*, just so long will the soul—like 'a horseman borne afar, who never sees the horse beneath his thigh'[3]—remain impotent either to exchange this unworthy pattern for a better or to redeem it by refining it in the crucibles of reflection and self-criticism.

The figure of the typical antinomian latter-day Western historian, caught fast in bondage to an invisible pattern whose dominion over him was secure just because he believed himself to be proof against ever entertaining any such idea, was, of course, a living witness to a relativity of historical thought that was the looking-glass through which we forced our entry into the vista of our present Study.[4] This captive mammoth was a unique twentieth-century relic of a now old-fashioned-looking Western intellectual fauna which, save for this single surviving representative, had become extinct because its *habitus* had been too nicely adapted by the goddess Natural Selection to the temporary exigencies of an eighteenth-century Western intellectual environment. The eighteenth-century dogma, still cherished by so many twentieth-century Western historians, that no sense was to be made of human affairs, had been gradually whittled away, as we have seen, by the progressive encroachments of Science during the intervening quarter of a millennium. Yet Science's overt conquests at the expense of a would-be antinomian school of historians were not so damaging to this school's thesis as its own subconscious thraldom to mental patterns that displayed the tell-tale imprint of a particular time and place.

This relativity of an unacknowledged pattern of thought, which was so conspicuous, and so crippling, an infirmity of eighteenth-century-

[1] Matt. xii. 44; Luke xi. 25.
[2] 'The danger of subconscious and primitive theorising should not require further argument. Our choice is not between theory and no theory but between workmanlike theory and theory that is not workmanlike' (Schumpeter, J. A.: *Business Cycles* (New York 1939, McGraw-Hill, 2 vols.), vol. i, p. 32, n. 1).
[3] Jalāl-ad-Dīn Rūmī: *Mathnawī*, Book I, ll. 1109 seqq., translated by Nicholson, R. A., in *Rumi, Poet and Mystic* (London 1950, Allen & Unwin), p. 106.
[4] See I. i. 1–16.

minded twentieth-century historians had been adroitly turned to account by a spirited historian-philosopher in an attempt to vindicate the historians' antediluvian Antinomianism by casting discredit on their *bête noire* in the shape of 'laws of Nature' in the affairs of Man in Process of Civilization.

'So-called sciences of the Human Mind, whether total or partial (I refer to such studies as those on the Theory of Knowledge, of Morals, of Politics, of Economics, and so forth). . . are designed as accounts of one unchanging subject-matter, the Mind of Man as it always has been and always will be. . . .

'This assumption is present . . . in Montesquieu, but it also lies at the back of all the philosophical work of the eighteenth century, not to mention earlier periods. The Cartesian innate ideas are the ways of thinking which are natural to the Human Mind as such, everywhere and always. The Lockian human understanding is something assumed to be everywhere the same, though imperfectly developed in children, idiots, and savages. The Kantian mind which, as Intuition, is the source of Space and Time, as Understanding the source of the Categories, and as Reason the source of the ideas of God, Freedom, and Immortality, is a purely human mind, but Kant unquestioningly assumes it to be the only kind of human mind that exists or ever has existed. Even so sceptical a thinker as Hume accepts this assumption. . . . Hume never shows the slightest suspicion that the Human Nature [which] he is analysing in his philosophical work is the nature of a Western European in the early eighteenth century, and that the very same enterprise, if undertaken at a widely different time or place, might have yielded widely different results. He always assumes that *our* reasoning faculty, *our* tastes and sentiments, and so forth, are something perfectly uniform and invariable, underlying and conditioning all historical changes. . . .

'A positive science of Mind will, no doubt, be able to establish uniformities and recurrences, but it can have no guarantee that the laws [which] it establishes will hold good beyond the historical period from which its facts are drawn. Such a science (as we have lately been taught with regard to what is called Classical Economics) can do no more than describe in a general way certain characteristics of the historical age in which it is constructed. If it tries to overcome this limitation by drawing on a wider field, relying on Ancient History, Modern Anthropology, and so on, for a larger basis of facts, it will still never be more than a generalised description of certain phases in Human History. It will never be a non-historical Science of Mind. . . .

'Little acquaintance with [so-called sciences of the Human Mind] is demanded in order to see that they are nothing of the sort, but only inventories of the wealth achieved by the Human Mind at a certain stage in its history. The *Republic* of Plato is an account, not of the unchanging ideal of political life, but of the Greek ideal as Plato received it and reinterpreted it. The *Ethics* of Aristotle describes, not an eternal morality, but the morality of the Greek gentleman. Hobbes's *Leviathan* expounds the political ideas of seventeenth-century absolutism in their English form. Kant's ethical theory expresses the moral convictions of German pietism; his *Critique of Pure Reason* analyses the conceptions and principles of Newtonian science in their relation to the philosophical problems of the day.'[1]

[1] Collingwood, R. G.: *The Idea of History* (Oxford 1946, Clarendon Press), pp. 229, 82–83, 223–4, 229.

All this is both true and well said, and we may observe in parenthesis that it is as pertinent a critique of the work of professedly antinomian historians as it is of attempts to discern 'laws of Nature' governing human affairs. A Chinese antinomian confrère and contemporary of the Western antinomian historian Herbert Fisher would have labelled his book, not 'A History of Europe', but 'A History of the Middle Kingdom'.[1] Yet a diversity of inscriptions on title-pages, which would thus illustrate the relativity of antinomian historians' outlooks to their own social milieux, would also testify, in the same breath, to the uniformity of antinomian historians' delusions about the workings of their own minds; for these two diverse titles are, both alike, specifications of patterns in the affairs of Man in Process of Civilization, and, in thus committing himself on his title-page to a pattern, whatever the pattern may be, either historian will have 'escaped his own notice' (to enlist an Ancient Greek turn of phrase) in making a public recantation of his boasted inability to discern in History any pattern, rhythm, or plot. Nor could our Chinese or Western historian-sceptic succeed in salvaging his scepticism by describing his work expressly as being 'A History without a Pattern'; for, supposing that this vaunted 'patternlessness' could be genuinely conceived of and that the idea could then be successfully put into execution, the result could be nothing but just one pattern the more. In this light we can see that Collingwood's act of sceptical faith in taking the shimmer of relativity in the foreground of historical thought[2] at its face value cannot be the last word; and indeed every sceptic who has the honesty to be thoroughgoing brings his negations tumbling to the ground by sawing clean through the branch on which the sceptic-sawyer is perching.

Overrunning the combative philosopher's échelon of advanced positions in the successive zones of Economics, Politics, and Morals without lingering, at this stage, to mop them up, let us now press our counter-offensive home into the zone of the Theory of Knowledge, which is Scepticism's last ditch where it will decisively stand or fall; and, in conducting this operation, let us take a leaf out of the tactical note-book of a nameless genius who, according to an amusing legend, once initiated his mates into the secret of how to win 'hands down' in a contest over some long since forgotten issue between the employees on the Italian State Railways and the Ministry of Communications at Rome.

When the leaders of the aggrieved *ferroviarii* were nervously debating whether they should take the risk of depleting their trade-union funds, and perhaps even falling foul of the law, by instructing their followers to strike work, one ingenious mind suggested an alternative course of action that would be certain to bring the railwaymen's adversaries to their knees without putting the workers in the wrong or even costing them a penny. 'Instead of going on strike', he suggested, 'let us simply carry out the official regulations'; and this elegant solution of the railwaymen's problem had only to be propounded in order to be accepted, *nemine contradicente*, as the unquestionably advantageous line

---

[1] See the rescript, cited in I. i. 161, which was addressed in A.D. 1793 by the Oecumenical Emperor Ch'ien Lung to the parochial princeling *in partibus barbaricis*, George III of Britain.   [2] See I. i. 16.

of tactics to pursue. Its elegance lay in the fact—too familiar to have registered itself in any ordinary railwayman's consciousness—that the continued operation of the Italian State Railways was dependent on the continued observance of a tacit 'gentleman's agreement' between the employees and the authorities that the regulations officially in force were to be tactfully ignored. So, by simply carrying out their legal duties for once in a way, the railwaymen could instantaneously bring the traffic on the railways to a standstill without either forfeiting their pay or rendering themselves liable to prosecution. No sooner said than done. When the moment arrived for the morning express train to leave Milan for Rome, and the guard duly blew his whistle, the driver correctly waited to hear the same blast twice repeated at intervals of fifteen minutes; and, when the train then did get under way, the driver, correctly again, accommodated the train's speed to the walking-pace of a colleague who was likewise correctly carrying out the regulations by advancing, ten paces ahead of the buffers of the locomotive, waving a red flag held in his right hand to ensure the safety of the public while he was tapping the rails with a hammer held in his left hand to ensure the safety of the passengers. This sly 'cold war' could have only one outcome, and the end came quickly. On receipt of a telegraphic report from the stationmaster at Milan, the Ministry at Rome announced its unconditional surrender.

Translating the Italian railwaymen's tactics from an economic to an intellec ual arena, let us now try the effect of taking Fisher's dictum 'There can be no generalizations'[1] *au pied de la lettre*. We can perhaps now still legitimately utter the word 'battle' in recording the battle of Megiddo (*commissum circa* 1468 B.C.); but, now that we are conscientiously abiding by the regulation that 'History never repeats itself', we must, of course, find some other word to describe what happened at Marathon, and some other again to describe what happened at Waterloo; and, when we have shot all the bolts in our most copious dictionary of synonyms (though, strictly speaking, we shall be guilty of 'not playing the game' if we stoop to any such verbal subterfuge), we shall find ourselves constrained to keep silence for ever after on the subject of the affairs of *Homo Belligerans*. We can also perhaps now still legitimately pronounce the words 'Pope John I'; yet all the known synonyms of that ilk—'pontiff', 'prelate', 'primate', 'hierophant', 'Grand Lama', 'Mōbadhān Mōbadh', and what-not—will hardly legitimize for us the twenty-two (or is it twenty-three?) repetitions that are obstinately demanded of us *sub rosa* by a History that officially declines to repeat itself. But our plight is perhaps more serious than we have yet realized, for, if 'History never repeats itself', one single 'John' is the only 'John' whom it is permissible for us to name; and, though we may dishonestly eke out this iron ration by buying 'Jack', 'Jean', 'Euan', 'Evan', 'Ivan', 'Johann', and 'Yohanan' in a philological black market, famine will still be lying in wait for us round the corner when we are left with no unappropriated homonym for affixing to the next man in the queue. But what are we saying? For Adam, now that we think of it, was a man, and, since 'His-

---

[1] See the passage quoted on p. 195, above.

tory does not repeat itself', our common father must have been the last man as well as the first, without prejudice to the question of how we are to refer to Adam's children. At this point speech and thought alike fail us. We have effectively inhibited ourselves from thinking or writing either about History or about anything else; and, if the philosopher-historian who has ruled out 'uniformities and recurrences' from the realm of Reality[1] wishes to be given quarter, he had better now make up his mind to capitulate with the promptness that, according to the legend, was once the only salvation of the Italian Ministry of Communications.

The truth which confounds an honestly consistent sceptic is that the Human Intellect is so constituted as to be intrinsically incapable of ever thinking about anything at all except in terms of uniformities, recurrences, regularities, laws, rhythms, plots, and patterns of other kinds, while, conversely, of course, none of these patterns is conceivable as being anything but an arrangement of facts.

'The theories with which Science works cannot be conceived as existing apart from the facts of human experience, and men can apprehend facts only in terms of the notions with which their minds are furnished. . . . In scientific work these two blends, knowledge of fact and theoretical conceptions, keep stimulating, extending, and enriching each other. An investigator who starts with what purports to be an exposition of theory is tacitly using the facts by which the ideas have been moulded; and one who starts with what purports to be an exposition of facts is tacitly using the theoretical conceptions by which facts have been apprehended.'[2]

Thus *Homo Sapiens* is confined *a priori* to a choice between two alternative conclusions, and these two only, when he is confronted with the ultimately inescapable necessity of making up his mind about the credentials of his own mental patterns. Either we must conclude that, in so far as we do apparently manage to think about something, the pattern that we register in performing any act of thought is a pattern that is genuinely present in Reality, or else we must conclude that the pattern registered in our minds is an illusion and that, in other words, our thoughts are not reflections of 'things' but are mental figments without counterparts in any reality distinguishable from our consciousness. In this dilemma a sceptic who has the courage of his convictions must either retire from the field or else change sides; and, when it comes to the point, he will find that, for a philosopher, desertion, not withdrawal, is the honourable course because it is the only logical one; for, in acknowledging that he is a sceptic, our adversary has proclaimed that he is a thinker and has committed himself in the act, by an involuntary re-affirmation of a celebrated proposition of Descartes', to a declaration of faith in the archetype-pattern, 'I am'.[3]

---

[1] Collingwood, in the passage quoted on p. 198, above.
[2] Mitchell, W. C.: *Business Cycles: The Problem and its Setting* (New York 1927, National Bureau of Economic Research, Inc.), p. 59, n. 2.
[3] Exod. iii. 14; Exod. iii. 6 and 16; Matt. xxii. 32; Mark xii. 26–27; Luke xx. 37–38.

(d) THE GROUNDS OF THE LATE MODERN WESTERN
HISTORIANS' AGNOSTICISM

The antinomian latter-day Western historians' dogma that the history of Man in Process of Civilization is an unintelligibly chaotic congeries of brute facts thus proves to be a heresy from the standpoint, not merely of Western science, but of Human Thought itself; and this spectacle of 'the laws of Nature' standing entrenched and embedded in the very structure of Man's intellect forces us to ask ourselves what can have possessed any—even antediluvian—breed of Man to make him nail these heretical colours to his mast. The antinomian historians' response to the challenge of a decisive change of intellectual climate in their cultural environment was not merely reactionary but truculent. So far from seeking to earn an erasure of the stigma with which they had been branded by eighteenth-century Western philosophers,[1] they retorted by telling the world that 'their glory' was 'in their shame'.[2] Their response to the challenge of outlawry was to proclaim themselves to be the Antinomians that they were. Constituting themselves the grand jury in their own case, they found that the charge indicting them of making nonsense of History was a true bill, and then, proceeding to constitute themselves, in turn, the jury, they acquitted themselves with a self-indulgent verdict of 'not guilty', on the plea that to be convicted of making nonsense was as good as to be warranted 'scientific'.

On this point our comparison of the historians with the ducks in the Round Pond will hardly help us out; for the ducks, as we have seen, were not truculent; they were supine; and, in proudly refraining from fighting with the vagrant gulls for the crusts that were tossed to the birds by the general public, the ducks were rationally discounting in advance a never yet disappointed expectation that the subsistence allowance, annually voted to them by a benevolent Parliament, would continue to be issued to them by a dutiful Ministry of Works. By contrast, the historians had no such comfortable assurance that, if they allowed the affairs of Man in Process of Civilization to be snatched from under their noses, morsel by morsel, by their predatory rivals the social scientists, any providence, human or divine, was going to dish out to them any alternative means of subsistence. Indeed, on any rational calculation the chances were that, on the contrary, the historians' policy of non-violent non-co-operation with the social scientists' depredations at their expense would result in leaving them destitute. Thus for the historians, unlike the ducks, the attitude of being 'too proud to fight' was a luxury that they could not afford; yet, nevertheless, they were indulging in it. Like the ducks, they were refusing to scramble for bread falling like manna from Heaven. They were declining to defend their own birthright by taking a leaf out of their rivals' book. What had prompted these latter-day Western historians to play this foolhardily dangerous game of challenging the validity of the ineluctable laws of thought by refusing to entertain the contemporary Western scientists' hypothesis that there were 'laws of Nature' governing the history of Man in Process of Civilization? They

[1] See Teggart, in the passages quoted on p. 183, above.   [2] Phil. iii. 19.

would hardly thus have followed the Pharisees' forbidding example of passing sentence of ostracism on themselves[1] if they, in their turn, had not been moved by Pharisaïcally compulsive motives. Can we account for the idiosyncrasy of these antinomian historians by laying bare its intellectual grounds?

One argument that was sometimes propounded by latter-day Western historians to prove the impracticability of applying to human affairs those methods by which non-human affairs had been successfully brought under the jurisdiction of laws of Nature was to point out that, in the study of human affairs, hypotheses could not be verified by mounting 'controlled' experiments, since in real life, in sharp contrast to the utopian conditions of an Huxleian *Brave New World,* Man had never yet been conditioned to the amenability of a guinea-pig, but was still exhibiting all the contrariness of a most recalcitrantly wild animal.[2] This observation was, of course, correct, but the agnostic conclusion drawn from it was put out of court by the following considerations. In the first place a human wild animal that was fiercely refractory to the personal wills of other representatives of its kind might at the same time turn out to be tamely submissive to the impersonal yoke of custom and impressionably amenable to spells cast upon the conscious personality by both a personal and an impersonal layer of a subconscious psychic underworld. The second weakness of the argument was the postulate that a 'law of Nature' could never properly be certified as having been duly ascertained unless it had been verified by experiments arranged and executed so as to insulate the particular phenomena in which the regularities and recurrences constituting this hypothetical pattern, rhythm, plot, or law were alleged to reveal themselves. The acceptance of this postulate would have entailed the disfranchisement of a number of sciences which had been recognized, by the general consensus of a Collective Human Intellect, to have won a legitimate title to the name by having put their finger on systems of 'laws of Nature' that were generally admitted to be valid.

Since Primitive Man was no more amenable to being made a victim of controlled experiments than was Man in Process of Civilization, the science of Anthropology would have been the first to lose its franchise on the postulated test; and no doubt the historians would not have been sorry to find this opportunity of disallowing retrospectively a title to which they had implicitly given a grudging recognition by maintaining a disapprobatory silence. Fortunately, however, for the vulnerably human science of Anthropology, the impeccably inhuman science of Astronomy happened to be in the same boat. The courses of the stars[3] were no more amenable to the test of controlled experiments[4] than were the tides in the affairs of men;[5] and Astronomy and Anthropology must therefore either sink or swim together—sharing the same watery grave if an ability to insist on registering its subjects' finger-prints was to be taken as the

[1] For the etymology of the word 'Pharisees', see V. v. 73, with n. 4.
[2] See Darwin, Sir Charles: *The Next Million Years* (London 1952, Hart-Davis), chap. vii: 'Man—A Wild Animal' (pp. 115–33).
[3] Judges v. 20.   [4] See p. 172, above.
[5] Shakspeare: *Julius Caesar,* Act IV, scene iii, l. 217.

crucial test of a science's respectability, and riding the storm hand in hand if this proposed test was to be dismissed as an imposition that was invidious and unnecessary. In these circumstances it was manifest that Astronomy and Anthropology alike would retain, and not forfeit, their titles to being recognized as full-blooded sciences, since it was manifest that, if common sense were confronted with the choice of having to throw overboard either Astronomy's claim to be a science or the historians' forensic insistence on the indispensability of controlled experiments, then common sense would salvage Astronomy at the price of jettisoning the requirement that *soi-disants* 'laws of Nature' must have been verified by controlled experiments in order to qualify for being promulgated as the findings of a science. Astronomy was not only perhaps the oldest of all the sciences; she had also continued to retain her place of honour even in an age that had seen the sinister rise of a parvenu Atomic Physics; and this persistent and unabated brilliance of a venerable science in which the method of controlled experiment was inapplicable in the nature of the case was a practical vindication of the thesis that, in the study of phenomena, non-human and human alike, observation, unverified by experiment, was after all capable of effectively ascertaining 'laws of Nature'.

This question of principle, however, probably counted for much less among the considerations inclining a latter-day school of Western historians towards Antinomianism than the question whether the ascertainment of 'laws of Nature' in the affairs of Man in Process of Civilization was feasible in practice under the conditions with which these historians were confronted by the quantity of the data with which they had to deal. It was arguable that this quantity was too great, and also arguable that it was too small; and both these mutually exclusive arguments were used by different sects of contemporary Western historians who were all of the antinomian persuasion. Since those who argued that the data on the table were too numerous to be made to make sense appeared to be in a large majority over their confrères who arrived at an equally agnostic conclusion for the opposite reason, it will be convenient to examine this plea that the quantity of data was disablingly abundant before considering the alternative plea that it was disablingly scanty.

Since the eighteenth century of the Christian Era, when the Modern Western historians had incurred the censure of the Modern Western philosophers, the historians had in truth vastly increased the quantity of data within their purview by raking in enormous masses of them from two previously unexploited rubbish-heaps. On the one hand they had opened up the archives of Western public institutions such as the Papal Curia and the governments, central and local, of the Western World's parochial states; and on the other hand they had brought within their horizon the ordinary affairs of private people who had left their trails in the archives of firms and families. If the historians had been concerned to erase the stigma with which the philosophers had branded them, they would have noticed that, for the purpose of an apologia, their two simultaneous paper-chases were not equally promising.

The gravamen of the philosophers' indictment had been that the historians neglected what was susceptible of scientific study in order to attend exclusively to events that interfered with 'the natural order' by being 'unnatural', 'monstrous', 'accidental', and 'unusual';[1] and the sting of truth in this charge had been retrospectively pressed home under the historians' thin skin by the witty authors of *1066 and All That*[2] in their parody of a presentation of History which had actually once held the field. In dissociating themselves from History as it was being written by Western historians in the eighteenth century, the Western philosophers of that age had in effect been praying to be delivered 'from battle and murder and from sudden death' (in the words of the Litany in *The Book of Common Prayer* according to the use of the Church of England). Sudden death, murder, and battle, however, were the dominant theme not only of a pre-Rankean Western historiography but likewise of the documents that the nineteenth-century Western historians had been extracting from Western public archives; and the 'unnaturalness' and 'monstrousness' of this 'penny dreadful', 'Sunday paper' streak in human affairs were not mitigated by bringing the stuff out of the wholesalers' warehouses in bulk and retailing it to the public in an infinite number of infinitesimally small samples.

On the other hand the nineteenth-century historians were genuinely breaking new ground—and thereby effectively converting their shame into glory—when they broke their way out of the madhouse of sensational public events, in which their predecessors had been 'cabined, cribbed, confined, bound in'[3] by a conventional limitation of the usage of the word 'historic', and thereby won for themselves the freedom of the great open spaces of private life, in which ordinary people demonstrated daily to intellectual sight-seers that, when the human animal was given the run of a Yellowstone Park, he could wear a less repulsive countenance than he was condemned to exhibit in his public life, where he had to live under the pathological slum conditions of the zoological gardens in a metropolis. In claiming for History this wholesomely spacious parkland of private life, the historians were legitimately appropriating for their own purposes a field of human affairs which the economists and the sociologists were cultivating contemporaneously with fruitful results. It was a pity, as well as a paradox, that the historians should feel themselves inhibited from joining in the search for a 'natural order' by their acquisition of the very data that were enabling the sociologists and the economists to make some sense out of a human chaos by establishing two new sciences through the discovery of 'laws of Nature' reigning over virgin soil.

The historians' inhibition was paradoxical because, in all fields of study, both human and non-human, it had been the experience of a Collective Human Intellect that, the greater the quantity of the data, the greater was the precision with which 'laws of Nature' were ascertainable.[4] This finding holds good, as we have seen, wherever the quantity of the data is not either so small that nothing can be made of them beyond the

---

[1] See Teggart, quoted on p. 183, above.
[2] Sellar, W. C., and Yeatman, R. J.: *1066 and All That, A Memorable History of England* (London 1930, Methuen).
[3] Shakspeare: *Macbeth*, Act III, scene iv, l. 24.   [4] See I. i. 452–7.

establishment of the facts, or else so great that the only practicable way of coping with the data is the method, not of Science, but of Fiction. Western historians might perhaps be forgiven for having failed to find any rhyme or reason in fifteen decisive battles, twelve imāms, seven sages, four Georges, three ages,[1] and other casts in which the dramatis personae had been brought on to the stage in these exiguous numbers;[2] but, in contrast to the quantity of data yielded by public events, the quantity yielded by ordinary affairs of private people was of just that intermediate order of magnitude that permits 'laws of Nature' governing data to reveal themselves to the human eye. The number of annual harvests, for example, that had been reaped by Man in Process of Civilization between the date of the invention of Agriculture and the time of writing, midway through the twentieth century of the Christian Era, was probably something between 6,000 and 12,000. The number of 'middletowns' that had come and gone from the *floruit* of Heliopolis and Ur and Harappa to the *floruit* of Chicago and Magnitogorsk and Shanghai must have run, all told, into some scores of thousands. The economists and sociologists had been showing what could be done with data presenting themselves in these quantities. Why was it that the historians were not taking the same advantage of the same opportunity?

The historians seem to have missed this opportunity by falling into a snare and a delusion. The snare was an obsession with their own professional technique;[3] the delusion was a mistaken impression that the panorama of History was incomprehensibly complex.

'For students of modern history it was an important moment when the young German historian Ranke, looking at the Age of the Renaissance, took various authors of that period, who had written the chronicles of their own times, and by various forms of detective-work undermined their credibility. The novelty of his technique was perhaps exaggerated in the nineteenth-century,[4] but it established the fact that you were foolish

---

[1] A critique of the Late Modern Western historians' conventional periodization of the history of Man in Process of Civilization into an 'ancient', a 'medieval', and a 'modern' age will be found in I. i. 168–71.

[2] It was noteworthy, however, that, of the five numbers here cited, the last two only would be decidedly too small to reveal underlying regularities and uniformities by giving the play of Chance on the surface a sufficient scope for it to neutralize itself.
'The number usually need not be at all large for the chances to average out. With the typical example of spinning a coin, even a quite small number like ten will almost count as a large number in the sense that, if the coin is spun ten times, the number of heads will rarely be more than two away from five, which is the average number of heads. In most matters concerned with probability, three or four count as small numbers, ten as a fairly large number, and a hundred as a very large number' (Darwin, C. G.: *The Next Million Years* (London 1952, Hart-Davis), p. 90).
By the time when this authoritative pronouncement by one of the most eminent mathematical physicists of the present writer's generation was published, the writer had been spending some twenty-five years of his working life on mental operations with twenty-one specimens of the species 'civilizations' without having any assurance that this number was, in truth, large enough for his requirements. He was proportionately elated when he came to this passage in Sir Charles Darwin's book.

[3] See I. i. 1–8.

[4] Ranke had certainly been anticipated by a school of Chinese philologists and textual critics in the Far Eastern World in the age of the Manchu imperial régime (see pp. 58–59, above) and by a school of Greek documentarians in an Aristotelian and post-Aristotelian age of Hellenic history. If Ranke and his disciples had taken to heart the two historical facts that Aristotle had organized the manufacture of a digest of the constitutions of 158 parochial states, and that Craterus had assembled a corpus of Athenian official

to depend on the contemporary chroniclers and narrative-writers of the sixteenth century if you wished to know what really happened in that period—you must go to official documents.[1] . . . The intensity of criticism

documents recorded in inscriptions, there might have been little more spirit left in them than was left in the Queen of Sheba after she had made her inventory of King Solomon's apparatus (1 Kings x. 5).—A.J.T.

[1] Scholars go to official documents at their peril if they have not previously trained themselves for interpreting them by having taken a hand in the manufacture of them; and Modern Western documentarians who had neglected this precaution would have been well advised to take warning by the cautionary tale of Aristotle's anonymous research assistant who, in the compilation of the narrative section of *The Constitution of Athens*, had the temerity to discard Thucydides' account of the *coup d'état* in 411 B.C. that had brought into power the ephemeral régime of 'the Four Hundred'. In our post-Rankean Age of Western intellectual history we can recapture the conscientious young woman's thrill when her patient exploration of the papyri in the Record Office at Athens, or of the stelae on the Acropolis, was rewarded by her discovery of the series of official documents manufactured in the official year within which the episode of 'the Four Hundred' had occurred. 'Who could have dreamed', she must have cried, as she was excitedly announcing her discovery to her august master, 'that our documentary technique would vindicate itself as sensationally as this? By going to the official documents we have now demonstrated how foolish it is to depend on Thucydides if one wants to know what really happened in that period.' Here indeed, as Horace was one day to write, *bonus dormitat Homerus* (*Epistulae*, Book II, Ep. iii, l. 359); but a latter-day historian's detective-work would not be complete until he had established the identity of the 'napping Homer' in the case, and here the last laugh turns against, not Thucydides, but Aristotle; for it was Aristotle who was caught napping when he condescendingly put his own name to his ingenuous research-assistant's draft. The discrepancy between Thucydides' chronicle and the contemporary official documents which the young woman had pointed out to Aristotle was indeed just as glaring as she had reported it to be; but, unfortunately for Aristotle's reputation, the explanation that he had allowed his pupil to impose upon him was a mare's nest.

The true story of the *coup d'état* of 'the Four Hundred' *wie es eigentlich gewesen* ('in the famous words of Ranke') turned out after all to have been the tale told by Thucydides on the authority of participants and witnesses whose evidence he had sagaciously followed though he tactfully withheld their names. The discrepant documents in the Athenian public records were (if the young blue-stocking was not in error in assigning the date of their manufacture to the time when the Four Hundred were in power) untruthful and, by the same token, authentic. They were untruthful because they had been manufactured (if manufactured at that time), on instructions from 'the Four Hundred', for the serious practical purpose of covering their politician-fabricators' tracks by throwing dust in academically innocent eyes. Thucydides, of course, was not taken in; he had once been in politics himself, and he was alive to the disreputable tricks of the trade; but 'the Four Hundred' did score a notable posthumous success when their documentary dust-cloud (if the credit for having raised it could truly be claimed by them) put Aristotle off the scent—and this after the location of the truth had been revealed to any sharp-eyed huntsman by the good dog Thucydides' shrewdly pointing tail. This revindication of Thucydides' veracity was a feat of Modern Western detective-work to the credit of M. O. B. Cary (see *The Journal of Hellenic Studies*, vol. xxxiii (London 1913, Society for the Promotion of Hellenic Studies), pp. 1–18; vol. lxxii (1952), pp. 56–61).

This posthumous success of 'the Four Hundred's' documentary imposture fully recouped these politicians for an expenditure of time and thought which, if they did spend them, they could ill afford to spare for the luxury of whitewashing themselves in the midst of a crisis in which they were struggling for power and life. A documentary misrepresentation of the truth that took in Aristotle had certainly not been labour lost. All the same, the Four Hundred, being men of action, were, no doubt, acting on shorter views, and working for quicker returns, for this in any documentary hoax that they may have committed. The normal motive for manufacturing an official document is to produce some immediate practical effect in current politics. The intention may be to prevent something from happening, to make something happen, or to create a false impression about something that has happened, or not happened, already; there are divers practical purposes which the manufacture of official documents can be made to serve; but there is one purpose—one which, though theoretically possible, would hardly occur to anyone but an historian—which the historian would be wise to leave out of his reckoning: the manufacturer of official documents is never inspired by an academic concern to record the truth for the benefit of future historians; for, from the man of action's standpoint, the briefing of future historians is, at best, unprofitable and, at worst, imprudent.

This is a cardinal consideration which historians seldom bear in mind, though

and the awareness of the possible pitfalls increased in a remarkable manner as time went on. . . . The development of the scientific method in nineteenth-century historiography did not merely mean that this or that fact could be corrected, or the story told in greater detail, or the narrative amended at marginal points. It meant that total reconstructions proved to be necessary, as in the detective stories, where a single new fact might turn out to be a pivotal one; and what had been thought to be an accident might transform itself into an entirely different story of murder. In these circumstances, evidence which had seemed to mean one thing might prove to be capable of an entirely different construction.'[1]

This nineteenth-century experience had two psychological effects. The Modern Western historians' discovery for themselves of the classic technique of 'detective-work' gave them an unwarranted sense of masterly power; the dissolution of once hard-looking facts under corrosively acid documentary tests gave the same historians an undue sense of helpless impotence. The more confident they became of their technical ability to handle the facts, the less confident they remained of their intellectual ability to apprehend these facts, not to speak of making any sense out of them; and these two conflicting psychological forces found their resolution in a concentration on professional technique both as an end in itself and as a mental city of refuge;[2] for here were sands in which an ostrich could reassuringly bury his head when the sight of a pursuing Hound of Heaven had got upon the fugitive's nerves.

The snare of historical technique has been exposed by the Western Christian historian whom we have just quoted:

'We fall into certain habits of mind and easily become the slaves of them, when in reality we only adopted them for the purpose of a particular technique. It is as though people could be so long occupied in tearing flowers to pieces and studying their mechanism that they forget ever to stand back again and see the buttercup whole. It is possible that in the transition to the modern outlook the World was guided much less by any deliberated philosophy than is often assumed, and I think that few people could be said to have come to that modern outlook by an authentic process of thinking things out. Men are often the semi-conscious victims of habits of mind and processes of abstraction like those involved in technical historical study or in physical science. They decide that for purposes of analysis they will only take notice of things that can be weighed and measured, and then they forget the number they first started from and come to think that these are the only things that exist. . . .'[3]

politicians seldom fail to act on it. Among the official documents with which the writer of this Study happened to be acquainted, the Hossbach Memorandum of the 10th November, 1937, recording the minutes of a conference held in the Reichskanzlei, Berlin, on the 5th November, was perhaps the only one that, by any stretch of the imagination, could be supposed to have been manufactured out of deference to an academic ideal. At any rate, the writer of this Study could not think of any credible motive for putting this incriminating record on paper except a concern to facilitate the future task of the Nazi war-criminals' historian-prosecutors. This one academically exemplary official document was, however, a joker in a pack in which most other cards were severely practical in their design. It was not Hitler's Colonel Hossbach, but the Four Hundred's anonymous secretary, who was the typical representative of the official document manufacturers' profession, and it was surely significant that an ingenuous Hossbach should have been an ingenuous Ranke's fellow-countryman.—A.J.T.

[1] Butterfield, Herbert: *Christianity and History* (London 1949, Bell), pp. 12, 13, and 14–15.　　[2] See the passage of Butterfield's work quoted on p. 191, above.
[3] Butterfield, op. cit., p 21.

Yet, even so, insidious though these toils of technique might thus prove to be, the example of the social scientists suggests that the captivated historians need not have remained prisoners if a failure of nerve had not scared them into hugging their technological chains. After having been intimidated by an ever more sensitive 'awareness of the possible pitfalls' in a mental landscape in which a once solid Earth was melting into a dreamlike kaleidoscope of 'total reconstructions', these distracted latter-day Western historians were appalled by a nightmare in which they saw this Protean chaos solidifying again, only to confront the tormented observer with a novel universe of an incomprehensible complexity; and this prospect made the sheltering sands of technique look like the only practicable refuge from the mental hell of being compelled to play an eternal game of croquet with the unmanageable implements prescribed for the luckless players of the game in Lewis Carroll's fantasy *Alice through the Looking-glass*.

If the latter-day Western historians' own appreciation of their plight had been correct, this plight would have been desperate indeed; but fortunately their attempt to distinguish between Appearance and Reality happened to be an outright inversion of the truth. The nightmare vision of Reality from which they were seeking shelter in the sand-heap of technique was an illusion generated by this obscurantist technique itself. The apparent dissolution of a once stable world into a Protean chaos of infinitesimally small vagrant electrons, which would re-form into an infinitely complex universe if they were ever to re-form at all, was not the apocalypse of an appalling Reality; it was the illusory optical effect of a distortingly diffractive lens; and the nightmare could be dispelled in an instant by the simple salutary act of dropping this delusively sophisticated apparatus and reverting to the effective use of the naked eye.

The physical eye itself presents a living allegory of this tragi-comedy of an intellectual *malade imaginaire*:

'In an organ like the eye there are two points that are equally striking: the complexity of the structure and the simplicity of the way in which it works. . . . The eye is a machine composed of an infinite number of machines which are all extremely complex, yet eyesight is a simple fact. The eye has merely to open for eyesight to come into action. . . . It is this contrast between the complexity of the organ and the unity of its operation that is intellectually disconcerting. . . .

'As a general rule, when an object looks simple from one side and infinitely composite from the other side, the two aspects are far from being of equal importance or—to put it more precisely—far from being on a par with one another in degree of reality. In such cases the simplicity is intrinsic to the object itself, while the infinite complexity is an effect of views that we take of it as we reconnoitre it, of disparate symbols through which our senses or our intelligence represent the object to us, and, in a more general way, of elements of a different order with which we try to imitate the object artificially, but with which nevertheless it remains incommensurable because its nature is different from theirs.

'An artist of genius has painted a figure on his canvas. We can imitate his picture in mosaic, in pieces of many colours, and, the smaller and the more numerous these pieces are, and the greater the variety of their shades of colour, the better we shall be able to reproduce the curves and nuances of our model. But we should require an infinite number of infinitesimally minute components, presenting an infinite number of nuances, in order to obtain the exact equivalent of a figure which the artist has conceived as a simple thing, which he has sought to transfer to his canvas *en bloc*, and which approaches perfection in its presentation in the measure in which it reveals itself as being the projection of an intuition which is indivisible . . . because [in the artist's own work] there has really been no such thing as an assemblage of pieces in a mosaic. What has happened is that the picture—by which I mean the simple act projected on to the canvas—has spontaneously decomposed in our eyes, through the mere fact of having come within our perception, into thousands and thousands of little pieces which, in their re-composition, present the spectacle of a wonderful arrangement.

'In the same way the eye, with its marvellously complex structure, might be nothing more than the simple act of sight, in spite of its splitting up, as it does, for us into a mosaic of cells, whose order appears marvellous to us when once we have represented this totality to ourselves as being an assemblage.

'If I raise my hand from Point A to Point B, this movement presents itself to me in two aspects simultaneously. Felt from within, it is an act that is simple and indivisible; perceived from outside it is the course of a particular curve AB. In this line I can distinguish as many distinct positions as I choose, and the line itself can be defined as a particular co-ordination of these positions among themselves. But this innumerable host of positions and the order linking one position with another are automatic products of the indivisible act in which my hand has moved from A to B. . . .

'It is the same with the relation of the eye to the eyesight. . . . [So far from Nature's having] produced the simple act of seeing by performing a Herculean *tour de force* with an infinite number of infinitely complicated elements, it has cost her no more trouble to make an eye than it costs me to raise my hand. Nature's simple act has split up automatically into an infinite number of elements which will all be found co-ordinated with a single idea, as the movement of my hand has precipitated an infinite number of points which all prove to answer to a single equation.'[1]

In the light of Bergson's intuitions, we can see that the latter-day Western historians' nightmare was the illusory visual effect of an intoxicating technique. The Saint Vitus's dance of an infinite number of infinitesimally small data which these self-confounded intellectual technicians saw through their perversely granulated lens was a shadow play substituted by this distorting medium for the simplicity and integrity of real life. The previously unpublished data which Western research-workers had been eliciting from Western archives, private and public, in apparently overwhelming quantities were, in truth, not so many integral facts, but merely so many artificial fragments into which the integral facts had been arbitrarily pulverized by a nihilistic technique. While the shivered splinters had become unmanageably numerous and complicated, the intact bones remained intelligibly few and simple. The true crux of History, in fact, was that the significant known integral events in the history of Man in Process of Civilization were, not awkwardly abun-

---

[1] Bergson, H.: *L'Évolution Créatrice*, 24th ed. (Paris 1921, Alcan), pp. 96–100.

dant, but awkwardly scarce;[1] and the question on which the possibility of ascertaining 'laws of Nature' in this episode of history turned was the question whether the significant known integral events were actually numerous enough to provide a basis for generalizations.

This experience is described in the following testimony from the pen of a practised investigator of the working of 'laws of Nature' on the economic plane of latter-day Western social life:

'The volume of economic statistics is certainly imposing—it is even intimidating at first sight. But on closer inspection the mass proves to consist less of a multiplication of independent observations upon particular phenomena than of observations upon a vast variety of phenomena, and of the infinite detail in which certain processes must be observed. . . . As an investigator gets deeper into a quantitative analysis of business cycles, his first impression that the statistical data to be dealt with are embarrassingly abundant turns into a conviction that they are painfully inadequate.'[2]

The agnostics who put their finger on the scarcity of significant known events as their ground for denying the possibility of discerning 'laws of Nature' in the history of Man in Process of Civilization were thus at any rate nearer the mark—mistaken though they too might be—than their fellow agnostics whose identical denial was based on the contradictory thesis that the hoppers in their factory had been choked by a plethora of overproduction.

This case for agnosticism on the ground, not of a redundancy in the data, but of an insufficiency, is judiciously presented in the following passage from the pen of a distinguished twentieth-century Western historian:

'The reading public asks for a final interpretation of History, and for an answer to the question why civilisations rise and fall. Is there, as Hume thought, a tidal movement in human affairs and nothing more than this tidal ebb and flow? Is there no hope of stability or of unmixed achievement in the temporal sphere? Or can it be said that, in spite of ages of regression towards barbarism, historians are able to bring evidence of progress towards a desirable end?

'To these questions British historians are not very ready to give an answer, and, in general, the answers which are given are not put forward by the most learned or the most profound scholars. In the preface to his *History of Europe*, H. A. L. Fisher wrote that he had no ultimate philosophy of history. Such a view does not imply scepticism, or even lack of belief in the possibility of a final synthesis. The difficulty at present is that the *data* are insufficient.[3] To a historian the history of the World of Man is a very short history. The years of the astronomers and the geologists reach beyond a historian's reckoning; a small fraction only of these vast epochs is covered by the period during which Man, with knowledge

---

[1] See I. i. 455–6.
[2] Mitchell, W. C.: *Business Cycles: The Problem and Its Setting* (New York 1927, National Bureau of Economic Research, Inc.), pp. 203 and 205.
[3] 'It is not—to my mind—altogether paradoxical to say *also* that we know too much. I mean, we know so many facts which lend themselves to arrangement in patterns that we can make any number of such patterns; but we do not know enough to judge between these patterns or to be sure that we are doing more than pick out chance or superficial resemblances' (Sir Llewellyn Woodward in a letter of the 25th July, 1952, to the writer of this Study).

of the wheel, of fire, of pottery, and of edged tools, has set out to be master of his environment. Within this fragment of Time, the history of Lettered and Civilised Man fills an even smaller space. It is therefore not remarkable that a satisfactory clue has yet to be found to the meaning of the strange acts of the strangest of living creatures. Bede tells the story of the Northumbrian thane who compared the life of Man on Earth, in relation to the unknown immensity of Time, to a moment in which a bird might fly into the warmth of a hall in winter, and then be lost to sight again in the storm—*de hieme in hiemem regrediens*. Of this short space of Time men had knowledge; they knew nothing of what had gone before, nothing of what might follow after.[1]

'British historians are not necessarily without "care of knowing causes" if they refuse to commit themselves to any more definite judgment upon the pattern of History and the meaning of human existence.'[2]

---

[1] In the famous passage (Baeda: *Historia Ecclesiastica Gentis Anglorum*, Book II, chap. 13) that Sir Llewellyn Woodward has cited here so aptly to illustrate his own thesis, the actual terms in the comparison are, of course, not the brevity of the civilizations' Time-span up to date by contrast with the immensity of the Time-span posited by Anthropology, Geology, and Astronomy, but the brevity of a soul's visible life on Earth by comparison with the immeasurable magnitude of this same soul's mysterious non-terrestrial history. The relevant words are *vita hominum in terris, ad comparationem eius, quod incertum est, temporis* and *ita haec vita hominum ad modicum apparet; quid autem sequatur, quidve praecesserit, prorsus ignoramus*. The meaning of these words seems clear, and it is clinched by the context; for the debate in which these words are reported by Bede to have been spoken was a discussion in the *witenagemot* of the Kingdom of Northumbria, and the question at issue was whether to abide by a traditional Paganism or to be converted to Christianity; it was not the question whether the data for studying the history of Man in Process of Civilization were at present to be deemed insufficient— on a criterion to be found in the estimated scale of Anthropological, Geological, and Astronomical Time—for attempting to make sense of this post-primitive current episode of human affairs.

The subject of the Northumbrian notables' debate was, in short, not History, but Religion and Politics. If, however, we could imagine them discussing, either before or after their historic debate, the question raised by Sir Llewellyn Woodward, we can be sure, *a priori*, that, whether they had been speaking as still unconverted pagans or been speaking as recent converts to the Christian Faith, they would have been as confident of their ability to read the riddle of the terrestrial history of Mankind as they were shy of trying to read the riddle of the eternal destiny of a soul. On the lips of Bede's seventh-century Northumbrian thane, 'the unknown immensity of Time' did not mean the chronological aeons with which the twentieth-century Western geologists and astronomers credited the duration of a Physical Universe; it meant an Eternity that was not commensurate with Time in the astronomer's or the annalist's sense of that word. In the seventh-century *Weltanschauung* of a pagan Northumbrian warrior or a Christian Roman missionary, the Time-span of the histories of the civilizations was not dwarfed by the Time-span of the age of the Earth and the far greater age of the Stellar Cosmos, since these seventh-century Western minds had no idea that chronological periods of these latter orders of magnitude might have elapsed already and might be due to go on rolling into the future. In their cosier vista, as presented in both the Christian and the pagan myth, the Cosmos, the Earth, Terrestrial Life, Human Life, and Civilization had all come into existence and entered on their careers in the self-same week; and this imaginary date lay a shorter time back than the estimated date at which the twentieth-century Western historian placed the rise of the earliest civilizations at the culmination of a chronological prelude of almost unspeakably greater length. In this seventh-century *Weltanschauung* neither the history of the World of Man nor the, on this estimate, coeval history of the Stellar Cosmos presented a puzzle to which a satisfactory clue had not yet been found; and neither the pagan seventh-century Northumbrian nor the Christian seventh-century Roman inquirer would have hesitated to commit himself to a definite judgement upon a pattern of history whose meaning, so he devoutly believed, had been revealed to Man by God.

Thus, in citing Bede, Sir Llewellyn Woodward is taking a pre-Christian or Christian antithesis between Time and Eternity, not as a precise equivalent, but as a suggestive allegory, of a post-Christian antithesis between one Time-span of one order of chronological magnitude and another Time-span of a different order of magnitude in the same chronological dimension.—A.J.T.

[2] Woodward, E. L.: *British Historians* (London 1932, Collins, produced by Adprint

The prudent answer to this challenge, at the date at which it was delivered, was King Agrippa's 'Almost thou persuadest me'.[1] It is indisputable that the discovery of 'laws of Nature' by induction cannot be attempted with any prospect of success unless the investigator has at his command a minimum quantity of data to serve as instances for testing hypotheses by the empirical method of trial and error. When the number is less than the minimum—whatever this indispensable minimum may be held to be in the particular field that happens to be under investigation—the margin of possible error in the findings of tentative inductions becomes prohibitively wide; and, on this account, an importunately scientific-minded student of history might have found himself constrained to admit that an unconditional surrender was the only honest response to an agnostic-minded historian's challenge if this had been delivered, not in the first century of a post-Modern Age of Western history, but, let us say, some four hundred years earlier.

If in A.D. 1532, instead of in A.D. 1932 (the year in which Woodward's book was actually published), a seeker after 'laws of Nature' governing the history of Man in Process of Civilization had been taxed to declare the number of the data of the highest order of magnitude in his chosen field of study about which he could claim to possess effective knowledge, a Western scholar at that earlier date would have had to confess an inability to muster more than three data on the requisite scale; and this insufficient figure of three[2] could not have been bettered at the time by the intellectual heirs to the cultural heritages of any of the other living civilizations. A Western scholar's effective knowledge of civilizations other than his own would have been confined in A.D. 1532 to the Hellenic Civilization, to which the Western was affiliated, and the Syriac Civilization, from which the spark of creativity in Christianity had been derived. A knowledge of the same two extinct civilizations of the second generation would likewise have constituted the entire intellectual stock-in-trade of a contemporary scholar in Orthodox Christendom, in its Ottoman and its Russian provinces alike, and in the Islamic World of the day. A contemporary Far Eastern scholar's knowledge of civilizations other than his own would similarly have been limited to the Sinic and the Indic, while a contemporary Hindu scholar would have had no knowledge of any civilizations except his own and its Indic predecessor. As for the living civilizations of the New World, they were at that moment losing consciousness through being brutally knocked on the head by Castilian *conquistadores*.

On this showing, it is manifest that in A.D. 1532 an agnostic would have been justified in submitting that the data were at present not sufficient to warrant an attempt to discover 'laws of Nature' governing the history of Man in Process of Civilization; and at that date this agnostic argument would have been unanswerable, not only in Western

in the 'Britain in Pictures' series), p. 48. The quotation from this book has been made with the permission of the author and the publishers. See further the same historian's Raleigh Lecture, 'Some Considerations on the Present State of Historical Studies', read on the 17th May, 1950, and published in the *Proceedings of the British Academy*, vol. xxxvi.
[1] Acts xxvi. 28.
[2] See the passage of Sir Charles Darwin's work quoted on p. 206, n. 2, above.

Christendom, but in the contemporary academies of all the other living civilizations. By A.D. 1932, on the other hand—and that was the year in which the passage quoted above was, in fact, published—the facilities at the disposal of a scientific-minded student of History had been improved and enlarged, out of all recognition, by three achievements that the Western Civilization had accomplished in the course of its intervening Modern Age.

In the first place the explosive aggressiveness of the Western peoples in this age had—for the first time in recorded history—rounded up the whole of Mankind, over a literally world-wide range, into a single oecumenical society; and, while in the first chapter of this gradually unfolding story the unification had been carried out within a frankly Western framework and on the superficial planes of Economics and Politics, it was evident by A.D. 1932 that the leaven was then working its way down to the cultural and spiritual depths of life and that, on these deeper levels, the receptivity of the living non-Western societies to the radiation of Western techniques, institutions, and ideas was preparing the way for a cultural counter-offensive.[1] A culturally servile non-Western intelligentsia, that had originally been called into being, like Frankenstein's monster, to further its callous manufacturer's step-fatherly purposes,[2] had begun, by the twentieth century, to beget a happier and more fruitful freedmen-class of 'occidentalists' who were making it their mission to serve the need of the hour in the lives of their own societies by interpreting the intrusive Western culture in their own cultural terms and thereby giving the great non-Western majority of Mankind the means of exercising some discrimination in a retaliatory spoiling of the Egyptians. The 'occidentalists' were already beginning to appropriate, for the common use and benefit of Humanity at large, the cultural wealth that had been amassed by an acquisitive-minded West; and in the meanwhile this internationalized stock of honey had been notably increased by the labours of busy Western bees.

If the Modern Western historians had been the sole representatives of Modern Western intellectual enterprise, a robbery of the Western hive in A.D. 1932 would have proved disappointingly unrewarding for the 'occidentalists'; for, in those imaginary circumstances, the occidentalists' plunder in A.D. 1932 would still have been as exiguous as it would have been four hundred years earlier. As we have already noticed, the Late Modern and post-Modern Western historians had done nothing to increase the number of the data of a significantly high order of magnitude that the Modern Western student of the history of Man in Process of Civilization had inherited from his Medieval predecessors. Though the latter-day Western historians had been no less restlessly industrious than the contemporary Western apprentices in other intellectual trades, they had been spending their energies on grinding the already known significant data into details, to the exclusion of any attempt to make significant additions to knowledge by discovering new data on an illuminatingly large scale. While, however, the Western historians had thus been leaving undone those things which they ought

[1] See IX. viii. 464–80.   [2] See V. v. 154–9.

to have done, their proper study had been magnificently advanced by their proxies the contemporary Western orientalists[1] and archaeologists.[2]

Since the days of the pioneer Western Sinologist Matteo Ricci (*vivebat* A.D. 1552–1610) and the pioneer Western Arabist Edward Pococke I (*vivebat* A.D. 1604–91), Western orientalists had been making accessible to contemporary Western scholars,[3] and hence also to future non-Western occidentalists, an effective knowledge of all the living non-Western civilizations and all those extinct civilizations of the preceding generation to which one or other of the living non-Western civilizations happened to be affiliated. Meanwhile, since the 2nd July, 1798, which was the day on which Napoleon had landed in Egypt, a new-model army of Western archaeologists had gone into action shoulder to shoulder with the Western orientalists in an intellectual crusade against a parochial-minded native Western ignorance; and within the next 134 years they had not only brought into clear visibility, out of the twilight, a number of extinct civilizations—the Egyptiac, Babylonic, Mexic, Yucatec, and Andean—which had already lain just within the ken of Western scholarship thanks to a few monuments still standing above ground and a few fragmentary and garbled references in the known literary records of other civilizations; the archaeologists had also brought to light—and this was the crowning glory of their rapid series of sensational successes—a number of other extinct civilizations—the Sumeric, Hittite, Minoan, and Mayan, not to speak of an Indus Culture and a Shang Culture—whose oblivion had been so complete that, on the eve of the moment when they were thus brought back within the ken of the living by ringing strokes of pick and spade that simulated in real life the mythical music of a Last Trump, there was no human scholar alive who was aware that these miraculously resurgent forgotten civilizations had ever risen and fallen.

By these veritable miracles of intellectual faith and works, the Western archaeologists and the Western orientalists, between them, had increased the number of civilizations known to Western scholars seven-fold, from a trio to more than a score;[4] and this immense enlargement of the West's historical horizon which had been thus achieved by Western intellectual pioneers had been won by them, not merely for the West itself, but for an oecumenical Republic of Letters which was a twentieth-century offspring of the West's assault upon the World. How did this revolutionary transformation of a traditional intellectual situation affect the issue between the seeker after 'laws of Nature' in the history of Man

[1] See I. i. 345–6.
[2] See I. i. 129, n. 1, and 157.
[3] The alertness shown by both Voltaire and Gibbon in appreciating, mastering, and turning to account the new datum that had been brought within Western ken by the scholarship of seventeenth-century and eighteenth-century Jesuit Western Sinologists has been noticed in I. i. 346. Gibbon also made good use of the work of the pioneer Modern Western Arabists.
[4] In virtue of the archaeologists' contribution to Western knowledge of historical data of a significantly high order of magnitude, twentieth-century Western scholars enjoyed a still greater advantage over Gibbon and Voltaire than Voltaire and Gibbon, in their day, had enjoyed over Bossuet or over Hartmann Schedel, the compiler of the Nuremberg Chronicle (see p. 178, n. 5, above).

in Process of Civilization and the agnostic who argued that the quest was foredoomed to failure because the number of the effectively known significant data was insufficient?

The multiplication of the mustered number by seven was not, of course, in itself any guarantee that the social scientist's case had been won for him by the orientalist's and archaeologist's achievements; for the social scientist's original fund of significant knowledge had been so grotesquely incommensurate with his ambitious purpose that, even when the figure of significant data had been raised from three to twenty-one, it might still perhaps be contended that, for serving as a basis for induction, this seven times larger number was still not large enough. In the present writer's personal judgement, a stock of twenty-one significant data was just sufficient to warrant a search for 'laws of Nature' in the history of Man in Process of Civilization; and, twenty years after the publication of Sir Llewellyn Woodward's book, this judgement had been fortified by the authority of Sir Charles Darwin.[1] But the present writer would not have denied that the margin of practicability provided by a stock standing at this twentieth-century figure—twenty-one—was a narrow one, and, notwithstanding Sir Charles Darwin's comforting assurance that a number no higher than ten would prove sufficient for a comparative study and for the induction of 'laws of Nature', he would have gone so far as to concede that an agnostic who could not have failed to win his case in A.D. 1532 might still—even in spite of the orientalists' achievements during the ensuing two centuries and three-quarters—have had a chance of winning it as late as A.D. 1798, if his book had been out of the printer's hands before the 2nd July of that intellectually momentous year.

Thereafter, in the present writer's view, the intellectual battle on this field had been won for Science by the intervention of the archaeologists in the long-since-combatant orientalists' support. As he saw it, the archaeologists had played here the decisive part that the Prussians had once played on a military battlefield on which their British allies had been bearing the heat and burden of the day. At Waterloo an Anglo-Prussian conjunction of military forces had proved irresistible; and the united intellectual forces of the orientalists and the archaeologists had similarly put the historians to rout. Under a twentieth-century specta-tor's eyes, these picturesque antinomian warriors had gone down to as ignominious a defeat at the hands of the disciplined champions of Science as their prototypes the Egyptian Mamlūks had suffered on the 21st July, 1798, in the Battle of the Pyramids, when they had been mowed down by the well-timed fire of Napoleon's efficiently manœuvring Janissaries.[2] The impression made on the writer by the spectacle of this decisive intellectual battle was the experience that had moved him to attempt a study of History; and his answer to the challenge of the agnostics is presented, not solely in the present passage, but throughout the present work.[3]

[1] See p. 206, n. 2, above.
[2] Jabarti's graphic account of this battle has been quoted in IV. iv. 458–60.
[3] See I. i. 458–9.

(IV) THE OPENNESS OF THE QUESTION

Without prejudice to the eventual findings of our present inquiry into the relation between the respective roles of Law and Freedom in History, we may conclude, from the results at which we have arrived up to this point, that, in repudiating a belief in the reign of Law, Late Modern Western Man (*florebat circa* A.D. 1675–1875) had been guilty of hybris, and that, in divers variations on his antinomian theme, the sinner had carried it to divers degrees of enormity. In their unanimous repudiation of a belief in a 'Law of God', all Late Modern Western minds alike had been making the unwarrantably overweening assumption that they had a deeper insight into the secret of the Universe than the Prophets of Israel, Judah, and Iran and these seers' Christian and Muslim epigoni from Amos through Augustine to Ibn Khaldūn and Bossuet. In their sectarian repudiation of a belief in 'laws of Nature' as well, the antinomian school of Late Modern Western historians had been making a still more overweening assumption that was even more unwarrantable—so unwarrantable and so overweening that it had laid this school of historians open to conviction on a charge of heresy by a jury of scientists who had been the historians' fellow-travellers on the first stage of Western Man's spiritual exodus from the Kingdom of God. The Late Modern Western scientists who had kept the historians company in going the length of throwing over 'the Law of God' had still clung to the skirts of Indic and Hellenic philosophers who had promulgated 'laws of Nature' in the name of the goddess Reason; and the Late Modern Western historians had taken a solitary way[1] when they had defiantly made a virtue of their former fellow-travellers' charge against them that they had denied the validity of 'laws of Nature', as well as the validity of 'the Law of God', in the realm of the affairs of Man in Process of Civilization.

Hybris of any degree in any circumstances is everywhere and always wrong and dangerous; but it was at least comprehensible, though not on that account necessarily excusable, that the Late Modern and post-Modern generations of Western Man should have succumbed to the hybristic fancy of imagining themselves to be above the Law in the halcyon days that had dawned upon the Western World after the close of the Wars of Religion and the repulse of the second Ottoman assault upon Vienna. In that hour, Western Man had just seen the two giant figures of an Almighty God and a Grand Signor disappear simultaneously from a mental horizon above which both of them had once loomed so formidably large; and he had not paused to recollect the Hellenic poet Menander's admonition that 'all that injures issues from within'.[2] But the twentieth-century epigoni of the Bayles and Fontenelles had no case at all for retaining their late-seventeenth-century predecessors' complacency in an age which had seen the destructiveness of the Wars of Religion matched, and their atrociousness exceeded, in Wars of Nationality and Ideology that had once again rent the Western Society asunder and, in the act, had conjured up against her an accuser

---

[1] Milton: *Paradise Lost*, Book XII, l. 649.
[2] Menander, fragment 540, quoted in IV. iv. 120, n. 3.

more damaging than Islam and an adversary more puissant than the 'Osmanli. Communism was more damaging than Islam because it spoke to the West with the voice of the West's own conscience, and the Soviet Power was more puissant than the Ottoman because it made war on the West with Western material and spiritual weapons. These harrowing and terrifying new Western experiences had demonstrated unanswerably that a century of low tension which had opened for the Western Society with an Ottoman 'cease fire' under the walls of Vienna in A.D. 1683, and had closed for it in A.D. 1775 with the firing, at Concord, Massachusetts, of 'the shot heard round the World',[1] had, after all, been nothing more than a deceptive lull; and, after the successive warnings served on Western Man by History in A.D. 1775, 1792, 1914, 1917, 1933, and 1939, the rake had come to a point in his progress at which his ears ought to have been open to Menandrian saws that certain of his own poets had been saying.[2] Volney's 'La source de ses calamités . . . réside dans l'homme même' had anticipated Meredith's 'We are betrayed by what is false within';[3] and in these sentences a Late Modern Western Antinomianism had written its own self-indictment.

The moral question whether these experiences and admonitions would move Western Man to repent of his hybris was one that could be answered by nobody except the tragic hero himself; but, on the intellectual point at issue between latter-day Western historians and latter-day Western scientists, it seemed reasonable, in the circumstances of A.D. 1952, to ask the historians to meet the scientists to the extent of admitting that it might, after all, at least be an open question whether 'laws of Nature' were or were not to be found governing the affairs of Man in Process of Civilization. Indeed, the openness of the question was actually so patent, the need to look into it so pressing, and the aphasia afflicting the historians so invincible, that it seemed warrantable at this point for a student of History to make the requisite declaration on the historians' behalf.

If we do thus take the liberty taken by godparents in the ministration of the Christian Church's rite of baptism by declaring open for discussion the question whether 'laws of Nature' have any currency in the domain of History, we immediately find a string of supplementary questions unrolling itself.

What (if any) instances of 'laws of Nature' governing the affairs of Man in Process of Civilization are brought to light in fact by an empirical survey of the data? If 'laws of Nature' operative in the realm of History do emerge from our study, what are the possible explanations of their currency? Do such 'laws of Nature' governing human affairs turn out, when we understand them, to be inexorable? Or can their incidence on Human Life be brought under human control at least in some measure? Are there any tracts in the realm of History in which human affairs appear, on the evidence of the data, to be, not amenable to 'laws of Nature', but recalcitrant to them? And, if this, too, is one of the findings

---

[1] Emerson, R. W., in his quatrain inscribed on the spot where the first shot was fired in the American Revolutionary War. The historical significance of this war has been discussed in IV. iv. 165.

[2] Acts xvii. 28.

[3] See IV. iv. 120.

of an empirical survey, what are the possible explanations of Man's apparent freedom from the rule of 'laws of Nature' in certain circumstances? Is the appearance simply an illusion that arises because our data are insufficient or because our interpretation of them is inadequate? Or have we grounds for surmising that, however great our knowledge and our insight might be, we should never find 'laws of Nature' operative here, because these tracts of human affairs are genuinely exempt from Nature's jurisdiction? If, however, certain tracts of human affairs are genuinely exempt from 'laws of Nature', what are the powers that do reign over these Alsatias? Are they spiritually waste lands swept by wayward winds of Chance? Or are they spiritual arenas for the interplay of Challenge and Response in encounters between personalities?

It will be seen that these last two supplementary questions carry us beyond the bounds of 'laws of Nature' and bring us back face to face with 'the Law of God'. The riddle of the relation between God's Law and a human soul's freedom is the last, the most difficult, and the most crucial of all questions on our present agenda.

B. THE AMENABILITY OF HUMAN AFFAIRS TO 'LAWS OF NATURE'

(I) A SURVEY OF INSTANCES

(a) 'LAWS OF NATURE' IN THE ORDINARY AFFAIRS OF PRIVATE PEOPLE IN AN INDUSTRIAL WESTERN SOCIETY

OUR exploration of the problem of Law and Freedom in History has brought us to the point of assuming that the question whether 'laws of Nature' have or have not any footing in the history of Man in Process of Civilization may legitimately be treated as open for the purpose of making headway in our inquiry. In allowing ourselves to make this postulate, we have bound ourselves to put it to an empirical test. Let us start by making a survey of affairs of Man in Process of Civilization in which 'laws of Nature' do appear to be operative, and then—when we have looked into possible explanations of such phenomena, and into the subsequent question whether 'laws of Nature' are inexorable or controllable in the domain of human affairs, if they do have any currency there—let us go on to make a corresponding survey of affairs of Man in Process of Civilization in which 'laws of Nature' appear not to be operative, and let us look into possible explanations of such phenomena in turn.

In embarking on our survey of apparent evidences of an amenability of human affairs to 'laws of Nature', it might be convenient to take our first soundings in the ordinary affairs of private people, since in this tract, in which fishing rights had been venturesomely claimed and profitably exercised by latter-day Western historians, the number of the data was apt, as we have noticed,[1] to run into comparatively high figures, rising from thousands to hundreds of millions, and figures of these orders of magnitude are high enough, and at the same time not too high, to allow of accurate and subtle statistics. Statistically established uniformities and recurrences are capable, not only of being visualized in mathematical curves, but also of being verified by being put to the test of being taken as bases for prediction; and, in the Western World at a date some two hundred years after the outbreak of the Industrial Revolution in Great Britain in the latter part of the eighteenth century of the Christian Era, the possibility of accurately working out statistical expectations in the light of the statistical patterns presented by arrays of relevant accomplished facts had been amply demonstrated by the magnitude of the financial profits earned by entrepreneurs who had staked their capital on a faith that, in their social milieu, the ordinary affairs of private people were governed by 'laws of Nature' that were at least sufficiently regular to be both ascertainable and trustworthy.

There were two principal departments in the province of private people's ordinary affairs in which commercially profitable predictions, made on the basis of statistical patterns detected in the data of past his-

[1] See pp. 205–6, above.

tory, had come to be commonplaces of latter-day Western business activity. One of these two sources of profit from predictions based on past statistics was the business of catering for divers markets for goods and services; the other was the insurance business. Catering was, no doubt, coeval with Civilization itself, though the scale on which it had come to be practised in the Western World, and the narrowness to which the margins of error and profit had been reduced *pari passu*, in this Western social milieu, by the competitiveness of Western capitalistic enterprise in its adolescence, may have been without precedent in other civilizations' histories. As for the insurance business, the insurance of commercially valuable commodities other than merchant ships and their cargoes seems to have been a Late Modern Western innovation; and, when we glance at the divers ramifications of a latter-day Western insurance business, we find in them as many demonstrations that 'laws of Nature', operating regularly enough to afford possibilities of making financial profits from statistical predictions with narrow margins, were in force, not only in the realm of Non-Human Nature in which the risks of damage or destruction by the blind fury of storm or tempest were run by sailors in ships at sea, but also in fields in which a waywardly purposeful human intelligence and human will had some power arbitrarily to interfere with a Non-Human Nature's course.[1]

The proven profitability of the insurance business in quoting premiums for accepting risks on storm-damage to ships and crops, lightning-damage to ricks and buildings, frost-damage to waterpipes, and pest-damage to fruit-trees and livestock was neither so remarkable nor so significant as the likewise proven profitability of insurance policies into which the human factors of intelligence and will did enter in divers measures. The death, for example, that was the subject of the wager in a life policy[2] was an event which the human intelligence and will were

[1] This latter-day Western insurance business was conducted on the assumption that God, if He existed, was the god of the eighteenth-century deists, who could be counted upon to be content to reign, while leaving it to Nature to govern and leaving it to Man to harness Nature by exerting his intellectual ingenuity upon her. In the technical terminology of this business, 'an act of God' was an event which, in the business relations between the two parties to an insurance policy, was the counterpart of a miracle in the Jewish, Christian, and Muslim meaning of that term, because it was something that had not been foreseen or provided for in the policy, as a miracle was something incongruous with what had come to be taken as being the normal course of Nature. An earthquake, for example, would be 'an act of God' in the construing of a policy on the structure of a building which gave cover only against the risk of damage or destruction by fire; but it would not be 'an act of God' in the construing of a policy which did cover the risk of damage or destruction by earthquake as well. It will be seen that the sphere of God's operation, in the meaning of this quaint professional jargon, would be perpetually expanding or contracting in accordance with the variations in the terms of the contracts negotiated between underwriters and their clients.

[2] The latter-day Western life insurance business could never have been launched if the pioneer entrepreneurs in this field had not been able to lay hands on data for statistics that were both abundant enough and accurate enough to enable them, from the outset, to quote rates of premium in which the margin of allowance for the element of statistical uncertainty would be narrow enough to make it possible for the transaction to fulfil simultaneously the two commercially requisite conditions of being neither prohibitively expensive for the party seeking to be insured nor prohibitively hazardous for the party proposing to invest capital in covering the acceptance of risks.

This statistical stock-in-trade with which the pioneer Western life insurance companies started business consisted of the statistical patterns discernible in three sets of data: 'the Breslau Table' (*editum* A.D. 1693) compiled by Dr. Edmund Halley from records of deaths in the Silesian city of Breslau in the years A.D. 1687–91; 'the Northampton Table'

able in some cases to postpone, though they were powerless to avert it in the long run, while, in an age in which Western preventive medicine was making sensational advances, will and intelligence were showing themselves able to mitigate, and even to avert, sickness on the grand scale, without, of course, being able to prevent death through sickness from supervening in the last resort. When it came to accepting risks of accidents, the insurance business was venturing into a field on the borderline between the domain of a physical and a subconscious psychic life, that were both governed by ascertainably, and therefore predictably, working 'laws of Nature', and the domain of a personal intelligence and will that were free to pursue their own purposes. The risk of accidents being caused by personal carelessness and recklessness was manifestly far less easy to calculate than the risk of automatic physical and subconscious psychic responses proving inadequate to cope with an emergency occurring too suddenly to give the party's will and intelligence the time to come into action. Nevertheless, the insurance business had found it profitable to cover risks not only of accidents but of burglaries, which were conscious, deliberate, and often carefully planned personal acts.

The fact that commercial profits could be made out of insuring against risks of burglaries demonstrated that individual acts of human will might be subject to 'laws of Nature' that would be statistically ascertainable if the instances could be mustered in sufficient numbers; and this commercially successful establishment of a burglary branch of the insurance business in the history of a Late Modern Western Society was also an indication that the dominion of 'laws of Nature' over individual acts of will might prove not to be confined to the ordinary affairs of private people but to extend to those extraordinary public affairs which had been the conventional theme of History in all societies in process of civilization[1] until the nineteenth-century Western historians had expanded their horizon to include the ordinary affairs of private people in their panorama. The latter-day Western phenomenon of burglary insurance had this historical significance in the field of public affairs because burglaries were the counterparts in private life of acts of military aggression and diplomatic chicanery in public life—as a captured Tyrrhenian pirate

---

(*editum* A.D. 1783) compiled from records of deaths, recording the ages at death, in a parish comprising the greater part of the English city of Northampton in the years A.D. 1735–80; and 'the Carlisle Table' (*editum* A.D. 1815) compiled from censuses taken in A.D. 1780 and 1787 and from records of deaths in the years A.D. 1779–87 in two parishes of the English city of Carlisle.

When once the life insurance companies had begun to transact the business which this original fund of statistical information had enabled them to start, their own records began to provide them with a great and ever growing volume of data to serve them for the elaboration and refinement of their statistics with an eye to increasing their aggregate profits by transacting business on ever narrower margins. The first table to be constructed entirely from life insurance records was 'Morgan's Equitable Table' (*editum* A.D. 1834), which was based on the experience of the Equitable Life Assurance Society.

Accounts of these primordial foundations on which the Modern Western life insurance business's indispensable statistical apparatus was originally based will be found in Farren, E. J.: 'The History of Assurance', in *The Assurance Magazine*, vol. i (London 1851, Layton), pp. 42–46; Raynes, H. E.: *A History of British Assurance* (London 1948, Pitman), pp. 125–30; Anderson, J. L., and Dow, J. B.: *Actuarial Statistics* (Cambridge 1948, University Press, 2 vols.), vol. ii, pp. 158–60. The writer of this Study was directed to these authorities by the kindness of Mr. Thomas Wallas, the General Manager of the London and Lancashire Insurance Company, Ltd.   [1] See pp. 182–4, above.

once pointed out to a self-righteous Alexander the Great, if we are to give credence to a celebrated anecdote.[1] Meanwhile, in the field of private affairs, the recognition that individual acts of will had only to occur in sufficiently large numbers in order to become amenable to commercially lucrative statistical calculations was a discovery that had not had to wait for a latter-day Western insurance business to bring it to light. The economic demand that had been profitably catered for by the Egyptiac potter, the Nomad conductor of caravans, and the Syriac innkeeper, long before any Western manufacturing concern, omnibus, railway, or airways company, or hotel or restaurant proprietor had put in an appearance, was, of course, for the purpose of our present inquiry, a statistical quantum of the same quality as the insurance risk of burglary, inasmuch as it was a collectively regular, and therefore predictable, statistical pattern emerging from an aggregate of individually wayward, and therefore unpredictable, acts of personal will.

(b) 'LAWS OF NATURE' IN THE ECONOMIC AFFAIRS OF AN INDUSTRIAL WESTERN SOCIETY

The statistical patterns discernible in the fluctuations of demand and supply in the dealings between caterers and their customers were woven, in the social woof and weft of an Industrial Western Society, into a wider network of economic regularities, uniformities, and recurrences revealing themselves statistically in the aggregate effects of numerous personal acts which, individually, were too wayward to be predictable. At the time of writing, half way through the twentieth century of the Christian Era, the state of knowledge and the range of activities in this particular field were illuminating for the study of the questions whether the affairs of Man in Process of Civilization were or were not governed by any 'laws of Nature', and, if they were, then to what extent and degree. By this date the man in the street in an Occidental Babylon had already long since come to take for granted the reality of 'booms' and 'slumps' whose alternations had made or marred his private fortunes perhaps more than once in his own personal experience; but the pattern of these popularly recognized 'business cycles' had not yet been worked out in statistical terms with sufficient clarity or precision to have emboldened the in-

---

[1] 'If justice is eliminated, what are states but gangs of robbers writ large (*quid sunt regna nisi magna latrocinia*)? For, after all, what are gangs of robbers but states writ small? . . . The captured pirate's retort to Alexander the Great was as neat as it was true. When the king asked the man what he meant by infesting the sea, he gave the frank and truculent answer: "What do you mean, pray, by infesting the globe? The only difference is that, because I do it with one small ship, I am called a robber, while you are called an emperor because you do it with a great fleet." '—Saint Augustine: *De Civitate Dei*, Book IV, chap. 4, already quoted in VI. vii. 210, n. 1.

This truth had, of course, always been unpalatable to heads of states. Early in the year A.D. 1936, one of Hitler's subjects who had invited the writer of this Study to give a lecture in Berlin found himself constrained to translate orally to his Führer a passage in one of this prospective visitor's published works in which the Englishman had written that 'it was shocking to see the head of a state—even when he was the leader of a recently victorious revolutionary movement—shooting down his own former henchmen in the style of an American "gangster" ' on the 29th–30th June, 1934 (*Survey of International Affairs, 1934* (London 1935, Milford), p. 325). Hitler's comment on this was: 'That is not fair, because the gangsters do it for money, and I did not do it for that.' The naïveté of this line of defence was engaging, but it did not impugn the justice of the Tyrrhenian pirate's point.

surance companies to open up a new branch of their business by quoting premiums for insurance against the formidable risks arising from economic fluctuations.[1] On the other hand, scientific investigators had rushed in where business men were still fearing to tread; and, in Modern Western history, disinterested scientific research had been apt to be followed by a profitable industrial application of the results as surely as, in the field of contemporary Western colonial enterprise, the advent of the missionary had been followed by that of the trader and the soldier.

The still disinterestedly academic students of latter-day Western 'business cycles' seemed, *circa* A.D. 1952, to be agreed that these particular economic patterns were peculiar to a social milieu in which a monetary economy had driven a barter economy off the field, in which Agriculture had become socially subordinate to Commerce and Industry, and in which the process of manufacture (in defiance of the etymology of the word) had come to be performed by power supplied, not by the muscles of men and non-human animals, but by inanimate forces of Nature ranging from winds caught in the sails of ships and windmills to electrons liberated in plant capable of splitting atoms.

'Business cycles which affect the fortunes of the mass of people in a country, which succeed each other continuously, and which attain a semblance of regularity, do not become prominent in the economic history of a country until a large proportion of its people are living mainly by making and spending money incomes.'[2]

'The "cause", if we wish to use that term, of business cycles . . . is to be found in the habits and customs (institutions) of men which make up the money economy, with its money and credit, prices, private property, buying and selling, and so on—all loaded, so to speak, on the industrial process.'[3]

In the history of the Western Civilization, business cycles had made their epiphany *pari passu* with the prevalence of a money economy in which the incentive to economic action was a desire to earn profits reckoned in monetary values;[4] and this cyclic rhythm in the flow of economic activity was a phenomenon that appeared to be peculiar to Modern Western business organization.[5]

'Presumably this contention that business cycles arise from that peculiar form of economic organisation which has come to prevail in England within the last two centuries, and over much of the World in more recent times, would be admitted by most theorists.'[6]

'The conception of business cycles obtained from a survey of contemporary reports starts with the fundamental fact of rhythmical fluctua-

---

[1] The unwillingness of the insurance companies to do business in economic fluctuations up to date was probably due to an excessive uncertainty in the relevant statistics rather than to an excessive timidity or conservatism on the part of business men who had recently ventured no less spiritedly than profitably into the new field opened up for insurance by the mechanization of road traffic.

[2] Mitchell, W. C.: *Business Cycles, The Problem and its Setting* (New York 1927 (2nd impression 1930), National Bureau of Economic Research, Inc.), p. 458. The quotations from this book have been made with the permission of the author and the publishers.

[3] Frank, L. K.: 'A Theory of Business Cycles,' in *The Quarterly Journal of Economics*, vol. xxxvii (Cambridge, Mass. 1923, Harvard University Press), pp. 625–42, quoted by Mitchell in op. cit., p. 45.   [4] See Mitchell, op. cit., pp. 62 and 63.

[5] See ibid., p. 61.   [6] Ibid., p. 56.

tions in activity, and adds that these fluctuations are peculiar to countries organised on a business basis, that they appear in all such countries, that they tend to develop the same phase at nearly the same time in different countries, that they follow each other without intermissions, that they are affected by all sorts of non-business factors, that they represent predominant rather than universal changes in trend, and that, while they vary in intensity and duration, the variations are not so wide as to prevent our identifying different cases as belonging to a single class of phenomena.'[1]

In the intellectual history of an industrial Western Society the phenomenon of trade cycles had been discovered empirically from direct social observation before it had been confirmed statistically from patterns discernible in collections of data.[2] The earliest known description of it had been given in A.D. 1837 by a British observer, S. J. Loyd, *alias* Lord Overstone (*vivebat* A.D. 1796–1883), in the light of experience in Great Britain since the time of the Napoleonic Wars;[3] and there was nothing to suggest that this empirically demonstrated relativity of the phenomenon to the social milieu in which it presented itself was not one of its intrinsic features. In a book first published in A.D. 1927 an American student of business cycles declared his belief that 'the characteristics of business cycles may be expected to change as economic organisation develops'.[4] On the basis of 'business annals' compiled by another American scholar, W. L. Thorp,[5] from non-statistical evidence for the economic history of the West in its Industrial Age, a third American scholar[6] had descried, within the longer Time-span illuminated by this less precise but more widely ranging kind of information, a secular tendency towards a prolongation of the wave-length of 'business cycles' of the shortest kind. In the light of these data, F. C. Mills had calculated that the mean wavelength of a short cycle was 5·86 years in the early stages of industrialization, 4·09 years in a subsequent stage of rapid economic transition, and 6·39 years in a succeeding state of relative economic stability; and, in the judgement of the first of the three American scholars just cited, expressed in a book first published in A.D. 1927,[7] 'there can be little doubt that the average duration of business cycles has undergone secular changes in the countries for which Thorp has compiled the longest records'. In a book published in A.D. 1939 a German economist, in whose belief 'innovation' was 'the outstanding fact in the economic history of Capitalist Society'[8] and was at the same time the cause of the cyclic fluctuations in

---

[1] Mitchell, W. C.: *Business Cycles, the Problem and its Setting* (New York 1930, National Bureau of Economic Research, Inc.), pp. 458–9.
[2] See Hawtrey, R. G.: 'The Monetary Theory of the Trade Cycle and its Statistical Test', in *The Quarterly Journal of Economics*, vol. xli (Cambridge, Mass. 1927, Harvard University Press), p. 471. 'No statistical finding can ever prove or disprove a proposition which we have reason to believe by virtue of simpler and more fundamental facts' (Schumpeter, J. A.: *Business Cycles* (New York 1939, McGraw-Hill, 2 vols.), vol. i, p. 33).
[3] See Hawtrey, ibid., pp. 471–2.   [4] Mitchell, op. cit., p. 413.
[5] Thorp, W. L.: *Business Annals* (New York 1926, National Bureau of Economic Research, Inc.).
[6] Mills, F. C., in *The Journal of the American Statistical Association*, December 1926, pp. 447–57.
[7] Mitchell, W. C.: *Business Cycles, the Problem and its Setting* (New York 1930, National Bureau of Economic Research, Inc.), p. 415.
[8] Schumpeter, op. cit., vol. i, p. 86. The same authority, in op. cit., vol. i, p. 223, defines Capitalism as 'that form of private property economy in which innovations are

this society's economic life, made it clear that this thesis of his was restricted in its application to the social milieu of the Western World in its
Industrial Age,[1] and hazarded the guess that this particular social milieu
in this particular society might already be passing away by the time at
which he was writing.[2] In a book published in A.D. 1947 a Belgian economist had expressed the view that

'l'expansion contemporaine . . . ne peut être qu'un épisode de l'histoire de
l'humanité et doit se terminer un jour, soit devant des impossibilités
matérielles de continuer, soit parce que le complexe économique et social
provoque la désagrégation de l'effort, soit enfin parce que les aspirations
collectives se donnent un autre bout'.[3]

Yet, ephemeral though the social milieu of these pulsations in the flow
of economic activity might prove to be, and brief though the experience
of these peculiar phenomena, occurring in these peculiar circumstances,
had actually been up to date, the fathers of a Western economic science
had succeeded, within less than two hundred years of the outbreak of the
Industrial Revolution in Great Britain,[4] in descrying economic cycles of
divers wave-lengths in latter-day Western history, without allowing themselves to be inhibited by an age-old conundrum of Formal Logic that
was paralysing contemporary non-economic Western historians. The
Western economists satisfied the non-economic historians' most exacting
Rankean requirements in studying the course of history *wie es eigentlich
gewesen* and in taking due account of the element of uniqueness in each
single historical datum; but, unlike the non-economic historians, they did
not fail to grasp the not very novel or abstruse logical points that there
was also an element of uniformity common to one datum and another
and that this element of uniformity, so far from being proved illusory by
the coexistence of the element of uniqueness, was the background against
which the element of uniqueness showed up, and without which it
would have been invisible.[5]

This difference-in-likeness and likeness-in-difference was noted, for
example, by an investigator who had described a series of seven cycles in
the fluctuations of the incidence of unemployment in the economic history of the United Kingdom during the years A.D. 1850–1914:

'The general movement is . . . rhythmic, both in respect of wave-
lengths and of amplitude. . . . The rhythm is rough and imperfect.[6] All

---

carried out by means of borrowed money, which in general, though not by logical necessity, implies credit creation'.   [1] See Schumpeter, op. cit., vol. i, pp. 144 and 223.
    [2] See ibid., p. 145.
    [3] Dupriez, L. H.: *Les Mouvements Économiques Généraux* (Louvain 1947, Institut de
Recherches Économiques et Sociales, 2 vols.), vol. ii, p. 280.
    [4] In Schumpeter's opinion, the minimum span of known history that was required
for a study of cycles in Modern Western economic life was of the order of 250 years (op.
cit., vol. i, p. 220).
    [5] The truth is, of course, as has been pointed out by W. C. Mitchell in *Business Cycles,
the Problem and its Setting* (New York 1930, National Bureau of Economic Research,
Inc.), p. 382, that the problem presented by the simultaneous uniqueness and uniformity
of the specimens of a species is a general problem of thought, not a special problem
peculiar to thought about business cycles.
    [6] According to Mitchell, ibid., pp. 377 and 453–4, the statistical and the annalistic
evidence concurred in indicating that business cycles were 'cyclic' in the sense of being
measurable recurrences, but were not 'periodic' in the sense of being measurable recurrences with a uniformly regular wave-length.—A.J.T.

the recorded cycles are members of the same family, but among them there are no twins.'[1]

The same finding was reported by a student of the general economic history of Great Britain during the years A.D. 1790–1914:

'A reading of the evidence, statistical and qualitative, on the movements within the British economy in modern times, taken year by year, month by month, or week by week, leaves two enduring impressions. First, one is impressed with the uniqueness and variety of the story of economic life. The combinations of forces within the moving economy are, like those in political life, in an important sense always new and fresh. No year is quite like another year;[2] and after a time one gets to know them like old friends. . . . Second, one is impressed with the solid reality of the cyclical pattern which steadily recurs, in Britain and then—gradually widening—throughout the World,[3] from the end of the American Revolution to the outbreak of the First World War. No two cycles, of course, are quite the same; and one can trace, as well, certain long-period changes in the character of cycles. But it is evident that the whole evolution of Modern Society in the West occurred in a rhythmic pattern, which had consequences for social and political, as well as for economic, events.'[4]

This finding that the spectacle of likeness-in-difference is no peculiar feature of British nineteenth-century economic history, but is discernible in contemporary Western economic history as a whole, is endorsed by an impressive consensus of authoritative opinions. For instance, the authors of an essay in measuring business cycles find that

'Two conclusions emerge from this analysis. In the first place our tests, so far as they go, bear out the concept of business cycles as units of roughly concurrent fluctuations in many activities.[5] In the second place they demonstrate that, although cyclical measures of individual series usually vary greatly from one cycle to the next, there is a pronounced tendency towards repetition in the relations among the movements of different activities in successive business cycles. Our analysis of hundreds of time series is sufficiently advanced to give us full confidence in these conclusions. Later monographs will demonstrate . . . that business-cycle phenomena are far more regular than many historical-minded students believe.'[6]

'Strictly speaking, every business cycle is a unique historical episode. . . . Business cycles differ in their duration as wholes and in the relative

[1] Pigou, A. C.: *Industrial Fluctuations*, 2nd ed. (London 1929, Macmillan), pp. 12–13.

[2] 'Each one [instance in any series of instances of a phenomenon: 'fluctuations, crises, booms, depressions'] is a historic individual and never like any other, either in the way it comes about or in the picture it presents' (Schumpeter, op. cit., vol. i, p. 34).—A.J.T.

[3] According to Pigou, op. cit., p. 11, industrial fluctuations became oecumenical in their range from about A.D. 1872 onwards. 'Bare as they are and short their span, the annals reveal a secular trend towards territorial expansion of business relations and a concomitant trend towards economic unity', and this both within the United States and in the World at large, according to Mitchell, ibid., p. 446. Cp. p. 456.—A.J.T.

[4] Rostow, W. W.: *British Economy of the Nineteenth Century* (Oxford 1948, Clarendon Press), pp. 31–32.

[5] 'The swings of the different industries are not independent. . . . They are concordant in direction. We may fairly speak of common swings of expansion and contraction in the main body of industries taken separately, and not merely in the aggregate or average of industries. But . . . the amplitudes of the swings in different occupations are very far from concordant; some are much larger than others' (Pigou, A. C.: *Industrial Fluctuations*, 2nd ed. (London 1929, Macmillan), p. 13).—A.J.T.

[6] Burns, A. F., and Mitchell, W. C.: *Measuring Business Cycles* (New York 1946, National Bureau of Economic Research, Inc.), pp. 488–91.

duration of their component phases; they differ in industrial and geographical scope; they differ in intensity; they differ in the features which
attain prominence; they differ in the quickness and the uniformity with
which they sweep from one country to another. . . . [But] differences
among business cycles . . . afford no reason for doubting that these cycles
constitute a valid species of phenomena.'[1]

'A tendency toward alternations of prosperity and depression must have
considerable constancy and energy to stamp its pattern upon economic
history in a world where other factors of most unequal power are constantly present. . . .'[2] The quiet business forces working towards uniformity
of fortunes must be powerful indeed to impress a common pattern upon
the course of business cycles in many countries.'[3]

These findings reappear in a judicious surveyor's panoramic view:

'Each cycle, each period of prosperity or depression, has its special
features which are not present in any, or not in many, others. In a sense,
each cycle is an historical individual: each is embedded in a social-economic
structure of its own. Technological knowledge, methods of production,
degree of capital-intensity, number, quality, and age-distribution of the
population, habits and preferences of consumers, social institutions in the
widest sense including the legal framework of Society, practice in the
matter of interventions of the State and other public bodies in the economic
sphere, habits of payment, banking practices and so forth—all these factors change continuously and are not exactly the same in any two cases. . . .

'This . . . raises the question whether it is possible to make any general
statements at all as to the causes and conditions of cycles—in other words,
whether the same theory holds for the cycles in the first half of the nineteenth century and for those in the second quarter of the twentieth century, for the cycles in the industrial countries of Western Europe and the
United States and for those in the agricultural countries of Eastern Europe
and overseas. . . .

'We believe . . . that a very general theory of the most important aspects
of the Cycle can be evolved, which will not on the one hand be so formal
as to be useless for practical purposes, while, on the other hand, it will
have a very wide field of application. . . . The mere fact that each cycle is
an historical individual is not a sufficient argument against a general
theory. Are there two men who are in all respects alike? Does this dis-
similarity in many respects destroy the possibility and practical usefulness
of Anatomy, Physiology, etc.? That each cycle is unique in many respects
does not prevent all cycles from being similar in other respects, over and
above those similarities which constitute the fundamental elements of the
Cycle.'[4]

In this summing up, certain salient features emerge. Three points are
picked out by A. C. Pigou:[5] 'the first general characteristic of industrial
fluctuations is their wide international range; the second, the rough similarity among successive cycles; the third, the general concordance in
timing and direction between the wave movements of different occupations.' W. C. Mitchell's first and last word is that 'business history repeats

[1] Mitchell, W. C.: *Business Cycles, the Problem and its Setting* (New York 1930,
National Bureau of Economic Research, Inc.), pp. 354 and 383.
[2] Ibid., p. 421.   [3] Ibid., p. 450.
[4] Haberler, G.: *Prosperity and Depression: A Theoretical Analysis of Cyclical Movements*, 3rd ed. (Geneva 1941, League of Nations), pp. 275–6.
[5] Pigou, A. C.: *Industrial Fluctuations*, 2nd ed. (London 1929, Macmillan), p. vii.

itself, but always with a difference', which does not, however, make the search for uniformities either impracticable or useless.[1] Considering the paucity of the data at the inquirers' disposal so far, it was not surprising to find that some of the four or five different kinds of cycles which different investigators had claimed to have discovered should have been less widely accepted than others as being proven historical realities, or that there should have been still undecided controversies over many points concerning even those kinds of cycles that had won recognition by a general consensus of authoritative scholars; the remarkable and significant features in the history of a still adolescent Modern Western economic science had been the boldness with which a band of intellectual pioneers had made use of the still scanty data at their disposal for hazarding generalizations, and the extent of the fundamental agreement underlying their superficial domestic quarrels. The attitude prevalent among economists mid-way through the twentieth century is made clear in the following passage of a letter, dated the 2nd December, 1949, from Professor T. S. Ashton to the writer of this Study in answer to inquiries on these points:

'There is no doubt whatsoever of the existence of what may reasonably be called a trade or business cycle in the nineteenth century: all are agreed on that. It is equally clear that the booms and slumps occurred at the same time, or almost the same time, in all industrialised countries and in the less developed areas connected with these by trade. The only dispute is as to the periodicity.'

Of the four or five kinds of cycles in view, the best established at the time of writing seemed to be one with a wave-length of something between 11 and 7 years[2] or something between 10 and 7 years;[3] of 9·4 years reckoning from peak to peak (between the dates A.D. 1792 and A.D. 1913), and 9 years reckoning from trough to trough (between the dates A.D. 1788 and A.D. 1914), in a series discernible in the economic history of Great Britain;[4] and of 9·2 years on the average.[5]

A cycle with a wave-length of about four years on the average had been descried, by at least one observer, alternating with the nine-year cycle in Great Britain during the first phase of her Industrial Age; but, in this observer's view, these four-years cycles 'tend virtually to disappear from the array of trade cycles [in the history of Great Britain] after 1860', except for a special case in A.D. 1907;[6] and he accounts for this progressive submergence of four-years cycles by nine-years cycles in Great Britain

---

[1] See Mitchell, W. C.: *Business Cycles and their Causes*, being a new edition of the author's *Business Cycles, Part III* (Berkeley, Cal. 1941, University of California Press), pp. ix–xi.   [2] See Hawtrey, op. cit., p. 476.
[3] Professor T. S. Ashton in a personal letter of the 2nd December, 1949, to the writer of this Study. In this letter, Professor Ashton draws attention to 'clearly marked booms in England in 1818, 1825, 1836, 1845, 1856, 1866, 1873, 1882, 1889/90, 1899/1900, 1906, 1913, and so on'. According to Mitchell, *Business Cycles, The Problem and its Setting*, p. 334, 'the memorable cycles which culminated in 1882, in 1893, in 1907, in 1917 and in 1920 stand out clearly in all our curves'.   [4] See Rostow, op. cit., p. 38, n. 1.
[5] See Huntington, E.: *Mainsprings of Civilisation* (New York 1945, Wiley), p. 477. The cycle of this wave-length had been first brought to light by Clément Juglar in *Des Crises Commerciales et de leur Retour Périodique en France, en Angleterre, et aux États-Unis* (1st ed.: Paris 1862, Guillaumin; 2nd ed.: Paris 1889, Guillaumin).
[6] Rostow, op. cit., pp. 38–39.

by interpreting the four-years cycle as an 'inventory cycle' whose 'character stems from the nature of the merchant's trade', and 'which one
could, almost certainly, trace back into the eighteenth century, and perhaps even back to mediaeval times'.[1] He points out 'that, until about
the [eighteen-] fifties, the principal British exports were consumers' rather
than capital goods',[2] but that, 'from the late 1780's at least, . . . this
rhythm is woven into the longer and deeper rhythm of fluctuations in
long-term investment',[3] and that the sixth decade of the nineteenth century marks the date at which, in the economic life of Great Britain, long-
term investment in capital goods supplanted the production of consumers' goods as the country's major economic activity.[4] 'The two types
of fluctuations', however, 'did not pursue their course in separate and
discrete channels. They were linked in at least four ways.'[5]

Students of the economic history of the United States in the Industrial
Age had here descried a cycle with a wave-length of 42 or 43 months on
the average.[6]

'The average (and the model) American cycle seems to be made up of
two unequal segments, a two-year period of gradually increasing activity, and
a period, four to six months shorter, of less gradually shrinking activity.'[7]

The same school of American investigators had seen in this three-and-a-
half-years cycle in the United States one local variant of a kind, likewise
exemplified in the four-years cycle in Great Britain, of which there were
other local variants to be found in the contemporary economic histories
of France, Germany, and Austria[8]—the chronological locus of this short-
wave cycle lying within miminum and maximum limits of three and six
years.[9] On the other hand, in the opinion of a Belgian scholar,

'Pour qui dépasse le cadre de l'histoire des États-Unis, la distinction
entre le cycle de sept à dix ans et le cycle court de quarante mois ne trouve
plus aucun semblant de confirmation dans les faits: le cycle de quarante
mois n'existe simplement pas.'[10]

A British scholar,[11] who likewise discounts, as being dubious, the evidence for the existence 'of a purely commercial short wave of about $3\frac{1}{2}$
years', also makes the same reservation of judgement about the evidence
for the existence 'of longer waves of from 20 to 80 years' duration'.
'Long cycles of remarkably regular duration'—with a chronological locus
between minimum and maximum limits of fifteen and twenty years—
were descried nevertheless, by some investigators, in the history of
building construction in the United States;[12] and, in the general economic history of Great Britain between A.D. 1790 and A.D. 1914, five phases
of an average wave-length of just under twenty-five years were descried
by one of the investigators already quoted.[13]

---

[1] Rostow, op. cit., p. 41. Cp. pp. 39–40.   [2] Ibid., p. 41, n. 1.
[3] Ibid., p. 41.   [4] Ibid., pp. 42–43.   [5] Enumerated ibid., p. 43.
[6] Mitchell, *Business Cycles, the Problem and its Setting*, p. 341. See also Huntington,
op. cit., pp. 463–8.
[7] Mitchell, ibid., p. 337.   [8] See ibid., pp. 385 and 390–1.
[9] See ibid., p. 457.   [10] Dupriez, op. cit., vol. ii, p. 280.
[11] Professor T. S. Ashton, in the letter quoted above.
[12] See Burns, A. F., and Mitchell, W. C.: *Measuring Business Cycles* (New York 1946,
National Bureau of Economic Research, Inc.), p. 418.   [13] See Rostow, op. cit., p. 7.

These economic cycles of the order of magnitude of about a quarter of a century, which W. W. Rostow detects in a British setting, are articulated by him as follows:

(i) A.D. 1790–1815: A war-period of economic stagnation and of decline in real wages.[1]

(ii) A.D. 1815 to the end of the eighteen-forties: 'This was the period when the rates of increase in industrial production were at a maximum for the whole era to A.D. 1914';[2] and it was also a period in which 'real wages rose for a rapidly expanding population'.[3]

(iii) The end of the eighteen-forties to A.D. 1873: A war-period, gold-mining period, and railway-building period.[4]

(iv) A.D. 1873–1900: A counterpart of Period (ii), with a tendency, in investment, to concentrate on openings at home.[5]

(v) A.D. 1900–14: A counterpart of Period (iii), with a corresponding spurt in gold-mining and a tendency to invest abroad in economically virgin fields.[6]

It will be seen that the last four of these five phases of an average wave-length of just under 25 years coalesce into a pair of still longer cycles, one taking fifty-eight years (A.D. 1815–73) and an at least partially repetitive successor taking forty-one years (A.D. 1873–1914) if the year 1914 is to be regarded as marking this second cycle's close.

A chronological pattern not unlike that descried by W. W. Rostow in the history of Great Britain between the years A.D. 1790 and 1914 had been descried by A. Spiethoff in the contemporary history of the Western World as a whole during the years A.D. 1822 to 1913 inclusive, where the German investigator finds four phases of an average wave-length of twenty-three years, articulated as follows:[7]

(i) A.D. 1822–42: on the whole, depressed.

(ii) A.D. 1843–73: on the whole, prosperous.

(iii) A.D. 1874–94: on the whole, depressed.

(iv) A.D. 1895–1913: on the whole, prosperous.

It will be noticed that in Spiethoff's geographically wider vista, as in Rostow's geographically narrower one, there are four phases of an average wave-length of not much less than a quarter of a century[8] coalescing into a pair of longer cycles which, on Spiethoff's reckoning, take respectively fifty-two years (A.D. 1822–73 inclusive) and forty years (A.D. 1874–1913 inclusive).

The pair of cycles of an average wave-length of about half a century, which emerges from Spiethoff's and from Rostow's vista alike, represents a long-wave kind of cycle which was descried independently by a couple of Dutch scholars—J. van Gelderen, who published his findings in A.D. 1913, and G. de Wolff, who endorsed van Gelderen's findings in

[1] Ibid., p. 17.   [2] Ibid., p. 17.   [3] Ibid., p. 19.
[4] Ibid., pp. 20, 21, and 23.   [5] Ibid., p. 25.   [6] Ibid., p. 26.
[7] As summarized in Habeler, G.: *Prosperity and Depression: A Theoretical Analysis of Cyclical Movements*, 3rd ed. (Geneva 1941, League of Nations), p. 273. See also Schumpeter, op. cit., vol. i, p. 164.
[8] A twenty-five-years cycle was descried by S. S. Kuznets as well (see Mitchell, ibid., p. 226, and S. S. Kuznets himself in his *Secular Movements in Production and Prices* (New York and Boston 1930, Houghton Mifflin)).

A.D. 1924[1]—and by a Russian scholar, N. D. Kondratieff, who published his own findings in A.D. 1926.[2] Kondratieff articulates his long-wave cycles as follows:[3]

	Trough	Crest	Trough	Total duration
(i)	circa 1790	1810–17	1844–51	50/60 years
(ii)	1844–51	1870–75	1890–96	40/50 years
(iii)	1890–96	1914–20		

An attempt to correlate these forty/sixty-years 'Kondratieff cycles' with the nine/ten-years 'Juglar cycles' and the three-and-a-half-years 'Mitchell cycles' had been made by J. A. Schumpeter.[4] His suggestion was that each 'Kondratieff cycle' was a clutch of six 'Juglar cycles', and each 'Juglar cycle' a clutch of three 'Mitchell cycles'.

'We . . . postulate that each Kondratieff should contain an integral number of Juglars, and each Juglar an integral number of Kitchins.[5] The warrant for this is in the nature of the circumstances which give rise to multiplicity. If waves of innovations of shorter span play around a wave of a similar character but of longer span, the sequences of the phases of the latter will so determine the conditions under which the former rise and break as to make a higher unit out of them, even if the innovations which create them are entirely independent of the innovations which carry the longer wave. . . . For every time series the sweep of any cycle is the trend of the cycles of next lower order. . . . The three deepest and longest depressions of the Industrial Age—1825–30, 1873–8, 1929–34—were depressions in the cycles of all three wave-lengths alike. . . . Barring very few cases in which difficulties arise, it is possible to count off, historically as well as statistically, six Juglars to a Kondratieff and three Kitchins to a Juglar—[and this] not [just] as an average, but in every individual case.'[6]

Schumpeter's hypothesis had not, however, won the support of W. C. Mitchell.

'No arrangement of our monthly measures in groups of three consecutive cycles will produce an approximation to "Juglar cycles" of from nine to ten years.[7] . . . The evidence is better that business cycles vary substantially within periods of "Juglar cycles" than that they do so within the long-cycle periods.[8] . . . The trough dates of the "Juglar cycles" correspond roughly to the trough dates of severe business depressions.'[9]

But, in the estimation of W. C. Mitchell and his colleague A. F. Burns, it remained still an open question whether 'the periods separating severe depressions are genuine cyclical units,'[10] while the same two investigators' judgement on the 'Kondratieff cycles' was that the evidence told, on balance, against their claim to be realities.[11]

---

[1] See Mitchell, *Business Cycles, the Problem and its Setting*, p. 227.
[2] Kondratieff, N. D.: 'Die Langen Wellen der Konjunktur', in *Archiv für Sozialwissenschaft und Sozialpolitik*, December 1926; 'The Long Waves of Economic Life', in *Review of Economic Statistics*, November 1935.
[3] As summarized in Mitchell, ibid., pp. 227–8.
[4] Schumpeter, J. A.: 'The Analysis of Economic Change', in *The Review of Economic Statistics*, May 1935, p. 8.   [5] *Alias* Mitchells.—A.J.T.
[6] Schumpeter, J. A.: *Business Cycles* (New York 1939, McGraw-Hill, 2 vols.), vol. 1, pp. 172–4.
[7] Burns, A. F., and Mitchell, W. C.: *Measuring Business Cycles* (New York 1946, National Bureau of Economic Research, Inc.), p. 442.   [8] Ibid., p. 444.
[9] Ibid., p. 448.   [10] Ibid., p. 464. Cp. p. 460.   [11] See ibid., p. 465.

It will be seen that the believers in the three-and-a-half-years cycle and the believers in the nine-years cycle were each sceptical about the reality of the others' article of faith, and that both schools alike were still more sceptical about the reality of the 'Kondratieff cycle' with a reputed wavelength of about fifty years. At the same time it will be realized that, midway through the twentieth century, the data were still scanty indeed; for, even if the earliest occurrences of the phenomena themselves were anterior to the last decade of the eighteenth century, there was at any rate no adequate evidence for them earlier than that date; and it is manifest that, within the span of 160 years running from A.D. 1790 to A.D. 1950, there had not been time for the completion of more than forty-five three-and-a-half-years cycles, more than seventeen nine-and-one-fifth-years cycles, or more than three fifty-years cycles. Even if the count of instances of the shortest and therefore most numerously represented of these three kinds of cycles were to be multiplied by reckoning as so many separate data the simultaneous epiphanies of one and the same occurrence in different geographical provinces of the Western World, the total number would still stand in three figures.

'In the sense in which the term is used here—recurrences of prosperity, recession, depression, and revival in the business activities of countries taken as units—the total number of past business cycles may well be less than a thousand. For business cycles are phenomena peculiar to a certain form of economic organisation which has been dominant even in Western Europe for less than two centuries, and for briefer periods in other regions. And the average cycle has lasted five years, if we may trust our data. Of the whole number of cases to date, the 166 cycles we have measured form a significant fraction. . . . We should be glad to have a larger sample; but the present one constitutes an appreciable fraction of its "universe".'[1]

The exiguousness of the quantity of data obtainable during the first half of the twentieth century for the investigation of business cycles even of the shortest wave-lengths had deterred investigators from attempting to apply to fluctuations in economic human activities a method of 'periodogram analysis' that had been found to work in the natural sciences. In the, so far, brief history of an Industrial Western Society the series were still too short; it was still uncertain whether these series were strictly periodic; and it was also still uncertain whether, if there were genuine periodicities, these were maintaining themselves over long enough periods for 'periodogram analysis' to be feasible.[2] Yet, short of going to these mathematical lengths, the investigators of business cycles resorted to mathematical devices that would have horrified any conventionally heterodox contemporary Western historian.

'The procedure adopted in ascertaining secular trends is usually empirical in high degree. Starting with a time series plotted to convenient scale on a chart, the statistician seeks to find for that one series, within the period covered by his data, the line which best represents "the long-time tendencies" shown by the plotted curve. . . . The technical process usually

---

[1] Mitchell, W. C.: *Business Cycles, the Problem and its Setting* (New York 1930, National Bureau of Economic Research, Inc.), pp. 395–6 and 397.
[2] See Mitchell, ibid., pp. 259–60.

consists in (1) fitting a "mathematical curve" (for example, a straight line or a third-degree parabola) to the data, or to the logarithms of the data, by the method of least squares or of moments; (2) computing moving or progressive arithmetic means or moving medians, including in the averages whatever number of items seems to give satisfactory results; (3) first computing moving averages and then fitting trend lines to the results; (4) drawing a free-hand curve through the data representing the investigator's impression, formed from careful study, of the long-time tendency; or (5) using ratios between the paired items of series which are believed to have substantially the same secular trends.'[1]

The pioneers of a Western economic science had the courage of their convictions, and they were justified in their faith that economic history must make sense by the validity and the value of the intellectual results that they achieved by staking their intellectual fortunes on the rationality of their hypothesis and pushing their interrogations of the data to the third degree.

(c) 'LAWS OF NATURE' IN THE HISTORIES OF CIVILIZATIONS

1. *Struggles for Existence between Parochial States*

The War-and-Peace Cycle in Modern and post-Modern Western History

If, without taking our eyes off the Modern and post-Modern chapters of the history of the Western Civilization, we now focus them on the political, instead of the economic, plane of activity, we shall see that, in an epoch in which the outstanding economic phenomenon was the epiphany and dissemination of Industrialism, the outstanding political phenomenon was the earlier epiphany of a Balance of Power between parochial states and the progressive inclusion of an ever widening circle of states within the field of force governed by this unitary system of inter-state power politics.

The Modern Western political Balance of Power resembled its younger contemporary the Modern Western industrial economy not only in tending to expand progressively over an ever wider geographical area, but also in exhibiting a cyclic rhythm in its history. Alternating phases of war and peace were the political counterparts of alternating phases of economic prosperity and depression; and a confrontation of the political with the economic series of fluctuations in Modern Western history threw fresh light on those cycles with wave-lengths of about twenty-five years, and double cycles with wave-lengths of about half a century, for which the economic evidence was so inadequate that the more cautious economic investigators had returned verdicts of 'non-

---

[1] Mitchell, W. C.: *Business Cycles, the Problem and its Setting* (New York 1930, National Bureau of Economic Research, Inc.), p. 213, in chap. iii: 'The Contribution of Statistics', iii: 'The Analysis of Time Series', 3. 'The Problem of Secular Trends', (1) 'The Empirical Approach to the Problem'. Schumpeter (*Business Cycles*, vol. i, pp. 200–5), declares himself sceptical of 'fitted trends' except in so far as these follow a lead given by an empirical investigation of the historical facts. 'Trend analysis by means both of smoothing and of fitting may, from additional theoretical and historical information, derive a right of existence not naturally or generally its own' (p. 203). 'Such trends [as autonomous changes in taste, such as occurred with respect to alcoholic drinks or heavy foods] can in no case be found by formal methods' (p. 205).

proven' on these longer cycles' claims to be economic realities.[1] The political evidence bore out the view, entertained by judicious economic inquirers,[2] that the apparitions of economic 'long waves' might not be hallucinations but might be economic reflections of political realities that had already been 'a going concern' in the Modern Western World for some three hundred years before the outbreak of the Industrial Revolution in Great Britain.[3] In any case, whatever the political cycles' relations to the economic cycles might eventually prove to be, there were indications that the political cycles, like their economic counterparts, were changing in character in accordance with a secular trend. Recurrent Western wars, for example, were, as we shall see, apparently becoming progressively shorter and sharper, while conversely the alternatingly re-current spells of peace in Western political history had, as we shall also see, tended to occupy a progressively greater aggregate number of years in each successive peace-and-war cycle down to the outbreak of the general war of A.D. 1914–18, though at the same time these progressive chronological gains for Peace at War's expense were being offset by a progressive aggravation of the economic, the political, and (above all) the spiritual devastation produced by wars when these did recur.

In studying the evidence for the currency of 'laws of Nature' in the economic affairs of a latter-day Western Society, we have noticed that inquirers who believed such laws to be both current and ascertainable were also aware that their validity was confined to a monetary and in-dustrial economic régime which had not established itself, even in its birthplace in Great Britain, before the later decades of the eighteenth century and which might be expected eventually to pass out of existence after an ephemeral appearance, and a still briefer oecumenical ascen-dancy, on the stage of History.[4] At the time of writing, mid-way through the twentieth century, the Balance of Power had had a longer innings than Industrialism had had so far in the history of the Western Civiliza-tion, since the epiphany of the Modern Western Balance of Power had been coeval with the opening of the modern chapter of Western history in the last quarter of the fifteenth century, some three hundred years before Industrialism had made its appearance. On the other hand a mortality which, in the history of Western industrialism, was at this time still no more than an academic expectation, was perhaps already assert-ing its dominion over the Balance of Power between parochial Western states.

A post-Modern Age of Western history which had opened in the seventh and eighth decades of the nineteenth century[5] had seen the rhythm of a Modern Western war-and-peace cycle broken, in the course of its fourth beat, by the portent of one general war following hard at the heels of another, with an interval of only twenty-five years between the outbreaks in A.D. 1939 and in A.D. 1914, instead of the interval of 120 years or more which had separated A.D. 1914 from A.D. 1792 and A.D. 1792 from A.D. 1672. In the histories of civilizations that were already

[1] See pp. 230–2, above.
[2] For example, by W. W. Rostow, in the passage cited on p. 231, above.
[3] See pp. 286–7, below.   [4] See pp. 224–6, above.   [5] See I. i. 1, n. 2.

extinct, so that the twentieth-century Western historian had the advantage there of knowing the whole story, such 'non-stop' recurrences of major wars had been apt to portend historic catastrophes. When, in the second chapter of Hellenic history, the Decelean War of 413–404 B.C. had followed the Archidamian War of 431–421 B.C. after an interval of only eight years, the consequence of this Atheno-Peloponnesian double war had been the breakdown of the Hellenic Civilization. When the Hannibalic War of 218–201 B.C. had followed the First Romano-Punic War of 264–241 B.C. after an interval of only twenty-three years, the consequence of this Romano-Punic double war had been the first relapse of a broken down and disintegrating Hellenic Society after its first rally.[1] When the Great Romano-Sasanian War of A.D. 603–28 had followed the Great Romano-Sasanian War of A.D. 572–91 after an interval of only twelve years, the consequence had been the obliteration of a frontier between an Hellenic universal state and recalcitrant Iranian Power which, reckoning from the date of its original establishment by the Roman empire-builder Pompey in 64 B.C., had maintained itself for all but seven hundred years by the time when the momentary restoration of the territorial *status quo ante bellum* in A.D. 628 was undone, once for all, by an explosion of Primitive Muslim Arab military force that completed the liquidation of a post-Alexandrine Hellenic ascendancy south of Taurus and re-established in the shape of an Arab Caliphate the Syriac universal state which Alexander had overthrown in the shape of an Achaemenian Empire.

At a moment in the post-Modern chapter of Western history at which the denouement of the double Germano-Western War of A.D. 1914–18 and A.D. 1939–45 was not yet an accomplished fact, the approaching overturn of a Balance of Power which had maintained its precarious existence since its inauguration in the last decade of the fifteenth century had already been announced by a rise in the death-rate of Western or Westernizing Great Powers that had been as steep as it had been sudden; and this carnage was ominous, considering that the first law of every balance, political and physical alike, is that the instability of the equilibrium varies in inverse ratio to the number of its *points d'appui*. While a two-legged stool, chair, or table would be doomed by the unpracticality of its construction to fall over in a trice, a three-legged stool is capable of standing by itself, though a corpulent sitter would rest more securely on a four-legged chair and a careful housewife would prefer a six-legged to a four-legged table for carrying a display of her best china. Since politics are never static but are always dynamic, an apter analogy from the chances and changes of physical life is to be found in the superiority of a tricycle over a bicycle as a mount for a rider who finds difficulty in keeping his balance, and the superiority of a six-wheeled omnibus over a four-wheeled car as a vehicle for traversing the sands of the desert. In the light of these homely physical analogies, the rise and decline in the number of Western or Westernizing Great Powers between A.D. 1552 and A.D. 1952 was politically most significant.

From the first epiphany of a Modern Western system of international

[1] See V. vi. 290–1.

relations at the close of the fifteenth century down to the outbreak of the General War of A.D. 1914–18 more than four hundred years later, the precariousness of the international equilibrium in the political life of the Western World had been progressively reduced by a gradual increase in the number of participant Powers of the highest calibre.

In the first bout of Modern Western wars (*gerebatur* A.D. 1494–1559), in which the original constellation of Modern Western Great Powers had crystallized out of a Late Medieval nebula surrounding the city-state cosmos in Northern Italy, Southern and Western Germany, and the Netherlands, there had been a phase (*durabat* A.D. 1519–56)—and this the decisive phase—in which only two Powers of the very highest calibre had been face to face; and this preliminary duel between Valois and Hapsburg, which was the overture to the rhythmic fluctuations of a Balance of Power in the subsequent course of Western political history, was, in the last analysis, a civil war between Valois and Valois,[1] since, in this chapter of Hapsburg history, the heart of the Hapsburg Power was that portion of the heritage of the Burgundian-Valois Duke Charles the Bold which Charles' Hapsburg son-in-law Maximilian I had managed to retain in A.D. 1477–82 for his Burgundian-Valois wife Mary, and to retrieve in A.D. 1493. This Burgundian nucleus of the dominions of a Hapsburg great-grandson and namesake of Charles the Bold who happened to be King of Castile and Aragon[2] and subsequently Holy Roman Emperor,[3] as well as Count of an Imperial Burgundy and a French Flanders,[4] was the heart which pumped out the life-blood that nourished the Hapsburg Power's sinews of war; and, if Charles V's treasury and arsenal were thus French in their provenance in virtue of being furnished by a Flanders that was a French county, his court was French in its culture in virtue of having been moulded in the tradition of a Burgundy that was a French duchy.

The Burgundian-Valois House had been founded by an act of the French Crown as recently as A.D. 1363, when King John of France had conferred on his fourth son Philip the Bold a Duchy of Burgundy which had escheated to the French Crown through the extinction, in A.D. 1361, of the dukes of the Capetian French line; and the fortunes of this newly endowed Burgundian cadet branch of the House of Valois had been made by Philip the Bold's marriage in A.D. 1369 with the reigning Count of Flanders' daughter and heiress Margaret; for Flanders was a fief of the French Crown that was still more important than Burgundy; and this matrimonial alliance had resulted, on the death in A.D. 1384 of Margaret's father, Count Louis II of Flanders, without male heirs, in the union of the French fief of Burgundy with the French fiefs of

---

[1] See Fueter, E.: *Geschichte des Europäischen Staatensystems von 1492–1559* (Munich and Berlin 1919, Oldenbourg), pp. 101–3, for the thesis that the fundamental cause of conflict in this cycle was not a rivalry between the two national states of France and Spain. Fueter suggests that, after Francis I's victory over the Swiss at Marignano on the 13th–14th September, 1515, Spain might have acquiesced in a partition of Italy between herself and France if the union of the crowns of Castile and Aragon with the Hapsburg–Valois Power in A.D. 1516 had not resulted in the subordination of Spanish interests to Burgundian interests in the determination of the foreign policy of Charles V.

[2] Since the 23rd January, 1516.

[3] Since the 28th June, 1519.

[4] Since the 5th January, 1515.

Flanders, Artois, Nevers, and Rethel and the Imperial County of Burgundy into the bargain.[1]

The duel between Royal French Valois and Burgundian Ducal French Valois who were thinly disguised under a Hapsburg Imperial mask did not, however, result in a reunion of these two branches of the House of France which, in the political circumstances of the Western World of the day, would have brought with it a political reunification of Western Christendom under the oecumenical rule of a resuscitated Carolingian Empire; and, in proving to have been at least an 'undecisive contest', if not a 'temperate' one,[2] this opening round in a rhythmical series of Modern and post-Modern Western wars justified the inauguration of a Balance of Power involving the Western World as a whole[3] if the value of this political device is to be measured by its capacity to obtain for a society a maximum amount of political decentralization and maximum degree of cultural diversity at a minimum cost in terms of political friction and military conflict. Thereafter, as the further fluctuations of this Modern Western Balance followed their rhythmic course, they long continued on the whole to serve the interests of a *Homo Occidentalis* who was at once their perpetrator and their victim, if we may find an index of their beneficence in the concomitant net increase in the number of participant Great Powers from the figure of two, at which it had stood on the eve of the abdication of Charles V in A.D. 1555/6, to the figure of eight, at which it stood in A.D. 1914.

In the course of those three centuries and a half, the number of Great Powers in the Western World had gradually risen. It rose from two to three through the fission of the Burgundian-Valois-Hapsburg Power into a Spanish Hapsburg Monarchy and a Danubian Hapsburg Monarchy after the abdication of Charles V in A.D. 1555/6,[4] and then, during

---

[1] The Imperial County of Burgundy (Franche-Comté) had been inherited in A.D. 1347 by Jeanne, the wife of Count Louis II of Flanders and the daughter of another Jeanne who had been the wife of King Philip V of France and the daughter of Count Otto IV of Franche-Comté. Philip of France had married this older Jeanne in A.D. 1307, ten years before he himself had come to the French throne in A.D. 1317, and Franche-Comté had thus temporarily fallen into the possession of the French Crown; it had then passed into the hands of the Capetian duke of the French Duchy of Burgundy, Odo IV, in A.D. 1330 through his marriage with Margaret, the daughter of Jeanne the elder and sister of Jeanne the younger; thereafter, in A.D. 1347, it had been inherited by Jeanne the younger upon Duke Odo IV of Burgundy's death; and, through Jeanne the younger, it was subsequently inherited by her daughter Margaret upon the death of Jeanne the younger's husband and Margaret's father, Count Louis II of Flanders, in A.D. 1384.

[2] See Gibbon, E.: *The History of the Decline and Fall of the Roman Empire*, chap. xxxviii, *ad finem*: 'General Observations on the Fall of the Roman Empire in the West'.

[3] A local Balance of Power, involving the city-states of Northern and Central Italy, had been in operation during the quarter of a millennium running from the death of the Holy Roman Emperor Frederick II in A.D. 1250 to the invasion of Italy by King Charles VIII of France in A.D. 1494.

[4] The first step towards the construction of a Danubian Hapsburg Monarchy had been taken as early as A.D. 1522, when, by a treaty signed at Brussels on the 7th February of that year, Charles V had invested his brother Ferdinand with a regency over the hereditary possessions of the House of Hapsburg. The second step had been taken in A.D. 1526, when the Crowns of Hungary and Bohemia had been conferred on Ferdinand after the Hungarians' disastrous defeat by the 'Osmanlis at Mohacz (see II. ii. 177–9). The third step was taken when Ferdinand was elected Holy Roman Emperor, in succession to Charles V, on the 28th February, 1558.

The separate existence of a Spanish Hapsburg Monarchy may be dated from Philip II's succession to Charles V in A.D. 1556 in Spain and in the Burgundian dominions, which were thereby reduced to the status of Spanish dependencies.

the first of the regular cycles of war-and-peace in this series (*currebat* A.D. 1568–1672), the number rose again from three to five through the successful self-assertion of a United Northern Netherlands that had broken out of the Spanish Monarchy and a Sweden that had broken out of the Danish Monarchy.

During the second of these three regular cycles (*currebat* A.D. 1672–1792) the number threatened to fall as sharply as it had risen during the preceding cycle; for Spain, as well as the Netherlands and Sweden, now proved unequal to staying the course, while the sixteenth-century fission of the Hapsburg Power into a Spanish and an Austrian branch came into danger of being neutralized by an eighteenth-century union of the Spanish Monarchy with France to create a Bourbon Power which, in the hands of Louis XIV, would have outclassed all the other Powers of the Western World as decidedly as the undivided Hapsburg Power had out-classed its French rival before the abdication of Charles V. None of these possibilities, however, materialized; for the replacement of a Hapsburg by a Bourbon dynasty at Madrid did not, after all, 'abolish the Pyrenees';[1] a Bourbon Spain remained at least as separate from a Bourbon France after A.D. 1713 as a Hapsburg Spain had been, since A.D. 1556, from a Hapsburg Austria; and the casualties among the parvenues 'just-great' Powers were made good by replacements. A United Kingdom of England and Scotland took the place of a United Netherlands who had exhausted herself in winning a General War of A.D. 1672–1713 in which she had been the protagonist in the anti-French coalition; Prussia took the place of a Sweden who had exhausted herself in waging the Northern War of A.D. 1700–21; and, though an eighteenth-century Spain who succeeded in retaining her independence did not succeed in becoming a Great Power again, this gap in the ranks of the Great Powers of the Western World was filled by the enlistment of an Orthodox Christian Russia whose decisive victory over Sweden had demonstrated the effectiveness of her reception of the Western Civilization, at any rate on the military plane.

During the third cycle (*currebat* A.D. 1792–1914) a number which had thus remained constant during the seventeenth and eighteenth centuries at the figure of five was raised once more, and this time from five to eight, by the successive additions of a United Italy, a United States of North America, and a Westernizing Japan. A nineteenth-century Italy attained the stature of a 'just-great' Power that had been attained by a seventeenth-century Holland and Sweden. A twentieth-century Japan won her spurs by defeating Russia, as an eighteenth-century Russia had won hers by defeating Sweden. The United States emerged through a fission of an eighteenth-century British Empire which ultimately had the same effect of making two Great Powers out of one as the fission of the Hapsburg Power after the abdication of Charles V, though the secession of the United States from the British Empire was achieved by the force of arms with which Sweden and the United Netherlands had

---

[1] 'Il n'y a plus de Pyrénées' was Louis XIV's comment on the accession of his grand-son to the throne of Spain in A.D. 1700 according to Voltaire, *Le Siècle de Louis Quatorze*, chap. 28.

won their independence from Denmark and Spain, and not by the pacific and amicable process through which the Danubian and the Spanish Hapsburg Monarchy had parted company.[1]

Thus, on the eve of the outbreak of a General War of A.D. 1914–18 which was to open the fourth regular cycle in the series, it looked, in the light of the experience of the past 350 years, as if the current Balance of Power in the Western World had ensured its own perpetuation for an indefinite time ahead by progressively increasing the number of the bases on which it rested until it had come to stand steadily upon eight legs instead of shakily upon two; and this appearance of security was enhanced by the spectacle of a row of ninepins standing in between the legs; for the increase in the number of Great Powers in the Western system of international relations between A.D. 1556 and A.D. 1914 had been accompanied by an increase *pari passu* in the number of 'buffer states' on which the mutually frustrating jealousies of rival Great Powers around them had bestowed an independence that these pigmies would have been incapable of either winning or keeping by force of their own arms. Such 'buffer states' had emerged and survived in so far as the balanced pressures of their powerful neighbours upon one another had happened to create and preserve here and there some nook or cranny in which a militarily impotent minor state could nestle and thrive like a rock-plant in an interstice between the rugged faces of the untooled stones in a wall of cyclopean masonry.[2]

The United States, for example, in her military and political infancy, had been able to win her independence in the war of A.D. 1775–83 in North America thanks to a temporary neutralization of British sea-power by French sea-power, and had then been able to expand westwards across the Continent by securing the reversion of the Mississippi Basin through the Louisiana Purchase thanks to a preponderance of British sea-power over French sea-power in the General War of A.D. 1792–1815 which had made it impossible for Napoleon to take delivery for France of a Transatlantic territory which he had compelled Spain to retrocede to France on paper. The Latin American republics, in their turn, had owed their independence to a mistrust of the Continental European Powers that had moved Great Britain to co-operate with the United States by tacitly putting the sanction of British sea-power behind President Monroe's announcement of his doctrine on the 2nd December,

---

[1] The first step in the rise of the United States to the rank of a Great Power was the winning of her independence in the Revolutionary War of A.D. 1775–83. The second step was the development of her potential strength through the political acquisition and economic exploitation of a trans-continental territory (a stage corresponding to the geographical expansion of the Danubian Hapsburg Power in and after A.D. 1526). The third step was the maintenance of the Union by force of arms in the Civil War of A.D. 1861–5 (to which the counterpart in Hapsburg history was the Thirty Years War of A.D. 1618–48). The fourth step was the victory of the United States in the Spanish-American War of A.D. 1898, which drew the United States out of a political isolation that she had been maintaining since A.D. 1783, and involved her in commitments overseas.

[2] This generation of minor states as a by-product of the pressures exerted by rival Great Powers upon one another, when these pressures neutralize one another, is an outcome of the Balance of Power which has been noticed in this Study already, apropos of the emergence of the city-states of Northern and Central Italy in an interstice between the Holy Roman Empire and the Hildebrandine Papacy (see III. iii. 345–6; IV. iv. 524; and p. 294, below).

1823, in order to make sure that the current insurrections in the Spanish American Empire against the Spanish Crown should not end in a re-establishment of Spanish rule there through the arms and under the aegis of the Powers of the Holy Alliance. The Monroe Doctrine had prescribed that American communities which had declared and maintained their independence were not to be allowed to fall again under the control of any European Power; and, since at the time there were no Great Powers in the Western system of international relations that were not located in Europe, the Monroe Doctrine had been tantamount to a declaration that no Great Power was to be allowed to profit by the break-up of the Spanish Empire in the Americas. It was because the United States was not yet either able or willing to play the part of a Great Power in the European cockpit of Western power politics[1] that the Great Powers of the day acquiesced in her purchase, in A.D. 1803, of Louisiana from France; in her veto, in A.D. 1823, on the entry of any Great Power into the political vacuum created by the collapse of Spanish rule in the Americas; and in her annexation of the northern fringe of the former Spanish dominions in North America, from Texas to California inclusive, after waging a victorious war of aggression against the Spanish Empire's local successor-state, Mexico, in A.D. 1846–7.

A principle thus first established in Western history in respect of the Americas was promptly applied in the Near and Middle East when, on the morrow of the General War of A.D. 1792–1815, 'the Eastern Question' became interwoven with the older strands of Western diplomacy. The break-up of the Ottoman Empire, like the break-up of the Spanish Empire, created a political vacuum that would have been dangerous for the preservation of peace if the Great Powers had engaged in a scramble for Ottoman spoils with an eye to a competitive self-aggrandizement; and, just because this risk of a disturbance of the existing balance might have been impossible to counteract by any means less drastic than a resort to war, it was prudently parried by the concerted institution of a Near Eastern equivalent of the Monroe Doctrine which was none the less efficacious for not being explicitly enunciated.

The measure of the efficacity of this tacit Near Eastern Monroe Doctrine in practice is given by the contrast between the respective destinies of the territories lost by the Ottoman Empire after the year A.D. 1815 on the one hand and before that date on the other hand. While the Ottoman Empire's territorial losses between A.D. 1815 and the final débâcle in A.D. 1918 were far larger than the losses between the turn of the tide in Ottoman-Occidental relations in A.D. 1683 and the end of the Western General War of A.D. 1792–1815, the amount of ex-Ottoman territory that passed under the sovereignty of Western or Westernizing Great Powers in the course of the later of these two periods was trifling compared to the extent of the gains made by the same Powers at Ottoman expense between A.D. 1683 and A.D. 1815. After A.D. 1815 the only gains made by

---

[1] In the message in which President Monroe warned the Great Powers off the former Spanish dominions in the Americas, he was careful to assure them, in the same breath, that the policy of the United States in regard to Europe was one of benevolent non-interference.

Great Powers at the Ottoman Empire's direct expense[1] were the acquisition of the tiny Caucasian districts of Akhaltzik and Akhalkalaki after the Russo-Turkish War of A.D. 1828–9 by Russia[2] and the acquisition of Qars-Ardahan-Batum, Bosnia-Herzegovina, and Cyprus by Russia, Austria-Hungary, and Great Britain respectively after the Russo-Turkish War of A.D. 1877–8. All other territories lost by the Ottoman Empire after A.D. 1815 went to the making of the national states of Greece, Serbia, Rumania, Bulgaria, and Albania. The Hapsburg Monarchy did not even reacquire a Northern Serbia and a Western Wallachia that it had held from A.D. 1718 to A.D. 1739. By contrast, the territories permanently lost by the Ottoman Empire between A.D. 1683 and A.D. 1815[3] had all been acquired by one or other of the two adjoining Great Powers in the Western system. Between those two dates the Danubian Hapsburg Monarchy had acquired the whole of the Ottoman portion of Hungary and Croatia, together with the Bukovina, and Russia the whole northern and north-eastern hinterland of the Black Sea, from the east bank of the Pruth to the south bank of the Rion, that had formerly lain under Ottoman sovereignty or suzerainty.

These clusters of newly created minor states on the American and the Near Eastern fringes of the Western World were not, however, such remarkable by-products of a latter-day Western Balance of Power as the states of the same small calibre that emerged or survived nearer to the centre of the system, where the political pressure was more severe. The classic case here was the success with which, from A.D 1667 to A.D. 1945, first France and then Germany had been prevented from acquiring the Southern Netherlands by coalitions of Powers which had taken up arms to preserve the sovereignty of Spain, Austria, and Belgium in turn over this small but strategically important piece of territory. A corresponding play of the Balance of Power had enabled Portugal in the seventeenth century to anticipate the Spanish American countries' nineteenth-century achievement of breaking away from Spain, and had enabled Spain herself, as well as the United Netherlands and Sweden, in the eighteenth century to retain her independence after she had fallen out of the ranks of the Great Powers. On the eve of a General War of A.D. 1914–18 which was to open with Germany's unprovoked violation of the neutrality of Belgium, the existence of nine small neutral states in Western Europe—the three Low Countries, the three Scandinavian Countries, the two Iberian Countries, and Switzerland—looked like an even better augury for the future maintenance of a Western Balance of Power than the existence of eight Great Powers in the World at large at the same date.

Thus, at the time by when the Western Balance of Power had been 'a going concern' for rather more than four hundred years, the international

---

[1] The North African territories which France and Great Britain respectively brought under their control between A.D. 1830, the date of the beginning of the French conquest of Algeria, and A.D. 1881–2, which witnessed the establishment of a French protectorate over Tunisia and a British military occupation of Egypt, had already ceased to be Ottoman *de facto*, though they were still Ottoman *de jure*.

[2] See IX. viii. 193, n. 1.

[3] The Morea, which was conquered from the Ottoman Empire by Venice in and after A.D. 1684, had been reconquered in A.D. 1715.

outlook wore a deceptively promising appearance. Even if, as was being prophesied by the more sensational-minded publicists at the turn of the nineteenth and twentieth centuries, a Danubian Hapsburg Monarchy that had prolonged its life by coming to terms with Magyar nationalism in the Austro-Hungarian *Ausgleich* of A.D. 1867 were nevertheless to break up, after the death of the venerable King-Emperor Francis Joseph, under the pressure of Slav national movements which the partial settlement of A.D. 1867 had left unsatisfied, the effect on the general system of international relations in the Western World that was expected to follow from a local Danubian débâcle was merely a reduction of the number of the Great Powers from eight to seven. In A.D. 1912 even the boldest prophet would not have dreamed of forecasting that by A.D. 1952 the number would have been reduced, as it actually had been, from the figure of eight which it had reached at the turn of the nineteenth and twentieth centuries to the figure of two at which it had stood between A.D. 1519 and A.D. 1556;[1] yet this drastic reduction had taken place within a span of thirty-two years running from A.D. 1914 to A.D. 1945 inclusive.

The break-up of the Danubian Monarchy, which had duly resulted from the General War of A.D. 1914–18, had proved in the event to be only the first of half a dozen casualties. On the morrow of the General War of A.D. 1939–45 a Prussia-Germany which had gone from strength to strength, until she had come, twice in one life-time, within an ace of conquering the World, now lay not only prostrate but partitioned, with her eastern frontier pushed back westwards to the line at which it had stood eight hundred years earlier.[2] In Germany's Assyrian fate an Israelite prophet would have seen God's judgement on Germany's Assyrian crimes of deliberately inflicting on Mankind, twice in one life-time, the awful sufferings of a general war and cold-bloodedly violating, in the course of her two orgies of aggression, the neutrality of seven out of those nine West European minor states whose immunity from the blood-tax that was the price of counting as a Great Power had been the touch-stone of the moral worth of a latter-day Western system of international relations. Milder chastisements had requited the punier outrages committed by a National-Socialist Germany's accomplices, Italy and Japan; but the death that had likewise been the fate of the other Great Powers who had been less guiltily involved in the Western general wars of A.D. 1914–18 and A.D. 1939–45 could not be interpreted so convincingly as having been the wages of sin.[3] Great Britain and France, as well as Italy and Japan, had failed to stay the course, as the Netherlands and Sweden had failed two hundred years earlier, though the British Empire, like Prussia-Germany, had grown, during the two hundred years ending in A.D. 1914, to a stature at which these two Powers had

---

[1] The undivided Hapsburg Power which Charles V had held together before his abdication in A.D. 1555/6 had come into his hands by successive stages during the years A.D. 1515–19. On the 5th January, 1515, he had inherited the Burgundian dominions; on the 23rd January, 1516, he had succeeded King Ferdinand as King of Aragon and Castile; on the 12th January, 1519, he had succeeded Maximilian I as ruler of the hereditary dominions of the House of Hapsburg; on the 28th June, 1519, he had succeeded Maximilian I as Holy Roman Emperor.

[2] See II. ii. 169.   [3] Rom. vi. 2.

latterly overshadowed all the rest, while France had held the same position of pre-eminence from A.D. 1648 to A.D. 1815.

In A.D. 1952 the Soviet Union and the United States alone were still standing erect; and from a strategico-political standpoint the respective stances of these two Powers *vis-à-vis* one another were reminiscent of those of France and the Burgundian-Hapsburg Power some four hundred years earlier. In an arena which had expanded in the meanwhile beyond the bounds of Western Europe till it had come to be coextensive with the entire surface of the planet, a prize that had expanded *pari passu* beyond the bounds of Italy, until it had come to embrace the whole of the Old World outside the limits of Russia's present domain, was being contended for in A.D. 1952 between a Russia which enjoyed the advantages of interior lines, compact metropolitan territory, and centralized autocratic government, once enjoyed by France, and a United States whose overwhelming superiority in aggregate strength on paper, when the assets of her dependencies and her allies were added to her own, was largely offset in practice, like the strength of the Count-King-Emperor Charles V, by the liabilities that these assets brought in their train and by the wide dispersion of the scattered territories and populations whose resources America had to defend in order to be able to draw upon them. It was easier for a twentieth-century Russia, as it had been for a sixteenth-century France, to take her adversary by surprise, in making sudden sorties in divers directions, than it was for a twentieth-century United States to mobilize her own and her friends' forces effectively for the arduous task of containing her adversary all the way round a line of circumvallation which, scale for scale, was proportionate in its length to the line which Charles V had once set himself to hold. The strategico-political bearings of a confrontation of two Great Powers, and two only, were thus much the same *circa* A.D. 1952 as they had been *circa* A.D. 1552. Yet, in these geographically similar circumstances, the Western Balance of Power's expectation of life was, for ideological reasons, decidedly less promising in the twentieth century than it had been in the sixteenth.

If the division of power in the Western World between no more than two competitors during the years A.D. 1519–55 had resulted, not in an increase in the number from the dual to the plural but in the reduction of a duality to a unity, the most likely way in which this unification would have been achieved would have been through the negotiation of one more felicitous dynastic marriage; and, even if a miscarriage of matrimonial diplomacy had made it impossible to avoid resorting to the barbarous alternative of unification through force of arms, the unifying war would still have been a temperate one, like those 'undecisive contests' through which the number of the Great Powers was, not diminished, but augmented in the course which history actually took during the three centuries and a half running from A.D. 1556 to A.D. 1914. The Royal French Valois and the Imperial Burgundian Valois were divided by nothing more serious than a dynastic rivalry that could have been removed painlessly by a marriage and almost painlessly by a conquest. They were not estranged from one another by any impassable gulf of incompatible religious or ideological faith or practice, such as had come, by A.D. 1952, to be fixed between the U.S.S.R. and the U.S.A.

It is true that the ostensible point of difference between the twentieth-century American and the twentieth-century Russian *Weltanschauung* and way of life was not insuperable; for ostensibly the two Powers were at issue over the question of the ratio in which private economic enterprise and public economic enterprise ought to stand to one another in a predominantly industrial society; and this was a question to which the correct answer could not be any absolute 'right or wrong' or 'yes or no', but only an arguable and adjustable 'more or less'. In every phase of every civilization known to History, the economy had always been a combination of public with private enterprise in proportions that had varied continually in response to changes in the social circumstances; the determination of the best mixture for meeting the practical needs of a particular time and place was a question, not of principle touching the religious foundations of life, but of expediency in regulating its economic surface; and, if this had really been all that was at issue between the United States and the Soviet Union in A.D. 1952, their conflict need have been no more tragic than the quarrel between the Burgundian ducal branch and the French royal branch of the House of Valois. The duel in A.D. 1952 was more formidable than the duel in A.D. 1552 because in A.D. 1952 the ostensible economic issue, which was no more serious in itself than the dynastic issue had been, masked a moral issue between the principles and practice of a Totalitarian Autocracy on the one hand and those of a Parliamentary Democracy on the other, in which the then still unanswered question

> utrorum ad regna cadendum
> Omnibus humanis esset terrâque marique[1]

was a matter of life and death for every living human being.

Thus the reversion of the number of Great Powers in a latter-day Western international arena from a maximum figure of eight to a previous figure of two, after a run of some four hundred years of precariously maintained equilibrium between a larger number of gladiators, was an indication that the cyclic rhythm, which was the first law governing this international balance of political power, was itself governed by an over-riding law that convicted this system of mortality—as the gyrations that keep a spinning top temporarily in balance are subject to an oscillatory movement that inclines farther, with each gyration, until at last it brings the gyrations to a stop by bringing the top to the ground. This diagnosis was confirmed by other symptoms which pointed the same way as the drastic reduction in the number of the Great Powers between A.D. 1914 and A.D. 1945. All these symptoms, taken together, suggested that the cyclic rhythm which had been keeping the political Balance of Power going during the Modern and post-Modern chapters of Western history was being accompanied by a secular movement that was working steadily towards an eventual overturn of the unstable equilibrium between a plurality of parochial states and towards the replacement of this by an at

---

[1] Lucretius: *De Rerum Naturâ*, Book III, ll. 836–7.

least temporarily stable oecumenical régime in which political power would be a monopoly administered from some single centre.

On a political plane which was the field of cycles of war and peace, as on an economic plane which was the field of 'booms' and 'slumps', the strength of this secular tendency towards integration was indicated by the failure of a concomitant tendency towards geographical expansion to counteract it. By A.D. 1952 the world-wide extension of the tentacles of a Western Industrial System of Economy that had made its epiphany in Great Britain during the later decades of the eighteenth century had been matched by the attraction of all the states then still surviving on the surface of the planet into a Western system of international relations that had made its epiphany in the last decade of the fifteenth century as a local West European political vortex round the nucleus of a Late Medieval city-state cosmos in Italy. In A.D. 1952 the prize at stake in the contest between the United States and the Soviet Union was nothing less than the command over all other habitable lands and navigable sea-routes and airways; and the General War of A.D. 1939–45 had been already 'global', and no longer merely 'European'; for in this war the battlefields had not been confined to a Lombardy and a Flanders that had been the cockpits of latter-day Western warfare during its overture and its first three regular cycles (*currebant* A.D. 1494–1914), and had not been confined, either, to the wider Continental European arena of the General War of A.D. 1914–18, with its western front stretching from the North Sea to the Alps and its eastern front stretching from the Baltic to the Carpathians. The General War of A.D. 1939–45 had been literally 'a world war' in which one battlefield embracing Europe, the Mediterranean, and the Eastern Atlantic had been matched by another embracing the Western Pacific and the Far East.

This twentieth-century integration of international relations all round the globe into a single system, centring on a Balance of Power that had originated in Western Europe and had then progressively brought the rest of the Earth's surface within the field of its magnetic attraction, presented a striking contrast to the configuration of the field of force in earlier chapters of the same story. The overture (*currebat* A.D. 1494–1559) had ranged no wider than the areas involved in a competition for hegemony over Italy between nascent adjoining Great Powers in the Transalpine and Transmarine provinces of Western Europe; and even Flanders had then been only a secondary theatre of military operations, though the two Great Powers of the day actually marched with one another there, without being insulated on this front by any intervening political vacuum or buffer. The civil war between Catholics and Protestants in France (*gerebatur* A.D. 1562–98) went on its way more or less independently of the contemporary civil war between Dutch and Spaniards in the Spanish Hapsburg Monarchy (*gerebatur* A.D. 1568–1609). The civil war in England (*gerebatur* A.D. 1642–8) likewise followed its own course without becoming implicated in the contemporary civil war in the Holy Roman Empire (*gerebatur* A.D. 1618–48). The Americas and the Indies were drawn into the main vortex of Western warfare only in the course of the first regular cycle (*currebat* A.D. 1568–1672); and, though during the second regular cycle (*currebat* A.D. 1672–1792) the decisive military operations on Flemish and Lombard battlefields were usually accompanied by 'side-shows' in North America and in Continental India in which the same belligerents were engaged, the synchronization of the local conflicts in the West European and the overseas theatres of war was still inexact. As often as not, the eighteenth-century campaigns on American and Indian soil would open later or earlier and close later or earlier than the corresponding campaigns in Western Europe, so that there were years in which France and Great Britain were at war with one another in Europe while at peace with one another overseas, or conversely at war overseas while at peace in Europe.[1]

As for the wars which the eastern border-states of the Western World were waging with a Muscovite Orthodox Christian Power in the continental hinterland of the Baltic, and with an Ottoman Iranic Muslim Power in the Danube Basin and the Mediterranean, these sequels to the Crusades were at first carried on in virtual independence of the Western Powers' fratricidal warfare with one another. The move made by France in A.D. 1534–6[2] to redress the balance between herself and the Hapsburg Power by allying herself with the Hapsburgs' Ottoman adversary was an obviously expedient application of a Machiavellianly rational statecraft which struck a contemporary Western Christian public, including the French themselves, as being so shocking that France forebore to follow this policy up, notwithstanding the importance of the military and political advantages that she stood to gain by it and the extremity of the straits in which she found herself at the time;[3] and, as late as A.D. 1664, Louis XIV gave precedence to the oecumenical interests of Western Christendom over the parochial interests of France when he permitted French volunteers to help a rival Western Power in the shape of the Danubian Hapsburg Monarchy to stem an Ottoman invasion whose success would have been advantageous to France on a Machiavellian reckoning.[4] France did not exploit, as she could have done, the predica-

---

[1] For example, in the General War of A.D. 1672–1713 the respective war years were 1672–8, 1688–97, 1702–13 in Western Europe; 1690–7, 1702–10 in North America. In the epilogue to the General War of A.D. 1672–1713 the respective war years were 1733–5, 1740–8, 1756–63 in Western Europe; 1744–63, 1775–83 in North America; 1746–9, 1750–4, 1758–61, 1778–83 in India.
The synchronization of the local conflicts continued to be inexact in the third regular cycle (*currebat* A.D. 1792–1914). In the General War of A.D. 1792–1815 the respective war years were 1792–1802, 1803–14, 1815 in Europe; 1812–14 in North America; 1799–1805, 1816–18 in India. In the epilogue to the General War of A.D. 1792–1815 the respective war years were 1848–9, 1859, 1864, 1866, 1870–1 in Europe; 1861–7 in North America (taking account of the French expedition to Mexico, 1862–7); 1838–42, 1843, 1845–6, 1848–9, 1857–9, 1878–81 in India; 1839–41, 1853–6, 1875–8, 1882, in the Near and Middle East.
[2] In May 1534 France made a treaty with the Ottoman Corsair Khayr-ad-Dīn Barbarossa; in February 1536 she made a commercial treaty with the Porte that served as a cloak for a political entente.
[3] See Fueter, E.: *Geschichte des Europäischen Staatensystems von 1492–1559* (Munich and Berlin 1919, Oldenbourg), pp. 47–49. There was no sequel to the Franco-Ottoman combined naval operations of A.D. 1543/4, in which an Ottoman fleet was harboured in the French naval base at Toulon.
[4] A regular French expeditionary force, as well as a flow of French volunteers, came to the aid of the Venetians in A.D. 1668–9 during the last agonies of the siege of Candia, but this French support of Venice was less meritorious than the French support of the Danubian Monarchy against the same assailant, considering that Venice, unlike the Danubian Monarchy, could not be regarded by France at this date as

ment of a Hapsburg Power that was implicated in Western Christendom's border warfare with the 'Osmanlis as well as in the Hapsburgs' family quarrel with France; and, thanks to this French forbearance, whether it was deliberate or inadvertent,[1] the Danubian Hapsburg Monarchy, throughout the sixteenth, seventeenth, and eighteenth centuries, usually found itself able to avoid simultaneous engagements on its French and on its Ottoman front.

The same policy of limiting her military liabilities to a single front at a time was followed by Russia after she had become implicated in the Western Balance of Power at the turn of the seventeenth and eighteenth centuries; and, until after the close of the General War of A.D. 1792–1815, the insulation of the vortex round the frontier between Western Christendom and the Ottoman Empire from the vortex in the interior of the Western World usually proved to be practical politics. 'The Eastern Question' began to enter into the Western Balance of Power only when Napoleon's failure to expand a French ascendancy over the debris of a Medieval city-state cosmos into a French ascendancy over the whole of a Modern Western and Westernizing World[2] left a victorious Russia and a victorious Great Britain free to pursue a rivalry with one another in the Near and Middle East.

Even the vortex round the frontier between Western Christendom and Russian Orthodox Christendom did not coalesce completely with the vortex in the interior of the Western World till more than a hundred years after the date of Peter the Great's victory at Poltava in A.D. 1709 over Charles XII of Sweden. It was not so surprising that, before Russia had been received into the Western Society as a result of Peter's life-work, the Great Northern War of A.D. 1700–21 should have been waged without becoming implicated in the Western World's General War of A.D. 1672–1713, just as the Great Northern War of A.D. 1558–83 had been waged without being implicated either in the last cadences of the overture (*currebat* A.D. 1494–1568) to a latter-day Western series of cycles of War and Peace or in the first cadences of the first regular cycle in this series (*currebat* A.D. 1568–1672). It was more remarkable that the partitions of Poland-Lithuania in A.D. 1772–95 between Russia and the two eastern march-Powers of the Western World, and also even Russia's acquisition of Finland from the Scandinavian march-State of the Western World in the Russo-Swedish war of A.D. 1808–9, should still have taken place in the margin, and not in the centre, of the Western system of international relations. It is true that Russia was a belligerent in the Seven Years War from A.D. 1756 to A.D. 1762, and that her withdrawal from this war in A.D. 1762 may have marked a turning-point in the fortunes of Frederick the Great. Yet the first Western general war in which Russia played a principal part was the war of A.D. 1792–1815, and

---

a rival Power, while on the other hand the French might have hoped, if their intervention against the 'Osmanlis at Candia had been successful, to enter into Venice's heritage in at least a remnant of her dominion in Crete.

[1] According to Fueter, op. cit., p. 48, no special consideration was shown to the Danubian Hapsburg Monarchy or to Venice by other states of the Western comity in return for the public service which these two anti-Ottoman march-states were performing for Western Christendom as a whole.   [2] See V. v. 619–42.

even in this war it was not till A.D. 1812 that Russia's role came to be a decisive one. On the other hand, from A.D. 1812 onwards down to the War of A.D. 1939–45 inclusive, there was no general war in the Western World in which the part played by Russia was not one of first-class importance. There were, however, down to the eve of the outbreak of the General War of A.D. 1914–18, still certain local wars—fought in outlying regions only recently incorporated into a Westernizing World—which followed independent courses of their own without being drawn into the central vortex of the Western Society's international relations. The Russo-Japanese War of A.D. 1904–5 was one case in point; the Spanish-American War of A.D. 1898 and the British-Afrikander War of A.D. 1899–1902 were two other instances.

The geographical expansion of an originally West European system of international relations to a world-wide range had not, however, sufficed to counteract the play of a centripetal force that, since A.D. 1914, had made itself felt by reducing the number of the Great Powers in this system from eight to two; and this carnage revealed a secular tendency in the history of a latter-day Balance of Power in the Western World for this unstable equilibrium, fluctuating in recurrent cycles, to bring about its own eventual overturn through the inversion of a competition into a monopoly. This tendency might prove to be no peculiar feature either of this Western political balance or indeed of political balances as a species of the generic social structure represented by any Balance of Power between any competitors.

'The experiences of our age refute the notion, which has been governing people's thinking for more than a hundred years past, that a Balance of Power between freely competing units—be these states, businesses, artisans or what you will—is a system that can maintain itself in this condition of unstable equilibrium for an indefinite length of time. To-day, as in the past, this state of equilibrium in a competition that is free from monopolistic restrictions has a nisus to pass over into some form of monopoly or other.'[1]

This nisus was presumably traceable in the last analysis to the working of some law of human dynamics that came into play wherever and whenever a balance of human forces had been set up on any plane of social activity; where the plane of activity was politics and the parties to the encounter were parochial states, the particular mode of this general law's operation was a matter of common knowledge.

The difficulty of maintaining in perpetuity a political Balance of Power between parochial states was due, at bottom, to the sinfulness of the vein of Human Nature that was the raw material of statesmanship. In politics, men and women who in other walks of life might be conscientious workmen, faithful friends, and devoted parents were apt to behave as idolatrous tribesmen; and, in their worship of their tribal idols of collective power, pride, passion, prejudice, and covetousness, they were prone to break moral laws that they would never have dreamed of breaking, and to perpetrate crimes that they would never have dreamed

---

[1] Elias, N.: *Über den Prozess der Zivilisation*, vol. ii: *Wandlungen der Gesellschaft: Entwurf zu einer Theorie der Zivilisation* (Basel 1939, Haus zum Falken), p. 436.

of perpetrating, in their private affairs. This immoral temper was not an auspicious psychological setting for the execution of the delicate and laborious task of constantly adjusting a balance in answer to constant changes in the relative strengths of parties whose strengths were bound to change in virtue of their being, not inanimate objects, but living creatures. The tribesmen of a tribe that had forged ahead of its neighbours in population, wealth, technique, or other constituent elements of military and political power were apt to yield to the temptation to try to take advantage of their relative gain in collective strength in order to make a bid for collective aggrandizement; and such criminally childish collective ambitions were not easily discouraged by merely diplomatic counter-measures. When the parties whose interests were threatened by the baleful rise of a new Mars in the international constellation had resorted to the crude device of a reversal of alliances and the subtle device of a general self-denying ordinance binding all Great Powers alike to abstain from competing for the spoils of some derelict empire, there were not many other pacific cards left in a diplomatist's hand; in the history of every political Balance of Power between parochial states whose story was on record, it had invariably proved to be beyond the resources of Diplomacy to save the balance from being overturned without at least an occasional recourse to inter-state war; and the institution of War, which was, itself, an outcome and expression of the tribal spirit, had proved, time and again, to be unamenable to rational regulation and control and, when out of control, to be destructive.

War had proved to be deadly, not only for a political Balance of Power that it had been called in to redress, but also for the civilization in whose body politic the maintenance of a balance was being attempted; and this destructiveness of War was not just incidental to its clumsiness, but was inherent in its nature. A collectively organized resort to violence was, indeed, so rough and ready a method of attempting to adjust a political balance that, even when successfully used to restore equilibrium in one quarter, it usually also had the effect of producing a new derangement of the balance in some other quarter. A diplomatist driven to resort to War *faute de mieux* was in the unhappy quandary in which a watchmaker would find himself if he were instructed to mend a broken watch and were given no tools for doing the job except a sledge-hammer. War was, however, also destructive in its essence, quite apart from the incongruousness of its diplomatic use, and its destructiveness tended to grow greater progressively, at each fresh hammer stroke. The toll taken by War tended to rise with the passage of Time because, in any society in which War was an established institution, the service of Mars was apt to be the first charge on the society's energies; and the maintenance of a competition by means of War, in default of Diplomacy, between parochial states was therefore apt to drive the competing military Powers into devoting to War an ever increasing proportion of their strength. Even while a society was still in growth, the increase in the demands made by War would thus outstrip the increase in the society's capacity to satisfy them; the rate of the blood-tax would rise with every improvement in the technical ability to mobilize the society's non-human and human resources; and, even when the mounting strain of War had produced a social breakdown, a still belligerent society would still continue to devote to War an increasing proportion of a strength that would now be, not increasing, but diminishing.

In an earlier context[1] we have watched the Hellenic Civilization following this fatal road during its disintegration, and in that instance we know what fate it was to which an unconscionably belligerent society condemned itself. In the course of an Hellenic Time of Troubles the toll taken by War eventually rose to a height at which the Hellenic Society would have died, forthwith, of the mortal wounds that it had already inflicted on itself if the then imminent dissolution of the body social had not been postponed (without being ultimately averted) in consequence of a sudden overturn of the Balance of Power itself. In the Hellenic World within the fifty-three years 220–168 B.C. a Balance of Power between parochial states was inverted into a monopoly of power in the hands of a universal state through a swift succession of 'knock-out-blows' with which four out of five Great Powers were laid low by one victorious survivor.[2] This dramatic episode of Hellenic history bore an ominous likeness to the dramatic course of Western history since A.D. 1914; and both stories alike threw light on a mortality that seemed to be the inevitable doom of all Balances of Power.

While Balances of Power thus appear to be intrinsically unstable and transitory, it is still more clearly evident that they could not follow this secular course from their original installation to their eventual overturn if they were not kept going in the meanwhile, like spinning tops, by rhythmically alternating fluctuations. Our next task is therefore to analyse the regularly recurrent characteristics of the cycle as these present themselves in Modern Western, post-Alexandrine Hellenic, and post-Confucian Sinic history, and to put our analysis to an empirical test by identifying the successive occurrences of the operation of this cyclic 'law of Nature' in a Western, an Hellenic, and a Sinic international arena.

Considering the dominance of the part played by War in the working of a political balance among parochial states, it is not surprising to find that the most emphatic punctuation in a uniform sequence of events recurring in one repetitive cycle after another is the outbreak of a great war in which one Power that has forged ahead of all its rivals makes so formidable a bid for world dominion that it evokes an opposing coalition of all the other Powers implicated in this particular system of international relations.

The storm that thus breaks in the form of 'a general war'—as we may conveniently label a great war of the all-engulfing kind just indicated —has usually been brewing in the course of a spell of fair weather following the calming down of the last preceding atmospheric disturbance. The derangement of an established equilibrium that is registered so sensationally in the outbreak of a general war is usually the cumulative outcome of gradual processes of growth, decay, and divers other forms

[1] In III. iii. 150.
[2] See the quotation from Polybius in III. iii. 312–13, and also IV. iv. 210–14.

of change that Life is always experiencing in Time. An equilibrium retrospectively designed to serve as a response to one particular set of already past challenges is thus virtually bound, with the sheer passage of Time, to fall farther and farther out of gear with current facts and needs, as these change in the flow of the Time-stream; every one of these changes adds to the mounting strain on the established equilibrium by increasing the discrepancy between an Epimethean dispensation and a Promethean reality; and, while it may be arguable that the consequent tension would never have exploded into a general war, but for the disproportionate increase in the relative strength of one of the Great Powers, it will usually also be arguable that the aggressor would never have ventured to challenge his peers for the prize of world dominion if he had not been able to count on reinforcing his own strength, and masking the egotism of his own ambitions, by presenting himself as the champion of other forces which could likewise claim that an antiquated equilibrium was no longer giving them fair play.

The storm in which this cumulative tension eventually discharges itself sometimes breaks unheralded from a clear sky. Sometimes, on the other hand, it is preceded by premonitory showers that are ominous for observers who have eyes to see. A burst of short local minor wars is a characteristic prelude to a general war, though it is not a symptom that invariably displays itself.

When, with or without such a prelude, a general war does break out, its immediate outcome is apt to be negatively decisive without being positively constructive. The outstanding direct result is usually the defeat of the arch-aggressor; but, in this act of the play, he is apt to be temporarily foiled rather than permanently ham-strung or sincerely converted to a good-neighbourly state of mind and feeling; and the other, perhaps ultimately more important, problems that had found no solution within the framework of the old order are now apt to be shelved, rather than solved, in a patched-up peace that is improvised primarily in order to meet the urgent immediate need for giving the society a rest in which it may recover from its exhaustion.

Even if the urgency of restoring peace for its own sake did not thus force the peace-negotiators' pace, they would, no doubt, find it difficult or impossible to map out a blue print for the summary and comprehensive solution of problems that were not open to being solved either all at once or all in the council-chamber. The passage of Time, which, in the spell of peace preceding the general war, had maleficently created intractable problems by turning an accomplished settlement into an anachronism, now beneficently ripens these still unsolved problems to a point at which a solution of them at last becomes attainable. Yet, even when Time is thus working to facilitate Diplomacy, instead of working, as before, to aggravate the difficulties of the statesman's task, Diplomacy once again proves incapable of doing its job without again employing the instrument of War to carry its policy over the stiles of collective obtuseness and inertia. A spell of peace that gives a war-stricken society the necessary breathing-space is therefore apt to be followed by a further burst of warfare over the still unsettled issues on which the recent general war was fought; but this martial epilogue to a general war usually differs auspiciously from the antecedent general war itself in producing more constructive and more lasting solutions for the social problems with which both these bouts of warfare are concerned, and in achieving this at a lower cost in terms of destruction and exhaustion.[1]

Though this martial aftermath of a general war usually outclasses the martial prelude to the general war in its scale, it also usually resembles the prelude in taking the form of a burst of short wars, some, at least, of which are only local, in contrast to the protractedness and the ubiquity that are a general war's characteristically noxious features; and, though the peace-settlements following these supplementary lesser wars may be partial and piecemeal by comparison with the grand essay in comprehensive and definitive peace-making after the antecedent general war,[2] their aggregate effect is often to find more or less adequate and enduring solutions for the problems which have precipitated the general war and which have been left still unsolved by the abortive peace-making after it. Thereby the disturbed equilibrium is temporarily restored by more positive measures than the mere frustration of a single Great Power's bid for world dominion that is the negative achievement of the opposing coalition in a general war. For this reason the interval of general peace that elapses between the constructive settlement achieved in the martial epilogue to a general war and the outbreak of another general war as the result of the ultimate explosion of gradually pent up new forces is more genuinely peaceful, and hence also more creative, in its quality, even when it is not longer in its duration, than the breathing-space between the end of a general war and the beginning of its martial epilogue.

The foregoing analysis has brought to light the composition and structure of the uniform sequence of events constituting one war-and-peace cycle in a repetitive series of cycles of the kind. The uniformly recurring sequence consists of alternating bouts of War and spells of Peace; there are four of these altogether, namely two of each, but these couples are not pairs of twins; for, in both the couple of spells of Peace and the couple of paroxysms of War, one of the two beats is more sharply accentuated than the other. The tranquillity of the interval of general peace following the martial epilogue to a general war presents as sharp a contrast to the uneasiness of the breathing-space between the

---

[1] This sequence of events is not, of course, invariable, and, even when it does duly present itself, it does not always conform exactly to the standard pattern delineated here. In Modern Western history, for example, the Thirty Years War (*gerebatur* A.D. 1618–48) did set the seal on the frustration, in the foregoing general war (*gerebatur* A.D. 1568–1609), of the Hapsburgs' bid for World dominion; but, at any rate in the Central European theatre of hostilities, this conclusive confirmation of a previous military and political decision took, not a lighter, but a heavier toll than the general war had taken. Similarly, in post-Alexandrine Hellenic history, the toll taken by the supplementary wars of 90–80 B.C. was greater in Italy—and indeed in the Aegean Basin as well—than the toll taken by the civil disturbances and social revolutions of 133–111 B.C., which had taken the place of a general war in this chapter of Hellenic history, as the civil wars in the Spanish Hapsburg Empire and in France had taken the place of a general war in the chapter of Western history within which the Thirty Years War fell.

[2] Here again the Thirty Years War presents an exception to the normal rule, inasmuch as the peace-settlement of Westphalia, by which it was followed, was actually the first Modern Western essay in peace-making on an oecumenical scale.

general war itself and its martial epilogue as the mildness of this epilogue presents to the severity of the antecedent general war.

Now that we have plotted out the typical physiognomy of a war-and-peace cycle, our next step must be to set out in tabular form[1] the successive occurrences of this sequence of phenomena in the Modern and post-Modern chapters of Western history.

This table shows that, in the course of the four and a half centuries that had elapsed between the last decade of the fifteenth century of the Christian Era, when this particular Balance of Power had been installed in the Western World, and the year A.D. 1952, the repetitive cycle through which a precariously unstable equilibrium had been turbulently maintaining itself had so far revolved five times over, counting in the overture to the series as well as the still uncompleted fourth round of the subsequent cycles. The table also shows that this fourth cycle, as well as the overture, had departed from the norm represented by the three regular cycles that had occurred between A.D. 1568 and A.D. 1914, and that, among these three, the second and the third cycle were closer replicas of one another than the first cycle was of either of them.

The departures of the overture and the fourth cycle from the norm were not of the same kind; for the fourth cycle differed from the overture and from the preceding three regular cycles alike in its structure, whereas the overture resembled the regular cycles in its structure and differed from them only in its wave-length.

The structural novelty of the fourth cycle was, as we have seen,[2] the portentous one of capping one general war with another one of still greater severity, atrocity, and inconclusiveness, instead of following it up with a burst of milder, but nevertheless more conclusive, supplementary wars that, on the precedent of the uniform sequence of events in each of the preceding cycles, were to be expected as the sequel to a breathing-space. There was no such radical difference of structure between the three regular cycles and the overture. In the overture, as in the regular cycles, a breathing-space after a general war had duly been followed by supplementary wars which had duly been followed, in their turn, by a general peace. The difference in this case was merely a chronological one. The overture's duration of seventy-four years (*currebat* A.D. 1494–1568) had been not much longer than the maximum wave-length of a single 'Kondratieff cycle' on the economic plane of latter-day Western history, and not quite so long as the sum of a couple of minimum wave-lengths of the same economic 'long cycle',[3] whereas the duration of the second and third regular cycles (*currebant* A.D. 1672–1792 *et* A.D. 1792–1914), running, as it had done, to 120 years in the one case and 122 years in the other,[4] had been equal to the sum of a couple of maximum 'Kondratieff'

---

[1] See Table I, opposite.   [2] On p. 235, above.
[3] These 'Kondratieff cycles' with wave-lengths ranging between maxima of about sixty years and minima of about forty years have been noticed on pp. 231–2, above.
[4] These are the respective wave-lengths found for Cycles II and III by measuring the intervals between outbreaks of general wars; and the durations of 104 years and 74 years, found for Cycle I and for the overture respectively, are obtained by measurements on the same basis. This basis is the obvious one to take, since the outbreaks of general wars are, as we have observed, the most emphatic of all the punctuations marking out the uniform sequence of events composing each of these repetitive cycles. An alternative

TABLE I. *Successive Occurrences of the War-and-Peace Cycle in Modern and post-Modern Western History*

Phase	Overture (A.D. 1494–1568)	First Regular Cycle (A.D. 1568–1672)	Second Regular Cycle (A.D. 1672–1792)	Third Regular Cycle (A.D. 1792–1914)	Fourth Cycle (A.D. 1914–)
(i) Premonitory Wars (the Prelude) ·	..	..	1667–81[1]	..	1911–12[2]
(ii) *The General War* ·	1494–1525[3]	1568–1609[4]	1672–1713[5]	1792–1815[6]	1914–18
(iii) The Breathing-space ·	1525–36	1609–18	1713–33	1815–48	1918–39
(iv) Supplementary Wars (the Épilogue) ·	1536–59[7]	1618–48	1733–63[8]	1848–71[9]	1939–45[10]
(v) *The General Peace* ·	1559–68	1648–72	1763–92	1871–1914	..

[1] Louis XIV's attack on the Spanish Netherlands.

[2] The Turco-Italian War of 1911–12; The Turco-Balkan Wars of 1912–13.

[3] 1494–1503, 1510–16, and 1521–5.

[4] 1568–1609 in the Spanish Hapsburg Monarchy; 1562–98 in France.

[5] 1672–8, 1688–97, and 1702–13.

[6] 1792–1802, 1803–14, and 1815.

[7] 1536–8, 1542–4, [1544–6 and 1549–50, England v. France], [1546–52, Schmalkald League of Protestant Princes in the Holy Roman Empire v. Charles V], 1552–9.

[8] 1733–5, 1740–8, and 1756–63.

[9] 1848–9, 1853–6, 1859 [1861–5, civil war in the United States; 1862–7, French occupation of Mexico], 1864, 1866, and 1870–1.

[10] This recrudescent general war of 1939–45 was heralded by a splutter of premonitory wars: the Japanese attack on China, launched in Manchuria in 1931; the Italo-Abyssinian War of 1935–6; the War of 1936–9 in Spain; and the fateful one-day campaign in the Rhineland on the 7th March, 1936, which was to pay for its bloodlessness at compound interest in the holocausts of the years 1939–45.

wave-lengths, while the first regular cycle (*currebat* A.D. 1568–1672), with its duration of 104 years, had been equal to the sum of a couple of 'Kondratieff cycles' of average length.

It is also noticeable that the shortness of the total span of the overture by comparison with the spans of the three regular cycles was accounted for mainly by the abnormal shortness of its two spells of Peace, and that, by contrast, its two bouts of War were not appreciably shorter than those of the regular cycles. The breathing-space after the general war had lasted for 11 years in the overture, as compared with 9 years in the first cycle, 20 years in the second, and 33 years in the third; the general peace after the supplementary wars had lasted for 9 years in the overture, as compared with 24 years in the first cycle, 29 years in the second, and 43 years in the third. On the other hand the general war had continued for 31 years (A.D. 1494–1525) in the overture as compared with 41 years each (A.D. 1568–1609 and A.D. 1672–1713) in the first and second cycles, and 23 years (A.D. 1792–1815) in the third cycle, while the bout of supplementary wars had continued for 23 years (A.D. 1536–59) in the overture as compared with 30 years each (A.D. 1618–48 and A.D. 1733–63) in the first and second cycles and 23 years (A.D. 1848–71) in the third cycle.

Our table also brings out a tendency, which we have already noticed by anticipation,[1] for the number of war years in a cycle to diminish, and for the ratio between the numbers of war years and of peace years to change to the numerical advantage of the peace years, with each successive repetition of the sequence.

This tendency does not, it is true, pronounce itself so sharply when measured in terms of individual years as when measured in terms of the groups of years, representing alternate bouts of War and spells of Peace, into which the sequence has been analysed; for, though the overall length of the bout that we have labelled 'the general war' falls off strikingly from the figure of 41 years at which it stands in the first and second cycles to its 23 years in the third cycle and its 4 years in the fourth, these reductions of the span are partly offset by concurrent eliminations of intercalated peace years. No less than 15 peace years, for example, were intercalated in the general war of A.D. 1672–1713—consisting, as this did, of three constituent bouts separated by two truces lasting from A.D. 1678 to 1688 and from A.D. 1697 to 1702, whereas in the General War of A.D. 1792–1815 the truces following, in A.D. 1802–3, the abortive conclusion of peace at Amiens and preceding, in A.D. 1814–15, 'the Hundred Days' were matters, not of years, but of months, while the sole truce during the General War of A.D. 1914–18 was the fraternization on the first Christmas Day after the outbreak of hostilities. When, however, the overall figures have been duly corrected to allow for such intercalations of peace years and peace months, the tendency towards a diminution in the relative lengths of the war periods still stands out

---

basis would be to measure the intervals between restorations of general peace; and on this basis the length of Regular Cycle I would work out at 89 years (1559–1648), that of Cycle II at 115 years (1648–1763), and that of Cycle III at 108 years (1763–1871).
[1] On p. 235, above.

conspicuously in a comparison of the four-years' span of the General War of A.D. 1914–18 with the corrected figures of approximately 21 years for the General War of A.D. 1792–1815 and approximately 26 years for the General War of A.D. 1672–1713.[1]

At the same time a synoptic view of the later and the earlier general wars in this Western series also shows that, in the act of becoming shorter, Western general wars had been becoming more concentrated, more intense, and more relentless, and that, so far from the progressive shortening of the lengths of bouts of general warfare signifying an alleviation of the scourge of War, the progressive concentration of general warfare within an ever smaller number of years at an ever higher degree of intensity had resulted in the recurrent general wars working greater havoc in the life of the Western Civilization than they had worked when they had been carried on more desultorily over longer Time-spans. While it was true that under this older dispensation the plague of War had been more or less endemic in the Western body social, it was also true that a relatively mild perennial malady was in many ways more tolerable and less dangerous than a series of occasional sudden violent epidemics breaking in upon spells of relatively good health. This abrupt alternation of Total War with Total Peace was, indeed, manifestly more trying to the constitution of Society than an earlier condition in which the difference between spells of health and bouts of sickness had been less sharply accentuated. In the Early Modern Age of Western history the war-ridden society had been affected like a victim of chronic malaria, whose vitality is permanently lowered by his complaint without his life being brought into jeopardy. In the Late Modern Age the Western Society had been relieved of its malaria thanks to a gratifying improvement in the day-to-day performance of Western political preventive medicine, but the patient had been made to pay for this rise in his normal level of health by becoming subject to thunderbolt 'strokes' which were as unpredictably sudden as they were lethally violent.

While the deadliness of War had thus been increasing by geometrical progression with each further repetition of a Western war-and-peace cycle in which the bouts of War had been becoming shorter, and the spells of Peace longer, every time, the respective stances of the competing Powers had been as uniform, throughout the series of recurrent cycles, as the sequence of events in which, cycle by cycle, the resolution of political and military forces had recurrently worked itself out.

We have already noticed[2] that the Western international tableau of

---

[1] The average figure for the length of time by which each successive Western general war was becoming shorter than its immediate predecessor thus works out at eleven years as between the latest three general wars in this series according to the corrected calculations of their spans. When the writer was doing this sum on the morning of the 2nd August, 1950, he had at his elbow his original notes, written in A.D. 1929; and, considering that at that date the possibility of constructing an atom bomb was still beyond the mental horizon of a layman like himself, he was startled to read in his own handwriting, jotted down twenty-one years ago: 'Since the General War of A.D. 1914–1918 lasted little more than four years, we find, on following out the progression, that the next general war, which might be expected to break out about A.D. 2035, would be instantaneous in duration, i.e. annihilating in effect. This mathematical fantasy is borne out by all the empirical evidence available for a forecast in this year A.D. 1929.

[2] On p. 244, above.

A.D. 1952, in which the Soviet Union was striving to break out of a ring within which the United States was striving to contain her, was a reproduction of the tableau of A.D. 1552, with a twentieth-century Russia playing a sixteenth-century France's part and the United States playing Charles V's. We can now see that this disposition of forces was not peculiar to the situation existing at those two dates, at each of which the number of Great Powers had been no more than two. In every round with the sole exception of the first regular cycle (*currebat* A.D. 1568–1672), the aggressor Power had invariably been a continental Power in a central position occupying a compact territory with sally-ports opening into the back-yards of the countries that were the arenas of combat, the stakes of contention, and the prizes of victory.

In the overture (*currebat* A.D. 1494–1568) this role had been played by a France who marched with Italy along one land frontier and with Flanders along another; and, after a temporary eclipse that had been the penalty of her civil war of A.D. 1562–98, France had recaptured this role from a Spanish Hapsburg Monarchy that had acquired it, in France's temporary absence, during the General War of A.D. 1568–1609 which had inaugurated Regular Cycle I (*currebat* A.D. 1568–1672).[1] In the

---

[1] This General War of A.D. 1568–1609 took, like the contemporary warfare in France during the years A.D. 1562–98, the form of a civil war between conflicting local interests and religious persuasions as far as the two principal belligerents were concerned. This civil war between the Spanish Catholic and Dutch Protestant subjects of Philip II was converted into a general war by England's entry into the lists as one of Spain's adversaries. This English intervention gave an oecumenical significance to what would otherwise have remained a domestic conflict within the body politic of a single Great Power, because, if the Spanish Armada had conquered England in A.D. 1588 and had installed there a minoritarian Roman Catholic Government dependent on Spanish backing, this increase in the power of the Spanish Hapsburg Monarchy would presumably have ensured, not merely the eventual resubjugation of the Protestant insurgents in the Netherlands, but the temporary supremacy of Spain in the Western international arena, since Spain would then have been able to take full advantage of the opportunity, offered to her by the civil war in France, for bringing France too under a Spanish hegemony through the agency of a Roman Catholic Government in France that would likewise have had to look to Spain for support.

The insurrection of the Netherlands against the Spanish Crown in A.D. 1568 and the increasing provocation of the Spaniards by the Spaniards in and after A.D. 1572 gave the measure of the temporary paralysis of French power during the French civil war of A.D. 1562–98. The inability of Spain to profit by the chance of winning world dominion, with which the temporary eclipse of France had presented her, gave the measure of Spain's intrinsic permanent weakness under her temporary outward appearance of strength. Whenever France was her normal mighty self, her neighbours Spain, the Netherlands, and England, none of whom was a match for France singly, had a strong interest in holding together against the Central Power that was a menace to all of them alike. The marriages between Henry VIII and Catharine of Aragon in A.D. 1509 and between Philip II and Mary of England in A.D. 1554—like the Anglo-Spanish combined military operations in the Iberian Peninsula in A.D. 1811–13—were the reflection of a community of Spanish and English interests that was normal until France fell out of the competition for world dominion after A.D. 1815; and it was a fatality that both these matrimonial alliances should have been exceptions to a rule which made the political felicity of Hapsburg—if not of Spanish—marriages proverbial.

An even greater portent, however, than the breach between England and Spain during the French civil war of A.D. 1562–98 was the alacrity with which the English and the Dutch fell out with one another over the scramble for Spanish and Portuguese spoils overseas, and the tardiness with which they eventually made up their minds to call a truce to their feud with one another in face of a menace from a rehabilitated France which was more dangerous for both of them than the menace from Spain had ever been. The treaty made by England with France on the 29th May, 1527, on the morrow of the crushing defeat of the French at Pavia on the 24th February, 1525, was not, on any Machiavellian reckoning, a precedent that could justify the treaty made on the 1st June, 1670, on the morrow of the French invasion of the Spanish Netherlands in May 1667.

general wars of A.D. 1672–1713 and A.D. 1792–1815 France had played the aggressor's part once again; but in the meantime a Western World that had been engaging in these domestic conflicts with one hand had been enlarging its territorial domain with the other hand; and this change in the Western World's geographical scale and structure had eventually deprived France of her central position.

France's last chance of winning world dominion had passed away at Waterloo upon the final failure of her third bid for it in the General War of A.D. 1792–1815. Thereafter the Western World's continental centre of gravity had shifted eastward from France to Germany as a result of the reception of the Western culture first in a Russian and then in an Ottoman Orthodox Christendom. These sweeping cultural conquests, which had carried the eastern marches of a Westernizing World as far as Alexandria and Vladivostok, had also substituted the Near and Middle East for Italy and Flanders as the arena in which the stakes were held, the wars were fought, and the prizes were to be won; and this transformation of the Western World's geographical landscape had been reflected on the political and military plane in the transfer of the role of aggressive Central Power from France to Prussia-Germany in the course of the supplementary wars (*gerebantur* A.D. 1848–71) following the General War of A.D. 1792–1815. Germany's tenure of a role which she had thus captured from France was, however, to be very much briefer

Though Louis XIV's premonitory attack on the Spanish Netherlands in A.D. 1667 had moved the United Netherlands and England to make peace with one another in that year and to enter into an anti-French triple alliance, including Sweden, in A.D. 1668, France nevertheless had England for her ally against Holland for the first three years (A.D. 1672–4) of a general war in which a French attack on the Dutch was the first move in a fresh French attempt at win world dominion.

The Spanish danger to the liberties of Western parochial states was never so great as the French danger—not even at the height of the power of Philip II—for the Spanish Power was an idol with feet of clay in a Western international arena in which the economic sinews of war were coming progressively, with each further round in the game, to count for more and more by comparison with mere military valour. The descendants of the Iberian Western Christian barbarians who had defeated the Maghribi Berber Muslim barbarians in a contest for the spoils of an Andalusian Umayyad Caliphate that had collapsed in A.D. 1010 were born soldiers in the Gothic and the Vandal vein; and, in their socially parasitic profession, they displayed an impressive adaptability when, in the Western General War of A.D. 1494–1525, they mastered a new-fangled Swiss infantry technique which, in this phase of a Western art of war, was the talisman of victory. This Spanish stock of military material was, however, as inadequate in quantity as it was outstanding in quality; for the Christians in sixteenth-century Spain were no more than an 'ascendancy' in a population which mustered perhaps no more than seven million souls in all, as against the fifteen or sixteen million culturally and communally homogeneous inhabitants of a contemporary France; and the Muslim and Jewish subject communities were Spain's economic mainstay. Whereas the Castilian and Aragonese soldiery of a sixteenth-century Spain were shepherds and herdsmen in civil life, her agriculture, such as it was, was carried on by a Morisco and a Catalan peasantry in the valley of the Wādī'l-Kabīr and along the seaboard of the Mediterranean, while the Jews were the life of the trade and industry of the Spanish cities. Whereas France could feed her sixteen millions from home-grown cereals, Spain could not feed her seven millions without importing cereals from Sicily and from Northern Europe; and, as if these economic handicaps were not serious enough as they were, the Spanish 'ascendancy' did its worst to aggravate them by oppressing and evicting the Moorish and Jewish producers of Spanish wealth. Simultaneously, even the reservoir of Castilian Christian military man-power was depleted by the draining off of *conquistadores* to live happily ever after as rentiers taking toll of subject peasant populations in overrun Mexic and Andean worlds.

A brilliant portrait of sixteenth-century Spain has been painted by Eduard Fueter in his *Geschichte des Europäischen Staatensystems von 1492–1559* (Munich and Berlin 1919, Oldenbourg), pp. 79–103.

than her predecessor's. The slower tempo of the Modern Western
World's expansion during its earlier stages had enabled France to cling
to this role—albeit at the price of bringing ever direr disasters upon
herself—from A.D. 1494 to A.D. 1870, with no more than a temporary
eclipse *circa* A.D. 1562–98. But the Western Civilization's transit from
a Modern to a post-Modern Age of Western history at the very moment
at which Germany was supplanting France had been accompanied by
a sudden immense acceleration in the tempo of Western geographical
expansion; and a change of geographical scale which had wafted Germany into a commanding position by A.D. 1871 had by then already
begun to gather an impetus that in A.D. 1945 was to bring Germany
lower than France had ever yet fallen.

In a Western system of international relations which, in the meantime,
had continued to expand until it had attained a literally world-wide
range, a Germany who had bid for world dominion twice within one
lifetime, in a brace of general wars fought in swift succession (*gerebantur*
A.D. 1914–18 *et* A.D. 1939–45), had been compelled, in her turn, by A.D.
1945 to surrender the role of aggressive Central Power to a Soviet
Union who occupied a commanding position in a geographical setting
that was oecumenical now and no longer merely regional. In A.D. 1952,
when an arena of competition which had originally been confined to
Italy and Flanders had come to embrace the whole of the Old World
outside the Soviet Union's own borders, the Soviet Union possessed
sally-ports opening into the back-yards of Scandinavia, Western
Europe, the Near and Middle East, the sub-continent of India, South-
East Asia, Indonesia, China, Korea, and Japan. In the course of four
centuries the geographical scale of a Western system of international
relations had thus been enlarged to a stupendous degree; yet the lay-out
of the arena and the stance of the gladiators face to face within it was
recognizably the same in A.D. 1952 as it had been four hundred years
earlier.

The War-and-Peace Cycle in post-Alexandrine Hellenic History

We have now perhaps reached the limit to which we can carry our
analysis of the war-and-peace rhythm in the Modern and post-Modern
chapters of Western history; and in any case we have carried it far
enough to enable us, if we turn our attention to the post-Alexandrine
chapters of Hellenic history, to see at a glance that a war-and-peace
rhythm is discernible here too, and that some of the main features of it
are identical with features that we have already observed in our Western
example of the working of this particular law of Nature in the political
affairs of civilizations.

In the Hellenic, as in the Western, case the series of cycles begins
with an overture in which the parties to the competition are jockeying
with one another not merely for victory in the race but for the winning
of a place in the running; and this inaugural round of the cycle takes
the form of a civil war among Alexander's successors over the swollen
heritage of the Argeadae which is reminiscent of the civil war between
a royal branch and a Burgundian ducal branch of the French House of

Valois over the swollen heritage of the Valois dukes of Burgundy. In the Hellenic case, again, a sequence of alternating bouts of war and spells of peace, that makes its first epiphany in the overture, then repeats itself in a cycle of competition between the survivors of the ordeal to which the overture had subjected all competitors who had had the hardihood to enter the lists. We shall also notice in the Hellenic course of events a tendency, which we have noticed in the corresponding Western story, for regional vortices which at first behave like so many independent focuses of military and political force to coalesce into a single vortex drawing into itself the whole of the action in all quarters of the international arena. In the evolution of a Western Balance of Power we have watched such outlying vortices round the marches between Western Christendom and the Ottoman Empire and between Western Christendom and Muscovy coalescing with the central vortex round Italy and Flanders. In the Hellenic story we shall see a vortex round the coasts of the Aegean in the Levant and a vortex round Sicily and Magna Graecia in the western basin of the Mediterranean[1] coalescing into a vortex engulfing the Mediterranean Basin from end to end.

We shall also see the partial neutralization of the Great Powers' potency, through their respective successes in frustrating one another's ambitions, giving opportunities for minor states to come to birth and grow in the interstices between the rugged cyclopean boulders which the deliberately engineered traffic-blocks in the avalanche have brought into a precarious equilibrium. For example, a Rhodian tripolis, that found itself in a key position in the new world called into existence by Alexander's overthrow of the Achaemenidae, was able, in the course of the overture cycle, during the General War of 321–301 B.C., to hold out in 305 B.C. against the siege artillery of Demetrius Poliorcêtês with the help of the coalition of Alexander's other successors that was opposing Demetrius's father Antigonus Monophthalmus's bid for world dominion. An Aetolian Confederacy of Continental Greek cantons and city-states, a similar Achaean Confederacy in the Peloponnese, and an Attalid Principality in the immediate hinterland of the Continental Asiatic half of the original homeland of Hellenism all started their political careers in the course of the overture during the catastrophic sequel to a supplementary war which had followed, in 282–281 B.C., the General War of 321–301 B.C.; and the exhaustion of the Great Powers in the next general war (*in Oriente gerebatur* 266–241 B.C.) not only gave these four already established minor states opportunities of consolidating and extending their previous gains, but also enabled partisans of reform at Sparta to regenerate their commonwealth by the social revolution of 227 B.C., and advocates of a quiet life at Athens to recapture a precarious independence for their country in 229 B.C.

While all these features in a post-Alexandrine Hellenic international landscape are reminiscent of the corresponding features in the landscape of a Western World in its Early Modern Age, the Hellenic tragedy differed from the Western in giving rein to violence with an unparalleled lack of restraint; and this demonic mania, which reminded a twentieth-

---

[1] 'The Ponent' of the Medieval Western mariners.

century Western historian of the temper that had erupted in his own world in his own later day, brought upon a post-Alexandrine Hellenic Society, in the first recurrence of the war-and-peace cycle after the overture, the catastrophe of a double general war to which a latter-day Western Society had not condemned itself till it had passed through three regular cycles of the rhythm and had entered on a fourth round. The recklessness of a post-Alexandrine Hellenic Society's violence in the conduct of its international affairs explains how it came about that the promise of the overture to the symphony was promptly and rudely belied by the performance in the first ensuing movement. The first war-and-peace cycle after the overture witnessed a decisive and irretrievable overturn of a post-Alexandrine Hellenic Balance of Power through the liquidation of all but one of a number of Great Powers which, in the course of the overture (*in Oriente currebat* 321–266 B.C.), had risen, not just from two to three, as in the course of the corresponding chapter of Early Modern Western history (*currebat* A.D. 1494–1568), but from two to as many as five.

At the moment of Alexander's death on the 13th June, 323, there were two Great Powers, and two only, in an Hellenic World whose eastern bounds Alexander had carried forward within the last eleven years from the Anatolian hinterland of the east coast of the Aegean Sea to the banks of an eastern tributary of the Indus. Alexander himself had momentarily united under his personal rule the domain over which the Achaemenian Empire had extended at its widest with the domain of a Macedonian Power which his father Philip had built up in Continental European Greece[1] between 357 and 338 B.C. The only other Great Power existing at that moment within the horizon of a thus vastly expanded Hellenic World was a Carthaginian Empire which had controlled the southern half of the western basin of the Mediterranean, with its African and Iberian continental hinterlands, since the closing years of the sixth century B.C.,[2] and which Alexander had not had time to liquidate as he had liquidated an Achaemenian Empire of which the Carthaginian had been a colonial counterpart in the political geography of a Syriac World. After the settling of the dust raised by the two successive wars for the possession of Alexander's heritage which had ended respectively at Ipsus in 301 B.C. and at Corupedium in 281 B.C., no less than five Great Powers came into view in the arena.

The Carthaginian Empire was still standing, not only intact but to all appearance more puissant than ever, in a still semi-detached West Mediterranean theatre of colonial competition between an Hellenic and a Syriac Society.[3] Meanwhile, Alexander's ephemerally united heritage

---

[1] Sparta was the only Continental European Greek state that had been able to hold aloof from the League of Corinth that Philip had inaugurated in 338 B.C. as the constitutional instrument of a Macedonian hegemony.

[2] See IX. viii. 426–7, 428–9, 437–8, and 485–6.

[3] In thus managing to retain her rank as a Great Power in an Hellenic or Hellenizing World in spite of the sudden vast increase in the scale of Hellenic life at the transition from a pre-Alexandrine to a post-Alexandrine Age of Hellenic history, Carthage achieved something that Venice failed to achieve at the transition from a Late Medieval to an Early Modern Age of Western history. *Circa* 281 B.C. Carthage was a Great Power still, whereas Venice, *circa* A.D. 1559, was lucky to find herself still independent and in possession of an empire in the Levant and on the Italian mainland that was now dwarfed

had been partitioned into three now more or less securely established successor-states which, under their appearance of being new creations artificially carved out by capricious strokes of Macedonian military adventurers' swords, revealed themselves on closer inspection to be, like the Carthaginian Empire, old structures masked, unlike the Carthaginian Empire, behind new façades. A Ptolemaic Power based on the Lower Nile Valley was an avatar of the Egypt of Psammetichus I; a Seleucid Power based on the alluvium of the Lower Tigris-Euphrates Valley (*Graecè* Babylonia, *Arabicè* 'Irāq) was an avatar of the Achaemenian Empire of Cyrus; an Antigonid Power based on the lower valleys of the Vardar (Axius) and the Struma (Strymon) was an avatar of the Macedon of Philip II. The one genuinely new creation among the five Hellenic Great Powers that were in being at the end of the overture (*currebat* 321–266 B.C.) to the post-Alexandrine chapter of Hellenic history was a commonwealth which the city-state Rome had been building up in Central Italy between 340 and 290 B.C.[1]

By 168 B.C. this one new Power was also the only survivor among the five Powers that had been in the arena in 266 B.C. Of the four Powers that had enjoyed the advantage of standing on old foundations, Carthage, the Seleucid Monarchy, and Macedon had been felled to the ground by Roman blows in the years 201, 190, and 168, while Ptolemaic Egypt had been reduced to the status of a Roman protectorate when Roman diplomatic intervention had saved her in 170 B.C. from being annexed by Rome's defeated Seleucid adversary. This overturn of a post-Alexandrine Hellenic Balance of Power, and its replacement by an unchallengeable monopoly of power in the hands of Rome, was not incomparable, in its abruptness, to the overturn of a Balance of Power in Sinic history through Ts'in's destruction of her six peers between the years 230 and 221 B.C.; and an Hellenic violence reminiscent of the spirit of those Sinic 'contending states' accounts for the striking divergence between a course of Hellenic events in which an international Balance of Power was thus overturned before the completion of the first cycle after the overture and a course of Western events in which an international balance, inaugurated during a similar overture, had run

by the gigantic stature of Great Powers of a higher calibre that had loomed up all around her. This contrast between the respective fortunes of Carthage and Venice during these corresponding chapters of their histories is accounted for by two differences in their experiences. By A.D. 1559 Venice had long since met her Ottoman fate, whereas Carthage was not to meet her Roman fate till 264 B.C.; and by A.D. 1559 Venice had also felt the adverse economic effects of the Portuguese conquest of the Indies and the Spanish conquest of the Americas, whereas the Macedonian conquest of the Achaemenian Empire had no similar adverse economic effects on Carthage's monopoly of the African and Iberian hinterlands of her 'wooden curtain'.

[1] The Central Italian Roman Commonwealth that had been brought into being by 290 B.C. was as genuinely new as the Danubian Hapsburg Monarchy that came into being in A.D. 1526; for, though the Roman Central Italy which in 290 B.C. was an accomplished fact had been foreshadowed in an Etruscan imperialism in the seventh and sixth centuries B.C., these Etruscan attempts to bring the Greek settlements on the coast of Campania and the Latin settlements in the lower valley of the Tiber under the hegemony of the Etruscan settlements between the Tiber and the Arno had been as abortive as the divers ephemeral unions between Hungary, Bohemia, Poland, and the patrimony of the House of Hapsburg in South-East Germany which in their successive permutations and combinations had foreshadowed the establishment, in A.D. 1526, of a Danubian Hapsburg Monarchy that was to hold together for nearly four hundred years (see II. ii. 178–9).

through three subsequent regular cycles before it had begun to get out of hand.

The difference in temper between the Western gladiatorial combat of A.D. 1494–1559 and the Hellenic combat of 321–281 B.C. can be measured by the difference between the personal fates that overtook the principal adventurers in the two arenas. The military defeat suffered by Francis I at Pavia in A.D. 1525 was no less crushing than the overthrows of Antigonus at Ipsus in 301 B.C. and Lysimachus at Corupedium in 281 B.C., yet the worst that happened to Francis was to have to spend rather less than a year as a prisoner of war and to ransom himself at the price of undertaking to marry his adversary's sister and to renounce his claims to the Italian and Burgundian territories that were the stakes in his contest with Charles V. There was never any serious question of the destruction or even subjugation of a Kingdom of France which had brought upon itself this prostrating blow; and Francis had no sooner recovered his liberty and his throne than he broke the promises in exchange for which he had been released, and resumed a struggle that was fraught with no mortal danger either for his person or for his realm. Francis lived to die in his bed more than twenty-two years after the day on which he had been taken prisoner on the battlefield of Pavia. There is a piquant contrast between the impunity with which Francis thus played with fire and the experiences of an Antigonus and a Lysimachus, whose realms perished with them on the battlefield.

There were no such fatal casualties in the Western gladiatorial contest of A.D. 1494–1559; and the contrast between the characters of the Western and the Hellenic episode comes out still more sharply when we pass on to compare the respective fates of the victors. The worst that happened to Charles V was to become so weary of his Sisyphean task that he insisted on sloughing off his public burdens on to other shoulders and retiring into private life under conditions skilfully devised to give his body its long-overdue rest without prejudice to the long-neglected welfare of his soul. Like a discomfited Francis I, a disillusioned Charles V died in his bed; and this tame death did not overtake him till more than thirty-three years after a victory at Pavia whose aftermath had been still more ironically disappointing for the victor than it had been for his vanquished opponent. A more tragic destiny was in store for Charles V's Hellenic counterpart Seleucus Nicator, who, after overthrowing and slaying his last adversary, was foully murdered in his old age by a younger and more unscrupulous adventurer, to whom he had rashly given his confidence, before he had satisfied his heart's desire to set eyes once again on a Macedonian homeland which he had not seen for fifty-four years.

The mutual exhaustion of the belligerents in this last round (*debellatum* 282–281 B.C.) of the Wars of Alexander's Succession was so extreme that a Macedon from which an Alexander had gone forth, conquering and to conquer,[1] in 334 B.C. was overrun in 279 B.C. by barbarians from a North European hinterland who went on in 278 B.C. to cross the Dardanelles and break into the vast Asiatic dominions of Seleucus

[1] Rev. vi. 2.

Nicator's son and heir Antiochus I.[1] A poetic justice which, within a year of the murder of Nicator, thus brought the Macedonian Macbeth, Ptolemy the Thunderbolt, to his death in battle, in a vain attempt to defend the kingdom whose diadem he had usurped against the north-western barbarians' onslaught, had to be purchased by Macedon's tutelary genius at a veritably prohibitive price.

> Du treibst mir's gar zu toll,
> Ich fürcht', es breche!
> Nicht jeden Wochenschluss
> Macht Gott die Zeche.

This apprehensive exclamation, wrung from a Goethe who was observing, with his heart in his mouth, the criminal recklessness of his own contemporaries, might have been wrung, with no less reason, from a spectator of the international arena in either the Western World of the sixteenth century of the Christian Era or the Hellenic World of the Age of Alexander's successors; yet, in the less turbulent course of Western history, God's settlement of accounts with Man was relatively long delayed.

The fate that, in the Hellenic tragedy, a mad-dog militarist Pyrrhus had brought, by 272 B.C., before the close of the overture, on a small and backward kingdom on which he had irresponsibly attempted to force the untenable role of a Great Power was not brought on Sweden by Charles XII until after the corresponding Western tragedy had entered on the second of its regular recurrent cycles; and, though Epirus, after Pyrrhus had got himself killed at Argos in 272 B.C., was allowed to lapse into the tranquillity of a premature exhaustion, like Sweden after Charles XII's defiantly courted death in the trenches before Frederiksten in A.D. 1719,[2] this long since inoffensive little Continental Greek country was given over to pillage in cold blood by the Roman conqueror of

---

[1] In II. ii. 281, n. 1, it has been noticed that the Macedonians invited this barbarian invasion by their imprudence in first stimulating the European barbarians by an aggressive expansion at their expense in the reign of King Philip Amyntou (*regnabat* 359–336 B.C.) and then neglecting this reanimated barbarian frontier in order to turn their arms against the Achaemenidae and thereafter against one another. The equivalent event in Early Modern Western history would have been an invasion of Spain on the morrow of the Battle of St. Quentin (*commissum* 10 August, 1557) by a horde of resurgent Muwaḥḥid Berbers from the Atlas or Murābit Berbers from the Senegal, with an impetus that we must imagine to have carried these irrupting barbarians on beyond an overrun Spain into Italy in one direction and Mexico in the other. Castile did neglect her Berber frontier when, after the completion of the conquest of Granada in A.D. 1492, she failed to follow up her seizure of this last unsubjugated remnant of Andalusia by a seizure of North-West Africa that was the logical next step in the march of Castilian imperialism. Instead of concentrating all her military efforts on pushing forward to the natural frontier offered by the north shore of the Sahara, she made a few half-hearted descents upon North-West African ports while diverting the best part of her energies to a conquest of the Americas and to a competition with France for the hegemony over Italy. Spain, like Macedon, did pay a penalty for having thus looked back after having put her hand to the plough (Luke ix. 62); she exposed herself to the scourge of a piracy organized by Ottoman corsairs ensconced in North-West African naval bases on which Spain had neglected to secure her own hold. Yet this nuisance was trivial compared to the catastrophe that Macedon brought on herself in 279–276 B.C.

[2] Between A.D. 1494 and A.D. 1952 the only other actor of a leading part in the Western power game who had lost his life in battle had been one of Charles XII's predecessors on the throne of Sweden, Gustavus Adolphus. Napoleon, like Francis I, had died in his bed; Hitler had died in his bunker. By contrast, the deaths among eminent participants in a post-Alexandrine Hellenic power game are too numerous to record.

Macedon, Lucius Aemilius Paullus, in 167 B.C., 105 years after Pyrrhus's death, whereas in A.D. 1952, 233 years after the death of Charles XII, Sweden was still inviolate, though her fellow ephemeral Great Power Holland, as well as her two Scandinavian neighbours Denmark and Norway, had suffered at German hands in A.D. 1940 what Epirus had suffered at Roman hands in 167 B.C. In A.D. 1952 the ultimate military and political outcome of a Western Balance of Power that had been inaugurated in A.D. 1494 was still obscure; and, however ominously impenetrable might be the darkness that still shrouded the future, an already accomplished passage of 458 years testified that this Modern and post-Modern Western Balance of Power, whatever might be the denouement towards which it was heading, had at any rate already achieved a decidedly longer run than had been attained by an Hellenic Balance which Rome had overturned by establishing her sole supremacy in 168 B.C., not more than 153 years after the post-Alexandrine Balance had been inaugurated by the outbreak of the first fighting between Alexander's successors.

After these general considerations it will be convenient to set out the successive occurrences of the war-and-peace cycle in post-Alexandrine Hellenic history in a tabular form which we can then analyse in the light of our foregoing table of the corresponding Western phenomena.[1]

The most striking feature in the history of the post-Alexandrine Hellenic war-and-peace cycles that our present table throws into relief is the balefully decisive importance of the Reduplicated General War of 220–189 B.C.

Before the outbreak of this war, an Hellenic World whose area had been vastly expanded by the conquests of Alexander the Great had not constituted a single unitary field of international politics but had consisted of two distinct arenas—one in the Levant and the other in the Western Basin of the Mediterranean—in which the competition between Great Powers had been carried on more or less independently; in the course of the Reduplicated General War of 220–189 B.C. these two arenas coalesced into one; the political event in which this coalescence was registered was the treaty of alliance against Rome that King Philip V of Macedon rashly concluded with Hannibal in 215 B.C. During the preceding period each of the two arenas had been infested with an aggressor Power of its own: the role played by Egypt in the Levant had been played by Rome in the Ponent.[2] After the close of the general war of the first cycle

---

[1] See Tables I, p. 255, and II, pp. 268–9.

[2] It is noteworthy that both Rome in the first Romano-Punic War (*gerebatur* 264–241 B.C.) and Egypt in the contemporaneous general war in the Levant (*gerebatur* 266–241 B.C.) employed sea-power as the principal instrument of aggression, whereas, in the history of a Modern Western balance of power, the successive arch-aggressors—France, Germany, and Russia—were, all alike, land-powers who were comparatively weak at sea. In the First Romano-Punic war, Rome transformed herself, by a technological *tour de force*, from the land-power that had conquered Italy and had defeated Pyrrhus's attempt to undo her work there into a sea-power capable of conquering Sicily and invading North-West Africa from an Italian base of operations. This difference in the matter of armament between the typical Hellenic and the typical Western aggressor Power was the corollary of a corresponding difference in geographical structure between the Hellenic and the Western World. The Hellenic World, throughout its history, was centred on a landlocked sea—the Aegean Basin at the beginning of the story and eventually the Mediterranean Basin as a whole. The geographical expansion of the

(*in Levante gerebatur* 266–241 B.C.), Egypt not only fell out of the running but actually became the principal victim of aggression instead of continuing to be the principal perpetrator of it, whereas Rome was provoked by an abortive Carthaginian war of revenge and Macedonian war of aggrandizement into assuming in the Levant, from 200 B.C. onwards, the aggressor's role which she had begun to play in the Western Mediterranean in 264 B.C.

The Reduplicated General War of 220–189 B.C. did not, however, merely unify the military and political action on the stage of Hellenic history round the now all-overshadowing presence of Rome;[1] it also imported into the conduct of Hellenic warfare a new vein of atrocity for which the arch-aggressor Rome was not solely responsible.

Though, in this episode of Hellenic history, the overture (*currebat* 321–266 B.C.) and the general war in the first cycle (*in Levante gerebatur* 266–241 B.C.) had produced heavy casualties among war-lords by comparison with the corresponding acts in the Modern Western drama, this first phase of the Hellenic episode came in retrospect to seem mild by contrast with the sequel. Judged according to this subsequent standard, the General War of 266–241 B.C. had been as 'temperate' a contest as the Modern Western wars of the second regular cycle (*currebat* A.D. 1672–1792) on which Gibbon looked back with an unprescient complacency[2] until he was overtaken by the outbreak of the General War of A.D. 1792–1815. The comparative temperateness of Hellenic warfare in this phase can be gauged by the fact that the deliberately and persistently aggressive policy of Egypt, directed though it was against both the Seleucid Monarchy and Macedon simultaneously, drove these two assaulted Powers into taking concerted action for their common defence on one occasion only, so far as we know, and then only for a spell of some five or six years (260–255 B.C.). This must mean that neither Power felt the aggression of Egypt to be a serious threat to its own survival. The comparative temperateness of the General War of 266–241 B.C. in

Hellenic Society left the maritime structure of the Hellenic World intact, albeit enlarged in scale, even after the incorporation of South-West Asia and Northern India. By contrast, the Western World had originally been centred on one corner of the Eurasian Continent; and here again the geographical expansion of the society did not produce any immediate radical modification of its original structure, since the world-wide oceanic extension of the Western World, which began towards the close of the fifteenth century of the Christian Era, was balanced by an eastward extension into the interior of the Eurasian Continent. Owing to this progressive enlargement of the continental area of the Western World, the arch-aggressor Power in the Western arena had continued to be a land-power from the inauguration of the Modern Western balance of power in A.D. 1494 down to A.D. 1952. All the same, the new Western World overseas that had been called into existence by Western maritime enterprise had gradually come to play a progressively greater part in redressing the balance of the old Western World on the Eurasian Continent. Whereas the bullion imported by the Spaniards from the Americas into Western Europe during the overture (*currebat* A.D. 1494–1568) and the first regular cycle (*currebat* A.D. 1568–1672) of this Modern and post-Modern episode of Western history had not availed to save Spain from falling out of the running, the 'colonial wares' that the overseas annexes of the Western World had afterwards come to produce had played an appreciable part in deciding the issue of the General War of A.D. 1792–1815; and in the subsequent general wars of A.D. 1914–18 and A.D. 1939–45 the decisive contribution to the defeat of Germany had been made by the war potential of the United States.

[1] On this portent see the passage of Polybius—*Oecumenical History*, Book I, chaps. 1–4—quoted in III. iii. 312–13.   [2] See the passage cited on p. 238, n. 2, above.

TABLE II. *Successive Occurrences of the War-and-Peace Cycle in post-Alexandrine Hellenic History*

Phase	Overture (321–266 B.C.)		First Cycle (266–133 B.C.)		Second Cycle (133–49 B.C.)	Third Cycle (49–31 B.C.)
	Levant	Ponent	Levant	Ponent		
(i) Premonitory Wars (the Prelude)	··	··	276–273/2[1]	264–241[6]	135–131[2]	··
(ii) The General War	321–301[3]	340–290[4]	266–241[5]	241–218	133–111[7]	49–31[8]
(iii) The Breathing-space	301–282	290–280	241–220	219[11]	111–90[9]	··
(i) (bis) Reduplicated Premonitory Wars	··	··	224/3–222/1[10]			··
(ii) (bis) The Reduplicated General War	··	··	220–189[12]		··	··
(iii) (bis) The Reduplicated Breathing-space	··	··	189–171		90–80[16]	··
(iv) Supplementary Wars (the Epilogue)	282–281[13]	280–272[14]	171–146[15]		80–49[17]	··
(v) The General Peace	281–266	272–264	146–133			31 B.C.–A.D. 376[18]

[1] The first war between the Ptolemaic and the Seleucid Power for the possession of Coelê Syria and of the Mediterranean coasts of Anatolia from Cilicia to the Dardanelles.

[2] The first revolt of the plantation-slaves in Sicily (see V. v. 69–71).

[3] Antigonus Monophthalmus's bid for world dominion, and his defeat.

[4] The creation of a Roman Commonwealth embracing the whole of Central Italy. The half century that witnessed this Roman achievement saw the successive failure of a series of half-hearted attempts to re-establish in some form the Greek Great Power in Sicily and Southern Italy that had been a going concern in the days of the Deinomenidae (*dominabantur circa* 485–466 B.C.) and the Dionysii (*dominabantur* 405–344 B.C.). These abortive enterprises were the Corinthian 'honest broker' Timoleon's intervention in Sicily (344–339 B.C.); the Spartan King Archidamus's intervention in Southern Italy (342–338 B.C.); the Epirot King Alexander's intervention in Southern Italy (333–331 B.C.); the Spartan Prince Cleonymus's intervention in Southern Italy (303 B.C.); the career of the Thermaean adventurer Agathocles (*Syracusis dominabatur* 322–289 B.C.). These episodes have been noticed in III. iii.357,n.1, and in IV. iv. 589–91.

[5] 266–261, 'the Chremonidean War' between Macedon (rehabilitated since 276 B.C. by Antigonus Gonatas) and a coalition of the Ptolemaic Power and its Continental Greek satellites; 260–255, the war between the Ptolemaic Power and a coalition of the other two Levantine Great Powers, Macedon and the Seleucid Monarchy; 253–246/5, naval warfare between the Ptolemaic Power and Macedon; 246–241, the third war between the Ptolemaic and the Seleucid Power.

[6] The First Romano-Punic War.

[7] 133–111, the Gracchan agrarian revolution in Roman Italy; 132–130, Aristonicus's proletarian insurrection in the *gleichgeschaltet* principality of Pergamum.

[8] The second bout of Roman civil wars.

[9] This breathing-space was interrupted by the second revolt of the plantation-slaves in Sicily (104–100 B.C.). The Hellenic World was in almost continuous revolution from 133 to 31 B.C., and even the spells of relative quiescence were broken by eruptions.

[10] 224/3–222/1, the war in Continental European Greece between Sparta and a coalition of Macedon and the Achaean Confederacy; 221, the Seleucid King Antiochus III's first tentative attack on the barrier fortresses covering the Ptolemaic Empire's possessions in Coelē Syria.

[11] Hannibal's attack on, and conquest of, Saguntum.

[12] 220–217, the war in Continental European Greece between the Aetolian Confederacy and a coalition of Macedon and the Achaean Confederacy; 219–217, the fourth war between the Ptolemaic and the Seleucid Power; 218–201, the Hannibalic War; 215–205, the First Romano-Macedonian War; 202–198, the fifth war between the Ptolemaic and the Seleucid Power; 200–197, the Second Romano-Macedonian War; 191–189, the War between Rome and a coalition of the Aetolian Confederacy and the Seleucid Monarchy.

[13] The overthrow of Lysimachus by Seleucus Nícátōr.

[14] 280–272, the war in Southern Italy between Rome and a coalition of Tarentum and Epirus; 278–276, the war in Sicily between Carthage and Epirus.

[15] 171–168, the Third Romano-Macedonian War; 149–148, the Fourth Romano-Macedonian War; 149–146, the Third Romano-Punic War; 146, the Romano-Achaean War.

[16] The first bout of Roman civil wars.

[17] This general peace was interrupted by the insurrections of Spartacus in 73–71 B.C. and of Catiline in 63–62 B.C.

[18] The *Pax Romana*, under which the Hellenic World enjoyed political unity in a universal state constituted by the Roman Empire.

the Levant is also attested by the recuperation of the Hellenic Society during the breathing-space (*durabat* 241–220 B.C.) that followed; for these two decades saw the culmination of the Hellenic Civilization's first rally[1] since its breakdown in the Atheno-Peloponnesian War of 431–404 B.C.

Against the background of this false dawn the unprecedentedly severe lapse into atrocity which the onset of the Reduplicated General War of 220–189 B.C. brought with it was thrown into sinister relief. In an earlier context[2] we have already noticed that, when the proud and virile Macedonians first crossed swords with the war-scarred Romans in 200 B.C., the Macedonian high command felt it necessary to safeguard the *moral* of their magnificent troops against the shocking spectacle of the carnage inflicted by new weapons which the Romans had learnt to employ in the Romano-Carthaginian War of 218–201 B.C.; yet, during these crucial years, a relatively sensitive Macedonian King Philip V was bringing himself into odium through the inhumanity of his own style of war by contrast with the practice of Alexander's successors and their epigoni. At an abortive conference between the belligerents in the Second Romano-Macedonian War that was held in the winter of 198–197 B.C. in Malis on the eve of the campaign that was to result in a military decision at Cynoscephalae, the following indictment of Philip is reported to have been addressed to him to his face by an Aetolian spokesman, Alexander Isius:

Alexander complained that Philip was not making peace sincerely now and was not in the habit of making war honourably when war was the order of the day. . . . He abandoned any attempt to face his opponents in the field, but signalised his flight by burning and plundering the towns— a policy of avenging defeat by ruining the prizes of the victors. What an utter contrast to the standards observed by past wearers of a Macedonian crown! These sovereigns had fought one another continuously in the open country but had rarely destroyed and wrecked the towns. This was a fact of general knowledge, established by the war which Alexander the Great waged against Darius for the empire of Asia and again by the struggle of Alexander's successors over his inheritance, when they fought Antigonus for the possession of Asia in coalition. Moreover, the policy of the successors in the second generation, down to Pyrrhus, had been the same. They were ready enough to stake their fortunes in battle in the open country and they left nothing undone in their efforts to overcome one another by force of arms, but they used to spare the towns in order that the victors might enjoy the dominion over them and might receive due honours at the hands of their subjects. On the other hand, to destroy the objects of contention in the war while leaving the war itself still in train was the act of a madman and of one far gone in the malady; yet that was precisely what Philip was now doing.'[3]

By the turn of the third and second centuries B.C. there had indeed been an appalling deterioration, in the Levant as well as in the Western Mediterranean, in those standards of conduct in international relations that had prevailed in the Hellenic World during the preceding three or

---

[1] The symptoms of this rally have been surveyed in V. vi. 287–9.
[2] In II. ii. 163.   [3] Polybius: *Oecumenical History*, Book XVIII, chap. 3.

four generations. In the Reduplicated General War of 220–189 B.C. there was no reflorescence of the chivalry that had been shown on both sides during Demetrius Poliorcêtês' siege of Rhodes in 305–304 B.C. and that had afterwards been shown to Demetrius, after his final surrender in 285 B.C., by Seleucus Nicator; and, if in this post-Hannibalic chapter of Hellenic history there was nothing to compare with these earlier mitigations of the barbarity of War, *a fortiori* there was no counterpart of the social solidarity which, in the halcyon days of a delusively promising antecedent spell of peace, the Hellenic World had displayed when, in 227 B.C., kings, princes, and city-states had vied with one another in contributing to the relief of Rhodes after this ornament of a post-Alexandrine Hellenic World had been laid in ruins by an earthquake.[1]

A comparison of our two tables brings out the further fact that, in recurrences of cycles of War and Peace, inter-state wars and civil wars are equivalent to one another and are interchangeable. We have noticed already[2] that, in the Modern Western episode, a series of wars that came to be fought as inter-state wars between France, Spain, and other parochial states was inaugurated by a civil war between two branches of the French House of Valois. Conversely, in the post-Alexandrine Hellenic episode, a series of wars that was similarly inaugurated by a civil war between rival successors of the Macedonian Argead king Alexander the Great, and that then similarly passed over into inter-state wars between Egypt, Asia, Macedon, Rome, and Carthage, was not brought to an end by Rome's overthrow of the last surviving rival Power in 168 B.C., but ran on thereafter through a second cycle into a third cycle in the form of a succession of civil wars within the bosom of a now oecumenical Roman Commonwealth.

The War-and-Peace Cycle in post-Confucian Sinic History

If we now enlarge our field of historical vision by bringing into our synoptic view the episode of Sinic history traditionally known as the 'Period of the Contending States' (*Chan Kuo*), we shall detect correspondences between this post-Confucian chapter of Sinic history and both the post-Alexandrine chapter of Hellenic history and the Modern and post-Modern chapters of Western history—and this not only in the general features of the historical landscape but also in the particular structure of the successive war-and-peace cycles.

Like those other two series, this Sinic series of cycles was originally set in motion by a struggle for possession of the derelict heritage of a former Great Power in which there had been a breakdown of the central government. The heritages of Alexander the Great and of Charles the Bold, which had been the original apples of discord in the post-Alexandrine Hellenic and in the Modern Western episode, had their counterpart in the post-Confucian Sinic episode in the heritage of the state of Tsin,[3] which fell to pieces in the fifth century B.C. after having played a leading part in a previous chapter of Sinic history as one of two prin-

[1] See Polybius: *Oecumenical History*, Book V, chaps. 88–90.
[2] In the present volume on pp. 237–8, above.   [3] See V. vi. 293–4.

cipal competitors for the prize of hegemony in the Sinic World.[1] In the post-Confucian Sinic episode, again, the series of cycles had an overture in which the historically significant warfare took the form of civil war; and in the course of the first subsequent regular cycle the severity of the incidence of War upon Society was accentuated, in the Sinic World like-wise, by appalling increases in the effectiveness of weapons,[2] in the ruthlessness with which non-combatants, as well as defeated com-batants, were treated,[3] and in the magnitude of the political prizes of victory and penalties of defeat.[4] After it had exacerbated the evils of War to this intolerable degree, the Sinic episode was terminated, like the Hellenic, by the establishment of an oecumenical peace through the elimination of all the contending Powers except one single surviving victor.

A chronological analysis of this post-Confucian episode of Sinic his-tory reveals a series consisting of an overture and two subsequent cycles with respective wave-lengths of 78, 86, and 112 years.[5] In the overture the *Leitmotiv* was the break-up of the state of Tsin into three successor-states; in the first of the two ensuing cycles it was the abortive attempt of one of Tsin's three successor-states, Wei, to play the part of arch-aggressor Power; in the next cycle it was the assumption of the arch-aggressor's part by the state of Ts'in with such success that this cycle ended in the political unification of the Sinic World through the over-throw, by Ts'in, of all other Powers in the Sinic international arena.

In the overture (*currebat* 497[6]–419 B.C.) the most significant bouts of warfare took the form of civil wars.

[1] See IV. iv. 66 and V. vi. 292–3. Tsin's principal rival during this earlier chapter of Sinic history had been Ch'u.

[2] The adoption of the Eurasian Nomad military weapons, equipment, and tactics at the turn of the fourth and third centuries B.C. by Chao, a successor-state of Tsin which had inherited Tsin's wardenship of an anti-Nomad march, has been noticed in III. iii. 167, n. 1. This Sinic technical military innovation was the counterpart, in post-Con-fucian Sinic history, of the adoption of new weapons by the Romans during the Hanni-balic War and of the application to War of the new driving forces of Democracy and Industrialism in the Modern Western World in the seventh decade of the nineteenth century of the Christian Era (see IV. iv. 151–2). It is significant that the Sinic state that was the first to make this revolution in its military technique during the Sinic General War of 333–247 B.C. should also have been the state that, at a later stage of the same war, successfully repulsed the attacks of the state of Ts'in, which, by that time, had established its military ascendancy over all other Powers in the Sinic World. Chao's successful resistance to Ts'in's repeated attempts to conquer her during the years 270–258 B.C. caused this general war to end in an inconclusive peace and postponed the political unification of the Sinic World by force of Ts'in's arms for half a century (from 270 B.C. to 221 B.C.).

[3] See Franke, O.: *Geschichte des Chinesischen Reiches*, vol. i (Berlin and Leipzig 1930, de Gruyter), p. 194.

[4] See Maspéro, H.: *La Chine Antique* (Paris 1927, Boccard), pp. 390–1, quoted in V. vi. 295, for the observation that, during the post-Confucian paroxysm of a Sinic Time of Troubles, the contending states were fighting for existence, as distinct from the smaller stakes of independence or hegemony for which they had fought during the pre-Con-fucian paroxysm. Franke points out, however, in op. cit., vol. i, p. 178, that the con-ventional restriction of the term 'the Period of Contending States' to the post-Confucian paroxysm is an arbitary misnomer, considering that the murder of no less than 36 princes and the destruction of no less than 52 states between the years 722 and 481 B.C. is recorded by Confucius in his annals of that period of Sinic history. The post-Confucian series of war-and-peace cycles was the second of two paroxysms which, together, con-stitute the Sinic Time of Troubles. In previous contexts (in IV. iv. 65–66 and in V. vi. 292–5) we have dated the beginning of the Sinic Time of Troubles from the outbreak of the first great war between Tsin and Ch'u (*gerebatur* 634–628 B.C.).

[5] See Table III, opposite.

[6] This year, which saw the outbreak of the great civil war (*gerebatur* 497–490 B.C.) in

TABLE III. *Successive Occurrences of the War-and-Peace Cycle in post-Confucian Sinic History*

Phase	Overture (497–419 B.C.)[1]	First Cycle (419–333 B.C.)	Second Cycle (333–221 B.C.)
(i) Premonitory Wars (the Prelude)	..	..	..
(ii) The General War . . .	497–490	419–370	333–247
(iii) The Breathing Space . .	490–455	370–354	247–230
(iv) Supplementary Wars (the Epilogue)	455–453	354–340	230–221
(v) The General Peace . . .	453–419	340–333	221 B.C.–A.D. 184[2]

[1] These dates are reckoned in terms of the domestic history of the state of Ts'in. If we were reckoning in terms of the contemporary history of the state of Ch'u, we should have to date the beginning of the overture in 506 B.C. instead of dating it in 497 B.C., and the Time-span of the overture would then run to 87 years, as compared with the 86 years of the first regular cycle and the 112 years of the second regular cycle.

[2] The *Pax Sīnica* running from the establishment of a Sinic universal state by Ts'in She Hwang-ti to its dissolution in the last days of the Posterior Han.

During this overture a common tendency towards spontaneous disruption through the play of centrifugal domestic forces was at work in all the larger states of the Sinic World of the day. The anarchic effect of the institution of feudalism, which had previously made itself felt at the expense of a once oecumenical Chóu Power, and which had brought about the breakdown of the Sinic Civilization and the onset of a Sinic Time of Troubles before the close of the seventh century B.C., after the Chóu had become manifestly impotent to control their parochial vassals, was now making itself felt within the body politic of each of these parochial states that had been the beneficiaries of this centrifugal tendency in the preceding chapter of the story. The principal sufferers in the fifth century B.C. were the states that had exhausted themselves in the seventh and sixth centuries by taking leading parts in the competition for hegemony during that earlier paroxysm. Now, however, that it was the turn of the parochial states to undergo an ordeal which had already worsted the imperial Chóu, the local responses to this identical challenge were far from being uniform. The two parochial states which had played the most ambitious—and consequently the most exhausting—parts in the first paroxysm of the Sinic Time of Troubles (saeviebat 634–528 B.C.) were Tsin and Ch'u; and, after the failure first of Ch'u's final attempt to impose her hegemony by force of arms in the war of 538–528 B.C.[1] and then of Tsin's subsequent motion to deal a *coup de grâce* to Ch'u in 506 B.C.,[2] the authority of the central government was at a low ebb in both states. The sequels, however, were dramatically different in the two cases.

Ch'u's predicament was, to all appearances, by far the more serious of the two, for, whereas Tsin at this time was threatened only by domestic disruptive forces, Ch'u was the target of foreign attacks as well. In the very year, 506 B.C., in which Tsin found herself too feeble to strike, Ch'u was attacked and overrun by Wu—a *ci-devant* barbarian state in the Lower Yangtse Basin which had followed Ch'u's example in adopting the Sinic culture and turning to account the consequent potential enhancement of her military strength by intervening in the arena of Sinic power-politics. In this crisis in Ch'u's fortunes, Ch'u was saved by the recklessness of her parvenue adversary Wu and by the rise, in this adversary's rear, of another ambitious *ci-devant* barbarian state, the principality of Yüe in the country that was eventually to become the Chinese province of Chekiang. In 506 B.C. Yüe saved Ch'u from annihilation by attacking Wu from behind; and, though Wu subsequently took her revenge on Yüe by imposing her suzerainty upon her in 494 B.C.,[3] Wu was ruined by these successive triumphs over Ch'u and Yüe. They

---

the state of Tsin, marks the true beginning of the first war-and-peace cycle of the *Chan Kuo* period of Sinic history. Since this great civil war was the beginning of the break-up of Tsin, and since the break-up of Tsin was the historic event which set this new series of war-and-peace cycles in motion, 497 B.C. is manifestly a more significant date to take as marking the beginning of the *Chan Kuo* period than either 403 B.C., which saw the recognition *de jure* of a break-up of Tsin into three successor-states which by 403 B.C. had been an accomplished fact for half a century past, or 479 B.C., which is the traditional date for the death of Confucius (see V. vi. 294, with n. 3).

[1] See Maspéro, op. cit., pp. 348–51, and the present Study, V. vi. 293.
[2] See Maspéro, op. cit., pp. 352–3. [3] See ibid., p. 355.

tempted her to make a bid for hegemony; and, while she was engaged on an unsuccessful assault on Ts'i during the years 489–485 B.C.,[1] King Hui of Ch'u seized the opportunity to re-establish his kingdom on firm foundations between the years 488 and 481.[2] Thereafter, in 473, Ch'u was suddenly liberated from the menace of Wu through the destruction of Wu at a resurgent Yüe's hands. The combined effect of Ch'u's internal reconstruction during the years 488–481 B.C. and her liberation from external pressure in 473 B.C. was to enable Ch'u, not merely to survive, but to expand. Her success in meeting the challenge of internal disintegration which was being presented to all the major parochial states of the Sinic World in the fifth century B.C. was registered in her successive conquests of adjoining minor states in the central arena of the Sinic World. Ch'u annexed Ch'ên in 479 B.C., Ts'ai in 447 B.C., and K'i in 445 B.C.[3]

The effective reassertion of the central government's authority in the state of Ch'u in 388–381 B.C. had its counterpart in the state of Ts'i, which likewise survived an attack delivered by Wu and likewise overcame its disruptive domestic feudal forces—though in Ts'i's case at the price of an eventual change of dynasty in 379 B.C.[4] These triumphs over feudalism in Ts'i and Ch'u stand out in sharp contrast to the collapse of the central government's authority in the state of Tsin in 497–490 B.C. During those years Tsin was disrupted and devastated by a civil war between rival factions of feudal lords which the Crown was impotent to prevent. The outcome was the virtual partition of Tsin between the four feudal houses on the winning side; this partition was confirmed by the outcome of a supplementary civil war (*gerebatur* 455–453 B.C.)[5] in which one of the four nascent successor-states of Tsin was annihilated by a coalition between the other three. This partition of Tsin in 453 B.C. between the successor-states Chao, Wei, and Han *de facto* received recognition *de jure* in 403 B.C., and the royal house of Tsin was formally disestablished in 376 B.C., 130 years after its loss of effective power. This break-up of Tsin in the fifth century B.C. was an event of greater historical importance than the contemporary survival of Ch'u because it changed the politico-military configuration of the Sinic World and opened the way for the eventual triumph of Ts'in, Tsin's previously isolated and backward western neighbour.

This denouement of a post-Confucian Sinic drama, for which the ground had thus been prepared during the overture, was, however, delayed by an abortive but determined attempt on the part of Wei, one of the three successor-states of Tsin, to play, in the post-Confucian paroxysm of a Sinic Time of Troubles, the part that had been played in a pre-Confucian paroxysm by Tsin herself. Wei's bid for supremacy in the Sinic World was the *Leitmotiv* of the first regular war-and-peace cycle (*currebat* 419–333 B.C.) in the post-Confucian series.

In thus aspiring to a role to which Tsin had proved unequal, Wei was courting the disaster that eventually overtook her. The largest and strongest of the three successor-states of Tsin was not Wei, but Chao;

---

[1] See Maspéro, op. cit., p. 356.
[2] See Franke, op. cit., vol. i, p. 187.
[3] See ibid.
[4] See ibid., pp. 181–2.
[5] See ibid., p. 180; Maspéro, op. cit., p. 366.

and Chao had opportunities that were not open to either Wei or Han for extending her territory and improving her military technique, thanks to her geographical situation on the border between the Sinic World and the Great Eurasian Steppe.[1] By contrast, Wei had for her western neighbour not the Eurasian Nomad World but the potentially more formidable Sinic anti-Nomad march-state of Ts'in; and Wei's territory was not only smaller in the aggregate than Chao's; it was also divided into three geographically discontinuous fragments, one of which lay on the farther side of Chao's territory, and another on the farther side of Han's, while Han's metropolitan territory, which lay south of the Yellow River, was similarly insulated by both the territory of Wei and the remnant of the imperial patrimony of Chóu from a detached province, north of the river, which was wedged in between the territories of Wei and Chao.[2] This awkward geographical distribution of the former domain of Tsin condemned Wei to find herself perpetually at war with her two fellow successor-states in addition to the wars with other neighbours which she brought upon herself by her aggressive policy of expansion.

The general war (*gerebatur* 419–370 B.C.) with which this cycle opened consisted of a series of efforts on Wei's part to dominate her neighbours.[3] Wei's first move was to take advantage of the domestic troubles, common to all states in the Sinic World of the day, by which Wei's western neighbour Ts'in was paralysed during the years 415–384 B.C.[4] In the course of the years 419–409 B.C.[5] Wei reconquered from Ts'in a strategically important belt of territory inside the great loop of the Upper Yellow River which had been part of the original domain of Wei's parent state Tsin but had been conquered from Tsin by Ts'in during the pre-Confucian paroxysm of the Sinic Time of Troubles. This reconquest by Wei of 'the Country west of the River' (Ho-si) in 419–409 B.C. was followed up by a temporarily effective subjugation of Han; but in 386 B.C. Chao succeeded, with Ts'i's help, in resisting Wei's efforts to complete the reunification of Tsin's former domain by subjugating Chao likewise; and, though Wei inflicted defeats on Ts'i in 384, 380, and 378 B.C., and on Ch'u in 371 B.C., her bid for oecumenical supremacy was frustrated in 370 B.C. by the combined forces of Chao and Han after Han had doubled her area and resources in 375 B.C. by annexing her neighbour on the west, the state of Cheng.[6]

This negative outcome of the General War of 419–370 B.C. was confirmed by the outcome of the supplementary wars of 354–340 B.C.[7] This bout of warfare opened, significantly, with a campaign in which Wei lost to Ts'in part of the reconquered territory 'west of the River'. This reverse was the signal for a general attack on Wei; and, though Wei staved off her now inevitable fate by winning repeated victories against

[1] See Franke, op. cit., vol. i, pp. 180–1.
[2] See Maspéro, op. cit., pp. 369–70; Herrmann, A.: *Historical and Commercial Atlas of China* (Cambridge, Mass. 1935, Harvard University Press), p. 16; and xi, Map 26.
[3] See Maspéro, op. cit., pp. 392–3.   [4] See ibid., p. 377.
[5] See ibid., p. 392 and p. 369, n. 1.
[6] See ibid., op. cit., p. 369; Franke, op. cit., vol. i, p. 181.
[7] See Maspéro, op. cit., pp. 394–6.

heavy odds, she was eventually brought to the ground in 340 B.C. The most important result of this bout of supplementary wars in terms of the redistribution of territory was the permanent recapture from Wei by Ts'in of a portion of the long-disputed territory 'west of the River' which gave the hitherto mountain-locked 'Country within the Passes'[1] a sally-port into the great plain of the Lower Yellow River Basin; and this decisive shift of the frontier between Ts'in and Wei in Ts'in's favour was registered in changes of the sites of the capitals of the two states. In 350 B.C. the capital of Ts'in was moved eastward from its former location in the Middle Wei Valley to a point in the Lower Wei Valley, opposite the site of the future Si Ngan;[2] in 340 B.C. the capital of Wei was moved eastward from its now perilously exposed former location at Ngan-yi, which had been overrun by the Ts'in forces in 352 B.C., to the site of the future Kai-fêng.[3]

The second and last of the post-Confucian Sinic regular war-and-peace cycles (*currebat* 333–221 B.C.) saw the series brought to an end through the political unification of the whole Sinic World by force of Ts'in's arms. The opportunity for performing this feat was presented to Ts'in by Wei's failure to establish her supremacy during the preceding cycle. But Ts'in would not have been in a position to succeed in an enterprise in which Wei had thus failed if she had not previously fitted herself for the task by innovations in her military technique, administrative organization, and economic policy (above all, measures for increasing her agricultural productivity and, therewith, her man-power) which were more rational, more radical, and more ruthless than any contemporary reforms in any other existing Sinic state. This internal transformation of the state of Ts'in was carried out during the reigns of the princes Hien (*dominabatur* 384–361 B.C.) and his son Hiao (*dominabatur* 361–338 B.C.).[4] The moving spirit was Wei Yang (*alias* Kung-sun Yang, *alias* Shang Yang),[5] a cadet of the princely house of the ancient minor central state of Wei.[6] He had first taken service under the government of the state of the same name—one of the three successor-states of Tsin —which at this time had not only imposed its suzerainty upon Shang Yang's native state of Wei but was attempting to establish its supremacy over all other states in the Sinic World. After having rejected a previous overture from Ts'in, Shang Yang transferred his allegiance from Wei, the successor-state of Tsin, to Ts'in during the reign of Hiao; and, though the revolutionary character of his measures provoked opposition to which he succumbed after Hiao's death, he succeeded in permanently changing the face of Ts'in by carrying out enactments which could not have been repealed without bringing to a halt the aggressive military expansion that these drastic measures enabled Ts'in to achieve with

---

[1] For this expressive synonym for Ts'in, see VI. vii. 172, n. 3, and 173.
[2] See VI. vii. 211.   [3] See Franke, op. cit., vol. i, pp. 184–5.
[4] See ibid., pp. 183–5; Maspéro, op. cit., pp. 377–9; and the present Study, VI, vii. 351, 352, and 374.
[5] See *The Book of Lord Shang*, translated by Duyvendak, J. J. L. (London 1928, Probsthain).
[6] Not to be confused with the parvenue Wei that was one of the three fifth-century successor-states of Tsin. Though the two names are oral homonyms, they are conveyed visually in two different Sinic characters.

ever increasing success. Though the most conspicuous motif of the first post-Confucian Sinic regular war-and-peace cycle (*currebat* 419–333 B.C.) was the abortive attempt of Wei to win an oecumenical supremacy, the course of the succeeding cycle (*currebat* 333–321 B.C.) was to make it evident, in retrospect, that the most significant event in Sinic history during the first regular cycle had really been the internal reconstruction of Ts'in.

The great war (*gerebatur* 333–247 B.C.) that inaugurated the second of the post-Confucian Sinic regular war-and-peace cycles opened, like the great war in the first of the post-Alexandrine Hellenic cycles, with two contemporaneous but unrelated sets of hostilities in two different theatres, one in the Yellow River Basin and the other in the Yangtse Basin; and the action in 333 B.C. in the Yangtse Basin, which took one of those sensational turns that were characteristic of war and politics in these southern fringes of the Sinic World, must have seemed at the time to be by far the most significant public event of the year. In 333 B.C. Yüe attacked Ch'u and brought upon herself a crushing defeat which was the end of Yüe as a Great Power. The former territory of Wu, which Yüe had held since 473 B.C., was now annexed by Ch'u, while Yüe's home territory broke up into petty principalities which fell under Ch'u's suzerainty.[1] The sequel was to show, however, that this imposing apparent increase in the strength of Ch'u was of no avail against the scientifically developed strength which Ts'in was now putting forth in the Yellow River Basin.

The enhancement of Ts'in's strength through the reforms of Shang Yang had become sufficiently apparent already during the wars of 354–340 B.C. to evoke in 333 B.C. a collective security pact between the other six Great Powers in the Sinic World of the day—the three successor-states of Tsin, together with Ch'u, Ts'i, and Yen—in which the contracting parties undertook to come with one accord to the aid of any of their number who might be attacked by Ts'in.[2] The six thus admittedly threatened Powers continued, however, to fall out with one another, while Ts'in showed unfailing skill in fomenting their mutual antagonism and allaying their suspicions of Ts'in's own aggressive designs—even after these had been unmasked, time and again, in action which told its own tale for those who had eyes to see; and consequently, from the beginning of this second and last cycle of the series in 333 B.C. down to its close in 221 B.C., there was only one occasion on which Ts'in had to face the united forces of all six Powers in the field. Ts'in's policy, like Hitler's, was to take her intended victims 'one by one'; and, unlike Nazi Germany in a post-Modern Western World, Ts'in succeeded in carrying this transparently Machiavellian policy through to its long premeditated goal when in 221 B.C. she completed the forcible unification of the entire Sinic World under her own oecumenical rule.

---

[1] See Maspéro, op. cit., p. 400, with n. 1; Franke, op. cit., vol. i, pp. 188–9.

[2] The moving spirit was Su Ts'in, a professional statesman who retaliated by this diplomatic coup for the lack of appreciation of his abilities that had been shown by the government of his native state Ts'in. After having failed to find professional employment in Ts'in, Su Ts'in had been taken into the service of Yen and Chao (see Hirth, F.: *The Ancient History of China* (New York 1908, Columbia University Press), pp. 308–11).

Ts'in's first move in the Sinic General War of 333–247 B.C. was a campaign against Wei (*gerebatur* 332–328 B.C.) in which Ts'in, profiting by the vantage ground which she had won from Wei in the first campaign of the wars of 354–340 B.C., now conquered from Wei the rest of 'the Country west of the River' and other border districts into the bargain.[1] A counter-attack against Ts'in in 318 B.C. by the combined forces of all the other six Powers, reinforced by Eurasian Nomad mercenaries, resulted in the sanguinary defeat of the allies and the reduction of Wei and Han to the rank of impotent satellites of the victor Power;[2] and, after Ts'in had thus confirmed her hold on the passes opening eastward from the Wei Valley into the Lower Yellow River Basin,[3] she proceeded in 316 B.C. to anticipate Ch'u by seizing the command over the passes opening southward from the Wei Valley into the Upper Yangtse Basin and imposing her own suzerainty on the two contending local semi-barbarian states between which the vast and potentially productive territory that was eventually to become the Chinese province of Szechwan was at that time divided.[4] By 285 B.C. Ts'in's resources had been doubled by the thoroughgoing incorporation of this country into her body politic;[5] but Ts'in had not waited for this consummation in order to use the occupied territory as a jumping-off ground against Ch'u. In a series of offensives delivered in 312–311 B.C.,[6] in 302–292 B.C.,[7] and in 280–272 B.C.,[8] Ts'in annexed from Ch'u first the Han Valley and then the Middle Yangtse Basin, which was the homeland of the Ch'u Power. The capital city, Ying, fell in 278 B.C.[9] The first move in the last of these three campaigns was an encircling movement in which Ts'in 'mopped up' the barbarian no-man's-land beyond Ch'u's southwestern fringes.[10]

While Ts'in was thus wearing down Ch'u with her right hand, she still had strength to spare in her left hand to crush a coalition between Ts'i, Han, and Wei (*debellatum* 298–293 B.C.).[11] Ts'in made sweeping annexations in the heart of Wei between 286 B.C. and 275 B.C.[12]

Even now that Ts'in's ominous shadow had thus been cast right across the Sinic World, her prospective victims did not abstain from fighting one another to Ts'in's advantage. In 286 B.C. Wei, Ts'i, and Ch'u combined to partition Sung in revenge for conquests which Sung had made at the expense of all three allies in 318 B.C.[13] Thereafter, in 285–279 B.C., Ts'i was attacked and temporarily occupied by Yen with the support of Chao, Wei, Ch'u, and, of course, Ts'in,[14] who was the ultimate beneficiary from this fratricidal warfare through which the other surviving states were using up the last remnants of their strength.

Towards the close of the third decade of the third century B.C. it

[1] See Maspéro, op. cit., p. 398; Franke, op. cit., vol. i, p. 185.
[2] See Maspéro, op. cit., pp. 401–3; Franke, op. cit., vol. i, p. 186.
[3] See Maspéro, op. cit., p. 403.   [4] See Franke, op. cit., vol. i, p. 186.
[5] See ibid., p. 187.   [6] See Maspéro, op. cit., pp. 404–5.
[7] See ibid., pp. 410–11.   [8] See ibid., pp. 418–19.
[9] See ibid., p. 418; Franke, op. cit., vol. i, p. 194.   [10] See ibid., p. 194.
[11] See Hirth, op. cit., p. 318; Maspéro, op. cit., pp. 411–12.
[12] See Franke, op. cit., vol. i, p. 196.
[13] See Franke, ibid., p. 196; Maspéro, op. cit., p. 415; Hirth, op. cit., p. 319.
[14] See Franke, op. cit., vol. i, pp. 190 and 196; Maspéro, op. cit., pp. 415–18; Hirth, op. cit., p. 319.

looked as if an offensive which had been maintained by that time for some sixty years had now brought the arch-aggressor Power to within a stone's-throw of her goal of world conquest; but at this point Ts'in's career of aggression was checked, and thereafter the general war was brought to a conclusion just short of the decisive result that had now long since come to be eventually inevitable.

The principal cause of Ts'in's temporary frustration was the toughness of the state of Chao, which, like Ts'in herself, was a march-state of the Sinic World over against the Eurasian Nomad barbarians, and which had, as we have seen, been the first Sinic state to enhance her military efficiency by adopting the Nomads' armament and tactics. Though Ts'in had inflicted one defeat on Chao in 280 B.C.,[1] she suffered severe reverses when she returned to the attack in 270 B.C.[2] and again in 262–258 B.C.[3] The second cause of Ts'in's temporary discomfiture was the encouragement that Chao's spirited and effective self-defence gave to other threatened Powers. When, in 263 B.C., Ts'in had invaded the detached northern enclave of Han territory (the Shang-tang) in an interstice between the territories of Wei and Chao, and the central government of Han had proved impotent to defend this outlying province, the Shang-tang had offered its allegiance to Chao, and Chao had accepted this dangerous gift. This was Ts'in's *casus belli* against Chao in 262 B.C., and the first consequence was disastrous for both the protégés of Chao and their protectors. In 260 B.C. a strong force which Chao had thrown into the capital of the Shang-tang was compelled by a besieging Ts'in army to capitulate and was then massacred. In 258 B.C., however, when a Ts'in army laid siege to Han-tan, the capital of Chao itself, it failed to take this city and eventually suffered a disaster under its walls through the intervention of Wei on Chao's side.

Though Wei paid dearly thereafter for this audacity, Chao was saved, and the concerted diplomacy of four statesmen representing the states of Chao, Wei, Ts'i, and Ch'u[4] succeeded in dragging the war out to an inconclusive close in 247 B.C.[5] Their diplomacy was assisted—and this was the third cause of Ts'in's temporary discomfiture—by the falls of a statesman and a general who had been the joint authors of Ts'in's previous successes. The year 265 B.C. had seen the disgrace of the minister Wei Jan, who had been in charge of the government of Ts'in for the past thirty-one years.[6] The year 258 B.C. saw the suicide, by royal command, of Po K'i,[7] whom Wei Jan, upon his own accession to office, had appointed generalissimo of the Ts'in armies, and who had been the winner of Ts'in's subsequent military victories from the overthrow of the coalition in 293 B.C.[8] to the capture of the Shang-tang from Chao in 260 B.C. The offence that cost Po K'i his life was his refusal to

---

[1] See Hirth, op. cit., p. 319.
[2] See ibid.
[3] See Maspéro, op. cit., pp. 421–2; Hirth, op. cit., pp. 321–2.
[4] See Hirth, op. cit., pp. 321–2.
[5] See Maspéro, op. cit., p. 423.
[6] 296–265 B.C., according to Maspéro, op. cit., pp. 412–20. According to Hirth, op. cit., pp. 318–20, Wei Jan fell in 266 B.C. after having come into power in or after 298 B.C.
[7] See Maspéro, op. cit., p. 421; Hirth, op. cit., p. 322.
[8] See Hirth, op. cit., p. 318.

continue to serve under the unworthy successor of his former patron and partner Wei Jan.

This combination of circumstances postponed the date of the inevitable denouement; but, when, after a breathing-space of seventeen years (*currebat* 247–230 B.C.), Ts'in returned to the attack under the command of an implacable King Chêng (*accessit* 246 B.C.) who was to make himself the first emperor of a Sinic universal state under the title of Ts'in She Hwang-ti,[1] the bout of supplementary wars (*gerebantur* 230–221 B.C.)[2] was as dramatically short as the foregoing general war (*gerebatur* 333–247 B.C.) had been inordinately long.

Within these ten years 230–221 B.C. Ts'in destroyed and annexed all the six surviving other states, together with the surviving fragments of Yüe which had been under the suzerainty of Ch'u since 333 B.C.[3] Han, who was the first victim, submitted tamely to her extinction in 230 B.C., and of all the six, the only one to put up a strenuous resistance was Chao. The reduction of Chao cost Ts'in two years of hard fighting (*debellatum* 229–228 B.C.); and, even after the fall of the capital, Han-tan, in 228 B.C., an indomitable remnant of Chao's army withdrew northward into the highlands adjoining the border of the Eurasian Steppe, and set up there a refugee state Tai, as a remnant of Assyria's army had withdrawn to Harrān after the fall of Nineveh in 612 B.C. The year 226 B.C. saw the fall of Yen, save for its outlying north-eastern annex in Liao-tung, and the year 225 B.C. the fall of Wei. The subjugation of Ch'u, like that of Chao, required two campaigns (*gerebantur* 223–222 B.C.), in the second of which the Ts'in armies 'mopped up' the Yüe principalities as well as their suzerain. The same year 222 B.C. saw the destruction of the refugee remnants of Yen in Liao-tung and of Chao in Tai. In 221 B.C. the forcible political unification of the Sinic World at the hands of Ts'in was completed by the *Gleichschaltung* of Ts'i, which, after having passively watched its fellow victims being extinguished one by one, now submitted in its turn as tamely as Han had submitted in 230 B.C.[4]

A Synoptic View of the Currency of the War-and-Peace Cycle in the Histories of the Western, Hellenic, and Sinic Civilizations

If we plot out the series of war-and-peace cycles in Sinic history during the years 497–221 B.C. in the tabular form in which we have already presented the cycles in Hellenic history during the years 321 B.C.–31 B.C. and the cycles in Western history during the years A.D. 1494–1945, we shall observe a common pattern that is unmistakable; and this uniformity in the structure of three episodes in the mutually independent histories of three civilizations, of which the Western episode did not overlap

---

[1] The moving spirit in this last phase in the process of unification in the Sinic World was Ts'in She Hwang-ti's minister Li Sse (see Bodde, D.: *China's First Unifier* (Leiden 1938, Brill)).

[2] See Maspéro, op. cit., p. 424; Franke, op. cit., vol. i, pp. 198–9.

[3] See VI. vii. 167.

[4] After 221 B.C. the only Sinic parochial state that still retained a nominal independence as an enclave within the universal state established by Ts'in was the ancient central state Wei—the native state of the fourth-century statesman Shang Yang, whose revolutionary innovations in the state of Ts'in had been the secret of Ts'in's subsequent military and political achievements.

chronologically with either of the other two, while the Sinic and the Hellenic episode were out of step with one another to the extent of about 190 years,[1] suggests that the operation of a Balance of Power between rival parochial states is governed by its own particular 'laws of Nature' which reveal themselves regularly in different social milieux because they are inherent in a particular human predicament which has been these divers' societies common experience.

It would be open to us to extend our field of induction for ascertaining the purport of these particular 'laws' by taking further samples in addition to the three that we have now examined. Each of these three episodes is, indeed, a second chapter in a story whose first chapter we have left unanalysed. The continuity of the post-Confucian Sinic episode with a pre-Confucian chapter of the same story is manifest, since most of the dramatis personae in the two acts are identical, notwithstanding the change in both the cast itself and in the grouping of the actors on a gradually expanding stage that resulted from the break-up of the state of Tsin in the fifth century B.C. In the corresponding passages of Hellenic and Western history the continuity of the action is obscured at first sight in either case by a sweeping change in the cast and by a sudden and sensational increase in the size of the stage on which the tragedy is being played. Yet the post-Alexandrine Hellenic balance of power between Powers of a supra-city-state calibre was nevertheless historically continuous with a previous balance between city-states that had been in play from 478 to 338 B.C., and the latter-day Western balance, brought into play by the French invasion of Italy in A.D. 1494, was likewise historically continuous with a previous balance between Late Medieval city-states, or agglomerations of them, in Northern and Central Italy.

If we chose, we could proceed to analyse each of these earlier chapters in the three stories on the lines that we have now worked out. For example, we can discern that the pre-Alexandrine Hellenic balance of power was brought into play in 478 B.C. by the splitting of a Pan-Hellenic coalition which had been formed in 480 B.C. against the Achaemenian Empire, and that it was brought to an end in 338 B.C. by the formation of a new coalition against the same common adversary. Again, in the history of the pre-Confucian Sinic series of war-and-peace cycles, we can discern a cycle, running from 634 to 506 B.C., in which the *Leitmotiv* was an inconclusive struggle for hegemony between Ch'u and Tsin, and an overture to this cycle in which the decay of the oecumenical Chóu Power was giving ever larger opportunities for a number of local Powers to assert their independence and to enter into competition with one another. We can date the beginning of this overture from the

---

[1] Augustus's achievement of establishing a universal state in the Hellenic World in 31 B.C. had been anticipated in the Sinic World, 190 years earlier, by Ts'in She Hwang-ti's establishment of a universal state there in 221 B.C. Neither the post-Alexandrine nor any other episode in Hellenic history overlapped chronologically with any episode in Western history, since the Western Society sprang from the Hellenic Society's ruins, as the Hellenic, in its day, had sprung from the ruins of the Minoan. If we can trace the Western Civilization back to the close of the seventh century of the Christian Era, and the Hellenic back to the close of the twelfth century B.C., we shall reckon the 'interval' between them to have been of the chronological magnitude of about 1,800 years.

recognition by the Chóu Imperial Government in 680 B.C. of the hegemony with which the parochial state of Ts'i had been invested in 681
B.C. by four of the minor central states;[1] or, as an alternative initial date,
we can take the overrunning of the capital city of the Chóu by the
western barbarians in 771 B.C.[2]—a catastrophe which invited the Chóu
Power's parochial feudatories to assert *de facto* their independence of
a suzerain who had now flagrantly forfeited his claim to exercise his
authority over them by having shown himself incompetent to perform
any longer his oecumenical task of defending the common frontier of
the Sinic World against barbarian attacks. On a similar reckoning, the
beginning of the overture to the play of the Late Medieval balance of
power between Northern and Central Italian city-states could be dated
from the beginning of the process of political consolidation which reduced the number of states in Northern and Central Italy from seventy
or eighty to ten in the course of the fourteenth and fifteenth centuries
of the Christian Era,[3] while an alternative initial date for this episode of
Western history would be the death in A.D. 1250 of the Holy Roman
Emperor Frederick II—an event which had for its consequence the
reduction of the Holy Roman Empire to the condition of practical
impotence into which the Chóu Empire lapsed after the catastrophe of
771 B.C.

Our survey of war-and-peace cycles could, indeed, be carried far and
wide. In the Sumeric World, for example, there was a balance of power
between contending parochial states that was in play for centuries
before it was brought to an end by the establishment of a Sumeric
universal state in the shape of Ur-Engur's (*alias* Ur-Nammu's) Empire
of the Four Quarters, and in the Egyptiac World a twentieth-century
Western historian might guess, pending a recovery of the missing
records, that there must have been a similar prelude to Narmer's establishment of a United Kingdom.[4] Nor need we confine our investigations
to struggles in which the parties are contending states and in which the
denouement is the elimination of all the competitors save for the one
surviving victor Power whose victory converts her from a parochial state
into an oecumenical empire.

In examining the history of a post-Alexandrine Hellenic Balance of
Power, we have observed already[5] that, in the last two cycles of this
series, the bouts of warfare took the form of civil war and social revolution in place of the international warfare between parochial sovereign
states through which the same current of violence had discharged itself
before that vent had been stopped by the elimination, in the course of
the preceding cycle, of all the Great Powers of a post-Alexandrine
Hellenic World except Rome. We may now go on to remind ourselves
that this alternating rhythm of bouts of war and spells of peace did not
cease to manifest itself in the Hellenic World after the inauguration of
a *Pax Augusta* in 31 B.C., any more than it had ceased after the assertion
of Rome's oecumenical supremacy in the Reduplicated General War of

---

[1] See Maspéro, op. cit., pp. 299–300.
[2] See ibid., pp. 63–64; Hirth, op. cit., pp. 176–7.
[3] See III. iii. 355.   [4] See p. 687, below.   [5] See p. 271, above.

220–189 B.C. and the confirmation of this result in the supplementary wars of 171–146 B.C. In the forms of civil war, social revolution, and barbarian invasion, the rhythmic bouts of disorder continued to recur throughout the history of an Hellenic universal state which Augustus had founded and which Diocletian afterwards rehabilitated, until the onset of a final bout of such severity that this time the moribund society was unable to rally its depleted vital forces. There was the eruption of A.D. 66–70; the convulsion, ending with the accession of Diocletian in A.D. 284, whose beginning may be dated from the assassination of Alexander Severus in A.D. 235 or indeed from the death of Marcus Aurelius in A.D. 180; and the recurrent convulsion of A.D. 376–394, which proved fatal to the Empire in the West and which was followed in the Centre and the East by a likewise fatal seizure after Justinian's death in A.D. 565.

We could go on to analyse on the same lines the histories of other universal states that we have identified in this Study, and, besides taking account of social revolutions, civil wars, and barbarian invasions, we could also bring into our panorama the warfare with neighbouring Powers representing alien civilizations. The Roman Empire, for example, served from 64 B.C. to A.D. 632 as the warden of a post-Alexandrine Hellenic World's marches over against a resurgent Syriac Power clothed in the successive forms of the Arsacid and the Sasanid Empire;[1] and an Ottoman Empire which had provided the main body of Orthodox Christendom with an alien universal state found itself recurrently at war with Hungary and Hungary's successor the Hapsburg Monarchy in the Danube Basin, with Venice and with Spain in the Mediterranean, and with the Safawī Power in South-West Asia.

Our purpose, however, is, not to make an exhaustive survey of war-and-peace cycles, but to carry our investigation far enough to assemble adequate evidence for judging whether there is, or is not, any uniform common rhythm discernible in different series of such cycles that are sufficiently remote from one another in date and location to be reasonably regarded as being mutually independent; and for this positive purpose a wider expansion of our field of vision might be less illuminating than a closer comparative view of the three series that we have now examined in some detail. We may therefore conclude the present chapter by juxtaposing our three series with an eye to ascertaining whether the likeness between them, which we have already observed, is no more than a similarity in their general structure, or whether it extends to a chronological correspondence between the lengths of the Time-spans of the alternating bouts of warfare and spells of peace out of which this more or less uniform structure is built up in all three episodes.

The accompanying table[2] sets out, side by side, the data presented separately in the three preceding tables displaying successive occurrences of the war-and-peace cycle in Modern and post-Modern Western history, in post-Alexandrine Hellenic history, and in post-Confucian Sinic history respectively. In each of the three triple columns of dates in Table IV, the dates in the column on the left are the historical dates of

---

[1] See I. i. 75.   [2] Table IV, opposite.

the major alternating transitions from bouts of war to spells of peace and vice versa, as these stand in the preceding table recording the particular series—Western, Hellenic, or Sinic, as the case may be—which this column reproduces. Dates of transitions from peace to war are printed in roman type, dates of transitions from war to peace in italics. The

TABLE IV. *A Synoptic Table of the Dates marking Turning-points from Bouts of War to Spells of Peace and vice versa in the Modern and post-Modern Western, the post-Alexandrine Hellenic, and the post-Confucian Sinic Series of War-and-Peace Cycles*[1]

Historical Western Dates	Transposed Corresponding Dates[2]		Historical Hellenic Dates	Transposed Corresponding Dates[2]		Historical Sinic Dates	Transposed Corresponding Dates[2]	
	Hellenic	*Sinic*		*Western*	*Sinic*		*Western*	*Hellenic*
A.D.			B.C.			B.C.		
1477[3]	(1479	)	321	(323	)	..	..	..
1482[4]	*(1484*	*)*	*[316]*[5]	*(318*	*)*		..	..
1494	(1485	1493)	[315][6]	(306	307)	497	(496	505)
[1503]	*(1499*	*1500)*	*301*	*(297*	*300)*	*490*	*(487*	*491)*
[1521]	(1518	)	282	(279	)	..	(	)
1525	*(1519*	*)*	*281*	*(275*	*)*		(	)
1536	(1534	1535)	266	(264	265)	455	(454	456)
1559	*(1559*	*1537*)*	*241*	*(241*	*263*)*	*453*	*(431**	*431*)*
1568	(1580*	1571)	220	(232*	229)	419	(422	410)
1609	*(1611*	*1620*)*	*189*	*(191*	*180)*	*370*	*(381**	*379)*
1618	(1629*	1636*)	171	(182*	164)	354	(372*	361)
1648	*(1654*	*1650)*	*146*	*(152*	*150)*	*340*	*(342*	*336)*
1672	(1667	1657*)	133	(128	143)	333	(318*	323)
[1697]	*(1689*	*)*	*111*	*(103*	*)*		(	)
[1702]	(1709	)	90	(98	)	..	(	)
1713	*(1720*	*1743*)*	*80*	*(87*	*57*)*	*247*	*(277**	*270*)*
1733	(1751*	1760*)	49	(67*	40)	230	(257*	239)
1763	*(1769*	*1769)*	*31*	*(37*	*31)*	*221*	*(227*	*221)*

[1] Dates of turning-points from peace to war are printed in roman type, dates of turning-points from war to peace in italics. Dates enclosed in square brackets are those of minor turning-points.

[2] A transposed date is marked with an asterisk when it falls more than ten years wide of the corresponding historical date with which it is being brought into comparison.

[3] Date of the outbreak of war over the inheritance of the Burgundian Valois Duke Charles the Bold.

[4] Date of the peace-settlement partitioning the inheritance of Charles the Bold between the French Crown and the Burgundian Valois-Hapsburgs.

[5] Date of the liquidation of Eumenes.

[6] Date of the formation of the coalition against Antigonus Monophthalmus.

dates between square brackets in these left-hand columns are those of minor transitions which, in the tables, are identified in footnotes. The pair of dates between round brackets by which each of the dates in the left-hand columns is accompanied are transpositions of the corresponding dates in each of the other two series into terms of the historical series represented by the dates on the left hand of each triple column. An Hellenic date is transposed into a Western date by the addition of 1,800 years, and into a Sinic date by the subtraction of 190 years, on the reckoning that the Western Civilization emerged about 1,800 years later than the Hellenic (i.e. *circa* A.D. 675 as against *circa* 1125 B.C.) and that the Sinic episode resulted in the establishment of a universal state 190 years earlier than the date of the corresponding denouement in the Hellenic episode (i.e. in 221 B.C. as against 31 B.C.). On the same reckoning, a Western date is transposed into an Hellenic by the subtraction of 1,800, and into a Sinic by the subtraction of 1,990 years; a Sinic date into an Hellenic by the addition of 190 years, and into a Western by the addition of 1,990 years.

Transposed dates, calculated in accordance with these scales, which fall more than ten years wide of the corresponding historical date in the series with which they are being brought into comparison, are marked with an asterisk; and it will be seen that, out of 84 transposed dates within the round brackets in our table, 22 fall outside, and 62 inside, this range of chronological proximity to the historical dates of which they are the equivalents. It will also be seen that, while the conspicuous 'misses' thus amount to something more than 25 per cent. of the total number of 'shots', and the approximate 'hits' to something less than 75 per cent., the comparison between the three series which reveals this surprising degree of coincidence[1] is simply a comparison of turning-points marking alternations between bouts of war and spells of peace. As soon as we introduce the distinctions that we have drawn between 'general wars' and 'supplementary wars' and between 'breathing spaces' and spells of 'general peace', we shall see that, as often as not, the correspondences apparent in the present table do not extend to these qualitative differences between bouts and spells of different characters. For example, the chronological correspondence between the Western bout of war running from A.D. 1536 to A.D. 1559 and the Hellenic bout of war running from 266 B.C. to 241 B.C. is very close; but, whereas the Hellenic bout in question ranks as 'a general war' in our analysis, the corresponding Western bout ranks as a set of supplementary wars. Moreover, in several cases, a major turning-point in one series has for its counterpart in one of the two other series a turning-point that is merely a minor one.

Our table does, on the other hand, enable us to calculate the average Time-span of the intervals between turning-points marking major transitions from spells of peace to bouts of war and vice versa. In our confrontation of the Western and the Hellenic series, apart from the Sinic, there are thirteen of these intervals within a total Time-span amounting to 286 years (A.D. 1477–1763) in the Western series, and fifteen of them within a total Time-span amounting to 290 years (321 B.C.– 31 B.C.) in the Hellenic series. A division of the average length of these two Time-spans, which works out at 288 years, by the average of the two numbers of intervals, which works out at fourteen, gives us an

---

[1] The writer must confess that he was surprised to find this degree of chronological correspondence between the three series of dates—the more so because his conscience did not convict him of having procured 'a pre-established harmony' by any designing manipulation of the figures when he was compiling the three tables out of which the present table has been composed. The tables of war-and-peace cycles in Modern and post-Modern Western history and in post-Alexandrine Hellenic history were compiled by him in A.D. 1929; the table of war-and-peace cycles in post-Confucian Sinic history in A.D. 1950; and it was not till after he had compiled this third table that he thought of bringing the three tables together into a synoptic view.

average interval of 20·57 years between turning-points, and an average wave-length of 41·14 years between successive turning-points in one or other of the two directions either from peace to war or from war to peace. In our confrontation of all three series, there are eleven intervals between turning-points marking major transitions within a total Time-span of 269 years (A.D. 1494–1763) in the Western series and of 276 years (497 B.C.–221 B.C.) in the Sinic, while in the Hellenic series there are fifteen intervals between turning-points marking major transitions within a total Time-span of 284 years (315 B.C.–31 B.C.). A division of the average length of these three Time-spans, which works out at just over 276 years, by the average of the three numbers of intervals, which works out at twelve and one third, gives us an average interval of 22·38 years between turning-points and an average wave-length of 44·76 years between successive turning-points in the same direction.

These average figures are perhaps not of any great significance, considering that, in our analysis of the Western series of war-and-peace cycles, we have found that the overture was on a very much shorter Time-scale than any of the ensuing regular cycles, and also that, in the course of these, there was a tendency for the bouts of war to become shorter and the spells of peace longer. The approximate correspondence in wave-length between these regular Western war-and-peace cycles and the contemporary Western 'long' business cycles[1] may well prove more illuminating.[2] The total Time-span of these three cycles amounted to 346 years (A.D. 1568–1914), and within this period there were twelve intervals between major turning-points. The average length of an interval between turning-points in these three regular Western war-and-peace cycles was thus 28·83 years, while the average wave-length between successive turning-points in the same direction, either from peace to war or from war to peace, was 57·66 years. It will be seen that these two Time-spans are respectively of about the same order of magnitude as the twenty-two-to-twenty-five-years-long 'Rostow-Spiethoff' phases of alternating economic booms and depressions and as the 'Kondratieff' economic cycles with a wave-length of something between forty and sixty years.

2. The Disintegrations and Growths of Societies

'Laws of Nature' in the Disintegrations of Civilizations

In our foregoing investigation of war-and-peace cycles in three episodes occurring in the histories of three different civilizations, we have found indications suggesting that these rhythmical fluctuations were, in each episode, the products of a tension between two conflicting tendencies. A tendency to keep the balance perpetually in play by taking action to right it whenever it was in danger of being overturned was in each case countered, and eventually overcome, by a tendency for the recurrent wars through which a disturbed equilibrium was periodically readjusted to become progressively more severe in their incidence on Society until a point was reached at which the 'temperate and undecisive contests',

---

[1] See pp. 230–2, above.   [2] See p. 322, below.

which once, perhaps, had more or less satisfactorily fulfilled their regu-
lative purpose, came to defeat the intentions of statesmanship by escaping from its control and rankling into enormities which were bound,
sooner or later, to liquidate themselves either by destroying the society
on which they had come to prey or alternatively by moving a society
whose life was now at stake to terminate this series of ever more destructive wars between parochial states by allowing all the contending
pieces but one to be swept off the board.

   The self-amortization of a cyclic rhythm which thus proves to be the
dominant tendency in struggles for existence between parochial states
has previously come to our notice in our study of the disintegrations of
civilizations; and it is not surprising that there should be this visible
affinity between the respective rhythms of two historical processes that
are manifestly bound up with one another. Our study[1] of the breakdowns in which the disintegrations of civilizations have originated has
shown us that a frequent occasion, symptom, and even veritable cause of
breakdown has been the outbreak of a war between parochial states in
which a perennial evil that has previously been kept under control and
been practised with moderation now disconcertingly lights up, in one of
its periodical recurrences, to a degree of intensity that is so unprecedentedly severe as to constitute a deadly danger to the society's survival.
In the pre-Alexandrine chapter of Hellenic history, for example, the
Atheno-Peloponnesian 'reduplicated general war' of 431–404 B.C. was a
scourge of this unprecedentedly lethal kind, as contrasted with the relatively moderate warfare with one another in which the Athenian and the
Lacedaemonian faction in an Hellenic body politic had been indulging
down to that date since their split in 478 B.C. In the pre-Confucian chapter of Sinic history, similarly, the great war of 634–628 B.C., in which the
principal belligerents were Tsin and Ch'u, marked a corresponding climacteric crisis in a series of cycles of warfare between parochial states.

   In our examination of three series of this kind, we have also noticed[2]
that the replacement of a litter of contending parochial states by a single
oecumenical power is apt to be followed, not by an entire cessation of
recurrent outbreaks of anarchic violence, but by their translation from
the previous form of wars between parochial states into the alternative
form of civil wars and social disorders; and, if we thus find that the
establishment of a universal state does not inevitably bring to an end the
alternating rhythm of War and Peace generated by an antecedent Balance of Power between parochial states, it is more patently evident that
this achievement of constructive statesmanship, magnificent though it is,
does not avail to reverse, and so avert, a process of disintegration which
it temporarily arrests.

   We have observed[3] that—in the histories of civilizations down to the
time of writing—the disintegrations of civilizations, like the struggles for
existence between parochial states through which the breakdowns of
civilizations had been precipitated, had run their course in a series of
rhythmic fluctuations; and an empirical survey of ten examples—leaving

[1] In IV, *passim*, in vol. iv.   [2] On pp. 271 and 283, above.
[3] In V. vi. 278–321.

out of account a lost Minoan and an uncompleted Western record—has enabled us to ascertain[1] that the cyclic rhythm of Rout-and-Rally in which the dominant tendency towards disintegration has fought out its long battle with a resistance movement has been apt—apart from cases in which the domestic history of a society has been thrown out of its own course by the impact of an alien body social—to take a run of three-and-a-half beats—rout-rally-relapse-rally-relapse-rally-relapse—in accomplishing the historical journey from the breakdown of a civilization to its final unretrieved dissolution. The first rout throws the broken-down society into the first paroxysm of 'a Time of Troubles' which is relieved by the first rally, only to be followed by a second, and usually more violent, paroxysm that is brought on by a relapse. This relapse is followed, in its turn, by a second rally which is more robust and more durable than the first inasmuch as it manifests itself in the establishment of a universal state; and, when a further relapse eventually supervenes nevertheless, the universal state manages to stage a recovery. This third rally, however, is the last that the disintegrating Civilization finds the strength to make. When, thereafter, the universal state is smitten by a second paralytic stroke, this is the end, not only of this oecumenical body politic, but also of the body social whose life the universal state has prolonged by incapsulating it in a carapace.

It will be seen that the drama of Social Disintegration has—to judge from performances up to date—a more precise and regular plot than the drama of the Balance of Power. In this drama of Disintegration the number of the acts seems to be normally three-and-a-half. We may now go on to observe that the regularity of the structure of the plot of this play is matched by a uniformity in the length of the time that this plot takes to work itself out. If we study our table of universal states,[2] we shall find that—in cases in which the course of events is not disturbed by the impact of alien bodies social—a span of some four hundred years is apt to be occupied by the movement of rout, rally, relapse, and more effective rally running from the initial breakdown of the civilization to the termination of its Time of Troubles through the establishment of its universal state, and a further span of about the same length—some four hundred years again—by the ensuing movement of recurrent relapse, last rally, and final unretrieved relapse running from the establishment of the universal state to its dissolution. The standard Time-spans both of Times of Troubles and of universal states would thus appear to be of the order of four centuries each;[3] but a universal state is apt to die hard, even after it has been overtaken by the deadly second stroke. A Roman Empire which went to pieces in the socially backward western provinces on the morrow of the catastrophe at Adrianople in A.D. 378 did not go

---

[1] See ibid., especially pp. 278–87.
[2] Printed in vol. vi, on p. 327, and reproduced in vol. vii, as Table I, on p. 769.
[3] Ibn Khaldūn, whose survey of universal states was limited in range to the special class of empires founded by Nomads (see III. iii. 475), reckons the standard duration of an empire at *circa* 120 years, i.e. at a Time-span running to three generations of 40 years each (see his *Muqaddamāt*, French translation by de Slane, Baron McG. (Paris 1863–8, Imprimerie Impériale, 3 vols.), vol. i, pp. 348–50). This number of generations is, in truth, the normal term for Nomad empires *in partibus agricolarum* (see the present Study, III. iii. 24–25).

L

the same way in the central and eastern provinces until after the death of Justinian in A.D. 565. Similarly, a Han Empire which had met with its second stroke in A.D. 184, and which broke up thereafter into 'the Three Kingdoms', managed to reconstitute itself for a moment in the empire of the United Tsin (*imperabat* A.D. 280–317) before going into its final dissolution in the fourth century of the Christian Era.

In cases in which the dissolution of a broken-down civilization has been followed by the emergence of an affiliated civilization there has usually been an interval of some three hundred years between the date of the declining civilization's last, and fatal, stroke and the earliest date at which the rising civilization becomes visible above the historical horizon. Considering that this intervening chronological interregnum is apt to be filled to some extent by a 'die-hard' epilogue to the history of the moribund antecedent civilization's universal state,[1] we have to reckon that the process of disintegration may exceed its minimum Time-span of some eight hundred years, running from the initial breakdown of the society itself to the second breakdown of its universal state, by trespassing on a subsequent interregnum which gives scope for an epilogue of any length up to a limit of three hundred years. The maximum Time-span of the disintegration process thus turns out to be of the order, not of eight centuries, but of eleven.

Within the minimum Time-span of eight hundred years, the six intervals between turning-points, into which the three complete cycles of Rout-and-Rally can be analysed, fall into two groups, consisting of three intervals each, which are of approximately equal aggregate length. The first run of four centuries, constituting the Time of Troubles, is occupied by a down-swing between the original rout and the first rally, an up-swing between the first rally and the ensuing relapse, and a down-swing between this relapse and the second rally. This second rally, which occurs at the half-way point on the eight-hundred-years-long total course, brings with it the establishment of the universal state, and the second batch of four centuries, during which a *pax oecumenica* prevails, is occupied by an up-swing between the second rally and a further relapse, a down-swing between this further relapse and a final rally, and an up-swing between this final rally and a final unretrieved relapse in which the fabric of a long-since-disintegrating society now dissolves in a social interregnum. While either group of three intervals between turning-points is thus apt to occupy a span of four centuries in the aggregate, there is no indication in the historical evidence of any corresponding tendency, within each of these four-hundred-years-long spans, for the three intervals occupying it to be uniform with one another in their length. On the contrary, it looks as if the chronological articulation of these intervals within any four-hundred-years-long span were highly elastic; for in any one example of the series they are apt to differ from one another in duration, and these differences in their duration which thus present themselves within the history of each disintegrating civilization also seem to differ, from case to case, in the ratio in which they stand to one another. There does not seem to be any uniform ratio be-

[1] See V. vi. 210–13.

tween the different lengths of the successive intervals that is common to all the divers examples of this series of intervals in the histories of different civilizations.

'Laws of Nature' in the Growths of Civilizations

When we turn our attention from Social Disintegration to Social Growth, we shall recollect our finding, at a previous stage of this Study,[1] that Growth, as well as Disintegration, exhibits a cyclically rhythmic movement. Growth takes place whenever a challenge evokes a successful response that, in turn, evokes a fresh challenge that is not identical with the preceding challenge by which the creatively provocative response has been elicited. We have not found any intrinsic reason why this process should not repeat itself *ad infinitum*, even though a majority of the civilizations that had come to birth down to the time of writing might have failed, as a matter of historical fact, to maintain their growth by managing, for more than a small number of times in succession, to make a response that had been both an effective answer to the challenge that had called it forth and at the same time a fruitful mother of a new challenge demanding a new response.

We have seen, for example,[2] that in the history of the Hellenic Civilization the initial challenge of an anarchic barbarism, which was the legacy of the break-up of an antecedent Minoan Civilization's universal state, evoked an effective response in the shape of a new political institution, the city-state, which was perhaps created by ship's companies of refugees who were cast up upon the eastern shores of the Aegean Sea in the course of a post-Minoan interregnum (*durabat circa* 1425–1125 B.C.); and we have noticed in the same context that the very success of this response to a challenge on the political plane evoked, in its turn, a fresh challenge, this time on the economic plane, in the shape of the rising pressure of a population whose natural increase was now no longer being kept in check by battle, murder, and sudden death as drastically as it had been before the return of law and order accompanying the rise of city-states.

This challenge presented to the Hellenes by the pressure of population upon the means of subsistence, in a physical environment in which Nature set rigid limits to the increase of agricultural production, evoked, as we have seen, a number of alternative responses of unequal efficacy. There was the disastrous Spartan response of conquering the fields of the Spartans' Messenian next-door-neighbours within their common Hellenic homeland; there was the temporarily effective Corinthian and Chalcidian response of winning new fields for Hellenes to plough overseas in lands wrested from more backward peoples in the Western Basin of the Mediterranean; and there was the permanently effective Athenian response of increasing the aggregate productivity of this enlarged Hellenic World—after its geographical expansion had been brought to a halt by the concerted resistance of Phoenician and Tyrrhenian competitors[3]—

[1] In III. iii. 119–27.
[2] Ibid., pp. 120–2. See also I. i. 24–26; II. ii. 36–49; and III. iii. 139–40 and 197–8.
[3] See I. i. 24–25; II. ii. 38–42; III. iii. 122; and IX. viii. 436.

through an economic revolution in which an undifferentiated economic régime of subsistence farming was replaced by a differentiated régime of cash-crop farming and industrial production for export in exchange for imports of staple foods and raw materials.

This successful Hellenic response to the economic challenge of a rising pressure of population evoked, as we have also seen, a further challenge on the political plane;[1] for a now economically interdependent Hellenic World required a political régime of law and order on an oecumenical scale; the existing régime of parochial city-state dispensations, which had fostered the rise of an autarkic agricultural economy in each isolated patch of plain in an original Hellas round the shores of the Aegean and thereafter also in a Magna Graecia in the Western Mediterranean, no longer provided an adequate political structure for an Hellenic Society whose economic structure had now come to be unitary. This third challenge in Hellenic history—the challenge to transcend the city-state and to create a polity of oecumenical dimensions—was not met by the Hellenes in time to save the growth of the Hellenic Civilization from being cut short by a breakdown.

In the growth of the Western Civilization we can descry a concatenation of successive challenges evoking effective responses evoking new challenges which surpasses the Hellenic concatenation by running to as many as three completed links, as contrasted with the two which were all that a growing Hellenic Civilization succeeded in forging.

The initial challenge with which a nascent Western Society was confronted was the same challenge of an anarchic barbarism that had confronted a nascent Hellenic Society; the break-up of the Roman Empire and the break-up of 'the thalassocracy of Minos' bequeathed an identical legacy to their respective heirs; but the Franks' response to this identical challenge was not the same as the Hellenes'. Whereas the Hellenes had mastered anarchy by creating a parochial political institution in the shape of the city-state, the Franks mastered anarchy by creating an oecumenical ecclesiastical institution in the shape of the Hildebrandine Papacy;[2] and the meeting of an identical challenge along these different lines evoked a new challenge of a different character. A growing Western Civilization that had now achieved an oecumenical unity under the ecclesiastical aegis of the Papacy found itself in need of a politically and economically efficient parochial state; and this need was met by the resuscitation of the Hellenic institution of the city-state in a Medieval Western Italy and Flanders.[3]

These local materializations in the Western World of an Hellenic institution on its original miniature scale were not, however, more than a foretaste of the response which the Western Society had to make to the challenge that it was facing; for the late Medieval city-state cosmos[4] extending from Central and Northern Italy through Southern and Western Germany to Flanders did not embrace more than a fraction of the Western World of the day, and the city-state itself was not an institution that could be grafted, *tel quel*, on to the medieval feudal monarchies of

[1] See IV. iv. 206–14.   [2] See IV. iv. 512–32.
[3] See pp. 7–8, above.   [4] See III. iii. 299–300 and 341–8.

vastly larger geographical dimensions which were the typical parochial polities of the Western World taken as a whole. Accordingly, the locally effective response, in the shape of the resuscitation of the Hellenic city-state, which Italy and Flanders had made to the need for an efficient form of parochial polity, presented the rest of the Western World with a new challenge. Could the solution of the problem of creating efficient parochial organs of Western political and economic life, which had been attained in Italy and Flanders through the resuscitation of an Hellenic institution, be harvested for the Western World as a whole by translating this Italian and Flemish efficiency from the city-state to the nation-state scale?

This problem, in its turn, was solved, as we have seen, in England, first on the political plane through the successful injection of an Italianate efficiency into the Medieval Transalpine institution of parliamentary representative government,[1] and afterwards on the economic plane through the Industrial Revolution.[2] The Late Modern Western Industrial Revolution, however, like the Solonian Economic Revolution in Hellenic history, had the effect of replacing a parochial economic autarky by an oecumenical economic interdependence; and thus the Western Civilization found itself confronted, as a result of its successful response to a third challenge, with the same new challenge that had faced the Hellenic Civilization after its successful response to a second challenge in its history. Would a society that had now achieved economic interdependence on an oecumenical scale succeed in providing its unified body economic with the requisite unitary political framework? This challenge, which had been presented to the Hellenic Society before the close of the sixth century B.C. and had defeated it before the close of the fifth century B.C., had likewise been presented to the Western Society before the close of the eighteenth century of the Christian Era, when the eruption of Democracy and Industrialism had already threatened to put a demonic new driving force into the old institution of War. By the time of writing, mid-way through the twentieth century, this challenge had not yet been met by Western Man, but it had already become manifest to him that, if he were to be defeated by it, he would be unable to save his civilization from disaster.

These brief glances at the histories of the growths of the Western and the Hellenic Civilization suffice to show that there is no uniformity between them in respect of the number of the links in the concatenation of interlocking rounds of Challenge-and-Response through which social growth had been achieved in these two cases; and this negative conclusion would be neither confirmed nor impugned by an extension of our survey to the histories of other civilizations in their growth-stage; for, among these comparable cases, there was none in which the growth-stage itself had not been too brief, or in which a twentieth-century student's knowledge of the history of the society in this stage had not remained too scanty, to enable the historian to attempt an analysis even of the summary kind that we have just been making of this phase in the histories of the Western and Hellenic societies.

[1] See III. iii. 350–63.　　　　[2] See IV. iv. 167–73.

If there is thus no indication of there being any uniformity in the number of the chapters in the history of social growth as between one civilization and another, there is also no evidence of there being any standard length to which the Time-spans of the successive chapters conform.

If, with an eye to this latter point, we look once again at the history of the growth of the Western Civilization, it might appear, perhaps, at first glance, as if each of the interlocking rounds of Challenge-and-Response through which the process of growth had been achieved in this episode had had something like a regular wave-length running to approximately four hundred years. This was in fact the Time-interval between the date of the emergence in the Western World of the nation-state, round about the turn of the fifteenth and sixteenth centuries of the Christian Era, and the foregoing emergence of the Hildebrandine Papacy round about the turn of the eleventh and twelfth centuries; and this earlier landmark in the history of the Western Civilization's growth is likewise separated by an interval of about four hundred years from the date of the emergence of the Western Civilization itself round about the turn of the seventh and eighth centuries. This appearance of uniformity of wave-length as between successive rounds of Challenge-and-Response in the growth-phase of Western history is belied, however, by an ominous absence, round about the turn of the nineteenth and twentieth centuries, of anything resembling the emergence of an effective Western political organization on the oecumenical scale in response to the challenge presented to the Western Civilization by its own previous success in providing itself with an efficient parochial form of polity on the nation-state scale. If the growth-process were in truth not merely cyclic but also periodic in the sense of proceeding through cycles with a uniform wave-length, the Western Society's current problem of establishing some kind of oecumenical order on the political plane ought to have been visibly on the way to solution by the year A.D. 1952; and the Western Civilization's actual failure to solve this problem up to date must indicate either that the appearance of a uniform four-hundred-years-long wave-length in the growth-process was an illusion or else that, by A.D. 1952, the Western Civilization had broken down.

The former of these two possibly alternative, but not necessarily incompatible, inferences was borne out by the irregularity of the date at which the Medieval Western renaissance of the Hellenic city-state had occurred. So far from being separated in Time by an interval of anything of the order of four hundred years from the antecedent emergence of the Hildebrandine Papacy and from the subsequent emergence of the nation-state, the renaissance of the Hellenic city-state in the Western World followed hard at the heels of the epiphany of the Hildebrandine Papacy and was indeed one of its immediate incidental effects, considering that a temporary Balance of Power in the struggle between a waxing Papacy and a waning Holy Roman Empire was the constellation of forces that gave the Medieval Western city-states in an intervening no-man's-land in Northern and Central Italy their opportunity to raise their heads.[1]

Our reconnaissance of the history of the growth of the Western Civili-

[1] See III. iii. 345–6; IV. iv. 524; and p. 240, n. 2, above.

zation thus points to the negative conclusion that, in the process of social growth, the cyclic movement of Challenge-and-Response through which growth is achieved has no fixed uniform wave-length for the successive beats of the rhythm, any more than it has a fixed uniform number of beats beyond which the movement cannot go.

The upshot of our present inquiry therefore seems to be that the operation of 'laws of Nature' is as inconspicuous in the histories of the growths of Civilizations as it is conspicuous in the histories of their disintegrations; and in a later chapter we shall find grounds for thinking that this striking difference in appearances is not just an accidental and illusory effect of the fragmentariness of our information and the dullness of our understanding, but is inherent in an intrinsic difference in character between the growth-process and the disintegration-process themselves.

(d) 'THERE IS NO ARMOUR AGAINST FATE'[1]

In studying the operation of 'laws of Nature' in the histories of civilizations, we have found that the rhythm in which these laws reveal themselves is apt to be generated by a struggle between two tendencies of unequal strength. There is a dominant tendency at work which prevails in the long run against repeated—and, in the short run, repeatedly successful—counteracting moves in which the recalcitrant opposing tendency asserts itself. The struggle sets the pattern of the action; the persistence of the weaker tendency in refusing to resign itself to defeat accounts for the repetitions of the encounter in a series of successive cycles; the dominance of the stronger tendency makes itself felt by bringing the series to a close sooner or later, instead of letting it go on repeating itself *ad infinitum*, as, in theory, it might perhaps go on if the two forces at work were of exactly equal potency.

On these lines we have watched[2] struggles for existence between parochial states following—through three or four cycles of wars fought on one side for the overthrow, and on the other side for the maintenance, of a Balance of Power—a course that in each case eventually overturns the Balance and terminates the struggle by liquidating all the competitors except one, whose sole survival has the effect of replacing a bevy of contending states by a unitary oecumenical empire. We have likewise watched[3] the struggle between a broken-down society's tendency to disintegrate and an opposing effort to restore it to a lost state of health following, through three-and-a-half cycles of lapse and rally, a course that in each case eventually ends in a dissolution which is final inasmuch as, this time, the relapse is not even partially retrieved. In studying[4] the operation of 'laws of Nature' in the economic affairs of an Industrial Western Society we have found expert investigators of 'business cycles' surmising that these repetitive movements of divers wave-lengths might prove to be waves rippling the surface of waters that were, all the time, flowing in a current whose headway would eventually bring these rhythmical fluctuations to an end by dissipating the particular conjunction of

---

[1] Shirley, James: *Death the Leveller.* [2] On pp. 234–87, above.
[3] On pp. 287–91, above. [4] On pp. 223–34, above.

economic and social conditions—a system of free competition for earning profits reckoned in terms of money—in which the series of Late Modern and post-Modern Western 'business cycles' had taken its rise. In the same connexion we may remind ourselves of our finding[1] that, when and where a conflict between a disintegrating civilization and bands of recalcitrant barbarians beyond its pale had passed over from a war of movement into a stationary warfare along the *limes* of a universal state, the passage of Time had been apt to militate against the professional defenders of the *limes* to the advantage of its barbarian assailants, until in the end the sagging dam had burst and the gradually accumulated flood waters of Barbarism had descended in a sudden devastating spate on the domain of a society whose defence had become at last an intolerably heavy tax on its resources. We may further remind ourselves of our observation[2] of a tendency for the native bent of a civilization to reassert itself, sooner or later, against the deflecting effect of the renaissance of some incongruous element artificially resuscitated from the ossuary of a dead antecedent culture.

The foregoing observations are all illustrations of our more general finding[3] that cyclical movements in human history, like the physical revolutions of a cart-wheel, have a way of forwarding, through their own monotonously repetitive circular motion, another movement with a longer rhythm which, by contrast, can be seen to be a cumulative progress in one direction, even if we cannot be equally sure that this course has ever been set for it deliberately in execution of a plan. In each of the historical instances in which we have detected one of these finite series of cycles generated by a struggle between two tendencies of unequal strength, the stronger tendency of the two has been apt to bring the series to a close by eventually winning a decisive victory over its weaker opponent; but, of course, this denouement tells us no more about the winning tendency than that, in this particular episode, it has proved stronger than its opponent to a degree that has eventually availed to put an end to the unequal struggle. There is no warrant for interpreting these victories of one tendency over another *de facto Historiae* as victories *de jure Naturae*. Empirically observed matters of fact are not necessarily the outcomes of an inexorable fate; the *onus probandi* here lies with the determinist, not with the agnostic. The unwarranted assumption that the historical denouement whose historical occurrence has been recorded in retrospect must therefore have been predestined to occur, in the teeth of all possible variations in previous acts of the play, has been propounded as a *jeu d'esprit* in Lewis Carroll's fable of 'the time-machine';[4] but the English mathematician C. L. Dodgson left it to his German confrère Oswald Spengler to crystallize this airy conceit into the ponderous dogma under which a man of genius has perversely buried the brilliant findings of his intuitive insight. This undocumented Determinism is the bane of many passages of Spengler's work besides the one—already quoted in this study[5]—in which the Western culture's reassertion of its

---

[1] In VIII. viii. 16–44.   [2] On pp. 62–73, above.
[3] In IV. iv. 34–37.   [4] See V. vi. 214–15.
[5] Spengler, O.: *Der Untergang des Abendlandes*, vol. i (Munich 1920, Beck), p. 321, quoted on pp. 65–66, above.

native bent against a fifteenth-century Italian renaissance of Hellenic art and letters is delineated with what would be a fine sense of historical reality if only the philosopher-hierophant had been content to present his findings as the matters of fact which they are—without importing the *ex cathedrâ* judgement that they are also the fore-ordained acts of an ineluctable Destiny.

After thus taking warning from the spectacle of Spengler's self-stulti-fication against the error of reading the unproven operation of an hypothetical Destiny into secular tendencies in human affairs which have happened in the end to win decisive victories over a stubborn opposition, we may now proceed, without prejudice to a still open issue between Law and Freedom in History, to take note of certain other episodes in which some tendency has reasserted itself in the face of successive rebellions against it. Such resolutions of conflicting human forces, in which Spengler would see the hand of 'Fate', can be observed in the histories of the political fortunes of territories; in the histories of encounters between different civilizations; and in the histories of struggles between conflicting religious concepts, doctrines, and allegiances; and this rhythm is endemic in the history of Man, in which all those particular episodes are embraced.

There is a conspicuous rendering of this rhythm in the political history of North America since its incorporation into a Western World expanding overseas from a Western European nucleus.

The unitary physiography of North America, with its magnificent natural system of internal waterways providing means of through-communication from the delta of the Mississippi to the estuary of the St. Lawrence via the Great Lakes, manifestly gave this giant Northern Island of the Western Hemisphere a physical predisposition to become the unitary political dominion of some single one out of the litter of Modern West European national states that were in competition for the prizes of a Western Society's New World. The French pioneers of West European enterprise in North America were quick to perceive this geographical nisus towards political unity, and they went on to take deliberate and systematic steps to bring the whole of North America under the all-embracing rule of the French Crown by entrenching themselves at both extremities of the central waterway and establishing a chain of connecting links inland between these two maritime terminals.[1]

In the course of the hundred years ending in A.D. 1763 this grandly conceived and ambitiously initiated French enterprise was frustrated by two unforeseen developments to the disadvantage of France in her contest for the possession of North America with her rival Great Britain. In the first place the British colonies planted along the eastern seaboard outstripped French Canada and Louisiana in the growth of their population to an extent that more than made up for the handicap of a location —hemmed in between the Atlantic and the Appalachians—that was, in itself, much less favourable for expansion into the interior.[2] In the second place a French colonial population in North America that was now no

---

[1] See II. ii. 66–67. [2] See ibid.

match for the neighbouring British colonial population, if left to its own resources, was deprived of indispensable support from the mother country in Europe in the hour of need by the ascendancy that the British Navy had gained over the French. Through the combined and cumulative effect of these two shifts in the Balance of Power, the French Crown not only failed to achieve its ambition of bringing the whole of North America under its own rule, but actually lost all its holdings on North American soil in the Seven Years War. Yet the peace settlement of A.D. 1763, which ratified this outcome of a Franco-British war over North America that had been smouldering, off and on, for some seventy years in effect, appeared to have disappointed French ambitions without invalidating the geographico-political conception on which these had been based. In declaring against France's design to unite the whole of North America under the French flag, the course of Modern Western history up to date had apparently substantiated the French 'geopolitical' thesis that a unification under one flag or another was the political dispensation to which North America was predestined by her physiographical structure. The fortunes of war might now have decided that the unifying West European Power was to be, not France, but Great Britain; yet in A.D. 1763 this might have looked as if it were only a superficial modification of a course of political events which seemed still to be moving steadily towards a now more than ever apparently inevitable ultimate goal of unity.

Nevertheless, within not more than twenty years of the disappearance of the French flag from North America in A.D. 1763, the peace-settlement of A.D. 1783 was to indicate that the dominant tendency in this North American episode of Western history was, not the nisus towards political unification that was inherent in the giant island's physiography and that, in A.D. 1763, had been momentarily translated into an accomplished political fact, but an inclination to fall apart, in defiance of physiography, into two separate political domains on lines foreshadowed in the competitive plantation of English and French colonies on North American coasts in the seventeenth century of the Christian Era. The political map of North America after A.D. 1783 was, and remained, in its general pattern, the same map of a politically partitioned island that it had been before A.D. 1763, with the two originally separate political domains once again separate under interchanged flags,[1] whereas the map of a politically united North American island, which had been a political reality between A.D. 1763 and A.D. 1775, turned out to have been merely History's passing tribute to a Physiography whose political requirements History was evidently bent on defying. After having per-

---

[1] While the French flag had disappeared from North America and the United States flag had made its epiphany there, the British flag had kept a footing on the North American island by contriving to supplant the French flag in Canada before it was supplanted, in its turn, by the Stars and Stripes in the United States. An English traveller *en route* by rail from New York to Montreal in A.D. 1952 would have the historically pregnant experience, at the moment when his train crossed the border, of re-entering the dominions of the sovereign whose subject he was and at the same instant passing out of the domain of his own English mother tongue into eastern counties of the Province of Quebec in which the place-names might be English but the prevailing language was unquestionably French.

mitted the British flag to supplant the French flag at Quebec and Montreal, History promptly reasserted her ascendancy over Physiography by
seeing to it that the Stars and Stripes should replace the Union Jack
from New England to Georgia inclusive.

The new flag that History had thus introduced into the North American landscape to serve her own anti-unitarian caprice was never allowed
by her to defeat her intentions by achieving North America's physiographically manifest political destiny through any sly move behind
History's back. During the War of A.D. 1812–14, no less than during the
War of A.D. 1775–83, History kept a watchful eye open to make sure that
the United States of North America should not surreptitiously put
Canada into her pocket; and, in the course of the next hundred years
after the negotiation of the peace treaty of Ghent, Clio made sure that
the United States should continue to fulfil the North American designs
that this officious Muse had had in mind when she had called into being
the first Western sovereign independent national state to make its appearance on non-European ground; for, in the course of the nineteenth century, History led the people of the United States to lose all desire to
annex Canada at the very time when she was putting it into their power
to bring the whole of North America under the Stars and Stripes if they
had still had any lingering ambition to make a seventeenth-century
French dream come true.

This outcome of a tug-of-war in North America between two conflicting tendencies, making respectively for the political partition and
for the political unification of the island, is an interesting case because
the eventually frustrated nisus towards unity was favoured by physiographical forces which were as potent as they were obvious, whereas the
ultimately victorious inclination towards partition was History's 'dark
horse' in the field.

The 'fate' of North America to be partitioned into two separate political domains in spite of a physiographical structure which 'predestined'
this island to attain political unity has an historical parallel in the 'fate' of
the post-Diocletianic Roman Empire to lose possession of Italy, in the
teeth of the historical fact that Italy had been the base of operations from
which the Hellenic World had been knocked together into a universal
state by Roman arms.

In the course of the fifth century of the Christian Era a post-Diocletianic Roman Empire lost Italy *de facto* to a series of North European
barbarian war-lords—first to Ricimer (*dominabatur* A.D. 456–72), then
to Odovacer (*dominabatur* A.D. 476–93), and then to Theodoric (*dominabatur* A.D. 493–526)—and this was not surprising, considering that, in
the course of the thirty-seven years between A.D. 293, when Diocletian
had officially established his headquarters at Nicomedia, and A.D. 330,
when Constantine had celebrated the completion of his lay-out of a New
Rome on the Bosphorus,[1] the political capital of an Hellenic universal
state had already gravitated from an always eccentrically western location at Rome towards a borderline between the Central and the Oriental
provinces which had always been the locus of the Roman Empire's eco-

[1] See VI. vii. 217–18.

nomic centre of gravity. These facts were the politically pertinent facts when, in the fifth century, Italy slipped out of the Imperial Government's control; yet present political realities counted for less in determining the emotional reaction of Constantinople to the eclipse of the Imperial Government's authority in Italy in this age than the historic role once played by a Roman Italy in the creation of a Roman Empire in a past age which had long since become ancient history. The *de facto* sovereignty of barbarian war-lords in Italy was never recognized at Constantinople *de jure*; and the work of financial, economic, and military reconstruction, that a Constantinopolitan Imperial Government had gradually carried out during the fifth century in the Central and Oriental provinces,[1] had no sooner borne fruit in the accumulation of a reserve of public resources than this reserve was squandered by the sixth-century Constantinopolitan Emperor Justinian on the archaistic enterprise of re-subjugating Italy to the direct rule of a Roman Imperial Government.

This political objective was duly attained by Justinian at the cost of an eighteen-years-long war (*gerebatur* A.D. 535–53). But, within five years of the collapse of the last Gothic resistance to Roman arms on Italian soil in A.D. 563,[2] the laboriously reconquered Italian dominions of the Roman Imperial Crown were lost again to yet another war-band of barbarian invaders. The Lombard irruption into Italy, which broke upon her in A.D. 568, did not come to a standstill until it had robbed the Empire of the whole of Italy save for seven bridgeheads on the beaches[3] and a line of isolated inland fortresses,[4] strung along the road between Ravenna and Rome, which survived, like stepping-stones, amid an encompassing flood of Lombard invasion that had swirled round their walls on its torrential course from the Po Basin into the Abruzzi. This prompt resumption of the march of History in reply to Justinian's archaistically conceived counter-attack was even less surprising than the anticipation of a post-Justinianean Alboin's exploit by his pre-Justinianean forerunners Ricimer, Odovacer, and Theodoric; for Justinian's ephemeral conquest of Italy for a Constantinopolitan Roman Empire had been purchased at the threefold price of ruining the Empire's revenue-producing Oriental provinces, depopulating her military recruiting grounds in the Danubian provinces, and alienating the 'liberated' Italians by first devastating Italy in the act of exterminating the Ostrogoths and then wringing revenue out of her for the treasury of a Transadriatic Imperial Government to whose jurisdiction Italy had never been subject before her annexation to it by Justinian himself. In these circumstances it would have been a miracle if Justinian's conquest of Italy had had any enduring effect. The 'fate' of a post-Diocletianic Italy, unlike the 'fate' of a Modern North America, was, in fact, as clear as day from first to last, and even a

---

[1] See IV. iv. 324–6.

[2] The date of the capitulation of the Gothic garrisons of Brescia and Verona. The garrison of Compsae had capitulated in A.D. 555.

[3] The Exarchate of Ravenna, together with the adjoining Pentapolis; the Ager Romanus, together with the adjoining maritime city-state of Gaeta; the 'toe' and the 'heel' of Italy; and the three isolated maritime city-states Venice, Amalfi, and Naples.

[4] Of which Perugia was the most considerable.

Justinian could hardly have succeeded in remaining blind to it if he had not taken pains to reinforce a congenital myopia by putting on the blinkers of Archaism.

The 'fatality' of a post-Diocletianic Roman Empire's loss of Italy has its closest historical parallel in the loss of the Oriental provinces south of Taurus; for this loss, likewise, was no historical surprise. Though the Hellenic ascendancy in South-West Asia west of Euphrates was little less than a thousand years old by the time when, in the seventh century of the Christian Era, Arab *conquistadores* liquidated it almost as rapidly as Macedonian *conquistadores* had established it in the fourth century B.C., Hellenism had never succeeded south of Taurus—apart from a cluster of maritime Greek settlements on the Cilician Plain which had been planted in the pre-Alexandrine Age—in becoming anything more than an exotic alien culture, all but confined within the walls of a few Hellenic or Hellenized cities and only feebly radiating out from these into a still invincibly Syriac and Egyptiac agricultural countryside. Hellenism's capacity to achieve mass-conversions here had been put to the test by the Seleucid Hellenizer Antiochus IV Epiphanes (*regnabat* 175–163 B.C.) when he had set out to make Jerusalem as Hellenic as Antioch or Athens; and the resounding defeat of this cultural missionary enterprise had portended the ultimate total disappearance of the intrusive culture *in partibus Orientalium*. Indeed, the sporadic veneer of Hellenism which Epiphanes had so signally failed to transmute into solid timbers would have been stripped away before the opening of the Christian Era by Arab Nomad intruders from the Syrian Desert and Iranian Nomad intruders from Eurasia if Rome had not given Hellenism a further lease of life in South-West Asia and Egypt by stepping masterfully into the shoes of prematurely senile Seleucidae and Ptolemies. The wonder was that an anti-Hellenic resistance movement—which in Egypt had first gone into action as far back as the turn of the third and second centuries B.C.[1]—should not have found an effective retort to an Hellenic ascendancy earlier than the same fifth century of the Christian Era that saw Roman Italy fall under the dominion of barbarian war-lords.

The Hellenic ascendancy over the Syriac and Egyptiac societies had been imposed and maintained by force of arms; and, so long as the subjugated societies had reacted by replying in kind, they had been courting defeat. When the Jews and Egyptians had been encouraged by the success of their insurrections against the epigoni of their Macedonian conquerors to try conclusions with the Roman heirs of those *peritura regna*[2], they had found to their cost that this Roman second wave of Hellenic domination had a more formidable momentum than its Macedonian forerunner. The discomfiture of Epiphanes at the hands of the Maccabees had been avenged on a Palestinian Jewry by a Titus and a Hadrian; and thereafter, when the temporary breakdown of the *Pax Augusta* in the third century of the Christian Era had given a militant Oriental resistance movement a fresh opportunity for trying its fortune, Zenobia's successor-state of the Roman Empire had gone the way, not of Mu'āwīyah's

---

[1] See V. v. 68.
[2] Virgil: *Georgics*, Book II, l. 498.

some four hundred years later,[1] but of Samsigeramus's successor-state of the Seleucid Empire some three hundred years earlier. In the next chapter of the story after the overthrow of Zenobia by Aurelian, the mass-conversion of the population of the Oriental provinces to Christianity, which had been consummated during the pre-Diocletianic bout of anarchy, might have seemed at the moment to have done for Hellenism incidentally what Epiphanes had once tried to do for it deliberately without success; for in the Oriental provinces a triumphant Catholic Christian Church had captivated a subject native peasantry and an urban Hellenic 'ascendancy' alike; and, since Christianity had been making its triumphal progress in an Hellenic dress, it looked as if the Orientals had now at last inadvertently 'received', in association with Christianity, a Hellenism which they had so vehemently rejected when it had been offered to them unadulterated and undisguised. This conclusion was not belied by the first of the schisms that rent the Christian Church after the Imperial Government, *imperante Constantino*, had given the Church its countenance; for the strife between Athanasians and Arians was not a cultural conflict between Hellenes and Orientals but a family quarrel between two rival factions of philosophizing Alexandrian Greeks. The subsequent breach between Catholics and Nestorians did, on the other hand, split the population of the Oriental provinces on communal lines; and, in thus resuming the Oriental resistance movement against Hellenism in the form of a theological controversy within the bosom of the Christian Church, the Orientals had hit upon a new technique of cultural warfare which eventually prevailed over a Hellenism that had shown itself to be invincible so long as the Orientals had been content to fight it on ground of Hellenism's choosing, and not of theirs.[2]

The series of Oriental counter-attacks on Hellenism in the form of Christian theological movements that were branded as 'heresies' by a dominant minority of 'Melchites'[3] has come to our attention in divers contexts in this Study so many times already that in this place we may confine our observation of it to the point of noticing that this was one of those 'fateful' movements that advance towards an ultimate victory through successive defeats. When an Oriental resistance movement struck at Hellenism by way of a Nestorian Christian attack on a Catholic Christian Christology, an Hellenic Orthodoxy was still strong enough to be able to proscribe a Syriac Nestorianism within the frontiers of the Roman Empire—though not strong enough to prevent the banned Nestorians from finding a second home under a Sasanian political aegis, capturing the whole of the Christian community in the Sasanian dominions, and thereby winning for themselves the monopoly of a Christian mission-field extending overseas south-eastward into Southern India and overland north-eastward into Western China. When thereafter the same Oriental resistance movement struck a second stroke at Hellenism by way of a Monophysite Christian attack on a Catholic Christian

---

[1] The historical relation between Muʿāwīyah's and Zenobia's successor-states of the Roman Empire in the East has been noticed in I. i. 74, n. 4.

[2] See IX. viii. 413–14.

[3] This nickname for the Catholic Christians which was applied to them by the Monophysites was a Graecized form of a Syriac word signifying 'Imperialists'.

theology—thus making a Christology that was the antithesis of the Nestorian serve the self-same purpose as a weapon of cultural warfare— an Hellenic Orthodoxy this time failed to drive the anti-Hellenic insurrectionary movement beyond the frontiers and merely played into its hands by succeeding in driving it underground. Underground and on the run, the missionaries of Monophysitism won the allegiance, *en masse*, of the submerged Egyptiac and Syriac populations within the Roman Empire's borders, and they increased their following further by also winning the allegiance of the Armenians, who had been the first people in the World to adopt Christianity as their national religion.

These sweeping subterranean triumphs of a militantly anti-Hellenic Monophysitism unmasked an Hellenic 'ascendancy's' perennial weakness; for Hellenism had now come to be identified with an anti-Monophysite and anti-Nestorian Christian Orthodoxy, and it had become manifest that, within the bounds of the three Oriental Patriarchates of Alexandria, Jerusalem, and Antioch, 'the Melchites' were—as their invidious nickname indicated—no more than a dominant minority consisting of the sprinkling of Roman Imperial officials and soldiers stationed in these provinces, together with a handful of Hellenic townspeople and Hellenized landowners who looked to the Imperial authorities to maintain them in their position of privilege *vis-à-vis* a Monophysite Oriental peasantry. This native peasantry's overwhelming numerical preponderance over an intrusive Hellenic 'ascendancy' began to make its weight felt now that the people themselves were conscious of it thanks to their having acquired a Monophysite national church of their own to give them a heartening sense of solidarity, as well as an inspiring cause. Within thirty-one years of the breach between Orthodoxy and Monophysitism in A.D. 451, the Emperor Zeno had made public, in promulgating an 'Act of Theological Union' (*Henôtikon*) in A.D. 482, his conviction that the Imperial Government could no longer hope to retain its political hold over the economically indispensable Oriental provinces except at the price of theological appeasement; and, when the political exigencies of Justinian's vain enterprise of conquering Italy constrained this unstatesmanlike successor of Zeno's to abandon an appeasement of Monophysitism that was anathema to the Papacy, Justinian thereby consummated the alienation of his Oriental subjects without succeeding in his attempt to conciliate the Italians.

The moral secession of an Orthodox Christian Roman Empire's Monophysite Christian Oriental subjects now went with a run; in the Oriental provinces, as in Illyricum and Italy, the Constantinopolitan body politic had become a hollow shell by the date of Justinian's death (*decessit* A.D. 565); and there was no longer any prospect of its surviving the deluge which the archaist emperor had put in store for his own unhappy successors on the Imperial Throne. A shell that Khusrū II Parwīz so easily shattered and that Heraclius so painfully pieced together again would assuredly have fallen to pieces, past retrieving, thereafter, even if Monophysitism had been the last of the domestic Oriental heresies, and Khusrū's invasion the last of the foreign Oriental military assaults, to which the worm-eaten fabric of the Roman Imperial body politic had been exposed. In raising up a successor to Nestorius and Eutyches in the person of Muhammad, and in unleashing the Primitive Muslim Arab assailants of the Empire at the heels of their Zoroastrian Persian predecessors, History was giving herself unnecessary trouble for the sake of making assurance doubly sure.

A 'Fate' that condemned the Roman Empire to lose both Italy and its Oriental provinces irretrievably in the end, in spite of the Imperial Government's obstinately repeated attempts to halt and reverse the remorseless march of History, asserted its power over the Achaemenian and Mauryan empires by the contrary move of constraining them to re-establish themselves sooner or later in new shapes after the militant intrusion of the Hellenic Society into the Syriac and Indic societies' domains had prematurely overthrown, first the Syriac, and then the Indic, universal state, before either of these had attained the term of four hundred years that seems to be the standard life-span of a polity of this species.[1] We have identified an avatar of the Achaemenian Empire in the Arab Caliphate, and an avatar of the Mauryan Empire in the Guptan Empire.[2] In the tug-of-war between an intrusive Hellenic Society's effort to absorb the Syriac and Indic societies' frayed social tissue into her own body social and the nisus of the two invaded societies to expel the invader, however tardily and at however high a cost, in order to resume and complete the regular course of a disintegrating society's history, we have another example, on the political plane, of a trial of strength between conflicting social forces working itself out in a series of successive rounds.

If we now pass from the political plane to the religious, we shall find here a counterpart of North America's 'fate' to be partitioned between two sovereignties in the 'fate' of France and England to be partitioned between two ecclesiastical allegiances.

In another context[3] we have already noticed that, since the twelfth century of the Christian Era, the Roman Catholic Church in France had been engaged in a never more than temporarily successful struggle to re-establish the ecclesiastical unity of France as a Catholic country against an impulse towards secession which, from that time onward, kept on reasserting itself in some new form after each previous manifestation had been repressed. A revolt against Catholic Christianity which had taken the form of Catharism at its first outbreak in Southern France in the twelfth century was stamped out there in the thirteenth century in this form only to re-emerge in the same region in the sixteenth century in the form of Calvinism. Proscribed as Calvinism, it promptly reappeared as Jansenism, which was the nearest approach to Calvinism that was possible within the Catholic fold. Proscribed as Jansenism, it reappeared as Deism, Rationalism, Agnosticism, and Atheism. Every time that a repeatedly challenged Catholic Church seemed to have succeeded in reimposing a Catholic ecclesiastical unity upon France through an apparently conclusive victory over the dissenting movement of the day, the momentarily defeated forces of dissent thus baffled the victor by

[1] See p. 289, above.　　　[2] See I. i. 76–77 and 86–87.
[3] In IX. viii. 609–10.

re-entering the lists under a fresh banner and in a new-fangled panoply. More than seven hundred years after the savage repression of the Albigenses had been completed in A.D. 1229,[1] France was farther than she had been at the twelfth-century zenith of Catharism's fortunes in Languedoc from an ecclesiastical unity that the Catholic Church had re-established in France by *force majeure* no less than three times over in the meanwhile. The Protean stratagem of metamorphosis had invariably saved a repeatedly defeated movement of religious dissidence from ever being stamped out for good and all; and, at the time of writing, mid-way through the twentieth century of the Christian Era, it looked as if this historic wrestling match between Proteus and Menelaus in a French ecclesiastical arena would end, unlike the fabulous incident in the Odyssey,[2] in Menelaus, not Proteus, giving up the game and capitulating on his opponent's terms.

This irrepressibly recurring rebellion in France against ecclesiastical unity under the auspices of the Roman Church has its counterpart in England in a likewise irrepressible rebellion against ecclesiastical unity under the auspices of an Episcopalian Protestant Established Church of England. An anti-episcopalian Protestant secessionist movement, which had raised its head in the course of the last quarter of the sixteenth century and had put down Episcopacy from its seat in A.D. 1643, was quashed in the form of Puritanism in and after A.D. 1662, only to re-assert itself in the form of Methodism in the eighteenth century. An Episcopalian Established Church of England, whose prelates might have imagined in A.D. 1662 that they had succeeded in their day in achieving an ecclesiastical uniformity that their redoubtable predecessor, Archbishop Laud, had failed to achieve in his, was living in the same ephemeral fool's paradise as the 'Melchites' on the morrow of a proscription of Nestorianism which had been the signal for the more baffling onset of Monophysitism. In England, as in France, by the middle of the twentieth century, the ideal of an authoritarian ecclesiastical unity had been demonstrated to be a lost cause by the repeated stultification of successive attempts to carry it to a conclusive victory.

In other contexts, again, we have noted the 'fate' of a Judaic Monotheism to be perpetually beset by a repeatedly resurgent Polytheism, and the 'fate' of a kindred Judaic concept of the One True God's Transcendence to be no less perpetually beset by a repeatedly resurgent yearning for a God Incarnate.

Monotheism put down the worship of Ba'al and Ashtoreth only to find a jealous Yahweh's rigidly proscribed traditional divine associates slily creeping back into the fold of Jewish orthodoxy in the guise of personifications of the Lord's 'Word', 'Wisdom', and 'Angel',[3] and afterwards establishing themselves within the fold of Christian orthodoxy, from the outset and as of right, in the doctrine of the Holy Trinity and in the cults of God's Body and Blood, God's Mother, and the Saints. These re-encroachments of Polytheism on Monotheism in the Christian Church, which were more flagrant than the re-encroachments in Juda-

[1] See IV. iv. 369, n. 4.
[2] *Odyssey*, Book IV, ll. 363–570.   [3] See VII. vii. 718.

ism, evoked a whole-hearted reassertion of Monotheism in the shape of Islam and a less thoroughgoing reassertion of it in the shape of Protestantism; yet Protestantism confessed its nostalgia for the comfortable practices of an abandoned Roman Church by eventually rankling into Anglo-Catholicism, while a would-be meticulously monotheistic Islam was no more successful than Judaism or Protestantism or Catholicism in living up to its superhumanly etherial principles. Islam, in its turn, made the now familiar concessions to the Soul's irrepressible appetite for a plurality of gods. Even the Sunnah found its equivalent for a personified Word of God in an uncreated Qur'ān and acquiesced in a cult of saints which owed at least as much to the corresponding Christian practice as this owed to the cult of pagan Hellenic heroes and demigods, while a doubly heretical 'Alī Ilāhī sect had the courage of the Shī'ah's muffled convictions when it openly conferred upon 'Alī the apotheosis that Jesus had received from the Christian Church. The Christians' apotheosis of Jesus had been rejected as a relapse into Polytheism by 'Alī's own cousin and father-in-law the Prophet Muhammad. The yearning, manifest in the Shī'ah, to find a legitimate Islamic substitute for a proscribed Christian God Incarnate gives reason to Horace's dictum *Naturam expelles furcâ, tamen usque recurret*.[1]

These variations on the theme of a trial of strength between conflicting tendencies, in which the eventually defeated tendency kicks repeatedly against the pricks without succeeding in the long run in defying its 'fate', are all embraced in the drama of Man's 'fate' of having daily and hourly to purchase and re-purchase his right to Life and Freedom by perpetually responding to repeated challenges.

> Nur der verdient sich Freiheit, wie das Leben,
> Der täglich sie erobern muss.[2]

In our search for a criterion of the process of growth,[3] we have found it in a cumulative success in responding to challenges which is rewarded, not by an exemption from Challenge which would be tantamount to a discharge from the active service of Life, but by a transfer of the field of challenge from a Macrocosm where God challenges Man through the agency of Non-Human Nature or of Man's fellow human beings to a Microcosm where God challenges Man through the agency of Man's own soul by an ineffable epiphany of God the Challenger Himself.

(II) POSSIBLE EXPLANATIONS OF THE CURRENCY OF 'LAWS OF NATURE' IN HISTORY

The Emancipation of Man's Work from the Day-and-Night Cycle and from the Annual Cycle of the Seasons by Civilization

The evidence for the amenability of human affairs to 'laws of Nature' that has presented itself in the foregoing survey of historical facts seems sufficient to warrant, and indeed to demand, an inquiry into possible explanations of the appearance of regularities and recurrences too well

---

[1] Horace: *Epistulae*, Book I, Ep. x, l. 24.
[2] Goethe: *Faust*, ll. 11575-6, quoted in II. i. 277.   [3] In III. iii. 192-217.

attested to be convincingly explained away. If these repetitions and uniformities have to be accepted as being realities, there are two obvious main alternative possibilities to be explored. The human affairs with which we are concerned in the present Part of this Study are, we may here remind ourselves, Man's psychic and spiritual affairs, as contrasted with his bodily physique and physiology, which, for our present purpose, we are treating as part of his non-human environment. If human affairs in this pertinent restricted sense of the term are subject to 'laws of Nature', these laws that govern them may be either laws current in Man's non-human environment which impose themselves on human affairs from outside by *force majeure* without having any more intimate relation than this with Human Nature, or alternatively they may govern human affairs in virtue of being inherent in the psychic structure and working of Human Nature itself. It may be convenient to look into these two possibilities in the order in which we have just mentioned them.

We may perhaps venture to start by making the assumption that, in the non-human provinces of Nature, there are 'laws of Nature' that are not only operative but manifest. Post-Modern Western men of science seemed to take the reign of Law over Non-Human Nature for granted, and, so far as the present writer was aware, post-Modern Western historians had not carried their Antinomianism to the length of challenging the *savants* of the non-human sciences on these sciences' own ground. Nor again did the historians seem to dispute the thesis that, in Man's non-human environment, there were some uniformities, regularities, and recurrences that had an effect on human affairs. Some of the astronomical cycles in the physical motion of the Stellar Universe are obvious cases in point.

The Day-and-Night Cycle, for example, manifestly affects 'the everyday life of ordinary people' in all human societies of every species, since human beings have an ineradicable physiological need for sleep at least once in every twenty-four hours, and night-time is the time for sleep that is indicated to Man by the physiological laws governing his body. Though fish-spearers, burglars, bakers, monks,[1] and journalists may be con-

---

[1] The monks of a monastery on Mount Athos in which the writer had been spending the night as a guest in June 1912 courteously expressed to him, the morning after, their hope that his sleep had not been disturbed by their frequent nocturnal celebrations of the Liturgy. Wishing to return his hosts' courtesy in kind, the writer on his side expressed the hope that the monks did not find these never intermitted night-long vigils too painfully exhausting. 'Not at all', replied the monks, 'considering that we are able to sleep in the day-time.'—'And how do you manage to do that?' their English guest inquired. 'O, well, because we have fine estates in Rumili, with peasants on them to work them for us. You will remember our showing you yesterday our arsenal at the water's edge, stored with provisions of grain, oil, and wine. All that comes from our estates, and the peasants have to deliver it to us at the arsenal by water.'—'And how do the peasants live?' I asked. 'O, the peasants live like dogs', said the monks, 'but you can see for yourself what an admirable arrangement ours is. As the peasants work for us and fetch and carry for us, instead of our having to do any of this for ourselves, we can afford to sleep in the day-time and so keep ourselves fresh for praying at night, and this is really most advantageous, as you can imagine. After all, most people in the World—including, perhaps, Your Honour (τὸν λόγον σας)—are in this respect in the less favourable position of our peasants. Having, as they do have, to work all day, they are forced to spend the night in sleep instead of in prayer, in order to be fit for work again next morning; so at night-time the volume of prayers reaching God is at a minimum, and this means that God can give to a prayer offered up to Him during the night an amount of individual attention that would be out of the question in the day-time, when the great majority of

strained by the exigencies of arduous professions to exchange the time-table of the common run of Man and Beast for the time-table of foxes, owls, and bats by working at night and sleeping in the day-time, these night-workers, no less than other people, conform to the astronomical rhythm of the Day-and-Night Cycle in their own topsy-turvy way; they merely turn inside out the ordinary human way of keeping in step with the planet's periodic rotation round its own axis. As for the majority of Mankind who sleep by night and wake by day, you can see them keeping time with the alternations of light and darkness in country life and in city life alike. The Moreot peasant who comes down every morning from his village on the crag to his field in the plain, and climbs up again every evening from the kambos to the kastro, is dancing to the same astronomical tune—played by the Earth's rotatory rhythm—as the New York business man who commutes between New Canaan and Manhattan or the New Yorker's Constantinopolitan confrère who makes the shorter daily 'round trip' between Asia and Europe.[1] All the same, by the writer's day, Man in Process of Civilization had contrived to break the chains even of this physiologically imperative Day-and-Night Cycle. He had extricated himself from his servitude to this particular law of Physical Nature by inventing the double shift. An organizational device that was being practised already in a post-Minoan heroic age by Laestrygonian herdsmen, who had tumbled to it thanks to living far enough north to know summer days that ran into one another without any intervening nights,[2] had been adopted before the writer's day in all latitudes by the navigators of the high seas and by the industrial workers on the *terra firma* of a Westernizing planet. By this trick of putting Mycerinus[3] into commission, the scientific managers of a latter-day Western industry had translated an Egyptiac fairy tale into a prosaic reality.[4]

Another astronomical cycle to which Man had been a slave was the Annual Cycle of the Seasons; and, though this Summer-and-Winter Cycle did not impinge upon Man directly, as the Day-and-Night Cycle did, by communicating its rhythm to the human body's physiological demands, it had exercised a hardly less potent indirect dominion over Man's life through its direct dominion over a physical environment out of which Man had to wring his livelihood and, beyond that, to gather a surplus, above the minimum required for bare subsistence, to spend on war

---

Mankind are awake and in the running to gain a hearing for their prayers at odd moments of their working day. Yes, thanks to the endowments bequeathed to us by pious benefactors, we monks do find ourselves in a decidedly advantageous position.'

[1] In this comparison the relevant point for our present purpose is the regulation of the rural and the urban worker's daily round alike by the cyclic motion of the Earth's night-and-day clock. It is true, of course, that the journey which these two kinds of workers make, in one direction every morning and in the reverse direction every evening, is forced upon them by diverse considerations. The peasant is moved to commute by the insecurity of his field of work, the business man by its congestion; but this diversity of motive for an identical daily shuttling movement is irrelevant to our present inquiry.

[2] See *Odyssey*, Book X, ll. 81–86.

[3] The tale of Mycerinus is told by Herodotus in Book II, chap. 133.

[4] The successive shifts of hands, through which a latter-day Western plant was kept in operation for twenty-four hours in the day, had been anticipated in the successive watches through which a ship had been enabled to hold on her course for twenty-four hours in the day without having to be beached each night in order to allow the crew to sleep ashore.

against his fellow human beings in a World which, so far, had not succeeded in attaining to an all-embracing permanent political unity under the rule of a single effective World Government. The Cycle of the Seasons, generated by a daily rotating Earth's annually recurrent movement round an orbit centred on the Sun, had set the clock for Man's military as well as for his economic activities in food-gathering, hunting, fishing, agricultural, and pastoral societies.[1]

In the Age of the Civilizations, when the food-gathering and hunting societies had been either exterminated or driven into holes and corners, and when Farmer Cain had eventually established a decisive ascendancy over Shepherd Abel,[2] the husbandman's dance to the recurrent tune of the Seasons had impressed its rhythm deeply upon the feelings and ideas of all but a fraction of the survivors of a five-or-six-thousand-years-long struggle for existence between the warring votaries of diverse ways of making a living. Though, down to the date of writing, the husbandman's annual series of operations had been repeated perhaps no more than some five thousand or some ten thousand times even in the South-West Asian regions in which the agriculture of the Old World had been invented, the ἐνιαυτὸς δαίμων[3] had been able, within this brief Time-span, to erect in the Human Psyche's subconscious abyss a primordial image of such spiritual potency that, through this dark glass, Christian faith had caught its vision of a Suffering and Dying God. In the post-Christian Industrial Western World of the twentieth century of the Christian Era this vision still appeared, in Christian eyes, to be the most penetrating and illuminating of any that Man was known ever to have been granted so far. Yet in the same century the husbandman's economic dance to the astronomical tune of the Seasons, out of which this sublime religious imagery had been conjured, was in the act of losing a dominion over Human Life which, in a post-Modern Western astronomer's, or even geologist's, Time-perspective, could now be seen in retrospect to have been short-lived, even at the longest estimate, when measured on the Time-scale of the life-span of the Human Race in the primitive pre-agricultural chapter of human history.

An organizing technique that had been able to liberate an Industrial Western Man from his physiological servitude to the cycle of Day-and-Night had found it relatively easy also to liberate him from his economic servitude to the Cycle of the Seasons by manning, with double or triple shifts of human ants, an industrial plant built to run, not only for twenty-four hours in the day, but for 365 days in the year; and the same spirit of Western enterprise had even succeeded, for the benefit of some Western consumers, in circumventing the dominion of the Seasons over Agriculture. In a Western World that had extended its domain out of the

---

[1] This annual refrain of human labour had, of course, been played in divers variations that were reflections of as many diversities of climate and occupation. In some variations the hot season, in others the cold season, and in others again the wet season was the closed season for economic activities; and the annual maxima of economic and military activity were in some cases crowded into one and the same season, while in other cases they were 'staggered' over different times of year. All these variations on Man's yearly round, however, had a common master theme in an astronomical Cycle of the Seasons to which, in one way or another, each of the human year-cycles conformed.

[2] See III. iii. 13–22.   [3] See III. iii. 256–8.

Northern into the Southern Hemisphere and had invented cold storage and expeditious means of transport, any vegetable, fruit, or flower could be purchased at any season by any members of the public who had the money to make an 'effective demand' for it. A still more signal triumph of Man over Physical Nature was Western Man's discovery of ways and means for growing crops out of season without having to resort to the opposite hemisphere in order to perform this agricultural sleight of hand. He had learnt how to supplement the natural heat and light of the Sun by artificial lighting and heating; and this had also enabled him to push the cultivation of particularly valuable crops into colder latitudes than these could have braved in a state of nature without human nursing. Western Man's ingenuity had covered the irrigated lowlands of Southern California with a pall of 'smog' rising from a myriad frost-averting 'smudge-pots' interspersed among the ranks of many times their own number of orange trees, while in the Connecticut Valley it had covered the tobacco-plantations with acres of gauze to serve the same purpose of screening them from the blighting touch of winter. Perhaps the greatest of all such agricultural *tours de force* was the all-year-round production of southern fruits on the fringe of the Arctic Circle in an Iceland which had been transformed from a bleak wilderness into a market garden under glass through the tapping of an inexhaustible natural source of hot water welling up from a thousand geysers.

The Emancipation of a Psychological Business Cycle from a Physical Crop Cycle by the Industrial Revolution

The familiar annual round was possibly not the only astronomical cycle to which the Earth's flora was subject and to which Man was therefore indirectly enslaved in so far as he was dependent on Agriculture for winning his means of subsistence. The researches of latter-day Western meteorologists had brought to light indications of the currency of weather-cycles with a longer Time-span than the period of a single year. In an investigation of the eruptions of the Nomads out of 'the Desert' into 'the Sown' we have found some indirect evidence—in the shape of oscillations in the Balance of Power between the Nomads and their sedentary rivals in disputable borderlands—for the currency of a cycle with a span of as many as six hundred years, made up of two alternating bouts of humidity and aridity.[1] This inferential six-hundred-years-long climatic cycle was, however, at the time of writing, probably farther from being substantiated than were certain other apparent cycles of the same class, with wave-lengths running only into double or single figures reckoned in years, which had been descried by meteorologists in periodical fluctuations of the yield, not of the natural grasses of the Steppe on which the Nomad pastured his flocks and herds, but of the crops artificially sown and harvested by the husbandman in his cultivated fields.[2] The approximate correspondence in dates of peaks and troughs,

---

[1] See III. iii. 395-454.
[2] See Huntington, E.: *Mainsprings of Civilisation* (New York 1945, Wiley), p. 460, fig. 57: 'Cycles in Wheat Prices for Three Centuries (after Beveridge) and in Weather for a Century in Europe (after Brunt and others).' According to Huntington, ibid., 'the

as well as in wave-lengths, between certain series of these alleged crop-yield cycles and the contemporary series of 'Kitchin' cycles and 'Juglar' cycles in the economic history of an industrialized Western World had evoked the conjecture that the observed coincidence between these isor-rhythmic series of diverse orders might be, not a meaningless freak of Chance, but an indication that the crop series and the business series stood to one another in the relation of cause and effect.

If this conjecture had been confirmed by convincing evidence and by cogent reasoning, we should have had to add the Crop Cycle to the Year Cycle and the Day Cycle in compiling our list of instances of 'laws of Nature', current in Non-Human Nature, which had led or forced Mankind to dance to their tune; and no doubt the crop cycle too had exercised an at times tyrannical dominion over the lives of predominantly agricultural societies; but, among professional students of the business cycles current in a predominantly industrial Westernizing World, there was, at the time of writing, a preponderance of opinion, clear enough to be manifest even to the layman's eye, against accepting the suggestion that the currency of business cycles could be explained as an effect of a currency of crop cycles that was itself presumably an effect of periodic fluctuations in those meteorological conditions on which the weal or woe of cereal crops depended. In this judgement, W. C. Mitchell, T. S. Ashton,[1] R. G. Hawtrey,[2] J. A. Schumpeter,[3] and G. Haberler concur. Haberler points out that there is a wide disagreement among different exponents of the theory that business cycles are to be traced to agricultural causes,[4] and gives it as his own opinion that

'There can be no "agricultural theory" of the cycle in the sense of an alternative to, say, the monetary theory or the over-investment theory, any more than there can be an "invention theory" or an "earthquake theory". . . . It is conceivable that a good harvest may exercise now a stimulating and now a depressing influence according to the phase of the cycle and the portions of the Earth's surface and the World's population affected. Nor must it be readily assumed that a good wheat crop and a good cotton crop have the same kind of effects.[5]

Mitchell points out that

'Even the writers who regard changes in crop yields as the cause of business fluctuations . . . recognise that these fluctuations manifest themselves chiefly in commercial dealings, manufacturing activity, transportation, and financial operations.'[6]

At least two of the same authorities also agree in rejecting suggestions

most obvious approaches to agreement between Beveridge and Brunt fall near $3\frac{1}{2}$, 5, 8, $9\frac{1}{2}$, and 35 years.'
[1] In a personal letter to the present writer, dated the 2nd December, 1949.
[2] Hawtrey, R. G.: 'The Monetary Theory of the Trade Cycle and Its Statistical Test', in The Quarterly Journal of Economics, vol. xli (Cambridge, Mass. 1927, Harvard University Press), p. 473.
[3] Schumpeter, J. A.: Business Cycles (New York 1939, McGraw-Hill, 2 vols.), vol. i, pp. 177–8.
[4] See Haberler, G.: Prosperity and Depression, 3rd ed. (Geneva 1941, League of Nations), pp. 152 and 154.   [5] Ibid., pp. 163 and 164.
[6] Mitchell, W. C.: Business Cycles, the Problem and its Setting (New York 1927 (new impression 1930), Bureau of Economic Research, Inc.), p. 87.

that business cycles may be effects of periodic fluctuations in some other non-human medium than the weather of the Earth whose fluctuations presumably account for those of crop yields. Ashton and Mitchell mention, only to discard,[1] the brilliant pioneer Stanley Jevons' audacious astrological conjecture that business cycles might be effects of fluctuations in the radioactivity of the Sun advertised by the appearance and disappearance of sun-spots; and Mitchell goes on to reject in principle all theories of physical causation, on the ground that no physical theory can be reconciled with secular changes in the wave-length of the 'Kitchin' Cycle which he believes that he has detected in the course of this cycle's currency up to the date of his own investigations during the third decade of the twentieth century.[2]

There was a wider consensus, in which A. C. Pigou concurred with the authorities already cited, in support of the view that the independence of the Late Modern and post-Modern Western business cycles of divers wave-lengths from the dominion of either the crop-yield cycle or any other periodic rhythm in Non-Human Nature had been the outcome of a progressive emancipation; and, on this view, the Industrial Revolution in the Western World had been revolutionary in two senses. It had not only inaugurated a novel kind of economic technique and organization; it had at the same time progressively liberated economic life itself—*pari passu* with the progressive establishment of the preponderance of Industry over Agriculture—from a bondage to the meteorological cropyield cycle and to other alien forces, both non-human and human, to whose dominion Man's economic life had been subject in some measure under pre-industrial economic dispensations.[3]

A. C. Pigou, for example, in whose minoritarian view there had been a positive correlation between crop yields and pig-iron production in the United States[4] and an approximate correlation between crop yields and the volume of industrial activity in general in the Western World as a whole,[5] goes on to allow that, while 'crop changes are an important factor in determining industrial fluctuations',[6] their influence in this field had been diminished by the relative decline in the importance of Agriculture by comparison with Industry in a Westernizing World.[7]

'Harvest variations as a factor determining, whether by direct or by indirect process, fluctuations in industrial activity, are substantially less important [in the third decade of the twentieth century of the Christian Era] than they used to be fifty or a hundred years ago.'[8]

And Pigou's final conclusion is that statistical correlations between cropyield variations and business cycles

'do not warrant the opinion that crop variations are the sole, or even the

[1] See Mitchell, ibid., p. 13; Ashton, loc. cit.
[2] See Mitchell, ibid., p. 418.
[3] This comparative freedom from the dominion of external forces was the distinguishing characteristic of the Industrial Western Economy according to Mitchell, op. cit., pp. 80–81.
[4] See Pigou, A. C.: *Industrial Fluctuations*, 2nd ed. (London 1929, Macmillan), pp. 42–44.
[5] See ibid., p. 46.   [6] Ibid., p. 221.
[7] See ibid., p. 221.   [8] Ibid., p. 224.

main, determinants of such periodicity as there is in industrial fluctuations.'[1]

Ashton draws the same picture of a shift, accompanying the march of a Late Modern Western Industrial Revolution, in the Balance of Power between the non-human external forces and the human internal forces exercising dominion over Western Man's economic life.

'There is little doubt, I think, that the fluctuations of harvests were a major cause of variations in economic activity in the eighteenth century. But nearly all economists now agree that the cyclical movements of the nineteenth century at least can be attributed to oscillation in investment (i.e. the creation of capital goods or goods not in a form available for direct consumption). It is the human factor rather than physical environment that is responsible.'[2]

In W. W. Rostow's opinion[3] 'the domestic harvests played a significant part in British trade fluctuations' until A.D. 1850 beyond question, and probably till the eighteen-seventies.

The epiphany of the particular rhythmical economic fluctuations that had come to be known as business cycles had been contemporaneous with the rise and spread of the industrial type of economy. On the strength of evidence marshalled by W. R. Scott, 'it seems clear', in W. C. Mitchell's view,

'that the English crises of 1558–1720 were not business crises of the modern type, and that the intervals between these crises were not occupied by business cycles.'[4]

According to W. R. Scott himself, the vicissitudes in the economic history of England in the Early Modern Age of Western history were mostly caused by repercussions of forces operative on non-economic planes of life.

'It is when the forecast of the majority of traders is in error that a crisis results. The cause of the miscalculation may lie either mainly in the men who judge or in the events to be judged. . . . At later periods the importance of Man's judgment and calculation becomes marked in the period of speculative activity which precedes a crisis. But, prior to the development of banking, such intense activity is scarcely to be expected. . . . Analysing the crises up to 1720 . . . it will be seen that, owing to defective intelligence in the form of news or to bad government, the objective aspect tends to predominate.'[5]

The next chapter of the story may be told in Mitchell's, Ashton's, and Dupriez's words:

'Business cycles are much later in appearing than economic, or even strictly financial, crises. In England itself they seem not to have begun before the close of the eighteenth century. But, when they did appear, it was in the form of an extension—over all branches of industry—of difficulties not unlike those which had been suffered for more than a hundred

[1] Ibid., p. 233. [2] Ashton, loc. cit.
[3] Rostow, W. W.: *British Economy of the Nineteenth Century* (Oxford 1948, Clarendon Press), p. 50. [4] Mitchell, ibid., p. 80.
[5] Scott, W. R.: *The Constitution and Finance of English, Scottish, and Irish Joint-Stock Companies to 1720* (Cambridge 1910–12, University Press, 3 vols.), vol. i, pp. 469–71.

years by large capitalists, bankers and speculators in stocks. With this extension in scope came a shift in the relative importance of the causes. In the past the undermining of credit had usually been caused by war, by the making of peace, or by some violation of financial obligations on the part of Government. In the future it was to be caused more frequently by stresses engendered within the world of business itself. The reason for both changes lay in the gradual extension of the highly organised business enterprise from its earlier centres of foreign commerce, mining, finance, and banking over the wide field of manufacturing and domestic trade—an extension that accompanied the Industrial Revolution. . . . In proportion as the Industrial Revolution and its concomitant changes in the organisation of commerce and transportation spread to other countries, the latter began to develop the phenomena of business cycles already familiar in England.'[1]

'It is . . . clear that the booms and slumps occurred at the same time, or almost the same time, in all industrialised countries and in the less developed areas connected with these by trade.'[2]

'Dans le monde, par extensification géographique, comme dans la nation, par pénétration des sphères d'activité les moins industrielles, les spasmes de la conjoncture tendent à gagner du terrain et à se synchroniser.'[3]

In an oecumenical economy of Western origin in which Industry had established its ascendancy over Agriculture and in which this new-fangled predominantly industrial way of economic life had spread from its Western birthplace all over the face of the planet, the distinctive feature in the rhythm of economic activity was its autonomy.

'The waning, like the waxing, of prosperity . . . must be due, not to the influence of "disturbing causes" from outside, but to processes that run regularly within the world of business itself.'[4]

'The mysterious thing about [these fluctuations] is that they cannot be accounted for by such "external" causes as bad harvests due to weather conditions, diseases, general strikes, lock-outs, earthquakes, the sudden obstruction of international trade channels and the like. Severe decreases in the volume of production, real income, or level of employment as a result of crop failures, wars, earthquakes, and similar physical disturbances of the productive processes rarely affect the economic system as a whole, and certainly do not constitute depressions in the technical sense of business-cycle theory. By depressions in the technical sense we mean those long and conspicuous falls in the volume of production, real income, and employment which can only be explained by the operation of factors originating within the economic system itself, and in the first instance by an insufficiency of monetary demand and the absence of a sufficient margin between price and cost.'[5]

'For various reasons it seems desirable, in the explanation of the business cycle, to attach as little importance as possible to the influence of external disturbances. . . . The responses of the business system seem *prima facie* more important in shaping the business cycle than external shocks. Secondly, historical experience seems to demonstrate that the cyclical movement has a strong tendency to persist, even where there are

---

[1] Mitchell, W. C.: *Business Cycles and their Causes*, a new edition of Mitchell's *Business Cycles*, Part III (Berkeley, Cal. 1941, University of California Press), pp. 170-1.
[2] Ashton, loc. cit.
[3] Dupriez, L. H.: *Les Mouvements Économiques Généraux* (Louvain 1947, Institut de Recherches Économiques et Sociales, 2 vols.), vol. ii, p. 542.
[4] Mitchell, ibid., p. 26. Cf. pp. 2 and 71.   [5] Haberler, op. cit., p. 265.

no outstanding extraneous influences at work which can plausibly be held responsible. This suggests that there is an inherent instability in our economic system, a tendency to move in one direction or the other.'[1]

If the fluctuations that made themselves felt in the flow of an industrialized Western economic life were neither astronomical rhythms in the motion of the stellar universe, such as the Day Cycle and the Year Cycle, nor meteorological rhythms in the temperature and circulation of the atmosphere and the water-jacket of the Earth, such as made themselves felt in the crop-yield cycle, we have to identify the medium in which these business cycles were inherent; and, here again, our question is answered for us by a consensus of the authorities whom we have just cited as witnesses to the industrial Western economic system's autonomy. The medium in which the recurrent cycles of expansion and contraction in an industrial society's business activity revolve is the psychic and spiritual medium of Human Nature itself.

'Every economic fact has a psychological aspect. The subject matter of economic science is human behaviour—chiefly conscious and deliberate behaviour. . . . The psychology of human behaviour is therefore a constituent part of the subject-matter of economics. When we assume that an entrepreneur will increase his output if demand rises or cost is reduced, or that workmen will respond to changes in money wages but not so readily to changes in real wages, or that consumers will buy more of a given commodity if the price falls and less if they think it will fall further, or that people will hoard money if the value of money rises—all these assumptions are assumptions about human behaviour which presuppose a certain state of mind on the part of the human agents.'[2]

'Money making for the individual, business prosperity for the nation, are artificial ends of endeavour imposed by pecuniary institutions. Beneath one lie the individual's impulsive activities—his maze of instinctive reactions partly systematised into conscious wants, definite knowledge, and purposeful efforts. Beneath the other lie the vague and conflicting ideals of social welfare that members of each generation refashion after their own images. In this dim inner world lie the ultimate motives and meanings of action, and from it emerge the wavering standards by which men judge what is for them worth while.'[3]

'The "cause," if we wish to use that term, of business cycles . . . is to be found in the habits and customs (institutions) of men which make up the money economy, with its money and credit, prices, private property, buying and selling, and so on, all loaded, so to speak, on the industrial process.'[4]

In this psychic medium a sense of uncertainty about the future is a potent motive force.

'Every economic decision is part of an economic plan which extends

---

[1] Haberler, op. cit., p. 10. This passage must, however, be read in the light of one on the preceding page, in which the author declares his opinion that purely endogenous, as well as purely exogenous, explanations of the Business Cycle are unconvincing.
[2] Haberler, G.: *Prosperity and Depression: A Theoretical Analysis of Cyclical Movements*, 3rd ed. (Geneva 1941, League of Nations), p. 144.
[3] Mitchell, W. C.: *Business Cycles and their Causes*, pp. 190–1.
[4] Frank, L. K.: 'A Theory of Business Cycles,' in *The Quarterly Journal of Economics*, vol. xxxvii, August 1923 (Cambridge, Mass. 1923, Harvard University Press), p. 639, quoted on p. 224, above.

into the more or less distant future. In principle, there is therefore always an element of uncertainty in every activity. There are, however, certain cases where the element of uncertainty is especially great and conspicuous, such as the case of investment of resources in long processes and durable plant and the provision of funds for these purposes. The longer the processes in which capital is to be sunk, and the more durable the instruments and equipment to be constructed, the greater the element of uncertainty and risk of loss.'[1]

' "Uncertainty" . . . is . . . an all-pervading phase of every business undertaking. The tap root is uncertainty concerning what people will buy at what prices. . . . The fruits of uncertainty appear in the emotional aberrations of business judgments.[2] [Uncertainty about the future] gives hopeful or despondent moods a large share in shaping business decisions.[3] . . . These emotional states are . . . in part the product of suggestions.[4]. . . [Optimism] helps to produce conditions that both justify and intensify it.'[5]

'A significant part in building up the recorded rhythm of Industry is played by the mutual generation of errors of pessimism and errors of optimism.'[6]

Perhaps the most impressive testimony to the truth that business cycles are products of psychic causes in a psychic medium is the avowal that Stanley Jevons has been constrained by his intellectual probity to make in the teeth of his own penchant in favour of seeing in business cycles the effects of non-human causes. While he cannot resist commenting

'It seems to be very probable that the moods of the commercial mind, while constituting the principal part of the phenomena, may be controlled by outward events, especially the condition of the harvests',

this comment is merely a wistful pendant to a frank admission that

'periodic collapses are really mental in their nature, depending upon variations of despondency, hopefulness, excitement, disappointment and panic.'[7]

'In recent years it has become fashionable to lay stress on the element of expectation.'[8]

'As economic events depend on Man's actions, one has to investigate what determines these actions. They always refer to a more or less distant future. Hence, one must study those expectations about the future which govern the actions.'[9]

'The record of movements in prices and interest rates goes to show that fluctuations in the real demand for labour come about predominantly through changes in expectations' [and not through changes in real income].[10]

[1] Haberler, op. cit., p. 145.
[2] Mitchell, *Business Cycles, the Problem and its Setting*, pp. 156–7.
[3] 'Credit—the disposition of one man to trust another—is singularly varying' (Bagehot, quoted by Rostow in op. cit., p. 164).—A.J.T.
[4] Mitchell, *Business Cycles and their Causes*, p. 5. Cp. pp. 57–58.
[5] Ibid., p. 5. Cp. p. 25. Cp. also Bagehot, Walter: 'All people are most credulous when they are most happy' (*Lombard Street* (London 1931, John Murray), p. 151).
[6] Pigou, op. cit., p. 230.
[7] Jevons, W. Stanley: *Investigations in Currency and Finance*, 2nd ed. (London 1909, Macmillan), p. 184.
[8] Haberler, op. cit., p. 144, n. 2.
[9] Ohlin, B., in *The Economic Journal*, vol. xlvii (London 1937, Macmillan), p. 58.
[10] Pigou, op. cit., p. viii.

'A change in expectations . . . can be taken . . . to define the beginning of the down-turn.'[1]

These psychic disturbances that manifest themselves in the form of economic fluctuations may originate either in the subconscious abyss of the Psyche or on its conscious volitional surface, and from either of these two alternative possible psychic sources they may communicate themselves to the other psychic plane. For example,

'Deflation must not . . . be interpreted in the narrow sense of a deliberate act or policy on the part of the monetary authorities or commercial banks. . . . When the process has once got under way, a sort of automatic deflation or self-deflation of the economic system (in contradistinction to a deflation imposed on it by the monetary authorities) is just as much an effect as a cause.'[2]

Conversely, the dealings between consumer and producer begin at the consumer's end on the subconscious level but are raised to the conscious level in the producer's response to the consumer's challenge. In the first movement of this market dance

'the psychological categories important to the understanding of consumers' demand are habit, imitation, and suggestion—not reflective choice.'[3]

In the second movement

'production is guided by forecasts of what consumers will buy, supplemented by judgments concerning profitable methods of providing both consumers' goods and the endless variety of producers' goods which modern technique requires.'[4]

A progressive increase in the relative influence of conscious ideas, aims, plans, and decisions in the psychic causation of economic events seemed to have been one of the characteristic concomitants of the industrialization of Western economic life.

'The most significant items [among various factors determining the amplitude of industrial fluctuations] in a world of complex organisation . . . are the monetary and banking arrangements of the country, the policy of industrialists as regards spoiling the market, and the policy of workpeople as regards rigidity of wage-rates.'[5]

In a money economy in which private enterprise enjoys an ascendancy over public enterprise, the individual's desire to make money is the most obvious of the conscious and deliberate psychic driving forces behind the production machine.[6] 'Profit making is the central process among the congeries that constitute the activities of a business economy.'[7] As Pigou puts it, 'in the Modern World industry is closely enfolded in a garment of

---

[1] Rostow, op. cit., p. 56. Ibid., p. 163, the same scholar draws attention to 'the role of expectations about the future, operating through the institutions of credit', in Bagehot's theory of economic cycles.
[2] Haberler, op. cit., p. 323. The meaning which the author intends to convey in the last nine words here quoted seems to be 'is not only an effect but a cause'.
[3] Mitchell, *Business Cycles, the Problem and its Setting*, p. 165.   [4] Ibid., p. 164.
[5] Pigou, op. cit., p. 208.   [6] See Mitchell, ibid., pp. 65–66.
[7] Ibid., p. 183. Cp. Mitchell, *Business Cycles and their Causes*, p. 149.

money.'[1] In the particular form taken by a money economy in an in-dustrialized Western World, one gauge of the increasing relative im-portance of conscious over subconscious psychic motive power was the submergence of business cycles that were fluctuations in the demand for, and supply of, consumers' goods by business cycles that were fluctua-tions in the volume of investment in producers' goods. This change in the character of business cycles had occurred in Great Britain round about the sixth decade of the nineteenth century, as we have already noticed in another context.[2] In a full-blown Industrial Age, 'industrial booms have nearly always been characterised by large and conspicuous investment in construction of some kind;'[3] and this is evidently bound to be a deliberate form of action.

The role of Reason in generating the business cycles in the economic life of an industrialized Western World was rated at its highest in a 'monetary' theory of which the most eminent and most wholehearted exponent at the time of writing was R. G. Hawtrey. According to this theory, the rhythm of 'slumps' and 'booms' was produced by a mani-pulation of monetary levers in the bankers' hands. 'The banks cannot allow optimism to prevail when gold is deficient, or pessimism when gold is redundant.'[4] As one cause of business cycles among others, this 'monetary' cause was widely recognized as being, not merely authentic, but important. 'The crucial importance of the policy followed by the leading banks in determining whether a crisis shall become a panic' is underlined by W. C. Mitchell,[5] while Haberler, after agreeing that the monetary theory must be near to the heart of the explanation of cyclical movements in an industrial Western economy,[6] goes so far as to concede that a depression 'may be started by purely monetary forces without anything being wrong with the structure of production.'[7] In its most uncompromisingly absolute form, however, the monetary theory of busi-ness cycles had proved unacceptable to a majority of the authorities down to the time of writing. Haberler, for instance, goes on to express the opinion that deflationary measures deliberately taken by governments or banks are not an all-sufficing explanation of all economic down-turns;[8] Pigou finds that his 'personal judgment is adverse to the full claims of the monetary school';[9] in Mitchell's opinion[10] the state of the money market is not an infallible pointer to the general state of the body econo-mic; and Rostow's study of the economic history of Great Britain during the years A.D. 1790–1914 has led him to the conclusion that 'in no cycle, over this period [in Great Britain], does inelasticity in the supply of money appear to have been the decisive factor in determining the moment of the down-turn.'[11] Yet, even if the ultimate verdict on this

---

[1] Pigou, op. cit., p. 132.
[2] On p. 230, above, following W. W. Rostow.   [3] Pigou, op. cit., p. 14.
[4] Hawtrey, R. G.: 'The Monetary Theory of the Trade Cycle and its Statistical Test', in *The Quarterly Journal of Economics*, vol. xli (Cambridge, Mass. 1927, Harvard University Press), pp. 481–2.
[5] Mitchell, *Business Cycles and their Causes*, p. 126.
[6] Haberler, op. cit., pp. 14–15.   [7] Ibid., p. 323, n. 1.
[8] Ibid., p. 350. Cp. pp. 362–3.
[9] Pigou, op. cit., p. 219, summing up his critique of Hawtrey's theory on pp. 210–19.
[10] See Mitchell, *Business Cycles and their Causes*, pp. 7–8.
[11] Rostow, op. cit., p. 57.

ultra-rationalistic account of the psychology of business cycles were to be an adverse one on the whole, it seemed already certain that there would be a consensus in favour of looking for a psychological explanation of some kind, on one plane or other of psychic life, as opposed to a physical explanation of these fluctuations in the volume and profit of industrial economic activity in a latter-day Western World.

The Human Spirit's Educational Use of a Physical Generation Cycle as a Psychological Regulator of Social Change

The Crop-Yield Cycle that had been more or less authoritatively pronounced not to be the generator of the business cycles current in an industrialized world was a meteorological cycle of a longer wave-length than the astronomical Year Cycle or Day Cycle; but there was another physical cycle, with a longer wave-length again, which differed from both the Crop-Yield Cycle and the Annual Cycle of the Seasons, but resembled the Day-and-Night Cycle, in exerting its dominion over the Spirit of Man, not at two removes, through elements in his terrestrial environment out of which he made his living, but at one remove only, through a biological law which in this case was a law governing the physical self-perpetuation of the Human Race. This biological cycle was, of course, the Generation Cycle of birth, growth, life-work, procreation, and senescence leading up to a death which left the field clear for the time-expired individual human being's successors. The wave-length of this Generation Cycle varied between lower and upper limits of about a quarter and about a third of a century in response to differences in social customs and in the average expectation of life in different societies at divers times and places; and it was indisputable that the periodic breaks in the continuity of life arising from the recurrent replacement of representatives of one generation by representatives of another at each successive revolution of the Birth-and-Death Cycle produced a rhythm of their own in human affairs which made itself felt in the gait of human history. Have we here encountered a periodic rhythm which, though current in a biological medium, external to Man's psychic and spiritual nature, nevertheless held Man's psychic and spiritual nature under its sway and constrained the Soul to dance to Mortality's tune?

A sinister 'Dance of Death' which seems to mock Man's spiritual ideals and aspirations by cutting them off brutally with swiftly recurrent sweeps of an inhuman scythe had been apt to haunt men's imaginations in unsettled times, as, for example, at the transition from the medieval to the modern chapter of Western history on the evidence of contemporary German woodcuts,[1] and during a post-Minoan interregnum on the evidence of a passage in the *Iliad* that has been quoted already in this Study.[2] But Nature had a retort to both a Homeric pathos and a Teutonic morbidity which had been cast for her into biting verse by a poet-philosopher who had risen above all self-regarding emotional reactions to the spectacle of the procession of the generations of Man.

[1] e.g. the woodcut on fol. cclxiiii of the Nuremberg Chronicle, cited on p. 178, n. 6, above.
[2] *Iliad*, Book VI, ll. 146–9, quoted in III. iii. 257.

Denique si vocem Rerum Natura repente
mittat et hoc alicui nostrum sic increpet ipsa
'quid tibi tanto operest, mortalis, quod nimis aegris
luctibus indulges? quid mortem congemis ac fles? . . .'
iure, ut opinor, agat, iure increpet inciletque.
cedit enim rerum novitate extrusa vetustas
semper, et ex aliis aliud reparare necessest . . .
materies opus est ut crescant postera saecla,
quae tamen omnia te vitâ perfuncta sequentur;
nec minus ergo ante haec quam tu cecidere, cadentque.
sic alid ex alio numquam desistet oriri,
vitaque mancipio nulli datur, omnibus usu.[1]

The ordeal of Death, which was so tragic a catastrophe for each individual living creature, was evidently an indispensable contrivance for
an ambitious Natura Creatrix if she was ever to break out of the blind
alley of a deathless and therefore static unicellular organism into the
infinite variety of multicellular organic life. Nature's endowment of her
new creation with the gift of multiplicity-in-unity at the price of mortality
insured her against being committed to more than a limited liability
towards any single specimen or single species of her brood. It gave her a
perpetually recurrent opportunity to liquidate her proven miscarriages
and to follow up her more promising experiments. In fact, the epiphany
of Death in the history of Life on Earth, so far from convicting Nature of
ineptitude or impotence, was evidence that she had been successful in
retaining an initiative that was a synonym for creativity itself; for the
mortality of the creature was merely the obverse of Nature's unforfeited
freedom to carry on her work of creation by varying at will the ratio
between racial change and racial stability in the ever flowing series of her
offspring.

If this 'concede: necessest'[2] were the whole story of Death's role in
Nature's dealings with her creature Man, we might have ruefully to conclude that, in the working of the Generation Cycle, a rhythm in the flow
of Physical Life had in truth imposed its dominion on the Spirit of Man.
Before we accept this conclusion, however, we may recall that, in the
life of those higher living creatures, culminating in Man, which pro-
create and die, there are two alternative methods of transmitting, from
one generation to another, behaviour approved as valuable for future
representatives of the species. There can be a transmission of a racial
heritage of instincts and aptitudes through the physiological process of
procreation; and there can be a transmission of a social heritage of habits
and knowledge through the spiritual process of moral and intellectual
education in the broad unprofessional meaning of this word.[3] The second
of these methods of transmission, which was the younger of the two, had
been employed, as a second string to the older physiological device, by

[1] Lucretius, De Rerum Naturâ, Book III, ll. 931–4, 963–5, and 967–71.
[2] Lucretius, op. cit., Book III, l. 962.
[3] 'Just as biological evolution was rendered both possible and inevitable when material
organisation became self-reproducing, so conscious evolution was rendered both possible
and inevitable when social organisation became self-reproducing' (Huxley, Julian:
Evolutionary Ethics, the Romanes Lecture 1943, reprinted in Huxley, T. H. and J.:
Evolution and Ethics, 1893–1943 (London 1947, Pilot Press), p. 122).

the non-human higher animals; but Man had been unique in inverting these proportions in the relative use that he had made of these two facilities; for Man had made singularly little use of a sexual animal's physiological facility,[1] while on the other hand he had developed a social animal's educational facility on an enormous scale without apparently having come within range of exhausting a capacity that thus bade fair to go on serving him *ad infinitum*.[2]

This capacity for transmitting a social heritage through a spiritual channel of the Human Spirit's own making was manifestly Man's distinctive trait.[3] In the creation, preservation, improvement, and liquidation of all the pre-human multi-cellular terrestrial flora and fauna, Nature had used Death for her own purposes without asking her creatures' leave; but, in the ensuing human episode of the story, Man—impotent though he might be to win exemption from Nature's common law—had at any rate discovered a means of making an ineluctable Death serve Man's purposes as well as Nature's. A social animal which, in virtue of its sociality, had succeeded in scaling the precipitous ascent from Sub-Man's level to Man's had made use of Nature's Generation Cycle as an instrument for regulating the ratio between a social change and a social stability that, unlike the racial change and racial stability which had hitherto been Nature's prime concern, were elements in a spiritual world of Man's own. In thus making the Generation Cycle serve a social as well as a racial purpose, the Spirit of Man in the Age of the Primitive Societies had been doing what we have already watched it doing when, in the Age of the Civilizations, it seized the chance offered by an industrial revolution in Western Man's economic life in order to emancipate Man's economic activities from the dominion of astronomical and meteorological laws of Nature by bringing them under the rule of laws intrinsic to these human activities themselves. In these two achievements Man was progressively conjuring into existence an autonomous human province within Nature's realm; and this finding may help us to answer a question which we raised at the beginning of this chapter; for it suggests that, among the 'laws' whose currency we have detected in human history, laws of Non-Human Nature exercising a dominion over human affairs are likely to have been, not, of course, abrogated, but restricted in the scope of their incidence, by laws intrinsic to Human Nature in the psychic and spiritual meaning to which we are here confining our usage of the term. We can test this possibility by ascertaining whether it is in

[1] 'Indeed, there are grounds for suspecting that biological evolution has come to an end, so far as any sort of major advance is concerned' (Huxley, J., ibid., p. 123).

[2] 'Real advance is now on quite another and more active front—the acquisition and transmission of wisdom and experience' (Sinnott, E. W.: 'The Biological Basis of Democracy', in *The Yale Review*, vol. xxxv, pp. 61–73 (New Haven, Conn. 1945, Yale University Press), quoted in Huxley, op. cit., p. 184).

Man 'has invented a new mechanism of heredity—the transmission of Civilisation to his descendants by writing, teaching, artistic creation. . . . The essential feature of human evolution is . . . that it is a process dependent on Man's *social* life' (Waddington, C. H.: 'Human Ideals and Human Progress', in *The World Review*, August 1946, pp. 29–36, quoted in Huxley, op. cit., p. 185).

[3] 'With the advent of Man, major evolutionary change is, and will continue to be, mediated through a social, not through a biological, mechanism' (Huxley, J.: 'The Vindication of Darwinism', in Huxley, T. H. and J.: *Evolution and Ethics, 1893–1943* (London 1947, Pilot Press), p. 176).

harmony or in contradiction with historical facts. The business cycles in the history of an Industrialized Western Society, the war-and-peace cycles in the histories of the Western, Hellenic, and Sinic societies, and rhythms discernible in the growths and in the disintegrations of these and other civilizations are obvious test cases for us to explore.

In our consideration of business cycles in the present context, we have already come to the conclusion that, in the industrial phase of economic activity with which these cycles are associated, the laws of Nature whose currency can be detected are laws inherent in the life of the Human Psyche itself, and that, even if these psychic laws should prove not to be solely the laws of Reason which the pure monetary theory of business cycles was inclined to see in them exclusively, it was recognized by most authorities that some of them, at least, were laws governing the play of feelings welling up from the subconscious depths of the Psyche—particularly the expectant feelings of Hope and Fear. When we pass from the consideration of the forty-months-long 'Kitchin' business cycles and the nine-to-ten-years-long 'Juglar' business cycles to the twenty-three-to-twenty-five-years-long 'Rostow-Spiethoff' phases and the forty-to-sixty-years-long 'Kondratieff' business cycles[1] which had been keeping time with the contemporary war-and-peace cycles in latter-day Western history, and which might turn out to be reflections on the economic plane of these cycles on the political and military plane, it is evident that the alternating bouts of war and spells of peace with an average duration of 28·83 years, and the waves, with an average span of 57·66 years, between successive turning-points in the same direction, either from peace to war or from war to peace, out of which the three regular war-and-peace cycles in Modern and post-Modern Western history had been built up,[2] could be accounted for convincingly as products of the working of the Generation Cycle in the transmission of a social heritage.

It is manifest that the survivors of a generation that has been of military age during a bout of war will be shy, for the rest of their lives, of bringing a repetition of this tragic experience either upon themselves or upon their children, and that therefore the psychological resistance to any move towards the breaking of a peace that the living memory of a previous war has made so precious is likely to be prohibitively strong until a new generation that knows War only by hearsay has had time to grow up and to come into power. On the same showing, a bout of war, once precipitated, is likely to persist until the peace-bred generation that has light-heartedly run into war has been replaced, in its turn, by a war-worn generation whom these inexperienced war-mongers have sent to the shambles. Thus the alternating transitions from war to peace and from peace to war which succeed one another in the three Western regular war-and-peace cycles at intervals of an average span of 28·83 years could be explained as effects of the periodic breach that is made in the continuity of a social tradition every time that an experience has to be transmitted by the generation that has experienced it in its own life to a generation that has merely learnt of it at second hand. Yet this loss of compelling first-hand experience in the transition from one generation

---

[1] See pp. 230–2, above.   [2] See p. 287, above.

to its immediate successor, which might account for alternations of war and peace at intervals of about the average length of a generation, would not account for the distinction that an empirical survey of the historical evidence has led us to draw between 'general wars' and 'supplementary wars' and between the 'general peace' that is apt to follow a round of 'supplementary wars' and the 'breathing-space' that is apt to precede it; for the complete War-and-Peace Cycle constituted by the occurrence of a set of these four diverse phases in an unvarying regular order has a wave-length with a span, not just of approximately the length of a single generation cycle, but of approximately the aggregate length of four generation cycles, whether we measure this span from outbreak to outbreak of general wars or from the inauguration of one general peace to that of the next in the series. If we are to look for an explanation of the War-and-Peace Cycle in the working of some psychic law of Human Nature, and to find this psychic law in the periodic breaking of the continuity of a social heritage as this is transmitted by one generation to another, we shall not be able to account on these lines for a rhythm of the wave-length of the War-and-Peace Cycle unless we find that a cumulative psychic and social effect can be produced by a series of breaks between generations running beyond the singular into the plural.

We have only to remind ourselves of this consideration in order to recognize that a concatenation, not just of two generations, but of three, is apt to be the vehicle of social transformation in changes of Nationality, of Religion, and of Class. In all these three variations on the theme of social metamorphosis, it takes not only more than the experience-span of a single lifetime, but also more than a single breach of social continuity through the transmission of experience from one generation to another, to negotiate the passage from an inherited nationality, religion, or class to an adopted one.

In the field of changes of Nationality, this 'law' to the effect that it takes three generations for a family to achieve a social metamorphosis is aptly exemplified in an illustration of it that once came to the writer's personal notice. One day in the summer of A.D. 1932, at a public luncheon in the city of Troy, New York State, the writer, finding himself seated next to the local Director of Public Education, took the opportunity to ask his neighbour what, among all his manifold professional duties, was the job that he was finding the most interesting at the time. 'Organizing English lessons for grandparents' the Director promptly and unhesitatingly replied. 'And how, in an English-speaking country, does anybody manage to arrive at being a grandparent without having mastered the national language?' I thoughtlessly went on to inquire. 'Well, you see,' said the Director, 'Troy is the principal seat of the linen collar manufacturing industry in the United States, and, before the enactment of the United States Immigration Restriction Acts of 1921 and 1924, most of the labour-force here was recruited from foreign immigrants and their families. Now the immigrants who came from each of the principal emigrant-exporting countries had a way—which was natural enough in the new and strange surroundings in which they found themselves over here —of cleaving, as close as they could, to their own familiar past by continuing to consort with other birds of the same feather. Immigrants of the same national origin were not only apt to work side by side in the same factories; they were apt to live next door to one another in the same blocks of tenements; and so, when the time came for them to retire, most of them knew little more English than they had known when they had first landed on American shores. They did not have to know any more up to this point in the American chapter of their life, because they commanded the services of home-bred interpreters. Their children had arrived in America young enough to go to the public school before entering the factory in their turn, and the combination of an American education with, let us say, an Italian infancy had made them thoroughly bilingual; they talked English in the factory, street, and store and Italian in their parents' homes almost without noticing that they were constantly switching back and forth from one language to the other; and their effortless and ungrudging bilingualism was highly convenient for their old parents. Indeed, it abetted their parents' inclination, after their retirement, to forget even the smattering of English that they had once picked up during their working life in the factory. However, this is not the end of the story; for in due course the retired immigrants' children married and had children of their own, and, for these representatives of a third generation, English was the language of the home as well as the school. Since their own parents had married after having been educated in the United States, one of them would be of non-Italian origin as often as not, and then English would be the *lingua franca* in which the father and mother would communicate with one another. So the American-born children of bilingual parents would not know their grandparents' Italian mother tongue, and, moreover, would have no use for it. Why should they put themselves out in order to learn a foreign lingo that would convict them of an un-American origin which they were eager to slough off and consign to oblivion? So the grandparents found that their grandchildren could not be induced to communicate with them in the only language in which the grandparents were able to talk with any ease, and they were thus confronted suddenly, in their old age, with the appalling prospect of being unable to establish any human contact with their own living descendants. For Italians and other non-English-speaking Continental Europeans with a strong sense of family solidarity, this prospect was intolerable. For the first time in their lives they now had an incentive for mastering the hitherto unattractive language of their adopted country; and last year they thought of applying to me for help. Of course I was eager to arrange special classes for them; and, though it is notorious that the enterprise of learning a foreign language becomes more difficult progressively as one grows older, I can assure you that these English lessons for grandparents have been one of the most successful and rewarding pieces of work that we have ever taken in hand in our department.'

This tale of Troy shows how a series of three generations can achieve, through the cumulative effect of two successive caesuras, a social metamorphosis which could never have been achieved by representatives of a single generation within the span of a single lifetime. The process by which an Italian family transformed itself into an American family could not be analysed or described intelligibly in terms of any single life. An interaction between representatives of three successive generations was required in order to bring it about. The first generation of immigrants had to wait for the birth of grandchildren to move them seriously to embrace an alien nationality into which their grandchildren had been born. And, when we turn from changes of Nationality to consider changes of Religion and of Class, we find that, in these other two fields likewise, the family, not the individual, is the intelligible unit, and that, in the process of these changes likewise, the cumulative effect of two successive breaks between generations is needed in order to achieve the metamorphosis.

In a class-conscious Modern England which in A.D. 1952 was fast dissolving under the writer's eyes, it had usually taken three generations to make 'gentlefolk' out of a family of 'working-class' or even of 'lower-middle-class' antecedents; and in the field of Religion the standard wave-length of the process of conversion seems to have been the same. In the history of the eradication of Paganism in the Roman World, the intolerantly devout Christian-born Emperor Theodosius I followed the ex-pagan convert Constantine I on the Imperial Throne, not in the next generation, but in the next but one; and in the history of the eradication of Protestantism in an Early Modern Western France there was the same interval between the intolerantly devout Catholic-born Bourbon King Louis XIV and his ex-Calvinist Bourbon grandfather King Henry IV. In a post-Modern Western France at the turn of the nineteenth and twentieth centuries of the Christian Era it took the same number of generations to breed genuinely devout Catholics among the grandchildren of officially reconverted bourgeois agnostics or atheists who had re-embraced Catholicism on the cynically calculating consideration that this was a traditional form of virtual Paganism, native to the soil of France, which promised, if only the Church could re-enlist sufficient support, to serve as an effective institutional bulkhead against a rising tide of Socialism and other ideologies that threatened to do away with the economic inequality between the bourgeosie and the working class.[1] In the Syriac World, again, under the Umayyad Caliphate, it took three generations to breed genuinely devout Muslims among Mawlās[2] whose ex-Christian or ex-Zoroastrian grandfathers had officially embraced Islam in order to make themselves eligible for being adopted as clients by influential members of a Primitive Muslim Arab ruling class. The duration of the Umayyad régime, which stood for the conquerors' ascendency over the conquered, was determined by the three-generations-long period that had to elapse in order to bring the original converts' Muslim-born grandchildren on to the stage of History. The Umayyad agents of a libertarian Arab 'ascendancy' were supplanted by 'Abbasid exponents of a Muslim egalitarianism[3] when, in the name of Islamic principles and ideals, the genuinely devout Muslim grandchildren of cynical converts

---

[1] See the observations of a French authority in Toynbee, A. J., and Boulter, V. M.: *Survey of International Affairs, 1929* (London 1930, Milford), p. 480, n. 1.
[2] See VI. vii. 142–4.   [3] See VI. vii. 147–52.

tried conclusions with the Laodicean Muslim grandchildren of Laodicean Muslim Arab *conquistadores*.[1]

If a concatenation of three generation cycles thus proves to be the regular psychic vehicle of social change in the three fields of Religion, Class, and Nationality, it would not be surprising to find a concatenation of four generations playing a similar part in the field of International Politics. In another context[2] we have already found that, in the field of encounters between civilizations, the Time-interval between the creation of an intelligentsia and its revolt against its makers has had an average length of about 137 years—i.e. about twenty years more than the combined Time-span of four generations of average length—in a set of three or four instances; and it is not difficult to see how a concatenation of four generations might also determine the wave-length of the War-and-Peace Cycle, if we may assume that the agony of a general war makes a deeper impression on the Psyche than is made on it by a comparatively anodyne round of supplementary wars. While it might require no more than a single inter-generational caesura to efface the impression of a general war sufficiently to give the next generation the nerve to embark on supplementary wars of limited scope, it might require two or three caesuras to make the grandchildren or great-grandchildren of the perpetrators and victims of a previous general war so insensitive to their forebears' crimes and sufferings as to have the heart to re-perform the tragedy on the grand scale. A psychological process thus working itself out across two or three inter-generational caesuras would extend, on an average, over a time-span of something between $87\frac{1}{2}$ and $116\frac{2}{3}$ years; and, in the Modern and post-Modern ages of Western history, these are, as we have seen,[3] in fact the approximate maximum and minimum lengths of an interval between the outbreak of one general war and another which gives the measure of the wave-length of the War-and-Peace Cycle.[4]

The Subjection of Broken-down Civilizations to Laws of Subconscious Human Nature

This War-and-Peace Cycle, however, is neither the last nor the longest of the regularities and recurrences for which we have to seek an explanation; for each of these cycles running to a wave-length of anything from about 80 to about 120 years is merely one term in a series. In

---

[1] See VI. vii. 144. This is an exemplification of a 'law'—noticed in III. iii. 24–25 —that, in Nomad empires *in partibus agricolarum*, it usually takes three generations, reckoning from the date of the Nomad conquerors' eruption out of 'the Desert' on to 'the Sown', for the Nomad empire-builders to degenerate and for their 'human cattle' to recuperate. [2] See IX. viii. 341, n. 1.

[3] In this series of war-and-peace cycles the overture took 74 years (A.D. 1494–1568), the first regular cycle 104 years (A.D. 1568–1672), the second regular cycle 120 years (A.D. 1672–1792), the third regular cycle 122 years (A.D. 1792–1814). See Table I on p. 255, above.

[4] In the light of this tentative psychological explanation of the standard wave-length of the War-and-Peace Cycle, we can perhaps now see why a reduplicated general war— in which one general war is followed, after a single breathing-space, by another general war instead of by a round of relatively innocuous supplementary wars—should be so portentous an enormity. If it normally requires two or three inter-generational caesuras to nerve a society to plunge into a general war again, the reduplication of a general war after a single caesura is manifestly something contrary to Human Nature, and the penalty for this breach of a psychic law is likely to be as signal as the breach itself.

Western history a series of war-and-peace cycles which had started in A.D. 1494 was in its 458th year and its fourth cycle in A.D. 1952; in Hellenic history a series that had started in 321 B.C. had run through 290 years and three cycles before it had been wound up in 31 B.C.; in Sinic history, 459 (or 550) years and five cycles had elapsed before a series that had started in 680 (or 771) B.C. had been wound up in 221 B.C.[1] Moreover, each of the first two series was, as we have seen,[2] only the second chapter of an older and longer story. In the history of each of these civilizations, and of others as well, we can trace these series of war-and-peace cycles in the relations between parochial sovereign states back into the afflicted civilization's growth-phase; we can watch the general wars that the civilization periodically inflicts on itself progressively taking a greater toll of the war-making society's energies until, sooner or later, one of these catastrophes precipitates a social breakdown; and from that epoch-making point we can follow the series of war-and-peace cycles working itself out to its conclusion through a Time of Troubles whose standard length we have found empirically to be of the order of approximately four centuries. A Time of Troubles, however, is no more than one phase of a far longer process of social disintegration; Times of Troubles are apt to be followed by universal states, and these, too, seem to run to a standard length of about four hundred years, which they sometimes exceed when they encroach upon the ensuing interregnum that is apt to intervene between the dissolution of a disintegrating civilization and the emergence of a successor affiliated to it. Thus the total Time-span taken by a series of war-and-peace cycles may vary between a minimum of 400 years and a maximum of 600, or perhaps even more, while the total Time-span taken by the disintegration of a civilization may vary between a minimum of 800 years and a maximum of not much less than 1,100. Will a psychological explanation of regularities in human affairs, which has served us up to this point, avail to account for the uniform recurrence of social processes, phase for phase in an identical sequence and measure for measure on an identical Time-scale, when these processes uniformly recurring in the histories of divers civilizations expand over periods which are many times longer, not only than the individual experience of a single life-time, but also than the cumulative experience of a concatenation of three or four generation cycles? Considering that, on the level of personal consciousness, the span of continuous human experience is confined within the limits of a single life-time, our answer to our question would have been bound to be in the negative if, in our eyes, the intellectual and volitional surface of the Psyche had been the whole of the Psyche, as the Hellenic discoverers of the Intellect were prone to assume that it was.

It is true that even the fathers of Hellenic philosophy were not so thoroughly blinded by the dazzling light of a newly discovered Reason as to be altogether without an inkling of an irrational psychic life brewing below this brightly illuminated surface of the Psyche in the dark deeps of a subconscious abyss. Aristotle perceived and declared that 'the Intellect

---

[1] See Tables II and III, on pp. 268–9 and 273, above.
[2] See pp. 282–3, above.

by itself moves nothing';[1] and Plato had anticipated, and advanced beyond, this merely negative Aristotelian dictum in his myth of the Soul
as a charioteer driving two mettlesome steeds of diverse temperaments.[2]
All the same, it was left to the children of a Western Civilization, affiliated to the Hellenic, eventually to follow up these Hellenic surmises by
tardily embarking, in a post-Modern Age of Western history, on the
scientific exploration of a psychic underworld that had been familiar to
Indic and Sinic contemporaries of the Hellenic discoverers of the Intellect, and that had been the source of every poet's and prophet's inspiration in all times and places.

In the Western World in the writer's generation a Western science of
Psychology was still in its infancy; yet the pioneers had already carried
their reconnaissances far enough to enable C. G. Jung to report that the
subconscious abyss on whose surface each individual human personality's
conscious intellect and will were afloat was not an undifferentiated chaos
but was an articulated universe in which one layer of psychic activity
could be discerned below another. The nearest layer to the surface
appeared to be a Personal Subconscious deposited by a personality's
individual experiences in the course of his or her own life up to date;
the deepest layer to which the explorers had so far penetrated appeared to
be a Racial Subconscious that was not peculiar to any individual but was
common to all human beings, inasmuch as the Primordial Images
latent there reflected the common experiences of Mankind, deposited
during the infancy of the Human Race, if not at a stage before Man had
yet become completely human. On this showing, it was perhaps not unreasonable to surmise that, in between the uppermost and the lower-
most of the layers of the Subconscious that Western scientists had so far
succeeded in bringing within their ken, there might be intermediate
layers deposited neither by racial experience nor by personal experience,
but by corporate experience of a supra-personal but infra-racial range.
There might be layers of experience common to a family, common to a
community, or common to a society; and, if, at the next level above the
Primordial Images common to the whole Human Race, there should
indeed prove to be images expressing the peculiar êthos of a particular
society, the impress of these on the Psyche might account for the length
of the periods which certain social processes seemed to require in order
to work themselves out.[3]

For example, one such social image that was manifestly apt to imprint
itself deeply on the subconscious psychic life of the children of a civilization in process of growth was the idol of the parochial sovereign state;
and it can readily be imagined that, even after this idol had begun to
exact from its devotees human sacrifices as grim as any that the Canaan-
ites ever paid to Moloch or the Bengalis to Juggernaut, the victims of a
demon which these victims themselves had conjured up might well need
the poignant experience, not just of a single life-time and not just of one
concatenation of three generation cycles, but of a span of not less than

[1] Aristotle: *Ethica Nicomachea*, Z 2, pp. 1139 A–B, quoted in III. iii. 231, n. 1, and
on p. 395, below.
[2] Plato: *Phaedrus*, 246A–257B.
[3] This consideration has been anticipated in IX. viii. 115–16.

four hundred years, in order to bring themselves to the point of plucking this baneful idolatry out of their hearts and casting it from them. It can also readily be imagined that they might need, not just four hundred years, but eight hundred years or a thousand, to dissociate themselves from the civilization whose breakdown and disintegration a Time of Troubles had made manifest, and to open their hearts to receive the impress of some other society of the same species or of the different species represented by the higher religions. For the image of a civilization presumably makes a still more potent appeal to the Subconscious Psyche than the image of any of the parochial states into which civilizations are apt to be articulated on the political plane unless and until they eventually enter into a universal state. From the same angle of mental vision we can likewise understand how a universal state, once established, should sometimes succeed, in its turn, in retaining its hold over its ex-subjects', or even over its actual destroyers', hearts for generations or perhaps even for centuries after it has lost its usefulness as well as its power and has become almost as grievously heavy an incubus as the antecedent parochial states that it had been created to liquidate.[1]

'The relation between the external anxieties felt by the representatives of an adult generation—anxieties that are directly conditioned by the social position of the people who feel them—and the inward, automatically operating, anxieties of these people's children in the rising generation is unquestionably a phenomenon of importance over a wide field. . . . The stamp that is set by the procession of successive generations on both the psychic development of the individual and the course of historical change is something that we shall only begin to understand more adequately than we do at present when we have become more capable than we are to-day of taking our observations, and doing our historical thinking, in terms of long chains of generations.'[2]

If the social laws current in the histories of civilizations are indeed reflections of psychological laws governing some infra-personal layer of the Subconscious Psyche, this would also explain why these social laws should be, as we have found them to be, so much more clearly pronounced and more exactly regular in the disintegration-phase of a broken-down civilization's history than in its foregoing growth-phase.

Though the growth-phase, as well as the disintegration-phase, can be analysed into a series of bouts of Challenge-and-Response, we have found it impossible to discern any standard wave-length common to the successive bouts through which social growth takes place, whether we measure the intervals between successive presentations of challenges or the intervals between successive deliveries of effective responses, and we have also seen that in the growth-phase these successive challenges and successive responses are infinitely various. By contrast, we have found that the successive stages of the disintegration-phase are marked by repeated presentations of an identical challenge which continues to recur because the disintegrating society continues to fail to meet it;[3] and we

[1] See VI. vii. 7–46.
[2] Elias, N.: *Über den Prozess der Zivilisation*, vol. ii: *Wandlungen der Gesellschaft: Entwurf zu einer Theorie der Zivilisation* (Basel 1939, Haus zum Falken), p. 451.
[3] See V. v. 12–13.

have also found that, in all past cases of social disintegration that we have mustered in an empirical survey, the same successive stages all invariably occur in the same order, each stage taking approximately the same period of time in the history of one civilization as the corresponding stage in the history of another, so that the disintegration-phase as a whole presents the picture of a uniform process with a uniform total duration when we take a synoptic view of the divers examples of it provided by the histories of a dozen different broken-down civilizations. Indeed, as soon as a social breakdown has occurred and the process of social disintegration has set in, the tendency towards variety and differentiation that is characteristic of the growth-phase of a civilization is replaced by a nisus towards uniformity and identity that shows its power and persistence by triumphing sooner or later over interference from outside, as well as over recalcitrance from within.

We have observed, for example,[1] how, when first a Syriac and then an Indic universal state was cut short by the impact of an intrusive Hellenic Civilization prematurely, before it had completed a universal state's standard life-span of some four hundred years' duration, the smitten and submerged society could not or would not pass away until, in spite of the disturbing influence of an alien body social, it had duly completed the regular course of a broken-down society's disintegration by eventually re-entering into the interrupted phase and abiding in a reintegrated universal state long enough to make up, in the aggregate, a psychological equivalent of the length of time normally occupied by this phase in the standard pattern of the disintegration-process.[2] Disintegration did not culminate in dissolution in either of these two historic cases until the prematurely shattered universal state had re-established its structure and resumed its course, even though in Indic history the interrupted universal state had to wait for more than 450 years before it could find its opportunity to achieve an avatar of the Mauryan Empire in the shape of the Guptan Empire, while in Syriac history it had to wait for no less than 950 years for the Achaemenian Empire to re-emerge in the shape of the Arab Caliphate. These belated but insistent resumptions of a regular

---

[1] In I. i. 73–77.

[2] This 'psychological equivalent' of a normal continuous Time-span of approximately four hundred years' length does not, of course, add up to precisely the same figure in the aggregate when it is provided in two instalments separated from one another chronologically by the intrusion of an alien civilization. We should expect it to take a longer aggregate tale of years to produce a psychological effect in two instalments than to produce it in a single one; and in the Syriac case we find, in fact, that the effective durations of the Achaemenian Empire and the Arab Caliphate amount, in the aggregate, not just to 400 years, but to 522 (see Table I in vol. vi, p. 327, and also in vol. vii, p. 769, there). On the other hand the effective durations of the Mauryan and Guptan Empires amount to no more than 322 years (see ibid.); and, even if we were to equate the period of the *Pax Guptica* with the full length of time during which the Gupta Dynasty was officially regnant, we should barely arrive at an aggregate exceeding four hundred years for the two instalments here.

This at first sight surprisingly small aggregate duration of a *pax oecumenica* in Indic history is perhaps partly explained by the consideration that a psychological equivalent of it was also provided regionally, during the period of Hellenic intrusion, by the Bactrian Greek, Sakan, Kushan, and Andhran régimes to some extent. In this context we may observe that, during the corresponding Hellenic intrusion upon the Syriac World, the role of the Andhra Dynasty in Indic history was played in Syriac history by the Arsacidae and Sasanidae, and the role of the Bactrian Greek, Sakan, and Kushan princes by the Seleucidae.

course of disintegration, with a standard duration, that had been interrupted by the intrusion of an alien society, have their converse in the
belated but ineluctable dissolution of the Egyptiac Society after it had
set Fate at defiance by galvanizing its dead body social into a state of life-
in-death which it managed to maintain for as long a period—some two
thousand years in all—as the aggregate length of the preceding growth-
phase and disintegration-phase.[1] The moral of this fruitless Egyptiac
tour de force is

> Nec prorsum vitam ducendo demimus hilum
> tempore de mortis nec delibare valemus
> quo minus esse diu possimus forte perempti.
> proinde licet quot vis vivendo condere saecla:
> mors aeterna tamen nilo minus illa manebit,
> nec minus ille diu iam non erit, ex hodierno
> lumine qui finem vitai fecit, et ille
> mensibus atque annis qui multis occidit ante.[2]

Apparently a broken-down civilization that has travelled so far along the
path of disintegration as to have entered into a universal state has no
more power to achieve immortality by prolonging this phase of life-in-
death *in saecula saeculorum* than it has to anticipate the inevitable hour
by going into dissolution before it has served the full term which every
disintegrating civilization is doomed to serve in this phase of the disintegration process.

This striking contrast between the regularity and uniformity of the
phenomena of social disintegration and the irregularity and diversity of
the phenomena of social growth has been noted frequently in this Study
up to this point as a matter of manifest historical fact, without any attempt so far to account for it. In the present Part, which is concerned
with the relation between Law and Freedom in human affairs, it is incu-
bent on us to grapple with this problem; and a key to its solution may be
found in the difference between the respective natures of the conscious
personality on the surface of the Psyche and the subconscious levels of
psychic life underlying it.

The distinctive gift of Consciousness is a freedom to make choices—
between alternative courses of action for the Will, and between alternative ideas and beliefs for the Intellect; and, although this path of freedom
has an inner law and order of its own which is manifest from within to
the thinking, planning, and acting personality itself, the same path looks
capriciously disorderly when it is surveyed by a spectator from outside.
In the sight of an alien observer, 'the wind bloweth where it listeth';[3]
and, considering that a relative freedom is one of the characteristics of
the growth-phase in the history of a civilization, it is, after all, only to be
expected that, in so far as human beings are free in these circumstances
to determine their own future for themselves, the course which they
follow should be in truth, as it appears to be, a wayward one in the sense
of being recalcitrant to the rule of 'laws of Nature'.

The reign of Freedom, which thus keeps 'laws of Nature' at bay, is,

[1] See I. i. 136–9.   [2] Lucretius: *De Rerum Naturâ*, Book III, ll. 1087–94.
[3] John iii. 8.

however, precarious inasmuch as it depends upon the fulfilment of two conditions, both of which are evidently exacting and arduous. The first condition is that the conscious personality must keep the subconscious underworld of the Psyche under the Will's and the Reason's control; the second condition is that it must also contrive to 'dwell together in unity'[1] with the other conscious personalities with which it has to dwell on some terms or other in the mortal life of a *Homo Sapiens* who was a social animal before he was a human being, and was a sexual organism before he was a social animal. These two necessary conditions for the exercise of freedom are actually inseparable from one another; for, if it is true that, 'when knaves fall out, honest men come by their own',[2] it is no less true that, when persons fall out, the Subconscious Psyche escapes from the unwelcome control of each and all of them.

Plato's comparison of the demonic forces of the Subconscious to mettlesome steeds, and of the controlling Personality to a charioteer, is perhaps too flattering to the Soul. The Zen School of Mahayanian Buddhism may be nearer to the mark in likening the Subconscious to an ox and the Conscious Personality to a boy who has to win and keep control over the powerful and recalcitrant beast by cultivating the Orphic arts of tact and charm.[3] Mithraism, picturing the beast, not as an ox, but as a bull, draws the conclusion that he cannot be domesticated and must therefore be butchered if the Personality is to assert its freedom effectively, and this militant attitude towards the Subconscious Psyche, which is the antithesis of a Far Eastern *modus vivendi*, was bequeathed by Mithraism to Western Christendom.

'From the beginning the Chinese seem to have favoured a dynamic rather than a moral conception of the Universe. The specialisation of the Intellect never assumed so great an ascendancy as to pit Reasoning Man against Unreasoning Nature. Whereas the heroic attitude of the West tends to picture Man in constant warfare with the destructive powers of Nature, Chinese common sense prefers to convince the bull that a parallel movement is better in every way than mere opposition. In the West the dragon symbolises the power of evil or the force of regression, for the Western mind is rooted in the idea that Man's original nature is evil. In the East the dragon dwells on the highest mountains and is identified with clouds and flowing water, because the Eastern mind sees spiritual events as the interplay of natural elements. Hence the dragon, as symbol of the inexhaustible potential of natural energy, represents beneficent spiritual power.[4] So long as it is conceived along Miltonesque lines as representing

---

[1] Ps. cxxxiii. 1.

[2] Palmer, Samuel: *Moral Essays on Some of the Most Curious and Significant English, Scotch, and Foreign Proverbs* (London 1710, Bonwicke), p. 327.

[3] See Suzuki, D. T.: *The Ten Oxherding Pictures* (Kyoto 1948, Sekai Seiten Kanko Kyokai), quoted in VII. vii. 506.

[4] Was Goethe inspired by some picture, or pictorial image, of Chinese provenance when he wrote

Kennst du den Berg und seinen Wolkensteg?
Das Maultier sucht in Nebel seinen Weg,
In Höhlen wohnt der Drachen alte Brut,
Es stürzt der Fels und über ihn die Flut:
Kennst du ihn wohl?
    Dahin! Dahin
Geht unser Weg; O Vater, lass uns ziehn!

Was it merely a chronological coincidence that an eighteenth-century Western philo-

the power of Hell, it has to be combated as evil. Yet, if we only could regard the dragon as a superior power, it would possibly reveal to us the daemonic aspect of God.'[1]

A more prosaic variation on the same mythical theme is the picture of a man who has to drive to market neither Saint George's dragon nor Mithra's bull nor a Chinese sage's ox, but some sullenly obstinate animal, such as a camel, a mule, or a goat, or some perversely insubordinate animal, such as a pig. It is relatively easy for the man to survey the country, choose his market, and find the most direct road leading to this goal; but 'the Intellect by itself moves nothing';[2] the man would be going to market on a bootless errand if he failed to bring the pig along with him; and in any case his freedom does not run to the length of allowing him this choice; for he is tied to the pig by an undetachable umbilical cord, and he must therefore either contrive to take the pig with him or resign himself to never reaching his own objective. His choice lies, not between bringing the pig to market and leaving it behind in its sty, but merely between alternative methods of trying to get the pig to travel his way. If he is Mithraic-minded, he will cut the pig's throat, sling the carcass over his shoulder, and stagger forward with his back bowed down under the weight of Pilgrim's burden. If he is Prussian-minded, he will try to coerce the creature with a drill-sergeant's rod;[3] if he is Platonic-minded, he will try to drive it with a charioteer's firm but sympathetic handling of the reins; if he is Zen-minded, he will try to charm it, with Orphic strains, to travel of its own accord towards the magic flute-player's appointed goal for this pair of incongruous yet inseparable Siamese twins. The man has a wide choice of tactics for bringing the beast along with him; the one thing that he cannot do is to travel unencumbered by the creature's awkward company. His predicament has been portrayed, with the insight of genius, by Pascal.

'Il ne faut pas se méconnaître: nous sommes automate autant qu'esprit; et de là vient que l'instrument par lequel la persuasion se fait n'est pas la seule démonstration. . . . Les preuves ne convainquent que l'esprit; la coutume fait nos preuves les plus fortes et les plus crues; elle incline l'automate, qui entraîne l'esprit sans qu'il y pense. . . . Quand on ne croit que par la force de la conviction, et que l'automate est incliné à croire le contraire, ce n'est pas assez. Il faut donc faire croire nos deux pièces: l'esprit, par les raisons, qu'il suffit d'avoir vues une fois en sa vie; et l'automate, par la coutume, et en ne lui permettant pas de s'incliner au contraire. *Inclina cor meum, Deus.*'[4]

It is evident that, even if this life-long implication with a subconscious fellow-traveller were the only impediment to the progress of a personality

---

sophy discarded a traditional Christian belief in Original Sin in favour of a revolutionary faith in the perfectibility of Human Nature on the morrow of the initiation of a Late Modern Western Republic of Letters into the Sinic Weltanschauung by Jesuit Sino-logues at the turn of the seventeenth and eighteenth centuries? Or did these consecutive events in Western history stand to one another in a relation of cause and effect?—A.J.T.

[1] Baynes, H. G.: *Mythology of the Soul* (London 1940, Baillière, Tindall & Cox; 1949, Methuen), p. 872.

[2] Aristotle. cited on p. 328, n. 1, above.   [3] See IV. iv. 123-4.

[4] Pascal, Blaise: *Pensées*, No. 252 in Léon Brunschvicg's arrangement of the text. The quotation is from Ps. cxix. 36.

along the path of freedom, the task of perpetually vindicating this free-dom by keeping this obligatory subconscious companion in step with itself would be a heavy tax on a personality's spiritual resources; but, in this ceaseless contest between man and pig, the man also labours under one grievous handicap from which the pig is exempt and of which the pig also knows how to take full advantage. While there is only one pig, there is a host of drivers tethered to his sly tail; and, if the drivers fall out with one another and, in falling out, neutralize one another's efforts to control the pig, then the pig has a chance of capturing the initiative from each and all of them, and of taking his revenge by leading each and all of them by the nose. The worst of it—from the drivers' standpoint—is that, notwithstanding their common interest in keeping the pig in order, it is superhumanly difficult for the drivers to achieve and maintain the mutual harmony without which each of them will be impotent to carry out their identical task; for, though Man is a social animal, and indeed is this *ex officio originis*, his attempts to achieve harmony between will and will and between mind and mind have been as singularly unsuccessful as his attempts to discipline or civilize his subconscious mate, by contrast with Man's extraordinary success in discovering the secrets, and tapping the energies, of Physical Nature. Moreover, in his social life Man has been least unsuccessful within the narrow range of his personal relations; the social problem that has signally defeated him is, as we have seen,[1] the problem of harmonizing wills and minds over a wider range on which a majority of the relations are necessarily impersonal. On this wider range, on which Man is bound to lead his social life if he is not to renounce his ambition to master Physical Nature, Man has so far not hit upon any more effective or less perilous an expedient than to mechanize the relations be-tween wills and intellects by subjecting them to 'social drill' through the enlistment of a faculty of mimesis which is the antithesis of rational choice and is, indeed, native, not to the conscious surface of the Psyche, but to the underlying subconscious abyss. If the quarrelsome drivers of the pig can think of no better way of keeping the peace among themselves than to take a leaf out of a porcine copybook, it is no wonder that their best-laid plans for securing social harmony with one another should 'gang aft a-gley';[2] and it is, in fact, notorious that the institutional machinery through which Man has endeavoured to organize his life on a supra-personal range has been Man's most tragic and most deadly failure. In the life which Man has made for himself on Earth, his institutions, in contrast to his personal relations, are the veritable slums, and the taint of moral obliquity is still more distressing in the least ignoble of these social tenements of the Human Spirit—for instance, in the churches and the academies—than in such unquestionably malignant institutions as Sla-very and War.

Thus the gift of Consciousness, whose mission is to liberate the Human Spirit from 'laws of Nature' ruling over the subconscious abyss of the Psyche, is apt to defeat itself by misusing, as a weapon in a fratrici-dal conflict between one personality and another, the freedom that is its *raison d'être*; and the structure and working of the Human Psyche

---

[1] See IV. iv. 133–584.   [2] Burns, Robert: *To a Mouse.*

account for this tragic aberration without any need for recourse to Bossuet's[1] impious hypothesis of special interventions on the part of an omnipotent yet nevertheless jealous God to make sure that human wills shall reduce one another to impotence by cancelling one another out.

'History is so made that the end result always arises out of the conflict of many individual wills in which every will is itself the product of a host of special conditions of life. Consequently there exist innumerable intersecting forces, an infinite group of parallelograms of forces which give rise to one resultant product—the historical event. This again may itself be viewed as the product of a force acting as a Whole without consciousness or volition; for what every individual wills separately is frustrated by what everyone else wills, and the general upshot is something which no one willed.[2] And so the course of History has run along like a natural process; it also is subject essentially to the same laws of motion.'[3]

This acute observation by one of the twin founding fathers of a Communist Church had been elaborated by a later Western student of social laws of Human Nature.

'Historical change, taken as a whole, is not the working out of any "rational" plan; yet at the same time it is also not just a chaotic appearance and disappearance of forms subject to no kind of order. How is this possible? How can it happen, at all, in a human world, that formations should come into being that have not been intended by any single human being, yet which, nevertheless, are worlds away from those shapes without stability, development, or structure that are assumed by the clouds...?

'The answer to these questions is a simple one. The plans and the transactions, the feelings and the thoughts, of individual human beings are perpetually subject to interference, friendly or hostile, from one another. This interweaving of individual human plans and transactions, which is [one of the] fundamental [facts of human life], ... and which, moreover, goes on continuously from generation to generation, is something that has not, itself, ever been planned. It cannot be understood by reference to the plans and aims of individual human beings, or on the

---

[1] See the passage quoted on pp. 381–2, below.
[2] In the same passage, Engels credits his poignantly true story of the mutual frustration of human wills with an unconvincingly 'happy ending':
'From the fact that the wills of individuals—who desire what the constitution of their body, as well as external circumstances, in the last instance economic (either personal or social), determine them to desire—do not get what they wish, but are sunk into an average or common result, from all that one has no right to conclude that they equal zero. On the contrary, every will contributes to the result and is in so far forth included within it.'
This 'happy ending' to Engels' grim proposition rings hollow; for wills that 'do not get what they wish' do equal zero in terms of the achievement of a conscious personality's deliberate purpose; and Engels' statement can mean no more than that each frustrated will would have made a contribution to a resolution of forces if the forces here in play had been mechanical (as they are not) instead of being volitional (as they are).
What moved Engels to adulterate the pure milk of his word by throwing in a grain of comfort that has the triple demerit of being untrue, unconsoling, and incongruous? The belief that human history is subject to laws of Nature is one of the cardinal doctrines of the Communist faith. What has induced this secular theologian thus to blunt his theology's cutting edge? It looks as if Engels were here inadvertently contaminating the Communist conception that laws of Nature come into operation in human affairs through the mutual frustration of human wills with a reminiscence of the Christian conception that human wills can save themselves from frustration in so far, and only in so far, as they voluntarily conform themselves to the will of God.—A.J.T.
[3] Engels, F.: Letter of the 21st September, 1890, to J. Bloch, reprinted in Hook, S.: *Towards the Understanding of Karl Marx* (New York 1933, Day), pp. 334–5.

analogy of the pattern that these display. . . .[1] [On the other hand,] it has the power to produce changes and formations which no single human being has planned or created. This interdependence of human beings, one with another, gives rise to an order of a highly special character—and this order is more compelling and more powerful than the will and the reason of the individual human beings who bring it into existence. This order, consisting in a network of interwoven relations, is the power that governs the course of historical change; this is the principle that lies at the root of the process of Civilisation.

'This order is neither "rational"—if by "rational" is meant something that has come into being, like a machine, as a result of purposive thinking done by individual human beings—and it is not "irrational"either—if by "irrational" is meant something that has come into being in a way that is beyond our comprehension. . . . The law governing the phenomena of social interweaving is a distinctive system which is identical neither with the law of the "Spirit" (des "Geistes"), in the sense of individual thinking and planning, nor with the law of what we call "Nature", in spite of the fact that all these divers dimensions of Reality are indissolubly bound up with one another in action (funktionell).'[2]

Engels' 'force acting as a whole without consciousness or volition', which comes into play when wills illuminated by Consciousness frustrate one another, and which is governed by a social law that is neither the law of the Spirit nor the law of Physical Nature, is none other than the sub-conscious tide in the Psyche, which no sooner escapes from the control of some will and mind that have been carrying it whither it would not[3] than it relapses into an unchallenged obedience to a law which is the antithesis of Freedom and which is morally facile just because it dispenses its subject from the free spirit's agonizing responsibility for making choices.[4] The character of these laws of the Subconscious Psyche was being brought to light by post-Modern Western psychologists in the writer's day, and two features of it were already clearly discernible: by comparison with the volatility of conscious thought and volition, the gait of subconscious imaginative and emotional life was evidently as slow as it was regular. Even when a conscious personality was more or less in control of its subconscious underworld, its freedom of manœuvre would be limited by the necessity of humouring the êthos of an inseparable subconscious fellow-traveller who could not be forced, either by coaxing or by coercion or by the ultima ratio of resort to a Mithraic butcher's knife, to exceed his own dead-slow maximum pace or his own infinitesimal maximum capacity for swerving from an irrationally sacrosanct rut of routine. A fortiori, when the subconscious brute was exempt from the imposition of conscious control thanks to an incapacitating fratricidal strife among the host of conscious personalities between whom

---

[1] This passage will be found, in the original, on p. 476.—A.J.T.
[2] Elias, N.: Über den Prozess der Zivilisation, vol. ii: Wandlungen der Gesellschaft: Entwurf zu einer Theorie der Zivilisation (Basel 1939, Haus zum Falken), pp. 313–15.
[3] John xxi. 18.
[4] The penalty that conflicting wills bring upon themselves by frustrating one another is thus not merely their own dethronement; it is the re-enthronement of the Subconscious Psyche; and this disconcerting positive consequence of mutual frustration is not faced by Engels in the perfunctory consolations of Philosophy that he offers in the passage quoted on p. 335, n. 2, above.

this control had to be shared, it was only natural that Caliban should celebrate his release from an irksome servitude by moving at a slower and more regular gait than ever.

On this showing, a process of social disintegration running through a regular series of phases in an unvarying order, and moving at a set pace over periods of approximately identical length in all cases, can be seen to reflect the êthos of a Subconscious Human Nature so faithfully that the detection and recognition of this process can hardly be dismissed as the baseless conceit of a phantasy arbitrarily imposing a subjective standard pattern of its own on the histories of broken-down civilizations in their disintegration-phase. A student of the *ci-devant* intelligence that had been petrified into instinct in the psychic life of the bees had ascertained that, in this apian psychic universe, instinctive acts that fall into sequences of chapters have to be performed integrally if they are to be performed at all. No chapter can be omitted because it has become superfluous, or be repeated because it has not been performed effectively at the first essay, or be transposed from its established place in the series because a transposition would make for increased efficiency;[1] for the law that rules over the instinctive life of the bees is not the flexible law of rational experiment and reflection; it is the adamantine 'law of the Medes and Persians which altereth not',[2] however convincingly and insistently a change may be demanded by an empirical common sense.

These findings of an apian social science can be translated into the human language of Plato's simile of the charioteer and our own simile of the cart and the wheel. So long as the driver of a vehicle is seated on the box with the reins in his hands, no spectator who does not happen to be in the driver's confidence can foretell the equipage's destination, route, or speed; but, if a brawl between two rival coachmen scrambling for possession of the reins unintendedly gives the horses their head, an observer has only to acquaint himself with the horse-power of the draft animals and the relief of the *terrain* in order to be able to calculate exactly how many seconds will elapse and how many revolutions of the wheels will occur before the runaway horses land themselves and the carriage and its quarrelling occupants in the ditch. 'Fertur equis auriga neque audit currus habenas.'[3] For the purposes of this calculation it makes no difference whether the accident has overtaken the party at the outset of the journey or within sight of their destination, nor what route the map records nor what mileage the taximeter registers nor what passage of time the stopwatch reads down to the moment when the driver lost control and the catastrophe happened. All these antecedent data are irrelevant because, whatever they may be—and they may, of course, be widely diverse in different cases—the carriage and pair, when once left to their own devices, will take, in every case, an identical course and an identical time to go to perdition.

---

[1] See Hingston, R. W. G.: *Problems of Instinct and Intelligence* (London 1928, Arnold), chap. iv, pp. 38–53.
[2] Dan. vi. 8.   [3] Virgil: *Georgics*, Book I, l. 514.

(III) ARE LAWS OF NATURE CURRENT IN HISTORY INEXORABLE OR CONTROLLABLE?

If our foregoing survey has convinced us that human affairs are amenable to laws of Nature as a matter of fact, and that the currency of these laws in this realm is also explicable, at least to some extent, we may now go on to inquire whether laws of Nature current in human history are inexorable or controllable. If we here abide by our previous procedure of considering laws of Non-Human Nature first before we bring laws of Human Nature into our picture, we shall find that, as far as laws of Non-Human Nature are concerned, we have virtually answered our present question in the preceding chapter.

The short answer is that, though Man is powerless either to modify the terms of any law of Non-Human Nature or to suspend its operation, he can affect the incidence of these immutable and inexorable physical laws on human affairs by steering his own course on lines on which the laws of Non-Human Nature will be ministering to human purposes instead of frustrating them. It is true, for example, that no human being, by taking thought, can add one cubit unto his stature;[1] but it is also true that a biped on whose bodily height a 'ceiling' of little more than four cubits above ground level had been imposed by Physical Nature so long as the creature was standing with its feet on *terra firma*, had succeeded in raising this 'ceiling' to an altitude of several miles above sea-level for human beings whose intelligence and manual skill had enabled them to take to the air by making other laws of Non-Human Nature work for Man through the device of the internal combustion engine. We have already watched Man eluding the incidence of the Day-and-Night Cycle by equipping his ships and his industrial plants with large enough crews to keep the ship travelling, or the factory wheels turning, for twenty-four hours in the day by the device of dividing the crews into 'shifts' constantly relieving one another. We have likewise watched Man eluding the incidence of the Year Cycle by growing crops in the antipodes, inventing cold storage and rapid means of transport in bulk, and keeping the cold and the heat at bay by divers methods of artificial heating and cooling.

Western Man's success in modifying the incidence of laws of Non-Human Nature upon human activities had been registered in reductions in rates of insurance premium. Improvements in charts, followed up by the installation of wireless and radar on board ship, had diminished the risk of shipwreck through running aground or through crossing the path of a hurricane; the installation of lightning-conductors had diminished the risk of lightning damage to ships, ricks, and buildings; the smudge-pots of Southern California and the gauze screens of the Connecticut Valley had diminished the risk of frost damage to crops cultivated in a climate that would have been just too inclement to harbour them without Man's deft intervention in Flora's favour; the devices of inoculation, spraying, and baptism with pest-killers had diminished the danger of pest-damage to crops, trees, and flocks; while, in the life of the human husbandmen of this domesticated Flora, and shepherds of this

[1] Matt. vi. 27; Luke xii. 25.

domesticated Fauna, the incidence of disease had been diminished, and the expectation of life had been lengthened, by advances in preventive medicine which had proved most effective when they had taken the positive form of improvements in the physical and spiritual conditions of human life.

When we pass into the realm of laws of Human Nature, we find the same tale being told by reductions in rates of insurance premium here likewise. The risk of accidents on the road and in the factory had been reduced through a moral education in a sense of responsibility still more effectively than through the imposition of pains and penalties or through the installation of physical safety-devices. The risk of burglaries—which was more conspicuously refractory than the risk of accidents was to reduction either through precautions or through punishments—had been found to vary in inverse ratio with the general average level of moral probity, and this, in its turn, was apt to vary in some relation with the minimum level of material well-being in societies in which there was no more than an infinitesimally rare leaven of saints capable of rising wholly superior to their material circumstances.

On the economic plane it had been found that the volume of production per man-hour could be increased by the stimulation of the will to work more notably than by improvements in the skill of the workman or in the efficiency of his tools; and religious, ideological, and political motives for working with a will had sometimes proved more potent than economic incentives.

When we come to consider, for our purpose in this chapter, those alternating increases and decreases in Western economic activity that had come to be known as business cycles, we find the professional students of them drawing a distinction between the 'controllable' and the 'uncontrollable' factors,[1] and one school—namely, the exponents of the 'pure monetary theory'—going so far as to maintain that these fluctuations were due to a control deliberately exercised by the bankers over the activities of the traders and the manufacturers. A majority, however, of the experts in the writer's day evidently held that these deliberate acts, based on rationally calculated considerations of individual self-interest, on the part of persons occupying key positions of power in the economic system, counted for less in the generation of a rhythm of alternating booms and slumps than the uncontrolled play of imagination and feeling welling up from the subconscious lower levels of the Psyche.

'In rejecting some and accepting other schemes, the men of money are taking an important, though not a conspicuous, part in determining how labor shall be employed, what products shall be made, and what localities built up. Not all lenders, however, are able to make intelligent decisions. The great mass of small investors, and not a few of the large, lack the experience or ability or time to discriminate wisely between profitable and unprofitable schemes. . . . Investors who lack independent judgment are peculiarly subject to the influence of feeling in the matters where feeling is a dangerous guide. The alternating waves of confidence and timidity

[1] See, for example, Haberler, G.: *Prosperity and Depression* (3rd ed., Geneva 1941, League of Nations), p. 7.

which sweep over the market for securities are among the most characteristic phenomena of business cycles. Even those who are relied upon for advice are not wholly immune from the emotional contagion. Thus the guidance of economic activity by the investing class is only in part an intelligent review of plans by competent experts.'[1]

This picture of economic activity fluctuating under the ascendancy of almost blindly irrational subconscious psychic forces came into sharper focus when Economic Man was considered, not as a producer, but as a consumer.

'One reason why spending money is a backward art in comparison with making money [is that] the family continues to be the dominant unit of organisation for spending money, whereas for making money the family has been superseded largely by a more highly organised unit. The Housewife, who does a large fraction of the World's shopping, is not selected for her efficiency as a manager, is not dismissed for inefficiency, and has small chance of extending her sway over other households if she proves capable. . . . It is not surprising that what the World has learned in the art of consumption has been due less to the initiative of consumers than to the initiative of producers striving to win a market for their wares.'[2]

These considerations suggested that the fluctuations in the volume of business activity in an Industrial Western World might continue to escape control so long as the units of consumption continued to be households, and the units of production freely competing individuals, firms, trade-unions, and states whose conflicting wills largely cancelled one another out and, to that wide extent, left the economic arena open for the play of subconscious psychic forces. At the same time there seemed no reason why the Hebrew Patriarch Joseph's legendary success, as economic intendant of an Egyptiac World during the last days of a Hyksos régime, in making provision during years of abundance against coming years of scarcity should not be emulated on a 'global' scale in a latter-day Western World that had become coextensive with the entire habitable and traversable surface of the planet. By maintaining reserves of non-perishable commodities, by rendering perishable commodities non-perishable through deep-freezing, and by constantly rationing supplies of consumers' and producers' goods and purchasing power on a comprehensive long-term plan, there seemed no reason why some historic American or Russian Joseph should not one day bring the sum total of Mankind's economic life under a central control which, whether benevolent or malevolent, would assuredly outrange in its effectiveness the wildest flights of either Mosaic or Marxian fancy.

When we pass from business cycles with a forty-months-long or a nine-to-ten-years-long wave-length to a Generation Cycle with a wave-length of something between a quarter and a third of a century, we can see that, in a twentieth-century Westernizing World, the wastage to which any cultural heritage was perhaps bound to be subject in some measure in the course of its transmission from one generation to another was being reduced on the physical plane by typing, printing, photostating, and

---

[1] Mitchell, W. C.: *Business Cycles, the Problem and its Setting* (New York 1927 (reprinted 1930), National Bureau of Economic Research, Inc.), p. 163.   [2] Ibid., pp. 165–6.

other techniques for producing permanent visual records, and on the spiritual plane by improvements in education—in the broader meaning of the word—that were making a larger proportion of the total social heritage more fully available to a higher percentage of the total population in each successive rising generation. This diminution of the entries on the debit side of the Generation Cycle's account was, however, manifestly less difficult to achieve with the physical and spiritual means so far acquired by Man than it would be for Man deliberately to engineer an enhancement, or even merely to safeguard the maintenance, of the Generation Cycle's positive service to mortal men as a culturally profitable regulator of social change. In a rationally ordered world, in which a progressive improvement in record-taking and in education had reduced the wastage of Man's social heritage through the Generation Cycle to vanishing-point, it was conceivable that Mankind might one day wake up to find that, in the act of making itself master of the Generation Cycle, it had enslaved itself to the tyranny of an indelible tradition no less cramping than the indelible instincts into which, for ages past, a *ci-devant* Intelligence had been petrified in the Spartan-like universe of the Ants and the Bees.

When we pass on from the Generation Cycle to social processes with a vastly longer wave-length, such as a series of war-and-peace cycles running to three or four revolutions of 'the sorrowful wheel', or the disintegration of a broken-down civilization in the eight-or-ten-centuries-long course of a Time of Troubles and an ensuing universal state, our present question whether laws of Nature current in History are inexorable or controllable assumes a form in which—however academic it might have looked in Western eyes at any date during the two and a half centuries ending in A.D. 1914—this question was now insistently presenting itself to an increasing number of minds in the Western World on the morrow of what had been the second world war within living memory.

When a civilization had once broken down and entered on the path of disintegration, was it doomed already in advance to go on following this path to the point at which it would end in dissolution? Or was there a possibility of retracing one's steps—at any rate so long as the broken-down society had not yet slipped farther down than the upper and less precipitous slopes of the *descensus Averni*? In A.D. 1952 this question could no longer be ignored or dismissed by any citizen of a Western Society who had any sense of History (and this sense seemed to be becoming more acute, as it is apt to become in days of increasing distress and anxiety). At the same time there was no guarantee that an increasingly anxious post-Modern Western Man would be in any way better placed for finding an answer to the riddle of the Sphinx than his persistently self-complacent Late Modern Western forebears would have been if the same fateful question had ever rung in their ears.

Perhaps the strongest practical motive for the interest that was undoubtedly being taken by the writer's Western contemporaries in a synoptic study of the history of Man in Process of Civilization was an eagerness to take their historical bearings at a moment in the history of their own civilization which they felt to be a turning-point. In this crisis the Western peoples, and the American people perhaps above all, were manifestly conscious of a load of responsibility that was weighing upon them. 'See, I have set before thee this day Life and Good and Death and Evil.'[1] Mid-way through the twentieth century of the Christian Era, Westerners saw themselves confronted with choices which might perhaps decide the fate, not merely of their own society, but of all Mankind; and, in looking to past experience for light to guide them in taking momentous decisions, they were turning to the only human source of wisdom which had ever been at the disposal of Mankind—though wise men had also never failed to recognize that the lessons of experience could not be applied automatically to grind out cut-and-dried solutions for current problems. In the twentieth century, Western minds were seeking in Mankind's historical experience for such guidance as experience could be expected to give; but they could not turn to History for light on how they ought to act without first putting to the oracle the preliminary question: Did History give them any assurance that they were really free agents? The lesson of History, after all, might turn out to be, not that one choice would be better than another choice, but that their sense of being free to choose was merely a flatteringly oppressive illusion, and that in truth it was out of their power to affect their own future. A comparison of the unfinished history of the Western Civilization with the histories of other civilizations in which the whole story was already known from beginning to end might inform the living generation of Westerners that they were in a phase in which their future no longer lay even partially in their own hands. The lesson of History might be that there was nothing now for them to do except to recognize, and resign themselves to, a doom from which there was no possibility of escape.

Was there indeed a stage in the disintegration of a civilization at which it ceased to be possible for human intellects and wills to recover control and to make use of this recaptured power by taking rational steps to avert an irretrievable disaster? In the regularly recurring pattern of the disintegration-process there was at least one landmark that was so outstanding as to be unmistakable whenever it was reached, and this was the termination of a Time of Troubles through the establishment of a universal state as a result of the forcible liquidation of all previously contending parochial states save one. At stages in the course of disintegration before this mark was reached and passed, was a recovery still feasible? In answer to this first question, perhaps the most that could be said was that, among all the untoward developments that were characteristic of a Time of Troubles, there was no sign of any that would make a recovery inherently impossible, though no doubt it would always be harder to recover from a relapse after a rally than to recover from an original breakdown that had not yet been repeated. The second question that presented itself was whether there was likewise no ground for assuming a recovery to be impossible after the establishment of a universal state, and in this case we might find ourselves giving a decidedly pessimistic answer with rather more assurance than we might have felt in giving a tentatively optimistic

[1] Deut. xxx. 15. Cp. 19.

answer to an identical question regarding the prospects during a Time of Troubles.

When once a Time of Troubles has passed over into a universal state, there are manifest inherent obstacles to recuperation that are so serious that they may well be insurmountable. To begin with, it is difficult to imagine how a society could have purchased peace at this price without having involuntarily inflicted mortal wounds upon itself. The price of a *pax oecumenica* imposed through the establishment of a universal state is, after all, a sacrificial price; for it is nothing less than the elimination, by force of arms, of all the previously contending parochial states save one which, if it does not die of its wounds, has to pay for its survival by suffering a grievous derangement of its life; and, in this political hecatomb, the parochial *regna peritura* themselves are the least valuable of the treasures that are destroyed; for, in the process of becoming the idols of infatuated communities, these political Juggernauts have a way of centring round themselves many of the non-political elements in a now disintegrating civilization's life; and, by the time when the progressive exacerbation of the Time of Troubles has come to threaten the stricken society with imminent death, it is as impracticable to overthrow these idols without simultaneously shattering the treasures now inextricably associated with them as it is imperative to overthrow these idols, whatever the cost. 'Ubi solitudinem faciunt, pacem appellant'[1] is, for this reason, an indictment on which all architects of universal states are bound in the nature of the case to be found guilty; and, for our present purpose, it is beside the point to argue whether or not the stricture is morally just; for, however convincingly the defendant may plead that he has saved a suffering world from a greater evil at the cost of inflicting on it a lesser evil in a situation in which no third choice was open to him, he will find it difficult to rebut the charge that even this lesser evil to which he has thus made himself a party is in the first place irretrievable and in the second place necessarily fatal in the long run to the afflicted body social.

If we may employ the homely simile of the eggs and the omelette, and identify the eggs with our clutch of contending parochial states, we may say that, during a Time of Troubles, down to the moment when it is liquidated through the establishment of a universal state, some, at any rate, of the eggs are likely to have remained unbroken, however severely even these may have been battered; but, when once the cook has converted all that is left of the eggs into an omelette, he has put it beyond his own or anyone else's power ever to reconstruct the eggs again by the impossible feat of putting scrambled yolks back inside broken shells. Moreover, as we have noticed in another context,[2] the chef's successors will find it beyond their power to preserve even the scrambled relics of broken eggs unadulterated, though, in originally making the omelette, the cook was aiming solely at preserving at least some recognizable vestige of his drastically processed raw materials. Time soon shows that the omelette will not keep without an infusion of preservatives, and these indispensable condiments inevitably de-nature the omelette's texture

---

[1] Tacitus: *Agricola*, chap. 30.   [2] In VI. vii. 57–60.

and taste, so that the pursuit of a conservative policy produces an unintended innovatory effect which plays straight into the hands of an insidious Spirit of Change. In our foregoing study of universal states[1] our principal conclusion has been that the conservative-minded makers and masters of universal states work, willy-nilly, for future destroyers, supplanters, and heirs of the civilization which the empire-builders themselves have been striving to make immune against the assaults of decay and death.

On this showing, it looks as if the process of social disintegration is likely to become inexorably irreversible if and when the disintegrating society passes out of a Time of Troubles into a universal state; and this finding raises the further question: Is there any remedy, short of the fatal imposition of a universal state, for the progressively more and more destructive fratricidal warfare between contending parochial states which appears to be the commonest symptom of a social breakdown?

If we try to answer this question empirically, as we ought, in the light of the historical evidence presented by the histories of civilizations up to date, we shall have to report that, out of some fourteen clear cases of breakdown, we cannot point to one in which the malady of fratricidal warfare had been got rid of by any means less drastic than the eventual elimination of the war-making parochial states themselves; but, in accepting this formidable finding, we must not allow ourselves to be discouraged by it; for a loyalty to the empirical method of investigation that requires us to be frank also requires us at same time to be judicious. The inductive method of reasoning is, after all, even at best, notoriously an imperfect logical instrument for proving a negative proposition, and the smaller the number of the instances under review the weaker, of course, the argument is. Now, at the time of writing, the number of known specimens of societies of the species 'civilizations' amounted, on the largest admissible count, to something less than thirty, and the species itself was apparently not more than some 5,000 or 6,000 years old, which was a brief span by comparison with the 300,000 or 600,000 or 1,000,000 years during which societies of a primitive kind had been in existence since the days before a sub-human social animal had achieved its mutation into Man. Against this historical background it was evident that the experience of some fourteen civilizations over a span of some five or six millennia established no very strong presumption against the possibility that, in response to the challenge by which these pioneer civilizations had been worsted, some other representative of the infant species might succeed some day in opening up a hitherto unknown avenue for a fresh and unprecedented spiritual advance by finding some less prohibitively costly device than the forcible imposition of a universal state for curing the social disease of fratricidal warfare between parochial states.

If, with this possibility in mind, we now glance back, once again, at the histories of those civilizations which, by the time of writing, had trodden the whole length of the *via dolorosa* leading from breakdown to dissolution without having managed to stop short of taking the perhaps irretrievable step of passing into a universal state, we shall observe that

[1] In VI, *passim*, in vol. vii.

at least some of them had caught a Pisgah sight of a saving alternative solution, even though none of them had ever yet succeeded in translating this ideal into an achievement.

In the Hellenic World, for example, the vision of a Homonoia or Concord that might do what Force could never do towards healing a deadly strife between contending states and contending social classes, and even between contending civilizations, had unquestionably been caught by certain rare Hellenic souls[1] under the spiritual stress of a Time of Troubles that had set in at the outbreak of the Atheno-Peloponnesian War of 431–404 B.C.—even though this glimpse of a happier alternative possibility had not availed to save the Hellenic Society from continuing to tread the path of destruction to the point at which a temporary reprieve had been purchased, through the imposition of a Roman Peace, at the cost of making the Hellenes' descent of Avernus irretrievable. In a post-Modern Western World the same ideal had been embodied, in response to the challenge of two successive world wars, in two successive oecumenical institutions—in the League of Nations after the War of A.D. 1914–18, and in the United Nations Organization after the War of A.D. 1939–45. In Sinic history during the Sinic Society's first rally after its breakdown, Confucius's zeal for the revivification of a traditional code of conduct and ritual and Lao-tse's quietist belief in leaving a free field for the spontaneous operation of the subconscious psychic forces of Wu Wei[2] had both been inspired by a yearning to touch springs of feeling that might release a saving power of spiritual harmony; and in the Sinic, as in the Western, World this yearning had also found institutional expression. In 681–679/8 B.C., for example, at a date when the progressive assertion of rival parochial sovereignties *de facto* was already threatening the Sinic Society with the breakdown that it eventually brought upon itself in 634 B.C., an attempt was made to provide an effective substitute for a now shadowy oecumenical presidency of the Imperial House of Chóu by an international recognition of the hegemony of one of the leading parochial Powers of the day;[3] and at least two Powers in turn

[1] There could be no doubt that this idea which was at the same time an ideal had made its epiphany in the Hellenic World in the course of its Time of Troubles; the only point in dispute between latter-day Western scholars was the question: Whose soul was it that was to be given the credit for having caught the vision first? For the debate between the respective champions of Alexander of Macedon and Zeno of Citium, see V. vi. 6, n. 4. Since the publication of that volume of the present Study, the debate had been carried farther. Alexander's advocate, Sir W. Tarn, had expounded his theory more fully in his masterly work *Alexander the Great* (Cambridge 1948, University Press, 2 vols.); and, according to this exposition (in op. cit., vol. ii, pp. 447–8), Alexander's ideas about Brotherhood and Unity could be seen to be 'three facets of a single idea':

'The first is the statement that all men are brothers; Alexander was the first man known to us, at any rate in the West, to say so plainly and to apply it to the whole Human Race, without distinction of Greek or Barbarian. The second thing is his belief that he had a divine mission to be the harmonizer and reconciler of the World, to bring it to pass that all men, being brothers, should live together in Homonoia, in unity of heart and mind. . . . The third thing . . . was the desire, expressed in the libation and prayer at Opis, that all the peoples in his realm should be partners and not merely subjects.'

In *Classical Philology*, vol. xlv, No. 3, July 1950, Tarn's contentions had been disputed by Philip Merlan in a paper under the title 'Alexander the Great or Antiphon the Sophist?' in which the writer argues that 'the idea of the equality of all men, Greeks and Barbarians alike', had been 'proclaimed, a century before Alexander the Great', by the fifth-century Athenian man of letters Antiphon in his work called *Truth*.

[2] See III. iii. 187 and V. v. 416–19.

[3] The first hêgemôn in the series, Huan, the prince of the parochial state Ts'i, secured

duly exercised this authority in the name of the Chóu before this embryonic constitution for a Sinic League of Nations fell into abeyance.[1] Thereafter, there were occasional revivals—as, for instance, in 546 B.C.[2] —of the international conferences for the preservation of peace between parochial states which, between 679 and 628 B.C., had been convened under the successive hegemons' auspices. It was not until after the opening of the second chapter in a Sinic series of war-and-peace cycles that the contending states finally abandoned their half-hearted quest for some way of living peacefully side by side, and allowed their fratricidal warfare to degenerate into a sheer struggle for existence; and, even after the onset of this second paroxysm of a Sinic Time of Troubles, the moderating institution of hegemony seems to have been revived once or twice.[3]

These Sinic, Hellenic, and Western essays pointed to a possibility of preventing the perhaps inevitable friction between parochial states from grinding a body social to powder by recourse to some remedy less drastic than the shattering of these trouble-making idols at the cost of mortal injury to the suffering society itself. As an alternative to the forcible imposition of a universal state, which had invariably proved in the event to have been a lethal remedy for a mortal disease, might not some civilization some day succeed in responding to the challenge of breakdown by inducing the loyal subjects of still unliquidated parochial states voluntarily to subordinate their parochial patriotisms to an overriding allegiance to some paramount oecumenical institution which would be a political embodiment of the whole of the society and not just of one or other fragment of it? Would not some such new solution for an old political problem offer a more favourable expectation of life to the parochial states themselves, as well as to the society of which these were political articulations? Surely, if these parochial states ceased to be a menace to the survival of the society in virtue of ceasing to be objects of idolatrous worship, then their votaries need no longer have to face the agonizing choice of allowing their idolization of these parochial political institutions to break the society up or else acquiescing in the preservation of the society at the all but prohibitive price of allowing the parochial states, and all the treasures associated with them, to be liquidated in order to make way for a universal state imposed by force.

The objective on the political plane was to find a middle way between two mutually antithetical deadly extremes: a devastating strife between

---

the recognition of his hegemony by the states represented at a congress which he convened in 681 B.C. This arrangement was embodied in a formal diplomatic instrument in 679/8 B.C. (see Franke, O.: *Geschichte des Chinesischen Reiches*, vol. i (Berlin and Leipzig 1930, de Gruyter), p. 161).

[1] The two hêgemons whose hegemonies seem to be historical are the first two out of the five in the traditional list: Prince Huan of Ts'i (*dominabatur* 685–643 B.C.) and Prince Wên of Tsin (*dominabatur* 635–628 B.C.). In Franke's opinion (see op. cit., vol. i, p. 162) the hegemonies of the three last princes on the list are not so well attested by the historical evidence, and Franke suggests that these three were included in order to make up the tale of five, because of the significance of this number in the conventional system of Sinic thought. The Time-span of the Age of the Hegemonies in Sinic history would thus be 685–628 B.C. instead of 685–591 B.C., which is the traditional dating.

[2] See I. i. 89 and V. vi. 292.

[3] In this period there may have been some recognition of the hegemony of King Kou-tsien of Yüe (*regnabat circa* 500–470 B.C.) and of Prince Hiao of Ts'in (*dominabatur* 361–338 B.C.) according to Franke, op. cit., vol. i, pp. 162 and 177–8.

irreconcilable parochial states and a desolating oecumenical peace imposed through the delivery of a knock-out blow. The reward for success in running the gauntlet of these adamantine Symplegades, whose clashing jaws had crushed every vessel that had attempted to make the passage up to date, might be the Argonauts' legendary experience of bursting out of the perilous straits into a hitherto un-navigated open sea. If the children of one of the civilizations one day were to accomplish this feat of pioneering, such an achievement might well open a new chapter of history with a new spiritual climate. It was obvious, however, that this happy issue out of some of the afflictions that Man had been bringing on himself in the Age of the Civilizations could not be ensured by any talismanic blue-print of a federal constitution for an oecumenical polity. The precise constitutional arrangements best calculated to secure the saving harmony of multiplicity-in-unity and unity-in-multiplicity would necessarily vary according to the nature of the particular circumstances in which the challenge presented itself; and the most adroit and opportune political engineering applied to the structure of a body social could never serve as a substitute for the spiritual redemption of souls. Such proximate causes of breakdown and disintegration as the horizontal schism cleft in the Body Social by warfare between parochial states and the vertical schism cleft in it by strife between classes were in truth no more than political symptoms of a spiritual disease; and a wealth of experience had long since demonstrated beyond dispute that technically perfect institutions were of no avail to save froward souls from bringing themselves and one another to grief, whereas brethren who had attuned their wills to dwell together in unity would find no insuperable difficulty in making technically imperfect institutions work by short-circuiting a mimetic social drill through flashes of 'light caught from a leaping flame'[1] and by subordinating the things that are Caesar's to the things that are God's.[2]

If the prospects of Man in Process of Civilization, on his arduous climb up a precipitous cliff-face towards an unattained and invisible ledge above,[3] evidently depended above all on his ability to recover a lost control of the pitch, it was no less evident that this issue was going to be decided by the course of Man's relations, not just with his fellow men and with himself, but, above all, with God his Saviour.

---

[1] Plato's Letters, No. 7, 341 B–E, quoted in III. iii. 245.
[2] Matt. xxii. 21; Mark xii. 17; Luke xx. 25.
[3] See II. i. 192–4.

C. THE RECALCITRANCE OF HUMAN AFFAIRS TO LAWS OF NATURE

(I) A SURVEY OF INSTANCES

(a) THE VARIABILITY OF THE RATE OF CULTURAL CHANGE

1. *The Hypothesis of Invariability and the Evidence against it*

IN the preceding division of this Part we have come to the conclusion that there are laws of Nature to which human affairs are amenable; but the same empirical survey of historical facts that has borne witness to the currency of these laws has also informed us that they are not inexorable.

We have found that laws of Non-Human Nature which Man cannot abrogate or even modify can nevertheless be brought under human control in the sense that Man can elude the incidence of these laws when their operation would have frustrated his purposes, and court it when this will serve them. Though, for example, Man is powerless to change either the direction or the force of the winds, he can trim his sails to catch winds that will carry his ship towards the port for which he is making; he can design a rig that will enable him to take advantage of almost contrary winds by sailing in their eye; and, when he encounters a hurricane blowing dead against him, he can reef his sails and thus mitigate the impact of the blast. By adroitly steering the course of human affairs amid the play of non-human forces subject to rigid and therefore calculable and predictable laws, Man can prevent potentially adverse laws from hindering him and can constrain potentially favourable laws to help him in the execution of his plans; and, where the laws of Nature with which he is confronted are laws of the Human Psyche, Man can bring these laws, likewise, under human control in the sense that he can diminish the discord and increase the harmony in human life by reconciling personal wills that are bound to encounter one another in the life of a creature that had to become social before it could become human, and by bridging the gulf between each of these conscious personalities and the Subconscious Psyche with which any personality is bound to be mated in the life of a creature in whose soul the Spirit could never have moved except upon the face of the waters,[1] and which could never have been made to see the light except against the foil of the darkness.[2]

Such evidences of Man's ability to control his own affairs either by circumventing laws of Nature or by harnessing them raise the question whether there may not be some circumstances in which human affairs are not amenable to laws of Nature at all. We can explore this possibility by following the same empirical method of inquiry that we have just been employing in order to ascertain the extent of Nature's dominion over Man; and we may begin by inquiring into the rate of social change. If the tempo proves to be variable, this will be evidence, as far as it

---

[1] Gen. i. 2.　　　　　　　　　　　　　　[2] Gen. i. 4.

goes, that human affairs are recalcitrant to laws of Nature in the Time-dimension at least. We cannot, however, take the variability of the rate of social change for granted.

In studying the phenomena of social disintegration, we have found that the disintegration-process has run a regular course which it has followed uniformly in a dozen divers instances up to date. It has invariably opened with a Time of Troubles which has invariably passed over into a universal state; the transit from the outbreak of the Time of Troubles, signifying the civilization's breakdown, to the break-up of the universal state, signifying the civilization's dissolution, has invariably been accomplished within the compass of three and a half revolutions of a Rout-and-Rally Cycle; and this process has invariably taken a minimum period of eight centuries to work itself out, while its maximum period has never been as much as eleven hundred years. Moreover, the rules of this process have been proved by the apparent exceptions.

When a universal state has been interrupted, before it has completed its regular Time-span of some four hundred years' duration, by the impact of an alien body social, the assaulted society has declined to accept this intervention as a *coup de grâce* and has obstinately prolonged its own existence until it has found an opportunity to swing back into the regular course of the disintegration-process by resuming its interrupted universal state and, this time, abiding in it until this phase of social experience has produced the full psychological effect that it has been its function to produce according to the disintegration-process's hitherto standard pattern. This process that has thus refused to allow an external agency to prevent it from working itself out has likewise been intractable to attempts to tamper with it from within. A universal state that has completed the full normal period of its course may have perversely insisted on superfluously prolonging the tale of its years; but we have seen that in every case it has broken up in the end, however long it may have succeeded in postponing the evil day; and we have also seen that in every case this illegitimate epilogue has been barren of creative achievements. The vanity of all such attempts to set the laws of social disintegration at defiance testifies to the inexorability of these laws so impressively, and this law-bound process of social disintegration has loomed so large in the history of the societies of the species 'civilizations' during the first five or six thousand years of this species' existence, that we are moved to ask ourselves whether the time-keeping propensity which has thus displayed itself in the disintegration-process over a span of something between a minimum of about eight hundred and a maximum of about a thousand years may not govern the histories of civilizations, not only when these societies are disintegrating, but also when they are still in growth.

If the tempo of History should indeed prove to be constant in all circumstances, in the sense that the passage of each and every decade, century, or millennium could be shown to generate a definite and uniform quantum of psychological and social change, it would follow that, if we knew the value either of a quantum in the psycho-social series or of a span in the Time-series, we should be able to calculate the magnitude of the corresponding unknown quantity in the other series. Supposing, for example, that, in the history of civilization x, a generation β were known to be separated from a generation α by a Time-interval of, say, one hundred years, we ought then to be able to estimate the psychic and social distance between these two generations, even if their chronological relation to one another were the only information about them that we had on record. Conversely, if we knew the psychic and social difference between two generations, thanks to being informed about their respective manners and customs by undated records such as folk-tales handed down orally or the material evidence of stratified artifacts disinterred by archaeologists, we ought then to be able to estimate the chronological interval between them by inference, even if we had not inherited or recovered any table of dates to tell us their chronological relation to one another in plain figures. The assumption that a particular quantum of psycho-social change invariably takes the same span of Time in accomplishing itself had become so unquestionable an article of faith in the mind of at least one distinguished Modern Western student of Egyptiac history that he actually rejected the chronological data presented by Astronomy on the ground, not that this evidence was dubious in itself, but that to accept it would mean accepting, in consequence, the, to him, inadmissible proposition that the tempo of psycho-social change in the Egyptiac World must have been notably quicker during one period of two hundred years' length than it had been during an immediately preceding period of an approximately equal span.

'If we find that the heliacal rising of Sirius is noted in an Egyptian document as falling in a certain month of a certain year in the reign of a certain king, it would seem that by calculating the loss of days implied we could discover the year B.C. to which the given year corresponds. On this principle, by means of a statement in a papyrus found at Kahun, that Sothis rose heliacally on the first of the month Pharmouthi in the seventh year of Senusret III, it has been computed that this year was 1882 (1876) or 1876 (1872) B.C., while from the same data another computer has arrived at 1945 B.C. But there are many considerations which militate against an unreserved acceptance of either of these dates, in the present state of our knowledge. If the former date were accepted, the end of the XIIth Dynasty would fall in 1788 B.C.[1] But it will be admitted by all who have studied the material for the history of the time that to allow only two centuries for the period between Dynasties XII and XVIII is difficult. If there are resemblances in culture between the XIIth and the early reigns of the XVIIIth Dynasty which argue a comparative proximity in time, there are, on the other hand, differences which cannot be accounted for if the distance is to be measured by no more than two hundred years. The XIIth Dynasty itself lasted for two centuries. Are the changes observable during its continuance in any way comparable to those which had come

[1] The last (incomplete) year of the Twelfth Dynasty's régime would be, not 1788 B.C., but 1778 B.C., according to L. H. Wood's revision (in the *Bulletin of the American Schools of Oriental Research*, No. 99, October 1945 (New Haven 1945, A.S.O.R.), pp. 5–9) of W. F. Edgerton's chronology (in the *Journal of Near Eastern Studies*, vol. i (Chicago 1942, University of Chicago Press), pp. 306–14). R. A. Parker, in *The Calendars of Ancient Egypt* (Chicago 1950, University of Chicago Press), p. 69, makes the last year of the Twelfth Dynasty's régime 1786 B.C.—A.J.T.

about between its termination and the rise of the XVIIIth? The answer can only be a decided negative.'[1]

This answer might be correct; yet it would not avail, by reason of that, to prove the case which is here based upon it. It might be true that, during the interval between the end of the Twelfth Dynasty and the beginning of the Eighteenth Dynasty, the Egyptiac culture had changed more than it had changed while the Twelfth Dynasty had been on the throne; but it would not follow that the time taken by the greater of these two unequal quanta of change must have been proportionately longer than the time taken by the lesser quantum. So far from its being requisite to assume that the rate of change must have been constant, it would be surprising if the pace of change had in truth been the same in two periods which were so different from one another in their social circumstances. The second of the two was an anarchic interregnum in which we should expect the pace of change to accelerate, whereas the preceding period was a time of relative peace, order, and stability in which we should expect the pace of change to be sluggish. An expectation based on this difference in character between two periods would thus have anticipated the astronomical evidence indicating that the greater quantum of change during the second period took no longer a time to come to pass than the smaller quantum during the first period; and, in fact, by the time when the present chapter of this Study was being written in A.D. 1950, the consensus of Egyptologists had declared itself unmistakably in favour of accepting the chronological evidence of Astronomy without regard for an unconvincing hypothetical law to the effect that the tempo of psycho-social change is not subject to variation.

This judgement of common sense is strikingly vindicated by indisputable facts in a number of cases in which the spans of time taken by cultural changes comparable in character to the change from a Twelfth-Dynasty culture to an Eighteenth-Dynasty culture in Egyptiac history are known to us from chronological records that cannot be impugned by any subjective estimate of the time required for allowing these cultural changes to take place.

For example, we know for a fact that the remains of the Temple of Zeus at Olympia and of the Parthenon at Athens which are still standing in our day date from the fifth century B.C.; that the remains of Hadrian's Olympieum at Athens and of the Temple of the Sun at Ba'lbak date from the second century of the Christian Era; and that the Church of the Ayía Sophía at Constantinople dates from the sixth century of the Christian Era. Supposing, however, that we had no record of any of these dates, and that in the absence of direct evidence we tried to reconstruct the chronology by making an estimate of the Time-intervals between the dates of the three sets of buildings on the basis of Hall's assumption that the tempo of cultural change is invariable, we should be bound to guess that the Time-interval between the Olympieum and the Ayía Sophía—representing, as these two buildings do, two orders of architecture that are, not merely diverse, but antithetical in their styles,

[1] Hall, H. R.: 'Egyptian Chronology', in *The Cambridge Ancient History*, vol. i, 2nd ed. (Cambridge 1924, University Press), pp. 168-9.

inspiration, and êthos—must be notably longer than the Time-interval between the Parthenon and the Olympieum, considering that the Olympieum is manifestly a mere variation on the Parthenon's architectural theme. In reality, as we happen to know, beyond dispute, the Time-interval between the Parthenon and the Olympieum, so far from being notably shorter than the Time-interval between the Olympieum and the Ayía Sophía, was half as long again, and an estimate of the relative length of the intervals, based on the hypothesis of invariability in the tempo of change, would be utterly misleading.

If we turn our attention from ecclesiastical to naval architecture and apply the hypothesis of invariability in the tempo of change to the dating of successive types of battleship in the history of the British Navy, we shall find ourselves inveigled into inferring that the *Sovereign of the Seas* (launched in A.D. 1637) must have been separated from the *Queen* (launched in A.D. 1839)[1] by a notably shorter Time-interval than that separating the *Queen* from the *Royal Sovereign* (launched in A.D. 1891). On this *a priori* method of reckoning, no other conclusion would be plausible, considering that the *Queen* was a wooden three-masted square-rigged sailing ship with her guns mounted along her broadsides, whose points of difference from the *Sovereign of the Seas* were merely points of detail, whereas the *Royal Sovereign*, with her gun-turrets fore and aft and her iron hull, steel armour, pair of funnels, and propellers driven by steam, was a Martian sea-monster that would not have been recognized as being a ship, in any intelligible sense of the word, by any sailor in Codrington's squadron at Navarino on the 20th October, 1827.

We should be similarly misled if we were to put our trust in the same *a priori* principle in trying to estimate the relative Time-intervals between the equipment of a Roman soldier in the last days of the Roman Empire in the West, a Saxon soldier in the *comitatus* of the Holy Roman Emperor Otto I, and a Norman knight depicted on the Bayeux tapestry. Considering that the round shields and the gladiator's square-rimmed crested helmets with which Otto's soldiers are equipped are manifest variations on the equipment of Majorian's soldiers,[2] whereas William the Conqueror's soldiers are equipped with Sarmatian conical helmets

---

[1] 'As late as 1845 there was laid down at Devonport a *Sanspareil* designed upon the lines of the ship of the same name captured from the French in 1794, although, it is true, the vessel was never actually launched as a sailing line-of-battle ship, but, while yet upon the stocks, was lengthened, converted to a screw ship of 80 guns, and launched as such in 1851' (Clowes, W. L.: *The Royal Navy: A History*, vol. vi (London 1901, Sampson Low, Marston, & Co.), p. 191). 'The first [British] ship of the line to be designed, *ab initio*, for the screw was the *Agamemnon*, 80, which was laid down at Woolwich in 1849, and launched in 1852' (ibid., p. 198). 'The last [British] wooden battleship, though fitted with a screw, was the *Collingwood* of 1861' (Mr. Christopher Lloyd, of the Navy Records Society, in a letter of the 23rd January, 1951, in which he kindly gave this information to the Librarian of the R.I.I.A. in answer to an inquiry made on the present writer's behalf).

[2] No doubt we have to allow for the possibility that the portrayal of a tenth-century Western soldier's equipment may have been influenced by a perhaps unconscious conservatism that may have made it look more like a fifth-century Roman soldier's equipment than it actually was; but such conservatism cannot have gone so far as to blind Western artists in the Dark Ages to the visual evidence, for they did not ignore the new-fangled equipment of an eleventh-century knight; on the contrary, they evidently took a delight in reproducing it faithfully to the facts. On this showing it seems reasonable to assume that their protrayal of a tenth-century Western soldier's equipment is likewise essentially true to life.

and with kite-shaped shields, the hypothesis of invariability in the tempo of change would lead us, here too, to fly in the face of the chronological facts by guessing that the Time-interval between Otto I (*regnabat et imperabat* A.D. 936–73) and William the Conqueror (*ducebat et regnabat* A.D. 1035–87) must have been notably longer than the Time-interval between Majorian (*imperabat* A.D. 457–61) and Otto I.

In the three cases just cited, estimates based on the assumption that the tempo of change is invariable fall wide of the true chronological marks because in reality the tempo was not constant. In all these three cases a spell of relatively slow cultural change was succeeded rather abruptly by a spurt of relatively fast change. We may complete our exposition of the argument against the hypothesis of invariability in the tempo of change by citing an inverse case in which a spurt of fast change was succeeded by a spell of slow change.

Anyone who takes a synoptic view of the standard Western male (non-military and non-clerical) dress as worn in A.D. 1700 and in A.D. 1950 respectively will see at a glance that the coat, waistcoat, trousers, and umbrella of A.D. 1950 are merely variations on the coat, waistcoat, breeches, and sword of A.D. 1700. By contrast, the doublet and trunk-hose of A.D. 1600 are as different from the Western civilian costume of A.D. 1700 as the Western military equipment of A.D. 966 is from the Western military equipment of A.D. 1066. If a child ignorant of the dates were asked to guess, from a series of pictures of celebrated Western poets, which two of our three sets of costumes were separated from one another by a Time-interval of a century and a quarter, and which two by an interval of two centuries, the innocent child would assuredly guess that the century and a quarter was the interval between Pope (*natus* A.D. 1688) and T. S. Eliot (*natus* A.D. 1888), and that the two centuries was the interval between Shakespeare (*natus* A.D. 1564) and Pope (*natus* A.D. 1688).

These cautionary tales are warnings against the danger of confiding in an hypothesis of invariability in the tempo of change as a basis for trying to estimate, not only the Time-interval between an Egyptiac Middle Empire and New Empire, but also the length of time that it took for successive strata of the debris of human occupation to accumulate on some site whose history has to be reconstructed solely from the material evidence disinterred by the archaeologist's spade, in default of chronological data furnished by independent, decipherable, and authoritative written records.[1] If, for example, we were tempted to compute the dura-

---

[1] Such an attempt to work out an absolute chronology by inference from the thickness of strata of deposits has, of course, to be distinguished from an attempt to estimate the relative age and duration of the strata deposited on different sites within the same broad cultural field by comparing the likeness and differences between their respective contents, on the lines of C. F. A. Schaeffer's monumental and masterly *Stratigraphie Comparée et Chronologie de l'Asie Occidentale (iiie et iie Millénaires): Syrie, Palestine, Asie Mineure, Chypre, Perse et Caucase* (London 1948, Oxford University Press). In comparing the successive strata on different sites, Schaeffer is comparing entities that are legitimately comparable. The error in method lies in assuming that the tempo of change is constant and that it is therefore feasible to argue from the thickness of strata to duration of Time, or vice versa. Absolute chronological values cannot be assigned to strata of debris with any likelihood of accuracy unless two conditions are satisfied. In the first place the stratum that is to be dated must contain some object bearing evidence of having

tion of the Neolithic Age on the site of Cnossos by measuring the thickness of the Neolithic deposits and reckoning that these were laid down at a constant rate of so many feet per century, without allowing for the possibility that the rate of deposit might have been slower at the dawn of the Neolithic Age than on the eve of the Chalcolithic, we should be well advised, before we committed ourselves to this wild-goose chase, to take to heart the two pertinent facts that the cubic content of the archives deposited in Whitehall during the six war years A.D. 1939–45 was equal to that of all extant British archives deposited before September 1939, and that the cubic content of the mineral ore mined by Mankind during the quarter of a century ending in the year A.D. 1925 was equal to that of all the ore that had ever been mined down to the year A.D. 1900 inclusive.[1]

The second of these two facts ought to warn us against attempting to estimate age by measuring height, whether we are practising on a slag-heap or on a *tell*. This procedure might perhaps be legitimate if we were dealing with an ant-heap or with a termitary, since the insect societies which deposit these inanimate material traces of their life have been in stable equilibrium with their environment[2] for ages beginning long before the epiphany of the Human Race. It might even be legitimate to assume the rate of deposit to be a constant if we were dealing with primitive human societies in their latter-day Yin-state (the only state in which we have any knowledge of them)[3]—always supposing that we could lay hands on a primitive society, either still alive or else extinct yet still on record, which was uncontaminated by the radiation of any of the civilizations and which had deposited debris comparable in size and solidity, scale for scale, with a termite community's baetyl-like phalanstery. However that may be, the hypothesis of invariability in the tempo of change is manifestly not legitimate when we are dealing with civilizations, considering that the distinguishing mark of their rhythm is an

---

been manufactured during some particular reign or some other independently well-defined and limited unit of Time. In the second place the reign or other Time-unit with which the stratum has thus been identified must be assignable to some definite place in a chronological table continuous with the well-established chronology that begins in Egyptiac history *circa* 1580 B.C. with the inauguration of the New Empire by Amosis and which runs on thence without a break until it passes over into the Christian Era.

[1] These two statements of fact both have the sanction of high authority. The second of them was made by Professor C. K. Leith, of the University of Wisconsin, at a lecture at the Williamstown Institute of Politics in August 1925 at which the writer of this Study was present in the audience; the first was verified by the writer at a conference on war documentation at Amsterdam in September 1950 in conversation with Professor W. K. Hancock, the scholar in charge of the production of official histories of the acts of the divers departments of the Government of the United Kingdom during the War of A.D. 1939–45.

A reiteration of Leith's statement is on record in a book published eighteen years after the delivery of the lecture. 'The burst of industrialisation since the opening of the present century has intensified the use of minerals, both in volume and [in] variety. In this forty-years period of industrial expansion the World has used more of its mineral resources than in all preceding history' (Leith, C. K.: *World Minerals and World Peace* (Washington, D.C. 1943, The Brookings Institution), p. 1). Leith's estimate of the acceleration in the use of minerals in general is corroborated by another contemporary expert's estimate of the acceleration in the use of copper. 'The total world production from earliest times up to 1910 has been estimated at 21 million tons. In the years 1911–1930 a further 25 million tons have been extracted' (Högbom, I.: 'Mineral Production', in the *Proceedings of the Royal Swedish Institute for Engineering Research*, No. 117 (Stockholm 1932, Svenskabokhandelscentralen), p. 29).

[2] See III. iii. 106–10.   [3] See I. i. 179–80.

instability that is equally characteristic of their growths and of their disintegrations.

2. *Instances of Acceleration*

We may perhaps usefully follow up our opening attack on the hypothesis that the rate of cultural change is invariable by making a brief survey of instances, first of acceleration, then of retardation, and, in the third place, of an alternating rate.

A familiar example of acceleration is the phenomenon of Revolution within the family circle of a single society; for Revolution, in this commonest current Western usage of the term, proves on analysis—as we have found, in a previous context in this Study[1]—to be a social movement generated by an encounter between two communities which, though they belong to the same society, happen at the moment to be in different stages of evolution—military, political, economic, intellectual, or spiritual, as the case may be—differing markedly enough to stimulate the more backward of the two parties deliberately to quicken his pace with the intention of catching up, by a forced march, with his more forward neighbour and contemporary. In Late Modern Western history the classical example is the French people's revolutionary move, in and after A.D. 1789, to catch up with the constitutional progress, ahead of an eighteenth-century French *ancien régime*, that had been achieved in Great Britain and the United States by that date.

A rather more violent kind of revolution is generated by an encounter between marchmen on the fringe of a civilization and the more precociously cultivated denizens of the interior, when the marchmen set out to make good a cultural lag which in their case is apt to be greater than any cultural differentiation between one community in the interior and another. In Hellenic history the classical example is the Roman people's series of revolutionary moves to catch up, first with the constitutional progress of Athens, and afterwards with the social progress of Sparta. When Rome entered on her forced march in the fifth century B.C. she was, as we have seen,[2] some 140 or 150 years behind Athens, if we are right in equating the compilation of the Twelve Tables of Roman Law by the Decemviri *circa* 450 B.C. with the constitution that Solon worked out for Athens in and after 594 B.C. By the year 133 B.C., when Tiberius Gracchus launched in Italy a revolutionary programme of agrarian reform emulating the programme launched in Lacedaemon by King Agis IV in 243 B.C.,[3] the Roman marchmen of the Hellenic World had reduced their Time-lag behind the communities in the heart of Hellas from nearly 150 years to no more than 110; but it took the century of revolution and civil war which Tiberius Gracchus undesignedly precipitated to enable Rome to draw right abreast of the farthest advanced of her Hellenic contemporaries. In the course of this terrible century the *stasis* within the bosom of the Roman Commonwealth became identical with the final paroxysm of an Hellenic Time of Troubles; and the no longer distinguishable tasks of bringing international peace to the Hellenic World and internal peace to the sole surviving Hellenic

Great Power were both performed in the same act by an Augustus who combined a revolutionary dictatorship within the Roman body politic with a providential mission for the salvation of the Hellenic World in a personal union between the *deus ex machina* and the boss which made this Janus-headed statesman as great a hero in the eyes of Rome's intolerably oppressed subjects as it made him a villain in the eyes of a tardily chastened Roman senatorial aristocracy which had so long and so abominably abused its power.

This progressive acceleration of the Romans' pace in the course of Hellenic history is, of course, merely one outstanding example of the forced marches made by peoples on the fringes of a society's domain in order to catch up with more precociously cultivated peoples living nearer to the society's heart. In Minoan history, for instance, we catch glimpses—even through Archaeology's dark glass—of the Peloponnese progressively catching up with the Cyclades and Crete, Central Greece with the Peloponnese, and Thessaly with Central Greece.[1] When Thessaly passed out of her Neolithic into her Chalcolithic Age *circa* 2000 B.C., she was no less than 1,000 years behind the Peloponnese, the Cyclades, and Crete, which had all made the same transition *circa* 3000 B.C., and was 500 years behind even Central Greece, which had parted company from Thessaly by emerging from the Neolithic Age *circa* 2500 B.C. Thereafter, when Thessaly made the subsequent transition from the Chalcolithic Age to the Bronze Age *circa* 1580 B.C., she was only 620 years behind the Peloponnese, which had crossed the same line *circa* 2200 B.C., and no more than 820 years behind the Cyclades and Crete, which had crossed it *circa* 2400 B.C. At the end of the Minoan story, *circa* 1200 B.C., Thessaly plunged out of the civilization of the Bronze Age into the barbarism of the Iron Age[2] neck and neck with all the other provinces of a dissolving Minoan World—which means that, during the 380 years 1580–1200 B.C., Thessaly had covered the cultural distance which it had taken the Cyclades and Crete the 1200 years 2400–1200 B.C. to traverse. This series of comparative dates indicates that, in Thessaly in the time of the Minoan Civilization, there was a progressive acceleration of the cultural tempo in the course of eight hundred years ending at the turn of the thirteenth and twelfth centuries B.C.

Beyond the outermost marches of a civilization's geographical domain there lies a limbo tenanted by primitive societies whose children are potential converts to the culture of an adjoining civilization in its growth stage but become an alienated external proletariat when the civilization loses its attractiveness as the result of a breakdown.[3] In an earlier context[4] we have glanced at what happens to these transfrontier barbarians after the collapse of a universal state's military *limes* which has been

---

[1] See the chronological chart in Glotz, G.: *La Civilisation Égéene* (Paris 1923, La Renaissance du Livre), pp. 28–31. Glotz's dating of strata of debris in the Minoan World is based on the presence there of objects of Egyptiac provenance which have made it possible at least tentatively to translate the relative terms of Aegean stratigraphy into the absolute terms of Egyptiac chronology from the date of the Eighteenth Dynasty's inauguration onwards.   [2] See III. iii. 160–1.

[3] See V. v. 194–210.   [4] In VIII. viii. 45–72.

damming the barbarians back for generations or perhaps even for centuries. By the time when the sudden bursting of a barrage that has been
cultural as well as military brings the flood of Barbarism down in spate
upon the long sheltered but now at last defenceless remains of a garden-
city within the fallen ring-wall, the cultural differentiation between the
unreclaimed barbarians and the sophisticated citizens of a cosmopolis
has become so extreme that the effort of cultural acceleration required
of the barbarian invaders, if they are to make good their Time-lag behind
the conquered subjects of the vanished universal state, usually proves to
be beyond the limits of the Human Psyche's adaptability. The barbarians' fate is therefore often an ironical one. The more sensational
their military and political triumphs, the more demoralizing their
spiritual *bouleversement* is apt to be.

These encounters between marchmen just within the fringe of a
civilization's domain, or barbarians just beyond its pale, and the more
highly cultivated communities in the interior are variations on the same
historical theme as the encounters between representatives of two or
more different civilizations; and in our study of these we have noticed
that, when a civilization is hit by the impact of a more powerful and
aggressive society of its own kind, one of the defensive responses that
the children of the assaulted civilization are apt to make is the attempt
to fight the aggressor with his own weapons which we have labelled
'Herodianism'.[1] Since Time is of the essence of the Herodian's problem
if his policy is to be justified by success in making an assaulted society able
to hold its own before it has been overwhelmed, Herodianism necessarily calls for an effort of cultural acceleration; and this is assuredly the
explanation of the success of the Herodian movement which was an
abortive Scandinavian Civilization's prevailing reaction to the impact of
an early Medieval Western Christendom.

The writer of this Study vividly remembers the impression made on
him by a visit to the Nordiska Museet at Stockholm in the summer of
the year 1910. After passing through a series of rooms displaying *chefs-
d'œuvre* of the Scandinavian Palaeolithic, Neolithic, Bronze-Age, and
pre-Christian Iron-Age cultures, he was startled to find himself walking
through a room displaying Scandinavian-made products of the Early
Modern Age of Western history in the style of the Italian Renaissance.
Wondering how he could have failed to notice the Scandinavian-made
products of the Western Middle Ages, which must surely be on view in
their due place in the sequence, the English visitor retraced his steps—
to find that there was, sure enough, a Medieval room, but that its contents were so inconspicuous, by comparison with the trophies of the
pre-Christian ages, that after all it was quite easy to traverse it unawares.
Thus the visual impression made on a traveller through this series of
rooms in a museum of Scandinavian arts and crafts was that Scandinavia
had passed in a flash out of a Late Iron Age in which she had been
beginning to create a promising distinctive civilization of her own into
an Early Modern Age in which she had become an undistinguished
participant in a standardized Italianate Western Christian culture; and

[1] See IX. viii. 580–623.

this impression faithfully reflected the patent historical truth that the Scandinavian peoples' *tour de force* of grafting themselves on to the stem of an alien Western Christian Civilization had been achieved by a forced march.

Part of the price of this feat of acceleration had been the cultural impoverishment to which the Nordiska Museet bore witness; for the banality of the Italianate Modern Western paraphernalia attesting the Scandinavians' success at that stage in drawing abreast of the main body of Western Christendom was thrown into relief by the inimitable excellence of the products of ages anterior to Scandinavia's cultural conversion in the eleventh century of the Christian Era; and this excellence had been one of the fruits of a previous Time-lag which the Scandinavian converts to a Western Christian culture had subsequently made good. The products of a Scandinavian Palaeolithic Age, Neolithic Age, and Bronze Age had been excellent because a laggardly Scandinavian craftsmanship had been wont to go on cultivating and perfecting imported techniques and *motifs* long after these had been abandoned in favour of some new-fangled device in the culturally precocious regions in which these *motifs* and techniques had originated.[1] To retain the cultural advantages of laggardliness while achieving the *tour de force* of catching up with precocious neighbours was beyond the wit of the Scandinavian or any other school of culture; and, over and above a cultural acceleration's inescapable penalty of cultural impoverishment, the Scandinavian Herodians also had to pay the further penalty of spiritual demoralization[2] which had likewise been the price of the Romans' forced march to catch up with the Greeks,[3] and of the Vandals' forced march to catch up with the Romans.

After this glance at one instance of acceleration in the field of encounters between contemporaries, in which a long procession of Westernizing Herodians, extending from Hauk Erlendsson through Peter the Great to Mustafā Kemāl, had succeeded, through forced marches, in catching up, at least on the surface of life, with the current Western culture of their day, we may turn next to the field of renaissances in which dead cultures had been brought back to life through being conjured up by living societies; and in this field we shall see that an acceleration of cultural tempo is part and parcel of the response to the challenge from the *revenant* which we have labelled 'the Antaean rebound'.[4]

This lively reaction to the evocation of a ghost is evidence that the establishment of a psychic contact with the dead can be exhilarating; and this at first sight surprisingly stimulating emotional effect of so eerie an encounter is explained by the fact that the necromancer's communion with the dead gives him a chance of sharing in experiences which are still out of his reach in his own living world. This exciting possibility is opened up by the gruesome art of Necromancy because an experience that lies chronologically in the Past may be situate philosophically in the Future, in the sense of being something that the necromancer who has conjured it up out of a dead civilization's repertory has

---

[1] See II. ii. 342–3; III. iii. 138 and 157.
[3] See IV. iv. 505–10.
[2] See II. ii. 357–60.
[4] See pp. 140–8, above.

never yet experienced in his own life. If, for example, the *lacrimae rerum*[1] that Virgil has immortalized in his poetry have been distilled from the experience of an age of Hellenic history that is philosophically some five hundred years later than Dante's age in Western history, then, if Dante can succeed in entering into Virgil's thoughts and feelings, he will be anticipating a stage in the experience of his own living society that will not be reached there until, at earliest, the generation of Wordsworth, and perhaps not until a generation still unborn in A.D. 1952. This means that in psychic, as opposed to chronological, terms a Dante who has placed himself *en rapport* with a Virgil will be, not recoiling thirteen hundred years back into the Past, but shooting ahead five hundred years forward into the future. In other words, his feat of raising Virgil from the dead will have been a feat of cultural acceleration.

The most drastic of all known movements of cultural acceleration is the offspring of a mood of Futurism[2] in which the heirs of a disintegrating civilization reject their own cultural heritage in order to embrace an alien culture which attracts these purest of all revolutionaries to the extent to which it presents an antithesis to ancient cultural traditions when these have ceased to satisfy deep spiritual needs that insist on seeking satisfaction from some source or other. A classical example is the conversion of the Hellenic World during its universal state from its native cults of nature-worship, state-worship, and philosophy to incoming Oriental religions which now met with no serious rivals except one another for the allegiance of pagan Hellenic souls, and whose competition ended in the decisive victory of Christianity. This complete triumph of Christianity in the Hellenic World has a counterpart in the Sinic World in the partial triumph there of the Mahāyāna; and in both cases we find the spiritual revolution expressing itself visually in an aesthetic revolution that is no less thorough. In a dissolving Sinic Society the native Sinic art of the Han Age was rejected in favour of an Helleno-Indic art that was the Mahāyāna's aesthetic vehicle. In a dissolving Hellenic Society the Hellenic style was rejected in favour of the Byzantine.

If the latter, at any rate, of these two aesthetic revolutions was, as it would seem to have been, a conscious and deliberate act,[3] this would explain how it could happen that the four hundred years between Hadrian's and Justinian's day should have witnessed a change of style in the architecture of the Hellenic World that was incomparably more radical than any change that can be observed in the course of the six hundred years between Ictinus's day and Hadrian's.[4] On the aesthetic plane, as on the military plane,[5] Justinian's generation had deliberately taken the plunge out of a disintegrating Hellenic into a nascent Byzantine culture which the next generation was compelled to take on the economic and political planes willy-nilly by the deluge that descended after Justinian's death. This revolutionary breach of cultural continuity accounts for the striking acceleration in the rate of change in the style

---

[1] Virgil: *Aeneid*, Book I, l. 462.
[3] See IV. iv. 21 and 54–55.
[5] See III. iii. 163 and IV. iv. 445.

[2] See V. vi. 97–132.
[4] See pp. 351–2, above.

of architecture that is recorded visually in the contrast between the Ayía Sophía and the Olympieum; and in this Helleno-Byzantine illustration of the rapidity of the pace of cultural change during the social interregnum intervening between the histories of an antecedent civilization and its successor we have the answer to H. R. Hall's conundrum; for in Egyptiac history the interval between the end of the Twelfth Dynasty and the beginning of the Eighteenth Dynasty was likewise a social interregnum that can be recognized, on close inspection, as being the historical lesion that it is, in spite of the solidity with which a parted steel cable's frayed and flying ends have been posthumously spliced and welded together in the white heat of an explosion of cultural fanaticism.

In previous contexts[1] we have seen reasons for believing that, after the expiry of the mandate of a Middle Empire which had served as a disintegrating Egyptiac Society's universal state, the disintegration-process was heading towards the dissolution of the time-expired civilization and the eventual emergence of a new society affiliated to it, when this normal course of events was arrested and reversed by the abnormal effects of a fanatical hatred that had been aroused in Egyptiac souls by Hyksos barbarian invaders who had committed the, in Egyptiac eyes, unpardonable offence of acquiring a tincture of an alien culture before setting foot on Egyptian soil. The consequent anti-Hyksos *union sacrée* between an Egyptiac dominant minority and internal proletariat resulted in a resurrection of the Egyptiac universal state in the shape of the New Empire and in the consequent substitution of an Epimethean epilogue to Egyptiac history for the new civilization, distinct from the Egyptiac though affiliated to it, that was showing signs of coming to birth when the normal course of historical development was given a peculiar twist in this Egyptiac case. The social interregnum insulating a moribund Egyptiac Civilization that refused to die from an embryonic affiliated civilization that was denied the opportunity of being born was to that extent abortive; yet the breach of cultural continuity at this point, which was afterwards so studiously patched up and plastered over by the hands of archaistic-minded Egyptian Zealots under the régime of a post-Hyksos restoration, was nevertheless sharp enough to account for the empirically verifiable fact that the two centuries between the end of the Twelfth Dynasty and the beginning of the Eighteenth Dynasty witnessed a notably greater change of style in Egyptiac art than the immediately preceding two centuries during which the Twelfth Dynasty had been continuously in the saddle. So far from its being incredible that 'the changes observable during its [the Twelfth Dynasty's] continuance' should not be 'in any way comparable to those which had come about between its termination and the rise of the Eighteenth,'[2] it would be inexplicable if the second of these two periods of equal chronological length should not have witnessed a notably greater change of style than the first, considering that during the first the Egyptiac Civilization was in its universal state, whereas the second period was occupied by one of

---

[1] See I. i. 136–45; IV. iv. 85, 412; V. v. 2–3, 152, and 351–3.
[2] H. R. Hall, quoted on pp. 350–1, above.

those social interregna in which the current of history perceptibly quickens its pace.[1]

If we were challenged to find evidence for some general law governing the tempo of change in the realm of Life, the evidence that has proved irreconcilable with the hypothesis of invariability might perhaps lend itself more speciously to an hypothesis of secular acceleration.

In the history of Life on Earth, the Fauna had developed faster than the Flora; the vertebrates faster than the invertebrates; the mammals faster than the reptiles; Man through the transmission of a social heritage by means of education faster than the non-human animals through the transmission of a racial heritage by means of physical procreation;[2] Upper Palaeolithic Man faster than Lower Palaeolithic Man; and Man in Process of Civilization faster than a Primitive Man who had lapsed into a Yin-state in reaction from the Yang-effort of struggling up into becoming human. In a twentieth-century Westernizing World in which the pace of Man's intellectual and technological progress had been speeded up once again, and this time to an unprecedented degree, by a recent Western Industrial Revolution, it looked as if a crescendo that had been rising by geometrical progression, in a steeper and steeper curve, ever since Life's first epiphany, might now be on the point of culminating, in Human Life, in a pace at which men's racing thoughts and wills would no longer find themselves able either to coax or to drive their inseparable subconscious fellow-traveller in the depths of the Psyche to keep in the running; and the psychic catastrophe which this threat of psychic discord portended seemed at this stage to be not merely overtaking the surviving primitive societies and surviving non-Western civilizations that were being uprooted by the Western bulldozer's titanic impact; it now also appeared to be impending over the heads of the demonic Western chauffeurs of a potently mechanized Juggernaut's car.

'One of the phenomena that bring out, particularly clearly, the relation between the magnitude and pressure of the network of interdependence [linking together individual human beings in the Modern Western World] on the one hand and the psychic state of the individual on the other hand is what we call "the tempo" of our age. This [term] "tempo" is in reality nothing but an expression for indicating the multiplicity of the chains of the social network that find a node in every single social function and the pressure of the competition, emanating from this far-flung and densely populated net, that puts its "drive" into every single transaction.'[3]

We need not commit ourselves to the theory of a secular tendency towards acceleration in the march of Life which might seem at first sight

---

[1] See I. i. 43–44.
[2] See pp. 319–26, above. Julian Huxley points out that, in the jump from evolution on the inorganic level to Life, as well as in the subsequent jump from the transmission of a heritage by procreation to its transmission by education, 'the evolutionary process' had to pay for being 'much accelerated in time' by being 'immensely restricted in extent' (Huxley, J.: *Evolutionary Ethics*, the Romanes Lecture, 1943, reprinted in Huxley, T. H. and J.: *Evolution and Ethics, 1893–1943* (London 1947, Pilot Press), pp. 120–1 and 123).
[3] Elias, N.: *Über den Prozess der Zivilisation*, vol. ii: *Wandlungen der Gesellschaft: Entwurf zu einer Theorie der Zivilisation* (Basel 1939, Haus zum Falken), p. 337.

to be commended by the evidence that we have just been marshalling; for one manifestly weak point in the implicit argument is that the evidence, impressive though it looks when viewed *en gros*, does not cover, at the human climax of the story, more than the intellectual and technological sides of Man's nature and activity; and the formidably clear-cut picture of imminent and apparently inescapable disaster falls out of focus as soon as we begin to make it more true to real life by bringing Man's aesthetic and religious faculties and activities into the frame. The value of this specious hypothesis of a secular acceleration in the tempo of change lies, not in any intrinsic probability of its own, but in its testimony against the probability of the hypothesis that the tempo is invariable.

3. *Instances of Retardation*

Now that we have mustered these divers instances of acceleration in the tempo of cultural change, we shall not find it difficult to identify antithetical instances of retardation.

For example, the accelerations that declare themselves in revolutions within the family circle of a single society have their antithesis in the social enormities that are generated by a straggler's refusal to try to catch up with the progress of the main body.[1] A classical example of an enormity arising from a wilful retardation is the exacerbation of the Modern Western institution of Plantation Slavery in the Southern States of the American Union during the generation that elapsed between the peaceful abolition of Slavery throughout the British Empire in A.D. 1833 and its forcible abolition in the United States in A.D. 1863 at the cost of the Civil War of A.D. 1861–5.[2]

The acceleration that is demanded of marchmen when they are inducted into the life of more precocious communities in the interior, and into which the transfrontier barbarians are spurred at a hotter pace when they pour across a fallen *limes* into the derelict provinces of a universal state, has its antithesis in the retardation that is apt to be the price of migrating, in the opposite direction, from the heart of a society towards its extremities. Classical examples are the 'living museums'[3] in which a seventeenth-century Normandy, Ulster, England, and Holland, and a sixteenth-century Castile and Portugal, were still to be found in a twentieth-century Quebec, Appalachia, Charleston, Transvaal, Peru, and Macao. The moral *bouleversement* that registers a barbarian invader's inability to accelerate the pace of his cultural adaptation to the almost prohibitively extreme degree demanded by the suddenness of his translation from an unreclaimed wilderness into a derelict paradise has its antithesis in a previous arrest of this adolescent's psychic development that has registered his frustration when he has found himself barred out by a military *limes* whose sudden creation at the moment of a universal state's establishment is as portentous an event in an external proletariat's experience as the sudden collapse of the *limes* when the universal state eventually breaks up.

In the field of encounters in the Space-dimension an Herodianism

[1] See IV. iv. 136–7.   [2] See IV. iv. 137–41.   [3] See III. iii. 134–9.

that deliberately quickens its pace, in order to learn, before it is too late, how to keep an alien assailant at bay by fighting him with his own weapons, has its counterpart in a Zealotism that wilfully slows its pace down in the vain hope of thereby breaking off contact with a galloping adversary. In Jewry's reaction to the impact of Hellenism, classical examples of Zealotism are presented by the violent responses of the Maccabees and *sicarii* and the non-violent responses of the Pharisees, Scribes, and Rabbis;[1] and, in an Islamic Society's reaction to the impact of a Modern Western Civilization, the militant Maccabees and *sicarii* have their counterparts in the Wahhābīs, Sanūsīs, Idrīsīs, and Mahdists.[2] In the field of encounters in the Time-dimension an Antaean rebound that wins from Necromancy an anticipatory communion with the Future has its antithesis in an Atlantean stance in which a Necromancer who has yielded to the legendary Epimethean impulse of Lot's wife is petrified by the hypnotic stare of a resuscitated corpse's Medusan countenance into the rigidity of a pillar of salt pinned down by the incubus of the Past. A classical example is the retardation of the Orthodox Christian and Far Eastern civilizations on the political plane through the resuscitation of the Roman Empire in the shape of the East Roman Empire in the one case, and of the Han Empire in the shape of the T'ang Empire in the other,[3] and their retardation on the linguistic and literary plane through the resuscitation of the Hellenic and the Sinic Classics.[4]

The violent acceleration in the tempo of cultural change that is generated by Futurism when it repudiates a social heritage has its antithesis in a comparably extreme retardation that is induced by Archaism when it surrenders itself to the spell of the Past. We have already come across classical examples of this archaistic retardation on the linguistic and literary plane in the Neo-Attic and Neo-Sanskrit languages and literatures,[5] and on the visual aesthetic plane in a Western Neo-Gothic architecture[6] and in an Egyptiac revival, in the Age of the Twenty-sixth Dynasty, of the classic style of an Old Kingdom which had been obsolete for some two thousand years.[7] A Saïte régime that recoiled that distance back into the past in its search for aesthetic inspiration was the penultimate avatar of an Egyptiac universal state which had refused to be content with a universal state's standard lease of life; and such tortoise-paced 'Tithoni',[8] within whose creeping carapaces a senile body social continues to lead a lingering life-in-death, are enormities of the same genus as the 'fossils' of extinct civilizations exemplified in the Jews and the Parsees,[9] and as the live but arrested civilizations exemplified in the Spartans and the Esquimaux.[10] An arrest which had been the nemesis of superhuman previous exertions was perhaps the most dramatic instance of retardation in the histories of the civilizations up to date; and in the histories of the primitive societies this had its counterpart in Primitive Man's eventual lapse into a Yin-state that had been the nemesis of a social animal's previous *tour de force* of transmuting itself from Sub-Man into Man.

[1] See V. v. 68–76 and IX. viii. 584–5. [2] See V. v. 295–6 and 329, and IX. viii. 601–3.
[3] See pp. 15 and 16, above. [4] See pp. 62–78, above.
[5] See V. vi. 71–81. [6] See V. vi. 60. [7] See V. vi. 61–62.
[8] See VI. vii. 47–52. [9] See I. i. 35 and 51. [10] See III. iii. 1–88.

4. *Instances of an Alternating Rate of Change*

In our survey of evidences of variability in the tempo of change we have so far confined our attention to cases in which this variability has displayed itself in some single change of speed, whether upwards or downwards. Our survey would be incomplete if we did not also take account of cases in which there has been a concatenation of changes of speed in which the two antithetical movements of acceleration and retardation have alternated.

A conspicuous instance of an alternating change of speed is the rhythm of Withdrawal-and-Return which we have analysed in a previous Part.[1] The purpose, whether conscious or subconscious, of a potentially creative minority's temporary withdrawal from full participation in the contemporary common life of the society of which it is a member is to win for itself an opportunity of realizing its potentialities by forging ahead of the rank-and-file. Its disengagement from contact with its neighbours permits an acceleration of its own pace which it could never have achieved if it had been content to have its own pace set for it by the average pace of these pedestrian neighbours; and it is in the course of this individual spurt of acceleration that the minority succeeds or fails in bringing its creative potentialities to fruition. This, however, is not the end of the story; for, as we have seen, a creative minority's mission is to perform its work of creation, not just for itself, but for the benefit of the whole of the society to which it belongs. A creative withdrawal therefore will have missed fire if it is not followed by a redemptive return; and a re-entry into the ranks that the minority has temporarily deserted is necessarily accompanied by a retardation of its pace from the rate at which it has been travelling *in vacuo* to the slower rate at which it must now travel once more if it is to keep in step with neighbours whom it has to convert to the newly created idea or ideal or aptitude that it is bringing back with it from its lone reconnaissance. It will be seen that, on analysis, the movement of Withdrawal-and-Return turns out to follow a rhythm of three beats entailing two changes of speed, the first change upward and the second downward; and, as far as it is possible to portray a spiritual act in terms of the mechanical play of physical forces, we may compare the tripartite movement of a creative minority's withdrawal and return with the drill performed by the driver of a car when he changes gear by the threefold action of declutching, acceleration, and a re-engagement that reabates the momentarily free-running engine's racing speed by loading it once again with the retarding weight of the momentarily disengaged vehicle.

A concatenation of alternating changes of speed which runs, not just to two, but certainly to three and possibly to four, terms is to be found in the Modern Western history of the arts of shipbuilding and navigation. This story begins with a sudden acceleration which revolutionized both these arts in the West during the fifty years A.D. 1440–90; this spurt was followed by a technological retardation which persisted throughout the sixteenth, seventeenth, and eighteenth centuries; and

---

[1] In III. iii. 248–63.

this relatively long spell of comparative stagnation was then followed by another sudden acceleration which revolutionized the same arts once again during the fifty years A.D. 1840–90. In A.D. 1952 the next phase was still enigmatical because it was still in progress; but to a layman's eye it looked at this date as if the fresh technological advances achieved during the immediately preceding sixty years, remarkable though they might have seemed in any other historical context, might prove in retrospect not to compare in extent with the revolutionary achievements of a Victorian half-century. This series of alternating changes of pace in one sphere of technological activity in the history of one civilization is worth examining for the light that it may throw on the general question of the relation between Law and Freedom in History.

The key-notes of the fifteenth-century acceleration in the ship-wright's and the navigator's art were its suddenness and its speed.

'In the fifteenth century . . . there was a swift and momentous change in the building of ships. It was a great era of architecture. In the space of fifty years the sea-going sailing-ship developed from a single-master into a three-master carrying five or six sails.'[1]

And this technological revolution in the West not only gave its authors access to all quarters of the Globe by making them masters of Oceanic navigation; it also gave them an ascendancy over all non-Western mariners whom they encountered in any seas.[2]

'At the beginning of the fifteenth century the seaborne trade of Europe was carried in ships markedly inferior in design and workmanship to the vessels used in many parts of the East; but at the end of the sixteenth century the West European ships were the best in the World. They were, perhaps, less handy and less weatherly than the junks of the China seas, but in general, in their combination of seaworthiness, endurance, carrying capacity, and fighting power, they proved superior to anything else afloat.'[3]

This new-fangled Western type of vessel is the most characteristic emblem of a Modern Age of Western history (*currebat circa* A.D. 1475–1875) during which its unchallenged supremacy was proclaimed in its monopoly of the title 'ship', by which it came to be known *par excellence*. The 'ship's' distinctive virtue, in which it surpassed its successors as conspicuously as its predecessors, was its power to keep the sea for an almost unlimited length of time on end; and this virtue has been divined and lauded by a nineteenth-century Western man of letters who lived to see the 'ship' reach its peak of technical perfection, and all but lived on to see it disappear from the seas as suddenly as it had invaded them some four hundred years earlier.

'L'ancien navire de Christophe Colomb et de Ruyter est un des grands chefs-d'œuvre de l'homme. Il est inépuisable en force comme l'infini en

---

[1] Bassett-Lowke, J. W., and Holland, G.: *Ships and Men* (London 1946, Harrap), p. 46. The quotations from this book have been made with the permission of the publishers.
[2] This revolutionary change in an oecumenical balance of power is touched upon in Toynbee, A. J.: *Civilization on Trial* (London 1948, Oxford University Press), pp. 62–96: 'The Unification of the World and the Change in Historical Perspective.'
[3] Parry, J H.: *Europe and a Wider World, 1415–1715* (London 1949, Hutchinson), p. 21.

souffles, il emmagasine le vent dans sa voile, il est précis dans l'immense diffusion des vagues, il flotte et il règne.'[1]

This Modern Western ship was the offspring of a happy marriage between divers traditional builds and rigs, each of which had peculiar excellencies but also consequent limitations. The Western ship that was brought to birth between A.D. 1440 and A.D. 1490 was a felicitous harmonization of the strong points of an age-old Mediterranean oar-propelled 'long ship', *alias* galley, and a coeval Mediterranean square-rigged 'round-ship', *alias* 'carrack', with a lateen-rigged Indian-Ocean-faring 'caravel' whose forerunner is depicted in the visual records of an Egyptiac maritime expedition to the East African land of Punt in the reign of the Empress Hatshepsut (*imperabat* 1486–1468 B.C.), and with a massively built Atlantic-Ocean-faring sailing-ship which caught Caesar's eye in 56 B.C. when he occupied the territory of the insurgent Veneti around the city that afterwards came to be known as Vannes in Britanny.[2] The fifteenth-century Western harmonization of these far-fetched elements was felicitous in the sense that their diverse excellencies were combined in a new pattern in which their respective limitations were transcended.

The carrack—which was introduced from Mediterranean into Atlantic waters, and was there blended with the local indigenous Ocean-faring type of craft, at the turn of the fourteenth and fifteenth centuries[3]—had the right rig to serve as the main equipment of ships of the large dimensions to which the coming West European Indiamen must run, because the carrack's square rig allowed the sail to be broken up into units of a manageable size, and therefore allowed the total spread of sail to be progressively increased by multiplying the number of these units.[4] At the opening of the fifteenth century the standard Western square-rigged ship had only a single sail, since it had only a single mast, and this mast carried no top-sail.[5] By the middle of the century the standard number of masts had risen from one to three in West European Atlantic waters;[6] and, though the sixteenth-century addition of a fourth mast was discontinued in the seventeenth century and was not reintroduced until the nineteenth,[7] the spread of sail was nevertheless increased by the alternative method of progressively raising the number of tiers of sail on each mast to six and by supplementing the regular sails with studding sails. This advantage of the square rig was, however, offset by the drawback that it gave the navigator no choice but to sail before the wind;[8] and no doubt this was one reason why 'the square-rigged ship—the *nau*—played no considerable part in the early discoveries. The Portuguese preferred a borrowed alternative, the lateen caravel—a highly individual craft which betrayed Asiatic influence in its every line.'[9]

---

[1] Hugo, Victor: *Les Misérables*, Part II, Book II, chap. 3.
[2] See Caesar: *Bellum Gallicum*, Book III, chap. 13.
[3] See Bowen, F. C.: *From Carrack to Clipper* (London 1948, Staples Press), p. 8. Cp. ibid., p. 12.   [4] See Parry, op. cit., pp. 21–22.
[5] See ibid., p. 22.   [6] See Bowen, op. cit., p. 8. Cp. ibid., p. 13.
[7] See Clowes, G. S. L.: *Sailing Ships, their History and Development*: Part I: *Historical Notes* (London 1932, H.M. Stationery Office), p. 107. Cp. Parry, op. cit., p. 25, and Prestage, E.: *The Portuguese Pioneers* (London 1933, Black), p. 332.
[8] See Parry, op. cit., pp. 21–22.   [9] Ibid., p. 22.

The lateen sail had been invented in the Indian Ocean; and lateen caravels had been introduced into the Mediterranean by the Muslims and had been borrowed by the Portuguese from them.[1] In Prince Henry the Navigator's annual southward voyages of discovery down the Atlantic coast of Africa, which had begun in A.D. 1421, if not before,[2] caravels were 'first used in 1440, to judge by Azurara'.[3] The virtue of the lateen rig was that it enabled the navigator to beat to windward;[4] but in this rig there were two drawbacks to set against the advantage. One was that in a lateen-rigged vessel it was difficult to 'go about'—a manœuvre that might be seldom necessary in monsoon navigation, but that became a matter of serious concern when the lateen rig was introduced from the Indian Ocean into other waters.[5] The other drawback of the lateen rig was that the size and weight of lateen spars were so great in proportion to the size of the sail which they could carry, by comparison with the sail-carrying capacity of the square rig, that this defect of the lateen rig set limits to the maximum spread of canvas, and therefore to the maximum size of the vessel thus equipped.[6]

Out of these two piquantly diverse types of vessel, the Portuguese and Spanish shipwrights succeeded, before the end of the fifteenth century, in creating a new composite type with a mixed rig, the *caravela redonda*.[7] This was a three-masted vessel of barquentine rig, in the sense that it carried square sails on the fore-mast and lateen (not, of course, yet fore-and-aft) sails on the main-mast and the mizen-mast.[8] By an early date in the sixteenth century this type—with the main-mast as well as the fore-mast now square-rigged—had become the standard type throughout Western Christendom;[9] and, though the vessels used by Vasco da Gama are recorded to have been, not *caravelas redondas*, but *naus*,[10] we may presume that these late-fifteenth-century 'ships' resembled the late-fifteenth-century caravels in having a mixed rig, even if they differed from them in being of heavier tonnage[11] and clumsier build. In the course of the sixteenth century this clumsiness was fined down in the build of the galleon, which was a carrack with a *caravela redonda*'s mixed rig and with a Mediterranean galley's slim lines.[12] By A.D. 1485 the navigators of this full-blown Modern Western 'ship' had equipped themselves for finding their way over the high seas by mastering the art —invented by Arab navigators in the Indian Ocean—of reckoning their latitude by the co-ordinated use of the quadrant and a set of astronomical tables.[13] By the opening of the sixteenth century they had equipped them-

---

[1] See ibid., pp. 23-24.
[2] See Prestage, E.: *The Portuguese Pioneers* (London 1938, Black), p. 54.
[3] See ibid., p. 332. The reference is to Eannes de Azurara, G.: *Chronica do Descobrimento e Conquista de Guiné*, edited by Carreira and Santarem (Paris 1841, Aillaud); English translation by Beazley, C. R., and Prestage, E.: *The Chronicle of the Discovery and Conquest of Guinea* (London 1896-9, Hakluyt Society, 2 vols.).
[4] See Parry, op. cit., p. 23.
[5] See ibid., p. 23. [6] See ibid., p. 23.
[7] See Prestage, op. cit., p. 332; Parry, op. cit., p. 24.
[8] See Bowen, op. cit., p. 9; Parry, op. cit., pp. 24-25.
[9] See Parry, op. cit., p. 25. [10] See Prestage, op. cit., p. 332.
[11] According to Prestage, op. cit., p. 332, the tonnage of the Ocean-faring *caravelas redondas* ranged from 150 to 200 tons, as against a range of from 400 tons to 800/1,000 tons for Vasco da Gama's *naus*.
[12] See Bowen, op. cit., p. 7. [13] See Prestage, op. cit., pp. 315-18.

selves for holding their own against any human adversaries *en voyage* by the invention of opening up gun ports between-decks.[1]

'What is so remarkable about these ships is their wonderful development. They do not stand so very far distant in point of general structure and rig from the ships of Nelson's day;'[2]

and, by the same token, what is so remarkable about the half-century of acceleration in the Western arts of shipbuilding and navigation *circa* A.D. 1440–90 is that it was followed by three centuries of hardly less conspicuous retardation.

'[The] smug complacency [of the majority of British shipowners at the time of the revision of the Navigation Acts in A.D. 1845] had devastating effects on the shipbuilding industry itself, as well as disclosing an inertia that was out of step with the changing times; for we were passing, as a nation, out of an agrarian order into an industrial one, which made far greater demands on transport. How much progress had been made in naval architecture in the past two centuries? Certainly there had been many innovations and important improvements in the construction and the rig.[3] Labour-saving appliances, too, had been invented. But, if we confine ourselves to essentials, especially in respect of the hull, the progress is almost negligible. After all, there was little incentive towards better ship-design while there was little competition. . . .

'Builders were content to pursue the well-tried methods, and there is small evidence of creative originality. The Dumer's draughts of ship-plans for 1680 . . . show a method of ship-building which does not differ very appreciably from that employed a century later. The standard work on the architecture of the wooden ship was written by Frederick Hendrick Chapman, who became Chief Constructor and Admiral Superintendent of the Swedish Naval Dockyard at Karlskrona. This great designer, born in 1721, came of an old English family from Deptford, from whom he inherited his skill and enthusiasm for naval architecture. His *Architectura Navalis Mercatoria* and his *Treatise on Shipbuilding*, an amplification of the former work published in 1775, were freely quoted from in the official report of the Chatham Committee of Naval Architects of 1842–44.[4] There could be no more conclusive evidence than this of the "mark-time" in shipbuilding and ship-design. . . .

'The ordinary standard of merchant ships was not creditable. They were slow, unhandy, ill-equipped, and inferior in workmanship. Can one say they reflect two centuries of progress? Ship-design, like a spinning-top, rotated on a point. The opening of the nineteenth century saw no

---

[1] See Parry, op. cit., pp. 27–28; Bowen, op. cit., p. 14.

[2] Bassett-Lowke, J. W., and Holland, G.: *Ships and Men* (London 1946, Harrap), p. 48.

[3] The main innovation in the course of the three hundred years A.D. 1500–1800 had been the Dutch invention of the fore-and-aft rig, which was 'an immense advance upon the lateen for beating to windward'. In the non-square-rig part of the rig of big ships (as distinct from the small craft in which the fore-and-aft rig had been first developed), fore-and-aft sails were substituted for lateen sails by the Dutch towards the end of the seventeenth century (Parry, op. cit., pp. 133–4). 'The late seventeenth and early eighteenth centuries saw great improvements in the rig of sea-going ships, notably the introduction of fore-and-aft headsails working on the stays, and a little later the transformation of the cumbersome lateen mizen into the fore-and-after "spanker" ' (ibid., p. 186).—A.J.T.

[4] 'Vessels were built to the patterns laid down under the Stuarts right down to the death of George III, even to the start of Victoria's reign' (Abell, W.: *The Shipwright's Trade* (Cambridge 1948, University Press), p. 102).—A.J.T.

lively effort to improve ship-design, nor any of that competitive enter-prise that marked the race of the factory-owners for business.'[1]

Thus, at a date some four hundred years after the opening of the half-century, bestriding the transition from a Medieval to an Early Modern Age, that had witnessed a revolution in the build and rig of Western ships, it might have looked in retrospect as if a fifteenth-century burst of acceleration in the tempo of Western marine technology, which had given the West a subsequent Ocean-wide ascendancy, had been a unique bout of creativity in the long annals of a Western maritime practice that had been almost as stagnant during the Modern sequel to this short-lived golden age as it had been during the Medieval prelude to it. Yet at this very date the Western art of shipbuilding was actually on the eve of another burst of acceleration that was to produce as great a revolution as its predecessor; and this time the work of creation at high speed was to go forward along two parallel lines. On the one hand, artificially generated mechanical power was to be substituted for wind-power as the driving force by which ships were to be propelled; and contemporaneously, in response to the same challenge that had thus evoked the application of steam-power to navigation, the art of building the classic Modern Western sailing-ship was to awake from its long slumber in order to carry an old type to a new and previously undreamed-of degree of perfection at which, for some of the purposes of maritime traffic, the sailing-ship was to hold its own against the steamship throughout the doubly creative half-century A.D. 1840-90.

The new-fangled type of vessel that was to acquire its classic form in the course of the half-century beginning in A.D. 1840 had by that year only just emerged from the pioneer experimental stage of its develop-ment. Though William Symington's steamship *Charlotte Dundas* had plied on the Forth and the Clyde as early as A.D. 1802,[2] and the Atlantic had been crossed by steam-power reinforced with sail-power in A.D. 1819[3] and by unaided steam-power in A.D. 1827,[4] the era of mechanical navigation as 'a practical proposition' did not open earlier than the triennium A.D. 1838-40, which saw the launching of the first screw-propelled vessel, the *Archimedes*,[5] in A.D. 1838, the successive establish-ment of the Cunard, the Royal Mail, and the Peninsular and Oriental steamship navigation lines (the first two of the three in A.D. 1839 and the third in A.D. 1840),[6] and the crossing of the Atlantic under steam in A.D. 1838 by the *Sirius* and the *Great Western*, and in A.D. 1840 by a *Britannia* that was the first Cunarder to make the passage.[7]

'The power-ship opens a new era in water-transport. She is not evolu-tionary but revolutionary, for she represents a complete break with tradi-tion. Any compromise with the sailing-ship works to her disadvantage both in efficiency and aesthetically. . . . Not till conservative tradition had been scrapped could the power-ship evolve in accordance with her own needs. For the power-ship is modern, different, and original. Her life is not in the

---

[1] Bassett-Lowke, J. W., and Holland, G.: *Ships and Men* (London 1946, Harrap), pp. 124-6.
[2] See ibid., pp. 166-7.
[3] See ibid., p. 168.   [4] See ibid., p. 178.   [5] See ibid., p. 172.
[6] See ibid., p. 178.   [7] See ibid., pp. 174 and 170.

sails but [in] the engine-room. Her natural home is the port rather than the sea. She is tied to her fuel supplies and crosses the oceans sailing to a time-table. Her officers are composed of scientists and technicians, specialists confined to special departments—deck or engine-room—and her crews have specialised duties. The engine-room staff is proportionately bigger than the deck-staff, which grows less and less numerous.'[1]

The conquest of the Ocean by this new-fangled mechanically driven type of vessel in the course of the fifty years A.D. 1840–90 was indeed as great and rapid a revolution as the previous triumph of the Modern Western Ocean-faring sailing-ship some four hundred years earlier; but the distinctive virtue of the steamship, like the qualities of the carrack and the caravel, was offset by consequent limitations. In the act of liberating navigation from its age-long servitude to the vagaries of the winds, the revolutionary new invention of mechanical propulsion re-tethered *Homo Navigans* to the land, of which he had been virtually independent ever since he had substituted the sail for the oar. The steamship dispensed with wind-power at the price of tying itself to coaling-stations; and, however short the intervals at which she might reluctantly consent to break her voyage in order to refuel, she would still be constrained to convert commercially valuable cargo-space into bunker-space which was as unprofitable as the rowing-space which the invention of the sailing-ship had long since enabled the merchantman to eliminate. A high consumption of coal for each effective unit of coal-generated steam power had to be paid for in a reduction of cargo-space and in a shortening of the maximum possible length of unbroken voyage that made the archaic steamship's performance uneconomic by comparison with the classic sailing-ship's.

In mechanically propelled vessels using coal for fuel the solution of this problem had to wait for the invention of the compound engine, which was first installed in the Holt Line S.S. *Cleator* in A.D. 1863, and which in A.D. 1865 enabled the Holt Line S.S. *Agamemnon* to make a non-stop run of 8,500 miles from Liverpool to Mauritius.[2] Even after this triumph of marine engineering, auxiliary sail, which had been the steamship designer's earliest expedient for keeping down the rate of coal consumption, was rigged in the Cunard S.S. *Umbria* as late as A.D. 1884;[3] and sailing-ships which avoided the steamship's handicaps by continuing to rely on wind-power alone earned the highest profits in their commercial history during those mid-nineteenth-century decades in which the technique of steam-propulsion was still feeling its way towards full efficiency.[4] The sailing-ship's nineteenth-century *tour de force* of keeping in the running with her new mechanically propelled rival could hardly have been achieved, however, if, during the same fifty years A.D. 1840–90, that saw the steamship's crucial problems solved, the sleeping art of sailing-ship construction had not bestirred itself out of a three-hundred-years-long stagnation in order to enter on a fresh spurt of creativity. In tempo and in quality alike, the improvements made in the Modern Western sailing-ship in that half century could bear com-

---

[1] Bassett-Lowke and Holland, op. cit., p. 163.
[2] See ibid., p. 182.
[3] See ibid., p. 182.
[4] See ibid., p. 180.

parison with the contemporary progress that was being made in the outlandish mechanism of the new-fangled steamship,[1] and perhaps even with the fifteenth-century revolution in marine technology which had brought the Modern Western sailing-ship herself into being.

The designers of the 'clipper' ship in the eighteen-thirties and eighteen-forties abandoned the late-seventeenth-century models which their predecessors had been lazily copying for the last 150 years in order to introduce revolutionary changes of build which gave a higher speed to a sailing-ship of more than twice the previous standard tonnage;[2] and they were also no less alert than the architects of the steamship in turning an Industrial Revolution to account. The use of iron as a material for shipbuilding, which was introduced in A.D. 1829,[3] made it possible to reduce the weight of the hull by 35 per cent.[4] A composite construction, part iron and part wood, was employed for sailing-ships from A.D. 1851 to A.D. 1870 or thereabouts.[5] The first sailing-ships constructed wholly of iron were built for the Australia wool trade.[6] The year A.D. 1851 saw the first use of ropes made of wire instead of hemp,[7] and the early eighteen-eighties the first use of steel tubing instead of timber for masts and lower yards.[8] *Circa* A.D. 1884 the substitution of mild steel for iron as the material for the construction of large sailing-ships made possible a further reduction of weight—by 15 per cent., this time.[9] In and after A.D. 1887 donkey engines, driven by steam, were installed on sailing-ships to save man-power, and, with the same end in view, all tiers of sails above the top-gallants were then cut out.[10]

Though the overcoming of the steamship's original limitations through the successful experiment with the compound engine in A.D. 1863–5 had spelled a rejuvenated sailing-ship's eventual doom, the Modern Western sailing-ship actually attained its acme at a time when it was thus already under sentence of death at the hands of a now irresistible competitor. Just as the coaches and the canals had been brought to their highest point of efficiency in Great Britain on the eve of their being put out of action by the railways, and a Medieval Western Latin poetry had reached its zenith throughout Western Christendom on the eve of its being silenced by the voice of the vernacular tongues, so the Modern Western sailing-

[1] According to Schumpeter, J. A.: *Business Cycles* (New York 1939, McGraw-Hill, 2 vols.), vol. i, pp. 369–70, the innovations in the construction of Western sailing-ships from *circa* A.D. 1840 onwards were partly evoked by the new challenge presented to the sailing-ship by the steamship's epiphany.

[2] The new move in sailing-ship design which produced the 'clipper' started in the shipbuilding yards at Baltimore, and it seems to be a moot point whether the *Ann McKim*, launched there in A.D. 1832, or the *Scottish Maid*, launched in A.D. 1839, was the first ship that could fairly claim the new title (see Bowen, op. cit., p. 58). Ships on the lines of the Baltimore clippers, but with a tonnage of over 750 tons, began to take the sea from American yards in and after A.D. 1843 (see Clowes, op. cit., p. 103). The development of the new breed of sailing-ship was given an impetus by the discovery of gold in California in A.D. 1849, since at this date the cheapest and surest route thither from the Atlantic seaboard of North America was by sea round Cape Horn. The average tonnage of a clipper then rose from 1,000 tons to 2,000 tons plus or minus (Bassett-Lowke and Holland, op. cit., pp. 145–6).

[3] According to Bassett-Lowke and Holland, op. cit., p. 168, the first iron ship was built as early as A.D. 1821.

[4] See Clowes, op. cit., p. 104. [5] See ibid., p. 104.

[6] See ibid., p. 105. Cp. Bassett-Lowke and Holland, op. cit., p. 157.

[7] See Clowes, op. cit., p. 109. [8] See ibid., p. 109.

[9] See ibid., p. 107. [10] See Bassett-Lowke and Holland, op. cit., p. 159.

ship sang its swan song during the quarter of a century A.D. 1865–90, bestriding the transition from a Modern to a post-Modern Age of Western history, when it was on the point of being driven off the seas by the steamship. The tonnage of the sail-borne British merchant marine reached its peak in A.D. 1875.[1] The historic race between tea clippers from Foochow to London was run in A.D. 1866;[2] the historic race between wool clippers from Australia to London in A.D. 1887–8.[3] The *Thermopylae* was launched in A.D. 1868; the *Cutty Sark*—a composite-built ship with a tonnage of 2,100 tons—in A.D. 1869.[4] The largest sailing-ship ever launched—the *Preussen*, with a length of over 400 feet and a tonnage of over 5,000 tons gross—was built at Geestemünde, near Bremen, after the turn of the century, in A.D. 1902.[5]

The writer of this Study had the good fortune, as a child, to catch a last glimpse of the sailing-ship before she vanished from the seas, and to be initiated into the lore of her divers rigs by the former master of an East Indiaman, his great-uncle Captain Henry Toynbee (*vivebat* A.D. 1819–1909),[6] who had retired from the sea in A.D. 1866 without ever having seen service on a steamship or indeed on any build of sailing-vessel other than a full ship since his first voyage at a tender age on a barque. On summer holidays in the eighteen-nineties at St. Margaret's Bay on the English shore of the Straits of Dover, under the eye of the South Foreland lighthouse, the small boy learnt the rigs from the old sailor as the ships came gliding past: schooners and three-masted schooners and top-sail schooners (very common); brigantines and brigs (rather rare); barquentines and barques; and full-rigged ships ranging from classic three-masters to the four-masters and five-masters that were a nineteenth-century revival of a sixteenth-century fashion. He learnt to know and love them all, without ever suspecting that he would live to see the disappearance of this divine work of Man's hands which, in his uncle's confident eyes, was as much a part of the eternal order of Nature as the chalk cliff on which they were standing, or as the water which gave the measure of the distance from the shore to the passing ship. In the eighteen-nineties the sailing-ships plying through the Straits were still far more numerous than the steamships (though doubtless steam had by then long since outstripped sail in aggregate tonnage). As late as the summer of 1910, there used always to be several four-masted sailing-ships at anchor in Falmouth harbour, and in the summer of 1911 the wreck of one huge sailing-ship was lying huddled against

---

[1] See Schumpeter, J. A.: *Business Cycles* (New York 1939, McGraw-Hill, 2 vols.), vol. i, p. 369.   [2] See Bassett-Lowke and Holland, op. cit., p. 155.
[3] See ibid., p. 153.   [4] See ibid., pp. 152–3; Abell, op. cit., p. 142.
[5] See Bassett-Lowke and Holland, op. cit., p. 160.
[6] 'Captain Henry Toynbee was one of the most scientific navigators of his day. . . . "He was always sure of his longitude within five miles," writes one of his officers. And his wonderful landfalls were the admiration of his passengers.

'Toynbee . . . went to sea in 1833 at the age of fourteen as a midshipman in the East Indiaman *Dunvegan Castle*. . . . Toynbee's first command was the *Ellenborough*; and he had also commanded the *Gloriana* and *Marlborough* before he took over the *Hotspur*, the command of which he resigned in 1866 in order to succeed Admiral Fitzroy as Marine Superintendent of the Meteorological Office. He retired in 1888, and lived to be over ninety years of age, an example of all that an officer in our mercantile marine should be (Lubbock, Basil: *The Blackwall Frigates*, 2nd edition (Glasgow 1950, Brown, Son, & Ferguson), pp. 145–6).

the cliffs between the South Foreland and Dover. Yet, already, forty years back, sail was being driven by steam off one sea-route after another. The China tea clippers had been put out of business by the opening of the Suez Canal in A.D. 1869,[1] which had deprived them of their advantage over steamships trying to compete with them on the long voyage round the Cape; by A.D. 1875 all routes except the Australian had been captured by steamships;[2] and in A.D. 1881 the Australian route itself was conquered for steam by the S.S. *Aberdeen* with her triple expansion engines,[3] though the wool clippers went on fighting their losing battle till the end of the decade.[4] The interval between the first two world wars saw the process of extinguishing the sailing-ship completed.[5]

If a lay observer's eye is not mistaken, the close of the ninth decade of the nineteenth century, which marked the virtual end of a fifty-years-long struggle between a rejuvenated sailing-ship and a new-fangled steamship, also marked the end of the spurt of creative activity which the shipwright's art had been making during those same fifty years in both these competing lines. While the standard battleship and merchant-ship of A.D. 1890 had no more recognizable affinity with those of A.D. 1840 than a basilisk has with an angel fish, the standard battleship and merchantship of A.D. 1950 bore as close a resemblance to those of A.D. 1890 as the standard battleship and merchantship of A.D. 1840 had borne to those of A.D. 1640. No doubt the sixty years A.D. 1890–1950 had also brought with them further innovations and improvements. The introduction of turbine engines driven by steam generated by burning oil instead of coal had been a change of perhaps the same order of magnitude as the substitution of fore-and-aft sails for lateen sails in the Modern Western ship at the turn of the seventeenth and eighteenth centuries,[6] while the invention of radio-telegraphy and the installation of the apparatus on board ship just after the end of the First World War, and the invention of radar and its installation after the Second World War, were perhaps as great landmarks in the history of the Western art of navigation as the eighteenth-century solution of the problem of calculating longitudes through the perfecting of the chronometer.[7] Yet, however notable these changes might be in themselves, they looked insignificant by comparison with the swiftness and greatness of the revolution that had been accomplished between A.D. 1840 and A.D. 1890. To a lay observer born in A.D. 1889 and looking back in the year 1952, it seemed clear that his own lifetime had been, in the history of shipbuilding, a period of retardation in the tempo of change by comparison with the pace of the forced march during the immediately preceding half century.

If this impression was correct, then a series of alternating accelerations and retardations which had begun with the acceleration *circa* A.D.

[1] See Clowes, op. cit., p. 105; Abell, op. cit., pp. 141–2.
[2] See Bassett-Lowke and Holland, op. cit., p. 182.
[3] See ibid., p. 182.   [4] See Clowes, op. cit., p. 106.
[5] See Bassett-Lowke and Holland, op. cit., pp. 160–1. In *The Times* of the 25th January, 1951, a photograph will be found of 'the *Pamir* and *Passat*, the last two sailing barques to take part in the traditional grain race from Australia to England, lying at Penarth Docks. They will be taken in tow to Antwerp for breaking up.'
[6] See p. 368, n. 3, above.
[7] See Prestage, op. cit., p. 324.

1440 had run through a first retardation into a second acceleration and thence into a second retardation in the course of some five centuries.

This glance at the history of the Western shipwright's art concludes our survey of evidences of variability in the rate of social change; and these evidences—which have presented themselves in divers phases of the histories of a number of different civilizations—are so many indications that a recalcitrance to laws of Nature is no less characteristic of Human Nature than an amenability to them. Indeed, if we now look again at the pattern of the disintegration-process, in which we have found our classic example of regularity, we shall see that a varying rate of change is one of this regular process's uniformly recurring features. There is a particularly sudden and extreme change of tempo at the transition from a Time of Troubles to a universal state; for the second paroxysm of a Time of Troubles, which is precipitated by the first relapse and is pulled up short by the second rally, is the most feverishly fast-moving episode in the story, whereas there is no episode in it so slow-moving as the first spell of oecumenical peace which supervenes. This rebellious variability in the rate of change is not, however, the only irregularity in the gait of History which suggests that, after all, Man may not be completely subject to Nature's orders.

(b) THE DIVERSITY OF CORRESPONDING EPISODES IN THE HISTORIES OF DIFFERENT CIVILIZATIONS

1. *A Diversity in the Duration of the Growth-Phases of Civilizations*

Evidences of human recalcitrance to laws of Nature multiply when we place the records of the life-histories of civilizations side by side and take a synoptic view of them. Two breaches of uniformity that stand out conspicuously are a quantitative diversity in the duration of the growth-phases of those civilizations whose growth-spans we are able to measure, and a no less striking qualitative diversity in the relations of Religion to the rises and falls of civilizations in different generations.[1]

The diversity in the length of measurable growth-spans is extreme, as can be seen by anyone who runs his eye down Table V at the end of the present volume.

In compiling this table we have had to leave out of account the seven civilizations of the first generation (the Egyptiac, Sumeric, Minoan, Indus Culture, Shang Culture, Andean, and Mayan), since each of these arose out of the mutation of some primitive society[2] at a stage of social development earlier than the invention of techniques for keeping records; and, though we may know, or guess, the nature of the challenges from Physical Nature by which these mutations were evolved,[3] we have no means of even approximately estimating the dates at which they occurred. In the history of the Egyptiac Civilization, for example, the evidence, as it stood in A.D. 1952, did not suffice to indicate whether the age of 'the Old Kingdom' was to be equated with the growth-phase of the Egyptiac Society, or whether an investigator was to see here a uni-

---

[1] See Table IV: Primitive Societies, Civilizations, Higher Religions, in vol. vii, *ad fin.*
[2] See II. i. 188.   [3] See II. i. 302–30.

versal state representing the last phase in the disintegration of a society whose antecedent Time of Troubles, breakdown, and growth-phase were still buried in oblivion.[1] In our present search for approximately ascertainable measurements of growth-spans, our field is therefore limited to the group of 'affiliated' civilizations; and in A.D. 1952 there were seventeen known specimens of these (reckoning the Sinic Civilization as one, now that the progress of archaeological discovery had deprived it of its title to rank as a primary civilization by bringing its Shang predecessor to light).

The epiphany of an 'affiliated' civilization ought to be less difficult to date, since we may expect to see it emerge out of an interregnum following the break-up of a universal state representing the last phase in the history of an antecedent civilization. There were, nevertheless, at least three 'affiliated' civilizations—the Yucatec, Mexic, and Sinic—whose epiphanies were almost as difficult to date as those of the primary civilizations in the dim and flickering light of the archaeological evidence at the disposal of an historian mid-way through the twentieth century of the Christian Era. In their pioneer attempts to link the Mayan Society's impressively exact, but self-contained and insulated, chronological records with the post-Amosan chronology of the Old World, Modern Western scholars had divided into two schools whose respective datings differed by no less than a quarter of a millennium; and this discrepancy was reflected in a corresponding uncertainty about the chronology of the growth-phases of the affiliated Yucatec and Mexic civilizations. As for the dating of the epiphany of the Sinic Civilization, Western scholars were confronted here with a discrepancy within the Sinic tradition itself, in which, for the period before the year 841 B.C., the standard chronology was challenged by the testimony of the so-called 'Bamboo Books'.[2] These two conflicting Sinic chronologies were as much as seventy-two years apart in their dating of the overthrow of the Shang Power by the Chóu invader Wu Wang; and, even if we were to opt in favour of the Bamboo Books' date 1050 B.C. against the standard chronology's date 1122 B.C., we might still find ourselves uncertain how to interpret this event in terms of the replacement of an antecedent Shang Society by an affiliated Sinic. Was the Shang Power whose latest capital at Mo the archaeologists had disinterred[3] since the publication of the first three volumes of the present Study in A.D. 1934 a universal state in the sense in which we have been using the term? And was the Chóu Power that replaced the Shang Power a semi-barbarian successor-state like the Achaean Power that asserted itself at Mycenae after the sack of Cnossos, or the Ostrogoth Power that established itself at Ravenna after the collapse of the Roman Imperial Government's rule over the Roman Empire's western provinces? These moot points of historical interpretation conspired with the discrepancy between conflicting chronological systems to baffle an historian seeking in A.D. 1952 to date the Sinic Civilization's epiphany.

[1] See pp. 682–92, below.
[2] See Hirth, F.: *The Ancient History of China* (New York 1908, Columbia University Press), p. 176.   [3] See VI. vii. 213, n. 1.

Moreover, there was at least one 'affiliated' civilization—the Western —whose epiphany could be dated but whose growth-span nevertheless could not be measured in A.D. 1952 because at that date it was still impossible to tell whether this civilization had or had not yet broken down.[1]

Subject to these still unclarified uncertainties, it was possible in A.D. 1952 to draw up the accompanying table[2] of the approximate Time-spans of the growth of the 'affiliated' civilizations in a descending order of duration.

In this table there are, no doubt, certain traces of regularity. For example, apart from the two extremes represented by the Western Civilization and the Mexic Civilization respectively, the Time-spans appear to fall into five groups: one of about 600 to 700 years length (in four instances); one of about 400 years (in three instances); one of about 300 years (in two instances); one of about 175 to 200 years (in four instances); and one of about 100 years (in two instances). It also seems unlikely to be merely an accident that two civilizations so closely resembling one another in their structure as the Hellenic Civilization and the Medieval Western city-state cosmos should have an identical Time-span. Such appearances of regularity, however, are insignificant by comparison with the magnitude of the differences in a spread of Time-spans ranging in length from 850 years or more to zero; and some of the greatest of these chronological differences are to be found between the respective spans of twin societies that are affiliated to the same predecessor and are coeval in their epiphanies. The Hellenic Society's growth-span of some 700 years presents as great a contrast to the twin Syriac Society's span of some 200 years as the Western Society's span of 875 years or more presents to the twin Orthodox Christian Society's span of some 300 years.

2. *A Diversity in the Relations of Religion to the Rises and Falls of Civilizations in Different Generations*

In a previous context[3] we have observed that every social interregnum between civilizations of different generations that had occurred in the history of this species of society up to date had been marked by flashes of religious light; but we have also observed that these successive flashes had been strikingly unequal in the degree of their luminosity. The higher religions which had made their epiphany during the falls of the secondary civilizations had brought into the world a spiritual illumination which seemed beyond compare with the fainter light cast either by the rudimentary higher religions that had appeared during the falls of the primary civilizations or by the secondary higher religions that had been appearing during the falls of the tertiary civilizations.[4] This difference in degree of spiritual power was so great that it amounted to a difference in kind and quality; and there could be no clearer intimation than this that the rotation of the sorrowful wheel of Human Life on

---

[1] See XII, *passim*, below.
[2] Table V at the end of the present volume.
[3] In VII. vii. 420–5.   [4] See Table IV in vol. vii, *ad fin.*

Earth was something more than one of those vain repetitions of the Heathen[1] through which Man is convicted of being in penal servitude to laws of Nature.

(II) POSSIBLE EXPLANATIONS OF THE INOPERATIVENESS OF LAWS OF NATURE IN SOME PHASES OF HUMAN AFFAIRS

Now that we have encountered some phases in which human affairs have all the appearance of being recalcitrant to laws of Nature, we shall find ourselves looking for possible explanations of a partial inoperativeness of these laws in the field of Human Life, where we have previously found impressive evidences of their currency. Divers alternative possibilities suggest themselves. This appearance of recalcitrance might be merely an illusion, due to ignorance, which would be dispelled if we were precisely informed of all the relevant facts. Or, supposing that an advance in our knowledge had made it certain that this appearance was a faithful reflection of Reality, then a genuine recalcitrance of human affairs to laws of Nature might perhaps be explicable as being either an effect of the play of Chance or a product of creative responses to challenges. Let us look further into each of these three possibilities.

The interpretation of the appearances of freedom in Human Life as mere mirages induced by sheer ignorance was one possible explanation that a twentieth-century Western inquirer was not entitled to rule out, since in that age a post-Modern Western intellect was only on the verge of discovering laws of Nature reigning in the Human Psyche's subconscious abyss, while at the same date the actual quantity of recorded statistical evidence bearing upon laws of Nature in the affairs of Man in Process of Civilization was still minute by comparison with the potential quantity of the evidence in the same field that might accumulate in the future.

The number of civilizations that were known to have existed up to date—leaving out of the reckoning those that had been abortive or had been arrested—amounted to no more than twenty-one, and these represented no more than three generations, so far, spread over no more than five or six thousand years, reckoning from the probable era of the species' epiphany down to the time of writing. In previous contexts[2] we have observed that, if we were to reckon the duration of the Age of the Civilizations up to date at the maximum figure of 6,000 years and were to halve the figure of 1,000,000 million years at which twentieth-century Western scientists had estimated the Human Race's present expectation of life on its native planet (always supposing that the race did not exterminate itself long before reaching the end of Nature's rope), there would be time during these next 500,000 million years for no less than 1,743,000,000 further civilizations to come and go if they were to continue to come and go at the same rate as during the first 6,000 years of the history of this species of Society. For an historian this was an in-

[1] Matt. vi. 7.   [2] In I. i. 456–64 and VII. vii. 453–4, and on p. 344, above.

timidating calculation, notwithstanding the evidence indicating that the tempo of social change was by no means uniform as a matter of fact. Within the writer's own infinitesimally short experience between the time when he was drafting his first systematic notes for this Study in A.D. 1927–9 and the time in A.D. 1950 when he was approaching the completion of the writing of the text, previously unknown facts had been brought to light—for example, in the realm of pre-Sinic archaeology and in the realm of Sumeric chronology—which were no mere points of detail but were 'integral' facts throwing fresh light on the whole study of History. The spectre of ignorance haunted the writer at the close of his work as insistently as at the beginning; and it was always in his mind that future students of History, equipped with vastly ampler funds of relevant knowledge, might smile at his faith in a pittance of knowledge that, by comparison with what they knew, would look as tiny as a squirrel's winter store. A faith that had moved him to carry out his own reconnaissance did not blind him to the possibility—improbable though he personally felt this to be—that the appearance of freedom in human affairs might be dissipated one day by a progressive increase in the candle-power of Science's dry light.

If a haze of Ignorance was thus one of the contingencies that had to be reckoned with, was it also necessary to allow for the play of Chance? The answer to this second question could be given out of hand, without any question here of having to await the verdict of a still untold tale of 500,000 million years; for the settling of the historian's accounts with Chance was a matter, not of fact-finding, but of reasoning; and Reason pronounces that Chance is not an absolute positive concept, but a negative and therefore necessarily a relative one, and that accordingly to see in Chance an ultimate explanation of any phenomenon would be as naïve an error as to mistake a sign-post for the goal to which it pointed. Just as the label 'Heterodoxy' merely indicates the existence of another 'doxy' labelled 'Orthodoxy',[1] and the name 'Neustria' merely indicates the existence of another country labelled 'Austrasia',[2] so the labelling of a phenomenon as an outcome of the play of Chance merely indicates that this phenomenon does not display the pattern of some particular kind of order that the thinker happens to have in mind—and perhaps also to expect, or even desire, to find—at the moment when he indicates its absence in the case in point by holding Chance responsible for the production of the phenomenon that has to be accounted for. To attribute a child's paternity to Chance is thus merely a form of words for stating that this child cannot be credited with some other paternity that might have been expected to be proved; but this negative label does not tell us what the child's true paternity is; nor can this or any other verbiage act as a spell to perform the miracle of begetting a child without recourse to any father at all. The patronymic 'child of Chance' merely informs us that the foundling is not the child of so-and-so; and this negative finding

---

[1] A theologian with a sense of humour who was asked by a lady at a dinner party to explain the difference between Orthodoxy and Heterodoxy is said to have answered her: 'Well, Orthodoxy is *my* doxy and Heterodoxy is *your* doxy.'

[2] See II. ii. 167, n. 2.

leaves us just where we were; for it leaves still unanswered our original
question asking who the child's true father is.

> All nature is but art, unknown to thee;
> All chance, direction which thou canst not see.[1]

This relativity, and consequent inconclusiveness, of the concept of
Chance has come to our attention already in this Study in other contexts;[2] and, in order to make sure, once again, of making this logical
point clear, we will quote, once again, a French philosopher's lucid exposition of it.

'If, at a venture, I select a volume in my library, I may replace it on the
shelves, after taking a glance at it, with the remark "This isn't verse". But
is this really what I perceived when I was turning the pages? Clearly not.
I did not see, and I never shall see, an absence of verse. What I did see
was prose. But, as it is poetry that I am wanting, I express what I find in
terms of what I am looking for; and, instead of saying "Here is some
prose", I say "This isn't verse". Inversely, if it takes my fancy to read
some prose and I stumble on a volume of verse, I shall exclaim "This isn't
prose"; and in using these words I shall be translating the data of my
perception, which shows me verse, into the language of my expectation
and my interest, which are set upon the idea of prose and therefore will
not hear of anything else. . . .

'An order is contingent, and appears so to us, in relation to the inverse
order, in the way in which verse is contingent in relation to prose, and
prose in relation to verse. . . . If we analyse the idea of Chance, which is
a near relation to the idea of Disorder, we shall find the same elements.
When the purely mechanical operation of the causes which bring the
roulette to a halt on a particular number makes me win and so behaves
as a good genius would have behaved if he had been looking after my
interests, and when the purely mechanical force of the wind snatches a tile
from the roof and flings it down on my head—thus acting as an evil genius
would have acted if he had been plotting against my life—in both cases
I find a mechanism in a place where I would have looked for—and ought,
it would seem, to have encountered—an intention; and that is what I
am expressing when I speak of "Chance". And in describing an anarchic
world, where the phenomena follow one another at the pleasure of their
caprice, I shall say, again, that this is the reign of "Chance", and I shall
mean by this that I find myself confronted by acts of will, or rather by
"decrees", when what I was looking for was mechanism. . . . The idea of
"Chance" simply objectifies the state of mind of someone whose expectation has been directed towards one of two species of order and who then
encounters the other. Chance and Disorder are, then, necessarily conceived of as relative.'[3]

In another context[4] we have noticed already that this mirage of
'Chance' and 'Disorder', even when it has been conjured up out of the
emotional underworld of the Psyche by some disappointment of expectations, can avail to obscure the regularities and uniformities of an
underlying positive order only so long as the number of instances of the

---

[1] Pope: *An Essay on Man*, *Ep.* i, ll. 289–90.
[2] In V. v. 419–21 and VII. vii. 544, n. 3.
[3] Bergson, Henri: *L'Évolution Créatrice*, 24th ed. (Paris 1921, Alcan), pp. 239–58,
quoted in V. v. 419, n. 4.   [4] On p. 206, n. 2, above.

phenomenon under consideration which the observer has at his command is less than ten or thereabouts.

If we take Bergson's elucidation of the concept of 'Chance' as our clue for unravelling the answer to our question whether the play of 'Chance' can be accepted as a possible explanation of an apparent recalcitrance of human affairs to laws of Nature, we shall have now to put two leading questions to ourselves: First, what is the species of order that we are expecting to find in human affairs? And, second, what is the other species of order with which we are actually confronted when we say that we find ourselves here in the presence of the reign of 'Chance'? In our foregoing inquiry into possible explanations of the manifest currency of laws of Nature in human history, our finding was that these laws governing human affairs were, for the most part, laws current in the Human Psyche's own subconscious underworld; and, if this is the species of order for which we are looking in this field, then the different order, found in fact to be reigning here, that we label 'Chance' because it is not what we had been expecting, must be one or other of three possible alternatives. It may be the order of Physical Nature as contrasted with Psychic Nature, or the order of human will as contrasted with the subconscious level of the Human Psyche, or the order of God's will as contrasted both with human wills and with the by-laws, psychic and physical alike, which the will of God has enacted.[1] These three alternatives would seem to exhaust the possible identities of the order, not identical with an expected subconscious psychic order, that we have left incognito in labelling it 'Chance'. Our negative label must mask some one of these three positive realities, since a label cannot be pasted on to a vacuum. We have already noticed that the 'Chance' which appears to come into play when conflicting human wills frustrate one another is a label masking the self-assertion of the laws of the Subconscious Psyche.[2] On this showing, the 'Chance' which appears to come into play when these laws of the Subconscious Psyche fail, in their turn, to answer to conscious expectations by asserting themselves must be a label masking the operation of some other positive force.

The possibility that 'Chance' in our present context might prove to be a label masking the order of Physical Nature diminishes to a vanishing point in the light of our inquiry into the amenability of human

---

[1] A belief in the reality of any of these three kinds of order, like a belief in the reality of the order of Subconscious Psychic Nature, is the offspring of experience wedded to faith. Without the faith that 'is the substance of things hoped for, the evidence of things not seen' (Heb. xi. 1), a human being's experience of Physical Nature, his experience of his fellow human beings, and even his experience of himself, would not guarantee the reality of any of these phenomena; and a belief in the reality of God and of His action in the Universe derives from the same twofold source. The experience of an encounter with God that was attributed to Jacob, Moses, and Samuel, and that was granted to the prophets of Israel, Judah, and Iran according to these prophets' own conviction, may not be experienced even by the prophets in more than one or two brief flashes in a lifetime, while the great majority of human beings may never have this experience at all at first hand; so that a belief in God will be an act of faith for the prophet himself for most of his life and for most of his followers for all of their lives. 'Blessed are they that have not seen, and yet have believed' (John xx. 29) is thus a truth that is conspicuously true of a belief in the reality of God; yet a belief in the reality of one's self, of other selves, and of Nature, Psychic or Physical, also requires a large measure of faith as well as of experience.   [2] See pp. 326–37, above.

affairs to laws of Nature; for we have found that, by comparison with the jurisdiction of the laws of the Subconscious Psyche, the jurisdiction of the laws of Physical Nature over human affairs has never been of much consequence; and we have also found that, whatever this jurisdiction may have amounted to originally, the human social animal has been singularly successful in discovering how to elude its incidence, and has been liberating himself in this way from Physical Nature's dominion at a pace that has been increasing by geometrical progression. We have watched human beings successfully conspiring to elude the incidence of the astronomical law of the Year Cycle that governs the yield of their domesticated plants and trees; we have watched them similarly eluding the incidence of a physiological law of the Day-and-Night Cycle;[1] and we have also seen them turning to human account even Nature's in-human device of a procession of generation cycles punctuated by the deaths of individuals, when human beings have overlaid Nature's own method of transmitting a racial heritage of instincts and aptitudes through the physiological process of procreation with the artificial human device of transmitting a social heritage of habits and knowledge through the spiritual process of moral and intellectual education.[2] On this show-ing, an apparent play of 'Chance' in human affairs is unlikely, if it looms at all large, to mask a reign of laws of Physical Nature; for, *pace* the astrologers, it seems much less likely that human affairs in which we do not discern the operation of laws of the Subconscious Psyche are governed, under the label of 'Chance', by hitherto unrecognized laws of Physical Nature than that they are governed either by hitherto un-recognized laws of the Subconscious Psyche itself or else by the will either of human beings or of God.

When human wills encounter one another without concurring in a common purpose to do God's will, they are prone, as we have seen, to frustrate one another, and their thus unintentionally concerted self-stultification reopens the way for the compulsive laws of the Subcon-scious Human Psyche to reassert themselves. When a human soul encounters God, what is the outcome of a meeting between wills of such immeasurably unequal potency?

Theologians who have pictured God in Man's image, through a failure to rise to a worship of God in spirit and in truth,[3] have sometimes fallen into the spiritual error of imagining that God exerts His irresistible power to make His own will prevail over Man's—either by ruthlessly over-riding it or by craftily bending it to conform to God's will unawares.[4] This picture of an iron law of God the Tyrant lurking under the mesh that God's guileless creatures label 'Chance' has been painted for us by Bossuet.

'Ne parlons plus de hasard ni de fortune, ou parlons-en seulement comme d'un nom dont nous couvrons notre ignorance. Ce qui est hasard à l'égard de nos conseils incertains est un dessein concerté dans un conseil plus haut, c'est-à-dire dans ce conseil éternel qui renferme toutes les causes et tous les effets dans un même ordre. De cette sorte tout concourt

---

[1] See pp. 306–10, above.   [2] See pp. 319–26, above.
[3] John iv. 24.   [4] See pp. 175–9, above.

à la même fin, et c'est faute d'entendre le tout que nous trouvons du hasard ou de l'irrégularité dans les rencontres particulières.'[1]

The orator's language is as brilliant as it is masterful, but the theologian's ideas of what God is and how God acts are as unconvincing as they are repellant to any drinker at the fountain-head of Christianity. As God is revealed in the Gospels, He is Love as well as Omnipotence; He is the Soul's father, redeemer, and illuminator, as well as its creator and its master;[2] and this Christian faith assures us that, when a soul encounters the God of whom this is the authentic Christian picture, Love suspends the fiat of Omnipotence in order to transmute a command into a challenge which confronts the human recipient of it with a free choice between Good and Evil and between Life and Death.[3] Such challenges from God may evoke in human souls creative responses that are genuinely free human acts; and this spiritual drama of Challenge-and-Response[4] is perhaps the key to an explanation of those human affairs in which human action wears the appearance of being at any rate partially exempt from the dominion of laws of Nature.

If we now recall some of our instances of an apparent recalcitrance of human affairs to laws of Nature, we shall find that these are also instances of a creative response to a challenge.

When, for example, a creative individual or minority distinguishes itself by breaking contact with the rank-and-file, forging ahead of them, and then re-entering into contact again, these distinctive moves, which are so many evidences of the minority's freedom of action, are at the same time so many stages in a response that the creative individual or minority has been stimulated to make in answer to some challenge that has been presented to all the members of the society, including the unresponsive rank-and-file, and also perhaps including other individuals or minorities who have made a choice of Evil instead of Good that brings Death instead of Life.[5]

If we now also look again at the history of the art of ship-building in the Modern and post-Modern ages of Western history, in which we have watched the sequence of an acceleration followed by a retardation occurring, not once only, as in the movement of Withdrawal-and-Return, but twice over, we shall find this duplication of the same sequence accounted for here by the presentation of two different challenges in succession.

The challenge that evoked the creation of the Modern Western 'ship' within the half-century A.D. 1440–90 was a political one. Towards the close of the Medieval Age of Western history, Western Christendom found itself not only conclusively foiled in its attempt to break out of its West European homeland south-eastward into Dār-al-Islām and Orthodox Christendom, but seriously threatened by a north-westward-heading counter-attack in which the military resources of Orthodox Christendom and Islam were brigaded under Ottoman auspices.[6] The dangerousness of Western Christendom's plight in the fifteenth century

[1] Bossuet, J.-B.: *Discours sur l'Histoire Universelle*, 3rd ed. (Paris 1700), Troisième Partie, chap. viii.   [2] See p. 175, above.
[3] Deut. xxx. 15–19.   [4] See II. i. 271–302.
[5] See I. i. 22–26 and III. iii. 217–377.   [6] See IX. viii. 216–72, 346–63, and 454–80.

was accentuated by geographical circumstances that had perhaps also been partly accountable for the launching of the ill-starred Crusades. The homeland of the Western Christian Society happened to lie at the tip of one of the peninsulas of the Great Eurasian Continent, and a society so precariously situated must sooner or later be pushed into the Ocean by the pressure of mightier forces thrusting outwards from the heart of the Old World if this besieged society did not succeed in fore-stalling disaster by breaking out of its West-European *cul-de-sac* into some larger *Lebensraum*. By the fifteenth century of the Christian Era the *peine forte et dure* of being crushed to death between the Devil and the Deep Sea had already brought to their last gasp the surviving repre-sentatives of an abortive Far Western Christian Civilization in 'the Celtic Fringe' of the Old World; and a Latin Christendom likewise had been exposed, since its birth, to this manifest destiny of all West European societies by which a Celtic Christendom was eventually to be overtaken. In the Crusades the Latin Christians—choosing the Mediter-ranean Sea as their war-path and faring across it in vessels of the tradi-tional Mediterranean builds—had been moved by a nostalgia for the cradle of their Christian faith[1] to defy Fate by breaking out of Western Europe into the Levant; and the eventual failure of this enterprise had not been followed by a return of the *status quo ante*. The retort to Medieval Western aggression had been in Egypt the replacement of effete 'Fātimids' by militarily efficient Mamlūks,[2] and in Orthodox Christendom the replacement of an effete East Roman Empire by 'Osmanlis who were still more efficient and far more aggressive than their Mamlūk cousins.[3]

These local revolutions which the West's own aggression had pre-cipitated had eclipsed the West's military and political prospects in the Levant, and had made her commercial prospects there dependent on the new Islamic Powers' goodwill. In what other direction was Western Christendom to look for an outlet? A once barbarian no-man's-land in Northern Europe had been eliminated before the end of the fourteenth century of the Christian Era by a parallel northward advance of Western and of Russian Orthodox Christendom which had carried their common frontier up to the shore of the Arctic Ocean;[4] and, when Western Chris-tendom had taken advantage of Russia's prostration by a tornado of Mongol invasion from the Eurasian Steppe in order to trespass on her Russian neighbour's domain in White Russia and the Ukraine, this east-ward aggression overland had been halted, in its turn, by the rise of Muscovy.[5] Mid-way through the fifteenth century, when the sea-route via the Mediterranean into the Levant and the land-route via Russia into the heart of the Eurasian Continent had both been effectively closed against any further Western expansion in either of these directions, the Atlantic Ocean was the sole remaining frontier of Western Christendom that was not beset by an impassable hostile human cordon; and the Atlantic was thus uninfested by human adversaries of the West only

---

[1] See I. i. 38; IX. viii. 346–63; and p. 100, above.
[2] See IV. iv. 447–50.   [3] See III. iii. 22–50.
[4] See II. ii. 168–9.   [5] See II. ii. 174–7; IX. viii. 126 and 398–403.

because it was, and always had been, believed by all denizens of the Old World to be an unharvested and unharvestable sea, setting an impassable physical western limit to the habitable portion of the Earth's surface. In the fifteenth century of the Christian Era the Atlantic was challenging the beleaguered peoples of Western Christendom by confronting them with a choice between two extreme alternatives. If they were not to be driven into the Atlantic in their turn, as they themselves had been driving the hapless Celtic Christians, they must convert Seneca's fancy[1] into fact by conquering an Ocean which not even a poet had ever seriously supposed to be conquerable by Man 'in real life'. The dual alarum of simultaneous challenges from the Atlantic and the 'Osmanli was the emergency that, within the half century A.D. 1440–90, stimulated Western shipwrights to create an Ocean-faring, globe-encircling sailing-ship, capable of keeping the sea continuously for months on end, of which the like had never before been designed or even imagined.

Why was this fifteenth-century outburst of creative energy in the Western shipwright's trade followed by a spell of relative stagnation lasting some three or four hundred years? Challenge-and-Response is the clue to the answer to this question likewise; for the creation of the Modern Western ship had been so effective a response to the military and political challenge presented to the West in the fifteenth century that the fifteenth-century Western shipwright's epigoni had little incentive for seeking to improve on their predecessors' work until they were eventually shaken out of their lethargy by a new challenge that was not military or political but was economic, and that did not impinge on the Western World from abroad but emerged from within.

The Modern Western ship had been an adequate solution for the Early Modern Western World's besetting problem of *Lebensraum*. It had enabled the Western peoples with one hand to acquire in the Americas what looked like an inexhaustible addition to their reserves of cultivable land, and with the other hand to seize for themselves a monopoly of all the existing Oceanic maritime trade in the World; and this sudden turning of the tables in their favour in their competition with the other living civilizations had not only given the Western peoples full military and political security; it had also amply satisfied their economic needs in an age in which they, as well as their contemporaries, were still living under the traditional economic dispensation of Man in Process of Civilization. In this dispensation—which, in the Lower Nile Valley and the Lower Tigris-Euphrates Basin, had already been a going concern at least as early as the end of the fourth millennium B.C.— agriculture was the staple source of livelihood and the standard occupation, while trade and manufacture were subsidiary and exceptional. In societies of this traditional type, towns and ports that lived by importing foodstuffs and raw materials and paying for these by exporting manufactured goods and by performing the economic services of providing and financing maritime and overland transportation, were few and far between; rarer still were the parasitic capitals of oecumenical empires— a Rome, a Constantinople, or a Peking—which used the lever of political

---

[1] See Seneca: *Medea*, ll. 364–79, quoted in II. i. 263, n. 1.

power to exact imports without making any economic return;[1] and the only other notable variation on the prevailing economic pattern of subsistence farming was an exchange of cereals and other products of agriculture for products of stockbreeding between the Nomads of the Steppes and their nearest sedentary neighbours. Classical examples of this unusual trade in commodities that were necessities, not luxuries, had been the importation of grain into the homeland of the Hellenic Civilization round the coasts of the Aegean out of the Russian agricultural hinterland of the Great Western Bay of the Eurasian Steppe from about the sixth century B.C. to about the third century of the Christian Era, and the importation of the same staff of life out of Sicily and Apulia into a sixteenth-century Spain[2] whose heart had been given over to breeding sheep for wool.[3]

The Western Society continued, like its contemporaries, to live under this traditional economic dispensation for some three centuries (*circa* A.D. 1475–1775) after it had won its economic victory over these other living civilizations in terms of the traditional economic values by monopolizing the Oceanic maritime trade in luxuries and impounding the World's largest still uncultivated reserve of cultivable land. During the last third or quarter of the eighteenth century, however, a new economic revolution—almost comparable in magnitude to the earlier revolution from food-gathering and hunting to agriculture and stock-breeding—declared itself in Great Britain and spread thence progressively to Belgium, Germany, and the Northern United States and eventually to Japan and other Westernizing countries beyond the original bounds of the Western World.

The two outstanding features of this fresh economic revolution were a sudden increase in population at a steeply accelerating rate and a concomitant rise of commerce and manufacturing industry to a decisive preponderance over agriculture as the standard occupations and staple sources of livelihood, no longer merely in tiny, rare, and insulated urban enclaves, but throughout whole countries and regions previously dedicated to subsistence farming. This sweeping subordination of agriculture and stockbreeding to industry was the more impressive considering that Western agriculture and Western stockbreeding, so far from remaining stagnant or regressing, were actually passing at this time through a simultaneous revolution in which their productivity, like the productivity of urban industry, was being notably increased by the jettisoning of traditional methods in favour of new experiments that were as rational as they were radical. The eighteenth-century technological revolution in agriculture[4] ran neck and neck with the eighteenth-century

---

[1] See VI. vii. 87–91, for the digging of the Grand Canal in China, after the political unification of the main body of the Far Eastern Society by the Sui Dynasty, in order to bring foodstuffs to a northern capital from a southern centre of agricultural production.

[2] See Fueter, E.: *Geschichte des Europäischen Staatensystems von 1492–1559* (Munich and Berlin 1919, Oldenbourg), p. 96.

[3] Klein, J.: *The Mesta: A Study in Spanish Economic History, 1273–1836* (Cambridge, Mass. 1930, Harvard University Press).

[4] See Ashton, T. S.: *The Industrial Revolution, 1760–1830* (London 1948, Oxford University Press), pp. 6–7.

technological revolution in industry, as the nineteenth-century creation of the 'clipper' sailing-ship ran neck and neck with the nineteenth-century creation of the steamship. If, in spite of this sudden spurt of progress, agriculture nevertheless failed to maintain its age-old primacy over industry in a Western and a Westernizing World, the reason was that the eighteenth-century agricultural revolution, by itself, would have been no adequate response—even in combination with the accompanying extension of the acreage under cultivation in Western Europe as well as overseas—to the Malthusian challenge which the eighteenth-century industrial revolution did prove able to meet.

The formidably steep and rapid increase in population, which declared itself in Great Britain first among the countries of the Modern Western World, seems to have been due to a reduction of the death-rate, thanks to an improvement in the standard of public health,[1] which was not offset by any countervailing fall in the birth-rate for the next five or six generations. In Great Britain the fall in the death-rate began to make itself felt *circa* A.D. 1740;[2] 'between 1740 and 1820 the death-rate fell almost continuously, from an estimated 35·8 for the ten years ending in 1740 to one of 21·1 for those ending in 1821';[3] but net rates of reproduction did not begin to fall off in either Great Britain or France before A.D. 1875–80, and not in other West European countries before A.D. 1905–10.[4] The net increase in the population of Western Europe through this Time-lag between the fall in the death-rate and the fall in the birth-rate was to reach its peak in A.D. 1890–1910.[5] By the time of writing of the book, published in A.D. 1947, in which these remarkable figures are presented, the average expectation of life in the Western World had risen from the span of thirty-five years, at which it had stood under the *ancien régime*, to a span of no less than sixty.[6]

This great spurt in the growth of population, first in Great Britain and then in other provinces of a Western and a Westernizing World, would have been an economic liability if the explosion of the Industrial Revolution had not responded to the challenge by converting this potential liability into an asset. The Industrial Revolution enabled an increasing population actually to raise its standard of living through a concomitant increase in the volume of economic production that more than kept pace with the increase in the number of mouths to be fed and bodies to be clothed and housed; and our familiarity with this achievement must not blind us to the truth that it was an amazing *tour de force*.

'The spectre of the pressure of population on the means of subsistence which oppressed the mind of Malthus in 1798 was no chimaera. . . . An increase of people . . . does not necessarily mean either a greater effective demand for manufactured goods or an increased production of these in

---

[1] As many as ten distinct influences operating in Great Britain, from about A.D. 1740 onwards, to reduce the incidence of death are enumerated by T. S. Ashton in *The Industrial Revolution, 1760–1830* (London 1948, Oxford University Press), p. 4.

[2] See Dupriez, L. H.: *Les Mouvements Économiques Généraux* (Louvain 1947, Institut de Recherches Économiques et Sociales, 2 vols.), vol. i, p. 304.

[3] Ashton, T. S.: *The Industrial Revolution, 1760–1830* (London 1948, Oxford University Press), p. 4.

[4] See Dupriez, op. cit., vol. i, p. 306.

[5] See ibid., vol. i, p. 303.   [6] See ibid., vol. i, p. 304.

the country concerned . . . it may just as well lead to a lower standard of life for all'[1]—

which, was, in fact, its consequence in Ireland, where the population increased in the late eighteenth and early nineteenth century *pari passu* with the simultaneous increase in the adjoining island. This Irish, and not the English, consequence was likewise the sequel to corresponding increases in the populations of China in the same age under a *Pax Manchuana*, and of India in the second half of the nineteenth century and the first half of the twentieth century under a *Pax Britannica.*

'There are to-day on the plains of India and China men and women, plague-ridden and hungry, living lives little better, to outward appearance, than those of the cattle that toil with them by day and share their places of sleep by night. Such . . . standards . . . are the lot of those who increase their numbers without passing through an industrial revolution. . . .[2]
'The central problem of the age [A.D. 1760–1830 in Great Britain] was how to feed and clothe and employ generations of children outnumbering by far those of any earlier time. Ireland was faced by the same problem. Failing to solve it, she lost in the 'forties about a fifth of her people by emigration or starvation and disease. If England had remained a nation of cultivators and craftsmen, she could hardly have escaped the same fate, and, at best, the weight of a growing population must have pressed down the spring of her spirit. She was delivered . . . by those who, seeking, no doubt, their own narrow ends, had the wit and resource to devise new instruments of production and new methods of administering industry.[3]. . . Britain might have learnt from bitter experience the fallacy of the view that, because with every pair of hands there is a mouth, therefore every expansion of numbers must lead to an increase of consumption, and so of output, if, after the middle of the nineteenth century, there had been no railways in America, no opening up of the prairies, and no steamships.'[4]

We can now see what the challenge was which, after a three-or-four hundred-years long interlude of comparative stagnation in the Western art of shipbuilding, evoked, during the half-century A.D. 1840–90, a burst of fresh creative activity—comparable to the previous burst in A.D. 1440–90—which brought forth the 'clipper' and the long-distance steamship in a twin birth. Under the goad of a sudden sharp increase in the pressure of population on the means of subsistence, a Modern Western Society which, so far from being resigned to seeing its standard of living fall, was bent upon raising it, had set out—in the footsteps of the Hellenic Society of the sixth century B.C.[5]—to convert an economy of subsistence farming into an economy of specialized production for export; and, for the first time in the history of Man in Process of Civilization, this economic revolution was now being put in train, not just within the walls of a handful of city-states, but throughout the body social of a hitherto preponderantly agricultural society. This revolutionary economic enterprise could not be carried through to success unless the *entrepreneurs* could multiply, many times over, a maritime carrying capacity that had met the comparatively modest requirements

[1] Ashton, op. cit., p. 6.   [2] Ibid., p. 161.
[3] Ibid., p. 161.   [4] Ibid., p. 6.
[5] See I. i. 24–25; II. ii. 38–42; III. iii. 122; IV. iv. 200–14; IX. viii. 429–30.

of the traditional economy; for these requirements had been limited to the transport of luxuries for a small governing class and of foodstuffs and raw materials for a few towns and ports specializing in commerce and industry. In order to make the revolutionary new economic régime work, maritime carrying capacity had to be expanded at short notice to cater for the transport of bulky and heavy primary commodities for consumption, not just by a few exceptional urban communities, but by the entire body social of a society that was making itself preponderantly industrial instead of remaining preponderantly agricultural.

Maritime carrying capacity could be expanded along three lines: by increasing the number of ships in commission, by increasing their size, and by increasing their speed and thus increasing the frequency of their voyages; and all three expedients were, in fact, resorted to in the Western World in face of the nineteenth-century Western maritime carrying-capacity crisis.

The line of least resistance was, of course, to shirk the arduous task of structural and mechanical innovation by simply increasing the number of ships of the customary size, build, and drive.

'The data available show that the changes in the size of vessels were not notable in England until after 1830, even though the proportion of the larger vessels to the total increased, especially after 1730. If we were to study the shipping of Europe as a whole, the changes in the size of merchant vessels would be less considerable than in the case of England alone. Down to 1850 no merchant vessels are recorded with a registered tonnage in excess of 1200 tons, and there were very few vessels in England in the group from 420 to 1199 tons. There were large numbers of vessels of that rate in the Mediterranean as early as 1500; there were proportionately more in Holland than in England, though the size of Dutch vessels was probably not as great as that of the larger Mediterranean carriers. Throughout the period [*circa* A.D. 1572–1830] the merchant fleets of the different countries included large numbers of very small vessels.'[1]

[1] Usher, A. P.: 'The Growth of English Shipping, 1572–1922', in *The Quarterly Journal of Economics*, vol. xlii (Cambridge, Mass. 1928, Harvard University Press), p. 476. 'There were changes in the proportions between the definitely small and the medium-sized vessels in all the countries, but less change in England than elsewhere, because the conditions in England were especially favourable to the persistence of small units in the carrying trade' (ibid., pp. 476–7). The average tonnage of a British merchantman had risen to a surprisingly small degree during the two centuries between the end of King James I's reign in A.D. 1625 and the end of King George III's in A.D. 1820. During James I's reign, the normal tonnage of English merchantmen had jumped from 100 tons to 300/500 tons, and between A.D. 1675 and A.D. 1680 sixteen East Indiamen had been built with tonnages ranging as high as 1,600 tons; but after A.D. 1702 the average figure for an East Indiaman had dropped back to 350/400 tons; and, though it had risen again in A.D. 1750 to a standard of 499 tons, and in A.D. 1786–90 to a new level of 1,200 tons, the average tonnage of British merchantmen of other ownership did not rise concomitantly. In the British merchant marine in A.D. 1810, apart from the East India Company's fleet, there were only twenty ships with a tonnage of more than 600 tons, and none with a tonnage of more than 1,000 tons (Abell, W.: *The Shipwright's Trade* (Cambridge 1948, University Press), pp. 99–100).

This virtual stationariness of the average size of the standard merchantman in the Western World in general, and in Great Britain more especially, over a period of some two hundred years ending *circa* A.D. 1830 is the more remarkable considering that, within the same period, the volume of British maritime trade was not static, but, on the contrary, was subject to perceptible fluctuations. 'The curve for the tonnage of the merchant fleet indicates that there were three periods of active growth: 1663–1730, 1770–1811, 1840–1910. The intervals between these periods, while not registering actual decline, were periods of relative stagnation, particularly the later intervals. The clearances in foreign trade disclose two periods of growth: 1663–1760 and 1801–1910' (Usher, op.

By contrast, from *circa* A.D. 1830 onwards, increases in the size of ships, requiring revolutionary changes in their build, and soon also in their drive, came to contribute far more than increases in the number of ships in commission towards the now steeply rising increase in the aggregate tonnage of the United Kingdom merchant marine, as can be seen from the following figures in the tables compiled by Usher.[1]

Year	Number of vessels	Register tonnage
1788	12,461	1,279,062
1830	19,174	2,201,592
1860	27,663	4,658,687
1890	21,591	7,978,538
1910	21,090	11,555,663

Percentage of Vessels in the United Kingdom Merchant Marine in Each of the Different Tonnage-Classes Distinguished in the Series of Columns Set Out Below

Year	Under 100 tons	100–419 tons	420–1,199 tons
1788	31·1	62·1	6·8
1830	25·2	62·4	12·4

Year	Under 100 tons	100–399 tons	400–1,199 tons	1,200–1,999 tons	2,000–3,999 tons	4,000 tons and over
1869	9·6	27·4	45·9	15·6	1·2	0·3

It is manifest that the almost six-fold increase in the United Kingdom merchant marine's aggregate register tonnage from a figure of 1,551,072 tons in A.D. 1799 to a figure of 9,304,108 tons in A.D. 1900 was mostly accounted for by an increase in the size of vessels, and not by an increase in their numbers, considering that, between the same two dates, that saw a 600 per cent. increase in aggregate tonnage, the numbers increased by hardly more than 50 per cent., from 12,461 in A.D. 1799 to 19,982 in A.D. 1900, after having reached and passed in A.D. 1860 a peak figure of 27,663.[2] It is no less evident that the increase in size could never have

cit., p. 474). 'The rapid growth in the seventeenth century is comparable to the growth of the late nineteenth century, which we have been inclined to think of as unexampled in the centuries preceding' (ibid., p. 472). Yet, in spite of the building of sixteen abnormally large East Indiamen during the years A.D. 1675–80, an increase in size evidently counted for much less than an increase in numbers in the doubling, between A.D. 1663 and 1688, of both the tonnage of the English merchant marine and the clearances in England's foreign trade (see the figures in Table I, on p. 467, and Table II, on p. 469, of Usher, op. cit.). 'It is important to note that the commercial growth of the late seventeenth century, as shown by both sets of data, was not accompanied by any large increase in population, whereas the increase in population was very considerable in the nineteenth century' (ibid., p. 474).

[1] The two sets of figures set out above are extracted respectively from Table I, on p. 467, and from Table IV, on p. 475, of Usher, op. cit. In Table I the figures for A.D. 1830, by comparison with those for A.D. 1788–1825, have been cut down by about 7 per cent. through the exclusion of lost vessels formerly carried on the register. The figures of tonnage for the years beginning with A.D. 1860, by comparison with those for A.D. 1830–50, have been raised by about 7·5 per cent. through a change in the rules for the measurement of tonnage that became effective in A.D. 1857.

[2] See Usher, op. cit., Table I, on p. 467.

been carried to the lengths attained in the event without an accompanying revolution in build.

'Some increase in size would have been possible without a change in materials. Wooden vessels could be built up to 4000, and possibly 5000, tons, but with rapidly increasing costs of construction and maintenance. Serious structural difficulties would have been encountered in building very large wooden vessels, because the stems and stern-posts must needs be single timbers, and there are fairly definite limits to the size of first-class timbers for these purposes. The introduction of iron and steel disposed effectively of all these problems. This radical change should be borne in mind in any discussion of the size of vessels in the earlier periods. The revolution in the character of the merchant fleet is a chapter in the history of the late nineteenth century—an outgrowth of the development of the iron ship.'[1]

The employment of iron made it feasible, as we have seen,[2] to build clippers of double the tonnage of the largest previous standard size of sailing-ship; yet, even when the problem of construction had thus been solved, there were limits to the possible tonnage of a sail-borne ship even of the square rig in which the total spread of sail could be increased, up to a point, by adding to the number of the tiers of sails and to the number of the masts; and the size of the nineteenth-century British merchantman, like that of the fifteenth-century Portuguese lateen-rigged caravel,[3] would have been confined, perforce, within the limits thus set by the technique of sail-drive, if revolutionary-minded nineteenth-century British shipwrights had not made the further innovation of propelling their new-fangled iron hulls by steam-power instead of by wind-power. The tonnage of British steamships, as distinct from the tonnage of all British merchantmen, whether steam-propelled or sail-borne, doubled between A.D. 1860 and A.D. 1868 according to Rostow;[4] and the ever more preponderant part that was being played by the increase in steam-propelled tonnage, as compared with the increase in wind-propelled tonnage, in the aggregate increase of United Kingdom merchant-marine tonnage, is reflected in the fact that the United Kingdom merchant marine's approximate carrying power, adjusted for steam, rose, according to Usher,[5] from 4,068,000 tons in A.D. 1850, when there was an aggregate register tonnage of 3,651,133 tons distributed among 25,984 vessels of both kinds, to 30,924,000 tons in A.D. 1900, when there was an aggregate register tonnage of 9,304,108 tons distributed among 19,982 vessels.[6]

It will be seen that, when nineteenth-century shipwrights were challenged, by the explosion of the Industrial Revolution, rapidly to cater for an enormous increase in marine carrying capacity which had to be conjured up somehow if an audaciously revolutionary economic enterprise was not to end in a catastrophic failure, the shipwrights solved the

[1] Usher, op. cit., pp. 477–8.   [2] On p. 371, n. 2, above.   [3] See p. 367, above.
[4] See Rostow, W. W.: *British Economy in the Nineteenth Century* (Oxford 1948, Clarendon Press), p. 23.   [5] In Usher, op. cit., Table I, on p. 467.
[6] In Schumpeter, J. A.: *Business Cycles* (New York 1939, McGraw-Hill, 2 vols.), vol. i, p. 268, the United Kingdom merchant marine's approximate carrying-power, adjusted for steam, is reckoned, as by Usher, at rather less than 31 million tons for A.D. 1900, but at rather more than 8 million tons for A.D. 1850.

crucial problem with which the Industrial Revolution had thus confronted them by enlisting new technical resources that the Industrial Revolution itself had placed at their disposal. The creativity displayed in the nineteenth-century shipwrights' response was proportionate to the severity of the challenge that evoked it. But, as soon as the problem of carrying capacity had been solved through the creation of a long-distance steamship whose speed could be progressively increased *pari passu* with progressive increases in its size, there was a slackening of the pressure that had been constantly stimulating the shipwrights' inventive faculties during the preceding fifty years; and this relaxation of tension would seem to explain why it was that, in shipbuilding, the rate of innovation during the sixty years A.D. 1890 to 1950 was markedly slower than it had been between A.D. 1840 and A.D. 1890, in spite of the fact that, during the six decades ending in A.D. 1950, the general progress of Western technology had been continuing to accelerate in a geometrical progression.

The sensitiveness, speed, and vigour of the Western shipwright's responses to two altogether different challenges within the four and a half centuries running from *circa* A.D. 1440 to *circa* A.D. 1890 are striking evidences of human freedom of action in response to a technological challenge; but Technology is, after all, the field where, if anywhere, evidences of human freedom are to be expected, considering that Man never comes so near to being master of a situation as when he is dealing with Non-Human Nature. Man seldom shows anything like the same mastery in his dealings either with the Subconscious Psyche underlying his personality or with the other personalities who are his fellow human beings; and it is therefore perhaps more remarkable if we find evidences of Challenge-and-Response giving birth to human freedom on the spiritual as well as on the technological plane. We do, in fact, find such evidences here too when we recall the part played by Challenge-and-Response in generating the diversity between corresponding episodes in the histories of different civilizations.

The diversity in the duration of the growth-phases of civilizations has manifestly been the consequence of a recurrent freedom of choice that brings with it, each time, both a chance of success and a risk of failure. As we have found in a previous context,[1] the process of social growth consists in a concatenation of acts of Challenge-and-Response in which a successful response to one challenge gives rise to another challenge which may be met by another successful response giving rise to yet another challenge in the series. It will be seen that, in each successive act, the recipients of the challenge of the hour are free to choose between a Good and an Evil that are fraught with Life and with Death;[2] and this means that each act raises afresh the issue 'to be or not to be'. In any such series of encounters between God the deliverer of the challenge and Man the recipient of it, there is manifestly nothing that makes it impossible for the spinning of a golden thread of challenge-met-by-successful-response-leading-to-further-challenge-met-by-further-successful-response to continue *ad infinitum*. It is equally manifest that, at the

<hr/>

[1] In III. iii. 119–20. [2] Deut. xxx. 15–19.

presentation of each successive challenge, there can be no assurance that the spinner will not fail, this time, to add another fathom's length to his life-line; for in each act Man is free to choose Death instead of Life; and, each time, his momentous choice depends on the uncertain issue of a spiritual struggle within his soul between an aspiration towards Grace and a gravitation towards Original Sin.

The severity of this perpetually recurring struggle is indicated by our finding that, out of twenty-two known civilizations,[1] there was only one that could not be certified to be either dead or in disintegration by the twentieth century of the Christian Era. It is true that these figures did not warrant any inferential estimate of a civilization's normal expectation of life, because this species of Society was at this date still so young, and the number of its representatives was still so few, that any attempt at a generalization must be subject to a stultifyingly wide margin of error. Yet, even if the statistics gave no legitimate ground for pessimism, it might be augured that each additional round might be likely to make the game more perilous, since a sinful Human Nature was apt to be tempted by every successful response to a challenge into succumbing either to the active sin of hybris or to the hardly less ruinous passive sin of resting on its oars.[2] If 'the greater the success, the greater the temptation' were in truth one of the laws to which the Human Psyche was subject, then it would seem to follow that an equilibrium which had to be unstable if it was to be a vehicle for the growth-process must be prone to become ever more precarious with each successive victory of Life over Death.

This besetting danger, which was the price of freedom, was advertised in the spectacle of disintegrating, petrified,[3] arrested,[4] and abortive[5] civilizations, and was illustrated in the history, not only of human societies, but of terrestrial life itself. Every species of living creature is an earnest of growth, inasmuch as it is the fruit of some past creative mutation of an antecedent species and might become in its turn the seed of some further creative mutation into yet another species; yet at the same time every living species 'is a halt', and it is this 'by definition', since it 'is essentially a created thing'.[6]

The tragic breakdown of the Hellenic Civilization in the flower of its growth was sensitively forecast in the premonitory arrest of the growth of the Attic art of the tragic drama in a generation that lived to see the Atheno-Peloponnesian War.

'Tragedy—as also Comedy—was at first mere improvisation. . . . Tragedy advanced by slow degrees; each new element that showed itself was in turn developed. Having passed through many changes it found its natural form, and there it stopped (ἐπαύσατο, ἐπεὶ ἔσχε τὴ ναύτῆς φύσιν).'[7]

The changes through which the Athenian tragic drama had passed

---

[1] On a count in which a Medieval Western City-state cosmos is given the status of a civilization distinct from the main body of the Western Society.
[2] See IV. iv. 245–61.   [3] See VI. vii. 4–6 and 47–52.
[4] See III. iii. 1–111.   [5] See II. ii. 322–60 and 388–91.
[6] Bergson, H.: *Les Deux Sources de la Morale et de la Religion* (Paris 1932, Alcan), p. 251, quoted in III. iii. 235.
[7] Aristotle: *Poetics*, chap. iv, § 12 (1449A), translated by Butcher, S. H.: *Aristotle's Theory of Poetry and Fine Art*, 3rd ed. (London 1902, Macmillan), pp. 18–19.

before its development was arrested had been rapid as well as radical; for a run of no more than three generations had seen the development begin and end; and the end and the beginning had both been abrupt. The 'natural form' attained by Attic tragedy at the hands of Sophocles and Euripides was conscientiously reproduced thereafter, without any further creative innovations, by their successors, not merely down to Aristotle's time, but until this genre of literature went out of cultivation in the Hellenic culture's latter days; and in the prelude to the story a traditional dramatic ritual, performed as a spell for ensuring the regular recurrence of an annual harvest and vintage, had, as far as we know, remained for centuries on end as static as the technique of agriculture itself until the genius commemorated in the historical or legendary name of Thespis transfigured this archaic religious institution into a rudimentary artistic vehicle for conveying the deepest feelings, problems, and interests of a flowering civilization. Considering that Aeschylus took over this new-born art in its swaddling clothes and handed it on to Sophocles all but full-grown, the three generations that saw the beginning and end of the growth of Attic tragedy virtually contract to the span of one single generation only.

How are we to account for a period of creativity hardly longer than the life-time of Aeschylus, when this brief spurt of growth has for its overture an aeon of the timeless ritual of the ἐνιαυτὸς δαίμων,[1] and for its epilogue an aeon of the conventional post-Euripidean Hellenic drama? The answer to this question is to be found in the history of the city-state of Athens in which the art of Tragedy was brought to life, like Pygmalion's statue, only to be turned to stone, like the Phaeacian galley,[2] in full career. The transfiguration of an Attic agricultural rite into a fine art was one of the expressions of a contemporaneous social and cultural transfiguration of Athens herself as a result of the Solonian revolution.[3] In accomplishing this revolution in her own life, Athens made herself 'the education of Hellas';[4] yet a title which conveyed the truth about the Athens of an age beginning with the generation of Solon at the turn of the seventh and sixth centuries B.C. and ending with the generation of Aeschylus (*vivebat* 525/524–456 B.C.) had ceased to be deserved by Athens before it was coined for her in 431–430 B.C. by Pericles; for by that date Athens, under the influence of no other leader than Pericles himself, had hardened into the repellent figure of 'a tyrant city'[5] who was selfishly misusing her power in Hellas in the narrow interests of her own citizens, and was jealously on her guard against the extension of an Athenian franchise that had now become a lucrative privilege. This moral fall of Athens had taken place during the half-century that had elapsed between the repulse of Xerxes's invasion of Continental European Greece and the outbreak of the Atheno-Peloponnesian War; and the act in which it is most expressively symbolized is the scrutiny and purgation of the official register of Athenian citizens in 445–444 B.C., on the occasion of a distribution of grain, presented to the Athenian people

[1] See III. iii. 256.
[2] See *Odyssey*: Book XIII, ll. 159–64.
[3] See IV. iv. 200–14.
[4] See I. i. 24–26.
[5] "Τυραννίδα ἔχετε τὴ ναρχήν" (Cleon, in a speech put in his mouth by Thucydides Book III, chap. 37).

by their ally Egypt, which prompted them to act on a restrictive law enacted, at Pericles' instance, six years earlier.[1] It is assuredly no accident that this symbolic date of Athens' spiritual narcosis should coincide with the artistic *floruit* of a Sophocles in whose hands the Attic art of Tragedy came to the end of a growth that had been so vigorous in the generation of Sophocles' own immediate predecessor Aeschylus. The hybris bred in Athenian souls by the triumphant success of Athenian responses to the Hellenic World's sixth-century ordeal of encirclement and fifth-century ordeal of invasion had blighted the Athenian people's moral growth; and the halt in the development of the Attic art of Tragedy was a consequence and an index of this spiritual disaster.

The element of freedom in human affairs which reveals itself in a diversity in the duration of the growth-phases of civilizations, and whose epiphany and atrophy we can see—in the history of the growth and petrifaction of the Attic art of Tragedy—as sharply focused as if we were gazing through a magnifying glass, is likewise revealed in a diversity in the relations of Religion to the rises and falls of civilizations in different generations; and in this field, as in that, we can discern that human freedom springs from an encounter in which Man is summoned to respond to a challenge presented by God.

The challenge of social breakdown, disintegration, and dissolution had been identical in the histories of the civilizations of each of the three generations of this species of society that had run their course so far, and, as between the divers representatives of a single generation, it had been identical *a fortiori*; yet the responses made to this spiritual challenge in the second generation had, as we have seen, been immensely more fruitful than any responses made in either the first generation or the third; and, among these responses in the second generation, it seemed unlikely to a latter-day Christian historian that either Hinduism or Islam would be placed on a spiritual par with either the Mahāyāna or Christianity by a judge who was wholly disinterested and at the same time fully qualified (if any such godlike human arbiter was anywhere to be found). This wide diversity in the responses to an identical challenge becomes intelligible if—and perhaps only if—we see in it the consequence of a freedom of choice which God had granted to human souls; and thus we see freedom springing from Challenge-and-Response in the most crucial of all the ordeals through which Man in Process of Civilization had been reminded of his Creator in the course of the five or six thousand years during which the human climber had been striving to scale this precipitous 'pitch' on the cliff-face of his terrestrial purgatory.[2]

[1] See Aristotle: *The Constitution of Athens*, chap. 27, *ad finem*; Plutarch: *Life of Pericles*, chap. 37. [2] See II. i. 192–3.

D. THE FREEDOM OF HUMAN SOULS THAT IS THE LAW OF GOD

IN the present Part of this Study we are trying to gain some insight into the relation between Law and Freedom in History; and, if we now reapproach this question in the light of the evidence that we have been gathering in the course of an empirical inquiry, we shall find that the question has already received an answer. How is Freedom related to Law? Our evidence declares that Man does not live under one law only; he lives under two laws, and one of these two is a Law of God which is Freedom itself under another and more illuminating name.

This 'perfect law of liberty'[1] is also a law of Love; for Man's freedom could only have been given to Man by a God who is Love in person,[2] and this divine gift can only be used by Man for freely choosing Good and Life instead of Death and Evil[3] if Man, on his side, loves God well enough to be moved by this responsive love of his to commit himself to God, by making God's will his own, as unreservedly as God has committed Himself to Man by giving Man the power of free choice.

> Our wills are ours, we know not how;
> Our wills are ours, to make them thine.[4]

'La sua voluntade è nostra pace';[5] and this self-surrender of Man's will to God's, which the Prophet Muhammad has preached in the lapidary word *islām*, is 'the glorious liberty of the children of God'.[6] 'History is, . . . above everything else, a call, a vocation, a dispensation to be heard and responded to by free human beings—in short, the interaction of God and Man';[7] and this truth has been partially divined by pre-Christian Hellenic philosophers and been faintly echoed in the utterances of post-Christian Western heresiarchs. Plato has testified that the Gods do not drive human beings, but steer them;[8] and Hegel's description of creation as a synthesis obtained through a settlement of accounts between a thesis and an antithesis is a recognizable academic abstract of the living truth, even though it makes nonsense of it by perversely depotentializing the creative act of God's and Man's mutual love into the logical procedure of an intellect that 'by itself, moves nothing'.[9]

Law and Freedom in History prove to be identical, in the sense that Man's freedom proves to be the law of a God who is identical with Love. But this finding does not dispose of our problem; for in answering our

---

[1] James i. 25.   [2] 1 John iv. 8.   [3] Deut. xxx. 15.
[4] Tennyson: *In Memoriam*, in the invocation.
[5] Dante: *La Divina Commedia*: 'Paradiso', Canto III, l. 85.   [6] Rom. viii. 21.
[7] Lampert, E.: *The Apocalypse of History* (London 1948, Faber), p. 45.
[8] Plato: *Critias*, 109 B–C: 'They tended us as herdsmen tend their flocks, live-stock and nurselings, except that they did not use physical force, as shepherds do when they drive beasts by beating them. The Gods led Mankind by steering them. They guided Mankind's course from astern, which is the way in which a living creature is most easily manipulated, and they used as their rudder the instrument of Persuasion to influence the Human Psyche in accordance with the Gods' own ideas.'
[9] Aristotle: *Ethica Nicomachea*, Z2, pp. 1139 A–B, quoted in III. iii. 231, n. 1, and on pp. 327–8, above.

original question we have raised a new one. In finding that Freedom is identical with one of two codes of Law, we have raised the question of the relation in which these two laws stand to one another; and at first sight the answer to this new question would seem to be that the Law of Love and the Law of Subconscious Human Nature, which both manifestly have jurisdiction over human affairs, are not only different but are contradictory, and are not only contradictory but are incompatible; for the law of the Subconscious Psyche, which our Western psychologists have located in the psychic abyss from which the Babylonian astrologers once projected it on to the stars in their courses, holds in spiritual bondage human souls whom God has called to work with Him in freedom. When one of two dispensations spells liberty, while the other spells servitude, are we not wantonly obscuring the truth and confusing the issue by using the same word 'law' to describe them both?

The more searchingly we compare these two 'laws', the wider the moral gulf between them seems to be. If we appraise the Law of Nature by the standard of the Law of Love, and see through Love's eyes everything that Nature has made, behold, it is very bad.[1]

> Ay, look: high Heaven and Earth ail from the prime foundation;
> All thoughts to rive the heart are here, and all are vain.'[2]

And, in the bitterness of his riven heart, Man explores divers possible explanations of a moral anomaly and enormity that he cannot explain away and cannot take for granted.

One of the conclusions that have been drawn by human spectators of the moral evil in the Universe is that this chamber of horrors cannot be any god's handiwork.

> Quod si iam rerum ignorem primordia quae sint,
> hoc tamen ex ipsis caeli rationibus ausim
> confirmare aliisque ex rebus reddere multis,
> nequaquam nobis divinitus esse paratam
> naturam rerum: tantâ stat praedita culpâ.[3]

To explain this evil universe as the undesigned outcome of a fortuitous concourse of indestructable atoms of matter is indeed the line of least resistance for an Epicurean in whose belief the gods are *rois fainéants*; but this Epicurean solution of the problem of Evil will not satisfy either a logician who sees through the word 'Chance' to an undesignated positive order lurking incognito under this negative label, or a Christian in whose belief God is the Love that has bestowed on Man a law that is Freedom. The Christian finds himself compelled to choose between two other alternatives, both of which are grievously disconcerting: Either the God who is Love must be also the creator of a manifestly ailing Universe, and therefore be either an incompetent demiurge or a malignant *mater saeva cupidinum*;[4] or, if the God of Love is not one aspect of a Janus-headed Godhead that, in another aspect, is Our Lady of the

---

[1] Gen. i. 31.
[2] Housman, A. E.: *The Shropshire Lad*, xlviii, quoted in V. vi. 139.
[3] Lucretius: *De Rerum Naturâ*, Book V, ll. 195–9. The grounds of this verdict are indicated in ll. 200–27.   [4] Horace: *Odes*, Book I, Ode xix, l. 1.

Jungle, πότνια θηρῶν, then the ailing Universe must have been created by another god who is not the God of Love. In the second century of the Christian Era the Catholic Christian Church impaled itself on the first of the two horns of this dilemma, while a Marcionite Christian Church impaled itself on the second.

Marcion was a posthumous disciple of the Apostle Paul who drew, with an un-Pauline rigour, the logical consequences of a Pauline distinction between opposing realms of Mosaic Law and of Christian Grace. Marcion's uncompromising jealousy for the immaculateness of the God who is Love made it impossible for him to remain in communion[1] with any fellow Christian

> Who trusted God was Love indeed,
>   And Love Creation's final law,
>   Tho' Nature, red in tooth and claw
> With ravin, shriek'd against his creed.[2]

Marcion broke with a Catholic Christianity because he had wrestled with the question

> Are God and Nature then at strife,
>   That Nature lends such evil dreams?[3]

and had given, for his part, the affirmative answer that William Blake's *anima naturaliter Marcionita* was to give to the same question some seventeen hundred years later.

> When the stars threw down their spears
> And watered Heaven with their tears,
> Did He smile His work to see?
> Did He that made the Lamb make thee?

Blake's and Marcion's solution for this moral enigma is to attribute the creation of an ailing Universe to a god who, so far from being identical with God the fount of Love and Father of the Saviour, is His antithesis inasmuch as the creator god's distinctive characteristic is the forbidding negative quality of being both unloving and unlovable. In Blake's, as in Marcion's, theology, God the Creator's role is to play the Erinyes to God the Redeemer's Orpheus.[4] While the Saviour God wins souls by love, without ever terrorizing them by threats of constraining them by force, the highest moral level to which a creator god depicted as a Prussian drill-sergeant *in excelsis* is deemed capable of rising is to exact outward conformity with the prescriptions of a cut-and-dried moral law by imposing savage penalties for formal breaches of it. He is spiritually impotent to move his human creatures by touching their heart-strings.

This melancholy taskmaster god whom Marcion identifies with a Mosaic Jehovah and whom Blake names 'Urizen' and nicknames 'Nobodaddy' would be bad enough if he performed his self-imposed duties

---

[1] Marcion founded a church of his own in A.D. 144, after his doctrine had been rejected by the Catholic Christian community at Rome. For the date, see Harnack, A. von: *Marcion, Das Evangelium vom Fremden Gott* (Leipzig 1921, Hinrichs), pp. 24 and 18*.
[2] Tennyson: *In Memoriam*, Section LVI, Stanza 4.
[3] Ibid., Section LV, Stanza 2.   [4] See IV. iv. 123–5.

competently even according to his own limited lights; but his work is a hideous failure; and this failure must be due either to incompetence or to malevolence. Even if the Creator were to be acquitted on the charge of wilful malice, he would have to be convicted of being either culpably unaware of his wantonly assumed responsibilities or else no less culpably indifferent to them; and either of these verdicts would be damning in the judgement of a decently human jury; for no human being who was not shockingly obtuse or callous could imagine himself ever having had the heart, if he had been creating morally irresponsible sentient living organisms, to victimize his own creatures by enduing them with the capacity to suffer when he was not endowing them with any capacity to turn suffering to moral account. It would have been still harder for him to imagine himself ever having implanted, in any morally responsible sentient living creatures of his, the capacity not only to suffer but to sin without having made sure in advance that he would never be driven by force of circumstances to lead these human beings into temptation and would always be sufficiently master of the situation to be able to deliver them from evil.

'That there is a "soul of good in things evil" is unquestionable; nor will any wise man deny the disciplinary value of pain and sorrow. But these considerations do not help us to see why the immense multitude of irresponsible sentient beings, which cannot profit by such discipline, should suffer; nor why, among the endless possibilities open to omnipotence—that of sinless, happy existence among the rest—the actuality in which sin and misery abound should be that selected.'[1]

When a human soul thus finds itself confronted with two numinous presences which are morally antithetical[2] to one another, yet which, none the less, both have to be recognized as being indubitably divine, the most obvious conclusion is that there must be, not one god, but two gods, in the Universe; and this argument came home *ad hominem* to the writer of this Study when, with the present chapter in mind, he was reading simultaneously Adolf von Harnack's *Marcion, the Gospel of the Stranger God*, and Thor Heyerdahl's *Kon-Tiki*.[3]

'They that go down to the sea in ships, that do business in great waters, these see the works of the Lord, and His wonders in the deep.'[4]

But they that go down to the sea, not in a ship, but on a balsa-log sieve, see works of God the Creator that are yet more wondrous and appalling than any that discover themselves to seafarers who 'plough across' the water, in latter-day Western style, 'with roaring engines and piston-strokes'.[5] 'The sea contains many surprises for him who has his floor on a level with the surface and drifts along slowly and noiselessly';[6] and in the experience of the crew of the *Kon-Tiki* most of these surprises were

---

[1] Huxley, T. H.: *Evolution and Ethics*, the Romanes Lecture, 1893, reprinted in Huxley, T. H. and J.: *Evolution and Ethics, 1893–1943* (London 1947, Pilot Press), p. 76.
[2] Marcion's principal recorded original work (published as a commentary on a Bible composed of expurgated versions of some of Saint Paul's Epistles and of the Gospel according to Saint Luke) bore the expressive title *Antitheses*.
[3] Heyerdahl, T.: *Kon-Tiki, Across the Pacific by Raft* (Chicago 1950, Rand McNally).
[4] Ps. cviii, vv. 23–24.
[5] Heyerdahl, op. cit., p. 117.   [6] Ibid., p. 117.

nightmares: the whale shark with a toadlike jaw four or five feet wide that came grinning like a bulldog;[1] the three luminous monsters larger than elephants;[2] the devilish green eyes of giant squids which shone in the dark like phosphorus;[3] and the ghastly life-and-death struggle between sharks, tunnies, and dolphins.[4] 'When we turned in on these evenings, in our mind's eye we saw greedy, open shark jaws and blood, and the smell of shark meat stuck in our nostrils';[5] yet these predatory monsters of the deep were bone of the bones and flesh of the flesh[6] of these horrified human spectators; for all terrene life is known to have originated in the sea, and the chemical composition of the human body betrays the marine origin of a perhaps not less predatory Mankind. Almost, Thor, thou persuadest me to be a Marcionite[7]—yet, though Man's heart may be moved by the *visio malefica* of Creation to curse a god who has brought these horrors into being, Man's head will forbid him to embrace a theology that breaks down under examination.

While Marcion is on strong ground in affirming that Creation is bound up with Evil, he is on weak ground in denying that Creation has anything to do either with Goodness or with Love; for the truth is that God's love is the source of Man's freedom, and that a freedom which gives vent for Creation thereby opens a door for Sin. The ordeals in which Man has to exercise his freedom to choose between Life and Death and between Good and Evil can be described, with equal faithfulness to truth, as challenges from God and as temptations from the Devil. We have watched the Devil unintentionally serving God's purpose by helping God to carry on His creative activity, and we have even wondered whether, under the disguise of a satanic malice, a divine love may not be operating through a Mephistopheles without whose left-handed assistance God's work might be brought to a halt by its own paradoxically paralysing perfection.[8] Every encounter between a human soul and God is thus inevitably fraught with possibilities of Evil as well as Good; and this chain that links Evil, as well as Good, to Love cannot be severed by the knife-edge of Marcion's logic. All morally sensitive hearts will sympathize with Marcion's zeal to keep the hem of a Divine Love's garment unspotted; yet the same fine feeling will make such hearts revolt against the logic of Marcion's consequent denigration of a Subconscious Psyche that animates Man and Beast alike, and that bears up human personalities on the surface of its abyss, as the unplumbed Pacific bore up Thor Heyerdahl's balsa-log raft. For this primal living creature that is the Great Mother of Life on Earth is not only the Kali whose obscene womb has spawned Leviathan and Behemoth, the Dragon and the Bull;[9] it is also the Pytho whose oracular omphalos—in 'that shady city of palm trees'[10] where 'Heaven lies about us in our infancy'[11]—is the fount of Poetry and Prophecy; and, if we believe that the voice of a God who is Love thus speaks to the Soul through the

---

[1] Ibid., p. 120.   [2] Ibid., pp. 118–19.
[3] Ibid., p. 118.   [4] Ibid., pp. 203–4.   [5] Ibid., p. 206.
[6] Gen. ii. 23.   [7] Acts xxvi. 28.   [8] See II. i. 271–99.
[9] See VII. vii. 506, and pp. 332–3, above.   [10] Vaughan, Henry: *The Retreat*.
[11] Wordsworth, William: *Ode on Intimations of Immortality from Recollections of Early Childhood*.

Subconscious in the divinely inspired accents of a Dante and a Deutero-Isaiah, we may venture on to believe that Love is also the God who has created the tentacles of the squid and the teeth of the whale-shark. 'For the creature was made subject to vanity, not willingly, but by reason of Him who hath subjected the same in hope.'[1]

In logic, this is evidently a harder saying than Marcion's *creatorem aut ignorasse aut noluisse aut potentem non esse*;[2] but in reality, as registered in the full gamut of our human experience, Marcion's vindication of God's love at the cost of denying His unity is no less evidently wider of the mark than Irenaeus's vindication of the identity of God the Almighty Creator with God the All-loving Redeemer at the cost of identifying with one another two epiphanies of the Godhead which are logically and morally irreconcilable from a human standpoint. And experience's testimony to the truth of a logical and moral paradox is strikingly vindicated by the findings of a science which cannot be suspected of having gone out of its way in order to ratify an Irenaean system of Christian theology. The travail of striving to reconcile two irreconcilable epiphanies of God, which torments the consciousness of the adult saint and scholar, is declared by at least one school of post-Modern Western psychological research to have already tormented a Subconscious Psyche in an antecedent struggle through which the future saint and scholar's moral personality has been originally acquired at a stage of early infancy in which God's future place in the Soul's universe has been occupied by the infant child's Mother.

'As the baby begins . . . early in the . . . second year of post-natal life . . . to draw a distinction between itself and outer reality, it is the Mother[3] who comes to represent the external world and to mediate its impacts on the child. But she dawns upon its growing consciousness under two opposite aspects. She is the child's chief object of love, and its fountain-head of satisfaction, security, and peace. But she is also Authority, the chief source of power mysteriously set over the child and arbitrarily thwarting some of the impulses along whose paths its new life quests outwards. The frustration of infantile impulse generates anger, hate, and destructive wishes—what the psychologists generally style aggression—directed against the thwarting authority. But this hated Authority is also the loved Mother. The infant is thus faced with the primal conflict. Two irreconcilable sets of impulses are directed towards the same object, and that object is the centre of its surrounding universe.'[4]

Thus, according to one psychological theory, the conscious moral conflict of maturity is subconsciously anticipated in early infancy; and, in the infantile, as in the adult, struggle, a spiritual victory exacts its spiritual price. 'Primitive Love conquers Primitive Hate by saddling it with the burden of primal guilt';[5] and Psychology thus endorses

---

[1] Rom. viii. 20.

[2] Marcion as interpreted by Tertullian in his *Adversus Marcionem*, Book IV, chap. 41 (see Harnack, op. cit., p. 95).

[3] 'And/or any efficient mother-substitute, such as a nurse who takes over the care of the baby, or a large part of it.'

[4] Huxley, J.: *Evolutionary Ethics*, the Romanes Lecture, 1943, reprinted in Huxley, T. H. and J.: *Evolution and Ethics, 1893–1943* (London 1947, Pilot Press), p. 107.

[5] Ibid., p. 110.

the Irenaean anti-Marcionite Christian finding that Love and Hate, Righteousness and Sinfulness, are indissolubly linked with one another through the chain of Creation.

'Without a mother, no strong love focussed on a personal object; without such love, no conflict of irreconcilable impulses; without such conflict, no guilt; and, without such guilt, no effective moral sense.'[1]

A latter-day Western psychology's discovery, in an infantile Subconscious Psyche, of two irreconcilable impressions of one Mother, who represents Authority as well as Love in her own indivisible person, testifies to the veracity of Irenaeus's intuition that the apparent coexistence of two gods, morally antithetical to one another, must be, not a faithful reflection of the divine reality, but a mirage reflecting merely a diffraction of the unitary image of the One True God in the prismatic lens of an imperfect human spiritual vision.[2] God the Lover and Redeemer of souls must, in spite of Marcionic appearances to the contrary, be identical, in an ineffable reality, with God the Creator of subconscious terrestrial life, as well as with God the Creator of a material cosmos whose mathematical perfection is not marred by any moral bar sinister on the inanimate level. This paradoxical truth that Love is inseparable from the Almighty Power put forth in Creation is visually portrayed in Medieval Western Christian *mappae mundi* in which the latent figure of Christ Crucified holds together and sustains the World; and this image does not become less true to reality if we replace the Greek cross on which the seventeenth-century Western mathematicians hung their analysis of a static universe by the Saint Andrew's cross, embodied in the three-dimensional form of an hour-glass, on which a twentieth-century Western mathematical physicist had learnt to hang his analysis of a universe travelling through Space-Time.

For finite human minds, it is morally inexplicable that God the Creator of Life on Earth should have anticipated the gait of His creature *Homo Faber* by feeling his way *gradatim et pedetemptim*. They can understand why Man should have had to serve an apprenticeship in flaking flints in order to learn how to build an atomic pile; but why did an Almighty God who is Love and Creativity in one not avail Himself of His power to create a Buddha and a Saint Francis *de toutes pièces*? Why did He elect to approach the creation of these spiritual masterpieces of His by the slow, laborious, clumsy, and apparently maleficent method of creating

---

[1] Ibid., p. 110.

[2] The psychological process by which the *Visio Beatifica* is distorted in a sinful soul's sight is perhaps adumbrated in the psychologists' account of the distortion of the image of a child's parents in the sight of the refractory infant child.

'It is characteristic of this first beginning of our ethical mechanism that it is in many respects unrealistic. The parents have to exercise control over the child, and in so doing will be strict, or even harsh, and will certainly sometimes *appear* cruel. But to their actual and real strictness is added an unreal quota and quality of unpleasantness in the shape of the child's own thwarted aggressiveness. Thus the dialectic of growth succeeds in intro-jecting a parent-figure very different from the real parent, since it is "endowed with all the crude and primitive aggressiveness of the child himself. In this way, it would appear, does the super-ego acquire its more alarming and barbaric features", and this is why the semi-conscious or unconscious core of the super-ego (which may persist even throughout life) is so harsh and so unnecessarily severe, calling all the time upon the Self to make atonement for its load of primal guilt' (Huxley, J.: 'Conclusions', in Huxley, T. H. and J., op. cit., p. 206. Cp. p. 195).

amoebas, cholera germs, sharks, and sabre-toothed tigers by the way?
'Did He that made the lamb make thee?' Can God, Marcion again
interpellates, be almighty if He is unable, or all-loving if He is unwilling,
to evoke sainthood except at the cost of a spiritual tension and struggle
fraught with the certainty of suffering and with the possibility of sin?
Is the rarely trodden path to sainthood only a higher and steeper reach
of the steep and arduous ascent climbed by every human infant that
acquires a moral personality at the cost of a psychic conflict? Human
minds cannot find a logically self-consistent answer to this riddle of
creation because they cannot view the travail of creation with the all-
comprehending vision of a Divine Creative Love which sees everything
that It has made, from the shark to the saint, and beholds that it is very
good.[1] Yet even a finite human understanding may surmise that the
history of Life on Earth describes a curve through Space-Time-Psyche
in which each of the imperfect and ephemeral successive living moments
out of which this curve is built up has its absolute value for the *Deus
Crucifixus* whose Cross is at once the sure evidence of God's love and
the firm frame on which the moving curve of His creation through
suffering hangs. 'Wie es eigentlich gewesen' is a mystery that may pass
the understanding of any creature afloat in the creative Time-stream;
but the historian's very consciousness of the relativity of his own infirm
standpoint is evidence that he has some inkling of an absolute ὅπου στῇ;
and perhaps even he may catch a fleeting glimpse of 'wie es geworden'
by clutching, for an instant, the skirts of 'I am'.[2] In such flashes of
illumination a human understanding may divine that the service performed for God by Evil as an instrument of creation in His hands is a
reality in God's creative work in Time which is transcended in those
higher spheres that are entered by a contrite Doctor Marianus in the
last act of the second part of Goethe's *Faust*; and this intuition is shared
with Christianity by Buddhism if the conception of *Nirvāna* is to be
interpreted as implying the extinction, not of Life itself, but of the
tragically creative experiences of Life-in-Time.[3]

In Life-in-Time, as human souls experience it in their passage through
This World, a finite human understanding, that cannot resolve an
apparent moral conflict between divers laws reigning within human
ken, can at least discern that, from the standpoint of creatures subject
to their dominion, these laws stand to one another in a hierarchical
relation, and that this hierarchy of laws is a Jacob's ladder up which
God is ever seeking to draw His Creatures towards Him, rung over rung.
This partial intuition of the role of Law in History, imperfect though it
be, throws some light on the relation between Law and Freedom if we
also take the view that 'Freedom', like 'Chance' and 'Heterodoxy', is a
relative concept, not an absolute one, and that, accordingly, Freedom
from the dominion of a law can be won only at the price of accepting the
dominion of some other law that is higher in the scale in the sense of
having power to liberate from the rule of the previously prevailing law
anyone able to live up to the rule of the new law and willing to live

---

[1] Gen. i. 31.   [2] Exod. iii. 13–15 (see V. vi. 42, n. 1).
[3] See V. vi. 18, n. 1.

under it. Freedom from the ineffectual law of an anarchic Iceland can be won only by submitting to a stern Norwegian King's Peace; freedom from the capricious law of Xerxes can be won only by submitting to the inexorable law of the Lycurgean *agôgê*;[1] freedom from the brutal law of Ishmael can be won only by submitting to an arbitrary law of Moses; freedom from the law of the Mosaic letter that killeth can be won only by embracing a law of Christ's spirit that giveth life.[2]

Since it is thus impossible to win freedom from the service of one law except by entering into the service of some higher law, the liberation that is achieved at each upward step from law to law is inevitably at the same time a sacrifice. The rise from the level of a law of inanimate Physical Nature to the level of a law of Subconscious Psychic Nature liberates Life at the cost of inflicting Death and of kindling sensations and passions that, in a retrospective view from a subsequently attained human standpoint, display a moral spectrum diffracted into Good and Bad. The rise from the level of a law of Subconscious Psychic Nature to the level of a law of Conscious Will liberates the Human Spirit at the cost of charging a creature hitherto as innocent as the lamb and the tiger with the crucial responsibility of having to make divine or satanic choices between Right and Wrong. Liberty from a lower law can never be purchased except at this cost of submitting to a higher law; and, when purchased at this cost, it can be preserved only at the price of eternal vigilance; for an empirically experienced hierarchical relation between these divers laws current in the Universe, which seems to certify that they are so many enactments of a single divine legislator, creates an agonizing conflict of laws for any of God's creatures that have accepted His challenge to transfer their allegiance from some lower law of His to some higher one.

'I delight in the Law of God after the Inward Man; but I see another law in my members, warring against the law of my mind, and bringing me into captivity to the Law of Sin which is in my members.'[3]

And Saint Paul's testimony from his personal experience was endorsed by a nineteenth-century Western man of science who had done as much as any man to write the laws of Nature large on his contemporaries' mental map.

'Cosmic Nature is no school of virtue, but the headquarters of the enemy of Ethical Nature. . . . Social progress means a checking of the cosmic process at every step and the substitution for it of another, which may be called the ethical process, the end of which is not the survival of those who

---

[1] This point is made by Herodotus (*Histories*, Book VII, chaps. 101–5) in an imaginary conversation which he puts into the mouths of Xerxes and the exiled King of Lacedaemon, Dâmarâtus, who is serving on Xerxes' staff during the Achaemenian Power's invasion of Continental European Greece in 480 B.C. The Spartan quisling is represented as saying to the Persian autocrat:

'Though the Lacedaemonians are free, their freedom is not absolute. They are subjects of a lord and master whose name is the Law; and they fear this master a great deal more than Your Majesty's subjects fear Your Majesty. At any rate, they never fail to carry out whatever orders this master may give them; and his orders are always the same: "The troops are forbidden to retreat in the face of the enemy, however great his numerical superiority; their orders are to remain at their posts and there conquer or die."'

[2] 2 Cor. iii. 6.   [3] Rom. vii. 22–23.

may happen to be the fittest, in respect of the whole of the conditions which obtain, but of those who are ethically the best. . . . The ethical process is in opposition to the principle of the cosmic process, and tends to the suppression of the qualities best fitted for success in that struggle. . . . What would become of the garden if the gardener treated all the weeds and slugs and birds and trespassers as he would like to be treated, if he were in their place? . . . The practice of that which is ethically best—what we call goodness or virtue—involves a course of conduct which, in all respects, is opposed to that which leads to success in the cosmic struggle for existence. In place of ruthless self-assertion it demands self-restraint. . . . It repudiates the gladiatorial theory of existence. . . . Man, as a "political animal", . . . is compelled to be perpetually on guard against the cosmic forces, whose ends are not his ends, without and within himself. . . . The ethical progress of Society depends, not on imitating the cosmic process, still less in running away from it, but in combating it. . . . The history of Civilisation details the steps by which men have succeeded in building up an artificial world within the Cosmos. . . . In virtue of his intelligence, the dwarf bends the titan to his will. . . . That which lies before the Human Race is a constant struggle to maintain and improve, in opposition to the State of Nature, the State of Art of an organised polity, in which, and by which, Man may develop a worthy civilisation, capable of maintaining and constantly improving itself, until the evolution of our globe shall have entered so far upon its downward course that the cosmic process resumes its sway and, once more, the State of Nature prevails over the surface of our planet.'[1]

If Freedom is to be taken as being a relative concept, and if all the mutually contrary and contradictory laws in an ascending hierarchy are in some sense laws of God, even though human minds cannot resolve an apparent moral conflict between God's Law of Love and God's Law of Subconscious Psychic Nature, is there any sense in which the Law of Love can be called God's Law without qualification, and in which the freedom to be found in God's service is, after all, not relative, but truly 'perfect'?[2] When we have heard Christ's challenge 'Take up the cross and follow me,'[3] can we credit His assurance 'My yoke is easy and my burden is light'?[4]

The answer to this question seems to be that 'the glorious freedom of the sons of God', which they enjoy under the Law of Love, is not merely the relative freedom of a release from the law of a compulsive Subconscious Psyche; it is also the perfect freedom possessed by God Himself, which an all-loving Creator has bestowed upon His creature Man at the sacrificial price of emptying Himself[5] of almighty power. Under a Law of Love which is the law of God's own Being, God's self-sacrifice challenges Man by setting before Man an ideal of spiritual perfection which Man has perfect freedom to accept or to reject. The Law of Love leaves Man as free to be a sinner as to be a saint. The one thing that Man

[1] Huxley, T. H.: *Evolution and Ethics*, the Romanes Lecture, 1893, and *Prolegomena*, 1894, reprinted in Huxley, T. H. and J.: *Evolution and Ethics, 1893–1943* (London, 1947, Pilot Press), pp. 78, 81, 51, 52, 81–82, 59, 82, 83, 83, 60.
[2] 'Whose service is perfect freedom.'—The Second Collect, for Peace, in the Order for Morning Prayer Daily throughout the Year, in *The Book of Common Prayer* according to the Use of the Church of England. [3] Mark x. 21.
[4] Matt. xi. 30. [5] Phil. ii. 7, as translated in the Revised Version.

can be sure that this law will never do to him is to make him take up the Cross against his will; for the Law of Love is the one law that can never be served involuntarily. There is not, and cannot be, any externally applied coercion to obey this law, or any externally imposed punishment for disobeying it. The punishment for disobedience is inherent in the act of disobedience itself; for, in using his God-given freedom to reject the ideal in which the Law of Love consists, a human soul that has been created 'to glorify God and fully to enjoy Him for ever'[1] is rejecting 'the true end of Man', and is running, self-driven, into the disaster that overtakes Man through the inexorable working of the Law of Sub-conscious Human Nature, if he fails to respond to God's challenge to rise to the service of the Law of Love by using his God-given freedom to choose what is the will of God for him. Moreover, even this self-inflicted disaster is no final judgement and no irrevocable doom, since mundane disaster brings with it the opportunity of learning through suffering for any sinner who repents of his sin and is moved by his penitence to seek the aid of God's grace.

Thus, on this highest visible pitch of a cliff-face up which the creature is being drawn by the call of his Creator to essay a perilous ascent, we catch a glimpse of God's hand reaching down to meet the upstretched hand of the struggling human climber; and, at the point where hands meet in the clasp of Love, Law and Freedom cease to be distinguish-able; for ' 'tis only he that loves not that is fettered by compulsion'.[2] Since the God who is Love is also Omnipotence, a soul that loves is liberated by the maker and master of all laws from a bondage to laws of the Subconscious Psyche which Babylonian souls used to project on to inexorable stars in their courses and which Hellenic souls used to per-sonify as malignant *kêres* and *daimones*; and a liberating truth which had once proved potent to set free[3] fast-fettered Hellenes and Babylonians might once again be taken to heart by the children of a post-Christian World which had been vainly seeking to ban those dread psychic prin-cipalities and powers[4] in the name of a Science that was as impotent to exorcize them as any pre-Christian magic.

[1] Answer to Question 1 in the Larger Catechism agreed upon by the Assembly of Divines at Westminster with the Assistance of Commissioners from the Church of Scotland . . . and approved Anno 1648 by the General Assembly of the Church of Scotland.
[2] Jalāl-ad-Dīn Rūmi: *Mathnawī*, Book I, ll. 1456 seqq., translated by R. A. Nicholson in *Rumi, Poet and Mystic* (London 1950, Allen & Unwin), p. 162.
[3] John viii. 32.   [4] Rom. viii. 38; Eph. iii. 10 and vi. 12.

XII

THE PROSPECTS OF THE WESTERN
CIVILIZATION

A. THE NEED FOR THIS INQUIRY

AS he took up his pen to write the present Part of this book, the
writer was conscious of a sense of distaste for this self-imposed
task which was due to something more than a natural shrinking from the
obvious hazards of a speculative subject.

On the 30th November, 1950, it was, of course, clear that the forecasts about the prospects of the Western Civilization that he was venturing to put on paper might be belied by events almost before the ink was
dry, and perhaps long before the manuscript could be printed and published.[1] Yet, if the risk of making himself ridiculous had been a governing consideration in the writer's mind, this would have deterred him
from ever embarking on any part of this Study; and, in committing himself to Part Twelve of the work after having already given eleven hostages to Fortune, he could take heart from the reflection that at this date
the prospects of the Western Civilization were at any rate very much less
obscure than they had been when, in the early months of the year 1929,
he had been drafting the original notes for this Part that were now lying
at his elbow.

In A.D. 1929, before the break on Wall Street, it was already possible
to discern the general direction in which the Western World was moving,
but it was far more difficult then than it was twenty-one years later to
picture the alternative possible routes along which this movement might
take its course. In 1929 it could already be foreseen, for example, that,
in a Westernizing World that had become coextensive with the entire
habitable surface of the Planet, a process of unification which, on the
economic, technological, and intellectual planes, was accelerating in a geometrical progression was bound to prevail on the military and political
planes likewise, sooner or later; yet in 1929 it was still impossible either
to guess how long it would take to arrive at this consummation or to
imagine how the unificatory process would overcome a passive and active
opposition which, at that date, were no less impressive than was the
contrary nisus towards unification. In 1929 an historian seemed to be in
presence here of a contest like the legendary race between the hound
who could never fail to catch his quarry and the fox who could never be
caught; and on the military and political plane this apparently insoluble
riddle of A.D. 1929 was illustrated by the situation of the Great Powers

---

[1] 'Lorsqu'il s'agit . . . d'un ensemble aussi complexe, la difficulté de reconstituer le
passé, même le plus récent, est toute comparable à la difficulté de construire l'avenir,
même le plus proche; ou, plutôt, c'est la même difficulté. Le prophète est dans le même
sac que l'historien. Laissons-les y.' (Valéry, Paul: 'La Crise de l'Esprit,' in *Variété*
(Paris 1924, Gallimard, Éditions de la Nouvelle Revue Française), p. 17).

as a group, and most pointedly by the particular situation of France. Though the Danubian Hapsburg Monarchy had become a total wreck in the War of A.D. 1914–18, the other seven of the eight Great Powers in existence at the outbreak of war had all survived, and, of these, Germany and Russia, which had both been prostrate in A.D. 1919, were manifestly both on the road to recovery ten years later. As for France, on the one hand it was manifest in A.D. 1929—and had indeed been evident since A.D. 1870–1—that she must resign herself, sooner or later, to losing the status of a first-class Power which she had enjoyed continuously ever since her decisive victory over an aggressive England in the fifteenth century; on the other hand it was no less manifest that she was still determined to play her traditional role of 'la Grande Nation', though she might be patently staggering under her present load and be hardly less patently anxious about her future.

Prospects that were thus so bafflingly ambiguous in A.D. 1929 were, by comparison, startlingly clear in A.D. 1950 for an observer who took as his criterion either France in particular or the Great Powers as a group.

By 1950 two decades of French history that had still been below the historian's horizon in 1929 had given a practical demonstration of the psychic alchemy by which 'a nation of patriots'[1] who had once prodigally sacrificed their lives on the goddess France's altar could transmute itself into a nation of 'defeatists'; and one of the most unpredictable, surprising, and significant metamorphoses in this sombrely miraculous transformation-scene was the inversion of French nationalists into French collaborators with a German attempt to reduce France to the status of being Germany's helot-in-chief *en permanence*. The French slogan, to the tune of which the Vichyssois had danced this German dance, had been 'la France seule'; for, under this parade of patriotically refusing to pull Great Britain's or any other foreign country's chestnuts out of the fire at the cost of burning French fingers, French 'defeatists' had indicated that they would reject all foreign proffers of help to throw off a German yoke to which France herself had submitted rather than endure the agony of remaining at war, like Norway, Holland, and Belgium, with an enemy who had overrun her metropolitan territory; and, though France had, in the end, been liberated in spite of herself, and had indeed anticipated the landing of the liberating American and British armies on French soil by throwing up a native resistance movement after the turn of the tide against Germany in a war from which France had previously contracted out, the Vichy chapter of French military, political, and psychological history had left a palpable mark on the spirit of a France who in A.D. 1950 was officially execrating the Vichy régime and all its works.

In 1950 there were Frenchmen who were resigned in advance to seeing France submit to a Russian yoke as she had submitted to a German yoke in A.D. 1940; and those other Frenchmen who were imbued with the spirit of the maquis rather than of Vichy agreed with their 'defeatist' compatriots in feeling that, in 1950, France could no longer stand

[1] Hayes, C. J. H.: *France, a Nation of Patriots* (New York 1930, Columbia University Press).

alone in the true sense in which these words expressed France's former political ideal of genuine national sovereign independence. In 1950 the more sanguine and constructive spirits in France saw their country's salvation in a merger of her once jealously vindicated separate national identity in a supra-national Western community that was to embrace at least all Western Europe and was perhaps eventually to bestride the Atlantic. In the hearts of Frenchmen who were 'good Europeans', as in those of Frenchmen who were 'defeatists', the ideal of parochial nationalism was thus dead; and this was a portent for the Western World as a whole; for, in a post-Medieval Western Society, France had been the archetype of the self-sufficiently sovereign independent national state; and therefore, if, in France, a five-hundred-years-old tradition of political parochialism had been broken between the years 1933 and 1940 by the irresistibly mightier force of an explosive German imperialism, it could be foreseen that tougher wills to retain a sovereign national independence might likewise be broken by the impact of forces mightier than a National-Socialist Germany.

Great Britain, for instance, had refused to give in when, in 1940, France's will to resist Germany had broken down; yet from 1931 to 1940 Great Britain had been France's fellow-traveller down the road of appeasement which France had followed to the bitter end; and, after 1940, Great Britain's happy issue out of afflictions to which she had then exposed herself at the eleventh hour—by then taking an heroic decision—had been due to the mighty reinforcement of her own inadequate national strength by the arms of a Soviet Union and a United States who were successively drawn into the war on the anti-Axis side thanks to a German and a Japanese miscalculation that were, either of them, egregious. The Second World War left Great Britain's two eventual allies alone still capable of playing the part of Great Powers in a struggle for existence between parochial states that had now become vastly more strenuous than it had been in A.D. 1929; America's and Russia's fellow victor Great Britain, no less than a defeated Germany, Japan, Italy, and France, had fallen out of the running; and a Second World War which had thus reduced the number of the Great Powers in a Westernizing World from seven to two had, in the act, forged a new weapon that might prove potent enough to break the spirit of parochial Powers even of a Russian or an American calibre. Even if the uranium atom bomb should fail to produce the same morally devastating effect on these two loose-limbed giants as it had produced on a congested and exhausted Japan, an inconscionable post-Modern Western Science still had up her sleeve a hydrogen atom bomb that could be guaranteed, if ever detonated, to blow even a United States or Soviet Union out of the water—at the cost, perhaps, of making the whole face of the Planet uninhabitable by human or any other living organisms.[1]

---

[1] The following comment on this passage, and on other passages to the same effect in the present Part of this Study, has been made by Professor William McNeill:

'I doubt the likelihood of total extinction of Civilization, still more of Mankind, as a result of a third world war. The will to resist and the capacity to conduct an organized campaign breaks down short of physical extinction; and the breaking point is removed farther from the point of physical extinction in proportion as the waging of war becomes

Thus in A.D. 1950 it was already far less open to doubt than it had been in A.D. 1929 that, in a struggle for supremacy between two titanic post-Christian Western idols—a Moloch Nationalism and a Juggernaut Technology—the treads of Juggernaut's irresistibly high-powered bull-dozer were going to trample over the antique plates of Moloch's brazen furnace; and this lesson from the experience of twenty-one sinisterly illuminating years had made experiments in prognostication less hazardous by pinning the still patently open questions within a framework of relatively sure prediction. On the 1st December, 1950, it was still impossible to foresee whether the third round in the struggle was going to be played out without another explosion of 'total war', and whether life on the planet would survive if a Third World War did break out within the bosom of an oecumenical human society that had now learnt how to split the atom. It could, however, now be foreseen that, if a Western Technology's victory over a Western Nationalism were to be consummated without the annihilation of the Human Race, the story would end in the monopoly of the technical means of annihilation in the hands of some single authority whose fiat would be virtually law, not merely in one island, continent, or hemisphere, but throughout the *Oikoumenê*—in whatever quarter of the globe this oecumenical authority's geographical base of operations might be located, and whatever the constitutional form in which its monopoly of world-power might be veiled or advertised. This concentration of political power might or might not be achieved by the 'knock-out blow' that had brought into being a *Pax Romana* and all the other 'universal states' so far known to History; the parochial *peritura regna* might be ostensibly preserved instead of being overtly liquidated; but, whatever course and shape the political unification of a post-Modern Westernizing World might take, it seemed safe to predict that the acquisition of atomic weapons would bring about the political unification of the *Oikoumenê* in one way or another—and this sooner rather than later—considering that a *Pax Romana* had been forced upon an Hellenic World, and a *Pax Hanica* upon a Sinic World, by the intolerableness of the alternative choice of continuing to suffer the consequences of wars between parochial states waged with unprecedented atrocity by new-fangled 'methods of barbarism'. If this revolutionary political effect could be produced by 'total war' fought with such comparatively humane and innocuous weapons as the spear, the bow, and the horse, it must assuredly be produced by atomic warfare *a fortiori*.

Thus in A.D. 1950 an intellectual prospector could enter on a mental exploration of the Western Civilization's future with rather more confidence that he could have felt in A.D. 1929; he need not feel now that he was sentencing himself to undertake a Psyche's task; and the writer's own distaste for his present subject ought therefore to have been appreciably diminished by the intervening passage of two enlightening addi-

a more complex activity, requiring the coordination of larger numbers of specialists both in and outside of the fighting forces. At the time of Germany's surrender in A.D. 1945 about 80 per cent. of Germany's industrial equipment was still intact, in spite of the bombing operations of the Allied Powers. This, however, does not mean that a particular battle-ground, such as Europe, could not be destroyed more or less completely by alien fighting forces whose bases of supply were situated elsewhere.'

tional decades of history if it had been merely a recoil from the risk of a
hazardous intellectual adventure. Why was it, then, that, so far from
diminishing, his distaste had been increasing steadily in the meantime?
The answer to this question was not obscure to the writer himself. The
reason was that this growing disinclination of his had in fact little or
nothing to do with the difficulty of estimating the Western Civilization's
prospects, but was rooted in a reluctance to throw overboard one of the
cardinal principles governing the writer's whole approach to his study of
History. He was distressed by a fear that, if he allowed himself to single
out any one civilization for special treatment, he might be abandoning a
standpoint from which alone it was, in his belief, possible to see in true
perspective the whole history of a species of Society of which the Western
Civilization was one, but only one, representative; and his belief in the
rightness of this non-Western standpoint had been confirmed, in his
personal judgement, by the results of two decades spent in trying to read
the map of history from a non-Western angle of vision.

One of the stimuli that had originally spurred the writer to embark
on the present Study was an intellectual revolt against a current Late
Modern Western convention of identifying a parvenue and provincial
Western Society's history with 'History', writ large, *sans phrase*. In the
writer's view this convention was the preposterous offspring of a distorting egocentric illusion[1] to which the children of a Western Civilization
had succumbed like the children of all other known civilizations and
known primitive societies. In a latter-day chapter of Western mental
history this blight of egocentricity had been the nemesis of an act of
hybris. Western minds had contracted their vision to the narrow limits
of a parochially Western horizon because they had despised and rejected
the cultural heritages of Christianity and Hellenism that had been bequeathed to them in the Bible and the Classics. This, in the writer's
belief, was an intellectual effect of Original Sin from which an historian
must thoroughly purge himself in order to win any hope of being able to
catch and communicate even a glimpse of the truth; and, if it was true
that an argument must find a point of departure in some axiom or other,
then the unavowed and unavowable axiom of egocentricity ought to be
ruled out by adopting the contrary axiom that all the representatives of
any species of human society are philosophically on a par with one
another.[2] This spiritual discipline, which no historian could afford to
neglect in any age of the history of any society, was incumbent *a fortiori*
on an historian of Western origin and upbringing in an age of Western
history in which the Western Civilization happened to be in the ascendant. The writer, for his part, had taken to heart this counter-axiom of
a philosophical parity between all societies of the same species; it had
justified his faith in it by serving him as his pole star for steering his
course through the first six parts of the present Study; and, though, in
a later Part,[3] the value of the civilizations known to have existed up to
date had been found to be unequal as a matter of historical fact on the
evidence of an assay in which the touchstone had been the part played

---

[1] See I. i. 158–64.   [2] See I. i. 175–7.
[3] See VII. vii. 422–3 and 444–9.

by the breakdowns and disintegrations of civilizations in the history of Religion, the result of this test had not been to re-exalt the Western Civilization to the pinnacle on which it had once been placed by a naïvely vulgar native Western egocentric prejudice; the finding had been that the civilizations of greatest mark and moment in the history of Religion had been civilizations of the second generation—the Syriac Civilization, the Indic, the Hellenic, the Sinic—and that, by comparison with these, the Western Civilization and its contemporaries of the third generation had been 'vain repetitions of the heathen'[1] from the standpoint of an observer who saw the guide-line of History in a progressive increase in the provision of spiritual opportunities for human souls in transit through This World.[2]

The writer's own adoption of this standpoint had confirmed and reinforced his original reluctance to single out the Western Civilization for special treatment. After having done his best, throughout the first eleven parts of this Study, to battle against a sin that beset his Western mind so easily,[3] was he to capitulate at the last moment to this tribal infirmity? Was he deliberately to redistort an historical perspective that he had been at such pains to correct? In deciding, in spite of such misgivings, to abide in A.D. 1950 by a plan originally drawn up in A.D. 1927–9, he was bowing to the logic of three facts which had lost none of their cogency during the intervening years.

The first of these facts was that, in the second quarter of the twentieth century of the Christian Era, the Western Civilization was perhaps the only extant representative of its species that did not show indisputable signs of being already in disintegration Of the seven other extant civilizations, five—namely the main body of Orthodox Christendom and its Russian offshoot, the main body of the Far Eastern Civilization and its Korean and Japanese offshoot, and in the fifth place the Hindu Civilization—had already not only entered into, but passed through, the universal state phase in a familiar rhythm of social disintegration;[4] and, though, on the strictest view, it might be held that, pending the epiphany of a universal state, disintegration could never be diagnosed with absolute certainty,[5] a scrutiny of the histories of the Iranic and Arabic Muslim civilizations revealed strong evidence of these two societies having broken down in the second decade of the sixteenth century of the

---

[1] Matt. vi. 7. [2] See VII. vii. 555–68.

[3] Heb. xii. 1. When a Westerner of the present writer's age and upbringing was conscious of being perpetually beset by his collective Western egocentricity, the difficulty of laying aside this sin must have been still greater for his younger Western contemporaries, since the writer himself had had the good fortune to be born into a generation which, in England, had still been educated on the Bible and the Greek and Latin Classics, and not on any native Western cultural pabulum. As a consequence of this fifteenth-century Italian education, the writer's spiritual home was, not a post-Christian Western World, but a pre-Christian Hellas; and, whenever he was moved to put his deeper and more intimate feelings into words, they found expression in Greek or Latin verse, and not in the English vernacular that happened to be his mother tongue. In the twentieth century of the Christian Era it was indeed hard for any living observer—Western or non-Western—to take an unbiased view of the Western Civilization and its prospects. A Western observer of the West would find it difficult to correct a bent towards his own collective Western ego without falling into the opposite inclination to lean over backwards.

[4] See Table I in vol. vi, p. 327, reprinted as Table I in vol. vii, p. 769, *ad fin.*

[5] See pp. 341–4, above.

Christian Era, when the Iranic Society had been split by an explosive recrudescence of Shi'ism, and when the ensuing struggle between the two fractions of this fissured body social had led an Ottoman Sunnī Iranic Muslim Power to conquer the sister Arabic Muslim Society. On this showing, the Western Civilization in the twentieth century of the Christian Era was apparently in the singular position of being the only one among all the known representatives of the species, extinct or extant, whose present state and future prospects might still be open questions. While all the others were either certainly dead or almost certainly *in articulo mortis*, the Western Society alone was possibly still in its growth-phase.[1]

This uncanny uniqueness of the contemporary situation of the West first struck the writer when he was putting on paper his original notes for the last portion of this Study in the early months of A.D. 1929; and the subject and title of the present Part were then immediately conjured up in his mind by a sudden reminiscence of a passage in *The Rime of the Ancient Mariner*. In his mind's eye he saw the picture of the stricken ship becalmed on the boundless expanse of the South Seas, with the crew prostrated by the torments of thirst; he saw the spectre bark shooting towards him from the horizon, on which the ribs of its skeleton hull had shown up sinisterly black against the blood-red disk of a setting sun; and, as the dreadful apparition drew near, he descried, on board, two demonic figures, one of which was Death, while the other was still more ghastly than her grim companion.

> Her lips were red, her looks were free,
> Her locks were yellow as gold:
> Her skin was as white as leprosy,
> The nightmare Life-in-Death was she,
> Who thicks men's blood with cold.[2]

He saw Life-in-Death winning the throw of the dice in her game with Death for the prize of the ship's crew; and his recollection of the poem ran on to bring before his eyes a vision of the dying sailors giving up the ghost one by one, till, on board the spellbound ship, the Ancient Mariner is left alone alive with his dead companions lying around him.

> The many men so beautiful!
> And they all dead did lie:
> And a thousand thousand slimy things
> Lived on: and so did I.[3]

When these words in which Life-in-Death's legendary victim describes his thoughts and feelings were ringing in the present writer's ears in A.D. 1929, he was conscious of a weird contrast between the Ancient Mariner's agony in his loneliness and the complacency of a post-Modern Western World whose own singular situation had evoked in the writer's mind these echoes of Coleridge's poetry. At that date the prospects of the Western Civilization appeared, on the whole, to be favourable. After

---

[1] See IV. iv. 38–39.
[2] Coleridge, S. T.: *The Rime of the Ancient Mariner*, Part III, Stanza xi.
[3] Ibid., Part IV, Stanza iv.

shuddering under the shock of the First World War, the Western body social seemed to have recovered its balance and to have resumed its rudely interrupted course. The spectre of an imminent break on Wall Street was then still hull-down below the horizon, and the tragic sequence of errors, crimes, and sufferings which this financial catastrophe in the United States was to bring in its train was still unsuspected, *a fortiori*. It looked, in fact, as if the Western ship had triumphantly weathered an unusually violent storm; and, if it had, what sense could be made of an irrational imagination's oracular impulse to identify the West's situation in A.D. 1929 with the Ancient Mariner's plight after the death of his companions? Need a once more prosperous Western Civilization take the other civilizations' deaths to heart? In A.D. 1929 it had been easier than it was in A.D. 1950 for Western common sense to dismiss this disturbing question.

One debating point that Common Sense could perhaps still make in A.D. 1950 was to suggest that, whatever the West's plight might now be, it was at any rate not singular, since it could not be distinguished from the plight of the two Islamic civilizations on any impartial interpretation of the evidence. If the evidence did not convict the West of being already in disintegration, then it would not convict the Islamic civilizations either; while, conversely, if it did convict these, then the West must stand convicted in their company. The Islamic civilizations, like the Western Civilization, were not yet in a universal state; yet the Western Civilization, like the Islamic civilizations, was showing signs of being already in a Time of Troubles. In a previous Part[1] we have detected, in the Modern and post-Modern chapters of Western history, the disintegration-rhythm of lapse-rally-relapse recording itself in a sixteenth-century outbreak of a paroxysm of Wars of Religion, in a lull lasting from the third quarter of the seventeenth century to the third quarter of the eighteenth,[2] and in a paroxysm of Wars of Nationality beginning with the outbreak of the American War of Independence.[3] If an impartial inquirer into the state of the extant civilizations in A.D. 1950 were to decide, notwithstanding this evidence, to give the Western Civilization the benefit of the doubt—on the ground that, whatever other symptoms of disintegration might be recognizable in recent Western history, it was at any rate still certain in A.D. 1950 that the West had not yet entered into a universal state—the same inquirer might perhaps feel bound to give the same benefit to the pair of Islamic civilizations on the same grounds. Yet, even if, in this point of not being yet demonstrably in disintegration, the Western Civilization's ambiguous situation were found to be shared with the West by two of its seven contemporaries, the second of the facts that seemed to qualify the Western Civilization for receiving special treatment in a study of History was a fact of Western history which had no parallel in the history of any other extant society.

This unique fact of Western history was that, in the course of some five centuries ending in A.D. 1950, the expansion of the Western Society and the radiation of the Western culture had brought all other extant civilizations and all extant primitive societies within a world-encompass-

---

[1] In V. vi. 312–21.   [2] See IV. iv. 142–50.   [3] See IV. iv. 165–7.

ing Western Civilization's ambit.[1] Already, some two hundred years before this date, the approaching unification of the entire *Oikoumenê* round a Western centre had been discerned and announced by a Western man of genius. In an *Esquisse d'un Plan de Géographie Politique* Turgot had put on record the propositions

'que chaque peuple qui a devancé les autres dans ses progrès est devenu une espèce de centre autour duquel s'est formé comme un monde politique composé des nations qu'il connaissait et dont il pouvait combiner les intérêts avec les siens; qu'il s'est formé plusieurs de ces mondes dans toute l'étendue du globe indépendants les uns des autres, et inconnus réciproquement; qu'en s'étendant sans cesse autour d'eux, il se sont rencontrés et confondus, jusqu'à ce qu'enfin la connaissance de tout l'univers, dont la politique saura combiner toutes les parties, ne formera plus qu'un seul monde politique, dont les limites sont confondues avec celles du monde physique.'[2]

By A.D. 1950 Turgot's prognostication had been vindicated by accomplished facts. By this date the two Islamic civilizations, which had not yet entered into the universal state phase, were no less compromisingly enmeshed in a Western net than the five non-Western civilizations which had passed through this phase already. Even the Russian Civilization, which, among these seven societies, had taken the lead, up to date, in making a fight for the preservation of its own identity, êthos, and genius, had found, as we have seen,[3] that the only practical way of trying to hold its own against the West was to master the technology which was the source of Modern Western Power and to step into a Western arena as a combatant arrayed in a panoply fashioned on the latest Western model. This world-wide ascendancy of a Western culture, at least on the plane of Technology, even over the non-Westerners who had dedicated themselves to the task of leading an anti-Western crusade, might prove to be a short-lived phenomenon; indeed, a glance at the history of a post-Alexandrine Hellenic Civilization's impact on the Oriental civilizations of the day—a history which had long since completed its course and was therefore on record from beginning to end—seemed to suggest that a Western ascendancy, in its turn, was likely to be liquidated in the long run by military, political, and religious counter-attacks of the kind that had once brought the ascendancy of Hellenism to an end. Yet this Hellenic precedent seemed also to suggest that even an eventual liquidation of a now prevailing Western ascendancy would come to pass in a world that had been unified within a framework of Western workmanship; and this unique role of a Modern Western Society as a unifying agency over a literally world-wide range of operations was the second fact that demanded—in A.D. 1950 no less than in A.D. 1929—a special consideration of the Western Civilization's prospects.

The third of the facts that seemed to make this inquiry imperative was the alarming fact that in the twentieth century of the Christian Era, perhaps for the first time in the history of the Human Race, all Mankind's

---

[1] See V. v. 152–3, and pp. 479–90, below.
[2] Turgot, A. R. J.: *Œuvres*, new ed. (Paris 1844, Guillaumin, 2 vols.), vol. ii, pp. 616–17.
[3] In IX. viii. 130–41.

eggs had been gathered into one precious yet precarious basket as a consequence of the Western Civilization's world-wide expansion.

> Gone are the days when madness was confined
> By seas or hills from spreading through Mankind:
> When, though a Nero fooled upon a string,
> Wisdom still reigned unruffled in Peking;
> And God in welcome smiled from Buddha's face,
> Though Calvin in Geneva preached of grace.
> For now our linked-up globe has shrunk so small,
> One Hitler in it means mad days for all.
> Through the whole World each wave of worry spreads,
> And Ipoh dreads the war that Ipsden dreads.[1]

Some degree of interdependence was, of course, nothing new in the history of human societies. The civilizations had, no doubt, begun to influence one another, as well as all the extant primitive societies, by their radioactivity at an early date after their first epiphany;[2] and these impersonal influences had been followed up by military and political assaults since the time when—at about the turn of the eighteenth and seventeenth centuries B.C.—an Egyptiac Middle Empire that had never collided with Hammurabi's reconstructed Sumeric Empire of the Four Quarters had been overrun, after Hammurabi's death, by Hyksos barbarian invaders who had imbibed a tincture of the Sumeric Civilization from Eurasian Nomads in their rear.[3] A latter-day Soviet Union's 'geopolitically' commanding position—with sally-ports opening on to the back-yards of all other extant civilizations located on *terra firma* in the Old World[4]—had been captured by Russia from Eurasian Nomads among whom the Mitanni had been the first to flood over the domains of adjoining moribund sedentary civilizations. The collisions with one another into which these sedentary civilizations had continued to fall since the Mitanni had implicated an Egyptiac Civilization in a Sumeric Civilization's fate had provided so many occasions for epiphanies of higher religions. At least twelve of these[5] had sprung from the impact made on six Oriental civilizations by an Hellenic Society which had radiated its culture as far as Japan in one direction and Britain in another. Yet none of these expansive movements, before the expansion of the Western Society, had ever been world-wide in the literal sense on the military and the political as well as on the commercial and the cultural plane. For example, the Roman Empire and the Han Empire had coexisted, not only on the face of the same planet but within the bounds of the same continent, for some two hundred years without ever coming into direct military or even political contact with one another—if the diplomatic mission from Marcus Aurelius, whose arrival in A.D. 166[6] is recorded in the Posterior Han Dynasty's annals, is to be written off as having been in reality perhaps no more than an isolated private commercial venture—and in this classic case even the convulsions of one of

[1] Skinner, Martyn: *Letters to Malaya*, I and II (London 1941, Putnam), pp. 34–35.
[2] See II. i. 187.   [3] See V. v. 351.
[4] See p. 260, above.   [5] See Table IV in VII. vii, p. 772, *ad fin.*
[6] See Franke, O.: *Geschichte des Chinesischen Reiches*, vol. i (Berlin and Leipzig 1930, de Gruyter), p. 404.

the two contemporary empires in its death agony did not impinge upon the survivor, as a post-Sumeric Völkerwanderung had impinged upon the Egyptiac World. When the Han Empire went to pieces at the turn of the second and third centuries of the Christian Era, the inhabitants of the Roman Empire remained unaware that an earth-shaking event was occurring at the opposite extremity of the Old World; and conversely, when, some two hundred years later, the Roman Empire in its turn went to pieces at a time when, in the Far East, a new society was beginning to emerge from the Han Empire's ruins, this nascent Far Eastern Civilization was not thrown back into chaos by the Roman Empire's fall. In the days of the Han Empire and the Roman Empire, human destinies had not yet been gathered into one basket, and so, though some eggs were constantly being broken, there were always others left intact.

The freedom which an Hellenic and a Sinic 'universal state' each still enjoyed to work out its own destiny without interference from the other appears the more remarkable when we recollect that neither of these 'oecumenical' empires was confined within the bounds of the single civilization that had brought it to birth. Each of them also embraced portions of the domains of other societies[1] and was consequently regarded by its inhabitants as being coextensive with Mankind itself. In a Westernizing World of A.D. 1950 which had not yet been united politically in a universal state, any such illusion would have been impossible for the members either of the supra-national community gravitating round the United States or of the community of the same order of magnitude gravitating round the Soviet Union; for, however tenuous might be the commercial contacts between these two groups of countries by comparison with the web of either group's internal trade, the competition between them in military technology and in political propaganda was so intense that the members of either were acutely aware all the time of the other community's existence and activity. The unification of the whole habitable and traversable surface of the planet, thanks to Western enterprise, had by this time gone so far on this plane of politico-military rivalry that there was reason to fear that, in this highly charged and at the same time highly conductive atmosphere, there might prove not to be room, even within the wide limits of a spaciously all-inclusive *Oikoumenê*, for both a sovereign independent Soviet Union and a sovereign independent United States, in spite of the auspicious fact that —in contrast to a Germany and a Japan who, between them, had detonated the Second World War—either of these giants was, on the economic plane, a 'satiated' power still possessing within its own boundaries immense reserves of undeveloped non-human resources and correspondingly immense opportunities of finding innocently productive employment for a growing population for as long a time as could be seen ahead. In A.D. 1950 the United States and the Soviet Union were enjoying freedom from want, but not freedom from fear.

If the charge with which an ever more high-powered Western technique and organization had thus loaded the now perilously conductive atmosphere of a not yet politically unified twentieth-century Western-

[1] See VI. vii. 63.

izing World were ever to be detonated by some carelessly or malignantly ignited spark, the resultant military, political, and spiritual explosion would sweep from end to end of the *Oikoumenê* as it vented itself with all the physical force of a post-Modern Western technology which had vastly heightened the destructiveness of the weapons at Man's command between A.D. 1929 and A.D. 1950 and was still, so far as the layman could learn, triumphantly advancing along the same suicidal course. A world-wide catastrophe might leave not a single egg unbroken in the solitary basket into which all human destinies had now been gathered.

In a Third World War fought with atomic or bacteriological weapons, it seemed, indeed, improbable that the Angel of Death would overlook even those nooks and corners of Man's terrestrial habitat which, till recently, had been either so uninviting or so inaccessible, or both, as to give their poor, weak, backward inhabitants a virtual immunity against the unwelcome attentions of 'civilized' militarists. In a talk given at Princeton[1] just three weeks before the enunciation of the Truman Doctrine of American support for Greece and Turkey against Russian pressure,[2] the writer had given play, half seriously and not wholly in joke, to the fancy that, if a Westernizing World were to allow itself to fall into a Third World War, the sequel might be a rendering, in real life, of one of Plato's myths in which the Athenian philosopher imagines the mountain-shepherds periodically issuing from their fastnesses in order to build up a new civilization on the vacated site of an old one that has perished in the latest of a number of periodic cataclysms.[3] In the imagery of a Collective Subconscious Psyche in the Age of the Civiliza-tions, 'shepherds' had come to symbolize the unspent and unspoiled primitive human potentialities for creation that God had still held in reserve after He had led a sophisticated majority of Mankind into the temptations that had worsted Cain the husbandman[4] and Cain's son Enoch the city-builder,[5] and their heir Tubal-Cain the smith.[6] When-ever Man in Process of Civilization had come to grief in essaying this most recent, and perhaps most hazardous, of all human enterprises up to date, he had always, so far, counted on being able to draw upon the reserve power latent in still primitive brethren of his whom he had driven out of those choicer portions of the Earth that he had appropriated as his own domain, 'to wander about in sheepskins and goatskins in deserts and in mountains';[7] and, in the past, these comparatively innocent sur-vivors of the children of Abel had heaped coals of fire on the heads of the children of Cain by coming to their murderers' rescue when the Cainites' sins had found them out. A shepherd from Ascra, on the foothills of Mount Helicon, had spoken the prologue to the tragedy of Hellenic history, and shepherds from the Negeb, on the fringes of the Arabian Desert, had stood by the cradle of Christianity in Bethlehem.[8] In his

---

[1] See Toynbee, A. J.: *Civilization on Trial* (London 1948, Oxford University Press), pp. 150–63.
[2] The Truman Doctrine was made public on the 12th March, 1947; the writer's talk, here mentioned, was delivered on the 20th February, 1947.
[3] See Plato: *Timaeus*, 21 E–23 C, quoted in IV. iv. 24–25.
[4] Gen. iv. 3.   [5] Gen. iv. 17.   [6] Gen. iv. 22.
[7] Heb. xi. 37–38.   [8] See V. vi. 174–5.

Platonizing *jeu d'esprit* the present writer had suggested in A.D. 1947 that, if the Western Civilization in which he and his audience were implicated were to inflict some major catastrophe on the *Oikoumenê*, the task of launching, all over again, a cultural enterprise that had been on foot for the last five or six thousand years might perhaps fall to Tibetans hitherto safely ensconced behind the ramparts of their plateau or to Esquimaux hitherto snugly nestling against an innocently inclement ice-cap that was a less vicious neighbour than any *homo homini lupus*.[1] Within the three and a half years that had elapsed between the delivery of that address and the writing of the present lines in the still peaceful pre-cincts of the same university town, these tentative fancies had been over-taken and ridden down by the march of historical events. At the moment of writing in December 1950, an invading Chinese Communist expedi-tionary force was reported to be *en route* for Lhasa, while Esquimaux who had formerly been happy in having no foe or friend except Physical Nature found themselves in the fairway of a transpolar bombing-route between the basins of the Volga and the Mississippi, and of a *ventre-à-terre* invasion-route, across the ice-floes of the Behring Straits, from the once sequestered habitat of the primitive denizens of the north-eastern tip of Russia-in-Asia into an Alaska that was divided from the main body of the Continental United States by nothing but a Canadian 'Polish Corridor'.

Thus a now ubiquitous Western Society held the fate of all Mankind in its hands at a moment when the West's own fate lay on the finger-tip of one man in Moscow and one man in Washington who, by pressing a button, could detonate an atom-bomb.

These were the facts that led the present writer reluctantly to endorse in A.D. 1950 the conclusion, reluctantly reached in A.D. 1929, that an inquiry into the prospects of the Western Civilization was a necessary part of a twentieth-century study of History.

[1] See V. vi. 161–2.

B. THE INCONCLUSIVENESS OF *A PRIORI* ANSWERS

(I) THE INCONCLUSIVENESS OF STATISTICS

WHAT were the Western Civilization's expectations of life in A.D. 1950 or 1952? On first thoughts a student of History, taking an observation in either of those years, might be inclined to rate the West's current expectations low, considering the well-known prodigality of Nature. The Western Civilization, after all, was one out of no more than twenty-one representatives of its species—or, at most, no more than thirty if the number were to be assessed at the highest possible figure by including four arrested civilizations and five abortive civilizations in the count. Was it rational to expect to see the twenty-first, or even the thirtieth, civilization on trial succeed in avoiding the failure that had been the history of all other civilizations up to date? Success would mean either finding some hitherto untravelled way for a civilization to go on living and growing *in saecula saeculorum*, or else creating a mutation that would generate a new species of society. Considering the number of failures that had been the price of each dearly bought success in the past history of the evolution of Life on Earth, it might appear improbable that, in the history of a species still so young as the civilizations were, any representative of the third generation would have been cast for the part of Fortunatus. Yet, if a twentieth-century inquirer's first thoughts did incline towards this pessimistic conclusion, his second thoughts were likely to enter the caveat that so momentous a question could not be disposed of so easily.

The thesis that, in the evolution of Life, it required many more than twenty or twenty-nine failures to pay for one success was, after all, an inference from empirical evidence; and the particular evidence from which this particular inference was drawn was the experience of Life, not at the human, but at a pre-human, level. The dicta that thirty issues of a species was a very small number, and that a species that could not yet muster more than thirty representatives was a very young species, might be justifiable in the mouths of naturalists studying spiders or beetles or perhaps some far more primitive manifestation of Life than these. It might be true that, when Nature had been engaged on the evolution of rudimentary organisms, she had been apt to coin hundreds and thousands and millions of specimens of a type in order to give herself the off-chance of making, at the millionth or the million-millionth strike of the die, a lucky hit that would produce either an execution of her design that was a close enough approximation to it to be worthy of being perpetuated or alternatively an adumbration of some novel and superior design which would render the type now on trial obsolete and therefore superfluous. At this relatively low level of Nature's creative activity, experience might indeed suggest that the twentieth or thirtieth representative of a type would have little chance of turning out to be the successful exponent of it. It might even be warrantable to draw from this limited experience the general inference that it was Nature's way, in all her creative work, to deal in prodigally large numbers. This generalization, however, might prove to be legitimate only in virtue of being barren; for it gave no clue for translating the abstract concept of 'a large number' into any single order of magnitude that could be warranted to hold good uniformly for all Nature's creative activities at all levels.

In the evolution of species of plants, insects, fishes, or other pre-human living organisms, twenty or thirty would have been, no doubt, not 'large numbers', but almost ridiculously small numbers; but, for the same creative purpose of Natura Creatrix, these same numbers might well be, not small, but large, when the species on which Nature was working was, not an organism, but a society, and when the living creatures whose fields of action intersected in this social arena[1] were, not spell-bound ants or bees, but human beings endowed with consciousness and freedom of choice. It was true that, even in this context, twenty or thirty were not very large numbers on the level of human societies of the primitive species; for, though the known number of representatives of this species did not run to millions or million-millions, it did run to hundreds and perhaps thousands.[2] The species now in question was not, however, the primitive human societies; it was the civilizations; and these differed so greatly from the primitive human societies—not to speak of any pre-human manifestation of Life—that any evidence derived from the experience of Life at these other levels would be irrelevant to an inquiry into a civilization's prospects. Second thoughts thus gravitated towards the negative conclusion that it was impossible to give any rational *a priori* answer to an inquiry into the Western Civilization's expectation of life because it was impossible to find any significant statistical basis on which an answer could be founded. While statistics lent no support to the egocentric illusion harboured by a Western Civilization which felt confident that the twenty-first civilization on trial was bound to triumph because this particular candidate happened to be the Western Civilization itself, statistics lent no support either to a dogma that, in the mintage of any species of any manifestation of Life whatsoever, twenty-one must be too low a figure to qualify for success. The statistical record of one species could not be invoked to lay down the law for the statistical prospects of any other species; and, where success or failure hung on the issue of Challenge-and-Response, success and failure were unpredictable. 'The wind bloweth where it listeth.'[3] 'The Kingdom of God cometh not with observation.'[4] 'The day of the Lord so cometh as a thief in the night',[5] and the hour at which the thief will come is never known beforehand by the householder.[6]

---

[1] See III. iii. 227–31. [2] See I. i. 148. [3] John iii. 8.
[4] Luke xvii. 20. [5] I Thess. v. 2. [6] Matt. xxiv. 43; Luke xii. 39.

(II) THE INCONCLUSIVENESS OF FEELINGS

When a twentieth-century Western inquirer into the prospects of the Western Civilization had recognized that a statistical approach to his problem was impracticable, he was still confronted by a pair of emotional *a priori* answers that he must take into consideration before proceeding to examine the testimony of the civilizations themselves, in order to see what light might be thrown on the prospects of the Western Civilization by a synoptic view of the recorded experiences of the twenty or thirty known representatives of the species. The two emotional answers were mutually contradictory; and the writer of this Study, who had been born into the Western World in A.D. 1889, had lived, by A.D. 1952, to see feeling in the West begin to lose faith in a self-complacent outlook which had previously been taken as a matter of course, and begin to revert to an alternative outlook that was, not merely different, but antithetical.

The outlook prevalent among people of the middle class in Great Britain at the earliest date in the last decade of the nineteenth century of the Christian Era at which the writer had begun to be aware of the psychological atmosphere of his social milieu was something that was best conveyed in caricature. In this milieu in the eighteen-nineties the feeling was:

'History is now at an end; this history is therefore final';[1]

and at this date this *Weltanschauung* was shared with an English middle class by the children of the German and the Northern American victors in the latest bout of Modern Western wars (*gerebantur circa* A.D. 1848–71). The beneficiaries from this aftermath of the General War of A.D. 1792–1815 had not, by then, begun to suspect, any more than their English 'opposite numbers' had, that the Modern Age of Western history had been wound up only to inaugurate a post-Modern Age pregnant with imminent experiences that were to be at least as tragic as any tragedies yet on record. At the close of the nineteenth century even a German middle class, that was then still permitting itself to indulge in criminally irresponsible day-dreams of more *frisch fröhlich* six-weeks' wars, was of the same mind as its North American and English 'opposite numbers' in its workaday sober senses. In these three provinces of a post-Modern Western World an unprecedentedly prosperous and comfortable Western middle class was taking it as a matter of course that the end of one age of one civilization's history was the end of History itself—at least so far as they and their kind were concerned. They were imagining that, for their benefit, a sane, safe, satisfactory Modern Life had miraculously come to stay as a timeless present. 'History is now at an end' was the inaudible slogan of the celebrations of Queen Victoria's Diamond Jubilee in A.D. 1897, which made a vivid and lasting impression upon the present writer's childish imagination; and 'this history is therefore final' was the invisible motto on the title-page of a topical publication—*Sixty Years a Queen*[2]—which was the same child's earliest source-

---

[1] Sellar, W. C., and Yeatman, R. J.: *1066 and All That* (London 1930, Methuen), p. viii.
[2] Maxwell, Bart., Sir H.: *Sixty Years a Queen* (London [1897], Harmsworth).

book of Western history in the nineteenth century. The assumption that the final product of those sixty years A.D. 1837–97 had come to stay was patently contrary to reason, considering that the pictures with which the text of *Sixty Years a Queen* was copiously illustrated presented a fascinatingly fast-moving pageant of change in every department of life, from Technology to Dress, in which change could clothe itself in visual form. In A.D. 1952 it was manifest in retrospect, even to the dullest eye, that this visual evidence had portended, not a perpetuation of the fleeting circumstances of late-nineteenth-century English middle-class life, but a revolutionary transformation of the ephemeral Victorian scene along the grim lines actually followed by the course of History within the next half-century. An oracular foreboding of the future was, indeed, uttered at the time by the Subconscious Psyche through an incongruous poetic medium. Yet Rudyard Kipling's *Recessional* made little impression on the contemporaries of a Late Victorian poet who had found himself writing these ominous lines at an imperious Muse's dictation. In the United Kingdom, as in Germany and in the Northern United States, the complacency of a post-Modern Western bourgeoisie remained unshaken till the outbreak of the first post-Modern general war in A.D. 1914.

English middle-class Conservatives for whom the Millennium had already arrived, and English middle-class Liberals for whom it lay only just round the corner, were, of course, aware that the English working class's share in the middle class's economic prosperity was shockingly small, and that British subjects in most of the colonies and dependencies of the United Kingdom were not enjoying a self-government that was the privilege of their fellow subjects in the United Kingdom itself and in a few other dominions of the British Crown; but these political and economic inequalities were discounted by Liberals as being something remediable and by Conservatives as being something inevitable. Citizens of the United States at the North were similarly aware, for their part, that their own economic prosperity was not shared by their fellow-citizens at the South, and that the fathers of these Southern contemporaries of theirs had seceded from the Union and had been brought back into it only by the *force majeure* of the North's crushing victory over the South in a terrible civil war. Citizens of the German Reich were aware that the inhabitants of a 'Reichsland' annexed from France after her crushing defeat in the Franco-Prussian War of A.D. 1870–1 were still French at heart and that the rest of a French nation which had not yet ceased to be a Great Power was still unreconciled to the amputation of the ceded departments. At the turn of the nineteenth and twentieth centuries France was still entertaining thoughts of a *revanche*, and the subject population in Alsace-Lorraine was still dreaming the same dream of an eventual liberation as other subject populations in Slesvik, Poland, Macedonia, and Ireland. These dissatisfied contemporaries of a sated German, British, and North American bourgeoisie were nursing national grievances and national aspirations which did not permit them to acquiesce in a comfortable belief that 'History' was 'at an end'; indeed they could not have continued, as they did continue, to keep alight the flickering flame of a forlorn hope if they had succumbed to a *Weltan-schauung* which, for them, would have spelled, not security, but despair. Yet their unwavering confidence that a, to them, intolerable established régime must be borne away, sooner or later, by Time's 'ever rolling stream' made little impression on the torpid imagination of 'the Ascendancy'. 'As a sheep before her shearers is dumb, so he openeth not his mouth';[1] and, though 'the Ascendancy' was under a delusion in mistaking for an intimation of consent a silence that was inspired by the watchword 'N'en parlons jamais, y pensons toujours',[2] there was in A.D. 1897 no living man or woman, even among the most sanguine-minded prophets of a nationalist or a socialist revolution, who dreamed that a demand for national self-determination was going to break up the Hapsburg, Hohenzollern, and Romanov empires and the United Kingdom of Great Britain and Ireland within the next twenty-five years, and going to spread, within another twenty-five years, from a few sore spots in Western Europe and in Orthodox Christendom to the uttermost parts of the Old World, or that a demand for social democracy was going to spread from the urban working class in a few precociously industrialized provinces of the Western World to the peasantry of Mexico and China. Gandhi (*natus* A.D. 1869) and Lenin (*natus* A.D. 1870) were then still unknown names; and the word 'Communism' then commemorated a lurid event in the past that had been the last eruption of History's now extinct volcano. This ominous outbreak of savagery in a Parisian underworld in A.D. 1871 was written off by optimistic post-Modern Western minds as an abnormal atavistic reaction to the shock of a startling military disaster, and there was no discernible fear of the recrudescence of a conflagration that had been smothered now for longer than a quarter of a century under a bourgeois Third Republic's wet blanket. In 1897 a Western bourgeois gentilhomme's sleep was not being seriously disturbed by prophetic nightmares.

This irrational faith had been fortified by experience, for the *fin-de-siècle* prosperity of the Western middle class was not a thing of yesterday. In Germany, it is true, the mirage of a golden age had not dawned on the bourgeoisie until A.D. 1871, when the victory of the German states over France and their unification in a Second Reich had been followed by a titanic local outburst of industrial development. There had been a contemporaneous local outburst of Industrialism in the North-Eastern United States after a victory of the North over the South in A.D. 1865 that had re-established and consolidated the Union; but in the United States the Golden Age had been inaugurated by a victory over Great Britain in A.D. 1783 through which the insurgent colonies had won the recognition of their independence; and in the history of Great Britain an inquirer bent on tracing the Golden Age back to its origins would have to look behind the General War of A.D. 1792–1815, which had made a victorious Britain the workshop of the World as well as the ruler of the waves, to 'the Glorious Revolution' of A.D. 1688 and perhaps

---

[1] Isa. liii. 7.
[2] The watchword suggested for the guidance of members of the rising generation in France, on the morrow of her loss of Alsace-Lorraine in A.D. 1871, by a French statesman of an older generation (? Paul Déroulède).

to the Restoration of the Monarchy in A.D. 1660. In the middle-class life of England, at any rate, the entries in Pepys' diary testify to a sense of security, comfort, and prosperity that was perhaps not attained in the middle-class life of the Lowlands of Scotland until after the suppression of the last and boldest Jacobite insurrection in A.D. 1745; and Pepys' incidental and *insouciant* expressions of confidence were deliberately echoed in bolder accents by Gibbon in 'General Observations on the Fall of the Roman Empire in the West'[1] which must have been finally passed for the press at some date in the first quarter of the year 1781,[2] when Gibbon's own country was in what this English historian will have felt to be a serious plight if he was appraising it by his own serene century's exacting standards.[3]

In this parenthesis in *The History of the Decline and Fall of the Roman Empire* Gibbon was inquiring 'whether Europe is still threatened with a repetition of those calamities which formerly oppressed the arms and institutions of Rome', and his conclusion was that the Late Modern Western Society of his day stood in no danger of being destroyed either by domestic civil war or by barbarian invasion. The perpetuation and progressive improvement of her present Golden Age were assured, as Gibbon saw it, by a political constitution which—in contrast to the debilitatingly despotic centralization of political authority in the Hellenic World under a *Pax Romana*—was a felicitous balance between parochial autonomy and oecumenical unity.

'In peace, the progress of knowledge and industry is accelerated by the emulation of so many active rivals;[4] in war, the European forces are exercised by temperate and undecisive contests. . . . It is the duty of a patriot to prefer and promote the exclusive interest and glory of his native country; but a philosopher may be permitted to enlarge his views, and to consider Europe as one great republic, whose various inhabitants have attained almost the same level of politeness and cultivation. The Balance of Power will continue to fluctuate and the prosperity of our own or the neighbouring kingdoms may be alternately exalted or depressed; but these partial events cannot essentially injure our general state of happiness, the system of arts and laws and manners which so advantageously distinguish, above the rest of Mankind, the Europeans and their colonies.'

Gibbon's optimistic appraisal of the Western Civilization's prospects in his day was no mere personal *parti pris*. Among the cultivated minority

---

[1] This passage of Gibbon's work has been quoted already in this Study in III. iii. 311; IV. iv. 148 and 283; V. v. 625, n. 1, and 644. It is so germane to the subject of the present Part of this Study, and at the same time so alien to the outlook of a Western student of History speculating on the prospects of the Western Civilization in A.D. 1952, that it has been reprinted with a running commentary in an annex on pp. 741–57, below.

[2] The first draft for this passage may have been written as early as A.D. 1772. See IV. iv. 148, n. 3, and compare III. iii. 311 and V. v. 644, n. 3.

[3] In the first quarter of the year 1781 Great Britain was at war with France and Spain and Holland, as well as with the Thirteen Colonies; the Northern Powers of Europe were maintaining an unfriendly 'armed neutrality' for which the term 'non-belligerency' had not yet been coined; and in the North American theatre of operations a campaign was about to open which was to decide the outcome of the war disastrously for the British cause.

[4] Compare the passage in Hume's essay *Of the Rise and Progress of the Arts and Sciences* quoted in II. i. 473–4, together with the references ibid., p. 474, n. 1, to variations on the same theme by Turgot, Eduard Meyer, and J. W. Headlam-Morley.—A.J.T.

in an eighteenth-century Western World there was a consensus in this sense, and the very passage of Gibbon's general observations that has just been quoted may have been a half-conscious echo of a kindred passage in Turgot's *Second Discours*, delivered at the Sorbonne on the 11th September, 1750, *sur les Avantages que l'Établissement du Christianisme a procurés au Genre Humain*.

'Tout se rapproche peu à peu de l'équilibre, et prend à la longue une situation plus fixe et plus tranquille. L'ambition, en formant les grands états des débris d'une foule de petits, met elle-même des bornes à ses ravages; la guerre ne désole plus que les frontières des empires; les villes et les campagnes commencent à respirer dans le sein de la paix; les liens de la société unissent un plus grand nombre d'hommes; la communication des lumières devient plus prompte et plus étendue; et les arts, les sciences, les mœurs avancent d'un pas plus rapide dans leur progrès. Ainsi que les tempêtes qui ont agité les flots de la mer, les maux inséparables des révolutions disparaissent: le bien reste, et l'humanité se perfectionne.'[1]

As for Gibbon's optimism, this was so robust that it inveigled a temperamentally sceptical eighteenth-century mind into committing itself to a credulous declaration of faith in the perpetual progress, not merely of the Western Civilization, but of Civilization in general.

'Since the first discovery of the arts, war, commerce, and religious zeal have diffused among the savages of the Old and New World those inestimable gifts: they have been successively propagated; they can never be lost. We may therefore acquiesce in the pleasing conclusion that every age of the World has increased and still increases the real wealth, the happiness, the knowledge, and perhaps the virtue, of the Human Race.'

The history of the decline and fall of the Roman Empire had been the last chapter in the history of the breakdown and disintegration of the Hellenic Civilization,[2] and this disaster that had swept away an imposing society had been within the knowledge of post-Hellenic Western Man ever since the first shoots of a new civilization, affiliated to the defunct Hellenic Society, had begun to sprout among the rubble of the fallen empire's ruins at the turn of the seventh and eighth centuries of the Christian Era. Gibbon had found the subject for a monumental work in this débâcle of a universal state which was also the débâcle of the culture which that oecumenical body politic had incapsulated; and, in the first paragraph of his first chapter, he had described it as 'a revolution which will ever be remembered, and is still felt by the nations of the Earth'. Can one contemplate a skull without being reminded of his own mortality? To a Western student of History in A.D. 1952 it was not at all surprising that Gibbon's subject should have impelled him to inquire whether his own Western Society might not be in danger of being overtaken, in its turn, by an antecedent Hellenic Society's fate. From a mid-twentieth-century Western angle of vision it did, however, appear amazing that, when Gibbon had once faced this question, he should have answered it, in transparent good faith, in the extravagantly optimistic terms of the sentences above quoted.

[1] Turgot, A. R. J.: *Œuvres* (Paris 1844, Guillaumin, 2 vols.), vol. ii, p. 599.
[2] See IV. iv. 58–63.

As the present writer was rereading this passage of Gibbon's history on the 11th December, 1950, his mind's eye conjured up a Late Medieval Florentine picture of saved souls in Heaven leaning lazily over a marble balustrade in order to make their bliss full and perfect by gazing down upon the torments of the damned in Hell; and, among the participants in this Satanic celestial recreation, a dreaming mind's roving glance singled out one figure whose ungainliness would have made it conspicuous, even if the uncouth effect had not been enhanced by an outlandishly un-medieval costume. There, in an uncongenial Dantesque Paradise to which he had unwittingly sentenced himself by embracing the irrational belief that 'History' was 'now at an end', stood Gibbon, in silver-buckled shoes, knee-breeches, tie-wig, and tricorne, looking down on wretched creatures, born under a different star, who had been floundering in the turbid waters of History in days before the flow of Time's 'ever rolling stream' had been cut off, for the benefit of the eighteenth-century English historian and his kind, by the advent of their secular Millennium in A.D. 1688.

In a pre-Gibbonian Early Modern Age a renaissance of Hellenic arts and letters had not been able to prevent an obstinately fanatical religious enthusiasm from beheading a King of England in A.D. 1649 or from defenestrating a Caesarean Majesty's envoys in A.D. 1618, or from celebrating Saint Bartholomew's Day, A.D. 1572, by a massacre of the adherents of one of two rival sects. In a pre-Modern 'Gothic Age'—into which Gibbon's historical vision ran together the Western 'Middle Ages' (*currebant* A.D. 1075–1475) and the Western 'Dark Ages' (*currebant* A.D. 675–1075) and a post-Hellenic social interregnum (*currebat* A.D. 375–675)—the human werewolf's inveterate crimes, follies, and misfortunes[1] had not even been relieved by a renascent gleam of intellectual and aesthetic light. That tale of eleven bestial centuries had been told off under the joint reign of Barbarism and Religion, whose triumph had been Gibbon's theme;[2] and, for two centuries after the official deposition of Barbarism by fifteenth-century Italian Hellenists, Religion had not only remained on the throne herself but had contrived to serve as a most effective deputy for her nominally dethroned colleague. Thus the history of the decline and fall of the Roman Empire—which Gibbon had pronounced to be 'the greatest, perhaps, and most awful scene in the history of Mankind'[3]—had been followed by no less than thirteen centuries, all told, in which History had persistently run true to her Gibbonian type; and then suddenly, rather less than a hundred years before the time at which Gibbon was writing, we are invited to believe that the noisome flow had inexplicably come to a halt and had left the historian and his contemporaries securely high and dry.

'God, I thank Thee that I am not as other men are.'[4] Gibbon's implicit faith in the uniqueness of his own advantageously distinguished generation's destiny is a classic example of the egocentric illusion;[5] and we are

---

[1] See Gibbon, E.: *The History of the Decline and Fall of the Roman Empire*, chap. iii (an echo of Bayle, P.: *Dictionnaire*, 4th ed. (Rotterdam 1720, Bohm, 4 vols.), iii. 1899 b).
[2] See Gibbon, op. cit., chap. lxxi.
[3] Ibid., chap. lxxi, in the first sentence of the last paragraph of this last chapter of the whole work.   [4] Luke xviii. 11.   [5] See I. i. 159.

left wondering how an eighteenth-century philosopher who was a merciless critic of 'Gothic' credulity could ever have come to harbour so incredible a belief as this. The answer must be that a conventional Christian *Weltanschauung* in Bossuet's vein, which Gibbon had repudiated on the level of his consciousness, had taken its revenge upon him by disappearing underground in order to evolve a secularized caricature of itself out of the sump of an outraged Subconscious Psyche.

This irrational eighteenth-century complacency about the present state and future prospects of a latter-day Western Society was not easily disturbed, though History lost no time in retorting to Gibbon's pontifical sentence of expulsion by recurring as inconscionably as Nature herself.[1] Gibbon had fallen into the naïve observational error of mistaking for the Millennium a spell of low ideological temperature (*durabat circa* A.D. 1660–1792) between two paroxysms of savage fratricidal warfare, owing to the lucky accident that his *magnum opus* happened to have been on the stocks when this low temperature had been at its nadir. The twenty years[2] (*circa* 1768–87) during which he had been writing *The History of the Decline and Fall of the Roman Empire* had elapsed within the lull (*durabat* A.D. 1763–92) between the martial aftermath of one general war—the most temperate and undecisive contest of its kind in Modern Western history—and the onset of another general war into which the newly kindled fire of Democracy was to put an ominously fervent drive.[3] Yet the experience of the General War of A.D. 1792–1815 and its aftermath did not save a latter-day Western bourgeoisie that was born into a subsequent lull (*durabat* A.D. 1871–1914) from hugging Gibbon's error; and, even after the great cataclysm of A.D. 1914–18, Gibbon's eulogy of a Modern Western international anarchy was re-edited in the form of an apologia by a distinguished English historian and public servant of the prediluvian generation, Sir James Headlam-Morley (*vivebat* A.D. 1863–1929)—as witness the following passage in an address delivered by him in April 1924.

'In our analysis of this [Western] culture the first great fact that we will notice is that, though undoubtedly there is a common history and common civilisation for all Western Europe, the people were not joined in any formal political union, nor has the country ever been subjected to one common government. For a moment, indeed, it looked as though Charlemagne would establish his authority over the whole area; that hope, as we know, was to be disappointed; his attempt to create a new empire failed, as all subsequent attempts have failed. Again and again attempts were made by the later Empire, by the rulers of Spain and France, to unite the whole of Western Europe in one great state or empire. Always we find the same thing: the appeal to local patriotism and personal liberty inspires a resistance which breaks down the efforts of every conqueror. And so there has been as a permanent characteristic of Europe that which critics call anarchy; for the absence of a common rule means struggle, fighting, and war, a ceaseless confusion between rival units of government [contending with one another] for territory and predominance.

---

[1] Horace: *Epistulae*, Book I, Ep. x, l. 24.
[2] See *The History of the Decline and Fall of the Roman Empire*, chap. lxxi, *ad finem*.
[3] See IV. iv. 150–1.

'This is a condition which to many is very shocking. Undoubtedly it implies a great expenditure of energy, a great destruction of wealth, at times a great loss of life. There are many, in consequence, who would have preferred to see the gradual establishment of some common government and who, to its disadvantage, contrast the history of Europe with that of Imperial Rome, or—at the present day—of the United States of America. There are many, from the days of Dante onwards, who have longed for that ordered government which might appear to be the true reflex and instrument of Divine Providence. How often do we hear it said that if, on the soil of America, English and Italians and Poles and Ruthenians and Germans and Scandinavians can all live side by side in peace and content-ment, why should they not do so in their original homes?

'I have not to-day to discuss ideals of the future; we are concerned with the past, and all that we have to do is to note the fact that this anarchy, this warfare, this rivalry, existed just at the time when the energies of the Continent were at their highest. Let us note also that the energies of the Mediterranean World—the vital force, artistic spirit, intellectual ingenuity —seem gradually but steadily to have decayed, and that the beginning of the decay coincided with the establishment of a common government.[1] May it not be that the friction and disorder was not in reality merely destruction of energy, but the cause by which the energy was produced?'[2]

It is strange to hear Gibbon's reassuring voice still echoing in an England that was now ringing with the dread sound of an apocalyptic trump. By A.D. 1924, however, the antithetical feeling, expressed in a different reading of the significance of an antecedent Hellenic Civiliza-tion's decline and fall, was already in the ascendant in a stricken Western World; and indeed Gibbon himself had lived to be overtaken by a re-vulsion of feeling about the prospects of the Western Civilization,though he did not live to make any corresponding revision of the text of his 'General Observations'.

At Lausanne, some two years after the night of the 27th June, 1787, on which he had written the closing words of the 'Decline and Fall' in his quiet garden in that peaceful Swiss city, an historian whose unsuspecting ear had failed to catch the undertones of a new ideological enthusiasm in the music of a temperate contest played in A.D. 1775–1783[3] was sud-denly shaken out of his complacency by the outbreak of the French Revolution, and he never recovered from the shock. He had flattered himself that a once rolling stream of Time had been frozen into a per-petual immobility, and now the rebellious waters had burst out again in an unprecedentedly boisterous flood. The horrifying cataclysm had swept away the sandy foundations of the hapless historian's confidence long before it became a menace to the independence and integrity of the Swiss Confederation, and the glimpse of Time's angry sea-horses tossing their white manes above the sky-line of the Jura was something more than Gibbon's nerves could stand. 'Altogether there was too much his-

---

[1] It will be noticed that Headlam-Morley here takes as marking the beginning of the disintegration of the Hellenic Civilization an event which, in this Study, has been taken as marking the second and most notable of the successive rallies by which the course of this disintegration was punctuated.—A.J.T.

[2] J. W. Headlam-Morley: 'The Cultural Unity of Western Europe', in *The New Past and other Essays on the Development of Civilization*, edited by E. H. Carter (Oxford 1925, Blackwell), pp. 88–89.   [3] See IV. iv. 165–7.

tory going on for a historian to feel quite safe.'[1] In May 1793 Gibbon fled from Lausanne for the insular asylum of which he was a native. Racing breathlessly round the wide arc described by the east bank of the Rhine while revolutionary French armies were battering the fortresses guarding the western approaches to the river, the historian-refugee managed to make his way to England via Holland; but his Muse had been silenced and his spirit broken; and he added nothing to his laurels before his death on the 16th January, 1794.

The verdict on an eighteenth-century Western Society's self-satisfaction was

'Woe unto you when all men shall speak well of you; for so did their fathers to the false prophets.'[2]

'I have said: Ye are gods, and all of you are children of the Most High; but ye shall die like men and fall like one of the princes.'[3]

Nemesis was the inevitable consequence of hybris in both Hellenic and Hebraic belief;[4] and the nemesis which a Modern Western Society invited by succumbing to a Gibbonian *Weltanschauung* was the death that had overtaken so many other representatives of the species. Intimations of mortality from experiences of the French Revolution might have been expected to have been the last testament of an English man of letters who had lived to see the French Revolution break out two years after he had finished writing *The History of the Decline and Fall of the Roman Empire*; but Gibbon left the message to be delivered, sixty years after his death, by a French aristocrat of perverse yet, in some points, prescient genius, Count J. A. de Gobineau (*vivebat* A.D. 1816–82),[5] who was born in the year following the close of the General War of A.D. 1792–1815, and who published his *Meisterwerk* late enough to include Western Industrialism as well as Western Democracy in his prophetic indictment, and to find the death's head that was to be his grand *pièce justificative* in the wreckage, not of Rome, but of Tiahuanaco.[6]

'Pour la vapeur et toutes les découvertes industrielles, je dirai aussi, comme de l'imprimerie, que ce sont de grands moyens; j'ajouterai que l'on a vu quelque fois des procédés nés de découvertes scientifiques se perpétuer à l'état de routine, quand le mouvement intellectuel qui les avait fait naître s'était arrêté pour toujours, et avait laissé perdre le secret théorique d'où ces procédés émanaient. Enfin, je rappellerai que le bien-être matériel n'a jamais été qu'une annexe extérieure de la civilisation, et qu'on n'a jamais entendu dire d'une société qu'elle avait vécu uniquement parce qu'elle connaissait les moyens d'aller vite et de se bien vêtir. . . .

'Nous croyons, nous, que notre civilisation ne périra jamais, parce que nous avons l'imprimerie, la vapeur, la poudre à canon. L'imprimerie, qui n'est pas moins connue au Tonquin, dans l'empire d'Annam et au Japon que dans l'Europe actuelle, a-t-elle, par hasard, donné aux peuples de ces contrées une civilisation même passable? . . .

---

[1] Young, G. M.: *Gibbon*, 2nd ed. (London 1948, Hart-Davis), p. 172.
[2] Luke vi. 26.   [3] Ps. lxxxii. 6–7.   [4] See IV. iv. 245–61.
[5] The political background of de Gobineau's racial theory of History has been indicated in II. i. 216–17.
[6] For Tiahuanaco, see the passage of a work by P. A. Means that has been quoted in the present Study in II. i. 322.

'Est-on bien en droit de . . . conclure, comme on le fait généralement avec trop de facilité, que notre civilisation ait la préexcellence sur toutes celles qui ont existé et existent en dehors d'elle? Oui et non. Oui, parce qu'elle doit à la prodigieuse diversité des éléments qui la composent, de reposer sur un esprit puissant de comparaison et d'analyse, qui lui rend plus facile l'appropriation de presque tout; oui, parce que cet éclectisme favorise ses développements dans les sens les plus divers; oui, encore, parce que, grâce aux conseils du génie germanique, trop utilitaire pour être destructeur [sic — A.J.T.], elle s'est fait une moralité dont les sages exigences étaient inconnues généralement jusqu'à elle. Mais, si l'on pousse cette idée de son mérite jusqu'à la déclarer supérieure absolument et sans réserve, je dis non, car précisément elle n'excelle en presque rien. . . .

'Toutes les civilisations qui nous ont précédés ont pensé, comme nous, s'être cramponnées au rocher du temps par leurs inoubliables découvertes. Toutes ont cru à leur immortalité. Les familles des Incas, dont les palanquins parcouraient avec rapidité ces admirables chaussées de cinq cents lieues de long qui unissent encore Cuzco à Quito, étaient convaincues certainement de l'éternité de leurs conquêtes. Les siècles, d'un coup d'aile, ont précipité leur empire, à côté de tant d'autres, dans le plus profond du néant.'[1]

In these passages de Gobineau draws from *les ruines*[2] a moral that gives the lie direct to Gibbon's. De Gobineau, however, was an erratic stumbling-block in a primly Philistine Victorian wilderness, and his maliciously paradoxical style of delivery was not well calculated to make these tart intimations of mortality carry far in the crassly non-conductive psychic medium of nineteenth-century Western bourgeois feelings. It required a more terrifying portent than the French Revolution, and a sharper stab than a disgruntled French aristocrat's gadfly sting, to produce an outright inversion of Western feelings about the Western Civilization's prospects. A French voice intoning a palinode to Gibbon's paean in Western ears that were at last attuned to receive this solemn warning was not to be heard before the morrow of the General War of A.D. 1914–18. The first effective counterblast to Gibbon's 'Observations' was an elegy from the pen of Paul Valéry that was first published in the spring of A.D. 1919 in an English translation.

'Nous autres, civilisations, nous savons maintenant que nous sommes mortelles.

'Nous avions entendu parler de mondes disparus tout entiers, d'empires coulés à pic avec tous leurs hommes et tous leurs engins; descendus au fond inexplorable des siècles avec leurs dieux et leurs lois, leurs académies et leurs sciences pures et appliquées, avec leurs grammaires, leurs dictionnaires, leurs classiques, leurs romantiques et leurs symbolistes, leurs critiques et les critiques de leurs critiques. Nous savions bien que toute la terre apparente est faite de cendre, que la cendre signifie quelque chose. Nous apercevions à travers l'épaisseur de l'histoire les fantômes d'immenses navires qui furent chargés de richesse et d'esprit. Nous ne pouvions pas les compter. Mais ces naufrages, après tout, n'étaient pas notre affaire. *Elam, Ninive, Babylone* étaient de beaux noms vagues, et la ruine totale de ces mondes avait aussi peu de signification pour nous que leur existence

---

[1] de Gobineau, le Comte J. A.: *Essai sur l'Inégalité des Races Humaines* (Paris 1853–5, Firmin-Didot, 4 vols.), vol. i, pp. 281, 276, 170, 281.
[2] Volney, C. F. C. de: *Les Ruines* (Paris 1791, Desenne).

même. Mais *France, Angleterre, Russie* . . . ce seraient aussi de beaux noms. *Lusitania* aussi est un beau nom. Et nous voyons maintenant que l'abîme de l'histoire est assez grand pour tout le monde. Nous sentons qu'une civilisation a la même fragilité qu'une vie. Les circonstances qui enverraient les œuvres de Keats et celles de Baudelaire rejoindre les œuvres de Ménandre ne sont plus du tout inconcevables; elles sont dans les journaux.'[1]

In chastened Western eyes, from which the scales had now fallen, the first vision of Reality was a recognition of the Western Civilization's mortality;[2] but the tardy dawning of enlightenment through suffering did not stop here; and the second vision was a conviction of sin which was a still more shattering spiritual experience than the recognition of mortality.

'Ce n'est pas tout. La brûlante leçon est plus complète encore. Il n'a pas suffi à notre génération d'apprendre par sa propre expérience comment les plus belles choses et les plus antiques et les plus formidables et les mieux ordonnées sont périssables *par accident*; elle a vu, dans l'ordre de la pensée, du sens commun et du sentiment, se produire des phéno-

---

[1] Valéry, Paul: 'La Crise de l'Esprit', in *Variété* (Paris 1924, Gallimard, Éditions de la Nouvelle Revue Française), pp. 11–12. The two letters composing this essay were written 'for translation into English' and were first published in the London Journal *The Athenaeum* on the 11th April and the 22nd May, 1919 (No. 4641, pp. 182–4; No. 4644, pp. 279–80).

[2] The present writer received his first intimation of the mortality of the Western Civilization in an experience (mentioned in this Study already in IV. iv. 282) at the south-eastern corner of the Island of Crete, *en route* from Khandrà to Palaíkastro, on the 19th March, 1912. Rounding the southern shoulder of a mountain, he was startled at suddenly finding himself face to face with the ruins of a country house in the Baroque style of architecture. If the date of this experience had been A.D. 1952 instead of being A.D. 1912, probably he would not have felt the same shock; for by A.D. 1952 a deserted and dilapidated seventeenth-century country house was no longer an unimaginable object in the landscape of the writer's native province of the Western World; but in A.D. 1912 every house of the kind in England would have been intact and have been inhabited—as likely as not, by descendants of the country squire who had had the house built for him some two or three hundred years back in the past. What was startling and disturbing for a Western observer in A.D. 1912 was to see a piece of architecture which, in his mental picture of his native country, was associated with the living world of his own generation standing here in Crete as starkly dead and deserted as the monuments of an Hellenic architecture at Gortyna and Praesus, and the monuments of a Minoan architecture at Cnossos and Phaestus, that he had been inspecting within the last few days in the course of his journey. This inevitable comparison awakened his imagination to the truth that, on this island, a civilization which was his own, and which on his own island was then still self-confidently alive, was already as dead as the civilizations that had come and gone in earlier generations of this species of society.

Gazing at what, at that date, was so portentous a spectacle for Western eyes, the English traveller realized that this house must have been built, on the eve of the Great Veneto-Ottoman War of Candia (*gerebatur* A.D. 1645–69), by some Venetian country gentleman or official, and that this seventeenth-century Venetian builder must have taken it just as much for granted as his English contemporaries, who were then building other houses in the same style on another island, that his new family mansion would continue to be occupied by his descendants for many generations to come. The Englishman then reflected that a Venetian rule in Crete that had been extinguished by Ottoman arms in A.D. 1669 had by that date been in existence for no less than 457 years—a span of time which, in A.D. 1912, was longer than that of the duration, up to date, of British rule in the oldest of the overseas possessions of the British Crown. The inference was inescapable. If the Venetian Empire had perished, the British Empire could not be immortal; and, if the Western Civilization, in which Great Britain as well as Venice lived and moved and had her being, had become extinct in a former Cretan province of its domain, there could be no province, on any shore of either the Mediterranean or the Atlantic, in which a Westerner would be justified in assuming that his civilization was invested with the incredible privilege of being exempt from the jurisdiction of Death the Leveller.

mènes extraordinaires, des réalisations brusques de paradoxes, des déceptions brutales de l'évidence.

'Je ne citerai qu'un exemple: les grandes vertus des peuples allemands ont engendré plus de maux que l'oisiveté jamais n'a créé de vices. Nous avons vu, de nos yeux vu, le travail consciencieux, l'instruction la plus solide, la discipline et l'application les plus sérieuses, adaptés à d'épouvantables desseins.

'Tant d'horreurs n'auraient pas été possibles sans tant de vertus. Il a fallu, sans doute, beaucoup de science pour tuer tant d'hommes, dissiper tant de biens, anéantir tant de villes en si peu de temps; mais il a fallu non moins de *qualités morales*. Savoir et Devoir, vous êtes donc suspects?'[1]

This keen-eyed castaway, peering down into the depths of Western Man's Subconscious Psyche from a revealing observation-post on the flotsam from a spiritual shipwreck, had anticipated the experience that Thor Heyerdahl and his comrades were to have when they peered down into the depths of the Pacific Ocean between the logs of their balsa-wood raft. This perilously intimate commerce with elemental Nature brought into view deep-sea monsters that had been invisible to the comfortable passengers on board a mechanically propelled Modern Western luxury liner;[2] and Valéry had the imagination to realize that there must be yet more horrifying depths below the depths so far surveyed by eyes receiving only a first lesson in enlightenment through suffering. The inhabitants of London needed the harsher ordeal of a Second World War to transfigure their mood from the hysterical *abandon* of Armistice Day, 1918, to the sober restraint of VE Day, 1945. An observer who, on both days, was out and about in the streets of London, in the neighbourhood of Buckingham Palace and Whitehall, could hardly fail to be struck by the contrast between the temper of a crowd who had jumped to the childish conclusion that they had seen the last of War in their time, and perhaps for all time, and the temper of the same crowd when another twenty-seven years of disillusioning experience had taught them to suspect that, in their time, world wars were not just meaninglessly hideous accidents in a normally rational and benign order of Nature, but were the very stuff of which the thread of contemporary world history was being spun. This lesson, which the Londoners were taking to heart in A.D. 1945, had been learnt by the French man of letters twenty-seven years earlier. At the moment of the sounding of the first cease-fire, Paul Valéry had been aware that he was witnessing the end of an act which was not the end of the tragedy—as he testifies in the following exordium of an address delivered by him at Zürich on the 15th November, 1922.

'L'orage vient de finir, et cependant nous sommes inquiets, anxieux, comme si l'orage allait éclater.

'Presque toutes les choses humaines demeurent dans une terrible incertitude. Nous considérons ce qui a disparu, nous sommes presque détruits par ce qui est détruit; nous ne savons pas ce qui va naître, et nous pouvons raisonnablement le craindre. Nous espérons vaguement, nous redoutons précisément; nos craintes sont infiniment plus précises que nos espérances;

---

[1] Valéry, op. cit., pp. 12–13.
[2] See Heyerdahl, Thor: *Kon-Tiki, Across the Pacific by Raft* (Chicago 1950, Rand McNally), p. 117, quoted on pp. 398–9, above.

nous confessons que la douceur de vivre est derrière nous, que l'abondance est derrière nous, mais le désarroi et le doute sont en nous et avec nous. Il n'y a pas de tête pensante, si sagace, si instruite qu'on la suppose, qui puisse se flatter de dominer ce malaise, d'échapper à cette impression de ténèbres, de mesurer la durée probable de cette période de troubles dans les échanges vitaux de l'humanité.

'Nous sommes une génération très infortunée à laquelle est échu de voir coïncider le moment de son passage dans la vie avec l'arrivée de ces grands et effrayants événements dont la résonance emplira toute notre vie.'[1]

In truth, the entr'acte during which these words of foreboding were written was to be followed by a second act of a post-Modern Western tragedy in which German virtues were to be the agents of far worse German wickedness than the worst that had come into action in the years A.D. 1914–18. The atrocities committed in hot blood by the armies of the Second Reich on the war-path through an invaded Belgium whose neutrality Germany had pledged herself to respect were to be eclipsed by the enormity of the cold-blooded atrocities that were to be perpetrated by Nazi gangsters on a home front, while the moral shock to Western feelings was to be in inverse ratio to the ghastliness of the crimes. Western consciences which in A.D. 1914 had still been tender enough to be startled and outraged had become too numb, twenty and thirty years later, for horror to keep pace with familiarity. Yet, where *saeva indignatio*[2] fell out of the race, intellectual integrity could still keep in the running, and this virginal virtue of the Human Spirit testified that, in bringing in a well-deserved verdict of 'guilty' against German prisoners at the bar of Divine Justice, the rest of the Western World was proclaiming its own guilt in the same breath; for, when a non-German majority of a Western community had done its best to clear itself of complicity in German crimes by making the most of the German people's peculiar aberrations from the main path of the Western Civilization's moral and political progress in the Modern Age, these non-German Westerners could not deny, in the last resort, that those horrifyingly aberrant Germans were still bone of their bones and flesh of their flesh.[3] A Western nation which, for good or evil, had played so central a part in Western history, since the first emergence of a nascent Western Civilization out of a post-Hellenic interregnum, could hardly have committed these flagrant crimes if the same criminality had not been festering foully below the surface of life in the Western World's non-German provinces. The twentieth-century German psyche was like one of those convex mirrors in which a gazer learns to read the character printed on his own countenance through seeing the salient features exaggerated in a revealing caricature. If a twentieth-century Germany was a monster, then, by the same token, a twentieth-century Western Civilization was

[1] Valéry, Paul: Extrait d'une conférence donnée à l'université de Zurich le 15 Novembre 1922, reprinted in *Variété*, pp. 33–34. See also Bridges, Robert: *The Testament of Beauty*, Book II, ll. 954 to the end, especially the last ten lines, recording the poet's feelings, charged with 'a profounder fear', 'amid the flimsy joy of the uproarious city'.
[2] 'Ubi saeva indignatio ulterius cor lacerare nequit' (Dean Swift's anticipatory epitaph on himself).   [3] Gen. ii. 23.

a Frankenstein guilty of having been the author of this German monster's being. There, in this monstrous exhibition of a Germany running amok, went France, England, and America likewise, but for the Grace of God —and not one of them could be sure of being saved when their sister Germany had been lost.

Thus already in A.D. 1922, and *a fortiori* in A.D. 1952, when the paroxysm by which the West had been seized in A.D. 1914 was another thirty years older, it was manifest that the West's direst malady was Sin and not Mortality.

'On peut dire que toutes les choses essentielles de ce monde ont été affectées par la guerre. . . . L'usure a dévoré quelque chose de plus profond que les parties renouvables de l'être. Vous savez quel trouble est celui de l'économie générale, celui de la politique des États, celui de la vie même des individus: la gêne, l'hésitation, l'appréhension universelles. *Mais parmi toutes ces choses blessées est l'esprit*. L'Esprit est en vérité cruelle-ment atteint; il se plaint dans le cœur des hommes de l'esprit et se juge tristement. Il doute profondément de soi-même.[1] . . . L'oscillation du navire a été si forte que les lampes les mieux suspendues se sont à la fin renversées.[2]

'Ainsi la Persépolis spirituelle n'est pas moins ravagée que la Suse matérielle. Tout ne s'est pas perdu, mais tout s'est senti périr.'[3]

This note of interrogation, on which a French man of letters con-cluded an inquiry into the prospects of the Western Civilization on the morrow of the first of the general wars that a Westernizing World in-flicted on itself in its post-Modern Age, was presented in a challenging visual form by a contemporary English caricaturist whose sardonic pictorial treatment of the same theme was not less effective than Paul Valéry's elegiac prose in bringing out an inherent tragedy.

In a serial triptych exhibited in London early in the inter-war period A.D. 1919–39, Max Beerbohm depicted, in his inimitable style, his notion of the Eighteenth, Nineteenth, and Twentieth Centuries' divers con-ceptions of their approaching successors.

In the first cartoon in the series, the Eighteenth Century, in the guise of a faultlessly frizzed and powdered man of the world, is looking down quizzically at the Nineteenth Century in the guise of a raw young man who is unable to hide his embarrassment under his disdainful senior's disgusted scrutiny. According to the Eighteenth Century's Gibbonian philosophy, History ought, of course, to have culminated in this Golden Age's unsurpassable self. The very suggestion that this definitive century might have a successor is a most offensive imputation upon its claim to have found and quaffed the elixir of immortality; and the present young pretender to a no longer open succession has added insult to injury by presenting himself as a figure of fun whose uncouthness is not a good joke when judged by eighteenth-century standards of good taste.

In terms of Sinic imagery with which we have made ourselves familiar in this Study, the Eighteenth Century is striking in this first cartoon the wry attitude of a complacently established Yin-state towards a diffidently

[1] Valéry, Paul: lecture of the 15th November, 1922, in *Variété*, p. 34.
[2] Valéry, Paul: 'La Crise de l'Esprit', in *Variété*, p. 16.   [3] Ibid., p. 13.

approaching Yang-activity. In the second cartoon the Nineteenth Century—here portrayed as a portly business man in Victorian dress whose rotundity and rubicundity give the measure of his prosperity—is shown beaming with a fatuous confidence as he pats on the back a still more rotund and rubicund reproduction of himself, attired in the self-same Victorian trousers, frock coat, and top hat; and in this mid-way tableau of the three a Sinic eye would no doubt see a picture of the Yang-activity no longer diffident and apologetic but flushed with an exhilarating sense of boundless achievement. The crack-brained inventor of a chimaerical steam-engine has justified his hopes, beyond his own wildest dreams, by getting up a hitherto unimaginably powerful head of steam. He has exploded a wizened Eighteenth Century's illusion of an already attained static perfection in order to substitute for this a dynamic ideal of perfectibility to be approached through a perhaps endless number of bigger and better editions of the sanguine Nineteenth Century itself.

In the third of the three cartoons, by contrast with the other two, there is only one figure on the stage on which the tragedy of Western history is being played out; and this solitary actor is an emaciated young man in a twentieth-century suit of clothes and with one arm in a sling. His clothes are of so dark a hue that you would take him to be in mourning, and the sombreness of his dress is matched by the obscurity of the prospect ahead of him. He is facing a curtain of night whose blackness is relieved only by the pale glimmer of an enormous question-mark; and this symbol of uncertainty, on which the wistful young man's apprehensive eyes are riveted, occupies the place where the spectator's eye looks to find the missing second living performer.

What is the question that is tormenting this tragic Twentieth Century that has just come through the shattering experience of being blown up in early manhood by a terrific explosion of the Nineteenth Century's recklessly over-heated boilers? Is he saying to himself that he, for his part, cannot even profess to have any notion of what a Twenty-First Century is going to be like? Or is he, perhaps, wondering whether he can even look forward to having any successor of any kind? A prospect which a Gibbonian Eighteenth Century has taken as an insufferable insult would be taken by a Valérian Twentieth Century as a comforting assurance; but, in venturing to consider this reassuring possibility, is not he (the unhappy questioner asks himself) indulging in a vice of 'wishful thinking' which has come to be rated a mortal sin in a disillusioned century's recension of the Decalogue? Is it not far more probable that a second and a third explosion will have blown the coffin-ship *Hesperus* and all her crew to pieces long before the arrival of New Year's Day, A.D. 2001, can give the signal for the next change of the watch?

In these two identical portrayals of a Western World's outlook on the morrow of the War of A.D. 1914–18, Max Beerbohm and Paul Valéry are giving as faithfully accurate a picture of the same world's outlook on the morrow of the War of A.D. 1939–45 as if the draughtsman had reined in his pencil, and the writer his pen, till he had lived through a second world war in one lifetime and had survived to witness the making and dropping of an atomic bomb.

If, however, we find this consensus between Valéry and Beerbohm impressive, what are we to make of it when Valéry and Gibbon, so far from speaking with one voice, declaim to us in irreconcilably discordant accents? When prophets disagree, are we to give credit to either of their opposing voices? The common-sense answer is that prophets talk the language of feeling, and that neither of the two antithetical attitudes which a Gibbon and a Valéry respectively represent is warranted by the facts. Gibbon's belief that, in his generation, the Western World had extricated itself, once for all, from the flow of History was decisively refuted, as we have seen, by revolutionary events that Gibbon himself lived to witness; but Gibbon's signal discomfiture is no evidence that an opposite appraisal of the Western Civilization's prospects is bound to prove correct. The symbol which a stricken Twentieth Century sees glimmering through the darkness ahead is not a skull-and-crossbones; it is a question-mark; and, though this cautionary signal will rightly give pause to a wayfarer who has been allowing himself to expect the light ahead of him to show green, the colour of the light that he is actually being shown is neither this beckoning green nor a forbidding red, but is a cryptically neutral yellow. Signs and portents which are good evidence that the wayfarer is in danger are no evidence at all that he is doomed to come to grief.

The truth is that Valéry's pessimism and Gibbon's optimism are, both alike, rationalizations of feelings that are irrationally subjective.

The only rational ground for Gibbon's complacent outlook was the ephemeral experience—out of date within Gibbon's own lifetime—of an exceptional spell of peace in the course of an exceptionally temperate passage of Modern Western history; but, if we were to try to account for Gibbon's complacency by seeing in it a rational inference from experience, we should hardly have begun to explain it. The deeper explanation of Gibbon's mood is to be found, not in any process of reasoning, but in an irrational egocentric illusion; and this most fantastic of all freaks of Maya is of course no peculiar aberration of one eighteenth-century Western philosopher's mentality.

The egocentric illusion has always beset every living organism in which an ego has ever asserted itself. In an earlier context we have made a survey of the breakdowns which human creatures, institutions, techniques, and ideals have brought upon themselves by the sin of self-idolization;[1] and we have observed[2] that there has never been a human personality, community, or society that has not been tempted to commit the fatuous impiety of trying to put itself in the place of its Creator by casting itself for the role of being 'the Chosen People' and 'the Heir of the World'.[3] The most damning characteristic of this Original Sin of Human Nature is its aptness to vary in the degree of its virulence in inverse ratio to the measure of any rational justification for succumbing to it. Self-idolization is most flagrantly in evidence, not as a self-

---

[1] See IV. iv. 261–465. [2] See IV. iv. 245–61.
[3] Rom. iv. 13.

adjudicated reward for success, but as a self-exculpating compensation for failure. For example, in encounters between divers civilizations, the party that is the more apt to fall into the self-hypnotization of Narcissus is the assaulted party, not the assailant. This mirage is the inspiration of a Zealotism[1] that is an assaulted party's negative reaction; and the same baneful vice of self-worship manifests itself in Tithonian universal states,[2] in petrified civilizations,[3] in the fossils of extinct civilizations,[4] in arrested civilizations,[5] and in primitive societies in their Yin-state.[6]

Such extreme manifestations of egocentricity are so many attempts to find escape in an inner asylum from an external reality with which the ego has failed to cope; and the most extreme manifestation of all is a Racialism which dreams of securing an automatic and inalienable salvation through the imaginary spiritual virtue of some particular physical make-up.[7] We can still say 'We have Abraham'—or Arminius—'to our father'[8] when we have no other word of hope or justification left; and this plea is, in fact, the last resort of spiritual bankrupts. Here, in self-esteem's last ditch, Zionists and National-Socialists meet; and here a de Gobineau rubs shoulders with a Gibbon; for the same ubiquitous ego-centric illusion is the common ground for the pessimism of a nineteenth-century French aristocrat who despairs of a Western Civilization that has bred out or killed out his own incomparable Nordic Race, and for the optimism of an eighteenth-century English man of letters who believes in the prospects of a Western Civilization that has culminated in his day in his own incomparably polite society. An illusion that captivates such incongruously mixed company must spring from an Original Sin common to all Human Nature, and not from any common element in the allegedly objective facts on which the rival claimants to a unique pre-eminence have sought to base their mutually incompatible pretensions.

Another indication that Gibbon's optimism about the prospects of the Western Civilization was not grounded in any rational appreciation of contemporary Western experience is the significant fact that the same experience has moved other Western participants in it to view the Western World, not as a Paradise Regained which must be, and can be, preserved, but as a City of Destruction from which a faithful remnant must flee before this Gomorrah's jerry-built towers fall about a blindly unrepentant majority's ears. The same landscape may take on irreconcilably different aspects from diametrically opposite standpoints. Where top-dog sees a heaven, under-dog will see a hell; and, in fact, while 'the best of all possible worlds' was being commended to a comfortably placed religious, political, social, and intellectual 'ascendancy' by a Leibnitz and a Gibbon, the Early Modern, Late Modern, and post-Modern chapters of Western history were seeing the same world being denounced, repudiated, and deserted in equal good faith by a long series of

---

[1] See IX. viii. 580–623.
[2] See VI. vii. 47–52.
[3] See I. i. 133–46.
[4] See I. i. 90–92.
[5] See III. iii. 1–111.
[6] See I. i. 179–180 and II. i. 192–3.
[7] See II. i. 207–49.
[8] Matt. iii. 9.

ardent secessionists. The Protestants revolted against a Roman Catholic Church which, in their eyes, had ceased to be *Una Sancta* to become the Scarlet Woman of the Apocalypse.[1] The English shook from their feet the dust[2] of a treacherous continent, and the Americans the dust of a treacherous hemisphere. And, when a Western internal proletariat had become as widespread as the 'capitalist' Western Civilization that, in the Communists' indictment of it, stood accused of having reduced the proletariat to misery, the seceding Communists found in Russia a non-Western base of operations for mounting an attack upon Capitalism in its Western birthplace and citadel. The irreconcilability of these conflicting appreciations of a Western Civilization's value showed that all of them were subjective, and their subjectivity convicted all of them of inconclusiveness.

Pessimism, of course, was no more proof than optimism against the possibility of being refuted by events. If Gibbon lived to see the outbreak of the French Revolution refute his unfounded optimistic conviction that History had come to an end in the eighteenth century, he was only suffering the same fate as his forebears the eleventh-century Western Millenarians,[3] whose no better founded pessimistic conviction that History was coming to an end on the thousandth anniversary of Christ's nativity—or, failing that, at any rate on the thousandth anniversary of the end of His mission on Earth—was no less conclusively refuted within their own lifetime by History's inconsiderate performance of sailing on serenely through each, in turn, of these nicely calculated successive terminal dates.

Nor did History merely insist on continuing to flow beyond the latest term that these Millenarians had prescribed for her. She completed their discomfiture by choosing the very date on which they had predicted that she was to go out of action as her date for opening a new chapter in the growth-phase of these eccentric Millenarian pessimists' own society. An eleventh century of the Christian Era which, in the event, did not bring with it the end of the history of all things, did doubly falsify the Millenarians' gloomy expectations by inaugurating, instead, the opening of a new chapter in the growth of the Western Civilization; and the fresh impetus acquired by this growing civilization in this critical passage of its history was actually comparable, in its vigour and creativity, to the classic flowering of the same civilization some four hundred years later. If it is a commonplace that the fifteenth century of the Christian Era saw the Western World move out of a 'medieval' into a 'modern' stage of its growth, it is no less clear that the eleventh century of Western history witnessed a similar transition to 'the Middle Ages' from 'the Dark Ages'.[4] Yet, in thus conclusively demonstrating the erroneousness of the eleventh-century Western Millenarians' application to their own times of a Primitive Christianity's belief in the imminence of Christ's Second Coming, the course of Western history did not eradicate this traditional expectation from the minds of the confuted Millenarians' descendants. In cultivated Western

[1] Rev. xvii. 3–6.   [2] Luke ix. 5. Cp. Matt. x. 14; Mark vi. 11.
[3] See I. i. 171, n. 1.   [4] See I. i. 171.

minds this belief did not fade out before the seventeenth century; in 'fundamentalist' Western Christian minds it was still alive in the present writer's lifetime.

The pessimist's error of mistaking dawn for nightfall may be rarer than the optimist's error of mistaking sunset for noon; yet the eleventh-century Western Christian Millenarians' misapprehension of the character of the age through which they were living has at least one striking counterpart in the Boeotian poet Hesiod's misapprehension of the prospects of his own Hellenic Civilization in the eighth century B.C. Hesiod believed that the Iron Age into which it had been his fate to be born was a worse age than all previous ages[1] of human history. In his eyes it was an age that was to see Honour and Justice, the slowest of the Gods to despair of Human Nature, at last break off their losing battle against triumphantly aggressive forces of evil and sorrowfully withdraw from the terrestrial arena, leaving human sinners and sufferers to their self-inflicted fate. The iron had entered into this eighth-century Hellenic prophet's soul.[2]

'O would that I had not tarried to live thereafter with the fifth race, but had either died before or had been born after; for now in these latter days is the Race of Iron. Never by day shall they rest from travail and sorrow, and never by night from the hand of the spoiler; and cruel are the cares which the Gods shall give them. The father shall not be of one mind with the children nor the children with the father, nor the guest with the host that receives him, nor friend with friend, nor shall brother cleave to brother as aforetime. Parents shall swiftly age and swiftly be dishonoured, and they shall reproach their children and chide them with cruel words. Wretches that know not the visitation of the Gods! Such as these would not repay their aging parents for their nurture. The righteous man or the good man or he that keeps his oath shall not find favour, but they shall honour rather the doer of wrong and the proud man insolent. Right shall rest in might of hand and Ruth shall be no more. The wicked shall do hurt to his better by use of crookèd words with oath to crown them. All the sons of sorrowful Man shall have Strife for their helpmate—harsh-voiced Strife of hateful countenance, rejoicing in evil.

'And then, at long last, shall those spirits go their way to Olympus from the wide-wayed Earth, with their beautiful faces veiled in white raiment, seeking the company of the immortals, and leaving behind them the company of men—even the spirits of Ruth and Retribution. Pain and grief are the portion that shall be left for mortal men, and there shall be no defence against the evil day.'[3]

The sincerity of Hesiod's cry of anguish is transparent; yet it is manifest in retrospect that Hesiod in the eighth century B.C. was misreading the signs of the times as egregiously as the Millenarians were to misread them in the eleventh century of the Christian Era. Hesiod's announcement of the withdrawal of Astraea was just as wide of the mark as the Millenarians' announcement of the approach of the Last Judgement;

---

[1] The diffraction of a post-Minoan heroic age in Hesiod's retrospective vision of it through two different lenses has been noticed in VIII. viii. 74–78.
[2] 'Ferrum pertransiit animam eius', Psalm cv. 18, as mistranslated in the Vulgate version (where it is numbered civ. 18).
[3] Hesiod: *Works and Days*, ll. 174–201.

for 'the Dark Night of the Soul' is a darkness that is the herald, not of Death, but of Dawn.

Thus feelings prove to be as inconclusive as statistics when we interrogate them as witnesses in an inquiry into the prospects of the Western Civilization; and, now that we have drawn blank in these two preliminary reconnaissances, it is time to have recourse to our well-tried empirical method of investigation.

C. THE TESTIMONY OF THE HISTORIES OF THE CIVILIZATIONS

(I) WESTERN EXPERIENCES WITH NON-WESTERN PRECEDENTS

IN earlier Parts of this Study we have tried to gain some insight into the causes of the breakdowns of civilizations and into the process of their disintegrations by making empirical surveys of relevant historical facts,[1] and in these surveys we have taken a synoptic view of evidence from the histories of all the civilizations known to us, including the Western. At the point which we have now reached in our present inquiry into the prospects of the Western Civilization mid-way through the twentieth century of the Christian Era, it may be useful to recall and review any conspicuous counterparts in Western history of phenomena in the histories of other civilizations which, in those histories, are recognizable symptoms of breakdown and disintegration.

In studying the breakdowns of civilizations, we found that the cause was, in every case, some failure of self-determination, and that, when human beings thus lost control over their own destinies, this social disaster usually turned out to have been the consequence of a moral aberration. A broken-down society, community, or individual would prove to have forfeited a salutary freedom of choice through having fallen into bondage to some idol of its own making. Mid-way through the twentieth century of the Christian Era the Western Society was manifestly given over to the worship of a number of idols that had been the bane of other civilizations in the past; but, among these, one stood out above all the rest, and this was the cult of the institution of Parochial Sovereignty embodied in parochial states that were being worshipped by their respective subjects as very gods[2] and that were demonstrating their demonic power over their devotees by exacting from them human sacrifices of ever greater enormity in cycles of fratricidal wars of a violence that was increasing in a geometrical progression.

This grimly prominent feature of post-Modern Western life was a terrifying portent on two accounts: first because this idolization of

[1] See IV. iv. 7–584; V. v. 15–568; and V. vi. 1–326.
[2] At some date during the latter part of the breathing-space between the general wars of A.D. 1914–18 and A.D. 1939–45, the writer of this Study heard the presiding officer of one of the livery companies of the City of London bear testimony which was convincing, because it was unselfconscious, to the primacy, in his *Weltanschauung*, of one of these tribe-worships. The occasion was a dinner at which the company was entertaining the delegates to an international congress that was in session in London at the time, and the presiding officer had risen to propose the toast 'Church and King'. Having it on his mind that a majority of his guests were foreigners who would not be familiar with an English tribal custom, the president prefaced the toast with an apology and an explanation. No doubt, he said, the order in which he had rehearsed the two institutions that were to be honoured conjointly in the toast that he was about to propose might seem to a foreigner not only quaint but perhaps even positively unseemly. He apologized for abiding, nevertheless, by the traditional order, and explained that he did so because it was the pride of the city companies to be meticulous in preserving antique usages, even when these had become so anachronistic as to be open to misconstruction by the uninitiated.

belligerent parochial sovereign states was the true, though unavowed, religion of a great majority of the inhabitants of the Westernizing World of the day[1] and, secondly, because this false and maleficent religion had been the death of no less than fourteen civilizations for certain, and perhaps of no less than sixteen, out of the twenty-one civilizations that had come into existence during the currency of this species of Society up to date.

Fratricidal warfare of ever increasing violence between parochial sovereign states had been by far the commonest cause of mortality among civilizations of all three generations.[2] In the first generation it had certainly been the destruction of the Sumeric[3] and the Andean[4] Civilization, and probably the destruction of the Minoan[5] as well. In the second generation it had destroyed the Babylonic,[6] the Indic,[7] the Syriac,[8] the Hellenic,[9] the Sinic,[10] the Mexic,[11] and the Yucatec.[12] In the third generation it had destroyed the Orthodox Christian Civilization, both in its main body[13] and in its Russian offshoot;[14] the Far Eastern Civilization in its Japanese offshoot;[15] the Hindu[16] and the Iranic.[17] Of the five remaining known representatives of the species of Society to which the Western Civilization belonged, we may suspect that the Hittite Civilization likewise had brought itself to ruin by fratricidal warfare at home before it had run full tilt against a petrified Egyptiac World and had subsequently succumbed to a barbarian Völkerwanderung;[18] and there were only four foundered civilizations whose evil genius had probably or certainly been an idol of a different clay. The evidence about the breakdown and disintegration of the Mayan Civilization that had been yielded by archaeological exploration so far was negative in the sense that it showed hardly a trace of any ravages of fratricidal warfare;[19] the more abundant evidence about the breakdowns of the Egyptiac Civilization and the Far Eastern Civilization in China indicated that the idol to which these had sacrificed their lives had been, not Parochial Sovereignty asserting itself in fratricidal warfare, but an oecumenical polity—'the Old Kingdom' in the one case[20] and in the other case the Sui and T'ang evocation of a ghost of the Han Empire[21]—which had brought with it the additional incubus of a more and more top-heavy and parasitic bureaucracy. The incubus of a parasitic Nomad institution *in partibus agricolarum*—the slave-ascendancy of the Egyptian Mamlūks[22]—may have been the death of the Arabic Civilization,[23] unless the fate of this society was a solitary instance of assassination by the hand of an alien assailant.[24]

An idol whose cult had thus proved fatal to fourteen or sixteen out of twenty-one representatives of the species of Society to which the Western Civilization belonged manifestly could not be worshipped by its latter-day Western devotees with impunity. This form of collective self-wor-

---

[1] See I. i. 442–5. [2] See V. v. 41–43 and 189. [3] See IV. iv. 64.
[4] See IV. iv. 105. [5] See IV. iv. 64–65. [6] See IV. iv. 101–3.
[7] See IV. iv. 66. [8] See IV. iv. 67–68. [9] See IV. iv. 62–63.
[10] See IV. iv. 65–66. [11] See IV. iv. 105–6. [12] See IV. iv. 105–6.
[13] See IV. iv. 72–73. [14] See IV. iv. 96. [15] See IV. iv. 94.
[16] See IV. iv. 99–100. [17] See IV. iv. 107. [18] See IV. iv. 108–12.
[19] See IV. iv. 108. [20] See I. i. 136–7 and 141–3, and III. iii. 212–15.
[21] See II. ii. 376; III. iii. 449; and VI. vii. 19. [22] See III. iii. 30–31.
[23] See IV. iv. 112. [24] See IV. iv. 113–14.

ship had, in fact, already been the death of a Western city-state cosmos which had disengaged itself from, and forged ahead of, the rest of the Western World in the Medieval Age of Western history.[1] In the unhappy experience of this abortive sub-society within a Western Christian body social, the Venetians' idolization of their own dead collective self from the fifteenth to the nineteenth century of the Christian Era[2] had, as we have seen, been a startlingly close counterpart of the Athenians' idolization of their dead collective self from the fourth century B.C. onwards;[3] and such examples from the history of the disintegration of a Western sub-society were not the only cases of this spiritual malady in the history of the Western World. While the Epimethean stance of Eire[4] might perhaps be discounted on the ground that this was a defensive reaction of a submerged relic of an originally alien Far Western Christian Civilization which was showing in this way its recalcitrance to the Western Civilization's attempt to assimilate it, the reaction of the Virginians and the South Carolinians to their defeat in the Civil War of A.D. 1861–5 in the United States[5] was an indubitable post-Modern Western instance of the Venetian-Athenian attitude; and, while this backward-turned posture was peculiarly incongruous with the forward-looking outlook normally characteristic of pioneers on new ground, the post-Bellum Epimetheanism of 'the Old South' of the United States was not so significant a portent for the prospects of the Western World as a whole as the Epimetheanism that had become rife in France after the General War of A.D. 1914–18 and, to a still greater degree, after the General War of A.D. 1939–45.

Moreover, in the Western World as a whole in the post-Modern chapter of its history, the devastating effects of the idolization of parochial sovereign states had been enhanced by the importation of a demonic 'drive' into the suicidal performances of these tribal gods' votaries. The restraining influence of an oecumenicalism on the ecclesiastical plane which the Western Civilization had inherited from its chrysalis the Western Christian Church had been removed by a lamentable victory of parochialism over oecumenicalism in Western life on this ecclesiastical plane at the transition to the Modern Age from the Middle Ages.[6] The capacity of the parochial sovereign states of a Modern Western World to ruin their common civilization by ruining one another had been enhanced by the importation into their statecraft of an Italian efficiency which had been the unfortunate legacy of a foundering Medieval Western city-state cosmos.[7] The impact of Nationalism upon the historic political map of a Late Modern Western World had imported a new ferocity into the fratricidal wars between Western parochial states by most inexpediently raising the stakes.[8] In the paroxysm of wars fought in the name of Nationalism coupled with some form of political ideology which had begun with the outbreak of the American Revolutionary War in A.D. 1775, the contests could no longer be kept 'temperate and undecisive' because the parochial states of the Western World were now fighting one another

---

[1] See III. iii. 299 and 342–50.
[2] See IV. iv. 274–89.
[3] See IV. iv. 263–74.
[4] See IV. iv. 291–6.
[5] See IV. iv. 289–91.
[6] See IV. iv. 214–22.
[7] See IV. iv. 198–200.
[8] See IV. iv. 185–90.

—as the Sinic parochial states had fought one another in the second and final paroxysm of a Sinic Time of Troubles—for their very existence, and no longer just for an inclination of the Balance of Power that would be too slight to menace the warring society's 'general state of happiness'.[1] The most serious of all these aggravations of an evil which was, at the best, a galloping consumption was, however, the impact of two recently begotten Western demons, Democracy and Industrialism, upon both Parochial Sovereignty[2] and an inter-state warfare[3] that could never be abolished so long as Parochial Sovereignty was permitted to survive.

An Industrial Revolution that had overtaken the Western World in the eighteenth century of the Christian Era was an unmistakable counterpart of the economic revolution that had overtaken the Hellenic World in the sixth century B.C.;[4] and this likeness was ominous inasmuch as the effect of either of these revolutions on the economic plane had been to increase the aggregate productivity of the society in which the revolution had taken place through the expedient of creating a single large-scale economic unit out of the hundreds of small-scale economic units of which the society had previously been composed. Communities that had previously made their living by subsistence farming had now combined to increase their output and their income by learning to produce specialized commodities —not only agricultural but now also industrial—for export in exchange for imports of raw materials and foodstuffs. Parochial communities that had formerly been economically autarkic had thus now become economically interdependent; and even the largest and wealthiest of them could no longer resume its former economic autarky, however keenly it might regret the loss of it, since the penalty would have been a prohibitively precipitous fall from a now customary standard of living (in the material sense of the term).[5] Thus the effect of the Western and the Hellenic economic revolution alike had been to give the society a new structure on the economic plane that was incongruous with its structure on the political plane. On the economic plane the society had now been unified, whereas on the political plane it had continued to be partitioned among a litter of parochial states. This incongruity had

---

[1] Gibbon, E.: 'General Observations on the Fall of the Roman Empire in the West', at the end of chap. xxxviii of *The History of the Decline and Fall of the Roman Empire.*
[2] See IV. iv. 156–85.   [3] See IV. iv. 141–55.
[4] See I. i. 24–25; IV. iv. 200–14; and IX. viii. 429–30.
[5] The progressive integration of the Western World on the economic plane as a result of the Industrial Revolution has been noticed already in another context (pp. 313–14, above). 'Bare as they are and short their span, the annals reveal', not only in the United States but likewise in the World at large, 'a secular trend towards territorial expansion of business relations and a concomitant trend towards economic unity' (Mitchell, W. C.: *Business Cycles and their Setting* (New York 1927 (reprinted 1930), N.B.E.R.,) p. 446. Cp. p. 456). 'The larger the agricultural element in a given nation, the less likely are that nation's business cycles to fit neatly into the international pattern over a long series of years. For two nations with large farming interests are not likely to have closely similar harvest fluctuations year after year' (ibid., p. 448). 'The quiet business forces working toward uniformity of fortunes must be powerful indeed to impress a common pattern upon the course of business cycles in many countries' (ibid., p. 450). 'Undoubtedly a larger proportion of the population' of Great Britain 'felt the impact of the trade cycle on their lives and fortunes in 1910 than in 1790' (Rostow, W. W.: *British Economy of the Nineteenth Century* (Oxford 1948, Clarendon Press), p. 44). We have already cited A. C. Pigou's dictum (in *Industrial Fluctuations*, 2nd ed. (London 1929, Macmillan), p. 11) that, by A.D. 1872, the industrial fluctuations in the economic activity of a Westernizing World had come to be oecumenical in their geographical range.

created a tension of a magnitude proportionate to its own; and the incongruity had been so extreme that the tension had become intolerable.

In the history of the Hellenic Civilization this tension had generated a Time of Troubles manifesting itself in two paroxysms of inter-state warfare, of which the second had been more devastating than the first;[1] and the idolization of the ephemeral institution of the city-state had died so hard in Hellenic hearts[2] that the troubles had lasted for four hundred years—from the outbreak of the Great Atheno-Peloponnesian War in 431 B.C. until the establishment of a *Pax Augusta* in 31 B.C.—before the rending tension had been relieved at last by a political revolution that had brought the political map of the Hellenic World into tardy conformity with a unitary economic map which had been in existence by then for at least five hundred years. The establishment of an Hellenic universal state to serve as a political framework for an Hellenic oecumenical economy had been achieved too late to save the life of the Hellenic Society; it had availed merely to bring it a temporary reprieve; and the expiry of this four-hundred-years-long period of grace had been the signal for the demise of a society which had inflicted mortal wounds on itself at least as early as the onset of the second paroxysm of its Time of Troubles in the Hannibalic War (*gerebatur* 218–201 B.C.). What was going to be the effect of the same tension, arising from the same incongruity, in the life of a Western World which, since the Industrial Revolution, had become, in its turn, a unity on the economic plane while continuing to be partitioned on the political plane among a litter of still, and indeed perhaps now more than ever, fanatically worshipped parochial sovereign states? Would the Western World, unlike the Hellenic World, succeed in arriving at some less belated and less radical solution of this problem than the *ultima ratio* of abolishing fratricidal warfare by abolishing the war-generating institution of Parochial Sovereignty through a liquidation of all existing parochial states and the establishment of a single universal state in their stead?

One discouraging symptom in Modern Western history had been the emergence there, first in Prussia and latterly in Germany at large, of a militarism that had been deadly in the histories of other civilizations. Militarism was a portentous moral evil because it was an abnormal one. The millions of human beings who had sacrificed wealth, happiness, and life itself in fighting the battles of some parochial state, whose subjects they had happened to be, had mostly gone to war, not because they had delighted in War for its own sake, but because they had more or less ruefully resigned themselves to war-making as an evil necessary for the preservation of another evil—Parochial Sovereignty—to which they had perversely said 'Be thou my good'.[3] In contrast to this normal negative human attitude towards the evil of War, militarism was a state of mind in which War had ceased to be looked upon merely as a means of serving an idolized state and had become an idol and an end in itself; and this cult of War was manifestly something contrary to Human Nature.

On this showing, it was disquieting for a Western historian to recall in

[1] See V. vi. 287–91. [2] See IV. iv. 303–20.
[3] Milton: *Paradise Lost*, Book IV, l. 110.

A.D. 1952 that a Modern Western militarism in its pristine Prussian form had made its first appearance—*regnantibus Frederico Gulielmo I et Frederico II*, A.D. 1713–86—in an age in which, of all ages of latter-day Western history, the evil of War had been at its minimum.[1] Yet this Western militarism, as it had been practised in Prussia in the days of Frederick the Great and even in the darker days of Bismarck, had been, like the Hellenic militarism practised at Sparta in the days of Cleomenes I, a vice that had still been kept within bounds by a surviving respect for at least some of a civilization's traditional conventions. The more devastating militarism of a post-Bismarckian Prussia-Germany which had brought upon the Western World the catastrophe of A.D. 1914–18 had been a Western counterpart of a Spartan spirit, exacerbated by the Great Atheno-Peloponnesian War of 431–404 B.C., which had found its nemesis in 371 B.C. at Leuctra, or of a Babylonic militarism practised in Assyria in the days of Asshurnazirpal II and Shalmaneser III (*regnabant* 883–824 B.C.). As for the mad-dog militarism of a National-Socialist Germany, this could only be compared with the last phase of the *furor Assyriacus*, after its temperature had been raised to the third degree by Tiglath-Pileser III (*regnabat* 746–727 B.C.).[2] It was true that, in A.D. 1952, it might look as if the fires of Western militarism had at least temporarily burnt themselves out, even in Germany, and at the same date it seemed improbable that even the virus of Russophobia would prove sufficiently inflammatory to kindle the same flame in the traditionally unpropitious atmosphere of the United States. Nevertheless, the fact that, no farther than seven years back, one of the principal nations of the Western World had been still waging an unprovoked war for war's sake, and this with all its might, was a fact of bad augury for the Western Civilization's prospects.

To set against these bad omens on a Western World's horizon in A.D. 1952 there were, on the other hand, certain more auspicious symptoms.

For example, the Epimethean self-worship of Venice and the other *ci-devant* city-states in Italy and Germany had yielded in the end to new allegiances in the course of the three or four generations running from A.D. 1789 to A.D. 1871; and, though at that stage the Venetians had merely exchanged their parochial loyalty to Venice for a parochial loyalty to Italy, and the Lübeckers their loyalty to Lübeck for a loyalty to Germany, the very fact that such old and, in their dotage, apparently hard-set idolatries had at least once been transcended gave some ground for hope that the descendants of those converts from the worship of a city-state to the worship of a nation-state might one day transfer their allegiance to a universal state between whose provinces war would be impracticable. It was also a good sign that, eighty-seven years after the forcible reincorporation of a Southern Confederacy into the United States, the descendants of bellicose Southern secessionists had become reconciled to a political destiny which had been imposed by force of arms upon their great-grandfathers.

Moreover, there was one ancient institution—no less evil than War itself—which the Western Civilization had plucked out and cast from it,

---

[1] See IV. iv. 142–50.   [2] See IV. iv. 473, n. 3.

albeit at the cost of a terrible civil war in one province of the Western World in which a 'peculiar institution' had been obstinately maintained for some thirty years after its abolition in the Western World at large.[1] A Western World which had succeeded in abolishing Slavery in the nineteenth century of the Christian Era might surely take heart from the memory of this unprecedented victory of a Christian ideal in a Western arena as it addressed itself in the twentieth century to Hêraklês' next labour, namely the attempt to abolish the coeval institution of War; for War and Slavery had been twin cancers of Civilization ever since this species of society had first emerged; and the nineteenth-century conquest of one of these two fell social diseases was therefore a good augury for the Western Society's prospects in its twentieth-century campaign against the disease of War.

The abolition of Slavery in a nineteenth-century Western World had also been a particularly notable triumph on two accounts. In the first place Slavery, like War, had been a potent cause of mortality among civilizations in the past. Slavery as an instrument of government and war had conspired with War itself to bring an Ottoman Civilization to grief;[2] Slavery as an instrument of specialization in economic production had similarly conspired with War to bring an Hellenic Civilization to grief during the second paroxysm of its Time of Troubles;[3] and a Modern Western Society's decisive victory over an evil that had thus proved almost as puissant as War in defeating other civilizations in the past was therefore impressive evidence of moral health in a latter-day Western body social. The second reason why the abolition of Slavery in a nineteenth-century Western World was noteworthy was because this evil in this century in this social milieu had been raised to a potency without precedent in any previous chapter of Western history by the impact of the new motive-power of Industrialism. On the cotton plantations in 'the Old South' of the United States, Slavery had been harnessed to the production of a crop supplying the raw material for a mechanized textile industry which was the master craft of Industrialism in that stage of its development. A victory over an ancient social institution into which a youthful Industrialism had put a demonic new 'drive' was a victory that might well be pregnant with future moral triumphs.

Moreover, a Western Society that in A.D. 1952 was still being worsted by War, eighty-seven years after its triumph over Slavery, could take heart from its record on other spiritual battlefields where the issue was still in the balance.

In its response to a challenge presented by the impact of Industrialism on the institution of Private Property,[4] the Western Society had already made some headway in Great Britain, the Scandinavian countries, New Zealand and Australia in forcing a passage between Scylla and Charybdis. The empirical compromises between Free Economic Enterprise and Socialism that were being worked out in those countries in that generation promised on the one hand to steer clear of an untempered economic individualism that would have driven all but a masterful minority to the wall if economic enterprise had been left uncontrolled in an age in which Industrialism had put a demonic 'drive' into it, while on the other hand this homoeopathic inoculation of a disordered body social with a moderate dose of socialism was a prophylactic against the danger of the society's succumbing to a totalitarianism that would have imposed on human beings the social justice of the ant-heap and the beehive at the cost of forcibly depriving them of Man's distinctive birthright of freedom.

In the same generation the Western Society had also been achieving some success in coping with the impact of Democracy upon Education.[1] In throwing open to the majority an intellectual treasure-house which had been a small minority's jealously guarded and oppressively exploited preserve since the dawn of Civilization,[2] the Modern Western spirit of Democracy had given Mankind a new hope at the cost of exposing it to a new danger. The danger lay in the opening which a rudimentary universal education gave for propaganda, and in the skill and unscrupulousness with which this opportunity had been seized by salesmen for advertising their wares and by news agencies, 'pressure groups', political parties, and the public relations departments of firms and governments for 'selling' their policies. The hope lay in the possibility that these exploiters of a semi-educated public would prove unable to 'condition' their victims so thoroughly as to succeed in preventing them from continuing their education; for, if only they could continue it, it might be expected to carry them to a point at which they would begin to become capable of detecting intellectual dishonesty and penalizing intellectual foul play.

Education was a two-edged sword which could be used at will, by the powers that wielded it, either for opening the minds of their fellow human beings to a liberating truth[3] or for subduing them to a cramping dogma. At the time of writing, when this mental strife between Enlightenment and Obscurantism was raging *aequo Marte* in the 'democratic' as well as the 'totalitarian' provinces of a Westernizing World,[4]

---

[1] See IV. iv. 192–8.   [2] See IV. iv. 418–21.   [3] John viii. 32.

[4] The extent to which people's opinion and feelings were being 'conditioned' in the West in the twentieth century of the Christian Era, even in a Western country that boasted of itself that it was democratic, had been brought home to the present writer by an amusing incident at an unofficial international conference convened at Kyoto in the autumn of A.D. 1929 by the Institute of Pacific Relations.

This conference was attended by representatives of a number of countries with frontages on the Pacific Ocean; and, when English-speaking Westerners from the United States, Canada, Australia, New Zealand, and the United Kingdom found themselves sitting round the same table with Chinese and Japanese colleagues, they put their heads together and decided with one accord to improve the shining hour by doing something, out of school, to advance their Oriental colleagues' education in the principles of 'Democracy'. To this end they planned a series of evening meetings at which distinguished 'Anglo-Saxon' speakers were to hold forth to a voluntary class of Oriental neophytes on divers aspects of this beatific Western institution, and they placed 'Public Opinion' at the head of their select list of edifying topics. On the appointed evening their Oriental colleagues courteously presented themselves, the distinguished Anglo-Saxon speaker spoke his lines, and the Anglo-Saxon chairman then called for questions in an intonation suggesting that he expected the response to be a negative one, while the Anglo-Saxon supporters of the chair sat back in a row and relaxed with the air of men who had accomplished a meritorious evening's work. The atmosphere changed, however, from one of drowsy complacency to one of expectant amusement when a little Chinese lady, sitting in the back row, asked permission, not to put a question, but to make a statement. What on earth could a middle-aged headmistress from Changsha, in the far interior of China, have to say?

'During the war', meaning the war of A.D. 1914–18, the little lady began, 'I was living

there was no reason to take it as a foregone conclusion that an insidious Propaganda would win a permanent victory anywhere over an innate Human Intelligence. The impact of Democracy upon Education, however, was not so formidable a challenge to the Spirit of Man as the impact of Civilization, reinforced by the 'drives' of both Democracy and Industrialism, on the Division of Labour and on an indispensable but perilous social drill which we have labelled 'mimesis';[1] yet these, again, were not the battlefields that were likely to prove decisive for the Western Civilization's destiny. The plane on which the decisive spiritual battle was likely to be fought was neither the military nor the political nor the social nor the economic nor the intellectual; for in A.D. 1952 the crucial questions confronting Western Man were all religious.

Had the fanatically positive Judaic, if not the unfanatically negative Indic, higher religions been discredited beyond repair by the incriminating historical record of an intolerance that had given the lie to their professions?[2] Was there any virtue in the religious toleration into which a Western World, disillusioned by the inconclusive savagery of the Wars of Religion, had subsided towards the close of the seventeenth century of the Christian Era, at the opening of a Late Modern Age of Western history?[3] How long would Western souls find it bearable to go on living in an empty, swept, and garnished house?[4] And, now that the discomfort of a spiritual vacuum had tempted them to open the door to such devils as Nationalism and Fascism and Communism, how was their vaunted latter-day conversion to a belief in tolerance likely to stand this test? Toleration had been easy to practise in a lukewarm age of Western history in which all varieties of Western Christianity had lost their former hold on Western hearts and minds, while these had not yet found any alternative objects for their frustrated devotion. Now that they had gone a whoring after other gods,[5] would an eighteenth-century toleration hold its own against a twentieth-century recrudescence of a seventeenth-century fanaticism which, in Gibbon's naïvely optimistic belief, had been exorcized once and for all from the precincts of a 'polite' society? And, even supposing that a fanatical intolerance were to bring upon itself, once again, when harnessed to the service of idolized parochial states, the discredit into which it had eventually fallen when it had raged in the service of warring Western Christian sects, might not this vice even then regain its hold on human hearts and minds once more by

in Blackheath'—and, at the mention of this familiar suburb of London, the Englishmen in the room all woke up with a start. 'I was living in Blackheath,' she went on, 'and travelling to my office in London every morning in a suburban train; so I could observe what newspapers my fellow-travellers were reading, and could listen to their comments on the news of the day. After a few days of this, I found myself able to tell each of them what his views would be before he had opened his mouth. "Now you have been reading *The Daily Mail*," I would say to one of them, "so your opinions on this morning's news will be such and such. You, though, have been reading *The Daily News*, so your opinions will be these". These predictions were fairly simple,' she said, 'so I thought I should like to tell you about this experience of mine, as a small contribution to a study of public opinion—at least, as this is understood in the West.'

This was enough. That same evening, before going to bed, the Anglo-Saxon committee for the education of Orientals in Democracy held an emergency meeting and cancelled the rest of their programme.

[1] See IV. iv. 232–45.
[2] See IV. iv. 222–7.
[3] See IV. iv. 227–8.
[4] Matt. xii. 44. Cp. Luke xi. 25.
[5] Judges ii. 17.

taking service, this time, with an idol standing, not for division, but for unity?

Wanderers in a Western wilderness, astray from their forefathers' One True God, who had been taught by a further bout of disillusioning experience that parochial states, like sectarian churches, were idols whose worship brought not peace but a sword,[1] might be tempted to seize upon a Collective Humanity as an alternative object for idolization.[2] A 'religion of Humanity' which had missed fire in the frigid mould of a Comtian Positivism had set the World ablaze when it had been fired from the canon's mouth of a Marxian Communism. Would a life-and-death struggle for the salvation of souls which Christianity had waged and won in its youth against an Hellenic worship of a Collective Humanity embodied in oecumenical cults of Dea Roma and Divus Caesar have to be fought out again, two thousand years later, against some latter-day embodiment of a worship of the same Leviathan? The Hellenic precedent raised the question without revealing the answer to a mid-twentieth-century inquirer into the Western Civilization's prospects.

If, in our review of Western experiences with non-Western precedents, we now pass on from the symptoms of breakdown to the symptoms of disintegration, we shall recall that, in our analysis of schism in the body social, we found unmistakable traces, in a latter-day Western World, of the epiphany of a dominant minority[3] and of an internal and an external proletariat.[4]

The Western World's external proletariat will make little demand upon our attention; for our general conclusion[5] that the barbarians had played no more than an insignificant part in the histories of the civilizations was conspicuously borne out by the situation on the Western World's anti-barbarian marches at the time of writing.[6] The fate of the surviving barbarians had been sealed, as far back as the seventeenth century of the Christian Era, by the success of two sedentary Powers in encircling a Eurasian Steppe that had been the most devastating source of barbarian eruptions for at least three thousand five hundred years; and, though neither the Russian nor the Manchu Power had been a Western polity, their combined achievement had redounded to the benefit of a Western Civilization that had been expanding all over the *Oikoumenê* thanks to a mastery, not of the Steppe, but of the Ocean. By A.D. 1952 the last surviving enclaves of still recalcitrant barbarians were all manifestly on the verge of being eliminated. By the same date, however, it could already be foreseen that the barbarians would not pass out of existence without leaving their mark on the life of their victorious antagonists.

At the very moment when a Western Society armed by a Western Science was conquering the barbarians in the flesh, Barbarism was taking its revenge by finding its way into the souls of its Western conquerors.[7] A regressive Western Neobarbarism, which, in the breathing-space between a First and a Second World War, had made so disconcerting an epiphany first in Italy and then in Germany,[8] was, of course, morally far

---

[1] Matt. x. 34.   [2] See IV. iv. 300–3.   [3] See V. v. 40–41 and 48–49.
[4] See V. v. 152–94 and 319–37.   [5] See I. i. 58–62 and VIII. viii, *passim.*
[6] See pp. 743–4, below.   [7] See pp. 744–5, below.
[8] See V. v. 334–7.

more evil and politically far more formidable than the relatively innocent pristine Barbarism into whose heritage it had entered; and this evil had not been exorcized from Western souls by the military overthrow of an Italian Fascism and a German National-Socialism; for this perverse Western manifestation of Original Sin was an occupational disease of a semi-educated urban lower middle class that was as ubiquitous as the Western Civilization itself,[1] and there was perhaps no province of the Western World in which this class was not in some danger of succumbing to this malady. In an inter-war Italy and Germany, the heart of the disease had shown itself to be a morbid state of public opinion and feeling that was sufficiently malignant, and at the same time sufficiently widespread, to give an opening in public life for criminal activities. In this odious atmosphere a villain could count on being able to win popularity and power for himself by making preposterously false charges against the innocent, since it was an atmosphere in which the innocent had only to be accused of impiety against the current idols of the market-place to find themselves permanently under a cloud, however conclusively they might have proved their integrity, while the unscrupulous had only to launch such accusations to find themselves the heroes of the hour, even when they had been convicted of having known their charges to be false before they had launched them. In A.D. 1952 a touch of this painfully familiar inter-war Italian and German atmosphere was perceptible in the United States; and, though, in a North American social milieu, this spiritual malaria might be expected to bring about its own cure by stimulating a host of antagonistic spiritual forces to deliver a vigorous counter-attack, it was nevertheless disquieting for all people of good will in a stricken and beleaguered Western Community that such symptoms should have manifested themselves at all in the one Western country that, after a Second World War, still remained capable of serving as the arsenal, citadel, and conning-tower of Democracy in the Western sense of the word.

In the same chapter of Western history a vanishing external proletariat was also leaving its mark on Western life in a more direct and concrete way; for the *ci-devant* barbarians were being eliminated for the most part, not by being physically exterminated, but by being transferred to the ranks of a Western internal proletariat which by this time had come to embrace a great majority of the living generation of Mankind.[2]

The thus forcibly domesticated *ci-devant* barbarians were actually one of the smallest of the contingents of which this vast twentieth-century Western internal proletariat was composed. A far larger quota of the human beings who had been reduced to the status implied in the word 'Natives'[3] by the sweep of a latter-day Western imperialism[4] were children of non-Western civilizations that had been caught, like the last of the barbarians, in a world-encompassing Western net. A third contingent—the most unhappy and therefore the most actively dissident of the three—consisted of *déracinés* of divers origins, Western as well as non-Western, who had suffered divers degrees of coercion. There were the descendants of African negroes who had been taken prisoners or kidnapped, been sold into slavery, and been forcibly transported beyond the Atlantic to the Americas;[1] there were the descendants of indentured Indian and Chinese coolies whose migration overseas had often in effect been just as involuntary as the African's, even though their virtual servitude might have been imposed on them under the legal cover of a formal contract. There were the descendants of transported West-European indentured servants and convicts[2] whose prospects had been less tragic than those of the Asiatic coolie or the African slave, since these temporarily disfranchised children of a Western household had been able to look forward to recovering their personal liberty after they had worked out the term of their sentence, and to finding themselves thereafter in as good a position as any voluntary emigrant of their own race to take advantage of opportunities offered by a new country. There were exiles whose banishment had been the penalty, not of real or imaginary crimes or misdemeanours, but of imputed heresies—religious, political, or ideological.[3] And there were emigrants who had chosen to go into a voluntary exile rather than continue to put up with a state of hopeless poverty to which the niggardliness of Nature or the injustice of their fellow men would have continued to condemn them if they had clung to an ancestral home.

There were other *déracinés* who had been uprooted without suffering a sea-change. The most flagrant examples of 'proletarianization' in a post-Modern Western World were 'the Poor Whites' in 'the Old South' of the United States and in the Union of South Africa, who, after having crossed the Ocean in order to better themselves, had sunk to the social and moral level of their more successful fellow colonists' imported or indigenous African helots.[4] There was an agricultural proletariat in Great Britain whose status had been depressed, not by the direct competition of helot 'Native' labour in their homeland, but by the ability of a West European country that had temporarily become 'the workshop of the World' to buy cheap mass-produced foodstuffs from overseas in exchange for exports of British manufactures. And there was an industrial urban proletariat[5] which, in Great Britain first of all, and thereafter in one country after another in a Western and a Westernizing World, had been drawn off the land into the city as a fall in the death-rate—bringing this down to ever lower levels over a Time-span of five or six generations before the restoration of the balance by a compensatory fall in the birth-rate—had made the creation of an unhappy urban proletariat the only alternative to the multiplication of an even more unhappy rural one.[6] This urban proletariat seemed in A.D. 1952 to be on the way to becoming as world-wide[7] as a Western standard of public health which was the ultimate cause of its epiphany, and as a Western style of Technology which was its staff of life; but there was another contingent of *déracinés* uprooted *in situ* which was the peculiar product of originally

1 See II. ii. 218.
3 See V. v. 159–60.
6 See pp. 385–7, above.

4 See V. v. 163.

2 See V. v. 161.
5 See V. v. 163–5.
7 See V. v. 155–6.

non-Western societies that had found themselves forced to conform in some degree to an alien Western way of life. An *intelligentsia*, called into existence to serve as a corps of interpreters between a proletarianized 'Native' society and an importunate Western 'ascendancy',[1] was, as we have observed, the most unhappy and the most explosive of the many ingredients of which a world-conquering Western Civilization's world-wide internal proletariat was composed.

The relations between a Western internal proletariat and a Western dominant minority were further aggravated by a 'colour-bar' in countries where there was an indigenous or imported proletariat that happened to have been stamped with the physique of a Black, Brown, or Yellow Race, and where the dominant minority had been recruited from Teutonic-speaking descendants of those White barbarians who had battened on the carcass of a dead Hellenic body social some fifteen hundred years back in the past. At the time of writing, the worst offenders were the Dutch-speaking lords and masters of the Union of South Africa; but the same fundamentally Fascist régime—making a class-distinction ineffaceable by identifying it with a race-distinction—was being maintained under the auspices of English-speaking cousins of the Afrikanders in Kenya Colony, in 'the Old South' of the United States, and in some respects—as, for instance, in a *de facto* segregation of domiciles—also in other sections of the North American Republic. Thus, in both a South African and a North American province of a latter-day Western World, a 'colour-bar' between divers communities sharing a common country was setting up, in a new social environment, the institution of Caste, which, in an Indic World that had been blighted by it, had likewise originated in a 'colour-bar' according to the tell-tale evidence of its Sanskrit name.[2]

In these circumstances it was not surprising to find a Western internal proletariat retorting to repression by exploding in outbreaks of retaliatory violence[3] reminiscent of the classical explosions during the second paroxysm of an Hellenic Time of Troubles.[4] The earliest of these outbreaks had occurred in an expanding Western Civilization's West European homeland; but the Anabaptist terror at Münster in A.D. 1543–5 and the successive Jacobin and Communard terrors in Paris in A.D. 1792–4 and in A.D. 1871 had been dwarfed in scale, though perhaps not surpassed in vindictiveness, by the insurrection of that vast majority of a latter-day Western internal proletariat which was of non-Western origin. The first of these anti-Western counter-attacks had been launched by Peter the Great, the Russian prototype of the Herodian saviour-king in a Westernizing World, in the Great Russo-Swedish War of A.D. 1700–21; but the consequent cession of the Baltic Provinces and the Karelian Isthmus by an eighteenth-century Western to an eighteenth-century Westernizing Power[5] was a trifling loss for the Western Community

---

[1] See V. v. 154–8.
[2] 'Colour' is the literal meaning of *Varna*, the Sanskrit word for which the Modern Western languages had found an equivalent in the Portuguese word *Casta*.
[3] See V. v. 167 and 170.   [4] See V. v. 177–80.
[5] See Gibbon's observations on this, and the present writer's comments on those observations, on pp. 752–4, below.

compared to the sweeping reversals of Western conquests during the fifth decade of the twentieth century.

In the General War of A.D. 1939–45, Russia had profited lucratively by her victorious alliance with the English-speaking Western Powers against a National-Socialist German Neobarbarism that had rankled into hideous life within the Western Society's bosom when in Germany a long since repressed abomination of desolation[1] had risen again, like an evil genius, from the depths of a collective Western subconscious psyche. In A.D. 1944–5 a Soviet Union, that had been compelled in A.D. 1918 to renounce Russian sovereignty over all Western territories that had been annexed by Russia since the days of Peter the Great, had re-established a Russian ascendancy over the Western World's East European marches; and this time Russia had succeeded in bringing under her domination a far larger portion of the Western Civilization's Continental European patrimony than had ever fallen under a Petrine Russia's rule. After the War of A.D. 1939–45, Russia had not only reannexed the Balticum and the Karelian Isthmus and suspended a sword of Damocles over Finland's head; she had enveloped the whole of Poland, Czechoslovakia, and Hungary, and large fractions of Germany and Austria, within her 'iron curtain'. These East European marches of the Western World were being kept under a Communist Russia's control by indigenous Communist parties with the backing of an undemobilized Russian Army; and this deft manœuvre of harnessing volunteer non-Russian running-dogs to the sledge of a Russian imperialism was being practised by the statesmen in the Kremlin not only in Europe but in Asia as well.

In Eastern Asia, Russia had been the beneficiary of Japanese conquests which had been as extensive as they had been short-lived; for, ephemeral though they had proved to be, these triumphs of a non-Western Great Power over Western empire-builders on Asiatic ground had irretrievably shattered the myth of Western invincibility. In the Philippines, Hong Kong, Malaya, Indonesia, Indo-China, and Burma in A.D. 1941, the Western strong man armed had met one who was stronger than he;[2] and the signal retribution that had afterwards overtaken a Japanese black dragon had not availed to set up a Western humpty-dumpty again in the esteem of his former Asian subjects. In their suicidal act of breaking the West's spell over Asian souls, the twentieth-century Japanese disciples of the Forty-Seven Rōnin had let loose, out of Aeolus's wind-bag, the long-pent-up spiritual force of Asian resentment against a Western ascendancy which had been all the more galling for being asserted on the cultural level as well as on the economic, the political, and the military; and an anti-Western crusade which had been half-hearted so long as it had had to be carried on by quislings in the service of a nakedly self-seeking Japanese nationalism had been resumed, after Japan's defeat, with a novel enthusiasm under the banner of a Communism in which a self-seeking Russian nationalism was artfully camouflaged. In 1952 it looked as if Chinese Communist armies that had, in effect, been fighting Russia's battles in Korea might have it in their

---

[1] Matt. xxiv. 15 and Mark xiii. 14, following Dan. xi. 31 and xii. 11.
[2] Luke xi. 21–22.

power to sweep off the Asiatic chess-board most of the Western pawns that had been precariously replaced on it in A.D. 1945.

The example of an insurgent Asia might be followed by an effervescent Africa whose soldiers had seen the World and taken stock of it in the South-East Asian and West European war-zones of a Second World War; and, as the spark ignited by Russian Communism travelled along a train of gun-powder long since laid by Western imperialism, it was not inconceivable that it might fire the native peasantry in a chain of Latin American republics, from Mexico to Paraguay inclusive, that had been planted on the volcanic soil of buried Andean and Central American worlds. A conflagration that had started in Mexico in A.D. 1910 by spontaneous combustion might spread to Peru and Bolivia if the flame were to be fanned by Communism's forced draught. In short, a world-wide proletarian revolt against a world-wide Western ascendancy had now become a possibility with which the West had to reckon; and, for a Western Society at bay, this prospect was daunting.

At the same time there were a number of less sensational, but not necessarily on that score less substantial, entries on the other side of the account.

The first point that might come to tell in a menaced Western Civilization's favour was the alloy of Russian nationalism in an Oecumenical Communism that professed, with a show of Pauline fervour, to have risen superior to all invidious distinctions between Jew and Greek or bond and free.[1] For this vein of insincerity, however adroitly it might be veiled, was a flaw in the physique of Communism which exposed it to the danger of death by thrombosis. At a moment when in Eastern Asia the Western cause was suffering grievous immediate adversity, a Western telepathist who could have looked into the hearts of the close-lipped statesmen in the Kremlin might have learnt that they were watching their Chinese allies' rather spectacular military successes against their common Western adversaries with not unmixed feelings. Would Chinese Communists elated by victories over the greatest Power in the Western camp be content to dance to Russia's tune thereafter? The future of Manchuria, Mongolia, and Sinkiang was, after all, of vastly greater importance for China and for Russia alike than the future of Indo-China, Hong Kong, and Formosa. The territorial issues between China and Russia were, in fact, both more momentous and more intractable than those between China and the West. Might not a Communist China, flushed with her demonstration of her ability to engage the United States in battle on equal terms, round on Russia with the cutting observation that, in accordance with the Marxian Religion of Humanity that both Russia and China professed, what was sauce for the American goose must be sauce for the Russian gander. A now hard-pressed Western World might perhaps live to see a Communist Russia's Asian Communist allies go a Communist Jugoslavia's way; and, at a moment when eager voices were being raised in the United States for a precipitate rearming of a Germany and a Japan who had been flying at the Western Community's throat only seven or eight years back, an English observer could look forward in his

[1] 1 Cor. xii. 13; Gal. iii. 28; Eph. vi. 8; Col. iii, 11.

imagination to a perhaps not distant day when the same voices would be
hailing Holy Russia as 'the White Man's hope'.

This no doubt at first sight unconvincing prognostication had a solid
basis in two indisputable facts. Russia was the only major province in the
patrimony of the White Race in which the population was increasing in
the twentieth century at the rate at which it had increased in the nineteenth century in Western Europe and North America; and Russia was
also the province of the White Race's patrimony which marched with the
Continental frontiers of China and India. If either or both of these two
sub-continents, which, in the twentieth century, each housed nearly one
quarter of the living generation of Mankind, were ever to succeed in
carrying the process of Westernization on the technological and organizational planes to a point at which Chinese or Indian 'man-power' would
begin to count—in contemporary Western terms of economic, political,
and military strength—in proportion to its immense strength in sheer
numbers, it was to be expected that a reinvigorated Samson would insist—under threat of pulling down the pillars of Humanity's house—on
a drastic revision of the grossly inequitable distribution of the World's
natural resources in territory, raw materials, and food producing capacity
which had been the consequence of the West European peoples' conquest of the Ocean in and after the fifteenth century of the Christian
Era. In such not inconceivable circumstances, Russia, in struggling to
preserve her own existence, might find herself involuntarily performing,
for a Western World snugly sheltering under her lee, the unrewarding
service of acting as a buffer that the main body of Orthodox Christendom
had once involuntarily performed for the same Western World when the
explosive quarter of the Continent had been, not China or India, but a
South-West Asia politically reunited under a dynamic Primitive Muslim Arab leadership.[1]

In A.D. 1952 it would, no doubt, have been folly for a Western World
that had been thrown on the defensive by a Russo-Chinese *entente* under
the banner of Communism to count upon any possibility of a future
breach between the two titanic non-Western Powers that were now co-
operating with one another in an anti-Western campaign. There was
perhaps more legitimate ground for encouragement in the fact that a
Western Community which had come into headlong collision with the
Chinese in Korea and which was desperately embroiled with the Viet-
namese in Indo-China had managed to come to terms with the Indonesians
after having crossed swords with them on the morrow of the 'liberation'
of the East Indian archipelago from the Japanese, and had voluntarily
abdicated its dominion over the Filipinos, Ceylonese, Burmans, Indians,
and Pakistanis by amicable agreements that had not been sullied by any
stain of bloodshed.

The voluntary liquidation of American rule in the Philippines was
perhaps not so remarkable—though an English observer could hardly
claim to be an impartial judge in this case—as the voluntary liquidation
of a British Rāj in India that was not only a hundred years older than the
American régime in a former dominion of the Spanish Crown but had

[1] See I. i. 156; II. ii. 376–9; and III. iii. 276, n. 1.

also come to count for far more in the life of the ruling Western country. When, on the 18th July, 1947,[1] Great Britain had completed the fulfilment of a pledge, first made on the 20th August, 1917,[2] to grant full self-government to India by stages at the fastest practicable pace, the Western country that had carried out this transfer of political power on this scale without having been constrained by any immediate *force majeure* had performed an act that was perhaps unprecedented and was certainly auspicious for the future, not merely of the Western Civilization, but of the Human Race.

In thus bestowing political independence on a sub-continent which they had originally brought under their rule by force of arms during a bout of anarchy at a late stage of a Hindu Civilization's disintegration, the British people had been inspired by an indelible memory of their disastrous failure in the eighteenth century to retain the allegiance of their own kinsmen and colonists in North America. This redoubtable lesson had burnt into their souls a conviction that it was as unwise as it was unwarrantable to attempt to rule other people by force when they could no longer be governed with their own consent, and that the right and statesmanlike course was always to grant self-government to a subject population that was demanding it in time to avoid the humiliation of being forced at last to concede it at the bayonet's point. This was the psychological background in British hearts and minds to the historic act of the 18th July, 1947; but so novel and difficult a political undertaking could hardly have been carried peacefully to success if the psychological atmosphere had not been propitious on both sides. The transformation of a British Rāj into the three independent Asian states of India, Pakistan, and Burma had been a joint achievement of the British people and their former Continental Asian subjects; and the Asian contribution had been a Hindu spirit of non-violence which had been blended with a Western spirit of non-violence—the living tradition of the Society of Friends—in the soul of the Mahatma Gandhi. The spiritual worth of this joint achievement and the genuineness of the co-operation between Westerners and Asians that had been the secret of its success were attested by the immediate transformation of a previous bitterness on the Asian side and a previous irritation on the Western side into a mutual esteem and friendship founded on a common sense of relief and satisfaction at having found, in concert, a happy issue out of a strange and awkward, but perhaps fatefully creative, encounter between the children of such diverse civilizations as the Western, the Hindu, the Islamic, and the Indic.[3]

This notable reconciliation between an Asia represented by various communities formerly subject to a British Rāj and a Western Society represented by British protagonists in the drama of Late Modern Western imperialism opened up a prospect that—in spite of a Communist

[1] This was the date on which the Royal Assent was given, at Westminster, to an India Independence Act enacted by the Parliament of the United Kingdom. The formal assumption of authority by the Governments of the Indian Union and Pakistan followed on the 15th August, 1947.

[2] In the House of Commons at Westminster by the Secretary of State for India, Mr. Edwin Montagu.

[3] For a diagnosis of the Hinayanian Buddhist communities in Ceylon, Burma, Siam, and Cambodia as fossils of an otherwise extinct Indic Civilization, see I. i.35.

enemy's assiduity in sowing tares in an expansive Western Civilization's Asiatic field—some part, at least, of the vast Asian contingent in an oecumenical Western internal proletariat that had been heading towards secession from a Western dominant minority might be moved to change its course in order to make for the alternative goal of entering into a social partnership on terms of political and psychological equality with its former Western masters. In that event, a world order, embracing the whole habitable and traversable surface of the planet, which had originally been established by Western force of civil and military technology on the inequitable basis of a Western minority's ascendancy over the rest of Mankind, might perhaps be saved from being shipwrecked on the rock of its own primal injustice through being converted into a common home for the whole Human Race, in which all members of the family would find themselves able to dwell together in unity[1] under the impartially hospitable roof of a house of many mansions.[2]

In Asia and in the North African province of an Islamic World the reconciliation of a world-encompassing Western Society's internal proletariat to its dominant minority seemed most likely to come about through the grant of local self-government to previously subject peoples within the framework of a political world order in which all states would enjoy an equal measure of liberty, while none of them would be free to exercise the licence of unlimited sovereign independence. The same open road to corporate membership in an oecumenical society seemed also to lie ahead of un-uprooted representatives of the Black Race in West Africa south of the Sahara whose continuing possession of their ancestral homes was guaranteed to them by the benevolence of a climate that made it impossible for any representatives of the White Race to enter in and dwell there[3] permanently. A reconciliation was manifestly more difficult in provinces of a Westernizing World in which the representatives of visually diverse races were citizens of the same country, working in the same fields and factories, and living in adjoining quarters of the same villages, towns, and cities. Yet the 'colour-bar' that had been a Dutch-speaking and English-speaking White dominant minority's inhuman response to this heart-searching challenge in South Africa and in North America north-east of the Rio Grande was not the only answer that had been found by European pioneers of the Western Civilization who had called into existence overseas new communities composed of diverse races.

The French, for example, had shown themselves ready to fraternize with any convert to the French version of the Modern Western culture, and the Spaniards and Portuguese to fraternize with any convert to the Roman Catholic version of a Western Christianity, whatever the colour of the proselyte's skin might happen to be;[4] and, though, in a post-Modern Age of Western history, the Romance-speaking representatives of the Western Civilization outside Europe might count for less than its Teutonic-speaking representatives, their older and more humane Western solutions for the problem of 'the clash of colour' were at any rate

---

[1] Ps. cxxxiii. 1.
[3] Matt. xii. 45; Luke xi. 26.
[2] John xiv. 2.
[4] See IX. viii. 565–6.

still in the field as alternatives to a 'colour-bar' which, so far from solving the problem, grievously aggravated it. The living examples of these happier alternative responses might perhaps still have some effect on the eventual handling of the race problem in English-speaking provinces of a Westernizing World in which the 'colour-bar' was a stumbling-block to Protestant as well as Catholic Christian consciences.

In the United States, in particular, at the time of writing, the tendency of a 'colour-bar' to harden into a caste-distinction on Indic lines was being resisted by the counter operation of the spirit of Christianity; and, though, at the time of writing, it was still impossible to tell whether this Christian counter-attack was a forlorn hope or whether it was 'the wave of the Future', it was at least a good omen that in the United States, as in India, the redeeming spirit had been at work on both sides. In the hearts of a dominant North American White majority a Christian conscience that had insisted on abolishing the evil institution of Negro Slavery at the cost of a civil war within the bosom of the White community had come to realize that a merely juridical emancipation was not enough, and had been moved by the Apostle's warning of the spiritual unprofitableness of good works, if these were not hallowed by Christian love,[1] to press on towards the more elusive goal of winning for a juridically emancipated Negro minority a social and psychological equality for lack of which the bare legal status of personal freedom had proved to be as bitter to the taste as Dead Sea fruit. This indefatigably sustained Christian endeavour on the part of a White minority that was the salt of this North American earth would, however, have been of little avail if a Christian spirit on a Coloured minority's side had not been ready to respond to a contrite White minority's Christian overtures. In other contexts[2] we have admired the spectacle of a Negro *anima naturaliter Christiana* taking to heart, in a New World that, for the African slave, had been a land, not of hope and glory, but of exile and servitude, a Christianity that had left no mark on the stony hearts of White slave-traders and slave-owners who had been its incongruous and impervious carriers. In North America, as in India, if the schism in the body social were eventually to be healed, the salvaging of a disintegrating civilization would, once again, have been Christianity's achievement.

A third arena in a Westernizing World in which Christianity had been battling with an inhumanity that had been making for social disruption was on the Western Society's home front, and on this front the critical sector was a Britain that had been the scene of the first eruption of a Late Modern Western Industrial Revolution. If, in the generation in which this visitation was conjuring into existence the English vanguard of an oecumenical industrial urban proletariat, John Wesley (*vivebat* A.D. 1703–91) had not devoted a long life to evangelizing an English under-world to which an eighteenth-century Established Church had heartlessly turned a blind eye, who can tell that the tribulations to which this pastor's sheep were subjected during the half-century following his death might not have goaded them into savagely militant insurrections of the kind that had once devastated a disintegrating Hellenic World in

---

[1] 1 Cor. xiii, *passim*.　　[2] See II. ii. 213–16 and 218–20, and V. v. 191–3.

the course of the second paroxysm of an Hellenic Time of Troubles in the second and the last century B.C. ?[1] It was thanks to the labours of Wesley and his fellow Christian evangelists in the eighteenth century of the Christian Era that in the nineteenth and twentieth centuries a slowly maturing political Labour Movement in Great Britain had not taken either an anti-clerical or an anti-constitutional turn.

The bloodless political revolution through which India had obtained her emancipation from a British Rāj on the morrow of the War of A.D. 1939–45 was not more remarkable than a simultaneous bloodless revolution in Great Britain through which a Western country, where power, wealth, and opportunity had been, within living memory, the close preserve of a scandalously small and odiously over-privileged minority, had now peacefully transformed itself, without vindictiveness on the majority's part and without rancour on the minority's, into a community in which a maximum of social justice had been secured at the cost of a minimal sacrifice of individual liberty. These two liberal and constructive non-violent revolutions—one in Great Britain and the other in India— on the morrow of a devastating war were achievements in which any living Englishman could take pride, for whatever party he might happen to have cast his parliamentary vote.[2]

---

[1] See V. v. 68–71.

[2] The writer of this Study, for example, who was not a member of the Labour Party, had found himself moved, on visits to the United States during the years A.D. 1947–52, to expound the ideals and commend the policy of the Labour Movement in the United Kingdom to middle-class American critics whose attitude towards British Labour was one of suspicion inclining towards hostility.

In the sight of these American onlookers this policy was obnoxious on two grounds. They deemed it in the first place socially superfluous, and in the second place politically untoward. It seemed to them superfluous because in the United States no regimentation or socialization had been required in order to enable the industrial workers as a group to share in a continuing general rise in the national standard of material living; it seemed dangerous because, in their expectation, even a modicum of socialism was bound to act as the thin end of a wedge which must eventually prise the last remnants of individual liberty out of the body social, and was consequently bound in the end to clamp the yoke of a totalitarian régime à la Russe on the necks of the whole nation, including the deluded industrial workers whose misguided socialist leaders had set this fatal train of events in motion. It was difficult at this date for an Englishman, even if he were in the forensically strong position of not being a member of the Labour Party himself, to convince his American interlocutors that the leaders of the British Labour Movement, as well as the rank-and-file, were as constitutional-minded as any British Conservative or any American Republican; that the British trade union organization had been built up in accordance with a national tradition of keeping elected representatives under their constituents' control; that the British working class set immense store by their trade unions, as going concerns which they had created for themselves and which had proved their value to them by enabling them over the course of decades to obtain notable successive improvements in their standard of living; that this trade union organization could only survive (as had been demonstrated by the fate of the Labour unions in a Communist Russia) in a social milieu in which Labour and Capital were free to bargain with one another; and that, if ever the logic of events were to force British Labour to choose between the preservation of their trade unions' right to negotiate and right to strike and the assertion of the absolute authority of a socialist state, a doctrinaire socialism, not a traditional trade unionism, was the cargo that would go by the board. It was no less difficult to convince middle-class Americans at this time that a modicum of socialism was, nevertheless, also indispensable if the minimum standard of living was to be raised substantially in a country whose aggregate national income and resources were as small as those of the United Kingdom were by comparison with those of the United States.

In putting these considerations before middle-class Americans the writer was always at pains to make it clear that his defence of British Labour policy was a defence of its application in Great Britain under current conditions of life in that particular country, and that he was not advocating it as a panacea for all countries in all circumstances. The United States, for example, with its vast already-developed national wealth and vast

The foregoing survey of facts telling against, as well as in favour of, the likelihood of the Western Civilization's coming to grief through the secession of an internal proletariat suggests two tentative conclusions. In the first place, the forces of reconciliation and recuperation that were in the field against the forces of schism and disintegration in the Western World at this stage in its history appeared to be stronger than any corresponding forces that might have been at work in the Hellenic World in the course of the second paroxysm of an Hellenic Time of Troubles in the second and the last century B.C. In the second place, this difference, to the Western World's advantage, between these two comparable passages of history appeared to be mainly due to the continuing operation of a spirit of Christianity that had not lost its hold over the hearts of latter-day Western men and women when their minds had eventually rejected an outworn creed in which the abiding spiritual truths of Christianity had been translated into the ephemeral language of a pagan Hellenic philosophy.[1]

This persistent vitality of a higher religion which had once provided a larval Western Civilization with its chrysalis was an element in the Western situation in the twentieth century of the Christian Era that had been conspicuously absent in an otherwise comparable Hellenic situation in the last two centuries B.C.; and it seemed not unreasonable to conjecture that there was some relation of cause and effect between this apparent invincibility of a living higher religion and the paucity and jejunity of the new crop of religions of the same species that were raising their heads in a Westernizing World at this time. The Bahā'īyah and the Ahmadī-yah[2] might be approximate counterparts, in the current chapter of Western history, of religions that had competed with Christianity for the conversion of an Hellenic World in its universal state; and Communism might resemble the Mahāyāna in being a religion that had been conjured out of a philosophy. But Communism had already fallen into the aberra-

reserve of still-untapped national resources, might, for all he knew, be able to make just as near an approach towards the democratic ideal of a classless society as had been made in A.D. 1945–51 in the United Kingdom under a Labour régime, without finding herself compelled to have any recourse to regimentation or socialization. However that might be, it was in any case an historical fact, as far as a foreign observer could judge, that, in the United States so far, there had been no appreciable signs of a tendency for an industrial urban proletariat to secede from Society. In the United States the industrial workers had not gone through the tribulations that in Great Britain had been their penalty for being the earliest representatives of their species to make their appearance in a Modern Western World. The North American industrial workers' minimum standard of living had always been fabulously high, as measured by even the highest contemporary West European standards; and any North American industrial worker who was energetic, able, and enterprising could still look forward—or at any rate still believed that he could still look forward—to finding opportunities of rising into the middle class by his own personal exertions. On this account, industrial workers in the United States mid-way through the twentieth century were perhaps still almost as much concerned to keep open their opportunities of attaining individually to a middle-class prosperity as they were to improve collectively a present state of life which they were inclined, one and all, to regard as transient. If this is a correct diagnosis of the mid-twentieth-century outlook of the industrial workers in the United States, this state of mind would manifestly be an effective insurance against any risk of a secession of the industrial proletariat in the leading Western industrial country of the age. A West European observer, however, would be moved at this point to ask himself whether, in the long run, North American conditions were not more likely in these respects to approximate to West European conditions than West European conditions were to approximate to North American.

[1] See VII. vii. 473–8. [2] See V. v. 174–6.

tion, to which the Mahāyāna had never succumbed, of lending itself to the mundane purposes of a militant state; and a sterility that had been the uniform nemesis of Zoroastrianism, Imāmī Shi'ism, and Sikhism when these abortive higher religions had prostituted themselves respectively to the service of the Sasanian Empire, the Safawī Empire, and the Khalsa[1] might be expected to blight a Communism that had prostituted itself to the service of the Soviet Union[2] at the very moment when it had embarked on the audacious spiritual enterprise of challenging not only a post-Christian Western Civilization but a Christianity that was the tap-root of the Western and the Russian Civilization alike.

Thus, while the symptoms of schism in the Western Civilization's body social were unmistakable, the patient's prospects were still enigmatic in A.D. 1952; and we shall find ourselves arriving again at this same pair of conclusions if we look into the contemporary state of Western souls. A sense of drift, for example, could be detected on the intellectual plane in the antinomianism of the post-Modern Western historians,[3] and on the economic and political planes both in a Liberal *laisser faire*[4] and in a Marxian determinism;[5] and any anti-Marxist who might be seeking comfort in the idea that a deterministic creed could not be a dynamic one would have been wise to recollect that Fatalism has a paradoxical power of acting as a spiritual tonic.[6] A sense of sin that Methodism had inculcated in the eighteenth century into the hearts of a despised and rejected urban proletariat was at work in the twentieth century in the hearts of Protestant Westerners of the middle class, to judge by the vogue of the revivalist enthusiasm that was being propagated in this soil by a 'Moral Rearmament' movement.[7] A sense of promiscuity was, of course, strongly marked in a Western Civilization that had become ubiquitous; but its most characteristic manifestations in a twentieth-century Westernizing World were not those tendencies towards pammixia and proletarianization that had loomed so large in the histories of civilizations whose geographical expansion had been an unequivocal symptom of cultural disintegration.

The notorious receptivity of empire-builders had been displayed by Modern Western representatives of the type for the most part in trivialities such as a partiality to exotic foods and beverages.[8] It was true that the advance-guard of the West European settlers on North American ground had gone considerably farther towards adopting in its entirety the barbarian way of life of the Red Indian 'natives' with whom they had fought and traded, but these barbarized pioneers of an expanding Western Civilization had ensured their own disappearance in the act of exterminating their barbarian 'opposite numbers'. As soon as they had accomplished their murderously romantic historical mission of clearing the North American barbarians out of the way, they themselves were swiftly sucked back into the prosaic Main Street of a pullulating Middletown.[9] The culture of this Middletown had lapsed into a conspicuous vulgarity and barbarism in the realm of Art;[10] yet an observer who might

---

[1] See V. v. 187–8.   [2] See V. v. 181–7.
[3] See pp. 173–216, above.   [4] See V. v. 414–15.
[5] See V. v. 426.   [6] See V. v. 615–18.   [7] See V. v. 439.
[8] See V. v. 444–5.   [9] See V. v. 479–80.   [10] See V. v. 481–2.

be inclined to see in this the token of a failure of creative power would have been wise to recollect that the vulgar Hellenic art of Gandhāra had given birth, in its day, to the etherially creative Mahayanian Buddhist art of China and Japan.[1]

An expanding Western Society had found it convenient to employ the Tuscan,[2] French,[3] and English[4] languages as *lingue franche* at successive stages of its progressive occupation of the *Oikoumenê*; but the inevitable debasement of these languages in this rough and ready usage had not disqualified either English, French, or Tuscan for continuing to be used as a vehicle of high poetry by poets who still spoke the language as their mother tongue. Latter-day Western history could also furnish examples of syncretism in religion. Since A.D. 1688 one of the attributes of the British Crown had been a simultaneous association with two—and, from A.D.1714 to A.D. 1837, actually with three—different denominations of a Protestant Western Christianity;[5] and this late-seventeenth-century constitutional combination of varieties of one of two branches of the Western Society's ancestral religion, which had marked the transition from a fanatical Early Modern to a latitudinarian Late Modern chapter of Western ecclesiastical history, had been surpassed in daring by the nineteenth-century infusion of an exotic Protestant Christianity into the ancestral Hinduism of the Brahmō Samāj and into the ancestral Taoism of the T'aip'ing.[6] Yet, however daring they might be, these and other syncretisms between an Occidental and an Oriental religion in Modern Western history had so far shown no sign of playing the momentous part that had been played in post-Alexandrine Hellenic history by Christianity, Mithraism, and the worships of Isis, Cybele, and Iuppiter Dolichenus.

In the life of a latter-day Western Society there were also some manifest exhibitions of Archaism and Futurism.

Archaism had displayed itself on the plane of institutions and ideas in Rousseau's cult of Primitive Human Nature[7] and in Hitler's cult of Barbarian Blood and Soil;[8] on the plane of visual art in a Neo-Gothic and a Neo-Colonial architecture which had been conspicuous in a pre-atomic Western urban landscape;[9] on the plane of language and literature in attempts to revive an antique Norse and an antique Irish;[10] and on the plane of religion in the nostalgia for a traditional Roman Catholic ritual that had been displayed in both Positivism and Anglo-Catholicism,[11] and in the nostalgia for a semi-fictitious Nordic barbarian ritual that had been displayed in Hauerism.[12] Yet this Hitlerian German attempt to revive a primitive pagan past was convicted of being nothing more than a passing extravaganza when it was measured by the standard of the Meiji Japanese revival of Shintō;[13] the preciosity of a selfconscious Anglo-Catholic and Positivist ritualism fell far short of achieving either a social or a moral effect that could be compared with the effects of the revival of traditional Roman religious observances by Augustus;[14] and it is significant

[1] See V. v. 482–3. [2] See V. v. 502. [3] See V. v. 503–6.
[4] See V. v. 507–12. [5] See V. v. 533–4.
[6] See V. v. 537. [7] See V. vi. 58. [8] See V. vi. 56–57.
[9] See V. vi. 60. [10] See V. vi. 64–67. [11] See V. vi. 83–84.
[12] See V. vi. 85. [13] See V. vi. 89–93. [14] See V. vi. 86–89.

that the linguistically selfconscious nineteenth-century Norwegians and Irish were descended neither from the original members of the Western Civilization nor from its barbarian proselytes, but from frustrated representatives of two abortive civilizations that had been blighted by premature encounters with a rising Roman Western Christian Civilization for which they had been no match.[1]

A glance at the contemporary exhibitions of Futurism in a latter-day Western Society's life told the same tale. On the plane of political institutions, the deliberate effacement of traditional boundaries through an artificial redrawing of the administrative map, *more Cleistheneo*,[2] had been exemplified in the remapping of an eighteenth-century France into departments and of a twentieth-century Germany into Gaue,[3] while, on the plane of the arts, there had been patent symptoms of Futurism in all provinces of a post-Modern Western World in music, dancing, painting, and sculpture.[4] Yet, though such manifestations of Futurism were discernible, it was also manifest that their effect, so far, had been slight.

In addition to these latter-day Western evidences—at whatever value their importance was to be appraised—of schism in the Soul and schism in the Body Social, we have found,[5] in a synoptic analysis of the rhythm of the disintegration-process, that the Western Civilization's latter-day history conformed to a pattern—a series of two paroxysms punctuated by one rally—that had been the regular rhythm of a Time of Troubles in the histories of civilizations that had run through the whole disintegration-process from breakdown to dissolution. The appearance of this sinister pattern in Western history was, in A.D. 1952, perhaps the most alarming of all current Western experiences with non-Western precedents. Yet, as we have already observed in another context,[6] the nebulous possibility that the Western Civilization might, at this date, be in the grip of the second paroxysm of a Time of Troubles was less significant than the plain fact that it had at least not yet entered into a universal state.

The inquiry that we have now completed thus suggests that the non-Western precedents for Western experiences were inconclusive. While we have found enough evidence to make it clear that authentic symptoms of breakdown and disintegration were discernible in the life of the Western Civilization mid-way through the twentieth century of the Christian Era, an assessment of this evidence has proved not to be so easy; and we might be in danger of exaggerating the significance of the facts if we were to allow ourselves to forget that, in the life of every living society, as in the life of every living organism, a tendency towards breakdown and disintegration is constantly asserting itself, and as constantly requiring to be resisted, even when the society is in the healthiest and most vigorous burst of its growth. The pertinent question was not whether the symptoms of breakdown and disintegration were present, but whether they were serious. Was the malady grave? Was it incurable? Was it lethal? And in A.D. 1952 these were questions to which no conclusive answer could be given when they were asked with reference to

[1] See II. ii. 322–60.   [2] See V. vi. 107–8.   [3] See V. vi. 108–9.
[4] See IV. iv. 51–52.   [5] See V. vi. 312–21.   [6] On pp. 411–12, above.

the prospects of the Western Civilization, because in A.D. 1952 the plot of this Occidental drama had not yet arrived at its denouement.

(II) UNPRECEDENTED WESTERN EXPERIENCES

In the pursuit of our inquiry into the prospects of the Western Civilization we decided to take testimony from the histories of all societies of the species, and in the preceding chapter we have called the roll of Western experiences with non-Western precedents. Our investigation would, however, be incomplete if we did not go on to consider evidence furnished by the history of the Western Civilization to which the histories of other civilizations present no parallels; and, as soon as we address ourselves to this remainder of our present undertaking, our attention will be caught and held by two commanding features in the social landscape of a latter-day Western World that have no visible counterparts in the landscapes of the other societies of the same species when, in our mind's eye, we conjure these up, side by side with the Western Society, in a synoptic view. The first of these apparently unprecedented Western experiences is the extent of the mastery that a Late Modern and post-Modern Western Man had acquired over Non-Human Nature; the second apparently distinctive Western experience is the constantly accelerating rapidity of the process of social change in the Western World in consequence of the no less constantly accelerating rapidity of Western Man's advance in his mastery over Non-Human Nature. It is true that these two at first sight seemingly unique experiences of a latter-day *Homo Occidentalis* turn out, on a closer view, to have been shared with him in some degree by all other avatars of Man in Process of Civilization, and in lesser degrees by all Mankind and perhaps even by all Life since the first epiphany of Life, human or pre-human, on the face of the planet. These differences of degree were, however, so great that they were tantamount to differences of kind, and this meant that the impression of being unique that these two latter-day Western experiences gave at first sight came nearer to the heart of the truth than the observation that both of them were actually shared by Western Man with the representatives of other species of Human Society and other forms of Terrestrial Life.

In an earlier context[1] we have noted that, since Mankind's passage from the Lower to the Upper Palaeolithic stage of a cumulative technological progress, the Human Race had been the lords of Creation on Earth in the sense that, from that time onwards, it had no longer been possible either for Inanimate Nature or for any non-human terrestrial living creature to exterminate Mankind or even to prevent them from continuing to increase their knowledge, their power, or their happiness. From that time onwards nothing on Earth, with one outstanding exception, had been capable any longer of thwarting Man's material and moral progress or of bringing him to ruin or destruction; but this one last unsubdued enemy and potential destroyer of Man was a formidable one, since he was, of course, none other than Man himself. Man's firmly established lordship over Creation had endowed him with a surplus of

[1] In VII. vii. 486.

power over and above his limited requirements for holding his own against Non-Human Nature; and it was open to him to use this surplus as he chose.

> The craft of his engines hath passed his dream,
> In haste to the good or the evil goal;[1]

and he had turned his face so perversely towards the evil goal of being his own enemy that, ever since his acquisition of this two-edged superfluity of material power, his crux had been the spiritual problem of dealing with himself, his fellow men, and God, not the technical problem of dealing with Non-Human Nature. Man's relation to a conquered Non-Human Nature now no longer had any importance for Man in itself, since his power to hold his own against this once formidable but now defeated adversary was something that, henceforward, he could take for granted. The importance of his Technology for him now lay in the surplus of power that he was able to extract from Non-Human Nature for use either for or against God and himself; but, by reason of the metamorphosis of a technological into a spiritual problem, the importance of Technology had actually become greater than ever; for its spiritual effects for good or for evil had increased and were increasing *pari passu* with each fresh advance in technological progress.

In the light of this tragic relation between Technology and Morality since a Fall that had been coeval and identical with Life's attainment of the level of Humanity, it might look as if, after all, there were nothing new in the spiritual challenge that a latter-day Western Man was presenting to himself by his continuing technological progress in the twentieth century of the Christian Era. In previous passages of Western history, as well as in the histories of other civilizations, human affairs had not infrequently been upset by sudden great advances in Man's command over Non-Human Nature; and this previous evidence was even sufficiently copious and illuminating to warrant the tentative formulation of a 'law' to the effect that, the greater the technological triumph, the greater the risk of spiritual devastation. The Western dawn of an Atomic Age had now, however, registered the point at which the stakes in the game of human life that Man must play willy nilly *ex officio humanitatis* had been raised to a degree that had made the change tantamount to a difference in kind; for the eruption of a Late Modern Western Industrial Revolution in Great Britain, less than two hundred years since, had brought with it a fresh increase in Man's power over Non-Human Nature that dwarfed the previous sum total of Man's cumulative achievements in a field of activity in which he had been as signally victorious over Non-Human Nature as he had been signally defeated by his own nature in the things of the spirit.

An unprecedented increase in Man's material power, which had begun with the harnessing of steam, generated by coal, to the service of manufacture and locomotion, had been mounting up in one feat of technological virtuosity after another. The physical driving force at Man's com-

---

[1] Sophocles: *Antigone*, ll. 365–6, translated by Gilbert Murray (quoted already in V. v. 61).

mand had been multiplied by the subsequent harnessing of mineral oil to drive an internal combustion engine, and by the discovery of a 'know-how' for converting Man's older servant water-power into electricity. The consequent possibility of producing cheaply an abundance of artificial light and heat had enabled Man to make himself at home within the Arctic Circle,[1] while the progress of Tropical Medicine and the discovery of a technique for air-conditioning had enabled the children of temperate latitudes to exploit the wealth and enjoy the amenities of the Tropics without any longer incurring a prohibitive risk of finding a grave there. After the invention of the steamship, the railway train, and the motor-car had 'annihilated distance' for travellers on the land and water surface of the planet, the invention of the submarine and the aeroplane had given Man's habitat a third dimension in both depth and height. The telegraph, telephone, gramophone, radio, television, and radar had 'annihilated distance' in a fourth dimension by enabling human beings to communicate with one another instantaneously round the whole circumference of the globe without having to meet one another in the flesh. And, finally, since the last days of a Second World War, the unprecedentedly fast and fertile technological progress of the Western World in the course of the preceding six generations had been crowned by a feat that had made even the intellectually and morally blindest men and women in the living generation suddenly aware of the fateful significance of all technological progress, not only in the Western World since the outbreak of a Late Modern Western Industrial Revolution, but in the World at large since the dawn of a Late Palaeolithic Age. The discovery of a 'know-how' for tapping the titanic force of atomic energy and applying this to the destruction of human lives and works had brought home to the imagination of Mankind in the mass some inkling of a tragic lesion in the affairs of men which more than one Western man of science had already diagnosed and reported.[2] A geometrically progressing Technology had now armed a perpetually reborn Original Sin with a weapon potent enough to enable a sinful Mankind to annihilate itself. 'The wages of Sin is Death.'[3] The fate of Hiroshima and Nagasaki had set these dread words ringing again in ears that, through a long familiarity with their sound, had long since grown deaf to their meaning.

In A.D. 1952, seven years after the detonation of an explosion that had been heard round the World, it was evident that an unprecedented human situation had now been created by the unprecedented potency to which Mankind's progressively accumulating surplus of material power had been raised, with an unparalleled rapidity, by the technological prowess of the Western Civilization in the latest chapter of its history. Man's acquisition of this degree of command over non-human forces had made it impossible for him any longer to evade the challenge of two

---

[1] The sudden provision of an abundance of cheap lighting in Northern Norway during the winter months of perpetual night through the generation of electricity out of the abundance of a previously unutilized local water-power was said to have been followed by a proportionately steep fall in the local rate of death by suicide.

[2] See, for example, the passage from Sir Alfred Ewing's address, on the 31st August, 1932, to the British Association for the Advancement of Science that has been quoted in III. iii. 211–12.   [3] Rom. vi. 23.

evils which Man himself had brought into the World in the act of providing himself with a new species of society. For some five or six thousand years ending on the 6th August, 1945, Man in Process of Civilization had been indulging in wars and class-conflicts between fractions of societies that had articulated themselves vertically into mosaics of parochial states and horizontally into layers of stratified classes. The strife generated by these fatal flaws in the structure of the civilizations had already been the death of perhaps twenty out of the twenty-one representatives of the species that had come into existence up to date. The vast and swift further technological progress that had since been made by the sole survivor was now threatening to bring destruction, not just upon one more civilization, but upon this species of Society itself and upon the species of living creature that had created it. The challenges of War and Class-Conflict had now been raised to a pitch of intensity at which the choice with which Mankind found itself confronted was the extreme choice of kill or cure. A latter-day Western Civilization's technological *tours de force* had, in fact, made War intolerable by making it manifestly suicidal,[1] and made Class-Conflict intolerable by making it apparently remediable.[2]

While the vast new impetus imparted by Western Man to Mankind's secular technological progress had thus precipitated a crisis in human affairs that had been pending since Primitive Man's entry into an Upper Palaeolithic Age, the correspondingly vast new acceleration of the pace of change that a Western technological revolution was now forcing upon Human Nature on every plane of activity had precipitated a crisis that had been pending since the first epiphany of Life on Earth. In a previous context[3] we have seen that an acceleration which was one of the keynotes of the current phase of Western history was the latest term in a serial crescendo movement that had been gathering momentum with each fresh advance in the evolution of terrestrial living organisms; and in this perspective the technological stimulus by which this movement had been carried forward in a human milieu looked like Man's translation, into his own rational purposive terms, of some nisus inherent in Life itself. In the same context, however, we have also seen that in the current phase of Western history the pace had been forced to a speed that had imported a new element into the situation. For the first time in the history of Mankind, not to speak of the history of pre-human forms of Terrestrial Life, the speed had risen to a height at which a quantum of change within a single lifetime that was beyond the adaptational capacity of a single life was being demanded of all living members of a Western Society that by this time had engulfed the whole living generation of Mankind.

A killing pace was not, of course, in itself, an altogether unknown tragedy in previous human experience. Ever since the time, some five or six thousand years back, when societies that were chronologically contemporary with one another had begun to become differentiated from one another culturally by the emergence of the civilizations above the

---

level of the primitive societies and by the distinctive individuality of the contours of each of these uprising cultural peaks, an abrupt encounter between two or more sharply diversified societies had been a perpetual possibility that had also frequently been realized as a matter of tragic historical fact. In such encounters between diverse contemporaries the weaker party was apt, as we have already observed,[1] to be confronted with the agonizing necessity of having to attempt to achieve an adaptation beyond the compass of its adaptational capacity as the only alternative choice to going under without a struggle; and, though we have not come across any instance of a civilization in its growth-phase having been broken down by a collision with a more potent alien society, we have noted a number of examples of civilizations already in disintegration receiving their *coup de grâce* from an alien hand.[2]

The Western Civilization, for example, had played either the murderous or the insidious aggressor's part in encounters with ten contemporary societies of its own species. It had assassinated the Mexic, Yucatec, and Andean civilizations, and had led the other seven the dance that Goethe's Mephistopheles leads Goethe's Faust.[3] The new element in the situation in a Westernizing World in A.D. 1952 was not the destructive or subversive effect that was the familiar consequence of any cultural encounter, but the fact that, in an *Oikoumenê* that was in process of being made into the common home of a single all-embracing society within a Western framework, the unifying Western Civilization had carried the acceleration of its own spontaneous internal change to a pitch at which it was now already victimizing itself by acting as its own Mephistopheles and was threatening to victimize itself more crudely than that by acting as its own Cortés or Pizarro. The pace of Western change had now become so fast that, even within the Western Civilization's own original Western patrimony, where this pace was being set from within and was not being forced upon the Subconscious Psyche by the pressure of any external agent, it was imposing an intolerable tax on the stamina of the best-trained native-born Western runners. *A fortiori*, this was a killing pace for that great majority of Mankind who were not native children of Hesperia's household but were alien conscripts in her immense internal proletariat.

At this critical moment in the history both of the West and of the World, when it would have been difficult in any circumstances for the Human Psyche to move fast enough and far enough along the path of psychological adaptation to a process of technological advance that was now rushing at a break-neck speed, the difficulty had been aggravated by revolutionary social and political changes that the revolutionary technological changes had brought with them.

Since the close of the fifteenth century of the Christian Era, the work of unifying the World within a Western framework had been mostly carried out by six West European countries—Portugal, Spain, Holland, France, Britain, and Belgium—and, within these countries, mainly by one class, the bourgeoisie; and, after the two Iberian pioneer countries in a Modern Western movement of world-wide Oceanic expansion had fallen out of the race, the British, French, Dutch, and Belgian middle

[1] In IX. viii. 88–629.   [2] See IV. iv. 76–114.   [3] See II. i. 272–99.

class had been left to share between them the bulk of the profits of this gigantic Western enterprise. In drawing profits and exercising power they had gradually acquired experience and undertaken responsibilities; and, though their Western competitors and non-Western commercial customers and political subjects might complain that these middle-class North-West European organizers of a Unitary World had been awarding to themselves unduly high fees for their unsolicited managerial services, the World's history since A.D. 1914 had demonstrated by the method of experiment that these services had come to be indispensable, whatever the fair charge for them might be estimated to be, and whatever agency might have the handling of the business of performing these services on commission. It had also been demonstrated that, whatever might be History's ultimate verdict on the conduct of a Unified World's affairs by its self-appointed previous British, French, Dutch, and Belgian managers, no other candidate had so far come forward who was, as yet, equally well qualified to execute delicate and exacting tasks that must be carried out with vision as well as with efficiency if a now oecumenical Western Society was to be saved from shipwreck.

By A.D. 1914 the North-West European bourgeoisie had knit the whole habitable and traversable surface of the planet together in a network of shipping, trade, and finance of which the nodes had come to be London, Paris, Amsterdam, and Brussels, and they had also bridged the cultural gulf between the Western Civilization and its contemporaries by building overseas empires that had brought Western and non-Western populations together under common governments operated and controlled by the West European imperial Powers who had organized them. No doubt, a world order that had been founded on so narrow a basis would have had to be placed on a broader basis sooner or later as a necessary alternative to a break-up that would have been a catastrophe for all parties in an age in which Technology had come to operate on an oecumenical range; but this doubtless ultimately inevitable transfer of profits, power, and responsibility would probably have taken place gradually, over a span of several generations and perhaps even more than one century, if a Westernizing World had continued to suffer no more severely from Civilization's historic maladies of War and Class-Conflict than it had been suffering during the century that had ended in A.D. 1914. If the World had gone on living at that tolerable nineteenth-century tempo the North-West European middle class would have had time to share their profits, power, responsibilities, and experience with a continually widening circle of successively co-opted new partners without being ruined by being called upon to adapt themselves to this necessary change at an impracticably headlong gait, while the new participants in North-West European middle-class experience, responsibilities, power, and profits would have had time, for their part, to digest the experience and to accept the responsibilities as a moral obligation bound up with the taking of the profits and the assumption of the power. Unhappily the Subconscious Psyche's failure to keep pace with the accelerating speed of technological innovation had forced an anyway inevitable change to take, not the auspicious course of orderly rational evolution, but the disastrous course of a revolution that was as uncircumspect as it was anarchic.

Between A.D. 1914 and A.D. 1945 the high tension between a conservative Psyche and a revolutionary Technology had discharged itself in two world wars in one lifetime; and this reduplicated catastrophe had 'put down the mighty from their seat and . . . exalted the humble and meek'[1] at a pace that was not less bewildering and overwhelming for suddenly exalted *novi homines*—a Bevin, a Nehru, a Truman, a Stalin—than it was for elder statesmen, proconsuls, financiers, and diplomatists who had been as suddenly deposed from a long-exercised office. In the course of little more than thirty years the North-West European middle class had had to concede a preponderance of political and economic power at home to the industrial workers, and simultaneously to hand over the whole of its previous political and economic power in its former Asiatic dominions to a native Asian *intelligentsia* whose left-handedly sincere way of flattering its European creators and employers by imitation had been to insist on taking their places as the masters in each once subject Asian people's own now emancipated national house. Within the same brief period of time a North-West European middle class that had thus been losing its predominance at home and its ascendancy in Asia had simultaneously been forfeiting its oecumenical economic and political influence to new supra-national Great Powers of an invincibly higher material calibre that had swiftly loomed up out of great open spaces where they had been able gradually to develop, unthwarted, on the fringes of an *Oikoumenê*[2] that since A.D. 1498 had been unified by, and till A.D. 1914 had been centred upon, a diminutive row of half a dozen nation-states along the Atlantic seaboard of Western Europe.

In A.D. 1952, when it was already possible to look back on this 'awful revolution'[3] as a decisively accomplished fact, the practical question of vital moment for the future of the West and of the World was whether the new holders of power and responsibility had grown in wisdom commensurately with their growth in stature.[4] People whose experience had been gained, and whose habits of feeling, thinking, and action had been formed, in the negative school of an opposition, in which they had been serving their apprenticeship for decades and even for generations, had now suddenly saddled themselves, or been saddled by the fiat of History, with the moral burden of onerous positive duties. A British industrial working class bred up in a century-old tradition of resisting exploitation by middle-class employers now had to 'make the country pay its way'. Indian nationalists bred up in a fifty-years-old tradition of rebelling against the rule of British imperialists now had to 'carry on the' *ci-devant* 'King-Emperor's government'. American politicians bred up in a one-century-and-three-quarters-old tradition of making it impossible for any American avatar of a British King George III to levy taxation without representation, and Russian autocrats bred up in a six-centuries-old tradi-

---

[1] Luke i. 52.
[2] See III. iii. 302–4.
[3] Gibbon, E.: 'General Observations on the Fall of the Roman Empire in the West,' at the end of chapter xxxviii of *The History of the Decline and Fall of the Roman Empire.*
[4] Luke ii. 52.

tion of making Holy Russia safe for an orthodox faith, had now 'to make the World go round' between them.

Would these rawly inexperienced new pilots succeed in keeping Mankind's battered and labouring ship off the rocks? This was the question that, in A.D. 1952, rose to the lips of a sixty-three-years-old middle-class North-West European observer who had been born into a seemingly rational and manageable world in which the feasible responsibility for keeping a world-wide Westernizing Society on an even keel had rested with his own kin and kind, and who had now lived on into an unfamiliar and disconcerting World in which his own kin and kind had become flies on a hazardously untended wheel that was spinning this way round and that way round at a venture, while two titans who alone now possessed the brawn-power to manipulate it were engaging in a quarrel over the dangerous competition between them for exercising the control. This question how a twentieth-century Westernizing World was likely to fare in the hands of its new masters is manifestly of the essence of our present inquiry into the Western Civilization's prospects. In trying to read this riddle we may manage to simplify to some degree a bafflingly complex intellectual task by giving separate consideration, first to Technology, War, and Government, and then to Technology, Class-Conflict, and Employment.

D. TECHNOLOGY, WAR, AND GOVERNMENT

(I) THE ORIGIN AND NATURE OF THE PROBLEM

THE problem with which the heirs of a Western Civilization were being confronted by the institution of War in A.D. 1952 had been set by the impact of an unprecedentedly potent latter-day Western technique on a literally world-wide Westernizing Society that was still articulated into a plurality of parochial states, since these states were still at liberty—and, because individually free, were collectively under pressure of a mutual fear and competition—to continue to go to war with one another as the penalty for being still severally sovereign and independent.

This problem was, as we have seen, by no means peculiar in itself to the Western World in the twentieth century of the Christian Era; it had likewise beset, in their day, all the civilizations that by this time were demonstrably extinct, fossilized, petrified, or moribund; but, as we have also observed, the extreme difference of degree between a latter-day Western and a previous human mastery over Non-Human Nature was tantamount to a difference in kind, because the additional 'drive' that it had put into the traditional institution of War had heightened the hazard of War for Humanity from a limited to an unlimited risk. In the situation as it was in A.D. 1952 the continuance of a possibility of War was no longer only a menace to the survival of another man-made institution, the now oecumenical Western Society. Since the invention of the atomic bomb and the incubation of further, and perhaps still more deadly, new weapons, War had also become a menace to the survival of all human beings implicated in this society—and, by the time of writing, the membership of the Western Civilization on the technological and military planes had come to include the entire living generation of the Human Race.

(II) THE SITUATION AFTER THE SECOND WORLD WAR

(a) A PROGRESSIVE CONCENTRATION OF POWER

On the morrow of the Second World War, a World that had now been unified within a Western framework found itself in the midst of a revolution generated and propelled by the double shock of two blows dealt by a Western technology that had been raised to an unprecedented degree of potency. The impact of Technology on the Human Psyche had detonated two world wars within twenty-five years of one another and had thereby reduced the number of the Great Powers in a Western system of international relations from eight to two within the thirty-one years 1914–45. The impact of Technology on Mankind's means of communication had brought these two surviving Great Powers within point-blank range of one another round the circumference of the globe by 'annihilating distance'. The situation thus created was so formidable, as well as so novel, that it called for a closer analysis.

The deadliness of the rate of the casualties among the Great Powers during these first thirty-one years of a new bout of Western warfare was grimly evident in retrospect. It was now clear that political and military power—and, by implication, economic power as well, in an industrialized and mechanized world—were being concentrated at a headlong pace; and the effect of a now manifest tendency upon its victims' minds and feelings was the sharper inasmuch as this dominant undercurrent of international affairs had been concealed, in and after the peace-settlement following the General War of A.D. 1914–18, by a short-lived tendency in the opposite direction that, at the time, had been conspicuous[1] just because it had been superficial.

By breaking up one Great Power, the Danubian Hapsburg Monarchy, and one *ci-devant* Great Power, the Ottoman Empire, and temporarily maiming and crippling two other Great Powers, Germany and Russia, the War of A.D. 1914–18 had permitted a previously dammed-back wave of Nationalism—rampant among politically un-unified and un-liberated peoples who had been dazzled by the historic success of the classical nation-states of Modern Western Europe[2]—to increase, at those four stricken Powers' expense, the number of the states of a medium and a small calibre in the Western international comity. During the preceding forty-three-years-long lull (*durabat* A.D. 1871–1914) between the end of the aftermath of the Revolutionary and Napoleonic Wars and the outbreak of the First World War, the political unification of Italy and of Germany had reduced the number of the lesser states in the Western system to a minimum and had indeed temporarily removed from the map all remaining states of a medium calibre with the sole exception of Spain. In the peace-settlement of A.D. 1919–21 this medium class of states had been reintroduced on to the political map by the reconstitution of Poland and by the aspiration of Brazil to have outgrown the stature of a small state even if she might not yet be deemed to have attained the dimensions of a Great Power.[3]

In the constitution of the League of Nations the success of the lesser states' self-assertion during the first decade after the close of the First World War had been registered in A.D. 1922 in the raising of the number of non-permanent seats on the Council from the provisional minority figure, originally agreed in A.D. 1919, of four, as against the minimum number of five permanent seats then reserved for Great Powers,[4] to the majority figure of six, as against four;[5] and in A.D. 1926 the Great Powers

---

[1] See Toynbee, A. J.: *The World after the Peace Conference* (London 1925, Milford), pp. 24–43, especially the comparative table, on pp. 32–34, of states, below the rank of Great Powers, which were playing an active part in international affairs before and after the War of A.D. 1914–18.

[2] See IV. iv. 185–90.

[3] See Toynbee, A. J., op. cit., pp. 35–36, and Toynbee, A. J., and Boulter, V. M.: *Survey of International Affairs, 1926* (London 1928, Milford), p. 21.

[4] See the original text of Article 4 of the Covenant of the League of Nations.

[5] See Toynbee, A. J., and Boulter, V. M.: *Survey of International Affairs, 1926* (London 1928, Milford), pp. 10–14.

on the Council had been prevented by the minor states' obstruction
from securing Germany's admission to membership in the League with
a permanent seat on the Council until they had consented to pay the
price of agreeing to the institution of three 'semi-permanent' seats for
the benefit of Poland and other medium-sized states of her kind.[1] The
Wilsonian illusion, thus created, that the comity of states was being
'democratized', had been fostered at the time by the self-restraint of the
three Great Powers—France, Great Britain, and the United States—
that had emerged from the First World War as temporary victors; for it
had been incompatible with these Powers' principles, and not imperative
for their interests, to treat the lesser states very high-handedly.

The brutal truth that had been hidden under this amiable but brittle
mask had, however, been quickly exposed by the resurgence of Germany
under a National-Socialist régime; and, after a criminal Power that had
taken full advantage of having been let off lightly in the Paris peace-
settlement of A.D. 1919–20 had paid in A.D. 1945 for her abominable
crimes by being first blasted, then invaded, and finally dismembered
like the Hapsburg Monarchy in A.D. 1918, it had become clear that the
significant event in the First World War had been the destruction of the
weakest of the Great Powers of the day, not the spawning of a litter of
new minor states. The temporary erection of minor states in a political
vacuum produced by the break-up or mutilation of former Great Powers,
so far from militating against the concentration of power, had created
an opportunity for it. The nominal 'liberation' of 'successor-states' had
indeed been illusory from first to last. They had been created to be
enslaved; for no other fate than enslavement could await minor states,
new or old, in a world in which the concentration of power was being
ordained inexorably by Technology's relentless progress.

In this world, states of anything less than the highest calibre were not
any longer either economically or militarily or politically 'viable'; their
presence on the map was an invitation to an aggressor, and the opportunity had been perceived by Hitler's intuitive genius and had been
exploited by his criminal lust for power as a key that was to open for
Germany her way to a world-wide domination. Hitler's strategy of
aggression had been to equip Germany with the material resources for
dominating the World by capturing the defenceless pawns that had
taken the *ci-devant* Hapsburg and Romanov Empires' places on a Central
and East European political chess-board; and his eventual catastrophic
failure to win for a Third German Reich this Hapsburg and Romanov
heritage had merely bequeathed to the Soviet Union the chance of
snatching out of a slain Third Reich's dead hands, and concentrating in
her own giant grasp, the whole of the Hohenzollern Empire's, as well as
the Hapsburg and Romanov Empires', legacy of 'successor-states' as far
west as the Elbe, Thuringia, and the Boehmerwald.

This progressive liquidation, since A.D. 1938, of the successor-states
of destroyed or mutilated Great Powers in Central and Eastern Europe
had indicated what the fate of all other successor-states in other regions
was likely to be. The only reason why West Germany and South-West

[1] See ibid., pp. 16–78.

Austria had not, by A.D. 1952, yet followed East Germany and North-East Austria into Russia's maw was that these two other fragments of a dismembered Third Reich had come meanwhile under the control of the United States and her West European allies Great Britain and France; and by this date it had become clear that the substitution of a United States protectorate for an untenable independence was the only insurance against Russian domination that promised to be effective in the long run for any state anywhere in the World.

This role, which was a new role for the United States in the Old World, was a familiar role of hers in the New World; for the substitution of a covert for an overt subjection through a process of nominal liberation was a tragi-comedy that, before being played in Central and Eastern Europe between A.D. 1918 and A.D. 1945, had been played in Latin America more than a hundred years earlier, between A.D. 1810 and A.D. 1823. From the days of the Holy Alliance to the days of the Third Reich, the Monroe Doctrine had saved the successor-states of the Spanish Empire in the Americas from falling under the domination of some other Continental European Power at the price of replacing a Spanish imperial administration by a United States political hegemony, that had been none the less effective for being exercised light-handedly, and by a no less alien economic ascendancy that had been enjoyed for a hundred years by the United Kingdom before this, too, had passed into North American hands. Since the reversal of the ratio of the relative strengths of the United States and Great Britain as a result of Great Britain's loss, and the United States' gain, in economic strength in the War of A.D. 1914–18, the underwriting of the Monroe Doctrine by British sea-power had ceased to be a necessity for the United States at the moment when it had ceased to be a possibility for the British Empire.

In a nineteenth-century Western World in which all the Great Powers except Great Britain had been situated on the European peninsula of the Eurasian Continent, the sea-power of the United Kingdom had incidentally screened the Americas in the act of screening the British Isles and the Transoceanic possessions of the British Crown against the danger of attack by any other Great Power then in existence. The temporarily favourable politico-geographical situation that had made it possible for the British Navy thus to provide strategic security for the entire English-speaking and overseas world had, however, ceased to exist when, at the turn of the nineteenth and twentieth centuries of the Christian Era, two new Great Powers—the United States herself and Japan —had arisen outside the British naval cordon round Continental Europe at the moment when, from within the cordon, British naval supremacy was being challenged by Germany; and the United Kingdom's inability, in these radically altered circumstances, to continue to give effective naval protection to the whole of the British Empire, not to speak of the United States and the Latin American republics, had been demonstrated in the course of half a century ending in A.D. 1945.

Even before the outbreak of the First World War, the challenge from Germany had constrained Great Britain to seek a reinforcement of her own naval strength—in the Pacific and the Indian Ocean by entering into an alliance with Japan in A.D. 1902 and in European waters by making an entente with France in A.D. 1904. In the Second World War, in which both the Japanese and the Italian Navy had gone into action on the anti-British side, even the countervailing aid of the by this time immense sea-power of the United States had not enabled British sea-power to save Hong Kong, Malaya, and the Dutch Empire in Indonesia from being temporarily overrun by the Japanese at a time when the whole strength of the British Navy was having to be employed nearer home on the three-fold task of holding the Levant, screening Great Britain herself from invasion, and keeping open the western approaches to the British Isles. In other words, the British Empire's tribulations during the Second World War had proved conclusively that, on the strategic plane, the British Empire was now no longer the unitary Power that it had been so long as the sea-power of the United Kingdom had been able effectively to protect the whole of the Empire, from its frontage on the North Sea and the English Channel to its frontage on the China Seas inclusive; and this dissolution of the British Empire's former strategic unity had been discounted on the political plane in advance. A British statesmanship that had never forgotten the lesson of Great Britain's disastrous intransigence towards her North American colonies in A.D. 1775–83 had been forestalling the violent break-up that had been the Spanish, the Ottoman, and the Danubian Hapsburg Empire's fate by transforming the British Empire into a Commonwealth of fully self-governing states since A.D. 1867, 1848, 1841, or even as early as 1791 if the local landmarks in the constitutional history of Canada are taken as indicators of the progress of political devolution in the British Empire as a whole.[1]

The voluntary, gradual, and pacific transformation of a once unitary empire into a free association between an ever-increasing number of fully self-governing states had been a triumph of good feeling and good sense which was perhaps almost unique in the political annals of Mankind in Process of Civilization up to date; and this political achievement reflected credit on the parties that had been willing to receive self-government in instalments, as well as on the party that had been willing to make progressive cessions of political power on its own initiative without waiting to be compelled. The creditableness of the political process in this British case could not, however, prevent the political effect of a dissolution of the British Empire by agreement from being much the same, in the stark terms of power politics, as the political effect of the break-up of the Spanish, Ottoman, and Danubian Hapsburg Empires by force. In this case, as in those, the effect had been the creation of a dangerous political vacuum which the champions of a dissolving Hapsburg Monarchy had diagnosed and deprecated when they had given it the pejorative nickname 'Balkanization', in allusion to the sequel to the previous break-up of the Ottoman Empire in Rumelia. The hard fact was that, by A.D. 1952, the sea-power of the United Kingdom

---

[1] A convenient list of the dates when responsible government was granted in the various British colonies with populations of West European origin will be found in Nathan, M.: *Empire Government* (London 1928, Allen & Unwin), pp. 47–48.

had ceased to be able, unaided, to protect the United Kingdom itself or what remained of its dependent empire, while the other now fully self-governing dominions of the British Crown, which had ceased to be able to count upon effective protection by the United Kingdom's Navy, had not become capable, unaided, of providing for their own security; and this meant that all continuing or former states members of the British Commonwealth, like all Continental European states west of the Soviet Union's 'iron curtain', must become protectorates of the United States as the only practicable alternative to their becoming satellites of the Soviet Union.

This was another way of saying that, in A.D. 1952, the Soviet Union and the United States found themselves confronting one another as the only two Great Powers still surviving on the face of the planet; and, in any international balance of power, two was bound, even at the best, to be an awkward number. It was true that in this current chapter of Western international history—in contrast to the situation during the chapter that had been opened in A.D. 1931 by Japan's initial act of aggression in Manchuria and had been closed in A.D. 1945 by the overthrow of both Japan and Germany—the two rival Great Powers were, both of them, economically 'sated' countries, either of which could find peaceful employment for the whole of its man-power, for many decades to come, in cultivating its own garden and developing the still untouched reserves of human and non-human resources within its own frontiers; and in this respect the international situation was less dangerous in A.D. 1952 than it had been before and during the Second World War, when Germany and Japan had been led into committing aggression by their belief that they could not continue to provide for a growing population at an acceptable standard of living within their own frontiers. By contrast, both the United States and the Soviet Union enjoyed, and admitted to enjoying, in A.D. 1952, a freedom from want that made both these surviving Great Powers immune to one of the historic motives for aggressiveness. Unfortunately, however, they did not, either of them, enjoy an equal freedom from the mutual fear that had been the other powerful motive for aggressiveness in the past; and their fear of one another was engendered and kept alive by the convergent operation of several different causes.

To begin with, the Russian and American peoples differed in êthos. The Russian people's habitual and characteristic temper was one of docile resignation, the American people's one of obstreperous impatience; and this difference of temper was reflected in a difference of attitude towards arbitrary government. The Russians acquiesced in this as an evil that some six hundred years of experience had schooled them to regard as inevitable, whereas the Americans' experience of successfully revolting against arbitrary government by ministers of a British King George III and successfully preventing any domestic recrudescence of arbitrary government during the first century and three quarters of the history of the United States had led them to think of arbitrary government as an evil which any people could banish if it had the will. In consequence, the Americans—including a middle-class-minded American industrial working class—saw their *summum bonum* in a liberty that they equated with equality, whereas a Russian Communist dominant minority saw their *summum bonum* in an equality that they equated with liberty. These temperamental and doctrinal differences made it difficult for the two peoples to understand, and therefore difficult for them to trust, one another; and this inevitable mutual distrust bred a no-less-inevitable mutual fear in the hearts of the two strong men armed, now that the arena in which they menaced one another had been transformed out of all recognition by the unprecedentedly rapid and far-reaching recent progress of Technology in Western hands.

(b) A METAMORPHOSIS OF THE *OIKOUMENÊ*

By the middle of the twentieth century of the Christian Era the progress of Technology had made a once wide world shrivel to dimensions so diminutive as to make it henceforth impossible for two gladiators to take their stand in this arena without finding themselves within pointblank range of one another—and this, *mirabile dictu*, simultaneously from the rear as well as from the front, since, in the act of diminishing the size of Mankind's habitat, the *Oikoumenê*, in terms of its conductivity for human purposes, Technology had also transformed the *Oikoumenê*'s shape.

The unprecedented vulnerability of the position of even the relatively least vulnerable Great Power in the World of A.D. 1952 was, indeed, a consequence of a recent revolutionary change in the strategico-political map. Within living memory, Man's World, in the sense of the habitable and traversable surface of the planet of which Man was a denizen, had at last become round in fact as well as in theory—or, if not yet fully round, at least already more than hemispherical.

The theoretical knowledge that the Earth was a globe and not a disk had, of course, been inherited by the Western Civilization from its Hellenic predecessor; and this theoretical globularity had been confirmed by an empirical demonstration when, in the course of Western Man's conquest of the Ocean at the opening of the Modern Age of Western history, Magellan's squadron, setting sail westward from Seville in A.D. 1519, had encountered in the Moluccas in A.D. 1521 Portuguese compatriots of its late commander's who had arrived there by setting sail eastward from Portugal, and when the *Vittoria* had clinched this proof by coming home to port in Seville, and thus completing the circumnavigation of the globe, in A.D. 1522. Yet even this empirical demonstration had been barren of any immediate appreciable practical consequences.

So long as a Modern Western World's footholds on the shores of the Pacific had remained under the rule of Spain, a mercantile community at Seville that had been determined to retain a monopoly of the trade between the Spanish Empire overseas and the metropolitan country had succeeded in confining the annual trade across the Pacific Ocean to a single 'round trip' in which a galleon (usually accompanied by a tender) from Manila had brought a cargo of Chinese wares to the port of

Acapulco on the Pacific coast of Mexico.[1] It had been only in the course
of the nineteenth century that this one sixteenth-century thread of Transpacific maritime commercial traffic had been multiplied in consequence
of the intervention of other Western Powers. From the eighteen-forties
onwards, the Western World's frontage on the American shores of the
Pacific had been extended northwards as a result of the overland expansion of both the United States and Canada from coast to coast. The
Mexican port of Acapulco had been reinforced by San Francisco, Portland, Seattle, and Vancouver, while, on the East Asian shores of the
Ocean, the Spanish port of Manila, the Portuguese settlement at Macao,
and the Dutch commercial establishment on Deshima[2] had been eclipsed
by Hong Kong, Shanghai, Tientsin, Nagasaki, Yokohama, and Dairen.
Yet, even when the one tenuous thread, linking Manila with the Spanish
dominions in the Americas, to which the Modern Western maritime
traffic across the Pacific had been confined for the first three hundred
years, had thus been transformed, during the nineteenth century, into
a multiple skein, the Oikoumenê had still retained, for practical purposes,
the flat and finite shape that it had worn since the days of Ptolemy,
Eratosthenes, and Hecataeus, and indeed since the pre-Hellenic dawn
of Civilization.

In the Old World, all civilizations of all generations up to date had
risen and fallen within a festoon-shaped zone that had been slung like
a hammock between a north-eastern peg in Eastern Asia slightly to the
north of the 45th parallel of northern latitude and a north-western peg
in Western Europe slightly to the north of the 60th parallel, with the
festoon's pendulous mid-point brushing the Equator at the Straits of
Malacca and sagging below it in Java. The divers sections of this
elongated home of the civilizations of the Old World had communicated
with one another through two socially and culturally conductive media
—a waterless inland sea, consisting of a chain of steppes and deserts
extending from Eastern Mongolia to the Western Sudan[3] via the Shā-
mīyah and the Desert of Sinai, and a chain of coastal and land-locked
waters extending from the Western Pacific to the Eastern Atlantic via
the Straits of Malacca, the portage linking the heads of the Persian Gulf
and Red Sea with the eastern extremity of the Mediterranean, and the
Straits of Gibraltar—and this pristine shape of the Oikoumenê had not
been changed when the western terminal of the longitudinal water-route
had been pushed westward, across the relatively narrow waters of the
Atlantic, from the west coast of the Continent to the two large off-shore
islands of North America and South America, or when the portage
previously interrupting the continuity of the voyage between the Continent's Atlantic and Pacific coasts had been circumvented in A.D. 1498
by da Gama and breached in A.D. 1869 by de Lesseps. At the turn of the
nineteenth and twentieth centuries of the Christian Era an Oikoumenê
whose eastern selvage had been extended southward from the east coast

---

[1] A.D. 1592 was the date at which the eastern terminal of the Spanish annual Transpacific voyage had been transferred to Acapulco from Callao. Officially the traffic had
been limited to this single sailing per annum. In practice there seems to have been a good
deal of illicit Transpacific trade after, as well as before, this date.

[2] See II. ii. 232-3. [3] See I. i. 64 and III. iii. 7-8.

of Asia to Australasia, and its western selvage westward from the west coasts of Europe and Africa to the west coasts of North and South America, had been still, in effect, just as flat and as finite as ever. It had merely been tied to the circumference of the globe, as if it had been an oblong strip of cloth, by a skein of threads attaching its eastern and western selvages to one another across the breadth of the Pacific; and, even when these threads had been drawn tight enough to convert the oblong strip into a band in the shape of an armlet by bringing the two selvages together, a tell-tale suture had remained visible as an International Date-Line intersecting the Pacific Ocean along a *tracée* which followed, with some local variations, the 180th meridian of longitude.

The establishment of this International Date-Line in A.D. 1884[1] had borne witness to two contemporary facts of human geography. On the one hand a circum-global maritime traffic-belt had now come to be sufficiently frequented to demand a global adjustment between the now contiguous extremities of a longitudinal series of regionally differentiated time-zones that could not extend in a continuous chain round the entire circumference of the globe without there being a chronometrical discrepancy, of the time-length of twenty-four hours, between the respective timings of the first and the last zone in the series at the line along which these two extremities now adjoined one another. On the other hand the Pacific Ocean had continued still to be decidedly the least-frequented section of a maritime traffic-belt that had come to encircle the globe by expanding eastward and westward simultaneously from a base-line along the Atlantic coast of Western Europe; and for this reason the heart of the Pacific had proved to be the least inconvenient locus on the traversable face of the globe for a conventional line at which west-bound travellers would add to, and east-bound travellers subtract from, their time-reckoning the twenty-four hours that, at some line or other, must be added or subtracted, according to the direction of the voyage, in order to cancel an inevitable twenty-four hours' discrepancy between necessarily contiguous extremities of a circum-global belt of differential time-zones.

Meanwhile, an *Oikoumenê* that had become round on the explorational plane in A.D. 1522, and on the chronometrical plane in A.D. 1884, had remained flat and finite on the strategico-political plane till A.D. 1941; for neither the passage of the Pacific on a voyage of exploration nor even the subsequent establishment of regularly frequented Transpacific traffic-lanes for merchant-ships had availed to reduce the Pacific to the dimensions of a basin in which navies based on opposite sides of its rim could manage to meet and fight. The turn of the nineteenth and twentieth centuries had seen this great Pacific gulf, breaking the continuity of the strategic map of a Westernizing World, still fixed—to all appearance as firmly as ever—in the locus of the International Date-Line; and a tacit assumption that the gulf not only was, but also would remain, an impassable one had been the common presupposition, on a fundamental point of fact, underlying the agreements reached at the Washington

---

[1] At the International Meridian Conference held in A.D. 1884 at Washington, D.C.

Naval Conference of A.D. 1921–2 between the Western naval Powers of the one part and Japan of the other.[1]

The basis of these agreements had been a reciprocal undertaking,[2] as between the United States, the British Empire, and Japan, to maintain the *status quo* with regard to fortifications and naval bases in certain specified territories and possessions of theirs in the Pacific area; for the effect of this reciprocal self-denying ordinance had been to insure Japan against the risk of seeing any potentially hostile foreign naval bases constructed within a closer range of her own home bases than the range of Pearl Harbour and Singapore; under the technical conditions of the moment, this provision had assured to the Japanese Navy the ability to maintain an unchallengeable regional supremacy in the Western Pacific; and, in return for the English-speaking naval Powers' consent to her thus preserving the security of her home territory through the retention of her command over the surrounding seas, Japan, for her part, had been willing to make a pair of counter-concessions without which the English-speaking Powers would not have been willing to make their own crucial concession to her.

In the first place, Japan had resigned herself to remaining markedly inferior to her two English-speaking competitors in absolute naval strength by agreeing[3] to maxima in the ratio of 525,000 tons each for them, as against 315,000 tons for herself, as the figures for the replacement of capital ship tonnage. In the second place, she had bound herself not to abuse her now virtually guaranteed naval supremacy in the Western Pacific by misusing it for the purpose of committing aggression either against the now defenceless West Pacific possessions of the English-speaking naval Powers (for instance, the Philippines and Hong Kong) or against a likewise defenceless China. Japan had entered into an agreement with the United States, the British Empire, and France in which the four parties had undertaken to respect one another's rights in relation to their insular possessions and dominions in the region of the Pacific Ocean,[4] and into an agreement with the same three parties, together with Belgium, Italy, the Netherlands, Portugal, and China, to respect China's sovereignty, independence, and territorial and administrative integrity and to refrain from taking advantage of anarchic conditions in China in order to take action there inimical to the security of the other contracting parties or damaging to the rights of their subjects or citizens.[5]

Twenty years after the date of the Washington Naval Conference the same assumption that the Pacific Ocean was still a strategically impassable gulf had nerved the Japanese Government to launch an attack on possessions of the United States, the British Commonwealth, and the

[1] See Toynbee, A. J.: *Survey of International Affairs, 1920–3* (London 1925, Milford), pp. 489–90.
[2] In Article 19 of the Treaty of the 6th February, 1922, for the Limitation of Naval Armament, between the United States, the British Empire, Japan, France, and Italy.
[3] In Article 4 of the Five-Power Treaty of the 6th February, 1922.
[4] In Article 1 of the Washington Treaty of the 13th December, 1921, between the United States, the British Empire, Japan, and France.
[5] The Washington Nine-Power Treaty of the 6th February, 1922, 'relating to the principles and policies to be followed in matters concerning China'.

Netherlands in the Pacific; but this audacious Japanese act of aggression had proved in the event to have been suicidal because the underlying assumption had proved, this time, no longer to hold good.

By A.D. 1941 the Japanese naval authorities must have come to believe in the possibility of the United States Navy's being able, from a base in Hawaii, at least to threaten the eastern flank of a Japanese advance southward in the Western Pacific; for there can be no other explanation of their surprise attack on the 7th December, 1941, upon the United States Pacific Fleet at Pearl Harbour. Their failure, however, to follow up their sensational success in this initial operation by attempting to occupy the Hawaiian Islands and to proceed thence to an attack upon the Pacific coast of the United States and Canada is presumptive evidence of an abiding conviction in Japanese minds that it would still be beyond the Japanese Navy's, and therefore likewise beyond the United States Navy's, power to conduct sustained naval operations on the grand scale across the breadth of the Pacific. It can never have entered into Japanese calculations, when the Japanese Government were taking their fateful decision to challenge the United States' sea-power, that the United States Navy would be able within less than four years to bring Japan to her knees by succeeding, as it did in A.D. 1942–5, in solving the unprecedentedly complex and difficult logistical problem of bringing a crushingly superior striking-power to bear upon Japan in a West Pacific theatre of naval operations that was more than 3,000 miles distant from Pearl Harbour and more than 4,500 miles distant from San Francisco.[1] Admiral Nimitz's achievement in dealing Japan a knock-out blow across the Pacific in A.D. 1945 was, indeed, as epoch-making an event in the history of the West and of the World as Magellan's achievement of making his way across the Pacific to the Philippines in A.D. 1521. The American seaman was, in effect, translating on to the far more exacting strategic plane the feat performed by his Portuguese forerunner on the relatively facile explorational plane 424 years earlier.

The capitulation of Japan on the 15th August, 1945, under the Transpacific pressure of United States sea-power signified the consummation of the revolutionary metamorphosis of a flat and finite *Oikoumenê* into a round one. After having been transformed from the shape of a card into the shape of an armlet when in A.D. 1884 its two selvages had been sewn together in a suture along the International Date-Line, the *Oikoumenê* had now been transformed again by the conversion of a sewn-up armlet into a welded ring; and this saturnine steel ring of unbroken strategic conductivity that had thus been clamped round the circumference of the globe in A.D. 1941–5 was threatening in A.D. 1952 to put the *Oikoumenê* through yet another metamorphosis by expanding into the shape of a great helm pulled down over the face of the globe from the North Pole to the southern edge of the Southern Temperate Zone.

In A.D. 1952 the problem of making direct flights, at least for warlike purposes, across the Arctic Circle was reported to be on the way to being solved, and this approaching fresh triumph of Western technology

---

[1] The distance to Yokohama was 3,445 miles from Hawaii and 4,750 miles from San Francisco.

would have the effect of putting the United States and the Soviet Union in jeopardy from one another on no less than three out of the four quarters of the compass. As a consequence of the latitudinal encirclement of the globe by the *Oikoumenê* through the United States Navy's strategic conquest of the Pacific in A.D. 1942–5, the two surviving Great Powers were already both in the same plight of simultaneously encircling and being encircled by one another—colliding, as they now did, on a front or rear in Eastern Asia, as well as on a rear or front in Europe.[1] The approaching conquest of the Arctic by the aeroplane was threatening soon to make the strategic position of both Powers even more precarious by now exposing both the United States' and the Soviet Union's northern flank to the new danger of trans-polar attack by air;[2] and, if this menace were to materialize, either Power would find itself in the desperate situation of having to provide concurrently for the defence of three fronts, each of which would be in danger of being turned from one flank as well as from the rear. Thus, in a now global *Oikoumenê* at the opening of the second half of the twentieth century of the Christian Era, either of the two still standing gladiators was in a posture to inflict upon, and to have inflicted upon him by, his adversary the shattering experience that once, at the crisis of the second paroxysm of an Hellenic Time of Troubles, had been inflicted upon the Romans by Hannibal and his brethren,

> ad confligendum venientibus undique Poenis
> omnia cum belli trepido concussa tumultu
> horrida contremuere sub altis aetheris oris
> in dubioque fuere utrorum ad regna cadendum
> omnibus humanis esset terrâque marique.[3]

Nor was this the end of a twentieth-century transformation-scene; for, in the act of enveloping the face of the globe, the *Oikoumenê* was contracting in scale, as measured by the speed of human means of communication, far faster than it was expanding in area, as measured by its extension over the physical surface of the planet. At the instant at which the *Oikoumenê* was assuming, on the strategic plane, the shape of a thirteenth-century Western helmet, this great helm was shrinking to the

---

[1] When the news of the Japanese attack on the United States fleet in Pearl Harbour reached England, an American visitor remarked to an English colleague of the present writer's, with whom he was discussing the news: 'It is all very well for you here in England to take this news so calmly! You can afford to, I suppose, considering that, in England, you are six thousand miles away from the front'. Forgetting, in the excitement of the moment, that the World had now become round and boundless, instead of being still flat and finite, this American commentator had consequently forgotten for the moment that a Britain which was six thousand miles and more to the east of the Japanese fleet's and air force's Pacific theatre of operations against Pearl Harbour was only twenty miles to the west of the German Luftwaffe's Continental bases of operations against Britain herself.

[2] The possibility that the ardent advance of Western Science might soon be going to set the North Pole on fire seems to have been overlooked by Senator Dandurand of Canada when, in A.D. 1924, in a debate on the draft Geneva Protocol for the Pacific Settlement of International Disputes, he had the hardihood to say about his native country: 'We live in a fire-proof house, far from inflammable materials. A vast ocean separates us from Europe.' In A.D. 1952 it was manifest that, as soon as the Arctic Circle became traversable by military aircraft, Canada's strategico-political situation would become much like what Belgium's had been in A.D. 1914 and in A.D. 1940.

[3] Lucretius: *De Rerum Naturâ*, Book III, ll. 833–7.

diminutive size of a thimble; and the strategic consequence of the coming reduction of 'the great open spaces' of Man's once immense terrestrial habitat to the dimensions of a Lilliput had already been visible to the mind's eye of a prophetically imaginative Victorian English mathematician.

' "What is the smallest *world* you would care to inhabit?" . . .

' "You don't mean to say you have been trying experiments in *that* direction!" I said.

' "Well, not *experiments* exactly. We do not profess to *construct* planets. But a scientific friend of mine, who has made several balloon-voyages, assures me he has visited a planet so small that he could walk right round it in twenty minutes! There had been a great battle, just before his visit, which had ended rather oddly: the vanquished army ran away at full speed, and in a very few minutes found themselves face-to-face with the victorious army, who were marching home again, and who were so frightened at finding themselves between *two* armies that they surrendered at once!" '[1]

At a date no more than half way through the twentieth century, current Western improvements in the technique of overland transport had not yet arrived at such a perilous pitch of efficiency as to have made it likely that a vanquished North Korean Army, if it had been thrown out of North Korea in a north-westerly direction by a victorious United Nations Army in A.D. 1952, would have cannoned into a dumbfounded American Army in Bavaria. The technique of maritime transport had, on the other hand, already been brought to a point at which a United Nations Army, if it were to be dislodged or withdrawn from South Korea in A.D. 1952, might be ferried round the globe in a trice to confront a Russian Army on the Elbe; and the contemporary progress in the technique of aerial transport had already left the utmost achievements of maritime and overland transport far behind. In A.D 1952 there was talk of aeroplanes which would be able to circumnavigate the Equator without having to break their flight in order to refuel, and which, when travelling from east to west, would be able to arrive before they had started by flying faster than the speed of the planet's eastward rotation round its axis; and presumably a single mechanical dragon of the kind could be freighted with bombs lethal enough to do execution on the appalling scale contemplated in the Book of the Revelation of Saint John the Divine. An *Oikoumenê* which had been so rapidly coalescing and contracting had, in fact, no less rapidly been transforming itself from a common home into a common abattoir for the Human Race.

Πάντες τῷ θανάτῳ τηρούμεθα καὶ τρεφόμεσθα,
ὡς ἀγέλη χοίρων σφαζομένων ἀλόγως.[2]

In contemplating the straits to which the Human Race had thus brought itself in the twentieth century of the Christian Era through the 'annihilation of distance' by a Western Civilization's prowess in Technology, an historian would recollect that this was not the first instance of an abrupt change of scale in the histories of the civilizations. In Western history itself, for example, there had been a previous change of the kind

---

[1] Lewis Carroll: *Sylvie and Bruno Concluded* (London 1889, Macmillan), pp. 169–70.
[2] Palladas of Alexandria in the *Anthologia Palatina*, Book X, No. 85.

some four hundred years back, when the old city-states of Italy and Flanders had been dwarfed by the sudden rise of nation-states along the Atlantic seaboard of Western Europe, and when these nation-states had suddenly extended Western Christendom's horizon by mastering the Ocean. There had been a corresponding dual change in Hellenic history after Alexander the Great's passage of the Dardanelles in 334 B.C., when the Hellenic World's horizon had been rapidly extended first eastward to India and then westward to the eastern shores of the Atlantic, while simultaneously the old Hellenic city-states had been dwarfed by new multi-municipal polities on the scale of the Seleucid and the Roman commonwealths.[1] The same pair of simultaneous and associated sudden changes of scale can be discerned in Sinic history at the time of the oubreak of the post-Confucian paroxysm of a Sinic Time of Troubles. From an historical standpoint the difference between these earlier instances of an abrupt change of scale in the histories of other civilizations and the current instance in Western history was one of degree; but this difference of degree was so great—whether measured in terms of Time or of Space or of Force—as to be tantamount, in practice, to a difference in kind.

In its current act of transforming itself by simultaneously coalescing and shrivelling, the *Oikoumenê* had reduced its strategico-political structure to an unprecedentedly stark simplicity. In A.D. 1952 there was, for practical purposes, only one surviving ocean, the Pacific; only one surviving continent, the Old World; only one surviving mediterranean sea, the Atlantic; only one surviving pair of islands, the Americas; and only a couple of surviving Great Powers, the Soviet Union and the United States. The 'heartland'[2] of the Continent and the more northerly of the two islands were the respective seats of the two Powers' metropolitan territories; the remainder of the habitable and traversable surface of the globe was a no-man's-land between the homelands of these two gladiators who were the only two still on their feet in a Western arena that had now become world-wide; and the comparative success or failure of the Soviet Union and the United States in a competition for gaining control over the human and non-human resources of the intervening no-man's-land seemed likely to be the decisive factor in determining the side to which the scales of an oecumenical Balance of Power would eventually incline. The circum-global range of this fateful no-man's-land on the strategico-political map of the World in A.D. 1952 was as significant a feature in the current situation as it was an unprecedented one.

In an earlier context[3] we have come across 'laws', operative in the play of the Balance of Power, that can be seen uniformly asserting themselves in divers episodes of history. In any system of international relations governed by the Balance of Power, it had been common form for the states at the centre to be pigmies by comparison with the relatively gigantic size of the states on the periphery, and for the central area, tenanted by the pigmy states, to be the arena into which the surrounding

[1] See IV. iv. 308–13.
[2] For this illuminating conception, see Mackinder, Sir H. J.: *Democratic Ideals and Reality* (London 1919, Constable), reissued in 1942 (New York 1942, Holt).
[3] In III. iii. 299–306 and 311–12.

giants descended to meet and do battle with one another. Since the particular constellation of states constituting a particular balance of power had usually been brought into existence by one of those abrupt changes of scale that we have just been calling to mind, the pigmies of today were apt to be the giants of yesterday, and the arena of today, in which today's contending giants were doing their worst to ruin the civilization that was their common mother, was apt to be yesterday's nursery-garden, in which the civilization of today had been brought up as a seedling before being bedded out farther afield.[1]

For example, the plain traversed by the Lower Yellow River, which in a post-Confucian Age of Sinic history was the principal battlefield of surrounding Great Powers that had arisen on the periphery of an expanding Sinic World, had previously been the domicile of the Chóu Dynasty and of a preceding Shang Dynasty's surviving successor-states, which in an earlier age had been the Great Powers of the Sinic World and the seed-beds of the culture that had come to prevail throughout the Sinic World in the subsequent Age of the peripheral Contending States. In Hellenic history corresponding roles were played by Continental European Greece and Sicily, and in Western history by Northern Italy and Flanders. Continental European Greece and Sicily, which in the third and second centuries B.C. were the battlefields of post-Alexandrine Hellenic Powers of the calibre of Egypt, Macedon, Carthage, Rome, and the Seleucid Monarchy, had been the domiciles of city-states that had been the Great Powers of a pre-Alexandrine Hellenic World and the seed-beds of an expanded Hellenic Civilization's post-Alexandrine phase of culture. Northern Italy, which from A.D. 1494 to A.D. 1866 was one of the two principal battlefields of the Great Powers of the Modern Age of Western history, and Flanders, which was their other principal battlefield down to A.D. 1918, had in a preceding constellation of forces been the domiciles of city-states that had been the Great Powers of a Medieval Western city-state cosmos and the seed-beds of the Western Civilization's Modern phase of culture.

It will be seen that these examples of *peripeteia*—the reversal of roles —in the play of the Balance of Power conform to a uniform pattern; and in Western history, by the time of writing, this pattern of events had repeated itself. In a twentieth-century Western World the nation-states that had been the Great Powers in the Modern chapter of Western history had been overtaken in their turn, since the transition to a post-Modern chapter, by the *peripeteia* which they themselves had inflicted once upon a time, at the preceding transition to the Modern chapter of Western history from a Medieval chapter, upon the city-states that had been the Western World's Great Powers in a foregoing Medieval Age. Since the onset of the series of world wars that had opened in A.D. 1914, France, Germany, Spain,[2] and Britain,[3] as well as Italy and Belgium,

[1] See I. i. 19, for the performance of this part by Northern Italy in a Medieval overture to a Modern chapter of Western history. See further II. ii. 263, and the passages in III. iii, cited on p. 486, n. 3.
[2] In the Civil War of A.D. 1936–9, which, under the guise of being a domestic conflict, had been a local prelude to the international war of A.D. 1939–45.
[3] In the attacks from the air to which she had been subject from A.D. 1940 to A.D. 1945.

had been suffering the ill-treatment that Lombardy and Flanders had suffered at French, Spanish, Austrian, Prussian, and British hands during the three war-and-peace cycles that had rolled over a Modern Western World in successive waves of calamity from A.D. 1494 to A.D. 1914.

Since A.D. 1914 the whole of the European nursery-garden of a Western culture that was now radiating into the whole of the rest of the *Oikoumenê* had become the Lombardy and Flanders of a literally world-wide constellation of forces in which the only surviving Great Powers were two states that were both non-European in their location and supra-national in their calibre; and this fate—physically and psychologically devastating though it was bound to be for the French and English and their like, now that their turn had come to suffer it—was nothing out of the ordinary in the sense that it was no exception to a 'law' of History exemplified in a number of earlier cases. The extraordinary feature in the strategico-military situation of a Westernizing World in A.D. 1952 was not that the European nursery-garden of a post-Modern Western culture had become the battlefield of a post-Modern Westernizing World's supra-national Great Powers; what was novel and anomalous was that, instead of being confined to the locality where its location was to be looked for in the light of all the historical precedents, the battlefield of a Westernizing World which had become literally world-wide had expanded—far beyond the limits of the Western Civilization's European patrimony—to embrace all the domains of all the civilizations that had risen and fallen up to date.

In the Old World the no-man's-land between the Soviet Union and the United States included the whole of the festoon-shaped zone extending from the Japanese Archipelago through Java to the British Isles that had contained the habitats of all civilizations originating in the Old World until the propagation of the Orthodox Christian Civilization into Russia at the close of the tenth century of the Christian Era and the propagation of the Western Civilization into the Americas at the close of the fifteenth century; and this globe-encompassing no-man's-land between two oecumenical Great Powers also embraced the habitats of the pre-Columbian civilizations of the New World in North America south-west of the Rio Grande and in a western strip of South America extending from Colombia to Bolivia. This conversion of all the nurseries of all the civilizations that had risen and fallen up to date into a common arena for a solitary pair of surviving Great Powers was an event that was, not merely unprecedented, but portentous. It seemed to signify that the latter-day expansion of the Western Civilization had been unique in two respects. Besides giving the *Oikoumenê* a spherical shape instead of a crescent shape in the act of expanding in the Space-dimension over the whole habitable and traversable face of the planet, a post-Modern Western Civilization had apparently been expanding in the Time-dimension as well by gathering up into its own heritage all the heritages of all the previous civilizations. All the eggs that all the representatives of this species of society had ever laid were thus now in the Western Civilization's basket, and this novel and hazardous concentration, in one target-area, of all the cultural treasures that Mankind had accumulated during the past five or six thousand years might be taken to indicate that the second half of the twentieth century of the Christian Era was to see the history, not only of the Western Civilization, but of Civilization itself, arrive at a crisis that might prove to be its climacteric.

In an historically as well as geographically unified *Oikoumenê*, it looked as if a competition for world-power between the Soviet Union and the United States might be decided in the long run by the suffrages of those three-quarters of the living generation of Mankind who, five or six thousand years after the dawn of Civilization, were still living in the Neolithic Age on the material plane of life, but who, within living memory, had begun to become aware that a higher material standard, opening up the possibility of a higher spiritual standard as well, had been demonstrated by the achievements of an industrialized Western Society to be attainable, under a latter-day Western technological dispensation, by a wider circle than the tiny minority which had monopolized the fruits of Civilization in all societies that had entered on the path of Civilization previously. In exercising a choice, now open to it, between an American and a Russian way of life, this hitherto submerged majority might be expected to choose whichever way of the two appeared in its eyes to promise better to satisfy this awakening majority's revolutionary aspiration to share in a hitherto dominant minority's traditional privileges; and the way of life for which the majority eventually opted on this criterion was likely to prevail throughout the *Oikoumenê*, as the progressive spread of a latter-day Western technological 'know-how' among Westernizing non-Western populations gradually enabled these to make their superiority in numbers tell in the conduct of Mankind's now common affairs.[1]

Yet, although the last word might lie with a hitherto submerged non-Western majority of Mankind, it nevertheless seemed probable that in the short run the decisive weight in the scales of a Russo-American balance would prove to be, not those three-quarters of the World's total present population, but that one-quarter of the World's total present industrial war-potential that in A.D. 1952 was still located in the Western Society's patrimony in Western Europe; for, in undergoing her melancholy metamorphosis from being the nursery-garden of a post-Modern Western culture to being one sector of a Westernizing World's battlefield, Western Europe had been losing her security, prosperity, and happiness without losing her economic, political, or military importance. In this circum-global battlefield the West European sector was a crucial one because it was the Insular Power's Continental bridgehead, and because, if this bridgehead on the tip of a Eurasian Continent's European Peninsula were to fall into the hands of the Continental Power domiciled in the Continent's 'heartland', the proportion between the respective shares of the World's total current industrial war-potential at the command of the two surviving rival Great Powers would be changed at a stroke from a present ratio of three to one in favour of the United

---

[1] The temper generated by militarization in the non-Western peasantry of a Westernizing *Oikoumenê* is examined on pp. 503–16, below.

States[1] to an approximate equality; and, although, to begin with, that half of the World's total industrial war-potential that in A.D. 1952 was located within the frontiers of the United States might be expected to count for more than the other half because it would be less difficult to organize and to manipulate as an organic unity, it was also to be expected that this organizational advantage on the side of the United States would be outweighed, as time went on, by an increasingly effective mobilization, under a Russian single command, of the resources of a Eurafrasian Continent whose aggregate resources, human as well as non-human, would doubtless prove far to exceed the aggregate resources of the American pair of islands.

(c) A TRANSMIGRATION OF THE MARTIAL SPIRIT

The Crescendo and Diminuendo of Militarism in Western Europe

The situation in which a Westernizing World on the morrow of a Second World War thus found itself on the strategico-political plane had its counterpart on the psychological plane; and, since the progress of Technology had no power to diminish the sway of feelings over the course of human affairs, but only power to put physical 'drive' into human action, our survey would remain incomplete if we did not take account of the spiritual, as well as the material, forces in the field. The effect of the current rapid increase in Mankind's material power, and of the recently consummated polarization of this power through its concentration at two points, and two only, on the face of a now global *Oikoumenê*, would depend on the feelings and calculations of the divers actors in a drama in which the action had become unprecedentedly high-powered without having ceased to be familiarly human. In a mid-twentieth-century Westernizing Society, the choices between Peace and War and between Parochialism and Oecumenicalism would be decided, not by a blindly mechanical play of non-human forces, but by the hopes, fears, recollections, and expectations of men and women domiciled in divers sections of an embryonic World Community.

In this psychological situation one crucial point was the temper of the people of Western Europe, since this *ci-devant* metropolitan area of a Westernizing World still contained, as we have noticed,[2] a large enough proportion of the World's total current industrial war-potential to determine the inclination of the Balance of Power as between the United States and the Soviet Union. In A.D. 1952 a Western Europe that had been in a perpetual ferment of aggressiveness, with the wide world for its arena, during more than four centuries ending in the catastrophe of A.D. 1914–18, was belatedly making involuntary psychological amends to its former victims by displaying markedly less martial spirit than any other region in the *Oikoumenê* of the day. After having at last converted even the Chinese, by the example of her own aggressiveness at their expense in the nineteenth century of the Christian Era, from a distaste for Militarism which had been ingrained in the Sinic tradition since

---

[1] This current superiority of the United States over the Soviet Union in the amount of industrial war-potential at its command is taken into account on pp. 529–30 and 531, below.   [2] On p. 489, above.

221 B.C., Western Europe mid-way through the twentieth century of the Christian Era had lost her own stomach for a warlike temper which she had thus perversely re-evoked in Chinese hearts; and this revolutionary psychological change in Western Europe marked the turn of a local tide that had been flowing, save for one pause in the eighteenth century, since the opening of the Modern chapter of Western history.

When, at the turn of the fifteenth and sixteenth centuries, the North Italian field of a Late Medieval Western Balance of Power between city-states had suddenly expanded to embrace the whole European domain of Western Christendom, the nation-states that were now replacing the city-states as the Great Powers in a larger constellation of forces had still followed the example of their Milanese, Venetian, and Florentine predecessors in fighting their battles mainly with mercenary troops—and these in numbers that were relatively small by comparison with the contemporary Western World's total stock of potential 'cannon-fodder'. In this Early Modern Western World the only peoples yet broken in to military service *en masse* were the seafaring populations of Venice and Genoa who furnished the man-power required for rowing their war-galleys.[1] In most of the Transmarine and Transalpine West European countries the only class yet militarized was a rural aristocracy that furnished a national heavy cavalry.

In sixteenth-century France, for instance, poverty conspired with martial spirit to send the younger sons of the nobility into the *gendarmerie*.[2] On the other hand the younger sons of a French peasantry that was able to make a living from agriculture found no need and felt no inclination to seek service in a national infantry;[3] the only French province that produced a native infantry in the sixteenth century was Gascony;[4] and in this age the French Government did not persevere in its discouraging attempts to build up a native infantry on a nation-wide scale,[5] because it was rich enough to hire a Swiss infantry which had established its ascendancy over the heavy cavalry of a Medieval Western Christendom since the eighth decade of the fifteenth century[6] and which had been constrained by poverty to raise its military proficiency to a professional pitch of excellence at which it could sell itself at a high price for mercenary service abroad.[7] Taking a cue from the Venetian Government,[8] the French Government in the sixteenth century recruited its light cavalry from mercenary Albanian 'stradioti';[9] and, for the reinforcement of armies operating in the Italian arena of Modern Western warfare, France could compete with other belligerents, non-Italian or Italian, for the services of the professional forces of the Italian principalities of Mantua, Ferrara, and Urbino,[10] which were pioneers in the state trading enterprise—afterwards taken over by German principalities catering for a wider market—of maintaining standing

---

[1] See Fueter, E.: *Geschichte des Europäischen Staatensystems von 1492–1559* (Munich and Berlin 1919, Oldenbourg), pp. 30–31, 163–4, and 228.
[2] See ibid., p. 54.   [3] See ibid., p. 53.   [4] See ibid., p. 59.
[5] See ibid., p. 59.   [6] See ibid., p. 18.
[7] The equipment, drill, and licensing of these Swiss mercenaries in the pre-Reformation generation of Early Modern Western history are described by Fueter, op. cit., pp. 10–18 and 234–6.   [8] See ibid., pp. 19 and 163.
[9] See ibid., p. 58.   [10] See ibid., pp. 231–2.

armies as profit-earning establishments to be hired at auction to the highest bidder.[1]

The Spanish light cavalry (*ginetes*),[2] French heavy cavalry (*gendarmerie*), and Gascon infantry were thus the only land-troops of any account in the Western World at the opening of the series of Modern and post-Modern Western war-and-peace cycles that sought service with their own national governments; and they too, like their Swiss contemporaries who sold their services abroad, were moved by mercenary motives as well as by a zest for bearing arms. In contrast to the spirit of the Governments of the Early Modern Western parochial states, which already delighted in war as ardently as any of their successors, a great majority of the population of Western Christendom was thus at this date still unmilitarized. While they were already being victimized by their rulers' warlike propensities, they had not yet become their rulers' accomplices in the public crime of making war for the love of it.

This initial unmilitary-mindedness of the peasantry and bourgeoisie of Modern Western Christendom is perhaps one explanation of the long survival there of the practice of treating military service as a professional career for 'expendable' foreign mercenaries rather than as a patriotic duty for respectable citizens. Scottish and Irish mercenaries were still employed, side by side with Swedish national forces, by Gustavus Adolphus in the Thirty Years War (*gerebatur* A.D. 1618–48), and German mercenaries by the Dutch and Venetian Governments in the Western General War of A.D. 1672–1713 and in the Veneto-Ottoman War of 1683–1715. The British Government employed hired Hessian conscripts as well as voluntarily enlisted native British professional troops in North America in its war with the insurgent people of the British colonies there in A.D. 1775–83; and as late as the time of the Crimean War (*gerebatur* A.D. 1854–6) it raised a foreign legion of German, Swiss, and Italian mercenaries amounting to nearly thirteen thousand men, all told.[3]

Even after the hired foreign mercenary had been superseded by the native professional soldier as the typical man-at-arms on Western parade-grounds, so ardent a militarist as Frederick the Great had reversed, as we have noticed already in another context,[4] his father's imprudent step of conscripting Prussian artisans as well as Prussian agricultural serfs;[5]

---

[1] The Rivieran principality of Monaco engaged in the corresponding state enterprise of maintaining a navy for hire (see Fueter, op. cit., p. 231) before it went in for the still more profitable public business of turning a sovereign independent city-state into an international gambling resort. [2] See ibid., p. 19.

[3] See Fortescue, J. W.: *A History of the British Army*, vol. xiii (London 1930, Macmillan), p. 227. When the writer of this Study was a child, he once met an old lady who told him that, in her own childhood, she had seen, encamped on the South Downs, the German mercenaries who, as she put it, had been hired to garrison Great Britain while the bulk of the small native British professional army of the day was on active service overseas. By the time of writing in A.D. 1951, the writer could not recollect his informant's identity, but the memory of what she had told him some fifty years or more ago was clear enough to send him in search of verification of it. The passage, cited in this footnote, of Fortescue's classical work shows that, out of close upon 10,000 German and Swiss mercenaries assembled in Great Britain from May 1855 onwards, about 6,000 were in fact retained there, while nearly 4,000 were sent to the seat of war.

[4] In IV. iv. 145–6.

[5] In an eighteenth-century Western World a selective conscription of the peasantry had been supplemented by the conscription of convicts and other 'social misfits'. The

and King Frederick William I himself would no more have dreamed than his son ever dreamed of attempting to impose military conscription upon the Prussian bourgeoisie. Nevertheless, the replacement of foreign mercenary volunteer or conscript professional troops by native volunteer or conscript professional troops, which had become the usual practice of a Late Modern Western World by Frederick the Great's day, was the prelude to the institution of compulsory universal service that was to be inaugurated, six years after Frederick's death, in a French *levée en masse*; and the raising of a native professional infantry, in imitation of, and substitution for, the rare, prized, and therefore costly Swiss, had been started by the Governments of contending Modern Western parochial states during a general war of A.D. 1494–1525 that had been the first war in the first war-and-peace cycle in the current Western series.

A sixteenth-century Austria who, like a sixteenth-century France, had no martial native source to tap for the meeting of her requirements in infantry,[1] and whose Government's poverty made it impossible for it to compete on equal terms with the French Government in the Swiss mercenary market,[2] had soon found a recruiting ground in adjoining German lands—in Bavaria, in Swabia, in Alsace—for Landsknechts who were passably good cheaper imitations of Swiss models;[3] and in a contemporary Spain the same necessitudinousness had been the mother of the same invention. On a Castilian Plateau which, like the Swiss highlands, was a predominantly pastoral country, the native herdsmen offered better material for making soldiers than the husbandmen who were numerically predominant in the populations of most sixteenth-century West European countries.[4] A Spanish 'gente armada y ordinada a la suiza' is mentioned as early as the 13th April, 1504, in correspondence between Their Catholic Majesties and the *gran capitán* Gonzalo de Córdoba;[5] by about the year A.D. 1520, this new-model Spanish infantry had made its début in the field of Western warfare;[6] and a Spanish copy had proved itself more versatile than its Swiss original in, for example, its capacity to storm fortresses besides fighting pitched battles.[7] A partial and gradual militarization of the population of Western Christendom, which had thus begun soon after the opening of the sixteenth century of the Christian Era with these German and Spanish national imitations of a Swiss model, had been the prelude to the wholesale militarization which had been inaugurated, some three hundred years later, in the French *levée en masse* of A.D. 1792.[8]

Napoleon's intemperately aggressive abuse of this newly forged French weapon had provoked a more thorough-going adoption and more efficient organization of compulsory universal military service in A.D. 1807–13 in an only temporarily crushed and humiliated Prussia; and

legislation of the day, which was the reflection of an oligarchic régime, had the effect of driving into the ranks of 'the criminal classes', and from these into the ranks of the armed forces, categories of offenders who might have been saved for Society if they could have had the benefit of the more humane Western legislation in force mid-way through the twentieth century.   [1] See Fueter, op. cit., p. 120.

[2] See ibid., p. 10.   [3] See ibid., p. 120.   [4] See ibid., p. 37.
[5] See ibid., p. 93.   [6] See ibid., p. 91.   [7] See ibid., p. 92.
[8] The tragically crucial importance of this revolutionary French step has been noticed in IV. iv. 150–1.

the political unification of Germany and Italy under the auspices of the
military-minded Houses of Hohenzollern and Savoy in the course of
the fifty-six years following the close of the Napoleonic Wars had
militarized Western Christian populations—in Tuscany, Saxony, the
former city-states of Frankfurt-am-Main, Bremen, Hamburg, and
Lübeck, and elsewhere—which had long since become unaccustomed
to bearing arms. The last members of Western Christendom to hold out
against the twentieth-century Franco-Prussian institution of compulsory
universal military service had been the English-speaking peoples; but in
the United States 'the draft' had been introduced and enforced on both
sides in the Civil War of A.D. 1861–5; in Australia and New Zealand
compulsory military service had been adopted in A.D. 1909, albeit
reluctantly and, as it turned out, only temporarily,[1] by two overseas
Western peoples who had come to fear that their thinly populated territories might be coveted today, and appropriated tomorrow, by the congested populations of Eastern Asia; and an institution which the United
States had found herself constrained to revive, and Great Britain to
introduce, *ad hoc* in the two first world wars had been retained in both
countries after the Second World War when the World had found itself
in a twilight state that was neither war nor peace as these had been
known in the past. Yet a still rising institutional tide of militarization
had hardly begun to reach the English-speaking peoples before the
psychological tide of martial-mindedness had begun to ebb in France.

The French psyche was, indeed, a psychological barometer on which
the readings at successive dates of Western history since A.D. 1494 had
been apt to give accurate forecasts of imminent rises and falls in the
strength of martial feeling in the Western World as a whole. The progressive militarization of Western Christendom in the course of the four
centuries beginning with a French King Charles VIII's invasion of Italy
had been registered in the French people's change of mood from the
peaceableness (perhaps due to their still lively memories of their sufferings in the Hundred Years War) that had been characteristic of a
majority of the French people in the first chapter of this tragic story to
the chauvinism that had come to be characteristic of a majority of them
by the Napoleonic Age. This adventitious aggressive spirit in France
had not been blunted by the horrors of the Grand Army's retreat from
Moscow in A.D. 1812 or by the experience of fighting on French soil in
A.D. 1814 or even by the humiliatingly decisive defeat, at Waterloo in
A.D. 1815, of a light-hearted attempt to reverse the military decision of
the preceding year. Thereafter, the French had still had in them the
spirit to seek psychological compensation for the loss of an abortive
Napoleonic French empire in Europe by embarking in A.D. 1830 on the
arduous aggressive military enterprise of conquering a substitute-empire
in North-West Africa; and a French aggressiveness which had thus survived a chastisement with whips at Waterloo had required the sharper
sting of a chastisement with scorpions at Sedan to make it wince and
wilt. The nemesis of a Napoleon I's militarism had not deterred French-

[1] Compulsion was suspended in Australia in A.D. 1929 and in New Zealand in A.D.
1930.

men of a later generation from placing their lives and fortunes in the hands of a Napoleon III; and, after having pandered to his subjects' still impenitently militaristic taste by leading them successively into a Roman adventure in A.D. 1849, a Russian adventure in A.D. 1854-6, an Austrian adventure in A.D. 1859, and a Mexican adventure in A.D. 1862-7, this second-rate practitioner of a dangerous trade had committed his country in A.D. 1870 to a Prussian adventure in which the agonies of the Hundred Years War had been concentrated within a Time-span of seven months. This terrible retribution upon France for a militarism to which her Government had been addicted since A.D. 1494, and her people since A.D. 1792, had been so shattering a psychological experience that French souls had never afterwards fully recovered from it.

Though in A.D. 1914 a conscript French national army had patriotically flown to arms to stem a fresh German invasion, and though for four years thereafter the French people had heroically endured casualties of a severity that was crushing for a country in which the population had ceased to increase, besides being grievous for millions of bereaved families, the French had emerged in A.D. 1918 from this deadly struggle for existence with a sharpened consciousness of having been caught by the malice or nemesis of History in a strategico-political position that was so perilously exposed that, sooner or later, it must prove untenable. History had condemned France in a post-Modern Age to have for her next-door neighbour a German national state that was at least as aggressive-minded as France had ever been at her worst, and that was now far more than a match for France in industrial war-potential, as well as in man-power. On the 11th November, 1918, the French had been aware that they would never have emerged on the winning side from a war with the Germany of that day if the combined strength of all the English-speaking peoples had not also been thrown into the anti-German scale; and from that moment onwards France's English-speaking allies and associates had started perversely to do their worst to break French hearts by serving public notice on France that she could not depend upon their being willing to come to her rescue again if the German peril were once more to loom up. In these cruelly unpropitious circumstances the French had entered an inter-war breathing-space in a mood of disillusionment and discouragement that had been registered in action eventually in France's collapse and capitulation in June 1940; and the ensuing passage of French history had been big with the future of the Western World as a whole.

The Vichyssois temper and régime had given a practical demonstration of a psychological process through which Nationalism, when carried to an extreme, could box the compass by turning into an equally extreme renunciation of a traditional will to maintain and assert a parochial sovereign independence. Frenchmen, responsible at the time for the government of their country, who, on the 16th June, 1940, had rejected with indignation Churchill's eleventh-hour offer of a voluntary political union on equal terms between a then all-but-conquered France and a then still unconquered United Kingdom, on the ground that this British offer was an insidious move to consummate the sacrifice of France for the United Kingdom's benefit, did not rebel when, six days afterwards, on the 22nd June, they were required to sign an armistice which placed France at the mercy of a National Socialist Germany, and did not refuse, after that, to accede to German demands for French collaboration with Germany's continuing war-effort against a Britain who, till yesterday, had been France's ally, though a German victory over Great Britain would have extinguished France's last hope of ever being liberated from the German yoke to which she had bowed her neck. The ostensibly nationalist Vichyssois slogan 'la France seule' was a euphemism for the unspeakable truth that France had placed herself at Germany's disposal and had accepted the shameful role of principal slave to a foreign tyrant nation that had attacked and conquered its neighbours in Continental Europe as a first step towards attacking and conquering the rest of the World with sinews of war that were to be reinforced thanks to the pliancy of Continental European victims who were to be bullied into becoming their German conquerors' accomplices.

It was true that a demoralized French nationalism would never have entered into a transaction of which it was manifestly ashamed if the alternative course demanded by a traditional standard of heroism had not been beyond the French people's powers of endurance under novel technological conditions of warfare which had keyed up a once familiar and tolerable ordeal to an unprecedented degree of severity; but this turn of a technological screw was not the whole explanation of the collapse of French *moral* that had declared itself in A.D. 1940. Part of the explanation also was that, for nationalist-minded souls, the psychological difficulty of acquiescing in the abrogation of a national sovereign independence by a foreign conqueror's exercise of an irresistible brute force was not so great as the psychological difficulty of taking the initiative in voluntarily surrendering some agreed part of the same national sovereign independence in order to enter into co-operation with people of other nations, on a footing of equality, in a loose confederation like the League of Nations or in a full federal union like the United States—and this though the difference between the respective effects of these two alternative ways of foregoing sovereignty was the extreme difference between purchasing security through co-operation and paying the penalty of subjection for the luxury of choosing the psychologically easier option of accepting a *fait accompli* imposed by *force majeure*.

The second factor that was reinforcing the effect of an advancing Technology in undermining a parochial patriotism was a victory of class-feeling over patriotism in a competition for precedence between two conflicting expressions of sectional corporate self-interest that were irreconcilable in the last resort. In a France that had been living under the régime of a *Front Populaire* from June 1936 to April 1938 a considerable portion of the middle class had apparently come, by A.D. 1940, to feel that the aggression of its working-class fellow-countrymen on a domestic front was a greater menace to the preservation of the middle class's most highly prized assets than the aggression, on an international front, of a Fascist Power which promised to protect a compliant French bourgeoisie's private property as a *quid pro quo* for the abrogation of their country's national sovereignty.[1]

If in France the Vichyssois policy and spirit had thus demonstrated that the experience of a First World War had made one once aggressively martial-minded Western nation willing to purchase peace 'at *any* price', the French people's British allies had been convicted of a willingness to purchase peace 'at *almost* any price'[2] by a policy and spirit of 'appeasement' (in a pejorative connotation of the word) that had been in the ascendant in Great Britain from the 18th September, 1931, when her inter-war temper had first been put to the test by the opening move in a new Japanese campaign of military aggression in the Far East, and the 10th May, 1940, when the British people had taken for their leader a statesman who had lost no time in putting their temper to the test again by his challenging offer to his countrymen of 'blood and toil and tears and sweat'[3] as the price that must be paid for the United Kingdom's present survival and future victory.

From June 1940 to August 1945 the British people had paid as appallingly heavy a price for the purchase of an inestimably valuable spiritual treasure as the French people had paid in A.D. 1914–18; and in A.D. 1952, some seven years after their release from this supreme ordeal, it had still to be seen whether the ultimate psychological effect of a Second World War on British *moral* would or would not prove to have been the same as the effect of a First World War had proved to have been on French *moral*. Would British souls that had been willing to purchase peace 'at *almost* any price' rather than have to face a Second World War be found willing to purchase it 'at *any* price' if a third world war were to descend upon them? There were, after all, limits to Human Nature's powers of endurance, even in communities of the toughest moral fibre fortified by the most Spartan martial tradition. If the spirit of France had flinched in June 1940 at the prospect of having to face casualties in the field even heavier than the French casualties in A.D. 1914–18 and having to see the whole of her metropolitan territory overrun by a temporarily victorious enemy, how was the spirit of Britain likely to react to the prospect of seeing a congested island subjected to an intensive bombardment with guided atomic missiles which would do incomparably greater execution than the heaviest of the blows recently delivered by Göring's *Luftwaffe*?

The answer to this question was no foregone conclusion, and any future follower, German or Russian, in Hitler's footsteps would be inviting the fate that Hitler had brought on himself and his ambitions if, like Hitler, he were to gamble on the answer to the question turning

---

[1] Similarly, in a China that had been living under the régime of a Kuomintang during the years A.D. 1928–48, a considerable section of the industrial working class and even of the peasantry had apparently come, by A.D. 1948, to feel that the incompetence and corruption of this ruling clique of a Chinese *intelligentsia* was a greater evil than the hegemony of the Soviet Union under which they would be allowing their country to fall if they acquiesced in the liquidation of the Kuomintang régime by a Chinese Communist Party.

[2] 'Not peace at *any* price, but peace at *almost any* price' (Mr. Eden in the House of Commons at Westminster on the 25th June, 1937).

[3] Mr. Churchill in the House of Commons at Westminster, 13th May, 1940.

out to be that the British no longer had any spirit left in them; yet, for all that, the question could not be denied a hearing in A.D. 1952; and the British people was not, of course, the only people in the World at this date about whom this importunate question had to be asked. If it was at least questionable whether a third world war would be endurable for the people of the United Kingdom, it was manifestly questionable *a fortiori* whether this tribulation would be endurable for Continental West European peoples who had undergone in the years A.D. 1940–5— and, in the Belgian, French, Italian, and Polish cases, in the years A.D. 1914–18 before that—an experience that was more harrowing, and very much more demoralizing, than the British people's ordeal of an aerial bombardment. These Continental West European victims of an inordinate German militarism had seen their countries partially or completely overrun and occupied by invading hostile armies, and they had found themselves at the mercy of an occupying alien enemy that had taken advantage of its power over them to distrain upon their material resources for the reinforcement of its own war effort against their surviving allies and to harness their energies to its own evil will by training upon them all the terrors of a post-Modern Western totalitarian police-state.

This institutional engine of militarism had been keyed up to a sinister efficiency on the home fronts of a Fascist Italy and a National-Socialist Germany; and, while in A.D. 1952 it was indisputably true that Western Europe as a whole had had its martial spirit damped by its devastating experiences since A.D. 1914, was this true without reservations of the two West European countries in which Fascist national governments had deliberately re-stoked the local fires of militarism after the First World War with the intention of profiting, in a Second World War, by a consequent marginal difference between the respective limits of their foreign victims' and their native instruments' capacity for continuing to stand the traditional test of an ordeal by battle? What had been the ultimate effect, on Italian and German souls, of the misdeeds that they had allowed their governments to require of them, and of the retribution that they had consequently allowed their governments to bring down upon their guilty heads? In what mood had the Italians emerged from the twenty-one years A.D. 1922–43, and the Germans from the twelve years A.D. 1933–45?

An observer in the year A.D. 1952 could predict with some assurance that the Italians would prove to have no more stomach for a Mussolinian militarism to which a majority of the nation had paid lip-service, not because they ever had it in them to go forth conquering and to conquer[1] any foreign people that was their match in technical equipment, but because they did not have in them the spirit to defy the will of a domestic tyrant from the Romagna. It was assuredly no accident that there was always an exceptionally strong local resistance to Fascism in a Piedmont that was also exceptional in being the one locality in a twentieth-century Italy that had preserved something of an earlier martial tradition. On this showing, it might be prophesied in A.D. 1952 that Italy would go the

[1] Rev. vi. 2.

same way as the rest of Western Europe. But could the same prophecy be made at the same date with the same confidence about Germany, where the traditional Prussian militarism that Hitler had stoked up to such incendiary effect manifestly had a far more wide-spread and far more tenacious hold on the souls of the people?

This question was one of grave concern to non-German West Europeans at a moment when, with their reluctant and half-hearted assent, the Americans were soliciting a German people that had attacked and overrun its neighbours twice in one lifetime to revive a martial tradition that, within living memory, had cost the rest of the World two world wars. At the time of writing, it was impossible to predict what the German response was going to be to a challenge presented to Germany by the current quarrel between the ex-victors in the latest of two wars that Germany had made and lost. Which of two features in the new situation would loom the larger in German eyes? The possibility for Germany of reacquiring political power by auctioning German military services to the higher bidder of the two parties that were now feverishly competing for so unquestionably valuable a military asset? Or the possibility of exposing herself to suffer a fate that would be even worse than the fate that she had brought upon herself in A.D. 1945, and indeed as bad as the fate that she had experienced in A.D. 1618–48, if she were now to become the battlefield of a war between foreign Powers by whom she had formerly been 'encircled'? On the morrow of the War of A.D. 1939–45 there were signs in Germany that some Germans, at any rate, had by this time had enough of sacrificing life, property, and conscience by submitting to serve as 'cannon-fodder' for successive German Governments to spend in successive wars of aggression ending in successive disastrous defeats; and the emergence of this mood in Germany after VE-Day, 1945, was, after all, something that was to be expected in the light of similar changes of heart which, at earlier dates, had come over other West European peoples who, in their day, had been addicted to Militarism no less strongly or persistently than the Germans.

The Germans' French victims, as we have already noticed, had lent themselves to Militarism for 376 years (A.D. 1494–1870), till they had been cured of it by a crushing German retort. A Swedish militarism that had been rampant since Gustavus Adolphus (*regnabat* A.D. 1611–32) had disembarked his expeditionary force on German soil on the 27–28th June, 1630, had been extinguished by a subsequent and consequent Swedish experience of being bled white by Charles XII (*regnabat* A.D. 1697–1718). A Spanish militarism that had been coeval with its French counterpart had evaporated after the Thirty Years War. 'Therefore say: "Thus saith the Lord God: . . . I will put a new spirit within you; and I will take the stony heart out of their flesh and will give them an heart of flesh".'[1] When this God-given change of heart had been vouchsafed, in recent Western experience, to the Spaniards and the Swedes and the French, it seemed unlikely that the Germans would be proof against an influence to which these other West European peoples had all yielded. Spanish, Swedish, and French hearts had been changed, sooner or later,

---

[1] Ezek. xi. 16 and 19.

by the experience of learning through suffering ($\pi\acute{a}\theta\epsilon\iota$ $\mu\acute{a}\theta os$);[1] and since A.D. 1914 the Germans had received, in their repeated punishment for a repeated sin, a double measure of this sovereign spiritual education. 'Whom the Lord loveth He chasteneth, and scourgeth every son whom He receiveth',[2] was a timeless truth that held out hope for the conversion of the Germans in the sixth decade of the twentieth century of the Christian Era.

No doubt the non-German West Europeans, in their dealings with their German neighbours at this critical time, might, while putting their trust in God, still feel inclined, *en attendant*, to keep their power dry.[3] Yet, notwithstanding the openness of this question concerning Germany, by the year A.D. 1952 it looked as if, in a Western Europe which had already been put to the torment of a Second World War, dispirited nations and exasperated social classes had been reduced, by the combined operation of the psychological forces analysed above, to a temper in which their moral capacity to offer resistance to a world-conqueror would be at a minimum.

The Significance of Hitler's Bid for World-Dominion

The opportunity for political crime on an oecumenical scale which had been opened up by a recession of Militarism in Western Europe had indeed been visible to Hitler as early as the morrow of the First World War.

Hitler had perceived that, in a World whose peoples were all now miserably war-weary and war-shy, world-dominion might be the easy prize of any nation that could still be coaxed, duped, doped, or flogged by an audacious demagogue or despot into being one degree less unwarlike than its neighbours. 'In the realm of the blind the one-eyed man is king.' On the strength of this intuition Hitler had cold-bloodedly remilitarized Germany and then attacked Poland, four small West European countries, and France; and the sensationally successful results of these successive criminal acts had testified to the correctness of Hitler's calculations up to that point. The German people, for the second time in one lifetime, had duly allowed themselves, not only to be used by a German Government as instruments for the commission of an international crime, but to be induced to play this criminal role with all their heart, soul, mind, and strength;[4] a Polish people that had remained exceptional in having lost nothing of its martial spirit had been overwhelmed by a German aggressor's crushing superiority on the plane of Military Technology; and the collapse of Hitler's West European victims had justified Hitler's thesis that, in the state of mind and feeling then prevalent in Western Europe, a small margin of superiority in martial spirit might earn for a boldly wicked aggressor a fabulous dividend in military conquests. Hitler was reported to have said, and this not in jest, that all good pacifists ought to wish him success because the con-

---

[1] Aeschylus: *Agamemnon*, l. 177, quoted in this Study, *passim*.
[2] Heb. xii. 6.
[3] 'Put your trust in God, my boys, and keep your powder dry' (Blacker, Valentine: *Oliver's Advice*). [4] Mark xii. 30.

centration of a monopoly of military and political power in Germany's hands was the only practical means, in the World as it was, of translating the ideals of Pacifism into reality. Hitler was, in truth, offering the World, at his own price, a commodity—freedom from fear of further world wars—of which Mankind stood in dire need, and for which they were therefore already prepared to pay dear.

In psychological principle, therefore, the business of world-conquest on which Hitler had embarked was as 'sound' as it was immoral; and, if in the event this would-be world-conqueror, so far from making Germany's and his own political fortune, brought down upon his Third Reich and upon himself a disaster that eclipsed the previous downfall of the Hohenzollern Reich and Dynasty, this was because Hitler was guilty of two fatal errors, of which the second, at any rate, might have been avoidable.

The builder of a Third Reich who had also been the creator of National Socialism had made the price of a *Pax Teutonica* so intolerably high in requiring submission to a Nazi German domination that, at the first glimmer of a prospect that this tyranny might ultimately be foiled and overthrown, resistance movements sprang up in even the tamest of the countries that Hitler's armies had overrun, while a British people which had allowed its governing class to practise 'appeasement' towards Japan, Italy, and Germany from A.D. 1931 to 1939 falsified the not irrational expectations that Hitler had founded on his observation of this decidedly un-martial and apparently persistent British temper by refusing to accept peace at Hitler's price even when the collapse and capitulation of France in A.D. 1940 had left Britain fighting on alone without any apparent prospect of staving off imminent defeat and subjugation.

Hitler's second fatal error was his abandonment of a hitherto brilliantly successful policy of administering his aggression to his victims in successive doses nicely calculated to be, each time, just not too large for a docile patient to swallow; and this error looks like a gratuitous one, since an historian cannot descry any contemporary change in the international situation that could have forced Hitler's hand in this crucial issue. By his seizure of Bohemia and Moravia on the night of the 15th–16th March, 1939, Hitler made it certain that, when he went on to attack Poland, he would find himself this time at war with Great Britain as well; by ensuring the belligerency of Great Britain, he converted a local war into a general war; by thus bringing on a general war, he ensured the eventual intervention of the United States (whatever assistance his Japanese accomplices might or might not eventually give in driving the United States into belligerency); and, by thus condemning Germany, sooner or later, to be smitten by the full force of an industrial war-potential in the United States that amounted to more than half the aggregate industrial war-potential of the whole World at the time, Hitler was condemning Germany to receive a knock-out blow. Moreover, as if this chain of inevitable and inevitably fatal consequences of a false step taken on the 15th March, 1939, was not enough to make sure of Hitler's frustrating his own purposes, he gratuitously attacked the Soviet Union after he had failed to subdue Great Britain and had succeeded in moving the United States to convert herself into 'the arsenal of Democracy'.

It will be seen that Hitler's eventual failure to impose peace on the World by force of arms was due, not to any flaw in his thesis that the World was ripe for conquest, but to an accidental combination of incidental errors in his measures for putting into execution a nefarious grand design that, in itself, was a feasible scheme for profiting by a correctly diagnosed psychological situation. A twentieth-century World, that had thus, in A.D. 1933–45, been reprieved, thanks only to a chapter of lucky accidents, from a fate which Mankind's patently increasing defeatism and submissiveness had almost provocatively invited, could hardly count upon any future would-be world-conqueror's being so clumsy as to let the same easy prey escape for the second time by allowing himself to blunder in his turn into an Hitlerian combination of egregious errors; and, if a future follower in Hitler's footsteps was unlikely to make Hitler's mistakes, he could, on the other hand, be sure of profiting by his Nazi forerunner's pioneer work in clearing the ground for a successor to cultivate; for, in failing by so narrow a margin to win the prize of world-dominion for himself, Hitler had left the prize dangling within the reach of any successor capable of pursuing the same aim of world-conquest with a little more patience, prudence, and tact.

The yeoman service that Hitler had performed for some future architect of a *Pax Oecumenica* was his historic achievement of forcing an oecumenical society that had already been devastated by one world war to inflict upon itself, within the lifetime of the generation that had been smitten by that shattering catastrophe, a Second World War that had brought still more grievous tribulations upon the World at large, and especially upon Europe. An Hitlerian 'revolution of destruction'[1] was an irrevocably accomplished fact by the time when Hitler came to grief; and the collapse of all Hitler's designs for the aggrandizement of Germany left this negative result of his criminal career intact. In A.D. 1952 it was manifest that, in failing to win world-dominion for his own abortive Third German Reich, Hitler had bequeathed, to any successor with the ability to take advantage of this opportunity, the legacy that Assyria had bequeathed to the Achaemenidae, Ts'in She Hwang-ti to Han Liu Pang, and Pompey and Caesar to Augustus.[2] Hitler, finding the peoples of a twentieth-century Westernizing World already psychologically devastated by the experience of one world war, had left them more than doubly devastated by a more harrowing repetition of the same experience within the same lifetime. A field that in A.D. 1914–18 had been scored by trenches and pitted with shell-holes had been ploughed up by bulldozers and effaced by bomb-craters in A.D. 1939–45. An *Oikoumenê* that in August 1914 had been under cultivation as a chequer-board of national allotments had now become a waste-land open to a unitary occupation. For a post-Hitlerian empire-builder, Hitler's derelict legacy was a gift of the Gods.

[1] Rauschning, H.: *Germany's Revolution of Destruction*, English translation (London 1939, Heinemann).
[2] See V. vi. 186–7.

The Temper generated by Militarization in the Non-Western Peasantry

At the time of writing, it could not be foreseen whether, after a failure for which Hitler had paid with his reputation as well as with his life, other adventurers would embark on an enterprise in which the magnitude of the risk was proportionate to that of the prize that would be the reward of success. It could, however, already be foreseen that, if Hitler did have successors, their calculations, like his, would largely turn on estimates of the marginal differences in the degree in which vestiges of a martial spirit still survived in the hearts of the divers peoples of a world in which a traditional heroism was everywhere being called in question by the revolutionary psychological effect of technological changes. For the purposes of our own present inquiry into the prospects of the Western Civilization at this date, we may find it illuminating to take our stand in a hypothetical post-Hitlerian aggressor's observation-post and try to read, through his eyes, a psychological map of the contemporary *Oikoumenê* on which the aggressor may be imagined to have plotted out, for his purposes, the local differences in the degree of the defeatism and submissiveness that he can count upon in the hearts of his intended instruments and victims.

In attempting such a psychological survey, we have to bear it in mind that even the most judicious aggressor might be prone to fall to some extent into Hitler's error of over-estimating the lengths to which he could go with impunity. Even in an Atomic Age, traditional virtues and ideals might be expected to die hard when, like martial valour and like patriotism, they had in them the momentum of a five-or-six-thousand-years-long tradition. In setting our standard of expectation in regard to the prospective behaviour of a Westernizing World in the second half of the twentieth century of the Christian Era, we shall be wise to recall such pertinent historical precedents as, for example, the alacrity with which, in 522 B.C., some of the peoples that had been passed under Assyria's harrow seized an opportunity—offered by the assassination of an occupant of the Achaemenian imperial throne who was the last legitimate representative of the Cyran Achaemenid line if he was not an impostor—to plunge their world into anarchy again and expose themselves once more to all the horrors suffered by their forebears in the eighth and seventh centuries B.C., in the hope of depriving themselves of the dearly bought blessings of a *Pax Achaemenia* and resubjecting themselves to the curse of a now manifestly anachronistic parochial sovereign independence. With this cautionary tale in our minds we may perhaps venture on a tentative appraisal of the diversities in the temper of the divers peoples of a Westernizing World on the morrow of its Second World War. Manifestly the crucial question here was whether the martial spirit which had been ebbing out of Western Europe had evaporated or had migrated to other regions of the *Oikoumenê*.

The second of these two possibilities required consideration because, by A.D. 1952, it had become clear that the thirty-eight years which had now passed since the outbreak of the First World War in A.D. 1914 had brought to pass a dramatically complete inversion, not only of Western

Europe's previous temper, but also of her corresponding previous role. A region out of which one wave of aggression at the heels of another had been surging up indefatigably and travelling to the uttermost parts of the Earth for some four centuries and a quarter, ending in A.D. 1914, had now become the battlefield of a World which, in that now past chapter of history, Western Europe had been knitting up with herself by innumerable acts of economic, political, and cultural victimization; and this recent revolution in Western Europe's strategico-political situation was one of the experiences that had made the mood of her inhabitants apprehensive and conciliatory instead of confident and truculent. This reversal of fortunes and feelings in Western Europe, which had become manifest to all politically conscious West Europeans, and indeed to all their politically conscious contemporaries, by A.D. 1952, had been perceptible on the morrow of the First World War to the sensitive spirit of a French man of letters in the light of his own people's tragic experience and limpid intelligence.

'Un frisson extraordinaire a couru la moelle de l'Europe. Elle a senti, par tous ses noyaux pensants, qu'elle ne se reconnaissait plus, qu'elle cessait de se ressembler, qu'elle allait perdre conscience — une conscience acquise par des siècles de malheurs supportables, par des milliers d'hommes du premier ordre, par des chances géographiques, ethniques, historiques, innombrables. . . .

'L'Europe va-t-elle garder sa prééminence dans tous les genres? L'Europe deviendra-t-elle *ce qu'elle est en réalité*, c'est-à-dire: un petit cap du continent asiatique? Ou bien l'Europe restera-t-elle *ce qu'elle paraît*, c'est-à-dire: la partie précieuse de l'univers terrestre, la perle de la sphère, le cerveau d'un vaste corps? . . .

'La balance qui penchait de notre côté, quoique nous paraissions plus légers, commence à nous faire doucement remonter — comme si nous avions sottement fait passer dans l'autre plateau le mystérieux appoint qui était avec nous. *Nous avons étourdiment rendu les forces proportionnelles aux masses!* . . . Notre science — devenue moyen de puissance, moyen de domination concrète, excitant de la richesse, appareil d'exploitation du capital planétaire — cesse d'être une "fin en soi" et une activité artistique. . . . L'utilité du savoir fait du savoir une *denrée* qui . . . se préparera sous des formes de plus en plus maniables ou comestibles; elle se distribuera à une clientèle de plus en plus nombreuse; elle deviendra chose du commerce, chose enfin qui s'imite et se produit un peu partout. . . . Donc, *la classification des régions habitables du monde tend à devenir telle que la grandeur matérielle brute, les éléments de statistique, les nombres — population, superficie, matières premières — déterminent enfin exclusivement ce classement des compartiments du globe.* . . .

'Le phénomène de la mise en exploitation du globe, le phénomène de l'égalisation des techniques et le phénomène démocratique, qui font prévoir une *deminutio capitis* de l'Europe, doivent-ils être pris comme décisions absolues du destin? Ou avons-nous quelque liberté *contre* cette menaçante conjuration des choses? C'est peut-être en cherchant cette liberté qu'on la crée.'[1]

On the morrow of a Second World War that had harrowed Western

[1] Valéry, Paul: 'La Crise de l'Esprit', in *Variété* (Paris 1924, Gallimard, Éditions de la Nouvelle Revue Française), pp. 13–14, 24, 30, 29, 30, and 32.

Europe far more cruelly than the War of A.D. 1914–18, it was evident that this cradle of the Western Civilization had indeed been overtaken by the fate that, on the morrow of the First World War, Paul Valéry had still been hoping against hope to see her succeed in keeping at bay. The knack of using the products and copying the procedures of a West European technology had by now been effectively acquired by other inhabitants of an *Oikoumenê* which had been unified by a secular movement of West European aggression; and, on the fringes of a world of which Western Europe had been the heart, a successfully propagated West European technique could command the brute force of an area of territory, a volume of non-human natural resources, and a head of population that this technique had never had, and would never have, at its disposal in the hands of its West European originators.

What use were Western Europe's pupils going to make of the power which their painful education had now placed in their hands? The wave of militarization, whose course since A.D. 1494 we have already traced within the narrow limits of Western Europe, had not come to rest at an expanding Western World's original boundaries or slackened the pace of its advance because the native Western peoples who had first set it travelling were now becoming war-weary as a consequence of having continued to indulge in recurrent bouts of warfare for more than four and a half centuries. Since the close of the seventeenth century of the Christian Era this ever advancing wave of militarization on Western lines had engulfed one after another of the once autonomous non-Western societies that had been drawn successively into an expanding Western Civilization's ambit; and in each case the introduction of this alien Western institutional process had had the same consequence as it had been having in the West since the opening of the overture to the current Western series of war-and-peace cycles. In the Western World at the turn of the fifteenth and sixteenth centuries of the Christian Era, the West European peasantry, with a few small local exceptions, had, as we have seen,[1] been strangers to the bearing of arms, and War had been the business of either a foreign mercenary infantry and light horse or a native feudal heavy cavalry; but we have also seen[2] that, since the General War of A.D. 1494–1525, there had been a sustained series of moves in all militant Western states to substitute native troops for foreign troops in all arms, conscripts for volunteers, and a universal compulsory service imposed on the whole population, without distinction between classes, for an earlier selective compulsory service in which the peasantry had been made to bear the brunt of the burden. These effects of modern militarization in the Western World itself were reproduced when the wave of militarization on Western lines spread to the once autonomous societies that were being swept into a Western net.

In these originally non-Western societies, as in the Western World itself in the past, the peasantry had as a rule been non-militant. The principal public service that had been required of them by their rulers had been to provide, out of their production of food and fibres, for the feeding and clothing of relatively small fighting forces consisting of

---

[1] On pp. 491–2, above.   [2] On pp. 492–4, above.

specialists for whom the bearing of arms at the public expense had been, not a *corvée*, but a privilege. These fighting forces might be recruited from transfrontier barbarians, such as the Gurkhas and Pathans who had served in the British Indian Army,[1] the Mongol bannermen, both tribal and professional,[2] who had been employed by the Manchu régime in China, or the Egyptian Mamlūks of Eurasian Nomad or Caucasian high-lander origin; they might be recruited from members of some alien civilization, like the British troops employed by the British Rāj in India, the Iranian Muslim troops employed by these British empire-builders' Timurid Mughal predecessors,[3] the Abyssinian Monophysite Christian mercenaries employed by the Muslim states in the Deccan which the Timurids eventually swallowed up,[4] or the Egyptian Mamlūks of Georgian Orthodox Christian origin; they might be recruited from the descendants of conquerors, drawn from one or other of the two external sources above mentioned, who had made themselves at home in the country, like the Manchu bannermen in China[5] or like the Rājpūt heavy cavalry of Hun and Gurjara origin who served the Mughal Raj as *foederati*, the Marāthā light horse of Saka origin who became the van-guard of an anti-Mughal Hindu counter-offensive, and the Jāt and Doghra fighting men, likewise of Saka origin, who became the back-bone of a Sikh Khālsā; or they might be recruited from a feudal class of indigenous origin, like the Japanese Samurai. Examples of professional troops recruited from a native peasantry are rare in the antediluvian chapters of the histories of the non-Western civilizations that were swamped by a Western deluge and whose military systems were conse-quently revolutionized by the impact of Western arms and influences. The highly selective compulsory levy of boys from the Orthodox Christian peasantry of the Ottoman Empire, which eventually became the principal source of recruitment for the Pādishāh's Slave-Household,[6] is one historic case of the kind; the enlistment of extramural Chinese volunteers in the professional banners of the Manchu Imperial Army[7] is another. The Streltsy ('Archers') raised by Ivan IV (*dominabatur* A.D. 1533–47; *imperabat* A.D. 1547–84) were Muscovite counterparts of the contemporary Janissaries.

With these three institutionally notable, but numerically inconsider-able, exceptions, the peasantry in the non-Western societies, like the peasantry in the Western World at the dawn of a Modern Age of Western military history, had, as the foregoing summary indicates, for the most part not been permitted, and *a fortiori* not been compelled, to bear arms before the military institutions of these non-Western societies were revo-lutionized, one after another, by the Western Civilization's impact. In all these encounters with the West except the Hindu World's and Rus-sian Orthodox Christendom's, the impact did not occur on the military plane until after an English Industrial Revolution had begun to make

[1] See VI. vii. 330–1. [2] See VI. vii. 332. [3] See VI. vii. 126–7.
[4] *Honoris causâ* we may cite the loyalty of the Abyssinian commandant of Asīrgarh in Khāndāsh, who committed suicide rather than surrender the fortress to Akbar in A.D. 1600 (see Smith, V. A.: *Akbar the Great Mogul*, 2nd ed. (Oxford 1919, Clarendon Press), pp. 278–80). [5] See VI. vii. 128–9.
[6] See III. iii. 37, n. 1. [7] See VI. vii. 129.

universal compulsory military service an economically practical possibility,[1] and until after this possibility had been translated into a portentous
accomplished fact in the fateful French *levée en masse* of A.D. 1792; and
therefore everywhere, except in Russia and India, the effect of the introduction of Western military institutions was to militarize *en masse* at one
stroke, without any transitional phase of selective conscription, a peasantry that had been non-militant up to that moment.

The Petrine Russian Army was exceptional in passing first through
the phase of selective conscription, which was the system in vogue in the
eighteenth century in the armies of the Continental European Western
states, before following a French lead into the subsequent Western
system of universal conscription. As for the British Indian Army, it
remained a select professional force of the eighteenth-century Western
type in its method of recruitment, and a force of privileged specialists of
the pre-Western type in its sources of recruitment, until it passed out of
British control upon its transfer in A.D. 1947 to the Governments of the
British Indian Empire's Indian and Pakistani successor-states. Throughout the British chapter of its history the Indian Army continued to be
recruited by voluntary enlistment and to be composed of troops drawn
partly from transfrontier barbarians and partly from the so-called martial
communities of barbarian origin in India itself. Its mainstays were the
Jāts, Doghras, and other breeds of Panjābī manhood which, in the ranks
of an early-nineteenth-century Sikh Army organized on Western lines
by ex-Napoleonic Western officers,[2] had been the latest, and sole formidable, Indian antagonists of the British in a competition of all against
all for the Mughal Empire's heritage.

The British Indian Army was perhaps the most conservative, as well
as the most efficient, of the non-Western fighting forces that had been
reorganized on a Western new model; yet, even in this decidedly old-
fashioned military institution, the necessity of 'Indianizing' the cadres as
a preliminary to handing the Army over to indigenous Indian successor-
states of an abdicating British Rāj had been taken as an opportunity for
making a breach in the traditional practice of recruiting the personnel
almost exclusively from certain privileged communities.[3] In the cadres
from which, between the years A.D. 1918 and A.D. 1947, the previous
British personnel was progressively withdrawn,[4] the replacements were

[1] Professor William McNeill comments: 'There are real economic obstacles to the
militarization of the World's peasantry. Where can a peasant country get modern arms?
It takes at least a generation to establish an industry capable of producing them locally;
and conditions for reduplication of the Russian *tour de force* cannot be assumed to be
present in countries like India and China necessarily or, I should say, even probably.'
In A.D. 1952 the answer seemed to be that the peasantry could get arms from one or
other of the two industrially potent Super-Powers that were competing, at this time, for
the peasantry's allegiance. A North Korean, Continental Chinese, and Communist
Annamese peasant soldiery was being armed from an 'arsenal of Communism' in the
Soviet Union, while a South Korean, Formosan Chinese, and anti-Communist Annamese peasant soldiery was being armed from an 'arsenal of Democracy' in the United
States.   [2] See IX. viii. 731.
[3] As late as A.D. 1930 divers communities domiciled in the Panjāb were still providing
54 per cent. of the combatant troops in the British Indian Army (see *Report of the Indian
Statutory Commission*, vol. i, Survey (London 1930, H.M. Stationery Office = Cmd.
3568), p. 96, and the instructive map of India facing this page).
[4] In A.D. 1923 a decision had been taken to 'Indianize' five infantry battalions, two
cavalry regiments, and one pioneer unit; in A.D. 1932 the decision was taken to 'Indianize'

no longer made solely from those indigenous Indian communities that had previously shared with alien British officers the privilege of manning their country's fighting force. Steps were deliberately taken to ensure that the elimination of the British element from a force that had hitherto been virtually an Anglo-Panjābī preserve should not have the effect of making it a Panjābī monopoly, at the risk of saddling India with a Panjābī Rāj—or pair of Panjābī successor-states, one Hindu and one Muslim —in place of a British Rāj. Pains were taken to make certain that indigenous Indian candidates for commissions should be drawn from all over the country, and the same new policy was applied to the recruitment of other ranks. The pace of this transformation of the Indian Army was greatly accelerated in the course of the Indian Army's expansion during the Second World War. In consequence, the militarization of India had entered, by A.D. 1947, on the same stage that the militarization of Russia had reached in the eighteenth century. Though the peasantry had not yet been subjected to a military service that was either compulsory or universal, their enrolment, by voluntary recruitment, in an army that had previously been a preserve for traditionally martial communities, indigenous and foreign, had set the Indian peasant's feet on the military road which the Russian peasant's feet had begun to tread after the way had been cleared in Russia by Peter's destruction of the Streltsy in A.D. 1698–9.[1]

This militarization of a previously non-militant peasantry, which had thus begun in Russia in A.D. 1699 and in India in A.D. 1918, had also been taking place in other quarters of the World. There is no need to retell in this place a story that has already been told in previous contexts.[2] It will suffice to recall that the militarization of the peasantry had been put in hand in Egypt after the destruction of the Mamlūks in A.D. 1811; in Turkey after the destruction of the Janissaries in A.D. 1826; in Japan after the voluntary abdication of the indigenous feudal lords (the *daimyō*) and their indigenous military retainers (the *samurai*) in A.D. 1868–9; in China after the deposition of the Manchu Dynasty, and disbanding of the Manchu Imperial banner regiments, in A.D. 1911; in Korea after her annexation by Japan in A.D. 1910. In the present context the only further observation that has to be made is that this revolutionary militarization of the peasantry had not been confined to the Old World. An eighteenth century that had seen the Russian peasant inducted into selective military service on the contemporary West European pattern had seen in Paraguay the warlike traditions of the *ci-devant* barbarian Guaraní reanimated by the policy of resourceful Jesuit philosopher-kings who had been prompted by their benevolence to make this pro-

one division of all arms and one cavalry brigade; and in the October of the latter year an Indian Military Academy for the training of Indian officers was opened at Dehra Dun; but the beginnings of the 'Indianization' of the British Indian Army went back to the last year of the First World War. From A.D. 1918 onwards a small number of vacancies in the Royal Military Academy at Sandhurst had been thrown open to Indian candidates, and, from A.D. 1928 onwards, vacancies had also been offered at Woolwich (the training institute for the British Royal Engineers and Artillery) and at Cranwell (the training institute for the British Royal Air Force). In A.D. 1931 the number of vacancies offered to Indian candidates at Sandhurst had been ten, while at Woolwich it had been three.

[1] See III. iii. 282, n. 1.   [2] In VI. vii. *passim* and IX. viii. *passim*.

vision for the defence of their Reductions against marauding *Mamelucos* from Brazil;[1] and, after the break-up of the Spanish Empire of the Indies into a score of mutually hostile successor-states, the forgotten wars which the Guaranís had fought in the seventeenth century as soldiers of the Society of Jesus, and in an earlier age as barbarian invaders of an Andean Empire of the Four Quarters, had been refought in the nineteenth century in Paraguay's deadly single-handed war of A.D. 1864–70 against the combined forces of Brazil, Uruguay, and Argentina, and in the twentieth century in her duel with Bolivia in A.D. 1930–35 for possession of the Gran Chaco. In Mexico, again, since the revolution in A.D. 1910 against an oligarchy of Creole Spanish and other alien origin, the descendants of once martial Toltecs and Chichimecs had exercised themselves, like a previously non-militant Chinese peasantry since the revolution in A.D. 1911 against a Manchu 'ascendancy', in chronic civil wars which had been 'undecisive', though unfortunately not 'temperate', contests.

This widespread militarization of a hitherto primitive and, for the most part, pacific peasantry, that, mid-way through the twentieth century of the Christian Era, still accounted for some three-quarters of the living generation of Mankind, was an event that could hardly fail, in the long run, to have some decisive effect on the destinies of a Westernizing World. Its most impressive feature was one that was manifestly pregnant with alternative possibilities, good and evil. In almost every case, these hitherto unmilitary peasants had no sooner been drilled and armed according to the latest Western fashion than they had astonished the World by defeating, and this with ease, old-fashioned warriors of the traditional type who had hitherto taken it for granted that the peasants were of no military account.

The Egyptian fallāhīn, who had been subjugated, oppressed, exploited, and despised by an interminable series of martial alien conquerors, proved their mettle by breaking the resistance of the Moreots, in those wild highlanders' native mountain lairs, in A.D. 1825, only one year after Mehmed 'Alī had begun to draft the fallāhīn in any appreciable numbers into his new-model army,[2] and some two thousand years after they had given their latest previous proof of a capacity to make good soldiers when, in the service of another Macedonian master of their country, Egyptian peasant phalangites had defeated Greek peasant phalangites in pitched battle at Raphia in 217 B.C.[3] This twice-performed achievement of the peasantry of Egypt had been capped by the peasantry of Japan when in A.D. 1877, only four years after the implementation in A.D. 1873[4] of the conscription law of A.D. 1870,[5] they had put down an insurrection of a dissident faction of the *samurai* of the self-assertive fief of Satsuma[6] against a Meiji régime that had been inaugurated in A.D. 1868–9.

The prowess of these Japanese peasant conscript soldiers in this early ordeal is the more noteworthy considering that, in A.D. 1873, they had

[1] See O'Neill, S.J., George: *Golden Years on the Paraguay: A History of the Jesuit Missions from 1600 to 1767* (London 1934, Burns Oates), pp. 89–91.
[2] See IX. viii. 242, n. 4.   [3] See V. v. 68, with n. 1.
[4] See Sansom, G. B.: *The Western World and Japan* (London 1950, Cresset Press), p. 342.   [5] See ibid., pp. 339 and 342.   [6] See ibid., pp. 347–50.

shown a distinct reluctance and apprehension[1] upon their receipt of the summons to take up a military calling from which they had been jealously excluded for at least a thousand years past, and considering further that, in the event, the first enemy whom they had been called upon to face in the field had been a war-band of those indigenous Japanese feudal warriors whom the Japanese peasant had been taught sedulously, throughout those last thousand years, to revere as his legitimate and invincible lords and masters. Even the parvenu element in a British Indian Army had had time, before the transfer of the *rāj* in A.D. 1947, to demonstrate, by gallant conduct in the General War of A.D. 1939–45, that it, too, had military virtue in it which, through the long age of inhibition, had been awaiting, undamped, the first opportunity to declare itself. For example, a Bihar Regiment, raised in A.D. 1941–2,[2] and a Madras Regiment, reformed in A.D. 1942, both distinguished themselves on the Burma front in warfare that was perhaps the severest ordeal to which any troops engaged in this Second World War were subjected in any theatre of operations.

The beneficial consequence of the peasant conscript's prompt and conclusive success in proving himself in action to be the traditional privileged warrior's military peer was the gain won by each of these military demonstrations for the civil cause of social justice. One of the conspicuous moral shortcomings of Civilization during the first five or six thousand years of its currency had been its endowment of a small minority with material and spiritual treasures at the expense of a large majority whose own share in the fruits of the whole body social's co-operative labours had been as inequitably inadequate as the minority's share had been inequitably excessive.[3] This moral flaw had reappeared in the histories of all the civilizations that had risen and fallen since the breakdown of the Egyptiac Civilization in the Age of the Pyramid-Builders;[4] so long as the flaw was allowed to persist, the institution of Civilization would remain morally unsound; and, in an aeon in which Mankind in Process of Civilization had not yet succeeded in extricating itself from the practice of War, it would perhaps have been too much to hope that a *misera plebs contribuens* should succeed in securing a long-since overdue modicum of social justice without having first vindicated its claim in an ordeal by battle. Nevertheless, it could be argued in A.D. 1952, on the evidence of disconcerting events, that militarization had by then already proved in practice to have been too high a price to pay for an approach towards egalitarianism. The course of Japanese history since A.D. 1877 aptly illustrated this point; for, while, on the one hand, the Japanese conscript peasant army instituted in the Meiji Era had proved to be the one effective institution for securing a minimum of social justice for a still conspicuously depressed majority in a Japanese Society that had continued,

---

[1] See Sansom, op. cit., p. 411.

[2] The First Bihar Regiment came into existence on the 15th September, 1941, when the Eleventh Battalion of the Nineteenth Hyderabad Regiment was converted into a regular battalion and redesignated. This was the first time that aboriginals were recruited into the Indian Army. The Second Battalion of the Bihar Regiment was raised on the 1st December, 1942, at Agra. Fifty per cent. of its recruits were from the aboriginal forest hill tribes of Chota Nagpur.

[3] See pp. 489, above, and p. 561, below.   [4] See I. i. 141–2.

in the main, to be authoritarian and oligarchic, this self-same Japanese conscript peasant army had been employed during the same period as an instrument of military aggression against Japan's neighbours by a Westernizing régime in Japan which had been unable or unwilling to think of any better device for raising the standard of living of a depressed peasantry within the national frontiers than the method—long since condemned by the judgement of History, but not yet discredited in human consciences—of taking tribute by force of arms from a still more deeply depressed peasantry in foreign parts.

An historian, contemplating this evil consequence—exemplified in recent Japanese history—of the success with which the peasant majority of Mankind was being militarized on Western lines, could find no comfort in the fact that an aggressive Militarism, evoked by this institutional process of militarization, had carried its Japanese addicts into disaster in A.D. 1945 in a military adventure in which a new-model military machine was being perversely used by its makers for the morally indefensible purpose of trying to raise the peasantry's standard of living in one country at the rest of the World's expense by force of arms; for in this case, as in others, Militarism had not recoiled upon its authors until after it had enabled them to inflict monstrous injury on Society at large. If the observer was to gauge the probable effects of the militarization of the peasantry upon a Westernizing World's prospects, he had to ask himself whether the hatching of Militarism from militarization, which had been the sequel to the history of militarization on Western lines in Japan, appeared to be the rule or the exception in a Westernizing World's current history.

There were, no doubt, here and there, peasant populations that could be militarized with impunity. The Egyptian peasant conscript army was perhaps a case in point; for the promise—or menace—implicit in the inaugural victory that it had won in an offensive campaign against the Moreots in A.D. 1825 had been belied by its signal failures to suppress the Mahdī Muhammad Ahmad's insurrection in the Sūdān in A.D. 1883-5 and to expel the Zionists from Palestine in A.D. 1948-9.[1] Thus in Egypt the militarization of the local peasantry bade fair to be as innocuous as it had been in the Kingdom of Naples.[2]

Was it this Egyptian experience or was it the Japanese experience that was to be taken as an index of the effect of militarization on the temper of the non-Western peasantry as a whole? At a moment when a North Korean and a Chinese conscript peasant army were fighting side by side

---

[1] The Egyptian Army crossed the Egypto-Palestinian frontier on the 15th May, 1948; an armistice agreement between the Egyptian and Israeli governments was signed on the 25th February, 1949.

[2] The significance of a conscript Egyptian peasant army's on the whole inglorious record is underlined by Professor William McNeill in the following comment: 'Among some peoples the psychological obstacles to militarization are tremendous. A nation without military traditions presents very refractory material. Egyptian fallāhs and Porto Rican jibaros are two cases, and some of the Indian peoples—the Bengalis, for example —must be similar. The military virtues cannot be called into existence at will, yet are very needful if an army is to fight effectively.' The military virtues can, however, manifest themselves spontaneously when they are given a chance, as is demonstrated by the records of the Bihar and Madras regiments of the Indian Army in the Second World War (see p. 510, above); and this Indian evidence is no less pertinent than the Egyptian evidence.

against a composite Western expeditionary force in a Korean theatre of military operations, while a Russian conscript peasant army in reserve was standing to arms both in Eastern Siberia and in Eastern Germany, it was evident that the temper and capacity of troops of this type would count for much in the shaping of a Westernizing World's destinies. What light was thrown on the peasant-soldier's qualities by his past performance? History indicated that, as might have been expected *a priori*, he was at his strongest in military situations calling for the exercise of the passive military virtues. He was stronger in endurance than in initiative, and stronger in defending his own country against an invader than in playing the invader's part himself.

In the history of a Westernized Russian peasant army, which was older, by more than a century, than other armies of the kind, the glorious passages, up to date, had all taken the form of ultimately successful wars of defence fought on Russian soil against an invader who, in the first phase of the war, had been apt to carry all before him. This had been the story of the Northern War of A.D. 1700–21, in which Peter the Great's callow peasant army had won its spurs in A.D. 1709 at Poltava, in the Ukraine, against Charles XII's far-ranging Swedes; the story of the foiling of Napoleon's invasion of Russia in A.D. 1812; and the story of the foiling of Hitler's invasion in A.D. 1940–4, when, in November 1942, the tide had been turned at the approaches to Stalingrad. On the other hand, in the Russo-Turkish wars of A.D. 1828–9 and A.D. 1877–8, in which the Tsar, by assuming Charles XII's and Napoleon's aggressive role, had thrust the Westernized Russian peasant army's classic defensive role upon this army's feebler Turkish counterpart, the noteworthy feature, on each occasion, had been, not Russia's victory in the second year's campaign, but her failure to overcome Turkey's resistance in the first campaigning season.

The extent of a nineteenth-century Russia's superiority over a nineteenth-century Turkey in military resources, as well as in experience of waging war on Western lines, had made an ultimate Russian victory a foregone conclusion in any trial of strength between the two Powers in that age; the length of the time that it had taken Russia, in both wars, to win her inevitable victory, and the heaviness of the price that she had found herself compelled to pay for it, had given the measure in which a conscript peasant army's *moral* and efficiency were apt to depreciate when this military instrument was transferred from the defensive role in which it felt itself at home to an aggressive role which it was accustomed to associate, not with glorious victories won by its own arms, but with shameful defeats incurred by enemy invaders of a patriot peasantry's own country. The beau role of offering a patriotic resistance to an invader was the moral advantage that had inspired a Turkish conscript peasant army to give so good an account of itself, against such heavy odds, in otherwise desperately adverse circumstances. A newly enrolled Turkish peasant-soldiery's achievement in the campaign of A.D. 1828, when it had succeeded in preventing the Russian Army from crossing the Balkan Range, had been particularly meritorious, considering that Sultan Mahmūd II had not been able to make any serious progress with the organization of his new-model army until after the destruction of the Janissaries on the 15th June, 1826.

The same conclusions emerge from the history of a Chinese conscript peasant army organized on Western lines since the overthrow of the Manchu régime in A.D. 1911. After twenty years devoted to preliminary domestic exercises in civil wars, the Chinese peasant-soldier had won his spurs in his stubborn defence of an area in Greater Shanghai against a Japanese assault from the 28th January to the 3rd March, 1932.[1] In psychology as well as in strategy this campaign had been reminiscent of the Russo-Turkish wars of A.D. 1828–9 and A.D. 1877–8, and it had been prophetic of China's ultimate victory over Japan in a defensive war on a sub-continental scale that was to drag on from A.D. 1937 to A.D. 1945. At Shanghai in A.D. 1932, as in the Balkans in the nineteenth century, the moral victory had been won by the belligerent who had managed by sheer endurance to postpone the hour of a defeat which he knew to be ultimately inevitable owing to the odds being overwhelmingly in his antagonist's favour, while this ultimate victor had been humiliated by having to take so long, and pay so high, to overcome the resistance of an antagonist who was notoriously not his match.

If a non-Western peasant-soldiery that had proved itself so stalwart in wars in defence of its own hearths and homes had thus been found to lose so much of its spirit when it was led into wars of aggression on foreign soil, was not this an historical fact that was of good augury for Mankind's prospects? Did it not mean that, though the non-Western World had been following Western Europe along the road of militarization, there might nevertheless be some hope that the baneful rankling of militarization into Militarism, which had been the ruin of Western Europe, might not, after all, be the destiny of the World at large? Any Western observer who might be tempted to look to this consideration for comfort in A.D 1952 would have been wise to temper his optimism by reminding himself that the quality in the non-Western peasantry which had made it possible to drill them so easily into becoming, for the most part, such unexpectedly good soldiers was a habit which would also impel them unquestioningly to obey the word of command, even when this bade them advance gloomily to the attack instead of bidding them stand cheerfully on the defensive. The soldierly trait in this peasantry's traditional êthos was an ingrained habit of submissiveness imprinted by an immemorially old experience of living in a state of serfdom on the verge of starvation; and a submissiveness that had not availed to beget a fighting-man when it had been mated with militarization in the soul of an Egyptian fallāh had borne a dragon's-tooth crop in the soul of this Egyptian peasant's Korean cousin.

A Western historian who, *en route* from Pusan to Seoul on the 15th November, 1929, has seen nothing in the Korean peasants, visible from his railway-carriage window, except a pathetic submissiveness mated with a comic unpracticality, had lived to chide himself, twenty-three years later, for having left out of account, in committing himself to that

---

[1] See Toynbee, A. J., and Boulter, V. M.: *Survey of International Affairs, 1932* (London 1933, Milford), pp. 480–95.

ill-judged appraisal, the combination of martial prowess and technological resourcefulness through which those ineffective-looking Koreans'
indomitable forebears had once countered and defeated a Japanese assault
upon their country in the Korean-Japanese War of A.D. 1592–8. This
admonitory testimony of Korean history had been ignored by the Western traveller in A.D. 1929, as his own words now rose against him to
testify.

'[The] inaudible music of the Korean landscape [this traveller had written in A.D. 1929] was not the serene and triumphant "music of the
spheres". It was an elegy in a minor key—a dirge over a country that was
in the autumn of its days. The rhythm was repeated in the movements of
the little people who were working conscienciously but languidly in the
fields or creeping along the roads. The little men and little women were
all dressed in white—appropriately to the country's mood, since white in
the East is usually the colour of mourning, yet in a manner obviously quite
unsuitable for the day's work. In other countries the husbandman girds
up his loins for the combat with Nature. But nobody could possibly gird
up those voluminous white robes; and what hours the women must spend
in washing out of them the mud imparted daily by those terraced fields in
which their wearers laboured! The last touch of quaintness was given by
the men's diminutive top-hats of black glazed gauze which were held in
position on the crown of the head by a ribbon tied under the chin. . . .
Yes, the poor Koreans were a joke. . . .

'Look at this scene at a country railway station where . . . the local
Japanese colony is seeing off the Japanese police-commandant and his
lady. . . . Where . . . are the Koreans? For there is nobody visible on this
Korean platform except the Japanese colony and ourselves. O, there they
are, a whole crowd of them, herded behind a barrier in the background.
The expression on their pathetic faces was not even faintly resentful. It
was wholly submissive. And, as I glanced from one row of faces to the
other, I felt as if I were a spectator of some comedy of manners, with the
Japanese playing "empire-builders" and the Koreans "ryots" or "fallāhīn". So the Koreans were Japan's Bengalis! And I could scarcely suppress an unmannerly guffaw as I suddenly thought of a colony of ants
bearing sway over their insect-cattle.'[1]

The wayfaring Occidental Philistine who had written these patro-
nizing words in A.D. 1929 had it is true, also written, in the same context,
that a 'ghostly music, audible all the time to the inward sense, would not
allow one to forget that', besides being a joke, the Koreans 'were a
tragedy'; and, in the light of an obvious analogy between Japanese rule
in Korea and a British Rāj in India which, in A.D. 1929, was already in
process of liquidation, he had also foreseen the passing of a Japanese
ascendancy.

'As I strolled up and down that platform, looking at the scene that was
being played before me there, the inaudible music of the Korean landscape
began to develop a secondary theme, which was an elegy over the prospects
of Japanese dominion. While the overtones were still sounding the dirge
of Korea's national past, this undertone sang the transitoriness of all
insular conquests on Continental ground.'[2]

[1] Toynbee, Arnold J.: *A Journey to China* (London 1931, Constable), pp. 185–6.
[2] Ibid., p. 187.

This twenty-three-years-old intimation of mortality was still pertinent in A.D. 1952, since by that date the ever accelerating shrinkage in the scale of the *Oikoumenê*, as measured in terms of human means of communication, had reduced the effective size of the Island of North America to about that of the British Isles or the Japanese Archipelago twenty-three years back. Yet, in catching in A.D. 1929 this glimpse of the irony in the destiny of an ephemeral Japanese rule in Korea, the observer had failed to penetrate to the inwardness of the tragedy in the destiny of Japan's Korean subjects. What he had seen had reminded him of the social insects, but he had failed to apprehend the meaning of this cue. He had failed to recollect that the inhuman or superhuman discipline to which the social insects had subjected themselves had enabled them to cultivate a super-Spartan Militarism;[1] that a discipline which had been the matrix of Militarism had been the fruit of habits of docility, industry, and endurance; that, for the inculcation of these ant-like or bee-like *mores* in the Human Psyche, the best school in the World had been the life and labour of a primitive peasantry working at a standard of living just above starvation-level; and that it was no accident that Frederick II's Prussian Janissaries, like Mehmed II's Ottoman Imperial Slave-Household before them, had been recruited from a subject peasantry and not from the wilful and wayward scions of a traditional privileged warrior class.

The traditional submissiveness of the peoples of Asia had, since time immemorial, taken the political form of passive obedience to arbitrary governments. and the cultural process of Westernization would have to go far beyond the rudimentary accomplishment of acquiring a Western military technique before the Asian peasant-soldier would begin to think of questioning, or, *a fortiori*, defying, orders from above to sacrifice his life even in an aggressive war that meant nothing to him personally. On the other hand the citizens of West European states who were accustomed to exercise at least some measure of control over their governments, through parliaments composed of their own elected representatives, would be apt to display their novel unwarlikeness in compelling their governments to submit, Vichy fashion, to a foreign aggressor rather than go to war for the traditional object of preserving their countries' sovereign independence at a cost in life, property, and welfare which the West European peoples might now no longer have the will to pay.

How far could mid-twentieth-century Asian governments go in exploiting their subjects' ingrained submissiveness for military purposes? On the evidence of recent history, they could go less far in a war of aggression abroad than in a defensive war fought on their own soil; yet History had demonstrated that they could make their peasant armies obey, however reluctantly, the order to march into battle even in a foreign campaign for which they had no heart. What were the limits of the Asian peasant-soldier's endurance in honouring his rulers' demands upon his self-sacrificing submissiveness? In Western eyes it might look as if the Chinese or Russian peasant-soldier had given his government a blank cheque drawn on his life; yet History had demonstrated that there

[1] See III. iii. 88–111.

was some limit—however remote this might be by Western standards—
beyond which neither a Chinese nor a Russian Government could venture, with impunity, to continue to turn the screw on their long-suffering
subjects. Chinese régimes, from the Ts'in Dynasty's to the Kuomintang's inclusive, that had had the temerity to give the screw just one turn
too many, had repeatedly paid for this excess by the forfeiture of their
mandate to bear rule; and in Russian history it had been the same story.

The Temper in the Soviet Union and in the United States

A Tsardom that had had the wisdom to take the sting out of the Rus-
sion people's sufferings, defeat, and humiliation in the Crimean War by
conceding the reforms of the eighteen-sixties had paid with its life for
its stiff-neckedness in refusing to forestall trouble once again by paying a
corresponding ransom for subsequent military reverses. The sufferings,
defeat, and humiliation that the Tsardom had brought upon the Russian people by an imperialistic policy in Korea that had precipitated the
Russo-Japanese War of A.D. 1904–5 had provoked the abortive Russian
Revolution of A.D. 1905; the far worse tribulations of the General War of
A.D. 1914 had cost the Tsardom its existence in the double revolution of
A.D. 1917; and the breakdown of the Russian people's endurance on
that occasion was noteworthy, considering that in A.D. 1917 the Russian
peasant army had been fighting in self-defence against invading armies
on Russian soil—a posture in which it had shown itself indomitable in
A.D. 1812 and in which it was to display the same invincibility in A.D.
1941–4.

It seemed, then, that there were limits—even in a manifestly defensive
war on home ground, and even without allowing for the unpredictable
effects of atomic weapons upon the most tenacious habit of endurance—
at which the *moral* of Russia or any other peasant country would collapse
under the strain of war waged on Western lines. Russia, like France, but
on a greater scale and to a more extreme degree, had suffered, twice in
one lifetime, the agonies of a war in her own country, inflicted on her by
a deliberately ruthless invader; and the fibre of Russian endurance could
not be so tough as to have remained unaffected by this experience.
Nevertheless, it seemed likely that the Government of the Soviet Union
would face the terrors of a war with the United States rather than make
any political concession to the United States that, in Russian eyes, would
be tantamount to submission to an American ascendancy; and it also
seemed likely that, if the Soviet Union did ever go to war with the United
States, it would be able to carry a traditionally submissive Russian people
with it, even if the initial military operations on the Russian side took the
form of invading and overrunning countries allied to the United States,
and not the form of resisting an American invasion of the territories of
the Soviet Union and its satellites. Even then, a Russian peasant-soldiery's habit of submissively obeying their rulers' most distasteful orders
might be expected to prevail over a war-weariness bred by recent and
poignant experiences of war in their own country.

If it was thus likely that there were circumstances in which the Soviet
Union could and would go to war with a Great Power of its own calibre,

was this also to be predicted of the United States? The question was a pertinent one, since there could not be a major war unless two Powers of first-class calibre were each prepared in the last resort to go to war with the other; and, when, at the opening of the latter half of the twentieth century, an inquirer put to himself the question whether the United States, as well as the Soviet Union, was willing to face a war with the one Power of her own calibre that was still on the map, he would find himself giving this question an affirmative answer.

Since the declaration of the independence of the United States, and perhaps since the first settlement of the oldest of the Thirteen Colonies, the American people had been one of the most unmilitary, yet at the same time one of the most martial, of the nations of the Western World. They had been unmilitary in the sense that they had disliked submitting themselves to military discipline and had had no Gallic ambition to see their country win military glory for such glory's own sake. They had been martial in the sense that, till the date of the closing of the frontier *circa* A.D. 1890, they had always numbered among them a contingent of frontiersmen accustomed, not only to bearing arms, but to using these at their own personal discretion in pursuit of their own private enterprises—a state of affairs which had become obsolete in Great Britain, even on the Anglo-Scottish Border, after the Union of the Crowns in A.D. 1603, and obsolete in most Continental West European countries since before the close of the fifteenth century. The martial spirit of ten generations of American frontiersmen would have been acknowledged by the North American Indians at any time since the first landing of White men from the British Isles on American coasts; by the English colonists' French rivals in the eighteenth century; and by their Mexican victims in the nineteenth century—and these encounters between the Anglo-American frontiersmen and their competitors for the possession of North America are also evidence that not only the frontiersmen, but the American people as a whole, were prepared, exceptionally and temporarily, to submit themselves to a military discipline without which the frontiersmen's personal spirit and prowess would have been unable to prevail against antagonists of their own cultural level.

The soldierly qualities latent in the American people as a whole had been revealed to their British adversaries in the wars of A.D. 1775–83 and 1812–14, and to their German adversaries in the wars of 1916–18 and 1941–5; but, up to date, by far the most impressive demonstration of American valour, discipline, generalship, and, not least, endurance had been given in a war in which Americans had been arrayed against Americans. The civil war of A.D. 1861–5 between the Union and the Confederacy had been the longest, the most stubborn, the costliest in casualties, and the most fertile in technological innovations of all wars in the Western World between the end of the Napoleonic Wars and the outbreak of the First World War; and this was a portent that the twentieth-century German militarists had twice overlooked to their own undoing.

Moreover, the two world wars that, within living memory, had harrowed Germany and Germany's Russian and West European victims, as severely as the American Civil War had harrowed the South, had left the United States virtually unscathed. The psychological effects that two world wars in one lifetime had produced on the *moral* of West Europeans had hardly made themselves felt on the American side of the Atlantic. This immunity from a living experience of war in their own country seemed likely to prevail over a traditional aversion from Militarism if the American people were to be faced, or to believe themselves to be faced, with a choice between submitting to the Russians and fighting them; and in A.D. 1952 it could not be doubted by any open-eyed observer that the American people would indeed be prepared to face the terrors of a war with the Soviet Union rather than make any concession to the Soviet Union that, in American eyes, would be tantamount to submission to a Russian ascendancy. On this point of being willing to fight another major war in the last resort—and it was a crucial point for the eventual decision of the still open question whether there was, or was not, to be a Third World War—the Americans and the Russians felt and thought alike in A.D. 1952, as far as could be judged by a West European observer.

The Psychological Consequences of Atomic Warfare

Yet there was no people in the World—not even the Russian people and not even the American—that was in a position to boast in advance that, in a third world war, it would be capable of staying the course; for, though War might be coeval with Civilization itself, an advancing Western technology's discovery of the 'know-how' for releasing atomic energy for military purposes had now aggravated the incidence of a familiar social evil to a degree at which it seemed no longer likely to produce its familiar psychological effects.

The new psychological situation, created by the invention of atomic weapons, which had made an aggravation in the degree of the severity of the incidence of War amount to a difference that was virtually one of kind, arose, of course, out of the consequent immense enhancement of War's lethal power.

In War as it had been traditionally waged, each individual combatant had gone into action fortified by the knowledge that the chances were in favour of his coming through alive and even unscathed, and that, the greater the courage, the cool-headedness, and the discipline that he and his companions in arms displayed, the lighter their casualties were likely to be. In the history of Hellenic warfare down to 371 B.C., the Lacedaemonians had notoriously kept their casualties low by keeping their martial spirit high;[1] and even the devoted three hundred Spartiates who had gone to their deaths at Thermopylae in the year 480 B.C. had sacrificed their lives in the consoling knowledge that neither their country nor even their families would die with them. In picking his three hundred devotees, King Leonidas is said to have been careful not to take any fighting man who did not leave a son at home behind him;[2] he and these three hundred companions were all aware that, even if no single one of them were to return alive (and only two of them did survive in the event), the total loss of a force of this number would not jeopardize the

[1] Xenophon: *Respublica Lacedaemoniorum*, chap. ix, quoted already in III. iii. 63.
[2] Herodotus, Book VII, chap. 205.

existence, or even cripple the fighting-power, of a Lacedaemonian Commonwealth whose combatant strength was estimated to have been, at this time, about eight thousand Spartiates, all as good soldiers as the three hundred, without counting the fighting men from the perioecic Lacedaemonian communities, who were 'good enough soldiers, even though they might not be the Spartiates' equals'.[1] As for the future of the Lacedaemonian body politic, the Lacedaemonian Government were said to have received an oracle from Delphi assuring them that, in the current war with the Achaemenian Empire, Lacedaemon would not be wiped out by the enemy if a King of Sparta were to forfeit his life, and this was afterwards supposed to have been one of the decisive considerations in Leonidas' mind when he took his decision to stand fast at Thermopylae and die there.[2] Leonidas and the rest of the three hundred thus believed, on the day on which they went to their deaths, that, if they did lose their lives, there would infallibly still be a Sparta in being to receive the news that they had died in carrying out their countrymen's orders; and this is, of course, the theme of the Cean poet Simonides' immortally ambiguous couplet.[3] They could also feel sure that these surviving countrymen of theirs would not forget either their deed or their names.[4]

The self-sacrifice of Leonidas and his three hundred in the year 480 B.C.[5] was thus rational, as well as heroic, under the technological conditions in which War was waged in that year and at any later date down

[1] See the words that Herodotus puts into the mouth of the exiled Spartan King Dâmarâtus, who was serving on Xerxes' staff, in Book VII, chap. 234.

[2] Herodotus, Book VII, chap. 220.

[3] Quoted by Herodotus in Book VII, chap. 228.

[4] Some thirty or forty years after the event a complete list of the names of the three hundred was obtained at Sparta by Herodotus (see Book VII, chap. 224).

[5] G. B. Grundy, the distinguished Modern Western historian of *The Great Persian War* (London 1901, Murray), argues, in his chapter on Thermopylae (pp. 257–317), that, when Leonidas, after receiving the intelligence that his position had been turned by an enemy force, took his decision to continue to hold his ground, between the mountains and the sea, with the Lacedaemonian, Theban, and Thespian contingents of his own force, amounting to rather more than one half of his total effectives, he was not wittingly and deliberately sacrificing his men's lives together with his own, but was dividing his force with the intention and expectation that the contingents which he was sending to the rear would not take the opportunity, as they actually did take it, for decamping, but would occupy and hold a position on the path over the mountains along which the enemy turning-movement was being made, in time to be able to bring to a halt the enemy's advance from this quarter, while Leonidas, with his half of the confederate army, continued to block the passage of the enemy's main body through the pass of Thermopylae itself.

This masterly and persuasive interpretation of what was in Leonidas' mind at that moment postpones the hour of the Lacedaemonian and Thespian contingents' witting and deliberate sacrifice of their lives without cheating these heroes of the glory of having performed their heroic act of self-sacrifice at a later hour of the same memorable day; for indisputably they did deliberately sacrifice their lives when, upon receipt of the news that the enemy turning-force had now succeeded in debouching out of the mountains on to the coastal plain in their rear, athwart their only possible line of retreat, they took their decision to retire to the famous hillock and make their last stand there, instead of taking a decision to lay down their arms, which was what the Thebans did in this now quite desperate situation.

Thus Grundy's theory, if accepted, leaves the Lacedaemonians and Thespians still eventually sacrificing their lives as deliberately as they are said to have sacrificed them according to the Herodotean rendering of the traditional story.

In the interests of his own reconstruction of the course of events, Grundy casts doubt on both the story of the oracle and the story that Leonidas did not take with him anyone who had not a son and the story that Leonidas did not take with him anyone who had not a son to leave behind him at Sparta. Yet the second, at least, of these two stories is surely credible, since Leonidas' expedition must, from the outset, have been one in which all participants will have faced the likelihood that they were going to lose

to the 6th August, A.D. 1945, when an atomic bomb was dropped on Hiroshima. Let us suppose, however, that the Babylonic, Egyptiac, and Syriac civilizations had been 2,425 years ahead of a latter-day Western Civilization in the development of Military Technology. The supposition is not fantastic, considering that, in some branches of Technology, these older civilizations were at least that much in advance; and, if we allow this licence to our imagination, we may find ourselves puzzled to estimate how Leonidas and his three hundred would have acted in circumstances that would have stultified most of the considerations that are attributed to them.

Suppose that Xerxes' invading army had not been constrained, as it was, by the state of Military Technology at the time, to kill Leonidas and his three hundred companions in hand-to-hand combat with swords and spears, or at short range with arrows; suppose that they had had a stock of two atomic bombs, one to drop on the Greek force at Thermopylae, and another to drop simultaneously on Sparta—or, better still, that they had had a single hydrogen bomb whose explosion would instantaneously have destroyed all life in Continental European Greece and in the Aegean Archipelago before the Achaemenian expeditionary force had started cautiously to advance from its assembly-point in the interior of Anatolia: in those then inconceivable circumstances there would have been no perpetuation of the three hundred devotees' families, since the sons whom they had left behind at home would have been killed at the same instant as their fathers; there would have been no Sparta to receive the news of the three hundred heroes' faithfulness unto death[1] and to remember their deed and their names; no Simonides to compose an epitaph; and no monumental mason to engrave it. The presupposition of the three hundred Spartiates' self-sacrifice was an assurance—which, in these hypothetical circumstances, would have been denied to them— that, in giving their lives, they were saving their country's existence; and this was likewise the theme of another epitaph composed by Simonides in commemoration, not of Spartiates who had fallen in defence of Sparta against Achaemenian aggression, but of Tegeatans who had fallen in defence of Tegea against Lacedaemonian aggression some years later.

Τῶνδε δι᾽ ἀνθρώπων ἀρετὰν οὐχ ἵκετο καπνός
αἰθέρα δαιομένης εὐρυχόροιο Τεγέας·
οἳ βούλοντο πόλιν μὲν ἐλευθερίᾳ τεθαλυῖαν
παισὶ λιπεῖν, αὐτοὶ δ᾽ ἐν προμάχοισι θανεῖν.[2]

their lives, even if they believed that the Lacedaemonian Government genuinely intended to reinforce Leonidas' little army, and even if they were unaware that the position at Thermopylae could be turned via a path over the mountains. On the last day, when the position had in fact been turned by the enemy before any reinforcements had reached the Hellenic army, the normal human reaction was either to decamp (as was done by the contingents which, according to Grundy's hypothesis, had been detached by Leonidas to check the advance of the enemy turning-force) or thereafter to surrender (as was done by the Thebans). Even if Leonidas did go into action that day, with little more than one half of his total force, with the intention of still holding his position while the other half of the force checked the enemy's turning-movement, the decision in these circumstances to continue to hold his ground instead of withdrawing while the coast was still clear was heroic enough; and the Spartan and Thespian survivors' subsequent decision to die fighting after the enemy turning-movement had been reported to have achieved success was just as heroic as it has always been deemed to be.   [1] Rev. ii. 10.

[2] *Anth. Pal. VII.* 512; Bergk, *P.L.G.*, 4th ed., iii. 459.

The point made in this poem is that the fallen Tegeatan fighting-men had been free to choose between preserving their lives and sacrificing them and that, in choosing to sacrifice them, they had chosen right because, at this price, they had purchased the preservation of treasures which, for them, were of far greater value. Suppose, however, that, instead of being inspired by a reasonable hope of being able to save Tegea from physical destruction and to hand her on to their children with her political independence still intact, these heroic Tegeatan fighting-men had known in advance that a Lacedaemonian atomic bomb would annihilate Tegea's masonry, independence, and progeny in the same flash as her combatant troops in the field, what would have been a Tegeatan warrior's psychological reaction then? 'Who dies, if England live?'[1] was a question to which, in a pre-atomic age, a noble soul had been able to give only one answer; but this time-honoured challenge had undergone a disconcerting mutation since the explosion at Hiroshima on the 6th August, 1945, and the question had now come to read: 'Who can die to make England live, if England has to die with him?' While few might be found to dispute that *pro patria mori* was *dulce et decorum*,[2] it was not indisputable that to die *with*, instead of *for*, one's country would be either gratifying or even meritorious.

No doubt this reformulation of the question does not dispose of the problem, for there is an element in heroism which is beyond Reason because it is above it. If we can imagine Leonidas and his three hundred being deprived, by an ante-dated advent of atomic warfare, of all the reasons that they may have given to themselves to rationalize a resolve to sacrifice their lives, we can still imagine them doing, nevertheless, exactly what they did. When, sixty-five years, or thereabouts, before the three hundred Spartiates gave their lives at Thermopylae, Cyrus's general Harpagus had been imposing Achaemenian rule on the south-west corner of Asia Minor, the fighting-men of Xanthus, 'when they had been defeated in the field and been driven within their city walls', had 'collected their women and children and property and slaves in the citadel', had 'made a holocaust of them by setting the citadel on fire, and' had 'then bound themselves by the most formidable mutual oaths [to seek their own deaths], and' had 'duly made a sortie and died fighting to the last man'.[3] On the same occasion the Xanthians' neighbours the Caunians had met the same challenge with the same response.[4] This was also to be the response of the Marmareis in 334 B.C.[5] and of the Tyrians in 332 B.C. to Alexander, of the Isaurians on the morrow of Alexander's death to Perdiccas,[6] of the Carthaginians in 146 B.C. to Scipio Aemilianus, of the Xanthians (once again) in 42 B.C. to Brutus,[7] of the Jews in A.D. 70 to

---

[1] Kipling, Rudyard: *For All We Have And Are.*
[2] Horace: *Carmina*, Book III, Ode ii, l. 13.
[3] Herodotus, Book I, chap. 176.
[4] See ibid.
[5] See Diodorus of Agyrium: *A Library of History*, Book XVII, chap. 28, cited by Bevan, E. R.: *The House of Seleucus* (London 1902, Arnold; 2 vols.), vol. i, p. 94, n. 2.
[6] See Diodorus of Agyrium: *A Library of History*, Book XVIII, chap. 22, cited by Bevan, loc. cit.
[7] See Appian of Alexandria: *The Roman Civil Wars*, Book IV, chap. 80. According to Appian, ibid., this was actually the third time that the Xanthians had chosen annihilation in preference to surrender—the second of their three performances of the heroic deed

Titus, and of the Suliots who blew themselves up or threw themselves and their children over a precipice in A.D. 1803 rather than surrender to 'Alī Tepelenli.[1] Nor can we omit from this role of honour those execrable Assyrians who died like heroes at Harrān in 610–609 B.C., two years after the destruction of the wasps' nest at Nineveh.

It is, however, significant that in Jerusalem in A.D. 70 a majority of the besieged would have countenanced overtures for forestalling extermination by surrender if they had not been terrorized by a minority of fanatics into participating in these Zealots' suicidal heroism—under pain, as the penalty for 'peace talk', of being stabbed to death by the dagger of a Jewish *sicarius* before any Roman legionary's sword could come within striking distance of them; and, though Josephus, who is the source of our information, is a hostile witness to the conduct of the Jewish Zealots, there is no reason to suspect him of having falsified the truth on this point.

It is also significant that the Christian martyrs, who gave their lives rather than commit what would have been, in their eyes, an act of disloyalty to God, died in the confident belief that their blood was the Church's seed;[2] that a Church which Christ Himself had founded would endure, not only till Christ's ministers on Earth had had time to go into all the World and preach the Gospel to every creature,[3] but to the end of Time; and that, though Heaven and Earth would pass away, Christ's words would not pass away[4]—as they believed that Christ Himself had declared after His resurrection and had then guaranteed by another positive act when He had ascended into Heaven, where He sitteth at the right hand of God the Father Almighty *in saecula saeculorum*. Though the citizens of this or that earthly commonwealth might have had the spirit, on occasion, to see their motherland perish with them, or even before them, rather than stoop to bow their necks to a foreign yoke, only the adherents of a religion that made no account of This World by comparison with an Other World could logically court, for the glory of God, a death that would be, not only their own death, but simultaneously the death of all life on the face of a planet that was their mundane home. It is all the more significant that the Early Christian martyrs, who did hold this transcendental belief, should have been inspired, not solely by a confidence that they were sacrificing their lives for the glory of God in a Heavenly Kingdom utterly beyond the reach of the most potent operations of a terrestrial human Technology, but also in part by a confidence that, by making this supreme personal sacrifice, they were promoting the propagation of Christ's Church Militant here on Earth—as Leonidas and his three hundred companions at Thermopylae had been confident that, by sacrificing their lives, they were furthering the mundane interests of the Commonwealth of Lacedaemon.

of mass self-immolation having been when they had refused to surrender to Alexander the Great.

[1] See Finlay, G.: *A History of Greece, B.C. 146 to A.D. 1864*, vol. vi (Oxford 1877, Clarendon Press), p. 51.

[2] See the passages from the works of Justin and Tertullian that have been quoted in V. vi. 202, nn. 2 and 3.

[3] Mark xvi. 15.   [4] Matt. xxiv. 35; Mark xiv. 31; Luke xxi. 33.

If it was thus true that even the Christian martyrs had been moved in part by a belief that their deaths would redound to the welfare on Earth of a Church and Faith that would live after them on Earth and would not die there with them, then we cannot know for certain what their psychological reaction would have been supposing that the Roman executioner's sword had been fraught with a hydrogen bomb's power to extinguish the Earthly Church Universal, throughout its geographical range at that day, from a Mesopotamian Edessa to a Baetican Gades and from an Egyptian Philae to a British Corstopitum. Would a martyr who knew in advance that this would be the earthly consequence of his own self-sacrifice have still gone unhesitatingly to his death with a serene confidence that he was doing God's indubitable will?

This was a hypothetical question that could never be answered conclusively by an historian living in A.D. 1952; but any human being at any date could comprehend that, if his martyrs-designate happened to be, not Christian transcendentalists, but post-Christian materialists who had deliberately invested in This World all their treasure, to the uttermost farthing,[1] it would be paradoxical to expect such self-made citizens of a 'Commonwealth of Swine'[2] to consent to sacrifice their lives for their treasure's sake if they knew in advance that, in the act, they would be bringing annihilation upon this mundane treasure as well as upon themselves; and this consideration was particularly pertinent to the circumstances of a Westernizing World mid-way through the twentieth century of the Christian Era; for in this world at this date—as, no doubt, in most times and places—both bona fide Christians and bona fide Spartans were rare indeed, while the Communist and Capitalist ideologies, whose respective champions were competing for the allegiance of all Mankind as eagerly and bitterly as if their beliefs and conduct had been poles apart, were in agreement with one another, and at variance with Christianity and with Spartanism alike, in setting up an exclusively mundane objective and ideal for Man, and differed from one another on this head only over the secondary question whether Man was to make a worldly success of himself as an individual or as a phalanstery.

What logic was there in asking a whole-hearted votary of either Capitalism or Communism to sacrifice his life for the sake of maintaining or improving a material mundane standard of living—not, of course, for his own personal benefit, *quod esset absurdum*, but even for the benefit of his family, tribe, or species—if the hydrogen bomb that was to take the prospective sacrificial victim's life was known by him in advance to be certain to extinguish in the self-same flash all possible beneficiaries of his proposed self-sacrifice? In this baleful light it looked as if an advancing Western technology's recent success in tapping atomic energy for use in War might have sapped the foundations of a traditional standard of heroism by stultifying some of the most compelling of the traditional motives for it.

[1] Matt. v. 26.
[2] Plato: *Respublica*, 372 D, cited in II. i. 193, n. 1; in II. ii. 23, n. 2; and on p. 612, below.

(III) ALTERNATIVE POSSIBLE APPROACHES TO WORLD ORDER

Our foregoing survey of the situation after the Second World War has shown that, at the opening of the second half of the twentieth century of the Christian Era, a Westernizing World found itself in a plight that can be summarily described as follows. Three recent achievements of Western technology—the coalescence and simultaneous shrinkage of the *Oikoumenê* and the invention of atomic weapons—had made it imperative for Man in Process of Civilization to abolish War; War could not be abolished unless the control of atomic energy employable for military purposes could be concentrated in the hands of some single political authority; this monopoly of the command of the master-weapon of the age would enable, and, in enabling, compel, the authority controlling atomic energy to assume the role of an oecumenical government; the seat of this oecumenical government must be either Washington or Moscow in the constellation of political forces that had emerged from the overthrow of Germany and Japan in A.D. 1945; but in A.D. 1952 neither the United States nor the Soviet Union was prepared voluntarily to place itself at the mercy of its sole surviving peer by submitting, without fighting, to seeing this rival arrogate to itself the world-wide political ascendency that would be conferred automatically on either Power by a monopoly of the control of atomic energy for military purposes.

What was to be the denouement of this political problem-play? The line of least psychological resistance would, no doubt, be a resort to the old-fashioned expedient of ordeal by battle. Now that four centuries and a half of recurrent warfare in a Western arena had left only two gladiators still erect and *aktionsfähig*, a third world war might be expected to elicit a knock-out blow that would leave only one Power alive, with no competitor now remaining in the lists to dispute the sole survivor's monopoly of a control of atomic energy that would carry world-dominion with it. This catastrophic denouement was evidently feasible, since a world war fought with atomic weapons would be likely to have at least as conclusive an ending as the first and second world wars, both of which had ended in the decisive defeat of one side, though both these wars had been waged with relatively ineffective pre-atomic armaments. It could therefore be predicted that a third world war between the two remaining Powers would prove to be the final round in a series of contests that, since A.D. 1914, had already reduced the number of the Powers in this arena to two from eight. The outcome of a third world war thus seemed likely to be the imposition of an oecumenical peace of the Roman kind by a victor whose victory would leave him with a monopoly of the control of atomic energy in his grasp.

This denouement was foreshadowed, not only by present facts, but by historical precedents, since, in the histories of other civilizations, a Time of Troubles had been apt to culminate in the delivery of a knock-out blow resulting in the establishment of a universal state; but the precedents also suggested that Mankind could not afford in A.D. 1952 to resign itself to sanctioning a reperformance of this familiar tragedy. Whenever, in the histories of other civilizations, a series of cycles of warfare had eventually been brought to a close by the destruction of all the contending Powers except one single survivor, this barbarous remedy for a desperate malady had not availed either to save the sick civilization's life or to rid a war-stricken world of war in perpetuity, because the cost of arriving at a world order by this rough road had been mortally heavy. In the past the forcible establishment of an oecumenical peace had been purchased by a war-stricken society only at the prohibitive price of its inflicting wounds upon itself from which it found itself unable to recover; and, if this had been the ultimate effect of imposing universal peace by violence in a pre-atomic age, what were the Western Civilization's prospects in the event of its falling into a third world war in which a knock-out blow would be delivered with the unprecedented violence that had now been imported into the conduct of War by the invention of atomic weapons?

If the Western Society took this traditional war-path now that it was equipped with unprecedentedly potent armaments, would it not be condemning itself to purchase an ephemeral peace at a price that would be prohibitive? Would not the spiritual ravages of War, which had always been much harder to repair than its physical ravages, be likely, this time, to exceed all imaginable measure? Would not the agonies inflicted by atomic warfare make even a once humane and generous-hearted victor turn savage? These were considerations that might well deter the most fanatical Russian mind from allowing itself to believe that a third world war was the necessary price for completing the conversion of Mankind to the Communist Faith, and, *a fortiori*, deter the most sanguine American mind from allowing itself to believe that, the sooner a third world war was fought and won, the sooner the American people would be rid of the distracting anxieties of international politics and be free once more to devote themselves to the normal pursuits of private life. A sober-minded observer could foresee that after a third war fought with atomic weapons there would no longer be any possibility of life as it had previously been lived either in the United States or in the Soviet Union.

In these perilous circumstances the best hope for the future of Mankind lay in the possibility that the governments and peoples of the United States and the Soviet Union might have the imagination, wisdom, tolerance, self-restraint, patience, and fortitude to seek and ensue the one alternative to a third world war that, at this stage, was practical politics: that is to say, a pacific partition of the *Oikoumenê* between these two surviving Powers for an indefinite time to come. All the virtues enumerated above would be required on both sides if this policy was to have any chance of success, since it was evident that a society which had tapped atomic energy could never rest easy until it had brought under the control of some single oecumenical authority a newly released titanic physical force which would be a menace to the existence of at least half the Human Race, or, more probably, to the existence of the whole of it, so long as two mutually independent and antagonistic

Powers each remained at liberty to use this appalling weapon in waging war against its neighbour. Yet, if this risk of a Third World War fought with atomic weapons was the consideration that made the establishment of some kind of world order imperative, it would be a *reductio ad absurdum* of Mankind's quest for freedom from fear if, in seeking the solid and lasting security against a social catastrophe that was to be found in the establishment of a unitary control over atomic energy, the governments and peoples of the two surviving Great Powers were to precipitate the very catastrophe that all Mankind was concerned to avert. If the establishment of a world order was imperative for the sake of avoiding an atomic war, the avoidance of an atomic war must be imperative *a fortiori*, as an end in itself.

In the circumstances of the time the greatest menace to the welfare and existence of the Human Race was not the invention of atomic weapons, but the rise in living human souls of a temper reminiscent of a mood once prevalent in an Early Modern Western World for about a hundred years beginning with the outbreak of the Western Wars of Religion in the seventh decade of the sixteenth century of the Christian Era. At the opening of the second half of the twentieth century there were Capitalists and Communists who, like their Catholic and Protestant forerunners, felt it to be impracticable as well as intolerable to acquiesce in leaving the allegiance of Society divided, for an indefinite time to come, between an orthodoxy that they identified with their own faith and a heresy that they identified with the ideology of their adversaries. The wrong-headedness of this attitude was betrayed by the conclusion, logically following from it, that Orthodoxy was called upon by duty and self-interest in unison to combat, suppress, and eliminate Heresy by the ruthless employment of every weapon at Orthodoxy's command. The history of the Western Wars of Religion bore witness that spiritual issues could not be settled by force of arms; and the acquisition of atomic weapons gave warning that it would not be open to Capitalists and Communists in a post-Modern Age of Western history to learn the futility of religious warfare, and the necessity for religious toleration, by an empirical method of prolonged trial and chastening error that had been practicable for Catholics and Protestants in an Early Modern Age in which gunpowder was the deadliest weapon at the command of wrong-headed crusaders.

In the nineteen-fifties, as in the fifteen-sixties, the advocate of a patience that could claim to be the highest form of fortitude laid himself open, no doubt, to the charge of being a contemptible procrastinator who could offer no prospect of being able ultimately to avert the 'showdown' that he was cravenly seeking to postpone; but in the nineteen-fifties, at any rate, this taunt did the Fabian policy an injustice; for it failed to take account of the positive advantage that Mankind stood to gain by a successful pursuit of a policy of playing for time in the particular social circumstances of the Westernizing World of the day. The vehemence of the animosity, at this date, between the respective adherents of Communism and of a traditional Western way of life was one of the psychological effects of the sudden coalescence and shrinkage of the *Oikoumenê* under the masterful impulsion of an ever faster advancing Western technology. It was an emotional reaction to the malaise that a Western and a Russian Society were both feeling as a result of finding themselves brought abruptly into an immediate physical contact with one another before either society had had time to become spiritually intimate with the other. Either party was having to accommodate itself to the sudden epiphany of a neighbour who had been a stranger to it during the centuries in which its own peculiar culture-pattern had been taking shape. What, on both sides, was now needed above all was time to allow a Subconscious Psyche, whose pace was the tortoise's gait, to adjust itself to the revolutionary situation created by the technological conjuring tricks of a Practical Intellect that had been racing ahead of its subconscious yoke-fellow at the pace of a march hare.[1]

This common-sense consideration is clearly brought out in the following passage from the pen of a nineteenth-century Chinese philosopher:

'Now that the ingenious inventions of the steamship and the railway are enabling the European peoples to reach every corner of the Earth and every strange tribe of Mankind, the beginning of a world unity is here. When scattered races and nations are brought together, then divers civilisations will also gradually become unified. Our ancient sages made a distinction between the *Tao* [the Way of Life] and the *Ch'i* [the Tools]. The ways of life cannot be immediately unified; they must first be brought together by the tools or implements of human invention. The steamship and the railroad are the carriages of the ways of life. . . .Therefore, these great inventions, which the Western Powers are using for their encroachment upon China, are the very things which the sages of a future age will utilise as the means for the unification of the ways of life of all the nations of the Earth.'[2]

This shrewd Chinese observation brings out the further point that the psychological discomfort, and consequent animosity, that had been caused by Technology's feat of 'annihilating' physical distance, were not peculiar to the relations between a twentieth-century Western Society and a contemporary Russian Society. The same psychological disturbance had been produced by the same technological revolution in the West's relations with a Chinese Society and with all the other living non-Western civilizations. There had been a simultaneous and similar disturbance in the relations of these living non-Western civilizations with one another in so far as they had been brought abruptly into closer contact with one another through the introduction of Western means of communication; and these divers twentieth-century psychological tensions were so many examples of regular consequences of encounters between contemporaries that, in a previous Part of this Study,[3] have also been illustrated from the histories of other arenas.

[1] See pp. 210–11, above.

[2] Wang T'ao (*natus* A.D. 1828), quoted by Hu Shih in *The Chinese Renaissance: The Haskell Lectures, 1933* (Chicago 1934, University Press), pp. 34–35. The contrast, in point of comparative effectiveness, between the respective careers of Wang T'ao and the contemporary Japanese pioneer of Westernization, Ito, is pointed out by Hu Shih, ibid., pp. 10–12. Cp. pp. 33–34.   [3] In IX. viii. 522–629.

Our foregoing study of encounters between contemporaries has lit up one truth that, in A.D. 1952, was most pertinent to the consideration of a Westernizing World's prospects. History showed that the psychological disturbance inevitably produced by an encounter was apt to be aggravated to a disastrous degree if either party sought impatiently to cut the Gordian knot by which he found himself unwelcomely tied to an uncongenial fellow-traveller, whereas the same disturbing effect of the same encounter might be turned to account as a supreme opportunity for an act of spiritual creation by evangelists who came to bring, not a sword, but peace, and who found their mission, not in striving to make one of two colliding cultures prevail over the other, but in seeking to make the challenge of an encounter yield the response of a new spiritual vision opening up the vista of a new way of life.

If this was indeed the truth, then the World's first need on the political plane in the sixth decade of the twentieth century of the Christian Era was a *détente* between the United States and the Soviet Union in the spirit of the *détente* which, at an equally critical moment of Hellenic history, the Roman and the Arsacid Power had jointly achieved in 23–20 B.C.—to their common credit and to the general benefit of a world whose fate had lain in the hands of those two Powers between them. In 23–20 B.C. the Roman and Arsacid governments virtually agreed to partition between them, *uti possidebant*, an Hellenic World which had been expanded by previous Macedonian conquests to embrace a Hittite, Syriac, Egyptiac, Babylonic, and Indic Society's domains in addition to the Hellenic Civilization's own patrimony.[1] Augustus was abandoning a Roman aspiration—inspired by a consciousness of Rome's decisive superiority over Parthia in military resources, and entertained since the year 53 B.C. by Crassus, Julius Caesar, and Mark Antony in succession—to reassert by force of Roman arms, as far eastward into the heart of the Continent as Alexander the Great had ever penetrated, an Hellenic ascendancy that, in the course of a century ending in 53 B.C., had been all but extinguished east of the Euphrates. In return for this tacit assurance that Rome was now renouncing an ambition whose achievement would have required the overthrow and destruction of the Parthian Empire, the Arsacid Government was now making it possible for Rome to forget her rankling resentment at the humiliating defeat of an aggressive Roman military adventure by giving back the captured standards and releasing the surviving prisoners of war that had been the trophies of a Parthian victory over an invading Roman army thirty years back.

It is true that the Romano-Parthian *détente* of 23–20 B.C. did not eliminate all the friction from the relations beween the two surviving Powers in a war-stricken Hellenic World. For another four centuries and more, Rome and Ctesiphon were to contend for the prize of paramountcy over a buffer state in Armenia which was to play the part played by Afghanistan in the relations between the British and Russian empires in the nineteenth century of the Christian Era. There were

[1] The outlying Indian province of this expanded Hellenic World was the only fraction of it which, at this date, was not under either Arsacid or Roman rule.

also to be other bones of contention between Rome and Parthia besides Armenia, and these divers chronic disputes were to erupt into occasional wars. Nevertheless, the *détente* of 23–20 B.C. was as auspicious as it was historic; for it set a tone which governed the relations between the Roman Empire and its eastern neighbour on the whole for not much less than six hundred years thereafter;[1] and the tradition of moderation that thus came to prevail in the relations between the western and the eastern Power in a partitioned Hellenic World was not easily overcome by the deliberately banned spirit of militancy.

When Trajan strained Roman resources almost to breaking-point by reverting to the Alexandrine Oriental ambitions of Mark Antony, Caesar, and Crassus, the Augustan policy of self-restraint was promptly readopted by Trajan's immediate successor Hadrian; and, after this Hadrianic liquidation of a Trajanic adventure, a 'temperate and undecisive' border warfare that continued occasionally to interrupt a normal state of peace was not converted into a holy war either by the hold that Zoroastianism gained over the later Arsacid princes of the Parthian line or by their Sasanid successors' act of officially establishing the Zoroastrian Church as the state church of their empire. The friction between the Roman trustees of Hellenism and the Iranian trustees of a temporarily submerged but never extinguished Syriac Civilization did not rankle into a life-and-death struggle until the two Powers fell into the reduplicated Romano-Persian war of A.D. 572–91 and A.D. 603–28; and it was only in the course of the second of the two bouts of this long-drawn-out struggle that a political conflict came to be inflamed into an ordeal by battle between the fanatical adherents of two rival faiths.

In the particular social circumstances of a Westernizing World in the twentieth century of the Christian Era, in which time was needed for the breeding of familiarity, the danger of an atomic world war, which loomed large in A.D. 1952, might be expected to recede if American and Russian statesmanship could contrive to keep the peace even for a much shorter period than the time for which it had been kept between the Roman and Parthian empires in virtue of the *détente* of 23–20 B.C.; but in this case, as in that, the task of statesmanship would not be easy.[2] A consideration that seemed likely to tell in favour of a preserva-

---

[1] From first to last the Euphratean frontier of the Roman Empire endured for nearly seven hundred years, running from Pompey's organization of the province of Syria in 64 B.C. to the irruption of the Primitive Muslim Arab barbarian invaders into the Roman and Sasanian empires simultaneously in and after A.D. 632 (see I. i. 75).

[2] Professor William McNeill comments: 'I feel that the Rome-Carthage relationship is a far more convincing parallel to contemporary conditions than the Rome-Parthia relationship. In the relations between Rome and Parthia mortal fear and the density of contact were, I believe, absent.' The present writer's comment on this comment is that it was not too much to expect of American and Russian statesmanship in the sixth decade of the twentieth century of the Christian Era that it should stabilize the relation between the United States and the Soviet Union on a Romano-Parthian basis and save it from degenerating into a Romano-Carthaginian 'irrepressible conflict'. Some of the obstacles to the achievement of the statesmen's task in the encounter between the United States and the Soviet Union are examined in the remainder of this chapter. These obstacles were manifestly formidable. Yet the present writer would submit that, when the obstacles had been looked in the face and had been estimated at their highest possible magnitude, it would still be a culpable surrender to despair—or, more culpable still, to mere impatience—if the statesmen were to resign themselves to the conclusion that a

tion of the peace was the current disparity between the two Powers' respective military resources.

In an age in which the sinews of war were technological and organizational experience and ability commanding man-power and non-human raw materials in quantities sufficient to ensure a full investment of the fund of human skill, the United States possessed in A.D. 1952 a superiority, in potential military strength, not only over the Soviet Union and her satellites, but over the whole World outside the United States' own frontiers;[1] and, though this present American superiority might, as has been noted,[2] be diminished, or even eventually converted into an inferiority, if the Russians were ever to succeed in fully developing the latent resources of the Soviet Union and in gaining effective control over the developed and latent resources of the rest of the Old World, the United States' present superiority seemed likely to last as far into the future as it was possible to see ahead, since the fund of skill which was the key to industrial power was, in the nature of things, an asset that it would take the Russians much longer to build up than material resources that could be converted into military strength only to the extent to which the skill to exploit them was forthcoming.[3]

On this showing, the present disparity between the United States and the Soviet Union in potential military strength seemed likely to endure. Yet it would have been rash to jump, on this account, to the conclusion that the Soviet Union would be willing or able in all circumstances to refrain from challenging her rival's decisively superior potential strength; for the competition between Rome and Parthia for paramountcy over Armenia after the *détente* of 23–20 B.C., and the competition between Athens and the Peloponnesian Confederacy for the accession of Corcyra after the peace settlement of 445 B.C., were warnings that, in any society that was partitioned politically between two Powers, and two only, a Balance of Power, even when this had been deliberately established by overt or tacit agreement, was in constant danger of being upset, even against the parties' will, by their falling into an involuntary yet unavoidable competition for the allegiance of forces, hitherto neutral, whose added weight might be expected to give the scales a decisive inclination to one side or the other—whichever of the two sides should succeed in securing this accession of strength for itself.

---

third world war could not be averted by a saving combination of the spiritual forces of wisdom, good will, and, above all, forbearance.

[1] Professor William McNeill comments: 'United States superiority is less than statistics of steel production would suggest, since, in the United States, more effort and material has to be devoted to civilian consumption, and more of military man-power and supply to services, than is required in the Soviet Union, where the lowness of the people's standard of living and the hardihood of their spirit makes them able to live and fight on a much smaller allowance of comforts and amenities than is demanded by Americans.'   [2] On pp. 488–9, above.

[3] 'Les atouts actuels de l'Europe ne paraissent pas reposer sur des nécessités physiques, mais sur un acquis historique qui ne peut lui échapper que par une évolution prolongée, et sur les qualités morales et intellectuelles de ses populations. Notre civilisation surindustrialisée ne peut avoir d'autres centres que l'Europe et les États-Unis, tant que les autres régions n'ont pas atteint le même degré de surindustrialisation, donc de technique, de capitalisation, de standard de vie; les courants ne peuvent donc être détournés que très insensiblement' (Dupriez, L. H.: *Les Mouvements Économiques Généraux* (Louvain 1947, University Press, 2 vols.), vol. i, p. 380).

In a twentieth-century *Oikoumenê* that, since A.D. 1947, had been virtually partitioned into an American and a Russian sphere of influence, there were at least two pawns on the board that imperilled the maintenance of peace between the two rival Powers through being assets on which neither Power's hold was secure, and consequently being objects for which the two Powers were bound to compete. One of these disputable assets was the industrial war-potential of Europe, which at this date amounted in the aggregate—including the Russian as well as the American sphere of Europe—to more than a quarter of the total industrial war-potential of the World; the other disputable asset was the man-power of the non-Western and non-Russian peasant countries in Asia, Africa, and Indian America (from Mexico to Paraguay inclusive), which amounted in the aggregate to about three-quarters of the living generation of Mankind. In A.D. 1952 each of these two assets was partly in American and partly in Russian hands; if either of them were to fall wholly into the hands of only one of the two competitors for possession, the effect might be to give the Russo-American balance a decisive inclination in the successful competitor's favour; and, in either field, the hold of one of the two competitors was precarious. While the United States had good reason for fearing that the secession of China from the American to the Russian camp in A.D. 1948–9 might be followed by further landslides in the same direction in other Asian or African countries, the Soviet Union had no less good reason for fearing that she might not be able permanently to retain her control over those eastern fringes of the Western Society's Continental European patrimony on which she had imposed her domination during the last phase of the Second World War. Thus either Power was vulnerable, on one of two critical fronts, to the danger of formidable encroachments at its expense on the rival Power's part; and the consequent instability of the current balance made it difficult to hold the political scales even, and proportionately difficult to keep the political temperature low.

A Russian observer, drawing an interim balance sheet in A.D. 1952, and entering in his credit column the accession of China over against an entry in his debit column recording the defection of Jugoslavia, might find it hard to say whether, on balance, the Soviet Union had been a loser or a gainer. If the triumph of Communism in China were indeed an augury of what was to come in the South-East Asian countries, in India, in Pakistan, in Persia, and in an Arab World extending westward from the oil-fields of 'Irāq and Sa'ūdī Arabia to the Atlantic seaboard of Morocco, this might seem in Russian eyes to be a winning card on a long view; for, in a competition for the allegiance of all Mankind between Communism and a traditional Western way of life, the suffrages of a peasant three-quarters of Mankind might be expected to be the determining factor in the long run; and, in appealing to this vast primitive electorate, Russia enjoyed advantages that America lacked.

The chief of these Russian advantages was that Russia herself, till yesterday, had been one of the primitive peasant countries at the mercy of a Western Society which had outstripped the rest of the World in its technological progress; and that, since yesterday, Russia had discovered a method of catching up with the Westerners by a forced march, and had by this means transformed her own economy at short notice with a success that had been registered in her victory in the Second World War over a Germany who, next to the United States, had been the strongest industrial Power in the Western World of the day. The Russians could thus use their own striking technological achievements under a Marxian dispensation as an impressive argument when they were commending Communism to other peasant peoples who still found themselves in the Russians' pre-Stalinian, or even in their pre-Petrine, plight of individual poverty and collective impotence. Russian propagandists could appeal in the same breath to an ancient Asian peasantry's new aspiration to raise its standard of living, and to a parvenu Asian intelligentsia's aspiration—which was as old and as young as this intelligentsia itself—to make itself mistress in its own house by throwing off the ascendancy of Western intruders who, for their own purposes in Asia, had called this Asian intelligentsia into being.[1]

At this point an alert Western counter-propagandist might try to put a spoke in the Russian propagandist's wheel by pointing out to the Asian intelligentsia that in reality the Russians were inviting them to exchange a Western ascendancy for a Russian ascendancy, and not for the national independence that the Russians were dangling before Asian eyes, and by simultaneously pointing out to the peasantry that in reality the Russians were inviting them to exchange the familiar woes of rack-rented tenants, not for the utopia of peasant proprietorship, but for the prison-house of a mechanized collective farm.[2] Such home truths, however, were likely to fall on deaf ears. The Asian peasants would not easily be deterred from making the common human blunder of exposing themselves to hitherto unknown evils in their eagerness to escape the known evils from which they were suffering at the moment. As for the Asian intellectuals, they might pay heed to a Western warning against a Russian imperialism if they happened to be natives of Manchuria, Outer Mongolia, or Soviet Central Asia, where this warning would evoke an echo in their memory of their own experience; but the voice of this handful of land-locked intellectuals would not carry far. In the experience of an overwhelming majority of the Asian intelligentsia of the day the typical alien imperialist was not a Russian; he was an Englishman, a Frenchman, a Dutchman, or some other variety of Frank. For the past 450 years the West European conquerors of the Ocean had been taking advantage of the conductivity of their physical medium of aggression to perpetrate indiscreet *actes de présence* in every corner of the *Oikoumenê*—'going to and fro in the Earth, and . . . walking up and down it'[3] with the assiduity of Satan himself. These ubiquitous Western mariners' Cossack contemporaries who had made the toilsome trek overland from the Urals to the Sea of Okhotsk had contrived hitherto to commit their aggression less conspicuously. In A.D. 1952 the Russian imperialist, in his missionary warfare with the Western imperialist, enjoyed the advantage of being relatively unknown

[1] See V. v. 154–8.   [2] See IX. viii. 674–5.   [3] Job ii. 2.

that had sometimes proved to be a winning card in American presidential elections. At this date the Russian candidate for the spoils of Imperialism was no more than a specious name to most of the peoples to whom Imperialism was now anathema.

By contrast, Eastern Europe was a region where, for the last two hundred years or so, the Russians had been acquiring the self-same bad reputation that, in the world at large, had been pre-empted by the Franks; and in A.D. 1952 a Russian observer, contemplating the entry of Jugoslavia's name on the debit side of his balance sheet, must have been ruefully conscious of Russia's weakness in this quarter. If Slavonic-speaking ex-Orthodox Serb Communists had broken with Slavonic-speaking ex-Orthodox Russian Communists—whose support was of vital importance to Jugoslavia in her dispute with the Western Powers over Trieste—because they could not bear the domineering behaviour of the Soviet Union Communist Party, how could the Soviet Union hope to win any voluntary adherents anywhere in Eastern Europe, or hope permanently to retain her hold on any East European countries if once she found herself reduced to holding them down by sheer physical force? The ominous symptom here, from Russia's point of view, was her unpopularity in East European countries that, as peasant countries, as Orthodox Christian countries, and as Slavonic-speaking countries, ought, on any *a priori* ideological theory, to have felt themselves drawn towards the Soviet Union rather than towards the West.

An Orthodox Christian Georgia, for example, had not been reconciled to Russian rule by the freak of chance that had saddled Russia with a Georgian dictator; a Bulgaria that was Slavonic-speaking as well as Orthodox Christian was apparently as recalcitrant to Russian domination in A.D. 1952 as she had shown herself to be on the morrow of her liberation from Ottoman rule by Russian arms in A.D. 1878; Slavonic-speaking Bosniak Muslims and Croat and Slovene Catholic Christians, who were apt to resent their Serb fellow Jugoslavs' ascendancy, had followed the Serbs' lead with alacrity in the stand that the Serbs had now taken against a Communist Russian imperialism. The Czechs had once looked confidingly to their Russian fellow Slavs to rescue them from the toils of Pan-Germanism; they had cherished this hope all through a century ending in A.D. 1945 with the arrival of a liberating Russian army in a Bohemia that, since the 15th March, 1939, had been a Third German Reich's 'Protectorate'; but the same Czechs had been quickly cured of their sentimental attachment to Russia by the experience of meeting Russians in the flesh in the role of representatives of an officially benevolent occupying Power. As for the Poles, the Magyars, and the Finns, History had demonstrated, long before A.D. 1945, that the Russians had no chance of reconciling them, and *a fortiori* none of assimilating them. The outcome of the Russian Empire's suzerainty over Finland from A.D. 1809 to A.D. 1918, and of her dominion over 'Congress Poland' from A.D. 1815 to A.D. 1915, indicated that a Slavonic-speaking Catholic Poland and an Ugrian-speaking Lutheran Finland were, both of them, proof against any attempts at Russification. As for the Ugrian-speaking Catholic and Calvinist Magyars, Russia had been their bugbear since A.D. 1849, when her military intervention in support of a Hapsburg Imperial Government at bay had enabled the Emperor Francis Joseph to put down a Magyar national insurrection with which he had been finding himself unable to cope unaided. After the Austro-Hungarian *Ausgleich* of A.D. 1867 Russia had come to figure in Magyar, as in Czech, imaginations as the champion of Panslavism; and, when invading Russian armies had arrived in Hungary in A.D. 1945 as the champions of Communism instead, this had not, of course, mollified the Magyars' by that time traditional Russophobia.

Nor could the Russians look forward to offsetting their general unpopularity in Eastern Europe by establishing an advanced post for Communism in Eastern Germany; for, in East German as well as West German minds, the Russian régime was bound to be abhorrent on account of its association with the partition of Germany, like Korea, between a Russian and an American hemisphere and with the annexation of Germany's eastern marches to Poland as far west as the Oder-Neisse Line. In the feelings of all Germans under all régimes after the Second World War, the Soviet Zone of Germany and the German territory annexed to Poland might be expected to fuse together into a monumental *Germania Irredenta*.

Thus, in a world that had been partitioned between the Soviet Union and the United States in A.D. 1947, either Power's hold on important portions of its provisional domain was decidedly precarious; this element of uncertainty made the current Russo-American Balance of Power unstable; this instability was inimical to the statesmen's task of keeping the peace until mutually alien societies, which the progress of Technology had suddenly brought into close quarters with one another, should have had time to become better acquainted; and, though the length of time required for allowing this psychological adjustment to work itself out seemed unlikely to be of the order of magnitude of the six centuries for which the Romano-Iranian frontier had endured after the Augustan *détente* of 23–20 B.C., it was nevertheless evident that a long period of precarious peace would be needed before there could be any practical possibility of placing this peace on the surer foundation of a genuinely good understanding between the Russian and the Western camp.

In the Western peoples' experience, in their intercourse with one another, the key to collective friendships between nations had been individual friendships between human beings whose personal comprehension of one another and goodwill towards one another had spun a network of human links across the psychological barriers set up by politico-military frontiers. In the light of this Western experience the Soviet Union's Western allies had taken the initiative, before the close of the Second World War, in proposing arrangements on a large scale for the promotion of personal intercourse between her nationals and theirs—especially in the promising form of an interchange of students. In the Westerners' belief it was not their fault that these overtures had not met with any response on the Russian side. They deplored the Soviet Government's evident unwillingness to let its subjects take advantage of these opportunities that were being offered to them of sampling the Western way of life at first hand for themselves; and, while they read in the Soviet Government's opposition to their proposals for intercourse a lack of confidence in the spiritual power of Communism to hold its own against the contemporary Western way of life in the judgement of Soviet citizens, if these were once given a chance of making a comparative personal trial of the two dispensations, this reading of the motives inspiring the Soviet Government's policy of seclusion was no comfort for those Westerners who saw no salvation for the World except in the achievement of a *détente* between the Western Society and its Russian neighbour. If the Politburo's belief in the hold of Communism upon the hearts and minds of Soviet citizens were ever to become robust enough to outweigh the Soviet Government's fear of allowing their subjects to see the Western World for themselves, then (so it would appear to Western minds) a positive approach would have been made towards the healing of a spiritual schism that was a menace to the prospects, not merely of the Western Civilization, but of Mankind itself, not excluding the garrison of a Communist camp.

In circumstances that were so plainly precarious but in other respects so enigmatically obscure, a dogmatic optimism was as unwarrantable as a dogmatic pessimism, and the living generation of Mankind had no choice but to reconcile itself as best it could to the disturbing knowledge that it was facing issues in which its very existence might be at stake, and that it was at the same time impossible at this stage to guess what the event would be.

In A.D. 1952 these perennial waifs on board Noah's Ark were in the situation in which Thor Heyerdahl and his five fellow vikings on board a balsa-log raft found themselves on the morning of the 7th August, 1947. On that fateful morning a westward-flowing current that had borne the raft *Kon-Tiki* 4,300 nautical miles across the breadth of the Pacific Ocean was now carrying her towards the Raroia Reef. Beyond the line of surf breaking over this barrier the approaching seafarers could descry the feathery tops of palm trees, and they knew that these palms bedecked idyllic isles set in a still lagoon; but between them and this haven where they would be[1] ran the foaming and thundering reef 'in one line from horizon to horizon',[2] and the set of the current and the wind gave the voyagers no chance of circumnavigation. They were heading perforce towards an inevitable ordeal; and, though they might know what were the alternatives awaiting any voyagers in this plight, they could not guess which of these alternatives was to be the ending of their own saga.

If the raft were to be broken up by the breakers, the crew would be torn to pieces by the knife-edged coral if they were not saved by speedy drowning from that more painful death. If the raft were to hold together, and if its crew were to succeed in holding on to it, until the breakers had defeated their own malice by washing the raft up on to the reef

[1] Psalm cvii. 30.
[2] Heyerdahl, Thor: *Kon-Tiki* (Chicago 1950, Rand McNally), p. 242.

high and dry, a shipwrecked crew might swim across the still lagoon beyond, and so reach one of the palm-crowned isles alive. If the moment of the raft's arrival at the reef should happen to coincide with the flood of one of those high tides that periodically submerged the reef to a depth that compelled the breakers temporarily to subside, the *Kon-Tiki* might, after all, clear the death-line in calm water, and so come through unscathed. In the event, a high tide did flow in to lift her battered frame off the reef into the lagoon[1] some days after the surf had cast her up on to a bare coral crest; but on the morning of the 7th August, 1947, no man on board the *Kon-Tiki* could tell which of these alternative destinies was going to be hers and theirs.

The experience of these six young Scandinavian seafarers on that day was an apt allegory of an ordeal that still lay ahead of Mankind at the opening of the second half of the twentieth century of the Christian Era. In A.D. 1952 an Ark of Civilization that had travelled a time-distance of some five or six thousand years across the ocean of History was now making, like the *Kon-Tiki*, for a reef which its crew would not be able to circumnavigate. This unavoidable danger ahead was the perilous line of transition between a world partitioned into an American and a Russian sphere and a world united under the control of the single political authority which, in an age of atomic weapons, must supersede the present division of authority sooner or later in one way or another. Was the eventual transition to be pacific or catastrophic, and, if catastrophic, how dire was the catastrophe to be? In A.D. 1952 no one in the World could foreknow the outcome of the ordeal towards which the World was then manifestly moving. One thing alone was certain, and this was that the spirit in which an inevitable ordeal would best be met was the spirit shown by Thor Heyerdahl and his companions at the moment when the *Kon-Tiki* struck the Raroia Reef.

(IV) POSSIBLE CONSTITUENT ELEMENTS OF A FUTURE WORLD ORDER

Without waiting for a facile wisdom after the event, an observer of world affairs in A.D. 1952 might perhaps usefully speculate on the shape of things to come so long as he confined his consideration of a future world order to elements that an oecumenical dispensation seemed likely to have in common with each of the two demi-mundane dispensations that had been crystallizing round the United States and round the Soviet Union since A.D. 1947.

If the construction of a world order had depended on the Technology in which Man was so accomplished an adept, and not on the Human Nature that Man found it so difficult to govern and guide, Mankind in A.D. 1952 could have contemplated the future with complacency; for a simultaneous coalescence and shrinkage of the *Oikoumenê* that had made it more dangerous than ever before to go on waging war had also made it less difficult than ever before to put Mankind in a position to preserve the peace by finding technological solutions for the administrative prob-

[1] See Heyerdahl, op. cit., pp. 273-4.

lem of bringing the whole of the *Oikoumenê* under the undivided control of a single oecumenical government.

In terms of facilities for human intercourse no point in the *Oikoumenê* was so remote from Washington in A.D. 1952 as Georgia and New Hampshire had been when, in A.D. 1792,[1] the Congress of the United States had provided for a four months' delay in the inauguration of a President after the election of his electors, in order to give the successful candidate the time that he would need for winding up his affairs at home and making his way to the seat of the Federal Government on horseback. For purposes of human intercourse the United States at the time of its establishment was of about the same size as the Achaemenian Empire in the fifth century B.C., when it took three months to travel to Susa, the imperial capital, from Ephesus, the Aegean terminus of the Great North-West Imperial Highway;[2] and the Roman Empire may be reckoned to have been of about the same size in human terms, if we may assume that the centurion who took charge of Saint Paul after the Apostle had appealed to Caesar would not have taken more than three months in conveying his prisoner from the Palestinian port of Caesarea to the Italian port of Puteoli if he had been able to book a direct passage and if he had been less unlucky in his weather.[3] In A.D. 1952 three months seemed an inordinate length of time to allow for any journey imaginable. Yet the Roman Empire, the Achaemenian Empire, and the United States in her pre-railroad age were effectively administered commonwealths, though in each of them a period of three months had to be allowed for making the journey from the frontier to the capital; and, in this pre-railroad age, a Darius, Alexander, Demetrius, Caesar, Constantine, and Napoleon were able repeatedly to confound their antagonists by the speed at which they managed to dart from one extremity to another of an *Oikoumenê* whose radius, in human terms, was a three months' journey for ordinary official travellers, and a proportionately longer time than that for anyone not entitled to travel by the public post.

While in point of conductivity an eighteenth-century United States had been a polity of the same order of magnitude as the Roman or the Achaemenian Empire, in point of constitution it had been more ambitious. In contrast to the Roman and Achaemenian imperial régimes, which had been content to impose upon their subjects an authoritarian government maintained by a professional army and administered by a professional civil service responsible to an individual autocrat, the Constitution of the United States had provided for democratic government in a polity of the Roman or Achaemenian size by combining the Medieval Western device of parliamentary representation of an electorate with the

---

[1] In an Act approved on the 1st March, 1792, the Congress of the United States laid down that the members of the Electoral College, provided in the Constitution (Art. II, § 1, par. 2) for electing the President, should themselves be elected on the Tuesday following the first Monday in the November of a presidential election year, and that the term of office of the President elected by the Electoral College should run from 'the fourth day of March next succeeding' the date of election. The initial date of the President's term of office was eventually advanced from the 4th March to the 20th January by the Twentieth Amendment to the Constitution, which was proclaimed on the 6th February, 1933—a date by which the United States had moved out of the Horse Age through the Railroad Age into the Air Age.

[2] See VI. vii. 82, n. 1.   [3] See Acts xxvii. 1–xxviii. 16.

Hellenic device of federalism. A representative system in which the people's control over the government was exercised at one remove would, no doubt, have seemed an anaemic dilution of Democracy to citizens of city-states like Florence or Athens, for whom Democracy had signified the direct participation of all the citizens in public affairs; and, for the sake of making a reality of this political ideal, most of these Hellenic and Medieval Western democracies had been content to see the size of their commonwealths limited for ever to the maximum within which a direct participation of the whole citizen body in the government was still practicable. When this was taken as the touchstone for testing the genuineness of Democracy, a country with the area and population of Attica in the fifth century B.C. was the largest that could be governed democratically in the Athenian and Florentine sense; for in Attica the points farthest from the capital—an Eleusis, a Marathon, a Sunium—were none of them farther away from Athens than a single day's journey on foot,[1] while a citizen body that, at a maximum estimate, may have approached a total strength of sixty thousand at its peak,[2] was unlikely, except on rare occasions, to present itself on the Pnyx in such force as to make the conduct of public business unmanageable.[3]

[1] On the 10th December, 1911, four students of the British Archaeological School at Athens, one of whom was the writer of this Study, verified this by walking from Sunium to Athens between the dawn and the dusk of a winter's day. Starting from Sunium at 6.30 a.m., our party reached Athens as night was falling. We should have arrived in daylight if, when approaching Vári, we had not wasted an hour or so by swerving off the track and scouring the south-eastern spurs of Hymettus in a vain search for the Cave of Pan. A citizen of fifth-century Athens whose home was at Sunium, Marathon, or Eleusis would, no doubt, have had to spend at least one night in the capital when he made the journey thither on foot in order to transact business there.

[2] That is, if M. N. Tod, in *The Cambridge Ancient History*, vol. v (Cambridge 1927, University Press), p. 11, is right in interpreting Thucydides' figures in *The History of the Atheno-Peloponnesian War*, Book II, chap. 13, to mean that the total number of male Athenian citizens of all classes, of the age of eighteen years and upwards, was something between 55,000 and 61,000 in 431 B.C. Whatever the figure actually was in 431 B.C., it may have been higher before 445 B.C., when some 5,000 men were struck off the register in execution of a law, passed in 451–450 B.C., restricting the Athenian franchise to the children of married couples in which both parents had been Athenian citizens at the time of the child's birth. We do not know the extent to which this reduction of the total by 5,000 in 445 B.C. had been offset by natural increase during the next fourteen years.

[3] In composing their nostalgic political utopias, in which Sparta was their ideal and Athens was their bugbear (see III. iii. 90–97), Plato and Aristotle agreed with one another in setting the optimum number of citizens for the citizen body of a city-state at a figure that was very much lower than the actual numerical strength of the Athenian citizen body in their day, when its strength was considerably smaller than it had been at its peak. In the *Republic* (423 A–D) Plato declares that, so long as his ideal city-state has the constitution that he has laid down for it in this dialogue, he does not mind if the number of citizens capable of bearing arms is no higher than a thousand; and he stipulates that, if the number is to be higher than that, it must not be raised to a figure at which the community will lose its unity. In *The Laws* (737 C–738 A) Plato takes as his criterion for the scale of his ideal city-state the need for the community's man-power to be sufficient to enable it to defend itself successfully if attacked by its neighbours, and on this criterion he opts for a figure of 5,040 citizens capable of bearing arms. Aristotle, in his discussion of the optimum magnitude in *The Politics* (1225 B–1226 B), refrains from committing himself to any precise figure and merely stipulates that the number of the citizens must not be so large as to make it impossible for them to be all personally acquainted with one another, or impossible for an announcer without a loud-speaker (κῆρυξ μὴ Στεντόρειος) to make himself heard by the whole assembly. A popular assembly even of this size would, of course, have been unmanageable if it had been the only organ of government. In a competently managed Hellenic democracy such as the Athenian in the sixth and fifth centuries B.C., the popular assembly was enabled to transact its business effectively thanks to an infusion of the representative system into the Cleisthenean Constitution of 508–507 B.C. Public business was pre-digested and presented, and its

The size of the territory of the Roman Commonwealth was perhaps hardly more than a third of the size of the territory of a contemporary Athens at the time when, at some date in the fifth century B.C., the Ager Romanus was divided into twenty districts in order to articulate a national popular assembly into as many companies of voters, each consisting of the citizens whose domicile lay in one of these 'tribal' districts;[1] and the maximum distance that any Roman citizen would have to travel from his home to the capital in order to take part in national public business remained well within Attic limits even after the territory of Rome had been enlarged by the addition of one new district (the Tribus Clustumina) up the left bank of the River Tiber[2] and four further new districts into which the territory of Veii, across the Tiber, was subsequently carved up after its conquest in 396 B.C.[3] When in 358 B.C. two more districts (the Pomptina and the Publilia) were carved out of conquered Volscian territory[4] in the lowlands south-east of the Alban Hills, Roman citizens now resident there might find it still just possible to

subsequent transaction in the popular assembly was controlled, by a grand jury, or general purposes committee, of the citizen body which was, not elected, but picked by lot, on a representative system in which the quota allocated to each local administrative district of Attica was proportionate to the fraction of the total citizen body that was estimated to be represented by the citizens resident in that district. Since this committee (the *Boulê*) was itself five hundred strong and was therefore, like the general assembly, too unwieldly to dispatch executive business in plenary session, it was divided into ten sections, which took it in turns to serve as an executive sub-committee for periods of thirty-six or thirty-five days each within the *Boulê*'s twelve months' term of office. This executive sub-committee had a chairman, picked by lot, who changed every twenty-four hours. The task of presiding over meetings of the *Boulê* and of the general assembly was entrusted to a presidential body of nine members, picked by lot *ad hoc*, with a chairman of their own, likewise picked by lot, from the nine sections of the *Boulê* that were not serving as the executive sub-committee at the moment (see Aristotle: *The Constitution of Athens*, chaps. 43–44).

[1] The date of the division of the Ager Romanus into the twenty 'tribal' districts is discussed by K. J. Beloch in his *Römische Geschichte bis zum Beginn der Punischen Kriege* (Berlin and Leipzig 1926, de Gruyter), pp. 270–1 and 298–302. The only certain chronological facts are that these first twenty 'tribal' districts must have been instituted before the addition of a twenty-first (the Clustumina), and that the territory of Crustumerium, out of which this twenty-first district was constituted, must have been annexed to the Ager Romanus before the annexation, in 396 B.C., of the territory of Veii, on the opposite bank of the river, which was subsequently carved up into four more districts (the twenty-second to the twenty-fifth inclusive). It can also be deduced from the lie of the land that the territory of Fidenae, along the left bank of the Tiber between the territory of Crustumerium and Rome, must have been annexed to the Ager Romanus before the annexation of Crustumerium, and Beloch (in op. cit., pp. 298–302) gives reasons for thinking that Fidenae was conquered by Rome in either 428 B.C. or 426 B.C. We do not know, however, whether this conquered Fidenate territory was included in one of the first twenty Roman 'tribal' districts or in the twenty-first district, i.e., the Clustumina.

Even, however, if the Ager Fidenas was already included in the Ager Romanus at the date at which the original twenty Roman 'tribal' districts were instituted, the aggregate area of the Ager Romanus at the time would have been no more than 861·5 square kilometres, as against 822 if at that time Fidenae was still independent (these figures will be found in Beloch, op. cit., p. 178). On the other hand the area of Attica, within her frontiers as they ran in the fifth century B.C., was as much as 2,440 square kilometres according to Beloch's reckoning in his *Die Bevölkerung der Griechisch-Römischen Welt* (Leipzig 1886, Duncker and Humblot), p. 56, if we include the island of Salamis, which had been colonized by Athenian citizens, but omit the two districts of Oropus and Eleutherae, adjoining the land-frontier between Attica and Boeotia. Thucydides describes the Oropians as 'subjects of Athens' (Book II, chap. 23; cp. Book IV, chap. 99), while it is not certain that the Eleuthereis possessed the full Athenian franchise (the status of the inhabitants of these two districts is discussed by G. de Sanctis in his *Atthis* (Turin 1912, Bocca), p. 333, n. 1).

[2] See Beloch, *Römische Geschischte*, pp. 159, 174, 265, and 270.
[3] See ibid., p. 607.   [4] See ibid., pp. 265 and 356–8.

exercise their public rights and duties in the capital by making, within the day, a journey that was rather longer than the journey from Sunium to Athens. This physical feat would certainly have been practicable for Roman citizens domiciled in two other new districts (the Maecia and the Scaptia) that were carved in 332 B.C.[1] out of territory, ceded to Rome in 338 B.C. by the Confederation of Latin City-States, between the two previously acquired outlying districts in the Pomptine Marshes and the metropolitan domain of the Roman Commonwealth containing the original twenty districts. A Roman citizen domiciled in another new district (the Oufentina), carved in 318 B.C. out of territory, ceded to Rome by Privernum,[2] in the Pomptine Marshes south-east of the two districts established there in 358 B.C., might have been able to reach Rome within the day by an athlete's *tour de force*; but the task would have defeated the classical Athenian long-distance runner Philippides himself if Philippides had been a Roman citizen domiciled in a district (the Falerna) that had been constituted in 332 B.C.[3] out of territory, ceded to Rome by Capua along the north bank of the Lower Volturnus, more than a hundred miles away from Rome as the aeroplane flies;[4] and, when in the course of the years 268–241 B.C. the territory inhabited by Roman citizens legally invested with the active rights of citizenship was progressively extended from the northern environs of Rome northward across the Appennines to the shores of the Adriatic, and when these fully enfranchised Sabines and Picentes were enrolled in 241 B.C. in a newly created Tribus Quirina and Tribus Velina,[5] the territory of the Roman Commonwealth flagrantly burst the bounds within which it was physically possible for every citizen to participate in the national government directly.

Thus, long before the time when the Roman Empire became co-extensive with the Hellenic World, and when local communities of transplanted or naturalized Roman citizens were scattered all over the territory of this Roman-built Hellenic universal state, an ever increasing majority of the total Roman citizen body had come to find itself unable in practice to exercise its rights and duties in the forum of Roman national politics simply because its domiciles were too far distant from a capital city that was the only place where, under Rome's city-state constitution, national public business could legitimately be transacted.[6]

---

[1] See Beloch, *Römische Geschichte*, pp. 164–5, 388, and 525.
[2] See ibid., pp. 390 and 526. [3] See ibid., p. 388.
[4] The writer flew over this stretch of country, from Ostia to the gap between Terracina and Monte Circello, on the 28th October, 1948, after having traversed it by train on the 14th November, 1911.
[5] See Beloch, op. cit., p. 265; eundem: *Der Italische Bund unter Roms Hegemonie* (Leipzig 1880, Teubner), pp. 76 and 122–3.
[6] As late as A.D. 69, when the *Pax Augusta* was a century old, and when a quarter of a millennium had passed since the date when Rome had made herself virtually mistress of the Hellenic World by overthrowing Macedon, the last other Hellenic Great Power capable of challenging Rome's supremacy, the Roman public was surprised at the discovery that the post of autocrat in constitutional disguise (*princeps*), which had long since become an indispensable organ in the government of the Roman Commonwealth, could be filled by a pronunciamiento on the part of Roman citizens serving in the garrisons of the imperial frontiers ('Finis Neronis . . . varios motus animorum non modo in urbe apud patres aut populum aut urbanum militem, sed omnes legiones ducesque conciverat, evolgato imperii arcano posse principem alibi quam Romae fieri' (Tacitus: *Histories*, Book I, chap. 4).

These outlying Roman citizens had to satisfy their Hellenic craving for direct participation in the government of a city-state by participating in the local government of the praefectura, forum, conciliabulum, colonia Romana, or municipium of which they were also citizens under a Boeotian system of dual citizenship that had been adopted by the Roman Commonwealth as well as by its post-Alexandrine contemporaries the Seleucid Monarchy and the Aetolian and Achaean confederacies;[1] but this municipal franchise was no compensation for the virtual disfranchisement that had been inflicted on them in the forum of Roman national politics, not by any narrow-hearted policy of making the control of the Roman national government a monopoly of a metropolitan minority of the citizen body,[2] but by the inability of pre-mechanical means of communication to enable the outlying citizens of the Roman Commonwealth to put in an appearance in the capital city when the territory inhabited by Roman citizens had become as extensive as it had actually come to be some two or three centuries before the Emperor Tiberius, upon his accession in A.D. 14, at last took cognizance of the stultification of Rome's city-state constitution by her territorial expansion in the long since overdue act of liquidating the anachronistic Roman national popular assemblies in the capital city.

It was, in fact, technologically impossible for the Roman citizen body in the first century of the Christian Era—and *a fortiori* in the third century, after the enfranchisement of almost all Rome's alien subjects in A.D. 212 by the Emperor Caracalla (*imperabat* A.D. 211–17)[3]—to take, in the government of a Pan-Hellenic Roman Empire, the direct part that the Athenian citizen body in the fifth century B.C. had been able to take in the government of Attica; and this would likewise have been impossible in the eighteenth century of the Christian Era for the citizen body of a United States whose populated territory was then still confined to the eastern seaboard of North America between the Atlantic and the Appalachian Mountains. On the other hand, by A.D. 1952 the progress made by Western technology within the 177 years that had elapsed since the Declaration of Independence had, in terms of human intercourse, reduced to the dimensions of a Periclean Attica a United States that now stretched from coast to coast of the North American island. On the 10th October, 1950, it took the writer of this Study a shorter time, by four hours, to fly from New York to Los Angeles than it had taken him to walk from Sunium to Athens on the 10th December, 1911. By A.D. 1952 it was possible for any politician in Washington, on any day of the year, to present himself, within the day, in person before an audience in any part of the United States; and, though it was not possible for him to be present in the flesh in every city, town, village, and homestead in the country at the self-same moment, it was possible at the self-same moment

---

[1] See IV. iv. 310–13.
[2] It was true that Roman citizens organized in local communities with the status of municipia had originally been saddled with the duties of Roman citizenship without enjoying the corresponding rights; but Roman citizens organized in local communities with the status of *coloniae Romanae* had always enjoyed these rights, besides being bound by those duties, subject to their being physically able to exercise these rights by making the journey to Rome.
[3] See V. vi. 7, n. 4; VI. vii. 156, n. 3; VI. vii. 375; and pp. 553–4, below.

for every inhabitant of all these homesteads, villages, towns, and cities to enjoy the edifying experience of listening to Cleon by radio and viewing him by television.

Thanks to these recent *chefs-d'œuvre* of Western Technology, it was in fact possible for all citizens of the United States at any moment to listen in and look in to the public discussion of political issues; and it was also possible for the spokesmen of any 'lobby' to take a more active part than this in American national politics by flying within the day from Portland, Oregon, or from San Diego, California, to Washington, D.C., and bringing Cleon to bay in his den on Capitol Hill before the demagogue had had time to forestall a Pacific Slope 'pressure group's' offensive by winging his own way to the Pacific Coast and cajoling a Californian or Oregonian audience face to face. It was true that the citizen body could not yet descend on Washington at a day's notice *en masse* pending the requisite multiplication of seats on aeroplanes and rooms in hotels. Yet, if in this respect the United States in A.D. 1952 might be deemed still to be not quite so close-knit, in terms of human intercourse, as Attica had been in 449 B.C., the United States was already closer-knit than Attica had ever been on the new plane of intercourse that the inventions of broadcasting and television had opened up. In Hellenic history there had never been a time when the entire population even of a Lilliputian Belbina, not to speak of a Brobdingnagian Attica, had been able to listen to the voice, and watch the countenance and gestures, of a politician talking to an assembly in the agora at the capital. On this plane the United States in A.D. 1952 was as diminutive in size, expressed in terms of human intercourse, as Abraham Lincoln's Springfield or as Demosthenes' Paeania; and the United States' size today gave the measure of the World's size tomorrow, since, if any one thing could be predicted with assurance in the apprehensive World of this date, it was that a rapidly growing fleet of aeroplanes, flying at a rapidly accelerating speed, would become capable of reaching their destinations in a rapidly diminishing number of minutes, and that a rapidly growing host of radio and television sets would become capable of picking up sights and sounds at a rapidly increasing distance from the points where these importunate instruments were located.

It will be seen that in A.D. 1952 world government was already within Mankind's grasp in so far as Technology could avail to thrust this now urgent political necessity into human hands. As soon, however, as we ascend—or descend—from the plane of Technology to the plane of Human Nature, we find the earthly paradise skilfully assembled by the ingenuity of *Homo Faber* being reduced to a fool's paradise by the perversity of *Homo Politicus*.

In A.D. 1952 a democratic world government that had now become technologically feasible was not within sight of becoming practical politics, because the ripe fruits of Technology could not be harvested without a change of heart of which, so far, there was little sign. In a coalescing and shrinking *Oikoumenê* whose human inhabitants were finding themselves at ever closer quarters with one another, an urgently needed, but not yet inaugurated, world order was still awaiting the fulfilment of a prophecy made in the Syriac World in the eighth century B.C. by the Judaean seer Isaiah:

'The wolf . . . shall dwell with the lamb and the leopard shall lie down with the kid, and the calf and the young lion and the fatling together; and a little child shall lead them. And the cow and the bear shall feed; their young ones shall lie down together; and the lion shall eat straw like the ox. And the sucking child shall play on the hole of the asp, and the weaned child shall put his hand on the cockatrice' den. They shall not hurt nor destroy in all My holy mountain; for the Earth shall be full of the knowledge of the Lord, as the waters cover the sea.'[1]

This Hebrew prophecy had not been left altogether unfulfilled by the Earth's non-human fauna; for it was a scientifically verified fact that the beasts of prey did have a habit of granting a truce to fellow creatures that were normally their quarry when a drought drove them all to the same still welling spring, or a forest fire to the same still unscorched glade, or a flood to the same still unsubmerged holy mountain; and these habitual signs of grace in the dumb animals' response to the challenge of emergencies threatening the lives of all creatures alike were the foil against which a Syriac prophet or a Western naturalist would contemplate the twentieth-century spectacle of human carnivores that still could not or would not bring themselves to enter into a Truce of God, even when they were being forced to rub shoulders with one another by the menacing rise of a tide of atomic science round the coasts of a shrinking *Oikoumenê*.

In A.D. 1952 the nearest approach to political co-operation that a Russian bear and an American eagle found themselves able to make to one another was their common participation in the activities of the United Nations Organization. The inability of the two surviving Great Powers to come closer together than this had been the limiting factor that had prevented the architects of the constitution of the U.N.O. from making of it anything more intimate than a forum for international debate between delegates of the governments of sovereign independent states, of which three, besides the two titans, were armed with a veto on resolutions passed by a majority of their fellow states-members. During the five years of its existence up to date, the U.N.O. had demonstrated its value, notwithstanding the severity of these limitations, by proving to be a decidedly more conductive means of political communication than 'the usual diplomatic channels'. Delegates of the United States Government and the Soviet Government could still continue to talk to one another here when the traditional channels of communication had become choked; and at Lake Success they were parleying in the presence, and with the participation, of delegates of governments of states of lesser calibre which, in this forum, had a constitutional right to make their own voices heard.

These were no mean services to the cause of peace and concord; and an oecumenical institution that provided these services was one with which Mankind could not afford to dispense in their perilous situation at the time. Yet these merits did not make the U.N.O. capable of be-

[1] Isa. xi. 6–9.

coming the embryo of a world government. The realities of the distribution of power in the World that had emerged from the Second World
War were not adequately reflected in the clumsiness of a constitution
that had embodied the unrealistic principle of 'one state one vote', and
that had then found no better means of bringing a fictitious 'equality of
states' into line with a harsh reality than the concession to five Powers of
a veto that was denied to their nominal peers. The best prospect in sight
for the U.N.O. was a possibility that it might evolve from being a forum
into becoming a confederacy; but there was a great gulf fixed between
any confederacy of sovereign independent parochial governments and
any federation of peoples with a central government claiming and
receiving the direct personal allegiance of each individual citizen of the
union; and it was notorious that the history of political institutions knew
of no case in which this gulf had been crossed by any other process than
a revolutionary leap.

On this showing, the U.N.O. seemed unlikely to be the institutional
nucleus out of which an eventually inevitable world government would
develop, though it seemed likely to remain an indispensable instrument
for the preservation of peace unless and until a unitary world government had grown out of some other germ. In A.D. 1952 the probability
seemed to be that, if and when an effective world government did come
into being, it would take shape through a development, not of the
U.N.O., but of one or other of two older and tougher political 'going
concerns' which, as a result of the outcome of a Second World War, had
already partitioned the *Oikoumenê* between them. The world government of the future seemed likely to stem either from the Government of
the United States, which in A.D. 1952 was already in effect the government of more than one-half of the *Oikoumenê*, or from the Government
of the Soviet Union, which at the same date was already in effect the
government of the rest of the Habitable and Traversable World.

If the living generation of Mankind had been free to choose

utrorum ad regna cadendum
omnibus humanis esset terrâque marique,[1]

there could be little doubt in a contemporary Western observer's mind
that a decisive majority of all living men and women that were competent
to make any judgement at all upon this issue, and an overwhelming
majority of such people in all Western countries, would have opted for
becoming subjects of the United States, and not subjects of the Soviet
Union, so long as these two Powers continued to divide between them
the dominion over the *Oikoumenê*; and there could be equally little
doubt that the same millions would also have prayed for the victory of
the United States in the event of a war between the two Powers for the
prize of world-wide supremacy that the elimination of one competitor
would leave exclusively in the surviving competitor's hands. In Western
eyes, at least, it seemed self-evident that, if Mankind were indeed to be
confronted with a choice between destroying itself or acquiescing in the
enforcement of peace by the fiat of some single Power, and if they were

---

[1] Lucretius: *De Rerum Naturâ*, Book III, ll. 836-7, quoted on p. 484, above.

then to be confronted with a choice between the United States and the Soviet Union as the only possible two candidates for this necessary yet invidious political mission, the United States would be preferable, out of all comparison, to the Soviet Union as the victor in this fateful competition for being the Power whose fiat the rest of Mankind was henceforth to obey.

The virtues that made the United States incomparably preferable to the Soviet Union as a candidate for this imperial role stood out conspicuously against a Communist Russian foil.

America's cardinal virtue in the sight of her present and prospective subjects was her transparently sincere reluctance to be drawn into playing this role at all. An appreciable portion of the living generation of American citizens, as well as all the ancestors of all American citizens who were not themselves immigrants, had been moved to pluck up their roots in the Old World and to start life again on the farther side of the Atlantic by a yearning, not to meddle in, but to extricate themselves from, the affairs of a Continent whose dust either they or their forebears had once demonstratively shaken from off their feet;[1] and the buoyancy of the hope with which the forebears had made their deliberate withdrawal from the Old World in the seventeenth, eighteenth, and nineteenth centuries was matched by the poignancy of the regret with which the living generation of Americans was making its compulsory twentieth-century return. The compulsion, as we have seen,[2] was taking the form of an 'annihilation of distance' through the progress of a Western technology; and the Americans themselves had done perhaps more than any other Western people to develop this peculiarly Western art in the direction in which its course was now running directly counter to its American adepts' cherished political aims and ideals. The flaming sword wielded by this inexorable angel of their own creation who was expelling the Americans from their utopian earthly paradise had been flaring in the skies since the invention of the aeroplane at the turn of the nineteenth and twentieth centuries. Yet nothing less cogent than the experience of finding themselves involved willy nilly in two world wars in one lifetime could have moved the American people between A.D. 1941 and A.D. 1947—as the Japanese people had been moved between A.D. 1853 and A.D. 1868 by the logic of comparably portentous events—to recognize that they could no longer safeguard their interests, independence, or even existence unless they broke with a traditional policy of isolation which still retained a hold on their hearts even when it was ceasing to convince their intellects. Shrinking, as they did, from involvement in international politics, the Americans shrank still more vehemently from being cast, as they were being cast by their inescapable preponderance in power, for the role of serving as their neighbours' leaders and masters; and their manifestly genuine regrets for a lost idyllic seclusion were their best credentials for commending them to foreign peoples over whom the force of circumstances was constraining them to assume authority.

'The truth is, and must be, that social life is happiest and most har-

---

[1] Matt. x. 14; Mark vi. 11; Luke ix. 5 and x. 11; Acts xiii. 51 and xviii. 6.
[2] On pp. 479–86, above.

monious where those who have to rule are the last people who would choose to be rulers, and is least happy and least harmonious where the rulers are of the opposite disposition.'[1]

On the morrow of the Second World War, Plato's dictum was as exculpatory for the Americans as it was damning for the Russians.[2]

The Americans' second outstanding virtue was their generosity. It has been noticed in a previous chapter,[3] as one of the auspicious features in the situation after the Second World War, that the Soviet Union, as well as the United States, was a 'sated' Power; but the economic and social situations of the two countries were identical only in the general sense that Russia, like America, was a country commanding vast still undeveloped human and non-human resources. In contrast to America, Russia had hardly yet begun to exploit her potentialities, and the developments that she had carried out at such cost in human effort and suffering during the twelve years immediately preceding the German assault upon her in A.D. 1941 had been largely sabotaged by her abominable Western invaders. Thereafter, the Russians had taken an unjust advantage of finding themselves on the winning side by recouping themselves for the Germans' destruction of Russian industrial plant by seizing and removing plant, not only from a guilty Germany, but from East and Central European countries that the Russians professed to be liberating from the Nazis, and from Chinese provinces in Manchuria that they professed to be liberating from the Japanese. This was a contrast indeed to the United States' post-war reconstruction policy of first making, on a vote passed in the House of Representatives at Washington on the 25th January, 1944, a major contribution to the resources placed at the disposal of the United Nations Relief and Rehabilitation Administration, and then following up this short-term emergency measure for the relief of the war-stricken peoples of the World by launching, on the 5th June, 1947, a long-term plan for reconstruction in Europe that was to be payable entirely out of the American tax-payer's pocket.

The Marshall Plan was perhaps not quite unprecedented. There was a classical precedent in a post-Alexandrine chapter of Hellenic history that had seen the states of the Hellenic World of the day vie with one another in the generosity of their gifts to the city-state of Rhodes after Rhodes had been smitten by an earthquake in 227 B.C.[4] This, however, had been a case of many countries contributing towards the relief of one country, whereas the Marshall Plan was a case of one country offering help to all the rest, and making this offer at a time when the donor was

---

[1] Plato: *Respublica*, 520 D, quoted in III. iii. 252.

[2] Damning, that is to say, for the Russians in the role of rulers, in which the Russians had always been at their worst. There had, however, been another role in which the Russians had always been at their best since the days of Borís and Gleb (*passorum* A.D. 1015), and that was the role of martyrs. The noble army of Russian martyrs, whose ranks had been perpetually recruited by one generation after another of intrepid volunteers from the eleventh century to the twentieth, bore witness to the historical fact that the tyrannical vein in the Russian êthos had always been under challenge from an antithetical Russian spirit of self-sacrificing love that had known no fear of 'them which kill the Body but are not able to kill the Soul' (Matt. x. 28; cp. Luke xii. 4–5). A student of Russian history, looking forward in A.D. 1952, would be slow to believe that this other vein in the Russian êthos had run dry   [3] On p. 478, above.

[4] See Polybius: *Oecumenical History*, Book V, chaps. 88–90, cited on p. 271, above.

already the strongest single Power in the World of the day. In the past it had been customary for dominant Powers, not to give, but to take,[1] and there had been no departure from this evil custom in the policy that the Soviet Union had been following. In setting a new moral standard for 'power politics' by launching the Marshall Plan, American statesmanship was putting Russian post-war actions to shame and Russian post-war intentions to an 'acid test',[2] and on both these counts Russian statesmanship made a poor showing in its response to this searching American challenge. In declining Marshall Aid for the peoples of the Soviet Union, the Soviet Government might be held to be acting within its rights, and foreign critics, at any rate, had no *locus standi* for objecting to a decision against which no effective protest had been made by the *misera plebs Sovietica* at whose expense their government's decision had been taken; but, in using her hold over her satellites in order to compel them too to reject the American offer, the Soviet Union was guilty of an abuse of power that was particularly flagrant in cases in which countries at her mercy whom she was forbidding to accept American assistance happened to be countries that were doubly in need of it because they had been stripped by the Soviet Government, since the end of the Second World War, of industrial plant which the war itself had spared.

It will be seen that Russia's behaviour would have made a present to America of the beau rôle even if America's behaviour had not been as handsome as in fact it was; and this contrast between the post-war records of the two surviving Great Powers comes out even more sharply when we pass from the economic plane to the political and the military. A post-war world that was craving for freedom from want had a still greater yearning for freedom from fear; and, while the fear inspired by the Soviet Union was as intense as it was ubiquitous, fathers of families in countries under the hegemony of the United States were not being kept awake at night by any fear that a United States Government that had them in its power might abuse this power by coercing them with the threat of taking their children's lives with atomic weapons which, in 'the Free World', were an American monopoly.

Citizens of West European countries were, however, now haunted by fears that some American decision, in which the West European peoples

[1] Imperial Powers which, like the Roman Empire in the Hellenic World and the British Rāj in India, had plumed themselves on their disinterestedness, had been apt to claim credit, not for having subsidized their subjects out of their own pockets, but for having (as Clive saw it) shown an astonishing moderation in leaving even a shred of wool on the backs of defenceless sheep whom the imperialists had been at liberty to sheer. It was true that, in the British dominions in India, Lord Cornwallis had restrained a British rapacity, and stamped out a British corruption, that had been running riot for a generation, and that in the Roman Empire Caesar and Augustus had put an end to the still more disgraceful orgies of Roman business men after these had run riot for longer than a century and a half; but such testimonials are not easy to distinguish from indictments. 'What shall we say then? Shall we continue in sin, that grace may abound? God forbid' (Rom. vi. 1–2).

[2] In A.D. 1947 the reigning government in Russia was a fair target for a telling phrase which in A.D. 1918 had been levelled primarily at the government then reigning in Germany by a President of the United States speaking on Russia's behalf. 'The treatment accorded to Russia by her sister nations in the months to come will be the acid test of their good will' (Point VI of President Wilson's Fourteen Points announced in his address at a joint session of the two houses of the Congress at Washington on the 8th January, 1918).

might have had no say, might inadvertently bring Russian atomic missiles hurtling down on Dutch, Danish, French, and British heads. Such West European fears of dire consequences descending upon Western Europe as unintended by-products of some impulsive American retort to some provocative Russian act of aggression were anxieties that might or might not be well founded, but their currency in Western Europe was a fact, and this psychological fact exposed a constitutional flaw in the structure of a commonwealth of Western nations in which all the partners, with the crucial exception of one partner whose 'fiat' was 'law', were exposed to the risk of being involved in a perhaps irretrievable catastrophe as a consequence of decisions in which they might have had no voice, on issues in which, for them, the stakes were life and death. It was proverbial that in a society articulated into a number of sovereign independent parochial states every people was apt to get the government that it deserved;[1] and even this political nemesis was not easy for human souls to bear, notwithstanding the undeniable justice of it. In a commonwealth of nations indissolubly associated under the hegemony of a paramount Power, the lot of all the subordinate participants was the intolerable injustice of getting a government that had been deserved, not by them, but by their predominant partner; and this was the plight of America's, as well as Russia's, satellites in A.D. 1952.

It was, moreover, a plight that could not be mitigated appreciably by resorting either to 'the usual diplomatic channels' or to the new forum provided by the United Nations Organization. Under the current unwritten constitution of a nascent Western Community, issues of vital or lethal moment to its West European, Canadian, and Australian citizens were being decided by the play of party politics in the domestic political arena of the United States. The non-American citizens of the Western Community had no institutional means of taking part in the working out of Western policy at this domestic American formative stage; and the most that their municipal governments could do on their behalf was to make the ineffective gesture of tabling motions pleading that a stable door should be locked after an apocalyptic steed had flown.[2]

By A.D. 1952 a celebrated American definition, dating from A.D. 1895, of the standing of the United States in the Western Hemisphere had come to be no less true of her standing in a world-wide *Oikoumenê* in which all countries were under the United States' hegemony save those that were under the Soviet Union's domination.

'To-day the United States is practically sovereign' ['in the United States' portion of a partitioned world', as an observer, quoting Olney's despatch in

---

[1] 'Toute nation a le gouvernement qu'elle mérite' (de Maistre, J.: *Lettres et Opuscules Inédits* (Paris 1851, Vaton), vol. i, p. 215, 15th August, 1811).

[2] By the end of the year A.D. 1950 these painful truths had been borne in upon the minds of the West European citizens of the Western Community by their experience of an international crisis over a local war in Korea that had been threatening to rankle into a war of world-wide dimensions. The contemporary reaction of a West European nationalist was expressed in caricature in the aphorism 'America was thus clearly top nation, and History came to a.' (Sellar, W. C., and Yeatman, R. J.: *1066 and All That* (London 1930, Methuen), p. 115). The reaction of a West European federalist, addressing himself to an American public, might be expressed in the slogan: 'No annihilation without representation.'

A.D. 1952, would be inclined to amend the text in substitution for the original words 'on this continent'], 'and its fiat is law upon the subjects to which it confines its interposition. Why? It is not because of the pure friendship or good will felt for it. It is not simply by reason of its high character as a civilised state, nor because wisdom and justice and equity are the invariable characteristics of the dealings of the United States. It is because, in addition to all other grounds, its infinite resources, combined with its isolated position, render it master of the situation and practically invulnerable as against any or all other Powers.'[1]

This dictum on the standing of the United States had not lost any of its cogency in coming to be applicable to a far wider sphere of hegemony than had been in the mind of the Secretary of State at Washington who had written those sentences in A.D. 1895; and, though a patriotic non-American citizen of a twentieth-century Western commonwealth of nations might be content to make the pertinent comment that the most lacerating American whips were, at any rate, less grievous instruments of political chastisement than even the least venomous Russian scorpions, 'a philosopher' might 'be permitted to enlarge his views'[2] by taking some meteorological observations. In the first place he would observe that the virtual monopoly, by a paramount Power, of the determination and execution of policies in which the lives and fortunes of satellite peoples were at stake was pregnant with a constitutional problem that could not be evaded; second, that, in the partitioned *Oikoumenê* of A.D. 1952, this problem was a live one both in the American and in the Russian sphere of hegemony or domination; third, that the problem would still present itself, and still demand a solution, if the two spheres were eventually to be amalgamated; and, fourth, that this problem could not be solved without recourse to some form of federal union.

The mere recital of these observations made it clear that the constitutional issues raised by the advent of a supra-national order on the political plane were unlikely to be settled easily or rapidly. One promising feature in the situation was that the United States and the Soviet Union—one or both of whom would have a decisive say in the constitutional development of a commonwealth of nations under its hegemony —were, as it happened, both of them morally committed to an approval of federalism in principle in virtue of having written it into their own constitutions.

The Constitution of the United States was the product of a deliberate choice of full federal union in preference to a looser form of political association—between states only, and not also between human beings— that had quickly been proved inadequate by painful experience; and the people of the thirteen original states-members of the Union had federated with one another on terms that had left a door open for the admission of new-comers. In the minds of latter-day citizens of a United States that had increased its membership from the original figure of thirteen states to an eventual figure of forty-eight between A.D. 1792 and A.D. 1912, a

[1] Secretary of State Richard Olney, in a dispatch of the 20th July, 1895, to the United States Ambassador to the Court of St. James's.
[2] Gibbon, Edward: *The History of the Decline and Fall of the Roman Empire*, 'General Observations on the Fall of the Roman Empire in the West', at the end of chap. xxxviii.

familiarity with the history of their country during those 120 years had associated the idea of federalism with the idea of progressively incorporating additional constituents; and against the historical background of this domestic American precedent a suggestion that the American people themselves might one day enter into a federation with other peoples would not be startling even to Americans who found it unpalatable. A federation between the peoples of the United States and other English-speaking countries would, indeed, be very closely in line with domestic American constitutional tradition. A proposal to extend a federation of English-speaking Western peoples to Continental West European peoples that were akin to the English-speaking peoples in their way of life without being linked with them by a community of language might, on the other hand, look, in American eyes, like a hitherto untried venture for which no adequate precedent was to be found in the domestic American experience of incorporating into the citizen body of the United States a small French-speaking population in Louisiana in A.D. 1803 and small Spanish-speaking populations in California and New Mexico in A.D. 1848. Yet the United States' next-door neighbour Canada was a successfully working model of a federation between two peoples, speaking different languages and professing different religions, who were approximately equal to one another in numbers; and another cue was offered by the letter of the law officially in force in the Soviet Union.

In Western eyes the federal constitution with which the Soviet Union had equipped itself might look suspiciously like a façade put up to mask the retention or re-establishment of a centralized despotism that had the momentum of six hundred years of Russian history behind it. The Petrine Russian Empire from which the Soviet Union had inherited its immense patrimony had been the heir of a Muscovite principality that, from the fourteenth century of the Christian Era onwards, had added field to field by extinguishing the independence of one after another of its neighbours. Was not the Union of Soviet Socialist Republics merely a disingenuous new title for a unitary autocracy of which no concealment had been made by Stalin's franker predecessors Peter the Great and Ivan the Terrible? As far as any Western observer could judge, this current Western critique of the constitution of the Soviet Union was fair comment on the whole. Yet there was one point in which the Bolsheviki's professed constitutional new departure appeared to have some substance, and this was a point in which Stalin's hand was credibly reported to have been at work. Thanks to his own Georgian origin, Stalin seems to have appreciated the strength of the nationalist opposition aroused among the non-Russian subjects of the former Russian Empire by a policy of Russification; and he seems to have drawn the conclusion that, if this policy were not repudiated and reversed by the Tsardom's Communist successors, the effect would be to alienate the non-Great-Russian citizens of the Soviet Union from a Communism which they would then write off as a new disguise for a familiar Russian imperialism.

Accordingly, when the constitution of the Soviet Union was being worked out during the years A.D. 1918–24,[1] the internal administrative

---

[1] The constitution in force in A.D. 1952 was that of the 6th December, 1936.

map of the former Russian Empire was entirely recast—and this apparently on Stalin's initiative—on lines that brought it into correspondence with the linguistic map; and the non-Great-Russian nationalities of the Union—including even the smallest and the most backward peoples in the Caucasus, the Urals, and Central Asia—were thus granted at least the boon of having their local administration and education conducted in their own mother tongues, however illusory their official autonomy might be in other respects. This Stalinian administrative map of the Soviet Union, drawn on a linguistic basis, was no Magna Carta. For example, the erection of an Autonomous Republic of Bashkiristan within the framework of a Russian Socialist Federative Soviet Republic in A.D. 1920 did nothing to abate the centralization at Moscow of the control of police, communications, economic affairs, and, indeed, all the effective levers of power; and, more than that, it did nothing in this case—under a local government on which the Bashkirs themselves were not represented—to check the continuation under the Soviet régime of the unedifying process of chicanery, expedited by brute force, through which, under the Tsardom, the Bashkirs' lands had been passing into Great Russian hands.[1] No doubt the Bashkirs, like the Five Civilized Indian Nations in the South-Eastern United States, were marked out for being made the victims of spoliation by the fact of their happening to lie in the fairway of a mighty tide of aggressive colonization; but the Bashkirs were not the only non-Russian people to suffer adversity under the Soviet régime. Thereafter, in the Great Purge of A.D. 1936, the non-Great-Russian personnel in the governments of some of the non-Great-Russian units on Stalin's administrative map was reported to have been liquidated,[2] and in the Russo-German War of A.D. 1941–5 both the Crimean Tatar Republic and the Kalmuck Republic on the Steppe between the Lower Don and the Lower Volga seem to have foundered on the charge that their peoples had been guilty of disloyalty to the Soviet cause.

It will be seen that Stalin's administrative map of the Soviet Union was not to be taken at its face value; but a moral commitment cannot be wiped out through being dishonoured by its makers; and, in the world that had emerged from the Second World War, Stalin's map might live to be translated, after all, from the limbo of camouflage into the realm of reality if, on either side of the dividing line between a Russian and an American demi-monde, the letter of the Soviet Union's federal constitution were one day to be applied in the spirit of the Pan American Union of Republics and the British Commonwealth of Nations.

On the constitutional plane neither of these two political associations between a number of fully self-governing parochial states was a stage on any road leading towards world government, since the basis of both associations was the scrupulousness of the associated states' reciprocal respect for one another's independence. The members of the Pan American Union were not moving towards a federation between these

[1] See Pipes, R. E.: 'The First Experiment in Soviet National Policy: The Bashkir Republic, 1917–1920', in *The Russian Review*, October 1950 (New York), pp. 303–19.
[2] See Toynbee, A. J., and Boulter, V. M.: *Survey of International Affairs, 1937*, vol. i (London 1938, Milford), pp. 13–20.

successor-states of four different West European Powers' colonial empires,[1] and the members of the British Commonwealth had been positively moving away from the former political unity of an old-fashioned British Empire governed from Westminster. The British Commonwealth was, in fact, an *entente* between mutually independent states that had disengaged themselves from a unitary empire, while the Pan American Union was an *entente* between mutually independent states that had never been united politically in the past and were not moving towards unity now. Yet, just because the weaker parties to the association were aware—as they were in either case—that the strongest member of the partnership had no intention of misusing his superior strength in order to impose his will upon the rest, both the Pan American Union and the British Commonwealth had achieved a felicitous relation of psychological parity between states of widely different calibre whose peoples not only spoke different languages but were also divided from one another by the more formidable barrier of a diversity in their ways of life. In this favourable psychological climate it had proved possible for Great Britain and Ceylon, the Indian Union and New Zealand, the United States and Guatemala, Brazil and Hayti, freely to co-operate with one another as moral equals; and the spirit animating these *ententes* might be enlisted in the cause of federation.

Though the practical possibility of federation, either with the United States or with the Soviet Union, was limited by the notorious fact that, hitherto, so intimate a form of political association had proved practicable only between communities closely akin to one another in their ways of life, the cultural and social circumstances of the time gave scope, within these limits, for federal union on a considerable scale. Federation with the Soviet Union did not, it is true, seem likely, in the dubious judgement of a Western observer, to prove an attractive proposition either to the Soviet Union's Orthodox Christian satellites to the south of her or to her Western Christian satellites to the west of her; but a federal union between the United States, the other English-speaking peoples, and the Continental West European peoples would already have been within sight above the horizon of practical politics if an affinity in culture and a community of interests had been the sole, or even the decisive, considerations. The obstacle—and it was a formidable one— was a human political animal's proneness to give prejudice the precedence over common sense and to allow itself to be swayed by feelings instead of taking rational decisions on the merits of a constitutional case. An American people which had once had to fight in order to win its independence would be reluctant to pool its sovereignty in a federal partnership with other peoples, even if the candidates for partnership were peoples of like passions with itself[2] and also even if the principal partner were assured that her own representation in the prospective federal government would be proportionate, not merely to the relative numerical strength of her population, but to an index figure registering

---

[1] The United States was a successor-state of the British Empire, Brazil of the Portuguese, and Hayti of the French. All the other seventeen members of the Pan American Union were successor-states of the Spanish Empire.   [2] Acts xiv. 15.

the United States' overwhelming preponderance over the rest of the Western World in economic productivity. On the other side, West European satellites of the United States might be reluctant, for their part, to sacrifice a shadow of sovereignty that they still retained in a dependent relation which actually left them at the United States' mercy; and, for the sake of clinging to this shadow, they might refrain from making any attempt to win the substance of an equitable share in the joint conduct of common affairs which could be obtained only at the price of pooling, in a federal union with the United States, a sovereignty which, in this form, could be revalidated within limits corresponding to current political and economic realities.

The mulish perversity of Human Nature that thus threatened to assert itself on both sides, if and when a proposal for federation was brought forward, was an obstacle that could not be expected to yield easily or quickly to common sense and goodwill; yet there were historical precedents which indicated that, in any commonwealth of nations that had originated in the establishment of one dominant Power's paramountcy over a cluster of satellites, the passage of time would be likely to bring with it a gradual approach towards political equality through the progressive enfranchisement of the imperial people's former subjects or subordinates.[1]

In the history of a Roman Commonwealth whose *arcanum imperii* had been its liberality in conferring the Roman citizenship upon aliens who had fallen under Rome's rule or hegemony, successive narrow-hearted reactions against this characteristic manifestation of a Roman political genius had all, in turn, been successively transcended sooner or later. Between 338 B.C. and 241 B.C. the inhabitants of about one quarter of Cisappennine Italy, extending along the south-west coast as far down as Cumae, and along the north-east coast as far up as Pesaro, had been progressively incorporated into the Roman citizen body, and this politic generosity had enabled Rome to establish her dominion over the whole peninsula. The door that had thus been held open for a century had then been closed and had been kept bolted and barred thereafter for the next 150 years; but in 90–89 B.C. the rest of Rome's Italian satellites had extorted the Roman franchise from the paramount Power by force of arms; and, when, after this tardy further step forward, the reactionaries had brought the process of enfranchisement to a halt again, this time along the line of the River Po, the door had been broken open by Caesar and had never been closed again. Caesar's enfranchisement of Rome's Transpadane satellites in 49 B.C. restarted a process which this time never came completely to a halt till in A.D. 212 it reached its term in Caracalla's enfranchisement of virtually all the residue of Rome's then still unenfranchised subjects throughout an empire that embraced all but a fragment of the Hellenic World; and the readiness of the Roman citizen body at this stage to share its political privileges with the rest of the inhabitants of an Hellenic *Oikoumenê* that had been united politically under Rome's aegis seems to have been matched by a readiness on the part even of ancient and famous non-Roman Hellenic communities now

---

[1] See, for example, VI. vii. 146–58.

to accept Roman citizenship at the cost of, at long last, merging in an oecumenical body politic a parochial identity which they had been jealously preserving through the ages. In earlier chapters of Hellenic history there had been at least two critical occasions—the first in 431 B.C. and the second in 228 B.C.[1]—on which Athens and Sparta had remorselessly sacrificed the Hellenic Society's prospects of attaining an urgently needed political unity to their own parochial corporate egotism. There is no record of the re-emergence of this spirit in either Spartan or Athenian hearts on the historic occasion at the turn of the second and third centuries of the Christian Era.[2]

In the history of the Caliphate a corresponding evolution was accomplished more swiftly. Little more than a hundred years elapsed between the political reunification of the Syriac World by the arms of Primitive Muslim Arab *conquistadores* in the fourth and fifth decades of the seventh century of the Christian Era and the *Gleichschaltung* of the Arab Muslim 'ascendancy' with their non-Arab ex-Christian and ex-Zoroastrian converts and clients as a result of the Khurāsānī Iranian Muslim marchmen's victorious insurrection against the Umayyad régime in A.D. 750.[3]

These precedents from Syriac and Hellenic history were good auguries for the prospect that, in a post-Modern chapter of Western history, a supra-national commonwealth originally based on the hegemony of a paramount Power over its satellites might eventually be put on the sounder basis of a constitutional partnership in which all the people of all the partner states would have their fair share in the conduct of common affairs. A constitutional development on these lines seemed as probable in the long run as it was desirable, but in A.D. 1952 this was not the first business on Mankind's political agenda. The rock immediately ahead was a sooner or later inevitable transition from a present political partition of the *Oikoumenê* between two rival Powers to a

---

[1] See III. iii. 340–1 and IV. iv. 265.

[2] Professor William McNeill comments: 'Was Roman citizenship still a privilege by the time of Caracalla? Or was it a burden? Some historians think that the franchise was extended to all free men for the purpose of making them liable to the citizens' taxes on inheritances, etc., [in addition to the subjects' taxes, to which they were liable already]. In any case the willingness of the existing citizen body to see new-comers allotted to its ranks will hardly have counted. The act of enfranchisement was surely an administrative act of a bureaucracy which was by then more or less immune from public opinion—at least in most matters.'

The present writer's reply would be, in general, that bureaucratic or autocratic governments, as well as elected representative governments, are amenable to public feeling and opinion—though their reaction to it may sometimes be slower, and though they may perhaps be able to go rather farther in the dangerous game of flouting it without being called to order. In regard to the case in question, his reply, in particular, would be that this enfranchisement of virtually the whole of the still remaining non-citizen element in the population of the Roman Empire was followed by the growth of a corporate sense of imperial patriotism which eventually expressed itself in the coining of the new word 'Romania' to denote a now undivided and homogeneous Roman imperial people's oecumenical fatherland. This sequel to the Act of A.D. 212 suggests that this Act was well timed in the sense of having been enacted at a date at which the public feeling of the divers elements in the population of the Empire was ripe for it; and if it had not been 'practical politics' in this sense in A.D. 212 it would not, so the writer would guess, have been possible to enact it in that year merely because of its fiscal attractiveness in the professional eyes of an imperial bureaucracy. The writer would also guess that even as recently as the reign of Hadrian (*imperabat* A.D. 117–38) it would not yet have been 'practical politics' to enact the provisions of the *Constitutio Antoniniana* of A.D. 212, however attractive the measure might have been to the bureaucracy already at this earlier date.   [3] See II. ii. 141 and VI. vii. 147–52.

future political unification of the *Oikoumenê* under the control of some unitary political authority; and the first concern of the living generation of Mankind was that this perilous transit should be accomplished without a third world war.

In an age of atomic warfare there were no peoples for whom this was not a matter of life and death in a world whose unification was already an accomplished fact on the military plane, but there were three peoples that had also incurred a special measure of moral responsibility for seeing to it that an urgently needed world order should be established without another catastrophe. In bringing about, between them, the defeat of Germany in the World War of A.D. 1939–45, the peoples of Great Britain, the Soviet Union, and the United States had taken it upon themselves on behalf of Mankind to reject Hitler's offer of a lasting peace at Hitler's price. If in A.D. 1940–1 Hitler had been allowed by these three Powers to have his way, peace would have been imposed on the World by the establishment of a *Pax Germanica* that would have relieved Mankind from the fear of another world war for as far ahead into the future as any human eye could see. Hitler's price for this boon had been so exorbitant that the three victor Powers' decision to reject his offer was likely to win for them the blessings of Posterity supposing that they were now to succeed, between them, in bestowing the same boon on Mankind at an appreciably lower cost in the coin of standardization, regimentation, injustice, and tyranny. On the other hand, these same victors over Hitler would bring down upon their own heads Posterity's curses if they were to allow a third world war to rankle out of their victory. In denying to Mankind the opportunity of enjoying the substantial benefits of an odious *Pax Germanica*, the peoples of the United States, the Soviet Union, and Great Britain had taken upon themselves a binding moral obligation to provide Mankind with a better world order than Hitler's without inflicting on Mankind the third world war that a German victory would have spared them.

Should the ex-victors now fail to accomplish this self-imposed task, they must expect to share with the Germans the execrations of an intolerably tormented Mankind so long as any memory survived of Mankind's history in the twentieth century of the Christian Era. On the other hand, if, between them, they were to succeed in piloting Noah's Ark intact into the still waters of the lagoon beyond the perilous reef, they could look forward to being remembered throughout the rest of the Human Race's term of life on Earth as the heroes who, by an unprecedented moral triumph over the perversity of their own human nature, had closed a chapter of human history branded with the ghastly mark of Cain[1] as the abominable Age of Civilization, Human Sacrifice, Slavery, and War, and had opened the way for Mankind to acquit itself better than before in its perennial struggle with an innate Original Sin. A generation which, in A.D. 1952, was thus bound over to render a strict account of a morally onerous stewardship might take heart from the words of an Athenian philosopher who had witnessed the breakdown of the Hellenic Civilization.

[1] Gen. iv. 15, 17, and 22.

'In the struggle that will decide whether good or evil is to prevail in us, the issue is immeasurably greater than at first sight it might seem to be. . . . We must do everything that lies in our power to attain to Virtue and Wisdom in This Life. The prize is so splendid and the hope is so great.'[1]

(V) PROBABLE FUNCTIONS OF A FUTURE WORLD ORDER

Supposing that a world government were to be established, what would its functions be? Presumably these functions would be much the same whether the establishment of this prospective world government were to be achieved pacifically or at the cost of a third world war, and whether it were to remain fixed in its initial form of a domination or hegemony exercised by a paramount Power or were eventually to acquire a federal constitution in which all the people in a supra-national commonwealth might hope to receive something like their fair share in the conduct of common affairs. Evidently the choice between these divers alternative roads might make a world of difference to the possibility of a world government's being able to perform its functions satisfactorily, whatever these functions might be; but the functions themselves would presumably have been determined in advance by the play of those historical forces that, in A.D. 1952, seemed to be making the establishment of some kind of world government, at some price, inevitable. Was the nature of these future functions then perhaps already discernible?

A world government would be the government of a universal state; and the specific characteristics of universal states, as well as the generic characteristics of states of all the divers historic species, were revealed in the history of Man in Process of Civilization within the last five or six thousand years.

A state was an institution in which part of the psychic power-charge of an individual human being was impounded and combined with parts of the power-charges of other men and women to constitute a pool of power at the disposal of persons controlling and operating a government. A state might be defined as a piece of social mechanism designed for the twin purposes of accumulating power and of applying it; and the preservation of the power of a state was consequently bound to be the first concern of the persons, whoever these might be, who had one of these political pools of power at their command. The most dangerous threat to the survival of any parochial state had always been the existence of other parochial states within striking distance of it, and therefore the most urgent business of any parochial sovereign government had been to maintain its own power against encroachments on the part of other parochial governments in the same politico-military arena and, if possible, also to increase its own power at the expense of each and all of its neighbours. At the same time, every parochial government had always had to fight for the preservation of its power on a domestic front as well as on a foreign front, since, even when it was not being threatened by

[1] Plato: *Respublica*, 608 B, and *Phaedo*, 114 C, quoted in V. vi. 168.

the aggressiveness of some foreign Power, a government would still have to reckon with the perennial recalcitrance of its own subjects; and, while it might be true that even in the smallest and weakest state the most powerful private individual would be impotent to resist the government's will so long as he was trying to resist it in isolation from his fellows, it was an obvious move for a number of individuals to take a leaf out of the state's own book by making common cause among themselves in order to pit against the pooled power of the state the pooled power of a family, clan, fief, faction, class, or interest.

In view of this possibility of a concerted private challenge to a state's corporate power, the concern felt by every government for the preservation of its power would force any government to set limits to its subjects' freedom of private enterprise. A government could not afford to allow any individual subject, and *a fortiori* not any organized group of subjects, to enjoy an unregulated licence to accumulate and apply power on their own private account, even in private relations with one another in which the state's interests were not involved directly and were perhaps not involved ostensibly at all. In order to safeguard its authority against threats to it on the domestic front, every government found it necessary to impose laws on its subjects and to see to it that these laws were effectively enforced. States had learnt, for example, that they could not afford to let their subjects take the law into their own hands, or even to let them keep it in their own hands in spheres in which the application and execution of the law had traditionally been, not a public, but a private, affair regulated by non-state institutions like the Blood Feud and the Wergeld. Equity demanded, of course, that a law drafted, promulgated, and enforced in the name of a state by the persons controlling and operating that state's government should not discriminate either to the advantage or to the detriment of any particular member or group of members of the political community, and should not be devised to serve the selfish interests of the ruling group of members constituting the government. In practice, even those states that had achieved the highest standards of justice so far known in the history of Civilization had never been able to preserve their legislation from being affected to some extent by the current domestic balance of power. It would, indeed, probably have been possible for a competent student of human affairs, possessed of full information about the content and application of the laws of any state at any date, to reconstruct, by inference, the domestic balance of power prevailing in that state at that time.

Thus, during the first five or six thousand years of the currency of this institution, a struggle—in which the government of every state that had ever existed had been constantly engaged—for the preservation and increase of a state's power had led, in the lives of parochial states, to a concentration of governmental activity on two functions: the function of competing with foreign Powers by waging war with them for objects unattainable by diplomacy and the function of regulating the private relations between the state's own subjects by legislation in which the current domestic balance of power was invariably reflected to some extent. The existence of states had thus been bound up with the perpetuation of two social evils, namely warfare between states and conflict between classes; and the wickedness that had thus proved to be inseparable from an institution which had been found to be indispensable by Man in Process of Civilization had been pilloried in the Christian doctrine that the incubus imposed by the existence of states upon the lives of human beings during their terrestrial pilgrimage was a consequence of, and self-inflicted punishment for, Mankind's Original Sin. This Christian proposition had, no doubt, latterly become a hard saying for politically sanguine-minded *ci-devant* Christian citizens of Modern Western states adorned with parliamentary representative institutions; yet in A.D. 1952 this doctrine still accurately represented the genuine attitude (as distinct from any officially prescribed theory) of all that vast majority of Mankind in Russia, Asia, Africa, and Indian America that was still subject, at this date, to the rule of authoritarian régimes.

These two activities—War and Police—through which a state asserted its power abroad and at home respectively, were characteristic, not only of parochial states, but of states of every species, including those universal states that, in the instances on record up to date, had come into existence, in the course of the disintegration of broken-down civilizations, through the eventual liquidation of litters of parochial states which had failed to keep their warfare with one another within non-lethal limits. Although, however, the revolutionary substitution of a single universal state for a multitude of parochial states had not ever put either of the two traditional functions of a government altogether out of court, it had been apt to make both the war-function and the police-function less imperative. Functions whose ultimate purpose was the state's own self-preservation would be less imperative for a universal state than for its parochial predecessors because, *ex hypothesi*, a universal state would have no adversaries of its own calibre to face within the bounds of its own world, and because the same antecedent Time of Troubles that had eliminated all states in this particular society save the single survivor could also be trusted to have broken the spirit of private individuals, factions, classes, and interests.

In a domestic field that had come to be coextensive with the entire domain of a disintegrating society, the oecumenical government of a universal state that had come into existence in the traditional catastrophic way had been apt to find the familiar task of asserting its own authority less pressing than the novel task of saving a disintegrating society from going into a final dissolution in which the universal state now embodying this society would be bound to perish with it.[1] In the pursuit of this more far-sighted concept of its own self-interest an oecumenical government might, no doubt, be prone still to see the salvation of Society in a policy of conserving the vested interests of a dominant minority and repressing the unrest of a dissatisfied proletariat. Yet, even if the oecumenical rulers' conception of the interests and welfare of Society might still appear to be prejudiced, one-sided, and inequitable in the eyes of a philosopher, the salvation of Society was, at least in principle and intention, an altruistic objective for the government of any state to

[1] See VI. vii. 57–61.

pursue; and the addition of this altruistic aim to a government's avowed agenda, over and above the original self-regarding aim of striving to maintain the state's own power, was therefore a landmark in political history.[1]

This positive concern of Mankind's rulers for Mankind's welfare had been born into the World at the births of universal states, and till recently it had always displayed the image and superscription,[2] and shared the fortunes, of one or other of those representatives of this type of polity that had risen and fallen up to date. The concern for welfare shown by oecumenical governments could not be more enlightened than these governments themselves were, and it could not survive their wrecks. In the dark night of Mankind's political life in the Age of the Civilizations, this flicker of light had accordingly come and gone with the universal states in which it had been momentarily kindled; yet the visionary gleam, intermittent though it had been, had never completely vanished from the *Oikoumenê* since the inauguration of a Sumeric Empire of the Four Quarters and an Egyptiac Middle Empire[3] at the close of the third millennium B.C.; and in the recent history of a post-Modern Western World the still awaited advent of a world government had been anticipated by a revival of the ideal of government for welfare in parochial states that were also still engaged in a familiar fratricidal struggle for existence. This post-Modern Western World at the time of writing presented the spectacle of a neck-and-neck race, at a speed that was already break-neck and that was still rapidly accelerating, between two ultimately incompatible conceptions of what the objective of a state ought to be. The Western parochial states of the day were war-and-police states and welfare-states simultaneously; and, though these Janus-faced parochial polities might perhaps be written off the political map

---

[1] This historic recognition that it was part of the duty of a government to concern itself with social welfare was undoubtedly a landmark in the political history of Man in Process of Civilization; but it is not so certain that it was an altogether new departure; for it might have been difficult to find, among the multitude of states known to History, any that had been concerned with the maintenance of its own power to the entire exclusion of all concern for the welfare of its subjects. It seems improbable that either force or habit or even the strongest combination of the two could avail for very long to keep a state in being if its subjects were once convinced that the sole object of their rulers was to misuse the state's coercive powers in order to promote the interests of a dominant minority at the expense of the rest of the community. When governments had indulged in activities that were patently anti-social, they had usually found it politic to refrain from carrying these activities to lengths at which they would constitute a serious tax upon their subjects' prosperity and happiness. For example, we have observed (in IV. iv. 144–50) that, in an eighteenth-century Western Society in which War was avowedly 'the sport of kings', the royal sportsmen took care to set discreet limits to the social costs of their anti-social pastime. The peoples could not be persuaded to sacrifice themselves for the sake of winning wars until they had been persuaded that the wars which they were being asked to fight were the peoples' own serious business in which the public welfare was at stake. On this showing, it seemed likely that some measure of concern for its subjects' welfare as well as some measure of concern for its own power must always have entered into the policy of any state that had ever succeeded in making itself a going concern. The most tyrannical government could perhaps never afford altogether to disregard its subjects' interests; and, conversely, the most benevolent government could perhaps never afford altogether to disregard its own self-preservation.

[2] Matt. xxii. 20; Mark xii. 16; Luke xx. 24.

[3] In IV. iv. 412–13 we have already noticed that under the political dispensation of the Middle Empire the Pharaonic autocracy was regarded as having its *raison d'être* in its services to Society, whereas the political dispensation of the Old Kingdom had found the *raison d'être* of Society in its services to the Pharaonic autocracy.

of the future as being patently *peritura regna*, this struggle within their bosoms between two competing and ultimately incompatible ideals was a new event of abiding interest because the struggle would be bequeathed by them to the world government, whatever this might be, that was to become the doomed parochial states' residuary legatee.

In the obscurity that at this time still veiled Mankind's political future, it could at any rate be foreseen that, if and when something in the nature of a world government did take shape, the task of maintaining its own power would cost it less effort and less anxiety than this had cost any universal state known to History. A single authority holding a world-wide monopoly of the control of atomic energy employable for military purposes would not be confronted by any rival of its own calibre, and it would also not have anything to fear from any residual pockets of recalcitrant barbarians in fastnesses encircled by a global polity that would already have embraced the rest of Mankind. A world government of the future would therefore be free to concentrate its efforts on the promotion of human welfare with a singleness of purpose that had not been feasible for any universal state in the history of any other society.

When a future world government eventually went into action in pursuit of this objective, what would be likely to be its first move? The pursuit of human welfare by political means would raise, as we shall see, for any political authority embarking on it the problem of striking a balance between the competing claims of individual freedom and social justice; but it might be prophesied that this would not be the first concern of a world government in the initial stage of its political operations. The best-intentioned world government would not have its hands free to work either for Justice or for Liberty or for a practical compromise between these two goals of human endeavour unless and until it had succeeded in making adequate provision for Police, in the broadest construction of the term, in a world in which all tools had now become edged tools and in which every act—deliberate or impulsive, wise or foolish—was now charged, no longer just with the innocuously feeble force of human muscles, but with the titanically high-powered 'drive' of machinery 'possessed' by atomic energy.

E. TECHNOLOGY, CLASS-CONFLICT, AND EMPLOYMENT

(I) THE ORIGIN AND NATURE OF THE PROBLEM

IF the meaning of the word 'employment' may be stretched to cover not only the amount and the distribution of work and leisure but also the spirit in which the work is done and the use to which the leisure is put, it would be true to say that the impact of an unprecedentedly potent latter-day Western technique on a literally world-wide Westernizing Society that was still articulated into a number of separate classes with widely different standards of living had confronted the heirs of the Western Civilization with a problem of employment comparable to the problem of government that has been discussed in the preceding chapter.

Like the problem of government, the problem of employment was nothing new in itself; for, if the primary cause of the breakdowns and disintegrations of other civilizations in the past had been a failure to get rid of war by a voluntary and timely expansion of the scope of government from a parochial to an oecumenical range, a secondary cause had been a failure to get rid of class-conflict by voluntary and timely changes in the distribution of the pressure and product of work and the enjoyment and use of leisure. In this field, however, as in that, the extreme difference in degree between a latter-day Western and a previous human mastery over Non-Human Nature was tantamount to a difference in kind. By putting an unprecedentedly powerful new 'drive' into economic production, a Modern Western technology had made a customary social injustice seem remediable and therefore feel intolerable. When the new-fangled cornucopia of a mechanized industry had churned out fabulous wealth—beyond the dreams of any class in any previous generation of this or any other society—for those Western *entrepreneurs* who had sown the seed and reaped the harvest of the Industrial Revolution, why should wealth and leisure still be monopolized by a privileged minority just as they had been before this Modern Western cornucopia had been invented?[1] Why should not this new-found abundance be shared with the Western capitalists by the Western industrial workers, and with the Western industrial workers by an Asian, African, and Indian-American peasantry that had been herded *en masse* into a world-embracing Western Society's internal proletariat?

This new dream of the possibility of abundance for all Mankind had generated unprecedentedly insistent and impatient demands for 'freedom from want'; the vehemence and ubiquity of these demands raised the

[1] This odious reign of arbitrary privilege had been accepted tranquilly, as part of an evidently unalterable order of Nature, by a Late Modern Western historian who had lived to see the beginning of the Industrial Revolution in his own country without having perceived its social implications.

'Such is the constitution of Civil Society that, whilst a few persons are distinguished by riches, by honours, and by knowledge, the body of the people is condemned to obscurity, ignorance, and poverty' (Gibbon, Edward: *The History of the Decline and Fall of the Roman Empire*, chap. ii).

question whether the productivity of the cornucopia was really in-exhaustible, as the importunity of the claims upon it assumed it to be; and this question could be answered only by solving an equation in which there were at least three unknown quantities.

The first of these unknown quantities was the extent of a latter-day Western technology's potential capacity to satisfy the rising demands of a Human Race which was continuing to multiply and was beginning to ask for leisure. What were the planet's reserves of irreplaceable material resources in the shape of minerals, and of replaceable material resources in the shape of water-power and crops and livestock and man-power and human skill? How far could the resources so far tapped be made to increase their yield by the application of more efficient methods of extraction and processing and utilization? And how far could Mankind's wasting assets in the shape of irreplaceable resources be set off by the tapping of alternative resources hitherto unexplored or at any rate un-exploited?

At the opening of the second half of the twentieth century of the Christian Era the current findings of Western Science suggested to a layman's mind that the Western technology's capacity was enormous; but at the same time the contemporary reactions of Human Nature to the impact of the Western technological revolution made it evident that there might prove to be practical limitations on this human plane to a productivity that might be virtually infinite in abstract terms of techno-logical potentiality. The production that had been rendered technically possible by a continuing and accelerating Industrial Revolution was a potentiality that could not be translated into a reality unless and until human hands could be found to hew the coal and stoke the fires and pull the levers with a will; but the price of the immensely enhanced power over Non-Human Nature that Western Man's mechanical prowess had now brought within Mankind's grasp was a proportionate increase in the regimentation of the workers and in the pressure of their work upon their life; and their inevitable resistance to these assaults on their personal freedom was bound to militate against the realization of those technological potentialities that had evoked the current demands for freedom from want.

What was the extent of the sacrifices of personal freedom that the workers would be prepared to make for the sake of increasing the size of the cake of which they were each now demanding a larger slice? How far would the urban industrial workers go in submitting to 'scientific management'? And how far would the primitive peasant majority of Mankind go in adopting Western scientific methods of agriculture and in accepting limitations on a traditionally sacrosanct right and duty of procreation? These questions are probed further in a later chapter,[1] and the outcome of our examination of them there need not be anticipated at this point except for reporting that, at the time of writing, it seemed premature to expect to find precise values for these two further unknown quantities in Mankind's current economic equation. At this stage the most that could be said was that the potential capacity of a latter-day

[1] On pp. 563-9 and 595-604, below.

Western technology to increase production perhaps virtually *ad infinitum* was running a race with the natural human refractoriness of the peasants and the industrial workers. The World's teeming peasantry was threatening to cancel the benefits of technological progress by continuing to raise the numbers of the World's population *pari passu* with each successive increase in the means of subsistence that Technology might achieve. The industrial workers were threatening to cancel the benefits of technological progress by restricting production through trade-union practices *pari passu* with each successive increase in the potentialities of productivity thanks to the triumphal march of scientific invention.

(II) THE SITUATION AFTER THE SECOND WORLD WAR

At the opening of the second half of the twentieth century of the Christian Era the outstanding feature in Mankind's situation on the economico-social plane in a world that was then undergoing a Western Industrial Revolution was a tug-of-war between a regimentation that was being imposed on Human Nature by the mechanization of the World's work and an obstinate human impulse to strive for freedom from regimentation, even if regimentation was the obligatory purchase-price of freedom from want.

The crux of the situation was the hard fact that, in Human Life, mechanization and police were as inseparable as Siamese twins. For Human Nature this was an unpalatable truth; yet any living observer of the age of sixty years or upwards who found himself shying at this truth would be compelled to look it in the face if, on any journey that he ever made by car, he compared the spectacle that now flashed past his eyes with his memory of what the traffic on the roads had been like in his childhood. Down to the close of the nineteenth century a trickle of horse-drawn and hand-pushed vehicles had been exempt from police control because it had been too slow and too thin to put life and limb in any serious jeopardy if drivers were left to their own devices. By contrast, on a twentieth-century road crowded with swift passenger-cars and ponderous lorries, travelling would have been, not merely perilous, but impracticable if the traffic had not been elaborately regulated, and if the regulations had not been strictly enforced. This change in the régime of the road, which we have noticed already in another context,[1] was an apt simile of the progressive encroachments on human freedom that were being imposed upon Mankind by a progressive increase in Man's command over Non-Human Nature and a consequent increase in the power-charge of men's actions in their encounters with one another.

An observer of this struggle between Technology's demand for discipline and Human Nature's recalcitrance to regimentation might find his impressions affected by the light in which he happened to be viewing the scene. From the technician's angle of vision the recalcitrant industrial workers' attitude might appear almost childishly unreasonable.

[1] In III. iii. 209–11.

Were these people really blind to a truth that was one of the truisms of Human Life? Had they never acquired the common knowledge that every desirable object has its price? Would they insist on demanding the 'freedom from want' which the technician's cornucopia could churn out, without reconciling themselves to the discipline that was the condition *sine qua non* for the successful performance of the technician's white magic? This indictment of the industrial workers' attitude might seem unanswerable to our observer so long as he was viewing the scene from the technician's standpoint; but as soon as he exchanged this for the historian's he might find himself seeing the same spectacle with different eyes. An historian would draw the spectator's attention to a string of historical facts. The Western Industrial Revolution had started in an eighteenth-century Great Britain; at that time and place an exceptionally high degree of freedom from regimentation on the economico-social plane had been enjoyed by at least a minority of the population, particularly by the Whig landlords and by the Nonconformist business men;[1] members of this economically free and powerful minority had been the creators of the industrial system of mechanized production; and the pre-industrial freedom of enterprise which these pioneers of Industrialism had inherited from a previous social dispensation had been the inspiration and life-blood of the new economico-social dispensation that their initiative had conjured into existence.

Moreover, the industrial *entrepreneurs'* pre-industrial spirit of freedom, which had been the *primum mobile* of the Industrial Revolution, continued to be its driving-force in the next chapter of the story; for, in the souls of the 'capitalists' who became the first masters of the new economic power-machine in virtue of having been its makers, this pristine êthos did not immediately succumb to the antithetical spirit of regimentation that was innate in their monstrous creature. While, however, the captains of Industry thus continued for a season to elude the fate of being crushed by a steam-roller of their own manufacture, this fate was the birthmark of the new urban industrial working class that the pioneers of Industrialism had called into existence to be the servitors of their new machines.[2] The industrial working class felt from the outset, in their full weight, the crushing effects upon human life of a triumphant Technology's success in mastering a previously intractable Non-Human Nature. In a previous context[3] we have watched Technology liberating Man's economic activities from the tyrannies of the cycle of Day-and-Night and the cycle of the Seasons; but, in the act of

[1] The return of the English Nonconformists to power on the economic plane after their exclusion from power on the political plane has been noticed in III. iii. 334 and 358, n. 1.
[2] This new industrial working class in the interior of the Western World had been cursed with the same congenital unhappiness as the new intelligentsia in the Russian and other non-Western societies that had been caught in the Western Civilization's net; and the cause of the unhappiness was evidently the same in the two cases. Either of these two new classes had been called into existence artificially and hastily for the purpose of performing a new social function for which there was an urgent demand; and the society that had commandeered the new class's professional services had not provided for its new servants' human needs. Both the Industrial Proletariat and the Intelligentsia were, in fact, proletarians in the original sense of being 'in' Society without being 'of' it. For the Intelligentsia, see V. v. 154–9; for the Proletariat, see I. i. 41, n. 3, and p. 597, below.
[3] On pp. 306–10, above.

setting Human Life free on one plane from an ancient servitude to the stars in their courses, Technology had been enslaving Man on another plane to Man himself by removing a buffer which Non-Human Nature had formerly interposed between the freedom of human souls and the impact on Man of Man's own collective material power.

In an agrarian economy out of which the new industrial working class had been uprooted, the incidence of Man's work upon Man's life had been rationed and regulated, not by a trial of strength between conflicting human wills championing divergent human interests, but by inexorably recurrent astronomical events—the fall of Night, the advent of Winter's frost or Summer's drought, the onset of the Monsoon— whose incidence *Homo Agricola* was impotent to elude. When these blindly beneficent non-human interruptions of Man's economic activity had been overcome by the invention of industrial plant capable of running without a pause for twenty-four hours in the day and for 365 days in the year, the workers in this plant found themselves under pressure of a new force—'heavy as frost, and deep almost as life'[1]—that bore harder on human souls than any tyranny of Inanimate Nature to which they had ever been exposed. This unfamiliar force that had substituted itself for the vanquished forces of Nature was Man's own collective material power. It lost nothing of its psychic 'drive' in being brought to bear upon the lives of its living victims along the driving-belt of a physical machine; and in this perspective an industrial working class's recalcitrance to the demands of a technique that promised, at the price of discipline, to set Mankind free from want might wear the appearance, not of a perverse impulse to hinder Mankind from breaking the bonds of Non-Human Nature, but of an heroic struggle to keep human souls free from regimentation by Leviathan.

The trade-union organization and procedure that were the new industrial working class's characteristic contributions to the structure of the Western Society were, indeed, legacies from the same pre-industrial paradise of private enterprise that had bred the êthos and activity of the industrial *entrepreneurs*. Looked at as instruments for enabling the workers to hold their own in their struggle with their employers, the trade unions were, in fact, creatures of the self-same social dispensation as their 'capitalist' antagonists. Privately Organized Labour, no less than Privately Organized Capital, stood or fell with a régime in which the terms of trade and the distribution of the product of economic activity were determined by bargaining between private parties in a public arena in which the local state confined its intervention to the negative role of holding the ring for these private competitors. Freedom of private economic enterprise was the air which trade unions, as well as 'capitalist' employers of labour, breathed; and this truth had been demonstrated by the common fate of both these gladiators in states which, in the interval between the First and the Second World War, had been captured by totalitarian régimes.

In Russia after the Communist Revolution of A.D. 1917 the liquida-

---

[1] Wordsworth, W.: *Ode on Intimations of Immortality from Recollections of Early Childhood.*

tion of the private employers of labour had been followed by a *Gleich-schaltung* of the trade unions; in Germany after the National-Socialist Revolution of A.D. 1933 the liquidation of the trade unions had been followed by a *Gleichschaltung* of the capitalists. Conversely, in Great Britain after the General Election of A.D. 1945, under a Labour government whose programme was to take the ownership of industrial enterprises out of private hands without trenching upon the sacrosanctity of personal freedom, the workers in the nationalized industries never thought of dissolving their trade unions or renouncing their right to promote their own private interests by means of collective bargaining backed by the sanction of collective strikes. In their dealings with the new public boards of management they plied these well-tried weapons as vigorously as they had ever plied them in their dealings with the state's private predecessors in the ownership of these particular means of production.

The diverse local histories of Great Britain, Germany, and Russia since A.D. 1917 thus presented, between them, a conclusive proof that the purpose for which the trade unions had originally been created, and for which they were still being maintained in all industrialized countries not yet captured by totalitarian political régimes, was to serve the workers as weapons in a struggle against regimentation; and, considering that the workers' will to freedom was thus not open to question, it was significant that the workers had not succeeded in finding any other effective means of resisting the pressure of a collective human material power than the desperate expedient of counter-regimenting themselves.[1] The pioneers of the trade-union movement had perceived from the outset that the workers' potential power of numbers was the one asset on their side that they could pit against the power derived by their employers from their control of the means of production. It had been obvious that this power of numbers could be made effective only through action that was both collective and disciplined; and thus the proletarian Western fathers of Trade Unionism, confronted by an aggressive Western capitalist dominant minority, had found themselves in the same dilemma as the non-Western fathers of Herodianism when these had been confronted by an aggressive Western World. The victims of aggression must either abandon the struggle or adopt their aggressive adversaries' weapons if they were to pursue the struggle with any hope of success; and accordingly the industrial workers had found themselves constrained to introduce their arch-enemy—regimentation—into the inner ward of their castle as an indispensable auxiliary in the defence of the outer ward against the assaults of the self-same adversary. They had had to impose regimentation upon themselves in order to resist its

---

[1] Professor William McNeill comments: 'Is there not a will to conform which is in constant tension with the will to freedom? I conceive of this tension as being parallel to the instinct of workmanship and the impulse to scamp work; and that most, if not all, men exhibit each of these contrary impulses in greater or lesser degree.'

The present writer would not deny the existence of this will to conform. He would merely suggest that in a mechanized twentieth-century Westernizing World the loyalty of the trade unionist, as against the skill of the craftsman, was the ideal towards which a perennial will to conform was steering a majority of the living generation of industrial workers.

imposition upon them by their employers, and this tragic paradox was a demonstration of a rampant Technology's unholy power to regiment human souls by hook or by crook.

The workers had been moved to resist regimentation by the same spirit of freedom, inherited from a pre-industrial past, that had inspired the *entrepreneurs* to make the Industrial Revolution and thereby to put the workers under pressure; and this pre-industrial êthos had been the psychic counterpart of an economic dispensation in which each individual worker had at least seen the results of his labours, even when he had not reaped the reward, and had therefore found himself able to work with zest—not because he had been able to count upon pocketing an equitable share of the profits of his own exertions, but because, even when he had been sweated and fleeced, his work had been intrinsically effective and significant and therefore psychologically satisfying. By contrast, under an industrial economic dispensation under which the pressure of the work upon the worker had, as we have seen, become overwhelming owing to the removal of ancient automatic safeguards, the *chefs-d'œuvre* of Technology that had swept those safeguards away had mechanized the processes of Industry to so high a degree, and had carried the Division of Labour to such extremes, that the factory hand's work had become intrinsically impersonal, monotonous, and infantile.

'We invent the machinery of mass-production, and, for the sake of cheapening the unit, we develop output on a gigantic scale. Almost automatically the machine delivers a stream of articles in the creation of which the workman has had little part. He has lost the joy of craftsmanship, the old satisfaction in something accomplished through the conscientious exercise of care and skill.'[1]

The effect of these psychologically untoward technological improvements had been, inevitably, to make a worker's attitude towards his work defensive and negative, like a schoolboy's attitude towards an uncongenial imposition.[2]

Thus the workers' resistance to regimentation at the hands of an external power had driven them into regimenting themselves. In fighting against the fate of being turned into robots in the factory, they had imposed on themselves the fate of serving as soldiers in a trade-union phalanx; and at the time of writing it was not easy to see how either fate could be exorcized, for by this time it was already evident that the external pressure on the industrial workers could not be relieved by the

[1] Sir Alfred Ewing in a presidential address delivered on the 31st August, 1932, at York, to the British Association for the Advancement of Science. Another passage of this address has been quoted already in this Study in III. iii. 211.

[2] Professor William McNeill comments: 'Is there not an instinct of workmanship that may act as an antidote to the trade unionist and civil servant spirit?' The present writer would not deny either the existence of this instinct or its pertinacity. He would merely suggest that, in a mechanized twentieth-century Westernizing World, Technology was tilting the balance adversely for the instinct of workmanship and favourably for a workers' resistance movement against the social effect of physical machinery which, at the current power of its 'drive', was threatening to serve as an instrument for placing the would-be craftsman at the mercy of a collective human social pressure instead of promising to serve as a tool for enabling him to express his own individuality in and through his work.

comparatively simple measure, on which such high hopes had once been set, of taking the means of production out of private hands.[1]

This was no radical remedy because, under the industrial dispensation, the private employer was in truth no longer the ultimate villain of the piece. Oppression by profiteering private employers or by rack-renting private landlords had, after all, been the lot of many workers in the histories of many societies, including the Western Society itself, in the days before the advent of a Western Machine Age; and before this Western Industrial Revolution, as well as after it, economic oppression had provoked resistance among its victims. Yet, under those pre-industrial dispensations, this resistance had never organized itself on trade-union lines and had never displayed the trade-union spirit; and the explanation of these new departures in the character of the resistance movement was that under the new industrial dispensation the personal oppressor who was the workers' familiar bugbear had been reduced, by his own revolutionary achievement, from his age-old status of being one of the principals in a conflict between two human antagonists to the novel status of being merely the personal agent of an impersonal force. The pressure against which the industrial workers were reacting could not be removed by eliminating the private employer, because this was a new pressure inherent in the new technique of machine industry. So costly an initial capital investment could not be made to yield an economically adequate return on the outlay unless the wheels were kept revolving at full speed, night and day, year in and year out; and, while it was true that a private owner of the plant would therefore be bound to press the human tenders of these Satanic mills to make the utmost exertions that the management could wring out of them, any public owner—municipality, community, or state alike—would be bound for the same reasons to do likewise.

Thus the change from private to public ownership could not abate a pressure that was being exerted on the industrial workers by the impersonal force of a mechanized technique; and, indeed, the representation of this impersonal oppressor by a public instead of a private agent made the trade unions' task of conducting the workers' resistance movement a more difficult one psychologically and politically. In contending with the *ci-devant* private employers before the bar of public opinion, the trade unions had been able to put their adversaries 'on the spot' by manœuvring them into the invidious role of harpies who were so bent upon grinding the faces of the poor that, rather than give the workers their due, they were prepared to deprive the public of essential economic services by forcing the workers to resort to a strike as their only practicable means of redress. It was not so easy to bring odium upon a public authority by accusing it of being actuated by motives of personal cupidity. A public authority was indeed as awkward

---

[1] This was not to say that in a mechanized society it was right or wise or feasible to leave Private Property uncurbed now that this traditional institution was being charged by the new social force of Industrialism with an unprecedentedly powerful new 'drive'. This point has been touched upon in IV. iv. 191–2. The measures for curbing Private Property, without abolishing it, that were being taken in Great Britain on the morrow of the Second World War are noticed on pp. 588–92, below.

an antagonist for a trade union as Peer Gynt's legendary obstructor the Böig.[1] The industrial workers' ultimate adversary was an impersonal collective human material power which was both more potent and more elusive than a personal villain; no man knew how to put asunder a Leviathan that the Western Industrial Revolution had joined together;[2] and this last enemy might well prove to be almost as tenacious as Death.[3] Indeed, the constant, and at the same time constantly accelerating, progress of Western technological invention—a progress of which the end was not, as yet, in sight—threatened to continue to key up the pressure on the industrial workers to ever higher degrees of severity; and the response of the workers to this mounting challenge seemed bound to be a progressive accentuation of the trade-union movement's characteristically defensive and negative êthos.

If this probable aggravation of the inauspicious elements in the industrial workers' spirit was a gloomy prospect, it was also an awe-inspiring spectacle to see the Western middle class beginning to take a road on which the Western working class's feet had been set long since. The period between the achievement of the Industrial Revolution and the outbreak of the First World War in A.D. 1914—a period that had lasted for about a century and a half in Great Britain and for about half a century in Germany and in the United States—had been the Western middle class's golden age; but the new era which the First World War had inaugurated had seen this Western middle class fall, in their turn, into the adversity to which the Industrial Revolution had condemned the industrial workers in the act of calling them into existence.

In the twentieth-century history of the Western middle class the liquidation of the bourgeoisie in Russia in and after the Bolshevik Revolution of A.D. 1917, which had been the first portent in a series, had not been the most significant one; for Russia was a recently and imperfectly Westernized country in which the Western social phenomenon of a bourgeoisie had been something exotic. The bourgeoisie in Germany that had been ruined after the War of A.D. 1914–18 by the social and economic consequences of Germany's military defeat had, by contrast, been part and parcel of the native Western middle class; but this local disaster might perhaps be interpreted as being the special nemesis of the German bourgeoisie's peculiar perversity, and might then be written off as one of those 'partial events' that could not 'essentially injure' the Western middle class's 'general state of happiness'.[4] A more accurate index of the fortunes and tendencies of the Western middle class in this age was to be found in the contemporary social histories of Great Britain and the other English-speaking countries, since in these countries the middle class was as deeply rooted as it was anywhere in the Western World, while, in contrast to its fate in the Continental Western countries, it had suffered less severely in

---

[1] Ibsen, Henrik: *Peer Gynt*, Act II, scene vii.
[2] Matt. xix. 6.   [3] 1 Cor. xv. 26.
[4] See Gibbon, Edward: *The History of the Decline and Fall of the Roman Empire*, 'General Observations on the Fall of the Roman Empire in the West', at the end of chap. xxxviii.

the English-speaking countries—and this even in Great Britain—from the direct impact even of the Second World War. The recent history of the middle class in the English-speaking countries thus seemed more likely to reveal the 'secular' trend of the Western middle class's current social evolution, in so far as it might be possible to identify this social trend by isolating it from contemporaneous military and political vicissitudes. It was therefore significant that in the English-speaking countries too—in Great Britain first and foremost, but also in the rest in divers degrees—this age had seen the middle class begin to lose both its nineteenth-century prosperity and its sanguine pre-industrial êthos. The psychological change was more portentous than the economic, since it was in virtue of its pre-industrial êthos that the middle class had made the industrial fortune that was now slipping out of its hands.

During the period between the Industrial Revolution and the outbreak of the First World War, the distinguishing psychological characteristic of the middle class, by contrast with the contemporary spirit of the clerical workers as well as the industrial working class, had been its unabated zest for work.

In the citadel of Capitalism on Manhattan Island there had been a trivial yet significant illustration of this difference of attitude as recently as the year A.D. 1949. In that year the financial houses on Wall Street were trying, without success, to induce their shorthand-typists, by offers of special remuneration at high overtime rates, to reconsider a collective decision to refuse henceforth to attend at their offices on Saturday mornings. The shorthand-typists' employers were eager to devote their own Saturday mornings to work for the sake of retaining the profits that they would forfeit if they were to submit to this shortening of their own working week; but they had ceased to be able to do their own work without having shorthand-typists in attendance to assist them, and they found themselves unable to persuade these indispensable collaborators in their business of money-making that the game of working on Saturdays was worth the candle. The shorthand-typists took the stand that one day's, or even one half-day's, additional leisure was worth more to them than any monetary inducement for withdrawing their demand for this amenity. Additional money in their pockets was of no use to them if they had to earn it at the price of forgoing the additional leisure without which they would have no time for spending it. In this choice between money and life, they opted for life at the cost of letting the money go, and their employers did not succeed in persuading them to change their minds. By A.D. 1952 it had begun to look as if, so far from the Wall Street shorthand-typists ever being brought round by a monetary inducement to the Wall Street financiers' point of view, the financiers might eventually be converted by economic adversity to the standpoint of the typists; for by this date even Wall Street was beginning to feel a breeze that had already chilled once sanguine hearts in Lombard Street.

In the twentieth century of the Christian Era the Western middle class's opportunities for doing profitable business were being progressively reduced in one Western centre of capitalist activity after another;

and these economic reverses were having depressing effects upon the middle-class êthos. The middle class's traditional zest for work was now being sapped by a progressive restriction of the field for private enterprise and a progressive regimentation of the remnant of private enterprise that was being permitted provisionally to survive. Inflation and taxation were conspiring to make nonsense of the sovereign middle-class virtues of strenuous earning and thrifty saving by robbing these ascetic activities of their sybaritic rewards. A rising cost of living was conspiring with a simultaneously rising standard of living to reduce the size of middle-class families. The loss of personal domestic service was threatening to undermine the middle class's professional efficiency. The loss of leisure was threatening to undermine its culture.

These blows that were raining down upon a twentieth-century Western middle class were hitting the man in the office less hard than the woman in the home; for, in order to make both ends meet when a falling income was failing to keep abreast of a rising budget, a middle-class housewife might find herself compelled—like so many working-class housewives in an earlier phase of the Industrial Age—to do two men's work by keeping house and earning a salary simultaneously. Neither a reduction in the size of middle-class families nor an improvement in domestic labour-saving contrivances could avail to save the middle-class married woman from being saddled with a burden of overwork from which her husband was exempted by a physical disability to bear children and by a degree of professional specialization which (in West European countries, though not in the United States) restricted his competence to be a help in the house. By contrast, his wife, who was still the only member of the family partnership who could bear and bring up the children and could make the house a home, had now also won for herself the opportunity of widening her horizon, or had exposed herself to the liability of adding to her labours, by taking on 'men's work' as well, thanks to the provision of higher education for girls as well as boys in Western countries within the last hundred years. In the very generation in which these new educational facilities had made it possible for middle-class women to take up professional careers in a world of affairs that had previously been the male sex's monopoly, the self-same social and economic revolution had deprived them, in their homes, of the paid help of domestic servants, and unpaid help of maiden aunts, sisters, and daughters, which had been enjoyed by middle-class married women of earlier generations who had had no duties or interests outside the domestic circle; and these two contemporaneous but antithetical changes in her circumstances had placed the highly educated and professionally competent twentieth-century Western wife and mother in a dilemma in which the acceptance of either of two alternatives spelled frustration. She found herself confronted with an unhappy choice between resigning herself to be a household drudge, without the leisure to turn her education to any account, and forcing herself to carry the intolerably heavy load of two simultaneous full-time jobs. In the Western middle class's twentieth-century crisis, as in the Western working class's nineteenth-century crisis, the wife and mother was, in fact, both the heroine and the victim of the tragedy.[1]

Meanwhile the Western middle-class woman's brother, husband, and son were in process of making a change of professional occupation which entailed a corresponding change of attitude and outlook. A nineteenth-century social and economic revolution in the life of the Western working class which had transported the manual worker from the field to the factory, and had transmuted his êthos from the husbandman's into the trade unionist's, was now finding its counterpart in the history of the Western middle class in a twentieth-century revolution which was turning private business men and professional men into employees of governments or of non-governmental business concerns that were almost equally impersonal because they were on an almost equally large scale;[2] and this change from being their own employers to being Leviathan's employees was producing a corresponding change of êthos in these middle-class workers' souls in their turn.

The twentieth-century Western middle class's progressive exodus out of private enterprise into public service or into its psychological equivalent in the service of giant non-governmental corporations had been bringing with it gains, as well as losses, for the Western Society. The principal gain—and this was a notable one—was the subordination of the egoistic motive of making personal economic profits to the altruistic motive of serving the public interest; and the social value of this change of personal objectives and moral ideals could be measured by the effects of corresponding changes in the histories of other civilizations in which the sequel was on record. In the histories of the Hellenic, Sinic, and Hindu civilizations, for example, the social rallies inaugurated by the establishment of universal states had been signalized and achieved—in so far as the credit for a complex corporate achievement can be assigned to any one of the contributing factors—by the redirection of a hitherto predatory class's ability and experience to serve social, instead of anti-social, ends.[3] Augustus and his successors had made good civil servants out of predatory Roman business men of the 'equestrian' class; Han Liu Pang and his successors had made them out of predatory feudal gentry bred by the contending Sinic parochial states; Cornwallis and his successors had made them out of predatory commercial agents of the British East India Company.

The beneficence of the social effects of these acts of moral redemption had been proportionate to the magnitude of the spiritual revolution in each case. Yet, in each case likewise, the social rally signalized in a universal state had been ephemeral; and a good civil service had so far

---

[1] At the cost of bearing this excessive burden, the women members of the Western Society in its post-Modern Age had won for themselves a position in which the World's work, outside as well as inside the home, would have come to a standstill if the women had gone on strike. The simultaneous entry of the women and the industrial workers upon the stage in this act of the drama of Western history had its parallel in Hellenic history in the likewise simultaneous entry of the women and the slaves upon the stage in a post-Alexandrine Age.

[2] Professor William McNeill comments: 'The transformation of the owner-manager-entrepreneur into the salaried manager is very striking in the United States and elsewhere, and is almost, if not quite, as significant as the rise of the civil service itself.'

[3] See V. v. 35–58.

never proved able to stage a recovery from more than a single relapse, and therefore never able to avert the ultimate dissolution of a disintegrating society. This ultimate failure of a mission that had achieved so striking an initial success was to be explained, in these previous cases, by the ambivalence of a civil-service êthos in which the sovereign virtue of moral integrity was counter-balanced by a lack of zest, a disinclination to take the initiative or to incur risks, and an impulse to play for personal safety which could militate against the public interest as severely as a thirst to acquire personal power and wealth; and these inauspicious defensive and negative characteristics of an historic civil-service êthos were all now being displayed by twentieth-century Western middle-class civil servants who, at the time of writing, were serving, in the administration of parochial *peritura regna*, an apprenticeship for their future task · of organizing and maintaining a world government.

When we look into the causes of a civil-service êthos which the twentieth-century Western civil servant thus shared with his professional counterparts in the histories of other civilizations, we find that this êthos was the response to the challenge of pressure exerted by a machine which bore no less hardly upon human souls for being constructed out of psychic instead of metallic materials. To tend the machinery of a highly organized state administering many millions of subjects was, indeed, as soul-destroying a task as stoking a furnace, minding a power-loom, or performing a repetitive set of scientifically managed physical movements in an assembly plant. The sheer magnitude of the scale of civil-service operations dwarfed and dominated any single concrete piece of civil-service business, with the consequence that, in any official action which a civil servant had to take, his decision was apt to be determined less by the actual merits of the case in point than by a calculation of the precedents which this or that course of action might or might not create.

This effect of the administrative machine in setting a negative rather than a positive impress on its servants' êthos was enhanced by the vein of caprice and tyranny in the êthos of any public administrative machine's sovereign lords and masters. One of the arch-fallacies in a nineteenth-century Western optimistic estimate of the capabilities of *Homo Politicus* had been the fatuous postulate that the occupational vices of an individual autocrat would be automatically exorcized by the trick of putting autocracy into commission. The truth was that an enlightened individual autocrat, however rare a bird he might have been, had proved himself, by occasional visitations, to be a bona fide natural species, whereas the legendary nineteenth-century enlightened parliament or electorate was as chimerical a figment of the imagination as Sinbad's Orc or Herodotus's Phoenix.

In their short history up to date, Western parliaments elected on a wide franchise had quickly betrayed their historical paternity by emulating the bad behaviour of an English King Henry VIII and a French King Louis XIV; these parliamentary corporate despots' constituents had been lax or incompetent in exercising their constitutional right and duty of bringing their elected representatives to book; the brunt of the consequent corporate abuse of power by parliaments had fallen upon their slave-household of civil servants; and the effect of this arbitrary parliamentary régime on the administrative action of these latter-day Western civil servants who found themselves in the plight of an Ottoman Pādishāh's *qullar* had been to set up a second impediment to the decision of cases on their merits; for if the first question that a conscientious civil servant must ask himself was 'What awkward precedents for the service might this decision create?' the second question that a cautious civil servant must ask himself was 'What awkward parliamentary questions for me might this decision evoke?' There were thus two irrelevant stumbling-blocks to be surmounted before the merits of a case could obtain consideration from the civil servant who would be called to account eventually over the outcome of whatever action had been taken or been withheld on his advice; and, since, in becoming a civil servant, he had not ceased to be a human being, it was inevitable that his conduct should be influenced by a personal anxiety to be in a strong position in any future reckoning, as well as by an impersonal concern not to compromise the interests of the public service by creating an unfortunate precedent.

It was also inevitable that civil servants should take personal advantage, against the public interest, of a notorious trait of parliamentary psychology. Civil servants had learnt from a long experience that, while a parliament was usually quick to notice and resent even the slightest damage to the public interest that might be traceable to a civil servant's recommendation of some positive action, the same corporate autocrat could usually be trusted not to visit upon a civil servant any proportionately condign punishment for a sin of omission, even when the sinner's failure to perform his public duty of recommending that positive action should be taken had been the cause of a public catastrophe. This bad habit of parliaments was as pertinent to the civil servant's professional work and personal interests as it was irrational in itself and inimical to the common weal; and a parliamentary practice of putting a premium upon sins of omission thus worked together with an administrative concern for the avoidance of awkward precedents to write 'Thou shalt not' into the exordium of each commandment in the civil servant's decalogue.

It would thus appear that, in the twentieth century, the psychic steam-roller of a ponderous public administration was crushing the business man turned civil servant as remorselessly as, in the nineteenth century, the metallic steam-roller of a ponderous industrial plant had crushed the husbandman turned machine-tender. A pressure that had made the industrial worker curl up like a hedgehog had made the civil servant mortify himself like a monk; two defensive reactions that were so widely diverse in their outward manifestations were nevertheless substantially identical in their psychological effect; and this pervasive psychological consequence of a penetrating technological revolution was inauspicious for the prospects of the Western Society in whose bosom this revolution had taken place.

While the breaking of the spirit of any class was, of course, bound to be damaging to the spiritual health of any body social in which this spiritual disaster occurred, the damage already suffered by the Western Society in consequence of the nineteenth-century tribulations of its working class might prove not to have been so grave as the further damage that the Western middle class's twentieth-century tribulations were now threatening to inflict upon an already ailing Western social constitution. The progressive depotentiation of the Western middle class's characteristic pre-industrial spirit was fraught with a serious threat to the stability, and even to the survival, of a world-wide Westernizing industrial society, because the Western middle class was the heart of this oecumenical body social;[1] it was the creative minority that had originally brought this body social into being and had subsequently kept it alive; and it had achieved all this in virtue of being animated by the pre-industrial êthos that was now showing signs of succumbing to the pressure of the same impersonal collective human material power that had already crushed the Western working class. 'A little leaven leaveneth the whole lump',[2] and 'salt is good';[3] 'but if the salt have lost his savour, wherewith shall it be seasoned?'[4]

In the cosmic imagery of an Atomic Age the pre-industrial temper of the Western middle class might be likened to the physical tone of the inner core of the Sun. In that titanic physical power-house in the current aeon, the temperature stood at a height at which the physical effect was a continual annihilation of atoms; this physical process was perpetually releasing a physical energy of enormous potency; and the discharge of this energy into the Sun's field of radiation might produce utterly diverse effects on any physical object that the out-streaming waves encountered in their passage, according to the distance of this object from the radiating energy's solar source and the corresponding degree of the energy's intensity at the moment when it made its impact.

A solar energy whose genial warmth had rendered it physically possible for Life to make its epiphany, and thereafter to maintain itself in being, on the surface of the planet Terra, might nevertheless one day fulfil the cosmological predictions of the Stoic school of Hellenic philosophers by melting the same planet into a gaseous vapour if a school of mid-twentieth-century Western cosmologists was right in predicting that the Sun was destined, in one of the future chapters of its history, to swell to a size at which it would envelop not only the Earth but also some, at least, of the remoter planets.[5] On the other hand, when, in a further chapter, subsequent to that, the Sun shrivelled and cooled into a 'black dwarf'—and this was believed by Western astronomers at this date to be the inevitable ultimate destiny of every star ever spawned in any nebula—the solar furnace would then have lost, utterly

---

[1] This indispensable role of the Western middle class in the life of a Westernizing World Society could have been conveyed by an Hellenic political scientist, without resort to a simile, by saying that the Western middle class was the πολίτευμα (i.e. the effective and responsible governing body) of an oecumenical πολιτεία.
[2] Gal. v. 9.   [3] Mark ix. 50; Luke xiv. 34.
[4] Luke xiv. 34; cp. Matt. v. 13 and Mark ix. 50.
[5] See Hoyle, Fred: *The Nature of the Universe* (Oxford 1950, Blackwell), p. 40.

and forever, its once seemingly inexhaustible capacity to radiate energy either for the weal or for the woe of terrestrial living creatures. 'Fear no more the heat of the Sun' would then be Everyman's posthumous consolation; and the exhaustion of the Sun's energy, which would thus have guaranteed any survivors among the dead star's planets against the danger of a repetition of a life-destroying conflagration, would also have extinguished all hope of any return of a genial warmth which, in the chapter before that, had given Life on Earth its opportunity.

This story—true or fabulous—of successive vicissitudes in the intensity, and consequently in the effect, of a physical energy radiating from the Sun might serve as a parable to expound the Western middle class's role in the Modern and post-Modern chapters of Western history. Here was an element in the Western body social whose radiant energy had threatened in the sixteenth century to consume all the non-Western civilizations on the face of the *Oikoumenê* in a veritably Zenonian cultural world-conflagration, and had then threatened in the nineteenth century to consume a native Western working class in the burning fiery furnace of an Industrial Revolution. Now that, in the twentieth century, the temperature of this Western middle-class psychic energy was being reduced to a milder degree through the conversion of the children of predatory buccaneers and *entrepreneurs* into conscientious civil servants and employees of giant non-governmental business concerns, had not the rest of Mankind, whom the fathers had ruthlessly ground down into a proletariat, good reason to rejoice at the children's change of heart? In the light of our parable we may be inclined to reply that the answer to this question must depend upon the length of the view that the observer of the Western middle class's metamorphosis might be able and willing to take. On a short view, the current abatement of the psychic temperature of the Western middle class was, on balance, possibly proving beneficial for the Western body social as a whole; but suppose that the welcome transformation of an incinerator into an incubator should prove to be merely one brief stage in a 'secular' cooling process that would eventually transform the incubator into a refrigerator, what, on this longer view, would be the significance of the 'secular' process for the Western Society's ultimate prospects?

The significance for the prospects of the current 'capitalist' system of Western economic life was not so difficult to gauge. The Western middle class's fund of pre-industrial psychic energy had been 'Capitalism's' driving force; and, if this energy was now being depotentiated and at the same time diverted from private enterprise into public service, this process unquestionably spelled Capitalism's doom.

'Capitalism is essentially a process of (endogamous) economic change ...: without innovations, no entrepreneurs; without entrepreneurial achievement, no capitalist returns and no capitalist propulsion. The atmosphere of industrial revolutions—of "progress"—is the only one in which Capitalism can survive. . . . Stabilised Capitalism is a contradiction in terms.'[1]

At the opening of the second half of the twentieth century of the

---

[1] Schumpeter, J. A.: *Business Cycles* (New York 1939, McGraw-Hill, 2 vols.), vol ii, p. 1033.

Christian Era it looked as if the regimentation inexorably imposed by a latter-day industrial Western technology might be taking the life out of a pre-industrial spirit of private enterprise in economic affairs by which the Western Industrial Revolution had originally been brought to birth; and this prospect opened up further questions, which were more enigmatic, as well as more important, than any questions about the future of the Western Capitalist system or the Western middle class. Would the technical system of mechanized industry be able to survive the social system of private enterprise which had brought it into operation originally and had kept it in operation hitherto?[1] And, if a Western mechanized industry were to prove unable to survive the death of Western private economic enterprise, would the Western Civilization itself be able to survive the death of a mechanized industry to which the Western Society had now given hostages by allowing its population to increase in the Machine Age far beyond the numbers that any non-industrial economy could support?

It was indisputable that the Industrial System, like any other technique, could work only so long as there was some fund of creative psychic energy to drive it, and that, hitherto, this psychic driving-power had been supplied to the Western industrial system by the energy of the Western middle class. The ultimate question therefore seemed to be whether there was some alternative source of psychic energy, employable for the same economic purposes, on which a Westernizing World could draw if the Western middle class's energy were to be depotentiated or diverted. If a practical alternative was within sight and within reach, the World could perhaps afford to look forward with equanimity to the possibility of the capitalist system's demise. On the other hand, if there was no such alternative on the horizon the outlook would be disconcerting; for Mankind might then have to reckon with the possibility that a Mechanized Technology might contain within itself the psychic seeds of its own decay. If mechanization spelled regimentation, and if this regimentation had taken the spirit out of a Western industrial working class and a Western middle class in succession, was it possible for any human hands to handle 'the accursed thing'[2] with impunity? The answer to this mid-twentieth-century question, whatever the answer might be, was pregnant with the Western Civilization's destiny.

(III) ALTERNATIVE POSSIBLE APPROACHES TO SOCIAL HARMONY

The social problem confronting Mankind on the morrow of a Second World War was being approached from different angles by divers members of a Westernizing Society that, on the economic plane, was already oecumenical in its range. One approach was being made in

[1] Professor William McNeill comments: 'I cannot think that there is much likelihood of a decay of established technology as a consequence of the decay of individual initiative. There may well be, however, a decrease in the *rate* at which new inventions are made and introduced, as bureaucratic habits of thought spread and harden themselves.'
[2] Joshua vi. 18.

North America, another in the Soviet Union, and a third in Western Europe.

The North American approach (which was shared with the peoples of the United States by the English-speaking element in the population of Canada) was inspired by the ideal of creating an Earthly Paradise in a New World. 'The lot is fallen unto me in a fair ground; yea, I have a goodly heritage.'[1] The motive that had moved the ancestors of the living generation of Americans to pull up their roots in the Old World and to make a fresh start in life on the farther side of the Atlantic had been a hope of being able to leave behind them the tares in their social heritage and to sow an American crop in which there should be nothing but wheat;[2] and in American eyes freedom for private enterprise in economic affairs was one of those good things in America's heritage from the Old World that were to be, not discarded, but transplanted. The American people believed in private economic enterprise whole-heartedly, and they were confident of being able, in their New World, to allow private economic enterprise to retain the freedom that was its life-breath without exposing themselves to the inconveniences and abuses that had been bred by private enterprise in the Old World when its freedom had there been left unrestricted.

In their New World the Americans claimed to have found a practical solution for a social problem which in the Old World had proved intractable. They claimed to have succeeded in getting rid of class-conflict in an industrial society, not by the inhuman and uneconomic crime of liquidating the middle class, but by building up a classless society on a middle-class footing. As middle-class Americans saw it, the American way of life had satisfied all reasonable demands for social justice that the industrial workers could make by raising the minimum standard of living in North America to at least the West-European middle-class level and by providing every industrial worker who chose to exert himself with opportunities for rising into the middle class, or at least with opportunities for educating his children into a middle-class career. The proof of a pudding is in the eating; and the social success of the American way of life was demonstrated (so its middle-class American advocates would contend) by the industrial workers' attitude. They were (it was asserted) much more eagerly concerned to change their momentary station in life for a better one than to spend their energies in striving for improvements in the conditions of the transitional station in which they happened at the moment to find themselves.[3]

The strong point in this North American approach to the social problem of an industrial society was its recognition of the truth that the energy which had set the wheels of a mechanized industry turning was the psychic energy generated by the pre-industrial êthos of the

---

[1] Ps. xvi. 6.   [2] See p. 545, above.

[3] Professor William McNeill comments: 'I feel that your description of the American response to the problem of class-conflict [as seen through middle-class American eyes in A.D. 1952] is valid only for the period before A.D. 1929. I feel that the differences between the United States and [Western] Europe are growing much narrower, and this in both economic and cultural organization and activity. In general the United States lags a bit behind the more advanced [West] European nations in its internal development, but surely it has been catching up, and doing so rapidly over the past generation.'

Western middle class. Middle-class Americans had grasped this truth, and they were determined at all costs to preserve the middle-class spirit of private enterprise by preserving the middle-class way of life, because they were alive to the danger that the energy which had originally made the Industrial Revolution and which was now keeping going the Industrial System of economic production might be paralysed by the rise and spread of the defensive, negative, unenthusiastic trade-union and civil-service êthos.

The weak points in the North American approach are all implicit in Horace's observation that 'coelum, non animum, mutant qui trans mare currunt'.[1] The American hope of being able to create an Earthly Paradise was founded, as we have noticed, on a belief in the possibility of being able to leave the Old World behind by making the transit of the Atlantic, and this belief was an illusion; for the Old World was not a physical continent whose dust the Pilgrim Fathers could shake off[2] as they took to their boats; it was the spiritual burden of Original Sin, which Christian had to carry with him to a stage in his progress that was far in advance of the farthest point normally attained by *l'homme moyen sensuel* on either side of the Atlantic.

The Old World in this haunting spiritual sense of the term had crossed the Atlantic into the New World of North America in the souls of the first settlers from Europe on North American soil; and Original Sin made havoc of the sanguine middle-class American belief that the claims of social justice could be satisfied by a guarantee to all men of an absolute minimum standard of living, however high that standard might be set; for human standards are never absolute and objective; they are always subjective and relative; and it is not in Human Nature for one man to be content with his own standard, whatever its height, if his neighbour's standard is conspicuously higher. The cause of class-conflict thus lay, not in the inadequacy of the absolute standard of the lowest class in the scale, but in the inequality between the standards of the lowest class and the highest; this law of Human Nature was no less valid west of the Atlantic than east of it; and, if the proof of the pudding was in the eating, there was another side to the attitude of the American industrial workers which militated against the contention that in North America the class-conflicts of the Old World had been exorcized by a new American way of life. It was both incontestable and significant that the height of the minimum standard of living enjoyed by industrial workers in North America, and the abundance of the opportunities open to them for rising into the middle class, had not made the North American working class proof against succumbing to trade-union practices and the trade-union êthos.

Moreover, an Old World that had invaded the New World of North America in the seventeenth century in the inward spiritual form of Original Sin had launched a second wave of invasion in the twentieth century in a form which, by comparison, was material and superficial, yet which nevertheless was importunately intrusive. The geographical

---

[1] Horace: *Epistulae*, Book I, Ep. xi, l. 27.
[2] Matt. x. 14; Mark vi. 11; Luke ix. 5 and x. 11; Acts xiii. 51 and xviii. 6.

coalescence and shrinkage of the *Oikoumenê* in the twentieth century as a result of a latter-day Western technological revolution[1] had put an end, even on the physical plane, to an isolation which, on that plane, had in truth been achieved partially and temporarily by West European settlers in North America whose boasted insularity had never, on the spiritual plane, been anything but a pure illusion.

The issue between an ideal of American insularity and an ideal of oecumenical human solidarity had been the most important issue in the history of the United States, and this was both a moral issue and a practical one. Was it possible to insulate the United States from the rest of the *Oikoumenê*? And, if it was possible, was it also right for Americans to make this one of the aims of their national policy?

The possibility of isolating the United States from the Old World had been open to question long before the Old World had closed in upon America on the physical plane as a consequence of twentieth-century Western Man's technological feat of 'annihilating distance'. The novel amplitude of the opportunity in the United States for rising in the social scale had, for example, been created by a stream of immigration from the Old World which had flowed, and this in an ever-increasing volume, for nearly a hundred years ending in A.D. 1914. Each annual influx of immigrants, as it poured into the sump of the American melting-pot, had buoyed up all the layers of immigrant population that had preceded it, and each of the annual contingents had been able to count upon being buoyed up, in its turn, by all the future annual influxes that were to follow. In the nineteenth century an American family's rise in the social scale had thus been almost automatic at every level in the structure of a social pyramid that was being jacked up and underpinned by the importation of a fresh layer of immigrant population year by year; and the same reservoir of population in the Old World that had ensured this rise by feeding an inflowing stream of immigration into the United States had also ensured a livelihood for the increasing population of the United States by providing a market for the increasing abundance of commodities that these new hands in a New World were producing through the exploitation of hitherto untapped American natural resources.

Thus, on the economic plane, the New World in North America had still been part and parcel of the Old World east of the Atlantic in the nineteenth century, even more conspicuously than in the eighteenth and the seventeenth. In the nineteenth century the United States had developed her new estate by importing man-power and capital from the Old World's surplus stores and exporting resultant American products to the Old World's markets; and, though successive approximations towards the achievement of North America's economic independence had been marked by the raising of the height of the United States' tariff wall during and after the Civil War and by the cutting down of the volume of immigration into the United States after the First World War, this approach towards autarky on the economic plane had been offset on the political plane by an increasing entanglement in inter-

[1] See pp. 479–90, above.

national politics that had been made dramatically manifest when the United States had found herself compelled to become a belligerent in two world wars in succession.

Looking back in A.D. 1952 over the history of the United States since the Declaration of Independence, an historian could see in retrospect that, on the political plane, the United States' long-protracted endeavour to keep out of the arena of Western international power politics had been a losing battle. Since A.D. 1941 the United States had become more deeply implicated in international politics than the Thirteen Colonies had been before they had severed their political connexion with Great Britain; and, while the question whether isolation was any longer a practical possibility was being answered for the American people in the negative by the *force majeure* of world-shaking events, the question whether Isolationism was a morally legitimate ideal was being answered in the same sense by the American people themselves in a national debate between the respective advocates of a policy of isolation and a policy of co-operation with like-minded peoples abroad for the establishment and maintenance of a world order. This domestic controversy in the United States was momentous for the oecumenical prospects of the Western Civilization, as well as for the national prospects of the United States herself.

The issue on which the American people had to take a decision had been ventilated, soon after the close of the Second World War, in a public discussion of the verbal question whether the twentieth century of the Christian Era should be described as 'the American Century' or as 'the Century of the Common Man'; for in spite of their brevity these two competing 'slogans'[1] brought out the essence of the issue when they were pitted against one another. Both slogans alike were inspired by the national American ideal of exorcizing the class-conflicts of the Old World by creating a classless society on a middle-class footing; their difference lay in a diversity between their respective conceptions of the range of the geographical field in which the endeavour to translate this ideal into an accomplished fact could and should be made; and even on this point the difference was not an irreconcilable discrepancy between incompatible programmes but was no more than a difference of emphasis. Yet a disagreement that was not irreconcilable was nevertheless crucial, for it raised the question whether the American ideal of creating an Earthly Paradise in a New World could and should be pursued within the political frontiers of the United States in isolation from the rest of the *Oikoumenê*, or whether it was neither morally right nor practically possible to draw the limits of the New World that was

---

[1] The original field of the competition in which these two slogans had been coined had been the domestic arena of American party politics. 'The American Century' had been coined (in an article published under this title in *The New York Times*, 4th March, 1941, pp. 14–15) by Mr. Harry Luce, who was one of the most successful living incarnations of a traditional American spirit of capitalist enterprise. 'The Century of the Common Man' had been coined (in a speech delivered at a 'Free World' dinner in New York on the 8th May, 1942), in reply to Mr. Luce's challenging slogan, by Mr. Henry A. Wallace, a leading champion of 'the New Deal' who had carried a traditional American spirit of liberal idealism to lengths at which this had eventually cost him the loss of his chance of being nominated as a candidate for the Presidency of the United States on the Democratic Party's ticket.

to be the site of the Earthly Paradise along any line short of the bounds of the *Oikoumenê* itself. Was the New World to be just a geographical expression, or was it to have a spiritual connotation? Was the new hope to be the monopoly of one fraction of Mankind that happened in the twentieth century to be domiciled within the frontiers of the United States thanks to the enterprise and foresight of its pilgrim forebears, or was it to be a hope in which the whole of Mankind could share? In working out their American way of life, had the American people been labouring for themselves alone, or had they been labouring for all Humanity?

A presciently affirmative answer to the second of these two questions had been given in the American people's name thirty-four years back by an American idealist speaking with the authoritative voice of a President of the United States. On the 30th May, 1917, fifty-four days after the date on which the United States had become a belligerent in the First World War, Woodrow Wilson had proclaimed America's conversion to an oecumenical interpretation of her mission in his Memorial Day address at the National Cemetery at Arlington.

'We have said in the beginning that we planned this great government that men who wished freedom might have a place of refuge and a place where their hope could be realised; and now, having established such a government, having preserved such a government, having vindicated the power of such a government, we are saying to all Mankind: "We did not set this government up in order that we might have a selfish and separate liberty, for we are now ready to come to your assistance and fight out upon the field of the World the cause of Human Liberty." '

In A.D. 1952 this great issue was being debated in the United States on a practical as well as on a moral level; Americans were asking themselves whether isolation was or was not now feasible, as well as whether Isolationism was morally right or wrong; but, in the contemporary American scene as this presented itself to at least one non-American observer, it seemed clear that the moral issue was paramount in American minds and that, unless and until Isolationism had been finally rejected by American consciences, American wills would not be disposed to capitulate to the importunate logic of events—however plainly manifest it might have become by this date that the American people would not have it in their power to construct an Earthly Paradise in North America in accordance with American specifications if they were to allow the collective economic, political, and military power of the Old World to be concentrated in the hands of a totalitarian government at Moscow whose blue-print for an Earthly Paradise was 'un-American' in every line. These practical considerations had, no doubt, been at work in American minds ever since the Japanese attack on Pearl Harbour had provided the crowning and conclusive proof that the United States could not contract out of international power politics by any unilateral action. Yet a thus forcibly enlightened regard for the United States' national self-interest had assuredly counted for less than an intuitive idealism in moving public feeling and opinion in the United States to support the Administration's historic decisions to join in founding the

United Nations Organization; to underwrite, in the proclamation of the Truman Doctrine, the territorial integrity and political independence of Greece and Turkey; to offer Marshall Aid to the peoples who had been hit the hardest by the Second World War; to make an improvement in the standard of living of the World's poverty-stricken peasantry an American concern (along the lines of President Truman's 'Point Four'); and to make the United States a party to the Atlantic Pact.

In any case there could be little doubt in A.D. 1952 of the direction in which American minds were moving, whatever the balance of motives might have been. Americans were coming to the conclusion that if they wanted the twentieth century to be 'the American Century' they must aim at making it 'the Century of the Common Man', not just within the frontiers of the United States, but throughout the *Oikoumenê*. It did not follow from this that the American approach to a solution of the problem of class-conflict would in fact prevail, or would even prove feasible, everywhere. It seemed unlikely, *a priori*, that an approach which reflected the American people's own exceptionally fortunate economic experience and exceptionally successful economic achievements would prove to be practicable, *tel quel*, in the widely different current economic and social circumstances of the majority of the living generation of Mankind; and the American approach was in fact being challenged by alternative approaches reflecting other achievements and other experiences. The American solution for the problem of class-conflict might or might not eventually prevail in the World at large; at the time of writing, its oecumenical prospects were still unpredictable; it could, however, already be predicted with some confidence that, unless the American solution did prove to have some general value for the World at large, it would not be able ultimately to prevail even within the narrow enceinte of a North American fastness.

The Russian approach to the problem of class-conflict was inspired, like the American, by the ideal of creating an Earthly Paradise, and took shape, like the American again, in a policy of getting rid of class-conflict by eliminating class-divisions; but here the likeness ended; for the Russian and American lines of attack on a common objective were poles apart. While the Americans were trying to eliminate class-divisions by bringing the industrial working-class on to a middle-class footing, the Russians had eliminated them within the frontiers of the Soviet Union by liquidating the middle class and by banning all freedom of private economic enterprise, not only for 'capitalists', but also (in political practice, though not in constitutional theory) for Trade Unionism as well.

In this Communist Russian policy there were strong points which the Soviet Union's Western rivals in a competition for world power could not afford to underrate; and the first and greatest of these Russian assets was the êthos of Communism itself. In the long run, perhaps, this 'ideology'—offering, as it did, a stone for bread[1]—might prove to be an unsatisfying substitute for Religion; and the disillusionment of one idealistic-minded Western convert after another who had embraced

[1] Matt. vii. 9; Luke xi. 11.

Communism in the belief that he had found in it Man's way of salvation was a portent which perhaps foreshadowed the eventual reaction of Mankind in the mass to the Marxian gospel. In the short run, on the other hand, Communism did offer to any soul whose house was empty, swept, and garnished[1] an immediate satisfaction for one of the deepest and most insistent of Man's religious needs by offering to the spiritual *déraciné* a purpose of high importance, transcending his own petty personal aims, as an object for his devotion. A Leviathan embodying the collective power and corporate interests of the Human Race was a more imposing idol than any of the individual mannikins whose trivial, ephemeral, and conflicting personal interests ranked as the ultimate goals of human endeavour under a post-Christian Western dispensation in which personal freedom had been cut loose from its religious origin, inspiration, significance, and sanction. Any hungry soul that was offered no objects for worship except these paltry Western idols and this imposing Russian one would be bound, when faced with that dismal choice, to opt for becoming a votary of Leviathan. The mission of converting the World to Communism was more inspiring, exhilarating, and edifying than the mission of keeping the World safe for the right to take profits or for the right to strike. 'Holy Russia' was a more rousing war-cry than 'Happy America'.

Another strong point in the Russian approach was that Russia's geographical position made it impossible for Russians to waste their energies, *more Americano*, by chasing the will-o'-the-wisp of Isolationism. The inextricable implication in the affairs of the rest of the *Oikoumenê* which was now overtaking the United States as a result of the *Oikoumenê*'s recent coalescence and shrinkage was a plight in which Russia had found herself since the dawn of Russian history. Isolationism was an ideal which could not be entertained by the inhabitants of a land-locked country. Russia marched with the domains of all the non-Russian civilizations of the Old World; and her frontier with the Western Society—which, in Russian experience, had been the most dangerous frontier of all—was a line drawn across an open plain where there was neither a mountain rampart nor a river moat to lighten the task of Russia's human defenders. The perilous exposure of her geographical location thus constrained 'Holy Russia', like the Biblical Israel with whom she was identified in her repressed but unexorcized Orthodox Christian tradition, to see herself as a Zion against whose Lord and His Anointed the Kings of the Earth would always be standing up and the rulers taking counsel together.[2] 'Why do the heathen so furiously rage together, and why do the people imagine a vain thing?'[3] They rage because the Chosen People are the depositories of a unique truth and unique righteousness which the froward hearts of the wicked are bent upon challenging. 'Holy Russia's' defence was not any 'natural frontier' like the now rapidly narrowing Atlantic Straits that had once insulated the United States; it was orthodoxy ('I will preach the law'[4]) supported by a faith in the inevitability of Truth's and Righteousness's ultimate

[1] Matt. xii. 44; Luke xi. 25.
[3] Ps. ii. 1.
[2] Ps. ii. 2.
[4] Ps. ii. 7.

triumph ('Thou shalt bruise them with a rod of iron and break them in pieces like a potter's vessel'[1]). Marx's Russian Khalīfah's proclamation to the capitalists was an echo of Muhammad's legendary message to Heraclius and Khusrū Parwīz: 'Be wise now therefore, O ye Kings; be learned, ye that are judges of the Earth.[2] . . . Kiss the Son lest He be angry, and so ye perish from the right way.'[3] Russian Communism's simultaneous proclamation to the Proletariat was: 'Blessed are all they that put their trust in Him.'[4]

A third strong point, in the short run, in the Communist Russian approach was the replacement of a traditional Eastern Orthodox Christianity by a Marxian post-Christian Western ideology as the current expression of Russia's perennial orthodoxy; for the Marxian ideology was a heresy in orthodox post-Christian Western eyes, and the anathematization of Marxism by a Western dominant minority was a testimony to its truth and righteousness in the sight of a now world-wide Western proletariat in which the peasant majority of Mankind had been brigaded together with the Western industrial workers.

Marxism interpreted by Lenin and Stalin and preached from the Kremlin made, in this exotic Russian dress, a potent appeal to the World's peasantry from China to Peru and from Mexico to Tropical Africa; for Russia herself had been, till yesterday, one of these poor and powerless peasant countries. In her social and economic situation Russia had a much closer affinity than the United States had with the depressed three-quarters of the Human Race for whose allegiance the two Powers were competing; and Russia could claim, with a specious appearance of veracity, that she had saved herself by her exertions and the rest of the Proletariat by her example. The heretical Western ideology which the Russians had made their own had enabled them to increase one great peasant country's collective power, and in the same act to raise its inhabitants' personal standards of living,[5] by acclimatizing a current Western technology through an industrial revolution—which, in Russia, had been made by the State in the Community's interest (as the Bolsheviks conceived of it) and not by private *entrepreneurs* in theirs. Soviet Communism's achievements, as presented in Soviet Communist propaganda, sounded impressive in the ears of non-Russian peasants and industrial workers who had no opportunity of checking the story that they were being told by the evidence of their own eyes; and even in the United States there were elements that might prove to be not altogether impervious to the Communist gospel.

In North America an oecumenical proletariat had been reproduced in miniature; for, in spite of tardy measures for the restriction of immigration from Europe and Africa and for the exclusion of immigration from a 'Barred Zone' of Asian countries,[6] the peasantry of the Old

---

[1] Ps. ii. 9. [2] Ps. ii. 10. [3] Ps. ii. 12.
[4] Ps. ii. 12. [5] See IX. viii. 684–9.
[6] See Toynbee, A. J., and Boulter, V. M.: *Survey of International Affairs, 1924* (London 1926, Milford), pp. 86–114 and 127–60. On the 27th June, 1952, when the writer was revising the present passage in his present work at Princeton, New Jersey, the McCarran-Walter Immigration Bill was enacted through being repassed by the Congress at Washington by more than the two-thirds majority of votes that was required in order to override President Truman's veto. This Act, which, on the whole, consolidated and

World was widely represented in the lower ranks of the American industrial working class; and the fusing power of 'the Melting Pot', in which America had put her trust as her solution for the problem of class-conflict, was counteracted by the institution of caste to the detriment of any American citizens of alien origin who differed markedly from their White fellow-citizens in physique. In a United States whose population was no longer being recruited by immigration in any appreciable volume, a Negro proletariat that was drifting away from Southern fields into Northern slums seemed destined to remain permanently battened down at the bottom of a social sump. The cutting off of the nineteenth-century stream of immigration was thus having the effect of generating, inside the Oceanic moats that were 'Fortress America's' natural frontiers, a penalized and alienated class in the American body social in which an enterprising director of Russian operations in a 'Cold War' might perhaps one day find the makings of a 'fifth column';[1] in this new American proletariat, in the technical sense of the term, the urban coloured population was merely the most conspicuous among a number of elements; and the middle class's sensitiveness to this potential danger in their midst was betrayed in their inclination to tolerate an odious practice of 'witch-hunting' that was a menace to traditional American civil liberties, and in their readiness to jump to the conclusion that any American citizen who had once been denounced by American 'witch-hunters' as an agent of Soviet Communism must be guilty even if proved innocent.

While this American nervousness was an index of the opportunities for Communist propaganda in an American mission-field, there were of course, weak points, as well as strong points, in the Russian Communist approach to a solution of Mankind's current social problems.

The most serious of these Russian weaknesses was the most obvious one. Soviet Communism had set out to put an end to the private exploitation of one individual human being by another, and, consistently with this aim, the fundamental law in the Soviet Communist social code was a veto on the private employment of labour; but the only practical means of liberating individual human beings from private exploitation by their fellows that Soviet Communism had been able to devise—or been willing to adopt—was the public exploitation of all individuals alike by the omnipotent rulers of a totalitarian state. The urban proletariat that a Western middle class had inadvertently called into existence in the course of their pursuit of their own private purposes had been manufactured deliberately in Russia by the Soviet Government for the sake of fulfilling the Marxian scriptures. A consequent weakness of Soviet Communist policy was that, in suppressing all individual liberty and thereby making sure of getting rid of the abuse

confirmed the already existing restrictive legislation, had at least the merit of abolishing, for the benefit of non-Communist Asian countries, the former invidious difference in status, for the purposes of the immigration law of the United States, between Asian countries on the one hand and European and African countries on the other.

[1] Professor McNeill comments: 'I believe it is true that, so far, Communism has made little progress among American Negroes; a better example would be the relative prominence of Jews in the ranks of the United States Communist Party.'

of private power to which the enjoyment of individual liberty might give rise, the Soviet Government had also cut the roots of an incentive to produce and to create which individual liberty alone could keep alive.

If the tasks of production and creation were ever to be taken wholly out of the hands of human beings and were to be assigned wholly to an impersonal 'Collective Man', the result could only be to bring production and creation to a standstill. The psychic driving-force of personal purposefulness and zest cannot be effectively replaced by the goads of governmental terrorism and coercion, and the rulers of the Soviet Union had tacitly confessed that they had learnt this lesson by experience when they had introduced their 'Stakhanovite' system of differential rewards for different degrees of efficiency in output, which was familiar in the West under the name of 'piece-work', and when they had sought to find an alternative to the monetary incentive for competition in honorary incentives of the kinds that had proved effective in Western monarchies under the *ancien régime* and subsequently in the recreational field of non-professional sport. Such concessions by Communism to Individualism may have tempered Communism's damping effects; yet these were no more than mitigations of a system that was intrinsically inimical to the application of human energies to economic purposes, and a non-Russian and non-Communist observer found it hard to see how, in the long run, on the economic and administrative (as distinct from the ideological) plane, a Communist totalitarian régime could avoid evoking an extreme manifestation of the defensive, negative, unenthusiastic trade-union and civil-service êthos. This prospect was a serious menace to the Soviet Union's chances of success in her competition with the United States, where even the trade-unionist industrial working class was infected with the American middle class's belief in the virtues of private enterprise and with its determination to keep this source of economic productivity and creativity alive.

The Soviet Union's present economic inferiority to the United States was as indisputable as it was depressing for believers in the Soviet Communist dispensation; and, though this inferiority was due, not merely to a difference of régime, but to the backwardness of Russian technology as appraised by Western standards, the Soviet Government had debarred themselves by the extravagance of their mendacity in their own domestic propaganda from making the valid and pertinent points that this technological backwardness of Russia's was at least as old as the seventeenth century and that, since the Bolsheviks' own advent to power in A.D. 1917, they had emulated the achievements of Peter the Great himself in notably diminishing the length of Russia's technological lag behind the contemporary progress of her Western neighbours.[1] Instead of claiming credit for their genuine and praiseworthy successes in narrowing the gap between Russia's and the West's technological and social performance, they had painted, for their subjects' edification, a fancy picture of an instantaneously attained Soviet Communist Earthly Paradise by comparison with which the contemporary Capitalist World was a howling wilderness. In consequence, the

[1] See IX. viii. 126–49.

Soviet Government were now living in constant fear of the possibility that their subjects might discover the very different truth; and the acuteness of their concern about this danger was betrayed by the rigour of their precautions for preventing personal intercourse between their subjects and the citizens of 'capitalist' countries.[1] Western psychological opportunities for propaganda in a Russian mission-field, if ever the iron curtain were to become rusty enough to be perforated, could be gauged by the degree of the Soviet Government's nervousness. The Soviet Government were taking individual lapses out of the Communist Faith in the Soviet Union just as hard as the American public were taking individual lapses into it in the United States.

The likeness between these contemporaneous American and Russian anxieties was significant because it was not fortuitous. The reason why both parties were taking so tragically any successes scored on their home front by their adversaries was that, in an *Oikoumenê* whose conductivity had been gaining in intensity in proportion to the progressive diminution of geographical distance measured in terms of human intercourse, it had now manifestly ceased to be feasible to attempt to create an Earthly Paradise in any artificially insulated province of what was already, on the psychic plane, One World. In the history of the Soviet Union the counterpart of an American Isolationism had been Stalin's slogan 'Socialism in One Country'; but, though this slogan had served Stalin's personal domestic purpose of defeating and ousting his rival Trotsky in a four-years-long struggle within the bosom of the Soviet Communist Party that had ended in Stalin's definitive victory in January 1928, it was no more fit than American Isolationism was to serve as a practical programme for a policy in the real world of the day; for in this world the Soviet Union and the United States were competing with one another at close quarters, and either party would be condemning itself to swift defeat and to eventual subjugation at its adversary's hands if it were ever to leave this adversary a free scope for sowing tares in the oecumenical mission-field[2] while it confined its own activities and attention to the cultivation of its own garden. The recent metamorphosis of the *Oikoumenê* through the magic of Western technology was forcing the Soviet Union and the United States to contend with one another in a world-wide arena.

The West European approach towards a solution of the problem of class-conflict, which was most in evidence in Great Britain and in the Scandinavian countries, differed from both the American and the Russian approach in being less doctrinaire than either of them. The British people, in particular, were now feeling their way towards a solution by compromise—an approach to political problems to which the British had become addicted as the result of a more-than-three-hundred-years-long apprenticeship in trial and error. In this span of their political history, intransigence had cost them the two catastrophes of the English Civil War and the secession of the Thirteen Colonies in North America, while the contrary tactics of compromise had enabled them to negotiate the gradual transformation of a unitary empire into a co-operative

[1] See pp. 534–5, above.   [2] Matt. xiii. 25.

commonwealth of nations and to carry out the domestic revolutions of A.D. 1688, 1832, and 1945 without either falling into civil disorders or sowing the seeds of inveterate resentment in the hearts of the class that happened to be the loser on each occasion. Since as early as the thirteenth century it had been one of the recognized principles of English statesmanship that it was the part of wisdom for the ruling element (*Graecè* πολίτευμα) in the body politic to forestall the danger of a *coup d'état* by voluntarily taking into partnership with itself any class, hitherto outside the privileged circle, which had accumulated sufficient power and experience to be now probably capable, in the last resort, of forcing an entry if it did not find an already open door. In A.D. 1945 the British middle class, which had profited by the agrarian landlords' acquiescence in its enfranchisement in A.D. 1832, had acquiesced in its turn in the industrial workers' advent to power; and this compromise between the politically conflicting interests of the middle class and the working class had been made feasible by a simultaneous compromise between the ideologically antithetical dispensations of Private Economic Enterprise and Socialism.

This institutional compromise was a common-sense recognition of the hard facts of the situation in which all West European peoples now found themselves. In countries that were in process of losing power and wealth to rising giants on the fringes of an expanding Western World[1] at the very time when the local industrial workers were demanding 'a new deal', it was manifestly impracticable for the West European middle class to follow the North American middle class's policy of offering to the working class the two amenities of a virtually middle-class standard of living and an abundance of individual opportunities for rising in the social scale as alternatives to governmental intervention for the promotion of social justice at the price of a regimentation that had proved to be unavoidable in any redistribution of private purchasing power through governmental action. On the other hand, in Great Britain, the Scandinavian countries, the Low Countries, and France civil liberties were so strongly entrenched and so highly prized by citizens of all classes that it would have been equally impracticable in any of these countries to carry governmental intervention on behalf of social justice to the Russian length of a régime of totalitarian autocracy. Accordingly the current Anglo-Scandinavian approach to the problem of class-conflict was an attempt to find a middle way between an American and a Russian extreme by experimenting in an illogical combination of a modicum of free private economic enterprise with a modicum of governmental planning and regimentation in the interests of social justice. In medical parlance this Anglo-Scandinavian Social Democracy might be described as a vaccine for giving immunity against the virus of Communism; and the efficacy of this West European preventive social medicine was certified by its irritating effect on Soviet Communist nerves. Next to the Trotskys and Titos whose deviationist Communism was a threat to a Stalinian orthodoxy within the Com-

---

[1] This dwarfing of Western Europe has been noticed in IV. iv. 308–13, and on p. 486, above.

munist fold, the Stalinists' principal bugbears were the Undéns and Attlees whose contemptible milk-and-water nostrum was breaking all the rules of a Marxian Historical Necessity by sterilizing the orthodox Communist Faith's mission-field in Western Europe.

This prosaic Anglo-Scandinavian policy of institutional compromise would ultimately be appraised on the practical test of its outcome in the long run, and in A.D. 1952 it would have been premature to try to anticipate History's future verdict on it; yet some, at any rate, of both its strong points and its weak points were by then already apparent.

Its strongest point was its consonance with the general experience of Man in Process of Civilization and with the particular requirements of the living generation of Mankind in an *Oikoumenê* in which a number of formerly segregated and diversified societies had been suddenly brought into close quarters with one another by advances in a Western technology that had been too swift to allow time for these now next-door neighbours to become culturally acclimatized to one another.

The policy of brewing a mixture between Socialism and Freedom of Private Economic Enterprise was justified by past experience, inasmuch as it would have been difficult for the best informed historian to cite significant examples of historical communities in which either of the two elements in this mid-twentieth-century British mixture had been wholly absent. Between the repellent anarchy of an abortive Scandinavian Civilization in Iceland and the uninviting regimentation of an Incaic Andean universal state, the constitutions of a vast majority of the communities that had risen and fallen up to date in societies in process of civilization had contained both an appreciable ingredient of Socialism and an appreciable ingredient of Personal Liberty. Communities that had allowed Individualism to run riot in private armies and private executions of private judgements founded on private laws had been as abnormal as communities that had allowed Socialism to go so far as to impose a community of wives and husbands or combs' and toothbrushes; and, while, in the mixture between the two dispensations that was the normal constitution of Society, there had been an infinite variety in the quotas of the two ingredients, and a perpetual dissension over the perennial question of what these quotas should be in any particular ephemeral set of kaleidoscopically changing social circumstances, the same two ingredients had regularly been present in the constitutions of most communities in the common run. In the solid setting of this historical background, mid-twentieth-century British social policy looked as realistic as it was empirical; and, if this conformity with past experience was its outstanding justification, its outstanding merit was its relevancy to present needs.

The philosophical implication of the current British institutional compromise was that the issue between Socialism and Private Enterprise on the economic plane—as, for example, over the question whether the telegraph and telephone service should be operated by the public post office or by private enterprise—was not a question of ideological principle on which it would be wrong not to take an intransigent stand, but was a question of practical expediency on which it would be wrong not to follow the pedestrian path of empiricism and give-and-take. This was a saving truth in a world which was faced with a genuine and crucial question of principle in the issue between a worship of God and a worship of Collective Human Power, and which had seen the power of Leviathan formidably reinforced by the onset of a soul-destroying Mechanized Technology. This was the battle in which the Spirit of Man must conquer or die in a twentieth-century oecumenical arena; and the living generation of Mankind had much to gain by adopting a British approach to current social problems that would leave human souls free to throw themselves into the momentous struggle on the religious plane without having their attention and energy diverted to fight on the economic plane over an issue of secondary importance.

The British approach was also sound common sense in a world in which peoples bringing with them sharply diverse cultural heritages had now been brought face to face with one another so suddenly by a technological 'annihilation of distance' that even the pace of the rapid and radical economic and social transformation which Technology was simultaneously bringing to pass throughout the *Oikoumenê* was not swift enough to give this jostling crowd of motley communities time to make mutual adjustments unless the period of grace could be prolonged by the exercise of Charity and Tolerance. Perhaps the two most promising features of the British approach were its flexibility and the coolness of its emotional temperature. In the British mixture between Socialism and Free Private Economic enterprise the proportions between the two ingredients could be agreed *ad hoc* in accordance with the particular requirements of a particular community at a particular time and place, and the proportions agreed today could be modified by a fresh agreement tomorrow in order to cater for changes overnight in methods of technique, in the size and distribution of national, sectional, and individual incomes, and in manners and customs. This flexibility of the British prescription for alleviating a social indisposition was unquestionably better adapted to provide for Mankind's still locally diverse and now everywhere rapidly changing current social needs than the rigid lines on the blue prints of rival Russian and American plans for social engineering, while the lowness of the temperature generated by a British social apothecary's work made it feasible to keep on perpetually experimenting in it without courting any serious risk of a catastrophic explosion.

When a British observer reached a conclusion that was so gratifying to British self-esteem, he had to ask himself whether—in spite of his not being an adherent of the Labour Party—he might nevertheless be a victim of a distorting national egocentric illusion; and, even if perchance his judgement were to be endorsed by non-British contemporary observers who could not be suspected of the same partiality, a disinterestedly favourable appreciation of the British approach might still be offset by a pessimistic estimate of the prospects of seeing a Twentieth-Century World take this salutary British middle course. The Anglo-Scandinavian experiment in Social Democracy was being made at a time when the margin of energy, wealth, and power required for embarking on a great new social venture had been wiped out in Western Europe by the cumulative effects of two world wars fought mainly on European battlefields; and, even if Great Britain were to succeed in making an enduring practical success of Social Democracy at home, it might be doubted whether, in the second half of the twentieth century, her influence would still be great enough—as it might have been a hundred years earlier, when she had been at the zenith of her power and prestige—to move other countries to follow her in experimenting in *ad hoc* mixtures of Socialism with Free Private Economic Enterprise.

If the peaceful domestic revolution in Great Britain in and after A.D. 1945 and the peaceful departure of the British from India in A.D. 1947 should come to be reckoned, in the judgement of Posterity, among the finest of the examples that the British people had ever set, then the timing of these two historic British acts might come to be lamented as one of the ironies of History. There could never have been a greater need for such examples of the unflamboyant virtues of reasonableness, self-restraint, conciliatoriness, and far-sightedness; but the practical effect of a good example is determined, not by the degree of the need, but by the degree of the readiness to follow it; and on this practical criterion these two British examples had possibly been given a hundred years too late. Yet, whether a distracted Twentieth-Century World did or did not prove willing to follow a British lead, it would find itself unable to elude the problem with which British statesmanship was wrestling in the United Kingdom on the morrow of a Second World War. In this chapter of British, Western, and human history the British people were groping after a practical solution of a theoretically insoluble problem by which the Human Social Animal was perennially beset. If Freedom and Justice were intrinsically incompatible ideals, as they were, and if nevertheless *Homo Politicus* could not afford to renounce either of them, as he could not, how was Jehu to drive in double harness two equally indispensable steeds that were pulling their human driver's chariot in two opposite directions? Any practical solution of this problem would be unlikely to be anything more than a local and temporary makeshift; yet the problem itself was so importunate and so crucial that even a makeshift solution in a single chapter of parochial history might prove to be something of general and permanent value for Man in his perpetual struggle with his own Human Nature.

(IV) POSSIBLE COSTS OF SOCIAL JUSTICE

Since social life is impossible for Man without some measure of both Personal Liberty and Social Justice, Human Society is a house perpetually divided against itself, which will not stand[1] unless the thrusts of these two conflicting dynamic ideals are shrewdly directed to making them hold the house together instead of pulling it to pieces. The temptingly simpler expedient of relying solely on one of the two opposing forces and eliminating the other is impracticable, because it is impossible for the Human Social Animal to dispense with either ideal. Personal

[1] Matt. xii. 25.

Liberty is an indispensable condition for any human achievement, good or evil, since human action can be undertaken only by individual minds and wills. At the same time, Social Justice is the sovereign rule of the game of human intercourse, and this rule can never be broken with impunity for the sake of giving scope to Personal Liberty, even when in other respects the exercise of Personal Liberty is achieving results that are indisputably good. An uncurbed Personal Liberty generates oligarchy by giving a free hand to a minority who, in an unrestricted competition of all against all, are more than a match for the rest of the community in physical strength, mental ability, wealth, or political power. On the other hand, Social Justice cannot be enforced up to the hilt except by completely suppressing Personal Liberty and instituting an absolute dictatorship.

In the history of Man in Process of Civilization, all known social constitutions had been pitched somewhere between these two theoretical extremes, with a bias, more or less strongly pronounced, in the one direction or in the other. The Soviet Communist régime in Russia, for example, had been expending almost all its zeal and alertness on guarding against the abuse of Personal Liberty through the private exploitation of one person by another, without being comparably sensitive to the evils of the dictatorship through which it was vindicating the demands of Social Justice.[1] By contrast, the Constitution of the United States had provided effective safeguards against dictatorship by its elaborate mechanism of checks and balances, without having shown a comparable concern to prevent freedom of personal enterprise from degenerating into freedom for one person to exploit another for his private profit.

Considering that, at the time of writing, both the United States and the Soviet Union were going concerns, it could be inferred that, in practice, neither of these two antithetical polities had pushed its own characteristic bias to the point of disequilibrium at which the house would come tumbling down upon its inmates' heads. In the working constitutions of both the Soviet Union and the United States, as in those of all other polities known to History, elements of both Personal Liberty and Social Justice were combined in diverse ratios; and in a mid-twentieth-century Westernizing World the mixture, whatever it might be, was invariably labelled 'Democracy', because this disinterred Attic blessèd word had come to be an obligatory shibboleth for every self-respecting political alchemist. In the Soviet Union in A.D. 1952 'Democracy' signified a substantial measure of Social Equality combined with a vestige of Personal Liberty that was the maximum compatible with the Communists' prescription for securing Social Justice. In the United States at the same date the same term 'Democracy' signified a substantial measure of Personal Liberty combined with as generous a modicum of Social Justice as an American indulgence of Personal Liberty allowed.

[1] Professor William McNeill points out that the Social Justice which, at this date, was being purchased in the Soviet Union at so high a price, in terms of a sacrifice of personal freedom, did not compare favourably with the Social Justice current at the time in the United Kingdom, or indeed in the United States, when the comparison was made in terms of the gamut of the differences in the personal incomes that different individuals in different occupational groups or classes were allowed to draw out of the total product of the community's collective work.

These diverse brews uniformly labelled 'Democracy' all had the elementary practical merit of making the wheels of a social mechanism revolve; yet the display of a reassuringly pretentious term of political art was a disingenuous device for concealing the cracks in the divers makeshifts over which the label bearing the bold imprint 'Democracy' had been pasted by rival bill-posting politicians. An intrinsic contradiction between Personal Liberty and Social Justice could not be reconciled at all by the mere repetition of a political catchword that was specious only because it was ambiguous, and it could not be reconciled more than superficially and provisionally by the more respectable and useful artifice of improvising makeshift political and economic measures for reconciling the two ideals in practice. The only genuine reconciliation between these conflicting ideals of Liberty and Equality was to be found in the mediating ideal of Fraternity;[1] and, if Man's social salvation depended on his prospects of translating this higher ideal into reality, he would find the politician's ingenuity a bruised reed,[2] since the achievement of Fraternity was beyond the reach of human beings so long as, in their struggles to achieve it, they trusted exclusively in their own powers. The Brotherhood of Man was an ideal that men could never translate into reality without acting on a saving belief in the common Fatherhood of God; and the implicit truth that human social problems could be solved only by lifting them from the social to the religious plane was as true in a twentieth-century Westernizing World as it had been true always and everywhere since the transfiguration of Sub-man into Man.

If in that world in that age Mankind's perennial social problem displayed any distinctive facet, this was to be found in the imperious intervention of a latter-day Western Technology; for, in the trembling balance in which Personal Liberty and Social Justice were being weighed against one another there and then, Technology's girder had been thrown, like Brennus's sword, into the anti-libertarian scale.

This finding could be illustrated and supported by taking an observation of a coming state of Society which was already within sight, though it might not yet be within reach. Let it be assumed, for the sake of the argument, that an almighty Technology has already accomplished the next major tasks on its agenda. By thrusting an atomic bomb into Man's hands Technology will have forced Man to abolish War and Civil Disorder and at the same time will have enabled Man to reduce the death-rate to an unprecedentedly low minimum by bestowing impartially on all classes in each community, and on all communities in the *Oikoumenê*, the benefits of preventive medicine. Let it further be assumed that these prodigious improvements in the conditions of Human Life by means of institutional changes have been carried out at a speed with which the

---

[1] The trio 'Liberty-Equality-Fraternity' had been deified by the authors of the French Revolution as a humanitarian substitute for a Christian theology's Holy Trinity. The incomprehensible persons of a hypothetical Godhead were to be replaced by three rational and practicable ideals. But this unacknowledged Christian inspiration of the ideas of 1789 was responsible for an *a priori* misreading of the true relation in which the three deified ideals stood to one another. In reality the trio was not a Nicene Trinity-in-Unity but was an Hegelian resolution of forces. Fraternity was the synthesis that could resolve a conflict between the thesis of Liberty and the counter-demands of an Equality that was Liberty's antithesis.   [2] 2 Kings xviii. 21.

consequently requisite cultural changes have failed to keep pace. These assumptions require us to imagine that the peasant three-quarters of Mankind will not yet have lost their immemorially old habit of reproducing their kind up to the limits of their means of subsistence; and this assumption in turn requires us to imagine them still to be expending on increases in their head of population all the additional means of subsistence that will have been placed in their hands by the establishment of a World Order that will have brought in its train the benefits of peace, police, hygiene, and the application of Science to the production of food.

Such prognostications would not be fantastic; they would merely be projections of current tendencies into the future. In China, for example, increases in the head of population had swallowed up increases in the means of subsistence which had been bestowed on the peasantry in China by the introduction of previously unknown food crops from the Americas in the sixteenth century of the Christian Era and by the establishment, in the seventeenth century, of a *Pax Manchuana*. Thanks to the naturalization of maize in China *circa* A.D. 1550, of sweet potatoes *circa* A.D. 1590, and of pea-nuts at the turn of the sixteenth and seventeenth centuries, the population had risen from the 63,599,541 indicated by the returns in the census of A.D. 1578 to an estimated figure of 108,300,000 in A.D. 1661—and this in spite of the fact that in the interval between these two dates this spurt in the growth of population had been partly offset by the mortality arising from Chinese civil disorders and Manchu military operations in the anarchic transition to the Manchu régime from the Ming.[1] Thereafter, under the Manchu Peace, the population had continued to rise to 143,411,559 in A.D. 1741 and to a figure of the order of 300 million by the time when, half-way through the nineteenth century, the decline of the Manchu régime in its turn had brought with it a fresh bout of anarchy that had taken another heavy toll of Chinese life. This prompt conversion of additional resources into additional population in China under the Ming and Manchu dispensations had been duplicated in a comparably portentous increase in the populations of India under a British Rāj and of Java under Dutch rule; and it was significant that all recent increases in Asian peasant populations were ultimately traceable to the oecumenical effects of Modern Western enterprise, since even in China, which had never come under the direct rule of any Western Power, the increase in the food-supply through the introduction of new crops had been a consequence of the West Europeans' discovery of the Americas.

If the effect of Modern Western enterprise in enabling Asian peoples to indulge their habit of increasing their populations up to the limit had been so great, yesterday and the day before, in the local and temporary incubators constituted by a Manchu, a Dutch, and a British Peace, it seemed safe to predict that the same effect of the same cause would be powerfully enhanced tomorrow if the whole *Oikoumenê* were to be united politically under an American Peace and if, within this global Earthly Paradise, the beneficent medical applications of a still advancing Western

[1] See Goodrich, L. C.: *A Short History of the Chinese People* (London 1948, Allen & Unwin), pp. 198–9.

Science were to continue to reduce the World's death-rate, besides continuing to increase the World's production of food. Though Science's magic cornucopia had produced an abundance that had falsified Malthus's pessimistic expectations up to date, the insuperable finiteness of the area of the Earth's surface must set a ceiling to the progressive increase in Mankind's food-supply that even Science could not transcend; and the pace of the Intellect in making scientific discoveries, and of the Will in applying them, was so much swifter than the pace of the Subconscious Psyche in adjusting its habits to conform with the necessities of successive new situations, into which it was perpetually being hustled by its volatile yoke-fellow, that it seemed at least as likely as not that Science's ceiling of global food production would be reached some time before the Peasantry's habit of breeding up to the limit would have been overcome.

The British people had taken not much less than 140 years to adjust their breeding habits to a rise in the population of Great Britain produced by a fall in the death-rate that had begun *circa* A.D. 1740;[1] and this had been the rate of change of habits in a then already predominantly commercial-minded community in which 'the cake of custom'[2] had been much less massive, less opaque, and less resistant than it yet was in the twentieth century in any of the peasant communities. It was, no doubt, conceivable that the Peasantry's custom of breeding up to the limits of subsistence might yield some day to the solvent of an exotic Western technology; for a Peasantry who by A.D. 1952 were already discovering that this Western talisman could endow them with something like a Western military efficiency,[3] at the price of their submitting to a Late Modern Western drill, might go on to discover that it could also endow them with something like a Western standard of living at the price of their adopting post-Modern Western methods of keeping the increase of population within bounds. Yet, even if there was thus some hope of the Peasantry's eventually making this revolutionary change of practice in this Malthusian field, the change here could hardly be counted upon to come quickly enough to forestall the onset of an already impending crisis.

In thus forecasting a posthumous fulfilment of Malthus's expectations, we should also have to forecast that, by the time at which the disconcerting gap between the World's food-supply and the Peasantry's breeding habits would have brought the Peasantry to the verge of famine, some oecumenical authority would have made itself responsible for looking after at least the elementary material needs of the whole living population of the planet. This prognostication, again, would be merely a projection of current tendencies, since, at the close of the Second World War, the quantities and kinds of the food required by the whole population of the World had actually been estimated, and the existing supplies been commandeered and allocated, to meet the minimum needs of the rice-eating, wheat-eating, and maize-eating provinces of the *Oikoumenê*,

---

[1] See pp. 386–7, above.
[2] Bagehot, W.: *Physics and Politics*, 10th ed. (London 1894, Kegan Paul), pp. 27 and 35, cited in II. i. 192.　　　　　　　　　　[3] See pp. 503–16, above.

by the United Nations Relief and Rehabilitation Administration. Even if we assume that the minimum standard of living that a future oecumenical authority would have undertaken to secure for the population of the World would have been no higher than the minimum standard for the population of England that had been contemplated in Queen Elizabeth's 'Poor Law' statute of A.D. 1601, a situation in which any authority would have assumed any responsibility for guaranteeing the whole living generation of Mankind against starvation in a world in which the production of food would have reached its ceiling would be a situation in which the begetting of children would have ceased to be the private affair of wives and husbands and have become the public concern of a ubiquitous impersonal disciplinary power.

If this situation were one day to arise, it would impose on Mankind one of the most drastic revolutions in human history since the first essays in Civilization; for hitherto men and women had not only been at liberty to beget children at their own discretion but had enjoyed this freedom when they had been destitute of all other rights and assets. This historic freedom was attested, as we have noticed in an earlier context,[1] by the etymology of the word 'proletariat'; for that technical term in the vocabulary of a Modern Western sociology was derived from a Latin word coined for the statistical purposes of the Roman census to describe a category of Roman citizens 'who had nothing but their children to enter in their returns as their contribution to the common weal'.[2] This Roman administrative terminology was an eloquent testimony to the truth that, in the history of Man in Process of Civilization up to date, no government—not even the most meticulous and most inquisitorial tyranny—had ever thought of contesting its subjects' freedom to reproduce their kind.

The nearest that governments had come hitherto towards intruding on this inner sanctum of private life had been to institute negative or positive rewards for the parents of large families if the public authorities were anxious to obtain an increase in their supplies of man-power or cannon-fodder; but they had no more dreamed of forbidding their subjects to restrict the size of their families than they had dreamed of compelling them, instead of merely inducing them, to multiply. Indeed, the freedom to beget or not to beget had been hitherto so uncontroversially sacrosanct that it had been tacitly taken for granted; and even as late as A.D. 1941 it had not occurred to President Roosevelt to raise the number of the axiomatic human freedoms consecrated in his charter from four to five by explicitly putting on record a wife's and husband's sacred right to determine the size of their own families.[3] It now looked as if the future might show that there had been an unintentional logic in Roosevelt's artless silence on this point, since it appeared that in the last resort—

[1] In I. i. 41, n. 3.
[2] 'Proletarii dicti sunt plebeii qui nihil rei publicae exhibeant sed tantum prolem sufficiant' (Nonius Marcellinus in his *Compendiosa Doctrina per Litteras*, quoted ibid.).
[3] This right was not challenged in principle by the ban on the procurement of abortion, or even by the ban on the advertisement and sale of artificial contraceptives, that was the law of the land in many countries at the time of writing; for, in theory at least, these bans still left husbands and wives free to limit the size of their families by the exercise of sexual self-control.

given the World's ultimate ceiling of food production and the Peasantry's traditional breeding habits—a novel 'freedom from want' could not be guaranteed to Mankind unless a familiar 'freedom to beget' were taken away from them. On this showing, the maintenance of a minimum oecumenical material standard of living would require a public interference with Personal Liberty that hitherto was unheard of; for, though it was true that in the past a minute fraction of Mankind had been either forcibly precluded from exercising its right of reproduction or had voluntarily abstained from exercising it, religious celibacy had always been considered to be an exceptional act of spiritual heroism, while the practice of making eunuchs had ranked with Human sacrifice, Prostitution, Slavery, and War as one of the blots on the pages of the history of Civilization.

If the time were indeed to come when the begetting of children would have to be regulated in conformity with imperious requirements of public policy instead of being left to chance in being left to the personal discretion of wives and husbands, how was this revolutionary future extension of the powers of authoritarian government into the intimacies of private life likely to be received on the one hand by the peasant majority of Mankind and on the other hand by a minority whom an Industrial Technology had emancipated from the peasant's bondage to unquestioned custom? The controversy between these two sections of Mankind that the Malthusian issue was bound to evoke was likely to be acute and acrimonious, since either section would have grievances against the other which would seem clamant in the aggrieved party's estimation. The peasantry would feel aggrieved at being threatened with the loss of their traditional freedom to reproduce their kind on the plea that this was the only alternative to starvation; for this sacrifice would be demanded of them at a time when the gulf between their own pauper standard of living and the industrial peoples' relatively lavish standard would have come to be greater than it had ever been before.

A progressive widening of this gulf was, in truth, one of the consequences that must be expected to follow from the course of events that we have been anticipating, if we are right in forecasting that, at the time when global food production would be reaching its ceiling, the peasantry would still be expending most of its additional supply of food on adding to the head of its population, and the industrialized peoples be expending most of their additional supply of commodities on raising a slowly increasing or even stationary population's standard of living. Considering that, by the time of writing, most of the industrialized peoples had already either reached or come within sight of reaching a new equilibrium in the movement of their population through the offsetting of an antecedent decrease in the death-rate by an eventual countervailing decrease in the birth-rate, it seemed likely that, among these peoples, this tendency would continue;[1] and, considering further that their standard of living had risen notably even during the period when their populations

---

[1] Professor William McNeill comments: 'The stabilization of population in the industrialized countries is surely less certain now, since the Second World War, than this passage implies.'

had been increasing very rapidly in consequence of a decrease in the
death-rate which at that time had not yet been offset by a countervailing
diminution in the number of births, it seemed likely that these peoples'
standard of living would rise still more steeply after their populations'
net rate of growth had fallen off (assuming that this new lower rate would
be, and would continue to be, not far from the economic optimum in the
sense of being the rate that in the current social and technological circumstances would best work together with the contemporary local rate
of increase in production to achieve the maximum of material prosperity).

In this situation in an *Oikoumenê* that would have been unified on the
psychological and moral planes while on the economic plane the local contrasts between diverse standards of living would have been accentuated,
the Peasantry would not see why, before they themselves were called
upon to renounce what, for them, was the most sacred and precious of all
human rights, an affluent minority of Mankind should not be called upon
to part with a larger quota of their provocative superfluity in order to
save an indigent majority from the stark choice between birth-control
and starvation; and this demand, which the Peasantry would present
with all the vehemence of a simple-minded good faith, would strike the
relatively comfortable and sophisticated Western minority as being even
more outrageously unreasonable than it was outrageously unjust.

What effrontery to demand that a Western élite which owed its enviable prosperity to its own ability, exertions, foresight, and self-control
should be penalized in order to pay for the inevitable nemesis of the
Peasantry's improvident incontinence! And what naïveté to imagine
that, even if the Western peoples could be cajoled or coerced into allowing their own standard of living—'the system of arts and laws and manners which so advantageously' distinguished them 'above the rest of
Mankind'[1]—to be reduced to the starveling level on which the Peasantry
had elected to remain, this sacrifice would extricate the Peasantry from
a plight for which they had only themselves to blame! A distribution of
the Western peoples' margin of material resources among the wilfully
indigent mass of Mankind would obtain for the Peasantry no more, at the
most, than a momentary postponement of an inevitable crisis, and it
would produce this futile result, not merely at the cost of depriving the
Western peoples of the fair reward for arduous good conduct, but also at
the cost of depriving Mankind at large, including the peasant majority,
of the possibilities of 'general happiness'[2] with which (so a Western
mind was apt to assume) the Western way of life, and this way alone, was
pregnant. If the peasants' way were to be allowed to prevail to the
Western peoples' undoing, this would in fact be a holocaust of the
rational hopes of Mankind on the altar of sentimentality. Surely this was
a case in which an enlightened altruism demanded of the Western peoples
that they should have the moral courage to insist on following the dictates
of an enlightened self-interest!

If and when this controversy broke out, it seemed likely to be carried

[1] Gibbon, E.: 'General Observations on the Fall of the Roman Empire in the West',
in *The History of the Decline and Fall of the Roman Empire*, at the end of chap. xxxviii.
[2] Gibbon, ibid.

from the planes of Economics and Politics on to the plane of Religion and this on several accounts. In the first place the Peasantry's current obstinate persistence in continuing to breed up to the limits of its food-supply was the social effect of a religious cause which could not be modified without a change in the Peasantry's religious attitude and outlook. The religious sanction that was now making the Peasantry's breeding habits so resistant to the arguments of a Western rationalism might not have been irrational in its origin, if we may hazard the conjecture that it had originated in a primitive state of society in which a household had been the optimum social and economic unit of agricultural production, and in which the perpetuation of each family had therefore been the key to keeping this Primitive Society in being. The epiphany of a latter-day Western industrial civilization was the new factor in Mankind's situation that had cut the rational roots of the Peasantry's by now traditional cult of *lares et penates*; for a Mechanized Technology had done away with the social and economic environment in which a worship of family continuity had made social and economic sense.

The persistence of the cult when there was no sense left in it was a consequence of the relative slowness of the Psyche's fastest pace on the subconscious level by comparison with the pace of the Intellect and Will, and it was to be apprehended that the Peasantry might cling to its ancestral deification of family continuity, at the ever more imminent risk of driving Humanity's ship on to Malthus's well and truly charted rock, unless and until the Peasantry's religion could be reoriented from an agrarian to an industrial *qiblah*. Now that the Industrial Revolution, through its 'annihilation of distance', had made one single family out of the whole of Mankind, the welfare and survival of the Human Race, instead of just the welfare and continuity of one household without regard for the rest of Mankind, had become the proper social objective of the religious commandment 'that he who loveth God love his brother also';[1] for a latter-day metamorphosis of the *Oikoumenê* through the progress of Technology had vindicated the truth of Saint Paul's proclamation to the Athenians that God had 'made of one blood all nations of men for to dwell on all the face of the Earth, and' had 'determined the times before appointed';[2] and the advent of this long-since heralded oecumenical dispensation would call for a spiritual revolution as radical as the forgotten spiritual revolution that must have accompanied the creation of neolithic husbandmen out of palaeolithic hunters, fishermen, and food-gatherers.

Without this fresh religious revolution in the souls of the Peasantry, it was hard to see how the World's otherwise inexorable Malthusian problem was to be solved; but the Peasantry was not the only party to the situation that would have to achieve a change of heart if Mankind was to find a happy issue out of an impending affliction; for, if it was true—as experience had shown it to be true—'that Man doth not live by bread only',[3] then a self-complacently prosperous Western minority of Man-

[1] 1 John iv. 21.
[2] Acts xvii. 26.
[3] Deut. viii. 3, quoted in Matt. iv. 4 and in Luke iv. 4.

kind still had something to learn, on its side, from the unworldly vein[1] in the êthos of a Peasantry which, in preference to hoarding the bread that it wrung from the ground in sorrow and in the sweat of its face,[2] had shared this hard-earned nutriment with an ever-increasing progeny in childlike obedience to Elohim's commandment to be fruitful and multiply and replenish the Earth and subdue it.[3] This traditional religious duty, which had been laid upon the peasantry at the moment when they were reclaiming their first tiny fields from an apparently boundless wilderness, might become a bane instead of a blessing for Mankind in an age that had seen the *Oikoumenê*'s last reserves of cultivable land brought under the plough in the Americas, Australia, Qāzāqstan, and Manchuria; but, inasmuch as this was also the age that had witnessed the rise of an acquisitive Western industrial civilization, it was no time for despising and rejecting the Peasantry's traditional virtue of subordinating the quest for material well-being to the pursuit of a non-material objective; for, in making nonsense of the Peasantry's ancestral worship of the Family, the Industrial Revolution had not discredited the abiding truth that Man is not merely a consumer but is also a soul, and that the Soul lives 'by every word that proceedeth out of the mouth of God'.[4] 'For what is a man profited if he shall gain the whole World and lose his own soul? Or what shall a man give in exchange for his soul?'[5]

A latter-day Western Man had brought himself into danger of losing his soul through his concentration on a sensationally successful endeavour to increase his production of material commodities; and it was ironical that the society which had put itself in this spiritual jeopardy should have been one which, by comparison with a contemporary peasantry in Asia, Africa, and Indian America, had already been in enjoyment of a lavish standard of living at the time when it had embarked on its eighteenth-century agricultural and industrial revolutions. The insatiability of the Westerners' acquisitiveness laid them open to a Western philosopher's indictment.

'The Indian scale of values has never been at all like ours. On the whole it is true to say that in India the love of God has always been put above the love of material things. India is a civilisation based on Religion, while ours is a civilisation based on wealth.'[6]

If an industrialized Western Society was to find salvation in spite of itself, it would find it in virtue of having all the time unconsciously been

---

[1] This unworldly vein was, of course, only one element in the êthos of a Peasantry that was saddled with as heavy a load of Original Sin as a contemporary Industrial Proletariat with whom it had in common a uniform Human Nature. The peasant êthos, like the urban êthos, had its selfish, exploitative, and materialistic side; and there were peasantries—for example, in the Flemish and French provinces of a Western World— in whose spiritual 'make-up' these unattractive characteristics were not perceptibly mitigated by the touch of archaic piety with which they were still apt to be combined in the character of the peasantries in the non-Western societies. A sentimentally idealized portrait of a non-Western peasantry, when painted with a Western brush, might be suspect of being a subjective expression of the painter's dissatisfaction with the shortcomings of his own society rather than an objective reproduction of the observed lineaments of the picture's professed subject. [2] Gen. iii. 17–19.
[3] Gen. i. 28. Cp. Gen. ix. 1 and 7. [4] Matt. iv. 4. Cp. Luke iv. 4. [5] Matt. xvi. 26.
[6] Stace, W. T.: *What are Our Values?* (Lincoln, Nebraska 1950, University of Nebraska Press), p. 54.

working not solely for its own material profit, but also for the benefit of a majority of its fellow men who were still living at the Peasantry's starveling level. Industrialism was a Western gift to Mankind at large which might be not the less beneficent for having been unintended; and the best hope for Mankind lay in a spiritually fruitful marriage of the Western engineer's insight with the Asian husbandman's. The peasant had to learn from the engineer that, in Human Life on Earth, a minimum of economic well-being was the necessary material condition (*Graecè χορηγία*) for spiritual achievement, while the engineer had to learn—or re-learn—from the peasant that the enterprise of increasing Man's command over Non-Human Nature had no value except as a means towards some end beyond itself, even if the particular end that had been the Peasantry's traditional objective were now an anachronism in the new world that the engineer had conjured into existence.

If these were the new religious issues that a future oecumenical Malthusian crisis might be expected to raise, it was also to be foreseen that this crisis would present a challenge to the old religious establishments, since the Peasantry's primitive worship of family continuity was part of the flotsam which the higher religions had picked up and swept along in their flood waters when they had come down upon Mankind in spate.[1] Even a Buddhism whose original, authentic, and essential mission had been to reveal to suffering human beings a way of escape from the sorrowful wheel of sensuous existence had not succeeded in keeping clear of an older cult of procreation which was its antithesis; and, if Siddhārtha Gautama's philosophy had thus been constrained to come to terms with the husbandman's religion, it was not surprising that Confucianism, Christianity, and Hinduism should have been captivated by it.

In these divers higher religions and philosophies the influence of the cult of procreation could be detected in different degrees. In the Roman Catholic variety of Western Christianity this influence had not penetrated so deep as to impose upon the ecclesiastical subjects of the Catholic Church the positive pre-Christian commandment to be fruitful and multiply; the influence of the primitive cult on the current Catholic Christian code of morals could be detected only in a ban upon artificial methods of birth-control that had been invented in the Western World in the twentieth century of the Christian Era; and a prohibition that could be criticized as an irrational concession to Conservatism could also be defended on its merits as a courageous stand against a morally undesirable sexual practice. But the pertinent fact for the purposes of an inquiry into the prospects of the Western Civilization was that, in all the higher religions alike, the cult of procreation had won a footing that was sufficiently strong to threaten—or promise—to bring a revolutionary public policy into collision with established religious traditions if the time were to come when the pressure of the World's population upon the World's food supply would compel an oecumenical public authority to grapple with the formidable task of trying to regulate the movement of the World's population.

In this not improbable event, what would the old religious estab-

[1] See VII. vii. 455.

lishments' reactions be? The still older cult of procreation that had ensconced itself among the higher religions' traditions would presumably impel the ecclesiastical authorities of the day to champion the peasant's cherished freedom to reproduce his kind; but how would they apply their traditional teaching in an unprecedented situation? In a world whose population would be pressing upon its food supply because this world would have been liberated at long last from the inveterate evils of War, Pestilence, and Famine,[1] the churches would assuredly recoil from even considering the diabolical proposal that, in order to make room in a teeming world for the Peasantry to go on breeding without restriction, one and all of those three dire scourges should be let loose again upon Mankind. The nemesis for opening Aeolus's windbag that had overtaken Odysseus' insubordinate crew had been grievous even when the fatal act had been committed in the heat of passion by mutineers who had been blind to the consequences of what they were doing.[2] To sow the storm in cold blood, with the deliberate intention of reaping the whirlwind, would be a crime that no responsible ecclesiastical authorities would be likely to contemplate.

It seemed even more unlikely that the churches would countenance any proposal to regulate the movement of population by resorting on the grand scale to the infamous neo-pagan 'scientific' method—once practised by German National Socialists—of forcibly sterilizing, as a matter of routine, all persons who happened to be so unfortunate as to fall within categories condemned by the fiat of the public authorities; and, if these two fantastically wicked alternatives may be left out of consideration in any sober forecast of the churches' future policy on this formidable question, we must imagine the issue being narrowed down, in ecclesiastical counsels, to a choice between divers voluntary means of controlling the number of births. Could the sexual continence that had hitherto been the rare achievement of religious celibates be required of *l'homme moyen sensuel* in the marital state? And, if this degree of self-discipline could not be expected of Human Nature in a non-monastic social and spiritual environment, what was to be Religion's ultimate attitude towards artificial methods of voluntary birth-control? Was it to continue to set its face against them? And, if it did still hold to the churches' twentieth-century view, was it to regard this as a precept which the individual soul ought to be free to follow or reject according to the dictates of its own conscience? Or were the churches to try to enlist the support of a coercive secular arm by calling upon the public authorities to keep on the statute book the legislation that had made the advertisement and sale of artificial contraceptives illegal?

At the time of writing, when this issue had not yet come to a head in a society that was then still heavily engaged in wrestling with the rampant social evils of Class-Conflict and War, it was not yet possible to anticipate the decisions that a still unborn generation would be likely to take in a situation that at the time of writing was still merely hypothetical. It was, however, already possible to foresee that the debate, whatever its outcome, would be conducted on the religious plane, since it was evi-

---

[1] See 2 Sam. xxiv. 13.   [2] *Odyssey*, Book X, ll. 20–79.

dent that this issue raised the religious question of the ultimate significance and purpose of Human Life on Earth.

(V) PROBABLE EMPLOYMENTS IN A FUTURE OECUMENICAL SOCIETY

(a) 'A COMMONWEALTH OF SWINE'

If we could imagine a future Oecumenical Society in which Mankind
had first rid itself of Civilization's congenital maladies, War and Class-
Conflict, and had then followed up this success by going on to solve a
Malthusian problem which the establishment of a world order would
have brought to a head, we might surmise that Mankind's next problem
after that would be the future role of Leisure in a mechanized society's
life.

Leisure had already played a part of capital importance in human
history; for, if Necessity had been the mother of Civilization, Leisure
had been its nurse. One of the distinctive features of Civilization had
been the astonishing rapidity of the pace at which this parvenu way of
life had developed its potentialities during the five or six thousand years
of its currency up to date by comparison with the tortoise-like tempo
of the primitive way of life which Mankind had been following for
hundreds of thousands of years before the earliest civilizations had made
their epiphany; and this unprecedented impetus had been imparted to
the civilizations by an able, purposeful, and virtuous minority of a
privileged minority whose privilege had been the enjoyment of leisure.
All the unique achievements of men and women in the realm of Art and
all the cumulative achievements of Man in the realm of Science and
Technology had been fruits of the profitably employed leisure of this
creative minority within a minority; but in a post-industrial Westernizing World it could no longer be taken for granted that the growth of
Civilization would continue to be fostered by the employment of
leisure for these creative purposes; for the Industrial Revolution had
upset—and this in several different ways—the previous equilibrium
between Leisure and Life.

The first and most momentous of these changes had been a psychological one. The mechanization of work in an industrialized society had
set up in the industrial worker's psyche a tension between his feelings
towards his work and his feelings towards his leisure to which neither
the peasant majority nor the privileged minority of the body social had
been subject in a pre-industrial age in which Man's rations of work and
leisure had not been dictated to Man by Man but had been given to
Man by Non-Human Nature.[1] In an agrarian society a cycle of the
seasons that had been the husbandman's calendar had consequently also
settled for a leisured minority the allocation of their time between holding court and going on the war-path or between sitting in parliament
and going shooting, fishing, and hunting; and the Peasantry and their
rulers alike had taken both Work and Leisure for granted as inevitably

[1] See p. 565, above.

alternating phases in a Yin-and-Yang rhythm beaten out by the perpetually recurring astronomical cycles of Day-and-Night and the Seasons. Each experience of either phase was both a relief from the last bout, and at the same time a prelude to the next bout, of an alternate phase that was psychologically complementary rather than antithetical to the phase that happened at the moment to be in course. But this pre-industrial interdependence and consequent parity between the psychological values of Work and Leisure had been deranged when the worker had been transformed from a husbandman whose time-table was set for him by Nature into a tender of machines with power-driven wheels that could go on turning in season and out of season; for the chronic industrial warfare which the worker had now found himself compelled to wage in order to prevent his new masters the machines from working him to death had instilled into him, as we have seen,[1] a negative, defensive, hostile feeling towards a toil that his peasant forebears had taken as a matter of course; and this new attitude towards Work had brought with it a new attitude towards Leisure; for, if Work was intrinsically evil, then Leisure must have an absolute value in itself.

Human Nature's reaction against the routine of the factory and the office had indeed gone so far as to make the value of freedom from an excessive pressure of work count for more than the value of the remuneration that the manual or clerical worker could earn by working at full stretch; and this order of preferences, which in A.D. 1949 had been the conscious motive of the Wall Street typists' refusal to come to work on Saturdays,[2] had been implicit from the outset in the restrictive practices that Trade Unionism had worked out for itself; for these were methods of purchasing relief from the pressure of work by the sacrifice of potential earnings. This rating of leisure—at least in the negative form of an exemption from an excessive pressure of mechanized work— at a higher value than money-making was a preference which, in the first chapter of post-industrial Western history, had been a distinguishing mark of the industrial and clerical workers and a prime cause of dispute between them and their employers; and this attitude had begun to communicate itself from the working class to a hitherto pre-industrial-minded middle class in a subsequent chapter in which the working class's more and more effectively insistent demand for social justice was being met by a more and more drastic redistribution of purchasing power through the differentially graded taxation of middle-class incomes. By the sixth decade of the twentieth century of the Christian Era the Western middle class had begun to follow the working class's example by opting for leisure in preference to profits at a level of income—and this level was progressively being lowered—at which the greater part of any additional earnings would be taken from the nominal recipient by the tax-collector.

At the same time the so far unchecked advance of Technology at a constantly accelerating pace was playing a sardonic practical joke on its human victims; for, while the ceaseless turning of the never tiring wheels was threatening to work them to death, it was simultaneously

[1] On pp. 563–9, above.   [2] See p. 570, above.

threatening, in consequence, to throw them into technological unemployment, without ever allowing them to make up their minds which of these two contradictory scourges of Industrialism was the greater menace to human welfare and happiness. The industrial workers had no sooner reacted against the pressure of mechanization by insisting upon their right to leisure than their inhuman tyrant and tormentor Technology began to drive them into insisting upon their right to work by taking them at their word and forcing leisure upon them; and, although the trade-union practices that had been devised for putting a brake upon the killing 'drive' of mechanized industrial work also served the workers' further purpose of spinning out the residue of the employment that was now being snatched out of human hands by progressive improvements in the machinery that these hands were tending, this rear-guard action of Trade Unionism in a fight to make an inexorably dwindling amount of work still go round was manifestly a losing battle.

Technology and Trade Unionism, between them, were thus generating an abundance of Leisure that was unprecedented; and the manifest irresistibility of this tendency was making it possible to cast the occupational horoscope of a future Oecumenical Society that would have rid itself of War and Class-Conflict and have found some acceptable way of regulating the movement of population. In this Earthly Paradise Regained, a régime of full employment would also be a régime in which the ration of work that could be doled out to each individual would occupy so small a fraction of his day that he would have almost as much leisure on his hands as if he had been a member of the privileged minority in some antediluvian agrarian society. In such circumstances the use made of Leisure would evidently be even more important than it had been in a pre-industrial chapter of human history in which *Homo Faber* had still been such a tiro in his Technology that the number of man-hours which he had yet been able to liberate for Leisure had been minute by comparison with the number that he had still been compelled to devote to Work.

If there was a prospect of such revolutionary changes as these in the amount of the leisure acquired by, or thrust upon, Man, as well as in Man's attitude toward Leisure in its relation to Work, what effects on Human Life might this revolution be expected to have?

In an industrialized Western Society in which an excessive acquisitiveness had been the besetting sin of its middle-class moving spirits, there was one negative effect that was manifestly good in itself as far as it went. By the time when the middle class, as well as the working class, had begun to value Leisure more highly than earnings, it was beginning to look as if the mechanism of the Industrial System of economic production included a providential automatic brake that might perhaps avail to save *Homo Faber Mechanicus* from his demonic self. In making the Industrial Revolution, Western Man's acquisitive-mindedness had perhaps unintentionally been working out a cure for itself by first making work odious and then making this now already odious work also unremunerative. If a shark-like Western appetite for acquisition was thus having its edge taken off by the pressure and the insipidity of routine-work in a mechanized society and by the ruthless efficiency of the tax-collector in a welfare state in reaping where he had not sown and gathering where he had not strawed,[1] this was surely a blessing in disguise for a *Homo Occidentalis* whose characteristic temptation had been to sell his soul if that was the market price of worldly prosperity. A society in which a minority had been allowed and encouraged to enrich themselves without restriction was surely a less estimable society than one in which a more equitable distribution of wealth was being secured at a cost of restricting the opportunities for enrichment and perhaps thereby diminishing, through the diminution of incentives to earn, the aggregate amount of the wealth that was now being less inequitably distributed.[2]

So far, so good; yet a mid-twentieth-century observer could not hail the reluctant transfer of psychic energy from money-making to the enjoyment of leisure as an unquestionable blessing, even for a Western Man whose nineteenth-century god had been Mammon, without taking into account the use to which the frustrated Mammon-worshipper was going to put the leisure for which he was now opting in preference to making money for the tax-collector to redistribute. This question had been raised in a notable address delivered, some twenty years before the time of going to press, by a philosophic spokesman of those magician-engineers whose cornucopia had 'been shaken over all the Earth, scattering everywhere an endowment of previously unpossessed and unimagined capacities and powers'.[3] Speaking at York on the 31st August, 1932, to the British Association for the Advancement of Science, their president, Sir Alfred Ewing, had ended on the following note:

'We must admit that there is a sinister side even to the peaceful activities of those who in good faith and with the best intentions make it their business to adapt the resources of Nature to the use and convenience of Man. Where shall we look for a remedy? I cannot tell. Some may envisage a distant utopia in which there will be perfect adjustment of labour and the fruits of labour, a fair spreading of employment and of wages and of all the commodities that machines produce. Even so the question will remain. How is Man to spend the leisure he has won by handing over nearly all his burden to an untiring mechanical slave? Dare he hope for such spiritual betterment as will qualify him to use it well? God grant [that] he may strive for that and attain it. It is only by seeking [that] he will find. I cannot think that Man is destined to atrophy and cease through cultivating what, after all, is one of his most God-like faculties—the creative ingenuity of the engineer.'

The pertinence of Sir Alfred Ewing's question about Mankind's spiritual prospects in a world that was being mechanized by a Western technique was brought home to a student of the Hellenic Classics by the reminiscence of a passage in a treatise on *Sublimity in Style* which had been written during the reprieve that a disintegrating Hellenic Society had won for itself through an Augustan rally of its retreating forces.[4]

---

[1] Matt. xxv. 24 and 26; Luke xix. 21-22.
[2] This point is made by W. T. Stace in *What are our Values?* (Lincoln, Nebraska 1950, University of Nebraska Press), p. 58.   [3] Quoted already in III. iii. 211.
[4] Down to the time of writing, Western scholars had been unable to determine whether this work had been written in the third century of the Christian Era or in the first.

The Hellenic Civilization had been distinguished by its relative indifference to a quest for economic gain that had become the master passion of the Western Civilization in the first chapter of its Industrial Age; and therefore, if, even in the Hellenic World, an observer living in an age of social recovery had been struck and distressed by the spectacle of the spiritual impoverishment of his generation through their passion for material enrichment, the same distressing effect might be expected, *a fortiori*, to follow from the working of the same sinister cause in a demonically acquisitive post-Modern Western Society.

In the last extant chapter of *Sublimity in Style* the author professes to be reporting a recent conversation between himself and a philosopher in which they had been disputing about the causes to which this contemporary spiritual decadence was to be ascribed. The philosopher argues, like Tacitus in his *Dialogus de Oratoribus*,[1] that the literary decadence in which this spiritual decadence is reflected can be adequately explained as being a consequence of the loss of political liberty; but this political explanation is rejected by the author, who sees in it merely an example of Human Nature's notorious proneness to seek an alibi for itself by blaming external circumstances. In his alternative explanation of the spiritual decadence of his day the author puts his finger on the demoralizing effect of an oecumenical peace. World Peace demoralizes its beneficiaries by releasing their energies for expenditure on 'total war' (ἀπεριόριστος πόλεμος) in the non-military fields of money-making and pleasure-seeking, and, in the author's view, as he expounds it, these are the spiritual maladies that have reduced this generation's spiritual stature. He raises the question whether the loss of political liberty may not be a blessing in disguise for a generation that has sunk to so low a spiritual level; for, if characters like these were given a free hand, an Ishmaelitish acquisitiveness would bring down a deluge of evils upon the *Oikoumenê*.

'One of the cancers (δαπανῶν) of the spiritual life in souls born into the present generation is the low spiritual tension (ῥαθυμίαν) in which all but a few chosen spirits among us pass their days. In our work and in our recreation alike our only objective is popularity and enjoyment. We feel no concern to win the true spiritual treasure that is to be found in putting one's heart into what one is doing and in winning a recognition that is truly worth having.'

These findings of an Hellenic literary critic at some date during the first spell of a Roman Peace were endorsed, at the dawn of the Modern Age of Western history, by one of the foremost pioneers of a distinctively Western scientific spirit. The following passage is to be found in *The Advancement of Learning*,[2] which was published by Francis Bacon in A.D. 1605.

'. . . For as it has been well observed, that the arts which flourish in times while virtue is in growth, are military; and while virtue is in state, are liberal; and while virtue is in declination, are voluptuary: so I doubt that this age of the World is somewhat upon the descent of the wheel. With

---

[1] Cited in V. vi. 80–81.   [2] Book II, chap. x, § 13.

arts voluptuary I couple practices joculary; for the deceiving of the senses is one of the pleasures of the senses.'

If the writer of these prescient words could have revisited the Western World three and a half centuries after the date at which he had written them, he might have been surprised to observe how accurately he had gauged the trend of the spiritual curve in which Western souls had begun to descend from Heroism towards Frivolity. Mid-way through the twentieth century of the Christian Era it was notorious—and significant—that the United States, where the Western industrial working class had come nearer than it had come in any European country towards being assimilated to the middle class in its material standard of living and in its opportunities for material advancement, was also the Western country in which, on the cultural, in contrast to the economic, plane, the middle class, for its part, had gone farthest down the *descensus Averni* which Bacon had foreboded. Yet the same middle class was slipping down the same steep place[1] in other Western countries likewise; and unwarily envious West European spectators of the use to which 'the common man' in the United States was putting his relatively ample margin of wealth and leisure at this date were apt to betray their own hankering after the frivolity that they were professedly castigating in an American whipping-boy when they maliciously described the American scene as a fun-fair patronized by grown-up children whose main interest in life was to play with mechanical toys. This caricature was perhaps not inaccurate as far as it went; for joy-riding could not be more felicitously described than as a 'practice joculary', nor television more felicitously than as an 'art voluptuary' designed to please the senses by deceiving them.[2] Yet any contemporary American critic of American *mores* could silence the carping West European visitor with a crushing 'De te fabula narratur';[3] for the reality that was being caricatured in some of the

[1] Matt. viii. 32; Mark v. 13; Luke viii. 33.
[2] On the evening of the day on which he had written this sentence in the morning, the writer received a timely intimation that this might not be the last word that would have to be said about the cultural effects of the wholesale installation of television in the United States. That same evening he heard a shrewd American observer of the American political scene tell an English audience that, if they wished to understand the current movement of American feeling on international affairs, they must not ignore the effect of the rapid current spread of the network of an American television service. Television, he explained, had now made it possible for the American public to see the countenances and gestures, as well as to hear the voices, of the delegates to the Council and the Assembly of the United Nations Organization at Lake Success; every owner of a television set who tuned in to the sessions of these international bodies received a vivid impression of the contrast in manners, and in the inner êthos that these outward manners betrayed, between the Russian delegates and their Western colleagues; and this impression was making a potent effect on American public opinion because the proceedings at Lake Success had effectively caught and held the interest of American 'viewers'. When a meeting at Lake Success came on, 'viewers' would tune in to it, even if this meant their having to break away from looking at a classic boxing-match or at a popular vaudeville.
This piece of information aptly illustrated two points that had to be taken into account in any attempt to estimate the Western Civilization's prospects. In the first place it showed that Television was already beginning to play its part in a political unification of the *Oikoumenê* through a technological 'annihilation of distance' that has been noticed in XII. D (ii) (*b*), above. In the second place it showed that a new instrument, which in the first flush of its novelty had been treated as a toy, might quickly be turned to account for serving a more serious purpose.
[3] Horace: *Satires*, Book I, Satire 1, ll. 69–70.

extravagances of American life was a contemporary Western *Weltanschauung* that was shared with North America by Western Europe. The United States at this time was, in fact, performing the salutary service of an automatic confessional for the Western World at large. She was serving as a convex mirror in which any Western observer, from either side of the Atlantic, could become acquainted with some of his own spiritual deformities by beholding them here revealingly magnified.

It was, in truth, no mere accidental coincidence that the current symptoms of cultural proletarianization in the life of a Western middle class in the United States should have been contemporaneous with the raising, in the same country, of a Western industrial working class's material standard of life to what was virtually a middle-class level. One of the elements in a higher material standard of living was, as we have seen, a larger ration of leisure. This increase of leisure was simultaneously being bestowed upon the industrial working class in Western Europe as one consequence of a radical revision of rates of wages and hours of work; and it was only to be expected that the progress towards social justice that was thus now being made in the Western World as a whole, along a West European as well as a North American line of approach, should have the, at first sight, paradoxical immediate effect of precipitating a fall in the mean level of Western culture.

This undesirable effect was to be expected in the first instance, not because Leisure was now still being bestowed, as it had always been, without regard to the recipient's capacity or incapacity for making use of it, but because it had also always taken even the choicest spirits time to learn how to make good use of any new gift. The pearls that were now being redistributed among a majority instead of remaining the monopoly of a minority were not being taken away from a minority consisting exclusively of connoisseurs in order to be cast before a majority consisting exclusively of swine who knew no better than to trample these precious offerings under their feet.[1] The misuse of Leisure by a majority of its possessors was, notoriously, no new thing. In the days when Leisure had been a monopoly of a minority, a majority of that minority had always misused it, as we have already observed.[2] Only a minority of that minority had made the creative use of Leisure that had been the mainspring of Civilization. The reason why, nevertheless, a redistribution of Leisure was likely to result in a lowering of the level of culture was that even the creative minority of a leisured minority had needed time to mature. The inestimably precious spiritual treasures that this minority had eventually created had been ripe fruits of self-education and self-discipline,[3] and these had been the cumulative spiritual achievement of a series of consecutive generations. This was the secret of cultural creativity; and it was something that could not be transmitted by print-

---

[1] Matt. vii. 6.   [2] On p. 604, above.

[3] The importance of the part that had been played by self-discipline in the creation of a Western Christian culture was indicated in the history of the word 'clerk', which, before its meaning had been depreciated to signify a worker who worked in an office and not in a factory, had once signified a possessor and trustee of culture, and had stood for this because, in Western Christendom, the original possessors and trustees of culture had been the clergy and, among them, above all, a disciplined minority that was enrolled in the monastic orders.

ing and distributing a sheet of directions for use. It was a secret that all new recipients of the gift of Leisure had to discover for themselves; and it could not be discovered in a day.

If this was the historic and intrinsic relation between Leisure and Culture, how were the Western Civilization's prospects likely to be affected by a current sacrifice of Culture on the altar of Social Justice? At a crisis in its history the Western Society was clipping the wings of a creative minority of a leisured minority and was lavishing leisure on a majority that had not yet had time to grow a new creative core. The immediate cultural effect of this equitable social revolution was as plain as it was deplorable.

'Over against the ever more amazing inventions of Science we see a kind of childishness creeping over our thoughts, our modes of expression, our art, our music, our morals. We talk in words from a very limited vocabulary, we produce pictures and statues of a more than ungainly "neo-primitiveness", we croon nigger songs while we push one another round a room in dances that need no brain, no zest, and no vitality for their successful performance. Many of our buildings have as their chief merits the fact that they can be rushed up quickly and finished within a few weeks. We tear over the Earth's surface along roads of brick-box straightness, past rows of houses of brick-box exactitude and hideousness, in order to get somewhere, it does not much matter where, in record time. Finally, the novels we read, apparently with pleasure, for there are many of them, show men and women as ill-conducted children whose one concern is that which they share with the animal world.

'There is to me something grim and horrible in an essentially mature civilisation playing at savage immaturity when it knows better. We cannot go back to the beginning of things any more than a mature mind can change into that of a child.'[1]

These words spoken in A.D. 1933 by the headmistress of a distinguished school in London made a powerful impression at the time upon the writer of this Study; for, in the village in the North Riding of Yorkshire where he was reading the report in the press, he had neighbours who, at that moment, were giving hospitality to relatives of theirs who had been thrown out of work in Leeds by an 'economic blizzard' that was then sweeping over the face of an Industrialized World, and he had been hearing these countryfolk describe the impressions that their town-bred cousins had been making on them. The description had been forcible and vivid; for the good-natured hosts had been amazed and horrified by their progressive discovery of their unfortunate guests' extraordinary manners and customs.

'Why, they don't know how to cook and they don't know how to sew and they don't know how to cure a ham; and then, in the evenings, they can't even sit at home and talk, because they have nothing in their heads to talk about. Their only notion of enjoying themselves is to take the bus to Malton and kill time at an "entertainment"—"the pictures" or something of the kind.'

[1] Miss E. Strudwick, the Headmistress of St. Paul's Girls' School, Hammersmith, London, England, in a presidential address delivered on the 17th June, 1933, at Liverpool, at a Conference of the British Association of Head Mistresses. The text quoted here has been taken from the report in *The Manchester Guardian* of the 19th June, 1933.

In taking their town-bred guests' inability to entertain themselves as the crowning and damning evidence of their urban neobarbarism, these country cousins were touching the heart of a spiritual malady from which all classes of a contemporary industrialized society were suffering in all provinces of a mechanically standardized *Oikoumenê*. The malevolent sorceress Technology had inveigled her victims into putting themselves in her power by selling them new lamps for old. She had bribed them with 'the pictures' and 'the wireless' into selling her their souls; and the outcome of this ruinous cultural 'new deal' was the spiritual wilderness which Plato had dismissed as a 'Commonwealth of Swine'[1] and Aldous Huxley had satirized as a 'Brave New World'.

In a Westernizing World mid-way through the twentieth century of the Christian Era this Huxleian anti-utopia was a very present reality. The guests at Circe's banquet had soon found themselves penned in Circe's sty.[2] Their plight was plain beyond all dispute; the open question—and it was a vital one—was the length of their term of humiliating metamorphosis and irksome incarceration. In succumbing to the enchantment of a latter-day Western technology, had Mankind sentenced itself to languish in 'Brave New World' for the rest of its days on Earth? Or was there in the offing some still unenchanted Odysseus who, with Hermes' aid, might have it in his power to release his unfortunate comrades from duress and bring them back to their lost human shape? Was this sordid 'Commonwealth of Swine' the destiny that had been lying in wait for Mankind on a hitherto invisible ledge that had been the goal of human endeavours while Mankind had been striving to scale the climbers' pitch called 'Civilization'?[3] If so, the fate of any climber who succeeded in attaining his objective on this pitch would be still more cruel than the doom of his fellows who had been falling to meet their deaths on a lower ledge that had been their common point of departure on this latest human enterprise. To wallow for ages in a 'Commonwealth of Swine' as a reward for having achieved Civilization would be as ironical a fate as the last phase of the primitive human societies that had been lying torpid for ages as their reward for having raised themselves from a sub-human level. An aeon of quarantine in Circe's sty might be the price that Mankind was doomed to pay for the boon of getting rid of War and Class-Conflict.

Was this a fate to which the Human Race was likely to resign itself? Would Human Nature really be content to 'live happily ever after' in a 'Brave New World' in which the only change from the monotony of a life spent on a frivolous employment of Leisure would be a modicum of mechanical work performed under restrictive trade-union rules in an unenthusiastic civil-service spirit? Even if a majority in each successive generation could be dragooned, drugged, hypnotized, or cajoled into living and dying like 'the beasts that perish',[4] the stewards of a 'Commonwealth of Swine' would still have to reckon with a creative minority that had been the salt of the Earth[5] in a pre-Porcine Age of human

---

[1] Plato: *Respublica*, 372 D, cited in II. i. 193, n. 1; in II. ii. 23, n. 2; and on p. 523, above.
[2] See *Odyssey* X, ll. 233–40, quoted in II. ii. 23.   [3] See II. i. 192–4.
[4] Ps. xlix. 12 and 20.   [5] Matt. v. 13. Cp. Mark ix. 50 and Luke xiv. 34–35.

history. The stewards would have to be past-masters in the technique of eugenics if they were to succeed in breeding out of Human Nature this angelically or demonically dynamic spiritual strain; and such mastery would probably prove to be beyond their capacity, for it could hardly be achieved without enlisting the aid of a creative intellectual activity which would be anathema in official circles in Hyampolis. Yet, if the managers of 'Brave New World' could not contrive to prevent the dynamic strain in the Spirit of Man from continuing to incarnate itself in a diasporà of untamed and untamable men and women, the security of their dehumanized commonwealth would never be complete; for the fatal flaw in the mechanism of a 'Brave New World' was its failure to provide a safety-valve for a spirit that would endure torture to the death rather than obey 'Brave New World's' first commandment: 'Et surtout, pas trop de zèle!'[1]

The trouble that this spirit was likely to give to the ruling authorities in an oecumenical Hyampolis was foreshadowed in the history of the Roman Imperial Government's long losing battle with the Christian martyrs; for martyrdom was a response to the challenge of a régime that was keeping the peace at the price of taking the savour out of Human Life;[2] and the attractiveness of Christian martyrdom to zealous souls under a Roman Imperial dispensation was the more significant in view of the fact that, under a Roman Peace that was not literally world-wide, Christian martyrdom was not the only opportunity open to Roman citizens or subjects for putting all their heart and all their soul and all their strength and all their mind[3] into the service of a cause that was worthy of being served with a wholehearted devotion. An alternative career in which they could sacrifice themselves like men instead of leading the life of human swine was offered to Roman citizens and subjects in the military police that held the cordon of the Roman Empire's anti-barbarian frontiers; and the *esprit de corps* of this magnificent force required its members to live up to a standard of professional conduct, in the performance of their military duty,[4] which the Christian Church

---

[1] Attributed to Voltaire.

[2] The Roman Empire was, and was intended by its makers and masters to be, a 'Brave New World' inasmuch as its *raison d'être* was to prevent the recurrence of War and Class-Conflict at whatever cost in terms of repression of creativity. The Roman Imperial Government was suspicious of any move—even on a non-political plane—that might conceivably disturb the existing equilibrium. This apprehensive, defensive, repressive official attitude is illustrated in the story—*ben trovato, se non vero*—of the unfortunate subject of the Emperor Tiberius who, after succeeding in inventing a malleable kind of unbreakable glass, offered his invention to the Emperor in the hope of receiving a reward as a public benefactor. The Emperor's reaction was to give orders—after ascertaining that the secret of the process was, so far, known to no one beyond the inventor himself—that the new invention should be suppressed and the inventor be put to death as a dangerous character whose misguided activities were a threat to the stability of Society because his unbreakable glass, if ever put on the market, would bring about a catastrophic fall in the prices of the metals and would thereby precipitate an economic crisis. This story is told by Petronius Arbiter in his *Caena Trimalchionis*, chap. 51; by the Elder Pliny in his *Naturalis Historia*, Book XXXVI, chap. 26 (66), § 195; and in a garbled form by Dio Cassius in his *History of Rome*, Book LVII, chap. 21, *ad finem*. The emperor who is the villain of the story is anonymous ('Caesar') in Petronius's version, but the other two authorities both name Tiberius. The writer was directed to these sources by his sister Professor J. M. C. Toynbee.

[3] Luke x. 27. Cp. Matt. xxii. 37. These passages in the Gospels are reminiscences of Deut. vi. 5; x. 12; xxx. 6.

[4] Among the many well-known illustrations of the standard of conduct that was demanded and attained in the Imperial Roman Army, we may cite the gallantry of the

itself did not disdain to commend to its own members as a shining example.[1] A pagan cult of the Eagles that drew this tribute of admiration from Christian worshippers of God was the Roman Imperial régime's officially approved vent for spiritual energies that refused to live at low tension and insisted on exerting themselves to full capacity. Yet this politic provision of an outlet for a zeal that was an ineradicable and irrepressible element in Human Nature was proved inadequate by the epiphany of martyrs who insisted on laying down their lives, not in battle with barbarians in defence of the Hellenic World, but in defiance of Caesar himself for the glory of the One True God.

When a 'Brave New World' had thus bred martyrs with whom it could not cope in a Roman Empire where there was a military police to provide an alternative outlet for zeal, it seemed likely, *a fortiori*, to breed martyrs in a literally world-wide commonwealth in which no opportunities would be left for risking life and winning honour in the defence of Civilization against outer barbarians. In a twentieth-century *Oikoumenê* the vindication of spiritual freedom was the living generation's most urgent business, and the arena in which this spiritual battle would be lost or won would be a field of Leisure that in a fully mechanized world might come to be all but co-extensive with the field of Life itself.

(b) 'THE ARGONAUTS OF THE WESTERN PACIFIC'

What, in this field, was Hermes' sovereign antidote to Circe's nefarious magic? One negative answer to this question could be given without hesitation. The remedy for a frivolous misuse of an inordinately ample leisure could not lie in re-evoking the evil spirits of greed and lust for

Syrian soldier Sabinus, with his eleven comrades (see Josephus: *A History of the Romano-Jewish War*, Book VI, §§ 54–67), and of the Bithynian centurion Julianus (see Josephus, ibid., §§ 81–90), during the Roman siege of Jerusalem in A.D. 70.

Professor William McNeill comments: 'I wonder whether the Roman soldier's experience can bear comparison with the Christian's conversion? Regular professional soldiers of my acquaintance are men attracted by pay and relatively easy conditions of work, not dedicated souls. I am inclined to imagine the Roman soldier as something like [that], and his occasional heroism as a psychological reaction against his normal "soldiering on the job"—a break-through of the instinct of workmanship, if you like.'

A non-American observer of American life in A.D. 1952 might point to the United States Marine Corps as an arm of the United States armed forces of the day that was animated by the same spirit of self-dedication as the Roman professional army in the Imperial Age. Neither a United States marine nor a Roman legionary was required to play the hero all day and every day; and many a member of either force might live out his term of service without ever having his *moral* put to the test of a practical ordeal. The rareness of the occasions for heroism is of the essence of any professional military service; the crucial question is whether, if and when the occasion does come, the troops have it in them to rise to it; and in this respect the professed Christian in the interior of the Roman Empire was in the same situation as the professional soldier on its frontiers. A professor of the Christian faith might live and die without ever being called upon to make the hard choice between apostasy and martyrdom; and in his case, as in the soldier's, the crucial question was how he would behave if and when the choice between honour and life ever did present itself for him personally. On this showing, there does perhaps, after all, seem to be something in common between the Early Christian's and the contemporary Roman Soldier's situation, attitude of mind, and standard of conduct; and, whatever may be the judgement of Modern Western historians on this point, it is attested by testimonials extant in the surviving literature of the Early Christian Church that the Christians themselves felt the standard of conduct in the Roman Army of the day to be closely enough akin to Christian ideals to be taken by Christians as an inspiring example for themselves.

[1] See the instances cited from Adolf Harnack's *Militia Christi* in VI. vii. 338–44.

power which had possessed Man in Process of Civilization; for that cure would be worse than the disease. The rebellious prisoner of 'Brave New World' would be stultifying his own efforts and ideals if he sought to make his escape by casting himself down the precipice which he had just scaled at so great a cost. The only line of escape that would be worth pursuing would be one leading, not downward, but upward. What upward openings, then, were within the prisoner's sight and reach? If the most promising prelude to action is a recourse to the oracle of experience, the obvious first step for a hard beset twentieth-century *Homo Mechanicus* to take was to look into the experience of the primitive societies; for (strange though this might sound to twentieth-century Western ears) the spiritual problem of unemployment arising from a solution of the economic problem of scarcity had been encountered up to date, not by societies in process of civilization, but by primitive societies living on the margin of the *Oikoumenê*, where the pressure of the struggle for existence had always been at its lowest.[1] Primitive experience of a problem beyond Civilization's ken could be studied in the legend of the Lotus-Eaters[2] and in the fable of the Doasyoulikes[3] and in the true history of the 'Argonauts of the Western Pacific'.[4] Twentieth-century Melanesians had found a solution for the problem of total leisure by which their mythical counterparts had been worsted; and the experience and achievements of these primitive islanders were not without interest for their sophisticated Western contemporaries now that the same problem was overtaking these in their turn.

The Trobriand Islanders' first attempt to occupy an inordinately increasing leisure had failed to keep pace with the progressive aggravation of their problem.

[1] The Australian Blackfellows, for example, had proved to be at an advantage in this respect over the pioneers of Civilization who had eventually overtaken and all but exterminated them in their antipodean Ultima Thulê—as had once been discovered, to his surprise, by an airman who had fallen in with a vagrant food-gathering tribe of aborigines as a result of having had to make a forced landing at a remote spot in the interior of the Northern Territory. Wishing to give his unsophisticated hosts an overwhelming impression of his superiority in power and skill, the castaway took up his rifle, which had come down with him intact, and picked off one of the innumerable black swans that were riding on the waters of a lake on whose shore the wandering Blackfellows were encamped. He had duly demonstrated Civilization's power of taking life at long range, yet it was evident that the Blackfellows had not after all been impressed, and his chagrin and bewilderment must have been manifest on his countenance, for his considerate hosts lost no time in giving him a demonstration of the proper way to do the job. As soon as the rest of the swans, who had risen in flight from the water at the sound of the rifle-shot, had recovered from their alarm and had settled again, an aged Blackfellow daubed his hair with mud, crowned the daub with a bunch of waterplants, stuck a hollow reed into each of his nostrils, waded gently into the water, and disappeared under the surface. All that was now visible was a bunch of water plants, apparently drifting in the wind among the swans, with the ends of two broken reeds protruding from the water a few inches away. The swans were not alarmed, nor did the survivors take alarm when, one by one, some six or seven of their number softly and silently vanished under water and did not reappear. After a few seconds the old Blackfellow re-emerged from the lake bringing with him the six or seven swans whom he had caught and killed by seizing their legs, pulling them down, and drowning them. The Blackfellows' method of food-gathering was so crushingly superior to the rifleman's that, after all, it was no wonder that his rifle-shot had failed to hit its intended psychological mark. For this tribe, the problem of scarcity was non-existent so long as there was a mud-banked, reed-fringed, swan-covered lake in their universe.

[2] See *Odyssey*, Book IX, ll. 92–102, quoted in II. ii. 22–23.
[3] See II. ii. 25–31.
[4] See Malinowski, B.: *Argonauts of the Western Pacific* (London 1922, Routledge).

When the sensational productivity of a happy marriage between the yam and the local soil and climate had first plunged the human husbandmen into technological unemployment, they had tried to consume their redundant time and energy by devising ingenious non-economic refinements on their utilitarian agricultural operations.

'In gardening . . . the natives produce much more than they actually require, and in any average year they harvest perhaps twice as much as they can eat. . . . They produce this surplus in a manner which entails much more work than is strictly necessary for obtaining the crops. Much time and labour is given up to aesthetic purposes, to making the gardens tidy, clean, cleared of all debris; to building fine solid fences; to providing specially strong and big yam-poles. All these things are to some extent required for the growth of the plant; but there can be no doubt that the natives push their conscientiousness far beyond the limit of the purely necessary. The non-utilitarian element in their garden work is still more clearly perceptible in the various tasks which they carry out entirely for the sake of ornamentation in connexion with magical ceremonies and in obedience to tribal usage. . . .

'All, or almost all, the fruits of his work, and certainly any surplus which he can achieve by extra effort, goes, not to the man himself, but to his relatives-in-law. . . . But, although he thus derives practically no personal benefit in the utilitarian sense from his harvest, the gardener receives much praise and renown from its size and quality, and that in a direct and circumstantial manner. For all the crops, after being harvested, are displayed for some time afterwards in the gardens, piled up in neat conical heaps under small shelters made of yam vine. . . .Their yam houses are built so that the quantity of the food can be gauged, and its quality ascertained, through the wide interstices between the beams. . . . The yams are so arranged that the best specimens come to the outside and are well visible. . . . They will boast that . . . half of the yams will rot away in the storehouses and be thrown on . . . the rubbish heap at the back of the houses to make room for the new harvest. Here . . . we meet the typical idea that the main aim of accumulating food is to keep it exhibited in the yam houses till it rots and then can be replaced by a new étalage.'[1]

Such ingenious methods as these for spinning out a stint of work had never been devised by any contemporary Western trade-unionist; but, in the Trobriand Islands, Adam's task was so fantastically productive that the islanders were hopelessly defeated in their efforts to lose their race against it. Do what they would, they could not make their agricultural work occupy more than half of their working time;[2] and at this critical point they gave proof of a power of imagination, amounting to genius, by finding a new occupation which did effectively consume all their surplus leisure, and which achieved this without leading them into mischief. The achievement was a remarkable one, considering that 'Satan finds some mischief still for idle hands to do',[3] and that the désœuvrés Trobriand Islanders would not have had far to look for a bad example. They could have found it in their neighbours the Dobuans; for, in Dobu Island, Nature had been as niggardly to Man as she had

---

[1] Malinowski, B.: *Argonauts of the Western Pacific* (London 1922, Routledge), pp. 58–59, 61, 168, and 169. [2] See ibid., p. 58.
[3] Watts, Isaac: *Divine Songs for Children*, xx: 'Against Idleness and Mischief'.

been bountiful in the Trobriand Islands; in Dobu, population pressed hard upon resources;[1] and 'from this island, in olden days, fierce and daring cannibal and head-hunting expeditions were periodically launched to the dread of the neighbouring tribes. . . . Districts . . . over a hundred miles away by sail never felt safe from the Dobuans.'[2] If the Trobriand Islanders had given ear to Satan's promptings, they might have found their solution for a problem of surplus leisure arising from a chronic excess of food production in a vicious Dobuan practice to which the Dobuans themselves had resorted as a remedy for the opposite evil of a chronic shortage in their home-grown food-supply. The Trobriand Islanders did follow the Dobuans' example in taking to long-distance voyages,[3] but not in making head-hunting and cannibalism the objects of their seafaring. They invented an alternative object, which was as engrossing as it was harmless, in the institution of the Kula.[4]

The Kula was a continual long-distance maritime exchange of objects which—like the garlands of greenstuff that had once been the prizes for victory in the four classic oecumenical sporting events in the Hellenic World—had an economic value that was derisory and a psychological value that was inestimable. The international exchange of these objects was conducted in a closed maritime circuit, round which articles of two kinds (necklaces of red shell and bracelets of white shell), and these two kinds only, were constantly travelling in opposite directions and being exchanged for one another *en route*.

'Every movement of the Kula articles, every detail of the transactions, is fixed and regulated by a set of traditional rules and conventions, and some acts of the Kula are accompanied by an elaborate magical ritual and public ceremonies.'[5]

This ceremonial exchange of economically worthless treasures in a perpetually recurrent cycle was an occupation on which the Trobriand Islanders could be sure of being able to spend the whole of their spare time, even if their agriculture were one day to attain a degree of technical efficiency at which the maximum time that it could take up would approximate to zero.

The Trobriand Islanders' invention of this invincible leisure-consuming institution was a moral as well as an imaginative triumph; for the Kula was so irresistibly attractive an employment for a Melanesian human nature that even the abominable Dobuans were drawn into the Kula ring; and, though these proselytes operated this borrowed institution in the peculiar spirit of their own repulsive culture,[6] their sharp practice in this ceremonial trade in non-economic commodities was at least a less objectionable offence against a Melanesian international code of good manners than their previous practice of sea-raiding to supply themselves with man-meat and human heads. The conversion of the

---

[1] Benedict, Ruth: *Patterns of Culture* (London 1934, Routledge), p. 130.
[2] Malinowski, op. cit., p. 39.
[3] The Dobuans seem to have been the pioneer 'Argonauts of the Western Pacific', to judge by the fact 'that their language is spoken as a *lingua franca* all over the d'Entre-castreaux Archipelago, in the Amphletts, and as far north as the Trobriands' (ibid., pp. 39–40).   [4] See ibid., *passim*, but especially pp. 81–84.
[5] Ibid., p. 81.   [6] See Benedict, op. cit., pp. 154–9.

Dobuans from head-hunting to the Kula was a measure of the Trobriand Islanders' success in finding a satisfying alternative activity to the curse of hard labour—which had proved itself, by the awkwardness of the vacuum that it left when it was lifted, to have been a blessing in disguise to the progeny of a sinful Adam.

The Kula was a virtuoso's solution for a problem that the Trobriand Islanders' amateurish British contemporaries were seeking to solve by eating city dinners, dancing attendance on the hunting, fishing, shooting, and social seasons, and looking on at horse and dog races and cricket and football matches; but the justness of this comparison was a reminder that the Kula and its contemporary Western counterparts were not solutions that could satisfy the Soul's spiritual aspirations; for these effectively time-killing occupations had been kept morally innocent only at the price of being made spiritually fatuous; creation, not mere recreation, was the true end of Man; and, since the creative spark in Man had happily shown itself to be inextinguishable, neither the Kula nor a grosser contemporary Western regimen of bread and circuses[1] could bring true spiritual salvation to the spellbound prisoners in Circe's sty.

(c) THE SPIRITUAL ODYSSEY OF THE WESTERN WORLD

Where then would a prospectively out-of-work Mankind have to look for a better employment of a morally perilous leisure than was to be found in either a Kula or a Lord Mayor's Show? Two of the Human Soul's higher faculties were Thought and Art; and the past exercise of these two faculties by Man in Process of Civilization had demonstrated that their fields of activity were boundless. In any future society that had sense and grace as well as leisure, the moving spirits would assuredly see to it that their fellow men's and women's intellectual and aesthetic capacities were given the best opportunities for coming to flower that an enlightened education could provide. Yet it seemed unlikely—as far as could be foreseen before this cultural experiment had been tried—that Thought and Art would prove to be activities in which a majority of Mankind could find their lifework; for Thought and Art appeared to be intrinsically esoteric in their nature, in the sense of requiring for their cultivation an innate spiritual gift with which only a minority was endowed; and this rare endowment was no talisman of spiritual perfection. 'To the purely spiritual, the intellectual but stand in a sort of corporeal relation'.[2] If the solution for Man's problem of total leisure lay in expending it in the service of some high calling to which all men would find themselves able to devote their lives, then Mankind must turn again for salvation to Religion; for the one employment of total Leisure that offered an infinite spiritual scope to Everyman was the use of this challenging gift for the glory of the God who had bestowed it.

Whatever the religious future of a Westernizing World might prove to be, a post-Christian chapter of Western history had already made it clear that, in some form, a banished Religion was going to return in any event; for it had not proved so easy, after all, to give the Hound of

---

[1] 'Panem et circenses' (*Juvenal*: Satire X, l. 81).
[2] Melville, H.: *Moby Dick*, chap. xlvi.

Heaven[1] the slip. Rather than relinquish His pursuit of His spiritual prey,[2] He had resumed it in the guise of a hell hound; and a liberal-minded and rationalist-minded society which had facilely assumed that it had rid itself of fanaticism for ever by exorcizing it on the ecclesiastical plane had lived to see it break out again with seven-fold virulence on political and economic planes on which the complacent watchman had been off his guard.

Mid-way through the twentieth century of the Christian Era it was already evident that the choice before Western Man was, not whether he was to be religious or irreligious, but whether his spiritual allegiance was to be given to this religion or to that; and in a scientific-minded society this choice between competing religions was limited virtually to two alternatives. A twentieth-century Western World might either return to a Christian worship of the God who is Love as well as Power, or it might succumb to a Narcissan worship of Man's own hypnotizing image. In an age in which Human Technology had so decisively and sensationally subjugated Non-Human Nature, it was no longer possible for Man to find a third alternative in a return to the worship of a Magna Mater who had been the principal object of Man's worship before the higher religions had made their epiphany in the wake of Civilization's higher technology. A generation that had discovered how to 'annihilate distance' and how to split the atom might be more prone than any of its predecessors to fall into the deadly error of deifying Man, but it had effectively debarred itself from recapturing a primitive vision of Non-Human Nature as the Great Mother of gods and men.

A Physical Universe that a Western Science had stripped naked and dissected could no longer be mistaken for a Theotókos. At the most she might be personified poetically as one of God's daughters; and the error of according to her some of the worship due exclusively to God Himself was a pitfall into which a twentieth-century Western worshipper of the One True God would have no excuse for falling, considering that, in a seventh-century Mecca, the Prophet Muhammed, at a time when his prophetic mission had been at its nadir, had manfully overcome a momentary temptation to compromise with the traditional idolatry of his compatriots by associating the three goddesses of the Ka'bah—Manat, Allat, and al-'Uzzā—with the worship of an Allah whose daughters these goddesses had been deemed to be.[3] The One True God and His creature Man were the sole two possible alternative objects of worship for a *Homo Faber Mechanicus*; and the choice between these two competitors for victory, in the final round of a struggle for existence between religions that was coeval with Mankind, had been brought to a crisis by a triumph of Human Technology over Non-Human Nature which had conclusively discredited the primitive worship of a Magna Mater.

Now that a conquered Material Universe was out of the running, Man Himself was the greatest power of which Man had any indisputable

[1] Thompson, Francis: *The Hound of Heaven.*
[2] Blake, William: *The Everlasting Gospel, β,* l. 27.
[3] For the tradition of this incident, see Andrae, T.: *Mohammed: The Man and his Faith* (New York 1936, Scribner), pp. 21–23.

direct experience; and the critical question was whether a scientifically warrantable worship of a visible and tangible human idol would now follow up a victory over the scientifically exploded worship of Cybele by also putting to rout a worship of God—considering that a faith which was 'the substance of things hoped for, the evidence of things not seen',[1] was the only justification for worshipping a God whom no man had seen at any time.[2] 'Through faith we understand that the worlds were framed by the word of God, so that things which are seen were not made of things which do appear';[3] but this faith was not countenanced by Science; and, long before Man had been led into a temptation to worship the Human Mind by the intellectually triumphant sequel to a seventeenth-century Western Scientific Revolution, Man-worship had already come to be the characteristic idolatry of Man in Process of Civilization, since one aspect of Civilization had been Man's progressive conquest of Non-Human Nature.

The response to the challenge of this first wave of Man-worship had been the epiphany of the higher religions; and it had been no accident that these had made their appearance and won their footing at times and places at which human beings had temporarily learnt the salutary lesson of disillusionment with Civilization from the suffering that had been inflicted on them by the breakdowns and disintegrations of the civilizations of an early generation. The spiritually educative effects of this creative experience of suffering had, however, afterwards been overwhelmed by the impetus of the triumphant resurgence of Civilization in the Modern Age of a Western Society's history. The evidence of things not seen had been rejected, and the substance of things hoped for had been devalued, by a Modern Western Man from whom a Westernizing majority of Mankind had latterly been learning to take its cue. Was this the last word in the story? The four principal surviving higher religions—the Mahāyāna, Hinduism, Christianity, and Islam— had all consistently spoken with one voice in proclaiming the truth that Man was not God. Was their consensus on this negative yet crucial point now to be overruled in a second reading of the bill? A Christian Church Militant had started its career by challenging a cult of Dea Roma and Divus Caesar that had been one of the most respectable and beneficent expressions of Man-worship so far devised. Were the heirs of the Christian martyrs who had given their lives to win the Church's battle against the deification of an Hellenic universal state now to capitulate to the worship of Leviathan in the cruder and wickeder latter-day Western forms of Fascism and Communism? The key to an answer to this question was to be found in the significance and prospects of a current domestic controversy within the bosom of the neo-pagan church whose religion was the worship of Humanity.

In an earlier chapter of this Part[4] we have already noticed that the real issue between Communism and a traditional Western way of life was not the economic issue between Socialism and Freedom for Private Economic Enterprise which was the ostensible subject of contention. We

[1] Heb. xi. 1.   [2] 1 John iv. 12.
[3] Heb. xi. 3.   [4] On p. 584, above.

have seen that this economic issue masked a religious one that was of much greater account and was therefore much more difficult to settle, and we have identified this religious issue as a conflict between two incompatible versions of the cult of a human idol. Communism was preaching that Man's divinity lay in Man's collective material power, while Liberalism was preaching that it lay in men's individual and personal freedom; and we have already committed ourselves to the forecast that, in a struggle for the spiritual allegiance of Mankind in which the only two competitors in the lists were the Communists' idol Leviathan and the Liberals' idol Homunculus, Leviathan could not fail to win the day.

The Liberals had, in fact, virtually admitted defeat when they had stooped to alloying their Liberalism with Nationalism; for this partial apostasy was not merely a confession that their proper godling Homunculus was an unsatisfying object of worship; it was also a confession that the Communists' idol Leviathan was verily the one true god, since, on the road from Liberalism to Communism, Nationalism was a half-way house at which there could be no permanent abiding place for the harassed *ci-devant* Liberal traveller. In becoming a nationalist the Liberal had in fact inadvertently but irrevocably become a fellow-traveller with his Communist adversary, since Nationalism, in unison with Communism and in contrast to Liberalism, was a worship of Collective Man, and the only substantial difference between these two varieties of the cult of Leviathan was that Communism was a worship of the collective human beast in its oecumenical entirety, whereas Nationalism was a worship of it in fragments chipped off to constitute parochial states. When even in the mundane sphere of economic and political and military affairs these idolized parochial states had already become untenable anachronisms, it was hard to believe that they could long continue to command the ideological allegiance of ex-Christians who, if their hearts were set on worshipping Collective Man, could find ready to hand, in Communism, an alternative form of Leviathan-worship that was more satisfying, more rational, and more practical.

The encounter between a Communist and a Liberal ideology on a twentieth-century Western religious battlefield was not unlike the encounter between the French gendarmes and the Genoese crossbowmen in the first phase of the Battle of Crécy. The two contingents of a twentieth-century man-worshipping army were in the field against the same God-worshipping adversaries; but, before either or both of them could join battle with their common theist enemy, they had first to settle accounts with one another; and, in this preliminary heat, the Communist devotees of Leviathan, in their attitude towards the Liberal patrons of Homunculus, were showing all the impatience and contempt that the French Knights had displayed in dealing with the French Crown's Genoese mercenaries on the 26th August, 1346. In twentieth-century Communist eyes the Liberal Western advocates of Individual Liberty were as ineffective in combat as the Genoese crossbowmen had been found by their French employers to be when their bowstrings had gone slack as a result of an improvident exposure to the rain. These useless troops in the van of the atheist army's order of battle were now standing in the way of a Marxian task-force that had the weapons and the will to bring the battle to a decision by charging home. To Communist minds the only open question was whether the Liberals had been making fools of themselves unintentionally in allowing their weapons to be put out of action by the weather and in taking up a position in which they were now nothing but a nuisance to their own side, or whether their ostensible ineptitude was in reality a cunning camouflage for a treacherous collusion with theists who, in theory, were Liberalism's and Communism's common enemies. The Communist answer to this question would be the verdict on Liberalism in the court of Marxian history; but for current practical purposes the question was academic; for the Marxian heavy cavalry had already made up their minds that they must clear the field for a decisive assault upon their ultimate adversaries the theists by riding the obstructive Liberals down; and, whether the prospective victims of this military necessity were fools or whether they were knaves, the necessity was in either case imperative.

In the face of the Communists' implacable determination to sweep the Liberals out of their path, the Liberals were in a sorry plight; for the negative Liberal ideal of civil liberty for individual men and women was as ineffective a weapon as an unstrung crossbow to pit against the positive Communist ideal of a self-sacrificing devotion to the service of a Collective Humanity. The apparent grandeur of the Communist ideal made the Liberal ideal appear trivial; yet there was one unquestionably genuine fact with which these appearances did not tally, and this was that in their allegiance to a seemingly trivial ideal the Liberals were thoroughly in earnest. Their belief in individual liberty, and the willingness of at least a few zealous souls to demonstrate their sincerity by going to the length of dying for this belief in the last resort at the hands of National Socialist German and Communist Russian and Chinese persecutors, were the one article of faith and the one spark of the martyrs' fiery spirit that were unquestionably still alive in a post-Christian Western World which had deliberately repudiated its title to the name 'Western Christendom'.[1] Considering how feeble this latter-day Western ideal of personal liberty appeared to be when it was held up to scorn against the foil of Communism's zeal for the welfare of the Human Race, it might seem strange that it should have retained so singular a hold upon the feelings of an otherwise prosaically utilitarian-minded society. What was the explanation of this mystery?

In attempting to explain the strength of a twentieth-century Western feeling for Liberty, an historian's first move would be to look into its origins; and he would begin his retrospective investigation by pointing out that the Liberals were allowing the Communists to do them a gross injustice in allowing them to state the issue between Liberalism and Communism in economic terms. The right of private *entrepreneurs* to take their profits might indeed seem a less worthy cause to champion than the right of Mankind to make its collective economic interests prevail over the selfish economic aims of a few able or privileged individuals; but this

[1] See I. i. 34.

exclusively economic interpretation of Liberalism was, of course, a travesty of it. The freedom which the Western Liberals had most at heart was not a freedom for the rich to make profits at the expense of the poor; it was a freedom for anyone of any class to express an unpopular opinion, advocate an unpopular policy, and co-operate for these unpopular purposes with other representatives of a like-minded minority of the community. This civil liberty was the freedom for which the members of a twentieth-century Western Society were prepared to fight and die; and they set this supreme value on civil liberty because they were aware that it was the palladium of Democracy; but this was only the latest chapter in the story; for civil liberty had been prized in the West long before the selfconscious resuscitation of a defunct Hellenic political ideal at the beginning of the Modern Age of Western history.[1]

The Western cult of civil liberty was not only older than a Modern Western democracy; it was also older than a Medieval Western parliamentarism, as was witnessed in the English rendering of Western constitutional history by the chronological fact that King John's signature of Magna Carta in A.D. 1215 had preceded by thirty-nine years the summoning of the first rudiment of a representative parliament in A.D. 1254. A passion for personal liberty on the political plane had in fact been a Modern Western democracy's priceless heritage from a Medieval Western aristocracy; but the feudal barons had not been the creators of this Western ideal of liberty, and politics had not been the plane on which it had first risen above the Western World's horizon. The Western ideal of personal liberty had made its epiphany on the religious plane, and this before the first rudiments of a Western Civilization had begun to take shape out of the chaos of a post-Hellenic interregnum; for this Western belief in personal liberty was part of the Western Society's spiritual heritage from Christianity, and its provenance was attested by 'the visionary gleam' of a halo of unearthly light that still made this ideal glow and shine, and so still made it thrill the hearts of men and women with its radiance, even after it had been debased into a prosaic twentieth-century Western secular concern to preserve the freedom of business men to make economic profits.

> Not in entire forgetfulness,
> And not in utter nakedness,
> But trailing clouds of glory do we come
> From God, who is our home.[2]

A latter-day Western belief in the value of personal liberty was a faded vestige of an original Christian belief in the brotherhood of Man; and this Christian belief in the brotherhood of Man was a corollary of a Christian discovery—or revelation—of the fatherhood of God, for which the First Epistle General of John was the *locus classicus*.

'Behold what manner of love the Father hath bestowed upon us, that we should be called the sons of God. . . . And this commandment have we from him, that he who loveth God love his brother also.'[3]

---

[1] See pp. 3 and 7–8, above.
[2] Wordsworth, William: *Ode on Intimations of Immortality from Recollections of Early Childhood.*
[3] 1 John iii. 1 and iv. 21.

A belief in the absolute and inestimable value of personal liberty, which was neither intellectually nor morally defensible when Liberty was claimed as the divine right of an impiously deified Homunculus, would take on a very different colour if this miserable pretender to the divinity of his Creator were to be salvaged from the worship of himself by again receiving 'the spirit of adoption whereby we cry "Abba, Father!"';[1] for 'the glorious liberty of the children of God', into which 'the creature itself also shall be delivered from the bondage of corruption',[2] was a cause in which Christians, vindicating it against the tyranny of an idolatrous worship of Leviathan, could lay down their lives, if need be, with a sure conviction that this was a worthy cause for martyrdom.

If we have accounted correctly for the abiding sincerity and earnestness of a twentieth-century Western belief in personal liberty by tracing this belief back to its historic Christian origin, we have perhaps performed for a hard-pressed Liberalism a service that might have saved the lives of the unfortunate Genoese soldiers on the field of Crécy if they could have done the same thing for themselves on the morning of the 26th August, 1346. We have rearmed our Liberal crossbowman by restoring the tone of his perished Christian bow-string; and, in thus effectively reconditioning his paralysed weapon, we have given him the power to turn the tables on his Communist assailant; for a crossbow in working order is more than a match for antique swords and lances. The historian's intervention with his time-machine[3] will, in fact, have given the battle a new turn. The mail-clad horsemen will make their charge with the same recklessly confident *élan* as ever, but this time their shrift will be short, for they will never arrive within range of the expectant longbowmen's shafts; they will meet their deaths *en route* at the hands of the interloping crossbowmen whom they had imagined to be at their mercy and had been expecting to trample under foot. They will be slain by bolts shot at point-blank range from unexpectedly restrung arbalests.

This military simile was an enlightening allegory of the religious issue that a post-Christian Liberalism was being forced to face under the mounting pressure of a post-Christian Communism's challenge. On the neo-pagan terms on which this spiritual battle had been joined, Liberalism was hopelessly outmatched; for Communism had been able to put the *élan* of its heritage of Christian enthusiasm into its worship of the idol Leviathan, while Liberalism had condemned itself to unstring its bow by taking as its counter-idol an Homunculus whose pretension to divinity was so patently spurious as to be incapable of kindling any glimmer of Christian zeal. This contemptible little idol might have been adequate for meeting a Western Society's ideological requirements during a comfortable nineteenth-century vacation, when Islam's once loud challenge to the Western World had fallen silent before any Western ear had yet begun to catch the first sound of a Communist Russian heavy cavalry's oncoming horse-hoofs; but by the middle of the twentieth century, when this new horde of charging Oriental cataphracts was bearing down, full tilt, upon a shaken Occidental infantry, it had become manifest that a nineteenth-century belief in civil liberty

[1] Rom. viii. 15.   [2] Rom. viii. 21.   [3] See V. vi. 214–15.

was no adequate armament for meeting the impetuous attack of the most formidable assailant that the Franks had yet encountered. The Communist onslaught had thus forced upon its Western victims a drastic choice between two extreme alternatives. Either the Westerners must resign themselves to seeing the defeat of a Western ideal of personal liberty that had been depotentiated in the process of being secularized, or else they must reinstate this now gravely imperilled ideal in its original Christian setting, since it was only through being reconsecrated that the ideal of Liberty could be revalidated. In forcing this choice upon a post-Christian Western Society, a post-Christian Russian Society was unintentionally doing an inestimably valuable service to its unloved sister; for it was thrusting into its Western adversary's unnerved hand the one spiritual weapon that had the power to turn the balance in the hitherto weaker combatant's favour. In a struggle between the two conflicting ideals of Freedom and Totalitarianism in which the cause of Freedom was at a desperate disadvantage so long as Freedom meant nothing more than a secular civil liberty, the idol Leviathan might still be triumphantly defied and defeated by souls contending for the liberty of Conscience and risking martyrdom for the glory of God.

If a latter-day Western Liberalism was to be retransfigured into the religion that was the fountain-light of all its day and the master-light of all its seeing,[1] it would have to carry out both a negative and a positive spiritual exercise.

Its negative task would be to recapture a saving humility. The first lesson in humility, for a society that had won a dominion over non-Human Nature by enthroning Natural Science in a dethroned Religion's seat, would be to acknowledge and confess the spiritual impotence of a Mechanized Technology that had proved itself capable of moving physical mountains;[2] and the palinode that was now demanded of the Western scientific intellect could not be evaded by the gesture of replacing a Newtonian 'God the Engineer' by an Einsteinian 'God the Mathematician'.[3] This perfunctory twentieth-century Western etherialization of a complacent eighteenth-century Western deism would not be enough to restore sick Western souls to spiritual health; for, though

---

[1] Wordsworth, op. cit.

[2] The writer can remember an occasion in one of the museums in London when he was gazing, as a child, at a beautiful fragment of Medieval Western stained glass and was listening to his mother's comment that this was the one Medieval Western art of which the Modern Western World had lost the secret. This remark made a lasting impression on his mind, because, for this mind at that age, an admission of the possibility of retrogression, even in one single art, had been as disquieting as it had been novel. In his subsequent musings over this recollection of early childhood, the writer gradually came to perceive that, while the loss of any technique was something portentous in a social milieu in which Technology was *in excelsis*, the Modern Western World's loss of the Medieval Western technique of making stained glass was particularly significant. It was indeed no accident that this particular technique should have been the first to have slipped out of a Modern Western virtuoso's hand; for, of all Medieval Western techniques, the making of stained glass had been the one in which Technology had been the most dependent for its success upon its marriage with Spirituality; and the repudiation of a Medieval Western spirituality had been the price of the sensational advance of a secularized Modern Western science.

[3] 'We have already considered with disfavour the possibility of the Universe having been planned by a biologist or an engineer; from the intrinsic evidence of His creation, the Great Architect of the Universe now begins to appear as a pure mathematician' (Jeans, Sir James: *The Mysterious Universe* (Cambridge 1930, University Press), p. 134).

these second thoughts of Western minds might be commended as the beginning of wisdom,[1] they would not exempt Western hearts from the duty and ordeal of conversion. Abashed Western intellects must follow the Hellenic example set by Socrates when he turned away from the study of an outer physical universe to the exploration of an inner spiritual one.[2] Contrite Western souls must accept a contemporary Asian verdict that 'Western science is ignorant of the distinction between worldly knowledge and godly knowledge'[3] and a classical Hellenic verdict that 'omnia . . . ista sagacitas hominum, non sapientia, invenit'.[4]

'The first scientific quest was concerned, not with the nature of the Objective Universe, but with the central problem of human fate.[5] Dream-interpretation, Divination and Astrology, the three great branches of Primitive Science, all attempted to answer the most poignant questions about the fundamental nature of Man. These questions still remain unanswered. . . . We know very well that the specific quest of the early intuitive sciences was not taken over by the scientific disciplines which superseded them. . . . Because of the immense success and prestige of the scientific *Weltanschauung*, it was hardly noticed until recently that these central problems of the Human Soul had been omitted from the fields of Modern Science and Philosophy. . . . It would be idle to contend that extraverted Science and Religion do not serve real human ends. Their social, ethical, and cultural values are manifest. But the Soul of Man is still athirst for the essential things which were left behind in the pre-scientific limbo—things which have lain dormant but are not dead. In the Unconscious they await the day of resurrection, ready to break through whenever the spiritual quest is undertaken anew, clothed perhaps in strange archaic garb, and whispering their primordial longings to our dreaming minds.'[6]

The negative act of spiritual purification through humility would be a necessary preliminary to this positive act of replenishing an empty Western cistern from well-springs in which the living waters of Religion had never run dry; and these sources for a renewal of Western Man's spiritual life were unlikely to be found either in Western or in Russian geological formations; for History and Scripture had testified with a conclusive unanimity that the parts of Caesar and Christ could never both be played by the same person or same people. If either the Americans or the Russians were to cast themselves for the Caesarean role of putting a distracted *Oikoumenê* into political and material order, they would thereby be disqualifying themselves for becoming candidates for the privilege of being chosen to be the prophets of a spiritual revival, while the West European peoples would have to face the hard truth that their recent forfeiture of their ephemeral power did not carry with it any guarantee that these ex-*conquistadores*, ex-proconsuls, and ex-*entre-*

---

[1] Ps. cxi. 10; Prov. i. 7 and ix. 10.
[2] See Plato: *Phaedo*, 96–97, quoted in III. iii. 186–7.
[3] P. Rámanáthan, Solicitor General of Ceylon: 'The Miscarriage of Life in the West', in *The Hibbert Journal*, vol. vii, No. 1 (London 1909, Williams & Norgate), p. 12.
[4] Seneca: *Epistulae Morales ad Lucilium*, Ep. xc, § 11.
[5] See N. K. Chadwick: *Poetry and Prophecy* (Cambridge 1942, University Press), pp. 91–94, quoted in VII. vii. 761.—A.J.T.
[6] Baynes, H. G.: *Mythology of the Soul* (London 1940, Baillière, Tindall, & Cox; 1949, Methuen), pp. 646 and 647–8.

preneurs would be compensated for their material losses by the receipt of a consolation prize in the shape of a prophet's mantle opportunely descending upon their shivering shoulders to cover their unwonted nakedness. After having provided a Westernizing World with its leaven, its workshop, and its cockpit in swift succession, Western Europe under a future *Pax Americana* seemed likely to settle down, like Greece under a *Pax Romana*, into the uninspiring role of a museum for conserving the relics of a departed greatness; and in the era of a Marshall Plan and a Festival of Britain, as in the days of the Antonines and Aulus Gellius, *ex Oriente lux.*

This had been the theme of the friars' chant in the Temple of Jupiter that had fallen on Gibbon's ears on the 15th October, 1764;[1] and, though the impenetrable complacency of an eighteenth-century Zeitgeist, in which Gibbon's talent had been lapped, had not permitted even this master mind to perceive that the subject on which his muse was inviting him to write was Man's mysterious spiritual ascent on the wings of material catastrophe,[2] and not the familiar vanity of Man's mundane ambitions,[3] the learning that comes only through suffering had begun to enlighten far more commonplace souls than Gibbon's within less than two centuries after the great historian had failed to catch the undertones of 'the bare-footed fryars'' descant. The friars' unfading song had outlasted the Forum's brief clamour and the Campo Vaccino's long silence; and by the beginning of the sixth decade of the twentieth century of the Christian Era a disoriented Western moth had already begun to hover wistfully round an unextinguished Oriental candle, according to the testimony of at least one contemporary Western psychiatrist, reporting his own clinical experience.

'Despite intellectual resistance, the Unconscious of the West turns irresistibly to the East; for there the "heliocentric" structure of the Self has long been realised, and the greater psychological depth and insight of Oriental philosophy comes directly from this recognition. . . . Allusions to Eastern ideas are liable to occur in a [Western] patient's material just at the critical juncture where the one thing needful is to be able to see things differently. These people are seriously seeking a more comprehensive view of themselves and of the Universe than that provided by their own background. Naturally, only those who have felt cramped and stultified by the traditional [Western] view of the Soul, which divided it arbitrarily into black and white, will be prompted to subject authoritative moral categories to psychological understanding. But, once the sheep and the goats have escaped from their respective folds, they can never again be herded into authoritarian enclosures. . . . Our tendency to think of instincts as separate and distinct entities makes it difficult to understand Psychology in terms of elementary dynamic principles; but the Unconscious still thinks in the grand manner of Ancient China: "There are

---

[1] *The Autobiographies of Edward Gibbon*, edited by Murray, J. (London 1896, Murray), p. 302. This experience of Gibbon's is discussed in the present Study in II. ii. 210, n. 1; IV. iv. 58–63; and XIII. x. 98–107. [2] See VII. vii. 423–5 and 551–5.

[3] Ecclesiastes had reduced this topic to a truism by his immortal statement of it in the twelve words of his immortal statement of it in the twelve words of his first chapter, and, though the *tour de force* of making these dry bones live (Ezek. xxxvii. 1–10) was to be achieved by Shelley in the fourteen lines of his *Ozymandias of Egypt*, this feat was beyond the compass of Gibbon's ponderous genius.

three elements: Heaven, Earth and Man". The age-long veneration of the swan, the goose, and the stork is the evidence of Man's constant need to find some reconciling symbol which could unite this elementary opposition in his nature. . . . The Chinese naturalistic conception . . . reduces the terrors of the moral conflict, in which the Soul swings dizzily between salvation and perdition, to the play of natural forces—Yang and Yin.'[1]

In a Westernizing World mid-way through the twentieth century of the Christian Era, the time was indeed ripe for the onset of a new Yang-movement to carry Western souls back from their long obsession with an extraverted Physical Science towards a fresh quest for the divine Dweller in the Innermost.[2] In the chapter of Western history that was now coming to a close, Western souls had disqualified themselves for the pursuit of this quest; for 'der Gott der mir im Busen wohnt'[3] does not act in a material medium; His activity is the passivity of Wu Wei in which His spiritual energy is at its acme;[4] He would not be Himself if He made His epiphany in the physical energy of the external universe of His creation; and therefore a Modern Western *Homo Faber Mechanicus* could fancy that he had no use for this *Deus Absconditus*[5] so long as he was preoccupied with his own victorious assault upon his material environment. But now, at the moment when this act of material conquest was being consummated by the extraordinary prowess of a scientific Western technology, the conqueror had been confronted by the ironical discovery that the very completeness of his triumph had placed in jeopardy, not merely the Earthly Paradise that he had seemed to be on the verge of recapturing, but perhaps even the survival of Life on Earth, which had never before been under threat of being extinguished by Man's maleficence.

The devastating agency that Western Man had thus let loose to his own mortal peril was not the physical force generated by splitting an atom; it was the spiritual force generated by a schism in the Soul; but, happily for Mankind's prospects in both This World and an Other World, the inadvertently liberated *jinn* was not evil in its essence; its titanic power was capable of working as much good, if it were rightly guided, as it was bound to work evil if it were allowed to run riot; and now, primed and poised for action, demonic or angelic, this potent spirit was awaiting a sign from the alchemist who had unintentionally liberated it from the alembic in which he had been conducting his excessively ingenious physical experiments. If he was to give himself a chance of self-preservation, the distractingly possessed *majnūn* technologist must now recognize, and act upon, the truth that, 'of all tools used in the shadow of the Moon, men are [the] most apt to get out of order'.[6] He must throw aside the physical tools with which he had been mastering his material environment, in order to concentrate his efforts on the now

---

[1] Baynes, H. G.: *Mythology of the Soul* (London 1940, Baillière, Tindall, & Cox; 1949, Methuen), pp. 505, 896, 698, and 872.
[2] See the picture with this title by George Frederic Watts in the Tate Gallery, Millbank, London.
[3] Goethe: *Faust*, l. 1566, quoted in II. i. 279.   [4] See III. iii. 187.
[5] 'Vere tu es Deus absconditus, Deus Israel salvator' (Isa. xlv. 15, in the Vulgate Latin text).   [6] Melville, H.: *Moby Dick*, chap. xlvi.

far more urgent task of re-conquering an inner spiritual world that had slipped out of his control while he had been engrossed in his unduly pro-longed child's-play with clockwork; for this spiritual world was the field in which lay buried his pearl of great price[1]—his master tool consisting of his Self; and 'what shall a man give in exchange for his soul?'[2] A Western Man who had all but gained the whole World could not recapture his lost self till he had made his peace with his fellow men and women, with his Subconscious Human Nature, and with his God; and he must first turn again to worship a *Latens Deitas*[3] if he was to have any hope of achieving an eventual reconciliation with his fellows and with himself. He must reorient his spiritual outlook by once more taking for his *qiblah* his father Abraham's Mecca in place of his prospector Bentham's New Jerusalem.

If this act of reconversion was what was required of Western souls seeking, at the eleventh hour, to find salvation, was it possible to esti-mate how far they had already travelled by this date on their spiritual Odyssey, and what experiences they had been encountering on the way? By the time when, under the surface of Western Man's spiritual life, the Subconscious Psyche was somnambulantly veering eastward, a van-guard of more alert—or more apprehensive—Western spirits had been racing so far ahead that they had already reached a critical divide in the road. *Hic locus est partis ubi se via findit in ambas*;[4] and this parting of the ways was critical because of the contrast between the two spiritual *ter-rains* into which the forking branches led; for one of them was as invit-ingly sheltering as the other was deterrently bleak.

In this valley of decision,[5] where the prodigal found himself confronted by the two frowning baetyls that had been waiting for his arrival there to bear witness against him,[6] his temptation was to retreat into the bosom of some established church enshrining some historic higher religion.

> Rock of Ages, cleft for me,
> Let me hide myself in Thee.[7]

In the spiritual life of the Western World mid-way through the twentieth century of the Christian Era there were already unmistakable signs of a movement of withdrawal that had been detected, and been stigmatized as 'the second bout of religiosity' ('*die zweite Religiosität*'), by a Western philosopher writing on the morrow of a First World War.[8] In the disin-tegration of the Hellenic Civilization, this tendency to seek shelter in a reversion to traditional religious observances had begun to be perceptible in the second century B.C., after the onset of the second paroxysm of an

---

[1] Matt. xiii. 46.   [2] Matt. xvi. 26.

[3] 'Adoro te devote, latens Deitas'—the first line of the hymn, attributed to Saint Thomas Aquinas that, in a Catholic Western Christian church, was sung during pro-cessions on Corpus Christi Day.

[4] Virgil: *Aeneid*, Book VI, l. 540.

[5] Joel iii. 14.   [6] Auden, W. H.: *The Two Witnesses*.

[7] In the writer of this hymn, A. M. Toplady, Western Man's subconscious psyche was as prescient as it was complacent in the author of *The History of the Decline and Fall of the Roman Empire*. Toplady published *Rock of Ages* in A.D. 1775, a year before the date of the publication of the first volume of Gibbon's work.

[8] See Spengler, O.: *Der Untergang des Abendlandes*, vol. ii (Munich 1922, Beck), pp. 381–3.

Hellenic Time of Troubles;[1] in the disintegration of the Sinic Civilization, it had come to a head under the *Pax Hanica*.[2]

'The second bout of religiosity is the inevitable counterpart of Caesar-
ism, which is the final political constitution of all disintegrating civilisations in their last phase (*später Zivilisationen*).[3]. . . The creations of this
[latter-day] piety have no more originality about them than is to be found
in the form of the Roman Imperium. There is no constructive activity, no
development of any idea. The phenomenon resembles the [optical] effect
of the dispersal of a mist that has been shrouding a landscape: the old
familiar forms begin to reappear—hazily at first, and then in clearer and
clearer outline. The content of religiosity in this second bout is, once
again, just what it was in the first authentic early bout, save for a difference
of nuance in the experience and expression of it. The first symptom is the
disappearance of Rationalism; the next symptom is the emergence of the
forms of the Early Age of Growth (*der Frühzeit*); the last symptom is the
resurrection of the whole universe of the primitive religions, which had
been compelled to give way to the grandiose forms of an Early [Higher]
Religion (*des Frühglaubens*), and which now bursts out again, with an
impetus that will not be denied, in a proletarian syncretism[4] which is
a never failing feature of every civilisation (*Kultur*) in this phase.'[5]

This vista of spiritual regression becomes attractive to self-deconsecrated souls even in the heyday of Rationalism, before their first experience of the nemesis of Rationalism has begun to shake their nerve.

'Materialism would not be complete if it did not feel a need now and
again to escape from its psychological tension by letting itself fall into
mythopoeic moods, by indulging in some kind of religious ritual, and by
finding relief from an internal pressure in allowing itself to savour the
charm of something irrational, something alien, something bizarre and,
in the last resort, something sheerly silly.'[6]

This gravitational pull will become doubly strong when the truant
from the fold of an established religion has experienced—like Gibbon at
Lausanne after the outbreak of the French Revolution—the shock of
suddenly finding himself on the brink of a catastrophe that he had never
foreboded. In this unhappy plight the impulse to take cover by retreating
into the abyss of the Subconscious Psyche's beatifically infantile *Nirvāna*
out of the storm-swept eyrie of an adult consciousness is as natural as the
instinct of an unweaned baby kangaroo to wriggle back into its mother's
pouch at its first alarming encounter with the challenging presence of a
dangerous world outside. Yet, however natural the promptings of spiritual cowardice may be, they are seldom either admirable or expedient;
and a post-Christian Western Society's temptation to seek refuge from
the consequences of its own technological handiwork by begging for
readmittance into the fold of a conventional Christian orthodoxy was
neither morally nor intellectually defensible. The impulse to indulge in
'a second bout' of traditional religion is, indeed, merely a manifestation,

---

[1] See V. v. 534 and 545–9.   [2] See V. v. 535 and 549.
[3] In Spengler's terminology, *Zivilisation* signifies a civilization in its disintegration-
phase, and *Kultur* a civilization in its growth-phase.—A.J.T.
[4] See V. v. 527–68 in the present Study.—A.J.T.
[5] Spengler, op. cit., vol. ii, pp. 382–3.   [6] Ibid., p. 381.

on the religious plane,[1] of an Archaism which, on all planes, we have found, in an earlier context, to be a bolt-hole that is always a trap because it invariably proves to be a blind alley.

Archaistic religious movements are intellectually indefensible because the antecedent Rationalism that has driven a traditional religious faith off the field does not in reality just come and go like the fog with which Spengler misleadingly equates Rationalism in his simile. It would be nearer to the truth to identify the fog with the alien matter which a higher religion, after its descent from Heaven, picks up and carries along with it on its terrestrial journey.[2] The onset of Rationalism will then assume the appearance of a process, not of obfuscation, but of enlightenment (*Aufklärung*); and it is a harder task for Psyche to undo the effects of enlightenment by reassembling the mental fog that the advent of Rationalism has once dispersed than it has been for her, in that antecedent chapter of her mental history, to disperse the fog by directing upon it the rays of enlightenment. This unaccommodating truth has been proclaimed, with an authority derived from personal experience, by a Muslim theologian-mystic who had the courage to face the loss of his religion for the sake of winning an opportunity of recovering it through an act of trans-figuration.

'There is no hope in returning to a traditional faith after it has once been abandoned, since the essential condition in the holder of a traditional faith is that he should not know that he is a traditionalist. Whenever he knows that, the glass of his traditional faith is broken. That is a breaking that cannot be mended, and a separating that cannot be united by any sewing or putting together, except it be melted in the fire and given another new form.'[3]

Souls that have once had the experience of intellectual enlightenment can never thereafter find spiritual salvation by committing intellectual suicide; and, though the quest of recapturing their lost faith is in itself both intellectually and morally legitimate, agnostics who embark on this quest will not find themselves able to worship God again in spirit and in truth[4] if they seek to open for themselves a homeward spiritual path by deliberately closing their mind's critical eye and by making a virtue of refusing henceforth to follow an argument fearlessly wherever it may lead them. In a would-be return to Religion, the path of intellectual dishonesty can lead only to worshipping we know not what;[5] for Reason, like Faith, is a goddess with whom Man cannot take the liberty of playing fast and loose—as though these mighty *numina* were cringing curs whom a capricious human master could break in to complying slavishly with his wayward mood. Faith and Reason cannot be alternately dismissed with a kick and then called back to heel with a whistle to suit Man's volatile fancy or changing convenience.

[1] See V. vi. 83–94.   [2] See VII. vii. 455–6.
[3] Ghazzālī, Abū Hāmid al-: *Al-Munqidh min al-Dalāl* ['The Preservative from Error'] (Cairo A.H. 1303), translated by D. B. Macdonald in *The Religious Life and Attitude in Islam* (Chicago 1909, University of Chicago Press), p. 180. In C. Barbier de Meynard's French translation of the complete text of al-Ghazzālī's *Munqidh* in *Journal Asiatique*, seventh series, vol. ix (Paris 1877, Imprimerie Nationale), this passage will be found on pp. 19–20.
[4] John iv. 23–24.   [5] John iv. 22.

If a once conventionally orthodox Muslim religious genius had been able to divine that it was intellectually impracticable to re-embrace a lost traditional religious faith *telle quelle*, it ought to be manifest to an ex-Christian soul that the temptation to take spiritual cover is morally reprehensible; for the attempt to put Christianity into action must mean trying to follow Christ's example; and the impulse of an ex-Christian on the run to find a hiding-place in Christ's riven side ran directly counter to the spirit and significance of Christ's incarnation. The essential and distinctive Christian belief about the nature and action of God was that a Person of the Trinity 'who, being in the form of God, counted it not a prize to be on an equality with God',[1] had been moved, by the Love that He was,[2] to divest Himself of His divine impassibility in order to come down from Heaven and be made man and suffer death for the sake of us men and our salvation.

'[He] emptied Himself (ἑαυτὸν ἐκένωσε), taking the form of a servant, being made in the likeness of men; and, being found in fashion as a man, He humbled Himself and became obedient unto death, even the death of the cross.'[3]

The example set by Christ for Christians was an example, not of shrinking from the suffering inherent in Human Nature, but of accepting it for the sake of saving human beings whom their Creator loved with a love that led Him to die for them as His brethren.

If a belief and an ideal that were the heart of Christianity did not give pause to an unnerved ex-Christian rationalist in panic flight back to the shelter of a traditional Christian orthodoxy, the fugitive might perhaps find an alternative example to fortify his *moral* in the history of another higher religion which latterly had been brought within the ken of Western minds as a result of the technological unification of the *Oikoumenê*.

The Mahāyāna, which shared with Christianity, Islam, and Hinduism the historic role of being one of the four surviving oecumenical higher religions, had sprung from a Buddhist philosophy which had concentrated on ethics to the exclusion of metaphysics and had valued ethics for their practical utility in offering to sentient beings a way of escape from suffering. In divining that the experience of pain was an inseparable concomitant of consciousness and will, the Buddha had shown a penetrating psychological insight. The moral weakness of the philosophy founded on the Buddha's teaching was that, in its compassionate concern to liberate Life from suffering, it was willing to condemn Life to lose its savour by counselling it to relapse into a beatific subconsciousness; and Buddhism fell into this spiritual error because it allowed itself to ignore the truth that, in extinguishing pain at this price, Man was also renouncing his highest capacities for good. In an Hellenic spiritual environment, Gautama's contemporary Aeschylus had divined that, for Human Nature, suffering was the necessary price of learning;[4] and Christianity was to add the revelation that suffering was also the necessary means of grace. The Indic philosophy had started on its course by precluding itself from

---

[1] Phil. ii. 6, Revised Version.   [2] 1 John iv. 8 and 16.
[3] Phil. ii. 7–8, Revised Version.
[4] πάθει μάθος.—Aeschylus: *Agamemnon*, l. 177, quoted in this Study *passim*.

taking cognizance of suffering's spiritual and intellectual value; and, considering the unpropitiousness of this start, it is remarkable and significant that, in the next chapter of the history of Buddhism's spiritual development, one sect of Buddhists should have discovered for themselves, by experience, that the evasion of suffering at any price was not a spiritual objective whose pursuit was a spiritually satisfying way of life.

The spiritual fruit of this Christian lesson of Buddhist experience was, as we have noticed in other contexts,[1] the transfiguration of a philosophy of escape into a religion of salvation through the rejection of the Hinayanian arhat's self-centred ideal of getting rid of his suffering self by anaesthetizing his own consciousness and the adoption, instead, of the Mahayanian bodhisattva's self-sacrificing ideal of helping his fellow living beings to make the arduous passage to the arhat's goal at the cost of postponing his own entry into his rest.[2] The bodhisattva's concern to rid himself of himself counts with him for so much less than his compassion for his kind that Love moves him to tarry, for an aeon if need be, in an excruciating state of consciousness after he has won his own right of entry into *Nirvāna* by the perfect performance of an arhat's spiritual exercises. The bodhisattva has it in his power to release himself from suffering by crossing the threshold of *Nirvāna* at any moment that he might choose, and the one desire that still fetters him to the pains of sentient life is the self-transcendent desire to put his own dearly bought experience at his fellows' disposal by serving them as their psychopompus.[3] The transit from the Hīnayāna to the Mahāyāna is thus nothing less than a spiritual revolution, and a Christian disciple of Buddhism would not quarrel with the Mahayanian sect of Buddhists for calling the ideal of the bodhisattva 'the Great Way', and the ideal of the arhat 'the Little Way', of interpreting the Buddha's teaching; for the bodhisattva's ideal was an imitation of Christ that was not the less authentic for being undesigned.[4]

The ideal of the bodhisattva was assuredly an example that the Western World could not afford to disregard in a generation in which it was in retreat towards the inviting shelter of a traditional form of Christianity; for the characteristic virtue of a bodhisattva was his fortitude in withstanding a perpetual temptation to desert his self-assigned post in a world of painful action in order to take the short cut to oblivion that lay perpetually open to him. In the latter half of the twentieth century of the Christian Era such fortitude as this was the first spiritual necessity for Western souls on the religious plane as well as on the political. In his politics, as we have seen,[5] Western Man's task in this chapter of Western history was to school himself to 'living dangerously', without yielding to the temptation of trying to resolve the tension either by capitulating or by committing aggression, in an *Oikoumenê* that had been overtaken by the invention of the atomic bomb before it had achieved political unity. In

---

[1] In V. v. 133–6 and 552; V. vi. 148 and 164, n. 3; and VII. vii. 733.
[2] Ps. xcv. 11.   [3] See IX. viii. 628.
[4] See VII. vii. 733. The rise of the Mahāyāna is accounted for by a yearning, in Buddhist souls, for the Christian graces of love and self-sacrifice for which a Primitive Buddhist philosophy found no place.
[5] On pp. 525–9, above.

his religious life in the same age, a comparable endurance in the exercise of self-command was the spiritual feat that was required of him.

Western souls, apprised by experience of the limits and the nemesis of Rationalism, must school themselves, in their consequent quest for reconciliation with God, to the prospect of finding themselves commanded by Conscience to check their panic impulse to try to force a premature entry into the Promised Land. They must repress their eagerness to take sanctuary again on soil hallowed by the tombs of the Patriarchs. They must even face the prospect that Conscience's injunction might sentence them to end their days in the Wilderness, like the generation of Israelites who after their exodus from Egypt had had to wander in the Wilderness for forty years until not a man of them was left alive save Caleb the son of Jephunneh and Joshua the son of Nun;[1] and they must steel themselves by recalling that in that generation the sternest test of fortitude had been reserved for the Israelite in whom God had been best pleased; for Moses' last experience in This Life had been a tantalizing Pisgah sight[2] of a Promised Land which his own feet were never to tread. 'I have caused thee to see it with thine eyes, but thou shalt not go over thither'[3] had been the last words of the Lord that had fallen on a dying Moses' ears.[4]

The temptation to run for shelter and the duty of riding the storm have been eloquently described by a nineteenth-century Western man of letters who divined, with the intuition of a poet, a truth that his generation came and went too early to have learnt from experience.

'All deep earnest thinking is but the intrepid effort of the Soul to keep the open independence of her sea, while the wildest winds of Heaven and Earth conspire to cast her on the treacherous, slavish shore. But, as in landlessness alone resides the highest truth, shoreless, indefinite as God—so, better is it to perish in that howling infinite than be ingloriously dashed upon the lee, even if that were safety.'[5]

The writer of this Study, who happened to have been born into a generation in whose time this ordeal had come to be a common Western experience, once had a personal intimation of the truth uttered by Herman Melville. In the summer of A.D. 1936, in a time of physical sickness and spiritual travail, he dreamed, during a spell of sleep in a wakeful night, that he was clasping the foot of the crucifix hanging over the high altar

---

[1] Num. xiv. 26–35 and xxvi. 64–65.
[2] Deut. xxxiv. 1.   [3] Deut. xxxiv. 4.
[4] A few weeks after he had written this passage, the writer came across a characteristically sincere and noble exposition of the same idea by a Western scholar-banker of an older generation, Walter Leaf (*vivebat* A.D. 1852–1927), with whom the writer had the good fortune to become personally acquainted after the publication of Leaf's *Troy, A Study in Homeric Geography* (London 1912, Macmillan), when Leaf was preparing for the press his *Homer and History* (London 1915, Macmillan).

'I am sure that we are working together to win a new form in which all the hearts of men will again be able to join in common worship, as they have hardly been able to do for many years. But the time does not seem near yet; and meanwhile a great deal of painful lonely groping has to be done by each one for himself. New faiths, like children, must be brought forth in sorrow, and many souls will have to pass through struggles greater than they can bear. . . . I feel that the minds of all men are slowly working their way from Trouble to Truth' (Walter Leaf, letters written on the 1st and the 4th April, 1894, to Charlotte M. Symonds, before their marriage on the 22nd May, 1894, in *Walter Leaf* (London 1932, John Murray), by Charlotte M. Leaf, pp. 180 and 182).

[5] Melville, Herman: *Moby Dick*, chap. xxiii.

of the Abbey of Ampleforth and was hearing a voice saying to him
Amplexus expecta ('Cling and wait').

An impetuous spiritual traveller on the road back to Religion from
Agnosticism might be inclined to interpret this dream as an irresolute
soul's subconscious apologia; and the postponement of a decision that
was ripe for being taken would indeed convict the procrastinator of a
culpable weakness of will; but the judgement on Fabius must be founded
on a right reading of his situation and his motive; and in the spiritual
circumstances of a twentieth-century Western Society an ex-agnostic
who took *expectans expectavi*[1] for his watchword, without allowing himself to cry 'Make haste, O Lord, to help me',[2] would be clear of the imputation of irresoluteness if his motive for resisting the temptation to
pray for a shortening of the term of his trial was a resolve to face and act
upon the truth that in a latter-day Western spiritual Odyssey the dire
passage of Time was a necessary means of grace in virtue of its being an
inevitable source of suffering.

This spiritual necessity for a painful period of probation could have
been short-circuited with impunity only if it had been possible for a
twentieth-century Western *ci-devant* Christian agnostic to take a traditional form of Christianity as he found it; but this would have meant
taking it back as he had left it; and that would have been no solution for
either the agnostic's or the Church's contemporary problem; for the progressive decay of a belief in, and an allegiance to, an ancestral religion,
which had been the note of a Western Society's spiritual history since
the latter decades of the seventeenth century of the Christian Era, had
not been due solely to Modern Western Man's perversity nor even solely
to his bewitchment by his intellect's entrancing scientific discoveries
and by this fascinating science's lucrative technological fruits. The responsibility for Modern Western Man's apostasy was shared with the
apostate by a Western Christian Church that had eventually alienated
its long-suffering votaries by its grievous sins of both heart and head.[3]

The moral scandal through which the Western Church had forfeited
Western Man's esteem had been a schism that it had allowed to rankle
into the savage Western Wars of Religion (*saeviebant* A.D. 1562–1660);
and the morally shattering effect of this resort to military force in pursuance of an ecclesiastical feud has been noticed in this Study in earlier
contexts.[4] The intellectual scandal which had consummated a Western
Church Militant's self-stultification in Western eyes had been its reaction to a Modern Western movement of intellectual enlightenment
(*Aufklärung*) for which the Wars of Religion had opened the door and the
subsequent Scientific Revolution had paved the way. The Western
Christian churches' response to an intellectual challenge which their
moral iniquity had brought upon them had been to discredit themselves
intellectually as well. They had taken the stand that their traditional
creed, including the whole cumulus of accretions acquired from pre-
Christian pagan religions and from Hellenic science and philosophy, was

---

[1] Ps. xxxix. i, in the Vulgate Latin text; Ps. xl. i, in the English A.V.
[2] Ps. xl. 16.　　　　　　　　　　　　　　　　　　　[3] See IV. iv. 583–4.
[4] See IV. iv. 142–3, 150, 184, 227–8, and 643–5; V. v. 669–71; and V. vi. 317.

an organic unity in which all articles of belief were equally sacrosanct; and they had fought as stubbornly to retain an exploded Ptolemaic astronomy, Aristotelian theology, and Isiac or Cybelene mythology as if this pre-Christian flotsam[1] had been as close to the heart of Christianity as the truth that God is Love and as God's witness to this truth in Christ's incarnation and crucifixion. These were the issues on which the Western Christian churches' once obedient flock had parted company with their ecclesiastical shepherds.

'The diseased have ye not strengthened, neither have ye healed that which was sick, neither have ye bound up that which was broken, neither have ye brought again that which was driven away, neither have ye sought that which was lost; but with force and with cruelty have ye ruled them.'[2]

And, though, by the middle of the twentieth century, a quarter of a millennium had passed since the flock had begun to scatter, the issues that had driven sheep and shepherds apart were still standing like a wall between them.

It was true that in the meantime the churches had ceased to assert their creeds and claims by force of arms; yet they had persisted in making War an instrument of ecclesiastical policy so long as they had been able to persuade any secular governments to put their armed forces at the churchmen's service. The churches had also been jettisoning one after another of their non-Christian intellectual paraphernalia; yet they had clung to them till they had become untenable and had abandoned them with the reluctance of a mother throwing her child to the wolves or of a senile mundane empire recognizing the independence of disaffected and insurgent provinces which it has shown itself impotent either to reconcile or to re-subdue. The estranging issues thus still remained open 250 years or more after the date at which they had come to a head; and, whatever God's eventual judgement on unfaithful shepherds and truant sheep might be, it was manifest, even to human eyes, in the writer's generation (*vivebat* A.D. 1889–   ), that a change of heart was required on both sides. The streams must be cleansed of the mud that had fouled the waters, and the land must be cleared of the jungle that had overgrown the pastures, before the flocks could return without being confronted immediately with a choice between scattering again and staying to die of hunger and thirst.

At this point a champion of a traditional orthodoxy might be moved to ask by what authority this process of purification was to be carried out. Supposing that churchmen were to concede that a purification was necessary, must they not also insist that this task was the Church's prerogative? Would semi-penitent agnostics have the effrontery to claim that they would be better hands at winnowing the chaff out of the wheat than the official heirs of an unbroken apostolic succession? Would the prodigal have the hardihood to stipulate that his re-entry into his father's house must be conditional on its being guaranteed to him in advance that the Church would submit its time-honoured traditions to his philistine judgement? These questions would be legitimate and pertinent enough to require an answer; and the present writer's personal answer

[1] See VII. vii. 455–6.   [2] Ezek. xxxiv. 4.

to them would be that the task of winnowing the chaff out of the traditional form of Christianity—or any other living higher religion—was a task to which both the two human parties to the case would find their own unaided judgement and insight unequal. An agnostic who could show a valid scientific warrant for challenging the Church's apostolic authority would be plunging out of his own depth if he then went on to claim for himself an alternative scientific authority to replace a traditional ecclesiastical chart by a revolutionary lay blue-print; for a petrified higher religion could not be requickened by methods that might serve for reconditioning an obsolete industrial plant. A futuristic reconstruction of Christianity by reconverted agnostics and an archaistic restoration of it by trustees of a traditional orthodoxy would both be impracticable for the same reason; and the reason was that no human hands could anticipate the operation of the Holy Spirit.[1]

If it were then to be asked how the dayspring from on high had ever come to visit human souls through God's tender mercy,[2] the answer would be that 'whom the Lord loveth He chasteneth, and scourgeth every son whom he receiveth', and that, 'if ye endure chastening, God dealeth with you as sons.'[3] If Christianity was to be requickened in agnostic Western souls through a winnowing of the chaff out of the wheat,[4] this palingenesia could be achieved only through suffering; and suffering is an experience that takes Time—and takes it at a length which is proportionate to the measure of the chastening that is required for the sufferer's salvation. If this is the truth, then what was required, above all things, of homeward-faring agnostic Western souls in the twentieth century of the Christian Era was the creative endurance exemplified in the age-long ministries of the bodhisattvas. Resisting the temptation to hide themselves in the rock, and facing the blast of the rushing mighty wind[5] that bloweth where it listeth,[6] these pilgrims through the Valley of the Shadow of Death[7] must let suffering do its unhurrying work within them till, in the fullness of times and seasons which it was not for them to know,[8] they should receive power[9] through the anguish of being born of the spirit.[10]

(d) THE 'LAW' OF PSYCHOLOGICAL COMPENSATION

A reader who has had the patience to follow the foregoing argument from its opening in a prospect of technological unemployment to its close in a vigil in expectation of a Day of Pentecost may be inclined to ask the sceptic's question 'How can these things be?'[11]

In a world whose economic and political life had been caught in the grip of regimentation, how could there be any hope of a spiritual revival on the religious plane? Does not this speculation conflict with previous findings in this Study? Have not the chapters dealing with encounters between contemporaries led to the conclusion that every culture is an organic whole in which all the parts prove, on trial, to be interdependent, however independent of one another some of them may seem to be at

---

[1] Acts ii. 1–4. [2] Luke i. 78. [3] Heb. xii. 6–7.
[4] Matt. iii. 12. [5] Acts ii. 2. [6] John iii. 8. [7] Ps. xxiii. 4.
[8] Acts i. 7. [9] Acts i. 8. [10] John iii. 8. [11] John iii. 9.

first sight?[1] And have we not noticed[2] that, among the processes or tendencies that are thus apt to spread from one part of a body social to another, mechanization is apt to be particularly infectious? In previous chapters of the present Part of this Study[3] we have been watching the spread of regimentation from the economic to the political plane of life in an Industrialized Western Society. What ground could there be there for expecting to see the process of infection come to a halt at this point, if a body social is the highly conductive medium that we have found it to be? We have quoted Bergson's authority for the possibility that 'la mécanique, en se développant, pourra se retourner contre la mystique';[4] and this was surely what was to be expected if we have been on the right track in our findings that the fabric of Society is highly conductive. Has this finding now to be disavowed? Or, if it holds good, does it not open up a different prospect for the Western Society than the vista that we have been sketching? Does it not suggest that, in a chapter of Western history that was on the horizon in A.D. 1952, the religious plane of life, so far from being likely to be a scene of spiritual travail coming to flower in spiritual creation, was likely to succumb to the arid social climate of regimentation which had come to prevail on the economic and political planes already? If it is in truth the nature of any culture to be all of a piece, could the religious life of the Western World have any chance of escaping the blight of a creeping paralysis which had fastened upon its economic life in the restrictive practices of Trade Unionism and on its political life in the êthos of a conscientious but unenthusiastic civil service?

The answer to this hypothetical objection would be that it had sprung from a misconception arising from the ambiguity of the phrase 'all of a piece'; for a fabric might be said to be all of a piece so long as it was a seamless web, even if the threads interwoven in it were of diverse stuffs, diverse twists, and diverse colours, while alternatively the same phrase might be used to describe a web whose texture was homogeneous in the sense that the interwoven threads were uniform with one another. If the latter and ampler of these two senses had been the one in which we had found the structure of a body social to be 'all of a piece', this finding would indeed have been incompatible with a vista of the Western Civilization's prospects in which a regimentation of its life on the economic and political planes might still leave room on the religious plane for freedom and creativity; but this is not in fact the true account of our finding. The truth is that the interdependence which we have observed in the relation between the several parts of a body social is the interdependence of interwoven elements that differ from one another in kind; and our forecast of the Western Civilization's prospects, so far from being in contradiction with this observation, has been partly founded upon it. Our observation that all the elements of a culture are apt to be interdependent was the ground for our prediction that some revolutionary change in the Western Society's religious life was likely to occur as a result of the revolu-

---

[1] For this thesis, see IX. viii. 530–64.
[2] In IV. iv. 125–7. [3] On pp. 561–604, above.
[4] Bergson, H.: *Les Deux Sources de la Morale et de la Religion* (Paris 1932, Alcan), p. 252, quoted in this Study in IV. iv. 126.

tionary changes produced in the Western Society's economic and political life by the psychological effects of the mechanization of its technology; but changes that are inter-related and concomitant do not, on that account, all have to take a single uniform course.

Indeed, so far from the regimentation of Western life on the economic and political planes being likely to induce a regimentation of Western life on the religious plane as well, it seemed likely to militate against this; for one of the devices by which Life achieves the *tour de force* of keeping itself alive is by compensating for a deficit or a surplus in one department by accumulating a surplus or incurring a deficit in another. Considering the importance of this 'law's' role in Life's perpetual struggle for survival, we should expect *a priori* that, in a social milieu in which, as in the twentieth-century Western case in point, there is a deficit of freedom or surplus of regimentation in Economics and Politics, the combined effect of the working of 'the law of interdependence' and 'the law of compensation' would be to produce a surplus of freedom or deficit of regimentation in Religion. This had, for example, been the history of the Hellenic Civilization in its universal state. After the wars and social conflicts of an Hellenic Time of Troubles had been effectively suppressed by the imposition of an Augustan Peace, the psychic energy that had thus been deprived of its former vent in Politics and Economics had found a new vent in Religion. The dullness of a world in which War had been banished to anti-barbarian frontiers beyond the horizon,[1] and in which the sterilization of Politics had taken the heart out of public speaking,[2] had been effectively relieved on the religious plane by a compensatory outbreak of Christian martyrdom. This psychological compensation had been effective because there could be no surer way of making Life worth living again than to rediscover a cause for which it was worth sacrificing it. It will be seen that this chapter of Hellenic history was a precedent that was significant for Western prospects.

One lesson of this Hellenic episode was that in Life there is always an irreducible minimum of psychic energy that will insist on discharging itself through some channel or other; but it is equally true, as we have observed in an earlier context,[3] that there is also a maximum limit to the quantity of psychic energy which Life has at its disposal; and from this it follows that, if a reinforcement of energy is required for putting a greater drive into one activity, the requisite additional supply will have to be obtained by making economies of energy in other quarters. Life's device for economizing energy is mechanization. For example, by making the beating of the heart and the alternating inflation and deflation of the lungs automatic in the human body, Life had released human thought and will for other uses than the continual maintenance of physical vitality from moment to moment. If a conscious act of thought and act of will had never ceased to be required for the initiation of each successive breath and successive heart-beat, no human being would ever have had any margin of intellectual or volitional energy to spare for doing anything else than just keeping alive; or, to state the point more accurately, no sub-human being would ever have succeeded in becoming human. On

---

[1] See VI. vii. 122–3.   [2] See V. vi. 80–81.   [3] In IV. iv. 125.

the analogy of this creative effect of the economy of energy in the life of Man's body physical, we might surmise that, in the life of his body social, Religion would be likely to be starved so long as thought and will were pre-occupied with Economics (as they had been in the West since the Industrial Revolution) and with Politics (as they had been in the West since the Western renaissance of a deified Hellenic state);[1] and we might infer from this that the regimentation that was now being imposed on the Western Society's economic and political life would be likely to liberate Western souls for fulfilling the true end of Man by glorifying God and enjoying Him once again.

This happier spiritual prospect was at least a possibility in which a dispirited generation of Western men and women might catch a beckoning gleam of kindly light; and, with this possibility in view, an historian recalling the history of the emergence of the Western Civilization out of a post-Hellenic interregnum would recollect that, in that episode, a psychic energy that had been transferred from Economics to Religion during an antecedent Hellenic Civilization's disintegration had eventually produced, as an incidental economic by-product of a life in which Religion had come to be the lode-star, economic effects which had been beyond the compass of a Roman oecumenical government commanding the total resources of a great society and the skill, experience, and good will of an admirable professional civil service. A decline and fall of agriculture in Italy, which the imperial Roman régime had proved as impotent to arrest as had their republican predecessors the Gracchi, was not only arrested but was reversed by monks of the Benedictine Order following the rule of a founder who had prescribed for his spiritual sons a daily stint of manual labour as an alternative way of serving God that would provide a psychologically wholesome foil to the singing of the Liturgy.[2]

This first chapter of Western history might perhaps repeat itself in a chapter that, in A.D. 1952, still lay unwritten in the womb of the Future. The transfer of psychic energy to Religion from Economics might once again save *Homo Economicus* from himself by saving him from the necessity of artificially reducing his economic productivity as the only means at his command for defending himself against the noxious effects of an excessive economic appetite. In previous chapters[3] we have noticed that the demonic physical 'drive' which Modern Western Man had put into his economic activities through the mechanization of his technology had manufactured a psychological brake for itself by generating the trade-union spirit in the industrial working class and the civil-service spirit in the middle class. These defensive psychic mechanisms had proved effective for the negative purpose for which they had been mounted; but they had protected *Homo Faber Mechanicus* against the tyranny of his clockwork at the cost of taking the heart out of his handiwork, and they had taken the heart out of his handiwork at the cost of depotentiating economic activities on which the mechanization of Technology had placed too grievously heavy a psychic load. It might be that, in the long

---

[1] See X. ix. 7–15.
[2] See III. iii. 266, with the passages quoted there, in footnotes 2 and 3, from Saint Benedict's Rule.　　　　　　　　　　　　　　[3] On pp. 563–74 and 604–6, above.

run the transfer of energy from Economics to Religion would justify itself from the chartered accountant's, as well as from the spiritual pastor's, point of view.

If the transfer of energy from Religion to Economics at the opening of the Modern Age of Western history had shot a bolt that had subsequently come home to roost like a boomerang in the economic field, it was conceivable that a re-transfer of energy from Economics to Religion at the opening of a post-Modern Age might ultimately come to a self-stultified Western *Homo Economicus*'s rescue. Under the aegis of Religion, Western Man might find himself able to handle with spiritual impunity the material power thrust into his hands by the mechanization of Western technology. A neo-pagan Frankenstein who had been enslaved by the monster that he had made might live to become this monstrous mechanism's once more Christian master; for, if the Western Society's progressive economic self-defeat since the Industrial Revolution had proved the truth of the saying in the Gospels that 'from him that hath not, even that he hath shall be taken away from him',[1] this saying was inseparable from its context 'that unto every one which hath shall be given', and this complementary *logion* was illustrated in the legend of Solomon's choice in his dream by night at Gibeon.[2] When the dreamer had responded to God's challenging invitation 'Ask what I shall give thee' by asking God to give his servant an understanding heart to judge God's people, he had been rewarded for his unselfseeking choice of a spiritual gift by being given, over and above this, the mundane riches and honour for which he had not asked. This Syriac legend might be taken by Western souls as a parable of the choice before them in the twentieth century of the Christian Era.

[1] Luke xix. 26. Cp. Luke viii. 18; Matt. xiii. 12; Mark iv. 25.
[2] 1 Kings iii. 4–15.

F. THE STRAITS AHEAD

IF the foregoing appreciation of the prospects of the Western Civilization in A.D. 1952 has not fallen altogether wide of the mark, the general conclusion that is to be drawn from it is not obscure. At this date the feat that had to be performed by Western navigators on the face of the waters of History was to pilot their vessel, without disaster, through perilous straits in the hope of making their way into more open waters beyond; and in this post-Christian Odyssey there was more than one passage to be negotiated and more than one kind of ordeal to be faced.

In terms of our Mediterranean maritime simile, we may compare the social and spiritual enterprise to which these Western adventurers were committed in the twentieth century of the Christian Era with the navigational task confronting Hellenic mariners in the sixth century B.C. who had bidden farewell to their Ionian homeland and had set sail westward rather than submit to the alien dominion of un-Hellenic-minded Achaemenidae. Following in Odysseus' wake, these Phocaean seafarers would have first to negotiate the straits between Sicily and Italy without approaching either an Italian shore where they would be pounced upon by the monster Scylla or a Sicilian shore where they would be engulfed by the whirlpool Charybdis; but, if, by managing to steer their course along the narrow fairway through this first danger-zone, they should succeed in making the friendly port of Marseilles, they would not there find themselves at rest in the haven where they would be;[1] for their bold and skilful negotiation of the Straits of Messina would merely have carried them from the inner basin into the outer basin of the Mediterranean, without having liberated them from the imprisoning shores of their landlocked native sea.

If they were to reach the boundless waters of a globe-encompassing Ocean, these voyagers must put to sea again from the sheltering harbour of their mother country's daughter city in order to make for the Straits of Gibraltar between the Pillars of Hercules, where this pair of menacing mountains, towering above the African and the European shore and threatening, from either flank, to fall upon any ship audacious enough to run the gauntlet without their leave, were visible embodiments of Imperial Carthage's decree that no Hellenic vessel was ever to sail on through this golden gate leading out from the landlocked waters into the main. And here woe betide the Hellenic mariner who allowed himself to be intimidated by his adversary's veto into following the Theban Pindar's poor-spirited advice to his Agrigentine patron Thêrôn.

'And now Thêrôn's achievements have carried him to the limit: they have brought him to the Pillars of Hercules on his long voyage from home; and what lies beyond this terminus is out of bounds (ἄβατον) for all men, wise or witless. I will not pursue this venture. I should deserve to lose my senses if I did this senseless thing!'[2]

[1] Ps. cvii. 30.
[2] Pindar: *Odes in Honour of Victors in the Olympic Games*, Ode iii, ll. 43–45.

Ne plus ultra! These were the very words that a forbidding Carthaginian statesmanship had been intending to extort from defeatist Hellenic lips; and, so long as this self-imposed Hellenic psychological
inhibition held, no Hellenic explorer would ever sail on to test the truth of
a later poet's intuition that the untried passage of the Ocean would prove
to be the avenue to a New World.[1] More than two thousand years were
to pass before Columbus's victorious defiance of the veto once imposed
by a jealous Carthage was to be commemorated, in the device of 'the
dollar sign', by the first sovereign on whose globe-encircling dominions
the Sun could never set.[2] On coins minted for Charles V out of American
bullion, the antistrophic words *Plus ultra!* were triumphantly inscribed
on a scroll displayed behind the minatory pair of pillars;[3] and the moral
was one which a twentieth-century Odysseus ought to take to heart if
this series of episodes in the history of the art of navigation was an apt
parable of the spiritual voyage on which his sails were set.

In the interpretation of this parable in terms of the Western Civilization's prospects, the finding of a passage between Scylla and Charybdis
signified the negotiation of the Western World's immediate problem of
finding some way of avoiding self-destruction without falling into self-
stultification. Mid-way through the twentieth century of the Christian
Era the Western Society was in imminent danger of destroying itself by
failing to stop making War now that a demonic drive had been put into
War by the progress of a Western physical science; and it was in hardly
less imminent danger of stultifying itself by seeking asylum from War
and Class-Conflict in Circe's pig-sty. If post-Christian Western souls
did succeed in threading their way between these two immediate perils,
they would owe their happy issue out of this affliction to an inspiration to
take Religion as the mark on which they were once more to set their
course; but an impulse to return to Religion would not in itself suffice to
bring the Western pilgrims' ships out of inland waters into open sea; for
the call of Religion was being uttered in diverse tongues;[4] and the questions to which the agnostic Western pioneer in search of a Christian
oracle would have, at his own peril, to find an answer for himself, were:

'Are all apostles? Are all prophets? Are all teachers? . . . Have all the
gifts of healing? . . . Do all interpret?'[5]

In this spiritual ordeal the forbidding Pillars of Hercules were a pair
of rival authoritarian and dogmatic faiths, both of which alike were offer-

---

[1] Seneca: *Medea*, ll. 364–79, quoted in II. i. 263, n. 1.
[2] See IX. viii. 428, n. 9.
[3] See Raymond, Wayte: *The Silver Dollars of North and South America* (New York
1939, Wayte Raymond, Inc.) for photographs of dollars coined for the Spanish Crown,
over a series of reigns ranging from Charles V's (*regnabat* A.D. 1516–56) to the break-up
of the Spanish Empire of the Indies in the nineteenth century of the Christian Era,
which display the pair of pillars with the motto *Plus ultra*. On 46 of the 67 specimens
(not counting 'necessity coins') of 'pillar type' coins here reproduced, including the
earliest in the series, Charles V's coin from Santo Domingo (p. 18, No. 1), the two words
are inscribed on a single scroll linking the pillars (and passing behind an heraldic shield
inserted between the pillars on coins of this type minted for the Bourbons). On fifteen
specimens, each of the two pillars is wreathed in a separate scroll of its own, with 'Plus'
inscribed on the left-hand scroll and 'Ultra' on the right-hand scroll. On six specimens,
including Philip II's dollar minted in Peru (reproduced in Supplement, p. 3, No. A 1),
the motto is inscribed behind or above the pillars without being mounted on a scroll.
[4] 1 Cor. xii. 28.   [5] 1 Cor. xii. 29–30.

ing to the storm-tossed voyager an everlasting *Nirvāna* in their stony bosoms and were threatening him with the eternal punishment that had been inflicted on the Flying Dutchman if he were to be so impious and so fool-hardy as to reject their offer and sail on past them out into the blue. From the one shore this ultimatum was being delivered to Western souls by a Christian heresy in which the stone of Communism had been substituted for the bread[1] of the Gospel, and from the other shore by a Christian Orthodoxy in which the body of Christ,[2] who had 'come that they might have life, and that they might have it more abundantly',[3] had been petrified into a pillar of salt[4] by a backward-looking ecclesiastical tradition. To dare the passage between these two frowning Pillars of Hercules was a venture that might daunt even a mariner whose *moral* had been fortified by a previous success in making his way safely between Scylla and Charybdis. But, if, at this supremely critical point in his voyage, the pilgrim were to feel his heart failing, he might recover his courage and initiative by taking his oracle from Paul's First Epistle to the Corinthians:

'Covet earnestly the best gifts; and yet show I unto you a more excellent way.'[5]

If a contrite humility was the first of the Christian virtues that were necessary for the Western pilgrim's salvation, an indomitable endurance was the second. What was required of him at this hour was to hold on his course and to trust in God's grace; and, if he prayed God to grant him a pilot for the perilous passage, he would find the bodhisattva psychopompus whom he was seeking in a Francesco Bernardone of Assisi, who was the most god-like soul that had been born into the Western World so far. A disciple of Saint Francis who followed faithfully enough in the saint's footsteps to participate in the saint's gift of receiving Christ's stigmata would know, with the knowledge that comes only through suffering, that his sacrifice had been accepted by the Lord.[6] *Asperges me hyssopo et mundabor.*[7]

---

[1] Matt. vii. 9; Luke xi. 11. [2] 1 Cor. xii. 27; Eph. iv. 12.
[3] John x. 10. [4] Gen. xix. 26. [5] 1 Cor. xii. 31.
[6] Gen. iv. 3–7.
[7] Ps. l. 9, in the Vulgate Latin text; Ps. li. 7, in the English Authorized Version.

THE CONFLICTING THEORIES OF SURVIVAL AND REVIVAL AS ALTERNATIVE EXPLANATIONS OF THE EMERGENCE OF THE MEDIEVAL ITALIAN CITY-STATES

DURING the post-Napoleonic decades of the nineteenth century of the Christian Era, when Italians who had been arbitrarily resubjected to an *ancien régime* were demanding their national unity and independence in the name of the French ideas of A.D. 1789, one of the forms in which this demand was expressed was a claim to the restoration of the constitutional liberties that had once been won and enjoyed by the Medieval Italian urban communes; and a feeling that the strength of this claim would be proportionate to the length of their ancestors' historical tenure of these allegedly prescriptive political rights moved a tendencious school of Romantic Italian historians, taking their cue from Savigny, the German historian of the renaissance of Roman Law in the West, to maintain that the communes which had begun to make their mark on the stage of Early Medieval Italian history in the eleventh century of the Christian Era were no new arrivals there and then, but were none other than the original city-states of a pre-Roman and Roman Italy which, on this hypothesis, had mutely survived the Hellenic Civilization's lapse into social anarchy in the third century of the same era, its subsequent last rally under the crushing aegis of a Diocletianic totalitarian régime, and its final dissolution in an interregnum preceding the emergence of a nascent Western Christian Hellenistic Society. According to this romantic thesis the 'ancient' Italian city-states had continued, through all these vicissitudes, to be going concerns. They had temporarily been 'off the record' without ever having lost their identity, and the epiphany of the Medieval communes in the eleventh century was not the 'ancient' city-states' rebirth, but merely their re-emergence.[1]

Considering that a progressive decay of constitutional self-government is the dominant note of Hellenic political history throughout the span of more than six hundred years intervening between the generation of Philip of Macedon and the generation of Diocletian of Doclea, the burden of proof surely rests on the shoulders of the advocates of a thesis that the self-governing institutions of the Italian city-states resisted the elsewhere victorious forces of disintegration so successfully that they managed to survive even the final series of devastating catastrophes that gave the Hellenic Civilization its *coup de grâce*.[2] In this instance the *argumentum ex silentio* is one that decidedly requires an answer. Yet

---

[1] See Goetz, W.: *Sitzungsberichte der Bayerischen Akademie der Wissenschaften*, philosophisch-historische Abteilung, Jahrgang 1944, Heft 1 (Munich 1944, Beck), pp. 5 and 105–6.

[2] This point is rightly emphasized by Goetz, op. cit., pp. 108–9.

this argument remains unrefuted; and the formidable negative case against the thesis that the Medieval Italian communes were derived from the 'ancient' Italian city-states without any breach of historical continuity is confirmed by a positive consideration which would appear to be conclusive.

In the Medieval Italian communes the civic magistrates bore the title 'consuls'; and the advocates of the thesis that a Medieval Italian civic self-government goes back, without a break, to 'ancient' origins will be hard put to it to explain how and why and when the cities of Italy had come to adopt a piece of constitutional nomenclature which, in 'ancient' times, had been foreign to all of them with the sole exception of Rome. After Rome had made herself the queen of Italy and the rest of the Hellenic World through the prowess of Roman armies led by Roman consuls, no state-member of a Roman commonwealth of city-states would ever have ventured to call its municipal magistrates 'consuls' in lieu of the traditional local title, whatever this might happen to be. If the civic institutions of the Medieval Italian communes had really been handed down from days before the Roman conquest, then their supreme magistrates would still have borne the title *meddices tutici* in ex-Oscan-speaking communities and the title *praetores* or *dictator* in ex-Latin-speaking communities. If their institutions had been of Roman origin, then their magistrates would have been called *duumviri* or *quattuorviri*. If they had dated from the last century of the Principate they would have been called *curator*. If they had dated from the post-Diocletianic Age they would have been called *defensor civitatis*. But they could never have been given the Roman title 'consuls' until the official abolition of the Roman Consulate by the Emperor Justinian in A.D. 541[1] had become so immemorially old an accomplished fact that the term had had time to fade out of the field of practical politics into an academic limbo of historical memories. Then, and not till then, this term 'consul' would have come to be at the disposal of any academic-minded constitution-maker who might be attracted by it—and it would, of course, possess the supreme attraction of being associated historically with memories of the greatest age in the history of the most potent of all Hellenic city-states.

This tell-tale internal evidence inherent in the history of the title 'consuls' is confirmed by external evidence testifying that, in the parts of Italy conquered by the Lombards in and after A.D. 568, the last vestiges of civic self-government were effaced by new institutions for governing the cities through officers appointed by, and answerable to, the kings and dukes who ruled over the Lombard successor-states of the Constantinopolitan Roman Empire on Italian ground; and these new Lombard royal and ducal officials in Italian cities bore such new titles as 'counts', 'viscounts (*locopositi*)', *missi, gastaldi*, 'Schultheisse', *iudices, decani*. During the interval of four hundred years between the completion of the Lombard conquests and the rise of the Medieval Italian city-states, the surviving contemporary documents and other records show no trace of the currency either of the Medieval Italian title

[1] See V. vi. 111 and 224.

'consuls' or of any of the pre-Lombard titles of Italian civic magistracies dating from the Roman or pre-Roman Age.[1]

This testimony borne by indisputable facts in the field of constitutional nomenclature tells conclusively in favour of the view that the communes which made their epiphany in Italy in the eleventh century of the Christian Era were walking ghosts of the 'ancient' Italian city-states and were not living survivals of them; for the use of the word 'consuls' to designate their magistrates shows that the eleventh-century Italian constitution-makers were playing at a resuscitation of 'ancient' republican institutions, consecrated in their tradition of the glories of 'Ancient Rome', with the same deliberate and selfconscious pedantry as was to be displayed, in their day, by the authors of the French constitution of the 25th December, 1799.

This vein of antiquarianism, which betrays the lack of any genuine continuity between the Medieval Western Italian city-states and the Late Hellenic city-states that had previously occupied some of the same sites on Italian ground, was not, of course, the creative source of the revival of a defunct Hellenic political institution in the life of a growing Western Civilization. Even in Italy the consciousness of a Roman past was exceedingly nebulous from the eighth to the thirteenth century of the Christian Era,[2] and these centuries included the period of gestation preceding the re-birth of the City-State in Italy. Down to the thirteenth century this successful Medieval Western revival of the Hellenic City-State was an unconscious, not a conscious, response to the challenge of new needs[3] (in contrast to the abortive Medieval Western revival of the Roman Empire, which was selfconscious at every stage). The preponderance of the part played in this particular renaissance by the subconscious depths of the Psyche is indicated by the fact that Italy—where a gleam of selfconsciousness is registered in the coining of the antiquarian title 'consuls'—was only one of a number of localities in a Medieval Western Christendom in which the resuscitation of the Hellenic institution of the City-State occurred more or less simultaneously. This was a Pan-Hesperian movement in which Flanders, Germany, France, the Iberian Peninsula, and England were implicated, as well as Italy. The demands for greater security of person and property which evoked the first rudiments of Western civic self-government were rife in Transalpine Western Europe perhaps at least as early as in Italy.[4] In presenting such demands, are we to suppose that 'the townsfolk of Northern France, Flanders, and Italy were taking their stand on Ancient Roman ideals? Is it not much more likely that the pressure of an emergency which was the same everywhere was the stimulus that evoked the same demands in all these places?'[5] And, if it comes to that, are we to imagine that the Lombard *nobiles* of the Italian city of Savona and the likewise Lombard *arimanni* of the Italian city of Mantua, who obtained charters from the Margrave of Savona and

---

[1] Goetz, op. cit., pp. 7–8. Cp. ibid., p. 113.
[2] See ibid., pp. 107 and 113–14.
[3] See ibid., pp. 108 and 113–15.
[4] See ibid., p. 116, n. 1.
[5] Ibid., p. 116. Cp. ibid., pp. 108, 111, and 118.

from the Holy Roman Emperor respectively in the year A.D. 1014, 'really retained any recollection of Roman civic franchises? Is it [their incentive] not much more likely to have been an urgent need for protection against the arbitrary proceedings of the great rural potentates?'[1]

[1] Goetz, op. cit., p. 116.

POINTS OF LIKENESS AND DIFFERENCE BE-
TWEEN THE RENAISSANCES OF THE SINIC
AND HELLENIC UNIVERSAL STATES

A HAN EMPIRE that had served as the Sinic Society's universal state
and a Roman Empire that had performed a corresponding service for
the Hellenic Society were both alike eventually raised from the dead
to minister to the needs of new societies that had sprung up among the
Sinic and Hellenic worlds' ruins; and, in both cases alike, these feats
of necromancy were performed after the derelict domain of the defunct
society and its fallen universal state had been irradiated by a higher
religion whose spark of creativity was of alien cultural origin, and had
also been invaded by barbarian war-bands from a no-man's-land beyond
the fallen universal state's *limes*. In both cases, again, the interloping
barbarians consisted partly of local sedentary peoples and partly of
Eurasian Nomads;[1] and, in both, the interloping higher religion was
introduced by subjects of the declining universal state, and members
of the disintegrating society's internal proletariat, who had this alien
spiritual treasure to impart because they were the offspring of *ci-devant*
members of another society—the Indic Society in the one case and the
Syriac in the other—who had not renounced their pristine cultural
allegiance when they had been incorporated into an alien oecumenical
empire by military force. These points of likeness between the two
episodes of history which we are here examining synoptically are so
remarkable that they challenge us to search for the causes of the no
less remarkable points of difference which the resemblances throw into
sharp relief.

The most striking of these differences is also the one that was fraught
with the most momentous historical consequences. The Han Empire
found its avatar in a single polity—established by the Sui and consolidated by the T'ang—which was not only an intentional resuscitation
of the defunct Sinic universal state but was also actually a genuine
reincarnation of it, at least in a geographical sense, in virtue of the Sui
Power's success in establishing its undisputed dominion over the entire
area that had once been occupied by the Sinic Society and by a Han
Empire under whose aegis the Sinic World had been united politically
in the concluding chapter of Sinic history.[2] On the other hand the
Roman Empire was resuscitated in two separate and mutually hostile
avatars, either of which claimed to be the sole genuine reincarnation
of the defunct Hellenic universal state and consequently found itself
constrained to denounce its rival as an impostor.

These two competing ghosts of the Roman Empire were severally
evoked in different fragments of former Roman territory at different

[1] The Eurasian Nomad barbarian invasion of a moribund Sinic World has been
noticed in V. v. 272–3.　　　　　　　　　　　　　[2] See V. v. 356, n. 6.

dates. Leo Syrus established his East Roman Empire in Anatolia after foiling the Arabs' second attempt to capture Constantinople (*iterum obsidebatur* A.D. 717–18); the Carolingians established their Holy Roman Empire under the lee of the Roman Empire's former frontier along the Rhine in the course of the sixty-eight years that elapsed between Charles Martel's repulse of the Arabs at Tours in A.D. 732 and Charlemagne's coronation at Rome in A.D. 800. The Roman Empire was thus resuscitated as a split personality; and, even so, the aggregate area of the actual domains of the two rival *soi-disants* Roman Empires that made their successive appearances on the political map in the eighth century of the Christian Era did not cover, between them, anything like the entire area of the Roman Empire *imperante Hadriano* (A.D. 117–38) or even *imperante Diocletiano* (A.D. 284–305). The Arabs' conquest of the Visigothic successor-state of the Roman Empire in the Iberian Peninsula in A.D. 711–13 had completed the liberation of all provinces of the Syriac World that had ever been annexed to the Hellenic World by force of Macedonian and Roman arms; and the military reverses which the Arabs suffered thereafter in A.D. 717 and in A.D. 732 merely prevented them from engulfing a Hellenized Hittite World in Anatolia and the adjoining Greek and Italian homelands of the defunct Hellenic Civilization, without resulting in the re-establishment of even a simulacrum of Roman rule over the former Roman provinces south of the Taurus and of the Pyrenees.

Moreover, the two rival eighth-century avatars of the Roman Empire were insulated from one another overland by the effects of successive eruptions of Eurasian Nomadism out of the Great Western Bay of the Eurasian Steppe into the Balkan Peninsula; and, though the Avars on the Alföld were extirpated by Charlemagne in A.D. 791, this Austrasian 'Roman Emperor's' success in thus disposing of one intrusive Nomad horde was purchased at the price of enlarging the domain of another. Charlemagne found himself constrained to divide the territorial spoils of the Avars with the Bulgars, and the elimination of the Avars thus left the Bulgars astride the Middle as well as the Lower Danube, while it did not relieve the Balkan Peninsula of the presence of pagan Slav sedentary barbarians whom the Avars had parked there as their 'human cattle' when they were restocking a ranch that had been depopulated by the ravages of the Avars' Nomad forerunners, the Huns, and by the simultaneous drafts drawn on Illyrian military man-power by the Roman Emperor Justinian in pursuance of an anti-barbarian *revanche* that had defeated its own ultimate purposes.

This partition of two salvaged fragments of former Roman imperial territory between two rival ghosts of the defunct Hellenic universal state is a tale of comparative failure which gives the measure of the success achieved by the Sui and the T'ang in reuniting the whole former territory of a defunct Sinic universal state under the undivided rule of a single reincarnation of the Han Empire; and the historical consequences of this difference between the outcomes of these evocations of ghosts of a Sinic and an Hellenic universal state were truly momentous. The Sui and T'ang empire-builders' success in establishing and maintaining a single oecumenical empire embracing the whole former domain of the extinct universal state of which this new empire was intended to be an avatar was a political achievement which ensured that the Sinic Civilization should be succeeded by a single undivided Far Eastern Society.[1] Conversely the Syrian and Carolingian dynasties' common failure to reincarnate a single unchallenged avatar of the Roman Empire was a political reverse which ensured that the Hellenic Civilization should be succeeded by one Christian Hellenistic Society in Anatolia and by another in the West.[2]

In the light of these portentous failures to re-establish either the political unity of the Roman Empire or the cultural unity of the Hellenic Society in the former geographical domain of the Hellenic World, the culturally fruitful political achievement of the Sui and T'ang Power stands out impressively; and this impression will be enhanced when we make a closer inspection of this great event's historical antecedents; since these will be found to forbid the assumption that, because this act of political reunification was successfully accomplished, it must therefore have been either a foregone conclusion or even an easy task.

By the time when the North and the South of a nascent Far Eastern World were united politically by the Sui Power in A.D. 589, the political separation between them had lasted, without a break, for no less than 272 years,[3] and the previous political unity that had dissolved in A.D. 317 had been both ephemeral and unsubstantial. Even in name the oecumenical empire of 'the United Tsin' had existed for no more than thirty-seven years (A.D. 280–317); and the façade of political unity that had been erected by Sse-ma Yen (alias Wu-ti) in A.D. 280 and had been maintained by his successors during the 'United Tsin' Dynasty's brief régime had been purchased by them at the fatal price of losing hold, de facto, of the dynasty's own original patrimony in the North which had been their base of operations for this anachronistic reunification of the Sinic World a hundred years after the fall of the Posterior Han. This concentration of the military energies of one of the Han Empire's three indigenous successor-states on the fratricidal objective of suppressing the other two came as a godsend to Eurasian Nomad laeti who had been establishing themselves inside the Great Wall, by a process of more or less peaceful infiltration, ever since the first beginnings of the Han Power's decline; for this internecine Sinic civil war gave these barbarian interlopers their patiently awaited opportunity to shake off

---

[1] The eventual supplementation of the main body of this Far Eastern Society in China by a branch in Korea and Japan was the result of a subsequent process which was one, not of division, but of multiplication.

[2] Even after the differentiation between an Orthodox Christian and a Western Christian Hellenistic Civilization had declared itself in the generation of Leo Syrus and had accentuated itself in the generation of Charlemagne and had exacerbated itself in the generation of Photius (see I. i. 66–67), History's decree *nisi* need not, even then, necessarily have been made absolute—as it was made in fact in the generation of Michael Cerularius—to judge by the different denouement of another historical drama after it had arrived at the same dramatic situation. The differentiation between an Arab Muslim and an Iranic Muslim successor of a defunct Syriac Civilization was at least arrested, even if it was not permanently overcome, through the political union of five-sixths of the Arabic World with one-third of the Iranic World as a result of Ottoman conquests of Arabic territories in the sixteenth century of the Christian Era (see I. i. 388–400).

[3] See V. v. 356, n. 6.

the control of the sedentary Power on whose domain they were tres-passers.[1] When we have discounted an attempt to re-establish the Han Empire at the turn of the third and fourth centuries of the Christian Era which had such unfortunate consequences, we shall realize that, in effect, the political separation between North and South that was brought to an end by Sui Wên-ti in A.D. 589 had prevailed, by that date, not merely for 272 years, but for no less than four hundred years if we ignore the interlude of the United Tsin and carry our reckoning back to the date of the Posterior Han Dynasty's death agonies, which had set in before the close of the second century of the Christian Era. The feat performed by Yang Kien (alias Sui Wên-ti) in thus overcoming a political disunity, which, by his day, was entrenched in the accu-mulated inertia of four centuries of use and wont, was only surpassed by the succeeding T'ang Dynasty's feat of consolidating the unity of the long severed northern and southern halves of the Far Eastern World which the Sui had so dexterously joined together.[2]

Both the Sui and the T'ang were heirs of the Eurasian Nomad bar-barian successor-states of the Han Empire[3] which had overtly asserted their independence in the hinterland of the Great Wall at the beginning of the fourth century of the Christian Era after the fiasco of the osten-sible political reunification of the Sinic World under the United Tsin; and, if we bear in mind this barbarian heritage of the dynasties respon-sible for the renaissance of the Sinic universal state in the history of the subsequent Far Eastern Civilization in its original political shape of a single oecumenical empire embracing the entire domain of the former Sinic Society, we shall be able to discern what the corresponding course of events would have been in the aftermath of the histories of the Hellenic Civilization and of a Roman Empire that had played the part of an Hellenic universal state.

To reconstruct a corresponding denouement here, we should not only have to imagine Charlemagne emulating, as he did, the achieve-ment of the Sui's predecessors the Pe Chóu, who had provided the Sui with their base of operations for uniting the South of the Far Eastern World with the North in A.D. 589 by having already reunited a pre-viously partitioned North in A.D. 577; we should have to imagine Charlemagne, after his reunion of the Roman Empire's Lombard successor-state with its Frankish successor-state in A.D. 772–4, being supplanted by a usurper of native Gallo-Roman descent who then went on—by conquest or marriage or diplomacy—to reunite the contem-

[1] See V. v. 272–3. In thus purchasing a transitory political reunification of the South with the North of the Sinic World at the cost of opening the door for barbarian usurpers to make themselves masters of an archaistically ambitious Imperial Power's home terri-tories, the United Tsin were making the same mistake that Justinian was to make when he purchased for the Roman Empire a transitory reconquest of Italy at the cost of losing the Balkan Peninsula to the Avars and their droves of Slavs (see V. vi. 286), and that Michael Palaiológhos was to make when he purchased for the East Roman Empire's Nicaean Greek Orthodox Christian successor-state a burdensome re-occupation of Constantinople at the cost of losing Western Anatolia to Turkish Muslim war-bands set in motion by the dissolution of the Saljūq Sultanate of Qōnīyeh.

[2] Matt. xix. 6.

[3] These barbarian antecedents of theirs are underlined by Franke, O.: *Geschichte des Chinesischen Reiches*, vol. ii (Berlin and Leipzig 1936, de Gruyter), p. 250. On this point, see also the present Study, V. v. 273, 356, n. 6, and 477–8.

porary East Roman reincarnation of the Roman Empire in Anatolia and Constantinople with Charlemagne's reincarnation of the Roman Empire in Gaul and Italy. But, to make our imaginary correspondence of post-Roman history with post-Han history complete, we must also endow the eighth-century East Roman Empire, which we are imagining Charlemagne's hypothetical Gallo-Roman supplanter to have annexed, with a vastly wider dominion than the modest combination of an Anatolian citadel with a Constantinopolitan bridgehead that had actually been inherited by Charlemagne's contemporaries Constantine VI and his mother Irene from their predecessor Leo Syrus. We must imagine the East Roman Empire of Charlemagne's day to have been coextensive with the Roman Empire within the frontiers that had been recovered for it by Justinian, and we must imagine Justinian to have succeeded completely in attaining his objective of reconquering the Roman Empire's Visigothic, as well as its Ostrogothic and Vandal, successor-state. This series of imaginary successes would have to be substituted for so many historical failures in the political history of a post-Hellenic inter-regnum in order to credit Charlemagne's hypothetical supplanter with an imaginary achievement of the same order of magnitude as the actual performance of the Chinese empire-builder Sui Wên-ti; and, even then, we should find that we had not succeeded in bringing Charlemagne's imaginary Gallo-Roman heir completely into line with his mighty Far Eastern counterpart; for the combination of actually unachieved successes which we have placed to the credit of Charlemagne's imaginary heir still leaves the English successor-states of the Roman Empire in Britain beyond our preposterously exaggerated imaginary limits of the Holy Roman Empire, whereas the whole former domain of the Han Empire was duly reassembled in the realm that Sui Wên-ti actually brought into being.

The residual discrepancy resulting from the recalcitrant independence of Mercia and the other barbarian successor-states of the Roman Empire in Britain might perhaps be glozed over, but we must not flatter ourselves by supposing that, if we were to ignore this minor point, we should find ourselves at the end of our imaginary rewriting of post-Roman history if we were seriously intent on bringing it into line with the post-Han history of the Far East; for an avatar of the Han Empire that had been integrally reconstructed by Sui Wên-ti was preserved all but intact for the next 553 years (A.D. 589–1142) under successive Sui, T'ang, and Sung régimes,[1] whereas Charlemagne's diadochi and epigoni actually proved incompetent to hold together even the fraction of the Roman Empire's former domain that Charlemagne had managed to reassemble. To bring the course of Far Eastern history into conformity with the course of Western history, we must imagine the year A.D. 589

---

[1] A stricter count would limit the duration of the Far Eastern avatar of a Sinic universal state to a span of some three hundred years, since the main body of the Far Eastern World went through a spell of political disruption between the onset of the T'ang Dynasty's death-agonies in the last quarter of the ninth century of the Christian Era (see IV. iv. 86 and 87–88) and the establishment of the Sung Dynasty in A.D. 960 (see V. vi. 306); and during this bout of anarchy sixteen border districts were ceded, between the years A.D. 927 and 937, to the Khitan transfrontier barbarians (see II. ii. 121; IV. iv. 86; V. v. 308; and V. vi. 307).

witnessing in the Far East, not the consummation of the Pe Chóu Dynasty's reunification of the North in A.D. 577 through Sui Wên-ti's unification of North and South, but the undoing of the local achievement of A.D. 577 in the North through a relapse of the North into the state of political disintegration in which it had been languishing before A.D. 577 since the break-up, in A.D. 534, of the 'Wei' empire in which the North had been reunited *circa* A.D. 410/439[1] as a result of the To Pa Eurasian Nomad barbarian principality's success in progressively swallowing up all the other barbarian successor-states of the Han Empire which had come to the surface in the North since the beginning of the fourth century.[2]

If we may assume that we have now taken the full measure of the difference between the respective courses of post-Han history and post-Roman history that has to be taken into account in order to see the equally evident points of likeness between the same two stories in their true perspective, we may now go on to inquire into the causes of this partial diversity of two lines of development that are at the same time partially similar. We shall find ourselves able to identify one geographical cause and one political.

The geographical cause is to be found in a physiographical difference between the Sinic and the Hellenic World which is reflected in the respective structures of the Han and the Roman Empire.

The Sinic Civilization[3] was a continental culture, and its geographical expansion was carried out overland up to 'the natural frontiers' of an East Asian sub-continent which was delimited by the southern shore of the Eurasian Steppe, the western shore of the Pacific Ocean, and the eastern escarpment of the Tibetan Plateau almost as definitely as the Indian sub-continent was delimited by the southern escarpment of the Tibetan Plateau, the eastern escarpment of the Iranian Plateau, and the northern shores of the Indian Ocean. In the expansion of the Sinic Civilization, the extirpation or assimilation of the sedentary barbarian highlanders previously inhabiting the northern fringes of the latter-day provinces of Shensi and Shansi had brought the Sinic World into immediate contact with the Eurasian Nomad World; and the risk of being invaded by the Nomads, to which the Sinic Society had thereby laid itself open, was not effectively parried by the expedient of reinforcing a 'natural' frontier in this quarter by the construction of those artificial fortifications that were eventually consolidated by Ts'in She Hwang-ti into one continuous Great Wall.[4] Yet, though this rather wantonly incurred peril from a seething pot towards the North[5] was not counteracted by these immense anti-Nomad defensive works, it was discounted, as the sequel was to show, by a vast overland extension of the Sinic Society's domain in another direction. A progressive subjugation of the sedentary barbarians beyond the south-western fringes of the Sinic World of the third century B.C. was initiated by Ts'in She Hwangti and was carried to completion rather more than a hundred

[1] See Herrmann, A.: *Historical and Commercial Atlas of China* (Cambridge, Mass. 1935, Harvard University Press), p. 29, Map IV.　　[2] See V. v. 356, n. 6.
[3] See Maps 25 and 26 in vol. xi.　　[4] See II. ii. 119–20 and V. v. 142.
[5] Jer. i. 13–15. Cp. iv. 6–7; v. 16–17; vi. 1 and 22–25; x. 22; xxv. 9.

years later by the Ts'in emperor's Han successors when they eventually pushed their advancing frontier over the crest of the Yangtse Basin's southern watershed down to the 'natural' frontier presented by the East Asian sub-continent's southern coast;[1] and this rounding-off of the Sinic universal state's domain towards the south-west, which was achieved by the Emperor Han Wuti in 111 B.C., was to prove its value four hundred years later, when in A.D. 311 the burst of a long-lowering Eurasian Nomad storm-cloud was proclaimed in the sack of 'the United Tsin's' historic capital, Loyang, by the Hiongnu founders of a barbarian successor-state which they sought to dignify with the name 'Pe Han'.[2]

This catastrophe of A.D. 311 gave a then senile Sinic Society a shock which was perhaps even more severe than the shock given to it by the previous sack of Loyang in A.D. 191, which had announced the beginning of the Posterior Han Dynasty's death-agonies; for in A.D. 191 the outrage had at least been committed by native Sinic hands, whereas the sacrilege of A.D. 311 was the deed of barely disguised *ci-devant* barbarians. The sack of Loyang in A.D. 191 had been followed in A.D. 221 by the dissolution of the Han Empire into the three indigenous successor-states, known as 'the Three Kingdoms', which had partitioned the Sinic World between them until its transitory political reunification under the United Tsin. The more appalling repetition of the catastrophe in A.D. 311 did not, however, sound the death-knell of the so-called 'Tsin'. Though they had now lost to the Nomad barbarian interlopers their own original territory in the upper and lower basins of the Yellow River, which had been the Sinic Civilization's original cradle before becoming the metropolitan territory of its universal state, the 'Tsin' were still masters of the Yangtse Basin and the Southern Seaboard, thanks to their completion of the reunification of the partitioned domain of the Han in A.D. 280.[3] In A.D. 318 the 'Tsin' turned to account their still unchallenged possession of this vast reserve of territory in the South by re-establishing their government in a new capital in the Lower Yangtse Basin in the city that eventually came to be known as Nanking.

By this politic migration the Tsin succeeded in prolonging the period of their rule for another century;[4] and, when they fell at last in A.D. 420,

---

[1] See V. v. 141-2 and 147.   [2] i.e. 'Northern Han'.

[3] In A.D. 280 the Tsin had annexed the Kingdom of Wu, which had held the Middle and Lower Yangtse Basin and the Southern Seaboard. The Kingdom of Shu, which had held the Upper Yangtse Basin (the latter-day province of Szechwan), had been annexed by the Northern Kingdom of Wei in A.D. 263, two years before the replacement of this Wei Dynasty by the Tsin Dynasty in the North in A.D. 265.

[4] This migration would not have achieved the political success that it did achieve if it had not had its economic counterpart in the effective development of the agricultural potentialities of the refugee régime's Southern fastness.

'The unity of China under the Western Tsin Dynasty (A.D. 265–317), which succeeded the Three Kingdoms, did not last long. Less than fifty years after its inauguration, the Tsin emperors had to retire to the south of the Yangtse River in the face of victorious rebellions on the part of the peasants in the northern provinces, who were in some districts the descendants of "barbarians" from what is now Chinese Turkistan and Mongolia, who had settled south of the Great Wall several centuries before. This period marks the change from "Western" Tsin to "Eastern" Tsin (A.D. 317–420). . . . The transition from "Western" to "Eastern" Tsin and subsequent events in the interval before China was unified again under the Sui Dynasty in A.D. 589 involved a tremendous

the Southern Empire which they had established did not fall with them, but passed intact to succeeding dynasties known as the Sung (*imperabant* A.D. 420–79), Ts'i (*imperabant* A.D. 479–501), and Liang (*imperabant* A.D. 502–55). It was not till A.D. 555, 244 years after the sack of Loyang by the Hiongnu in A.D. 311, that any part of the South came under the rule of a northern state of Eurasian Nomad barbarian origin. In A.D. 555[1] the Liang Empire's capital, Kiangling, on the Middle Yangtse, was captured by the armies of the 'Western Wei' fraction of the To Pa Northern Empire; but the consequent break-up of a Southern Empire, which, by that time, had been a going concern for an unbroken period of little less than a quarter of a millennium, resulted at the moment in only a partial southward extension of northern barbarian rule. In A.D. 555 the middle and upper basins of the Yangtse were duly annexed by the 'Western Wei', to pass thereafter from the 'Western Wei's' To Pa hands into the 'Pe Chóu's' Hiongnu hands[2] in A.D. 557,[3] and from the Pe Chóu's barbarian hands into the Sui's Chinese hands[4] in A.D. 581; but, in the Lower Yangtse Valley and on the Southern Seaboard, an attenuated Southern Empire survived under the Ch'en Dynasty (*imperabant* A.D. 557[5]–89) until the extinction of the Ch'en by the Sui in A.D. 589 at last reunited the whole former domain of the Han Empire under the rule of an oecumenical Power incubated in the North.

If we ask ourselves why this conquest of the South by heirs of the Eurasian Nomad conquerors of the North was so long delayed, the first answer is that the Prior Han Dynasty, in rounding off their domain towards the south-west, had created a 'Solid South' which was to prove impregnable to Nomad assaults.[6] In contrast to a long-since dry and open North, in which Man had won his victory over Water[7] as early as the Shang Age, even a latterly likewise tamed and regulated Yangtse Basin still presented a network of waterways to hamper the advance of the Nomad cavalry; and, if some enterprising squadrons were to suc-

---

change in the socio-economic history of the nation. The risings of "barbarian" settlers, who were mostly serfs working on land owned by Chinese "mandarin" lords, as well as the rebellions of discontented Chinese peasants, drove a vast number of Chinese of the upper classes, as well as retinues of their supporters, to the south of the Yangtse River. When the "barbarian" dynasties set up in their northern homes had lasted over a generation, hopes of regaining the northern domain were practically given up in the latter years of the Eastern Tsin, and the Chinese refugees in the Lower Yangtse Valley prepared for a permanent stay. . . . Such an impetus and necessity for migration had hitherto never been so keenly felt in the history of the Chinese people. The result . . . was the beginning of a period of rapid development of the fertile Yangtse Valley, which ultimately made it the Key Economic Area in China, replacing the Ching-Wei Basin and Lower Yellow River Valley. This brought about a sharp transformation of Chinese culture' (Chi, Ch'ao-ting: *Key Economic Areas in Chinese History as Revealed in the Development of Public Works for Water-Control* (London 1936, Allen & Unwin), pp. 107–8 and 110).

[1] This is the date given by Franke, O.: *Geschichte des Chinesischen Reiches*, vol. ii (Berlin and Leipzig 1936, de Gruyter), p. 175. In op. cit., vol. cit., p. 229, however, the same scholar dates the same event as having happened before the close of the year A.D. 554.

[2] For the Hun origin of Yü-wên T'ai, the barbarian mayor of the *ci-devant* barbarian Western Wei Dynasty's palace who laid the foundations of the parvenu Power that subsequently took the name 'Pe Chóu', see Franke, op. cit., vol. cit., pp. 226–7.

[3] See ibid., p. 235.   [4] See ibid., p. 180.   [5] See ibid., p. 176.

[6] This point has been noticed already in VI. vii. 357, n. 4.

[7] See II. i. 318–21.

ceed in threading their southward way through this watery maze and floundering out again without having been bogged, they would then straightway find themselves confronted with a broad belt of forest-clad highlands over which they would have to force a passage if they were bent on descending upon their Sinic victims' last ditch on the South China Coast. The strength of this Sinic 'Festung Südland' was demonstrated in A.D. 383, when a supreme effort to conquer the refugee 'Tsin' Dynasty's Southern Empire was made by a northern barbarian empire-builder of Tibetan origin, 'Ts'in' Fu Kien (*imperabat* A.D. 350–85),[1] who had momentarily united under his own rule all the barbarian successor-states of the former 'United Tsin' Empire in the North. This barbarian invasion of the South in A.D. 383 met with a crushing disaster before it had penetrated beyond the basin of the River Huai;[2] and the barbarian rulers of the North learnt this lesson so well that, as we have seen, the indigenous Southern Empire survived thereafter for 172 years (A.D. 383–555) intact, and for 206 years (A.D. 383–589) in an attenuated form, till it was eventually united with the North by a Northern Power with barbarian antecedents in whose êthos a hereditary barbarism had been winnowed out, by the date of the Sui Dynasty's accession to power in A.D. 581, through the persistent counter-influence of a still radioactive Sinic culture that had been playing upon the barbarian interlopers in the North for no less than four hundred years by the date of the Sui's conquest of the Ch'en.

Thus the continental physiography of the Sinic World enabled Han empire-builders to provide the Sinic culture with a natural fortress in the South which proved impregnable to the Eurasian Nomad barbarian conquerors of the North. In contrast to the physical structure of the Sinic World, the physiography of the Hellenic World was not continental but maritime, and the corresponding structure of the Roman Empire partly accounts for the Hellenic universal state's relative ill-success in foiling its barbarian invaders.

Whereas the Sinic Civilization had spread from river basin to river basin—originating in the Basin of the Yellow River and expanding into the Basin of the Yangtse—the Hellenic Civilization had spread from the shores of a lesser inland sea round the circumference of a greater one. It had come to birth between the Asiatic and European shores of the Aegean;[3] and in the penultimate phase of its decline[4] it had been unified politically by Roman empire-builders within the framework of a 'thalassocracy' commanding the entire perimeter of the Mediter-

[1] See Franke, O.: *Geschichte des Chinesischen Reiches*, vol. ii (Berlin and Leipzig 1936, de Gruyter), pp. 80–101.
[2] See ibid., pp. 95–97. The date of this decisive battle, which was fought in the angle between the Huai and its tributary the Fei, is given as A.D. 387, not 383, by C. P. Fitzgerald in *China, A Short Cultural History* (London 1935, Cresset Press), p. 257.
[3] See IX. viii. 711–12.
[4] The first attempt to provide the Hellenic World with a universal state had been made within the confines of Hellenism's Aegean cradle; but by the year 478 B.C., which saw the establishment of this abortive Athenian 'thalassocracy', the Hellenic World had already expanded far beyond these original limits; and, when, in 415 B.C., the Athenians sought to make their 'thalassocracy' coextensive with the contemporary domain of Hellenism by attempting to conquer Sicily, this enterprise proved to be so much beyond their strength that it led them into a disaster which was ultimately fatal to their 'thalassocracy' even within its more modest previous Aegean bounds.

ranean.[1] Though Roman roads and Roman legions left a deeper impression on the mind of Posterity than Roman shipping-lanes and naval patrols, the Roman Empire was in truth a pool of water surrounded by a hollow ring of land,[2] in contrast to the structure of the Han Empire, which was a plain of ploughland flanked on one side by a moated highland citadel.[3]

When we compare this maritime structure of the Roman Empire with the continental structure of the Han Empire, we can see that the Pan-Hellenic 'thalassocracy' had two politico-geographical weaknesses from which the Pan-Sinic terrene empire was exempt.

In the first place a Power that ruled the shores of the Mediterranean in virtue of ruling its waves could not extend its rule inland in any direction very far beyond the range of action of naval landing-parties, and therefore, in most directions, was constrained to draw the line of its *limes* along an alinement that fell far short of the nearest 'natural frontier'. The halo of impregnability with which the semi-official panegyrists of the Roman Empire sought to crown its landward defences during its illusory 'Indian Summer'[4] was rudely dissipated by the historical sequel; and the Emperor Hadrian had already seen through it as early as the year A.D. 117, when the death of a frustrated Roman Alexander had given this Roman Antipater his chance of liquidating a Trajanic adventure by reverting to a sober Augustan policy of territorial retrenchment. The Romans failed to find either a natural frontier or a satisfactory artificial substitute, not only in the South-West Asian hinterland of the Mediterranean,[5] but in its European hinterland as well.[6] The only two natural frontiers that they did succeed in reaching were the First Cataract in the Nile Valley—where they had merely to take over a line that an Augustan-minded Pharaoh, Psammetichus I, had laid down for them[7] more than six hundred years before Augustus's own occupation of Psammetichan Egypt after the Battle of Actium— and the Atlantic coast of Continental Europe between the Straits of Gibraltar and the Delta of the Rhine; but the Roman hold on this Continental European natural frontier was never confirmed by an integral occupation of its natural outworks in the British Isles. Though Claudius and his successors realized that the occupation of Britain was a necessary complement to that of Gaul, Lower Germany, and the north-west corner of the Iberian Peninsula, they were never willing to face the truth that, so long as their occupation of Britain stopped short at the line of the Solway and the Tyne, or even at the line of the Clyde and the Forth, without going on to embrace Caledonia and Ireland, they were condemning themselves to an increase in their military liabilities instead of securing a diminution of them.

The Romans' failure to round off their conquest of Britain by pushing

---

[1] See VI. vii. 216–17.   [2] See VI. vii. 217.
[3] The plain—consisting of the Wei Basin 'within the Passes' and the Lower Yellow River Basin to the east of that mountain barrier—corresponded physiographically to the western and eastern basins of the Mediterranean in the structure of the Roman Empire. The 'Festung Südland', perched on the southern watershed of the Yangtse Basin behind a network of waterways, corresponded to the Roman dominions in North-West Africa.
[4] See the panegyrics cited in VI. vii. 43–44 and 45–46.
[5] See IX. viii. 411–13.   [6] See V. v. 591–5.   [7] See II. ii. 116.

on to the natural frontiers that here lay close within their reach was more significant, and more ominous, than their failure to find a satisfactory frontier in the great open spaces of Continental Northern Europe and South-West Asia. Their performance in Britain argued an inability or unwillingness to mobilize even a limited additional quantum of energy or resources or both when this quantum amounted to no more than an inconsiderable fraction of Rome's total latent strength, and when a temporary exertion of this marginal effort promised to bring her a permanent relief from strain. The weakness that the Romans thus exhibited in Britain was also displayed by them in North-West Africa; and their failure here is particularly pertinent to our present inquiry because, as has been pointed out,[1] North-West Africa corresponded, in the geographical structure of the Roman Empire, to that southern hinterland of the Sinic World in which a Sinic universal state at bay eventually found 'a natural citadel' thanks to the successful exploitation of this region's politico-geographical potentialities by the conscientiously thorough-going labours of Prior Han empire-builders.

In terms of human geography North-West Africa was an island; for, wherever its coasts were not laved by the waters of the Mediterranean Sea and the Atlantic Ocean, they were brushed by the sands of the Sahara; and this desert, as the Romans had found it, had been a more effective insulator than the conductive waters of the Western Mediterranean, since the Sahara remained recalcitrant even to the steppe-conquering technique of the Afrasian Nomads until the Romans themselves placed a Sahara-conquering weapon in their Afrasian Nomad barbarian adversaries' hands by introducing the camel into North-West Africa from Arabia.[2] The conquest of the Sahara by indigenous North-West African Zanāta Berber Nomads,[3] who had learnt the use of the camel from Nafūsa and Lawāta Berber Nomad immigrants from Tripolitania,[4] was not, however, consummated before the overthrow of the Roman régime in North-West Africa in A.D. 429–39 by the co-operation of an intrusive barbarian war-band, composed of Alan Eurasian Nomads and semi-nomadicized Vandals, with indigenous barbarian war-bands recruited from the never subjugated sedentary barbarian North-West African highlanders. This long-delayed but, in the event, irresistibly overwhelming assault on Roman North-West Africa by the combined forces of convergent barbarian aggressors was the penalty of the Romans' failure to exploit the Maghrib's potentialities as 'a natural fastness' by subjugating the Berber highlanders up to 'the natural frontier' offered to Rome by the dry shore of a then still untenanted Sahara.[5] The Romans' sole achievement in this field was a precarious pacification of the isolated massif of the Aurès; but they did not ever effectively occupy more than the eastern half of the Algerian Tall, and, *a fortiori*, they hardly touched the Moroccan Rīf and never took even a first step towards subduing the Atlas.

This Roman record in North-West Africa was a very different story

---

[1] See p. 658, n. 3, above.
[2] See Gautier, E. F.: *Les Siècles Obscurs du Maghreb* (Paris 1927, Payot), pp. 162, 184, and 199–200.　　　　　　　　　　　　　　[3] See ibid., pp. 197–8.
[4] See ibid., pp. 209–10.　　　　　[5] This failure has been noticed in V. v. 205.

from the Han Empire's record in South China; for, though, in this case likewise, the subjugation of the local sedentary barbarian highlanders was by no means complete, it went sufficiently far to rule out all possibility of dangerous combinations between unsubdued southern barbarian highlanders and invading northern barbarian Nomads in the crisis in which the strength of the Sinic World's southern citadel was put to the test in the fourth century of the Christian Era, whereas, in Roman North-West Africa, a local eruption of unsubdued barbarian highlanders had been one of the regular incidents in each of the successive paroxysms of simultaneous concentric barbarian attacks on the perimeter of the Roman Empire's hollow ring. The *Bellum Gildonicum* had broken out in A.D. 398, thirty-one years before Genseric's passage into North-West Africa from the European shore of the Straits of Gibraltar; and in the previous paroxysm in the third century of the Christian Era there had been a similar outbreak of dissident local Berbers taking up arms on their own initiative.[1]

Another politico-geographical weakness of the Roman Empire was that, if once an aggressive external enemy had succeeded in breaking through its inevitably long-drawn-out and ill-sited artificial frontier defences, the Roman armies found themselves hampered by the narrowness of their manœuvring room in their attempts to foil the invader by a strategy of defence in depth[2] which proved the salvation of the Han Power's feeble 'Tsin' epigoni in A.D. 383.[3] When once an assailant had broken through the Roman *limes*, the odds would be heavily against the Roman defence force in its subsequent efforts to prevent the invader from reaching the coast; for the whole terrene perimeter of the Roman Empire was so thin—even in those Gallic and Anatolian sectors which were of twice the tenuous standard thickness[4]—that any breach of the *limes* would bring the Mediterranean within the invader's range; and, when once he had debouched on its shores, the conductivity of this central pool of politically neutral navigable water would give any pawn that launched a keel on it the range and versatility of a queen, and would offer these facilities for a sudden vast increase in mobility to Gothic, Vandal, or Arab piratical craft with the same undiscriminating hospitality that it had shown to Roman warships and to Alexandrian merchantmen. The maritime physiography of the Hellenic World thus militated against a latter-day Roman Empire at bay[5] as powerfully as it had once told in favour of Roman empire-builders who had made Rome's imperial fortune when their audacity in taking to an element on which their Carthaginian adversaries had previously reigned supreme had justified itself by its success in breaking through a sea-borne Punic 'wooden curtain'.[6]

These weaknesses in the structure of the Roman Empire proved, in the event, to outweigh, in combination, one fortuitous advantage over the Han Empire which the Roman Empire enjoyed thanks to an accident

[1] See V. v. 219.
[2] The Diocletianic Restoration's substitution of a system of defence in depth for a broken cordon along the *limes* has been noticed in VI. vii. 322–3.
[3] See p. 655, above.   [4] See VI. vii. 217.
[5] See VI. vii. 93.   [6] See IX. viii. 428–9.

of physical geography. We have seen that the Han Empire was exposed at point-blank range to the blast of Eurasian Nomad explosion along the enormous length of a Great Wall whose masonry was all that stood between the nucleus of the Sinic universal state in the Yellow River Basin and the huge reservoir of Nomad energy in and beyond Gobi. By contrast, the Roman Empire was nowhere in immediate contact with the Eurasian Steppe except at the tip of the Steppe's Great Western Bay where the Iron Gates barred the way farther westward into the isolated enclave of steppe-land in the Hungarian Alföld.[1] Yet one band of Alan Eurasian Nomads, whose point of departure was this far-flung western outpost of their native Eurasia, capped their initial feat of breaking through the Continental European *limes* of the Roman Empire by making their way, not only overland into the south-western extremity of the Continent, but on across the waters of the Western Mediterranean into the Romans' North-West African island, in the train of the Vandal war-lord Genseric. And, after thus making their sea-passage without mishap in A.D. 429, these outlandish invaders from beyond the extreme opposite sector of the vast Roman perimeter brought their long trek to a triumphant termination by entering Carthage itself within ten years of their audacious landing on African ground.

This brilliant success of Vandal-led Alan Nomads at the Roman Empire's expense in North-West Africa in A.D. 429–39 throws into piquant relief the blackness of the disaster that overtook the Tibetan-led Hiongnu and Sienpi Nomad assailants of the Sinic World's moated southern fortress at the very first ditch that these ill-starred barbarian aggressors tried to cross. The water-jump in the Huai Basin was the outermost of all the Sinic southern fortress's defences. How was it that the regulated waterways of a Far Eastern river-basin availed in A.D. 383 to foil the Nomad cavalry who, at the opposite end of the Old World only forty-six years later, were to commit themselves with impunity to the less familiar waters of 'the salt estranging sea' when they ventured to take ship from Europe to Africa in A.D. 429?

These versatile Alano-Vandal 'horse-marines' did not merely escape mishap in making a single sea-passage from Europe to Africa; when once they had taken to the sea they immediately made themselves so much at home on this previously unfamiliar element that, from a newly conquered North-West African base of operations, they succeeded in wresting back out of Roman hands the naval command of the Western Mediterranean which the Romans had wrested out of Carthaginian hands seven hundred years back, in the First Punic War (*gerebatur* 264–241 B.C.). How was it that the Alano-Vandals were able to master the sea when the Hunno-Tibetans had been worsted by a river?

The surprising answer to this irrepressible question seems to be that the art of marine navigation was less difficult for these centaurs to acquire than the steeple-chaser's knack of leaping clear from bank to bank of a fresh-water ditch. The Eurasian Nomad's strange inability to cope with inland waterways was indeed eventually to prove his undoing

[1] See III. iii. 401–2.

when this fatal flaw in his efficiency was discovered and exploited by the Cossacks;[1] and the rare amphibious prowess of 'Water Sakas', who turned to account on the Indus a fluvial waterman's skill that they had acquired on the Oxus,[2] was manifestly one of those exceptions that prove a rule. If this reading of the historical evidence is correct, it requires us to discard, as a misleading illusion, the visual impression produced by a synoptic view of the physiographical maps of the Han Empire and the Roman Empire when we place these two pictures side by side. If, in ignorance of the historical facts, we were to ask ourselves which of these two strikingly diverse physiographical structures might be expected to offer the greater facilities to mounted invaders, the obvious *a priori* answer would be that a continental empire built round the basins of two rivers with a common watershed would be as easy for an invading cavalry to overrun as it would be difficult for these horsemen to conquer the transmarine provinces of a maritime empire built round the basins of two interconnecting bays of one continuous inland sea. Yet this *a priori* answer is given the lie by the historical fact that the Alano-Vandals brilliantly succeeded in conquering a transmarine North-West Africa in A.D. 429–39, whereas the Hunno-Tibetans were ignominiously repulsed in A.D. 383 on the banks of the River Huai.

The outcome of the contest between an Alano-Vandal attack and a Roman defence in North-West Africa in the fourth decade of the fifth century of the Christian Era was decided, as we have already observed, by the cumulative effect of one feature of the Roman Empire's physiographical structure and one politico-military legacy of an antecedent chapter of Roman imperial history. The Alano-Vandals were sped on their way from Central Europe to North-West Africa by the conductivity of the invaded oecumenical empire's central sea; but their subsequent conquest of Rome's North-West African dominions would certainly not have been completed so quickly, and might perhaps never have been completed at all, if, in the course of the 575 years that had elapsed, by the date of the Alano-Vandal landing in Africa in A.D. 429, since Rome's first annexation of territory in Africa in 146 B.C., the Romans had emulated the thoroughness of the Prior Han empire-builders' work in Southern China by effectively subjugating all the North-West African highlands up to the natural frontiers afforded by this virtual island's Saharan desert coasts. The conjuncture that ensured the rapid and complete extinction of Roman rule in North-West Africa after the advent of the Alano-Vandals in A.D. 429 was the survival of a still unsubjugated local barbarian enemy at the gates, ready to join hands with the exotic Eurasian barbarian new arrivals. The alliance between the interloping horsemen and the indigenous highlanders was as decisive as it was inevitable.

Thus Rome failed to furnish a senile Hellenic World with a defensible fortress in a North-West Africa which, in the physiographical structure of the Roman Empire, was the morphological counterpart of the New South in the structure of the Han Empire. On the other hand, Rome did succeed in creating an imperfect, yet locally effective, functional counterpart of the Sinic World's never violated southern fortress in an Anatolia[1] which had no morphological affinity at all with the Sinic World's latter-day southern extension, though it had a partial affinity on this physiographical plane with the Sinic World's original nucleus in the North.

Both the extent and the limits of this physiographical correspondence between Anatolia and Northern China come to light when we remind ourselves that the chain of mountain-girt fluvial plains, extending from the Wei Basin on the west to the Lower Yellow River Basin on the east, had played, in the genesis and growth of the Sinic Civilization, the part played in the genesis and growth of the Hellenic Civilization by a chain of landlocked seas extending from the Aegean on the south to the Sea of Azov on the north.[2] The Aegean reach of this saline inland waterway had been the original home of a maritime Hellenic Society which had come to birth between the Aegean's Asiatic and European shores; and the Asiatic half of the birthplace of Hellenism—which was to figure on a pre-Diocletianic Roman imperial administrative map as the province of 'Asia'—occupied the western extremity of the Anatolian Peninsula up to the western fringes of the Central Steppe. Thus the Anatolian citadel of a post-Diocletianic Roman Empire included the Asiatic half of the Hellenic World's original nucleus; but, on the other hand, it did not include the European half of this homeland of Hellenism, while it did include a Central and an Eastern Anatolia which, so far from having been parts of the Hellenic Civilization's original patrimony, had been the homelands of a Hittite Civilization which had neither been annexed to the Hellenic Society's political domain nor exposed to an intensive play of Hellenic cultural radiation until after the overthrow of the Achaemenian Empire by Alexander the Great. The Anatolian citadel of the Roman Empire was thus composed of one-half of the original homeland of Hellenism in combination with the whole of the original homeland of the Hittite Civilization; and we have already noticed in previous contexts[3] that, in the eventual structures of both a Hellenistic Orthodox Christian World and an East Roman avatar of the Roman Empire, the centre of gravity came to rest in a *ci-devant* Hittite Central and Eastern Anatolia that were occupied by the East Roman Empire's Anatolic and Armeniac army corps districts, and not in a *ci-devant* Hellenic Western Anatolia, where a Thracensian army corps district occupied the area once covered by the Roman province of Asia.

In Late Roman Imperial history an Anatolia whose cultural heritage was thus partly Hellenic but predominantly Hittite was the scene of decisive events corresponding on the politico-military plane to the historic defeat in A.D. 383 of the Hunno-Tibetan barbarian assailants of the Sinic southern fortress; and the salvaging of Anatolia in the fifth century of the Christian Era was as signal an achievement of contemporary Roman imperial statesmanship as the loss of North-West Africa was a nemesis of local Roman sins of omission in the past.

[1] See VI. vii. 357, n. 4.   [2] See IX. viii. 711-12.
[3] In II. ii. 79–80 and IV. iv. 342.

By the end of the fourth century, Roman rule in Anatolia was already in jeopardy from a local juxtaposition of those two varieties of Barbarism that were to provide the ingredients for so explosive a mixture in North-West Africa twenty-nine years later. The never subjugated Berber highlanders had their fourth-century Anatolian indigenous barbarian counterparts in Isaurian highlanders who had shaken off a precariously established Roman control,[1] while counterparts of the future Alano-Vandal conquerors of North-West Africa, in the shape of Alano-Gothic *laeti*, had been imported into Anatolia already by the deliberate action of the Roman imperial authorities themselves. Yet, in the event, this ominous situation in Anatolia was saved by a Constantinopolitan Imperial Government's success in forestalling Gainas the Goth's plotted *coup* in A.D. 400 and Aspar the Alan's plotted *coup* in A.D. 471; the Gothic *laeti* in Anatolia were extirpated before it had occurred, either to these imported carnivores or to the native Isaurian representatives of the breed, that the wolf and the jackal in partnership would have it in their power to make the stricken deer their prey; and the indigenous Anatolian barbarians, who thus missed their opportunity of becoming co-partners of local Visigothic *laeti* in establishing an Anatolian barbarian successor-state of the Roman Empire, allowed themselves to be enlisted, instead, in the Roman Imperial Army and eventually to be used by a Constantinopolitan Imperial Government for the reconquest of an Ostrogothic successor-state of the Roman Empire in Italy.[2]

This series of energetic Roman acts of state, which were as prescient as they were strong-minded, successfully exorcized a sinister possibility that, in the course of the fifth century of the Christian Era, Anatolia might become the site of an Alano-Gothico-Isaurian barbarian principality corresponding to the actual fifth-century Alano-Vandalo-Berber successor-state of the Roman Empire in North-West Africa and to the fourth-century Tibetan, Hiongnu, To Pa, and Sienpi successor-states of a Sinic oecumenical empire in the Yellow River Basin. Late Imperial Roman statesmanship did not, indeed, rise to the height of saving the whole of the cradle of Hellenism from being swamped, like the cradle of the Sinic Civilization, by an influx of barbarism. Justinian's improvident expenditure of an irreplaceable residue of Illyrian man-power on the indulgence of his perverse ambition to reconquer Italy had to be paid for before the close of the sixth century by a stampede of the Avars' Slav 'human cattle' into a Continental European Greece which had been saved from becoming the prey of the Visigoth war-lord Alaric by Stilicho's generalship in A.D. 396 and by the diplomacy of Constantinopolitan ministers of state who had unobtrusively sped a departing barbarian guest in A.D. 410. But, though the European half of the cradle of Hellenism thus suffered, in a post-Justinianean deluge, the fate that overtook the entire cradle of the Sinic Civilization after the débâcle of the United Tsin, the Asiatic half of the Hellenic Society's original patrimony was saved from the same doom by the defeat of the Arabs' attempts to capture Constantinople in A.D. 673–7 and A.D. 717–18, and by the miscarriage in A.D. 823 of a formidable insurrection of Slav

[1] See IV. iv. 325 and V. v. 206, n. 1. [2] See IV. iv. 324–5 and VI. vii. 335–7.

laeti who had been planted in Anatolia to till fields left fallow there by the extermination of these Slavs' Gothic predecessors in A.D. 400.[1]

The preservation of this citadel of Hellenism in Anatolia during the social interregnum that followed the dissolution of the Hellenic Society elsewhere was a feat of the same kind as the preservation of a citadel of the Sinic culture in Southern China during the interregnum that followed the dissolution of the Sinic Society in the Yellow River Basin; and this common achievement on the politico-geographical plane is, as we have seen, one of two distinctive common assets which account, between them, for the remarkable robustness of both the T'ang Empire and the East Roman Empire by comparison with such anaemic ghosts as the Holy Roman Empire and the Chóu Empire. The two exceptionally stalwart *revenants'* other special common achievement was, as we have also already noticed, the revival of a professional lay civil service. We may now go on to observe that, of the two achievements, this institutional feat was by far the more efficacious in assisting the wraith of a dead oecumenical empire to clothe itself in flesh and blood. The truth is that the part played in the two miracles of reincarnation by an inviolate South Chinese fortress in the one case and by an inviolate Anatolian fortress in the other case was only a passive one. The mere survival of a cultural asylum would have been of no avail in itself if it had not served to give sanctuary to an imperial corporation by whose action a suspended imperial administration's paralysed, but never fatally dislocated, heart could be conjured into beating again; and, when we compare the relative success of the Han régime's and the Roman régime's residuary legatees in weathering this ordeal of hibernation, we shall find that the Han imperial civil service far surpassed its Roman counterpart in both the extent and the success of its performance.

During a post-Roman interregnum the anarchy into which the central and eastern provinces followed the western provinces after the murder of the Emperor Maurice in A.D. 602 put out of action, here too, an imperial administrative machine that in the western provinces had already ceased to function some two hundred years earlier; and, even when an eventual break of political continuity in the central provinces, which had lasted, when it had come, for not less than four generations, had been followed at length by Leo Syrus's evocation of an East Roman ghost of the Roman Empire in Anatolia in A.D. 717, another 147 years had still to pass before this local simulacrum of the Roman Empire was to be endowed with a local simulacrum of the Roman civil service[2]

[1] The largest settlements of Slav *laeti* in Anatolia of which a record survives took place during the first reign of the Heraclian Emperor Justinian II (*imperabat* A.D. 685–95 *et* 704–11) (see Vasiliev, A. A.: *Histoire de l'Empire Byzantin* (Paris 1932, Picard, 2 vols.), vol. i, pp. 288–9). Thomas the Slav, who was the leader of the great Anatolian insurrection of A.D. 821–3, was the offspring of a Slav family settled at Gaziura (Toqat) in the Armeniac army-corps district, and the Anatolian Slavs were one of the dissident elements in Anatolia that joined his standard. The insurrection was not, however, confined to the Slav element in the population of Anatolia, and Thomas was aiming at a more ambitious objective than the establishment of an Anatolian Slav successor-state of the East Roman Empire. His aim was to make himself master of the East Roman Empire itself, and this was why he wasted his strength on a fruitless siege of Constantinople.

[2] The conspicuous absence of an administrative renaissance of the Diocletianic Roman Imperial régime in the administrative organization of Leo Syrus's East Roman Empire has been noticed in VI. vii. 357, n. 4.

thanks to the foundation of the Caesar Bardas' college in the Magnaura in A.D. 864.[1] By comparison with this undistinguished post-Roman administrative record in the limited area once occupied by the Roman Empire's central provinces, the heirs of the Han imperial civil service gave a far better account of themselves. To begin with, they maintained their corporate life and remained on active service without any break at all in the Sinic World's southern citadel, to administer a southern remnant of the Sinic universal state, under its successive 'Eastern Tsin', Sung, Ts'i, Liang, and Ch'en dynasties, from the date of the installation of a refugee Imperial Government at Nanking in A.D. 318 down to the date of the political reunification of the entire former domain of the Han Empire through the conquest of the Ch'en by the Sui in A.D. 589.[2] Thereafter, this never incapacitated southern residue of the Sinic imperial civil service was able, in virtue of having survived as a going concern in the South, to provide the Northern political necromancer T'ang T'ai Tsung with the fund of professional man-power that he required in order to create a unitary oecumenical civil service for his resuscitated unitary oecumenical empire.[3] This seventh-century Far Eastern feat of necromancy had a Northern as well as a Southern historical background; and in this Northern episode the heirs of the Han imperial civil service had acquitted themselves like men in a role that had demanded far greater heroism than their contemporary performance in the South, highly creditable to them though this southern performance was.

T'ai Ts'ung would never have been able to reintroduce the Han tradition of imperial administration into a politically dominant North from a newly annexed South, nor indeed have been capable even of conceiving in his own mind the ambitious project of incubating this administrative renaissance, if the great T'ang statesman himself, and his predecessors of barbarian origin who had been ruling the North ever since the collapse of the United Tsin régime there at the beginning of the fourth century of the Christian Era, had not already been profoundly Sinified in the course of the 278 years that had elapsed between the sack of Loyang by the Hiongnu in A.D. 311 and the annexation of the Ch'en Dynasty's attenuated Southern Empire by Sui Wên-ti in A.D. 589. The founder of the Hiongnu successor-state of the United Tsin Empire, Liu Yuan ('*imperabat*' A.D. 304–10), was already so far Sinified that he sought to legitimize his usurpation by claiming descent from the founder of the authentic Imperial Han Dynasty, Han Liu Pang, and styling his own dynasty 'Pe Han' ('Northern Han') accordingly.[4] The deliberate self-Sinification of *ci-devant* barbarian intruders

---

[1] See IV. iv. 345.　　　　　　　　　　　　　　　　[2] See VI. vii. 369.
[3] See VI. vii. 365, n. 4.
[4] See Franke, O.: *Geschichte des Chinesischen Reiches*, vol. ii (Berlin and Leipzig 1936, de Gruyter), pp. 40–45, and the present Study, V. v. 273. This practice of adopting the name of some dynasty of the Chóu Age of Sinic history, which had been canonized posthumously as classical, had perhaps been invented by Liu Yuan's alleged ancestor Liu Pang himself; for Liu Pang had taken over the dynastic title 'Han' with the territory (ruled, in the Chóu Age, by a local dynasty of that name) which had happened to be the first scrap of the spoils of the Ts'in Empire to come into Liu Pang's possession (see VI. vii. 172). After the fall of the thus self-styled Imperial Han Dynasty, their practice was imitated in the nomenclature of almost all succeeding dynasties—indigenous and bar-

on the sacred soil of the original homeland of the Sinic culture in the North was thus coeval with the first overt establishment there of barbarian successor-states of the United Tsin; and this Herodian movement reached its totalitarian climax in the Sinomane measures taken in A.D. 494–6 by an ex-barbarian ruler of a temporarily reunited North whose To Pa provenance was disguised under the dynastic name 'Wei' and the throne-name Hiao Wên-ti.[1]

This intensive and progressive Sinification of the immigrant barbarian squatters in the North, who established successor-states of the United Tsin Empire there in and after the beginning of the fourth century of the Christian Era, is the cultural background of the administrative unification of the South with the North of a nascent Far Eastern World in the seventh century by the joint endeavours of a T'ang heir of these Sinophil barbarian war-lords in the North and a Confucian imperial civil service which had succeeded in preserving its continuity during a post-Han social interregnum and which welcomed an opportunity of co-operating with the Northern ruler of a reunited empire in giving practical effect to cultural and administrative ideals that T'ai T'sung shared with the litterati. The survival of the Sinic culture in the South during this age is adequately explained, as we have seen, by the impregnability of the southern fortress which had been provided for a senile Sinic Society by far-sighted and energetic Prior Han empire-builders. But how are we to explain the same Sinic culture's contemporary survival in the North, where the open plains of the Wei Basin and the Lower Yellow River Basin had been swept by the icy blast of a Eurasian Nomad whirlwind in spite of the massive artificial windbreak that had been erected, for the protection of this northern homeland of the Sinic culture, by the Titans who had built the Great Wall? An answer to this question may perhaps be yielded by a further pursuit of our comparative study of post-Sinic and post-Hellenic history.

If we explore this synoptic view, the first point that we shall notice is that, in the first phase of the interregnum following the break-up of a Sinic universal state, all the fragments of a now dissolved Han Empire's former domain still remained provisionally exempt, during a period of grace which lasted for more than a century, from seeing the calamity of partition capped by the still more grievous calamity of falling under barbarian rule. In the Age of the Three Kingdoms (*dimicabant* A.D. 221–263/80), the Northern successor-state of the Han Empire, as well as its two southern rivals, was a work of native Sinic hands; and here, at the very outset, the courses of these two comparable episodes of post-Sinic history and post-Hellenic history diverged on lines which placed the Sinic Society at a relative advantage over its Hellenic contemporary; for a corresponding chapter of Hellenic history that had the same opening quickly took a different turn.

When in A.D. 395 a post-Diocletianic Roman Empire was divided into two indigenous successor-states as a consequence of Theodosius I's

barian, parochial and oecumenical, alike—down to the end of Sinic history and throughout the subsequent course of Far Eastern history until the abolition of the imperial régime in China in A.D. 1911.   [1] See V. v. 477–8.

concern to provide an appanage for either of his two sons Arcadius and Honorius, this bi-partition of the Roman Empire was carried out smoothly and peacefully, in auspicious contrast to the bout of political and social disorder in the Sinic World at the turn of the second and third centuries of the Christian Era which was the price of the tri-partition of the Han Empire in that generation. Yet, on the morrow of the division of the Roman Empire into an appanage for Arcadius in the central and eastern provinces and an appanage for Honorius in the western provinces, the western indigenous successor-state of Theodo-sius's unitary Roman Empire fell a prey to barbarian war-lords whose power spread so far and wide and increased so rapidly, both in the provinces and at the centre, that in A.D. 476, only eighty-one years after Theodosius's death, the last successor of Honorius was compelled to abdicate by a barbarian gangster who, in virtue of being accepted as their leader by the barbarian mercenary troops in Italy, was already master, *de facto*, of all the territory still remaining under the effective control of the government ruling in the name of Honorius's successors, while the outlying fragments of this shattered western indigenous successor-state of the Roman Empire that had not already passed out of local Roman hands by A.D. 476 went the same way as Italy when in A.D. 481[1] the Scirian usurper Odovacer added the ex-emperor Nepos' principality in Dalmatia to the Italian dominions which Odovacer had already taken over from the ex-emperor Romulus 'Augustulus', and when in A.D. 486 the Salian Frankish war-lord Clovis wrested the Seine Basin out of Syagrius's hands.

In the next chapter of our synoptic history, we again find an identical movement working itself out on different lines in the Sinic and in the Hellenic case. The identical movement in this chapter was an endeavour on the part of one of the indigenous successor-states of a divided oecumenical empire to re-establish a lost imperial unity by force of arms. The United Tsin's successful reunification (*stabat* A.D. 280–317) of the whole former domain of the Han Empire has its counterpart in the partial success of the Constantinopolitan Emperor Justinian (*imperabat* A.D. 527–65) in reuniting African, Italian, and Spanish fragments of a defunct Honorian indigenous successor-state of the Roman Empire with an Arcadian indigenous successor-state that was still a going concern. These two endeavours had not only a similar general aim but also a similar general sequel; for in both cases the attempt to re-establish a lost imperial unity so cruelly taxed the human and material stamina of the indigenous successor-state whose resources were expended on the pursuit of this ambitious politico-military aim that the successors of Justinian and Sse-ma Yen (alias Tsin Wu-ti) not only found themselves unable to maintain the imperial unity that their predecessors had re-established at so heavy a cost, but also had to witness the collapse of their régime even in their own metropolitan territories. Justinian's successors paid for Justinian's excesses by seeing his and their momentarily swollen dominions reduced to the confines

---

[1] See Bury, J. B.: *A History of the Later Roman Empire from Arcadius to Irene, 395 A.D.–800 A.D.*, 1st ed. (London 1889, Macmillan, 2 vols.), vol. i, p. 279.

of Anatolia through the loss of their South-East European provinces to the Slavs and of their Oriental provinces to the Arabs, while the successors of Tsin Wu-ti lost to barbarian successor-states the entire domain of the northern indigenous successor-state of the Han Empire which had been the Tsin dynasty's original base of operations, and were forced to transfer their capital to a recently annexed South over which they still retained their hold after they had ceased to reign over a reunited Sinic universal state.

In these respects the Justinianean chapter of Hellenic history and the United Tsin chapter of Sinic history ran on parallel lines; but this resemblance was accompanied by differences which had their origin in the preceding divergence between the Sinic and the Hellenic course of events. In order to translate the course of Hellenic history in the Justinianean Age into the corresponding Sinic terms, we should have to imagine that in the foregoing post-Theodosian Age the Honorian indigenous successor-state of a unitary Roman Empire had not only been as successful as the Arcadian indigenous successor-state was in crushing the attempts of barbarian war-lords to make it their prey, but had lived on through the fifth century of the Christian Era into the sixth century in order to achieve—and this completely—from a seat of government at Milan or Trier the reunification of the Theodosian Empire which was actually achieved in part by Justinian from a seat of government at Constantinople; and we should then have to imagine an Honorian Empire which had shown this impressive capacity for survival and recuperation suddenly suffering after all, at the end of this imaginary Roman imperial story in the sixth century, the fate which it actually suffered in the fifth century when its dominions were divided up among a host of usurping barbarian war-lords.

When we see the northern indigenous successor-state of the Han Empire eventually meeting this Honorian fate, our first thought is likely to be that the auspiciously un-Honorian path which this northernmost of 'the Three Kingdoms' had managed to follow during the preceding hundred years had not, after all, made any difference in the end. What had it profited the North, in the long run, first to keep the local reins of government out of barbarian hands and then to reunite the whole former domain of the Han Empire under its own indigenous régime, if in the third chapter of the story it was destined to be overtaken, as it was overtaken, by the doom which descended upon an Honorian indigenous successor-state of the Roman Empire no later than the morrow of its establishment? Any such first impression that the former northern provinces of the Han Empire under a belatedly established barbarian régime were no better off than the former western provinces of the Roman Empire under a promptly established barbarian régime will, however, give way to very different second thoughts when we go on to look at the third chapter of our synoptic history; for in a barbarian-ruled western fragment of the Hellenic World there was no sequel corresponding to the brilliant recovery of an apparently moribund culture in a barbarian-ruled northern fragment of the Sinic World.

The cultural sequel in the Far East to the establishment of barbarian successor-states of the United Tsin was, as we have seen, a Sinification of these barbarian war-lords and their followers which reached its climax in the reign of the To Pa chief who took so seriously his Sinic duties as the 'Wei' Emperor Hiao Wên-ti (*imperabat* A.D. 490–9). The thorough-going reception of his Sinic subjects' culture in A.D. 494–6 by this To Pa successor of the United Tsin was the logical sequel to the assumption of the imperial title by Hiao Wên-ti's ancestor To Pa Kuei in A.D. 398[1] and to the conversion of the To Pa horde itself from a Nomad to a sedentary way of life by Kuei's grandfather Shi-i-kien (*dominabatur* A.D. 338–76);[2] and, during the century intervening between Kuei's reign and Hiao Wên-ti's, Kuei's presumptuously Herodian gesture had been justified politically by his barbarian 'Wei' Dynasty's success in extinguishing all rival barbarian successor-states of the United Tsin Empire and enlarging the borders of a thus politically reunited North of the Sinic World by stretching out a long arm towards the Tarim Basin.[3]

This was, it is true, the limit of the To Pa Power's political achievement; for, when Hiao Wên-ti sought to crown his predecessors' successes by uniting the South with an already reunited North, he suffered in A.D. 495, at the hands of the Ts'i, as decisive a defeat at the first ditch of the southern fortress in the Huai Basin[4] as had been inflicted on his Tibetan forerunner Fu Kien in A.D. 383 by the Ts'i Dynasty's forerunners the refugee Tsin.[5] Yet, though either of these successive disastrous outcomes of a Northern barbarian invasion of the South of the Sinic World had the same consequence as far as the South was concerned, the repercussions in the North were different in the two cases. In the South, the impregnability against Northern barbarian attack which the southern citadel of the Sinic culture displayed first in A.D. 383 and then in A.D. 495 gave the refugee culture, on either occasion, another hundred years of grace; and thanks to these successive reprieves the South was exempted from ever having to undergo the supreme ordeal of proving its mettle under even a belated experience of the *ci-devant* barbarian rule to which the North had succumbed as early as A.D. 317, since the Northern Power that did eventually reunite the South with the North in A.D. 589 was one which by that date had, as we have seen,[6] already winnowed out the chaff of an intrusive Barbarism from the grain of an unmildewed local store of native Sinic culture. In the North, on the other hand, the effects of the two decisive battles of A.D. 383 and A.D. 495 were diverse instead of being similar and cumulative.

In the North, as we have seen, the barbarian war-lord Fu Kien's 'Ts'in' régime had been so deeply discredited by his disaster in A.D. 383 on the banks of the Huai that this local Tibetan barbarian successor-state of the United Tsin Empire immediately fell to pieces[7] and, in crumbling, opened the way for a rival To Pa Tungus barbarian suc-

---

[1] See Franke, O.: *Geschichte des Chinesischen Reiches*, vol. ii (Berlin and Leipzig 1936, de Gruyter), pp. 108–9.   [2] See ibid., pp. 86.
[3] See ibid., pp. 149–50.   [4] See ibid., p. 160.
[5] See p. 657, above.   [6] On p. 657, above.
[7] See Franke, op. cit., vol. ii, pp. 98–101.

cessor-state to occupy the vacuum. The To Pa eventually reunited the whole of the North under their own rule between the year A.D. 385, in which Shi-i-Kien's grandson To Pa Kuei had declared his barbarian principality's independence under the high-sounding Sinic name 'Wei',[1] and the year A.D. 439, in which the last of the other surviving barbarian principalities in the North was extinguished.[2] In contrast to these Northern repercussions of the decisive battle in the Huai Basin in A.D. 383, the no less decisive battle in the same theatre in A.D. 495 did not bring to the ground the To Pa barbarian 'Wei' reproduction of the Tibetan barbarian 'Ts'in' realm. The unitary Wei régime in the North survived for another thirty-nine years; its eventual bi-partition in A.D. 534 was followed, within another forty-three years, by the reconstitution of a unitary Northern Empire under the régime of the Pe Chóu in A.D. 577; and this political reunification of the North was followed in its turn, within twelve years, by a third, and this time at last successful, endeavour on the part of a Northern war-lord to conquer the South. An enterprise that had proved to be beyond a Tibetan Ts'in Fu Kien's strength in A.D. 383, and still beyond a To Pa Wei Hiao Wên-ti's strength in A.D. 495, was thus eventually achieved in A.D. 589 by a Chinese Sui Wên-ti who had supplanted his Hiongnu Pe Chóu master in the North in A.D. 581.

In this perspective the histories of the former northern provinces of the Han Empire during a post-Han interregnum and the former western provinces of the Roman Empire during a post-Roman interregnum take on very diverse appearances. When we look in a post-Roman Western Europe for a counterpart of the Wei Empire in a post-Han Northern China, the Merovingian Power will be the closest match that we shall find. Like the To Pa under the Wei régime, the Franks under the Merovingian régime progressively swallowed up the neighbouring barbarian successor-states of the Roman Empire that had been carved out by rival barbarian war-bands. Clovis himself annexed the Alemannic principality in Alsace and Swabia in A.D. 496 and threw the Visigoths out of Gaul in A.D. 507; in A.D. 528 Clovis's successor Theodoric I stretched out his arm into a then still barbarian interior of the Continent as far eastward as Thuringia; and the Burgundian principality in the upper basin of the Rhône and the Saône was definitively annexed to an expanding Frankish realm in A.D. 532–4. If there is any period in the Merovingian Frankish annals that invites comparison with the half-century of To Pa history, ending in the year A.D. 495, during which the Wei régime was at its zenith, we shall find this Merovingian equivalent 'in good King Dagobert's palmy days'.[3] As soon, however, as we confront the Merovingian and the Wei dispensations with one another, as they were in these periods of their respective *floruits*, we become aware of the immensity of the Wei régime's relative superiority.

[1] See ibid., p. 105.
[2] See Herrmann, A.: *Historical and Commercial Atlas of China* (Cambridge, Mass. 1935, Harvard University Press), p. 29, Map IV.
[3] Barham, R. H.: *The Ingoldsby Legends*, Second Series: 'The Lay of Saint Medard', line 1.

The first point of diversity that strikes the eye is a difference in the degree of success in the enterprise of empire-building. Whereas the Wei Power had succeeded in reuniting the whole northern third of the Han Empire's former domain under its own exclusive rule by A.D. 439, and was able thereafter to hold these dominions together till A.D. 534, the Merovingian Power never succeeded in reuniting under its own rule more than a Gallic splinter of a western fragment of the former domain of the Roman Empire. The Franks left it to their Lombard fellow barbarians to undo Justinian's work in Italy, and to their Arab fellow barbarians to undo the same ineffectual Roman spendthrift's work in Africa and to complete in the Iberian Peninsula the work of liquidating Visigothia which Clovis, the founder of the Merovingian Dynasty's fortunes, had begun in Gaul some two hundred years earlier. But this balance sheet of relative successes and failures in acquiring political dominion over territory is a crude test of relative total achievement, and to get to the heart of the matter we must lift our comparison from the political to the cultural plane. It is here that the contrast between the sterling Sinism of a Hiao Wên-ti (*imperabat* A.D. 490–9) and the transparent barbarism of a Dagobert I (*regnabat* A.D. 629–39) brings to light the full measure of the breadth of the gulf between these two barbarian essays in writing an epilogue to the history of a fallen civilization.

So far from finding an adequate counterpart in the Merovingian Frankish dispensation at its apogee, the Wei dispensation at its apogee, when it achieved on the political plane an integral reunification of one-third of the former domain of the Han Empire, was performing a feat which, in the western portion of the former domain of the Roman Empire, was not performed by the Franks until after the Merovingians had been supplanted by the Carolingians. And even a Carolingian Frankish dispensation that might venture to challenge comparison with the Wei dispensation on the political plane could not hold a candle to it on the cultural plane—not even in the light of the Carolingian linguistic and literary renaissance.[1]

Manifestly this immense difference in the cultural outcome of our synoptic history of a post-Han Northern China and a post-Roman Western Europe must be traceable to the operation, in Northern China in the post-Han Age, of some potent force, making for the resurgence of a classical culture there, which was not in action in the post-Roman Age in Western Europe; and this force that availed to decide the destiny of the Far East was none other than the pertinacity of a corporation of masters of Confucian arts in holding their ground, not only within the cosily sheltered precincts of a politically inviolate southern citadel where a Confucian licentiate could continue to practise his administrative profession, but also in the bleakly exposed waste land of a North that had fallen under barbarian rule.

'The gist of the political history of the Far west [of the former Sinic World during the post-Sinic interregnum] is to be found in the vicissitudes of fortune in struggles between military leaders of [barbarian] war-bands

[1] See p. 63, above.

—Sienpi, Tanguts, Tibetans, and Huns—in which the Chinese element can hardly be said to have played an independent role. Every petty captain of mercenaries who enjoys an official status and has troops at his command becomes the ruler of a piece of territory, makes himself independent, and founds a state in which all the [traditional Sinic] imperial pomp and circumstance—a distinctive dynastic era, the supreme sacrificial rites, the traditional offices of state, and the rest—is faithfully reproduced. And thus, while the political power of the Chinese population in the North dwindles to the vanishing point of a complete insignificance, the formal institutions of the Sinic State succeed in subjugating every [barbarian] people and every [barbarian] ruler, in the teeth of all other spiritual influences, in virtue of their being enjoined by Confucian doctrine. . . . Confucianism was the force to which the [Sinic] universal state (*Weltstaat*) owed its salvation and its renaissance.'[1]

This northern triumph of the official Sinic imperial philosophy of state is the more impressive in view of the unparalleled strength of those 'other spiritual influences' with which Confucianism had to contend in a northern arena; for the same Sinic corporation of Confucian licentiates that was endowed, in the Han Empire's inviolate southern citadel, with a local asylum, for which they would have been envied by post-Diocletianic Roman imperial civil servants, had to hold their ground in the North against a convergent drum-fire of radioactive alien spiritual influences that their Roman confrères were never called upon to face in any quarter.

A Sinic World under a Han imperial régime and an Hellenic World under a Roman imperial régime were both exposed, like other disintegrating civilizations in their universal states, to the impact of alien spiritual influences of two kinds—higher religions organized in universal churches making their epiphany among an internal proletariat, and the barbarian êthos of an external proletariat's Heroic Age—but the distribution of the incidence of this twofold impact was quite different in the two particular cases with which we are concerned at the moment. The Hellenic World in its universal state was attacked by Barbarism and Religion[2] from opposite quarters of the compass; and, though the two attacking forces' fields of fire did eventually come to overlap in the last phase of the assaulted civilization's débâcle, there was never a stage of the battle at which the defence had to contend with both invaders at once on one and the same sector of the perimeter of Hellenism's beleaguered fortress.

The province of the Hellenic World in which Christianity made its earliest lodgement in the greatest force, and entrenched itself thereafter most strongly, was an Anatolia which Saint Paul and his fellow missionaries rapidly overran from a base of spiritual operations at Antioch;[3] but this precociously Christianized province of Hellenism in Anatolia

[1] Franke, O.: *Geschichte des Chinesischen Reiches*, vol. ii (Berlin and Leipzig 1936, de Gruyter), pp. 112 and 55.
[2] Gibbon, Edward: *The History of the Decline and Fall of the Roman Empire*, chap. lxxi (already quoted in this Study in I. i. 42 and IV. iv. 58).
[3] In VI. vii. 93–95, we have noticed that, in making this conquest of Anatolia from a North Syrian base, Saint Paul was brilliantly succeeding on the religious plane in an enterprise which the Seleucidae had previously attempted on the military and political plane with signal ill-success.

did not come within the range of barbarian infiltration from Northern Europe and the Great Western Bay of the Eurasian Steppe until long after Hellenism and Christianity in Anatolia had already negotiated an *entente* with one another; and Hellenism's local success in making Anatolia into a citadel for itself in the fifth century of the Christian Era[1] was partly due to the support which Hellenism received here in this crisis from a Church that, in Anatolia, had long since been converted from Hellenism's adversary into its ally. The measures taken by a Constantinopolitan Imperial Government to forestall Gothic and Alan attempts to give Anatolia the alternative destiny of becoming one of the Roman Empire's barbarian successor-states thus proved effective partly because Hellenism never found itself constrained in Anatolia to contend with two alien enemies at once; and in the western provinces of the Empire, where a contemporary Honorian imperial régime failed to save itself from being supplanted by barbarian usurpers, the only vestiges of Hellenism that survived were actually such elements of the moribund pagan culture as had already been incorporated into the cultural heritage of Christianity in this area during the brief interval that had elapsed in this western theatre of operations between the belated achievement of an *entente* between Hellenism and Christianity and the victory there of the local barbarian war-lords over the Roman Empire's Honorian indigenous successor-state.[2]

The wide dispersal of the geographical distribution of the two pressures of Christianity and Barbarism on the perimeter of the Hellenic World, together with the difference in the timing of the religious and the barbarian attack on Anatolia (in contrast to the virtual simultaneity of the same two alien invaders' victories over Hellenism in the western provinces), manifestly told in Hellenism's favour in its fight to save its Anatolian citadel from falling. In the corresponding episode of Sinic history the strategic circumstances were more adverse to the prospects of the defence; for Barbarism's and Religion's assaults on the Sinic World were delivered not only at the same moment but on the same front. The North had to bear the brunt of both on the morrow of the débâcle of the Han Empire at the turn of the second and third centuries of the Christian Era; and a hundred years later, on the morrow of the débâcle of the United Tsin Empire at the beginning of the fourth century, the simultaneous offensives of Nomadism and the Mahāyāna against the same northern front of the Sinic World were resumed with a redoubled intensity. In sharp contrast to this twofold ordeal to which the North was subjected for some four hundred years ending in A.D. 589, the southern citadel of the Sinic culture in the same age suffered little more heavily from the Mahāyāna's spiritual infiltration than from the Nomads' attempts at military invasion.

---

[1] See the present Annex, pp. 662–5, above.

[2] 'Unlike Christian Byzantium, Christian Rome represents only a brief interlude between Paganism and Barbarism. There were only eighteen years between Theodosius's closing of the temples and the first sack of the Eternal City by the Barbarians. The great age of the Western Fathers from Ambrose to Augustine was crammed into a single generation, and Saint Augustine died with the Vandals at the gate' (Dawson, Christopher: *Religion and the Rise of Western Culture* (London 1950, Sheed & Ward), p. 28).

It is true that on the throne of the Southern Empire, in the last phase but one before its political reunification with the North, we are confronted by the almost Açoka-like figure of the convert-emperor Liang Wu-ti (*imperabat* A.D. 502–49), who proved the sincerity of his devotion to his Mahayanian faith by repeatedly attempting to retire from the World without regard to the public responsibilities inherent in his imperial office. And, though Liang Wu-ti's politically awkward Mahayanian Buddhist piety was manifestly an unusual phenomenon in the political life of Southern China in this imperial devotee's age, it is true on the other hand that, in the South as well as in the North, the Mahāyāna's Indo-Hellenic ecclesiastical art made a total conquest of the aesthetic faculties of Far Eastern souls that were much less prone to dedicate themselves whole-heartedly to the Mahāyāna's Indic unworldliness. Nor did either the artistic or the spiritual ray of the Mahāyāna's radiation into a Sinic Society's southern citadel play exclusively upon northern approaches where those water-barriers that so effectively baffled a predatory Nomad cavalry proved impotent to arrest an etherial vehicle of salvation. The Mahāyāna also took South China in the rear by availing itself of an alternative southern approach along an Oceanic water-route which was taken over in the fifth century of the Christian Era by Indian apprentices of Hellenic navigators who had begun to open up the sea-routes from the Red Sea coast of Egypt to India towards the end of the second century B.C.,[1] when the Prior Han empire-builders were on the point of arriving at their 'natural frontier' on the South China coast, and who had made their first land-fall on Sinic *terra firma* in A.D. 166,[2] just in time to catch a glimpse of the Posterior Han Empire before its collapse.[3] Yet even this far-flung encircling movement did not place the Mahāyāna in a position to penetrate the South of the Sinic World with the impetus that carried it into the heart of the North.

The Mahāyāna's overland route from its Indian cradle to its Far Eastern mission-field has already been surveyed in previous passages of this work.[4] We have watched an esoteric philosophy turning into a popular religion as it travelled from North-West India to North-East Iran, from North-East Iran to the Oxus–Jaxartes Basin, and from the Oxus–Jaxartes Basin to the Tarim Basin; and from the Tarim Basin we have seen a nascent Mahāyāna being transmitted to the internal proletariat of the Sinic Society as a lasting and momentous religious consequence of a transitory and inconclusive series of border wars between the Kushan and the Posterior Han Power in which the Tarim Basin more than once changed hands between the two contending empires round about the turn of the first and second centuries of the Christian Era.[5] The temporary reincorporation of the Tarim Basin into the Sinic

[1] See Herrmann, A.: *Historical and Commercial Atlas of China* (Cambridge, Mass. 1935, Harvard University Press), pp. 26–27, and the present Study, V. vi. 448, n. 1.
[2] See Fitzgerald, C. P.: *China, A Short Cultural History* (London 1935, Cresset Press), pp. 193–4.
[3] A.D. 166 was the year in which the Confucian civil servants of the Han régime formed an abortive association for the purpose of combating the influence of the eunuchs who were bringing the Han Empire to ruin (see VI. vii. 371, n. 3).
[4] See IV. iv. 65, n. 4; V. v. 133–46; and IX. viii. 90 and 91.
[5] See V. v. 142–5 and IX. viii. 95.

universal state, and of its Iranian inhabitants into the Sinic Society's internal proletariat, at this date opened the way for the Mahāyāna to travel on eastwards in search of the fortune that awaited it in a wider world.

The subterranean proletarian channels through which the Mahāyāna permeated were social counterparts of those masterpieces of hydraulic engineering, called *qanāt* or *kārīz*, through which, in the thirsty climate of Central Asia, the life-giving waters of the mountain springs were conveyed over vast distances underground in order, at the end of their long hidden course, to emerge at last on the surface of the plain and there to transfigure a desert into a garden through the far-borne waters' fruitful marriage with a soil whose latent fertility had been awaiting this magic rite of baptism. The geographical route along which a spiritually rejuvenating Indo-Hellenic higher religion made its way to the Far East was the narrow corridor of Sinically cultivated territory between the southward-looking inner face of the western extremity of the Great Wall and the northward-pointed foot of the northern escarpment of the great Tibetan Plateau. In crossing the watershed between the Upper Yellow River Basin and the Wei tributary of the Lower Yellow River on the eve of the Han Empire's débâcle, the Mahāyāna impinged on the northern cradle of the Sinic Civilization, rose to the surface of a Sinic Society whose social crust was at that moment caving in, burst into spiritual flower, and at the same time encountered the barbarians who were likewise taking advantage of the collapse of the Sinic dominant minority's universal state in order to break into the Wei Basin and the Lower Yellow River Basin out of a Eurasian Steppe from which those homelands of the Sinic culture were now no longer screened by any effective defence of the Great Wall.

This simultaneous invasion of the North of the Sinic World by the Eurasian Nomads and by the Mahāyāna plunged the Confucian litterati there into a sea of troubles. The breakdown of the Han régime had already been a disaster for them in itself, since it had deprived them, outside the bounds of the southern citadel, of the authority and emoluments deriving from a monopoly of the imperial civil service which they had been enjoying since the reign of their first imperial patron Han Wuti (*imperabat* 140–87 B.C.).[1] To accentuate their discomfiture, these unemployed Confucian civil servants now lost whatever moral influence they might previously have been able to exert on the internal proletariat of the Sinic Society; for the collapse of a Sinic oecumenical empire which threw these representatives of a *ci-devant* Sinic dominant minority out of official employment also brought appalling tribulations on the rank-and-file of a Sinic body social that had been relieved of the relatively efficient and benevolent rule of the Confucian litterati only to fall into the rough and clumsy hands of parvenu barbarian war-lords; and these cruel experiences moved the masses to look to non-Confucian quarters for relief and solace. A third blow suffered by the Confucian litterati in the North was their new barbarian masters' disinclination to re-employ them in the administrative service of the Han Empire's nascent barbarian successor-states.

---

[1] See V. v. 418–19, 654–5, and 708; and VI. vii. 355.

This unfriendliness of the barbarians towards the Confucians seems to have had two psychological roots. In the first place the barbarian usurpers of Sinic imperial prerogatives were well aware that the *ci-devant* imperial civil servants—whose interests, traditions, and principles conspired to make them 'die-hard' legitimists—were bound to be unfriendly to régimes whose pretensions they did not acknowledge; and the barbarians' consequent lack of confidence in the Confucians' loyalty made them anxious to dispense with these Confucians' services if they could find effectively trained Buddhist or Taoist substitutes for them.[1] In the second place the fascination which was exerted on the imagination of these, as well as other, militarily triumphant barbarians by a culture whose spiritual superiority was not effaced by its military defeat was counteracted to some extent, in this case as in others of the kind, by the victorious barbarian's usual desire[2] to distinguish his lordly self from his contemptibly servile subjects by wearing and airing the cultural badges of an unorthodox religion and an heroic poetry; and, in the sphere of religion, a Mahāyāna that was as alien an intruder on Sinic soil as the barbarian war-lord himself seemed to offer this military conqueror the distinctive religious emblem that he required.

Thus the Confucian ex-civil servants of an indigenous Sinic imperial régime who were left stranded in the North by the ebb of the imperial power after the fall of the Posterior Han, and *a fortiori* after the fall of the United Tsin, were constrained to watch their once docile Northern Sinic sheep straying out of a now dilapidated Confucian fold in search of some alternative spiritual shelter against the steppe-wind's icy blast, and at the same time to watch the once effectively barred-out barbarians who had now invaded the sacrosanct Sinic imperial paddock looking about them in Buddhist and Taoist quarters for new shepherds to employ in rounding up the scattered flock. In lieu of a Confucian philosophy which, like other philosophies, was a closed book to the unsophisticated and cold comfort to the afflicted,[3] the common run of Sinic provincials in the North under an oppressive barbarian tyranny turned for comfort to a higher religion which offered a prospect of release from the painfulness of life;[4] and such members of a Sinic internal proletariat as were not gathered into the bosom of the Mahāyāna fell into the net of an indigenous Taoist Church which had managed in the wilderness to survive a four-centuries-long Confucian ascendancy, and whose prelates now shrewdly observed and slyly imitated the methods of appeal by which the Mahāyāna was rapidly making its fortune on Far Eastern ground.[5] These two religious by-paths along which a suffering Sinic rank-and-file sought ways of spiritual release turned out also to be avenues to worldly advancement owing to the barbarian usurpers' policy of seeking civil servants who would be literate without being Confucian; and the ousted Confucian litterati thus had the double mortification of seeing apostasy to an alien Mahāyāna and to

[1] See the passage quoted, in VI. vii. 371, from Fitzgerald, C. P.: *China, A Short Cultural History* (London 1935, Cresset Press), p. 275.
[2] See V. v. 229–34, et seqq. [3] See V. v. 557–68.
[4] See Fitzgerald, op. cit., p. 259, quoted in VI. vii. 371–2.
[5] See V. v. 146–7, 178, n. 1, and 557.

a charlatan Taoism rewarded by appointment to offices of state from which Confucian licentiates were now *ex officio* debarred after having formerly been *ex officio* the only candidates eligible.

It is not surprising that, in these discouraging circumstances, a large number—perhaps a majority—of the Confucian litterati in the North should have taken the easy and attractive option of migrating to an inviolate southern citadel of the Sinic World in order to pursue their professional career in the administrative service of the refugee Tsin Dynasty and its southern successors.[1] The astonishing thing is that any of them should have elected to stay out in the cold; and it seems at first sight positively miraculous that this steadfast, but tiny, remnant[2] should eventually have captivated the barbarian rulers who had deliberately put these Confucian ex-imperial civil servants out of business.

In the sequel, as this progressively unfolded itself in the North in the course of the 278 years running from the sack of Loyang in A.D. 311 to the *Gleichschaltung* of a residue of the Southern Empire by the Chinese Northern war-lord Sui Wên-ti in A.D. 589, the disestablished remnant of the corporation of Confucian litterati in the North won their first victory when they subtly prevailed upon the local barbarian usurpers voluntarily to mould their illegitimate successor-states into likenesses of the Sinic imperial régime that they had supplanted by force; and an inevitable corollary of this change of countenance on the barbarians' part was, of course, the reinstatement in office of Confucian licentiates who were the sole repositories of Sinic *arcana imperii*.[3] These reinstated northern survivors of the Sinic imperial civil service were not, however, content with their success in thus inducing the barbarians who had dismissed them to re-employ them. To their mind, the re-establishment of the Confucian form of government was incomplete so long as the Confucian officiants in these civil rites were performing their ritual duties in the name of mere *mulūk at-tawā'if*.[4]

So soon as the re-established Confucian civil servants in the North were confident that their *ci-devant*-barbarian pupils in the Confucian lore had thoroughly taken their education to heart, they felt that the time had come to crown their long and patient work of rehabilitation by employing barbarian converts on whom they could now at last rely as instruments for achieving an ultimate aim of which they had never lost sight. The political reunification in A.D. 589 of the South with the North of the former domain of the Sinic universal state might look, from the Northern Barbarians' standpoint, like an attainment, by the

[1] See Fitzgerald, op. cit., p. 275, quoted in VI. vii. 371.

[2] By the year A.D. 405 the surviving non-Buddhist element in the population of the North had dwindled to a ratio of about 10 per cent., including the Confucians' Taoist competitors as well as the Confucians themselves, according to the Confucian historians' own admission (see Fitzgerald, op. cit., p. 276, quoted in VI. vii. 371).

[3] Tacitus: *Annals*, Book II, chap. 36, § 2; *Histories*, Book I, chap. 4, § 2. On this point see Fitzgerald, op. cit., p. 286, quoted in VI. vii. 372.

[4] The inadequacy of this half-way house was brought home to the resurgent Confucian litterati when they followed up their local reinstatement in the Northern Barbarian principalities by opening a counter-offensive against their now discomfited Buddhist competitors. 'In A.D. 446 the ruler of Wei, the Northern Empire, [at the instance of his Confucian advisers,] issued an edict against the Buddhists; but, as his rival in the [Southern] Chinese Empire was prepared to receive them, the monks were able to escape its effects' (Fitzgerald, op. cit., pp. 275–6).

barbarians' Chinese legatee Sui Wên-ti, of a barbarian objective that had eluded the grasp of a To Pa Wei Hiao Wên-ti before him, and of a Tibetan Ts'in Fu Kien before Wei Hiao Wên-ti; but, from the standpoint of the Confucian litterati in North and South alike, this same historic act of union looked like a reattainment—through the use of a now Chinese-controlled Northern Empire of barbarian origin—of a Confucian objective which, once before, had been attained—on that occasion only to be lost as soon as gained—by the unreinforced native Sinic efforts of the United Tsin.

What is the explanation of this apparent miracle? When we trace back the causes of the political reunification of the domain of the Han Empire in A.D. 589 as far as an historical analysis can follow them, we find ourselves led back to two acts of state that were both performed by the Prior Han Emperor Wuti (*imperabat* 140–87 B.C.): his endowment of the Sinic World with an impregnable southern citadel, through his southward expansion of his dominions up to the natural frontier presented by the South China Coast, and his investiture of the Confucian school of Sinic philosophers with a monopoly of the Sinic imperial civil service. In the light of the inquiry which we have now carried out, we shall pronounce that, of these two mighty deeds, the decisive act was, not an act of conquest that was Wuti's own exclusive achievement, but an institutional measure which would have been beyond the power even of this mightiest of all the Han Emperors if he had not been using his power merely to fulfil, in the fullness of time, the long disappointed hopes of a sage who had lived and died some four hundred years before Han Wuti's day. In short, the ultimate credit for the epoch-making renaissance of the Sinic universal state in the year A.D. 589 is shared by Han Wuti with Confucius.

The marriage of the Han imperial civil service with the Confucian school of philosophy which Han Wuti thus solemnized was the crucial event in Sinic history to which Hellenic history can show no parallel.[1] If Han Wuti's Hellenic counterpart is to be seen in the Roman Emperor Trajan, we can imagine this Roman empire-builder perhaps dreaming of equipping his Hellenic World with an equivalent of Han Wuti's southern citadel by setting himself to complete the Roman conquest of North-West Africa up to the natural frontier offered by the north shore of a Saharan sand-sea;[2] but we cannot imagine this prosaic-minded

---

[1] This capital point of difference between the respective courses of Sinic and Hellenic history has been noticed in VI. vii. 354–7.

[2] There is no indication that this dream ever did flit across Trajan's mind, but there is evidence that, if it ever did, it would have been doomed before birth to remain abortive, supposing that the dreamer had sought to translate it into reality; for before the end of Trajan's reign the Hellenic universal state was showing symptoms of severe strain and stress as a result of Trajan's mobilization of its resources for the pursuit of a Central European and a South-West Asian military objective, even without the aggravation of a third military enterprise on a North-West African front. After Trajan had followed up his incomplete and ephemeral annexation of an outstanding Dacian enclave of Central European barbarism by an attempt to arrive at a definitive settlement of the Roman Empire's 'eastern question', his momentary conquest of the Euphrates–Tigris Basin from Armenia to Mesênê was immediately undone by insurrections in his rear not only in the newly annexed territories but in provinces west of Euphrates which had been under Roman rule since the time of Pompey or earlier; and these unexpected and alarming complications in the East were accompanied in the West by threats of

practical soldier and administrator ever hitting upon the idea of solemnizing a marriage between a Stoic school of philosophy and a Roman imperial civil service, any more than we can imagine Trajan's third successor Marcus, in whose person the Roman imperial diadem was actually worn by a Stoic philosopher-king, summoning up either the zest or the energy or the *savoir faire* to attempt to translate into reality an ideal which Marcus, unlike Trajan, might well have entertained. In any case it is an historical fact that the Roman imperial civil service never did come to be identified either with Stoicism or with any other school of Hellenic philosophy; and, in thus remaining a mere professional corporation, this Roman civil service failed to qualify itself for outliving the oecumenical empire whose administration was its sole *raison d'être* from the beginning to the end of its professionally hide-bound existence. When the Roman Empire's Honorian indigenous successor-state was torn to shreds by contending predatory barbarians, the imperial civil servants whom this political catastrophe threw into technological unemployment had no choice open to them beyond the two courses of going out of business altogether and of finding alternative employment in the service of a Christian Church[1] which did not cease to be a going

a strike on the part of colonial communities of Roman citizens whose limited supply of man-power was no longer equal to meeting Trajan's inordinate drafts upon it. The representations made to Trajan in Mesopotamia by the representatives of the western municipalities, like those made to Alexander in the Panjab by his Macedonian veterans, were all the more compelling for being respectful; and Trajan would have found himself constrained, like Alexander, to bow to them, if Death's timely visitation had not permitted him to bequeath to Hadrian the urgent dirty work of liquidating a now patently over-ambitious South-West Asian military adventure.

In these unpropitious circumstances an attempt to subdue the vast virgin barbarian fastness in the Atlas would manifestly have been out of the question; and, indeed, if Trajan's grim North-West African cavalry-general Lusius Quietus had been given the task of completing the pacification of his own homeland, a Nomad Berber light horse that had acquitted itself brilliantly on the Mesopotamian plains might have fared ill in mountain-warfare against its sedentary Berber kinsfolk in the Atlas highlands.

The slenderness of the Roman Empire's reserves of war-potential in Trajan's day was exposed, as it was, without any need for a North-West African test, by the Central European and South-West Asian tests to which Trajan did, in fact, subject it; and this exposure gives the measure of the disparity in strength between the Roman Empire in the Age of the Principate and the Han Empire in the Age of the Prior Han Dynasty. For the Emperor Han Wuti, who successfully rounded off the Han Empire's southern marches up to the natural frontier presented by the South China Coast, was also the Prior Han emperor who committed the Sinic universal state to a war to the death against the Hiongnu Nomad lords of the eastern half of the Great Eurasian Steppe; and, though Wuti himself did not live to see this hazardous and exacting enterprise carried to completion, his eventual successor Han Yuanti did succeed, within a hundred years of the launching of Wuti's first attack *circa* 133 B.C., in gaining at least that measure of victory over the Hiongnu that Trajan succeeded in gaining over the Dacians (see V. v. 144–5 and 271).

However imperfect and transitory this Sinic triumph over a Eurasian Nomadism might be, the relative magnitude of the Sinic achievement here may be gauged from the significant fact that neither Trajan nor any other Roman empire-builder ever attempted to emulate Han Wuti's audacious attack on the Eurasian Nomads even within the confines of the Steppe's extreme Western Bay, any more than the Romans ever attempted to complete the pacification of North-West Africa by embarking on the enterprise of subjugating the Atlas and the Rif. The Sarmatians were never threatened, at Roman hands, with the fate that the Han Power inflicted on the Hiongnu; and we may guess that, if any Roman emperor had been so rash as to attack the Sarmatians, he would only have brought upon himself a repetition of the humiliation which had been suffered by the Achaemenian emperor Darius the Great when he had attacked the Sarmatians' local predecessors the Scyths.

[1] This transfiguration of frustrated Roman civil servants into creative Fathers of the Christian Church has been noticed in VI. vii. 369–70.

concern in the West when the western indigenous successor-state of the Roman Empire fell about the distracted imperial civil servants' ears.

In sharp contrast to this dilemma, from which there was no escape for Roman imperial civil servants in the Roman Empire's derelict western provinces, the Sinic imperial civil servants in the Sinic universal state's derelict northern provinces had no need to look for hospitality to an alien church in order to provide themselves with an alternative institutional framework when there had ceased to be even a fraction of an oecumenical empire for them to administer. It is true that these Sinic imperial administrators showed themselves just as blind as all but a handful of their Roman counterparts to the opportunity for a *beau geste* that was seized, according to the legend, by a Pannonian Roman soldier who impetuously divided his cloak with a beggar before the soldier's pursuing barbarian adversary had time to tear a surprisingly sanctified *sagum* from a suddenly transfigured warrior's shoulders. Like Saint Martin's civilian Roman contemporaries, the Sinic civil servants did wait stolidly to see themselves ignominiously stripped of their official robes of office; yet, in allowing themselves to incur this humiliating common experience, they were not exposing themselves, as their Roman confrères were, to face winter cold and barbarian scorn stark naked.

A Confucian civil servant who had been deprived of his official robe remained clad in his philosopher's shirt; and this respectable garment protectively covered his nakedness. With an all but deified hero-sage still to revere and confide in as his infallible master, and with a cloud of fellow witnesses,[1] past as well as present, to testify to the efficacity of a Confucian faith that had justified itself first in the glorious Wutian outcome of a four-hundred-years-long initial ordeal, the professionally unemployed passed-master of Confucian arts could bide his time, after the downfall of the United Tsin régime, without losing a *moral* which had carried his elder brethren, in their day, through their weary wanderings in the wilderness of a Sinic Time of Troubles and its first aftermath during the four centuries that had elapsed between Confucius's death and Wuti's belated advent. A patience that had once been crowned with such a dazzling ultimate reward could be practised in a second emergency with a new leaven of hope to lighten the old burden of fortitude; and, for a still living school of Confucian philosophers, this waiting game, so long as they had the strength of mind to play it, was bound, as we have seen, to be a winning game as well. After the political reunification of the whole former domain of the Sinic universal state by Sui Wên-ti in A.D. 589, the *manes* of Confucius were to see that disappointed sage's overweening pretensions posthumously vindicated for the second time; and T'ai Ts'ung's homage must have been even sweeter than Wuti's to Confucius's demurely jubilant ghost.

[1] Heb. xii. 1.

THE ROLE OF 'THE OLD KINGDOM' IN EGYPTIAC HISTORY

WHAT is 'the Old Kingdom's' role in Egyptiac history? In this Study up to this point we have assumed that 'the Old Kingdom' was the political expression of the growth stage of the Egyptiac Civilization; but this assumption cannot be endorsed without verification, considering that, in the growth stage of other civilizations, the constellation of political forces that usually presents itself to the historian's eye is, not an oecumenical empire, but a litter of parochial states, while, in the few cases in which we do find an oecumenical empire on the scene at this stage, it can be accounted for as the product of a renaissance. The oecumenical and at the same time ineffectively ramshackle structure of the Carolingian, the Chóu, and the Khatti Empire, for example, is what we should expect, *a priori*, to find in an oecumenical polity which had been brought into being through the evocation of a ghost at a stage in the necromantic society's history at which it would have been incapable of achieving, or indeed of conceiving, so ambitious a programme of political construction by an independent exercise of its own creative powers without the aid of the Black Art. The ineffectiveness of the three empires above mentioned is thus self-explanatory. We have then still to explain the establishment of an efficient oecumenical polity such as, for example, the T'ang Empire or the East Roman Empire at an early stage in a civilization's growth; and, where an explanation that accounts for the facts on the hypothesis of a renaissance is not forthcoming, as it is in these two cases,[1] when we are thus confronted with the emergence of an efficient oecumenical polity at what would appear to be an early stage of a civilization's growth, we must look elsewhere for the solution of an historical problem that cannot be either ignored or evaded. A so-far unsolved problem of the kind is presented by the effective political union of Lower with Upper Egypt, to constitute 'the Old Kingdom', at a stage of Egyptiac history which is an early one according to the provisional analysis of the structure of Egyptiac history which we have been using as our working hypothesis in this Study up to the present point; for on this hypothesis 'the Old Kingdom' cannot be accounted for, like the East Roman Empire and the T'ang Empire, as a ghost of the universal state of an antecedent civilization effectively re-embodied in a reconstituted imperial civil service, since no such antecedent civilization or oecumenical empire figures either in the Egyptiac tradition or in the dossier of our Modern Western Egyptologists.

Does the enigma thus presented by 'the Old Kingdom' in our present vista of Egyptiac history require us to view Egyptiac history in a new perspective? And might a fresh avenue of interpretation be opened up

---

[1] See pp. 15 and 20, above.

by a recognition of the possibility that, in contenting ourselves with the view of Egyptiac history which we have taken so far, we may have been neglecting one of our own precepts? At the outset of this Study[1] we took note of the risk of error to which a student of History would be exposing himself if he were to allow his vision of an historical landscape to be governed by the fleeting distribution of the light and shade at the moment when the scene happened to be under his observation. The comparative abundance or scarcity of the evidence at an historian's disposal for the study of this and that past episode is determined for him by freaks of Chance which bear no relation whatsoever to those episodes' relative intrinsic importance or unimportance; and we should therefore be positively courting error if, in our mental reconstruction of the course of past history, we were to treat the capriciously irrational quotas of the intellectual materials at our disposal for our professional work as if these were trustworthy indexes of the true proportions of the past realities which we were seeking to bring into the focus of our present consciousness.

In administering this prefatory warning to ourselves, we commended it by citing, as an example of the consequences of ignoring it, the disproportionate concentration of the attention of Modern Western scholars on the Ptolemaic successor-state of the Achaemenian Empire, to the comparative neglect of its Seleucid sister commonwealth, and we pointed out that the consequent distortion of historical vision was the result of an unconsidered subservience to blind workings of Chance through which 'the natural museum' of Upper Egypt happened to be included among the shreds of ex-Achaemenian territory which, in the scramble for the spoils of Alexander's conquests, Ptolemy Lâgou decided to seize and managed to hold. Ptolemy's choice of Egypt for his personal prize was determined by shrewd 'geopolitical' calculations which, of course, had no connexion whatsoever with those peculiar local qualities in the climate and soil of a post-pluvial Upper Egypt that were to make the Sa'īd a veritable archaeologist's paradise. Ptolemy's objective in seizing Upper Egypt was to appropriate its revenues, and, even if he might have been gratified to learn that he was also incidentally acquiring a ready-made record office in which the debris of his dynasty's acts would automatically accumulate into a collection of material evidence that moth and rust would not corrupt before thievish Modern Western archaeologists would be moved by a Faustian curiosity to break through and steal,[2] we may take it as certain that this consideration would have counted for nothing in his decisions if he had come to the conclusion that Egypt was a less desirable prey than the South-West Asian territories which he actually decided to abandon to Seleucus as a bone for this confederate of his to pick with their formidable common rival Antigonus.

This example provided an excellent illustration of our point; but we might have illustrated it equally well without looking so far afield from Upper Egypt as Lower Asia, and without descending so far in the Time-scale of Egyptiac history as the Ptolemaic Age. If we had confined our

---

[1] In I. i. 5–7.   [2] Matt. vi. 19–20; Luke xii. 33.

chronological horizon to 'the Predynastic Age' and our geographical horizon to the Lower Nile Valley, we could have made our point no less effectively by citing the contrast, in the archaeologist's historically misleading inventory, between the preservative powers of a dry-as-dust Sa'īd and the destructive powers of a water-logged Delta; and, had we clinched our argument by adducing this illustration as well, we might have saved ourselves from what may prove to have been an hallucination in our subsequent interpretation of Egyptiac history.

The premiss of this interpretation was an assumption that the emergence of the Egyptiac Civilization could be equated, for practical purposes, with the conquest of Lower Egypt by the Upper Egyptian militarist empire-builder Narmer; and this assumption was based on the fact that in our Modern Western archaeologists' Upper Egyptian 'natural museum' the earliest extant monuments of the apparatus of the Egyptiac culture—and, in particular, the earliest specimens of its script —are attributable to this epoch. The weak point in this chain of reasoning is its unspoken and uncriticized prior assumption that an array of evidence derived almost exclusively from Upper Egypt can be treated with assurance as if it were good evidence, not merely for the local history of Upper Egypt itself, but also for the oecumenical history of the Egyptiac World as a whole. This prior assumption ignores the possibility that a relatively mature Egyptiac culture which, in our Upper Egyptian 'natural museum', has left no evidence of its existence dating back appreciably earlier than Narmer's day, may have had a previous history —and this perhaps a long one—in a Lower Egyptian 'natural destructor' of the debris of human activities.[1] And this possibility opens up the further one that the sudden appearance of, for example, an already mature Egyptiac script[2] in the Sa'īd at the transition from 'the Predynastic Age' to Narmer's new era may be evidence, not that the Egyptiac culture suddenly came to birth in Narmer's day, but that a more advanced form of the Egyptiac culture was suddenly introduced into Upper Egypt from Lower Egypt as a consequence of Narmer's sudden forcible political unification of the two lands.

The magnitude of the possible error to which we expose ourselves in ignoring these considerations can be gauged by imagining, for the sake of the argument, that the unknown historical relation between the Sa'īd and the Delta in the Egyptiac World may have been analogous to the known historical relation, in the Andean World, between the Plateau and the Coast.

In the history of an Andean World that consisted, like the Egyptiac World, of two physiographically diverse cultural provinces,[3] we happen to know that the Andean culture originated in the coastal province and

---

[1] See Wilson, J. A.: *The Burden of Egypt* (Chicago 1951, University Press), p. 16.

[2] In the earliest specimens of the Egyptiac script that had been discovered by Modern Western archaeologists down to the time of writing, the characters were already being used, not as 'pictograms' giving a visual representation of objects or ideas, but as 'phonemes', in which the sound of the spoken Egyptian word corresponding to the original visual meaning of the character was associated with the character for the conveyance of this sound in other contexts. 'At the very beginning of history, Egyptian hieroglyphic writing appeared on stone and clay with this rebus-principle already accepted' (Wilson, op. cit., p. 38).   [3] See II. i. 322–3.

that this was the scene of successive experiences of growth, breakdown, and disintegration through which the Andean Civilization passed before its coastal birthplace was eventually united politically with a culturally parvenu highland province to constitute an Andean oecumenical empire as a result of the conquest of the lowland coastal states Chimu and Nazca by the highlander militarist Pachacutec (*imperabat circa* A.D. 1400–48).[1] The reason why we are able to see Andean history now in this true perspective is because, in Peru, the coastal province that was the true birthplace of the culture happened, like the Sa'īd in the Egyptiac World, to be 'a natural museum' in which climate and soil conspired to preserve the incriminating material evidence of Civilization instead of conspiring to destroy it; and, by the time of writing, this Peruvian 'natural museum' had been explored by the enterprise of experienced twentieth-century Western Americanists with a skill and energy that would have done credit to the pioneer nineteenth-century Western Egyptologists. The bearing of these triumphs of Archaeology in Peru on the interpretation of Egyptiac history was indicated by the revolutionary violence of the change in the interpretation of Andean history which these Peruvian archaeological discoveries had dictated.

Before the archaeologists started operations in Peru, Modern Western knowledge of Andean history had been virtually confined to evidence concerning the Empire of the Incas; and, while this evidence had partly consisted in the massive material monuments of cyclopean architecture constructed by these empire-building highlanders and their neighbours and predecessors on the Plateau, the main source of information at the disposal of Western scholars at that stage had been the Incaic imperial tradition preserved in Castilian literary dress and more or less misleadingly travestied in the process.[2] In the picture presented in this tradition the rise and fall of the Incaic Power were equated with the beginning and end of Andean history; and, while Modern Western scholarship correctly divined, on the strength of the internal evidence, that little credence was to be given to a version of the Incaic tradition, picked up by the seventeenth-century Spanish Jesuit historian Fernando Montesinos,[3] which professed to carry the record of Incaic history back to a high antiquity, this well-justified rejection of an apocryphal prelude to genuine Incaic history was merely a negative result of historical criticism, and the most acute analysis of the Incaic traditional evidence would never have brought to light the authentic early history of the Andean Civilization in a coastal province of the Andean World where neither the Incas nor their predecessors in the highland province had played any decisive part before the fifteenth century of the Christian Era.

The true perspective of Andean history could only be brought to light by the instrument of Archaeology; and, when an archaeological

---

[1] See I. i. 121–2.

[2] The life and work of the Herodian half-breed Garcilaso de la Vega have been noticed in IX. viii. 597.

[3] A critique of Montesinos' *Memorias Antiguas Historiales y Políticas del Perú* will be found in Baudin, L.: *L'Empire Socialiste des Inka* (Paris 1928, Institut d'Ethnologie), pp. 17–18. Montesinos wrote this book in A.D. 1652, in the fifth generation after the Spanish conquest of the Andean Empire of the Four Quarters.

searchlight was eventually brought into action, it showed up the falsity of the picture that the Incaic tradition had presented; for even that portion of the traditional Incaic story that was not now proved false in itself was now proved to have been placed in a most misleadingly false perspective. While the traditional account of the foundation of the Incaic Empire according to the shorter of the two irreconcilable traditional schemes of chronology might still be accepted as being more or less true as far as it went, it was now shown to be, not the alpha and omega of Andean history, but merely the last chapter in the story of the Andean Civilization's disintegration.

If we were to apply this Andean analogy to our interpretation of Egyptiac history, we should find ourselves having to reckon with the possibility that the picture which we had accepted here so far might be little less misleading than an Incaic tradition which had been exploded by an archaeological bomb. The corresponding Upper Egyptian tradition was, no doubt, unlikely ever to be discredited in this conclusively objective way, because the Delta, unlike the coastal province of the Andean World, was unlikely to yield up positive archaeological evidence of the part that it had played in history. Nevertheless, the Upper Egyptian tradition which, in the absence of Deltaic archaeological evidence, had hitherto held the field was at least impugned by the sensational overthrow of the Incaic tradition at the archaeologists' hands; for an egocentricity that led the Incaic makers and masters of an Andean universal state to telescope the whole drama of Andean history into the single last act in which the Incas themselves happened to hold the stage is, as we know, a common infirmity of Human Nature; and it would be surprising if there had been no alloy of the same human weakness in the character of the Upper Egyptian makers and masters of 'the Old Kingdom' of the Two Lands. The inference to be drawn from this presumption of a taint of Original Sin would be that 'the Old Kingdom' in Egyptiac history, like 'the Empire of the Four Quarters' in Andean history, might in truth have been merely the last chapter of a long story, or, in other words, might have been, like 'the Empire of the Four Quarters', a universal state in the technical sense in which that term is used in this Study.

When once this idea has been suggested by the external evidence, it becomes manifest that there is also internal evidence which likewise testifies in favour of it.

In the first place 'the Old Kingdom' actually was a universal state in the literal sense of the words, inasmuch as it was an oecumenical empire embracing the whole domain of the Egyptiac World of the day. In the second place it exhibits the constitution and êthos of a universal state if 'totalitarianism' is to be regarded as one of the distinctive characteristics of this species of polity. While 'the Middle Empire', in which we have hitherto seen the Egyptiac universal state, and 'the New Empire', in which we have seen a recrudescence of it, both certainly pass muster on this test, 'the Old Kingdom' qualifies even more conspicuously for recognition as being another representative of the same species, considering that 'totalitarianism' probably asserted itself more rapidly in 'the Old Kingdom' than in 'the Middle Empire',[1] and certainly went to greater lengths in 'the Old Kingdom' than in either of its two successors.[2] There was no phase of Egyptiac history after the fall of 'the Old Kingdom' in which any Pharaoh could have said 'L'État, c'est moi' with the same plenitude of veracity that would have animated the Early Modern Western *Roi Soleil*'s celebrated words if they had been uttered by one of the Pyramid-Builders. In other contexts we have seen how the Pyramid-Builders broke the Egyptiac Society's back,[3] and how the mark made by this inordinate abuse of power on the Egyptiac Society's folk-memory bit so deep and smarted so sorely as to make it impossible for any of those titanic egoists' successors ever to emulate their total inhumanity *vis-à-vis* their subjects.[4] In our first reading of Egyptiac history we identified the catastrophe inflicted on the Egyptiac Society by the Pyramid-Builders with the breakdown of the Egyptiac Civilization. On second thoughts we might be inclined to see in it, not the first blow, but the *coup de grâce*, and to look for the breakdown in some forgotten disaster in 'the Predynastic Age' which had passed into oblivion simply because the historical evidence happened to have been swallowed up in a Deltaic Serbonian Bog.

On the analogy of what we know about the causes of the breakdowns and disintegrations of other civilizations, we might conjecture that the Egyptiac Civilization ruined itself, like so many societies of its kind, through a failure to keep within bounds the destructiveness of a chronic warfare between parochial sovereign states;[5] and on this line of interpretation we might see in the gruesome scenes carved on the palette of Narmer[6] a record of the knock-out blow that brought an Egyptiac Time of Troubles to its tardy close. The measure of the incidence of an evil is apt to be reflected in the scale of the price that its victims bring themselves to pay for the sake of escaping from it; and the plenitude of the power that, under the régime of the Old Kingdom, was invested in a Pharaoh reigning on Earth as a god incarnate suggests that the suffering inflicted on the Egyptiac World by political disunity in a predynastic age of unrecorded warfare between contending parochial states was probably proportionate in its severity to the exorbitancy of the price which this society is known to have consented to pay in the next chapter of the story for an oecumenical peace which had come to be recognized as a necessity of Egyptiac life.

If we were to find ourselves convinced by the argument of our present *retractatio* of our previous interpretation of Egyptiac history, we should

---

[1] Wilson, op. cit., pp. 45–47, conjectures that the dogma that Pharaoh was not a man, but was a god incarnate on Earth, was officially adopted after the establishment of the United Kingdom in order to ground a political union which had originally been brought about by force upon a moral consent springing from a religious faith. He suggests that this institution took root in the time of the first two dynasties.

[2] See IV. iv. 408–14.

[3] See I. i. 136–7 and 141–2, and III. iii. 212–15.

[4] See IV. iv. 412–14.

[5] In the later Predynastic Age of Egyptiac history, 'Archaeology produces a great amount of arrowheads and mace-heads, and the skeletons of the Predynastic Egyptians show an extraordinary number of broken bones. Apparently, communities had come into competitive contact with other communities, so that there was already that warfare which built little states into larger states' (Wilson, op. cit., p. 25).

[6] See IV. iv. 502–4.

then have to revise that interpretation in two respects. We should have to suppose that 'the Middle Empire', like 'the New Empire', was a recrudescence of a universal state, and that a phenomenon which we had already detected in Egyptiac history in one occurrence had actually occurred not merely once but twice. And we should then have to regard the chapter of Egyptiac history that intervened between the fall of 'the Old Kingdom' and the rise of 'the Middle Empire' as having been, not a Time of Troubles following the breakdown of a civilization and ending in the establishment of a universal state, but an interregnum following the dissolution of a universal state and ending in this case, not in the emergence of a new civilization, but in the recrudescence of a universal state that had gone into dissolution without having lost its capacity to reconstitute itself. Such recrudescences of universal states after they had once gone to pieces might not represent the 'normal' course of History according to a standard of normality based on what had been perhaps the more usual denouement of the histories of the disintegrations of civilizations during the five or six thousand years within which a score of societies of this species had been rising and falling up to date; yet it would not be surprising to find an additional instance of the phenomenon of recrudescence in an Egyptiac history which had already shown itself peculiar by providing the historical investigator with one specimen of this unusual turn of events at a later stage in its long course. When once we have interpreted 'the New Empire' as being a recrudescence of 'the Middle Empire', there is no intellectual stumbling-block to hinder us from similarly interpreting 'the Middle Empire' as being a recrudescence of an 'Old Kingdom' which, on this revised interpretation, we should then identify as having been the original Egyptiac universal state.

We have, however, still to ask ourselves whether a view of 'the Old Kingdom's' role in Egyptiac history that is suggested by the deification of an oecumenical Pharaoh and by material evidences of the previous ravages of warfare in a Late Predynastic Age is compatible with all the phenomena that have to be taken into account in an appreciation of a period of Egyptiac history extending from the date of the unification of Lower Egypt with Upper Egypt under the First Dynasty to the dissolution of the United Kingdom under the Sixth Dynasty. In the survey of other oecumenical empires from which our concept of a universal state has been derived, we have found that one of the outstanding features of this institution is a negative one. The dominant minority that has pieced together, in a universal state, the fragments of a society that has been broken up by the same dominant minority's fratricidal strife in a foregoing Time of Troubles is conspicuously destitute of the creativity which, before the breakdown, has been displayed by its predecessors when they have been leading the rank-and-file by the persuasive arts of Orpheus instead of dragooning them with a Prussian drill-sergeant's rod.[1] If there is any creative activity in the body social of a disintegrating society in its universal state, this makes its appearance among the Internal Proletariat; it works from below upwards; and, if the Dominant Minority is ever stirred by this fresh breath of life, it

[1] See IV. iv. 122–31.

yields to it grudgingly and late in the day. Does the record of an Egyptiac dominant minority conform to this pattern of behaviour in the Age of 'the Old Kingdom'? If the first two dynasties in the history of an Egyptiac United Kingdom had been followed immediately by the Fifth and Sixth, we could have certified that, on the test of the dominant minority's being destitute of creativity, 'the Old Kingdom' would have qualified for classification as a universal state; but the performance of the Third and Fourth Dynasties—which has, of course, likewise to be taken into account—does not fit into this picture.

At first sight, indeed, it might look as if the First and Second Dynasties, too, were convicted of creativity by the sudden epiphany, at the inauguration of the United Kingdom, of an Egyptiac script at an advanced stage of development.[1] This invention, without which the problem of administering an oecumenical empire on the scale of the Egyptiac United Kingdom might well have been insoluble, must have been the fruit of a creative activity of a high potency at some time and place, but the creative act will not be debited to the Thinites' account. While, in the absence of records from the Delta, it is no more possible to prove than it is to disprove that the Egyptiac script was an independent invention of the people of Lower Egypt in the predynastic days before the political unification of the two lands, there is the alternative possibility that the idea of a script consisting of phonemes derived from pictograms may have come to the Egyptiac Society from the Sumeric World; for in the first place the archaeological record, as it stood in A.D. 1951, indicated that in Sumer the art of writing had appeared earlier than in Egypt and had developed gradually from rudimentary beginnings, whereas in Egypt it seemed to have made a sudden epiphany at an advanced stage,[2] while in the second place there were certain other elements of culture in Egypt in the Late Predynastic and the Early Dynastic Age which were undisputedly Sumeric in origin: for example, the cylinder seal; a panelled brick architecture; an antithetic composition of groups of figures; the portrayal of composite monsters and animals with intertwined necks; and the use of boats of a distinctively Sumeric build.[3] These Sumeric influences, which had declared themselves in the Egyptiac World during the last two centuries of the Predynastic Age, continued to dominate the Egyptiac culture under the first two dynasties;[4] and, though they may not be so important as to impugn the Egyptiac Civilization's claim to originality,[5] they do absolve the First and Second dynasties from any imputation of creativity.

On the other hand the Fourth Dynasty, if not the Third, is convicted of creativity by an apparently sudden effacement of these Sumeric

---

[1] See p. 684, n. 2, above.   [2] See Wilson, op. cit., p. 38.
[3] See ibid., p. 37, and the present Study, IX. viii. 453, n. 2.
[4] See Wilson, op. cit., pp. 39 and 50.
[5] Wilson contends that, for some 1,800 years out of the 2,000 years that may have elapsed between the genesis of the Merimdian predynastic culture and the establishment of the United Kingdom, 'the development of Egyptian culture was internal' (op. cit., p. 37). Egypt's 'debt to the influence of Mesopotamia was very great, but the inner spiritual urge to a new way of life was the essential factor—really the only motivating factor—in the great change' in the Egyptiac way of life at the transition from the Predynastic Age to the Age of 'the Old Kingdom' (ibid., p. 40).

influences, after a reign of perhaps not less than six centuries' duration according to Wilson's chronology,[1] through the abrupt creation of a new style of culture that was distinctively Egyptiac.[2] The initiative in this burst of creative activity manifestly came from above, not from below; its pace seems to have been extraordinarily swift, if the speed of the development of Architecture is a fair sample of it;[3] and this sudden swift advance was made on a broad front: in the provinces of Medical Science[4] and the Philosophy of Religion[5] as well as in the visual arts. In the province of Architecture, which was the master art of the time and place,

'this sudden development seems to have been entirely native within Egypt. It was called forth by two devotions: the acceptance of the dogma that the King was a god and thus deserving of a supreme offering of energies, and the excitement of a new adventure in Art and Technique.'[6]

And, while the piling up of colossal buildings in honour of a god incarnate—an oecumenical monarch who was an object of worship because he was a guarantor of peace through unity—is something that might be interpreted as one of the familiar phenomena of a universal state, on a par with the big buildings of 'the New Empire' of Egypt under the Nineteenth Dynasty and of the Roman Empire in its post-Diocletianic Age,[7] 'the excitement of a new adventure in Art and Technique' is a mark, not of a temporary rally in a long-drawn-out losing battle against the forces of social disintegration, but of an early stage of social growth. Moreover, the distinctive feature of the pyramids built by pharaohs of the Third and Fourth Dynasties, as contrasted with pyramids of a later age, is not the inordinate physical bulk that they have in common with the fallen colossus of Ramses II at Thebes or with the Baths of Diocletian at Rome, but the beautiful exactness of workmanship[8] that they have in common with the Parthenon at Athens and with the Green Mosque at Brusa.

On this showing, we are bound, in reconsidering our analysis of the structure of Egyptiac history, to conclude that, whether or not there was a flowering of creativity in the Early Predynastic Age, there un-

---

[1] See Wilson, op. cit., p. vii.   [2] See ibid., pp. 39, 44, and 78.

[3] Under the first two dynasties the Egyptians were content, with one or two exceptions, to go on using a Sumeric building material in a Sumeric style of architecture, in spite of the fact that in Egypt, in contrast to Shinar, brick was not the only building material within the architect's reach. Though, in Egypt, 'stone was abundant and easy to work' (Wilson, op. cit., p. 50), 'the first significant structure of stone' (ibid., p. 70) was the Third Dynasty Pharaoh Djoser's Step Pyramid at Saqqārah, and 'the stone of this structure was cut into small bricks, laid as if the stone blocks were mud bricks, and panelled in the same way as the previous brick tombs were' (p. 51). The rise from a Sumeroid brick architecture to the climax of an Egyptiac stone architecture in the Pyramid of Khufu was, by contrast, 'astonishingly fast. The first serious stone masonry may have been about 100 or 125 years before Khufu; . . . Djoser's Step Pyramid was about 75 years before Khufu. In that brief span the Egyptians had learnt how to handle tremendous masses of stone. . . . They abandoned the handling of stone as if it were brick and treated the new material for its own qualities of mass and durability. And they learnt how to finish off myriads of blocks with a perfection that presented a single unified mass' (ibid., p. 70).

[4] See ibid., pp. 56–58.   [5] See ibid., pp. 58–60.
[6] Ibid., p. 70.   [7] See IV. iv. 638.
[8] See Wilson, op. cit., pp. 54–55, citing Edwards, I. E. S.: *The Pyramids of Egypt* (London 1947, Penguin).

questionably was one in the Age of the Third and Fourth dynasties;[1] and then we shall also find ourselves further bound to conclude that, whether or not there was a social breakdown, leading to a Time of Troubles, in the Late Predynastic Age preceding the establishment of the United Kingdom under the First Dynasty, there was unquestionably a breakdown after the running out of the Fourth Dynasty, and a Time of Troubles between this breakdown and the political reunification of the Egyptiac World by a Theban Mentuhotep[2] *circa* 2050 B.C. So, after all, we shall not find ourselves able to account for the decline and fall of the Old Kingdom under the Fifth and Sixth dynasties entirely as a belated but eventually inevitable nemesis of wounds inflicted by the Egyptiac Society on its own body in an age before a temporary reprieve had been won for it by the First Dynasty's feat of imposing an oecumenical peace. We shall have to find the chief cause of this decline and fall where we have found it in earlier passages in this Study,[3] and that is in the egotism which was the dark reverse side of the Pyramid-Builders' dazzling creativity; for this egotism brought in its train a nemesis that worked itself out in the full light of history.

The official concentration of political power in the hands of a Pharaoh whose practical capacity to transact business could not in truth surpass the limits of the ordinary human nature of this bogus god found its nemesis in a decentralization of power, *de facto*, which Pharaoh might ignore but found himself impotent to arrest. The expenditure of an economic surplus—acquired by a politically united Egyptiac Society through the corporate achievement of systematically reclaiming a Nilotic jungle-swamp—upon building the Pyramids, and then setting apart lavish assignments of land revenues for the maintenance of successive Pharaohs' mortuary cults, found its nemesis in an economic breakdown that conjured penury out of abundance. The dedication of 'a new adventure in Art and Technique' to the perpetuation of a life-in-death for dead pharaohs found its nemesis in the freezing of the living plasma of a new-born Egyptiac style of art into a rigid convention[4] as swiftly as the lava welling out of the crater of a volcano is frozen in the act of flowing down the mountain's side. And all these divers unhappy consequences of the deification of a human ruler eventually stung Egyptian hearts into a moral revolt against the injustice of a régime of privilege that had been

---

[1] The cause of this flowering in this age was still a mystery at the time of writing. Wilson, in op. cit., p. 61, raises the questions: 'Did a new government bring into being new ruling classes and therefore new social classes? Did a single government, controlling the land from the First Cataract to the Mediterranean, so improve the economic standard of the nation that there was a newly rich class and a notable increase in population? These are highly important questions, but we cannot answer any of them.' Yet, while these questions remained unanswerable apropos of the history of an Egyptiac 'Old Kingdom', they could be answered in the affirmative apropos of a Roman Empire in Hellenic history and of a Han Empire in Sinic history, and it could be reported that, in those two cases, in which the answers to Dr. Wilson's questions were known, a prima facie promising conjunction of political unity with economic development had not availed to kindle a new flame of creative activity.

[2] See Drioton, É., and Vandier, J.: *L'Égypte* (Paris 1946, Presses Universitaires de France), pp. 271–3; Winlock, H. E.: *The Rise and Fall of the Middle Kingdom in Thebes* (New York 1947, Macmillan), pp. 22–32.

[3] See I. i. 136–7 and 141–2, and III. iii. 212–15.

[4] On this point, see Wilson, op. cit., pp. 66–67.

carried to monstrous lengths. In its moral atmosphere the anarchic chapter of Egyptiac history between the dissolution of 'the Old Kingdom' and the establishment of 'the Middle Empire' is much more reminiscent of the Time of Troubles between the breakdown of the Hellenic Civilization and the establishment of the Roman Empire than it is of the interregnum between the dissolution of the Roman Empire and the emergence of Christian Hellenistic societies affiliated to the Hellenic Civilization.

In view of these well-authenticated positive facts, we must abide by our original finding that, in the structure of Egyptiac history, the Age of the Pyramid-Builders is an authentic age of growth, in spite of its being an episode in the life of an 'Old Kingdom' which bears marks of being the universal state of a disintegrating society. We must recognize, in fact, that 'the Old Kingdom' is enigmatically Janus-faced.

THE RELATION, IN RENAISSANCES OF UNIVERSAL STATES, BETWEEN EFFECTIVENESS OF EVOCATION AND DEGREE OF GEOGRAPHICAL DISPLACEMENT

In a preceding Annex to this chapter,[1] in which we have compared the renaissances of the Sinic and Hellenic universal states, we have found that the renaissance of the Sinic universal state in the main body of the Far Eastern World was remarkably more effective than was the renaissance of the Hellenic universal state in either Western or Orthodox Christendom, and also that, as between these two renaissances of the Roman Empire in the histories of the two Christian Hellenistic civilizations, its renaissance in the shape of an East Roman Empire in the main body of Orthodox Christendom fell less far short than its renaissance in the shape of a Holy Roman Empire in the West fell short of the standard of effectiveness set by the renaissance of the Ts'in and Han Empire in the shape of the Sui and T'ang Empire. These findings suggest, as far as they go—and they are, of course, based on a consideration of only three cases—that the effectiveness of the evocation of an antecedent society's universal state varies in direct ratio with the tenacity of the original universal state in surviving, or with its persistence in rallying, during the death agonies of the moribund society of which it was a tardy political embodiment, and in inverse ratio with the degree of the geographical displacement of the domain of the affiliated civilization, in whose history the renaissance takes place, from the domain of its defunct predecessor.

In Sinic and Far Eastern history the dissolution of the Posterior Han Empire at the turn of the second and third centuries of the Christian Era was ephemerally retrieved during the years A.D. 280–317 by a reunion of the whole of its former territory under the rule of 'the United Tsin'; and, when, thereafter, a nascent Far Eastern Society emerged out of a post-Sinic interregnum, its domain was virtually coextensive with its Sinic predecessor's, even though, within this domain, the Yellow River Basin, which had been the Sinic Civilization's cradle, was now rivalled in importance by a Yangtse Basin which had been incorporated into the Sinic World only in the course of its Time of Troubles and its universal state. In Hellenic and Orthodox Christian history a Roman Empire which had dissolved at the turn of the fourth and fifth centuries of the Christian Era in the West survived till the turn of the sixth and seventh centuries in the central and eastern provinces with a tenacity comparable to the persistence of a temporarily dissolved Sinic universal state in reconstituting itself for a further spell under the auspices of the United Tsin. On the other hand the domain of the Orthodox Christian Society that emerged thereafter out of a post-Hellenic interregnum,

[1] On pp. 649–81, above.

unlike the domain of the Far Eastern Society, was not coextensive with the domain of the antecedent society to which it was affiliated. The cradle of the Hellenic Civilization had been the basin of the Aegean Sea;[1] but for some two hundred years after the emergence of an Orthodox Christendom the whole of Continental European Greece and the Morea, save for a few isolated fortresses, was in the hands of pagan Slav interlopers, while Continental Asiatic Greece and the islands of the Archipelago, though they were inside the Orthodox Christian fold, were playing a subordinate part in the nascent civilization's history. Orthodox Christendom's cradle lay on the Anatolian Plateau, and the antecedent civilization to whose domain it approximately corresponded was not the Hellenic but the Hittite. The only important common ground between a nascent Orthodox Christendom and a pre-Alexandrine Hellas was the coastline and immediate hinterland of the Black Sea Straits—above all, of course, an Orthodox Christian imperial capital at a Constantinople which had once been the Hellenic city-state founded by Megarian colonists at Byzantium. This province of the Hellenic World beyond the Dardanelles had, however, lain outside the original domain of Hellas round the Aegean, and the planting of Hellenic colonies along the coasts of the Dardanelles and the Bosphorus had not begun before the turn of the eighth and seventh centuries B.C.

As for the relations between the Hellenic Civilization and Western Christendom, the earliness of the date of the break-up of the Roman Empire in the West was matched by the extent of the displacement of the cradle of Western Christendom from the Hellenic World's Aegean homeland. The cradle of Western Christendom lay in Gaul, north-west of the Alps and astride the Rhine, in territory that had not been incorporated into the Hellenic World until the eve of the establishment of the Roman Empire; and in the early centuries of Western history the Mediterranean seaboard of Gaul in Provence and Languedoc, which had been won for Hellenism by Roman arms a century earlier than the interior and had been penetrated, long before that, by Hellenic influences radiating from Marseilles, played no more important a part than was played in Orthodox Christian history by a *ci-devant* Roman province of Asia that had become the East Roman Empire's Thracensian army-corps district.

We have now to inquire whether the historical 'law' which we have inferred from a synoptic examination of these three cases stands or falls if we bring into the picture the other cases known to us. In another context[2] we have classified fifteen 'related' civilizations[3]—reckoning the offshoots of the Far Eastern and Orthodox Christian civilizations separately from their main bodies—on the criterion of the degree of their geographical displacement from the antecedent societies to which they are affiliated. Does this widening of our horizon discredit or vindicate our tentative 'law' to the effect that the evocation of the ghost of an antecedent civilization's universal state in the history of an affiliated

---

[1] See IX. viii. 419 and 711–12.   [2] In I. i. 132.

[3] The Sinic Civilization should be added to this list if we are right in concluding, in the light of the progress of archaeological discovery since the time when the first six volumes of this Study were being written, that this Sinic Society had a predecessor in the shape of the Shang Culture.

civilization varies in its effectiveness in inverse ratio to the degree of the geographical displacement of the affiliated society's cradle from its predecessor's? If we now go on to complete our survey, we shall find our tentative 'law' vindicated on the whole.

For example, in the history of the offshoot of the Far Eastern Civilization in Japan, on ground lying right outside the domain of the antecedent Sinic Civilization, even at its widest extent, a ghost of the Sinic universal state that had been successfully resuscitated in the main body of the Far Eastern Society in the shape of the Sui and T''ang Empire was duly introduced into Japan *tel quel*; but, as we have seen,[1] this unimaginatively exact replica of the T''ang régime was too exotic a plant in Japan to strike root there effectively; and accordingly a resuscitation of the Han régime that was against nature even in China was soon reduced in Japan to a political façade thinly masking a free play of native Japanese political forces on original lines of their own.

The offshoot of Orthodox Christendom in Russia resembled the offshoot of the Far Eastern Civilization in Japan in lying right outside the geographical limits of the antecedent civilization, even at their widest; and here Moscow's claim to be 'the Third Rome'[2] was not belied by her performance so conclusively as Kyoto's claim (if ever made) to be 'the third Ch'ang Ngan'. Yet, though a Muscovite Tsardom was a more effective avatar of the Roman Empire than a Western 'Holy Roman Empire' ever contrived to be, the native Russian element in its êthos, which was the source of its vitality, made it a much less exact replica of its Roman model than was reproduced in an East Roman Empire which had retained the authentic 'Second Rome' to serve as its own imperial capital.

If we pass on to take a synoptic view of the two Islamic societies affiliated to the Syriac Civilization, we shall find our 'law' holding good here again. In an Arabic Muslim World whose cradle included Syria itself, a reintegrated Syriac universal state, in the shape of an 'Abbasid Caliphate, was revived, in a beleaguered fortress which had Syria for its glacis and Egypt for its donjon, within less than three and a half years after the extinction of the original 'Abbasid Caliphate in its residual metropolitan territory in 'Irāq.[3] On the other hand, in an Ottoman extension of the Iranic Muslim World into Anatolian territory that had not been embraced in the domain of the Syriac Civilization at any time since its inclusion, from 547 B.C. to 334 B.C., in the dominions of the Achaemenian Empire, the Caliphate enjoyed so little prestige that, as we have seen,[4] Sultan Selīm I, the Ottoman conqueror who overthrew the Egyptian Mamlūk power and annexed its dominions, never took the trouble to usurp the title of Caliph from the last scion of the Mamlūks' Cairene 'Abbasid puppets; and Istanbul's potential claim to be 'the Third Baghdad' was not exploited by Ottoman statesmanship till the rapid break-up of the Ottoman Empire after the Great Russo-Turkish War of A.D. 1768–74 moved the Porte to bring its dusty title to the Caliphate out of its muniment room as a long-neglected political asset which might perhaps be used to offset the Ottoman Empire's grievous

---

[1] In II. ii. 158–9.
[2] See VI. vii. 31–40.
[3] See VI. vii. 20.
[4] In VI. vii. 21–27 and on p. 103, above.

losses of territory and power by helping to preserve some residue of Ottoman political influence over former Muslim subjects of the Porte who had now passed under non-Muslim rule, and to extend this influence over other Muslims, likewise living under non-Muslim rule, who had never at any time been subjects of the Ottoman Empire, even at its widest extent.

We can see, again, that the régime of the Kassite barbarian kings and their indigenous successors, in a Babylonia that was coextensive with an antecedent Sumeric Civilization's cradle in the Land of Shinar, ran much truer to the type of the Empire of Sumer and Akkad, which had been the Sumeric Civilization's universal state, than did the régime of a Hittite barbarian Empire of Khatti on an Anatolian Plateau that had been only on the fringe of the Sumeric World even at the Empire of Sumer and Akkad's apogee.

While our 'law' has thus stood the test of an empirical survey so far, there is at least one case in which the 'law' seems to break down. In the history of a Hindu Society whose cradle was as nearly coincident with an antecedent Indic Civilization's as the Far Eastern Society's cradle was with an antecedent Sinic Civilization's, we should expect to find some avatar of the Mauryan Empire comparable in effectiveness to the Sui and T'ang avatar of the Ts'in and Han Empire; but an inspection of Hindu history reveals no political renaissance of the kind.[1]

As for the histories of the sister societies affiliated to the Minoan Civilization, we should expect an Hellenic World whose cradle partially coincided with the Minoan World's to be the scene of an avatar of 'the thalassocracy of Minos' to which we should find no such effective counterpart in a Syriac World whose cradle lay completely outside the bounds of the Minoan World, even at its widest extent, save for the Minoan settlement at Ugarit on Ras ash-Shamrah. Actually we do find something that might be taken for a Syriac avatar of 'the thalassocracy of Minos' in the maritime predominance of the Phoenicians in the Mediterranean in the archaic age of Syriac and Hellenic history, while, on the other hand, no such avatar is to be found in Hellenic history. The thalassocracy in the Aegean Basin that was established by Athens in the fifth century B.C. shows no trace of having been the ghost of a dead Minoan universal state. This abortive Athenian first attempt at the creation of an Hellenic universal state shows all the signs of having been an original response to a contemporary challenge.[2]

On this showing, we must conclude that the 'law' which we have been examining in this Annex holds good in a majority of the cases in point, but is by no means universally valid.

---

[1] This non-conformity of Hindu history to our tentative 'law' would be offset by the conformity of Sinic history, if the Sinic Society should prove to have been affiliated to a predecessor in the shape of the Shang Culture; for the cradle of the Chóu barbarians, whose overthrow of the Shang Power gave the Sinic Civilization its opportunity for coming to birth, lay in 'the Country within the Passes' in the Middle Basin of the Yellow River (see VI. vii. 170), not within the homeland of the Shang Culture in the Lower Basin of the Yellow River, and we have noticed (on p. 682, above) that the Chóu Empire wears the appearance of being, like the Khatti Empire and 'the Holy Roman Empire', an attempt, though a clumsy one, to resuscitate the universal state of a defunct antecedent civilization.　　　　　[2] See IX. viii. 435–6 and 522–5.

ARE THE RELATIONS OF THE FINE ARTS AND THE MATHEMATICAL AND NATURAL SCIENCES TO THE SOCIAL MILIEU DIVERSE OR SIMILAR?

In the chapter to which this Annex attaches,[1] we have taken, in passing, a synoptic glance at the relations in which three varieties of human activity stand respectively to a social milieu—located in some particular time and place—which is the field of all these three activities alike; and we have formed the opinion that the relation is a different one in each of the three cases.

While activities in the realm of social human affairs, as exemplified in Politics and in Law, would manifestly be stultifying themselves if they did not try to provide parochial and ephemeral solutions for social human problems that are nothing if not local and temporary, activities in the realm of Non-Human Nature, as exemplified theoretically in Mathematics and in Natural Science and practically in Technology, would be stultifying themselves no less signally if they did not extend their view backwards and outwards beyond the narrow and fleeting bounds of Here and Now to take account of the whole sum of knowledge and 'know-how' accessible to their professors and practitioners. On the other hand, the Fine Arts, as exemplified in Literature and in the Visual Arts, enjoy a relative freedom from the trammels of Time and Space in virtue of their source in the subconscious abyss of the Psyche; for 'the Primordial Images' which the Arts translate into the temporary and local symbolism of some particular social milieu had known 'no variableness, neither shadow of turning',[2] during the five or six thousand years within which human societies of the species labelled 'civilizations' had been coming and going down to the time of writing, half-way through the twentieth century of the Christian Era; and therefore the oracles, drawn from this unvarying subterranean source, which it was the mission of the Fine Arts to deliver to intelligences and wills domiciled in the kaleidoscopic social milieux on Life's conscious volitional surface, were not only independent of the particular Here and Now in which any system of government or law was bound to be imprisoned, but were likewise free from the hardly less narrow confines of a cumulative intellectual inheritance which was the social prison-house of Mathematics, Natural Science, and Technology.

In the history of Modern Western thought the difference between the respective relations of the Fine Arts and the Mathematical and Natural Sciences to the social milieu was brought out in the course of the seventeenth-century controversy in France and England over the respective merits of 'the Ancients' (i.e. the creators and exponents of

---

[1] Pp. 48–82 above. [2] Jas. i. 17.

the Hellenic culture, seen through the medium of the surviving works of Classical Greek and Latin literature and art) and 'the Moderns' (i.e. the representatives of a Western culture in transition from its Early Modern to its Late Modern phase). Both parties to this debate perceived that the Fine Arts were, for some reason,[1] exempt from the necessity—or debarred from the opportunity—of progressing by a process of cumulative growth which was the servitude—or privilege—of Mathematics, Natural Science, and Technology; and the more temperate and judicious spirits among the champions of the Moderns' cause made a virtue of conceding this point to their opponents. It was frankly admitted by Fontenelle, for example, in *Une Digression sur les Anciens et les Modernes*:[2]

'Pour ce qui est de l'Éloquence et de la Poësie, qui sont le sujet de la principale contestation entre les Anciens et les Modernes . . . je crois que les Anciens en ont pû atteindre la perfection, parceque . . . l'Éloquence et la Poësie ne demandent qu'un certain nombre de vûes assez borné, par rapport à d'autres arts, et elle[s] dépendent principalement de la vivacité de l'imagination.[3] Or les hommes peuvent avoir amassé en peu de siècles un petit nombre de vûes, et la vivacité de l'imagination n'a pas besoin d'une longue suite d'expériences, ni d'une grande quantité de règles pour avoir toute la perfection dont elle est capable. . . . Comme l'Éloquence et la Poësie sont assez bornées, il faut qu'il y ait un temps où elles soient portées à leur dernière perfection, et je tiens que, pour l'Éloquence et pour l'Histoire, ce tems a été le siècle d'Auguste. Je n'imagine rien au dessus de Ciceron et de Titelive. Ce n'est pas qu'ils n'ayent leurs défauts, mais je ne crois pas qu'on puisse avoir moins de défauts avec autant de grandes qualitez, et l'on sait assez que c'est la seule manière dont on puisse dire que les hommes soient parfaits sur quelque chose. . . .

'Mais la Phisique, la Medecine, les Mathematiques sont composées d'un nombre infini de vûes, et dépendent de la justesse du raisonnement, qui se perfectionne avec une extrême lenteur, et se perfectionne toûjours. Il faut même souvent qu'elles soient aidées par des expériences que le hazard seul fait naître, et qu'il n'améne pas à point nommé. Il est évident que tout cela n'a point de fin, et que les derniers phisiciens ou mathematiciens devront naturellement être les plus habiles.'[4]

The same concession to the claims of the Ancients in the realm of the Fine Arts was made by the ablest of the English champions of the Moderns, William Wotton, in his *Reflections upon Ancient and Modern Learning*.[5]

[1] The autonomy on the social plane which the Fine Arts enjoyed in virtue of their source in the subconscious abyss of the Psyche was divined intuitively by the Modern Western thinkers of that generation more than two hundred years before 'the Collective Subconscious' was discovered empirically by the cumulative intellectual labours of Modern Western Science.

[2] First edition, January 1688 (see Bury, J. B.: *The Idea of Progress* (London 1924, Macmillan), p. 101).

[3] Fontenelle's 'limited number of ideas within a narrow horizon' which are animated by 'the liveliness of the Imagination' are synonyms, in non-technical phraseology, for Jung's 'Primordial Images'.—A.J.T.

[4] Fontenelle, B. le B. de: *Pöesies Pastorales, avec un Traité sur la Nature de l'Eglogue et une Digression sur les Anciens et les Modernes*, 4th ed. (Amsterdam 1716, Etienne Roger), pp. 142, 140, 143–4, and 140.

[5] See the second edition (London 1697, Leake), pp. 23–24. The first edition of Wotton's book was published in A.D. 1694.

The consensus on this point between the victorious advocates of the case for the Moderns and their discomfited opponents might have been expected to have settled this question, at least, definitively. Yet, between the close of this seventeenth-century *Kulturkampf* and the time at which this Study was being written, some 250 years later, the controversy over this issue had been reopened again from two sides. On the one side Oswald Spengler, in a work published on the morrow of the War of A.D. 1914–18, had put forward the thesis that Mathematics, Natural Science, and Technology, notwithstanding their proud pretensions to be objective, were in fact just as much at the mercy of the influences and exigencies of diverse social milieux as any activities in the realm of social human affairs.[1] On the other hand, Shelley[2] had won Bury's applause[3] for having resuscitated a suggestion—thrown out tentatively, in the course of the seventeenth-century debate, by Charles Perrault, but not taken up by such circumspect advocates of the Moderns' cause as Fontenelle and Wotton—that the Fine Arts did, after all, progressively improve in the same fashion as Mathematics, Science, and Technology.

Spengler's thesis was enunciated by its author in characteristically dogmatic language:

'There is not and cannot be any such thing as Number-in-Itself. There is a plurality of worlds of numbers because there is a plurality of civilizations. . . . The notion of a universally valid Science which is true for all civilizations is an illusion.'[4]

The grain of truth in these misleadingly unqualified statements is the fact that each particular historical way of life or culture is in some sense a whole whose parts are sensitively and subtly interdependent. This truth has presented itself to us forcibly in our study of encounters between societies that are one anothers' contemporaries.[5] We have found that, when some single element in one culture is modified by the impact of another culture, the effects of this modification of the assaulted culture in one point are apt to spread through the entire body social and to make themselves felt at points which might seem, at first sight, to have no connexion with the point in which the change has been introduced first. This intimate interdependence has proved, in the light of such convincing evidence, to be so characteristic a feature of the structure of Human Society that it would indeed be surprising if one particular group of activities, represented by Mathematics, Natural Science, and Technology, should turn out to be entirely unaffected by a tendency that appears to be one of the general 'laws' of social life; and we may find ourselves able to come to an understanding with Spengler when we catch him slipping out of his pontifical vestments and condescending to explain to us that the distinctive quality of each individual civilization, on which he has been insisting, is to be interpreted, not as an absolute

---

[1] See the passage quoted in III. iii. 380–2.
[2] In his Introduction to *The Revolt of Islam*.
[3] In *The Idea of Progress*, p. 124.
[4] Spengler, O.: *Der Untergang des Abendlandes*, vol. i (Munich 1920, Beck), pp. 85 and 532, quoted in this Study ibid.   [5] See IX. viii, *passim*.

difference of essence, but as a gradational difference of emphasis, *habitus*, or penchant.[1]

We can, for example, agree with Spengler in holding that the predominant penchant that gives a particular culture its distinctive style may impart to all the men and women who have been brought up in the atmosphere of that culture, whatever the native psychic orientation of each individual may happen to be, a uniform inclination either towards or away from the mathematical, scientific, and technological approach to life, or, short of that, may at least incline them, within the bounds of this broad field of activity in the realm of Non-Human Nature, to address themselves to one branch of Mathematics, Science, or Technology rather than to another. In this sense and within these limits it may be true, as Spengler contends,[2] that the 'Apollinean' spirit of an Hellenic upbringing would foster a static-minded *Weltanschauung* which, in the province of Mathematics, would find its most congenial expression in Geometry, whereas the 'Faustian' spirit of a Western upbringing would foster a dynamic-minded *Weltanschauung* which, within the same mathematical field of intellectual activity, would find its most congenial expression in Algebra and the Calculus. But of course, in assenting to this more judiciously formulated version of Spengler's proposition, we are admitting nothing beyond the indisputable facts that there are diverse schools or fashions of education (in the widest meaning of that word) and that the uniform impress of any such educational *habitus* is bound to leave its mark on all individual human beings whose fate it may be to be put through that particular cultural mill, even when the penchant of the society into which a particular individual happens to have been born is at variance with that individual's native personal bent. In admitting this much, we are not committing ourselves to the nonsense implicit in the pontifical version of Spengler's thesis, in which the philosopher-hierophant goes so far as to assert that 'there is not and cannot be any such thing as Number-in-itself' and that 'the notion of a universally valid Science . . . is an illusion'.

It would, indeed, be as fantastic to suggest that Geometry and the Calculus are diverse, alternative, and incompatible systems of Mathematics as it would be reasonable to say that these are different aspects of one identical object of mathematical study that can properly be called 'Number-in-Itself'. We may go on to observe that the several provinces of this realm of Mathematical Science have been opened up at different times and places by divers members of a single mathematical fraternity whose choices of their particular fields of mathematical research have been always influenced, and sometimes virtually determined, by a mental penchant or *habitus* imparted to the individual mathematician by his social milieu. In going thus far, however, we must be careful to steer clear of the nonsense that Spengler makes of his own thesis when he propounds it in its extreme form; for Spengler is manifestly flying in the face of the facts when he suggests that a pioneer in the realm of Mathematics cannot occupy the whole kingdom simultaneously, but

[1] See Spengler, op. cit., vol. i, p. 156, quoted in this Study in III. iii. 383-4.
[2] Ibid., pp. 380-3, quoted in III. iii. 388-9.

must evacuate the province of Euclidean Geometry as the price of gaining an entry into the province of a Cartesian Calculus, or alternatively must renounce all hope of mastering the Calculus if he is unwilling to relinquish his hold upon Geometry.

The divers provinces of Mathematics, Natural Science, and Technology that have been successively conquered by the Collective Intellect of Mankind do not stand to one another in the same relation as the divers systems of government or law that succeed one another in the history of a human society. A new ministry, new ruler, new dynasty, new régime, or new state cannot come into power without replacing a predecessor; a new law cannot be enacted without abrogating the law previously in force on the same subject. In short, successively established political and legal institutions cannot coexist side by side. They are mutually exclusive because they are incompatible, and they are incompatible because each of them has, as we have seen, to be geared to the particular circumstances of some local and temporary social situation. There is no room in the dimension of social life for more than one such situation at a time, and therefore there is no room there, either, for more than one institution at a time, since every institution's *raison d'être* is to provide a solution for some social problem here and now. Thus, on the plane of social affairs, all human experience testifies with one accord that

> Time, like an ever rolling stream,
> Bears all its sons away;
> They fly forgotten, as a dream
> Dies at the opening day.[1]

But a 'law of Sin and Death',[2] which reigns inexorably in this social human realm of government, legislation, and the rest, has no dominion over the abstract non-human realm of Mathematics. In the struggle for mastery between Time and Man in this bloodless intellectual arena, Man has succeeded in making Time Man's servant instead of allowing Time to make Man Time's victim. The monument of Man's victory over Time here is a Collective Human Intellect's cumulative achievement; and this exception to Time's rule, which Watts overlooked and Spengler ignored, had long since been divined by Fontenelle and been noted by Gibbon.

'The Mathematics are distinguished by a peculiar privilege that, in the course of ages, they may always advance and can never recede.'[3]

If we are right in thinking that we have now disposed of Spengler's contention that Mathematics are subject to the same law of social relativity as social human affairs,[4] we may now go on to examine Perrault's contention that the Fine Arts are subject to the same law of cumulative growth as Mathematics.

---

[1] Watts, Isaac, quoted in I. i. 459.
[2] Rom. viii. 2.
[3] Gibbon, Edward: *The History of the Decline and Fall of the Roman Empire*, chap. lii.
[4] This thesis of Spengler's receives short shrift at Collingwood's hands (see Collingwood, R. G.: *The Idea of History* (Oxford 1946, Clarendon Press), pp. 225–6).

While Perrault[1] anticipated Fontenelle and Wotton in conceding that the general superiority which the champions of the Moderns' cause claimed for 'the Moderns' over 'the Ancients' might not be demonstrable in the provinces of Poetry and Eloquence, he made this concession expressly 'for the sake of peace'[2] and perceptibly against the grain; for Perrault himself was a poet; and, though his poetry was doomed to be judged inferior by all standards, whether 'Modern' or 'Ancient', he was vain enough to fancy that he had a personal stake in the question of the relative merits of 'the Moderns' and 'the Ancients' in the field of his own art. His advocacy of the Moderns' cause in the domain of the Fine Arts was therefore not altogether disinterested, and his argument, ingenious though it might be,[3] was eventually exploded by one of the twentieth-century Western scientific achievements of a progress which, in the field of Science, was to vindicate Perrault's championship of the Moderns in the act of confuting the seventeenth-century Western poet on the particular issue which he had most at heart.

Perrault's argument ran as follows:

'Pourquoy, voulés-vous . . . que l'Eloquence et la Poësie n'ayent pas eu besoin d'autant de siecles pour se perfectionner que la Physique et l'Astronomie? Le cœur de l'homme qu'il faut connoistre pour le persuader et pour luy plaire, est il plus aisé à penetrer que les secrets de la Nature, et n'a-t-il pas de tout temps esté regardé comme le plus creux de tous les abismes, où l'on découvre tous les jours quelque chose de nouveau, et dont il n'y a que Dieu seul qui puisse sonder toute la profondeur? . . . Je pourrois vous faire voir ce que j'avance en examinant toutes les passions l'une après l'autre, et vous convaincre qu'il y a mille sentimens delicats sur chacune d'elles dans les ouvrages de nos auteurs, dans leurs traitez de morale, dans leurs tragedies, dans leurs romans, et dans leurs pièces d'eloquence, qui ne se rencontrent point chez les Anciens. Dans les seules tragedies de Corneille il y a plus de pensées fines et delicates sur l'ambition, sur la vengeance, sur la jalousie, qu'il n'y en a dans tous des livres de l'antiquité.'[4]

These were Perrault's grounds for his contention that there might be a possibility of cumulative achievement in Poetry as well as in Mathematics; and, if there had been any cogency in the minor Modern Western poet's case, his suit would have been won for him by the posthumous support that he received from one of the immortals. In reflecting on the sources of his own inspiration, Shelley once observed[5] that he had found 'common sources of those elements which it is the province of the poet to embody and combine' in 'the beautiful and majestic scenery of the Earth' and in 'the poetry of Ancient Greece and

---

[1] Perrault, Ch.: *Paralelle des Anciens et des Modernes en ce qui Regarde les Arts et les Sciences* (Paris 1688–96, Coignard, 4 Parts).

[2] 'Nous conclurons, si vous l'avez agreable, que dans tous les arts et dans toutes les sciences, à la reserve de l'Eloquence et de la Poësie, les Modernes sont de beaucoup superieurs aux Anciens, comme je croy l'avoir prouvé suffisamment, et qu'à l'égard de l'Eloquence et de la Poësie, quoy qu'il n'y ait aucune raison d'en juger autrement, il faut pour le bien de la paix ne rien decider sur cet article' (Perrault, op. cit., Part iv, Cinquiéme et Dernier Dialogue, pp. 292–3).

[3] A summary of it will be found in Bury, *The Idea of Progress*, pp. 86–87.

[4] Perrault, op. cit., Part ii, Troisiéme Dialogue, pp. 29–31. Cp. p. 294 and Part iii, Quatriéme Dialogue, pp. 23, 155, and 279.

[5] In his Introduction to *The Revolt of Islam*, composed in A.D. 1817.

Rome and Modern Italy and our own country', which had been to him, 'like External Nature, a passion and an enjoyment'; and this personal experience suggested to Shelley's mind that

'in this sense there may be such a thing as perfectibility in works of fiction, notwithstanding the concession, often made by the advocates of human improvement, that perfectibility is a term applicable only to Science.'[1]

In endorsing a suggestion which Shelley had thus thrown out in passing, Bury drew out the implications of Shelley's argument in the following terms:

'In other words, all the increases of human experience from age to age, all the speculative adventures of the Intellect, provide the artist in each succeeding generation with more abundant sources for aesthetic treatment. As years go on, Life in its widest sense offers more and more materials "which it is the province of the poet to embody and combine". This is evidently true; and would it not seem to follow that Literature is not excluded from participating in the common development of Civilisation?'[2]

Bury's expansion of Shelley's argument is a legitimate interpretation of Shelley's words which would assuredly have been certified as correct by the poet himself if he could have lived to read Bury's book. Yet, in invoking Poetry in the same breath as External Nature, and describing their effect on his soul as being 'passion' and 'enjoyment', Shelley was unconsciously testifying that the sources of the Wild West Wind that was his tempestuous inspiration were, not 'the speculative adventures of the Intellect', but 'the Eternal Deep' from whose Primordial Images Wordsworth derived his intimations of Immortality. From the same testimony it could be divined that the tale of the years that it had taken 'Life in its widest sense' to accomplish Psyche's task of accumulating the 'materials' for the fund of experience on which every inspired poet drew amounted to an aeon of an utterly different order of magnitude from the brief span of some twenty-six centuries or thereabouts that was the extent of Shelley's own chronological distance from the anonymous authors of an Homeric Greek Epic which was the chronologically re-motest poetry within Shelley's conscious ken. The 'passion' and 'enjoyment' that were kindled in Shelley's soul by the works of his brother poets did not find their fuel in any 'increases of human experience' during the few thousand years within which a few representatives of the recently created species of Human Society labelled 'civilizations' had been rising and falling. It would be as fantastic to look for the sources of any great poet's inspiration there as it would be to fancy that a blast-furnace could have been stoked with the contents of a charcoal-burner's basket. 'The visionary gleam' of which the poet catches his beatific glimpse in External Nature and in the poetry of his brother poets alike is the glow of a spiritual fire fed by mighty coal-seams that have been slowly compacted in the womb of Mother Earth out of the debris of forests deeply buried there countless ages ago.

---

[1] Shelley, ibid., in a footnote.　　[2] Bury, *The Idea of Progress*, p. 124.

A thousand ages in Thy sight
Are like an evening gone,
Short as the watch that ends the night
Before the rising Sun.

No doubt, in God's sight, the aeons in which the human historian has to reckon the longevity of the Human Psyche's primordial abyss will approach no nearer than the brief annals of recorded human history to being comparable with an Eternity with which all Time is incommensurate and into which none of God's creatures can ever enter without being first transfigured by God's grace; yet it is neither inaccurate nor impious to ascribe a godlike timelessness to a subconscious underworld of the Psyche that is merely one of God's creatures, when we find ourselves impotent to plumb the thoughts of 'the human heart by which we live', or to compass the range of 'an eye that hath kept watch o'er Man's mortality', by applying to the Primordial Images the yard-measure of the Intellect. The surface of a planet which in God's sight may loom no larger than an orange would appear to be of an infinitely vast extent to the mind of any human surveyor who set out to measure the Earth's circumference with a measuring-rod of the dimensions of a match.

If these considerations move us to reject Perrault's thesis as well as Spengler's, we shall be confirmed in our acceptance of Fontenelle's and Gibbon's thesis that it is the privilege of Mathematics, Natural Science, and Technology to be capable of progress on a Time-scale set by the pace of the conscious Intellect, and the privilege of the Fine Arts to be exempt from a servitude to Time which is the price of a capacity for cumulative achievement. We shall also be able to repay part of our debt to Fontenelle by underpinning his intuition with one of the empirical discoveries made by Science in the course of its progress between Fontenelle's day and ours. For, within the quarter of a century that had elapsed between the year in which Bury had endorsed Shelley's tentative approval of Perrault's argument and the year in which the present lines were being written, Jung had demonstrated that the Fine Arts draw their inspiration from creative depths of subconscious experience at which, on the Intellect's Lilliputian scale of time-reckoning, there 'is no variableness, neither shadow of turning',[1] in the ageless presences of the Primordial Images.

[1] Jas. i. 17.

'CLASSICAL' LANGUAGES AND LITERATURES

THE most striking point about the usage of any language or literature that has been canonized as 'classical' is that it is not the mother tongue of any of the members of the society in which it is being cultivated in virtue of having been given this status; and this salient feature of 'the classics' is as characteristic as it is prominent; for a 'classical' language or literature is *ex hypothesi* a 'dead' one which has been brought back to life artificially through the deliberate and selfconscious cultural achievement of a renaissance.

In the polyglot population of the Western World, for example, there was no people whose mother tongue was Ancient Greek or Latin at the time of the literary renaissance of Hellenism at the beginning of the Modern Age of Western history. The Romance-speaking Western peoples, whose mother tongues were derived from Latin as a matter of philological fact, were just as incapable of understanding, speaking, or reading Latin by the light of nature as were their fellow Westerners whose mother tongues were twigs of the Celtic, Teutonic, Slavonic, or Letto-Lithuanian branches of the Indo-European family of languages; and those Western peoples whose non-Indo-European mother tongues —Basque, Magyar, Estonian, and Finnish—had not even the remotest linguistic affinity with either Latin or Greek showed no less enthusiasm than was shown by their Indo-European-speaking neighbours for a revival of the study of the Hellenic literature in the original Greek, as well as in an imitative Latin, which became one of the common cultural enterprises of the Western peoples in and after the fifteenth century of the Christian Era.

The same point comes out in a survey of the currency of other classical languages and literatures in other societies. In an Arabic Muslim World a Classical Arabic language and literature were cultivated by peoples whose mother tongues were varieties of the Berber form of Hamitic speech, as well as by those whose mother tongues were dialects of a current vernacular Arabic. In an Iranic Muslim World both a Classical Arabic and a Classical Persian language and literature were cultivated by peoples whose mother tongues were members of the Turkish and Indo-Aryan families, as well as by peoples whose mother tongues were Irano-Aryan vernaculars linguistically akin to Classical Persian. In a Hindu World a Classical Sanskrit language and literature were cultivated by Indians whose mother tongues were members of the Tamil and other non-Indo-European families, as well as by Indians whose mother tongues were Indo-Aryan vernaculars of Sanskrit origin. In a Far Eastern World a Classical Sinic language which had been standardized (for the eye, though not for the tongue and ear) by Ts'in She Hwang-ti, the founder of the Sinic universal state, and which had consequently become the exclusive vehicle for conveying the Confucian classics, was cultivated, as the key to the classical literature which it enshrined, by peoples whose mother tongues were Korean and Japanese, as well as by peoples whose mother tongues belonged, as Annamese belonged, to the Sino-Siamese family, or were actually derived, as the latter-day Chinese spoken vernaculars were, from the particular language belonging to the Chinese branch of the Sino-Siamese family which had been canonized as 'classical'.

When we extend our survey to languages and literatures that were cultivated as 'classical' by civilizations of the second generation, the same picture presents itself again. In a Babylonic World the Classical Sumerian language and literature, like their Classical Greek counterparts in the Modern Western World, were cultivated by peoples whose diverse mother tongues—in this case, Semitic, Elamite, and Urartian—had in common the single negative characteristic of having no affinity with the language that had been canonized as 'classical'; and the Classical Akkadian language and literature, that were parasites on the Sumerian as the Latin were on the Ancient Greek, were cultivated, side by side with the Sumerian, by the non-Semitic-speaking Elamite and Urartian peoples of the Babylonic World as well as by the speakers of Babylonian and Assyrian Semitic vernaculars of Akkadian origin. The same Classical Sumerian and Classical Akkadian languages and literatures were likewise cultivated in a polyglot Hittite World whose peoples' Asianic and Indo-European mother tongues had no affinity with either Sumerian or Akkadian. We may also observe that in the corpse of an Egyptiac body social which was galvanized into a long-drawn-out life-in-death by the repeated stimulus of successive stabs administered by a series of alien intruders—Hyksos, Assyrians, Persians, Hellenes—a Classical Egyptian language and literature were cultivated, until the advent of Christianity, not only by latter-day Egyptians whose mother tongue was of Classical Egyptian origin, but also by Libyans whose mother tongue belonged to a different branch of the Hamitic family and by polyglot Ethiopians among whom an earlier Hamitic-speaking stratum of population had been partly submerged under successive waves of invaders from the heart of Tropical Africa whose mother tongues were not akin to Classical Egyptian even remotely.[1]

Thus, wherever we find any language or literature being cultivated as classical, we almost invariably[2] also find that it is current in this classical usage among people who do not speak this language, or any language derived from it, as their mother tongue. Yet this trait, though almost invariably present, is nevertheless not a distinctive hall-mark that can be taken as the differentia of languages and literatures that have become 'classical'; for there are other categories, besides, in which the self-same feature presents itself. *Lingue franche*,[3] the official languages of

---

[1] See II. ii. 114–15.
[2] 'Invariably' has to be qualified by 'almost', in view of the fact that, in Orthodox Christendom, the revival and cultivation of Ancient Greek as a classical language is virtually confined to Modern-Greek-speaking Orthodox Christians. A possible explanation of this exception to what seems to be the general rule is offered on pp. 713–17, below.
[3] See V. v. 483–527.

universal states,[1] and the liturgical languages and literatures of universal churches[2] are three categories which share with 'classical' languages and literatures the characteristic of being cultivated by peoples who have not inherited them as their mother tongues; and we must look farther for the points of difference that distinguish 'classical' languages and literatures from these.

One such point of difference is that, whereas a classical language or literature is, by definition, a ghost that has been raised from Sheol after a *vitai pausa*[3] during which it has not been current, a *lingua franca* or an official language or a liturgical language or literature must have been, not merely alive, but aggressively radioactive, at the time when it won its status, and must also have maintained and preserved this status, after winning it, without any break of continuity from the beginning to the end of its career. These common characteristics of a *lingua franca*, an official language, and a liturgical language or literature, which a classical language or literature does not share with them, all derive from the fact that languages and literatures in these three categories are propagated by 'men of action'—merchants, empire-builders, deportees, or missionaries, as the case may be—to meet the practical needs of some current form of intercourse between contemporaries such as trade or administration or communal worship, whereas classical languages and literatures are propagated by scholars whose purpose is to enrich the culture of the society into which they have been born by making accessible in their own world the cultural treasures of an antecedent civilization which, in their belief, are superior to their own society's corresponding native products.

This distinction between a practical-minded utilitarianism and a scholarly-minded idealism must not, however, be pressed too far; for on a closer scrutiny we shall find that it is not a difference of kind but is merely one of degree. A scholar who would repudiate any suggestion that he was animated by a 'utilitarian' purpose would be equally unwilling to admit that his activities were useless; and in a previous context[4] we have already noticed that a ghost is never evoked simply for its own sake; the necromancer is always moved to act by the practical motive of seeking, through the exercise of his black art, to find a solution for some pressing current problem in the life of his own society. Moreover, when a ghost has been successfully raised, this *jinn* is apt to make the fortune of the magician who has enslaved him. A classical education has frequently been the passport to an eligible career in the administrative service of a state. In the Far Eastern World, Greek Orthodox Christendom, and the Arabic Muslim World, a proficiency in the Sinic, the Ancient Greek, and the Classical Arabic language and literature respectively was the indispensable qualification for enrolment in the imperial civil service of a resuscitated universal state,[5] while in the Iranic, Early Hindu, and Modern Western worlds the administrators of parochial states were similarly recruited from candidates whose qualification

---

[1] See VI. vii. 239–53. [2] See VI. vii. 254–5.
[3] Lucretius: *De Rerum Naturâ*, Book III, ll. 860 and 930.
[4] On pp. 119–20, above.
[5] The three universal states here in question were, of course, the Sui and T'ang Empire, the East Roman Empire, and the Cairene 'Abbasid Caliphate.

was a proficiency in the Arabic, Persian, Sanskrit, Ancient Greek, and Latin classical languages and literatures.

The canonized dead language, which thus opens the door to a career in the public service in the political life of a society which has taken to cultivating this element of an extinct antecedent culture, may once have served as an official language of the antecedent civilization's universal state. The Ancient Chinese language that had been standardized visually by Ts'in She Hwang-ti had subsequently served as the official language of the Empire of the Ts'in and Han before being given the status of a classical language in a latter-day Far Eastern World. Latin and Ancient Greek had served as the official languages of the Roman Empire before Ancient Greek in Orthodox Christendom, and both Ancient Greek and Latin in the Western World, were canonized and cultivated as classical. Sumerian and Akkadian had served as the official languages of the Empire of the Four Quarters, from the days of its Sumerian founder Ur-Engur (*alias* Ur-Nammu) of Ur down to the days of its Amorite restorer Hammurabi of Babylon, before becoming classical in the eyes of a latter-day Babylonic Society. A Sanskrit that had been brought back into currency in an Indic World by a feat of linguistic archaism[1] had subsequently served as the official language of the Guptan Empire before being adopted as classical by a latter-day Hindu Society.

This use of a language as the official language of a universal state can never overlap chronologically with its eventual apotheosis as a classical language in the life of an affiliated society, since a universal state is always carried to destruction in the final dissolution of the disintegrating society that, in its last phase, has come to be embodied politically in an oecumenical empire of this type,[2] and therefore a language that has once served as the official language of a universal state is bound to have lost this function before gaining the status of a classical language as the result of a linguistic and literary renaissance in the life of an affiliated society that has come to birth eventually after a social interregnum. On the other hand the use of a language as the liturgical language of a universal church may well overlap chronologically with the use of the same language as a classical language canonized in a renaissance, since a church, unlike a universal state, is apt to survive the social interregnum between the dissolution of an old civilization and the emergence of a new one;[3] and there are in fact a number of instances of the simultaneous cultivation of the same language in these two different roles. Cases in point are the simultaneous currency of Sanskrit as the liturgical language of the Hindu Church and as the classical language of the Hindu Civilization; of Arabic as the liturgical language of the Islamic Church and as a classical language of the Arabic and Iranic Muslim civilizations; of the standardized visual form of Ancient Chinese as the liturgical language of the Taoist and Far Eastern Mahayanian Buddhist churches and as the classical language of the Far Eastern Civilization; of Ancient Greek as the liturgical language of the Greek Orthodox Christian Church and as the classical language of Modern-Greek-speaking Orthodox Christians; and of

---

[1] See V. vi. 75–77.
[2] See I. i. 53 and VI. vii. 1–379.
[3] See I. i. 56 and 59, and VII. vii. 392–419.

Latin as the liturgical language of the Western Catholic Church and as one of the two classical languages of the Western Civilization.

In some of these cases this simultaneous use of the same dead language in two different roles did not produce any sense of incongruity and therefore did not generate any cultural friction. No effect of the kind followed from, for example, the dual role played by Arabic, since the liturgy of the Islamic Church and the secular Arabic literature that came to be canonized as classical had a common fountain-head in the Qur'ān.[1] The dual role of Sanskrit was likewise eased by a pre-established harmony, since the Sanskrit epic had been transfigured, long before it had become one of the classics of the Hindu World, into one of the holy scriptures of Hinduism, and this not merely through the interpolation of the *Bhagavad Gītā*, but through a permeation of the secular native substance of the *Mahābhārata* by a religious leaven.[2] In the Sinic and Hellenic worlds, as in the Indic World, the secular language and literature that were eventually to be canonized and cultivated as classical in the latter-day life of an affiliated civilization had already been going concerns before the epiphany of a universal church in the underworld of an internal proletariat; but in these cases the church was either unable or unwilling, or both unable and unwilling, to swallow an existing secular literature and digest it.

A nascent church did, nevertheless, in both these cases, adopt the language or languages in which the existing secular literature had been written, since in the Sinic World at the time of the epiphany of the Mahayanian and Taoist churches and in the Hellenic World at the time of the epiphany of the Christian Church even the most militant 'futurist' innovator would never have dreamed of using any language but Ancient Chinese in the one case and Ancient Greek and Latin in the other case as the medium for any serious literary work, either secular or religious; and, if a Buddhist, Taoist, or Christian missionary had attempted to boycott languages that were current, not only as vehicles of an ancient and revered secular literature, but also as *lingue franche*, he would have defeated his own purpose by eschewing the only linguistic media that were both universally familiar and universally esteemed in his day in the world that was his mission-field. But, when a church thus found itself constrained to use a current oecumenical language as its literary vehicle without being able or being willing, as the case might be, to capture, appropriate, and transfigure the secular literature that had already been written in this language either in its current form or in some older dialect, the inevitable result was the production of a new corpus of religious literature—a liturgy, holy scriptures, commentaries on the scriptures, and treatises on theology—in rivalry with the already existing corpus of secular literature in the same language.

[1] It is true that the Qur'ān was not the only source of a subsequent secular Arabic literature's inspiration. It was also inspired in part by a pre-Islamic lyric poetry that was one of the spontaneous cultural products of an heroic age of the Arab transfrontier barbarians adjoining the Syrian *limes* of the Roman Empire (see V. v. 234). The Qur'an itself, however, had already drawn inspiration from this same pre-Islamic source; so there was no clear-cut division between a pagan source of an Arabic used in a secular Arabic literature and an Islamic source of an Arabic used in the Islamic Church's liturgy.　　　　[2] See V. v. 596–9 and 604–6.

The consequent coexistence of two competing literatures in the same language was bound to cause friction between their respective votaries, and such friction duly made itself felt when this situation arose in a moribund Sinic World in the Age of the Posterior Han and in a moribund Hellenic World in the Age of the post-Diocletianic Roman imperial régime. Thereafter, when a once dominant minority by whom the secular literature had been kept alive had been wiped out, as it was in the former domain of the Hellenic Civilization, or, short of that, had been driven into a corner, as it was in the former domain of the Sinic Civilization,[1] the friction diminished as the cultivation of the secular literature dwindled towards vanishing point, leaving the religious literature temporarily in almost unchallenged possession of the field; but, if and when a neglected and half-forgotten secular literature recovered its vitality through a renaissance of it in the history of an affiliated civilization—as happened in the Far Eastern World in and after the Age of the T'ang, in Greek Orthodox Christendom in and after the generation of Photius, and in the Western World in and after the fifteenth century of the Christian Era—the friction was bound to recur.

In its recurrence as the sequel to a renaissance, as well as in its original occurrence in the last days of an antecedent civilization, this friction between two literatures conveyed in one language was apt to be accentuated by any appreciable difference of nuance between the particular forms of the common language in which the secular literature and the religious literature were respectively embodied. We have already noticed[2] that, in Greek Orthodox Christendom by the fifteenth century of the Christian Era, when a school of Byzantine imitators of Hellenic historians had been at work for not much less than four hundred years, at least two of their number had become sensitive to the difference between a post-Alexandrine Attic κοινή and the undiluted Attic Greek of a Thucydides and Ionic Greek of an Herodotus; and, although, as we have also seen, a Khalkokondhýlis and a Kritópoulos flew ambitiously higher than a Léon Dhiakónos or a Nikítas Khoniátis, only to fall ludicrously lower, their dawning glimmer of a finer aesthetic sense lit the way for more sure-footed Italian and Transalpine Western followers in these Greek Orthodox Christian pioneers' shambling footsteps. So far from coming to grief, these Modern Western literary mountebanks achieved an amazing virtuosity in keeping their precarious footing on a slippery path, thanks to an infinite capacity for taking pains which a nineteenth-century Western vernacular poet was to immortalize in his fantasy of *A Grammarian's Funeral*. But, the more accurately these Western Humanists performed their self-imposed *tour de force* of aping the styles of Ancient Greek and Latin classical authors, the more exquisitely were their over-refined aesthetic sensibilities excruciated by the barbarism of a 'Low Latin' that was the sacrosanct language of the Vulgate version of the Bible, the Roman liturgy, and the works of the Latin Fathers of a Western Catholic Christian Church.

'Joannes Petrus Maffeus, S.J., (*vivebat* A.D. 1536–1603) was one of the

---

[1] See VI. vii. 357, n. 4, 367, and 370–2; and pp. 649–81, above.
[2] On pp. 60–61, above.

best of the Jesuit writers. He wrote in Latin, and prided himself on the purity and elegance of his style. His two principal works are *Historiarum Indicarum Libri XVI* (Florence 1585) and *Vita Ignatii Loyolae* (Venice 1585). The first of these took twelve years to complete; but, as the author is said to have spent hours, even days, in modelling a single sentence, the wonder is that he ever did complete it. So great was Maffeus's reverence for *la belle Latinité* that he used to repeat his breviary in Greek, so as to avoid contaminating his style.'[1]

This sixteenth-century extravaganza was surpassed by the pedantry of at least one nineteenth-century Western scholar who succeeded in sharpening his sensibilities to a still finer point. When the writer of this Study first went up to Oxford as an undergraduate in the autumn of A.D. 1907, one of the tutorial fellows of his college, who had by then devoted the best part of a lifetime to the hot-house cultivation of *Litterae Graecae et Latinae*, was alleged to have refined his taste to such an exquisite degree that he had eventually rendered himself incapable of enduring the torture which he had diligently trained himself to suffer from reading even the common run of 'classical' pagan Greek and Latin authors, not to speak of a 'post-classical' Christian Greek and Latin literature. By the year 1907 this scholar was reported to have carried his progressive mental self-mutilation to an extreme at which the only authors in any tongue that he could any longer bear to read were four Latin poets, namely Virgil, Horace, Ovid, and the humanist-fakir himself. For fear of forgetting one day to slip a printed copy of one or other of the first three of these still unproscribed classics into his pocket, he used to inscribe Latin verses of his own composition on his shirt-cuffs as an iron ration to insure him against the risk of dying of aesthetic starvation. The fate that did overtake him was the sadder one of mental inanition.

The irreconcilably divided spiritual allegiance of a less fanatically humanist Maffeus betrays the tension between a would-be *revenant* Hellenism and its votaries' ingrained Christian spiritual heritage, which, in a tug-of-war for the possession of Maffeus's soul, had demonstrated the tenacity of its grip by drawing this ardent Hellenist into the ranks of a Spartanly disciplined Society of Jesus. The renaissance of a classical language and literature in the history of a civilization which had been hatched out of a chrysalis-church inevitably confronted the humanist—in the West, in Greek Orthodox Christendom, and in the Far Eastern World alike—with the insoluble problem of trying to serve two masters.[2] The tension thus produced by the resuscitation of a pagan classical literature was, of course, no more of a novelty than was the resuscitated literature itself. In the cases in question, the Fathers of a Christian, a Mahayanian, and a Taoist Church had been caught on the horns of the same dilemma in the last phase of the history of an antecedent civilization, when they had found themselves constrained to conduct their propaganda campaign against an outworn paganism in an irreplaceable pagan

---

[1] Payne, C. H., in Du Jarric (S.J.), P.: *Akbar and the Jesuits*, English translation (London 1926, Routledge), Introduction, p. xxv, n. 1.
[2] Matt. vi. 24; Luke xvi. 13.

linguistic and literary medium.[1] When this tension recurs as the result of a renaissance, it may prove, in spite of appearances, to be in this

[1] Unless they were to resign themselves to confining their preaching to the proletariat and renouncing all hope of penetrating the ranks of a dominant minority, the missionaries of the higher religions had to present their case to a cultivated pagan public in a literary guise which readers of this class would find at least familiar, if not congenial. The difficulty of persuading a sophisticated audience to give a hearing to an outlandish gospel would be great enough in any case; and the apostles to 'the high-brows' would have deprived themselves in advance of all prospect of success if they had gone out of their way to antagonize their shy spiritual quarry at the outset by wantonly making the form of their creed as *rébarbatif* as the substance of it could hardly fail to seem to an aesthetically sensitive Hellenically-cultivated mind ('si quando . . . prophetam legere coepissem, sermo horrebat incultus'—Saint Jerome, *Ep.* xxii ad Eustochium, chap. 30). These diplomatic considerations, however, were not the Fathers' only motive, and indeed not even their strongest one, for resorting to the use of a cultural instrument which their church had officially condemned as frivolous at its best and, at its worst, pernicious. The evangelists of a cultivated pagan society were moved to address this audience in its own idiom chiefly because these evangelists themselves were mostly converts from these very pagan circles. Their conversion to an alien proletarian religion had not availed to break the spell of a pagan cultural heritage that was their birthright; and, when they used their pagan literary equipment for a religious missionary purpose, they were acting, not on calculation in cold blood, but spontaneously, *con amore.*

The abiding value of a pagan culture for Christian converts from a cultivated pagan milieu was demonstrated by the severity of the blow which Julian succeeded in dealing to the Christian community in the Hellenic World of his day by his shrewdly malicious stroke of making a professing Christian ineligible, *ex officio religionis*, for holding a teacher's official licence (see V. v. 682). The Christian victims of this sly manœuvre in a 'cold' religious war were so hard hit by their exclusion from a pagan field of cultural activity, and were at the same time so well versed in a literature which was the common heirloom of both parties, that, according to the story (as told by Gibbon, Edward: *The History of the Decline and Fall of the Roman Empire*, chap. xxiii, following Sozomen), Christian men of letters 'had recourse to the expedient of composing books for their own schools. Within a few months Apollinaris produced his Christian imitations of Homer (a sacred history in twenty-four books), Pindar, Euripides, and Menander; and Sozomen is satisfied that they equalled, or excelled, the originals'.

Julian's stroke was a shrewd one because the Christians' unwillingness to dispense with a pagan cultural instrument not only laid them open to a public exposure as hypocrites but also secretly vexed their own consciences and continued to vex them even when Julian was no longer there to taunt them with their inconsistency. At a time when Julian was dead and his Hellenic paganism was moribund, a Saint Jerome suffered the same inward spiritual discomfort from a tension between a Christianity to which he had dedicated himself and a pagan cultural heritage which he had failed to pluck out and cast from him ('bibliothecâ . . . carere non poteram'—Saint Jerome, ibid.) as a Father Maffeus was to suffer, in his day, from a corresponding tension between a Humanism to which he had dedicated himself and a Christianity from which he had found himself unable to break loose. Jerome's psychological conflict came to the surface of his consciousness in the celebrated dream in which he fancied that he was hailed before the heavenly tribunal of Christ; was convicted by his divine judge of being still a Ciceronian and no Christian; and was reprieved only thanks to the intercession of the consistory and in consideration of an oath which he swore by Christ's name, binding himself never to read any profane literature any more: 'si legero, te negavi' (Hieronymus: *Epistulae*, No. xxii ad Eustochium, chap. 30). Paganism had to become not merely moribund but extinct before the Christian heirs of a pagan Hellenic culture could play their part as Hellenism's literary executors with an easy conscience.

This task of cultural conservation, which was thus voluntarily undertaken during a post-Hellenic social interregnum by a Christian clergy, was sometimes thrust upon their Buddhist and Taoist counterparts during a post-Sinic interregnum. 'In A.D. 409, for example, when the eighteen-year-old T'o-pa Ssŭ ascended his father's throne . . . [as the ruler of one of the barbarian successor-states of a United Tsin imperial régime], he commanded Ts'ui Hao (*vivebat* A.D. 381–450), a rising young scholar who later became famous as the Taoist foe of Buddhism, to give him a course in [Confucian classical] Chinese literature. This course, which took three years, included the Han vocabulary and exercise book *Chi chiu chang*, *The Classic of Filial Piety*, *The Analects*, *The Odes*, *The History*, *The Spring and Autumn Annals*, *The Book of Rites*, and *The Changes*' (Goodrich, L. C.: *A Short History of the Chinese People* (London 1948, Allen & Unwin), pp. 83–84). A convinced Taoist can hardly have relished the *corvée* of giving this command performance in the role of a professor of Confucianism; for, in a nascent Far Eastern World in Ts'ui Hao's day, 'Confucianism was not dead', as Stoicism and Neo-

milieu a superficial antagonism masking a covert co-operation between two ostensibly conflicting cultural forces.

This possibility is indicated by a difference, which we have already noticed in passing,[1] between the respective fortunes of resuscitated classical languages and literatures in the Far Eastern and Western worlds on the one hand and in Orthodox Christendom on the other. We have observed that, when a visually standardized Ancient Chinese classical language and literature were resuscitated in the Far East, and when an Ancient Greek and a Latin classical language and literature were similarly resuscitated in the West, the cultural coin that had thus been brought back into currency came into general circulation in all the linguistic provinces of a Western and a Far Eastern World; but we have also observed that in Orthodox Christendom the circulation of a resuscitated Ancient Greek classical language and literature never spread *proprio motu* beyond the Modern-Greek-speaking province of a polyglot Orthodox Christian World. The Georgian-speaking, Slavonic-speaking, and Rumanian-speaking Orthodox Christians never attempted to appropriate the secular cultural heritage of Hellenism except in so far as they may eventually have taken up the study of the Ancient Greek and Latin languages and literatures as a consequence of their eventual reception of a Modern Western culture on to which those classical Hellenic studies had been grafted by that time as a result of a fifteenth-century Italian Renaissance.

This difference in the respective ranges of the circulation of resuscitated classical languages and literatures within the ambits of the worlds in which they have been conjured back to life becomes intelligible on the hypothesis that a resuscitated classical language or literature finds difficulty in striking root on any ground that has not been prepared for its reception by the survival there of a religious liturgy and literature embodied in the same language. At any rate, it is a matter of historical fact that a Mahayanian Buddhist liturgy and literature conveyed in Sinic characters had already become current in the non-Chinese-speaking as well as in the Chinese-speaking provinces of a Far Eastern World before the reception there of a classical Sinic secular literature conveyed in the same visual medium, and that a Christian liturgy and literature conveyed in the Latin script and language had already become current in the non-Romance-speaking as well as in the Romance-speaking provinces of a Western World before the reception there of a classical Hellenic literature that was likewise conveyed in Latin before the West's reception of Ancient Greek, whereas in the Orthodox Christian World the use of Ancient Greek as a vehicle for a Christian liturgy and literature had been confined to the province in which Modern Greek was the local current vernacular. This conterminousness of the range of circulation of a resuscitated classical language and literature with the range of the same language in its surviving use for ecclesiastical purposes is so regular an occurrence that it cannot be explained away as a fortuitous coincidence;

platonism were in a nascent Western Christendom in Bede's day; 'it was merely quiescent' (Goodrich, ibid. Cp. the passage quoted in VI. vii. 372 from Fitzgerald, C. P.: *China, A Short Cultural History* (London 1935, Cresset Press), p. 286).
[1] On p. 705, above.

and the only other possible explanation is that the survival of an otherwise 'dead' language as 'a going concern' for ecclesiastical purposes is an indispensable antecedent condition for the successful recultivation of a 'dead' classical secular literature that has used the same 'dead' language as its vehicle.

On this showing, we must conclude that the linguistic liberality of the Eastern Orthodox Church was as inimical to the eventual cultivation of a classical secular Ancient Greek literature, in those provinces of Orthodox Christendom in which Ancient Greek was not imposed as the local ecclesiastical language, as the Western Catholic Church's illiberal insistence on an oecumenical use of Latin, as the exclusively authorized and uniformly required ecclesiastical language for all spiritual subjects of the Holy See, was favourable to the eventual cultivation of a classical secular Latin literature in all provinces of Western Christendom, whatever the local vernacular might happen to be.[1]

It is noteworthy, for example, that the fruits of the renaissance of Ancient Greek linguistic and literary studies at Constantinople in the ninth century of the Christian Era were not disseminated into an adjacent Orthodox Christian Bulgaria, though the Bulgarian Tsar Symeon (*imperabat* A.D. 893–927) had been brought up in Constantinople and had been educated there, not only in a School of Slavonic Studies founded by Photius, but also, apparently, in the School of Hellenic Studies founded by the Caesar Bardas,[2] where he had acquired a taste for the works of Demosthenes and Aristotle.[3] Why was it that a Bulgar autocrat who had become so enthusiastic a Hellenist that he had been nicknamed 'the semi-Greek'[4] was unable or unwilling to introduce his beloved Hellenic studies into his own country? In this Bulgarian case the answer to our question is ambiguous, since the Bulgarian and East Roman Empires were embroiled with one another by a political conflict[5] which came to a head in Symeon's day and which would probably have blighted the prospects of Hellenic studies in Bulgaria even if the ecclesiastical language with which a then recently converted Bulgaria had been endowed had been the Greek Orthodox Church's own Attic Greek κοινή and not the Macedonian Slavonic dialect that had been equipped with an alphabet and been turned to ecclesiastical account by the Salonican Greek missionary-philologist Saint Cyril.[6] It is perhaps significant, all the same, that Symeon's cultural work in Bulgaria even at the beginning of his reign, before his political breach with the East Roman Imperial Government, took the form, not of introducing into Bulgaria the study of the Ancient Greek language and literature in the originals, but of translating into the Slavonic a number of Ancient Greek classics, of which the majority were Christian and not pagan works.[7] The test case, however, is not the Bulgarian case but the Russian.

---

[1] The contrast between the diverse linguistic policies of the Eastern Orthodox Church and the Western Catholic Church has been noticed in IV. iv. 374–7.

[2] See IV. iv. 382.

[3] See Runciman, S.: *A History of the First Bulgarian Empire* (London 1930, Bell), p. 137.

[4] See IV. iv. 382.

[5] See IV. iv. 377–91.

[6] See IV. iv. 376–7.

[7] See IV. iv. 382, following Runciman, op. cit., p. 139: 'The Presbyter Gregory

In Russia's, in contrast to Bulgaria's, encounter with the East Roman Empire and conversion to Orthodox Christianity, there was no political complication to interfere with the reception of Hellenism in its original Ancient Greek dress by a converted Slavonic-speaking people. The acknowledgement of the East Roman Empire's political suzerainty, which was implicit in a submission to the Oecumenical Patriarchate's ecclesiastical jurisdiction, did not stick in the throats of Varangian princes at Kiev and Novgorod who well knew that their principalities were *de facto* safely beyond the reach of even Basil the Bulgar-killer's long arm. While Bulgaria lay on the East Roman Empire's threshold, Russia was insulated from the East Roman Empire by the twofold physical barrier of the Black Sea and the Great Western Bay of the Eurasian Steppe. The Russians therefore had nothing to fear from exposing themselves *de jure* to an East Roman political pretension which in their case could never have any serious practical effect; and they felt so sure of their political security that in the ecclesiastical sphere they submitted not only to being enrolled among the Oecumenical Patriarch's spiritual subjects but to leaving in this Constantinopolitan Greek prelate's hands the appointment of the local head of the Russian national church, and allowing him to exercise this right of patronage by always installing a Greek in preference to a Russian.[1]

The Metropolitans of Kiev were, with only two exceptions, Greek appointees of the Oecumenical Patriarch's from *circa* A.D. 1037/9 until the Kievan Russian World was overwhelmed by the impact of the Mongols in and after A.D. 1237;[2] during the same two centuries about half the bishops in Russian Orthodox Christendom were Greeks as well;[3] and Russia's consequent ecclesiastical intercourse with the East Roman Empire 'was most fertile for spiritual culture'.[4] Yet in Russia, as in Bulgaria, literature written in Ancient Greek was acclimatized, not in the original, but only in translation; and the range of the Greek works selected for translation into Macedonian Slavonic for the edification of Bulgar and Russian converts to Orthodox Christianity approximately coincided with the contents of 'the library of an average Greek monastery'.[5] 'At first the main bulk of the translated literature belonged to the Christian Antiquity of the fourth and fifth centuries';[6] and, though it is true that, of the two or three dozen translations from the Greek which show linguistic signs of having been made before the Mongol conquest of Russia in the thirteenth century of the Christian Era, 'most are the works of secular or half-secular literature',[7] it is significant that, out of these, only one—Josephus's *History of the Great Romano-Jewish War*—is a non-Christian author's work, and not one a pagan author's, while some of them are not works of the Hellenic Age at all, but are medieval. For instance, a translation of the Medieval Greek Epic—written in a mix-

translated the chronicle of John Malalas, and also a romantic tale of Troy for "the book-loving prince".'

[1] See Fedotov, G. P.: *The Russian Religious Mind: Kievan Christianity* (Cambridge, Mass. 1946, Harvard University Press), pp. 57–58 and 401–2.
[2] See Vernadsky, G.: *Kievan Russia* (New Haven, Conn. 1948, Yale University Press), pp. 69, 79, and 350.
[3] See ibid., p. 350.
[4] Fedotov, op. cit., p. 57.
[5] Ibid., p. 49.
[6] Ibid., p. 48.
[7] Ibid., p. 50.

ture of Modern and Ancient Greek—whose hero was Digénis (Dhiyénis) Akrítas[1] was included in this earliest batch.[2] As for the secular works subsequently translated from the Greek, these amounted to no more than a tiny fraction of the total bulk of the literature that had been translated by the sixteenth century; and this batch consisted of one Late Hellenic chronicle, one Early Byzantine chronicle, and some fragments of works on grammar and logic. Here again, there is not one pagan Greek classic in the list.

How are we to account for this signal failure of the classical Hellenic literature to strike root in a Russia whose reception of Orthodox Christianity had exposed the Slavonic-speaking converts to the influence of their Greek-speaking co-religionists? In this case, as we have seen, no political obstacle loomed up across the path of cultural intercourse; and by the date of Russia's conversion the literary renaissance of Hellenism in Greek Orthodox Christendom was already in full swing. Why should a Medieval Greek renaissance of Hellenism have failed to capture Russia as a Medieval Italian renaissance of Hellenism eventually captured Hungary, Poland, and Scandinavia? The key to an explanation of this puzzle is perhaps to be found in the practice of translating Greek into Slavonic, instead of studying works of Greek literature in the original; for, notwithstanding the power and prestige enjoyed by the Greek Metropolitans of Kiev,

'the knowledge of Greek seems to have been not much extended among Russians. In the *Chronicles* or in the *Lives* of Saints we never find them speaking Greek, nor is there any mention of the Greek language being taught in schools. What is still more significant, there have been preserved no Greek manuscripts written in Russia, no Greek quotations or even single words in Greek letters in Russian manuscripts. It appears that Greek was for the Russians a language of practical intercourse with foreigners and not an instrument of culture. Studying the theological and scientific fund of the most learned Russian authors, one cannot discover among their sources direct Greek originals. . . . Everything in their writings can be explained on the ground of the existent literature of translations.'[3]

The formidable intellectual enterprise of mastering Greek had thus been made superfluous for the Russians thanks to the linguistic liberality of the Orthodox Church and the philological ability of Saint Cyril, the Greek Apostle to the Slavs. Yet this exemption from an intellectual labour was a doubtful blessing, since, in being let off a task, these Slavonic-speaking Christians were at the same time being denied an opportunity. If they had been compelled to take Orthodox Christianity in its original Greek dress, a mastery of the Attic Greek κοινή in its ecclesiastical use would have provided them with the necessary stepping-stone for mounting to the higher attainment of cultivating the pagan Hellenic literature written in an earlier form of the same Attic Greek dialect, and passing on thence to an Ionic Greek Herodotean prose and an Epic Greek Homeric poetry. A Greek Orthodox Christian who had

[1] See V. v. 252–9. [2] See Fedotov, op. cit., p. 50.
[3] Ibid., pp. 58–59.

mastered his church's liturgy and literature in the original Ancient Greek could not be confronted with the pagan classical literature written in the same language without finding himself both easily able to understand it and potently affected by its aesthetic charm and its intellectual power; but this ghost of a dead Hellenic literary culture would be impotent to haunt a Slav Orthodox Christian who had contentedly remained ignorant of Greek because all that he needed to know of the Orthodox Christian liturgy and literature had been adequately translated for him out of the original Greek into a dialect of his own Slavonic mother tongue.

Whatever the explanation may be, it is an indisputable fact that, in the Orthodox Christian World, a renaissance of the Ancient Greek language and literature that was both vigorous and persistent in the geographical province within which the Orthodox Christian Church had continued to use Ancient Greek as its literary vehicle failed to make any headway in those provinces in which the Orthodox Christian liturgy and literature were translated out of Greek into Georgian or into Slavonic. On the other hand, this diversity of ecclesiastical languages did not prevent the spread of another resuscitated element of Hellenism which was not a literature but a political institution, and which therefore, unlike the Ancient Greek classics, was not dependent on a linguistic vehicle for its dissemination. In contrast to the ghost of a dead Hellenic literary culture, the ghost of a dead Hellenic universal state in its post-Diocletianic totalitarian last phase did not remain confined within the ambit of a Modern-Greek-speaking province of Orthodox Christendom where it, too, had originally been raised. After having made its first reappearance in the shape of the East Roman Empire, it proceeded, as we have seen, to haunt one after another of the non-Greek-speaking peoples who were successively converted to the Orthodox Christian Religion and Civilization. After Constantinople had seen her pretension to be 'the Second Rome' made good by a Leo III and a Constantine V (*imperabant* A.D. 717–75), she lived to see a Bulgar Symeon in A.D. 925, a Vlach Asen and Cuman Terteri after A.D. 1204,[1] a Serb Stephen Dushan in A.D. 1346, and a Russian Ivan IV in A.D. 1547 each attempt in turn to steal her title from her by inaugurating 'a Third Rome' at Preslav, Trnovo, Skoplje, and Moscow in succession.[2] Thus, unlike the Byzantine renaissance of the Ancient Greek language and literature, the Byzantine renaissance of the Hellenic universal state knew no geographical bounds short of those of Orthodox Christendom itself; and it transcended even these when, from a base of operations in the East Roman Empire's Norman successor-state in Sicily and Apulia, it was launched by Frederick II Hohenstaufen on its triumphal career of conquest in the Western World.[3]

---

[1] See VI. vii. 34.   [2] See VI. vii. 31–36.   [3] See pp. 10–11, above.

R. G. COLLINGWOOD'S VIEW OF THE HISTORIAN'S RELATION TO THE OBJECTS THAT HE STUDIES

IN the passage to which this Annex attaches,[1] we have quoted Collingwood's dictum:

'Western Civilisation expresses, and indeed achieves, its individuality, not by distinguishing itself from Hellenic Civilisation, but by identifying itself therewith.'[2]

These words can only be construed to mean that in 'the Renaissance' of Hellenism the Western World was doing what is done by a man who expresses and achieves his individuality, not by distinguishing himself from Napoleon, but by identifying himself with him; and this is in fact an accurate statement of what the makers of the Renaissance professed to be trying to do and claimed to have accomplished. The difference between a Humanist and a lunatic is in fact one of degree. The lunatic has 'bet his life' on his illusion, whereas the Humanist has taken care not to go to quite that fatal length.

For good or evil, the Modern Western Humanists were not plagued with the lunatic's devastatingly whole-hearted sincerity; they were, as Spengler depicts them,[3] *poseurs* in whose activities there was a saving, and at the same time damning, element of make-believe. Their identification of themselves with 'the Ancients' was kept within the bounds of a few innocuous conceits. They aped the language and style of the classical Latin and Ancient Greek writers;[4] they sometimes Latinized or Graecized their own barbarophone personal names; and for the occasion of a fancy-dress party or a pageant they would dress up in what they imagined to be classical costume; but they reserved the permanent assumption of the imperator's lorica or the orator's toga for their posthumous apotheosis in bronze or marble, and the same prudent unwillingness to sacrifice their physical comfort on the altar of their Hellenomania can be detected in their architecture. In discarding a grotesque Gothic in favour of a classical Vitruvian canon, they never carried their Hellenic purism to the length of renouncing fireplaces, chimneys, and glazed windows. This judicious discrimination in the pursuit of their

---

[1] p. 64, above.

[2] Collingwood, R. G.: *The Idea of History* (Oxford 1946, Clarendon Press), p. 163.

[3] In the passage quoted on pp. 65–66, above.

[4] This aping of an alien idiom might, however, cease to be a conceit through becoming a second nature; and the writer of this Study could testify from his own personal experience to the genuineness of a cultural metamorphosis in which he might otherwise have seen nothing more than a rather tiresome pose. As a result of his good fortune in having received a Late Medieval Italian education at the College of Saint Mary de Winton prope Winton and at Balliol College, Oxford, in the years A.D. 1902–11, he had acquired, and retained in after life, an articulateness in Greek and Latin of which he was destitute in his vernacular mother tongue. Whenever his feelings were deeply moved, they used to discharge themselves by finding expression in Greek or Latin verse which welled up spontaneously from the subconscious depths of his psyche.

follies saved the Humanists from the madhouse, but it also condemned them to be hustled off the stage of Modern Western history after a vogue which lasted no longer than two hundred years in the Transalpine provinces of an Occidental pseudo-Hellas. A seventeenth-century controversy between the champions of 'the Ancients' and 'the Moderns' had resulted, as we have seen,[1] in the exorcizing of the Renaissance and the reassertion, in the Modern Western World, of the Western Civilization's own native bent about a quarter of a millennium before the date at which Collingwood pronounced that the Western Civilization had identified itself with the Hellenic and had thereby expressed and achieved its own individuality.

In the same passage[2] Collingwood also asserts that, in performing this alleged feat of identifying itself with Hellenism, the Western Civilization has done 'exactly' [*sic*] what is done by 'the historian who studies a civilization other than his own'; and this assertion, too, takes the reader aback by coming into headlong collision with reality; for, however like a lunatic the historian may look in any other respect, he does at any rate hold the diametrically opposite view to the lunatic's view about his relation to Napoleon. The one mistake about Napoleon that an historian is sure not to make is to mistake the Napoleon whom he is studying for the historian himself.

It would, of course, be unlikely *a priori* that a thinker who, like Collingwood, was an eminent historian, as well as an eminent philosopher, really intended to say what he actually says in this startling passage. The context in which these assertions occur is a criticism of the present writer's idea of History as seen through Collingwood's eyes, and these statements of Collingwood's own ideas are thrown out here just in passing. More carefully considered statements of his views are to be looked for in the essays, published in the same volume as epilegomena to *The Idea of History*, in which Collingwood's first concern is, not the criticism of other people's ideas, but the exposition of his own; and, if Collingwood had lived to revise these sibylline leaves of his for publication, we may be sure that he would have sorted out and cleared up any inconsistencies between them, and may guess that in bringing his divers statements into harmony he might have reconsidered some of his premises. This was, of course, a task which no one but Collingwood himself could have undertaken; and, in using a posthumously published edition of his work in which the editor has perforce left the content (as distinct from the layout and some of the form) of the book in the unfinished state in which it happened to be when the brilliant author of it was overtaken by a premature death,[3] the student who wishes to profit from this skilfully salvaged intellectual treasure must do his best, in the face of inevitably uneliminated inconsistencies, to divine which exposition it is, where divers expositions conflict, that most faithfully reflects Collingwood's thought at its zenith.

In the case in point—in which we are seeking to ascertain what Collingwood really meant by saying that an historian identified himself

---

[1] On pp. 68–69, above.   [2] Collingwood, op. cit., p. 163.
[3] See the Editor's preface to Collingwood, op. cit., p. v.

with the object of his study—the passage quoted above is manifestly less authoritative than another,[1] in which Collingwood answers an imaginary critic's objection that Collingwood's theory implies 'an immediate identity between the historian and his object'—'say Thomas Becket'—by putting it that

'for Becket, in so far as he was a thinking mind, being Becket was also knowing that he was Becket; and for myself, on the same showing, to be Becket is to know that I am Becket, that is, to know that I am my present self re-enacting Becket's thought, myself being in that sense Becket.'

To credit the lunatic's statement 'I am somebody other than myself' with having the meaning of the sane man's statement 'I am myself thinking thoughts that somebody else has already once thought' is to strain the interpretation of plain words to a degree that Collingwood would not readily have tolerated if the torturer had been anyone but himself. A forced interpretation that vindicates the historian's sanity is, nevertheless, proved to be Collingwood's true meaning by the testimony of other passages whose cumulative weight of evidence is decisive.

'All thinking is critical thinking; the thought which re-enacts past thoughts [sic], therefore, criticises them in re-enacting them.[2]. . . The historian . . . re-enacts past thought [sic] . . . in the context of his own knowledge and therefore, in re-enacting it, criticises it.[3]. . . This re-enactment . . . is not a passive surrender to the spell of another's mind; it is a labour of active and therefore critical thinking.[4]. . . Unless he knows that he is thinking historically, he is not thinking historically.[5]. . . Historical thinking is always reflexion; for reflexion is thinking about the act of thinking, and . . . all historical thinking is of that kind.'[6]

By this time it has become clear that Collingwood's historian is not, after all, going to be certified as insane. Yet his acquittal on the charge of lunacy leaves him still open to a hardly less serious charge of eccentricity, to which he exposes himself by insisting on confining his field of action within limits that look capriciously arbitrary to Philistine eyes.

'All history is the history of thought.[7]. . . Of everything other than thought, there can be no history.[8]. . . In order . . . that any particular act of thought should become subject-matter for history, it must be an act not only of thought but of reflective thought.[9]. . . Reflective acts may be roughly described as the acts which we do on purpose, and these are the only acts which can become the subject-matter of history.'[10]

It will be noticed that the acts of reflective thought which are declared by Collingwood on one page to be the only possible subject-matter for history are equated by him on the next page with 'the acts which we do on purpose'; and here it looks to the historian-Philistine as if the historian-philosopher has slipped unintentionally and unconsciously into practising a sophist's sleight of hand; for, unless some undeclared esoteric construction is to be placed upon the meaning of Collingwood's words, 'the acts which we do on purpose' include acts of other kinds—

[1] Collingwood, op. cit., pp. 296–7.
[2] Ibid., p. 216.   [3] Ibid., p. 215.   [4] Ibid.
[5] Ibid., p. 289.   [6] Ibid., p. 307.   [7] Ibid., p. 215.
[8] Ibid., p. 304.   [9] Ibid., p. 308.   [10] Ibid., p. 309.

for instance, acts of will—besides acts of reflective thought; and acts of other kinds—for instance, acts of impulse as well as acts of will—play a much larger part than any acts of reflective thought in the action that is the subject-matter of History as we find this 'in real life' when we look at the actual practice of historians without allowing a philosopher's *a priori* dictum to hypnotize us into ignoring the realities.

In another passage,[1] in which Collingwood speaks of the historian as 'investigating actions' and consistently defines an 'action' as being an event that has something 'in it which can only be described in terms of thought', in contrast to 'everything belonging to it which can be described in terms of bodies and their movements', the philosopher takes, as an illustration of his meaning, Caesar's action in crossing the Rubicon. The least philosophical-minded of historians would assuredly agree with Collingwood that the physical movements made by Caesar and his troops, when they transported themselves from the north to the south bank of a river, were only a trivial element in the action that is both the object of the historian's study and the fount of the River Rubicon's fame; and the historian would also agree that the psychic element in Caesar's action, which is recognized, by a general consensus, as being the significant element in it, can be described in terms of thought in one of its aspects; but he would demur to Collingwood's assertion that this non-physical element 'can only [*sic*] be described in terms of thought'; for the 'thought' which Collingwood cites to prove his point is 'Caesar's defiance of Republican law, or the clash of constitutional policy between himself and his assassins',[2] and in the ordinary usage of words these events would not be called acts of 'thought'; they would be called an act of will on Caesar's part and a resulting conflict of wills between the author of this act and other dramatis personae in an interplay between Caesar and the constitutionalists which Caesar's initial act had set in motion.

This is not the only passage in which Collingwood's equation of the historian's subject-matter with 'thought' compels him to describe a familiar historical event in language which, if the words that the philosopher uses are to be taken in their normal meaning, will strike the reader as being quaintly inadequate.

For example, when 'the historian of politics or warfare' is trying to understand Caesar's actions, he is trying, according to Collingwood, 'to discover what thoughts [*sic*] in Caesar's mind determined him to do them'.[3] Caesar is an unusually favourable subject for Collingwood's verbal treatment, since History knows few men of action of his calibre in whose psychic 'make-up' the intellectual element has counted for so much; yet even in Caesar's history the historian's main concern is not, in reality, with the thoughts in Caesar's mind; for even in a Caesar's psychic spectrum it is the 'affective' and the 'conative', not the 'cognitive', activities that loom largest in the historian's field of vision. In the historian's endeavours to understand Caesar's actions, Caesar's thoughts are *les cadets de ses soucis*; Caesar's feelings, ambitions, purposes, and decisions are the first things about Caesar that the historian seeks to

[1] Ibid., p. 213.   [2] Ibid.   [3] Ibid., p. 215.

discover. If he were to start by trying to discover Caesar's thoughts and were to content himself with leaving it at that, the historian would then be leaving himself still in the dark. This is why Collingwood's phrase makes the impression of artificiality that it does make on the mind of Collingwood's reader; and the same impression is made by Collingwood's formula for Brutus:

'When an historian asks "Why did Brutus stab Caesar?" he means "What did Brutus think [*sic*], which made him decide to stab Caesar?" '

If Collingwood's imaginary historian were given the chance to explain his meaning in the language that came natural to him, he would not say, 'What did Brutus think?' He would say, 'What did Brutus feel?'

When Collingwood substitutes some stock character—'a politician' or 'a military commander'—for his historic Brutus or Caesar, the effect of the application of his formula is quainter still.

'If it were possible to say of any man that he acted with no idea whatever what would come of it, but did the first thing that came into his head and merely waited to see the consequences, it would follow that such a man was no politician, and that his action was merely the intrusion into political life of a blind and irrational force.'[1]

The truth here is, of course, exactly contrary to Collingwood's assertion. In real life such a man as Collingwood describes would be no politician if he did not [*sic*] behave in the intellectually horrifying way that the philosopher deprecates. President Wilson, for instance, proved himself to be no politician, and tragically brought himself to grief, by answering all too well to Collingwood's specification. This 'intellectual' who had been the president of a university before becoming President of the United States is one of the rare examples of a prominent actor on the political stage who would have been a strong candidate for Collingwood's degree of master of political arts. And, if blind and irrational forces were in truth outside the pale of political history, most published works on political history, from Thucydides' *History of the Atheno-Peloponnesian War*[2] to D. C. Somervell's *British Politics since 1900*,[3] would have to be thrown on the scrap-heap. Yet, in Collingwood's own words, 'it would be generally admitted that politics is a thing that can be historically studied'.[4]

How has Collingwood got himself into this tangle? He has entangled himself by giving a wrong explanation of a commonplace truth. 'The reason', he goes on to assert, why it is possible to study politics historically 'is that politics affords a plain instance of purposive action'; and since this assertion flies in the face of historical facts it is not surprising that it should reduce *ad absurdum* an idea of History that is founded on it.

The same false premise, applied to the history of warfare, leads Collingwood into the equally untenable position of maintaining that if a military commander's acts were not done on purpose 'there can be no

---

[1] Collingwood, op. cit., pp. 309–10.
[2] Scaptêsŷlê, date uncertain, publisher unrecorded.
[3] London 1950, Dakers.   [4] Collingwood, op. cit., p. 309.

history of them'.[1] An open-minded student of military history will find this dictum of Collingwood's less convincing than the picture of Bagration's generalship in Tolstoy's *War and Peace*.

We need not, however, *subpoena* either Tolstoy or Somervell or Thucydides to rise up in judgement against[2] Collingwood, since we can win our case more expeditiously by appealing from Collingwood theorizing about history as a philosopher to the same Collingwood studying and writing history as an historian. An equal eminence in two fields of intellectual activity was the distinctive mark of Collingwood's genius, and his characteristic achievement as an historian was his masterly employment of Archaeology in History's service. 'Everything belonging to' an event 'which can be described in terms of bodies and their movements'[3] was grist to Collingwood the historian's mill, though it might be chaff to Collingwood the philosopher's winnowing fan; and, in virtue of their rare archaeological merits, Collingwood's own historical works would fail still more ignominiously than Thucydides' or Gibbon's to pass the test of Collingwood's idea of History.

How has this historian-philosopher arrived at an idea of History which he has confuted by 'direct action' of his own? Collingwood's confutation of Collingwood is as irresistible as Doctor Johnson's confutation of Bishop Berkeley. The historian has given a conclusive kick to a philosopher's stone that is a plain man's stumbling-block. How has the philosopher ever come to erect the artificial obstacle which the historian in the same philosopher's skin has unceremoniously removed from our path? An answer to this question may perhaps be elicited from the following arrestingly paradoxical passage.

'If the discovery of Pythagoras concerning the square on the hypotenuse is a thought which we today can think for ourselves, a thought that constitutes a permanent addition to mathematical knowledge, the discovery of Augustus, that a monarchy could be grafted upon the Republican constitution of Rome by developing the implications of *proconsulare imperium* and *tribunicia potestas*, is equally a thought which the student of Roman history can think for himself, a permanent addition to political ideas. If Mr. Whitehead is justified in calling the right-angled triangle an eternal object, the same phrase is applicable to the Roman constitution and the Augustan modification of it. This is an eternal object because it can be apprehended by historical thought at any time; time makes no difference to it in this respect, just as it makes no difference to the triangle.'[4]

In this passage Collingwood shocks even an unphilosophic-minded reader by placing a political improvisation on all fours with a mathematical proposition on the score of its being 'a permanent addition to political ideas'. The mathematical theorem which came into the focus of human consciousness for the first time in Pythagoras' mind, according to the Hellenic tradition, was in truth 'a permanent addition to mathematical knowledge' in the sense that, when once this element in an eternally valid system of mathematical truth had been brought within the pale of a Collective Human Intellect, it was open, ever afterwards, to any other

---

1 Ibid., p. 310.   2 Matt. xii. 42.
3 Ibid., p. 213.   4 Ibid., pp. 217-18.

individual mind to apprehend the theorem for itself, and use it for the purposes of its own mathematical thought, on the sole condition of having access to a cumulative body of mathematical knowledge that was one of the common possessions of Mankind. On the other hand, if a President of the United States who happened, like President Wilson, to be a better historian than politician were to act on Collingwood's thesis that Augustus's discovery was 'a permanent addition to political ideas', he would quickly run into trouble that will never overtake the mathematician who acts on the assumption that Pythagoras' discovery was 'a permanent addition to mathematical knowledge'.

In a Western international arena on the morrow of a Second World War, let us imagine a President Wilson *redivivus* coming to the conclusion that Mankind can be saved from committing the crime and folly of race-suicide only by the prompt establishment of an effective oecumenical government. His next thought will be that, in the existing oecumenical constellation of political forces, the Presidency of the United States is the one well-established vantage-point from which it might be just possible to achieve the Herculean task of reducing a world-wide political anarchy to a world-wide political order. His next thought after that will be that the Presidency's powers, as laid down in the Constitution of the United States and as customarily interpreted in American political practice, are at present quite inadequate for the accomplishment of this urgent and arduous political labour. And this thought, in turn, will lead on to the further consideration that, however desirable it may be that the powers of the Presidency of the United States should be enlarged to the requisite extent, and however ardently this change in the Constitution of the United States may be desired by the vast majority of Mankind who are not American citizens, the change cannot be made without the acquiescence of at least a sufficient majority in the Senate and People of the United States to make a presidential dictatorship workable for practical purposes. But how can the Senate and People be induced to play their indispensable part? Clearly it would not be practical politics just to put the cards on the table and, in the light of them, make a naïve appeal to Reason and to Virtue; for the most adult-minded electorate and most experienced representative body could not be expected to make so great a readjustment of its political feelings and ideas at such short notice. Again, it would not be practical politics to try coercion; for, even if the inevitable resistance could be overcome, the struggle would generate a friction that would bring the high-handed usurper's benevolent activities to a standstill. In a fix in which neither Force nor Reason will break the deadlock, the only remaining alternative is to try cajolery; and at this stage in his brown study our imaginary historian-president will recollect that this was the device by which the problem now confronting him was solved, in other ages and in other worlds, by an Augustus and a Muʿāwīyah and a Han Liu Pang.

So far so good; but in the political arena, in contrast to the intellectual forum, to apprehend a proposition is not the same thing as to put it into effect; for a practical proposition, unlike a theoretical one, has to be translated into action, and this action will be successful only in so far as it is geared to the actualities of Here and Now. The fineness of their sense of these all-important actualities was the common gift that was the secret of Augustus's and Mu'āwīyah's and Liu Pang's common success; and their possession of this gift explains why it was that Augustus and Liu Pang succeeded in solving problems that had defeated their more brilliant forerunners Divus Julius and Ts'in She Hwang-ti.[1] The very brilliance of their ideas had been the undoing of those two men of genius, for it had enticed them to fly straight into the light, like moths plunging into the flame of a candle. The clarity with which they perceived their goal had made them so impatient of approaching it by any roundabout road that, instead of being content to feel their way between the natural obstacles, they had tried to ride roughshod over the perilous broken ground of actualities that were none the less actual for being irrational. Caesar the God invited assassination by allowing his partisans to make the provocative gesture of paying him royal honours; Augustus the politician discovered 'that a monarchy could be grafted upon the constitution of Rome by developing the implications of *proconsulare imperium* and *tribunicia potestas*'; but this Augustan 'modification' of the republican constitution of Rome was the antithesis of the 'eternal object' that had been Divus Julius's will-o'-the-wisp; and, if any twentieth-century dictator-aspirant were to follow Collingwood's prescription by trying to 're-enact' Augustus's 'experience for himself',[2] he would soon find himself in queer street; for, just because Augustus's sly policy fitted Augustus's own political milieu like a glove, it was bound, if tried in any other political milieu, to prove there an egregious misfit. Since a sensitiveness to the exigencies of his own Here and Now was the secret of Augustus's success, the only profitable lesson that a twentieth-century American aspirant to an oecumenical dictatorship could learn from 'the crafty nephew of Julius'[3] would be the hint that his cue was to develop with equal tact, care, and patience the implications of the presidential prerogative in the written and the customary constitution of the United States. A cue that, taken in these general terms, might put him on the road towards an Augustan success would infallibly lead him into a Julian disaster if he were ever to try to translate it from the general into the particular by setting out to develop the implications of *proconsulare imperium* and *tribunicia potestas* in the second half of the twentieth century of the Christian Era at Washington, D.C.

Collingwood's contention that Augustus's political contrivance is 'a permanent addition to political ideas' and 'an eternal object' thus proves to be untenable; and it is, indeed, implicitly contradicted by Collingwood himself in another passage published in the same book.

'The *Republic* of Plato is an account, not of the unchanging ideal of political life, but of the Greek ideal as Plato received it and reinterpreted it. The *Ethics* of Aristotle describes, not an eternal morality, but the morality of the Greek gentleman. Hobbes's *Leviathan* expounds the political ideas of seventeenth-century absolutism in their English form.

---

[1] See V. vi. 186–9.   [2] Collingwood, op. cit., p. 163.
[3] Bryce, quoted in I. i. 343.

Kant's ethical theory expresses the moral convictions of German pietism; his *Critique of Pure Reason* analyses the conceptions and principles of Newtonian Science, in their relation to the philosophical problems of the day.'[1]

Here the historian in Collingwood joins forces with the philosopher in him to proclaim the relativity of political, ethical, and even metaphysical thought to the local and temporary social milieu in which the thinker is living and working; and the unphilosophic historian will break no lance with Collingwood over this issue; he will, though, find himself all the more curious to discern how it can be that an historian-philosopher who so resolutely refuses the status of 'an eternal object' to a product of political thought can at the same time venture to confer this enviable status upon a product of political action. An act of thought—even when its object is the parochial, ephemeral, and contingent world of politics— is at any rate more nearly akin to an act of thought in the realm of Mathematics than it is akin to an act of state in the realm of practical political activity. To dub Augustus's principate 'an eternal object', while describing Plato's *Republic* as a progress report on the state of political science up to the date of its publication, is a paradox that demands an explanation.

What motive has led Collingwood to commit himself to this *tour de force*? He has set his readers a puzzle, but he has also supplied them with the key. It is evident that, in Collingwood's view, the perfect kind of knowledge is the mathematician's relation to the objects that he studies. This mathematical kind of knowledge is Collingwood's ideal; and in the emotional thermometer of his feelings the prestige of Mathematics attains so high a degree that the best turn that Collingwood can think of doing to the historian is to demonstrate, if he can, that the historian's kind of knowledge is a knowledge of this mathematical sort. If this diagnosis is correct, Collingwood's idea of History—like any other idea entertained by any other philosopher, however intellectually austere he may be doing his best to be—carries a human charge of emotion in it. The emotional 'affect' that is just perceptible in this passage may be presumed to be latent elsewhere; and, if the presence of this emotional nigger can in truth be detected in Collingwood's intellectual wood-pile, we have here identified the villain who has betrayed the philosopher's thought into confusions that have landed him in intellectually untenable positions. In the equation of an Augustan principate with a Pythagorean theorem we can detect two intellectual flaws in Collingwood's idea of History that can both be traced to this 'affective' origin. One of these is a failure to distinguish between the historian's and the mathematician's diverse interests in the same mathematical proposition; the other flaw is a failure to distinguish between the historian's way of apprehending the thought in a mathematical proposition and the same historian's way of apprehending a mathematical or any other act of thought in its historical setting in real life, where acts of thought are always found to be intertwined with acts of will and acts of feeling in a psychic rope in which the intellectual strand is sometimes conspicuous mainly by its virtual

[1] Collingwood, op. cit., p. 229, quoted on p. 198, above.

absence. These distinctions that the philosopher has ignored to his cost must now be investigated by the historian at his peril.

The difference between the historian's interest and the mathematician's in taking cognizance of the same mathematical proposition is not difficult to descry. When a mathematician is confronted with a mathematical proposition, he asks himself two questions: first, 'Is it true?' and, second, 'If it *is* true, then what position does this particular piece of mathematical truth occupy in the structure of the general system of mathematical truth in so far as this system and its structure are known to me?' For these professional purposes of the mathematician's, it does not matter when, where, or how this particular mathematical truth first happened to become known to the mind of some individual human being. Let the memory of Pythagoras' life and work 'fly forgotten as a dream'; the proposition which an historian associates with Pythagoras' name would lose none of its mathematical validity through becoming a proposition without a history. Its mathematical validity is conferred on it solely and wholly by an apprehension of its truth in the mind of a mathematician who is thinking it at the moment. This is the sense in which it is 'the eternal object' that Whitehead has proclaimed it to be. It is an element in a system of mathematical truth which is intrinsically self-consistent, coherent, and constant; and these intrinsic characteristics of this system of truth are not affected by the historical fact that a knowledge of it, accumulated in 'the collective consciousness' of the Human Race, has been, and is still being, acquired piecemeal by the successive intellectual exertions of individual human minds. In other words, the eternity of any object of thought that is successively entertained by the minds of a series of mathematicians has its converse, condition, and price in the impersonality with which this object is entertained by one mind after another without establishing any human link between them.

In thinking a proposition which Pythagoras is said to have been the first human being to have thought, a latter-day mathematician is not 're-enacting' Pythagoras' 'experience for himself';[1] for the experience shared with Pythagoras by this historical successor of his is the bare intellectual act of thinking an impersonally mathematical thought,[2]

[1] Collingwood, ibid., p. 163.
[2] This point is made by Collingwood himself in another context: 'Even thought itself, in its immediacy as the unique act of thought with its unique context in the life of an individual thinker, . . . cannot be re-enacted; if it could, Time itself would be cancelled and the historian would be the person about whom he thinks, living over again in all respects the same. The historian cannot apprehend the individual act of thought in its individuality, just as it actually happened. What he apprehends . . . is the act of thought itself, in its survival and revival at different times and in different persons' (ibid., p. 303). This is Collingwood's exegesis of his own previous contention that 'the process of argument which I go through is not a process resembling Plato's, it actually is Plato's . . . if I not only read his argument but understand it—follow it in my own mind by re-arguing it with and for myself' (ibid., p. 301; cp. p. 215).
We shall concur with Collingwood's considered view that, while the thought that is thought on the two occasions is identical, it can only be so in so far as it is impersonal; but we must apply to this conclusion of Collingwood's the distinction that we have drawn between the historian's purpose and the mathematician's or natural scientist's. It is true that the rethinking of a thought does not bring a later thinker of it into personal communion with an earlier thinker of it, and it is also true that a mathematical or scientific thinker is not seeking to conjure any ulterior personal communion out of the impersonal mathematical or scientific thought into which he does effectively enter. On the other

whereas Pythagoras' actual experience included the sensation of suddenly seeing the light, the belief that his was the first human mind that had ever seen it, and the emotional exultation of feeling himself to be an intellectual pioneer. All these non-mathematical elements in a mathematician's actual experience are expressed in Archimêdês' exclamation ηὕρηκα; yet the latter-day student of hydrostatics is deaf to a cry which, coming as it does from Archimêdês' heart, never fails to thrill the heart of the historian, however faintly the sound may echo in the historian's ears across an ever widening gulf of fleeting Time.

There is indeed a piquant difference between the mathematician's impersonal way of looking at a proposition and the way in which the same proposition interests the historian. When the historian is confronted with it, he does not ask himself, 'Is this mathematically true?' He asks himself, 'What can this mathematical proposition tell me about the personality and life of Pythagoras and about the history of his social milieu—the thoughts, feelings, aims, and characters of Pythagoras and his contemporaries, predecessors, and successors in Samos and in Croton, in the Hellenic World at large, and in the other societies that were this society's successors, predecessors, and contemporaries? So long as the mathematical proposition associated with Pythagoras gives him some light on the answers to these historical questions, it is of no professional consequence to the historian whether the proposition happens to be mathematically true or false; for a mathematically true proposition might prove to be barren of historical information, while a mathematically false proposition might prove to be an historian's gold mine.

Since everything that has been said about Mathematics in this Annex is likewise true of Natural Science, the case of Astrology will serve to illustrate our point. In Collingwood's and Toynbee's day in Western scientific circles, Astrology was in deep disgrace. It was perpetually being cited as the classical example of a pseudo-science whose falsity had been exposed and whose prestige had been exploded;[1] yet, in this selfsame generation, masterly studies of astrological beliefs for historical purposes had been throwing floods of light on the *Weltanschauung* and *Gefühlsart* of the children of the Babylonic Civilization who had invented —or discovered—Astrology in the eighth century B.C.[2] and the children

hand the historian, even if he fails fully to apprehend this impersonal mathematical thought, may nevertheless succeed in utilizing it for his own ulterior purpose of making a psychic passage across the gulf of Time and Space that lies between him and some earlier thinker of the same thought with whom he is seeking to make contact (see pp. 729 and 730, below).

[1] There was, of course, a long time-lag between the date, before the close of the seventeenth century of the Christian Era, at which Modern Western men of science ceased to believe that astrological propositions were true and the consummation of Astrology's ruin as a practical going concern in non-scientific circles in the West and elsewhere. In A.D. 1952 a glance at any issue of any organ of the popular press in England would inform an historian that at this date Astrology, so far from having been sent to Jericho, was fast occupying a spiritual vacuum created by the waning of Western Man's belief in the truth of Astrology's old rival, Christianity. A more surprising phenomenon, of which there were indications at this date, was an incipient readmission of this long-since scientifically discredited science into the Eden of scientific truth from which it had once been ignominiously expelled. The tree of knowledge on to which Astrology was being grafted this time was not its ungrateful natural daughter Astronomy, but an indulgent adoptive mother—Psychology.

[2] See V. v. 56–57.

of contemporary and posterior civilizations, down to and including Collingwood's and Toynbee's own seventeenth-century forebears in the West, who had fallen like ninepins to the fascination of this professedly scientific system of ideas.

'The human interest' which attaches to the history of astrological beliefs, and which is just as well served by a study of them if they happen to be scientifically false as if they happen to be scientifically true, is the hidden treasure[1] that is the historian's lodestone. Nothing else except the quest for this trove would induce the historian to give his mind to scientific and mathematical propositions which for the historian have no intrinsic professional interest either *a priori* or even in consequence of the historian's being told by a *savant* that the *savant* believes them to be true—and, perhaps, not only true but momentous—in the inhuman realm of scientific and mathematical reality.

It will be seen that the mathematician's and the historian's respective professional interests in the same mathematical proposition are mutually exclusive; and consequently either party's interest is at best boring to the other party and at worst exasperating to him. The historian has no professional use for a system of mathematical or scientific truth if he is asked to study it for its own sake; for he is not concerned to certify the permanence of 'a permanent addition to mathematical knowledge' in thinking this mathematical thought for himself, any more than he is concerned to certify the permanence of 'a permanent addition to political ideas' in entering into the thoughts and aims of Augustus. If he sets himself to think thoughts that were once entertained by the mind of either an Augustus or a Pythagoras, his purpose is to utilize the political calculation or the mathematical theorem as an intellectual spring-board from which his imagination can make an attempt, by taking a flying leap, to establish psychic communications with other human souls whose intellects have thought the same thought at other times and places. Conversely, the mathematician or natural scientist has no professional use for the history of mathematical or scientific beliefs.

It is true that the beliefs which mathematicians and scientists will be found to be holding at any date will always also be found to be the historical product of beliefs held by their predecessors, some of which will have been retained, and others discarded, by these past thinkers' present epigoni; and this is an aspect of mathematical and scientific beliefs that is of greater professional interest to an historian than the mathematician's or scientist's professional question whether these beliefs happen to be intrinsically true or false. At any date at which the historian takes a sounding, he is apt to find the mathematicians and scientists of that generation indebted to the past beliefs that they have discarded, not much less deeply than to those that they have retained; but the historian is also apt to find himself being astonished by his own mathematical and scientific contemporaries' ingratitude. If they are confronted with one of their predecessors' beliefs, their first question is not, 'What do we owe to it?' but, 'Is it true or false?' And, if once they have pronounced it to be false according to their own present lights, they suffer

[1] Matt. xiii. 44.

no natural human sentiment of gratitude to restrain them from ruthlessly consigning this discarded belief to the scrap-heap, as a nuisance of which they must resolutely rid their minds for fear that it might breed intellectual confusion and error there if they were to dwell on it at the prompting of their own better feelings.

When once men of science have thus condemned some previously orthodox belief, it is idle for the historian to upbraid them for this impiety towards their predecessors. He will meet with no success in his endeavour to prick these hard hearts to compunction. The mathematician's and the scientist's judgement on the history of Mathematics and Science runs on the lines of the Caliph 'Umar's legendary dispatch to his lieutenant 'Amr b. al-'Ās in reply to 'Amr's request for instructions for the disposal of a Ptolemaic Library at Alexandria in which the treasures of an Hellenic literary culture had been accumulating for the best part of a millennium by the date of the Arab conquest of Egypt. 'If these writings of the Greeks agree with the Book of God, they are useless and need not be preserved; if they disagree, they are pernicious and ought to be destroyed'[1] is the minute which 'Umar is said to have made on 'Amr's query. 'If these tenets held by our predecessors agree with those held by us today, they are useless and need not be preserved; if they disagree, they are pernicious and ought to be destroyed' is the answer which, in fact and not in fiction, the historian evokes from the mathematician and the scientist when he begs them to take a pious interest in the genesis of their own current beliefs.

If we have now sufficiently explored the difference between the historian's and the mathematician's or scientist's respective interests in the same mathematical or scientific proposition, we may pass on to an examination of the difference between the historian's way of apprehending a thought that has been thought in other minds before his, and his way of apprehending the manifold human experience in which every act of thought is actually implicated in real life.

We have observed already[2] that the historian, when he is thinking for himself a thought that has also been entertained by some other person's mind in some other time and place, is not interested in the naked thought for its own sake; he is interested in it as a possible spring-board from which he may perhaps find himself able to take a flying leap into psychic communion with that other person who, in his own act of entertaining the same thought, was certainly animated by feelings associated with his act of thinking, and was perhaps also meditating, planning, or executing some associated act of will for the weal or woe of his contemporaries. This interest, which is a genuine historian's abiding ultimate interest,

---

[1] Gibbon, Edward: The History of the Decline and Fall of the Roman Empire, chap. li, paraphrasing the thirteenth-century Jacobite Monophysite Patriarch of Antioch, Abu'l-Faraj (alias Mar Gregor of Malaṭīyeh, alias Bar Hebraeus). Gibbon's paraphrase is based on a passage on p. 114 of Edward Pocock's Latin translation (Oxford 1663, printed by H. Hall, Printer to the University) of 'Abulpharagius's' own Arabic translation, from the original Syriac text, of the political part of his chronicle of universal history, both political and ecclesiastical. The title of this Arabic version is Tārīkh Mukhtaṣar al-Duwal (Historia Compendiosa Dynastiarum). The story has been cited in VI. vi. 111–12.

[2] On p. 729, above.

could not have been described more accurately than it has been described by Collingwood in the following words:

'To the historian, the activities whose history he is studying are not spectacles to be watched, but experiences to be lived through in his own mind; they are objective, or known to him, only because they are also subjective, or activities of his own;'[1]

and if it were indeed true of Toynbee, as Collingwood believes it to be, that

'he regards History as a mere spectacle, something consisting of facts observed and recorded by the historian, phenomena presented externally to his gaze, not experiences into which he must enter and which he must make his own,'

then—q.e.d.—Toynbee would have been convicted by Collingwood of being no historian.

This personal question is, of course, a trivial piece of private business; and in any case the only line of defence that would be likely to appeal to the defendant's readers would be for him to whisper *Circumspice* and then at once move on to the next piece of public business on the agenda —and this is the momentous question: How far is it actually possible for the historian to perform that feat of living through other people's experience which is agreed on all hands to be the historian's proper aim? Collingwood's answer is that it is possible for the historian to achieve this aim completely; but if he is able to give this simple and satisfactory reply this is only because, as we have noticed already,[2] Collingwood defines the area of the historian's field of sympathetic magic in terms that strike an historian-philistine as being arbitrarily restrictive. 'All history is the history of thought[3]. . . . Of everything other than thought, there can be no history[4]. . . . The record of immediate experience, with its flow of sensations and feelings, . . . is not history',[5] Collingwood maintains; and in thus defining and limiting the historian's field he is alleviating, by the exercise of a royal prerogative, the weight of the load that the imperious philosopher has legitimately imposed on the historian's devoted shoulders. When Collingwood admonishes the historian that 'he must always remember that the event' which he is studying 'was an action, and that his main task is to think himself into this action',[6] he reduces this Psyche's Task to finite dimensions by a ruling that is as merciful as it is arbitrary. 'To think himself into this action' is to be interpreted, Collingwood rules, as meaning 'to discern the thought [*sic*] of its agent'. The same restrictive interpretation is applied again when Collingwood reminds the historian that 'the events of history are never mere phenomena, never mere spectacles for contemplation, but things which the historian looks, not at, but through';[7] for, after thus demanding of the historian's vision that it should pierce, and not just strike, its target, he scales down his demand, here too, by defining the

---

[1] Collingwood, op. cit., p. 218. Cp. p. 293.
[2] On pp. 720–2, above.
[3] Collingwood, op. cit., p. 215.
[4] Ibid., p. 304.
[5] Ibid.
[6] Ibid., p. 213.
[7] Ibid., p. 214.

objective of this arduous penetration as being 'to discern the thought [*sic*] within' the objects under fire.

If it were indeed true that 'thought' was the sole possible element in human experience that the historian's psyche can apprehend, and therefore the sole legitimate target for the historian's proper aim of penetrating through the phenomena to the psychic inwardness of events, the historian's task, however exacting, would at least be straightforward, since, as we have seen, it is practicable for the same thought to be entertained by the minds of different persons, and there is one body of thought —namely mathematical and scientific thought—that is a thoroughly impersonal product and possession of a 'Collective Human Consciousness'. Unhappily for the historian, this doctrine of Collingwood the philosopher's is a dogma which is belied by the experience and practice of historians, including Collingwood himself on the evidence of his own published historical works. In real life, thought is never to be found apart from the non-intellectual strands in the composite rope of human experience; and, if Collingwood is right—as he is right—in requiring of the historian that he must 'enter into' other people's experiences and 'live through' them, he is wrong in instructing the historian to ignore all strands of experience except the intellectual strand.

The historian, for his part, must therefore resist the temptation to close with this relatively easy option. He must take to heart Collingwood's commandment 'Thou shalt get inside events'; but he must obey this commandment more rigorously than Yahweh requires of him. If he is to participate in other people's experiences, he must participate, not only in their thoughts, but also in their emotions and in their volitions; and his task will not have been achieved even when he has participated in the total individual experience of some single personality; for any act of will implies and duly produces an encounter between the person who performs the act and at least one other person whose action the act of will is intended to influence. An experience that embraces acts of will must, *ex hypothesi*, also embrace encounters; and this *a priori* conclusion is, of course, borne out by our own experience in this Study, in which we have been led by an empirical method of inquiry to find, below the surface of this phenomenon of encounters between personalities, the mysterious fount of spiritual creativity.[1] The historian must obey Collingwood's commandment over a wider field of experience than the intellectual allotment of which, alone, Collingwood takes cognizance; and from this it follows that the historian must discover for himself some additional means of establishing psychic communications with the human objects of his study beyond a re-performance of acts of thought which is the sole means suggested by Collingwood for attaining an arbitrarily limited objective.

The inadequacy of Collingwood's prescription for an historian's *modus operandi* is not, of course, equally obvious in all cases. It is least obvious where the intellectual strand in the experience in which the historian has to participate is the most important strand in this experience in the unanimous opinion of the historian and the subject of

[1] See II. i. 271–99, and pp. 395–405, above.

the particular experience that is the historian's object of study in the case in point. A classic instance of this type of case is that experience of Pythagoras' which Collingwood has cited. In Pythagoras' and Posterity's opinion alike, the important element in this experience is the thought that the area of the square on the hypotenuse of a right-angled triangle is equal to the sum of the areas of the squares on this triangle's other two sides. Pythagoras himself would have been the first to pronounce that the thrill of exultation accompanying the mathematical pioneer's experience of intellectual discovery was a piece of private business that cannot compare in importance with the momentousness of the associated impersonal mathematical thought. Yet however austerely that exultant feeling may be depreciated by the historian's and Pythagoras' consentient intellects, their concordant hearts cannot help leaping up at the recollection of it, to thrill rebelliously in unison. Even when the gist of an experience is a mathematical theorem, an irrepressible explosion of concomitant feeling proclaims that Thought is not the whole of Life and that Nature will keep on coming back at you however energetically you may have pitched her out.[1]

If Collingwood's prescription thus proves inadequate to the historian's need even when the experience in which the historian has to participate is Pythagoras the mathematician's, how is the poor historian likely to fare in coping with some experience of Timur Lenk the ogre's? In the ghastly history of human affairs, Pythagoras' experience of the thrill of discovering a theorem inside the city-wall of Croton is, after all, an event of a rarer and less characteristic kind than Tamerlane's experience of the thrill of building minarets out of five thousand human heads outside the city-wall of Zirih;[2] and how is the conscientious historian to 'enter into' and 'live through' that? The pertinent difference between this experience of Tamerlane's and that experience of Pythagoras' is that the strand of thought, which looms so large in Pythagoras' experience, is so exiguous in Tamerlane's experience as to be barely discernible, whereas the exuberance of Tamerlane's feelings on this gruesome occasion must have been veritably Gargantuan. By comparison, the thrill experienced by Pythagoras was a barely perceptible emotional tremor. Since 'the activities whose history' the historian 'is studying . . . are objective, or known to him, only because they are subjective, or activities of his own',[3] he has to make Tamerlane's experience 'an integral part of his own . . . by re-enacting' it 'for himself';[4] and at this point, if the historian is a truly conscientious workman, the shadow of the madhouse once again falls athwart his thorny path.

How is a scrupulous historian to set about the job? We have to picture him studying a gazetteer to find some easily accessible town whose population will suffice to provide him with about twice the number of heads (to be on the safe side) that he requires for making a pile of the same order of magnitude as Tamerlane's historic pile at Zirih. He selects Princeton, New Jersey; takes the afternoon train from

[1] Horace: *Epistulae*, Book I, Ep. x, l. 24.
[2] See IV. iv. 500.
[3] Collingwood, op. cit., p. 218.
[4] Ibid., p. 163.

New York; gives himself a good night's rest at the inn or the tavern; raises his temper to the requisite pitch by meditating for five minutes on the last demand-note served on him by the Bureau of Internal Revenue; rushes out in a thoroughly Tamerlanian rage into the quiet unsuspecting streets; and has not bagged more than half a dozen heads towards his target of five thousand before he finds himself in the police court being asked by the magistrate what he means by it. When he explains that he has not been committing a *crime passionel* but has been simply taking seriously his professional duties as Tamerlane's historian under Collingwood's marching orders, an enlightened Department of Justice sends him, not to the electric chair, but to the asylum. What a theme for Edward Lear!

In the eyes of an outraged society, the homicidal maniac has got off lightly; yet, even as it is, this professionally scrupulous historian's fate is sad enough from the victim's personal standpoint. Is there any way out of such an awkward dilemma? Can our devoted historian find some means of doing his professional duty by Tamerlane without making all that havoc of his own life, not to speak of his neighbours'? Yes, it is open to him to participate in Tamerlane's experience without 're-enacting' it in real life if he can bring himself to use his imagination. This alternative course likewise has its price. The historian who does his job by using his imagination is exposing himself to the censure meted out by Plato to painters and poets who have brought this sly faculty into play in their own professional activities. Yet to be castigated by Plato is, after all, a lesser evil than to be certified insane.

'Your painter,' Plato half-seriously complains, 'will paint for you a shoe-maker, carpenter, and every other kind of artisan without ever having been initiated into the technique of any of these trades; yet, all the same, if he is a good artist, he will be able to take in a child or a feeble-minded adult by painting him a carpenter that he will mistake for a real carpenter if he is given a distant view of the picture. . . . [In fact,] when someone tells us, about someone else, that in him he has met a man who is a master of all trades and actually has a more accurate knowledge of each single one of them than can be claimed by any of that particular trade's professional practitioners, our conclusion will be that our interlocutor is a simpleton and that he must have come across a cheat who took his victim in so completely by tricks of mimicry that he succeeded in giving him the impression that he was a universal genius—owing to the victim's inability to distinguish between mimicry and knowledge and ignorance. . . .

'Well, this calls for an inquiry into "high-brow" poetry (τραγῳδίαν) and its presiding genius Homer, because there are people who tell us that these poets are masters of all the arts and of all the problems of ethics and of theology. A good poet, the argument runs, must *ex hypothesi* be a con-noisseur of his subject if he is to write about it properly—if he were not a connoisseur, he would not be able to write at all. The question for inquiry is whether the poets may not be adepts at mimicry who have taken in these sponsors of theirs by a confidence trick which has been so well played that the victims of it, when they see the poets' works, do not tumble to it that these products are at three removes' distance from reality and are easy for an ignoramus to fabricate because these works of the poets' are not realities at all but are mere phantasms. . . .

'Let us now be generous to Homer or any confrère of his whom we may choose to interrogate. Let us confine our interrogation to a single question. We will not ask him: "If you are really a doctor and not just a mimic of the medical profession's patter, what evidence can you produce, master poet, ancient or modern, of cures performed by yourself?" . . . But we are justified in questioning Homer about the greatest and the noblest of the activities on which he has the assurance to hold forth—I mean, War and Generalship and Government and Education. "Well now, Homer," we may justifiably say to the poet, "If you are really not at three removes' distance from the truth in the relation in which you stand to human conduct at its best (ἀρετῆς πέρι)—if you are not one of those fabricators of simulacra whom we have labelled mimics—if you are really at no more than two removes' distance from the truth and are really an expert in the science of ethics, private and public, give us an instance of a state whose government has shown an improvement thanks to you". . . . Name a war, fought in Homer's lifetime, that is recorded to have been efficiently conducted thanks to Homer's leadership or counsel. . . . Is there any suggestion that Homer ever gathered round him in his own lifetime a school of disciples who felt it a privilege to be in personal touch with him and who handed down to Posterity the tradition of an Homeric way of life? . . .

'Well, [on this showing,] must not our verdict on Homer and all his successors in the poetic line be that they are mimics of simulacra of human conduct at its best and of any other subject that they may elect to adorn? I think we must conclude that they are quite out of touch with the truth, and must therefore place them in the same category as the painter, whom we were considering just now, who, without himself having been initiated into the technique of shoemaking, will make for you what will look like a shoemaker to eyes that judge merely by colours and shapes because their owners are no better initiated than the painter who has thus imposed on them. . . . On this analogy, we shall describe what the poet does by putting it that, without himself having been initiated into any technique except the art of mimicry, he tints his nouns and verbs with colours stolen from the divers trades and thereby makes, on birds of his feather who judge merely by words, an invariable impression of talking admirably about anything that he elects to talk about—shoemaking or generalship or what you will—so long as he does his business in metre and rhythm and harmony. It is these stage properties of his that do the trick for him in virtue of the extraordinary fascination that they exercise. If you strip off the literary colouring from a poet's ideas and make him express them in naked prose—well, I do not need to tell you what the impression then will be. . . . You have seen what happens to a face that is in the flush of youth without possessing any intrinsic beauty. You know what that face comes to look like when the bloom has faded.'[1]

If Plato means his readers to take this passage at all seriously, he has committed himself to approving our over-scrupulous historian's legendary escapade. If Plato had heard the news of our mythical 'incident' at Princeton, New Jersey, and had had the courage of his own professed convictions, he would have appeared in court to testify on behalf of the defence that the prisoner in the dock would have been committing a cold-blooded fraud on the public if he had undertaken to produce and publish a work purporting to be a history of Tamerlane without attempting bona fide to make Tamerlane's experience 'an

[1] Plato: *Respublica*, 598 B–601 B.

integral part of his own . . . by re-enacting' it 'for himself '. If our historian has any sense, however, he will be less grateful to Plato for this courageous defence of his conscientious head-hunting expedition than for his disclosure of a trick for doing an historian's professional business without having to go to these embarrassing extremes. Plato, if he likes, may give this trick the bad name of 'confidence trick', and may stigmatize as 'mimicry' something that the historian, the poet, or the painter, for their part, might prefer to call 'imagination'. But the philosopher's magisterial censure is a cheap price to pay for the benefits of the same philosopher's unintentional 'tip'—as will be evident if we come to our hard-pressed historian's rescue with Lewis Carroll's benevolent 'time-machine'.[1]

Let us make sure that our historian has taken Plato's back-handed hint to give his imagination free play, and then let us see him off again on his journey from New York to Princeton. He buys his ticket, catches his train, registers at his hotel, and works up his feelings by thinking of a recent income-tax demand-note, all just as before; but at this critical point, instead of rushing out into the streets, yataghan in hand, and decapitating the first foot-passengers that he meets, like a Spartiate Cleomenes in the streets of a Ptolemaic Alexandria,[2] he stalks out into the garden, walking-stick in hand, and decapitates the first dandelions that catch his eye—and, if the useful occupation of weed-killing fails to strike in him the requisite Tamerlanian spark, he can proceed to make a glorious massacre of the sun-flowers and handsomely indemnify the hotel management for their pecuniary loss without any risk of finding himself on the wrong side of the Law. If he then goes back indoors, sits down at his writing-desk, and indites his history of Tamerlane's life and works, his ingenuous reader (*teste Platone*) will never know that the heads which the historian duly cut off, in order to put himself in the proper mood for doing his job, were not human, but only floral. We can be reasonably confident of the plausibility of the impression that Timur Lenk's unscrupulously unhomicidal imaginative historiographer will contrive to make, since we have no evidence that Christopher Marlowe ever took any more drastic steps than those suggested here when he was working himself up to write his *Tamburlaine the Great*.

But what is this faculty of Imagination which makes it possible, after all, for an historian to participate in Timur Lenk's experience without his having to re-experience it in real life? Are the historian, the painter, and the poet really practising on the public the fraud of which Plato accuses them half in earnest? Are they really palming off appearance as reality, and getting something for nothing out of their professional activities at the price of sacrificing their moral integrity? The truth is that the exercise of the Imagination is something that is quite as familiar as it is mysterious. It is not just a professional trick of a literary and artistic trade; it is an indispensable means of social intercourse between ordinary people in every-day life; and, since Sub-Man had to become a social animal before he could become fully human,[3] it is no exaggera-

<hr>

[1] See V. vi. 214.   [2] See V. vi. 391.   [3] See I. i. 173.

tion to say that a constant use of the Imagination is one of the primary
necessities of life for the Human Race, and that, if Mankind were to
take Plato's castigation seriously enough to pluck this vital faculty out
and cast it from them, they would be sentencing themselves to the
doom of the legendary Kilkenny Cats.

While Plato pillories the Imagination by stigmatizing its exercise as
a fraud practised by painters and poets on the public, Collingwood
saves the historian's reputation, according to Collingwood's own lights,
by ruling out any psychic activity other than thought about thought
from his definition of what constitutes the historian's legitimate business. In thus committing himself to a doctrine that cannot be reconciled
with the facts, Collingwood has fallen a victim to a common human
infirmity. Each of us is prone to exaggerate the importance of the organ
or faculty or activity—hand, ear, or eye; sensation, intuition, or feeling;
will or thought—that happens to be the principal instrument or medium
of his own dealings, personal or professional, with his fellow human
beings; and Collingwood the historian has been led up this prim garden
path by Collingwood the philosopher. An idolization of thought is the
philosopher's idolatrous sacrifice on the altar of his professional patriotism;[1] but it is as true in the Academy as it is in the world outside its
garden walls that 'patriotism is not enough';[2] for there are always more
things in Heaven and Earth than are dreamt of in the philosophy of
any of our Horatios.[3]

---

[1] Collingwood has also laid a wreath on the Imagination's cenotaph, but he has
nullified the signature of this tribute by the terms in which he has composed his inscription. The idea, he declares (op. cit., p. 249) that governs an historian's work 'is the idea of
the Historical Imagination as a self-dependent, self-determining, and self-justifying form
of—thought [sic]'.

[2] Edith Cavell at Brussels on the 12th October, 1915.

[3] Shakspeare: *Hamlet*, Act I, scene 5.

WAS THERE A RENAISSANCE OF MINOAN RELIGION IN HELLENIC HISTORY?

In the pre-Alexandrine Age of Hellenic history there were several religious movements that were felt by the Hellenes at the time to be, in some sense, exotic. The chief instances were the worship of Dionysus, the rites, poems, and ideas associated with the name of Orpheus, and the Pythagorean School of Philosophy. If some, at any rate, of the elements in these divers religious practices, experiences, and beliefs were un-Hellenic in reality, there were two different possible quarters from which they might have made their way into Hellenic life. Either they might have been introduced through the radiation of some living contemporary non-Hellenic culture or cultures with which the Hellenic World was already in contact in the pre-Alexandrine Age—as it is notorious that a number of alien religious influences were introduced subsequently, in the sequel to the overthrow of the Achaemenian Empire by Alexander—or alternatively such un-Hellenic religious phenomena in a pre-Alexandrine Hellas might have been, not importations from living contemporary societies, but evocations of ghosts from the dead past of an antecedent civilization to which the Hellenic was affiliated. The hypothesis of an Hellenic renaissance of Minoan religion has been found convincing—at least as far as the worship of Dionysus is concerned—by one of the most eminent of the twentieth-century Western authorities on the subject.

'The ecstatic cult of Dionysos, which spread all over Greece in the Archaic Age, was a powerful religious movement. I venture to think that its strength is better understood if we assume that it was not an importation of a completely foreign god and form of religion but the revival of old Minoan and Mycenaean religious ideas, and perhaps also rites, which had for a time fallen into the background. The ideas peculiar to the Minoan religion were suppressed under the overwhelming onset of the gods and religious ideas which the [Achaean barbarian] conquerors brought with them; but, just as the old gods did not vanish but mingled with the new-comers, so the old religious ideas persisted in secret. When the opportunity arose they emerged once more to cause a religious revolution, the occasion being the acceptance of a foreign cult with kindred ideas of a mystic character. This was the Thracian worship of Dionysos combined with the Phrygian form of the same cult, which had already been transformed through the influence of the native religion of Asia Minor, which in its turn also contained elements of Minoan origin, identical with or similar to Minoan ideas which still survived in Greece.'[1]

In the historical perspective of a latter-day Western historian, this hypothetical renaissance, in Hellenic history, of supposedly repressed elements of Minoan religion would have counterparts in the historic

---

[1] Nilsson, M. P.: *The Minoan-Mycenaean Religion and its Survival in Greek Religion* (London 1927, Milford), p. 504.

renaissances, in Orthodox and in Western Christian history, of a Judaism embedded in a Christianity that was these two Hellenistic civilizations' religious heritage from their Hellenic predecessor. This analogy,
however, so far from corroborating Nilsson's view, actually militates
against it *a priori*; for the hypothesis that there has been a renaissance
of some element of an antecedent civilization's religion in the history
of an affiliated civilization pre-supposes the survival, through an intervening social interregnum, of a religious tradition in which the eventually resuscitated element of an earlier religion has been latent all the
time; and in a previous context[1] we have found reason to believe that
a religious link of this kind, such as is provided by a chrysalis church,
between two civilizations of different generations is the distinctive mark
of the historical relation between a civilization of the second generation
and one of the third—as, for example, the Orthodox and Western
Christian civilizations were affiliated to the Hellenic through the link
provided by Christianity. By contrast, the normal link between a
civilization of the first generation, such as the Minoan, and a successor
in the second generation, such as the Hellenic, seems to be, not a
chrysalis church, but an external proletariat; and in a previous inquiry,
after we had raised the question whether a religious legacy from a
Minoan past was to be detected in 'Orphism',[2] our judgement inclined
tentatively towards the alternative view[3] that the un-Hellenic elements
in 'Orphism', if such there were, were not revivals of a Minoan past,
but were importations into Hellas from the contemporary Syriac and
Indic worlds.

Between the date of publication of the fifth volume of this Study in
A.D. 1939 and the date of writing of the present Annex in A.D. 1950,
our doubts about the hypothesis of an Hellenic renaissance of Minoan
religion had been confirmed by the authoritative verdict of a lucid-
minded scholar who had re-examined all the extant historical evidence
regarding 'the arts of Orpheus' by a stringently scientific method.[4]
Professor Linforth's most significant conclusion is the negative one that
there is no cogent evidence for there ever having been anything in the
nature of an institutionally organized 'Orphic Church', or even anything
in the nature of a systematic body of Orphic doctrine;[5] and he finds
no 'trustworthy support' for the view, which had received some
countenance in previous works of scholarship,[6]

'that the teletae and the poem of the dismemberment [of Dionysus] were
actually the work of Onomacritus, and that therefore "the Orphic Religion" originated in Athens, or was introduced into Athens, in the time of
Peisistratus.'[7]

In the dry light of Linforth's salutarily ruthless criticism of theories
without warrant in the sources, the supposed evidence for the presence
of Syriac and Indic elements in pre-Alexandrine Orphic rites, poems,

---

[1] In VII. vii. 392–419. [2] See I. i. 95–100.
[3] See V. v. 82–87 and 697–8.
[4] Linforth, I. M.: *The Arts of Orpheus* (Berkeley, Cal. 1941, University of California
Press). [5] See ibid., pp. 288, 291, 304–5, and 356.
[6] See the references in V. v. 697–8. [7] Linforth, op. cit., p. 353.

and ideas dwindles almost to the vanishing-point at which the supposed evidence for the presence there of Minoan elements quite disappears from view.

Scepticism can, of course, be carried to an extreme at which it becomes more paradoxical than credulity; and, if there were incontrovertible evidence, as there seems in fact to be,[1] that in a pre-Alexandrine Hellenic World a belief in the transmigration of souls under stress of *Karma*,[2] and a prescription for winning release from a melancholy round of successive reincarnations, were current in Pythagorean, Orphic, or any other philosophical or religious circles, it would seem decidedly more improbable that these practices and doctrines had been worked out in the Hellenic World independently than that they had been derived by the Hellenes from the Indic World through the culturally conductive medium of the Achaemenian Empire.[3] Moreover, whatever the source or sources of the philosophy of Pythagoras and of the 'miscellaneous' and 'disparate'[4] 'arts of Orpheus'[5] may have been, it has still to be explained why a pre-Alexandrine Hellenic Society should ever have welcomed and promoted movements that were certainly felt to have in them at least a touch of something alien. An explanation suggested in a previous passage of this Study[6] was that 'Orphism' proved attractive to Hellenic souls because it promised to fill a fearful spiritual void; and, since the publication of Linforth's book, this idea, at least, can be entertained with somewhat greater assurance, since it has received the *nihil obstat* of a scholar who has placed so many other once cherished notions on a scientific censor's index.

'If we look for a wider unity in the things that bore the name of Orpheus, we may perhaps find that they are the expression of a particular aspect of the religious instinct among the Greeks. The practice of the public cults involved little or no religious speculation and was not developed to meet the deeper religious needs of the individual. Greek poetry—epic, lyric, and dramatic—full as it was of gods and myths and profound thought on the relations between gods and men, was secular rather than hieratic. Philosophy, though it touched Religion at many points and became more and more a guide for the moral life, was primarily intellectual and divorced from religious practice. Meantime, the common human need required a religion in which practice and belief would be united, a religion which would allay the concern which men individually felt for their spiritual welfare, in this life and the next. This need was met by the things that bore the name of Orpheus, the comfortable rites of the mysteries, with the doctrines that were implicit in them, and the poems which gave expression to the doctrines and supplied authority for the rites.'[7]

---

[1] As, for example, in Pindar's Second Olympian Ode, ll. 62–91 (according to the numbering in Christ's edition), and in the myth at the end of the Tenth Book of Plato's *Republic*. If the inspiration of these passages was not Orphic, it must have been Pythagorean.

[2] The Indic conception of *Karma* has been noticed in V. v. 432–3.

[3] If the philosophy of the Buddha was indeed the original source of these pre-Alexandrine Hellenic notions, it had suffered lamentable spiritual damage *en route*. For instance, the perfect freedom of an Indic *Nirvāna*, which was the etherial goal of the would-be arhat, had been jettisoned in favour of the sensuous delights of an Egyptiac Elysium.

[4] Linforth, op. cit., p. 291.   [5] Ibid., p. 296.
[6] In V. v. 86.   [7] Linforth, op. cit., p. 305.

A CRITIQUE OF GIBBON'S GENERAL OBSERVATIONS ON THE FALL OF THE ROMAN EMPIRE IN THE WEST

IN the chapter to which this annex attaches, three passages of this analytical parenthesis in Gibbon's narrative have been quoted as classical expressions of an eighteenth-century Western spirit of complacency.[1] Gibbon's analysis, however, throws light, not only on the outlook of a cultivated minority in the Western World of his day, but also on the prospects of his generation's and his society's successors mid-way through the twentieth century, after the lapse of some 170 years or more since the date—some time between A.D. 1772 and A.D. 1781[2]—when Gibbon's 'General Observations' were drafted. The last six of the ten paragraphs of which these observations consist are devoted to a comparison, point by point, between the state of the Hellenic Society at the time of the fall of the Roman Empire in the West, in the fifth century of the Christian Era, and the state of the Western Society at the time when Gibbon was writing—which was during the lull between the close of the Seven Years War in A.D. 1763 and the outbreak of the Revolutionary and Napoleonic Wars in A.D. 1792. The points that Gibbon brings up as topics for comparison are so well chosen, and his estimates, point by point, of the Western Civilization's prospects in his day are so illuminating for any mind attempting to make corresponding estimates five or six generations later,[3] that, in the present Annex to a Part of this Study dealing with the prospects of the Western Civilization in the twentieth century, the writer has reprinted the synoptic paragraphs of Gibbon's observations with a twentieth-century commentary on each of them, in the belief that he could have found no more effective way of prosecuting his own inquiry.

The fifth paragraph of Gibbon's observations, which opens with a passage quoted already in the main body of the present Part,[4] may now be reprinted in full.

'This awful revolution may be usefully applied to the instruction of the present age. It is the duty of a patriot to prefer and promote the exclusive interest and glory of his native country: but a philosopher may be permitted to enlarge his views, and to consider Europe as one great republic, whose various inhabitants have attained almost the same level of politeness and cultivation. The Balance of Power will continue to fluctuate, and the prosperity of our own or the neighbouring kingdoms may be alternately exalted or depressed; but these partial events cannot essentially injure our general state of happiness, the system of arts, and laws, and manners,

---

[1] See pp. 424 and 425, above.
[2] See IV. iv. 148, n. 3.
[3] The original notes for the present Annex were drafted, not in A.D. 1950, but in A.D. 1929.
[4] On p. 424, above.

which so advantageously distinguish, above the rest of Mankind, the Europeans and their colonies. The savage nations of the globe are the common enemies of Civilised Society; and we may inquire, with anxious curiosity, whether Europe is still threatened with a repetition of those calamities which formerly oppressed the arms and institutions of Rome. Perhaps the same reflections will illustrate the fall of that mighty empire, and explain the probable causes of our actual security.'

In this paragraph Gibbon enunciates the argument that governs the remainder of his observations: The Western World is now not exposed to the possibility of a breakdown from within; the only danger by which it might conceivably still be threatened is that of another attack by barbarians from the outer darkness; and, since this danger does not now appear to be a serious one, the Western World may consider itself secure.

The major premiss of this argument—a premise which Gibbon simply takes for granted—would be challenged by a twentieth-century Western inquirer who had lived to see the history of his own society demonstrate, in its turn, that 'we are betrayed by what is false within.'[1] In the light of this first-hand experience it was easier for a twentieth-century Western historian than it had been for his eighteenth-century predecessor to see that the breakdowns of all the civilizations that had broken down by Gibbon's time, not to speak of a date some 170 years later, had been due to inward spiritual failures and not to outward physical blows. We need not labour a point that we have already illustrated at length in an empirical survey.[2] If Gibbon had taken this point, he would have divined that the decline and fall of the Roman Empire had been no more than an episode, and this a late one, in the decline and fall of the Hellenic Civilization; and he would have detected the cause of the downfall, not in 'the triumph of Barbarism and Religion' in the Roman Empire in the fourth and fifth centuries of the Christian Era, but in the fratricidal warfare between the parochial city-states of Hellas in the fifth century B.C.[3]

After filing this notice of dissent we may go on to Paragraph Six:

'The Romans were ignorant of the extent of their danger and the number of their enemies. Beyond the Rhine and Danube the northern countries of Europe and Asia were filled with innumerable tribes of hunters and shepherds, poor, voracious, and turbulent; bold in arms, and impatient to ravish the fruits of industry. The Barbarian World was agitated by the rapid impulse of war; and the peace of Gaul or Italy was shaken by the distant revolutions of China. The Huns, who fled before a victorious enemy, directed their march towards the West; and the torrent was swelled by the gradual accession of captives and allies. The flying tribes who yielded to the Huns assumed in *their* turn the spirit of conquest; the endless column of barbarians pressed on the Roman Empire with accumulated weight; and, if the foremost were destroyed, the vacant space was instantly replenished by new assailants. Such formidable emigrations no longer issue from the North; and the long repose, which has been imputed to the decrease of population, is the happy consequence of the progress of arts and agriculture. Instead of some rude villages thinly scattered among its woods and morasses, Germany now produces a list of

---

[1] George Meredith, quoted in IV. iv. 120 and VI. vii. 46, n. 6.
[2] In IV. iv. 119–584.   [3] See IV. iv. 58–63.

two thousand three hundred walled towns; the Christian kingdoms of Denmark, Sweden, and Poland have been successively established; and the Hanse merchants, with the Teutonic knights, have extended their colonies along the coast of the Baltic as far as the Gulf of Finland. From the Gulf of Finland to the Eastern Ocean, Russia now assumes the form of a powerful and civilised empire. The plough, the loom, and the forge are introduced on the banks of the Volga, the Oby, and the Lena; and the fiercest of the Tartar hordes have been taught to tremble and obey. The reign of Independent Barbarism is now contracted to a narrow span; and the remnant of Calmucks or Uzbecks, whose forces may be almost numbered, cannot seriously excite the apprehensions of the great republic of Europe.[1] Yet this apparent security should not tempt us to forget that new enemies and unknown dangers may *possibly* arise from some obscure people, scarcely visible in the map of the World. The Arabs or Saracens, who spread their conquests from India to Spain, had languished in poverty and contempt till Mohamet breathed into those savage bodies the soul of enthusiasm.'

A twentieth-century Western observer would find no difficulty in agreeing with Gibbon that the Western World was unlikely ever again to be successfully invaded by barbarians from any no-man's-land beyond its borders; for, if Gibbon had lived to see the offensive power of the Eurasian Nomads broken at last, after a 3,500-years-long series of explosions, by the Manchus' overthrow of the Zungar Calmucks in A.D. 1755[2] and the flight of the Torgut Calmucks in A.D. 1771 from a Great Western Bay of the Eurasian Steppe where the Russians had reasserted the ascendancy of a sedentary civilization, Gibbon's twentieth-century successors had lived to see the last of the barbarians—in the highlands as well as on the steppes—followed up and subjugated in the last of their fastnesses.[3] Gibbon's doubts about the stability of the Manchu Empire were to be proved prescient by the swiftness of its decline and fall after the death of Gibbon's own contemporary the Emperor Ch'ien Lung (*imperabat* A.D. 1735–96); but the beneficiaries from this decay of the Manchu power were not to be the Calmucks or any other Eurasian Nomads; they were to be Russia along the disintegrating empire's continental frontiers and the maritime Powers of the Western World along its coasts; and a twentieth-century Western observer might feel justified in venturing to leave out of his reckoning Gibbon's *caveat* 'that new enemies and unknown dangers' might '*possibly* arise from some obscure people, scarcely visible in the map of the World'. This conclusion, however, would bring with it no sense of security to a twentieth-century Western historian who dissented from Gibbon's thesis that the barbarians had been responsible for the overthrow of the Roman Empire;

---

[1] [in the original, [6]]. 'The French and English editors of the Genealogical History of the Tartars have subjoined a curious, though imperfect, description of their present state. We might question the independence of the Calmucks, or Eluths, since they have been recently vanquished by the Chinese, who, in the year 1759, subdued the lesser Bucharia, and advanced into the country of Badakshan, near the sources of the Oxus (*Mémoires sur les Chinois*, tom. i, pp. 325–400). But these conquests are precarious, nor will I venture to ensure the safety of the Chinese Empire.'
[2] See Courant, M.: *L'Asie Centrale aux xviie et xviiie Siècles: Empire Kalmouk ou Empire Mantchou?* (Paris 1912, Rey), pp. 101–17.
[3] See V. v. 332–4, and pp. 450–1, above.

and, if the twentieth-century Western inquirer held the opposing view that the Roman Empire itself was merely a symptom of the decline and fall of an Hellenic Civilization which had been betrayed from within, and this four hundred years before the tardy estabishment of a *Pax Augusta*, then this latter-day Western investigator would find no consolation in being able to endorse Gibbon's judgement that the Western Civilization was unlikely ever to be overthrown by barbarian arms. He would find this conclusion cold comfort because he would find it irrelevant to his and Gibbon's common problem.

In attempting to estimate the Western Civilization's prospects, the twentieth-century Western student of History might be expected to concentrate his attention on the question whether a betrayal by something false within—which had been, as he saw it, the true cause of the Hellenic Civilization's downfall—was or was not likely to bring the Western Civilization to the same tragic end; and in this inquiry the elimination of a former menace from the Barbarians would be beside the point for several telling reasons. In the first place a ubiquitously expanding Western Society's external proletariat had been eliminated, for the most part, not through being annihilated, but through being transferred from the external to the internal proletariat's ranks, and this Western internal proletariat had been reinforced simultaneously by the conscription into it, *en masse*, of the populations of all the extant non-Western civilizations.[1] In the second place the possibility that the Western Civilization, like the Hellenic, might be betrayed by something false within had been brought home by the appalling experience of seeing a vanishing barbarian's most evilly barbarous propensities reappearing—in reproductions that were far more sinister than the original—among superficially Westernized children of non-Western civilizations that had been caught in the Western net and—most terrifying portent of all[2]—among native sons and heirs of the Western Civilization's promise.[3]

Gibbon had been gratified to observe that 'the fiercest of the Tartar hordes have now been taught to tremble and obey' by Russian converts to the Western Civilization who, by mastering a Western technique, had made themselves into efficient wardens of anti-Nomad marches, to the Western World's advantage as well as to Russia's. It had not occurred to Gibbon that the introduction of 'the plough, the loom, and the forge . . . on the banks of the Volga, the Oby, and the Lena', which in his time was serving the Western World's convenience by making the Nomads tremble and obey, might be employed one day by the same now irrevocably Western-fingered Russian hands for the inconvenient purpose of putting the same fear and trembling into Western hearts.

A fortiori, it had not occurred to an English historian who was a contemporary of King Frederick II of Prussia that a Germany producing 'a list of two thousand three hundred walled towns' might present a greater threat to the Western World, if Germany's rulers and leaders repudiated the moral standards of the Western Civilization, than 'rude villages scattered among' Germany's 'woods and morasses', in a no-man's-land

---

[1] See V. v. 152–3, and pp. 413–15, 451–2, and 489, above.
[2] See pp. 450–1, above.   [3] Heb. vi. 17 and xi. 9.

beyond the *limes* of the Roman Empire, had ever presented to an Hellenic World which had been successfully defended against primitive barbarian German assaults by this Roman military rampart for some four hundred years, and which might never have succumbed, and indeed never even have been exposed, to a German peril if, four hundred years before the date at which the Roman *limes* was established, Hellas had not been betrayed by something false within. The unreclaimed barbarian beyond the pale is a negligible danger to a civilization by comparison with the apostate son and heir[1] who has deliberately looked back after having put his hand to the plough;[2] and Frederick's unprincipled attack on the dominions of Maria Theresa in A.D. 1740, within Gibbon's own lifetime, was the first step in a German *descensus Averni* which was to reach the bottom of the infernal pit in A.D. 1933–45. If a Western people which had played so capital a part as the Germans had played in the long and hard task of building up a Western Christian Civilization could fall so low as this, no guarantee of immunity against future aggression by a straightforward barbarism from abroad could make up to the Western World for its now proven exposure to betrayal by a morally perverse barbarism within its own bosom.[3]

'The empire of Rome was firmly established by the singular and perfect coalition of its members. The subject nations, resigning the hope, and even the wish, of independence, embraced the character of Roman citizens; and the provinces of the West were reluctantly torn by the Barbarians from the bosom of their mother-country.[4] But this union was purchased by the loss of national freedom and military spirit; and the servile provinces, destitute of life and motion, expected their safety from the mercenary troops and governors who were directed by the orders of a distant court. The happiness of an hundred millions depended on the personal merit of one or two men, perhaps children, whose minds were corrupted by education, luxury, and despotic power. The deepest wounds were inflicted on the empire during the minorities of the sons and grandsons of Theodosius; and, after those incapable princes seemed to attain the age of manhood, they abandoned the church to the bishops, the state to the eunuchs, and the provinces to the Barbarians. Europe is now divided into twelve powerful, though unequal, kingdoms, three respectable commonwealths, and a variety of smaller, though independent, states; the

---

[1] On this point, see V. v. 334–7, where it is illustrated by the citation of an Italian neobarbarism which had not yet been eclipsed by a still darker German neobarbarism at the time when that passage of this book was written.   [2] Luke ix. 62.

[3] 'Vevey [1875].
'There is a perfect little woman here, mother of a fair-haired child, niece of Gortschakoff. She smokes cigarettes, very small, very elegantly. She told me that Ignatieff never by any chance told the truth. It is a proverb in Russia: "Il ment comme Ignatieff".
'She was mentioning the overthrow of previous civilisations by barbaric forces; and we came to the conclusion that it was unlikely that the Tartars, who seem the only available barbarians, would stamp out the civilisation, extended as it is over the World. She expressed her belief that the dark force is developed with the brightness of prosperity all-pervading now; and then suggested that what could provide a force strong, ignorant, barbarian, and widespread, is the lower populations of the various nations of Europe grouped in some such society as the International inbred with communistic and destructive notions' (*Journals and Letters of Reginald Viscount Esher*, ed. by M. V. Brett, vol. i (London 1934, Nicholson & Watson), p. 34). This passage was brought to the present writer's attention by his friend J. L. Hammond on the 3rd September, 1934.

[4] [in the original, 7] 'The prudent reader will determine how far this general proposition is weakened by the revolt of the Isaurians, the independence of Britain and Armorica, the Moorish tribes, or the Bagaudae of Gaul and Spain.'

chances of royal and ministerial talents are multiplied, at least, with the number of its rulers; and a Julian, or Semiramis, may reign in the North, while Arcadius and Honorius again slumber on the thrones of the South. The abuses of tyranny are restrained by the mutual influence of fear and shame; republics have acquired order and stability; monarchies have imbibed the principles of freedom, or, at least, of moderation; and some sense of honour and justice is introduced into the most defective constitutions by the general manners of the times. In peace, the progress of knowledge and industry is accelerated by the emulation of so many active rivals: in war, the European forces are exercised by temperate and undecisive contests. If a savage conqueror should issue from the deserts of Tartary, he must repeatedly vanquish the robust peasants of Russia, the numerous armies of Germany, the gallant nobles of France, and the intrepid freemen of Britain; who, perhaps, might confederate for their common defence. Should the victorious Barbarians carry slavery and desolation as far as the Atlantic Ocean, ten thousand vessels would transport beyond their pursuit the remains of Civilised Society; and Europe would revive and flourish in the American World, which is already filled with her colonies and institutions.'[1]

In this brilliant appreciation of the cost, in loss of liberty, initiative, and variety, which is the price of gaining unity and fraternity under the aegis of an oecumenical empire, Gibbon is implicitly contradicting his own major thesis that the Antonine Age had been the Golden Age of Hellenic history. Yet even in the present passage he shows no sign of any awareness of the obvious truth that, if, in the generation of Augustus, the Hellenic World did bring itself to buy unity and fraternity at an exorbitant price, this purchase must have come, by Augustus's day, to be a matter of life and death for the Hellenic World. In other words, Gibbon fails to recognize the two historical truths that the *Pax Augusta* was a disintegrating Hellenic Society's tardy response to the challenge of a four-hundred-years-long Time of Troubles and that the weak points, as well as the strong points, of the Roman Empire only become intelligible when they are viewed against this historical background; and his blindness to these two truths is the penalty for an antecedent failure to recognize a prior truth; for he has also failed to recognize that an Hellenic Time of Troubles which had preceded and evoked the organization of a Roman Peace had arisen out of the breakdown, in the fifth century B.C., of a felicitous but also precarious equilibrium between the two conflicting social forces of oecumenicalism and parochialism which had been a counterpart, in fifth-century Hellas, of the delicate equilibrium between the same two forces in the Western World of Gibbon's day.

The virtues of this régime of diversity-in-unity, which have been indicated by Gibbon in an introductory paragraph already quoted in this Annex, are enlarged upon in the present paragraph with the same masterly touch. Yet, in spite of the fact that the parallel between a classical Hellas and an eighteenth-century Western Christendom is explicitly

[1] [in the original, 8] 'America now contains about six millions of European blood and descent; and their numbers, at least in the North, are continually increasing. Whatever may be the changes of their political situation, they must preserve the manners of Europe; and we may reflect with some pleasure that the English language will probably be diffused over an immense and populous continent.'

pointed out in the works of two of Gibbon's own contemporaries, Hume[1] and Turgot,[2] Gibbon himself has not drawn the obvious moral for the prospects of his own civilization from the tragic historical fact that the once beneficent diversity-in-unity of a Classical Hellenic body social— whose parochial sovereign states had brought themselves to 'confederate for their common defence' in the crisis of 480–479 B.C.—eventually fell so desperately out of joint that a long-tormented Hellenic society came, at last, to acquiesce in the hardly less desperate remedy of replacing a dislocated constellation of parochial Powers by one single universal state. In the light of this tragic episode of Hellenic history, it would be no paradox to suggest that the foundation of the Roman Empire was a more 'awful revolution' than its fall. Yet, familiar though Gibbon was with the plot of this pre-Augustan Hellenic tragedy, he seems never to have inferred from it the possibility that the diversity-in-unity of an eighteenth-century Western body social might be exposed to the same danger of going awry.[3]

Another disagreeable contingency that Gibbon overlooks in this passage is the possibility that the effect of social conductivity may be equivocal. He perceives that the Western body social of his day is conductive in virtue of the unity underlying the diversity in its constitution, but he tacitly makes the assumption that the political qualities which one member of a Western family of states will acquire from another can only be those that happen to be desirable in his estimation. The same assumption was still being made, a hundred years and more after Gibbon's time, by British, American, French, and Belgian practitioners of a parliamentary representative form of constitutional government which its votaries labelled 'Democracy'.[4] At the turn of the nineteenth and twentieth centuries it was being taken for granted in 'democratic' Western countries that 'Democracy' was destined to supplant all other forms of government, not only in still 'undemocratic' Western countries, but in the World at large. But after the lapse of yet another half-century this optimistic assumption had come to seem naïve to Western observers who had seen the tide of 'Democracy', in the Western meaning of the word, begin to ebb on the morrow of a First World War which had been fought and won in order 'to make the World safe for Democracy', in the words of President Wilson's accurate description of the Western Allied and Associated Powers' principal war-aim.[5] Since A.D. 1919 'the general manners of the times' had been furthering the propagation, from one state to another, of the principles and practice, not of parliamentary democracy, but of Communist and Fascist totalitarianism; and in the

[1] In his essay *Of the Rise and Progress of the Arts and Sciences*, quoted in II. i. 473–4. Hume had been anticipated by Sprat, T.: *The History of the Royal Society* (London 1667, Martyn), pp. 22–23.
[2] In his *Second Discours sur les Progrès Successifs de l'Esprit Humain*, delivered on the 11th December, 1750, which has been cited ibid.
[3] This inference was obvious to a Western observer taking his bearings some 170 years after Gibbon's time, when a constitutional weakness in the structure of a Modern Western body social, to which Gibbon's genius had been blind, had become too flagrant to escape the notice of even the dullest understanding. There is, of course, no need to be a genius in order to be wise after the event.   [4] See I. i. 2.
[5] President Woodrow Wilson in his address to the Congress of the United States on the 2nd April, 1917.

mouth of a believer in constitutional government this statement of an indisputable historical fact was tantamount to a confession that, in these latter days, the abuses of tyranny were proving more infectious than the principles of freedom or even of moderation. In a dolorous twentieth century any citizen of a Western community that was then still partitioned among a host of warring parochial states would have been content to see Arcadius and Honorius slumber harmlessly on their thrones without itching to see their sleep disturbed by the pernicious activities of wakeful neighbours; for in an age in which Gibbon's Julian had turned out to be a Phocas, and his Semiramis a Sennacherib, political dynamism was at a discount.[1]

Gibbon's dictum that 'in war the European forces are exercised by temperate and undecisive contests' conveyed in one sentence to the ears of Gibbons's successors in A.D. 1952 the full measure of the change for the worse in the Western Civilization's prospects since Gibbon's day. We need not enlarge here on a point that we have already taken to heart in a number of previous contexts.[2] Since A.D. 1914 Europe had become a Westernizing World's battlefield.[3] We need only add that, since the inter-war dates at which those earlier passages of the present Study had been published, the disillusioning flow of Time had also brought with it a refutation of Gibbon's complementary thesis that 'in peace the progress of knowledge and industry is accelerated by the emulation of so many active rivals'; for the suspension of hostilities at the close of a Second World War had been anticipated by the dropping of two atomic bombs; and this horrifying triumph of a marvellous post-Modern Western scientific technique had marked the beginning of the end of an era of free scientific research and discussion which had now brought forth this satanic *chef-d'œuvre* after two and a half centuries of gestation.

This epoch of Western history had opened at the turn of the seventeenth and eighteenth centuries of the Christian Era with the liberation of scientific inquiry from the intellectual bonds of a Christian theology that had been clamped upon it some thirteen hundred years earlier under the auspices of the Christian Roman Emperor Theodosius I (*imperabat* A.D. 379–95); and, during a subsequent quarter of a millennium in which Science had been enjoying a freedom that was her life-breath, her vota-

---

[1] 'Benevolent government is rarely associated with a ruler whose mind is over-alert and intelligence over-developed. Benevolence is most commonly found in rulers who are easy-going or who behave as if they were. The worst defect in the alert-minded ruler is that he lays burdens upon his subjects which are greater than they can bear; and he does this because his mental vision outranges theirs and because his insight penetrates to the ends of things at the beginnings—with disastrous consequences for them. The Prophet says: "Go the pace of the weakest among you"; and in this context the exponent of the Divine Law prescribes in the case of rulers that excess of intelligence should be avoided . . . because it produces oppression and bad government and makes demands upon the people which are contrary to their nature. . . . It is evident from this that intellectuality and intelligence is a fault in an administrator, because this is an excess of mental activity—just as dull-wittedness is an excess of mental torpidity. The two extremes are to be deprecated in every attribute of Human Nature. The ideal is the Golden Mean. . . . And for this reason a man who is over-intellectual has Satanic attributes attributed to him and is called "Satan", "possessed by Satan", and so on' (Ibn Khaldūn: *Muqaddamāt*, Book I, chap. xxiv).
[2] See, for example, III. iii. 311; IV. iv. 148, 189, and 283.
[3] See III. iii. 303–4, and *Civilization on Trial* (London 1948, Oxford University Press), pp. 97–125: 'The Dwarfing of Europe'.

ries had never suspected that their liberation from the theological censorship of an oecumenical church was to be followed after a season by their subjection to the political control of a litter of sovereign independent parochial states. This twentieth-century forfeiture of a Western Science's intellectual freedom was the penalty for a Western Technology's practical success; for Science had been supplying Technology with edged tools; these tools were bound to be used and misused as weapons in a world that was partitioned among parochial states prone to go to war with one another; and, when Science had once furnished Technology with the 'know-how' for forging a weapon of the potency of the atomic bomb, any parochial government that possessed or aspired to acquire this 'know-how' was bound, on categorically imperative grounds of military security, to make this deadly knowledge a state secret and in consequence to bring the intellectual activities of atomic scientists under politico-military control.

Thus, on the morrow of 'V-J Day', A.D. 1945, the scientific workers of the Western World had woken up to find themselves conscripted into the secret service of this or that parochial state, whichever state might happen to be able to claim this or that scientist as its subject. And this political enslavement proved to have been only the milder of two calamities that had overtaken the men of science on that day of horror. The subjection of their scientific work to a political control was bound, no doubt, in the long run, to sterilize their flow of intellectual creativity; but this strangulation of their intellects by the dead hand of the secret police was a light affliction[1] compared with the *peine forte et dure* that was being inflicted on their consciences by a crushing sense of guilt and remorse. From the close of the seventeenth century of the Christian Era till the 15th August, 1945, a post-Christian school of Late Modern Western physical scientists had been casting upon the waters[2] a series of socially and morally subversive intellectual discoveries in a blind belief that any increase in Man's knowledge of, and command over, Physical Nature was an absolute good which was bound to bring in profitable returns, without regard to the human effect of this new inhuman knowledge and power upon the social milieu into which it was being spawned. In the ears of these prodigally irresponsible devotees of a renascent Athena, the explosion at Hiroshima on the 6th August, 1945, had reverberated with the sound of the Last Trump. A blast that had rent the veil under which they had been content hitherto to leave their goddess's ambiguous countenance hidden had suddenly confronted them with reality and convicted them of sin; and an inward spiritual monitor that might help a mortified soul to work out its personal salvation in the long run was a harsher taskmaster in the short run than the merely external tyranny of the security police.

In these circumstances, Gibbon's thesis that, during suspensions of international hostilities, the progress of knowledge and industry is accelerated by international competition could no longer carry conviction. But in the context of Gibbon's General Observations this thesis is only a parenthesis. The particular virtue of political diversity-in-unity that is

[1] 2 Cor. iv. 17.   [2] Eccl. xi. 1.

Gibbon's principal theme in this paragraph is the military effect of 'temperate and undecisive contests' between Western parochial states in exercising them for the common military task of meeting 'the Yellow Peril', if the Nomads should ever again break westwards out of the Great Eurasian Steppe. In the improbable event of these hypothetical aggressors from the heartland of the Old World overcoming the resistance of each and all of the mutually independent sedentary peoples living between the European shore of the Steppe and the Atlantic coast of Europe, Gibbon imagines 'the remains of Civilised Society' seeking and finding asylum in an America which by his time had already become a second home of the Western Civilization.

By Gibbon's time a series of waves of refugees, as well as *conquistadores*, from Western Europe had, in truth, already broken on the coasts of a New World where these *déracinés* had found themselves able to strike fresh root, and this stream of Transatlantic migration was to flow on, in greater volume and at a faster pace, for another 140 years after the date at which Gibbon was writing. But neither the Pilgrim Fathers nor 'the Forty-Eighters' were victims of 'the Tartar hordes'; and, if in A.D. 1952 'the remains of Civilised Society' on the European Peninsula of Asia were hoping once again—and this for the third time in one lifetime— that America was going to play the part of arsenal and citadel of Democracy on behalf of European peoples 'who perhaps might confederate for their common defence', this was not because the European homeland of the Western Civilization was having to face the prospect of another Nomad attack. This once perennial peril had never loomed up again since A.D. 1237–41, when the dreaded advance of Bātū Khan's expeditionary force had moved the herring-fishermen of Friesland and Gothland to stay ashore, mounting guard over their homes and families, while the whole season's catch of the year 1238 glutted the market in a snugly insular England.[1] In the general wars of A.D. 1914–18 and 1939–45 the aggressors whose ambitions had been frustrated by the intervention of the United States had been, not Nomad Mongols, but urban Germans; and, though in December 1950 Mongol cavalry were operating in Korea as auxiliaries of an intervening Chinese Communist army, it was not the Mongols, but the Russians, who were playing the aggressor's part in this fateful year. Thus a persisting partition of the Western World among a litter of warring parochial states, in which Gibbon had seen a salutary insurance against the chimaerical danger of a resurgence of the Nomads, had actually opened the way for a betrayal of the West European sanctuary of Western culture to an enemy within the gates. In Gibbon's order of battle against a Nomad offensive, 'the robust peasants of Russia' are posted in the first line of the defending forces, and 'the numerous armies of Germany' in the second. How will a historian-strategist fare when

---

[1] 'Unde Gothiam et Frisiam inhabitantes, impetus eorum pertimentes, in Angliam, ut moris est eorum, apud Gernemue [Yarmouth], tempore allecis capiendi, quo suas naves solebant onerare, non venerunt. Hinc erat quod allec eo anno in Angliâ quasi pro nihilo prae abundantiâ habitum, sub quadragenario vel quinquagenario numero, licet optimum esset, pro uno argento in partibus a mari etiam longinquis vendebantur' (Matthew Paris: *Chronica Maiora*, sub anno A.D. 1238, in H. R. Luard's edition, vol. iii (London 1876, Longman, Trübner, Parkes, Macmillan, Black, & Thom), p. 488).

forces detailed for the defence betray their trust by delivering the attack? And what chance would Europe have of reviving and flourishing in an American city of refuge if the Power that had driven 'the remains of Civilised Society' out of the Old World and across the Atlantic was, not 'the Tartar hordes', but a sedentary people equipped with the most recently invented engines of a Western military technique?

Experience indicated that Gibbon's confidence in the inviolability of an American asylum for the Western Civilization would have been justified if—but only if—the aggressor's part had been played in reality by those arrested Nomad riders who had been cast for it in Gibbon's imagination. If the Continental Power that was under suspicion in A.D. 1952 of entertaining designs of world-wide conquest had been, once again, the Mongols, the peoples of the Western World would assuredly have had better reason this time for counting on the survival of their own distinctive culture than they had had in A.D. 1238, when they had been facing the prospect of a Mongol occupation of the West European peninsula of Asia without having any reassuring Transatlantic asylum at their backs. In A.D. 1952 they could have taken comfort in reminding themselves that in A.D. 1281 the forces of a Mongol Empire, which at that date had been mistress of the Continent from the shores of the Pacific Ocean to the shores of the Persian Gulf and the Baltic Sea, had been thrown back ignominiously from the beaches of Japan;[1] for a cavalry Power which had proved impotent to conquer a cluster of small islands separated from the Continent by only a hundred miles of sea at the nearest point would have had no prospect, if she had occupied the European coastline of the Continent that the Germans held in June 1940, of being able to conquer the great island of North America on the farther side of a nearly two-thousand-miles-broad Atlantic Ocean, or even the sister island of South America, which was divided by not less than sixteen hundred miles of sea from the Continent at the Straits of Dakar, where the westward bulge of Africa approached closest to the eastward bulge of Brazil. Indeed, the fiasco of Qubilay Khan's attempt on Japan suggests that even the twenty-miles-wide Straits of Dover, which had foiled Napoleon and foiled Hitler when the local Continental war-lord of the day had had the whole of Europe under his command, might have proved impassable for Qubilay Khan in spite of his commanding the Asiatic mass as well as the European extremity of the Continent. But the historic immunity of the isles from conquest by Continental war-lords had been due to the comparative innocuousness of even a sedentary community's most formidable weapons of offence until a hundred years and more after the date at which Gibbon had been writing; and no one who had lived through the war of A.D. 1939–45 could be blind to the truth that, since then, times had changed. The weapons with which Hitler had come within an ace of conquering Britain, and with which the combined forces of the United States and the British Commonwealth had succeeded thereafter in conquering Hitler's vaunted *Festung Europa*, were indications that in a future world war the conquest of North America might not be beyond the reach of a Power controlling the aggregate resources of the Old World

[1] See IV. iv. 93.

and capable of forging this incomparably vast store of war potential into unprecedentedly potent weapons through a mastery of an ever improving Western technology.

The significance of the Western World's progress in military technology is examined by Gibbon in the paragraph that follows next.

'Cold, poverty, and a life of danger and fatigue fortify the strength and courage of Barbarians. In every age they have oppressed the polite and peaceful nations of China, India, and Persia, who neglected, and still neglect, to counterbalance these natural powers by the resources of military art. The warlike states of Antiquity, Greece, Macedonia, and Rome, educated a race of soldiers; exercised their bodies, disciplined their courage, multiplied their forces by regular evolutions, and converted the iron which they possessed into strong and serviceable weapons. But this superiority insensibly declined with their laws and manners: and the feeble policy of Constantine and his successors armed and instructed, for the ruin of the empire, the rude valour of the Barbarian mercenaries. The military art has been changed by the invention of gunpowder, which enables Man to command the two most powerful agents of Nature, air and fire. Mathematics, chymistry, mechanics, architecture have been applied to the service of war; and the adverse parties oppose to each other the most elaborate modes of attack and of defence. Historians may indignantly observe that the preparations of a siege would found and maintain a flourishing colony;[1] yet we cannot be displeased that the subversion of a city should be a work of cost and difficulty; or that an industrious people should be protected by those arts which survive and supply the decay of military virtue. Cannon and fortifications now form an impregnable barrier against the Tartar horse; and Europe is secure from any future irruption of Barbarians, since, before they can conquer, they must cease to be barbarous. Their gradual advances in the science of war would always be accompanied, as we may learn from the example of Russia, with a proportionable improvement in the arts of peace and civil policy; and they themselves must deserve a place among the polished nations whom they subdue.'

In this paragraph Gibbon first suggests a second reason why a latter-day Western Civilization is unlikely ever to succumb to a Nomad conqueror, and then goes on to make an anticipatory reply to our critique of the immediately preceding paragraph of his General Observations. Our Western Civilization can count on never being extinguished by an eruption of the Eurasian Nomads, not only because 'the Tartar horse' would be incapable of pursuing across the Atlantic the ten thousand vessels that would transport to the Americas the refugees from a conquered Europe, but also because these Nomad barbarians would not even be capable of conquering the European peninsula of the Continent

---

1 [in the original, 9]. ' "On avoit fait venir [for the siege of Turin] 140 pièces de canon; et il est à remarquer que chaque gros canon monté revient à environ 2,000 écus: il y avoit 110,000 boulets; 106,000 cartouches d'une façon, et 300,000 d'une autre; 21,000 bombes; 27,700 grenades, 15,000 sacs à terre, 30,000 instruments pour le pionnage; 1,200,000 livres de poudre. Ajoutez à ces munitions le plomb, le fer, et le fer-blanc, les cordages, tout ce qui sert aux mineurs, le souphre, le salpêtre, les outils de toute espèce. Il est certain que les frais de tous ces préparatifs de destruction suffiroient pour fonder et pour faire fleurir la plus nombreuse colonie." — Voltaire, Siècle de Louis XIV, chap. xx, in his Works, tom. xi, p. 391.'

against defenders armed with Modern Western weapons. After thus completing the otiose task of flogging a dead Tartar horse, Gibbon makes the admission that the Nomads are not the only potential barbarian invaders on a Western World's eastern horizon, and that, even if we may assume that the Nomads could never succeed either in launching an ocean-going navy or in assembling a siege train of heavy artillery, there might be sedentary barbarians capable of mastering, for the purpose of aggression against the West, all the latest devices of Western military technology that the Western peoples, on their side, would have at their own disposal for the purpose of self-defence. Gibbon avowedly has in mind the metamorphosis of Russia in and after the reign of Peter the Great; and his reading of this passage of Russian history emboldens his optimism to venture on the highest of all its flights. 'Europe is secure from any future irruption of Barbarians, since, before they can conquer, they must cease to be barbarous': *si monumentum requiris*, look at Russia and be of good cheer!

What would have been Gibbon's second thoughts about this most 'doubtful' and most 'fallacious' of all his speculative grounds for optimism if he could have lived to see this particular argument tested by the experience of another 170 years? The fallacy, of course, lies in failing to distinguish the intellectual culture that takes practical effect in Technology from the spiritual culture that takes effect in morals. The flaw in Gibbon's argument here is to be found in his equivocal phrase 'the arts of peace and civil policy'. If this phrase could reasonably be construed as meaning no more than civil as contrasted with military engineering, then the minor argument of this sentence could perhaps be salvaged at the cost of jettisoning the major argument of the whole passage. It might be true, at any rate in the peculiar circumstances of latter-day Western life, that Technology was indivisible. Military engineering might be incapable of ever rising very high if it were not based on a firm civil foundation. But this truth—if it were indeed the truth—about Technology had no bearing on any question of morals, since it was not true that morals and Technology were indivisible from one another. On the contrary, we have found reason to believe that they go their different ways—Technology being a cumulative and collective acquisition of Mankind's, whereas the battle between good and evil has to be fought over again in the soul of each child that is born into the World.[1]

Gibbon's case for optimism in this context thus proves to be founded on nothing more substantial than the ambiguity of a 'portmanteau' phrase which, by verbally confounding with one another the two mutually independent movements of moral and material progress, serves to give the false impression that these actually run in double harness. This is never true even within the bosom of a single society, where there is a nisus towards a harmony between the different elements constituting what is, after all, a single culture-pattern. *A fortiori*, there is no reason to expect that the moral standards of a civilization will keep company with its technique when this is being radiated out into an alien social milieu; for our study of encounters between different societies has shown that—

[1] See III. iii. 154–74; VII. vii. 556 and 701–11; and pp. 697–704, above.

whether both parties are civilizations[1] or whether one party is a civilization in its universal state and the other party a barbarian war-band beyond the *limes*[2]—the invariable effect of any impact on an alien body
social is to diffract the integral culture-ray of the impinging civilization
into its constituent elements; and we have also observed that, whenever
this process of cultural diffraction occurs, the technical and economic
radiation of the impinging civilization is apt to travel faster and penetrate farther than its political and cultural radiation.

In ignoring these manifest lessons of History, Gibbon is practising on
himself the same trick that a contemporary Russian courtier once practised on a German Empress of Russia whom Gibbon has delighted to
honour under the pseudonym 'Semiramis'; for, if, as Gibbon's major
argument requires, the phrase 'arts of peace and civil policy' is to be
construed as meaning morals as well as Non-Military Technology, the
answer to Gibbon is that, while Russia, from the time of Peter the Great
onwards, did indeed make advances in Technology *accelerando*, her advances in public morals, in and after the reign of the Empress Catherine
the Great, were no more substantial than 'Potemkin villages'. Since
morals, and not Technology, must be taken to be the true criterion of
any conquering Barbarians' title 'to deserve a place among the polished
nations whom they subdue', Gibbon was adding insult to injury in ad-
vising conquered Estonians and Latvians to console themselves with the
reflection that the Russians' proven ability to conquer these 'polished'
Western nations with borrowed Western weapons was good evidence
that their conquerors had become their peers in a 'politeness' which was
the eighteenth-century Western equivalent of a twentieth-century Western 'civilization'.[3]

The last two paragraphs of Gibbon's General Observations may be
quoted together, since they are open to a common criticism that has been
anticipated in our critique of the paragraph immediately preceding them.

'Should these speculations be found doubtful or fallacious, there still
remains a more humble source of comfort and hope. The discoveries of
ancient and modern navigators, and the domestic history or tradition of
the most enlightened nations, represent the *human savage* naked both in
mind and body, and destitute of laws, of arts, of ideas, and almost of language.[4] From this abject condition, perhaps the primitive and universal

---

[1] See IX. viii. *passim.* [2] See VIII. viii. *passim.*

[3] An older contemporary of the present writer's who was a scion of one of the families
of the *ci-devant* Baltic German landed aristocracy had heard, as a child, his father tell a
story that is historically significant just by reason of its triviality. Some time about
three-quarters of the way through the nineteenth century of the Christian Era, this
Baltic Baron was travelling out of an Orthodox Christian Great Russia into the Protestant
Baltic provinces of the Russian Empire in the company of one or two native Russian
nobles. At the provincial boundary they changed carriages (they were travelling by road),
and, as they were climbing into the Baltic carriage that had been awaiting them, the
coachman happened to take out his handkerchief and blow his nose. The boyars, who
were visiting the Baltic provinces for the first time, had been expecting surprises, but at
this first exhibition of Baltic 'politeness' they were overwhelmed. 'Well,' they exclaimed
to their Baltic host, 'What a country! Even a coachman here has a handkerchief! Why,
this is Europe!'

[4] [in the original, ¹⁰]. 'It would be an easy, though tedious, task to produce the
authorities of poets, philosophers, and historians. I shall therefore content myself with
appealing to the decisive and authentic testimony of Diodorus Siculus (tom. i, Book I,
pp. 11, 12; Book III, p. 184, &c., ed. Wesseling). The Ichthyophagi, who in his time

state of Man, he has gradually arisen to command the animals, to fertilise the Earth, to traverse the Ocean, and to measure the Heavens. His progress in the improvement and exercise of his mental and corporeal faculties[1] has been irregular and various; infinitely slow in the beginning, and increasing by degrees with redoubled velocity: ages of laborious ascent have been followed by a moment of rapid downfall; and the several climates of the globe have felt the vicissitudes of light and darkness. Yet the experience of four thousand years should enlarge our hopes and diminish our apprehensions: we cannot determine to what height the Human Species may aspire in their advances towards perfection; but it may safely be presumed that no people, unless the face of Nature is changed, will relapse into their original barbarism. The improvements of Society may be viewed under a threefold aspect. 1. The poet or philosopher illustrates his age and country by the efforts of a *single* mind; but these superior powers of Reason or Fancy are rare and spontaneous productions; and the genius of Homer or Cicero or Newton would excite less admiration if they could be created by the will of a prince or the lessons of a preceptor. 2. The benefits of law and policy, of trade and manufactures, of arts and sciences, are more solid and permanent; and *many* individuals may be qualified, by education and discipline, to promote, in their respective stations, the interest of the community. But this general order is the effect of skill and labour; and the complex machinery may be decayed by time or injured by violence. 3. Fortunately for Mankind, the more useful, or, at least, more necessary, arts can be performed without superior talents or national subordination; without the powers of *one* or the union of *many*. Each village, each family, each individual must always possess both ability and inclination to perpetuate the use of fire[2] and of metals; the propagation and service of domestic animals; the methods of hunting and fishing; the rudiments of navigation; the imperfect cultivation of corn or other nutritive grain; and the simple practice of the mechanic trades. Private genius and public industry may be extirpated, but these hardy plants survive the tempest and strike an everlasting root into the most unfavourable soil. The splendid days of Augustus and Trajan were eclipsed by a cloud of ignorance; and the Barbarians subverted the laws and palaces of Rome. But the scythe, the invention or emblem of Saturn,[3] still continued annually to mow the harvests of Italy; and the human feasts of the Laestrigons[4] have never been renewed on the coast of Campania.

'Since the first discovery of the arts, war, commerce, and religious zeal have diffused, among the savages of the Old and New World, those inestimable gifts: they have been successively propagated; they can never

wandered along the shores of the Red Sea, can only be compared to the natives of New Holland (*Dampier's Voyages*, vol. i, pp. 464–69). Fancy, or perhaps Reason, may still suppose an extreme and absolute state of Nature far below the level of these savages, who had acquired some arts and instruments.'

[1] [in the original, 11]. 'See the learned and rational work of the President Goguet, *De l'Origine des Loix, des Arts, et des Sciences*. He traces from facts or conjectures (tom. i, pp. 147–337, edit. 12mo.) the first and most difficult steps of human invention.'

[2] [12]. 'It is certain, however strange, that many nations have been ignorant of the use of fire. Even the ingenious natives of Otaheite, who are destitute of metals, have not invented any earthen vessels capable of sustaining the action of fire and of communicating the heat to the liquids which they contain.'

[3] [13]. 'Plutarch, *Quaestiones Romanae*, in tom. ii, p. 275. Macrobius, *Saturnalia*, Book I, ch. viii, p. 152, edit. London. The arrival of Saturn (or his religious worship) in a ship may indicate that the savage coast of Latium was first discovered and civilised by the Phoenicians.'

[4] [14]. 'In the ninth and tenth books of the Odyssey, Homer has embellished the tales of fearful and credulous sailors who transformed the cannibals of Italy and Sicily into monstrous giants.'

be lost. We may therefore acquiesce in the pleasing conclusion that every age of the World has increased, and still increases, the real wealth, the happiness, the knowledge, and perhaps the virtue, of the Human Race.'[1]

In these concluding paragraphs Gibbon—prudently recollecting certain considerations that had emerged from a celebrated controversy between the respective champions of the Ancients and the Moderns[2]—is at pains to refrain from drawing too optimistic a conclusion from the cumulativeness and collectiveness of Mankind's progress in Technology. He readily admits that the wind of individual genius bloweth where it listeth;[3] and he goes so far as to concede that the corporate culture-pattern of a civilization may be precarious. He is content to follow Turgot[4] in making for Technology the relatively modest claim that the humbler skills providing an agrarian society's fundamental necessities of life 'can never be lost';[5] and twentieth-century Western sociologists and economists would perhaps find little to quarrel with in this Gibbonian thesis. Yet a Western historian who had lived to see the moral collapse of the Western Civilization in the twentieth century would hesitate to follow Gibbon in assuming it to be self-evident that a recrudescence of cannibalism in the Western World was quite so unlikely as a discontinuance of agriculture there; and, in agreeing that 'the imperfect cultivation of corn or other nutritive grain and the simple practice of the mechanic trades' are 'hardy plants' which 'survive the tempest and strike an everlasting root into the most unfavourable soil', a twentieth-century Western Christian would certainly not 'acquiesce in the pleasing conclusion that every age of the World has increased, and still increases, . . . the happiness, . . . and perhaps the virtue', as well as 'the knowledge, . . . of the Human Race.' Indeed, on the morrow of a Second World War that had laid Europe and Eastern Asia in ruins, a Western historian writing in A.D. 1952 might also be inclined to dispute even the proposition that 'the real wealth' of Mankind was inevitably increased by the progress of a Technology that could be used just as effectively for destruction as for production.

Gibbon's unargued assumption that progress in Technology and pro-

---

[1] [15]. 'The merit of discovery has too often been stained with avarice, cruelty, and fanaticism; and the intercourse of nations has produced the communication of disease and prejudice. A singular exception is due to the virtue of our own times and country. The five great voyages, successively undertaken by the command of his present Majesty, were inspired by the pure and generous love of Science and of Mankind. The same prince, adapting his benefactions to the different stages of Society, has founded a school of painting in his capital, and has introduced into the islands of the South Sea the vegetables and animals most useful to human life.'

[2] See pp. 62–73, above.   [3] John iii. 8.

[4] 'Les arts mécaniques n'ont jamais souffert la même éclipse que les lettres et les sciences spéculatives.'—Turgot, A. R. J.: 'Plan du Second Discours sur l'Histoire Universelle dont l'Objet sera les Progrès de l'Esprit Humain,' in Œuvres, nouvelle édition, (Paris 1844, Guillaumin, 2 vols.), vol. ii, p. 666. Compare eundem, 'Second Discours sur les Avantages que l'Établissement du Christianisme a procurés au Genre Humain', delivered at the Sorbonne on the 11th September, 1750, ibid., vol. ii, p. 608, cited already in this Study in III. iii. 159, n. 3.

[5] Among the higher intellectual activities, the same claim is made for mathematics alone by Gibbon in another context: 'The mathematics are distinguished by a peculiar privilege, that, in the course of ages, they may always advance and can never recede' (The History of the Decline and Fall of the Roman Empire, chap. lii, quoted on p. 701, above).

gress in morals must run neck and neck, as a matter of course, had been so effectively refuted by the experience of 170 more years of Western history that it could not fail to be evident to a Western historian, taking an observation in A.D. 1952, that progress in Technology, so far from being a guarantee of progress in virtue and happiness, was a challenge to it. Each time that Man increased the potency of his material tools, he was increasing the gravity of the moral consequences of his acts and was thereby raising the minimum standard of the goodness required of him if his growing power was not to turn to his destruction; and, while it was true that, in so far as a human soul succeeded in meeting Technology's spiritual challenge, technological progress might be credited with having been at least the blind and unintentional stimulus of this spiritual achievement, it was also true, as we have observed, that each individual soul had to fight the same ever recurring spiritual battle for itself under a mounting pressure from a Technology whose collective and therefore cumulative progress was bearing ever harder on each individual human spirit. In the intolerably mechanized 'Brave New World' conjured into existence by the Western Civilization in its post-Modern Age it was hard indeed for any human soul to resist the temptation of becoming a fiend without succumbing to the opposite temptation of becoming a robot.[1] This was the Human Race's predicament as twentieth-century Western eyes saw it, and from this observation no facilely pleasing conclusion could be drawn.

[1] See pp. 563–77, above.

TABLE V. *The Time-spans of the Growth-phases of the Affiliated Civilizations*

Civilization	Date of Epiphany	Date of Breakdown[1]	Span of Growth-phase (in approximate number of years)
Western	circa A.D. 675	post A.D. 1550[2]	875 at least
Medieval Western City-State Cosmos	circa A.D. 675	A.D. 1378[3]	700±
Hellenic	circa 1125 B.C.	431 B.C.	700±
Indic	circa 1375 B.C.	circa 725 B.C.[4]	650±
Far Eastern in Japan	A.D. 554[5]	A.D. 1185	631
Babylonic	circa 1375 B.C.	circa 1000 B.C.[6]	400±
Far Eastern in China	circa A.D. 475	A.D. 878[7]	400±
Hindu	circa A.D. 775	A.D. 1175	400±
Orthodox Christian, main body	circa A.D. 675	A.D. 977	300±
Yucatec { either or }	circa A.D. 900[8] / circa A.D. 1150[10]	A.D. 1201[9] / A.D. 1451[11]	300±
[Mexic	circa A.D. 900[12]	circa A.D. 1150[13]	250±]
Syriac	circa 1125 B.C.	circa 937 B.C.[14]	200±
Iranic	circa A.D. 1275	A.D. 1511[15]	200±
Arabic	circa A.D. 1275	A.D. 1516–17[16]	200±
[Sinic	circa 825 B.C.[17]	circa 634 B.C.	200±]
Hittite	circa 1375 B.C.	circa 1200 B.C.	175±
Orthodox Christian in Russia	circa A.D. 989[18]	circa A.D. 1075	100±
Sinic	circa 750 B.C.[19]	634 B.C.	100±
Mexic	circa A.D. 1150[20]	circa A.D. 1150	zero

[1] See IV. iv. 56–114, and Table I in vol. vi, p. 327, reprinted as Table I in vol. vii, p. 769.

[2] The only statement that could be made with assurance in A.D. 1952 regarding the phase in which the Western Society was living at that date was that, so far, it had not entered into a universal state; and, if it is legitimate to infer from the uniformity of the pattern of the disintegration-process that a broken-down civilization would be unlikely to arrive at a universal state without having previously passed through a Time of Troubles with the standard Time-span of some four centuries, it would seem to follow that, if the Western Civilization had broken down (which was still an open question), this catastrophe could not have overtaken it earlier—at the earliest—than about half-way through the sixteenth century.

[3] The date of the outbreak of the Veneto-Genoese War of Chioggia, which was the counterpart, in the history of the Medieval Western city-state cosmos, of the Atheno-Peloponnesian War that broke out in 431 B.C. in the Hellenic World.

[4] This date is an inference from the date of the establishment of an Indic universal state by Chandragupta Maurya in 322 B.C.

[5] This is the date of the introduction of the Mahāyāna into Japan from Korea (see Murdoch, J.: *History of Japan*, vol. i (London 1910, Kegan Paul), p. 111). Literacy in the Sinic characters and classics is recorded to have been introduced into Japan from Korea as early as A.D. 404 (see ibid., p. 44). If this record is correct, and if this cultural event, rather than the introduction of the Mahāyāna, were to be taken as marking the planting of an offshoot of the Far Eastern culture in Japan, then the growth-phase of Japanese history—running, as it then would run, to 781 years—would be the longest of any in our list except the Western Civilization's.

[6] The approximate date of the flood-tide of the influx of Aramaean and Chaldaean Nomad barbarians from the North Arabian Steppe into both Babylonia and Mesopotamia. The Babylonic Civilization was brought to ruin by the militarism to which the Assyrians succumbed as the price of their arduous victory over the Aramaean invaders (see II. ii. 133–5).

[7] The date of the sack of Khānfū (see IV. iv. 87).

[8] Following Spinden's chronology, which dates the end of 'the First Empire' of the Mayas *circa* A.D. 600 (see I. i. 125, nn. 3 and 4).

[9] Following Spinden's and Gann's chronology (see I. i. 124, n. 2).

[10] Following Thompson's chronology (see I. i. 125, n. 3).

[11] Following Thompson's chronology (see I. i. 124, n. 2).

[12] Following Spinden's chronology.

[13] This date is an inference from the fact that the Aztecs were on the eve of establishing a universal state in Central America when the Spaniards arrived on the scene in A.D. 1519.

[14] The approximate date of the death of Solomon (see IV. iv. 68).

[15] The date of the Shī'ī revolt against the Ottoman Power in Anatolia.

[16] The date of the Ottoman conquest of the dominions of the Egyptian Mamlūks.

[17] Following the standard Sinic chronology, which dates the overthrow of the Shang Power by Wu Wang in 1122 B.C.

[18] The date of the conversion of Russia to Orthodox Christianity.

[19] Following the chronology of the Bamboo Books, which dates the overthrow of the Shang Power by Wu Wang in 1050 B.C.

[20] Following Thompson's chronology, which dates the end of 'the First Empire' of the Mayas in the first half of the ninth century of the Christian Era (see I. i. 125, n. 3).

PRINTED IN
GREAT BRITAIN
AT THE
UNIVERSITY PRESS
OXFORD
BY
CHARLES BATEY
PRINTER
TO THE
UNIVERSITY